Other books by the author

Inflation, Saving and Growth in Developing Economies
Regional Growth and Unemployment in the United Kingdom (*with R. Di...*
Financing Economic Development
Balance-of-Payments Theory and the United Kingdom Experience (Fourth Edition *with H. Gibson*)
Nicholas Kaldor
UK Industrialisation and Deindustrialisation (Third Edition *with S. Bazen*)
The Performance and Prospects of the Pacific Island Economies in the World Economy
Economic Growth and the Balance-of-Payments Constraint (*with J. McCombie*)
The Economics of Growth and Development: Selected Essays, Vol. 1
Macroeconomic Issues from a Keynesian Perspective: Selected Essays, Vol. 2
The Euro and 'Regional' Divergence in Europe
The Nature of Economic Growth: An Alternative Framework for Understanding the Performance of Nations
Trade, the Balance of Payments and Exchange Rate Policy in Developing Countries
Essays on Balance of Payments Constrained Growth: Theory and Evidence (*with J. McCombie*)
Trade Liberalisation and The Poverty of Nations (*with P. Pacheco-López*)

Edited works

Keynes and International Monetary Relations
Keynes and Laissez-Faire
Keynes and the Bloomsbury Group (*with D. Crabtree*)
Keynes as a Policy Adviser
Keynes and Economic Development
Keynes and the Role of the State (*with D. Crabtree*)
European Factor Mobility: Trends and Consequences (*with I. Gordon*)
The Essential Kaldor (*with F. Targetti*)
Further Essays in Economic Theory and Policy, Volume 9, Collected Economic Papers of N. Kaldor
    (*with F. Targetti*)
Causes of Growth and Stagnation in the World Economy (the Mattioli Lectures of N. Kaldor *with F. Targetti*)
Economic Dynamics, Trade and Growth: Essays on Harrodian Themes (*with G. Rampa and L. Stella*)

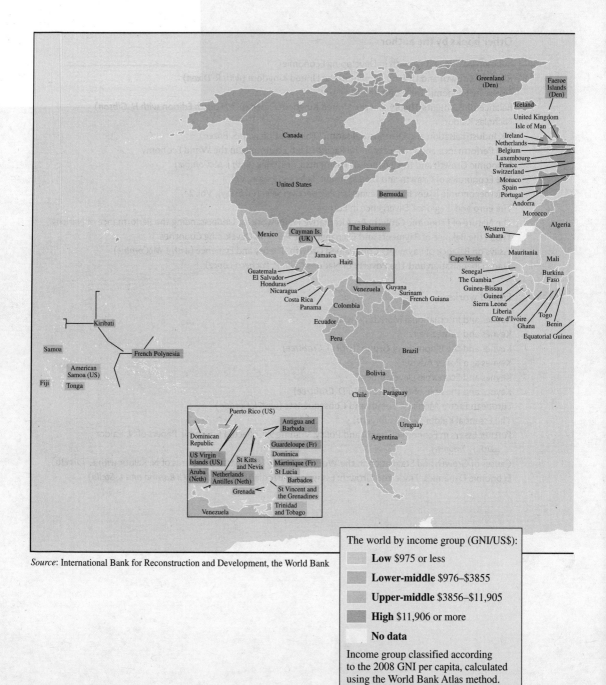

Greenland
(Den)

Faeroe
Islands
(Den)

Iceland

United Kingdom
Isle of Man

Ireland
Netherlands
Belgium
Luxembourg
France
Switzerland
Monaco
Spain
Portugal
Andorra

Morocco

Canada

United States

Bermuda

The Bahamas

Western
Sahara

Algeria

Mexico

Cayman Is.
(UK)

Jamaica

Haiti

Mauritania

Mali

Cape Verde

Guatemala
El Salvador
Honduras
Nicaragua
Costa Rica
Panama

Venezuela
Colombia

Guyana
Surinam
French Guiana

Senegal
The Gambia
Guinea-Bissau
Guinea
Sierra Leone
Liberia
Côte d'Ivoire

Burkina
Faso

Togo
Benin
Ghana

Equatorial Guinea

Ecuador

Peru

Brazil

Kiribati

French Polynesia

Samoa

American
Samoa (US)

Fiji
Tonga

Bolivia

Chile
Paraguay

Uruguay

Argentina

Puerto Rico (US)

Antigua and
Barbuda

Dominican
Republic

Guardeloupe (Fr)
Dominica
Martinique (Fr)
St Lucia
Barbados
St Vincent and
the Grenadines

US Virgin
Islands (US)

St Kitts
and Nevis

Aruba
(Neth)

Netherlands
Antilles (Neth)

Grenada

Venezuela

Trinidad
and Tobago

The world by income group (GNI/US$):

Low $975 or less

Lower-middle $976–$3855

Upper-middle $3856–$11,905

High $11,906 or more

No data

Income group classified according
to the 2008 GNI per capita, calculated
using the World Bank Atlas method.

Source: International Bank for Reconstruction and Development, the World Bank

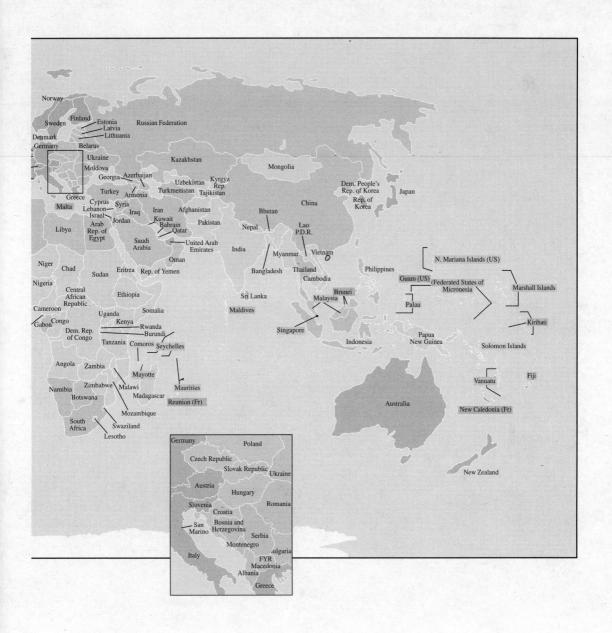

ECONOMICS OF DEVELOPMENT

THEORY AND EVIDENCE

NINTH EDITION

A. P. Thirlwall

Professor of Applied Economics, University of Kent

Reprinted in 2014, 2016

© A. P. Thirlwall 1972, 1978, 1983, 1989, 1994, 1999, 2003, 2006, 2011

First edition 1972
Second edition 1978
Third edition 1983
Fourth edition 1989
Fifth edition 1994
Sixth edition 1999
Seventh edition 2003
Eighth edition 2006
Ninth edition 2011

Published by
PALGRAVE MACMILLAN

Palgrave Macmillan in the UK is an imprint of Macmillan Publishers Limited, registered in England, company number 785998, of Houndmills, Basingstoke, Hampshire RG21 6XS.

Palgrave Macmillan in the US is a division of St Martin's Press LLC, 175 Fifth Avenue, New York, NY 10010.

Palgrave Macmillan is the global academic imprint of the above companies and has companies and representatives throughout the world.

Palgrave® and Macmillan® are registered trademarks in the United States, the United Kingdom, Europe and other countries.

ISBN 978–0–230–39444–5

A catalogue record for this book is available from the British Library.

A catalog record for this book is available from the Library of Congress.

Printed and bound in India by Replika Press Pvt. Ltd.

**This edition is manufactured in India and is authorized for
sale only in India, Bangladesh, Pakistan, Nepal, Bhutan and Sri Lanka**

To Penélope
for
Oliver Anthony
with love

A PERSONAL MESSAGE FROM THE AUTHOR

(Courtesy of Spencer Scott of the University of Kent photographic unit)

The economic and social development of poor countries, and reducing divisions in the world economy between rich are poor, are two of the greatest challenges facing mankind. Vast differences in income and wealth between countries and peoples are not only morally indefensible but also a grave threat to peace and stability in the world.

The great English economist John Maynard Keynes once described what drew him to economics; it was, he said, 'its intellectual rigour combined with its potentiality for good'. He treated the subject of economics as a moral science, the purpose of which is to understand economic behaviour and thereby to be able to design policies to make the world a more civilized place in which to live. It is this 'potentiality for good' that attracts to development economics so many of today's top economists.

I have written this textbook on the economics of development so that students can apply their knowledge of economics to the plight of poor countries in the hope that they will better understand the divided world in which we live and think about issues of development in whatever capacity they may subsequently work.

I have been teaching development economics for over forty years and have encountered thousands of students in different parts of the world and from different countries, many of whom have gone on to work in the development field – as employees in international institutions and non-governmental organizations concerned with economic and social development, or as teachers and researchers in poor countries. If new generations of students studying development economics are inspired to do the same, this volume will have achieved its purpose.

I hope you will enjoy the book, and that when you reach the end you will feel that the study of the economics of development has enriched your experience as an economist and citizen of the world.

Wherever you live, I wish you good luck in your studies.

Tony Thirlwall

BRIEF CONTENTS

Part I   Development and underdevelopment

1   The study of economic development   3

2   The development gap and the measurement of poverty   25

3   The characteristics of underdevelopment and structural
    change   70

4   The role of institutions in economic development   117

5   Theories of economic growth: why growth rates differ between countries   130

Part II   Factors in the development process

6   The role of agriculture and surplus labour for industrialization   179

7   Capital accumulation, technical progress and techniques of production   227

Part III   The perpetuation of underdevelopment

8   Dualism, centre–periphery models and the process of cumulative causation   261

9   Population and development   284

Part IV   The role of the state, the allocation of resources, and
sustainable development

10 Resource allocation in developing countries, and sustainable development   305

11 Project appraisal, social cost–benefit analysis and shadow wages   330

12 Development and the environment   351

Part V   Financing economic development

13 Financing development from domestic resources   385

14 Foreign assistance, aid, debt and development   437

Part VI International trade, the balance of payments and development

15 Trade theory, trade policy and economic development   501

16 The balance of payments, international monetary assistance and
    development   561

CONTENTS

List of Figures   xxii
List of Tables   xxv
List of Case Examples   xxvii
Preface   xxviii
Universal Declaration of Human Rights   xxxiii
Acknowledgements   xxxiv

Part I Development and underdevelopment

1 The study of economic development   3
  Introduction   4
  Development economics as a subject   5
  Academic interest in development   6
  A new international economic order   11
  Globalization and interdependence of the world economy   14
  The meaning of development and the challenge of development economics 18
  The perpetuation of underdevelopment   20
  Summary   22
  Discussion questions   22
  Websites   23

2 The development gap and the measurement of poverty   25
  Introduction   26
  The development gap and income distribution in the
      world economy   27
  Measures of inequality and historical trends   27
  International inequality (unweighted and weighted)   34
  Global (or world) inequality   36
  The measurement and comparability of per capita income   37
  Purchasing power parity (PPP)   38
  Per capita income as an index of development   40
  Measuring poverty   42
  Meeting the Millennium Poverty Reduction Target   45

Tackling poverty from the 'grass roots'   47
Human Poverty Index and Human Development Index   52
Can the poor countries ever catch up?   53
Summary   67
Discussion questions   67
Notes   68
Websites on poverty and income distribution   69

**3 The characteristics of underdevelopment and structural
    change**   **70**
Introduction   71
The dominance of agriculture and petty services   71
Low level of capital accumulation   73
Rapid population growth   75
Exports dominated by primary commodities   76
The curse of natural resources   77
Weak institutional structures   78
Other dimensions of the development gap   80
Inequality: vertical and horizontal   84
Growth and distribution   90
Poverty-weighted growth rates   91
Nutrition and health   92
Famine   97
Food production   100
Stages of development and structural change   101
Rostow's stages of growth   104
Diversification   108
Industrialization and growth   108
Kaldor's growth laws   110
Summary   114
Discussion questions   114
Notes   115
Websites on health, nutrition, famine, education, structural change
    and income distribution   116

4 The role of institutions in economic development   **117**
Introduction   118
The role of institutions   118
Measuring institutions and the debate on institutions versus
    geography   121
The role of democracy   125
Summary   127
Discussion questions   128
Note   129
Websites on institutions and market behaviour   129

5 Theories of economic growth: why growth rates differ between countries   130

Introduction   131

Classical growth theory   132

The Harrod–Domar growth model   140

Neoclassical growth theory   146

The production function approach to the analysis of growth   150

Production function studies of developing countries   158

'New' (endogenous) growth theory and the macrodeterminants of growth   162

'Growth diagnostics' and binding constraints on growth   171

Summary   173

Discussion questions   174

Notes   174

Websites on growth theory   175

Part II Factors in the development process

6 The role of agriculture and surplus labour for industrialization   179

Introduction   180

The role of agriculture in development   180

Barriers to agricultural development   183

Land reform   189

The supply response of agriculture   191

Transforming traditional agriculture   193

The growth of the money economy   196

Finance for traditional agriculture   198

The interdependence of agriculture and industry   199

Economic development with unlimited supplies of labour   200

A model of the complementarity between agriculture and industry   204

Rural–urban migration and urban unemployment   207

Disguised unemployment: types and measurement   210

Incentives and the costs of labour transfer   215

Summary   217

Appendix: the functioning of markets in agrarian societies   218

The land market   218

The labour market   221

Credit markets   222

Interlocked markets   224

Institutions and decision-making in agriculture   224

Discussion questions   225

Notes   225

Websites on agriculture   226

7 Capital accumulation, technical progress and techniques of production   227

Introduction   228

The role of capital in development   228

Technical progress   231

Capital- and labour-saving technical progress   232
How societies progress technologically   234
Learning   236
Investment in human capital: education   236
Women's education   240
Infrastructure investment   242
Technology and the developing countries   243
Techniques of production   245
The conflict between employment and output and employment and saving in
     the choice of techniques   249
Employment versus output   249
Employment versus saving   251
Wages and the capital intensity of production   252
Different classes' propensity to consume   253
Support of the unemployed   253
Are consumption and investment distinct?   254
Taxes and subsidies   254
Future policy   255
Summary   256
Discussion questions   257
Notes   257
Websites on technology and investment   258
Website on choice of techniques   258

Part III   The perpetuation of underdevelopment

8   Dualism, centre–periphery models and the process of
     cumulative causation   **261**
     Introduction   262
     Dualism   262
     The process of cumulative causation   264
     Regional inequalities   267
     International inequality and centre–periphery models   269
     Two models of 'regional' growth rate differences: Prebisch and Kaldor   271
     The new economic geography   276
     Theories of dependence and unequal exchange   278
     Unequal exchange   280
     Summary   281
     Discussion questions   282
     Notes   283

9   **Population and development**   **284**
     Introduction   285
     Facts about world population   285
     The determinants of fertility   288
     The costs and benefits of population growth   291

Population and the growth of cities   294
Simon's challenge   295
The 'optimum' population   297
A model of the low-level equilibrium trap   299
Summary   301
Discussion questions   302
Notes   302
Websites on population   302

Part IV The role of the state, the allocation of resources, and sustainable development

10 Resource allocation in developing countries, and sustainable development   305
Introduction   306
The market mechanism and market failures   306
The role of the state   308
Corruption   311
Failed states   316
Development plans   316
The allocation of resources: the broad policy choices   317
Industry versus agriculture   319
The comparative cost doctrine   319
Present versus future consumption   320
Choice of techniques   322
Balanced versus unbalanced growth   322
Investment criteria   326
Summary   327
Discussion questions   328
Notes   328
Websites on government and corruption   329

11 Project appraisal, social cost–benefit analysis and shadow wages   330
Introduction   331
Project appraisal   331
Financial appraisal   332
Economic appraisal   333
Divergences between market prices and social values   334
Economic prices for goods   335
Non-traded goods and conversion factors   336
Traded goods   338
Shadow prices for factors of production   338
The social rate of discount   339
The social cost of investment   339
The shadow wage rate   340
A closer examination of the change in consumption in industry and agriculture   342
The valuation of production forgone and the increase in consumption   343

A numerical calculation of the shadow wage   343
Social appraisal   344
The equivalence of the Little–Mirrlees formulation of the shadow wage and the
    UNIDO approach   346
Is it worth valuing all goods at world prices?   347
The application of the Little–Mirrlees and UNIDO approaches to
    project appraisal   347
Summary   349
Discussion questions   349
Notes   350
Websites on project appraisal   350

12   Development and the environment   **351**
Introduction   352
A model of the environment and economic activity   353
The market-based approach to environmental analysis   354
Externalities   355
Common property rights   358
The discount rate   359
The harvesting of renewable resources   360
Non-renewable resources   361
Other environmental values   363
Measuring environmental values   364
National income accounting   366
Risk and uncertainty   367
Economic growth and the environment   368
Sustainable development   369
Natural capital, equity and environmental values   370
Economic thought and the environment   373
Climate change and the Stern Review   373
Climate change and the poor   376
International agencies, agreements and the environment   377
Summary   379
Discussion questions   380
Notes   380
Websites on the environment   381

Part V   Financing economic development

13   Financing development from domestic resources   **385**
Introduction   386
Forms of saving   387
The prior-savings approach   392
The capacity to save   393
The willingness to save   395
Financial systems and economic development   397

The informal financial sector 398
Monetization and money market integration 399
Developing a banking system 400
Rural financial intermediaries and micro-credit 402
Development banks 405
Financial intermediaries 406
Financial liberalization 407
Fiscal policy and taxation 413
Tax reform in developing countries 419
Inflation, saving and growth 420
The Keynesian approach to the financing of development 420
Reconciling the prior-saving and forced-saving approaches to development 424
The quantity theory approach to the financing of development 424
The dangers of inflation 427
Inflation targeting 428
Inflation and growth: the empirical evidence 428
The inflationary experience 430
The structuralist–monetarist debate in Latin America 433
Summary 434
Discussion questions 435
Notes 436
Websites on banking and finance 436

14 Foreign assistance, aid, debt and development **437**
Introduction 438
The role of foreign borrowing 438
Dual-gap analysis and foreign borrowing 439
Models of capital imports and growth 442
Capital imports, domestic saving and the capital–output ratio 444
Types of international capital flows 445
The debate over international assistance to developing countries 445
The motives for official assistance 446
The critics of international aid 447
The macroeconomic impact of aid 449
The total net flow of financial resources to developing countries 453
Official development assistance (ODA) 454
Total net flow of financial resources from DAC countries 456
UK assistance to developing countries 456
The recipients of official assistance 459
Aid tying 463
Remittances 464
Multilateral assistance 465
World Bank activities 466
Structural adjustment lending 468
Poverty Reduction Strategy Papers 471
Estimating the aid component of international assistance 471

The distribution of international assistance   475
Schemes for increasing the flow of revenue   476
Foreign direct investment and multinational corporations   478
International debt and debt–service problems   481
Optimal borrowing and sustainable debt   486
The debt crisis of the 1980s   488
Debt relief   489
The highly indebted poor country initiative (HIPC)   490
Debt rescheduling   492
Debt–service capping   493
Debt buy-backs and debt swaps   493
Long-term solutions   494
Summary   495
Discussion questions   496
Notes   496
Websites on aid, remittances, debt and FDI   497

Part VI International trade, the balance of payments and development

15 **Trade theory, trade policy and economic development**   **501**
Introduction   502
Trade and growth   502
The gains from trade   505
The static gains from trade   506
The dynamic gains from trade   509
Trade as a vent for surplus   510
Theory of customs unions and free trade areas   510
Free trade enthusiasm in the modern era   514
Measurement and process of trade liberalization   515
Models of export-led growth   517
What you export matters   520
Trade liberalization and export growth   521
Trade liberalization, import growth and the balance of payments   522
Trade liberalization and economic performance   524
Trade liberalization, poverty and domestic inequality   526
Trade liberalization and international inequality   532
Disadvantages of free trade for development   533
Theory of protection: tariffs versus subsidies   535
Effective protection   537
Import substitution versus export promotion   539
The Prebisch doctrine   540
Technical progress and the terms of trade   540
The income elasticity of demand for products and the balance of payments   542
Recent trends in the terms of trade   543
Fair trade not free trade   546
Trade strategy for development   548

International commodity agreements 551
Trade versus aid 556
Summary 558
Discussion questions 559
Notes 559
Websites on trade 560

16 The balance of payments, international monetary assistance and development **561**
Introduction 562
Balance-of-payments-constrained growth 562
The terms of trade 565
The exchange rate and devaluation 566
The IMF supply-side approach to devaluation 568
The growth of world income and structural change 569
Application of the balance-of-payments-constrained growth model 569
Capital flows 571
Exchange-rate systems for developing countries 573
The East Asian financial crisis: a cautionary tale 577
The international monetary system and developing countries 583
How the IMF works 585
Ordinary drawing rights 586
Extended Fund Facility (EFF) 586
Special facilities 587
Other IMF activities 592
Criticisms of the IMF 593
The results of IMF programmes 595
Special Drawing Rights and the developing countries 596
Summary 599
Discussion questions 600
Notes 600
Websites on balance of payments and the IMF 601

References and Further Reading 602
Name Index 636
Subject Index 643
Geographic Index 673

LIST OF FIGURES

2.1	Lorenz curve diagram	34
2.2	Distribution of world income (percentage of total, with quintiles of population ranked by income)	38
2.3	Percentage of people in the world at different poverty levels, 2005	45
3.1	The law of diminishing returns	72
3.2	Natural resources and economic growth	77
3.3	Relation between productivity and energy intake	93
3.4	The distribution of the labour force 2005 (%)	103
3.5	The distribution of output 2005 (%)	103
3.6	Association between growth of industry and growth of GDP	108
5.1	Ricardo's model of the economy	137
5.2	Adjustment of g_w and g_n	144
5.3	The 'labour-intensive' form of the neoclassical production function	148
5.4	Equilibrium capital–labour ratio and output per head	148
5.5	The production function	151
5.6	Production function diagram	152
5.7	The effect of increasing returns	152
5.8	Kaldor's technical progress function	165
6.1	Marginal product of successive units of labour added to the land	201
6.2	Tendency towards diminishing returns	202
6.3	Industrial/capitalist sector	202
6.4	Industrial terms of trade and agricultural growth rate	205
6.5	Industrial terms of trade and industrial growth rate	206
6.6	Growth equilibrium and disequilibrium	206
6.7	Disguised unemployment	210
6.8	The dynamic surplus	212
6.9	Effect of labour withdrawal	213
6.10	Maximum sustainable labour	214
6.11	The possibility of negative marginal product	215
6.12	Backward-bending supply curve	215
6.13	The social valuation of labour	216
7.1	Capital-saving technical progress	232
7.2	Labour-saving technical progress	233
7.3	Neutral technical progress	233

7.4	Optimal choice of technique	245
7.5	Different wages: same technique	247
7.6	Efficiency frontier	250
7.7	Employment versus saving	251
7.8	Preserving the level of saving through taxation	255
8.1	Region A	265
8.2	Region B	265
8.3	Convergent–divergent growth	275
8.4	The theory of unequal exchange	281
9.1	Past and projected world population, AD 1–2150	287
9.2	Past and projected population growth rates	287
9.3	Past and projected fertility	288
9.4	Fertility rate and female literacy, 1990	289
9.5	Population momentum	291
9.6	Maximization of average product	298
9.7	The 'optimum' population	298
9.8	Low-level equilibrium trap	300
9.9	Leibenstein's approach	301
10.1	Welfare maximization	307
10.2	Functions of the state	315
10.3	Induced decision-making	324
11.1	The optimal shadow wage	340
12.1	Environmental indicators at different country income levels	352
12.2	A simple model of the relationships between the economy and the environment	353
12.3	Marginal benefits and environmental costs of a dam	356
12.4	Taxation, marginal benefits and costs of a dam	357
12.5	Relation between the growth and stock of a renewable resource	360
12.6	Economic rent and the use of a non-renewable resource	362
12.7	Sources of CO_2 emissions	375
13.1	The Keynesian absolute income hypothesis	393
13.2	The McKinnon–Shaw argument	408
13.3	Inflation tax	425
13.4	Inflation and per capita income growth, 1960–92 (pooled annual observations, 127 countries)	429
13.5	Effects of different inflation rates on growth	429
14.1	Official development assistance (ODA), 1950–2010	454
14.2	Ratio of ODA to GNI, 1960–2005	455
14.3	Estimated workers' remittances to developing countries by region in 2005 (US$ billion)	464
14.4	Debt–export ratio and growth	487
15.1	The relation between export growth and GDP growth across 133 countries, 1995–2006	503
15.2	Gains from trade	507
15.3	Gains and losses within a customs union	512
15.4	The share of world trade in world output, 1960–2006	514

15.5	The trade-off between growth and the balance of payments	524
15.6	Welfare gains and losses from protection	536
15.7	Tariffs and subsidies	537
15.8	Movements in the terms of trade	541
15.9	Asymmetrical cycles	541
15.10	Nominal and real price indices of non-food primary commodities, 1862–1999	544
15.11	Keynes's commod-control scheme	552
15.12	Price compensation and export earnings	555

LIST OF TABLES

2.1	Income per capita and population, 2007	29
2.2	A comparison of Gini ratios	35
2.3	Absolute poverty and poverty rates 1981–2005 (at PPP 2005)	44
2.4	Poverty gap index ($\times$100) by region, 1981–2005	46
2.5	Growth and poverty across the globe, 1990–2015	47
2.6	Human Development Index 2007 and its components	54
2.7	Human Poverty Index	63
2.8	Explaining growth of per capita GDP, 1960–88	65
3.1	Distribution of employment, by sector (percentage)	71
3.2	Savings and investment as a percentage of GDP, 2009	73
3.3	Population growth, 2000–2007 (% per annum)	76
3.4	Primary commodities as a percentage of total exports, 2007	76
3.5	Participation in education	84
3.6	Income inequality, selected economies, 1990s	86
3.7	Health indicators	96
3.8	The shares of output in GDP by region	104
5.1	Contribution of factor inputs and total productivity growth to industrial growth in Kenya, Tanzania, Zambia and Zimbabwe, 1964–81	159
5.2	Contribution of factor inputs and total productivity growth to economic growth in 68 developing countries, 1960–87	159
5.3	Growth of output and total factor productivity in the East Asian 'dragons', 1966–90 (%)	160
5.4	Sources of growth in China, 1953–94 (%)	160
5.5	Sources of growth by region of the world, 1960–94	161
5.6	The macrodeterminants of growth	167
6.1	Agricultural productivity, agriculture value-added per worker, 2005 ($)	183
A6.1	Land concentration and farm size in Asia and Latin America	219
7.1	Returns on investment in education (%), by continent, early 1990s	239
7.2	Returns on investment in education (%), by level of per capita income, early 1990s	240
7.3	Educational provision and literacy, females relative to males, 2005	241
7.4	Capital–labour substitution possibilities	250
8.1	Regional disparities within developed and developing countries	268
9.1	Population statistics	286

9.2	Total fertility rate (births per woman)	290
10.1	Transparency International's corruption perception index, 2008	312
10.2	Consumption benefits with different investment ratios over different planning horizons	321
11.1	Numerical example of the calculation of NPV	333
11.2	Values of the consumption distribution weight (d) for marginal changes in consumption	345
11.3	Comparison of the Little–Mirrlees and UNIDO approaches to project appraisal	348
12.1	Energy use and CO_2 emissions, 2006	375
13.1	Investment and savings as a percentage of GDP	389
13.2	Interest sensitivity of saving	397
13.3	Tax effort indices estimated over 1985–95	416
13.4	Inflation	431
14.1	Estimates of investment-savings and import–export gaps assuming a 5% growth of GDP, 2010–2015 ($ million)	442
14.2	Total net flow of financial resources from DAC countries to developing countries and multilateral organizations, by type of flow ($ million)	453
14.3	ODA and total net flow of financial resources from DAC countries to developing countries and multilateral agencies, 2007	455
14.4	Total net flow of financial resources from the United Kingdom to developing countries and multilateral agencies, 2007	456
14.5	The recipients of aid, 2007	459
14.6	Concessional and non-concessional flows by multilateral organizations, US$ million, at current prices and exchange rates	465
14.7	Distribution of World Bank lending, 2007	468
14.8	Grant element in loans at different discount rates	473
14.9	DAC members' ODA terms, 2007	475
14.10	FDI net inflows to top ten developing countries	479
14.11	Balance-of-payments effects of private foreign investment	481
14.12	The debt burden of developing countries, 2007	482
15.1	World market shares of manufactured exports of developing regions, 1981 and 2006	504
15.2	Income inequality in selected developing countries measured by the Gini ratio	530
16.1	Application of the balance-of-payments-constrained growth model to developing countries	570
16.2	Estimates of extended version of dynamic Harrod foreign trade multiplier, 1970–90 (annual percentage average)	572
16.3	Types of exchange-rate regime	574
16.4	Countries classified by exchange-rate regime	578
16.5	Balance of payments on current account, 1992–98 ($ million and % of GDP)	580
16.6	External financing of deficits in Asia-5 countries, 1994–97 ($ billion)	581
16.7	Outstanding IMF credit by facility and policy, 2000–2008	587
16.8	Access limits to IMF facilities, 2008 (% of member's quota)	589

LIST OF CASE EXAMPLES

1.1	Millennium Development Goals and Targets	13
2.1	The voices of the poor	48
2.2	Poor people's exposure to risk	50
3.1	Savings and investment in India and China: a comparison	74
3.2	Inequalities between groups can fuel conflict and tension	89
3.3	AIDS and life expectancy	95
3.4	China's industrial revolution	109
3.5	Testing Kaldor's growth laws across African countries	113
5.1	Findings of the Commission on Growth and Development	172
6.1	Land reform	190
6.2	Time for a second Green Revolution	194
6.3	The challenge of agricultural reform in India	196
7.1	Main messages from *World Development Report 2005* on investment	230
7.2	Bridging the technology divide	244
13.1	Vietnam's Bank on Wheels	401
13.2	Financial liberalization in Indonesia and Kenya, mid-1990s	412
14.1	Successes and failures of aid, 1970–1990s	448
14.2	Sectorwide development cooperation, mid-1990s	452
14.3	DFID Mission Statement	457
14.4	Rethinking conditionality	458
14.5	The IMF and the World Bank – what's the difference?	469
14.6	The highly indebted poor country initiative	491
14.7	How debt relief fits into a poverty-reduction strategy: Uganda's Poverty Action Fund	492
15.1	Globalization and manufacturing employment	527
15.2	Unfair trade in cotton	546
16.1	IMF lending facilities	589
16.2	Promoting financial system soundness	592

PREFACE

This book is a sequel to the eighth edition of *Growth and Development: with Special Reference to Developing Economies* published in 2006. Since the first edition of the book was published in 1972, it has been widely used as a text for courses in economic growth and development in both developed and developing countries, and has been translated into Greek and Chinese. This new 'edition' and new format of the book has given me the opportunity to substantially revise the content of the book, adding new chapters, updating statistics, and rewriting chapters to include new theoretical ideas and institutional material in order to improve the exposition to aid students and teachers alike.

But the purpose of the book remains the same: to introduce students to the exciting and challenging subject of development economics, which draws on several branches of economics in order to elucidate and understand the development difficulties facing the economies of the world's poor countries. This does not mean that the book provides a recipe or blueprint for development: far from it. There can be no general recipes of this nature, and even if there were, they would have to include more than economic ingredients.

The book combines description and analysis, with an emphasis on the elaboration of simple and useful theoretical economic models for an understanding of the issues that comprise the subject matter of development economics. I make no apology for the use of conventional economic theory. I concur with Theodore Schultz, the Nobel Prize-winning economist, who has said of development economics:

> This branch of economics has suffered from several intellectual mistakes. The major mistake has been the presumption that standard economic theory is inadequate for understanding low-income countries and that a separate economic theory is needed. Models for this purpose were widely acclaimed until it became evident that they were at best intellectual curiosities. The reaction of some economists was to turn to cultural and social explanations for the alleged poor economic performance of low income countries. Quite understandably, cultural and behavioural scholars are uneasy about this use of their studies. Fortunately the intellectual tide has begun to turn. Increasing numbers of economists have come to realise that standard economic theory is just as applicable to scarcity problems that confront low income countries as to the corresponding problems of high income countries.
>
> (T. W. Schultz, 'The Economics of Being Poor', *Journal of Political Economy*, August 1980)

This is not to say, of course, that *all* standard theory is useful and relevant for an understanding of the development process. In particular, the relevance of static equilibrium theory may be questioned. Nor is it possible to ignore non-economic factors in the growth and development process. The fact is, however, that the desire for material improvement in developing countries is very strong, and, in the final analysis, growth and development must be considered an economic process in the important practical sense that it is unlikely to proceed very far in the absence of an increase in the quantity and quality of the resources available for production. The book lays particular emphasis on the economic obstacles to development and the economic means by which developing countries may raise their rate of growth of output and living standards in order to reduce poverty.

For those new to the book, or for those now using the eighth edition, I outline below the main contents of each chapter and the changes introduced into this new edition.

The material in **Part I** of the book, 'Development and underdevelopment', consists of four major chapters which provide a basis for an understanding of the nature of poverty and underdevelopment in low-income countries, and therefore constitutes an important background for the rest of the book.

Chapter 1 addresses the subject matter of development economics, the meaning of development and the challenge of development economics. The globalization and interdependence of the world economy is emphasized, and there is a discussion of the call for a new international order, including a statement of the Millennium Development Goals.

Chapter 2 portrays the magnitude of the development gap between rich and poor countries in the world economy and discusses the measurement of poverty, including the attempt by the United Nations Development Programme (UNDP) to construct a Human Poverty Index and Human Development Index. There is discussion of the World Bank's approach to tackling poverty based on the ideas of empowering the poor and extending their capabilities as discussed in the *World Development Report* 2000/2001. New research is also reviewed on whether the global and international distribution of income is widening or narrowing.

Chapter 3 outlines the characteristics of underdevelopment and gives quantitative evidence of various dimensions of the development gap with respect to employment and unemployment, education, health, nutrition and the distribution of income within countries. The major characteristics of underdevelopment identified include the dominance of low-productivity agriculture and lack of industrialization, low levels of capital accumulation, rapid population growth, an export trade dominated by primary products, the 'curse of natural resources' and weak governance and institutions. These topics are discussed more fully in later chapters. The process of structural change is also addressed, as is the notion of industrialization as the engine of growth.

Chapter 4 is a new chapter which discusses the role of institutions in the development process. The importance of property rights and the rule of law is particularly emphasized, and the various institutions for regulating markets and providing social insurance. The important work of Rodrik on democracy is reviewed, and also the pioneering work of Acemoglu, Johnson and Robinson on the relationship between institutional development in colonized countries in the past and institutions today, and the debate on the importance of institutions versus geography in explaining differences in economic development.

Chapter 5 introduces students to various theories of economic growth. There are sections on classical growth theory (Adam Smith, Malthus, Ricardo and Marx), the Harrod–Domar growth model, neoclassical growth theory, and the 'new' endogenous growth theory which now dominates the literature on the applied economics of growth, with its stress on the importance of physical and human capital formation and research and development effort as the prime determinants of growth. Many empirical studies are surveyed, with regard to both the production function approach to understanding the growth process and to the macrodeterminants of growth approach using 'new' growth theory. There is a new section based on the work of Hausmann, Rodrik and others on growth accelerations, and the concept of 'growth diagnostics' and binding constraints on growth. If you find the technical details too difficult, you should proceed straight to Chapter 6 – but you will be missing a lot!

Part 2 of the book, 'Factors in the development process', contains two chapters: one on the role of agriculture and surplus labour for industrialization; the other on capital accumulation, technical progress and techniques of production.

Chapter 6 deals with the different contributions that agriculture makes to the development process, one of which is a source of cheap labour for industry. Particular attention is paid to the influential Lewis model of economic development with unlimited supplies of labour. There is explicit treatment, following on from Lewis, of the interaction and complementarity between agriculture and industry, with a number of interesting insights into the importance of demand expansion from agriculture as a stimulus to industrial growth and of achieving an equilibrium terms of trade between the two sectors. There is also a discussion of barriers to raising agricultural productivity, highlighted by the World Bank's *World Development Report 2008*. There is a new Appendix on how markets function in the rural agricultural sector, and how the land, labour and credit markets interlock, based on uncertainty of agricultural output and the risk aversion of agents.

Chapter 7 is on the role of capital accumulation and technical progress in the development process and contains sections on the importance of infrastructure investment and empirical estimates of the rates of return to human capital. The choice of appropriate techniques of production is also explored, and the potential conflicts involved in moving towards the use of more labour-intensive techniques – between employment and output on the one hand and between employment and saving on the other. The role played by multinational corporations in dictating technological choice is also examined.

Part 3 of the book, 'The perpetuation of underdevelopment', focuses on factors that can perpetuate underdevelopment, including poverty itself (causing a vicious circle) and rapid population growth.

Chapter 8 is on dualism and Myrdal's concept of the process of circular and cumulative causation. This chapter describes the mechanisms by which economic divisions between regions and between countries tend to be perpetuated and widened. The chapter includes the early centre–periphery models of Prebisch and Kaldor, together with discussion of the new economic geography pioneered by Krugman. The views of Marxist writers, including Emmanuel's model of unequal exchange, are also presented.

Chapter 9 is on population and development and attempts to evaluate the debate on whether population expansion is a growth-inducing or growth-retarding force. Particular attention is devoted to the early work of Enke and to the recent work of Simon. The facts on population growth are clearly outlined, with a discussion of the determinants of fertility.

Part 4 of the book covers the broad topic 'The role of the state, the allocation of resources and sustainable development'.

Chapter 10 is on resource allocation in developing countries and considers the market mechanism versus the role of the state. Market imperfections, market failures and corruption are highlighted, as are the limited capabilities of the state, drawing on the extensive analysis contained in the World Bank's *World Development Report*, 1997. Some of the broader issues of development strategy are also considered, including the case for planning. There is a new section on failed states.

Chapter 11 is devoted exclusively to social cost–benefit analysis, highlighting the distinction between the financial, economic and social appraisal of projects. The main emphasis is on comparing and contrasting the approaches of Little and Mirrlees (using world prices) on the one hand and the United Nations (using domestic prices and the shadow exchange) on the other. Attention is given to the relation between the shadow exchange rate and the standard conversion factor rates used by Little and Mirrlees for the repricing of non-traded goods. The chapter contains a lengthy discussion of the determination of the shadow wage rate, and how to take account of the distributional effects of project choice.

Chapter 12, written by my colleague Dr John Peirson, discusses how environmental issues may be incorporated into social cost–benefit analysis, and the new and important concept of sustainable development which is the subject of the World Bank's *World Development Reports 1992, 2002* and *2010*. There are new sections on the Stern Review on climate change, and the impact of climate change on the poor.

Part 5 of the book, 'Financing of economic development', covers both domestic and foreign resources.

Chapter 13 deals with the financing of development from domestic resources. There is a full discussion of the theory of financial liberalization, together with critiques and empirical evidence of the relation between real interest rates, saving, investment and growth. There is new material on the financial system in developing countries and the relationship between financial development and economic development. Fiscal policy and taxation are also discussed, together with the topic of forced saving through inflation. New research is reported on the relation between inflation and growth, and there is a new section on inflation targeting.

Chapter 14 is on the finance of development from external resources. All the statistics relating to foreign resource inflows have been updated, including a new section on remittances from abroad. The whole aid debate is reviewed, and the impact of aid on development. There are new sections on the macroeconomic impact of aid and the critics of aid. Structural adjustment lending by the World Bank, and the role of foreign direct investment in the development process, are both examined. The debt-servicing problems created by foreign borrowing are thoroughly surveyed, and there is extensive discussion of the debt crisis of the 1980s, which still lingers today, together with the latest schemes designed to reduce the debt burden of highly indebted countries.

Part 6 of the book covers the topic 'Trade, the balance of payments and development'.

Chapter 15 is on trade theory, trade policy and economic development. The static and dynamic gains from trade are thoroughly explored (including the theory of customs unions and free trade areas), as are the ways in which the present pattern of trade works to the relative disadvantage of poor countries. The tendency of the terms of trade to deteriorate, and for balance of payments difficulties to arise, is stressed. There are new sections on the theory and practice of trade liberalization, and the impact that trade liberalization has had on export growth, import growth, the balance of payments, economic growth, domestic income inequality and international inequality. What trade policies poor countries should pursue are also examined, and the arguments given for various forms of protection.

Chapter 16 is on the balance of payments and development, and discusses the important concept of balance-of-payments-constrained growth and the various policy responses to this constraint at the national and international level. The latter involves a consideration of the extensive facilities afforded by the International Monetary Fund (IMF) for balance-of-payments support. Some of the criticisms levelled at the IMF are also considered. There is an analysis of the different types of exchange-rate systems that developing countries can adopt, and lessons to be drawn from the financial crisis in East Asia in 1997. The chapter ends with a discussion of Special Drawing Rights as a potential form of international assistance to developing countries.

This new edition continues to provide the addresses of **websites**, chapter by chapter, to guide students to relevant information and data on the Internet. By the time the next edition of this book becomes due in 2016, the facts pertaining to developing countries will again be out of date, and no doubt there will have been new institutional changes and innovations in thinking about development strategy. To keep abreast with what is going on, students are encouraged to consult such publications as the World Bank's *World Development Report*, the IMF's *Finance and Development* (published quarterly in several different languages), *The Human Development Report* published by the United Nations Development Programme and *The Least Developed Countries Report* and *Trade and Development Report* published by the United Nations Conference on Trade and Development, as well as journals such as *World Development, Journal of Development Studies, Journal of Development Economics, Journal of International Development, Economic Development and Cultural Change, Oxford Development Studies* and the *World Bank Economic Review*.

I am deeply grateful to the economics editor of Palgrave Macmillan, Jaime Marshall, for encouraging me to write this new version of the book that has now been going for nearly 40 years. It needed a new image and substantial rewriting. I owe an enormous debt of gratitude to his assistant, Aléta Bezuidenhout, for supporting me along the way, to Elizabeth Stone for her expert copy-editing, and to all the production team at Palgrave Macmillan, who helped in various ways.

But most of all, my thanks go to my partner, Penélope Pacheco-López, for all her technical assistance in preparing the tables, checking references and typing, not to mention her wise advice. Without her, the book would never have seen the light of day, and I dedicate it to her and our new son, Oliver Anthony.

Visit the author's website: www.kent.ac.uk/economics/staff/profiles/tony-thirlwall.html.

UNIVERSAL DECLARATION OF HUMAN RIGHTS

Everyone has the right to a standard of living adequate for the health and well-being of himself and of his family, including food, clothing, housing and medical care and the necessary social services and the right to security in the event of unemployment, sickness, disability, widowhood, old age or other lack of livelihood in circumstances beyond his control.

(Article 25 adopted by the UN General Assembly, 10 December 1948)

ACKNOWLEDGEMENTS

The author and publishers wish to thank the following organizations for permission to use material previously contained in their publications: *The Times* Newspaper Group; the *Financial Times*; the *Guardian* newspaper; University of Sussex; the American Economic Association; Pergamon Press; and Edward Elgar from my book *Trade Liberalization and the Poverty of Nations* (with Penélope Pacheco-López).

Photographic acknowledgements

1. Gunnar Myrdal (UN Photo)
2. Muhammad Yunus (Getty Images)
3. Robert Solow (Photograph by Donna Coveney/MIT, reproduced by kind permission of Professor Solow)
4. Amartya Sen (reproduced by kind permission of Professor Sen)
5. Dani Rodrik (reproduced by kind permission of Professor Rodrik)
6. Hans Singer (Gary Edwards/Institute of Development Studies)
7. Raúl Prebisch (reproduced by kind permission of Doctor Eliana Diaz Prebisch)
8. Nicholas Kaldor (reproduced by kind permission of the Estate of Professor Kaldor)
9. Walt Rostow (Time & Life Pictures/Getty Images)
10. Adam Smith (Time & Life Pictures/Getty Images)
11. Thomas Malthus (Getty Images)
12. Karl Marx (Getty Images)
13. Arthur Lewis (Getty Images)
14. David Ricardo (Getty Images)
15. Roy Harrod (Getty Images)
16. Joseph Stiglitz (AFP/Getty Images)

I

DEVELOPMENT AND UNDERDEVELOPMENT

1

THE STUDY OF ECONOMIC DEVELOPMENT

- **Introduction**
- **Development economics as a subject**
- **Academic interest in development**
- **A new international economic order**
- **Globalization and interdependence of the world economy**
- **The meaning of development and the challenge of development economics**
- **The perpetuation of underdevelopment**
- **Summary**
- **Discussion questions**
- **Websites**

Introduction

I ask the reader (especially the young student) to consider, behind a veil of ignorance (Rawls, 1972), what sort of world they would prefer to have been born into. A world in which 1.4 billion people live on less than $1.25 a day (the official World Bank poverty line), 2.5 billion live on less than $2 a day, and with only a 5 per cent chance of living a luxurious lifestyle or in a fairer world which provides a decent living standard for everyone wherever they are born – whether in Norway, the richest country, or Burundi, the poorest? Whatever answer you give, you will have shown an interest in **development economics**, which seeks to understand and explain why some countries are poor and others rich, and how to reduce poverty in poor countries to give everyone on the planet a minimum standard of life and freedom from hunger and fear of the future.

Development economics as it is understood and taught today is a relatively new sub-discipline of economics dating from the early years after the Second World War; but in fact the economic progress of nations has always been at the heart of economic enquiry, at least since the time of the great classical economists of the late eighteenth century and the first half of the nineteenth century – Adam Smith, Thomas Malthus, David Ricardo, John Stuart Mill and Karl Marx. These writers were all concerned with understanding the growth and development process of countries and the factors determining the distribution of income between classes of people. Modern development economics has in many ways revived the old interests of the classical economists concerning the importance of saving, investment, capital accumulation and the mobilization of surplus labour for structural change out of agriculture into manufacturing industry and service activities.

In this chapter we start by considering development economics as a subject – and academic interest in development issues – and why there has been a revival of development economics in the last 60 years, with many of the world's best economists researching and writing on development matters. One of the major contributory factors has been the poorer countries of the world calling for a fairer deal from the functioning of the world economy, which they view as being biased against them. This demand for a **new international economic order** has been endorsed by all the major multilateral agencies established after the Second World War to oversee international relations and a smoother functioning of the world economy after the economic chaos of the pre-war era: the United Nations and its several affiliates, the World Bank for Reconstruction and Development and the International Monetary Fund. We shall discuss what a new international economic order might consist of, and the components of the **Millennium Development Goals** laid down in 2000, to be achieved by 2015. Is the world on track?

Another major factor responsible for the growing interest and concern with developing countries, and the process of economic development itself, has been the increased **globalization** of the world economy, which has led to a greater **interdependence** between countries of the world. We shall consider what globalization means, and what forms interdependence takes.

We then turn to the meaning of development and the challenge of development economics, focusing particularly on the ideas of Denis Goulet and Amartya Sen, who argue powerfully and persuasively that economic development must mean much more than just a rise in the average level of per capita income of a country. A concept of development is required that embraces all of the economic and social objectives and values that countries strive for – not simply material progress but, in particular, the self-esteem of peoples and nations, and freedom.

We end the chapter by considering the perpetuation of underdevelopment and poverty; that is, the forces in the world economy that historically have produced and continue today to create divisions between rich and poor countries, and even widen them. Differences in the structure of production between countries, unequal trade, the dependency of poor countries on rich countries, and the operation of international institutions can all interact to produce 'vicious circles' of poverty and relative stagnation for countries that get left behind in the development 'race'.

Development economics as a subject

The study of development economics as a separate subject in economics is a relatively new phenomenon. For the student today it will be difficult to appreciate that as recently as 60 years ago a course in development economics was a rare feature of an undergraduate programme in economics, and that textbooks on economic development were few and far between. Today, no respectable department of economics is without at least one course in economic development; there are scores of texts and thousands of case studies and articles on the subject.

The political and public concern with the poorer nations of the world is of equally recent origin. The majority of the national and international bodies that exist today to promote development, such as national development banks, the World Bank and its affiliates, and agencies of the United Nations, were established after the Second World War. Before the war, when most of today's poor countries were still colonies, there was much less focus on the economic and social problems of the developing (dependent) economies than there is today. Perhaps the facts were not so well known, or perhaps the attention of most people was focused on depression and unemployment in the developed countries. Whatever the reason for this neglect, the situation today is very different. The development of the Third World (the collective name for the developing countries), meaning above all the eradication of primary poverty, is now regarded as one of the greatest social and economic challenges facing mankind, together with environmental pollution and climate change. As the Pearson Report (1969) remarked a generation ago, 'the widening gap between the developed and the developing countries has become the central problem of our times'.

What accounts for this change in attitude and upsurge of interest in the economics of development and the economies of poor countries? A number of factors can be pinpointed, which interrelate with one another.

- First, in the wake of the great depression of the 1930s, and in the aftermath of war, there was renewed interest among professional economists in the growth and development process and in the theory and practice of planning.
- Second, the poor countries themselves have become increasingly aware of their own backwardness, which has led to a natural desire for more rapid economic progress.
- Third, the absolute numbers of poor people are considerably greater now than in the past, and greater awareness has struck a humanitarian chord in the world at large.
- Fourth, there has been a growing recognition by all concerned of the interdependence between countries in the world economy. The Cold War between the capitalist West and the communist East led the major developed countries to show a growing economic and political interest in poor and ideologically uncommitted nations. The political and military ramifications and dangers of a world divided into rich and poor countries are even more serious now than they were in the past. The recognition of interdependence has also been heightened in recent years by the process of globalization making all countries more vulnerable to shocks and financial crises, which spread through trade and capital movements.

Academic interest in development

As mentioned in the introduction to this chapter, academic interest in the mechanics of growth and development is a *renewed* interest rather than an entirely new preoccupation of economists. The progress and material well-being of people and nations have traditionally been at the centre of economic writing and enquiry. It constituted one of the major areas of interest of the classical economists. Adam Smith, David Ricardo, Thomas Malthus, John Stuart Mill and Karl Marx all dealt at some length (albeit with divergent opinions on many issues) with the causes and consequences of economic advance (see Chapter 5). It is entirely natural that thinkers of the day should comment on the contemporary scene. There is perhaps an analogy here between the preoccupation of the classical economists at the time of Britain's industrial revolution in the eighteenth and nineteenth centuries and the concern of many economists today with the economics of development and world poverty, the nature of which has been brought to the attention of the world so dramatically in recent decades. The list of modern-day economists who have turned their fertile minds to the study of economic development reads like a *Who's Who* of economics. Distinguished economists (past and present) that immediately come to mind are Pranab Bardhan, Jagdish Bhagwati, Hollis Chenery, Paul Collier, Partha Dasgupta, Albert Hirschman, Harry Johnson, Nicholas Kaldor, Michal Kalecki, Paul Krugman, Simon Kuznets, Harvey Leibenstein, Arthur Lewis, James Mirrlees, Gunnar Myrdal, Raúl Prebisch, Dani Rodrik, Joan Robinson, Paul Rosenstein-Rodan, Walt Rostow, Jeffrey Sachs, Theodore Schultz, Amartya Sen, Hans Singer, Nicholas Stern, Joseph Stiglitz and Jan Tinbergen (my apologies to those I have left out!).

Development also represents a challenge equivalent to that of the depression and mass unemployment in the 1930s, which attracted so many brilliant minds to economics, John Maynard Keynes among them. But the nature of the challenge is of course very different. In the case of unemployment in the 1930s, there was an orthodox theory with which to grapple; the task was to formulate a theory to fit the facts and to offer policy prescriptions. As it turned out, the solution to the problem was to be costless: expand demand by creating credit and bring idle resources into play. Fancy, an economic problem solved costlessly – there is such a thing as a 'free lunch'!

The challenge of development is very different. There is no divorce between theory and the observed facts. The mainsprings of growth and development are well known: increases in the quantity and quality of resources of all kinds. Countries are poor because they lack resources or the willingness and ability to bring them into use. The problems posed by underdevelopment cannot be solved without cost. It would be reassuring to think, however, that advances in growth theory, coupled with more detailed understanding of the sources of growth and the refinement of techniques for resource allocation, have all increased the possibility of more rapid economic progress than hitherto. Certainly, particular theoretical models and techniques have been used extensively in some countries, presumably in this belief. For example, models for calculating investment requirements to achieve a target rate of growth invariably form an integral part of a development plan; and now the so-called 'new' growth theory (see Chapter 5) provides the rationale and impetus for improving the quality of investment through education, research and development, and infrastructure investment. Good governance must also play a vital role.

The question is often posed as to what lessons, if any, the present developing countries can draw from the first-hand observations of the classical writers or, more directly, from the development experience of the present advanced nations. One obvious lesson is that while development can be regarded as a natural process, it is also a lengthy one, at least left to itself. It is easy to forget that it took Europe the best part of three centuries to progress from a subsistence state to economic maturity. Much of development economics is concerned with the timescale of development, and how to speed up the process of development in a way that is consistent with freedom and democracy. Later in the present millennium, when primary poverty in most countries will, one hopes, have been eradicated, courses in development economics will undoubtedly take a different form. The emphasis will be on inter-country comparisons rather than on the process of development as such and on the growth pains accompanying the transition from a primarily agrarian to an industrial or service economy.

As far as classical economic theory is concerned, the gloomy prognostication of Ricardo, Malthus and Mill that progress will ultimately end in stagnation would seem to be unfounded. It has certainly been confounded by experience. Population growth and diminishing returns in agriculture have not been uniformly depressive to the extent that Ricardo and Malthus supposed. Rising productivity and per capita incomes appear quite compatible with the growth of population and the extension of agriculture. Classical development economics greatly underestimated the beneficial role of technical progress and international trade in the development process. It is these two factors above all others which seem to have confounded the pessimism of much of classical theory. With access to superior technology there is hope, and some evidence, that material progress in today's developing countries will be much more rapid than in countries at a similar stage of development 150 years ago. The pool of technology on which to draw, and the scope for its assimilation, is enormous. Used with discretion, it must be considered as the main means of increasing welfare.

The role of trade, however, is more problematic. Much will depend on how rapidly the developing countries can alter their industrial structure, and on movements in the terms of trade. Currently, the developing countries are probably in an inferior position compared with the present advanced countries at a comparable stage of their economic history. There are potential dynamic gains from trade, but the static efficiency gains are weak based on primary production, and the terms of trade in most commodities are worse. The gains from trade accrue mainly to the rich industrialized countries, notwithstanding the rapid increase that periodically takes place in some commodity prices as witnessed in recent years. The fact that the gains from trade are unequally distributed does not, of course, destroy the potential link between trade and growth, or constitute an argument against trade. Rather, it represents a challenge for altering the structure of trade and the terms on which it takes place.

Then there is the question of planning. Classical economists were generally opposed to interference with the market mechanism, believing that the free play of market forces would maximize the social good. But fashions change in economics, and after the Second World War there was a much greater acceptance of interference with the market mechanism, so that planning in developing countries was seen by many as one of the main means by which economic development could be accelerated. In many countries the experience of planning has not been favourable, however, and planning has come into disrepute, not least because of the economic disarray of the rigidly planned economies of the old Soviet Union and Eastern Europe. It should never be forgotten, however, that no country in the world ever made such a swift economic advance in such a short space of time as the Soviet Union did after 1918, through a planned allocation of resources that favoured investment at the expense of consumption. The fact that planning may be operated too rigidly, or for too long and go wrong, should not be allowed to obscure the fact that it also has merits, and that unfettered free enterprise can also lead to economic disaster and social deprivation. There can be market failure as well as government failure. What is required in most developing countries is a judicious mix of public and private enterprise, with the use of markets combined with different types of government involvement, for the maximization of social welfare. The state has a role to play in economic development (see Chapter 10).

Planning requires a certain amount of model building, and this too has been inspired by economists. The most common type of model, which forms the basis of much of the model-building that developing countries practise, is to calculate the investment requirements necessary to achieve a target rate of growth of per capita income – commonly referred to as a Harrod–Domar model (see Chapter 5). Neither the models of Harrod (1939) or Domar (1947) were designed for the purpose to which they are now put in developing countries, but their growth equations have proved to be an indispensable component of macroeconomic planning. We shall consider in Chapter 10 the strengths and weaknesses of using this type of aggregate model in development planning, and the arguments for and against planning in general.

As a result of the apparent failure of development planning and the slow progress made by many developing countries in the 1970s, the status of the discipline of development economics began to be called into question in the 1980s and several obituaries of the subject were written (see, e.g., Hirschman, 1981; Little, 1982; Lal, 1983). I will concentrate here on the worries expressed by Hirschman, the practitioner who first rang the alarm bells most vigorously. Hirschman argues that development economics was originally born out of a rejection of monoeconomics (that is, the universality of neoclassical economics) on the one hand and of neo-Marxism on the other, which asserted that economic relations between developed and less developed countries could only lead to the development of underdevelopment. The two themes at the forefront of the rejection of monoeconomics were (1) the existence of a massive amount of surplus labour in agriculture in developing countries and (2) backwardness or late industrialization – the latter requiring active state intervention. In terms of policy, the major strategic themes emphasized and pursued by developing countries were the mobilization of underemployed manpower, rapid capital accumulation and industrialization, for all of which planning was thought to be necessary.

Hirschman's first explanation of the alleged demise of development economics is the resurgence of neoclassical orthodoxy and rejection of the view that there is a separate economics applicable to poor countries, as distinct from the developed ones. The defence of monoeconomics has been buttressed by the observed success of some ostensibly free market developing countries, such as South Korea, Hong Kong, Taiwan and Singapore (the so-called 'East Asian miracle' countries), and the failure of planning in others.

Early development economics not only asserted the need for a separate economics applicable to developing countries, but also believed that the integration of developing countries into the world economy would bring material benefits to rich and poor alike. Hirschman's second explanation of the alleged demise of development economics is that the subject has not only been attacked by the neoclassical school, but also by neo-Marxists who reject the claim of mutual benefit. Thus development economics has been squeezed, as if in a vice, from both ends of the politico-economic spectrum.

What can be said in response? It is not difficult to defend the traditional preoccupations of development theory and development policy. Amartya Sen (1983) and Syed Naqvi (1996) show that the focus on **mobilizing surplus labour, capital accumulation and industrialization** has not been misplaced. It can be seen from the international evidence that many high-growth countries (and this is particularly true of South-East Asian countries, including China) have drawn extensively on surplus labour from the rural sector; that investment and growth are highly correlated across countries; and that the best growth performers are those countries where the share of industrial output in gross domestic product (GDP) is rising most rapidly. Those defending the rejection of monoeconomics have not retreated into their shells, and very few economists would disagree that there is mutual benefit to be had from country interaction. It is not conceivable that the majority of developing countries would be absolutely better off if they were isolated and autarchic, although this is not to say that some 'delinking' and strategic protection may not be desirable and that the gains from globalization and interdependence could not be more equitably distributed across countries.

But is there a separate 'development economics'? Most observers would still argue that poor countries differ from the rich in such a way that different concepts, models and theories are required to understand their functioning in many respects. While it might be argued that the basic microeconomic assumptions about how people behave are similar for all countries, developing countries still differ *structurally* from rich ones and therefore require different models. The differences between the two sets of countries are large, particularly in relation to resource allocation and matters relating to long-term growth. It is not accidental that social cost–benefit analysis has been largely developed and refined within the context of developing countries, nor that developing countries have been the breeding ground for theories of tendencies towards disequilibrium in economic and social systems – models of virtuous and vicious circles and centre–periphery models of growth and development. But as Arthur Lewis, one of the fathers of development economics, once said in his presidential lecture to the American Economic Association, the central task of development economics is to provide a general framework for an understanding of the pace and rhythm of growth and development. As he put it: 'the economists' dream would be to have a single theory of growth that took an economy from the lowest level . . . past the dividing line . . . up to the level of Western Europe and beyond . . . or to have at least one good theory for the developing economy . . . to the dividing line' (Lewis, 1984). That is what development economics is all about. **Development economics is the only branch of economics that attempts to understand and explain the nature of the development process** (Naqvi, 1996).

But even if the need for a separate development economics could not be established, would this jeopardize the status of the subject? It might be argued that in the interests of scientific respectability there is a strong case for thinking of economics as a unified body of theory and doctrine, and not a subject of compartments. What leads to compartmentalization is the wide diversity of subject areas, which then gives rise to the descriptive labels of monetary economics, labour economics, regional economics and so on, but all these sub-disciplines employ a large measure of theory that is common to economics as a whole.

What distinguishes the sub-discipline is first and foremost the area of application and only secondarily the distinctive theory. A favourite definition of economics is that 'economics is what economists do'. By analogy, 'development economics is what development economists do'. The development literature indicates that they do a number of things that other economists do not do, and in the process they both invent new models, and adapt and modify existing theory in the light of circumstances. Any contribution that a sub-discipline makes by way of theoretical development enriches economics as a whole, and may well have application elsewhere. New models, concepts and ideas invented by development economists include the following:

- The concept of the low-level equilibrium trap
- The theory of the 'big push'
- Dynamic externalities
- Models of dualism
- The theory of circular and cumulative causation

- The concept of dependency
- Growth pole analysis
- Models of population and growth
- Models of rural–urban migration
- Refinements to social cost–benefit analysis
- The notion of immiserising growth
- Models of structural inflation
- The concept of dual-gap analysis
- The theory of missing markets
- The study of rent-seeking; and so on.

None of these innovations has been borrowed from other branches of economics, but other branches of economics have borrowed liberally from the expanding tool kit forged by development economists. International economics is no longer taught within the straitjacket of equilibrium economics. Labour economics has taken on board the concepts of dualism and dual labour markets, while structural inflation and dual-gap analysis are part of the language of macroeconomics. As Bardhan (1993) concludes:

> While the problems of the world's poor remain as overwhelming as ever, studying them has generated enough analytical ideas and thrown up enough challenges to the dominant paradigm to make all of us in the profession somewhat wiser, and at least somewhat more conscious of the possibilities and limitations of our existing methods of analysis.

Finally, how should one respond to the charge that development economics has not produced the results expected of it? As Hirschman (1981) puts it, the developing countries were 'expected to perform like wind-up toys and "lumber through" the various stages of development single-mindedly . . . these countries were perceived to have only *interests* and no passions'. If the expectations have not materialized, this probably has more to do with the expectations being unrealistic than with deficiencies in the theory and practice of development economics. This in turn may have something to do with economists in general losing their historical sense and perspective. The process of development is a long, protracted process. It took over 200 years for the present developed countries to progress from Rostow's traditional stage of economic development to economic maturity and high mass consumption. Arthur Lewis (1984) bemoans the loss of historical perspective, which he attributes to the poor training of economists:

> If our subject is lowering its sights, this may be because the demise of economic history in economics departments has brought us a generation of economists with no historical background. This is in marked contrast with the development economists of the 1950s, practically all of whom had some historical training, and guided by Gerschenkron and Rostow, looked to history for enlightenment on the processes of development.

Students beware: Learn your history!

Where do we stand today? At present there is a resurgence of academic interest in the growth and development process, inspired by the 'new' endogenous growth theory and the increased availability of large data sets that facilitate interesting and rigorous econometric work on the major determinants of inter-country growth performance. Paul Krugman (1992) has described the 1950s and 1960s as the years of 'high development theory', when many important models of development were formulated but were lost sight of because they were not formulated rigorously enough. Now the ideas are being brought back into play by more skilled theoreticians. The central core of ideas that emerged in the 1950s and 1960s, which were largely swept away during the neoclassical counter-revolution, but which Krugman believes still remain valid, were **external economies, increasing returns, complementarity between sectors** and **linkages**. It is these ideas that have been recaptured by the 'new' endogenous growth theory (and which remained alive outside the mainstream in the works of such economists as Nicholas Kaldor and Kenneth Arrow – see Chapter 5).

'New' growth theory provides an answer to the question of why per capita income differences in the world economy seem to be as persistent as ever when conventional neoclassical growth theory predicts convergence. The answer is that there are many externalities that prevent the marginal product of capital from falling as countries get richer, so that the level of investment matters for growth, and growth is endogenous in this sense – not simply determined by an exogenously given rate of technical progress, common to all countries. Indeed, technical progress is also largely endogenous, determined by research and development (R&D) and education. This theory tells us what sustains growth, but it does not address the question of what it is that gets growth started. To answer this we need to go to the roots of economic development, which initially lie in the performance of the rural economy and agriculture (see Chapter 6).

A new international economic order

Another major factor accounting for the upsurge of interest in the growth and development process has been the poor nations' own increased awareness of their inferior economic and political status in the world, and their desire for material improvement and greater political recognition through economic strength. This was precipitated by decolonization in the 1950s and 1960s and increased contact with the developed nations, and has been strengthened from within by rising expectations as development has proceeded. Development is wanted to provide people with the basic necessities of life; for their own sake, and to provide a degree of self-esteem and freedom for people, which is precluded by poverty. Wealth and material possessions may not necessarily provide greater happiness but they widen the choices that individuals have, which is an important aspect of freedom and welfare. The developing countries have also called for a fairer deal from the functioning of the world economy, which they view, with some justification, as biased in favour of countries that are already rich.

The official call for a **new international economic order** was first made during the Sixth Special Session of the United Nations General Assembly in 1974. The United Nations pledged itself

> to work urgently for the establishment of a new international economic order based on equity, sovereign equality, common interest and cooperation among all states, irrespective of their economic and social systems, which shall correct inequalities and redress existing injustices, make it possible to eliminate the widening gap between the developed and the developing countries and ensure steadily accelerating economic and social development and peace and justice for present and future generations.

The programme of action called for such things as:

- Improved terms of trade for the exports of poor countries
- Greater access to the markets of developed countries for manufactured goods
- Greater financial assistance and the alleviation of past debt
- Reform of the International Monetary Fund and a greater say in decision-making on international bodies concerned with trade and development issues

- An international food programme
- Greater technical cooperation.

The call for a new international economic order has been reiterated several times by various UN agencies. In 1975 the United Nations Industrial Development Organization (UNIDO) produced the **Lima Declaration**, which set a target for the developing countries to secure a 25 per cent share of world manufacturing production by the year 2000 compared with the share then of 10 per cent. The target was just met, thanks to rapid industrial growth in East Asia and the Pacific, and the share now stands at 29 per cent. On the monetary front, in 1980 the **Arusha Declaration** demanded a UN Conference on International Money and Finance to create a new international monetary order 'capable of achieving monetary stability, restoring acceptable levels of employment and sustainable growth' and 'supportive of a process of global development'. This goal has not been achieved.

In 1995 a UN World Development Summit was held in Copenhagen, focusing on social development and employment issues. The **Copenhagen Declaration** made several commitments:

- Full employment, equality between men and women, and universal access to education and health care should be basic priorities
- Overall development aid should be increased for spending in areas of social policy
- Developed countries should allocate 20 per cent of their aid to basic social projects and in return developing countries should spend at least 20 per cent of their budgets on social needs
- The IMF and the World Bank should pay more attention to social factors when designing programmes.

Progress in these areas has been slow.

The United Nations Conference on Trade and Development (UNCTAD) regularly calls for new policy initiatives in the four major areas of debt relief, international aid, commodity policy and trade promotion for developing countries.

Millennium Development Goals

The latest commitment endorsed by the World Bank and the United Nations (UN) is for the percentage of the world's population living in absolute poverty to be halved by the year 2015 compared with the level in 1990. Using the poverty rate of $1.25 a day, this means a reduction from 41.6 per cent to 20.8 per cent. In 2005 the level was 25.2 per cent, although it is much higher than this in particular countries (see Table 2.3 in Chapter 2). In addition several other development goals and targets have been set, outlined fully in Case example 1.1 below. They relate to:

- Enrolling all children in primary school by 2015
- Making progress towards gender equality, particularly in education
- Reducing child mortality
- Reducing maternal mortality
- Providing universal access to reproductive health services
- Implementing national strategies for sustainable development and to reverse the loss of environmental resources.

Each of the goals addresses an aspect of poverty, and all are mutually reinforcing. For example, higher school enrolment, especially for girls, reduces poverty and mortality. Better basic health care will increase school enrolment and reduce poverty. Many poor people earn their living from the environment, so a better environment will help poor people.

On average, the poverty rate tends to fall by about 1 per cent for every 1 per cent increase in per capita income. A 50 per cent reduction in the poverty rate compared with 1990 therefore requires a 50 per cent increase in per capita income between 1990 and 2015, or approximately 2 per cent per annum. Many countries are on track, and the global target of a 20.8 per cent poverty rate in 2015 looks like being met, but several African countries are off-track, and world hunger will still remain above target.

On the other Millennium Development Goals, progress is mixed. With regard to universal primary education, it looks as if about 60 countries will not reach the target by 2015, again mainly in Africa. The gender gap in education between boys and girls is narrowing, but will not be eliminated in most countries by 2015. Child mortality is still high. Ten million children in poor countries die before their fifth birthday. The mortality rate is falling slowly, but will not have been reduced by two-thirds by 2015. Likewise, maternal death rate reduction is way off target. Half a million women die in pregnancy and childbirth in poor countries every year, and the mortality rate is hardly falling. Progress in combating HIV/AIDS, malaria and other major diseases is more encouraging, and there may be an absolute reduction in the incidence of these diseases by 2015 if current trends continue. Finally, with regard to the state of the environment, and particularly with respect to access to sanitation and safe water, progress has been very slow. Lack of sanitation, polluted water and poor hygiene still kill nearly 8 million children a year. Lack of progress in this field makes some of the other Millennium Development Goals more difficult to achieve (see World Bank, *Global Monitoring Report*).

Case example 1.1	Millennium Development Goals and Targets

Goal 1: Eradicate extreme poverty and hunger

Target 1: Halve, between 1990 and 2015, the proportion of people whose income is less than $1 a day (now $1.25 a day).

Target 2: Halve, between 1990 and 2015, the proportion of people who suffer from hunger.

Goal 2: Achieve universal primary education

Target 3: Ensure that, by 2015, children everywhere, boys and girls alike, will be able to complete a full course of primary schooling.

Goal 3: Promote gender equality and empower women

Target 4: Eliminate gender disparity in primary and secondary education, preferably by 2005 and in all levels of education no later than 2015.

Goal 4: Reduce child mortality

Target 5: Reduce by two-thirds, between 1990 and 2015, the under-five mortality rate.

Goal 5: Improve maternal health

Target 6: Reduce by three-quarters, between 1990 and 2015, the maternal mortality ratio.

continued overleaf

| Case example 1.1 | Millennium Development Goals and Targets – *continued* |

Goal 6: Combat HIV/AIDS, malaria and other diseases

Target 7: Have halted by 2015 and begun to reverse the spread of HIV/AIDS.

Target 8: Have halted by 2015 and begun to reverse the incidence of malaria and other major diseases.

Goal 7: Ensure environmental sustainability

Target 9: Integrate the principles of sustainable development into country policies and programmes and reverse the loss of environmental resources.

Target 10: Halve by 2015 the proportion of people without sustainable access to safe drinking water.

Target 11: Have achieved by 2020 a significant improvement in the lives of at least 100 million slum dwellers.

Goal 8: Develop a global partnership for development

Target 12: Develop further an open, rule-based, predictable, non-discriminatory trading and financial system (includes a commitment to good governance, development, and poverty reduction – both nationally and internationally).

Target 13: Address the special needs of the least developed countries (includes tariff- and quota-free access for exports, enhanced programme of debt relief for and cancellation of official bilateral debt, and more generous official development assistance for countries committed to poverty reduction).

Target 14: Address the special needs of landlocked countries and small island developing states (through the Programme of Action for the Sustainable Development of Small Island Developing States and 22nd General Assembly provisions).

Target 15: Deal comprehensively with the debt problems of developing countries through national and international measures in order to make debt sustainable in the long term.

Target 16: In cooperation with developing countries, develop and implement strategies for decent and productive work for youth.

Target 17: In cooperation with pharmaceutical companies, provide access to affordable essential drugs in developing countries.

Target 18: In cooperation with the private sector, make available the benefits of new technologies, especially information and communications technologies.

Source: UNDP, *Human Development Report 2002* (New York: Oxford University Press, 2002).

Globalization and interdependence of the world economy

A third major factor responsible for the growing concern with Third World development is the increased **globalization** of the world economy leading to a greater interdependence between countries of the world. There have been three major eras of globalization in the last 150 years. The first was from 1870 to the First World War (1914), which witnessed large-scale capital flows and labour migration from Europe to the American continent and the colonies. The second started after the Second World War with the freeing of trade. The third phase started in the 1980s based on technological advances in communications and transport. Fischer (2003) has given a useful, succinct definition of globalization:

> the ongoing process of greater economic interdependence among countries reflected in the increasing amount of cross-border trade in goods and services, the increasing volume of international financial flows and increasing flows of labour.

As far as the interdependence between developed and developing countries is concerned, developing countries depend on developed countries for resource flows and technology, while developed countries depend heavily on developing countries for raw materials, food and oil, and as markets for industrial goods. The term globalization refers to all those forces operating in the world economy that increase interdependence and at the same time make countries more and more dependent on forces outside of their control, as time, space and borders diminish in importance. Foremost among these forces are:

- The widening and freeing of trade. Over 30 per cent of the world's output of goods and services is now traded.
- The growth of global capital markets and the greater flow of short-term speculative capital: over 2 trillion dollars are exchanged on the world's currency markets every day.
- More foreign direct investment (FDI) by giant multinational corporations with greater power and assets than many national governments.
- The growth of global value chains with firms sourcing inputs from the cheapest international markets.
- The greater movement of people than ever before, breaking down cultural barriers – but also leading to the spread of disease (e.g. AIDS) and international crime in drugs, prostitution and arms.
- The spread of information technology (IT), which can exacerbate contagion in financial markets.
- New institutions, such as the World Trade Organization (WTO), with authority over national governments, and new multilateral agreements on trade, services, intellectual property, which reduce national autonomy.

All these aspects of globalization and interdependence make countries more vulnerable to shocks such as: world recessions and downturns in world trade as occurred in the early 1980s and precipitated the debt crisis; financial crises, such as the Asian crisis of 1997, and the banking crisis in the US in 2007/2008 which became contagious and spread like a disease affecting not only the countries of origin but other parts of the world too; and commodity price rises (including the price of oil) which in 2008 more than doubled for several basic foods, such as maize and rice, leading to food riots in several poor countries. In recent years there have been major protests at meetings of the WTO and the World Economic Forum in Davos (Switzerland) by groups concerned with the damage done by globalization, particularly to the poorer countries in the world economy which tend to be most exposed to, and suffer most from, the forces of competition and global capital movements. Competitive markets may be the best guarantee of efficiency, but not necessarily of equity. As the *Human Development Report* of the United Nations Development Programme (UNDP) (1999) put it:

> The challenge of globalisation in the new century is not to stop the expansion of global markets. The challenge is to find the rules and institutions for stronger governance – local, national, regional and global – to preserve the advantages of global markets and competition, but also to provide enough space for human, community and environmental resources to ensure that globalisation works for people – not just for profits.

So far, more progress has been made in promoting the institutions of globalization than in protecting people against the consequences of globalization. The UNDP calls for globalization tempered by:

• **Ethics** – less violation of human rights
• **Equity** – less disparity within and between nations
• **Inclusion** – less marginalization of people and countries
• **Human security** – less instability of countries and less vulnerability of people
• **Sustainability** – less environmental destruction
• **Development** – less poverty and deprivation.

When the actions of any one country, or group of countries, result in consequences for others (good or bad), the effects become a type of **public good** or **externality**. The task of the international community in these circumstances is to maximize the spread of public 'goods' which confer positive externalities (e.g. technology, information, health care) and to minimize the spread of public 'bads' (e.g. disease, pollution, financial contagion). It is in the self-interest of the international community to assist developing countries in particular, not only because they are poor but also to enable them to make their contribution to the provision of essential global public 'goods' (and to minimize the production of public 'bads', e.g. AIDS in Africa).

Globalization and interdependence particularly means that the malfunctioning of one set of economies impairs the functioning of others. This was never more evident than in the world economy in the 1980s, when the rising price of energy and the debt crisis led to mounting economic chaos. The 1980 Brandt Report, entitled *North–South: A Programme for Survival* (1980), and its sequel *Common Crisis: North–South Co-operation for World Recovery* (Brandt Commission, 1983), stressed the mutual benefit to all countries of a sustained programme of development in the Third World, and documented the prevailing adverse trends in the world economy, which pointed to a sombre future if not tackled cooperatively:

• Growing poverty and hunger in the Third World
• Rising unemployment with inflation
• International monetary disorder
• Chronic balance of payments deficits and mounting debts in most Third World countries
• Protectionism, and tensions between countries competing for energy, food and raw materials.

Nothing much has changed since the 1980s. Poverty and hunger are still rife in the world. Tens of millions of people in poor countries lack productive employment. There is international monetary disorder. There are chronic global imbalances of payments between countries, and international debt continues to grow. And there are growing tensions between countries for energy, food and raw materials, which surfaced dramatically in 2007/8 with the price of oil reaching over $150 a barrel, and the price of many raw materials and food more than doubling.

Development economics addresses itself to many of the issues contributing to disarray in the world economy.

There is not only a moral case for greater efforts to raise living standards in Third World countries, but a purely practical case that it is in the interests of the developed countries themselves. The ability of poor countries to sustain their growth and development means a greater demand for the goods and services of developed countries, which generates output and employment directly and also helps to maintain the balance-of-payments stability of these countries, which is so crucial if there is to be a reciprocal demand for the goods of developing countries. Any constraint on demand in the system arising from, say, poor agricultural performance in poor countries, or a balance-of-payments constraint on demand in developed countries, will impair the functioning of the whole system and reduce the rate of progress below potential. Herein lies the importance of the transfer of resources to poor countries to maintain their momentum of development (global Keynesianism), and of international monetary reform to smooth the burden of balance-of-payments adjustment and to shift more of the burden of adjustment from the deficit to the surplus countries.

The Brandt Report called for a short-term emergency programme as a prelude to longer-term action, consisting of four major elements:

1. A large-scale transfer of resources to developing countries
2. An international energy strategy to minimize the dislocation caused by sudden and rapid increases in the price of oil
3. A global food programme
4. A start on some major reforms in the international monetary system.

To date, very little has been done.

In the longer term the Brandt Report called for:

- A 20-year programme to meet the basic needs of poor countries, involving additional resource transfers of $4 billion a year ($10 billion at 2009 prices)
- A major effort to improve agricultural productivity to end mass hunger and malnutrition
- Commodity schemes to stabilize the terms of trade for primary commodities
- Easier access to world markets for the exports of developing countries
- Programmes for energy conservation
- The development of more appropriate technologies for poor countries
- An international progressive income tax, and levies on trade and arms production, to be used by a new World Development Fund (to fund development programmes rather than projects)
- A link between the creation of new international money and aid to developing countries
- Policies to recycle balance-of-payments surpluses (as accumulated by the Arab oil exporting countries since 1973 and China since the 1990s, for example) to deficit countries to remove balance-of-payments constraints on demand and remove the risk of a slide into international protectionism.

We could add to this list new forms of global governance to cope with the consequences of globalization, which at the same time also represent the interests of those countries that suffer most from the effects of globalization: the poor and marginalized.

We shall discuss many of these issues in the course of this book. Such a programme of action would be of mutual benefit to all parties, rich and poor. It would create investment confidence, which is the crucial ingredient maintaining the dynamics of any economic system; it would also stimulate trade and investment, and help the prospects of sustained growth in the world economy.

It would be wrong to give the impression, however, that the developed countries' concern with world poverty is motivated exclusively by the selfish realization that their own survival depends on economic and political harmony, which cannot thrive in a world perpetually divided into rich and poor. There has also been an affirmation by many developed countries of a **moral obligation** towards poorer nations. Not all aid and development assistance is politically inspired. Particularly over the last four decades, the developed countries have shown a genuine humanitarian concern over the plight of Third World countries, which has resulted in the establishment and support of several institutions to assist developing countries, and which led the period 1960–70 to be named the 'First Development Decade'.

We are now in the Fifth Development Decade, and the pledge to assist developing countries out of humanitarian concern has been reaffirmed. The goal of a greater degree of income equality between the citizens of a nation seems to be gaining support, albeit slowly, as an objective among nations. Moreover the propagation of this ideal is not confined to the supranational institutions that have been especially established to further it. Recent years have witnessed the spontaneous creation of several national pressure groups in different parts of the world, whose platform is the abolition of world poverty; and the Church, which remained silent and inactive for so long, periodically makes its voice heard. Aid from voluntary agencies to developing countries now amounts to over $5 billion annually. But whatever the motive for concern, the reality of world poverty and underdevelopment cannot be ignored. Furthermore, primary poverty in developing countries is likely to persist for many years to come. The economist has a special responsibility to contribute to an understanding of the economic difficulties that poor countries face and to point to possible solutions. This textbook is devoted to that end.

We start by considering the meaning of development and the perpetuation of underdevelopment. Then in Chapters 2 and 3 we consider the measurement of poverty, the magnitude of the development gap in the world economy, and the major characteristics of underdevelopment, particularly the employment situation, the income distribution, the level of nutrition and other basic needs such as education and health care.

The meaning of development and the challenge of development economics

Development implies change, and this is one sense in which the term 'development' is used; that is, to describe the process of economic and social transformation within countries. This process often follows a well-ordered sequence and exhibits common characteristics across countries, which we shall discuss later in the chapter. But if development becomes an objective of policy, the important question arises: development for what? Not so long ago the concept of development, defined in the sense of an objective or a desired state of affairs, was conceived of almost exclusively in terms of growth targets, with very little regard to the beneficiaries of growth or the composition of output. Societies are not indifferent, however, to the distributional consequences of economic policy, to the type of output that is produced, or to the economic environment in which it is produced. A concept of development is required that embraces the major economic and social objectives and values that societies strive for. This is not easy. One attempt is by Goulet (1971, 2006), who distinguishes three basic components or core values in this wider meaning of development, which he calls **life-sustenance, self-esteem** and **freedom**.

Life-sustenance is concerned with the provision of basic needs, which we shall discuss in Chapter 3. The basic needs approach to development was initiated by the World Bank in the 1970s. No country may be regarded as fully developed if it cannot provide all its people with such basic needs as housing, clothing, food and minimal education. A major objective of development must be to raise people out of primary poverty and to provide basic needs simultaneously.

Self-esteem is concerned with the feeling of self-respect and independence. No country can be regarded as fully developed if it is exploited by others and does not have the power and influence to conduct relations on equal terms. Developing countries seek development for self-esteem; to eradicate the feeling of dominance and dependence that is associated with inferior economic status.

Freedom refers to freedom from the three evils of 'want, ignorance and squalor' so that people are more able to determine their own destiny. No person is free if they cannot choose; if they are imprisoned by living on the margin of subsistence with no education and no skills. The advantage of material development is that it expands the range of human choice open to individuals and societies at large.

All three of these core components are interrelated. Lack of self-esteem and freedom result from low levels of life sustenance, and both lack of self-esteem and economic imprisonment become links in a circular, self-perpetuating chain of poverty by producing a sense of fatalism and acceptance of the established order – the 'accommodation to poverty' as Galbraith (1980) once called it.

Goulet's three core components of development are also related to Amartya Sen's vision of development (Sen, 1983, 1984, 1999), defined in terms of the expansion of **entitlements** and **capabilities,** the former giving life sustenance and self-esteem; the latter giving **freedom**. Sen defines entitlements as 'the set of alternative commodity bundles that a person can command in a society using the totality of rights and obligations that he or she faces', and entitlements generate the capability to do certain things. Economic development should be thought of in terms of the expansion of entitlements and capabilities, which are not necessarily well captured by aggregate measures of output growth. For most people, entitlements depend on their ability to sell their labour and on the price of commodities. It is not only the market mechanism that determines entitlements, however, but also such factors as power relations in society, the spatial distribution of resources in society, such as schools and health care, and what individuals can extract from the state.

In the final analysis, Sen views **freedom** as the primary objective of development, as well as the principal means of achieving development. Development consists of the removal of various types of 'unfreedoms' that leave people with little choice and opportunity. Major categories of 'unfreedom' include famine and undernourishment, poor health and lack of basic needs; lack of political liberty and basic civil rights, and economic insecurity. Development should be regarded as a process of expanding the real freedoms that people enjoy. The growth of per capita income is only a means to that end. The ideas and views of Amartya Sen, who won the Nobel Prize for Economics in 1998 for his work on the interface between welfare and development economics, have been enormously influential within the international community and can be most recently seen in the World Bank's *World Development Report 2000/2001* which is devoted to the topic of how to expand the entitlements, capabilities and freedom of poor people (see Chapter 2).

The focus and stress on expanding entitlements and capabilities for *all* people is a natural extension of the earlier switch in development thinking away from growth maximization to concern with the structure of production and consumption and the distribution of income. Sen's dissent is that income is often a very inadequate measure of entitlements, which he tries to illustrate with reference to the incidence of famines across the world. He finds that most famines have been associated with a lack of entitlements, not with a lack of food.

Amartya Sen

Born 1933, Santiniketan, Bengal, India. Professor of Economics, Delhi University, the London School of Economics, Oxford, Cambridge and Harvard Universities. Important contributions to many branches of development economics, including choice of techniques, project appraisal, the measurement of welfare, and the analysis of famines. The foremost economist working on the interface between development and welfare economics. Sen sees development as 'freedom' – the title of one of his books. Awarded the Nobel Prize for Economics 1998.

Using Goulet's and Sen's concept of development, therefore, and in answer to the question 'development for what?', we can say that **development has occurred when there has been an improvement in basic needs, when economic progress has contributed to a greater sense of self-esteem for the country and individuals within it, and when material advancement has expanded people's entitlements, capabilities and freedoms**. The fact that many of these ingredients of development are not measurable does not detract from their importance: the condition of being developed is as much a state of mind as a physical condition measurable by economic indices alone.

The challenge of development economics lies in the formulation of economic theory, and in the application of policy, in order to understand better and to meet these core components of development. Clearly the range of issues that development economics is concerned with is quite distinctive and because of this the subject has developed its own *modus vivendi* (way of doing things), although drawing liberally on economic theory, as do other branches of economics.

If it is to be useful, however, a great deal of conventional economic theory must be adapted to suit the conditions prevailing in developing countries, and many of the assumptions that underlie conventional economic models have to be modified, if not abandoned, if they are to yield fruitful insights into the development process. Static equilibrium theory, for example, is ill-suited to the analysis of growth and change and of growing inequalities in the distribution of income between individuals and countries. It is probably also true, as Todaro and Smith (2008) strongly argue, that economics needs to be viewed in the much broader perspective of the overall social system of a country (which includes values, beliefs, attitudes towards effort and risk-taking, religion and the class system) if development mistakes are to be avoided that stem from implementing policy based on economic theory alone.

The perpetuation of underdevelopment

The study of economic development helps us to understand the nature and causes of poverty in low-income countries, and the transformation of societies from primarily rural to primarily industrial, with the vast bulk of resources utilized in industrial activities and in service activities that serve the industrial sector. But why have some countries hardly participated in this process or have been left behind? The first industrial revolution gave the present developed countries an initial advantage, which they then sustained through the existence of various cumulative forces against those left behind (see Chang, 2002; Reinert, 2007). Since the 1960s there has been a second industrial revolution, which has propelled another bloc of countries (the so-called 'newly industrialized countries' of South-East Asia and Latin America) into a virtually industrialized state, and many others into a semi-industrialized state. But many countries are still left behind in a semi-feudal state, including the very poorest, which have now become the prime focus of concern of the World Bank and other development agencies.

There are many theories of the perpetuation of underdevelopment but none seems to have universal validity. The condition of agriculture is of foremost importance. It was, first of all, settled agriculture that laid the basis for the great civilizations of the past, and it was the increase in agricultural productivity in England in the eighteenth century that laid the basis for, and sustained, the first industrial revolution. If there is one overriding factor that explains why some countries developed before others, and why some countries are still backward without a significant industrial sector, it lies in the condition of agriculture, which in the early stages of development is the sector that must release factors of production for other activities and provide the purchasing power over industrial goods.

The condition of agriculture depends on many factors, institutional as well as economic, and physical conditions are also of key importance. Climate particularly affects the conditions of production. Heat debilitates human beings. Extremes of heat and humidity also reduce the quality of the soil and contribute to the low productivity of certain crops. It cannot be coincidence that almost all developing countries are situated in tropical or subtropical climatic regions and that development 'took off' in the temperate zones.

The condition of agriculture has not been helped by what Lipton (1977) called **urban bias**, which in many countries has starved agriculture of resources. This has happened because ruling elites generally originate from, or identify with, the non-rural environment, and because policymakers have been led astray both by empirical evidence that shows a high correlation between levels of development and industrialization, and by early development models that stressed investment in industry.

Many other internal conditions have acted as barriers to progress in poor countries; barriers that interacted in a vicious circle. In some countries population size and growth presents a problem, combined with low levels of human capital formation. The latter in turn perpetuates poverty, which is associated with high birth rates and large family size. This is a form of 'accommodation to poverty' (Galbraith, 1980), which then perpetuates low living standards in a circular process. Other countries may lack the psychological conditions required for modernization, built on individualism and the competitive spirit, coupled with a strong work ethic, rationalism and scientific thought, which characterized the industrial revolutions of eighteenth- and nineteenth-century Europe, and which played a large part in the emergence of the newly industrialized South-East Asian countries in the latter half of the twentieth century.

External relations between countries also play a part in the poverty perpetuation process, and this has given rise to **structuralist** and **dependency** theories of underdevelopment. It seems to be the general lesson of history that once one set of countries gains an economic advantage, the advantage will be sustained through a process of what Myrdal (1957) has called 'circular and cumulative causation', working through the media of factor mobility and trade. (For a full discussion see Chapter 8.) Favoured regions denude the backward regions of capital and skilled labour, and they trade in commodities whose characteristics guarantee that the gains from trade accrue to them. **Colonialism** was an extreme form of dependency, and many of the countries exploited during the colonial era are still poor today. On the other hand, a number of countries that were never colonized, such as Ethiopia and Thailand, are equally backward.

Dependence can take more subtle forms, however, based on the international division of labour, for example, which leads to unequal exchange relations between rich and poor, with the poor dependent on the rich for capital and technology to equip their industrial sectors. The current indebtedness of the less developed countries, the 'increasing price' that poor countries have to pay for development inputs relative to the price they receive for their exports, and the growing number of poor people are manifestations of this dependency. There are exceptions to the thesis of 'circular and cumulative causation', but in most cases it requires a strong exogenous shock to break out of a vicious circle of poverty and dependency.

Some of these issues will be discussed in Part 3 of this book, but Chapter 2 focuses attention on the magnitude of poverty in developing countries and the world distribution of income.

Summary

- Development economics is a challenging and exciting sub-discipline of economics which addresses the fundamental issues of why some countries are poor and others rich; why some countries grow faster than others over long periods, and what is the best way to tackle poverty in poor countries.
- Interest in the progress of nations is not new. It was the fundamental preoccupation of all the great classical economists such as Adam Smith, Thomas Malthus, David Ricardo, John Stuart Mill and Karl Marx – but the subject matter of development economics has witnessed a revival since the Second World War.
- Revival of interest in development economics has been the result of several factors such as: increased awareness of world poverty; developing countries asking for a fairer deal from the functioning of the world economy; the call for a new international economic order, and the increased globalization and interdependence of the world economy. The Millennium Development Goals set out explicit targets for poverty reduction, education and health (among other things) to be achieved by 2015.
- Economic development means more than a rise in the average level of income per head of a country. A definition of economic (and social) development must embrace a variety of goals and values that societies strive for, particularly self-esteem and freedom for people based on their entitlements and capabilities (to use the terminology of Amartya Sen).
- Economic development presents a major challenge to development economists and policy-makers. This is because there are structural forces at work within countries and in the world economy which tend to perpetuate underdevelopment and poverty and cause countries to get caught in 'vicious circles' related to unequal trade between countries and the dependence of poor countries on the rich for aid and investment.

Chapter 1	Discussion questions

1 What constitutes the study of development economics?

2 Do you think there is a case for a separate subject of development economics, and what are the arguments against it?

Chapter 1	Discussion questions – *continued*

3   What accounts for the political and academic interest in Third World development?

4   Why was the status of the discipline of development economics called into question in the 1980s?

5   How would you define the process of economic development?

6   What do the developing countries want from a 'new international economic order'?

7   Do you think that the Millennium Development Goals are achievable?

8   What forces perpetuate underdevelopment?

9   What lessons, if any, can poor countries learn from the development experience of today's industrialized countries?

10   What is meant by 'globalization' and the mutual interdependence between rich and poor countries?

11   What do you see as the major challenges confronting development economics and the developing countries?

Websites

The study of development economics requires a good deal of reading and familiarity with case-study material, as well as access to statistical sources. Below is a list of general Internet sites that can be accessed with links to topics, countries, regions and international organizations. Other sites on specific topics will be given at the end of other chapters.

Institutes of Development Studies

Canadian International Development Agency (Virtual Library on International Development) http://w3.acdi-cida.gc.ca/virtual.nsf

Institute of Development Studies, University of Sussex (British Library for Development Studies) www.ids.ac.uk/blds/index.html

School of Development Studies, University of East Anglia www.uea.ac.uk/dev/

International organizations

World Bank www.worldbank.org

International Monetary Fund www.imf.org

United Nations Conference on Trade and Development (UNCTAD) www.unctad.org

United Nations Development Programme (UNDP) www.undp.org

Food and Agricultural Organization (FAO) www.fao.org

World Trade Organization (WTO) www.wto.org

World Health Organization (WHO) www.who.int

United Nations Industrial Development Organization (UNIDO) www.unido.org

International Labour Organization (ILO) www.ilo.org

African Development Bank http://afdb.org
Asian Development Bank www.adb.org
Inter-American Development Bank www.iadb.org
World Development Movement www.wdm.org.uk
Centre for Global Development (Washington) www.cgdev.org
Non-Governmental Organizations Global Network www.ngo.org
Heritage Foundation www.heritage.org

Databases

Penn World Tables (accessed through the National Bureau of Economic Research) www.nber.org/
   pub/pwt56.html
Economic Growth Resources (Jon Temple, Bristol University) www.bris.ac.uk/Depts/Economics/
   Growth
World Bank http://econ.worldbank.org/prr/globalisation
IMF/World Bank Library Network http://jotis

Globalization

Department for International Development, UK www.globalisation.gov.uk
Centre for Research on Globalization http://www.globalresearch.ca
The Globalization Website http://www.emory.edu/soc/globalization/
Institute for International Economics http://www.iie.com/research/globalization.htm
New Economics Foundation www.neweconomics.org

2

THE DEVELOPMENT GAP AND THE MEASUREMENT OF POVERTY

- Introduction
- The development gap and income distribution in the world economy
- Measures of inequality and historical trends
- International inequality (unweighted and weighted)
- Global (or world) inequality
- The measurement and comparability of per capita income
- Purchasing power parity (PPP)
- Per capita income as an index of development
- Measuring poverty
- Meeting the Millennium Poverty Reduction Target
- Tackling poverty from the 'grass roots'
- Human Poverty Index and Human Development Index

- Can the poor countries ever catch up?
- Summary
- Discussion questions
- Notes
- Websites on poverty and income distribution

Introduction

This chapter focuses on three major topics: first the development gap in the world economy and the measurement of the world distribution of income; secondly, the measurement of global poverty and the problems associated with the use of per capita income as a measure of development, and thirdly the construction of alternative measures of economic and social development including the Human Development Index (HDI) and the Human Poverty Index (HPI) constructed by the United Nations Development Programme (UNDP).

To measure the development gap, and the degree of income inequality across countries of the world, we consider: the absolute gap between the richest and poorest country (the range); the relative gap between the richest and poorest countries; the dispersion of income per capita around the average level of per capita income for all countries, and lastly the Gini ratio which is derived from the Lorenz curve of the income distribution. Using the Gini ratio, we distinguish between **international inequality**, which takes each country's per capita income as just one observation (regardless of the distribution of income within countries) and **global inequality**, which takes account not only of the distribution of income between countries but also within countries (using household survey data). We show that international and global inequality have both been rising since the beginning of the nineteenth century, but the major cause of global inequality is inequality between nations, not inequality within nations.

It is important to recognize, however, that when measuring income inequality and poverty, the measures of income per head in US$ at the official exchange rates are not necessarily a good measure of the purchasing power of local currencies (or what is called purchasing power parity or PPP) because official exchange rates do not take account of the much cheaper price of non-traded goods in poor countries relative to richer countries. We show how PPP is measured, and discuss in general the comparability of per capita incomes between countries, and the use of per capita income as an index of development.

Turning to the measurement of poverty, we discuss the World Bank's criterion of absolute poverty, which is $1.25 a day at PPP, and give the **head count index** of the numbers living below this level of income across different regions of the world. The concept of the **poverty gap** is also discussed because the head count index does not take account of how far below the poverty line people live. Another method of measuring poverty is the **food energy method**, which measures the income necessary to buy a certain nutritional intake in different countries.

The World Bank claims that it puts poverty reduction at the heart of all the work that it does, and in its *World Development Report 2000* it proposed a three-pronged strategy for poverty reduction: promoting opportunity; facilitating empowerment and enhancing security. The meaning of these concepts is discussed in this chapter. Growth, of course, is central to poverty reduction, but how fast the poverty rate falls with growth (to meet the Millennium Development Goal, for example) depends on the elasticity of the poverty rate with respect to growth.

To overcome the limitations of taking a single measure of per capita income as an index of development, the UNDP constructs annually a Human Development Index and Human Poverty Index. The HDI is based on three variables: life expectancy at birth, educational attainment (enrolment and literacy), and the standard of living measured at PPP. The HPI is also based on three variables: the percentage of the population not expected to survive to the age of 40; the adult illiteracy rate, and a deprivation index based on the percentage of the population without access to safe water and the percentage of underweight children under the age of five. The rankings of countries by their level of per capita income are not the same as the rankings of countries by the HDI or HPI indices because some countries devote more resources to social expenditure than others, particularly on education and health.

Finally we consider the question of whether poor countries are ever likely to catch up with the rich, and we reach the pessimistic conclusion that it will take the average poor country at least 100 years to achieve current living standards in developed countries and probably 300 years for poor countries to equalize living standards with developed countries if they manage to grow, say, 1 per cent faster than the rich countries. But this, of course, cannot be taken for granted.

The development gap and income distribution in the world economy

By any measure one cares to take, the evidence is unequivocal that the world's income is distributed extremely unequally between nations and people. There are many ways of classifying these divisions in the world economy. First, at a very basic level there is the division between rich industrialized countries, mainly concentrated in the northern hemisphere, and poorer non-industrialized (or semi-industrialized) countries in the southern hemisphere – often referred to in the development literature as the North–South divide.

Secondly, there is the division between continents: between the developed continents of Europe and North America on the one hand, and the continents of Asia, Africa and Latin America on the other. But the countries of Asia, Africa and Latin America are by no means homogeneous. They have many characteristics, and obstacles to development, in common, but there is also much that divides them, not least their economic performance since the 1960s, with South-East Asia, China and India forging ahead, Africa left behind, and Latin America in the middle (often prone to financial crises).

Thirdly, the World Bank, which was established by the Bretton Woods Agreement in 1944 as a Development Agency to lend to poor countries, classifies countries in its annual *World Development Report* into three broad categories: low-income, middle-income and high-income countries, with the middle-income countries split into lower middle-income and upper middle-income. Table 2.1 gives the level of per capita income in 2007 for all countries in the world with a population of more than one million, and at the bottom of the table the average levels of per capita income are given for the low-, middle- and high-income countries. Ignoring for the moment measurement difficulties (see later) we see that for the low-income countries, containing nearly one billion people, the average level of income per head is only $484 per annum; for the lower- to middle-income countries, containing 3.6 billion people, the level of per capita income is a meagre $1,832, while for the high-income countries the figure is $38,194. The poorest country is Burundi with $124. The richest country is Norway with $82,814 (all measured at official exchange rates).

Measures of inequality and historical trends

(i) One measure of dispersion is **the range** or **absolute income gap** between the richest and poorest countries. This gap is almost bound to grow over time if both the rich and poorest countries experience positive growth. For example, if the richest country, Norway, grows at 1 per cent, this adds roughly $800 to the level of per capita income in Norway, which is seven times more than the present level of per capita income in the poorest country, Burundi. Burundi would have to grow at more than 700 per cent for the absolute gap between itself and Norway to narrow.

But even the gap between the richest and poorest country is an understatement of the degree of income inequality in the world economy because it compares only the *average* income for poor and rich countries. If the income per head of the poorest people in poor countries is compared with the income per head of the richest people in rich countries, the absolute gap is even wider.

(ii) A second measure of dispersion, or division in the world economy, is the **relative income gap**, which is the ratio of the richest country (or group of countries) to the poorest country (or group of countries). At present, the ratio of income per head of the richest to the poorest country is approximately 700:1, and the ratio of income per head in the low-income countries to the high-income countries is approximately 80:1 (i.e. \$38,194//484). This relative income gap is unprecedented historically. A necessary condition for the relative income gap to narrow is that the poorest countries grow faster than the richest.

(iii) Third, a well-known statistical measure of dispersion is the **standard deviation**, or the square root of the variance, which measures the average sum of the squared deviations of each country's per capita income from the average (or mean) income for all countries. Formally, the standard deviation (SD) is measured as:

$$SD = \sqrt{\frac{\sum_{i=1}^{n}(Y_i - \overline{Y})^2}{n}}$$

where Y_i is the per capita income of country i; $\overline{Y}$ is the average level of per capita income of the whole sample, and n is the number of countries. In the growth and development literature, movements in this ratio, up or down, are referred to as sigma (σ) divergence or convergence, respectively.

(iv) Fourth, there is the **coefficient of variation**, which is the standard deviation (SD) divided by the mean of the sample ($\overline{Y}$). This normalizes the standard deviation because there is a positive correlation between the mean and standard deviation.

(v) But the most widely used measure of income inequality is the so-called **Gini ratio**, derived from the **Lorenz curve**, which in this field of enquiry relates to the distribution of income in relation to the distribution of population across countries or groups of countries. Three measures or concepts of inequality need to be clearly distinguished in using the Gini ratio. First, there is **international inequality**, with each country treated as a single unit and given equal weight in the measure. Secondly, there is international inequality, with each country treated as a single unit but **weighted by its size of population**, Thirdly, there is **world or global inequality** which takes the individual person (or household), not the country, as the unit of measurement, and therefore takes into account not only differences in income *between* countries, but also between people *within* countries. Each measure has its own purpose, and there is no theoretical reason why the measures should move together (although, in practice, they tend to, taking a long historical perspective).

Before describing how the Lorenz curve is constructed, and the Gini ratio is measured, however, it needs to be said in advance that a single statistic does not say what is happening *within* the distribution, and, in particular, what is happening at the extremes of the distribution. Ratios of extremes, such as the income of the poorest 10 per cent of the world's population compared with the richest 10 per cent, or income of the poorest countries compared with the richest, can say as much, if not more, about income inequality and social justice than any integral measure.

Table 2.1   Income per capita and population, 2007

	Population	Gross national income per capita		PPP gross national income per capita	
	millions	$	rank	$	rank
Albania	3	3,554	74	7,350	68
Algeria	34	3,917	72	7,650	67
Angola	18	2,876	84	4,400	89
Argentina	40	6,510	52	12,970	45
Armenia	3	3,087	80	5,740	80
Australia	21	37,365	16	33,400	19
Austria	8	44,134	11	36,750	11
Azerbaijan	9	3,259	77	6,630	76
Bangladesh	158	466	133	1,340	126
Belarus	10	4,624	64	10,790	57
Belgium	11	43,075	12	35,320	14
Benin	8	647	126	1,410	124
Bhutan	1	1,518	100	4,050	94
Bolivia	10	1,360	103	3,960	95
Bosnia and Herzegovina	4	4,139	68	8,010	66
Botswana	2	6,235	53	12,760	46
Brazil	190	6,886	50	9,510	61
Bulgaria	8	4,965	62	10,790	56
Burkina Faso	15	457	134	1,120	133
Burundi	8	124	152	370	149
Cambodia	14	554	129	1,720	120
Cameroon	19	1,112	105	2,120	111
Canada	33	39,978	15	35,500	13
Central African Rep.	4	392	135	710	145
Chad	11	540	130	1,220	127
Chile	17	8,754	45	12,280	51
China	1,318	2,413	88	5,430	82
Colombia	44	4,545	66	8,260	65
Comoros	1	743	121	1,170	130
Congo, Dem. Rep.	62	149	151	290	150
Congo, Rep.	4	1,562	99	2,700	103
Costa Rica	4	5,708	58	10,510	59
Côte d'Ivoire	20	940	114	1,550	122
Croatia	4	12,862	35	17,840	34
Cyprus	1	24,145	25	24,040	27
Czech Rep.	10	15,545	31	22,160	30
Denmark	5	58,102	3	36,800	10

continued overleaf

Table 2.1   Income per capita and population, 2007 – *continued*

	Population	Gross national income per capita		PPP gross national income per capita	
	millions	$	rank	$	rank
Djibouti	1	1,072	106	2,240	110
Dominican Rep.	10	4,034	69	7,340	69
Ecuador	13	3,279	76	7,100	72
Egypt, Arab Rep.	80	1,644	95	5,090	84
El Salvador	6	3,241	79	6,330	77
Equatorial Guinea	1	10,392	40	16,230	38
Eritrea	5	282	146	620	147
Estonia	1	14,448	33	18,830	33
Ethiopia	79	247	148	780	141
Fiji	1	3,926	71	4,210	90
Finland	5	46,581	8	34,760	15
France	62	42,189	13	33,850	18
Gabon	1	7,063	49	12,320	49
Gambia, The	2	369	141	1,200	128
Georgia	4	2,322	90	4,680	86
Germany	82	40,716	14	34,740	17
Ghana	23	649	125	1,350	125
Greece	11	27,321	24	27,830	22
Guatemala	13	2,526	86	4,550	87
Guinea	10	468	132	1,100	134
Guinea-Bissau	2	243	149	510	148
Guyana	1	1,365	102	2,330	109
Haiti	10	637	127	1,060	135
Honduras	7	1,638	96	3,610	97
Hong Kong, China	7	31,065	22	43,960	6
Hungary	10	12,821	36	17,470	35
India	1,125	1,041	108	2,740	102
Indonesia	226	1,836	93	3,560	98
Iran, Islamic Rep.	71	3,985	70	10,840	55
Ireland	4	50,131	5	37,700	8
Israel	7	22,830	27	26,310	24
Italy	59	35,208	19	30,190	21
Jamaica	3	4,560	65	7,170	70
Japan	128	35,456	18	34,750	16
Jordan	6	3,032	81	5,300	83
Kazakhstan	15	5,926	56	9,510	62
Kenya	38	721	122	1,550	123
Korea, Rep.	48	21,693	28	26,880	23

Table 2.1 Income per capita and population, 2007 – *continued*

	Population	Gross national income per capita		PPP gross national income per capita	
	millions	$	rank	$	rank
Kuwait	3	46,964	7		
Kyrgyz Rep.	5	705	123	1,980	113
Lao PDR	6	679	124	1,920	114
Latvia	2	12,220	37	16,770	37
Lebanon	4	6,217	55	10,910	54
Lesotho	2	1,041	109	1,880	115
Liberia	4	154	150	280	151
Libya	6	9,702	41	14,710	40
Lithuania	3	11,044	38	17,090	36
Macao, China	1	35,949	17	52,260	2
Macedonia, FYR	2	3,750	73	9,050	64
Madagascar	19	392	136	980	138
Malawi	14	256	147	760	142
Malaysia	27	6,882	51	13,230	43
Mali	12	604	128	1,180	129
Mauritania	3	881	117	2,000	112
Mauritius	1	5,436	59	11,410	52
Mexico	105	9,581	42	13,910	42
Moldova	4	1,314	104	2,900	101
Mongolia	3	1,476	101	3,170	99
Montenegro	1	6,232	54	12,560	47
Morocco	31	2,402	89	4,050	93
Mozambique	21	340	143	730	143
Namibia	2	4,139	67	6,070	79
Nepal	28	370	140	1,060	136
Netherlands	16	47,685	6	39,470	7
New Zealand	4	29,784	23	25,380	26
Nicaragua	6	998	112	2,510	106
Niger	14	299	145	630	146
Nigeria	148	1,050	107	1,850	117
Norway	5	82,814	1	53,650	1
Pakistan	162	895	115	2,540	104
Panama	3	5,435	60	10,610	58
Papua New Guinea	6	888	116	1,870	116
Paraguay	6	2,035	91	4,520	88
Peru	29	3,470	75	7,070	73
Philippines	89	1,765	94	3,660	96

continued overleaf

Table 2.1   Income per capita and population, 2007 – *continued*

	Population	Gross national income per capita		PPP gross national income per capita	
	millions	$	rank	$	rank
Poland	38	10,807	39	15,600	39
Portugal	11	20,098	29	21,790	31
Romania	22	7,694	47	12,350	48
Russian Federation	142	8,857	44	14,330	41
Rwanda	9	359	142	920	139
Saudi Arabia	24	15,888	30	22,950	28
Senegal	12	942	113	1,720	119
Serbia	7	5,214	61	9,830	60
Sierra Leone	5	300	144	720	144
Singapore	5	33,873	20	46,820	3
Slovak Rep.	5	13,298	34	19,220	32
Slovenia	2	22,919	26	26,230	25
South Africa	48	5,741	57	9,460	63
Spain	45	31,195	21	30,750	63
Sri Lanka	20	1,599	98	4,200	92
Sudan	40	1,031	110	1,790	118
Suriname	1	4,769	63	6,950	74
Swaziland	1	2,568	85	4,880	85
Sweden	9	50,714	4	37,490	9
Switzerland	8	61,387	2	44,410	5
Syrian Arab Rep.	21	1,944	92	4,200	91
Tajikistan	7	535	131	1,700	121
Tanzania	41	391	137	1,130	132
Thailand	67	2,919	83	6,110	78
Timor-Leste	1	1,624	97	3,110	100
Togo	6	390	138	810	140
Trinidad and Tobago	1	14,940	32	22,420	29
Tunisia	10	3,252	78	7,140	71
Turkey	73	8,886	43	12,970	44
Turkmenistan	5	2,454	87	5,650	81
Uganda	31	381	139	1,050	137
Ukraine	47	3,023	82	6,830	75
United Kingdom	61	45,969	9	35,540	12
United States	301	45,893	10	45,890	4
Uruguay	3	7,184	48	11,300	53
Uzbekistan	27	833	118	2,430	108
Venezuela, RB	27	8,392	46	12,290	50
Vietnam	85	784	120	2,530	105

Table 2.1   Income per capita and population, 2007 – *continued*

	Population	Gross national income per capita		PPP gross national income per capita	
	millions	$	rank	$	rank
Yemen, Rep.	22	1,012	111	2,440	107
Zambia	12	814	119	1,130	131
World	**6,614**	**8,252**			
Low income	**953**	**484**		**1,332**	
Middle income	**4,601**	**2,968**		**5,719**	
Lower middle income	3,660	1,832		4,225	
Upper middle income	941	7,386		11,564	
Low & middle income	**5,553**	**2,544**		**4,964**	
East Asia & Pacific	1,917	2,233		4,928	
Europe & Central Asia	440	6,897		11,278	
Latin America & Caribbean	559	6,358		9,789	
Middle East & North Africa	319	3,038		7,308	
South Asia	1,520	950		2,538	
Sub-Saharan Africa	798	1,017		1,901	
High income	**1,061**	**38,194**		**36,349**	
Least developed countries	**797**	**533**		**1,252**	

Source: World Bank, *World Development Indicators*, June 2009, online (Washington: World Bank).

In fact, the Gini ratio may indicate convergence or less inequality, while the ratio of extremes is increasing.

Consider now Figure 2.1. On the vertical axis is measured the percentage of income, and on the horizontal axis is measured the percentage of population. To draw the distribution of income (the Lorenz curve) first rank each country, groups of countries, or groups of individuals in ascending order according to the ratio of the percentage of income they receive and the percentage of population they represent; then cumulate the observations, and plot them on the diagram. To give a simple example, suppose we take the World Bank's division of countries into low income, middle income and high income, and that low-income countries contain 20 per cent of the world's population and receive only 2 per cent of world income; middle-income countries contain 64 per cent of the world's population and receive 23 per cent of world income, and rich countries contain 16 per cent of the world's population and receive 75 per cent of world income. The cumulative distribution of income in relation to population would then be 2/20, then 25/84 (when middle-income country figures are added), and finally 100/100 when the rich countries are added. These points are plotted in Figure 2.1 and the curve joining them is the Lorenz curve. The diagonal 45-degree line on the diagram shows an equal distribution of income. The position of the Lorenz curve in relation to the 45-degree line therefore gives a visual impression of the degree of inequality. The closer the Lorenz curve, the more equal the distribution, and the more 'bowed' the curve the more unequal the distribution. The Gini ratio is calculated as the area between the Lorenz curve and the 45-degree line divided by the area of the triangle it lies within. If the Lorenz curve is coincident with the 45-degree line, the Gini coefficient would be zero – complete equality. If one person received all the world's income, the Lorenz curve would follow the horizontal and vertical

Figure 2.1 Lorenz curve diagram

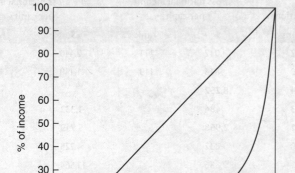

axes and the Gini coefficient would be one. When we examine international and global inequality, what we find is that through time, at least since the early 1900s, the Lorenz curve has been shifting outwards, and the Gini ratio has been rising, although according to some investigators it may recently have levelled off, albeit at a high level. A central estimate for the current level of international inequality would be a Gini ratio of 0.55, and for a global inequality a Gini ratio of 0.65. But, as we shall come to see, estimates vary depending on such factors as the sample of countries taken; how income is measured – whether by per capita income or household income – and whether income is measured at official exchange rates or at purchasing power parity rates (PPP).

There have been many recent studies measuring and summarizing what has been happening to international and global inequality historically (e.g. Milanovic, 2005; Bourguignon and Morrisson, 2002), and particularly since the 1950s (e.g. Norwegian Institute of Economic Affairs, 2000; Sala-í-Martin, 2002; Maddison, 2003; Ghose, 2004; Wade, 2004; Sutcliffe, 2004; Svedberg, 2004, and Milanovic, 2005). What does the evidence show? We distinguish between international inequality (unweighted and weighted by population) and global (or world) inequality.

International inequality (unweighted and weighted)

The unweighted Gini ratio of international inequality takes each country as one unit, regardless of population size, and assumes that each person within the country has the same average income. The distribution of income within the country is not considered. It is countries that are the focus, not people. The ratio is basically, therefore, a measure of whether or not countries are converging with each other, not whether the distribution of income across individuals in the world is becoming more or less equal. What does the evidence show? Using the best historical data available (Maddison, 2001; Bourguignon and Morrisson, 2002) for 26 countries covering nearly 80 per cent of the world's population, the Gini ratio in 1820 was approximately 0.2. This is very low by current standards. Two hundred years ago, international differences in income per head were not great. Maddison (2003) and Easterlin (2000) show that the ratio of per capita income of the richest to the poorest country in 1820 was only 3:1, compared with nearly 700:1 today. Table 2.2 shows the evolution of the unweighted Gini ratio through time, rising consistently to 0.54 in 2000 – a more than doubling of income inequality in the space of nearly 200 years. Some of the increase may be spurious due to the larger sample of countries used to calculate the ratio, but Milanovic shows that for the same 26 countries as used for the 1820 calculations, the Gini ratio still rises to just over 0.5 in 2000. For the period since the Second World War, the Gini ratio shows as increase for a consistent set of over 100 countries from 0.45 in 1952 to 0.54 in 2000: an increase of 20 per cent. There is no evidence of declining international inequality; that poor countries have grown faster on average than rich countries. On the contrary, they have been growing slower.

Turning now to the population-weighted measure of international inequality, Table 2.2 tells a slightly different story. It shows the Gini ratio peaking in1952 at 0.57 and declining to 0.50 in 2000. This implies that poor countries with large populations must have been growing faster on average than richer countries with smaller populations. In the 1950s and 1960s this was due to the fast growth of some of the big Latin American countries, such as Brazil and Mexico, and of Japan and South Korea, all using trade protection of one form or another. In the 1980s and 1990s the decline in the weighted Gini ratio has been largely due to the rapid growth of a small number of poor populous Asian countries, especially India and China. Ghose (2004), in his study of 96 countries over the period 1981 to 1997, finds that the weighted Gini ratio fell by 0.7 per cent per annum, but only 17 of the 76 developing countries in the sample converged on the per capita income of the 20 developed countries. The majority of poor developing countries diverged. Despite the fall in the ratio since 1952, it is still high and much higher than the estimate of 0.12 in 1820. In other words, for a large part of the last two centuries, the world's poorest and most populous countries

Table 2.2 A comparison of Gini ratios

	International inequality		Global (or world) inequality		
Year	Unweighted	Population weighted	Milanovic (2005)	Bourguignon and Morrisson (2002)	Sala-í-Martin (2002)
1820	0.20	0.12		0.50	
1870	0.29	0.26		0.56	
1890	0.31	0.30		0.59	
1913	0.37	0.37		0.61	
1929	0.35	0.40		0.62	
1938	0.35	0.40			
1952	0.45	0.57		0.64	
1960	0.46	0.55		0.64	
1978	0.47	0.54		0.66	0.66 (1970)
1988	0.50	0.53	0.62		0.65
1993	0.53	0.52	0.65	0.66 (1992)	0.64
1998	–	–	0.64		0.63
2000	0.54	0.50			0.63

Source: Adapted from Milanovic, 2005, Table 11.1.

have fared badly compared with the smaller, rich countries of the world. China and India are now reversing the trend, but for how long remains to be seen.

Global (or world) inequality

The Gini ratio of global (or world) inequality takes into account not only differences in average per capita income between countries, but also differences in income per capita within countries. Because internal income distributions are never equal, the measure of global inequality is bound to be higher than the unweighted measure of international inequality. It also means that changes in the global distribution of income are an amalgam of forces including: what is happening to the distribution of income between countries; what is happening to population growth in rich and poor countries; and what is happening to the distribution of income within countries. What does the evidence show? As far as the historical record is concerned, Bourguignon and Morrisson (2002) have tried to measure inequality among world citizens back to 1820 using a sample of 33 countries (or groups of countries) and measuring domestic income inequality by taking decile income shares (with the top decile of income earners divided into two). The results are shown in Table 2.2. It can be seen that the global Gini ratio in 1820 was already 0.5, more than double the level of international inequality, implying that domestic inequality was as great, if not greater, than international inequality. Through time, global inequality has increased, but because of rising international inequality, not because of even greater inequality within countries. On the contrary, income inequality in many countries shows a decrease historically, particularly in the richer countries of the world. Bourguignon and Morrisson calculate that within-country inequality accounted for 80 per cent of global inequality in the first half of the nineteenth century, when most countries were more or less at the same income level, but by 1950 within-country inequality accounted for only 40 per cent of global inequality because of the increase in inequality between countries. Today, the contribution is about 20 per cent. The Gini ratio of global inequality seems to have peaked in the late 1970s at 0.66, and has more or less stayed stable since then. At least the changes look minor compared with the unequivocal increase since 1820. But conflicting forces are still at work. International inequality is still increasing, but at a slower rate than in the past because of the fast growth of China and India; income distribution within some countries is narrowing, but in China and India the income distribution is widening particularly between the rural and urban sectors. This is probably now the greatest force preventing a fall in the global distribution of income.

Sala-i-Martin (2002) covers the more recent period from 1970 and 1998, taking the income distribution of 125 countries and aggregating them. Despite the much larger sample, the calculated global Gini ratios are remarkably similar to those of Bourguignon and Morrisson. The estimate for 1970 is 0.66 (see Table 2.2), gradually falling to 0.63 in 1998. The explanation for the slight fall is that the lower 'tail' of the aggregated income distribution has shifted rightwards more dramatically than the upper 'tail', largely due to developments in China and India. Fast growth in these two countries has lifted millions of people above the poverty line, and has reduced the relative income gap with richer countries, and this has been enough to just offset the worsening income distribution within China and India, as mentioned earlier. Still, we have evidence again of global inequality on a vast scale.

Milanovic (2005) has also undertaken the Herculean task of bringing together 360 household sample surveys of income and expenditure for nearly 100 countries for the years 1988, 1993 and 1998, covering 80 to 90 per cent of the world's population. There are 86 countries with samples for all three years, containing 84 per cent of the world's population. For this common sample of countries, the calculated global Gini ratio using household income or expenditure measured at purchasing power parity (PPP) is 0.62 in 1988; 0.65 in 1993, and 0.64 in 1998. For the full sample of countries (102 in 1988; 121 in 1993, and 122 in 1998) the Gini ratios are exactly the same as for the common sample. These estimates are remarkably similar to those of Sala-í-Martin, despite the difference in samples, and the measure of income. The mean income or expenditure from household surveys will be less than per capita income (or GDP per head) because the former excludes taxes and the provision of public goods. Nonetheless, Milanovic shows that if all survey incomes are scaled up by the ratio between GDP per capita and the survey mean, the Gini ratios hardly differ: 0.64 in 1988; 0.66 in 1993, and 0.64 in 1998. Of the total global inequality estimated, between 70 and 80 per cent is attributed to differences in the mean income between countries, leaving the minor part to be explained by inequality within countries. These results are confirmed by Edward (2006) using national consumption distributions and collating them into a global distribution measured at PPP in US$ for 1993 and 2001. The global Gini ratio is estimated at 0.610 for 1993 and 0.614 for 2001. Just over 80 per cent of this inequality is the result of between-country differences.

All the evidence and studies show a massive degree of inequality in the world distribution of income, which is not improving. This development gap naturally extends into other aspects of human welfare such as health; nutrition; life expectancy; education; employment opportunities, etc., as we shall come to see later in this chapter and in Chapter 3. The UNDP has described the world as 'gargantuan in its excesses and grotesque in its human and economic inequalities'.[1] This is, of course, a normative statement, but economists should not be afraid of making normative statements, as Basu (2006) does when he argues that 'the hiatus between the richest and the poorest people is too large, and the extent of poverty on earth is unacceptable. I like to believe that there will come a time when, looking back at today's world, human beings will wonder how primitive we were that we tolerated this.'

Many other statistics can be given to illustrate the grotesque inequalities that exist. The richest 1 per cent of people in the world receive as much income as the bottom 60 per cent. Or, to put it another way, the 60 million richest people receive as much income as 2.7 billion poor. The total income of the richest 25 million Americans is equal to the total income of 2 billion of the world's poorest people. The assets of the world's 400 billionaires (mostly in rich countries) exceed the total amount of income of nearly one-half of the world's total population.

The most evocative graph comes from Wade (2001), who divides the world's population up into equal 20 per cent shares (quintiles) from poorest to richest, and then shows the percentage of income that each share receives. Interestingly, and ironically, the picture resembles a champagne glass with a very narrow stem in the hands of the poor and a wide open bowl (containing the champagne) in the hands of the rich (Figure 2.2).

Below we discuss some technical problems concerning the measurement and comparability of per capita income across countries, and the measurement of poverty itself.

The measurement and comparability of per capita income

When using per capita income (PCY) figures to measure poverty, to classify countries into rich and poor and to compare the rate of development in different countries over time, the difficulties of measuring real per capita income and real living standards between countries must be continually borne in mind. There are two issues to discuss. The first concerns the problems associated with national income accounting, particularly in developing countries. The second is the need to convert each country's per capita income in *domestic* currency into a common unit of account

Figure 2.2   Distribution of world income (percentage of total, with quintiles of population ranked by income)

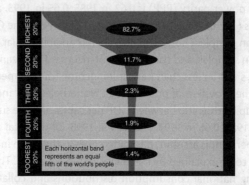

(e.g. the US$) so as to be able to make meaningful international comparisons of living standards. This leads to the topic of **purchasing-power parity** (**PPP**) estimates of PCY.

Turning first to national income accounting, the first point to bear in mind is that only goods that are produced and sold at a price in the market are included in the value of national income, measured by either the output or the expenditure method. Much output in developing countries never reaches the market, particularly in the rural sector where production is for subsistence purposes. If no allowance is made for the subsistence sector, this will bias downwards the calculation of national income, and therefore PCY. This point also implies that growth rates will tend to have an upward bias as a result of the extension of the money economy and the shift of economic activities from the household and subsistence sector to the market place. Part of the observed trend of faster GDP growth in developing countries since the 1960s may be partly a statistical illusion arising from the changing balance between the informal subsistence sector and the modern exchange sector.

Secondly, there is the sheer practical difficulty of measuring money national income in a rural economy where communications are bad, illiteracy is rife, and accounting procedures are rudimentary. Differences in the extent of the subsistence economy between developing countries, and differences in the ease and difficulty of collecting data, may markedly influence estimates of national income, and therefore of per capita income differences, between these countries and the rest of the world. Attempts are made in developing countries to make some allowance for production that never reaches the market place, but the estimates are likely to be subject to a wide margin of error.

Some testimony to the role that the subsistence sector must play in the economies of most developing countries is provided by the inconceivability that 60 per cent of the world's population could remain alive on the equivalent of $1,000 per annum. But this is not the whole story.

Purchasing power parity (PPP)

The other part of the story, and probably the major part, concerns the understatement of living standards in developing countries when their national incomes measured in local currencies are converted into US$ (as the common unit of account) at the official rate of exchange. If the US$ is used as the unit of account, the national per capita income of country X in US$ is given by

$$\frac{\text{GNP}_X}{\text{Population}} \div \text{Exchange rate}$$

For example, if the GNP of country X is 100 billion rupees, its population is 5 million, and there are 10 rupees to the dollar, then the per capita income of country X in dollars is

$$\frac{100 \text{ billion}}{5 \text{ million}} \div 10 = \$2,000$$

But if the living standards of the two countries are to be compared by this method, it must be assumed that 10 rupees in country X buys the same living standard as \$1 in the USA. It is well known, however, that official exchange rates between two countries' currencies are not good measures of the PPP between countries, especially between countries at different levels of development. The reason is that exchange rates are largely determined by the supply of and demand for currencies based on goods and assets that are traded (the prices of which tend to be equalized internationally) but living standards depend also on the prices of non-traded goods, which are largely determined by unit labour costs, and these tend to be lower the poorer the country. As a general rule, it can be said that the lower the level of development and the poorer the country, the lower the price of non-traded goods relative to traded goods and the more the use of the official exchange rate will *understate* the living standards of the developing country measured in US\$.

Let us give a simple example. The motor car is an internationally traded good. Suppose that the dollar price of a particular model of car is \$10,000 and there are 10 rupees to the dollar. Ignoring transport costs, tariffs and so on, the price of the car in India will be \$10,000 × 10 = 100,000 rupees, otherwise a profit will be made by dealers buying in the cheapest market and selling in the most expensive. The forces of demand and supply (and arbitrage) will equalize the price of traded goods. But let us now consider a non-traded good such as a haircut. Suppose a haircut in the USA costs \$10. At the official exchange rate of 10 rupees to the dollar, a haircut in India should be 100 rupees. But suppose that in fact it is only 25 rupees. This would mean that as far as haircuts are concerned, the value of the rupee is underestimated by a factor of four. The PPP rate of exchange for haircuts alone is \$10 ÷ 25 rupees, or \$1 = 2.5 rupees. If the national income of country X measured in rupees was divided by 2.5 instead of 10, the national income of country X in dollars, and therefore PCY in dollars, would now be four times higher: \$8,000 per head instead of \$2,000 per head as in the example above.

As development proceeds, the ratio of the price of non-traded goods to traded goods tends to rise as wage levels in the non-traded goods sector rise but productivity growth is slow – slower than in the traded goods sector. **To make meaningful international comparisons of income and living standards, therefore, what is required is a measure of PPP, or a *real* exchange rate, between countries.**

There are several methods of constructing PPP ratios in order to make binary comparisons (one country with another) or 'multilateral' comparisons in which the currency of any one of a group of countries can act as the unit of account without altering the ratios of living standards between countries.

The most common way of constructing a PPP ratio between two countries (say India and the USA) is to take a representative, comparable basket of goods and services in both countries, and then take the weighted average of prices, where the weights (w_i) reflect the proportion of expenditure on each good in total expenditure. The PPP rate of exchange between India and the USA is therefore:

$$PPP = \frac{w_{il}P_{il}}{w_{iUS}P_{iUS}},$$

where P_{il} is the price of the good in India and P_{iUS} is the price of the good in the USA.

The difference between estimates of PCY measured at the official exchange rate and PPP esti-mates of PCY is shown in Table 2.1. By comparing the figures and ranks in columns two and three, it can be seen that the difference is quite dramatic, and in general the difference is greater the poorer the country. In India, for example, the PPP estimate of PCY is $2,740 compared with an estimated $470 at the official exchange rate. In Kenya the figure is $1,041 compared with $721.

In the high-income countries, however, there is hardly any difference between the two esti-mates. Norway enjoys the highest standard of living in the world, with the USA a close second using the PPP method.

Irving Kravis and his associates (1975, 1978) have also developed a method of making **mul-tilateral** comparisons of real per capita income across countries, allowing a direct comparison between any two countries using *any* country's currency as the unit of account (not necessarily the US$). This pioneering work of Kravis is now regularly extended and updated by his collabo-rators Summers and Heston (1988, 1991), who have produced international comparisons of *real* income per capita for all the major countries of the world since 1990, which can be compared with the World Bank estimates of per capita income based on official rates of exchange with the US$. The two are markedly different.

Per capita income as an index of development

Now let us turn to the question of the use of per capita income figures as an index of development and for making a distinction between developed and developing countries, as well as between rich and poor. While there may be an association between poverty and underdevelopment and riches and development, there are a number of reasons why some care must be taken when using per capita income figures alone as a measure or indicator of development (unless underdevelopment is *defined* as poverty and development as riches). Apart from the difficulty of measuring income in many countries and the difficulty of making inter-country comparisons, using a single per capita income figure to separate developed from developing countries is inevitably somewhat arbitrary, because it ignores such factors as the distribution of income within countries, differences in devel-opment potential and other physical indicators of the quality of life. It is not so much a question of whether or not low-income countries should be labelled 'underdeveloped' or 'developing', but what income level should be used as the criterion for separating the developed from the develop-ing countries, and whether all high-income countries should necessarily be labelled 'developed'. In many ways it should be the *nature* and *characteristics* of the countries that determine which income level should be used as the dividing line. It also makes sense to categorize separately the oil-rich countries, which have high per capita incomes but cannot be regarded as developed by the criteria discussed in Chapter 1.

Acronyms abound to describe the different stages of development. Perhaps the most amusing set is attributable to the Brazilian economist Roberto Campos, who distinguishes five categories of countries: the HICs, PICs, NICs, MICs and DICs. These stand for hardly industrialized countries, partly industrialized countries, newly industrialized countries, mature industrialized countries and decadent industrialized countries! The HICs and the PICs would certainly cover all the low-income countries and at least the lower half of the middle-income countries. The NICs cover most of the upper half of the middle-income countries – Brazil, Mexico, Hong Kong and Singapore being prime examples. The MICs and DICs cover most of those countries classified as 'industrial market economies', with the exception of New Zealand and Australia, which have become rich through agriculture.

But bearing in mind the arbitrariness of per capita income, it is still very convenient to have a readily available and easily understandable criterion for classifying countries, and perhaps per capita income is the best single index we have. It also has one positive advantage, namely that it focuses on the *raison d'être* of development: raising living standards and eradicating poverty. And in the last resort per capita income is not a bad proxy for the social and economic structure of most societies. If developing countries are defined on the basis of a per capita income level so as to include most of the countries of Asia, Africa and Latin America, striking similarities are found between the characteristics and development obstacles of many of the countries in these continents. These include:

- A high proportion of the labour force engaged in agriculture with low agricultural productivity
- A high proportion of domestic expenditure on food and necessities
- An export trade dominated by primary products and an import trade dominated by manufactured goods
- A low level of technology and poor human capital
- A high birth rate coupled with a falling death rate
- Savings undertaken by a small percentage of the population.

There are, of course, some countries that on a per capita income basis are classified as developed and possess many of the above-mentioned characteristics (e.g. some oil-producing countries), but the exceptions are few, and the reverse of this situation is almost inconceivable. Also these countries have many social problems in common, such as growing unemployment in urban areas, inegalitarian income distributions, and poor health and standards of education – about which we shall say more later.

In general, therefore, it can be said that per capita income may be used as a starting point for classifying *levels* of development, and can certainly be used to identify the *need* for development. The only major reservation that we shall have to consider later concerns the case of geographically dual economies, where an aggregate per capita income figure can disguise as great a need for the development of a sizeable region within the country as the need for the development of the country itself.

There is a difference, however, between using per capita income as a guideline for classifying countries into developed or underdeveloped at a point *in time* and using the growth of per capita income as an index of development *over time*. The difficulty of using per capita income for the latter purpose is the obvious one that if, in a particular period, per capita income did not grow because population growth matched the growth of a country's total income, one would be forced into the odd position of denying that a country had developed even though its national product had increased. This is an inherent weakness of linking the concept of development to a measure of living standards.

This leads on to the distinction between **growth** and **development**. Development without growth is hardly conceivable, but growth is possible without development. The upswing of the trade cycle is the most obvious example of the possibility of growth without development; and examples of abortive 'take-offs' are not hard to find where countries have grown rapidly for a short time and then reverted to relative stagnation. Historically, Argentina is a case in point. On the other hand, development is hardly possible without growth; but development is possible, as we have suggested, without a rise in per capita income. It would be a strange, rather purposeless, type of development, however, that left per capita income unchanged, unless the stationary per capita income was only temporary and a strong foundation was being laid for progress in the future.

For the ultimate rationale of development must be to improve living standards and welfare, and while an increase in measured per capita income may not be a sufficient condition for an increase in individual welfare, it is a necessary condition in the absence of radical institutional innovations, such as an increase in public goods.

An increase in income is not a sufficient condition for an increase in welfare, because an increase in income can involve costs as well as benefits. It may have been generated at the expense of leisure or by the production of goods not immediately consumable. **If development is looked upon as a means of improving the welfare of present generations, probably the best index to take would be consumption per man-hour worked**. This index, in contrast to an index of per capita income, focuses directly on the immediate utility derived from consumption goods in relation to the disutility of the work effort involved in their production.

Measuring poverty

The World Bank defines poverty as the inability of people to attain a minimum standard of living.[2] This definition gives rise to three questions. How do we measure the standard of living? What is meant by a *minimum* standard of living? How can we express the overall extent of poverty in a single measure?

The most obvious measure of living standards is an individual's (or household's) real income or expenditure (with an allowance made for output produced for own consumption). The same level of real income and expenditure in different countries, however, may be associated with different levels of nutrition, life expectancy, infant mortality, schooling and so on, which must be considered as an integral part of 'the standard of living'. Measures of living standards based on per capita income, therefore, may need to be supplemented by further measures that include these other variables. Later in this chapter we discuss the attempt by the UNDP to construct a **Human Poverty Index** and a **Human Development Index**, which take some of these factors into account.

To separate the poor from the not so poor, an arbitrary per capita income figure has to be taken that is sufficient to provide a minimum acceptable level of consumption. There are two main ways of setting a consumption poverty line in order to measure poverty and make comparison across countries: the **PPP method** and the **food energy method**. As we have seen above, a country's PPP is defined as the number of units of the country's currency required to buy the same amount of goods and services in the domestic market as a dollar in the USA. The World Bank publishes the PPP levels of per capita income for all countries (see Table 2.1). For the measurement of poverty, to give an example, the PPP poverty line could be set at, say, $40 per month or $480 per annum. By definition, people on this PPP poverty line in any country have the purchasing power to obtain the same level of consumption of any person on the poverty line in any other country. But the composition of the consumption bundle is very likely to differ. The PPP poverty line is not explicitly linked to nutritional intakes derived from different consumption bundles, so there are likely to be inter-country differences in nutrition on the PPP poverty line.

The **food energy method** of setting a consumption poverty line is one way of dealing with this problem by defining a minimum internationally agreed calorie intake line, and converting consumption bundles into calorie intakes using the nutritional values of consumption goods (with non-food goods having a zero value). The problem here, however, is that consumers in different countries may choose different combinations of food and other goods which then require different incomes to meet nutritional requirements. Indeed, the nature of the society and the stage of development reached may *require* different combinations. What are regarded as optional extras in some countries may be necessities in others. The United Nation's Food and Agriculture Organization (FAO) defines undernourishment as 'food intake that is continuously insufficient to meet dietary energy requirements'.

A consumption-based poverty line can therefore be thought of as comprising two elements: an objective measure of the expenditure necessary to buy a minimum level of nutrition; and a subjective additional amount that varies from country to country, reflecting the cost to individuals of participating in the everyday life of society.

All this is in theory. In practice, to measure the extent of absolute poverty in the world, the World Bank takes two main criteria: $1.25 a day and $2 a day at 1995 prices. The $1.25 a day criterion used to be the $1.08 a day (or roughly $1 a day) criterion widely cited in earlier poverty studies, but the figure was revised by the World Bank in 2008 because of new estimates of the comparative cost of living across countries (see Chen and Ravallion, 2008). The new estimates draw on 675 household surveys in 116 countries over the period 1979 to 2006. The $1.25 a day line at PPP is the average of the national poverty lines for the poorest 15 countries in the sample, namely: Malawi, Mali, Ethiopia, Sierra Leone, Niger, Uganda, Gambia, Rwanda, Guinea-Bissau, Tanzania, Tajikistan, Mozambique, Chad, Nepal and Ghana. The $1.25 a day line is regarded, therefore, as the minimum subsistence level across the globe. The $2 a day line is the median poverty line found amongst developing countries as a whole.

Given the poverty line, the simplest way to measure the amount of poverty is by the **head count index**, which simply adds up the number of people who fall below the poverty line (which can also be expressed as a proportion of the total population, giving the **Poverty Rate**). The most recent estimates for different continents over time, and in total, are given in Table 2.3. In 2005, the number of people living on less than $1.25 a day was nearly 1.4 billion or one-quarter of the world's population, and the number living on less than $2 a day was 2.56 billion or approximately 40 per cent of the world's population. These are staggering statistics. There has been a large fall since 1981 in the numbers living on less than $1.25 a day, but this is more than accounted for by the reduction of poverty in China. There has been virtually no change since the early 1990s in the number of those living on less than $2 a day. If we look by continent, poverty has fallen rapidly in East Asia and the Pacific, but has been rising in absolute terms in South Asia, Latin America and the Caribbean, and sub-Saharan Africa. Poverty is most concentrated in Africa where over 50 per cent of the population are living in absolute poverty and 73 per cent are living on less than $2 a day.

Figure 2.3 gives a graphical representation of the number of people in the world living above and below different levels of per capita income, including $10 a day. Eighty per cent of the world's population subsists on less than $10 a day. Students reading this book might like to try the experiment of living on such a meagre sum and see how they fare!

Paul Collier (2007) has called those living on less than $1 a day **the Bottom Billion**. On the new estimates of absolute poverty, the 'bottom billion' have become the 'bottom 1.4 billion' caught in the four 'poverty traps' he identifies: the conflict trap (civil wars); the natural resources trap (the curse of natural resources – see Chapter 3, p. 77); the trap of being landlocked with bad neighbours, and the trap of bad governance in a small country.

One weakness of the headcount index, however, is that it ignores the *extent* to which the poor fall *below* the poverty line, so that comparison between countries, or over time, using only the headcount index or the poverty rate, do not tell the full story. To overcome this weakness, the concept of the **Poverty Gap** is used and measured. This measures the proportionate gap between the average level of income below the poverty line and the poverty line itself. For example, if

Table 2.3 Absolute poverty and poverty rates 1981–2005 (at PPP 2005)

| | Absolute poverty (millions) | | | | | | | | | Poverty rate (%) | | | | | | | | |
| | $1 a day | | | $1.25 a day | | | $2 a day | | | $1 a day | | | $1.25 a day | | | $2 a day | | |
Region	1981	1990	2005	1981	1990	2005	1981	1990	2005	1981	1990	2005	1981	1990	2005	1981	1990	2005
East Asia and Pacific	921.7	623.4	175.6	1,071.5	873.3	316.2	1,277.7	1,273.7	728.7	66.8	39.1	9.3	77.7	54.7	16.8	92.6	79.8	38.7
of which China	730.4	499.1	106.1	835.1	693.2	207.7	972.1	960.8	473.7	73.5	44.0	8.1	84.0	60.2	15.9	97.8	84.6	36.3
Eastern Europe and Central Asia	3.0	4.1	10.2	7.1	9.1	17.3	35.0	31.9	41.9	0.7	0.9	2.2	1.7	2.0	3.7	8.3	6.9	8.9
Latin America and Caribbean	28.0	29.0	30.7	42.0	42.9	46.1	82.3	86.3	91.3	7.7	6.6	5.6	11.5	9.8	8.4	22.5	19.7	16.6
Middle East and North Africa	5.6	3.8	4.7	13.7	9.7	11.0	46.3	44.4	51.5	3.3	1.7	1.6	7.9	4.3	3.6	26.7	19.7	16.9
South Asia	387.3	381.2	350.5	548.3	579.2	595.6	799.5	926.0	1,091.5	41.9	34.0	23.7	59.4	51.7	40.3	86.5	82.7	73.9
of which India	296.1	282.5	266.5	420.5	435.5	455.8	608.9	701.6	827.7	42.1	33.3	24.3	59.8	51.3	41.6	86.6	82.6	75.6
Sub-Saharan Africa	169.4	245.2	304.2	213.7	299.1	390.6	294.2	393.6	556.7	42.6	47.5	39.9	53.7	57.9	51.2	74.0	76.2	73.0
Total	1,515.0	1,286.7	876.0	1,896.2	1,813.4	1,376.7	2,535.1	2,755.9	2,561.5	41.4	29.5	16.1	51.8	41.6	25.2	69.2	63.2	47.0
Total excluding China	784.5	787.6	769.9	1,061.1	1,130.2	1,169.0	1,563.3	1,795.1	2,087.9	29.4	24.4	18.6	39.8	35.0	28.2	58.6	55.6	50.3

Figure 2.3 Percentage of people in the world at different poverty levels, 2005

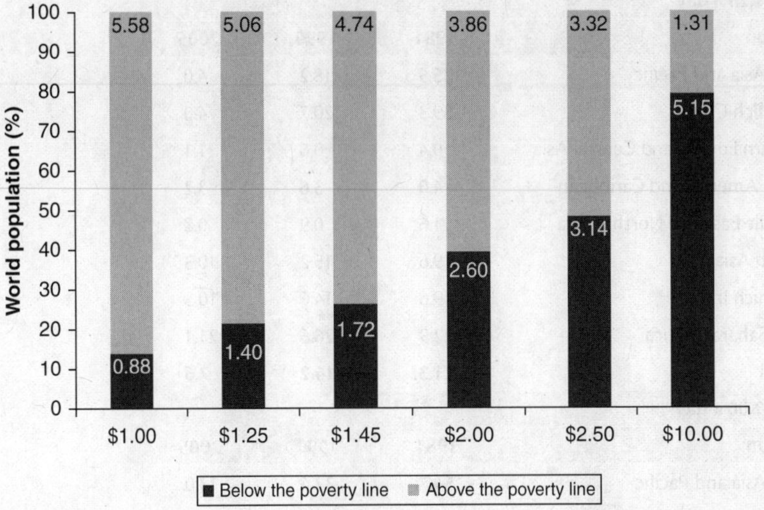

Source: World Bank, 2008.

the poverty line is $1.25 a day and the average income of the poor below this line is $1 a day, then the poverty gap is ($1.25 − $1)/1.25 = 0.2 or 20 per cent. Table 2.4 gives estimates of the poverty gap for different 'continents' in 1981, 1990 and 2005, using both the $1.25 and $2 a day criterion. The aggregate poverty gap in 2005 at $1.25 a day is 7.6 per cent and 18.6 per cent using $2 a day, but notice the big difference between regions. While the gap in East Asia and Pacific is only 4 per cent in 2005 at $1.25 a day, it is over 20 per cent in Africa. At $2 a day, the gap for Africa is 37 per cent. This represents 9 per cent of GDP. In other words, 9 per cent of GDP would have to be redistributed to raise everyone in Africa above the $2 a day level. That would be a huge task.

The focus of the World Bank is now very much on poverty eradication. When Robert McNamara was President of the World Bank in the 1970s, he defined absolute poverty as 'a condition of life so degraded by disease, illiteracy, and malnutrition and squalor, as to deny its victims basic human necessities – [a condition] so limited as to prevent the realisation of the potential of the genes with which one was born'. In May 1992 the then President of the World Bank, Lewis Preston, declared that poverty reduction will be 'the benchmark by which our performance as a development institution will be measured'. And in the *World Development Report 2000/2001*, the President, James Wolfensohn, wrote: 'poverty amidst plenty is the world's greatest challenge. We at the Bank have made it our mission to fight poverty with passion and professionalism, putting it at the centre of all the work that we do.' As Collier (2007) also writes, 'an impoverished ghetto of 1 billion people [is] increasingly impossible for a comfortable world to tolerate'.

Meeting the Millennium Poverty Reduction Target

To meet the Millennium Goal of halving the proportion of people living in absolute poverty by 2015 compared with the level in 1990 requires a sustained growth in the level of per capita income. To calculate the growth required, the elasticity of the poverty rate with respect to the

Table 2.4   Poverty gap index (×100) by region, 1981–2005

(a) $1.25 a day			
Region	**1981**	**1990**	**2005**
East Asia and Pacific	35.5	18.2	4.0
of which China	39.3	20.7	4.0
Eastern Europe and Central Asia	0.4	0.6	1.1
Latin America and Caribbean	4.0	3.6	3.2
Middle East and North Africa	1.6	0.9	0.8
South Asia	19.6	15.2	10.3
of which India	19.6	14.6	10.5
Sub-Saharan Africa	22.9	26.6	21.1
Total	**21.3**	**14.2**	**7.6**
(b) $2.00 a day			
Region	**1981**	**1990**	**2005**
East Asia and Pacific	54.7	37.4	13.0
of which China	59.3	40.9	12.2
Eastern Europe and Central Asia	1.9	2.0	3.0
Latin America and Caribbean	8.9	7.8	6.7
Middle East and North Africa	7.4	4.8	4.0
South Asia	40.7	35.7	28.7
of which India	40.8	35.3	29.5
Sub-Saharan Africa	38.8	42.2	37.0
Total	**36.5**	**29.1**	**18.6**

Source: Chen and Ravallion, 2008.

level of per capita income needs to be determined. This can be estimated using the equation below:

$$\log P_i = a + b \log PCY_i \tag{2.1}$$

where P_i is the headcount poverty rate for country i, PCY_i is the level of per capita income, and b is the elasticity of the poverty rate. Besley and Burgess (2003) calculate this elasticity for developing countries as a whole and for different continents. The results are shown in Table 2.5. The elasticity for the whole sample of countries is 0.73 which means that the poverty rate declines by 0.73 per cent for every one per cent increase in per capita income (given the distribution of income). Let us give an example. Suppose the poverty rate in 1990 was 50 per cent, and the goal is to reduce it to 25 per cent by 2015; that is, by 50 per cent. With an elasticity of 0.73, this would require per capita income growth of approximately 70 per cent (i.e. 50 per cent/0.73), or roughly 3 per cent per annum over 25 years. If population growth is 1.5 per cent per annum, this means GDP growth of 4.5 per cent per annum. This is relatively high, but not out of line for some countries in the recent past. In fact, it can be seen from the poverty rates in Table 2.3 that East Asia and Pacific has already reached this Millennium Development goal. In 1990, the $1.25 a day poverty rate was 54.7 per cent and in 2005 it was 16.8 per cent. Some countries outside East Asia and Pacific are also

Table 2.5   Growth and poverty across the globe, 1990–2015

	Whole sample	East Asia and Pacific	Eastern Europe & Central Asia	Latin America and Caribbean	Middle East and North Africa	South Asia	Sub-Saharan Africa
Elasticity of poverty with respect to income per capita	−0.73	−1.00	−1.14	−0.73	−0.72	−0.59	−0.49
Annual growth rate needed to halve world poverty by 2015 (%)	3.8	2.7	2.4	3.8	3.8	4.7	5.6
Historical growth 1960–1990 (%)	1.7	3.3	2.0	1.3	4.3	1.9	0.2

Source: Besley and Burgess, 2003.

on track to meet the goal, but many are not, particularly in Africa and South Asia. In the latter region, for example, the poverty rate was still 40.3 per cent in 2005 compared with 51.7 per cent in 1990. The target is roughly 25 per cent in 2015, so it still has 15 percentage points to fall or 35 per cent (i.e. (15/40) × 100). If the elasticity of the poverty rate with respect to growth is 0.59 (as calculated in Table 2.5), this requires growth of PCY of 35 per cent / 0.59 ∼ 60 per cent, or an average of 6 per cent per annum over ten years; and even higher GDP growth. Even faster growth rates would be required for Africa, with a bigger fall required and a lower elasticity of poverty to growth. According to Chen and Ravallion (2008), the annual rate of poverty reduction from 1981 to 2005 outside of China has been −0.44 percentage points a year, so the world outside China will not meet the Millennium Development Goal of halving poverty by 2015 compared with 1990. The 1990 poverty rate was 35 per cent, which gives a target rate of 17.5 per cent. The 2005 poverty rate was 28.2 per cent. A 0.44 percentage point reduction from 2005 to 2015 would give a reduction of 4.4 percentage points or a fall from 28.2 to 23.8, which is still 6.3 percentage points above the target.

The depressing conclusion to be reached is that many countries, particularly in Africa, will not achieve the Millennium Poverty Reduction Target – the required growth rates are too high – unless poverty is tackled at the 'grass roots' by income and wealth redistribution and institutional change. This is the World Bank's 'new' approach to tackling poverty.

Tackling poverty from the 'grass roots'

Poverty not only means low income and consumption, and low levels of human development in terms of education and health care, but also feelings of powerlessness, vulnerability and fear because poor people are not free, and are exposed to greater risk, living on the margin of subsistence.

What it means to be poor is well illustrated from the World Bank's study *The Voices of the Poor*, which asked 60,000 poor people in 60 countries to articulate their feelings about their physical and mental state. The answers are contained in Case example 2.1, which are both moving and revealing. Feelings of helplessness, humiliation and lack of self-esteem are paramount.

The World Bank proposes a three-pronged strategy for poverty reduction: **promoting opportunity; facilitating empowerment** and **enhancing security**.

Promoting opportunity is partly about expanding economic opportunities for poor people through the process of economic growth, and partly about expanding the asset base of poor people and increasing the return on those assets. The major causes of individual poverty can be linked to a lack of assets and/or a low return on assets. Important assets to enable people to grow out of poverty include (1) natural assets, such as land; (2) human assets, such as education and health; (3) financial assets, including access to credit, and (4) social assets, such as networks of contacts. The return on assets once acquired depends on the institutional framework of a country, the performance of the economy, and what is happening in the world economy. The state has a role to play in expanding poor people's assets because markets do not work well for poor people owing to lack of access, power and collateral. The state can help in three major ways: first by using its power to redistribute resources; secondly through institutional reforms to deliver services more effectively, particularly in the fields of health and education; and thirdly by facilitating the engagement of poor people in programmes which help them to acquire assets, such as land and credit.

Case example 2.1	The voices of the poor

Poor people in 60 countries were asked to analyse and share their ideas of well-being (a good experience of life) and 'ill-being' (a bad experience of life).

Well-being was variously described as happiness, harmony, peace, freedom from anxiety, and peace of mind. In Russia people say 'well-being is a life free from daily worries about lack of money'. In Bangladesh, 'to have a life free from anxiety'. In Brazil, 'not having to go through so many rough spots'.

People describe ill-being as lack of material things, as bad experiences, and as bad feelings about oneself. A group of young men in Jamaica ranks lack of self-confidence as the second biggest impact of poverty: 'Poverty means we don't believe in self, we hardly travel out of the community – so frustrated, just locked up in a house all day.'

Although the nature of ill-being and poverty varies among locations and people – something that policy responses must take into account – there is a striking commonality across countries. Not surprisingly, material well-being turns out to be very important. Lack of food, shelter, and clothing is mentioned everywhere as critical. In Kenya a man says: 'Don't ask me what poverty is because you have met it outside my house. Look at the house and count the number of holes. Look at my utensils and the clothes I am wearing. Look at everything and write what you see. What you see is poverty.'

Alongside the material, physical well-being features prominently in the characterizations of poverty. And the two meld together when lack of food leads to ill health – or when ill health leads to an inability to earn income. People speak about the importance of looking well fed. In Ethiopia poor people say, 'We are skinny', 'We are deprived and pale', and speak of a life that 'makes you older than your age'.

Security of income is also closely tied to health. But insecurity extends beyond ill health. Crime and violence are often mentioned by poor people. In Ethiopia women say, 'We live hour to hour', worrying about whether it will rain. An Argentine says, 'You have work, and you are fine. If not, you starve. That's how it is.'

Two social aspects of ill-being and poverty also emerged. For many poor people, well-being means the freedom of choice and action and the power to control one's

| Case example 2.1 | The voices of the poor – *continued* |

life. A young woman in Jamaica says that poverty is 'like living in jail, living in bondage, waiting to be free'.

Linked to these feelings are definitions of well-being as social well-being and comments on the stigma of poverty. As an old woman in Bulgaria says, 'To be well means to see your grandchildren happy and well dressed and to know that your children have settled down; to be able to give them food and money whenever they come to see you, and not to ask them for help and money.' A Somali proverb captures the other side: 'Prolonged sickness and persistent poverty cause people to hate you.'

The following quotations are an illustration of what living in poverty means:

Certainly our farming is little; all the products, things bought from stores, are expensive; it is hard to live, we work and earn little money, buy few things or products; products are scarce, there is no money and we feel poor.

(From a discussion group of poor men and women, Ecuador)

We face a calamity when my husband falls ill. Our life comes to a halt until he recovers and goes back to work.

(Poor woman, Zawyet Sultan, Egypt)

Poverty is humiliation, the sense of being dependent on them, and of being forced to accept rudeness, insults, and indifference when we seek help.

(Poor woman, Latvia)

Source: World Bank, 2000.

A growing economy is absolutely crucial for poverty reduction as emphasized recently by the World Bank's Commission on Growth and Development headed by the Nobel Prize-winning economist Michael Spence (World Bank, 2008). Poverty cannot be reduced in a stagnant economy. The Commission finds a strong negative association across countries between the average growth of income and consumption and the *share* of people living on less than $1 per day. A one percentage point growth of income below the average is associated with a 2 percentage point increase in the share of people living in poverty.

On the other hand, similar rates of growth of countries are associated with different rates of poverty reduction. This is the result of existing inequalities in the distribution of income, assets and access to opportunities. Growth is much more effective in reducing poverty where the income distribution is more equal than where there are big inequalities. The World Bank estimates that when inequality is low, growth reduces poverty by nearly twice as much as when inequality is high. If income inequality remains unchanged in Latin America and sub-Saharan Africa, the Bank's poverty targets will not be met even if per capita income grows at 4 per cent per annum to the year 2015 (which itself is optimistic).

Facilitating empowerment is a new departure in the thinking of the World Bank compared with its 1990 *Report*. Empowering poor people means strengthening the participation of poor people in decision-making; eliminating various forms of discrimination – ethnic, religious, sexual – and making state institutions more accountable and responsive to poor people. The great challenge here is to tackle the institutional structures of poor countries that continue to marginalize, discriminate against, and disenfranchise vulnerable sections of society. The law, the church, bureaucrats and local elites, and customs and traditions, all play a part. The state has a role to play in helping to empower people by (1) curbing corruption and harassment, and using the power of the state to redistribute resources for actions benefiting the poor; (2) ensuring that the legal system is fair and accessible to the poor; (3) making sure that the delivery of local services is not captured by local elites; (4) encouraging the participation of poor people in the political process; and (5) galvanizing political support for public action against poverty.

Enhancing security means reducing poor people's vulnerability to the various forms of insecurity that affect people's lives such as economic shocks, natural disasters, crop failures, ill health, violence, wars, etc., and helping people to cope with these adverse shocks when they occur. The wide range of risks that poor people are exposed to is highlighted in Case example 2.2. This vulnerability to risk requires a range of insurance mechanisms for managing risk such as: health and old-age insurance; unemployment insurance and workforce programmes; social funds and cash transfers; microfinance programmes; insurance against crop failures and price instability, and so on.

The World Bank points out, however, that promoting opportunities, facilitating empowerment and enhancing security are *necessary* conditions for tackling poverty, but not *sufficient* conditions in an interdependent, global economy. International action is also required to help poor people in at least five ways:

- Promoting global financial stability and reducing the risks of economic crisis
- Opening up markets (particularly in developed countries) to the goods of poor countries
- Encouraging the production of international public goods that benefit poor people; for example the control of disease, agricultural research and the dissemination of knowledge
- More foreign aid and debt relief
- Giving a greater voice to poor countries and peoples in the global forums and multilateral institutions of the world such as the World Bank, IMF and WTO.

Case example 2.2	**Poor people's exposure to risk**

Poor people are exposed to a wide range of risks.

Illness and injury

Poor people often live and work in environments that expose them to greater risk of illness or injury, and they have less access to health care. Their health risks are strongly connected to the availability of food, which is affected by almost all the risks the poor face (natural disasters, wars, harvest failures and food price fluctuations). Communicable diseases are concentrated among the poor, with respiratory infections the leading cause of death. A recent study of poverty in India found that the poor are 4.5 times as likely to contract tuberculosis as the rich and twice as likely to lose a child before the age of two.

Illness and injury in the household have both direct costs (for prevention, care and cure) and opportunity costs (lost income or schooling while ill). The timing, duration and frequency of illness also affect its impact. A study of South India found that households can compensate for an illness during the slack agricultural season, but illness during the peak season leads to a heavy loss of income, especially on small farms, usually necessitating costly informal borrowing.

| Case example 2.2 | **Poor people's exposure to risk** – *continued* |

Old age

Many risks are associated with ageing: illness, social isolation, inability to continue working and uncertainty about whether transfers will provide an adequate living. The incidence of poverty among the elderly varies significantly. In most Latin American countries the proportion of people in poverty is lower for the elderly than for the population at large. In contrast, in many countries of the former Soviet Union the incidence of poverty is above average among the elderly, particularly among people 75 and older. Women, because of their longer life expectancy, constitute the majority of the elderly, and they tend to be more prone to poverty in old age than men. The number of elderly people in the developing world will increase significantly in coming decades with the rapid demographic transition.

Consultations with poor people show that income security is a prime concern of the elderly, followed closely by access to health services, suitable housing and the quality of family and community life. Isolation, loneliness, and fear all too often mark old people's lives.

Crime and domestic violence

Crime and domestic violence reduce earnings and make it harder to escape poverty. While the rich can hire private security guards and fortify their homes, the poor have few means to protect themselves against crime. In São Paulo, Brazil, in 1992 the murder rate for adolescent males in poor neighbourhoods was 11 times that in wealthier ones. Poor people frequently voice their fear of violence and the resulting powerlessness: 'I do not know whom to trust, the police or the criminals.'

Crime also hurts poor people indirectly. Children exposed to violence may perform worse in school. A study of urban communities in Ecuador, Hungary, the Philippines and Zambia showed that difficult economic conditions lead to destruction of social capital as involvement in community organizations declines, informal ties among residents weaken, and gang violence, vandalism and crime increase. Violence and crime may thus deprive poor people of two of their best means of reducing vulnerability: human and social capital.

Unemployment and other labour market risks

Labour market risks include unemployment, falling wages, and having to take up precarious and low-quality jobs in the informal sector as a result of macroeconomic crises or policy reform. The first workers to be laid off during cutbacks in public sector jobs are usually those with low skills, who then join the ranks of the urban poor; a pattern observed in Africa and Latin America during the structural adjustment reforms of the 1980s and early 1990s. The East Asian crisis also had pronounced effects on labour markets, with real wages and non-agricultural employment falling in all affected countries. As state enterprises in Eastern Europe and the countries of the former Soviet Union were privatized, poverty increased among displaced workers with low education and obsolete skills, not qualified to work in emerging industries.

continued overleaf

| Case example 2.2 | Poor people's exposure to risk – *continued* |

Fluctuations in demand for labour often disproportionately affect women and young workers. Most public sector retrenchment programmes have affected women's employment more than men's, and women are more likely than men to work for small firms, which tend to be more sensitive to demand fluctuations. As incomes fall, poor households try to increase their labour market participation, especially for women and children.

Harvest failure and food price fluctuations

Weather-related uncertainties (mainly rainfall), plant disease and pests create harvest risk for all farmers, but technologies for reducing such risks (irrigation, pesticides, disease-resistant varieties) are less available in poor areas. In 1994–6 less than 20 per cent of all cropland was irrigated in low- and middle-income countries (only 4 per cent of such land was irrigated in sub-Saharan Africa).

Fluctuations in food prices are a related risk. Since poor households spend a large part of their income on food, even small price increases can severely affect food intake. Households that meet their food needs through subsistence agriculture are less vulnerable than households that have to buy all their food.

Liberalization of markets often boosts the price of staples – a benefit to small farmers if they are net sellers of food. Hurt are the urban poor and the landless rural poor, as net food buyers, and farmers who engage in seasonal switching, selling food after the harvest when food is plentiful and cheap and buying it when it is scarce and expensive. Where transport facilities are good, traders can step in and equalize prices over the year through arbitrage, but such infrastructure is lacking in many areas.

Source: World Bank, 2000.

Human Poverty Index and Human Development Index

To overcome the limitation of taking a single measure of PCY as an index of development and the problem of using PCY as a measure of living standards, the UNDP has developed two alternative indices by which to compare the level of development and the progress of countries: **the Human Development Index (HDI)** and the **Human Poverty Index (HPI)**. These indices give alternative measures of the economic well-being of nations that do not necessarily accord with the usual measure: the level of per capita income. As the UNDP says in its *Human Development Report* (2004) 'although GNP growth is absolutely necessary to meet all essential human objectives, countries differ in the way that they translate growth into human development'. The UNDP defines human development as 'a process of enlarging people's choices'. This depends not only on income but also on other social indicators such as life expectancy, education, literacy and health provision.

We consider first the HDI because the UNDP uses this index to rank countries. The **HDI** is based on three variables:

- Life expectancy at birth
- Educational attainment, measured by a combination of adult literacy (two-thirds weight) and combined primary, secondary and tertiary school enrolment ratios (one-third weight)
- Standard of living measured by real PCY at PPP.

These variables are shown in the first four columns of Table 2.6. To construct the index, fixed minimum and maximum values are taken for each of the variables. For life expectancy at birth the range is 25–85 years. For adult literacy the range is 0–100 per cent. For real per capita GDP the range is $100–40,000. For any component of the HDI, the individual indices can be computed according to the general formula:

$$\text{Index} = \frac{\text{Actual value} - \text{Minimum value}}{\text{Maximum value} - \text{Minimum value}} \tag{2.2}$$

Each index thus ranges from 0 to 1. If the actual value of the variable is the minimum, the index is zero. If the actual value is equal to the maximum value, the index is one. Let us take the example of life expectancy in India (country 134). The life expectancy is 63.4 years, and if we put this value into (2.2) we get $(63.4 - 25)/(85 - 25) = 38.4/60 = 0.64$.[3]

The three indices are shown in columns (5), (6) and (7) of Table 2.6. The HDI is an average of the three indices and is given in column (8), with countries ranked from highest to lowest. The ranking of countries by HDI is then compared with the ranking by PCY in column (9). Among the developing countries, some are shown to have much higher HDIs than PCY, and vice versa. In the former category are countries such as Cuba, Myanmar, Ecuador and many countries of the former Soviet Union, while in the latter category are many of the oil-producing countries, such as Saudi Arabia, Iran, Angola and Equatorial Guinea, and South Africa and Botswana.

The **HPI** is based on three main indices:

- The percentage of the population not expected to survive to the age of 40 (P_1)
- The adult illiteracy rate (P_2)
- A deprivation index based on an average of two variables: the percentage of the population without access to safe water and the percentage of underweight children under five years old (P_3).

The formula for the HPI is given by:

$$\text{HPI} = [1/3(P_1^3 + P_2^3 + P_3^3) - 3]^{1/3} \tag{2.3}$$

Illustrative results for 22 Low Human Development Countries are shown in Table 2.7.

The statistics from the HPI show the extent of deprivation and suffering, and various aspects of human poverty. At the beginning of the twenty-first century, over 1 billion people lack access to safe water, nearly 1 billion people are illiterate, and half a billion will die before the age of 40. The UNDP calculates, however, that the cost of eradicating poverty across the globe is relatively small compared with global income, and that political commitment, not financial resources, is the real obstacle to poverty eradication. Basic social services could be made available to all people in developing countries at a cost of $60 billion over 10 years. A further $60 billion over 20 years could eradicate income poverty across the world. A total cost of $120 billion is 0.2 per cent of the global world income of $60,000 billion.

Can the poor countries ever catch up?

If living standards are largely determined by the level and growth of productivity, the interesting question is whether the developing countries will ever catch up with the performance of the rich industrialized countries. There are at least three possible mechanisms by which **catch-up** may occur.

Table 2.6 Human Development Index 2007 and its components

HDI rank	Human Development Index value 2007	Life expectancy at birth (years) 2007	Adult literacy rate (% aged 15 and above) 1999–2007	Combined gross enrolment ratio in education (%) 2007	GDP per capita (PPP US$) 2007	Life expectancy index 2007	Education index 2007	GDP index 2007	GDP per capita rank minus HDI rank*
Very high human development									
1 Norway	0.971	80.5	–	98.6	53,433	0.925	0.989	1.000	4
2 Australia	0.970	81.4	–	114.2	34,923	0.940	0.993	0.977	20
3 Iceland	0.969	81.7	–	96.0	35,742	0.946	0.980	0.981	16
4 Canada	0.966	80.6	–	99.3	35,812	0.927	0.991	0.982	14
5 Ireland	0.965	79.7	–	97.6	44,613	0.911	0.985	1.000	5
6 Netherlands	0.964	79.8	–	97.5	38,694	0.914	0.985	0.994	8
7 Sweden	0.963	80.8	–	94.3	36,712	0.930	0.974	0.986	9
8 France	0.961	81.0	–	95.4	33,674	0.933	0.978	0.971	17
9 Switzerland	0.960	81.7	–	82.7	40,658	0.945	0.936	1.000	4
10 Japan	0.960	82.7	–	86.6	33,632	0.961	0.949	0.971	16
11 Luxembourg	0.960	79.4	–	94.4	79,485	0.906	0.975	1.000	–9
12 Finland	0.959	79.5	–	101.4	34,526	0.908	0.993	0.975	11
13 United States	0.956	79.1	–	92.4	45,592	0.902	0.968	1.000	–4
14 Austria	0.955	79.9	–	90.5	34,370	0.915	0.962	0.989	1
15 Spain	0.955	80.7	97.9	96.5	31,560	0.929	0.975	0.960	12
16 Denmark	0.955	78.2	–	101.3	36,130	0.887	0.993	0.983	1
17 Belgium	0.953	79.5	–	94.3	34,638	0.908	0.974	0.977	4
18 Italy	0.951	81.1	98.9	91.8	30,353	0.935	0.965	0.954	11
19 Liechtenstein	0.951	–	–	86.8	85,382	0.903	0.949	1.000	–18
20 New Zealand	0.950	80.1	–	107.5	27,336	0.919	0.993	0.936	12
21 United Kingdom	0.947	79.3	–	89.2	35,130	0.906	0.957	0.978	–1
22 Germany	0.947	79.8	–	88.1	34,401	0.913	0.954	0.975	2
23 Singapore	0.944	80.2	94.4	–	49,704	0.920	0.913	1.00	–16

24 Hong Kong, China (SAR)	0.944	82.2	–	74.4	42,306	0.953	0.879	1.000	–13
25 Greece	0.942	79.1	97.1	101.6	28,517	0.902	0.981	0.944	6
26 Korea (Republic of)	0.937	79.2	–	98.5	24,801	0.904	0.988	0.920	9
27 Israel	0.935	80.7	97.1	89.9	26,315	0.928	0.947	0.930	7
28 Andorra	0.934	–	–	65.1	41,235	0.925	0.877	1.000	–16
29 Slovenia	0.929	78.2	99.7	92.8	26,753	0.886	0.969	0.933	4
30 Brunei Darussalam	0.920	77.0	94.9	77.7	50,200	0.867	0.891	1.000	–24
31 Kuwait	0.916	77.5	94.5	72.6	47,812	0.875	0.872	0.920	–23
32 Cyprus	0.914	79.6	97.7	77.6	24,789	0.910	0.910	0.920	4
33 Qatar	0.910	75.5	93.1	80.4	74,882	0.841	0.888	1.000	–30
34 Portugal	0.909	78.6	94.9	88.8	22,765	0.893	0.929	0.906	8
35 United Arab Emirates	0.903	77.3	90.9	71.4	54,626	0.872	0.838	1.000	–31
36 Czech Republic	0.903	76.4	–	83.4	24,144	0.856	0.938	0.916	1
37 Barbados	0.903	77.0	–	92.9	17,956	0.867	0.975	0.866	11
38 Malta	0.902	79.6	92.4	81.3	23,080	0.910	0.887	0.908	1
High human development									
39 Bahrain	0.895	75.6	88.8	90.4	29,723	0.843	0.893	0.950	–9
40 Estonia	0.883	72.9	99.8	91.2	20,361	0.799	0.964	0.887	3
41 Poland	0.880	75.5	99.3	87.7	15,987	0.842	0.952	0.847	12
42 Slovakia	0.880	74.6	–	80.5	20,076	0.827	0.928	0.885	3
43 Hungary	0.879	73.3	98.9	90.2	18,755	0.805	0.960	0.874	3
44 Chile	0.878	78.5	96.5	82.5	13,880	0.891	0.919	0.823	15
45 Croatia	0.871	76.0	98.7	77.2	16,027	0.850	0.916	0.847	7
46 Lithuania	0.870	71.8	99.7	92.3	17,575	0.780	0.968	0.893	3
47 Antigua and Barbuda	0.868	–	99.0	–	18,691	0.786	0.945	0.873	0
48 Latvia	0.866	72.3	99.8	90.2	16,377	0.788	0.961	0.851	3

continued overleaf

Table 2.6 Human Development Index 2007 and its components – *continued*

HDI rank	Human Development Index value 2007	Life expectancy at birth (years) 2007	Adult literacy rate (% aged 15 and above) 1999–2007[a]	Combined gross enrolment ratio in education (%) 2007	GDP per capita (PPP US$) 2007	Life expectancy index 2007	Education index 2007	GDP index 2007	GDP per capita rank minus HDI rank[a]
49 Argentina	0.866	75.2	97.6	88.6	13,238	0.836	0.946	0.815	13
50 Uruguay	0.865	76.1	979.9	90.9	11,216	0.852	0.955	0.788	20
51 Cuba	0.863	78.5	99.8	100.8	6,876	0.891	0.993	0.706	44
52 Bahamas	0.856	73.2	–	71.8	20,253	0.804	0.878	0.886	−8
53 Mexico	0.854	76.0	92.8	80.2	14,104	0.850	0.886	0.826	5
54 Costa Rica	0.854	78.7	95.9	73.0	10,842	0.896	0.883	0.782	19
55 Libyan Arab Jamahiriya	0.847	73.8	86.8	95.8	14,364	0.814	0.898	0.829	2
56 Oman	0.846	75.5	84.4	68.2	22,816	0.841	0.790	0.906	−15
57 Seychelles	0.845	–	91.8	82.2	16,394	0.797	0.886	0.851	−7
58 Venezuela (Bolivarian Republic of)	0.844	73.6	95.2	85.9	12,156	0.811	0.921	0.801	7
59 Saudi Arabia	0.843	72.7	85.0	78.5	22,935	0.794	0.828	0.907	−19
60 Panama	0.840	75.5	93.4	79.7	11,391	0.842	0.888	0.790	7
61 Bulgaria	0.840	73.1	98.3	82.4	11,222	0.802	0.930	0.788	8
62 Saint Kitts and Nevis	0.838	–	97.8	73.1	14,481	0.787	0.896	0.830	−6
63 Romania	0.837	72.5	97.6	79.2	12,369	0.792	0.915	0.804	1
64 Trinidad and Tobago	0.837	69.2	98.7	61.1	23,507	0.737	0.861	0.911	−26
65 Montenegro	0.834	74.0	96.4	74.5	11,699	0.817	0.891	0.795	1
66 Malaysia	0.829	74.1	91.9	71.5	13,518	0.819	0.851	0.819	−5
67 Serbia	0.826	73.9	96.4	74.5	10,248	0.816	0.891	0.773	8
68 Belarus	0.826	69.0	99.7	90.4	10,841	0.733	0.961	0.782	6
69 Saint Lucia	0.821	73.6	94.8	77.2	9,786	0.810	0.889	0.765	8
70 Albania	0.818	76.5	99.0	67.8	7,041	0.858	0.886	0.710	23

	HDI value	Life expectancy at birth (years)	Adult literacy rate (%)	Combined gross enrolment ratio (%)	GDP per capita (PPP US$)	Life expectancy index	Education index	GDP index	GDP per capita rank minus HDI rank
71 Russian Federation	0.817	66.2	99.5	81.9	14,690	0.686	0.933	0.833	−16
72 Macedonia (the Former Yugoslav Rep. of)	0.817	74.1	97.0	70.1	9,096	0.819	0.880	0.753	8
73 Dominica	0.814	–	88.0	78.5	7,893	0.865	0.848	0.729	10
74 Grenada	0.813	75.3	96.0	73.1	7,344	0.838	0.884	0.717	18
75 Brazil	0.813	72.2	90.0	87.2	9,567	0.787	0.891	0.761	4
76 Bosnia and Herzegovina	0.812	75.1	96.7	69.0	7,764	0.834	0.874	0.726	11
77 Colombia	0.807	72.7	92.7	79.0	8,587	0.795	0.881	0.743	4
78 Peru	0.806	73.0	89.6	88.1	7,836	0.800	0.819	0.728	7
79 Turkey	0.806	71.7	88.7	71.1	12,955	0.779	0.828	0.812	−16
80 Ecuador	0.806	75.0	91.0	–	7,449	0.833	0.866	0.719	11
81 Mauritius	0.804	72.1	87.4	76.9	11,296	0.785	0.839	0.789	−13
82 Kazakhstan	0.804	64.9	99.6	91.4	10,863	0.666	0.965	0.782	−10
83 Lebanon	0.803	71.9	89.6	78.0	10,109	0.781	0.857	0.770	−7
Medium human development									
84 Armenia	0.798	73.6	99.5	74.6	5,693	0.810	0.909	0.675	16
85 Ukraine	0.796	68.2	99.7	90.9	6,914	0.720	0.960	0.707	9
86 Azerbaijan	0.787	70.0	99.5	66.2	7,851	0.751	0.881	0.728	−2
87 Thailand	0.783	68.7	94.1	78.0	8,135	0.728	0.888	0.734	−5
88 Iran (Islamic Republic of)	0.782	71.2	82.3	73.2	10,955	0.769	0.793	0.784	−17
89 Georgia	0.778	71.6	100.0	76.7	4,662	0.777	0.916	0.641	21
90 Dominican Republic	0.777	72.4	89.1	73.5	6,706	0.790	0.839	0.702	7
91 Saint Vincent and the Grenadines	0.772	71.4	88.1	68.9	7,691	0.774	0.817	0.725	−2
92 China	0.772	72.9	93.3	68.7	5,383	0.799	0.851	0.665	10
93 Belize	0.772	76.0	75.1	78.3	6,734	0.851	0.762	0.703	3

continued overleaf

Table 2.6 Human Development Index 2007 and its components – *continued*

HDI rank	Human Development Index value 2007	Life expectancy at birth (years) 2007	Adult literacy rate (% aged 15 and above) 1999–2007[a]	Combined gross enrolment ratio in education (%) 2007	GDP per capita (PPP US$) 2007	Life expectancy index 2007	Education index 2007	GDP index 2007	GDP per capita rank minus HDI rank[*]
94 Samoa	0.771	71.4	98.7	74.1	4,467	0.773	0.905	0.634	19
95 Maldives	0.771	71.1	97.0	71.3	5,196	0.768	0.885	0.659	9
96 Jordan	0.770	72.4	91.1	78.7	4,901	0.790	0.870	0.650	11
97 Suriname	0.769	68.8	90.4	74.3	7,813	0.729	0.850	0.727	−11
98 Tunisia	0.769	73.8	77.7	76.2	7,520	0.813	0.772	0.721	−8
99 Tonga	0.768	71.7	99.2	78.0	3,748	0.778	0.920	0.605	21
100 Jamaica	0.766	71.7	86.0	78.1	6,079	0.778	0.834	0.686	−2
101 Paraguay	0.761	71.7	94.6	72.1	4,433	0.778	0.871	0.633	13
102 Sri Lanka	0.759	74.0	90.8	68.7	4,243	0.816	0.834	0.626	14
103 Gabon	0.755	60.1	86.2	80.7	15,167	0.584	0.843	0.838	−49
104 Algeria	0.754	72.2	75.4	73.6	7,740	0.787	0.748	0.726	−16
105 Philippines	0.751	71.6	93.4	79.6	3,406	0.777	0.888	0.589	19
106 El Salvador	0.747	71.3	82.0	74.0	5,804	0.771	0.794	0.678	−7
107 Syrian Arab Republic	0.742	74.1	83.1	65.7	4,511	0.818	0.773	0.636	5
108 Fiji	0.741	68.7	–	71.5	4,304	0.728	0.868	0.628	7
109 Turkmenistan	0.739	64.6	99.5	–	4,953	0.661	0.906	0.651	−3
110 Occupied Palestinian Territories	0.737	73.3	93.8	78.3	–	0.806	0.886	0.519	
111 Indonesia	0.734	70.	92.0	68.2	3,712	0.758	0.840	0.603	10
112 Honduras	0.732	72.0	83.6	74.8	3,796	0.783	0.806	0.607	7
113 Bolivia	0.729	65.4	90.7	86.0	4,206	0.673	0.892	0.624	4
114 Guyana	0.729	66.5	–	83.9	2,782	0.691	0.939	0.555	13
115 Mongolia	0.727	66.2	97.3	79.2	3,236	0.687	0.913	0.580	10
116 Vietnam	0.725	74.3	90.3	62.3	2,600	0.821	0.810	0.544	13

117 Moldova	0.720	68.3	99.2	71.6	2,551	0.722	0.899	0.541	14
118 Equatorial Guinea	0.719	49.9	87.0	62.0	30,627	0.415	0.787	0.955	−90
119 Uzbekistan	0.710	67.6	96.9	72.7	2,425	0.711	0.888	0.532	14
120 Kyrgyzstan	0.710	67.6	99.3	77.3	2,006	0.710	0.918	0.500	20
121 Cape Verde	0.708	71.1	83.8	68.1	3,041	0.769	0.786	0.570	5
122 Guatemala	0.704	70.1	73.2	70.5	4,562	0.752	0.723	0.638	−11
123 Egypt	0.703	69.9	66.4	76.4	5,349	0.749	0.697	0.664	−20
124 Nicaragua	0.699	72.7	78.0	72.1	2,570	0.795	0.760	0.542	6
125 Botswana	0.694	53.4	82.9	70.6	13,604	0.473	0.788	0.820	−65
126 Vanuatu	0.693	69.9	78.1	62.3	3,666	0.748	0.728	0.601	−4
127 Tajikistan	0.688	66.4	99.6	70.9	1,753	0.691	0.896	0.478	17
128 Namibia	0.686	60.4	88.0	67.2	5,155	0.590	0.811	0.658	−23
129 South Africa	0.683	51.5	88.0	76.8	9,757	0.442	0.843	0.765	−51
130 Morocco	0.654	71.0	55.6	61.0	4,108	0.767	0.574	0.620	−12
131 Sao Tome and Principe	0.651	65.4	87.9	68.1	1,638	0.673	0.813	0.467	17
132 Bhutan	0.619	65.7	52.8	54.1	4,837	0.678	0.533	0.647	−24
133 Lao People's Democratic Republic	0.619	64.6	72.7	59.6	2,165	0.659	0.683	0.513	2
134 India	0.612	63.4	66.0	61.0	2,753	0.639	0.643	0.553	−6
135 Solomon Islands	0.610	65.8	76.6	49.7	1,725	0.680	0.676	0.475	10
136 Congo	0.601	53.5	81.1	58.6	3,511	0.474	0.736	0.594	−13
137 Cambodia	0.593	60.6	76.3	58.5	1,802	0.593	0.704	0.483	6
138 Myanmar	0.586	61.2	89.9	56.3	904	0.603	0.787	0.368	29
139 Comoros	0.576	64.9	75.1	46.4	1,143	0.666	0.655	0.407	20
140 Yemen	0.575	62.5	58.9	54.4	2,335	0.624	0.574	0.526	−6
141 Pakistan	0.572	66.2	54.2	39.3	2,496	0.687	0.492	0.537	−9
142 Swaziland	0.572	45.3	79.6	60.1	4,789	0.339	0.731	0.646	−33
143 Angola	0.564	46.5	67.4	65.3	5,385	0.359	0.667	0.665	−42

continued overleaf

Table 2.6 Human Development Index 2007 and its components – continued

HDI rank	Human Development Index value 2007	Life expectancy at birth (years) 2007	Adult literacy rate (% aged 15 and above) 1999–2007[a]	Combined gross enrolment ratio in education (%) 2007	GDP per capita (PPP US$) 2007	Life expectancy index 2007	Education index 2007	GDP index 2007	GDP per capita rank minus HDI rank[*]
144 Nepal	0.553	66.3	56.5	60.8	1,049	0.688	0.579	0.392	21
145 Madagascar	0.543	59.9	70.7	61.3	932	0.582	0.676	0.373	21
146 Bangladesh	0.543	65.7	53.5	52.1	1,241	0.678	0.530	0.420	9
147 Kenya	0.541	53.6	73.6	59.6	1,542	0.477	0.690	0.457	2
148 Papua New Guinea	0.541	60.7	57.8	40.7	2,084	0.594	0.521	0.507	−10
149 Haiti	0.532	61.0	62.1	–	1,155	0.600	0.588	0.408	9
150 Sudan	0.531	57.9	60.9	39.9	2,086	0.548	0.539	0.507	−13
151 Tanzania (United Republic of)	0.530	55.0	72.3	57.3	1,208	0.500	0.673	0.416	6
152 Ghana	0.526	56.5	65.0	56.5	1,334	0.525	0.622	0.432	1
153 Cameroon	0.523	50.9	67.9	52.3	2,128	0.431	0.627	0.510	−17
154 Mauritania	0.520	56.6	55.8	50.6	1,927	0.526	0.541	0.494	−12
155 Djibouti	0.520	55.1	–	25.5	2,061	0.501	0.554	0.505	−16
156 Lesotho	0.514	44.9	82.2	61.5	1,541	0.332	0.753	0.457	−6
157 Uganda	0.514	51.9	73.6	62.3	1,059	0.449	0.698	0.394	6
158 Nigeria	0.511	47.7	72.0	53.0	1,969	0.378	0.657	0.497	−17
Low human development									
159 Togo	0.499	62.2	53.2	53.9	788	0.620	0.534	0.345	11
160 Malawi	0.493	52.4	71.8	61.9	761	0.456	0.685	0.339	12
161 Benin	0.492	61.0	40.5	52.4	1,312	0.601	0.445	0.430	−7
162 Timor-Leste	0.489	60.7	50.1	63.2	717	0.595	0.545	0.329	11
163 Côte d'Ivoire	0.484	56.8	48.7	37.5	1,690	0.531	0.450	0.472	−17
164 Zambia	0.481	44.5	70.6	63.3	1,358	0.326	0.682	0.435	−12
165 Eritrea	0.472	59.2	64.2	33.3	626	0.570	0.539	0.306	12

166 Senegal	0.464	55.4	41.9	41.2	1,666	0.506	0.417	0.469	−19
167 Rwanda	0.460	49.7	64.9	52.2	866	0.412	0.607	0.360	1
168 Gambia	0.456	55.7	–	46.8	1,225	0.511	0.439	0.418	−12
169 Liberia	0.442	57.9	55.5	57.6	362	0.548	0.562	0.215	10
170 Guinea	0.435	57.3	29.5	49.3	1,140	0.538	0.361	0.406	−10
171 Ethiopia	0.414	54.7	35.9	49.0	779	0.496	0.403	0.343	0
172 Mozambique	0.402	47.8	4.4	54.8	802	0.380	0.478	0.348	−3
173 Guinea-Bissau	0.396	47.5	64.6	36.6	477	0.375	0.552	0.261	5
174 Burundi	0.394	50.1	59.3	49.0	341	0.418	0.559	0.205	6
175 Chad	0.392	48.6	31.8	36.5	1,477	0.393	0.334	0.449	−24
176 Congo (Democratic Republic of the)	0.389	47.6	67.2	48.2	298	0.377	0.608	0.182	5
177 Burkina Faso	0.389	52.7	28.7	32.8	1,124	0.462	0.301	0.404	−16
178 Mali	0.371	48.1	26.2	46.9	1,083	0.385	0.331	0.398	−16
179 Central African Republic	0.369	46.7	48.6	28.6	713	0.361	0.419	0.328	−5
180 Sierra Leone	0.365	47.3	38.1	44.6	679	0.371	0.403	0.320	−5
181 Afghanistan	0.352	43.6	28.0	50.1	1,054	0.310	0.354	0.393	−17
182 Niger	0.340	50.8	28.7	27.2	627	0.431	0.282	0.307	−6
Arab States	0.719	68.5	71.2	66.2	8,202	0.726	0.695	0.736	–
Central and Eastern Europe and the CIS	0.821	69.7	97.6	79.5	12,185	0.745	0.916	0.802	–
East Asia and the Pacific	0.770	72.2	92.7	69.3	5,733	0.786	0.849	0.676	–
Latin America and the Caribbean	0.821	73.4	91.2	83.4	10,077	0.806	0.886	0.770	–
South Asia	0.612	64.1	64.2	58.0	2,905	0.651	0.621	0.562	–
Sub-Saharan Africa	0.514	51.5	62.9	53.5	2,031	0.441	0.597	0.503	–
OECD	0.932	79.0	–	89.1	32,647	0.900	0.966	–

continued overleaf

Table 2.6 Human Development Index 2007 and its components – *continued*

HDI rank	Human Development Index value 2007	Life expectancy at birth (years) 2007	Adult literacy rate (% aged 15 and above) 1999–2007[a]	Combined gross enrolment ratio in education (%) 2007	GDP per capita (PPP US$) 2007	Life expectancy index 2007	Education index 2007	GDP index 2007	GDP per capita rank minus HDI rank[*]
European Union (EU27)	0.937	79.0	–	91.0	29,956	0.899	–	0.952	–
GCC	0.868	74.0	86.8	77.0	30,415	0.816	0.835	0.954	–
Very high human development	0.955	80.1	–	92.5	37,272	0.918	–	0.988	–
Very high HD: OECD	–	80.1	–	92.9	37,122	0.919	–	0.988	–
Very high HD: non-OECD	–	79.7	–	–	41,887	0.912	–	1,000	–
High human development	0.833	72.4	94.1	82.4	12,569	0.790	0.902	0.807	–
Medium human development	0.686	66.9	80.9	63.3	3,963	0.698	0.744	0.614	–
Low human development	0.423	51.0	47.7	47.6	862	0.434	0.477	0.359	–
World	0.753	67.5	83.9	67.5	9,972	0.708	0.784	0.768	–

Note: *In column 9, a positive figure indicates that the HDI rank is higher than the PCY rank, and vice versa for a negative figure.

Source: *Human Development Report 2009* (New York: Oxford University Press).

Table 2.7 Human Poverty Index

HDI rank	Human Poverty Index		Probability of not surviving to age 40 (% of cohort) 2005–2010	Adult illiteracy rate (% aged 15 and above) 1999–2007	Population not using an improved water source (%) 2006	Children underweight for age (% aged under 5) 2000–2006
	Rank	Value (%)				
Low human development						
159 Togo	117	36.6	18.6	46.8	41	26
160 Malawi	90	28.2	32.6	28.2	24	19
161 Benin	126	43.2	19.2	59.5	35	23
162 Timor-Leste	122	40.8	18.0	49.9	38	46
163 Côte d'Ivoire	119	37.4	24.6	51.3	19	20
164 Zambia	110	35.5	42.9	29.4	42	20
165 Eritrea	103	33.7	18.2	35.8	40	40
166 Senegal	124	41.6	22.4	58.1	23	17
167 Rwanda	100	32.9	34.2	35.1	35	23
168 Gambia	123	40.9	21.8	–	14	20
169 Liberia	109	35.2	23.2	44.5	36	26
170 Guinea	129	50.5	23.7	70.5	30	26
171 Ethiopia	130	50.9	27.7	64.1	58	38
172 Mozambique	127	46.8	40.6	55.6	58	24
173 Guinea-Bissau	107	34.9	37.4	35.4	43	19
174 Burundi	116	36.4	33.7	40.7	29.	39
175 Chad	132	53.1	35.7	68.2	52	37
176 Congo (Democratic Republic of the)	120	38.0	37.3	32.8	54	31
177 Burkina Faso	131	51.8	26.9	71.3	28	37
178 Mali	133	54.5	32.5	73.8	40	33
179 Central African Republic	125	42.4	39.6	51.4	34	29
180 Sierra Leone	128	47.7	31.0	61.9	47	30
181 Afghanistan	135	59.8	40.7	72.0	78	39
182 Niger	134	55.8	29.0	71.3	58	44

Source: *Human Development Report 2009* (New York: Oxford University Press).

First, it is sometimes argued that the larger the gap between a poor country's technology, productivity and per capita income and the level of productivity in advanced countries, the greater the scope for a poor country to absorb existing technology and to catch up with richer countries. Technology is thought of as a public good, so for a given amount of technological investment a poor country can reap high returns because it has paid none of the development costs. Clearly, there also has to be the willingness and ability to invest and the capability to absorb new technology. A productivity gap is a necessary but not a sufficient condition for catch-up by this means.

Second, the process of development is characterized by a shift of resources from low-productivity agriculture to higher-productivity industrial and service activities. Other things being equal, this should also produce a move towards convergence to the extent that the resource shifts are greater in poor countries than in rich countries.

Third, mainstream neoclassical growth theory predicts convergence (see Chapter 5) because of the assumption of diminishing returns to capital. Rich countries with a lot of capital per head will have a lower productivity of capital than poor countries. Thus if tastes and preferences are the same, the same amount of saving and investment in poor countries should lead to faster growth than in rich countries.

The standard procedure for testing the convergence hypothesis is to do a simple correlation across countries between the rate of growth of per capita income (y) as the dependent variable and the *initial* level of per capita income (or productivity) as the independent variable, and to see whether the relation is significantly negative. If it is, this means that per capita income is growing faster in poor countries than in rich countries, which is a necessary condition for convergence to take place (often called **beta convergence** in the literature). One of the earliest studies of this type (Baumol, 1986) showed a strong inverse correlation between a country's productivity level and its average productivity growth among industrial countries and those at an intermediate stage of development, but no evidence of convergence as far as the poorer countries are concerned.

Zind (1991) focused on 89 developing countries and regressed the rate of growth of per capita income on the level of per capita income in 1960. He could find no evidence of overall convergence, but there was some evidence of convergence taking place between countries with per capita incomes in excess of $800 per annum. One reason appears to be that in these latter countries there was a positive relation between per capita income and the rate of growth of investment per capita.

Another study by Dowrick (1992) across 113 countries shows that while there is some evidence of catch-up in recent decades in the sense that growth rates have been negatively related to initial levels of productivity, other factors have caused per capita income growth to be faster the higher the level of per capita income, producing a *divergence* of living standards across the world.

Similarly, Pritchett (1997) takes 117 countries over the period of 1960–88 and regresses the rate of growth of per capita income on the initial level of per capita income relative to the leading country and finds no evidence of unconditional convergence, as shown in Table 2.8, because the coefficient of 0.4 is *positive*. It is interesting to note, however, that when differences in investment and schooling between countries are allowed for the coefficient becomes negative (-0.32), indicating conditional convergence. The problem is, however, that rich countries are able to save and invest more, and they devote more resources to education, which perpetuates their growth advantage. Columns (3) and (4) in Table 2.8 show a strong positive relation between the initial level of per capita income and the investment level on the one hand, and primary school enrolment

Table 2.8 Explaining growth of per capita GDP, 1960–88

Effect of	Unconditional divergence	Conditional convergence	The richer accumulate faster	
	Average growth of GDP per capita (1)	Average growth of GDP per capita (2)	Investment level (3)	Primary school enrolment (4)
Initial level of GDP per capita relative to leader	0.40	−0.32	4.43	14.57
Average level of investment	–	0.07	–	–
Average enrolment in primary school	–	0.03	–	–

Source: Pritchett, 1997.

on the other. Poor countries tend to grow more slowly than rich ones in spite of the potential advantages conferred by backwardness. When conditional convergence is found, however, it is not possible to distinguish between the various sources of catch-up; whether it is easy access to technology as a public good, resource shifts, or diminishing returns to capital. A negative sign on the initial per capita income variable could be picking up any one of these effects, or all three.

All this confirms what we found earlier: that there is no tendency for the international distribution of income to narrow, as measured by the Gini ratio. A necessary condition for the Gini ratio to fall is that poor countries grow faster than the rich, but this has not been happening overall. Some poor countries are narrowing the gap with the rich, but others are falling behind, leaving the overall distribution of income unchanged.

The interesting question then arises: can poor countries ever catch up, and how long will it take? Let us consider two issues:

- First, given the recent growth experience of the poor countries of roughly 3 per cent per annum, how long will it take for the average poor country to reach the current average living standards of rich developed countries?
- Secondly, how long will it take for poor countries to catch up with rich countries assuming that rich countries grow at 3 per cent per annum and poor countries were to raise their per capita growth to 4 per cent per annum. (Clearly a necessary condition for catch-up is that poor countries do grow faster than rich countries, otherwise convergence is impossible.)

We can answer both questions using the simple compound interest formula:

$$S = P(1 + r)^n$$

where P is the 'initial' income level, and S is the sum to which the income level grows at an annual compound rate of interest, r, over n years.

The answer to the first question, assuming that the current level of per capita income in poor countries (P) is $1,200 per annum, and in rich countries (S) it is $25,000, and the recent growth performance of poor countries (r) has been 2 per cent per annum, it would take 153 years for poor countries to reach the current standard of living of rich countries.[4]

The answer to the second question is that it would take nearly 300 years for the average poor country growing at 4 per cent per annum to catch up with the rich country growing at 3 per cent per annum, given the initial difference in the level of per capita incomes in 2010.[5]

The above calculations are sensitive to the initial income levels taken and the assumed future growth rates of poor and rich countries, but it is difficult not to reach the conclusion that the timescale of catch-up will be extremely prolonged.

It can be argued, of course, that world income equality is an impracticable ideal, and that the primary aim is not equality of living standards throughout the world but 'tolerable' living standards in all countries, which is a very different matter. This seems to be the position of the World Bank which argued in its *World Development Report 2000* that rising income inequality 'should not be seen as a negative', provided that incomes at the bottom do not fall, and the number of people in poverty falls or does not rise. The problem is to define 'tolerable' living standards, and to specify an acceptable income distribution at that average level of real income. The time scale involved to reach 'tolerable' living standards is clearly less than that required to eliminate the income gap entirely, but even so, if the average level of per capita income now enjoyed in the rich developed countries is regarded as the tolerable level, we estimate it will take over a century for the average poor country to attain it on current performance. Can these countries wait that long?

On the other hand, it is easily forgotten that the rich–poor country divide in the world economy is a relatively recent phenomenon. All countries were once at subsistence level, and as recently as 200 years ago, at the advent of the British industrial revolution, the absolute differences in living standards between countries cannot have been great. The average per capita income of the developing countries today is approximately $1,400 per annum, and this is not far below the average level of real per capita income in Western Europe in the mid-nineteenth century, measured at current prices. If we regard $1,400 as only barely above subsistence, the major part of the present income disparities between developed and developing countries must have arisen over the twentieth century. Some countries, through a combination of fortune and design, have managed to grow much faster than others. The overriding influence has been industrialization and the technological progress associated with it. The close association between industrialization and living standards spells out the clear policy message that to base a development policy on agricultural activities *alone* would be misguided, however attractive such aphorisms as 'back to the land' and 'small is beautiful' may sound to those disillusioned with the industrialization experience of the developing countries. Sutcliffe (1971) is right when he argues:

> It is understandable that vague memories of the oppression of the working class in nineteenth-century Britain, the contemporary horrors of American machine-age society, and the Stalinist attack on the Russian peasantry, should arouse feelings which are hostile to industrialization. Yet to oppose machines altogether, like Gandhi, or to argue that a long-run rise in the standard of living is possible without industrialization, are no more than forms of sentimentalism, especially when the condition of most of the population of the non-industrialized world is now both terrible and worsening. It is not sentimentalism to demand that the process of industrialization should be made as humane and as painless as possible and that the long term aims of equality at a higher standard of living should be constantly borne in mind as the process goes on.

The concentrated impact of industrialization on living standards in the Western world is dramatically emphasized by the observation that if 6,000 years of 'civilized' human existence prior to 1850 is viewed as a day, the last century or so represents little more than half an hour; yet in this 'half-hour' more real output has been produced in the developed countries than in the preceding period. It is true that living standards in most developing countries have risen faster since 1950 than at any time in the past; but so too have the living standards in the developed countries, and the gap between rich and poor countries continues to widen. Although development consists of more than a rise in per capita incomes, income disparities are the essence of the so-called 'development gap'.

Summary

- The development gap between rich and poor countries is huge. The absolute gap between the per capita income (PCY) of rich and poor countries is growing, and the ratio of the PCY of the high-income developed countries to the low-income developing countries is currently at a historical high of 80:1.
- The Gini ratio for international inequality has risen from 0.2 in 1820 to over 0.5. The Gini ratio for global inequality has risen from 0.5 in 1820 to over 0.6 today, and shows no sign of falling.
- This income gap and income inequality in the world economy manifests itself in other aspects of human welfare such as health, nutrition, life expectancy, education and employment opportunities (see Chapter 3). No wonder the UNDP has described the world as 'gargantuan in its excesses and grotesque in its human and economic inequalities'.
- The number of people living in the world on less than US$1.25 at PPP is 1.4 billion, and the number living on less than $2 a day is 2.5 billion, or approximately 40 per cent of the world's population. In Africa, 73 per cent of the population live on less than $2 a day.
- The average PCY of countries, even converted into PPP, is not always a good indicator of the development of a country because it ignores the distribution of income and various aspects of human development such as education and health.
- The UNDP constructs alternative measures of economic development and progress, the HDI and the HPI, which include measures of schooling, literacy, health, life expectancy etc. Countries rank differently by PCY, HDI and HPI.
- The World Bank attempts to tackle poverty from the 'grass roots' by promoting opportunity, facilitating empowerment and enhancing economic security.
- At current rates of PCY growth in poor countries it will take at least 100 years for the average poor country to reach current living standards enjoyed by developed countries, and 300 years for living standards to be equalized. This is some measure of the development 'gap'.

Chapter 2	Discussion questions

1 How would you measure the development gap in the world economy?

2 How would you construct a Lorenz curve and calculate the Gini ratio for the measurement of income inequality?

Chapter 2	Discussion questions – *continued*

3 What has been happening to the international and global distribution of income over time?

4 What difficulties arise in measuring and comparing the per capita incomes of poor countries using the US$ as the unit of account?

5 What do you understand by the concept of purchasing power parity (PPP), and how would you make PPP calculations of per capita income across countries?

6 What difficulties are encountered in the measurement of poverty?

7 How would you calculate the growth required in order to meet the Millennium Goal of halving the proportion of people living in poverty by 2015 (compared with the 1990 level)?

8 What is the World Bank's new thinking concerning the attack on world poverty?

9 What is the rationale for the UNDP to construct an HPI and HDI?

10 Are there any theoretical reasons for supposing that poor countries might catch up with the rich countries?

11 How would you analyse how fast poor countries have to grow to catch up with the rich countries?

Notes

1. UNDP (1997).
2. The 1990 and 2000/2001 *World Development Reports*, published by the World Bank, were devoted to a consideration of the measurement, magnitude and nature of poverty in developing countries, and how to tackle it.
3. The construction of the income index is slightly more complex. See UNDP (2001), technical note, p. 240.
4. Rearranging the formula for compound interest gives:

$$n = \frac{\log (S/P)}{\log (1+r)}$$

and applying the assumed values gives:

$$n = \frac{\log (\$25,000/\$1,200)}{\log (1.02)} = 153 \text{ years}$$

5. The solution is obtained from the expression:

$$S_r (1+r_r)^n = P_p(1+r_p)^n$$

where S_r is the initial income of the rich countries; P_p is the initial income of the poor countries; r_r is the assumed growth rate of the rich country (= 3 per cent) and r_p is the assumed growth rate of the poor country (= 4 per cent). Therefore:

$$n = \frac{\log\,(\$25{,}000/\$1{,}200)}{\log\,(1.04) - \log\,(1.03)} = 287 \text{ years}$$

Websites on poverty and income distribution

World Bank (Poverty Reduction Learning Network) www.prln.org; www.worldbank.org/poverty
UNCTAD/UNDP www.unctad-undp.org
UNDP (Human Development Report) http://hdr.undp.org
Inter-American Development Bank http://www.iadb.org/sds/pov/index-pov-e.htm
Oxfam www.oxfam.org.uk
War on Want www.waronwant.org

3

THE CHARACTERISTICS OF UNDERDEVELOPMENT AND STRUCTURAL CHANGE

- Introduction
- The dominance of agriculture and petty services
- Low level of capital accumulation
- Rapid population growth
- Exports dominated by primary commodities
- The curse of natural resources
- Weak institutional structures
- Other dimensions of the development gap
- Inequality: vertical and horizontal
- Growth and distribution
- Poverty-weighted growth rates
- Nutrition and health
- Famine
- Food production
- Stages of development and structural change
- Rostow's stages of growth
- Diversification
- Industrialization and growth
- Kaldor's growth laws
- Summary
- Discussion questions
- Notes
- Websites on health, nutrition, famine, education, structural change and income distribution

Introduction

This chapter is about the distinguishing characteristics of poor developing countries, and the process of structural change necessary for a rise in living standards. There cannot be an increase in living standards and a reduction in poverty without an increase in output per head of the working population or an increase in labour productivity. This is the sine qua non of development. Rich countries have high levels of labour productivity; poor countries have low levels of productivity. Why is productivity low in poor countries, and what are the major sources of productivity growth?

The major distinguishing characteristics of poor countries that contribute to low levels of productivity and poor economic performance are: the dominance of low-productivity agriculture and petty service activities in the economic structure; low levels of capital formation – both physical and human (education); rapid population growth and exports dominated by primary commodities. Some of these major characteristics of underdevelopment are both causes and effects of poverty; for example, low savings and investment, poor education and rapid population growth can be causes of poverty but also symptoms.

In addition to these major distinguishing features of poor countries, some suffer from what is called 'the curse of natural resources', which refers to the detrimental effects that high dependence on natural resource exploitation and exports can have on an economy, because of an overvalued exchange rate (the Dutch disease), corruption and rent-seeking behaviour.

Many poor countries possess weak institutional structures such as lack of property rights, absence of the rule of law and political instability, all of which act as disincentives to investment.

In this chapter we also discuss many other dimensions of poverty in poor countries such as unemployment, income inequality, poor nutrition and health, food production and famine, and the basic needs of people.

The chapter ends with a discussion of the **stages of growth** and development that countries go through, and the strong association that seems to exist between the progress of nations and the shift of resources from agriculture into industry and sophisticated service activities, known in the literature as **Kaldor's growth laws**. The fastest-growing developing countries today are those where the share of industry in GDP is rising the fastest; and this is no accident because manufactured goods have production and demand characteristics that make them the 'engine of growth'.

The dominance of agriculture and petty services

One of the major distinguishing characteristics of poor developing countries is the fact that their economies are dominated by agriculture and petty service activities. There is very little manufacturing industry in many of the poorest countries. Table 3.1 shows the distribution of employment by sectors of the economy in the low-income, middle-income and high-income countries. It can be seen that in the low-income countries, 61 per cent of the labour force still relies on agriculture

Table 3.1 Distribution of employment, by sector (percentage)

Countries	Agriculture	Industry	Services
Low income	61	19	20
Middle income	22	34	44
High income	4	26	70

Source: International Labour Organization, 2009.

to make a living. This compares with 22 per cent in the middle-income countries and 4 per cent in the high-income countries.

Most of those working on the land in poor countries are either subsistence farmers (producing only for themselves), tenant farmers (with no land rights and no incentive to increase output) or landless labourers (selling their labour in a daily labour market). Some high-productivity commercial agriculture does exist, but it forms a small proportion of total agricultural activity. The dominance of agriculture has a number of implications and poses a number of problems for developing countries. First of all, agriculture is a **diminishing returns** activity because cultivatable land is ultimately a fixed factor of production. There are only a few incontrovertible laws in economics, but one is that if a variable factor is added to a fixed factor its marginal product will eventually fall: **the law of diminishing returns**. This principle is illustrated in Figure 3.1.

As labour is added to the land, the marginal product of labour first of all rises because land requires a certain amount of labour for each unit of labour to work with maximum efficiency, but then the marginal product declines and could become zero (or even negative in extreme cases where there is so much labour on a fixed piece of land that everyone gets in each other's way, reducing total output!).

If the marginal product of labour falls below the subsistence level, the unit of labour will not be able to survive unless total output is shared. This may characterize family farms. If labour is hired, however, or works on commercial farms, no (profit-maximizing) employer will pay a wage above the marginal product of labour. We reach the conclusion that in a diminishing returns activity, such as agriculture, there is always a limit to employment set by the minimum subsistence wage. This can lead to unemployment, open or disguised (see Chapter 6), particularly in a society where the population is growing rapidly and there are limited alternative employment opportunities.

Secondly, on the demand side, the demand for most agricultural products (and other primary products derived from the land) is **income inelastic**. This means that the rise in demand is proportionately less than the rise in income, and the growth of demand for agricultural output is less than the growth of supply potential determined by the growth of the labour force plus the growth of labour productivity. For example, suppose that the agricultural labour force is growing at 2 per cent and labour productivity is growing at 1 per cent, so that the growth of productive potential is 3 per cent. Now suppose that income growth in the economy is 3 per cent but the income elasticity of demand for agricultural products is only one-half (0.5). The demand for output therefore grows by only 1.5 per cent. The gap between the growth of supply and demand is 1.5 per cent, which will manifest itself in unemployment.

There are thus two major causes of surplus labour in agriculture: one arises from the low income elasticity of demand for agricultural output; the other arises from the fact that agriculture is a diminishing returns activity so that there is a limit to the employment of (paid) labour

Figure 3.1   The law of diminishing returns

set by the minimum subsistence wage. What happens to this surplus labour? First, it may stay in the rural sector and work is spread, with each unit of labour working a suboptimal day. This is described as **disguised unemployment** (see Chapter 6). This, of course, depresses labour productivity and therefore per capita income. Second, the surplus agricultural labour may migrate to the towns to find alternative work. If work cannot be found in the formal sector of the economy, the labour attempts to make a living in the informal sector by providing petty services of various kinds: street trading, haircutting, shoe-shining, transport and so on. These are also very low-productivity activities.

Industry has very different characteristics from agriculture. It is not a diminishing returns activity. If anything, it is an increasing returns activity. All factors of production are variable, and no limit to employment is set by the marginal product of labour falling below the minimum (subsistence) wage. Secondly, the demand for most industrial goods is income elastic so that the demand for labour may rise faster than labour productivity, leading to increases in employment – at least in the early stages of industrialization. Also, there is greater scope for capital accumulation in industry, which enhances labour productivity. Overall, the productivity of labour in industry is much higher. As discussed later, there is a strong association across countries between the level of per capita income, and the share of resources devoted to industrial activities, and between the growth of industry and the growth of economies.

Low level of capital accumulation

A second major distinguishing characteristic of developing countries is their low level of capital accumulation – both physical and human. Physical capital refers to the plant, machinery and equipment used in the production of output. Human capital refers to the skills and expertise embodied in the labour force through education and training. (The role of education in the development process will be discussed later in this chapter.) Low levels of capital accumulation are a cause of low productivity and poverty, but are also a *function* of poverty, because capital accumulation requires investment and saving and it is not easy for poor societies to save. The process of development can be described as a generalized process of capital accumulation, but the levels and rates of capital accumulation in poor countries are low. The amount of physical capital that labour has to work with in a typical developing country is no more than one-twentieth of the level in Europe and North America. This reflects the cumulative effect over time of much higher savings and investment ratios in the rich countries. The savings and investment ratios for low-income, middle-income and high-income countries are shown in Table 3.2.

Domestic investment can differ from domestic saving owing to investment from abroad. The figures for low-income countries are distorted by China, which in 2009 saved over 50 per cent

Table 3.2 Savings and investment as a percentage of GDP, 2009

Countries	Gross domestic investment	Gross domestic savings
Low income[a]	24	17
Middle income	25	25
High income	20	21

Note: [a] Including China, which saved 55 per cent and invested 44 per cent of GDP.

Source: World Bank, 2009.

of its national income. If we exclude China, the savings ratio of the low-income countries is less than half that of the middle- and high-income countries, although their investment ratio is still relatively high because of capital inflows from abroad. These are not always stable, however.

The distinguished development economist, Sir Arthur Lewis, once described development as the process of transforming a country from a net 5 per cent saver and investor to a 12 per cent saver and investor.[1] Rostow, in his famous book *The Stages of Economic Growth* (1960), defines the **take-off** stage of self-sustaining growth in terms of a critical ratio of savings and investment to national income of 10–12 per cent (see p. 105 for a discussion of Rostow's model). What is the significance of this ratio? It has to do with a very simple growth formula, which originally came from the growth model of the famous British economist (Sir) Roy Harrod (see Chapter 5). The formula is

$$g = s/c \qquad\qquad (3.1)$$

where g is the growth of output ($\Delta Y/Y$), s is the savings ratio (S/Y) and c is the incremental capital–output ratio – that is, how much investment is associated with an increase in the flow of output by one unit ($I/\Delta Y$). Substituting these definitions of s and c into (3.1) shows that in an accounting sense the formula is an identity since in the national accounts $S = I$

$$\Delta Y/Y = (S/Y)/(I/\Delta Y) \qquad\qquad (3.2)$$

That is, if $S = I$, then $g = s/c$.

Now, for the level of per capita income to rise, output growth must exceed population growth. If population growth is 2 per cent per annum, output growth must exceed 2 per cent per annum. It can be seen from (3.1) that how much saving and investment as a proportion of national income is required for growth depends on the value of the incremental capital–output ratio (c). If 4 units of capital investment are required to produce a 1 unit flow of output year by year over the life of the investment, then $c = 4$, so s must exceed 8 per cent for the growth of output to exceed 2 per cent. A net rate of saving and investment to national income of at least 8 per cent or more is therefore necessary if there is to be sustained growth of per capita income. In most developing countries, the net savings and investment ratio is above this critical magnitude, but the fact remains that a major cause of low productivity and poverty in developing countries is the low level of capital that labour has to work with. In Case example 3.1 the difference in the savings and investment climate between India and China is highlighted and discussed.

| Case example 3.1 | **Savings and investment in India and China: a comparison** |

In 2000, India's population was 1,016 million, the second largest in the world after China's 1,275 million. These two countries contained 38 per cent of the world's population. By 2050, India is forecast to have the bigger population. By then, according to the United Nations population division, its population may be about 1,500 million. Comparisons between these two giants are irresistible. Both are performing well, by historical standards, but China is doing better on most measures of economic performance.

| Case example 3.1 | **Savings and investment in India and China: a comparison** – *continued* |

In 1980, real incomes per head were much the same in the two countries. By 2000, however, according to the World Bank, China's gross national income per head at purchasing power parity was close to 70 per cent higher than India's at $3,920. China's real gross domestic product per head rose 9 per cent a year in the 1990s, according to the World Bank, while India's rose 4.1 per cent. This is the difference between an increase of some 140 per cent and one of 50 per cent in incomes per head over a decade.

Behind China's superior growth lies a higher national savings rate. This reached 40 per cent of gross national product in 2000 against India's 24 per cent. The incremental capital–output ratio (which is the ratio of the investment rate to the growth rate) is much the same in both countries. This suggests that the efficiency with which capital is deployed is much the same in the two countries.

A World Bank study of the Indian investment climate, made in collaboration with the Confederation of Indian Industries, analyses the obstacles to the country's economic dynamism at the level of individual businesses. It helps explain China's relative attraction for foreign investors and its superior trade performance.

It takes ten permits to start a business in India against six in China, while the median time it takes is 90 days in India against 30 days in China. In India, a typical foreign power project requires 43 clearances at central government level and another 57 at state level. These obstacles are far smaller in China.

In restrictions on the hiring and firing of workers, India ranked 73rd out of 75 countries in the Global Competitiveness Report for 2001. China ranked 23rd. Bankruptcy is almost impossible for large businesses. Sixty per cent of liquidation processes before the Indian High Court have continued for more than ten years. Public administration is also poor. It takes an average of 10.6 days to clear goods at customs into India, against 7.8 into China.

As important as regulatory barriers to competition is India's poor infrastructure. Paved roads are only 56 per cent of the total, against over 80 per cent in China. Shipping a container of textiles to the USA costs 35 per cent more than from China. Because of power shortages, 69 per cent of Indian companies have their own generator, compared with just 30 per cent in China.

Source: Financial Times, 4 April 2003.

Rapid population growth

A third distinguishing feature of most developing countries is that they have a much faster rate of population growth than developed countries – in fact their population is growing faster than at any time in the world's history (see Chapter 9 for a full discussion). This can confer advantages, but it also imposes acute problems. Population growth in the developing countries as a whole averages 1.3 per cent per annum, resulting from a birth rate of 24 per 1,000 population (or 2.4 per cent) and a death rate of 11 per 1,000 population (or 1.1 per cent). The rapid acceleration of population growth compared with its historical trend is the result of a dramatic fall in the death rate without a commensurate fall in the birth rate. Population growth in developed countries averages no more than 0.7 per cent per annum. The population growth rate in low-income, middle-income and high-income countries is shown in Table 3.3. Population growth in low-income countries is three times higher than in high-income countries.

Table 3.3 Population growth, 2000–2007 (% per annum)

Low income	2.2
Middle income	1.0
High income	0.7

Source: World Bank, 2009.

Rapid population growth, like low capital accumulation, may be considered as both a cause and a consequence of poverty. High birth rates are themselves a function of poverty because child mortality is high in poor societies and parents wish to have large families to provide insurance in old age. High birth rates also go hand in hand with poor education, a lack of employment opportunities for women and ignorance of birth control techniques. Population growth, in turn, helps to perpetuate poverty if it reduces saving, dilutes capital per head and reduces the marginal product of labour in agriculture. The pressure of numbers may also put a strain on government expenditure, lead to congestion and overcrowding, impair the environment and put pressure on food supplies – all of which retard the development process, at least in the short run. In the longer run, population growth may stimulate investment and technical progress, and may not pose such a problem if there are complementary resources and factors of production available, but the short-run costs may outweigh the advantages for a considerable time.

Exports dominated by primary commodities

A fourth distinguishing characteristic of developing countries is that their trade tends to be dominated by the export of primary commodities and the import of manufactured goods. This has consequences for the terms of trade of developing countries, the distribution of the gains from trade between developed and developing countries, and the balance of payments situation – all of which may adversely affect real income per head. Table 3.4 shows primary commodities as a percentage of the total exports of different continents. The trade of Africa, the Middle East, Latin America and the Caribbean is still dominated by primary commodities. Only Asia and the Pacific have made headway in reducing dependence on commodity exports.

The **barter terms of trade** measures the ratio of export prices to import prices. There has been a historical tendency for the terms of trade of primary goods relative to manufactured goods to deteriorate over the last 100 years or so – by about 0.5 per cent per annum on average. This tendency is known in the literature as the **Prebisch–Singer thesis** (see Chapter 15). The commodity

Table 3.4 Primary commodities as a percentage of total exports, 2007

East Asia & Pacific	23
Latin America & Caribbean	46
Middle East & North Africa	84[a]
South Asia	34
Sub-Saharan Africa	70[a]

Note: [a] The figure corresponds to 2006.

Source: World Bank, World Development Indicators June 2009, online (http://data.worldbank.org/indicator).

price boom in 2007/8 must be seen against a background of a long-run deteriorating trend in real commodities prices (see Chapter 15, p. 544). The falling price of exports relative to imports reduces the real income of a country because more exports have to be exchanged to obtain a given quantity of imports.

A second point to note is that the income elasticity of demand for primary commodities in world trade is less than unity, while the income elasticity of demand for manufactured goods is greater than unity. This means that as world income grows, the demand for primary commodities grows at a slower rate, but if developing countries grow at the same rate as the world economy their demand for manufactured imports grows at a faster rate. As a consequence, developing countries specializing in the production and export of primary commodities suffer acute balance-of-payments difficulties. Often, the only means available to developing countries to adjust the balance of payments is to slow down their economies in order to reduce the growth of imports.

The prices of primary commodities are also more cyclically volatile than the prices of manufactured goods. This can also cause havoc with a country's balance of payments and its tax revenue if it relies heavily on trade taxes. The resulting instability makes planning difficult and may deter private domestic investment and investment from overseas.

For all these reasons, the structure of trade poses severe problems for many developing countries and may keep countries poorer than they would be if they were able to produce and export more industrial goods. It is not possible to understand the growth and development process – and the perpetuation of divisions in the world economy – without reference to the unequal trading relations between rich and poor countries and the balance-of-payments consequences of specializing in primary commodities.

The curse of natural resources

In general, it seems to be the case that the more natural resources a country has, the worse it performs. This phenomenon is referred to in the literature as the '**curse of natural resources**' (Sachs and Warner, 2001; Gylfason, 2001). This is illustrated in Figure 3.2, which shows a scatter diagram for 105 countries of the relationship between the growth of per capita income over the period 1965–98, and the share of the labour force employed in the primary sector. There is a very

Figure 3.2 Natural resources and economic growth

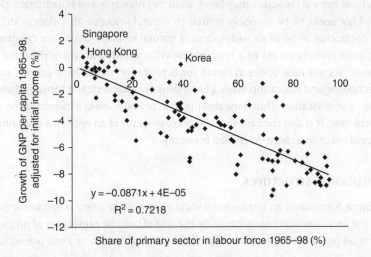

$y = -0.0871x + 4E-05$

$R^2 = 0.7218$

Share of primary sector in labour force 1965–98 (%)

strong negative relationship ($R^2 = 0.7218$), and the regression coefficient of -0.0871 indicates that a country with a primary sector share 11 percentage points above the average has experienced a growth of per capita income of one percentage point below the average (controlling for the initial level of per capita income). This represents a substantial loss of welfare.

The same negative pattern emerges when the growth of per capita income is regressed against the export of natural resources as a share of GDP; and the negative relation persists even when controlling for other variables such as differences in the level of investment between countries, and for climate and geography (Sachs and Warner, 2001). Most countries that have grown rapidly in recent decades started as resource poor, not resource rich. There are exceptions to this general rule – countries such as Malaysia, Thailand, Indonesia and Botswana, for example – but most of these exceptional countries have grown fast not through the exploitation of natural resources but through diversification into manufacturing industry.

What lies behind this 'curse of natural resources'? A number of interrelated factors can be mentioned which seem to have an adverse effect on many of the important determinants of development. Gylfason shows a negative relation across countries between the share of the primary sector in the labour force and export performance, domestic and foreign investment and education, and a positive relation with the size of external debt, the level of protection, corruption and income inequality. We have already seen why primary production can lead to poor export performance because many natural resources are income inelastic and suffer terms of trade deterioration, but why should natural resource-abundant countries neglect investment and education, and be more corrupt? There are two major explanations.

First, natural resource abundance may 'crowd-out' other activities through two mechanisms: (1) higher wages or earnings in the natural resources sector discouraging entrepreneurial activity and innovation in other sectors, and (2) revenues from natural resource exports keeping the exchange rate artificially high which makes the rest of the economy uncompetitive. This is known as the **Dutch disease** – so named because of the effect that the discovery of natural gas in Holland in the 1960s had on the exchange rate and other sectors of the economy. Sachs and Warner (2001) test this 'crowding-out' hypothesis across 99 countries and find a positive correlation between natural resource abundance and the domestic price level. The higher relative price level is then found to impede the export growth of manufactured goods. It could also be that a country rich in natural resources simply neglects to develop other sectors of the economy.

A second major explanation why natural resource abundance may lead to poor performance is that the **rents** from natural resources may be misused by politicians and bureaucrats. Democracy and the rule of law seem to be inversely related to natural resource abundance, and Gylfason (2001) shows corruption to be more widespread in natural resource-abundant countries. This is not surprising since limiting access to a resource provides a rent, and where the state owns the resource, bureaucrats will take bribes in return for exploitation rights. Rent earners may not be interested in schooling and education, having lined their own pockets, and those of their children, without acquiring an education. Thus, rent-seeking leads to low levels of expenditure on education and school enrolment. It is also the case that the primary sector of an economy does not have the same educational needs as a more diversified economy.

Weak institutional structures

Economies cannot function in an institutional vacuum, otherwise there is economic (and political) chaos. At the very minimum there has to be the rule of law, the protection of property rights, and constraints on power and corruption if private individuals are to be entrepreneurial, to take risks and invest. In many developing countries, the rule of law and the protection of property rights is still rudimentary, and politicians (and bureaucrats) abuse their powers. Many economists (e.g. Acemoglu, 2003; Rodrik, 2007) have recently argued that it is weak institutional structures that are the fundamental cause of underdevelopment because the character of institutions is the determinant of all the proximate causes of progress such as investment, technology, education and trade. There are several measures of institutional quality that economists focus on, and they will be discussed in detail in Chapter 4. Three main ones are: the extent of legal protection of private property, the quality of governance (including the strength of the rule of law) and the limits placed on political leaders. Attempts have been made to distinguish econometrically the relative importance of institutions compared with other factors (including geography) in explaining different levels of per capita income across the world, with interesting, but controversial, results. Rodrik et al. (2002) take a large sample of developed and developing countries, measuring the quality of institutions mainly by a composite indicator of a number of elements that capture protection afforded by property rights, and conclude 'Our results indicate that the quality of institutions overrides everything else. Controlling for institutions, geography has, at best, weak direct effects on income ... [s]imilarly trade ... has no direct positive effect on income.' Easterly and Levine (2002) also test the influence of institutions compared with geography and policy variables across 75 rich and poor countries and find that institutions seem to matter most as the determinant of per capita income. Even countries with 'bad policies' do well with good institutions. We will examine the evidence for this in more detail in the next chapter.

It is recognized, however, that the correlation found between institutions and economic development could reflect reverse causality, or omitted factors. We need to find a source of exogenous variation in institutions where institutions differ or change independently of other factors. Acemoglu et al. (2001) argue that the different experience of **colonization** is one exogenous source where at one extreme colonizers set up exclusively extractive institutions (to exploit minerals and other primary products) – such as slavery and forced labour – which neither gave property rights to inhabitants nor constrained the power of elites. This was the experience in Africa and Latin America. At the other extreme, colonizers created settler societies, replicating the European form of institutions protecting private property and controlling elites and politicians in countries such as Australia and New Zealand and in North America. But what determined why some countries were settled and others not? Acemoglu et al. argue that the major determinant was the mortality rate faced by the early settlers, and that there is both a strong negative correlation between past mortality rates and current institutional quality (because institutions persisted) and between past mortality and the current levels of per capita income. In fact, over 50 per cent of the variation in per capita income across the 75 countries is associated with variation in one particular index of institutional quality which measures 'protection against expropriation'. The authors conclude 'There is a high correlation between mortality rates faced by soldiers, bishops and sailors in the colonies and European settlements; between European settlements and early measures of institutions, and between early institutions and institutions today. We estimate large effects of institutions on income per capita using this source of variation.' They also say that 'this relationship is not driven by outliers, and is robust controlling for latitude, climate, current disease environment, religion, natural resources, soil quality, ethnolinguistic fragmentation, and current racial composition'. But this is where the controversy starts because presumably the mortality rates of the early settlers, which affected the nature of institutions, was strongly influenced by geography as it affects disease. In the same vein Sachs (2003) argues that the finding of Acemoglu et al. concerning the negative relation between mortality rates 200 years ago and per capita income today is simply picking up the pernicious effects of malaria (which still persists), not institutions. Development is not simply about good government and institutions. Institutions might make anti-poverty policies more effective, but that is all. Poor countries need resources to fight disease, to provide education and infrastructure, and all the other resource prerequisites of development. Sachs classifies three types of countries combining institutions and geography, which is a sensible approach:

- Countries where institutions, policies and geography are all reasonably favourable, e.g. the coastal regions of East Asia
- Countries with favourable geography, but weak institutions, e.g. many of the transition economies of Eastern Europe and the former Soviet Union
- Countries impoverished by a combination of unfavourable geography – such as landlocked countries and those plagued with disease – and poor governance, for example many of the countries of sub-Saharan Africa.

One manifestation of poor governance and weak institutions is **wars** both within countries (civil wars) and between countries. According to Oxfam (2007), conflicts in Africa since 1990 have cost the continent $150 billion, equivalent to the total amount of foreign aid received over the same period. The economic damage to economies is immense. In countries such as the Democratic Republic of the Congo, Burundi and Rwanda, for example, wars have reduced national output by over 20 per cent. This is the 'conflict trap' referred to by Collier (2007) in his book *The Bottom Billion*. In war-torn countries, inflation, debt and unemployment are all higher; public investment in education, health and infrastructure suffer; life expectancy is lower, and people are more prone to disease and malnourishment.

Other dimensions of the development gap

Deprivation in developing countries is not simply a matter of low levels of per capita income. There are many other dimensions to the development gap between rich and poor countries. Developing countries generally experience much higher levels of unemployment – open and disguised – than do developed countries. The levels of education, health and nutrition are often abysmally low, and income distribution tends to be much more inegalitarian. Policy in developing countries is increasingly concerned with these other features of the development gap. The **basic needs approach** to development, originally pioneered by the World Bank, is a reflection of this switch of emphasis from exclusive concern with per capita income to these wider development issues.

Unemployment

The developing countries contain a huge reservoir of surplus labour. For a long time, poor countries, particularly since the population explosion, have been characterized by underemployment or disguised unemployment in rural areas (see Chapter 6). What has happened in recent years is that disguised rural unemployment has transferred itself into **disguised** and **open unemployment** in the towns. Unemployment in the urban areas of developing countries is another dimension of the development problem and an increasingly serious one. The rationale for rural–urban migration will be considered later, but first it is appropriate to outline some of the facts on employment and unemployment. According to the International Labour Organization (ILO) in Geneva,

1 billion people in developing countries are either jobless or underemployed, which amounts to one-third of the total working-age population.[2]

This represents a colossal challenge, particularly as the workforce is expected to grow by another 1.5 billion by the year 2025. The ILO argues for a renewed commitment by developing countries to the goal of employment creation, and not to treat current unemployment levels as natural and the inevitable outcome of market forces, as if nothing can be done. The ILO estimates that at least one billion new jobs need to be created if the proportion of people living in poverty is to be halved by 2015. The World Bank devoted its 1995 *World Development Report* to the conditions of employment in developing countries, and it painted a sombre picture.[3] To stop unemployment rising there has to be employment growth of at least 2 per cent per annum, which requires output growth of at least 4 per cent per annum. Not many countries are able to grow this rapidly and consistently over time.

All this is very aggregative analysis. The issue still to be addressed is the emergence of increasing urban unemployment. The problem is not so much one of a deficiency of demand for labour in an aggregate demand sense. The causal factors relate to the incentives for labour to migrate from rural to urban areas, and the incapacity of the urban areas to provide employment owing to a lack of other necessary factors of production to work with labour, particularly capital. As far as migration is concerned, there are both push and pull factors at work.

The **push factors** have to do with the limited job opportunities in rural areas and a greater desire and ability to move, fostered by education and improved communications. The **pull factors** relate to the development of urban industrial activities that offer jobs at a higher real wage than can be earned in rural areas, so that even if a migrant is unemployed for part of the year, he or she may still be better off migrating to the town than working in the rural sector. If there is no work at all in the rural sector, the migrant loses nothing, except friends and the security of the extended family system. The rate of growth of job opportunities in the rural sector depends on the rate of growth of demand for the output of the rural sector and the rate at which jobs are being 'destroyed' by productivity growth.

As we saw in our previous example (p. 72), if the demand for agricultural output is growing at 1.5 per cent and productivity is growing at 1 per cent, then the growth of labour demand will be 0.5 per cent. But if the labour force is growing at 2 per cent there will be a 1.5 percentage point gap between the supply and demand for labour. If the level of disguised unemployment in the rural sector does not increase, this figure constitutes the potential volume of migrants. If the urban labour force is one-half of the size of the rural labour force, a 1.5 per cent migration of rural labour would represent a 3 per cent increase in the urban labour force owing to migration.

On average, this is about the extent of the influx from the rural sector into the urban areas of developing countries. On top of this there is the natural increase in the workforce in the urban areas of 2 per cent to consider. If job opportunities in the urban areas are increasing at only 3 per cent, then 2–3 per cent of the urban labour force will be added to the amount of urban unemployment year by year, forcing labour into the informal service sector. In that case, unemployment shows up as poverty.

Historically, the process of development has always been associated with, and characterized by, an exodus from the land, continuing over centuries. The uniqueness of the present situation is not the migration itself but its magnitude and speed. And the problem is that the urban sector cannot absorb the numbers involved. For any given technology, the rate at which the urban (industrial) sector can absorb migrants largely depends on the rate of capital formation. If labour and capital must be combined in fixed proportions, and the rate of capital accumulation is only 3 per cent, then the rate of increase in job opportunities can be only 3 per cent also. Unfortunately, however, as will be shown in Chapter 6, the problem is not necessarily solved by a faster rate of capital accumulation in the urban sector, because migration is not simply a function of the actual difference in real remuneration between the two sectors, but also of the level of job opportunities in the urban sector. If the rate of job creation increases, this may merely increase the flow of migrants with no reduction in unemployment. The solution would seem to be to create more job opportunities in the rural sector. This requires, however, not only the redirection of investment but also the extension of education and transport facilities, which in the past few years have themselves become powerful push factors in the migration process. Whereas formerly redundant labour might have remained underemployed on the family farm, nowadays education and easy transportation provide the incentive and the means to seek alternative employment opportunities. While education and improved communications are desirable in themselves, and facilitate development, their provision has augmented the flow of migrants from rural to urban areas.

The **pull factors** behind migration are not hard to identify. The opportunities for work and leisure provided by the industrial, urban environment contrast sharply with the conservatism and stultifying atmosphere of rural village life and naturally act as a magnet for those on low incomes or without work, especially the young. Given the much higher wages in the urban sector, even the prospect of long spells of unemployment in the towns does not detract from the incentive to migrate. Moreover the choice is not necessarily between remaining in the rural sector and migrating to the urban sector with the prospect of long periods of unemployment. The unemployed in the urban sector can often find work, or create work for themselves, on the fringes of the industrial sector – in particular in the **informal service sector** of the urban economy. The wages may be low, but some income is better than no income. In other words, unemployment in urban areas may take the form of underemployment, or become disguised, just as in the case of the rural sector – its manifestation being low income. This has led to the notion of an **income measure of unemployment**, which needs to be added to registered unemployment to obtain a true measure of unemployment and the availability of labour supply.

One way of measuring the extent of unemployment disguised in the form of low-productivity/low-income jobs is to take the difference between the actual labour employed at the substandard income and the labour that would be required to produce a given level of output or service at an acceptable level of income per head. Before measurement can take place, of course, the acceptable (standard) level of income has to be defined. It could be that level set as the 'poverty line', below which health and welfare become seriously impaired. The income measure of unemployment would thus be

$$U = L - L^* = \frac{O}{O/L} - \frac{O}{O/L^*}$$

where L is the actual labour employed, L^* is the labour consistent with an acceptable level of income per person employed, O/L is the actual level of productivity (or income per head), O/L^* is the acceptable level of income per employed person, and O is output. Let us work an example. Suppose that the annual flow of output of an activity or service, such as shoe-shines or haircuts, is $1 million and that the existing number employed is 5,000, giving a level of productivity of $200. Now suppose that the acceptable level of productivity to produce an acceptable level of income per person employed is $500 (roughly the new international poverty line of $1.25 a day). The income measure of unemployment is then

$$U = \frac{1,000,000}{200} - \frac{1,000,000}{500} = 3,000$$

that is, over one-half of the existing labour force is disguisedly unemployed in the sense that the level of output is not sufficient for those who currently work to maintain an adequate standard of living.

The above analysis of employment and unemployment trends in developing countries points to a number of policy implications that were also highlighted by the ILO as long ago as 1969, when it first sponsored missions to several countries to undertake a detailed diagnosis of the employment problem.[4] Certainly an adequate rate of output growth is required to employ workers entering the labour market for the first time and to absorb the effects of productivity growth, but much more is required. There is a case for the use of more labour-intensive techniques of production (see Chapter 7), and the issue of rural–urban migration needs to be tackled by promoting more employment opportunities outside the urban centres, particularly for young people. Without such measures, unemployment will continue to grow, especially in urban areas. Felipe and Hasan (2006) at the Asian Development Bank argue that employment creation, and combating unemployment, is the major development challenge facing Asian economies today because unemployment is a major cause of poverty and social unrest.

Education

Another dimension of the development gap is the difference in educational opportunities between rich and poor countries, which manifests itself in much lower primary, secondary and tertiary school enrolment rates in developing countries, much higher levels of illiteracy and lower levels of human capital formation in general. This has a number of adverse consequences for the growth and development process. Low levels of education and skills make it more difficult for countries to develop new industries and to absorb new technology, it makes people less adaptable and amenable to change and it impairs the ability to manage and administer enterprises and organizations at all levels.

Table 3.5 shows the relative underprovision of educational facilities and opportunities in many poor countries, and the low rate of literacy in the poorest countries. The first three columns show the percentage of the age group enrolled in primary, secondary and tertiary education. In the primary and secondary sectors, the percentage sometimes exceeds 100 per cent because the gross enrolment ratio is the ratio of *total* enrolment, *regardless of age*, to the population of the age group that officially corresponds to that level of education. The primary school age group may be 5–11 years, but children older than that are attending. The enrolment rate is also not the same as the completion rate, which is only 65 per cent in low-income countries, and only 60 per cent in Africa. Moreover, enrolment and completion do not necessarily mean receiving a good education. For economic development, it is not just the quantity of education that is important, but also the quality.

Notice, however, the huge discrepancy in the provision of secondary education, with less than one-half of the age group in low-income countries receiving any education beyond the age of 11. This amounts to approximately 265 million children not enrolled in secondary schools. It is estimated that over 300 million will be missing from both primary and secondary schools in 2015

Table 3.5 Participation in education

	School gross enrolment ratio			Adult literacy rate	
	% of relevant age group			% ages 15 and older	
	Primary 2006	Secondary 2006	Tertiary 2006	Female 2007	Male 2007
World	105	66	25	79	88
Low income	94	38	6	55	72
Middle income	111	70	24	80	90
Lower middle income	111	65	19	77	88
Upper middle income	111	91	42	93	95
Low & middle income	106	61	19	75	86
East Asia & Pacific	110	73	21	90	96
Europe & Central Asia	97	88	53	96	99
Latin America & Carib.	118	89	31	90	92
Middle East & N. Africa	105	71	25	65	82
South Asia	108	—	10	52	74
Sub-Saharan Africa	94	32	5	54	71
High income	101	101	67	99	99

Source: *World Development Indicators 2009*, online (http://data.worldbank.org/indicator).

without increases in expenditure on education. This requires a reorientation of priorities in poor countries (e.g. less expenditure on arms and wasteful subsidies, more aid from donor countries and more help from the World Bank). Poor countries currently spend approximately $100 billion on secondary education, but another $20 to $40 billion is needed if the Millennium Development Target is to be achieved.

The current deficiency in education in poor countries compared with rich countries manifests itself in high levels of adult illiteracy. One-third of adults in low-income countries cannot read or write; and a big gender gap is also evident. While just under 30 per cent of males are illiterate, about 50 per cent of females are illiterate. Among the poor countries, China performs well, but in many of the poorest countries in Africa female illiteracy is well over 50 per cent. The gender gap narrows as income rises, but it is still evident.

Developing countries neglect educational provision at their peril. Research shows a strong association across countries between levels of human capital formation, growth performance and poverty reduction. For example, Baldacci et al. (2005) find, using a panel data set for 120 developing countries over the period 1975 to 2000, that an increase in education spending of one per cent of GDP is associated, on average, with three extra years of schooling, and an increase in annual GDP growth of 1.5 percentage points after 15 years. This reduces the poverty headcount by 17 per cent. Further research on the link between education and growth is discussed in Chapters 5 and 7.

Inequality: vertical and horizontal

As well as the average per capita income being low in developing countries, the distribution of income, wealth and power is also typically very unequal, and much more unequal than in developed countries. All too often, the growth and development that takes place in poor countries benefits the richest few, and the vast mass of the population is left untouched. Rural and urban poverty are still widespread, and if anything the degree of income inequality within many developing countries is increasing. The way income is distributed across individuals and households is referred to as **vertical inequality**, and is the traditional measure of inequality that development policy focuses upon. There is also the concept, however, of **horizontal inequality** concerned with how different *groups* in society are treated, based on race, religion, language, class, gender and so on. The well-being of people can be affected as much by horizontal inequality as vertical inequality. First we will consider vertical inequality and then horizontal inequality.

It should come as no surprise that the transformation of economies from a primitive subsistence state into industrial societies, within a basically capitalist framework, should be accompanied in the early stages by widening disparities in the personal distribution of income. Some people are more industrious than others and more adept at accumulating wealth. Opportunities cannot, in the very nature of things, be equal for all. In the absence of strong redistributive taxation, income inequality will inevitably accompany industrialization because of the inequality of skills and wealth that differences in individual ability and initiative – and industrialization – produce.

The observation that income inequality increases with the level of development and then declines is often called the **Kuznets curve**, named after the famous development economist Simon Kuznets, who did pioneering research on structural change and income distribution in the 1950s and 1960s (e.g. Kuznets 1955, 1963) which earned him the Nobel Prize for economics in 1971. Kuznets showed that in many of the present developed countries, the degree of inequality first increased and then decreased in the later stages of industrialization, giving an inverted U-shaped curve. For the developing countries, the pioneering work of Adelman and Morris (1971), extended by Paukert (1973), also showed fairly conclusively that inequality increases up to a certain stage of development and then declines, graphically showing an inverted U-shape similar to the work of Kuznets for the developed countries. The greater degree of inequality in the developing countries appears largely due to the higher share of income received by the richest 5 per cent of income recipients – nearly 30 per cent of income in developing countries compared with 20 per cent in developed countries.

Deininger and Squire (1996) of the World Bank have surveyed 682 studies of income distribution in over 100 countries and calculated average Gini ratios for each country, together with the ratio of the share of income received by the top 20 per cent of income earners (top quintile) to that of the bottom 20 per cent of income earners (bottom quintile). The results are shown by continent in Table 3.6. It can be seen from the Gini ratios (multiplied by 100) that Latin America and the Caribbean, and Africa, have by far the largest degree of income inequality, with the Gini ratio well over 50 in many countries, for example Brazil (57.3), Mexico (53.8) and South Africa (62.3). In contrast, income inequality in Asia and the Pacific, and Eastern Europe, appears to be much less. In the two largest countries in the world measured by population – China and India – the Gini ratio is just over 30, much the same as for the high-income countries. Generally speaking, the higher the Gini ratio, the greater the ratio of income shares between the top and bottom 20 per cent of income earners. In South Africa that ratio is 32:1 and in Brazil 23:1.

There are several formidable barriers to narrowing the income distribution gap. First, there is the dualistic nature of many economies (see Chapter 8), perpetuated by feudal land-tenure systems and urban bias in the allocation of investment resources. Secondly, there is inequality in the provision of education facilities, and a particular lack of facilities in rural areas where

Table 3.6 Income inequality, selected economies, 1990s

Region and economy	Number of observations	Average Gini ratio	Ratio of top quintile's share of income to bottom quintile's share
Sub-Saharan Africa	40	44.71	11.61
Botswana	1	54.21	16.36
Cameroon	1	49.00	–
Central African Republic	1	55.00	–
Côte d'Ivoire	4	39.18	7.17
Gabon	2	61.23	19.79
Ghana	4	35.13	5.97
Guinea–Bissau	1	56.12	28.57
Kenya	1	54.39	18.24
Lesotho	1	56.02	20.90
Madagascar	1	43.44	8.52
Mauritania	1	42.53	13.12
Mauritius	3	40.67	6.62
Niger	1	36.10	5.90
Nigeria	3	38.55	8.67
Rwanda	1	28.90	4.01
Senegal	1	54.12	16.75
Seychelles	2	46.50	–
Sierra Leone	1	60.79	22.45
South Africa	1	62.30	32.11
Sudan	1	38.72	5.58
Tanzania	3	40.37	6.63
Uganda	2	36.89	6.01
Zambia	2	47.26	12.11
Zimbabwe	1	56.83	15.66
East Asia and the Pacific	123	36.18	7.15
China	12	32.68	5.17
Fiji	1	42.50	–
Hong Kong	7	41.58	9.46
Indonesia	11	33.49	5.22
Japan	23	34.82	7.06
Korea, Rep. of	14	34.19	6.29
Lao PDR	1	30.40	4.21
Malaysia	6	50.36	14.18
Philippines	7	47.62	12.00
Singapore	6	40.12	6.71
Taiwan (China)	26	29.62	4.67
Thailand	8	45.48	11.65
Vietnam	1	35.71	5.51

Table 3.6   Income inequality, selected economies, 1990s – *continued*

Region and economy	Number of observations	Average Gini ratio	Ratio of top quintile's share of income to bottom quintile's share
South Asia	60	34.06	5.50
Bangladesh	10	34.51	5.72
India	31	32.55	4.98
Nepal	1	30.06	4.34
Pakistan	9	31.50	4.68
Sri Lanka	9	41.71	7.98
Eastern Europe	101	26.01	4.05
Armenia	1	39.39	23.88
Belarus	1	28.53	4.30
Bulgaria	28	23.30	3.24
Czechoslovakia	12	22.25	3.08
Czech Republic	2	27.43	3.75
Estonia	3	34.66	6.62
Hungary	9	24.65	3.61
Kazakhstan	1	32.67	5.39
Kyrgyz Republic	1	35.32	6.31
Latvia	1	26.98	3.83
Lithuania	1	33.64	5.20
Moldova	1	34.43	6.06
Poland	17	25.69	3.75
Romania	3	25.83	3.79
Slovak Republic	2	20.50	2.76
Slovenia	2	27.08	3.77
Ukraine	1	25.71	3.71
USSR	5	26.94	4.06
Yugoslavia	10	32.62	5.63
Middle East and North Africa	20	40.77	7.14
Algeria	1	38.73	6.85
Egypt, Arab Rep. of	4	38.00	4.72
Iran, Islamic Rep. of	5	43.23	–
Jordan	3	39.19	7.39
Morocco	2	39.20	7.03
Tunisia	5	42.51	8.25
Latin America and the Caribbean	100	50.15	16.02
Barbados	2	47.18	17.56
Bolivia	1	42.04	8.58
Brazil	15	57.32	23.07
Chile	5	51.84	14.48
Colombia	7	51.51	13.94

continued overleaf

Table 3.6 Income inequality, selected economies, 1990s – *continued*

Region and economy	Number of observations	Average Gini ratio	Ratio of top quintile's share of income to bottom quintile's share
Costa Rica	9	46.00	13.13
Dominican Republic	4	46.94	11.06
Ecuador	1	43.00	9.82
El Salvador	1	48.40	10.64
Guatemala	3	55.68	20.82
Guyana	2	48.19	9.15
Honduras	7	54.49	27.74
Jamaica	9	42.90	8.75
Mexico	9	53.85	17.12
Nicaragua	1	50.32	13.12
Panama	4	52.43	22.64
Peru	4	47.99	9.21
Puerto Rico	3	51.11	22.20
Trinidad	4	46.21	18.31
Venezuela	9	44.42	10.93
Industrial countries and high-income developing countries	238	33.19	6.63
Australia	9	37.88	8.32
Bahamas	11	45.77	14.14
Belgium	4	27.01	4.26
Canada	23	31.27	5.54
Denmark	4	32.09	6.29
Finland	12	29.93	5.35
France	7	43.11	6.31
Germany	7	31.22	5.35
Greece	3	34.53	6.37
Ireland	3	36.31	8.91
Italy	15	34.93	4.94
Luxembourg	1	27.13	4.11
Netherlands	12	28.59	4.43
New Zealand	12	34.36	6.78
Norway	9	34.21	7.39
Portugal	4	37.44	7.44
Spain	8	27.90	4.34
Sweden	15	31.63	5.64
Turkey	3	50.36	15.22
United Kingdom	31	25.98	4.03
United States	45	35.28	8.46
Total	682	36.12	7.80

Source: Deininger and Squire, 1996.

the poorest are concentrated. Third, there is disguised rural unemployment, underemployment and open unemployment in urban areas created by rural–urban migration, a shortage of investment resources and inappropriate production techniques. Until development policy comes to grips with these problems, there will continue to be large pockets of absolute poverty and a marked degree of inequality in income distribution. When deciding on the allocation of investment resources and the choice of projects, a high weight must be given to projects that raise the income of the poorest if the income distribution is to be narrowed (see Chapter 11).

Now let us turn to horizontal inequality (HI), which is concerned with how economic differences, social demarcations and political power combine to produce differences in entitlements and capabilities for different groups in society. Groups may be defined in a number of ways, as already mentioned: by race, religion, gender, location, class, language and so on. Stewart (2001) develops the hypothesis that not only is HI responsible for much conflict within societies, but it also affects the development process in a number of ways. For example, some groups may be denied access to public goods such as education and health care. This impoverishes not only the group, but the economy at large. Certain regions may be deprived of infrastructure investment because of particular groups located in these regions, which not only damages the region but the progress of the whole economy. To be discriminated against on the basis of a particular group identity has psychological effects, and affects the core goals of development that were discussed in Chapter 1: life sustenance, self-esteem and freedom. Thus HI is an important dimension of well-being, and can have economic and political consequences highly detrimental to development. Despite this, international development policy is rarely focused on the narrowing of group divisions. HI would not matter so much if there was mobility between groups, or if individuals were free to choose which group they belonged to, but this is rarely the case in often highly stratified developing countries. Stewart (2001) gives examples of several case studies of the basis and consequences of horizontal inequality, for example, in Mexico, Brazil, Fiji, Malaysia and South Africa. The situation in several countries is given in Case example 3.2. It is clear that development policy needs to tackle horizontal inequality between groups, as well as vertical inequality with respect to the income distribution across individuals.

| Case example 3.2 | **Inequalities between groups can fuel conflict and tension** |

The root causes of violent conflict are rarely simple. But as the examples below show, a common theme is emerging from recent research into conflict: the role that socio-economic and political inequalities between groups can play in causing tensions and violence. Less research has been done on the role that cultural exclusions of groups may play (such as lack of recognition of languages or religious practices), but these are also issues that can lead to mobilization and protests and so may also be important root causes or triggers of conflict.

- Severe rioting against the Chinese in **Malaysia** in the late 1960s has been attributed largely to the animosity felt by the politically dominant but economically sidelined Bumiputera majority towards the economically dominant Chinese minority.

continued overleaf

| Case example 3.2 | **Inequalities between groups can fuel conflict and tension** – *continued* |

- Civil war in **Sri Lanka** since the early 1980s has been linked to tensions resulting from inequalities between the Tamil minority and Sinhalese majority. Colonial administrators had favoured the Tamil minority economically, but this advantage was sharply reversed once the Sinhalese gained power and increasingly sidelined the Tamil minority in such areas as educational opportunities, civil service recruitment and language policy.

- In **Uganda** the Bantu-speaking people (largely in the centre and south) have been economically dominant but politically sidelined compared with the non-Bantu-speaking people (largely in the north). These economic and political inequities have played a role in major conflicts, including the violence initiated by Idi Amin (1970s) and by the second Obote regime (1983–85).

- Indigenous people in the state of Chiapas, **Mexico**, have long suffered political and socio-economic deprivation. They have demanded greater political autonomy, improved socio-economic conditions and protection of their cultural heritage, culminating in uprisings against the Mexican state in four municipalities.

- In **South Africa** before 1994 the black majority was severely disadvantaged politically and socio-economically. That led to many uprisings between 1976 and the transfer of power in 1993.

- Catholics in **Northern Ireland** have suffered economic and political deprivation since the sixteenth century. The continuance of Northern Ireland as part of the United Kingdom in the 1920s ensured that Protestants would enjoy permanent political and economic dominance – fuelling demands by northern Catholics to become part of the predominantly Catholic Republic of Ireland. Violent conflict started in the late 1960s and began to ease in the 1990s following systematic efforts to reduce these inequalities.

- Constitutional crises and coups have occurred in **Fiji**, notably in 1987 and 1999, as economically sidelined indigenous Fijians have feared losing political control to the economically dominant Indian-origin Fijians.

- Increasing tensions between Muslims and Christians in Poso, Central Sulawesi, **Indonesia**, began surfacing in the mid-1990s as the Muslim community increasingly gained more than indigenous Christians from new economic policies.

- Since colonial times the indigenous people of **Guatemala** have suffered political and economic discrimination, contributing to the country's ongoing conflicts.

- The Maoist insurgency launched in **Nepal** in 1996 may be attributed to deep grievances stemming from the systematic marginalization and exclusion of certain ethnic groups, castes and women.

Source: UNDP, 2004.

Growth and distribution

The observation that income inequality increases with the level of development and then declines is not to say that faster economic growth within a country necessarily worsens the income distribution. Recent international evidence suggests that rapid structural transformation and fast economic growth have benefited the poor as much as the rich. Nor for that matter is inequality a necessary condition for growth because it generates more saving, as it is sometimes claimed. Naqvi (1995) looked in detail at 40 developing countries and found that high growth rates and distributive justice (as well as macroeconomic stability) have tended to move together. This is also the conclusion of Dollar and Kraay (2000), who examine the relation between growth and income distribution across 80 countries over 40 years. They find that the income of the poor (the bottom 20 per cent of the population) rises one-to-one with overall growth, and the relation is no different in poor countries than in rich ones. Nor has the poverty–growth relationship changed much over time. In other words, growth seems to benefit the poor as much as the rich, so that relative inequality (the Gini ratio) stays the same (although *absolute* inequality still widens, of course, because the same growth of income gives more dollars to a rich person than a poor person).

On the question of whether inequality promotes growth, the answer seems to be 'no'. If the Gini ratio is included in a cross-section equation to explain differences in growth between countries, the coefficient is normally negative, not positive (see Forbes, 2000). In other words, a more equal distribution of income is good for growth. Income equality is probably standing here as a proxy for such growth-inducing factors as good governance, civil society, equal property rights and equality of opportunity. The successful Asian 'tiger economies' have much more equal distributions of income than most other developing economies, and better governance.

Poverty-weighted growth rates

Whether progress is being made towards achieving the twin objectives of faster growth and a more equal distribution of income can be examined simultaneously by constructing **poverty-weighted indices of growth**.

GNP growth as conventionally measured is a weighted average of the growth of income of different groups of people, where the relevant weights are each group's share of total income. The measured growth rate pays no regard to the distribution of income. A high growth rate may be recorded, but this may have benefited only the rich. For example, suppose the bottom third of the population receive 10 per cent of income, the middle third receive 30 per cent of income, and the top third receive 60 per cent of income. GNP growth would be measured as

$$\% \text{ growth of GNP} = r_1(0.1) + r_2(0.3) + r_3(0.6)$$

where r_1, r_2 and r_3 are the respective rates of growth of income of the three groups. Suppose $r_1 = 1$ per cent, $r_2 = 1$ per cent and $r_3 = 10$ per cent. A GNP growth rate of 6.4 per cent would then be recorded, which looks very respectable but the position of the poorest will hardly have changed.

The idea of constructing poverty-weighted indices of growth is to give at least equal weight to all income groups in society, if not a greater weight to the poor, in order to obtain a better measure of the growth of overall welfare combining the growth of income with its distribution.

In the above example, for instance, if each group is given an equal weight of one-third, the measured growth of welfare becomes

$$\% \text{ growth of 'welfare'} = 1(0.33) + 1(0.33) + 10(0.33) = 4\%$$

which is much less than the rate of growth shown by the conventional measure of GNP growth when distributional considerations are taken into account.

A society could go further and say that it places no value or weight on income growth for the richest third of the population, and places all the weight on the lower-income groups with, say, a 60 per cent weight to the bottom third and a 40 per cent weight to the middle third. The growth of 'welfare' would then look derisory:

$$\% \text{ growth of 'welfare'} = 1(0.6) + 1(0.4) + 10(0) = 1\%$$

This approach has been experimented with by economists from the World Bank (see Ahluwalia et al., 1979) to compare countries, giving a 60 per cent weight to the lowest 40 per cent of the population, a 40 per cent weight to the middle 40 per cent and no weight to the top 20 per cent. In countries where the distribution of income had deteriorated, the poverty-weighted measure of the growth of welfare showed less improvement than GNP growth, and where the distribution of income had improved, the poverty-weighted growth rate showed more improvement than GNP growth.

Nutrition and health

Another dimension of the development gap between rich and poor countries is the poor level of nutrition and health among large sections of the population in developing countries. It has been estimated by the United Nations Food and Agriculture Organization (FAO) in Rome that over 1 billion people in the world suffer from various types of malnutrition, including over half of the world's 1.5 billion children. One billion people suffer protein–energy malnutrition, 1.3 billion suffer from anaemia (iron deficiency), 1.0 billion people have iodine deficiency, and 30 million children have vitamin A deficiency, causing blindness and death. Over 1 billion people have no reliable access to safe drinking water. Over 2 billion people have no access to proper toilet facilities. Nearly half the population of poor countries suffer from water-related diseases. Diarrhoea caused by unclean water claims the lives of 1.5 million children a year. This weakens the body, and the weaker and more undernourished children are, the more prone they are to infection and disease; and the more infections the greater the undernourishment due to loss of appetite, the difficulties of eating and the low absorption rate of food during digestion. Malnutrition among children is particularly serious because it stunts growth and mental development, and adds another twist to the vicious circle of poverty. Malnutrition is also a major cause of infant mortality, the rate of which is ten times higher in developing countries than in developed countries.

In his monumental and path-breaking book *An Inquiry into Well-Being and Destitution* (1993), the famous Indian economist Partha Dasgupta attempts to understand the common circumstances in which people are born in poor countries and in which they live and die in rural communities in these countries. He pays a lot of attention to the question of nutrition and its effects on health and work effort. The relation between low income and food intake is, of course, two-way. Low income is the major cause of malnutrition, which in turn is a cause of low income as it impairs work efficiency and productivity. Indices or measures of malnutrition can be based either on **nutritional requirements** in terms of different kinds of food or on **food energy**. Both affect labour productivity. The food requirements that nutritionists consider necessary for efficient working and healthy living are far greater than the levels achieved by the vast mass of the population living in developing countries. Calorie deficiency causes loss of body weight, tiredness, listlessness and a deterioration of mental faculties. Calories are also required for the absorption of protein: if the calorie requirement is met the protein requirement is normally met too, but not always. The condition 'Kwashiorkor' (associated with the bloated stomachs and staring eyes of the starving or malnourished children we see on our television screens) arises from protein deficiency because the calorie intake is in the form of low-protein tubers such as cassavas and yams. Protein is particularly important for brain development in the first three years of life, during which time the brain grows to 90 per cent of its full size. Brain damage due to protein deficiency is irreversible.

When it comes to the relation between nutrition and the capacity for physical effort, nutrition is generally defined in terms of the energy requirement. In this context, Dasgupta (1993) defines undernourishment as 'a state in which the physical functioning of a person is impaired to the point where she cannot maintain an adequate level of performance at physical work, or at resisting or recovering from the effects of any of a . . . variety of diseases'. The minimum amount of energy, or maintenance requirement (r), is the daily calorie requirement when a person is engaged in the minimal activities of eating and maintaining essential hygiene, with no allowance for work and play. According to nutritionists, r is 1.4 times the basal metabolic rate. The relation between productivity and energy intake is shown in Figure 3.3.

The interesting thing here is the slope of the line. In Figure 3.3 it is decreasing, but it could be linear or even increasing over certain ranges. When Bliss and Stern (1978) surveyed the literature they found the line to be linear in the region slightly to the right of r. More recent research confirms this[5] and shows substantial economic and social returns to investment in nutrition and health in terms of increased productivity on the job, increased productivity of time spent in school, and cost savings from treating the consequences of malnutrition and poor health. The costs of treating various forms of malnutrition are trivial relative to the tangible benefits, and to the costs of treating the consequences. To prevent malnutrition in children from the age of six months to three years, which is a child's most vulnerable period, can cost as little as $50 at current prices. The annual cost of preventing malnutrition is no more than the daily cost of treating its effects. Vitamin A deficiency is a cause of blindness. The annual cost of supporting a blind person is at least 1,000 times the annual ingredient cost of the vitamin A needed for prevention. Iodine deficiency is a cause of hypothyroidism (goitre), which leads to cretinism and deaf-mutism. The cost of iodate to prevent this is less than $0.01 per person per year. And so one could go on. Prevention is better than cure not only for the individual but also in a very real economic sense for the welfare of society as a whole.

Figure 3.3 Relation between productivity and energy intake

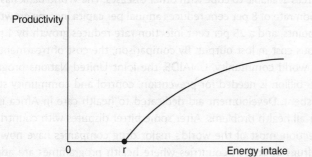

The World Bank has calculated that the cost to developing countries of deficiencies of vitamin A, iodine and iron amounts to 5 per cent of GDP owing to disabilities, deaths and reduced productivity. The cost of remedies would be no more than $1 billion. The Bank has now launched **micronutrient projects** in many poor countries to combat nutritional deficiencies that lead to blindness, mental retardation, learning difficulties and low work capacity.

Survival depends not only on nutrition but also on freedom from infection and disease. A major investment effort in this field would also yield substantial returns. These major infectious diseases blight the lives of millions of people in developing countries, particularly in Africa. The old enemies, which are still rampant, are tuberculosis and malaria. The new enemy is AIDS, which is starting to have a devastating effect on the economies of Africa.

Tuberculosis kills 3 million people a year. This is controllable. Treatment requires a combined dose of four powerful antibiotics a day for six to eight months. Close monitoring is required to make sure the daily dose is taken, but research in India by the World Health Organization (WHO) shows that if $200 million a year was spent there on effective control programmes, the economic return would be a colossal $750 million through reduction in the cost of treatment for sufferers and increased productivity.

Malaria kills 23 million people every year either directly or indirectly. The social and economic cost is enormous. Since 1970 it has reduced the GDP of Africa by over $100 billion. Despite this, malaria control receives only $300 million a year in aid from the international community. It is estimated that at least $1 billion is needed for effective control in order to distribute mosquito nets and to pay for medical treatment and vaccines. There is, however, hope for the future. Scientists working on the global genome project have unlocked the genetic code of both the malaria parasite and the mosquito species that transmits it. This paves the way for a new generation of vaccines, insecticides and repellents to combat malaria; provided, of course, that it is profitable for the drug companies to develop them.

But acquired immune deficiency syndrome (AIDS) is fast becoming the biggest killer. The UN forecasts that 70 million people will have died from AIDs by 2020. Worldwide, 50 million people are currently HIV (human immunodeficiency virus) and AIDS infected, and 35 million of these are in Africa. The numbers infected are increasing by 5 million a year, and nearly 3 million a year are dying. AIDS kills ten times more Africans than armed conflict. The social and economic consequences are manifold. In some of the countries worst affected, such as South Africa, Botswana, Zimbabwe and Zambia, life expectancy has been reduced to less than 40 years (see Case example 3.3). This is denuding countries of skilled and productive labour, including teachers, and leading to high levels of absenteeism at work. It is leaving millions of children orphaned and uneducated. The cost of treatment is putting a great strain on the health budget of countries, which reduces the resources available to cope with other diseases. The World Bank has estimated that an HIV/AIDS infection rate of 8 per cent reduces annual per capita income growth of countries by 0.4 percentage points, and a 25 per cent infection rate reduces growth by 1 percentage point. This is an enormous cost in lost output. By comparison, the cost of treatment would be easily affordable by the world community. UNAIDS, the joint United Nations programme on HIV/AIDS, estimates $15 billion is needed for prevention, control and community support yet only $5 billion is being spent. Development aid dedicated to health care in Africa is currently only $10 billion to cover all health problems. After some bitter disputes with countries and the WTO over patent protection, most of the world's major drug companies have now agreed to provide anti-retroviral drugs at cost in countries where health programmes are administered efficiently.

| Case example 3.3 | AIDS and life expectancy |

Life expectancy in much of sub-Saharan Africa will soon fall to levels not seen since the nineteenth century under the weight of the AIDS pandemic, according to research by the American government. Average lifespans will be reduced in 51 countries, mainly in Africa and the Caribbean, and the global catastrophe will become even worse if the disease begins to infect large numbers of people in China, India and South-East Asia, as experts predict.

In Botswana, where 39 per cent of the adult population are HIV positive, life expectancy would have been expected to rise to 74 years and five months in 2010, had there been no AIDS pandemic. It currently stands at 33 years and 11 months. The other countries in which life expectancy was lower than 40 in 2010 are Angola (35); Lesotho (36.5); Malawi (36.9); Mozambique (27.1); Namibia (33.8); Rwanda (38.7); South Africa (36.5); Swaziland (33.0); Zambia (34.4); and Zimbabwe (34.5).

AIDS has also reversed the decline in infant mortality that was seen across southern Africa in the 1980s and early 1990s, with rates in several countries, such as Swaziland and Zimbabwe, standing at close to double what they would have been without the pandemic. In four countries – Botswana, Zimbabwe, South Africa and Namibia – more infants will die of AIDS than of any other cause by 2010.

Peter Piot, executive director of UNAIDS, the United Nations HIV agency, said that AIDS was now responsible for the worst pandemic in history: 'More money is being spent than ever, but if you look at the number of positive people and treatment in the poorest countries, there is still a long way to go. To a certain extent, we have failed to stop the expansion of the epidemic.'

	Life expectancy (Age in years)	
	Without AIDS	**With AIDS**
Angola	41.3	35.0
Botswana	74.4	26.7
Lesotho	67.2	36.5
Malawi	59.4	36.9
Mozambique	42.5	27.1
Namibia	68.8	33.8
Rwanda	54.7	38.7
South Africa	68.5	36.5
Swaziland	74.6	33.0
Zambia	58.6	34.4
Zimbabwe	71.4	34.6

Source: *The Times*, 8 July 2002.

Apart from the big killers of tuberculosis, malaria and AIDS, there are many other tropical diseases that continue to disable tens of millions of people in tropical Asia, Africa and Latin America such as leprosy, river blindness, Chagas disease and lymphatic filariasis. With modern medicine and antibiotics there is now the opportunity to eliminate these diseases. There are still nearly 1 million leprosy sufferers, but this was reduced from 5 million as recently as 20 years ago through a combination of three antibiotics. Over 300,000 people suffer river blindness through a parasite spread by sandflies, but already the drug ivermectin has eliminated the transmission of the disease in 11 West African countries. Chagas disease is spread by bloodsucking bugs and infects 17 million people a year in Africa, killing 45,000 a year. Lymphatic filariasis is transmitted by mosquitos and infects 120 million people in over 70 countries, causing a range of symptoms from elephantiasis to kidney damage. To treat everyone for these diseases, it has been estimated that it would cost as little as $400 million a year (compared with the $15 billion budget for malaria, tuberculosis and AIDS) and save half a million lives.

Disease and malnutrition blight the lives of millions of men, women and children across the developing world. Small investments in nutrition and disease prevention would transform their quality of life and the productive potential of their countries, yet the world prefers to send robots to Mars!

The United Nations and other bodies are calling for an additional $20 billion a year of health aid to fight AIDS and other infectious diseases. This amounts to only $20 per head from the 1 billion citizens of rich countries: not much to improve the health and life-chances of fellow citizens in our so-called 'global community'.

The Sachs Report for the WHO recommends a Global Health Resource Fund with capital of $1.5 billion a year. The report estimates that 8 million lives could be saved at a total annual cost of $38 billion by 2015 – equal to only 0.1 per cent of the GDP of rich countries.[6]

Poor nutrition and disease, combined with rudimentary health facilities, leads to low life expectancy and a high incidence of infant mortality. Half a million women a year also die in pregnancy or childbirth. The Millennium Development Goal of reducing the maternal mortality rate by 75 per cent by 2015 will not be met. Table 3.7 presents some selected health-related statistics,

Table 3.7 Health indicators

	Health expenditure	Health expenditure per capita	Access to improved water source	Access to improved sanitation facilities	Infant mortality rate
	Total % of GDP (2007)	$ (2006)	% of population (2006)	% of population (2006)	per 1,000 live births (2006)
World	9.8	722	86	60	47
Low income	4.3	23	68	39	80
Middle income	5.4	140	89	60	35
Lower middle income	4.5	75	88	55	38
Upper middle income	6.3	412	95	83	21
Low & middle income	5.3	114	84	55	51
East Asia & Pacific	4.3	83	87	66	22
Europe & Central Asia	5.5	304	95	89	21
Latin America & Caribbean	7.0	374	91	78	22
Middle East & North Africa	5.7	133	89	77	32
South Asia	3.5	26	87	33	59
Sub-Saharan Africa	5.7	53	58	31	89
High income	11.2	4033	100	100	6

Source: *World Development Indicators 2009*, online (http://data.worldbank.org/indicator).

including total expenditure on health as a percentage of GDP; health expenditure per head of the population; the percentage of the population with access to safe water and sanitation, and the rate of infant mortality. Notice that while rich countries spend $4,000 per head per year on health, poor countries spend only $23. The lack of access to basic health facilities is reflected in the fact that the infant mortality rate in low-income countries is 80 per thousand live births compared with only 6 per thousand in high-income countries. Baldacci et al. (2005) calculate that an increase in health spending of 1 per cent of GDP is associated with an increase of 0.5 percentage points in the survival rate of children under 5 and a 0.5 per cent increase in per capita income growth.

The provision of health services, education, housing, sanitation, water supply and adequate nutrition came to be known in development circles in the 1970s (and supported by the World Bank) as the **basic needs approach** to economic development. The rationale of the approach was that the direct provision of such goods and services was likely to relieve absolute poverty more immediately than alternative strategies that would simply attempt to accelerate growth or would rely on raising the incomes and productivity of the poor. Five arguments were used to support this change in strategy:

- Growth strategies usually fail to benefit those intended
- The productivity and incomes of the poor depend in the first place on the direct provision of health and education facilities
- It may take a long time to increase the incomes of the poor so that they can afford basic needs
- The poor tend not to spend their income wisely, and certain facilities such as water supply and sanitation can be provided only publicly
- It is difficult to help all the poor in a uniform way in the absence of the provision of basic needs.

The basic needs approach has lost none of its rationale in the direct fight against poverty and disease in the world's poorest countries.

Famine

Throughout the ages, poor people in poor countries have experienced famine conditions which are a major cause of malnutrition and death. O'Grada (2007), in his comprehensive study of the causes and consequences of famines experienced in the past, and in most recent times, defines famine as 'a widespread lack of food leading directly to excess mortality from starvation or hunger-induced illness'. It is reckoned that about 70 million people died from famines in the twentieth century, and many more in previous centuries. Three of the greatest famines of the twentieth century were the famine in Russia in 1932–33 during the time of Stalin; the Great Bengal famine of 1942–44, and the famine in China in 1959–61 during the 'Great Leap Forward' when between 15 and 20 million people starved. More recently, Bangladesh suffered a severe famine from 1972 to 1974, and many African countries have suffered: Nigeria 1969–70; Ethiopia 1984–85; Sudan 1995; Malawi 2002 and Niger 2005. In general, however, today's high-profile famines shown vividly on our TV screens are small by historical standards, because knowledge of them is spread so easily and relief comes quickly.

Famine doesn't necessarily mean, however, that there has been a contraction in the supply of food, nor that those deprived of food are the ones who die. Others may die due to diseases that spread during famines especially amongst malnourished children and those forced into relief camps. Lack of food availability, or **food availability decline (FAD)**, was traditionally viewed as the cause of famine, but in practice there can be several causes of famine, not only the failure of crops and bad harvests due to extreme weather conditions or crop disease. Other causes include food blockades (which may occur because of war); civil unrest; hoarding of food; and speculation which drives up the price of food making it unaffordable for people.

The conventional view of the causes of famine was first challenged in a significant way by Amartya Sen in his powerful and persuasive book *Poverty and Famines* (1981a; see also Sen, 1981b). Sen's thesis is that famine depends not only (or even primarily) on the availability of food – that food has become scarce – but mainly on people's **entitlements** to food, particularly of vulnerable sections of the community. As Sen (1981b) puts it, 'starvation is a matter of some people not having enough food to eat, and not a matter of there being not enough food to eat'. The latter can be a cause of the former but not necessarily the most important cause. People's entitlements depend on their resource endowments and the ability to exchange those resource endowments for food. There may be 'direct endowment failures' or 'trade endowment failures'. Resource endowments largely depend on the ability of people to sell their labour, on the wages they receive and on the ownership of assets. The ability to exchange or trade those resource endowments for food depends on the price of food, which may rise through hoarding and speculation rather than a shortage of food per se. Clearly, therefore, entitlements may deteriorate independently of a general decline in the supply of food. Unemployment may rise; real wages and productivity may fall, and other people may become better off and demand more food (which also drives up the price).

Sen documents his theory drawing on the experience of the Great Bengal famine of 1943; the Ethiopian famine in Wollo of 1943, and the Bangladesh famine of 1974 (see also Ravallion, 1997). It appears that in all these cases, famine occurred without a significant fall in food availability per head. During the Great Bengal famine, for example, 3 million people died, yet in terms of the total availability of food grain, 1943 was not an abnormal year. Starvation occurred because people's entitlements to food fell as a result of: a rise in the price of food due to military procurement, the prices of other commodities falling as people switched to food (causing the incomes of other producers to fall), and, most importantly, hoarding and speculation. Sen documents how farmers and grain merchants converted 'a moderate shortfall in production . . . into an exceptional shortfall in market release', and concludes that the famine was mainly due to 'speculators' withdrawal and panic purchase of rice stocks . . . encouraged by administrative chaos'. Ravallion's 1997 study of the 1974 Bangladesh famine supports Sen's analysis that famine and excess mortality was the effect of a speculative crisis raising the price of rice out of the reach of the poor.

In other cases, famines have had different causes. In the big famines in Russia under Stalin in 1932–33 and China 1959–61, it was totalitarian regimes engaged in disastrous economic policies that managed to keep the consequences of their actions hidden. Elsewhere, wars and civil strife have been the cause.

Most economists now accept Sen's analysis, but it is not without its critics, and several questions still need answering, including the policy implications for preventing or relieving future famines. One criticism of Sen is that he understates the importance of aggregate food availability. As O'Grada (2007) says, there are very few 'pure' lack of entitlement famines. Most famines are accompanied by food availability declines of one form or another. It is partly the expected shortage of food that leads to hoarding and speculation. It is significant that most major famines are preceded by declines in food consumption per head, and farmers selling assets and livestock to acquire more food. In the great famine of China in 1959–61, grain production fell by nearly

30 per cent due to bad weather and agriculture being starved of resources by the government. And there was no government action to prevent starvation. In Niger in 2005, harvest failure was the main cause of famine, but in this case food aid materialized and kept mortality low.

Other critiques of Sen are that there is nothing particularly new in the analysis because if the price of food rises, for whatever reasons, it is obvious that people cannot afford to buy so much. Also, some people may prefer to go hungry for a time rather than sell assets to buy food. Another point made is that the health environment of people and the country is more important than entitlements because disease causes more deaths than starvation. There is some truth in this argument. O'Grada (2007) shows that infectious diseases account for most deaths during famines and affect particularly young children who are too weak to stave off measles, malaria and dysentery.

The questions that are relevant to what public action is required to prevent and relieve famine include:

- What are the major causes of entitlement failures?
- Is starvation only a matter of entitlement failures?
- What determines vulnerability to famines?
- Do markets and institutions within countries help or hinder the way shocks impact on entitlements?

On the last point, many famine situations in the past have been made worse by failures of public action through lack of social safety nets, stopping people migrating in search of food, or preventing the redistribution of food between regions of the country. Totalitarian regimes, a lack of democracy and the absence of a free press can make matters worse by allowing governments to hide the consequences of their actions, or lack of action (as the case may be).

Ravallion (1997) makes several suggestions for preventing and relieving future famines:

- Set up early warning systems to monitor such things as the price of food grains, employment and unemployment, real wages, asset sales by farmers, etc. – all things that affect people's endowments and their ability to exchange endowments for food. India has had early warning systems since the nineteenth century, which were strengthened after independence in 1949. Despite droughts, India has avoided serious famines – helped by the fact that India is also a democracy with a free press.
- Promote the domestic production of food even if famine is not caused primarily by food availability decline.
- Provide entitlements to people through cash handouts. It has been observed that private traders get food to famine victims quicker than government or aid agencies. This also avoids the need to herd famine victims into relief camps where disease can spread very easily and quickly.
- Provide entitlements through the provision of unskilled employment on public works programmes. The absence of famine in China since 1978 (and in other socialist countries) has been not so much the result of increased food production per head, but a shift in the entitlement system through guaranteed employment and social security provisions.
- The regulation of trade: control the export of food, and increase the import of food in times of famine.
- Hold buffer stocks of grain for release in periods of need. Such buffer stocks could be supported and financed by the international community in regions prone to famine.

- Improve the transport infrastructure to allow food to be moved more easily from place to place which would also improve food market integration and prevent large price differentials between different parts of the country.

Above all, public action requires programmes of **food security** which guarantee that people have access to enough food at all times, plus **nutrition programmes,** working through clinics targeted particularly at children and pregnant women.[7]

Food production

The world food problem is not caused by the world being physically incapable of producing enough food to feed its inhabitants adequately. The pessimism expressed by Thomas Malthus in 1798 that food supply would grow only arithmetically while the population would grow geometrically (see Chapter 5) has not been borne out in practice. Global food production has kept pace with population growth, and since 1950 has outstripped it by a substantial margin. World population has increased by 150 per cent while food production has increased by 300 per cent. Since 1970 the world production of cereals has increased from 1,000 million tons to over 2,000 million tons per annum. Cereal production per head of population has risen from 300 kg to 400 kg, while over the long term food prices relative to industrial goods' prices have fallen by over 50 per cent.

The world is probably capable of feeding itself ten times over if need be. There are pessimists, for example Lester Brown of the World Watch Institute in Washington, but there are also more measured assessments, such as that by Tim Dyson in his book *Population and Food* (1996). Dyson concludes that it will be perfectly possible to feed the population of 8 billion that is predicted for the year 2020: 'there is fair reason to expect that in the year 2020 world agriculture will be feeding the larger population no worse and probably a little better than it manages to do today'. The Green Revolution has not entirely run out of steam; genetically modified (GM) technology promises a new dawn; and productivity with the existing technology is way below its potential in many countries, particularly in Africa. For example, India successfully feeds twice as many people as Africa on 13 per cent of its land area, even though the growing conditions are roughly the same. Hunger and malnutrition for a large fraction of the world's population are likely to remain a problem of *distribution* rather than capacity.

Notwithstanding the increased global availability of food, the situation is still precarious for many individuals and countries. The United Nations' **World Food Programme** dispensed emergency relief to millions of people in more than 40 countries in the 1990s, made necessary by poor harvests, political upheaval or a shortage of foreign exchange to pay for imported food. Many developing countries are still far from self-sufficient in food, even in 'normal' times.

In 2007 and 2008 there was a serious food scare, with the prices of many basic commodities, such as rice, maize, wheat, sugar, soya beans and dairy products, rising dramatically. The price of rice, a staple consumption good for millions of poor people, rose by over 300 per cent in a year, and the price of wheat doubled. The overall food price index rose 40 per cent in 2007, and another 40 per cent in 2008. There were food riots in over 40 countries; not surprisingly, since the poor spend as much as 80 per cent of their income on food. Many factors were responsible for the sudden rise in prices, First, it must be remembered that both supply and demand for food are very inelastic in the short term so that any shock from the supply- or demand-side can lead to great volatility. On the supply side there were relatively poor harvests in some countries due to adverse weather conditions which drove up prices. The rising price of fuel increased the cost of production and distribution of goods. Stocks were already low, and more grain was used for bio-fuels. In 2007, 40 per cent of US maize was used to make ethanol. On the demand side, the rapid growth in fast growing countries, such as China and India, played a part, as well as speculation. In recent years, several big investment banks have launched agricultural commodity funds. In 2008, $150 billion was invested in these funds compared with $15 billion in 2004.

At the beginning of this third millennium, it seems incredible (indeed, intolerable) that year in and year out the lives of millions of people should be threatened and blighted by the vagaries of the weather and shocks of one form or another. There is an urgent need for agricultural reform in developing countries (see Chapter 6) and for a new world food programme.

Technically, it is well within the world's ability to increase agricultural production on an immense scale. What is required is the initiative and political will on the part of both the international community and the developing countries, to make the necessary radical changes. As far as the international development agencies are concerned, they could increase aid and investment for agricultural projects, especially where this could lead to a significant breakthrough in agricultural production. For example, an investment of $4 billion to eliminate the tsetse fly in infected areas of tropical Africa could open up 7 million square kilometres to livestock and crop production. Of the $103 billion of official development assistance (ODA) to developing countries, less than 20 per cent goes to agriculture. There must also be genuine international cooperation and agreement to guarantee world food supplies. One possibility would be a system of granaries strategically placed across the world under international supervision, which could store the food surpluses of the rich North and release them in times of need. This need not hinder the fundamental agricultural reforms necessary for achieving a greater degree of self-sufficiency in the long run.

Food availability and security is not only a question of agricultural policy, it is also a question of trade policy. Increased trade liberalization in agriculture, for example, is encouraging many small farmers to produce cash crops for export to the neglect of growing food for their own needs, and the profit from cash crops is not enough to purchase their food requirements. The return from cash crops is often low because so much buying power is concentrated in the hands of large multinational commodity buyers. Also, as the supply of cash crops increases their price falls. Trade liberalization in agriculture can thus have serious consequences for food security in many countries.

Stages of development and structural change

It is often argued that countries pass through certain phases during the course of development and that by identifying the particular characteristics of these phases, a country can be deemed to have reached a certain stage of development. The simplest stage theory is the sector thesis of Fisher (1939) and Clark (1940), who employed the distinction between primary, secondary and tertiary production as a basis of a theory of development. Countries are assumed to start as **primary** producers and then, as the basic necessities of life are met, resources shift into manufacturing or **secondary** activities. Finally, with rising income, more leisure and an increasingly saturated market for manufactured goods, resources move into **service** or **tertiary** activities producing 'commodities' with a high income elasticity of demand.

Naturally enough in this schema, the less developed countries are identified with primary production, the more developed countries with the production of manufactured goods, and the mature developed economies have a high percentage of their resources in the service sector.

There can be no dispute that resource shifts are an integral part of the development process, and that one of the main determinants of these shifts is a difference in the income elasticity of demand for commodities and changes in their elasticity as development proceeds. But just as care must be taken to equate (without qualification) development and welfare with the level of per capita income, caution must also be exercised in identifying different degrees of underdevelopment, industrialization and maturity, with some fairly rigid proportion of resources engaged in different types of activity. Such an association would ignore the doctrine of **comparative advantage**, which holds that countries will specialize in the production of those commodities in which they have a relative cost advantage, as determined by natural or acquired resource endowments. The fact that one country produces predominantly primary products while another produces mainly manufactured goods need not imply that they are at different stages of development, particularly if productivity in the primary sector matches productivity in the industrial sector. Such an association would also ignore the different types of service activities that may exist at different stages of a country's history. There are three broad categories of service activities. Newer service activities linked with the growth of leisure and high mass consumption tend to have a high income elasticity of demand; services linked to the growth of manufacturing also grow, but at a declining rate; and traditional services of pre-industrial times, such as domestic servants, decline. In short, tertiary production is an aggregation of many dissimilar service activities, some of which are related to low per capita incomes and some to high per capita incomes. Thus the same proportion of total resources devoted to services may be associated with very different levels of development.

Having said all this, however, the fact remains that there is a good deal of empirical support for the Fisher–Clark view that the pattern of development across countries evidences many common characteristics, especially the shift of resources from agriculture to industry.

Figure 3.4 plots the relation between the level of per capita income and the share of employment in agriculture, industry and services across 69 countries in the year 2005 using simple regression analysis. The broad thesis of Fisher and Clark is confirmed. On average, in the low-income countries, the share of employment in agriculture is over 40 per cent (and much higher in the very poorest countries of Africa), while only 15 per cent is employed in industry. By contrast, in the high-income countries, less than 5 per cent is employed in agriculture and nearly 30 per cent in industry. The proportion of the labour force employed in services rises inexorably, but the nature of the service activities is different, petty services in low-income countries, and sophisticated services in the high-income countries.

What is true of the sectoral distribution of the labour force is also true of the sectoral distribution of output, although the magnitude of the proportions differ in the lower income countries because productivity differs between sectors. Figure 3.5 shows the sectoral distribution of output across 141 countries in the year 2005 also by regressing the shares on per capita income. In the low-income countries, on average, the share of agriculture in total GDP is 30 per cent compared with an employment share of over 40 per cent, because productivity is lower in agriculture than in industry. Industry's share of output in poor countries is 20 per cent compared with an employment share of 15 per cent. The share of output and employment in services is roughly equal.

Figure 3.4   The distribution of the labour force 2005 (%)

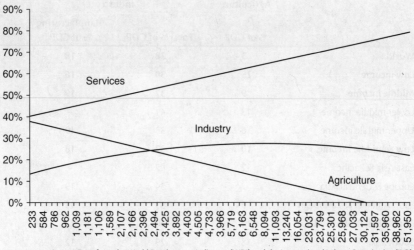

Source: Data from the *World Development Indicators* (WDI) and the *International Labour Organization* (ILO)
for 69 countries.

Figure 3.5   The distribution of output 2005 (%)

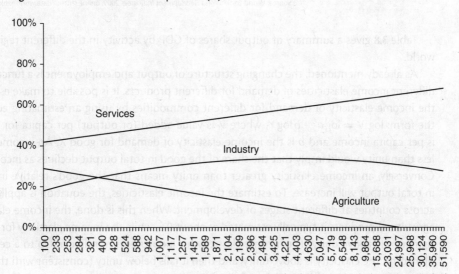

Source: Data from the *World Development Indicators* (WDI) and the *International Labour Organization* (ILO)
for 141 countries.

Notice also that while the share of agriculture falls continually, and the share of services increases continually, the share of employment and output in industry first rises and then falls as countries get richer. This is referred to as the process of **deindustrialization**. This process started in the developed countries many years ago (see Rowthorn and Ramswamy, 1999), but is now beginning to hit middle-income (and even some low-income) countries (see Pieper, 2003; Tregenna, 2009). Only in East Asia and the Pacific is the importance of industry increasing, while some African and Latin American countries are 'deindustrializing' before they have ever been properly industrialized!

Table 3.8 The shares of output in GDP by region

	Agriculture	Industry		Services
	% of GDP	Total % of GDP	Manufacturing % of GDP	% of GDP
World	3	28	18	69
Low income	25	30	16	46
Middle income	9	37	19	53
Lower middle income	13	41	–	46
Upper middle income	6	33	19	61
Low & middle income	10	37	18	53
East Asia & Pacific	12	47	–	41
Europe & Central Asia	7	34	19	60
Latin America & Caribbean	6	33	18	61
Middle East & North Africa	11	40	12	49
South Asia	18	29	17	53
Sub-Saharan Africa	15	32	14	53
Least developed countries	25	29	12	46

Source: World Bank, *World Development Indicators* 2009, online (http://data.worldbank.org/indicator).

Table 3.8 gives a summary of output shares of GDP by activity in the different regions of the world.

As already mentioned, the changing structure of output and employment is a function of the different income elasticities of demand for different products. It is possible to make estimates of the income elasticity of demand for different commodities by using an estimating equation of the form: $\log V = \log a + b \log Y$, where V is value-added (or output) per capita for good X, Y is per capita income and b is the income elasticity of demand for good X. An income elasticity less than unity would imply that the share of the good in total output declines as income grows. Conversely, an income elasticity greater than unity means that the good's relative importance in total output will increase. To estimate the income elasticities, the equation is applied to data across countries at different stages of development. When this is done, the income elasticity for agricultural products is typically estimated at about 0.5, while the income elasticity for services is significantly above unity. The income elasticity for industries is non-linear. Up to a certain level of income, the elasticity is above unity, and then it falls below unity (consistent with the share of industrial output first rising and then falling).[8]

Within the industrial sector, there are also differences in the income elasticity of demand for products, which cause the pattern of industry to change as development proceeds. The most notable demand shift is the relative switch from basic necessities and low value-added goods to high value-added consumer durables.

Rostow's stages of growth

Interest in stage theories of development was given a major impetus with the publication of Rostow's *The Stages of Economic Growth* (1960), which represents an attempt to provide an alternative to the Marxist interpretation of history – hence its subtitle, 'A Non-Communist Manifesto'.

Rostow presents a political theory as well as a descriptive economic study of the pattern of the growth and development of nations.

Walt Rostow

Born 1916, New York, USA. Died 2003. Professor of Economic History, MIT (1950–1961) and, after US government service in the 1960s during the Kennedy and Johnson administrations, Emeritus Professor of Political Economy, University of Texas, Austin. Famous for his best-selling, but controversial, book *The Stages of Economic Growth: A Non-Communist Manifesto* (1960), in which he identifies several necessary conditions for countries to take off into self-sustaining growth: important among them an agricultural revolution, an investment ratio at least 10 per cent of GDP, and an institutional environment conducive to entrepreneurship.

The essence of Rostow's thesis is that it is logically and practically possible to identify stages of development and to classify societies according to those stages. He distinguishes five such stages: **traditional**, **transitional**, **take-off**, **maturity** and **high mass consumption**.

All we need say about **traditional societies** is that for Rostow the whole of the pre-Newtonian world consisted of such societies; for example, the dynasties of China, the civilizations of the Middle East, the Mediterranean and medieval Europe, and so on. Traditional societies are characterized by a ceiling on productivity imposed by the limitations of science. Traditional societies are thus recognizable by a very high proportion of the workforce in subsistence agriculture, coupled with very little mobility or social change, great divisions of wealth and decentralized political power. Today few societies could be classed as traditional, except perhaps some of the primitive tribes of Amazonia or Papua New Guinea. Most societies emerged from the traditional stage some time ago, mainly under the impact of external challenge or the rise of nationalism. The exceptions to the pattern of emergence from the traditional state are those countries which Rostow describes as having been 'born free', such as the United States and certain British dominions. Here the preconditions of 'take-off' were laid in a more simple fashion by the construction of social overhead capital and the introduction of industry from abroad. But for the rest of the world, change was much more basic and fundamental, consisting not only of economic transformation but also a political and social transition from feudalism.

The stage between feudalism and take-off Rostow calls the **transitional stage**. The main economic requirement in the transition phase is that the level of investment should rise to at least 10 per cent of national income to ensure self-sustaining growth. The main direction of investment must be in transport and other social overhead capital to build up society's infrastructure. The preconditions for a rise in the investment ratio consist of the willingness of people to lend risk capital, the availability of entrepreneurs, and the willingness of society at large to operate an economic system geared to the factory and the principle of the division of labour. But a country shifting resources out of agriculture needs to feed itself, so an agricultural revolution is also necessary.

On the social front a new elite must emerge to fabricate the industrial society, and it must supersede in authority the land-based elite of the traditional society. Surpluses must be channelled by the new elite from agriculture to industry, and there must be a willingness to take risks and to respond to economic incentives. And because of the enormity of the task of transition, the establishment of an effective modern government is vital. The length of the transition phase depends on the speed with which local talent, energy and resources are devoted to modernization and the overthrow of the established order. In this respect, political leadership has an important part to play.

Then there is the stage of **take-off**. The characteristics of take-off are sometimes difficult to distinguish from the characteristics of the transition stage, and this has been a point of contention between Rostow and his critics. Nonetheless, let us describe the take-off stage as Rostow sees it – a 'stage' to which reference is constantly made in the development literature. Since the preconditions of take-off have been met in the transitional stage, the take-off stage is a short stage of development, during which economic growth becomes self-sustaining. Investment must rise to a level in excess of 10 per cent of national income in order for per capita income to rise sufficiently to guarantee adequate future levels of saving and investment. Also important is the establishment of what Rostow calls 'leading growth sectors'. Historically, domestic finance for take-off seems to have come from two main sources. The first was from a diversion of part of the product of agriculture by land reform and other means. The examples of Tsarist Russia and Meiji Japan are quoted, where government bonds were substituted for the landowner's claim to the flow of rent payments. A second source was from enterprising landlords voluntarily ploughing back rents into commerce and industry.

In practice the development of major export industries has sometimes led to take-off permitting substantial capital imports. Grain in the United States, Russia and Canada, timber in Sweden and, to a lesser extent, textiles in Britain are cited as examples. Countries such as the United States, Russia, Sweden and Canada also benefited during take-off from substantial inflows of foreign capital. The sector or sectors that gave rise to the take-off seem to have varied from country to country, but in many countries railway building seems to have been prominent. Certainly improvement of the internal means of communication is crucial for an expansion of markets and to facilitate exports, apart from any direct impact on such industries as coal, steel and engineering. But Rostow argues that any industry can play the role of leading sector in the take-off stage provided four conditions are met:

• The market for the product is expanding rapidly to provide a firm basis for the growth of output
• The leading sector generates secondary expansion
• The sector has an adequate and continual supply of capital from ploughed-back profits
• New techniques of production can be continually introduced into the sector, leading to increased productivity.

Rostow contends that the beginnings of take-off in most countries can be traced to a particular stimulus. Historically, this has taken many different forms, such as a technological innovation or, more commonly, political revolution, for example Germany in 1848, the Meiji restoration in Japan in 1868, China in 1949 and Indian independence in 1947. Rostow stresses, however, that there is no one single pattern or sequence of take-off. Thus there is no need for the developing countries today to repeat the course of events in, say, Britain, Russia or America. The crucial requirement is that the preconditions for take-off are met, otherwise take-off, whatever form it takes, will be abortive. Investment must rise to over 10 per cent of national income; one or more leading sectors must emerge; and there must exist or emerge a political, social and institutional framework that exploits the impulse to expand. The examples are given of the extensive railway building in Argentina before 1914, and in India, China and Canada before 1895, which failed to initiate take-off because the full transition from a traditional society had not been made. The dates of take-off for some of the present developed countries are given as follows: Britain 1783–1802; France 1840–60; the United States 1843–60; Germany 1850–73; Sweden 1868–90; Japan 1878–1900; Russia 1890–1914.

Then there is the stage of **maturity**, which Rostow defines as the period when society has effectively applied the range of modern technology to the bulk of its resources. During the period of maturity new leading sectors replace the old. By this criterion Rostow sees the development of the steel industry as one of the symbols of maturity. In this respect the United States, Germany, France and Britain entered the stage of maturity roughly together.

Accompanying changes in the industrial structure will be structural changes in society, such as changes in the distribution of the workforce, the growth of an urban population, an increase in the proportion of white-collar workers and a switch in industrial leadership from entrepreneur to manager.

Maturity also has important political features. This is the period when nations grow confident and exert themselves – witness Germany under Bismarck and Russia under Stalin. This is also the period when fundamental political choices have to be made by society on the use to which the greater wealth should be put. Should it be devoted to high mass consumption, the building of a welfare state, or imperialist ends? The balance between these possibilities has varied over time within countries, and between countries. Eventually, however, every nation will reach the stage of **high mass consumption** whatever the balance of choices at the stage of maturity. Since there is no likelihood of developing countries reaching this stage in the foreseeable future, however, and only a handful of rich countries have reached it already, we shall ignore this fifth stage here.

Instead, let us evaluate Rostow's thesis and consider the usefulness of this type of stage theory, apart from its use in providing a valuable description of the development process and pinpointing some of the key growth variables. Most criticisms have hinged on whether a valid and operationally meaningful distinction can be made between stages of development, especially between the so-called transitional stage and take-off, and between take-off and maturity. Critics have attempted to argue that the characteristics that Rostow distinguishes for his different stages are not unique to those stages. Thus the demarcation between take-off and transition is blurred because the changes that take place in the transition stage also seem to take place in the take-off phase, and similarly with the demarcation between take-off and maturity.

Despite these points of criticism, Rostow's stage theory still offers valuable insights into the development process. While the concept of a stage may be quibbled with, and stage theory dismissed as a blueprint for development, there are certain features of the development process that do follow a well-ordered sequence. Moreover, there are certain development prerequisites that countries neglect at their peril. The importance of agriculture in the early stages of development cannot be overemphasized, together with the provision of infrastructure and political stability, if the preconditions for take-off into self-sustaining growth are to be met. The role of investment is also highlighted: investment must reach a certain ratio of GDP (at least 10 per cent) if per capita income growth is to be positive. Finally, there is the transition from the rural to the industrial society with growth based on the development of leading sectors and foreign trade, which propels a society from take-off to the stage of maturity and eventually high mass consumption. The process of industrialization is crucial.

Diversification

Another feature of structural change is that, as well as resource shifts from agriculture to industry and services, the structure of production tends to become more diversified as countries develop, at least up to a fairly high level of per capita income – after which there is evidence that it becomes more specialized again. This is well documented in the work of Imbs and Wacziarg (2003) on 'stages of diversification' (see also Felipe, 2009). They take several different measures of industrial concentration (including the Gini ratio) and, using ILO and the United Nations Industrial Development Organization (UNIDO) data, show how the concentration of employment and value-added tends to fall as countries get richer up to about $9,000 per head (at 2000 prices) and then increases, giving a U-shaped curve. Obvious explanations for this pattern are that people's preferences widen as they get richer, and there are more risk-takers willing to undertake new investments, which increases diversification. But at later stages of development, international trade increases the degree of specialization due to agglomeration benefits (increasing returns) and falling transport costs.

Industrialization and growth

From a global perspective, there seems to be a close association across countries between living standards and the share of resources devoted to industrial activities, at least up to a certain point. In very poor countries there is virtually no industrial activity at all, while the middle- and high-income countries devote 20–40 per cent of resources to industry. Only three countries in the world have become rich on agriculture alone: Australia, New Zealand and Canada. In all other countries, living standards have risen rapidly only as resources have shifted out of agriculture into industry and sophisticated services.

Furthermore, research[9] also shows a close association across countries between the growth of industry and the growth of GDP; or more precisely, that GDP growth is the faster the greater the *excess* of industrial growth relative to GDP growth; that is, when the *share* of industry in total GDP is rising the fastest. Figure 3.6 shows this relationship across 131 developing countries over the period 2000–2005, with GDP growth measured on the vertical axis and the growth of industry

Figure 3.6   Association between growth of industry and growth of GDP

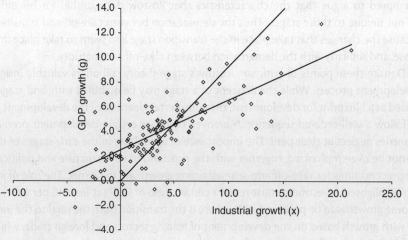

Source: Author's own calculations using UNSD database.

on the horizontal axis. The scatter points represent the individual country observations. A line through the points with a slope less than unity shows that the greater the excess of industrial growth over GDP growth, the faster GDP seems to be. The point where this line cuts the 45-degree line gives the average growth rate that divides countries into those where the share of industry is falling and are growing slowly, and those where the share of industry is rising and are growing fast. A linear equation fitted to the scatter points in Figure 3.6 gives the following regression result:

$$g = 2.529 + 0.394x \quad r^2 = 0.507$$

The equation says that a country with industrial growth one percentage point above the average for all countries will have GDP growth of 0.394 percentage points above the average; and the point where the regression line cuts the 45-degree line is approximately 4.5 per cent.[10] This rate of industry growth separates the slow-growing countries from the faster-growing countries.

The question is: what is special about industry, and particularly manufacturing industry, which accounts for these empirical associations, and which makes industry 'the engine of growth'? Since differences in the growth of GDP are largely accounted for by differences in the rate of growth of labour productivity, there must be an association between the growth of industry and the growth of labour productivity. This is to be expected for two main reasons. First, if there are increasing returns to scale in industry, both static and dynamic, a relation is to be expected between the growth of industrial output and the growth of labour productivity in industry. **Static economies of scale** refer to the economies of large-scale production whereby the mass production of commodities allows them to be produced at a lower average cost. **Dynamic economies of scale** refer to the induced effect that output growth has on capital accumulation and the embodiment of new technical progress in capital. Labour productivity also increases as output grows through 'learning by doing'. Second, if activities outside industry, such as agriculture and petty services, are subject to diminishing returns, with the marginal product of labour less than the average product, then if resources are drawn from these activities into industry as industry expands, the average product of labour will rise in non-industrial activities. Some of the characteristics of China's industrial revolution are outlined in Case example 3.4.

These relationships between industrial growth, productivity growth and GDP growth are known in the growth and development literature as **Kaldor's growth laws**, named after the famous Cambridge economist (Lord) Nicholas Kaldor, who first enunciated them in the 1960s (Kaldor, 1966, 1967).

| Case example 3.4 | **China's industrial revolution** |

Manufacturing growth in China over the past five years has been so rapid that virtually all manufacturers worldwide now have to take the country into account in their strategies.

- Output of factory goods in China has risen 5–10 per cent a year for a decade and China now accounts for an estimated 7 per cent of global manufacturing production, a proportion that is likely to expand greatly in the next few years.

continued overleaf

Case example 3.4	China's industrial revolution – *continued*

- Since the mid-1990s some $500bn (£274 bn) of foreign investment has gone to China, mostly into manufacturing.
- Foreign enterprises account for 10–15 per cent of the Chinese economy and the proportion is probably bigger in manufacturing.
- In 2003 China was the second most popular country for foreign investment after the USA, with telecommunications, automotive, electronics, energy and chemicals among the sectors showing the heaviest spending. Some observers believe that by 2007 a third of the world's electronics industry – in terms of overall output of goods and components – will be based in China.
- In some specialized fields of electronics China is already dominant. It is believed to account for about 70 per cent of world production of the 'motherboards' at the heart of personal computers, many of which were made in Taiwan until recently.
- Among the biggest individual manufacturing investors in China are Motorola, Siemens, Philips, General Electric, Nokia and BP. Each company has pumped in more than $1 bn.
- While most of China's rapid manufacturing expansion has been based on the availability of low-cost workers (often working for as little as 5 per cent of the wages of those in the main industrialized countries), the shortage of highly skilled engineering managers has become a serious problem.
- Chinese universities turn out about 400,000 qualified scientists and engineers a year, although the most pressing skills shortage is among senior engineers with management experience in foreign companies.
- One factor that will help to address this shortage is China's growing share of the world's research and development spending. According to the Organization for Economic Co-operation and Development, China is the world's third-biggest spender on R&D, behind the USA and Japan.
- R&D spending in China grew from 0.6 per cent of gross domestic product in 1996 to 1.1 per cent in 2001. About 60 per cent of R&D spending in 2001 came from domestic and foreign companies.

Source: Financial Times, 21 June 2004.

Kaldor's growth laws

There are three basic laws that have been widely tested in developed and developing countries using both cross-section (that is, across countries) and time-series data.

The **first law** is that there exists a strong positive correlation between the growth of manufacturing output (g_m) and the growth of GDP (g_{GDP}), that is

$$g_{GDP} = f_1(g_m) \quad f_1' > 0 \tag{3.3}$$

where f_1 is the functional relationship that is hypothesized to be positive.

The **second law** is that there exists a strong positive correlation between the growth of manufacturing output and the growth of productivity in manufacturing (p_m), that is

$$p_m = f_2(g_m) \quad f_2' > 0 \tag{3.4}$$

where f_2 is the functional relationship assumed to be positive. This law is also known as **Verdoorn's Law** after the Dutch economist P. J. Verdoorn, who in the 1940s first discovered such a relationship across Eastern European countries.

The **third law** is that there exists a strong positive relationship between the growth of manufacturing output and the growth of productivity outside of manufacturing (p_{nm}), that is

$$p_{nm} = f_3(g_m) \quad f_3' > 0 \tag{3.5}$$

where f_3 is the functional relationship assumed to be positive.

The most rigorous test of these laws is to take a cross-section of countries, or a cross-section of regions within a country, and to perform correlation and regression analyses for each equation. We will illustrate this with reference to an interesting study that applies the model across 28 regions of China taking average data for the period 1965–91 (Hansen and Zhang, 1996). See also Case example 3.5 for an application of the model to the countries of Africa.

Fitting equation (3.3) to the Chinese regional data gives the following regression result:

$$g_{GDP} = 1.79 + 0.56(g_m) \quad r^2 = 0.67$$

The r^2 measures the correlation between the two variables, so this equation says that 67 per cent of the difference in the growth rate of output between the 28 regions in China can be accounted for by variation in the growth of manufacturing output between regions. This is a high degree of explanatory power. The regression coefficient of 0.56 says that a region with manufacturing output growth of 1 per cent above the average for all regions will grow 0.56 per cent above the average for all regions.

But before the equation can be used to support the hypothesis of manufacturing industry as the engine of growth, some words of warning are in order. If industrial output is a large fraction of total output, the correlation will be spurious to a certain extent because the same variable appears on both sides of the equation. There are ways to overcome this problem, however. One is to regress the growth of output on the *difference* between industrial and non-industrial output growth. The other is to regress non-industrial output growth on industrial output growth. Also, for manufacturing industry to be regarded as special, it needs to be shown that there is no significant relationship between total output growth and the growth of other major sectors, such as agriculture or services.

Turning to the second law, fitting equation (3.4) to the regional data for China gave the following result:

$$p_m = -0.009 + 0.71 g_m \quad r^2 = 0.73$$

We see again that the correlation is very high, with 73 per cent of the difference in the growth of labour productivity between regions accounted for by differences in the growth of output itself. On average, a 1 per cent difference in the growth rate of output induces a 0.71 percentage point difference in the growth of labour productivity. This coefficient is referred to as the **Verdoorn**

coefficient. The coefficient here is higher than typically found in developed countries, which is normally about 0.5, but this may reflect the large economies of scale to be reaped in the early stages of development. Again, for manufacturing industry to be regarded as special, this second law (or Verdoorn's Law) should be weaker for other activities, which it will be in the absence of scale economies.

The third law is difficult to test directly because it is not easy to measure productivity growth in many activities outside manufacturing, particularly service activities where output can only be measured by inputs – for example, public services such as teaching, health, defence, the civil service and so on. It can be tested indirectly, however, by taking *overall* productivity growth (p_{GDP}) as the dependent variable to be explained and linking this to employment change in non-industrial activities (e_{nm}), holding constant the effect of output growth in industry (g_m). The equation to be estimated is thus

$$p_{GDP} = a_3 + b_3 (g_m) + c_3 (e_{mm}) \tag{3.6}$$

with the expectation that $c_3 < 0$.

Fitting (3.6) across the Chinese regions gives:

$$p_{GDP} = 0.02 + 0.49 \, g_m - 0.82 \, (e_{nm}) \quad r^2 = 0.70$$

The coefficient on e_{nm} is significantly negative so that the slower employment growth outside industry, the faster overall productivity grows.

The complete Kaldor model of the relationship between industrial growth and the development process also contains a number of subsidiary propositions. First, as the scope for absorbing labour from diminishing returns activities dries up, the overall growth of GDP will slow down. The successful newly industrializing countries in South-East Asia will not go on growing at close to 8 per cent per annum for ever! Second, there is the question of what determines the rate at which industry grows in the first place. In the early stages of development, it must be demand coming from the agricultural sector because this is what dominates the economy. In the later stages of development, however, it is export demand that drives the system. The internal market is often too small to reap economies of scale, and selling to the home market does not provide the foreign exchange to pay for necessary imported inputs. The most successful developing countries are those that have geared themselves to export markets. The third proposition is that the fast growth of exports and output can set up a **virtuous circle of growth** that other countries will find difficult to break into without exceptional enterprise or protection. This can lead to polarization between countries, which is the essential feature of the **centre–periphery models of growth and development** that will be discussed in Chapter 8.

Finally, there is the big policy question of how developing countries bring about structural change in favour of industrial activities if growth and development is to be accelerated. Should everything be left to market forces, or is there a role for government? The Cambridge development economist Ajit Singh tells the story of when he first went to Cambridge University as a student of Kaldor in the 1960s that Kaldor taught him three things: first, developing countries must industrialize; second, they can industrialize only by protection, and third, anyone who says otherwise is being dishonest! It is indeed worth remembering that none of today's developed countries developed on the basis of free trade. All countries protected and promoted their infant industries in one way or another (see Chang, 2002; Reinert, 2007). And it is a myth, of course, that the highly successful countries of South-East Asia have developed on the basis of minimalist state intervention and simply allowed markets to work freely (Wade, 1990). In Japan, South Korea, Singapore and other 'Asian Tigers' there has been heavy state involvement in the promotion of industry, often working through the banking system. The issue is not *whether* to protect, but *how* to protect and promote industry while preserving efficiency and international competitiveness. These are issues that will be addressed when we turn to the topic of trade and development in Chapter 15.

| Case example 3.5 | **Testing Kaldor's growth laws across African countries** |

One of the striking features about Africa since the 1980s is that there has been virtually no structural change. This is undoubtedly one of the explanations for its poor growth performance. Over the period 1980–96, the average growth of GDP was 2.09 per cent per annum. The growth of manufacturing output was 2.11 per cent, and the growth of agricultural and service output were both 2.07 per cent. On the other hand, some African countries grew faster than others (e.g. Uganda, Botswana, Mauritius, Equatorial Guinea, Swaziland and Cape Verde grew particularly fast). To what extent can this differential growth performance be explained by the differential performance of manufacturing industries?

Regressing GDP growth against the excess of manufacturing growth (g_m) over non-manufacturing growth (g_{nm}) across 45 countries (the side test of Kaldor's first law) gives:

$$g_{GDP} = 0.021 + 0.408 \, (g_m - g_{nm}) \quad r^2 = 0.188.$$

This suggests that a country with excess growth of manufacturing of one percentage point has experienced a GDP growth rate of 0.41 percentage point above average.

When GDP growth is regressed against the excess of agricultural growth over non-agricultural growth, there is a strong *negative* correlation.

Estimating Kaldor's second law gives a Verdoorn coefficient of 0.878, which suggests substantial increasing returns in industry.

Estimating Kaldor's third law gives:

$$p_T = 0.020 + 0.524 \, (g_i) - 1.606 \, (e_{ni}) \quad r^2 = 0.712$$

This shows that overall productivity growth (p_T) across African countries is positively related to the growth of industry (g_i), but negatively related to the growth of employment outside industry (e_{ni}).

These results support Kaldor's structural thesis that there is something special about industrial activity that makes it the 'engine of growth'.

Source: Wells and Thirlwall, 2003.

Summary

- Poverty and underdevelopment of poor countries are associated with many characteristics which combine to keep labour productivity low.
- The economic structure of poor countries tends to be dominated by low productivity agriculture and petty service activities. Still over 50 per cent of the labour force in many poor countries live and work in the rural sector where value-added per head is barely US$2 a day.
- Levels of saving and investment are low in poor countries because poor people naturally lack the capacity to save, and investment can be risky.
- Poor countries tend to have higher rates of population growth than rich countries and while this can confer some benefits, it can cause major difficulties by depressing saving, putting pressure on food supplies and the environment, and adding to unemployment.
- Some poor countries suffer the 'curse of natural resources'. Mineral and oil production can lead to corruption and rent-seeking behaviour and keep the exchange rate high, making the production and export of other goods uncompetitive.
- Unemployment is high in poor countries because there are limited employment opportunities on the land, and the growth of alternative employment opportunities is constrained by a lack of investment. Rural–urban migration exacerbates unemployment in the cities.
- Human capital formation is important for raising levels of productivity, but secondary school enrolment rates are low, and illiteracy is rife, particularly amongst women.
- Undernourishment and malnutrition also keep labour productivity low.
- Food production falls short of requirements in many poor countries, but, as Amartya Sen has shown, famines are not mainly caused by a lack of food availability, but rather a lack of entitlements to food.
- The distribution of income tends to be more unequal in poor countries than rich, and also power relations between sections of society. There is very often discrimination on the grounds of sex, religion, race and ethnic origin.
- Countries pass through stages of development – what Rostow describes as traditional; transitional; take-off; maturity, and high mass-consumption. Many poor countries are still in the transitional or early take-off stages. Certain preconditions must be met for full take-off, including an agricultural revolution; investment in infrastructure; the emergence of leading sectors in the economy; saving and investment of at least 10 per cent of GDP, and an institutional structure conducive to risk-taking and investment.
- Countries grow fast and living standards rise when resources shift into industrial activities because manufacturing industry experiences considerable static and dynamic returns to scale. This is the experience of history and the contemporary experience of the fast growing countries of the world today (Kaldor's growth laws).

Chapter 3	Discussion questions

1 What are the major reasons why some countries are rich and others poor?

2 What is the importance of the distinction between diminishing returns activities and increasing returns activities?

Chapter 3	Discussion questions – *continued*

3   Why have economists identified a certain ratio of investment to GDP as a necessary condition for self-sustaining growth?

4   What are the causes of growing urban unemployment in developing countries?

5   What is meant by 'income measure' of unemployment?

6   In what ways do poor education and poor health affect the performance of an economy?

7   Why is the distribution of income more unequal in developing countries than in developed countries?

8   Consider the view that the existence of famine and malnutrition is a distributional problem, not one of food shortage.

9   What do you understand by the 'basic needs approach' to development?

10 What major structural changes take place during the course of development?

11 What accounts for the fact that a close association exists between industrial growth and the growth of GDP?

12 What contribution does Rostow's stage theory make to an understanding of the development process?

Notes

1. 'Net' in the sense of making an allowance for investment to cover depreciation of worn-out plant and machinery.
2. International Labour Organization, *Annual Employment Report* (Geneva: ILO, 2008).
3. *World Development Report 1995: Workers in an Integrating World* (Oxford University Press for the World Bank, 1995).
4. See Thorbecke (1973) for a survey of the missions to Colombia, Kenya, Iran and Sri Lanka.
5. For a comprehensive survey, see Behrman (1993).
6. See the *Report of the Commission on Macroeconomics and Health* authored by Jeffrey Sachs for the WHO (2001).
7. See Drèze and Sen (1989) for the Hunger and Poverty project of the World Institute for Development Economics Research (WIDER).
8. For pioneering studies of structural change, see Chenery and Syrquin (1975), and Chenery, Robinson and Syrquin (1986). For a more recent assessment, see Naqvi (1995).
9. See, for example, the Symposium on Kaldor's growth laws, edited by Thirlwall, in the *Journal of Post Keynesian Economics*, Spring 1983; also Bairam (1991); Drakopoulos and Theodossiou (1991); Hansen and Zhang (1996), and Wells and Thirlwall (2007).
10. Setting $g = x$, and solving for x gives: $2.529/(1-0.394) = 4.5$ per cent.

Websites on health, nutrition, famine, education, structural change and income distribution

Food production and statistics

Food and Agricultural Organization www.fao.org
International Food Policy Research Institute www.ifpri.org
World Hunger Programme at Brown University, USA www.brown.edu/departments/world-Hunger-Program
World Food Programme www.wfp.org/index.html

Health

World Health Organization www.who.int
AIDS www.int/emc-hiv; www.worldbank.org/aidsecon
Pan American Health Organization www.paho.org

Labour market statistics

International Labour Organization http://laborsta.ilo.org

Income distribution

University of Texas Inequality Project http://utip.gov.utexas.edu

Education

UNESCO www.unesco.org
World Bank Education Data www.worldbank.org/education/edstats/
UNICEF Girl's Education www.unicef.org/girlseducation/

4

THE ROLE OF INSTITUTIONS IN ECONOMIC DEVELOPMENT

- Introduction
- The role of institutions
- Measuring institutions and the debate on institutions versus geography
- The role of democracy
- Summary
- Discussion questions
- Note
- Websites on institutions and market behaviour

Introduction

Growth and development cannot take place in an institutional vacuum. Economic maturity and the growth of markets require an institutional framework that allows transactions to take place in an orderly manner and in which agents know that the decisions they take and the contracts they make will be protected by law, and enforced. Savers, investors, consumers, entrepreneurs, workers and risk-takers of all kinds need a framework of rules if rational, optimizing decisions are to be made. They also need some guarantee of economic stability and certainty, which can be provided only by good governance and sound economic policy-making. The alternative to a lack of property rights, law and order and political stability is economic anarchy – and failed states (see Chapter 10).

This chapter deals with the role of formal institutions in general in providing an economic, political and social environment in which economies can flourish and prosper, and it considers some of the empirical evidence on the relationship between institutional development and economic development.

The role of institutions

The Nobel Prize-winning economist Douglass North first brought to the fore the role of institutions in economic development. The modern exponents of the 'primacy of institutions' are Dani Rodrik of Harvard University and Daron Acemoglu, Simon Johnson and James Robinson of the Massachusetts Institute of Technology. North says in his famous book *Institutions, Institutional Change and Economic Performance* (1990):

> I wish to assert a fundamental role for institutions in societies: they are the underlying determinants of the long-run performance of economies – Third World countries are poor because the institutional constraints define a set of pay-offs to political/economic activity that do not encourage productive activity.

North also said that 'the inability of societies to develop effective low-cost enforcement of contracts is the most important source of both historical stagnation and contemporary underdevelopment in the Third World', because the absence of secure property and contractual rights discourages investment and specialization. Mancur Olson (1982) makes the same point in his classic book *The Rise and Decline of Nations* (1992).

It is possible to give both general and narrower, more formal, definitions of institutions. North himself describes institutions very broadly as the 'formal and informal rules [or norms] governing human behaviour'. A similar broad definition is given by Lin and Nugent (1995) as 'a set of humanly devised behavioural rules that govern and shape the interaction of human beings, in part by helping them to form expectations of what other people do'. At a more formal, precise level, institutions can be defined in terms of the extent of property rights' protection; the degree to which laws and regulations are fairly enforced; the ability of the government to protect the individual against economic shocks and to provide social protection, and the extent of political corruption.

When economists undertake empirical work on the relation between institutional structure and economic performance, it is of course necessary to have quantitative measures of the important institutions being discussed and evaluated. Lumping all institutions together in a single index of 'institutional quality' would obscure the different channels through which institutions work.

The reason why institutional structures and rules of behaviour are a necessary condition for economic activity to flourish is that incentives and price signals, so vital to a market economy, cannot function properly without them. As Rodrik (2008) says: 'markets require institutions because they are not self-creating; self-regulating; self-stabilising, or self-legitimising'. Which institutions are important and which are not will differ across space and time according to the history of a country, its geography, stage of development and its political aspirations, that is, what sort of society its people want. In small rural communities where everyone knows each other, the scope for cheating, fraud and not honouring contracts is limited. Transaction costs associated with the costs of information, negotiation, monitoring, coordination and enforcement of contracts are low, and communities survive by adhering to norms of behaviour; but economic development is limited through a lack of specialization. In contrast, in large, modern, industrial societies, where transactions are impersonal, there is widespread scope for opportunistic behaviour (Bardhan and Udry, 1999). Transactions (and therefore production) costs may be very high without institutional structures that curtail such behaviour, such as the enforcement of property rights and the rule of law, the provision of limited liability, the guarantee of contracts, patent protection and so on. With low transaction costs, firms and markets can concentrate on the job of investment in the knowledge that property rights are secure.

There is no one set of institutions that will suit all countries, but there is a consensus among development economists that at least five main types of market-supporting institutions are necessary, if not sufficient, conditions for rapid economic progress (see Rodrik, 2000, 2008; Rodrik and Subramanian, 2008).

- property rights and legally binding contracts: market-creating institutions
- regulatory institutions: market-regulating institutions
- institutions for macroeconomic stability: market-stabilizing institutions
- social insurance institutions: market-legitimizing institutions
- institutions of conflict management: market-legitimizing institutions

Rodrik (2000) highlights the following institutional arrangements that are conspicuously absent in poor countries:

- a clearly defined system of property rights
- a regulatory apparatus curbing the worst forms of fraud, anti-competitive behaviour and moral hazard
- a moderately cohesive society exhibiting trust and social cooperation
- social and political institutions that mitigate risk and manage social conflict
- the rule of law and clean government

These five main prerequisites of a sound institutional structure for economic development are described briefly below.

Property rights and legally binding contracts. These are important because agents lack the incentive to invest and innovate if they do not have control over the return on the assets they accumulate. Intellectual property rights are particularly important to encourage invention. Control is more important than ownership. Formal property rights do not mean very much if there are not control rights; but control rights can spur entrepreneurial activity without clearly defined property rights (witness China).

Regulatory institutions. Markets fail if there is fraud or anti-competitive behaviour. Regulatory institutions are needed if markets are to function properly. When markets are liberalized, a regulatory framework is also required to avoid the consequences of risky behaviour, such as financial crises if the banking system is not properly regulated (as the world economy witnessed in 2008). Institutions to compensate for capital market imperfections and coordination failures must also be an integral part of a 'regulatory' framework for promoting innovation and growth. A good example of this is the way the state intervened to promote industrial development in Korea and Taiwan in the 1960s and 1970s. All successful economies have an array of regulatory institutions that oversee different markets such as the product market, financial markets and the labour market. Developing countries may need more regulatory institutions because market failures are more pervasive than in developed countries.

Institutions for macroeconomic stability. Monetary and fiscal policy institutions are necessary to provide an enabling environment in which private investment can flourish. Market economies are not self-regulating, and macroeconomic instability creates risk and uncertainty. The minimization of risk is vital if entrepreneurs are to take informed, long-term investment decisions. Financial markets are inherently unstable, which can have damaging real effects, and they need careful supervision. A central bank, a responsible banking system and fiscal prudence are all important ingredients of macroeconomic stability.

Social insurance institutions. These are necessary if individuals are to accept change. In rural, peasant societies on the margins of subsistence, change may spell disaster, but progress (particularly in agriculture) requires willingness to take risks. Insurance against unemployment, crop failures and price fluctuations for agricultural commodities are all important if traditional agriculture is to be transformed. Economic reforms of any type, particularly in the process of liberalizing markets, will meet resistance if not enough attention is paid to creating social security institutions to protect the vulnerable. Social stability and cohesion within a market economy in the process of structural change requires social insurance and safety nets.

Institutions of conflict management. Many developing countries have deep ethnic, tribal and religious divisions. Social conflict damages economies because it diverts resources from directly productive activities, and creates uncertainty, which deters investment. To minimize conflict requires a full range of institutions – the rule of law, a fair legal system, a political voice for minority groups – which make it clear that the potential winners of social conflict will not benefit and potential losers will be properly safeguarded.

The question is, how are good institutions acquired? Because of history and the diversity of countries, there is no one unique set of institutions that can be prescribed for every country: 'there is no single mapping between the market and the set of non-market institutions required to sustain it' (Rodrik, 2000). Rodrik likens institutions to technical progress that allows countries to transform inputs into higher levels of output, shifting outwards a country's production possibility frontier. But technological blueprints that operate well in one context may not be appropriate in another – and so it is with institutions. A 'market economy' cannot simply be transposed from one country to another, at least without some adaptation. As Rodrik and Subramanian (2008) put it: 'there is growing evidence that desirable institutional arrangements have a large element of context specificity arising from differences in historical trajectories, geography, political economy and other initial conditions; . . . institutional innovations do not necessarily travel well'.

Nor is it easy to bring about institutional change. There is a **collective action problem** that limits potential gainers from bringing about change in opposition to vested interests (Bardhan and Udry, 1999). One is the **free-rider problem** about sharing the cost of change; the other is the **bargaining problem** relating to sharing the potential benefits of change. It can be difficult for potential gainers to compensate potential losers, as in the case of land reform for example. In these circumstances, the state has a role to play in fostering institutional change and development without destroying markets, or allowing itself to be influenced by special interest groups or corrupted by rent-seeking behaviour on the part of politicians and bureaucrats.

Rodrik (2000) argues forcefully that 'institutions need to be developed locally, relying on hands-on experience, local knowledge and experimentation'. Some institutional blueprints for some specific purposes may be borrowed (e.g. forms of financial regulation) because they are straightforward to implement and save costs, but others need to be built from scratch. Building from the 'bottom up' requires **participatory political institutions** that can use and assess local knowledge, so that the institutions created have consent and legitimacy. Institutions imposed from the 'top down' usually fail. Rodrik finds an association across countries between democratic political structures and economic success; but other studies are more agnostic.

Measuring institutions and the debate on institutions versus geography

To do serious empirical work on the impact of institutions on growth and development requires a measure of institutional development. But some care needs to be taken because if measures of institutional *quality* are used, a correlation with economic performance is almost certain to be found because the measures themselves are partly a function of the stage of development and economic success. Institutional measures are required which are devoid of 'quality'. The statistical way of putting the same point is that the institutional variables used should be strictly *exogenous*; but we know in practice that institutional development is partly a function of growth and development itself, making many institutional variables *endogenous*. To cope with this difficulty one can either find instruments to proxy for present-day institutions (see below), or take the initial (or base) level of institutions as the independent variable, rather than the contemporaneous level. There are also other econometric difficulties in determining the impact of institutions. Many institutional variables are highly correlated with one another, so it is difficult to measure the separate influence of each, and many institutional measures are ordinal (they simply rank countries) rather than cardinal, which means that they do not measure the *magnitude* of the difference in the institutional variables between one country and another.

Several different measures of institutions have been used in empirical work:

- **An aggregate governance index**, which is an average of six measures of institutions developed by Kaufman et al. (1999). These measures include (1) *voice and accountability* – the extent to which citizens can choose their government and enjoy political rights, civil liberties and an independent press; (2) *political stability and absence of violence* – the likelihood that the government will not be overthrown by unconstitutional or violent means; (3) *government effectiveness* – the quality of public service delivery and competence and political independence of the civil service; (4) *regulatory burden* – the relative absence of government controls on goods markets, banking systems and international trade; (5) *rule of law* – the protection of persons and property against violence and theft, independent and effective judges, and contract enforcement; and (6) *freedom from graft* – public power is not abused for private gain or corruption. Each of these measures can be taken individually.
- **A measure of property rights and risk of expropriation** using the International Country Risk Guide (ICRG) and Business Environmental Risk Intelligence (BERI). These indices are used

by Keefer and Knack (1995). The ICRG index includes a measure of expropriation risk, rule of law, repudiation of contracts by governments, corruption in government and quality of bureaucracy. The BERI index includes contract enforceability, nationalization potential and bureaucratic delays.

- **An index of democracy, political rights and civil liberties,** e.g. the Freedom House Index of Political Rights and Civil Liberties (Gastil, 1983, 1986).
- **Political instability** as measured by the number of revolutions and coups, and by the number of assassinations (Barro, 1991).
- **An index of corruption** (Transparency International)
- **Economic freedom** (Heritage Foundation)
- **An index of social division**, e.g. ethnic diversity

Apart from Rodrik, the other foremost modern exponents of the view that institutions are of primary importance in understanding the development process, and why some countries are rich today and others poor, are Acemoglu et al. (2001, 2002). Acemoglu (2008) himself identifies three important characteristics of good institutions:

- The enforcement of property rights and the rule of law, so that individuals have the incentive to save, invest and take risks (as argued above)
- Constraints on those in positions of power so that they cannot expropriate the resources of a country for their own benefit
- Equal opportunities for all, so that everyone has the incentive to better themselves and to participate productively in society.

Acemoglu and his colleagues believe that the fundamental cause of differences in the levels of development across countries of the world lies in differences in the evolution of institutions (in particular, property rights), which has historical roots, and that it is possible to find an *exogenous* cause of variations in institutions today that is unrelated to the level of development itself (or geography); namely the way in which colonizers settled in countries in the seventeenth and eighteenth centuries. This is determined by the mortality rates of soldiers, sailors and missionaries in various parts of the world.

The model of institutional development proposed by Acemoglu et al. (2001) is that (potential) settler mortality determined the degree of settlement, the degree of settlement determined the type of early institutions, and that early institutions have determined current institutions and can explain current economic performance. In other words, mortality rates in countries during early colonial times can be used for predicting institutions and the level of per capita income across countries today.

Let us consider the theory in more detail, and then some of the evidence. The model is based on three basic premises. First, there were different colonization policies which created different types of institutions. At one extreme, in some countries (mainly in Africa) 'extractive states' were created with the main purpose of transferring as many resources as possible from the colony. Private property rights were not established and colonizers did not settle in large numbers. At the other extreme, in countries such as the USA and Australia, Europeans settled in large numbers and tried to replicate European institutions with a strong emphasis on private property, and checking the power of elites – political and vested interests. The second premise is that the colonization strategy depended to a large extent on the feasibility of settlement, and particularly the incidence of disease and mortality. Thirdly, the institutions created during the colonial period persisted after the colonies became independent.

The authors present a mass of evidence of how mortality rates affected the willingness to settle in the various colonies, and how the presence or absence of European settlers was a key determinant of the form colonization took. A great deal of historical evidence is also presented that the control structures set up during the colonial period in the 'extractive states' that were not settled, such as in Africa and parts of Latin America, have persisted to this day, while the institutions of protecting private property rights, and law and order that were established in settler countries such as Australia, Canada, the USA, Hong Kong and Singapore, have also persisted.

The measure of institutions today, used by Acemoglu et al., is a 'risk expropriation' index first used by Keefer and Knack (1995).[1] The index goes from 0 (lowest protection of property rights) to 10 (highest), measured for each country for each year. They test their model using 64 former colonies for which there are data on settler mortality in the nineteenth century, current protection against expropriation risk, and living standards for the period 1985–95. Using simple two-variable regressions shows: (1) a strong negative correlation between per capita income (PCY) today and settler mortality rates per 1,000 of population; (2) a strong positive relation between PCY and protection against expropriation risk today (the correlation coefficient exceeds 50 per cent), and (3) that the settler mortality rate explains 25 per cent of the variation in the expropriation risk index. When the endogeneity of the expropriation risk index (as the measure of institutional quality) is instrumented by the settler–mortality variable, a significant negative effect on the current level of per capita income of countries is found, even controlling for other variables that might be correlated with settler mortality such as the identity of the colonial power, natural resource endowments, soil quality, religion, temperature and humidity. In fact, the authors dismiss the effect of geography altogether (see below). Moreover, the strong results are not dependent on the heavily settled countries with good institutions, such as the USA, Canada, Australia and New Zealand, nor if African countries are excluded from the sample. When a dummy variable for Africa is used in the equation, it is not statistically significant, which leads the authors to conclude that Africa is poor not because of geography but because of poor institutions, inherited from the past because the colonial powers established 'extractive states'.

In a separate analysis, Acemoglu et al. (2002) try to support their theory by showing how the fortunes of countries between the sixteenth century and the present have changed because of '**institutional reversal**'. It is a fact that those countries that were relatively rich in 1500 are now relatively poor, and vice versa, and this is attributed to the two different types of institutional structures discussed above that were imposed on countries during colonial times. Economic prosperity in 1500 is measured by the rate of urbanization and population density. With either measure there is a negative relation between prosperity in 1500 and the level of PCY today. The explanation given is that in previously poor areas European colonialism led to the development of institutions of private property because the regions were sparsely populated, which enabled Europeans to settle in large numbers and develop new institutions to the benefit of all. By contrast, in previously prosperous areas, already more densely populated with powerful ruling elites, colonizers found it easier and more profitable to maintain or introduce extractive institutions. There was a ready workforce available and taxation was relatively easy. Besides, in the more densely populated regions there was more disease, and mortality rates were higher. The reversal of relative incomes took place in the eighteenth and nineteenth centuries, with societies with good institutions taking advantage of the opportunity to industrialize: 'the interaction between institutions and the opportunity to industrialise during the 19th century played a central role in the long-run development of the former colonies' (Acemoglu et al., 2002). The authors find a negative relation between measures of prosperity in 1500 and the risk of expropriation (insecure property rights) today. Some basic econometric results are: (i) a 10 percentage point lower rate of urbanization in 1500 is associated with double the level of PCY today, and (ii) a 10 per cent higher population density in 1500 is associated with a 4 per cent lower PCY today.

The authors again dismiss the role of geography because geography is a 'constant' and predicts the persistence of economic outcomes. If geography is the most important factor in development, the most (least) prosperous areas prior to colonization should have continued to be the most (least) prosperous, but this is not the case. Geography cannot explain the reversal of fortunes. The authors recognize what they call a 'sophisticated version' of the geography hypothesis; that certain geographic characteristics that were inimical to successful economic performance in 1500 became less important later on when new crops and new technologies made temperate zones more productive than the more prosperous tropical zones (where civilization started), and transport costs fell. But they argue that there is no evidence that the reversal of economic fortunes between sets of countries in the eighteenth and nineteenth centuries were associated with agriculture or a more favourable transport environment. Reversal was most closely related to industrialization. The authors conclude: 'if you want to understand why a country is poor today, you have to look at institutions rather than its geography'.

But institutions and geography cannot be separated so easily. Geography, and its effects on disease, affects the type of colonization and therefore the character of institutions. Acemoglu (2008) effectively concedes this when he says 'geographic factors also likely influenced the institutions that Europeans introduced'. Rodrik et al. (2004) (see also Rodrik and Subramanian, 2008) attempt to tackle this issue empirically. They estimate a series of regressions relating the income levels of countries to measures of geography, institutions (and also the degree of economic integration), taking account of the endogeneity of institutions. Institutional development is measured by a composite indicator of the strength of property rights and the rule of law. They reach the conclusion that:

> Quality of institutions is the only positive and significant determinant of income levels. Once institutions are controlled for, integration has no direct effect on income, while geography has but weak direct effects. These results are very robust.

Rodrik et al. (2004) claim that the quality of institutions overrides everything else, but also concede, like Acemoglu, that 'geography has a strong indirect effect through institutions by influencing their quality'. Thus, geography may be the ultimate determinant after all!

In fact, Sachs (2008) points out that the incidence of malaria itself is enough to account for the negative relation between the mortality rates of British soldiers in various parts of the world in the nineteenth century and low levels of per capita income today. Sachs is critical of the almost exclusive emphasis on institutions in explaining differences in economic performance between countries, as if nothing else matters: 'the barriers to economic development in the poorest countries today are more complex than institutional shortcomings . . . both institutions and resource endowments are critical, not just one or the other'.

Another critic is Bardhan (2005b), who argues that there are other institutions that matter besides property rights and the rule of law, particularly **coordinating institutions** to overcome coordination failures which are endemic in poor countries and require institutions to cope with them. They would remain important even if property rights were secure. In Bardhan's view, 'this preoccupation of the literature with the institutions of security and property rights, often to the exclusion of other important institutions, severely limits our understanding of the development process'. Bardhan doubts whether the mortality rate of colonial settlers really captures the major historical forces that determined the economic and social structure of colonies.

Think of the *differences* between countries today all with similar disease environments, such as Brazil, India or the Congo in Africa, let alone the countries that were never colonized, such as Ethiopia and Thailand. Countries had a history before colonization: Bardhan calls this **state antiquity**, a term that refers to whether a country had a unified state structure or not. By this criterion, Asia ranks higher than Latin America and Africa, and in the latter, as a result of colonial rule, the post-colonial state was often incongruent with the pre-colonial political structures and geographic boundaries. This has been a major source of political turmoil and instability. In statistical analysis, Bardhan finds the state antiquity variable a significant determinant of differences in per capita income today (as well as settler mortality rates).

The role of democracy

Apart from the institutions versus geography debate, most empirical work on the role of institutions in economic development has been conducted on political instability and on the impact of political structures and the role of democracy. The challenge for any government, whatever its structure, is to provide leadership in resolving collective action problems (Bardhan, 1993), which means a commitment to formulating and implementing development policies in the interests of all the people, to prevent groups going their own separate ways. Democracy can make this more difficult because politicians can succumb to vested interest groups and take short-term decisions. On the other hand, dictatorships may have no interest in maximizing total output, and may allocate resources very inefficiently. Democracy makes life difficult for corrupt elites. In the discussion of democracy and growth it is also important to distinguish between democracy defined as free, multi-party elections on the one hand and civil and economic liberties on the other (Alesina and Perotti, 1994). Some non-democratic regimes in the first sense (e.g. China) give their citizens a lot of economic rights, and vice versa.

Early work by Barro (1991) measured institutional quality by the number of revolutions and coups in countries and by the number of political assassinations. A negative relation was found between these measures and economic growth across a sample of 98 countries, controlling for other variables (see Chapter 5).

But political instability is not the same as the nature of the political system. Here we shall highlight two major studies on the role of democracy by Rodrik (2000) and Barro (1996a, 2008). Rodrik examines data for 90 countries over the period 1970–89, using the Freedom House Index of Political Rights and Civil Liberties (the Gastil index) as a measure of democracy which ranks countries on a scale zero to one. He draws four important conclusions:

• democracies deliver more predictable long-run growth rates
• democracies produce greater short-term stability
• democracies handle adverse shocks much better
• democracies promote a fairer distribution of income

Democracies produce better outcomes in these ways because they produce superior institutions better suited to local conditions. There is little evidence that the average growth rate is higher in democracies than in more autocratic regimes, but the variance around the average is significantly lower in democracies. One reason for this is because adjustment to shocks requires managing

social conflict, and democratic institutions are more efficient institutions for conflict management. Democracies deliver better institutional outcomes because they tend to create more equal
opportunities for people, especially in the fields of health, education and employment opportunity, which manifests itself in a higher share of wages in national income. In general, therefore,
democracy helps to build better institutions based on local knowledge: 'participatory and decen-
tralised political systems are the most effective ones we have for processing and aggregating local
knowledge. We can think of democracy as a meta-institution for building other good institutions'
(Rodrik, 2000). Barro (2008), on the other hand, is more circumspect about the impact of democracy. Most agree that democracy tends to follow economic development, rather than precede
it; what is debated is the role of democracy in sustaining development once it has started. Barro
argues that democracy can hamper growth in the early stages of development by the tendency of
majority voting to support programmes that redistribute income from rich to the poor, involving
tax increases and other distortions that reduce incentives. Also, democracies may give in to pressure groups that redistribute resources to themselves; for example agricultural lobbies, defence
contractors and trade unions. On the other hand, and very important, democracy is a check on
corrupt autocracies (dictators). In statistical work that examines the link between democracy and
growth, Barro measures the degree of democracy by the Gastil index of political rights in Gastil's
publication *Freedom in the World* (1983, 1986). The definition of political rights is: 'rights to participate meaningfully in the political process. In a democracy this means the right of all adults to vote
and compete for public office, and for elected representatives to have a decisive vote on public
policies.' Barro's results suggest that the relationship between democracy and growth across countries is weakly negative, but not statistically significant. The most interesting finding is that there
is evidence of non-linearity; that is, more democracy increases growth when political freedoms
are weak, but depresses growth when a moderate degree of freedom has been achieved (perhaps
because, as said above, democracies give in to pressure groups and engage in more redistribution). Barro concludes that 'democracy is not the key to economic growth; ... advanced Western
countries would contribute more to the welfare of poor nations by exporting their economic
systems, notably property rights and free markets, rather than their political systems, which typically developed after reasonable standards of living had been attained'. Barro's conclusion concurs
with that of Alesina and Perotti (1994) in their early survey of the political economy of growth
when they say: 'growth is influenced not so much by the nature of the political regime (democracy or dictatorship) as by the stability of the political regime ... transitions from dictatorship to
democracy, being associated with socio-economic instability, should be typically periods of low
growth'.

The historical evidence for the now-developed countries, as documented by Chang (2003),
would seem to support this broad conclusion. He considers six categories of institutions as they
were in the developed countries in the nineteenth century – democracy; bureaucracy (including the judiciary); property rights; corporate governance institutions; financial institutions; and
welfare and labour institutions – and reaches the following conclusion: First, the now-developed
countries did not develop on the basis of democracy. Universal suffrage only came in the twentieth century. Poor developing countries today are adopting suffrage at much lower levels of
income than in now-developed countries. Second, public offices and the judiciary were historically corrupt. Appointments were made not on merit, but through class or political connections,
and the judiciary often lacked independence, dispensing justice according to class and race.
Third, property rights, such as contract law, company law, bankruptcy law, tax law and land law
were all lax historically. So, too, were intellectual property rights. Chang remarks with respect

to patents, copyrights and trademarks: 'the protection fell well short of what is demanded in developing countries today'. Fourth, in most now-developed countries, modern corporate governance structures emerged after, rather than before, industrial development. There was no proper auditing of companies and no bankruptcy law, and competition laws did not properly exist until the twentieth century. Fifth, banking regulation in the nineteenth century was very perfunctory, and banks only became professional lending institutions, serving all the people, in the early twentieth century. Finally, social security institutions to protect against change were virtually non-existent.

The lessons of history are that many institutions deemed to be important for poor developing countries today emerged after, not before, economic development was taking place, and it took a long time for them to emerge in fully fledged form from the time of their perceived need. Chang is right to conclude, however, that this does not mean 'the clock should be turned back'; rather, that institutional development is not the sine qua non of economic development, and institutional reforms in developing countries should not be imposed from outside, but should be allowed to evolve naturally, internally.

This would accord with the central conclusion of Rodrik, namely everything we know about economic growth indicates that large-scale institutional transformation is not so necessary for getting growth started, but that it is very important for sustaining it. This conclusion is based on the pioneering research by Hausmann et al. (2005) on 'growth accelerations'. The secret of economic success in the early stages of development is to find the 'binding constraints' on growth using 'growth diagnostics' (see Chapter 5). This does not require wholesale institutional reform.

Summary

- Institutional structures and rules of behaviour are a necessary condition for economic activity to flourish because incentives and price signals in a market economy cannot function properly without them.
- There are at least five main types of market-supporting institutions that are necessary, if not sufficient, conditions for rapid economic progress: property rights and legally binding contracts; regulatory institutions; social insurance institutions; institutions for conflict management, and institutions to secure macroeconomic stability.
- Poor countries are often characterized by a lack of trust and the rule of law; weak institutions to mitigate risk and to manage social conflict; no clearly defined system of property rights; an inadequate regulatory apparatus to curb fraud and anti-competitive behaviour; and a lack of clean government.
- Without property rights and the rule of law, the incentive to invest, on which economic growth ultimately depends, is very weak.
- It is not easy to bring about institutional change. There is a collective action problem which limits potential gainers from bringing about change in opposition to vested interests, including the free-rider problem and the bargaining problem of distributing the gains.
- It is not easy to measure institutional development and its impact on economic performance because institutional development itself is endogenous to economic development. An exogenous measure of institutions is required.
- Several different measures of institutions have been used in empirical work, such as a measure of property rights and risk of expropriation; an aggregate governance index; an index

of democracy, political rights and civil liberties; an index of political instability; an index of corruption; an index of economic freedom, and an index of social division.

- The economists Acemoglu, Johnson and Robinson believe that the fundamental cause of differences in the level of development across countries in the world today is the historical evolution of institutions, and that in those parts of the world where conditions were harsh, in Africa for example, colonizers created 'extractive states' with no firm property rights, while in other parts (e.g. the USA and Australia) colonizers settled in large numbers and built institutions conducive to development. Disease and mortality rates in the nineteenth century are taken as an exogenous institutional variable. The role of geography (a constant) is dismissed.

- If geography was the most important factor in development, the most (least) prosperous areas prior to colonization should have continued to be the most (least) prosperous, but this is not the case. On the other hand, geography, and its effects on disease and mortality, affected the type of colonization and therefore the character of institutions. The role of geography is therefore controversial.

- Apart from the debate on institutions versus geography, most of the empirical work on the role of institutions in economic development has been conducted on the influence of democracy and political stability on economic performance.

- Rodrik finds that democracies deliver more predictable long-run growth rates, produce greater short-term stability, handle adverse shocks better and promote a fairer distribution of income than non-democratic states.

- Chang shows, however, that the lessons of history are that many of the institutions that are argued to be important for developing countries today emerged *after*, not before, economic development was taking place – for example, democracy and property rights, contract law, company law, bankruptcy law and tax law. His message is that institutions should be allowed to evolve naturally, internally, and not be imposed from outside.

Chapter 4	Discussion questions

1 Why are institutional structures and rules of behaviour a necessary condition for economic activity to flourish?

2 What institutions do you think are the most important for encouraging investment in developing countries?

3 What is the importance of local knowledge in building appropriate institutions?

4 What are the major empirical problems of testing the relationship between institutions and economic development?

5 Briefly describe the Acemoglu, Johnson and Robinson theory of the link between colonialism, institutions and economic development.

6 Is it possible to distinguish the role of institutions and geography in explaining differences in the level of development between countries?

7 In what ways can democracy help and hinder economic development?

Note

1. Keefer and Knack (1995) was an early study which examined the impact of property rights on economic growth across countries over the period 1974 to 1989 using composite indices of contract enforceability and risk of expropriation and found a strong positive effect of property rights; stronger than the effect of political instability or measures of civil liberties.

Websites on institutions and market behaviour

Transparency International www.transparency.org
Heritage Foundation www.heritage.org
Center for Global Development www.cgdev.org
Freedom House http://www.freedomhouse.org/template.cfm?page=1

5

THEORIES OF ECONOMIC GROWTH: WHY GROWTH RATES DIFFER BETWEEN COUNTRIES

- Introduction
- Classical growth theory
- The Harrod–Domar growth model
- Neoclassical growth theory
- The production function approach to the analysis of growth
- Production function studies of developing countries
- 'New' (endogenous) growth theory and the macrodeterminants of growth
- 'Growth diagnostics' and binding constraints on growth
- Summary
- Discussion questions
- Notes
- Websites on growth theory

Introduction

Growth and development theory is as old as economics itself. The great classical economists of the eighteenth and nineteenth centuries were, in a sense, all development economists writing about forces determining the progress of nations as the countries of Europe embarked on the process of industrialization. The most famous of the early classical economists was Adam Smith, who published a famous book in 1776 entitled *An Inquiry into the Nature and Causes of the Wealth of Nations*. This work is still widely cited today because Smith recognized how specialization in industrial activities could lead to increasing returns and big increases in labour productivity, compared with specialization in agriculture.

In this chapter we examine how theories of growth and development have evolved through time from the classical economists to modern-day thinking about factors which determine the pace of economic growth. Other great classical economists, apart from Smith, were Thomas Malthus, David Ricardo and John Stuart Mill, who were all pessimistic about the growth and development process because of the pressure of population on food supply and diminishing returns in agriculture, which they argued would reduce the rate of profit in industry. Eventually a stationary state would be reached. Even more pessimistic was Karl Marx, who predicted the collapse of capitalism itself.

Modern growth theory started with (Sir) Roy Harrod's famous 1939 paper 'An Essay in Dynamic Theory'. His main purpose was to make dynamic Keynes's static theory of income determination. In doing so he showed how unstable economies can be in the short run, and how, in the long run, it is possible for countries to experience either prolonged periods of secular stagnation if the supply of saving exceeds the demand for it, or structural unemployment if the growth of the labour force exceeds the growth of capital (as it does in most developing countries).

The neoclassical response to the Harrod model was Robert Solow's famous growth model (Solow, 1956) which attempts to show that if the prices of factors of production are flexible, and labour and capital are substitutable, it is possible for countries to achieve equilibrium growth at the so-called 'natural rate', determined by the growth of the labour force and labour-saving technical progress. What determines labour-force growth and technical progress is left unexplained. Because of the assumption of diminishing returns to capital, investment itself does not matter for long-run growth. The model also predicts that capital-scarce countries should grow faster than capital-rich countries, leading to a convergence of per capita incomes across the world, because the marginal product of capital should be higher in poor countries than in rich countries.

As we saw in Chapter 2, however, convergence of living standards across countries is not apparent, and this led in the 1980s to the development of so-called 'new' growth theory or endogenous growth theory which relaxes the assumption of diminishing returns to capital by redefining capital to include improvements in human capital and new techniques of production through research and development (R&D) expenditure. In these 'new' models, convergence is only conditional, and investment matters for long-run growth because the marginal product of capital does not decline as more investment takes place.

We not only look at theory, but also empirics, and see how the neoclassical production function has been used to analyse the sources of growth in developing countries, and how 'new' growth theorists treat their models empirically.

An attempt is made to illustrate the contemporary relevance of the theories discussed. We shall in fact discover that the wheel has turned full circle, and that the most recent theories of endogenous growth rehabilitate many of the ideas of the old classical economists, particularly

Adam Smith's emphasis on **increasing returns** associated with investment in manufacturing industry, and the general emphasis in both classical and Keynesian theory on the role of capital accumulation, and the embodiment of various forms of technical progress associated with it.

The chapter ends with a discussion of the topic of growth diagnostics and identifying binding constraints on growth.

Classical growth theory

The macroeconomic issues of the growth of output, and the distribution of income between wages and profits, were the major preoccupation of all the great classical economists, including Adam Smith, Thomas Malthus, David Ricardo and, last but not least, Karl Marx. This discussion starts with **Adam Smith**, because while Smith had a generally optimistic vision of the growth and development process, the later classical economists tended to have a more gloomy vision. This led the historian Thomas Carlyle to describe economics as a 'dismal science' – not a sentiment, I hope, that will be shared by students reading this book!

Adam Smith

Born 1723, Kirkcaldy, Scotland. Died 1790. Professor of Moral Philosophy, University of Glasgow. Often described as the 'father' of modern economics. Famous for two main books: *The Theory of Moral Sentiments* (1759) and *An Inquiry into the Nature and Causes of the Wealth of Nations* (1776). A strong advocate of free markets and free trade, but most important for recognizing the role that increasing returns play in the growth and development process based on the principle of the division of labour or specialization – a characteristic of manufacturing industry in particular.

Adam Smith and increasing returns

One of Smith's most important contributions was to introduce into economics the notion of **increasing returns**, based on the **division of labour**. He saw the division of labour (or gains from specialization) as the very basis of a social economy, otherwise everyone might as well be their own Robinson Crusoe producing everything they want for themselves. This notion of increasing returns, based on the division of labour, lay at the heart of his optimistic vision of economic progress as a self-generating process, in contrast to later classical economists who believed that economies would end up in a stationary state owing to diminishing returns in agriculture. It was also in contrast to Marx, who believed that capitalism would collapse through its own 'inner contradictions', by which he meant competition between capitalists reducing the rate of profit, and the alienation of workers.

Given the central importance of increasing returns, the essence of Smith's model is basically a very simple one, and many of the features he emphasizes will be a recurring theme in this and other chapters. The growth of output and living standards depends first and foremost on investment and capital accumulation. Investment, in turn, depends on savings out of profits generated by industry and agriculture and the degree of labour specialization (or division of labour). The division of labour determines the level of labour productivity, but **the division of labour is limited by the extent of the market**. The extent of the market, however, depends partly on the division of labour as the determinant of per capita income. We have here a circular cumulative interactive process, although not without constraints, as we shall see later.

The notion of increasing returns may on the surface appear to be relatively trivial, but it is of profound significance for the way economic processes are viewed. It is not possible to understand divisions in the world economy and so-called 'centre–periphery' models of growth and development (see Chapter 8) without distinguishing between activities that are subject to increasing returns on the one hand, and diminishing returns on the other. 'Increasing returns' means rising labour productivity and per capita income as output and employment expands, while 'diminishing returns' means falling labour productivity and per capita income and a limit to the employment of labour at the point where the marginal product of labour falls to the level of the subsistence wage. Beyond that point there will be no more employment opportunities, and there will be disguised unemployment (see Chapters 3 and 6). Increasing returns are prevalent in most industrial activities, while diminishing returns characterize land-based activities such as agriculture and mining, because land is a fixed factor of production – and one of the few incontrovertible laws of economics is that if a variable factor is added to a fixed factor its marginal product will eventually fall (the law of diminishing returns). Poor developing countries tend to specialize in diminishing returns activities, while the rich developed countries tend to specialize in increasing returns activities, and this is one of the basic explanations of the rich country–poor country divide in the world economy. As we see later, it is the concept of increasing returns (or more precisely, non-diminishing returns to capital) that lies at the heart of the new endogenous growth theory.

Adam Smith gives three sources of the increasing returns to be derived from the division of labour:

> This great increase in the quantity of work, which, in consequence of the division of labour, the same number of people are capable of performing, is owing to three different circumstances; first to the increase of dexterity in every particular workman [what we now call **learning by doing**]; secondly, to the saving of time which is commonly lost in passing from one species of work to another; and lastly, to the invention of a great number of machines which facilitate and abridge labour, and enable one man to do the work of many.

That is, specialization provides greater scope for capital accumulation by enabling complex processes to be broken up into simpler processes permitting the use of machinery. But the ability to specialize, or the division of labour, depends on the extent of the market. Smith uses the example of the production of pins. There is no point in installing sophisticated machinery to deal with the different processes of pin production if the market for pins is very small. It is only economical to use cost-saving machinery if the market is large. If the market is small, there would be surplus production. To quote Smith again:

> when the market is very small, no person can have any encouragement to dedicate himself entirely to one employment, for want of power to exchange all that surplus part of the produce of his own labour, which is over and above his own consumption, for such parts of the produce of other men's labour as he has occasion for.

Smith recognized, however, that increasing returns based on the division of labour were much more a feature of industry than agriculture:

> the nature of agriculture, indeed, does not admit of so many subdivisions of labour, nor of so complete a separation of one business from another, as manufactures. It is impossible to separate so entirely the business of the grazier from that of the corn farmer, as the trade of the carpenter is commonly separated from that of the smith.

This does not mean, of course, that agriculture is unimportant in the development process. On the contrary. Even though industry offers more scope for the division of labour, it would be difficult for industry to develop at all without an agricultural surplus, at least in the absence of imports. Smith recognized that an agricultural surplus is necessary to support an industrial population, and labour released by improved productivity in agriculture can be used for the production of non-agricultural goods. So agriculture is certainly important for industrialization from the supply side. On the demand side, it is the agricultural surplus that gives rise to the demand for other goods, which can be purchased with the excess supply of agricultural goods. As Smith put it: 'those, therefore, who have the command of more food than they themselves can consume, are always willing to exchange the surplus – for gratification of this other kind [manufactured goods]'. We have here a model of reciprocal demand between agriculture and industry, with industry demanding food from agriculture to feed workers, and agriculture exchanging its surplus for industrial goods. Balanced growth between agriculture and industry is essential for the growth and development process to proceed without impediment. Many later models of economic development reflect this insight (see Chapters 6 and 10).

The division of labour is limited by the size of the market. This is a central axiom of Smith's model. The size of the market will be partly limited by restrictions on trade; hence Smith's advocacy of free trade and laissez-faire, internally and externally. Goods must be able to be exchanged freely between industry and agriculture. But demand for industrial goods can also come from abroad, and Smith recognized the role of exports in the development process:

> without an extensive foreign market, [manufactures] could not well flourish, either in countries so moderately extensive as to afford but a narrow home market; or in countries where the communication between one province and another was so difficult as to render it impossible for the goods of any particular place to enjoy the whole of that home market which the country could afford.

The subject of trade and growth, and models of export-led growth, is discussed in detail in Chapter 15.

Smith's model of development is driven by capital accumulation generated by profits from industry; and the stimulus to invest, as in all classical models, comes from the rate of profit. If the rate of profit falls, the desire to invest diminishes. Smith was somewhat ambiguous about what happens to the rate of profit as development proceeds. On the one hand he recognized that as the economy's capital stock grows, the profit rate will tend to fall due to competition between capitalists and rising wages. On the other hand, new investment opportunities raise the rate of return. Thus, the rate of profit may rise or fall in the course of development depending on whether investment is in old or new technology. If there is any tendency towards a stationary state in which the rate of profit falls to zero so that there is no further incentive to invest, it is a long way off in Smith's model, in contrast to the models of Malthus, Ricardo and Marx, in which a fall in the rate of profit is seen as inevitable.

Before turning to these models, which focus on some of the more depressing features inherent in the development process, it needs to be mentioned that Smith's vision of development as a cumulative interactive process based on the division of labour and increasing returns in industry lay effectively dormant until an American economist, Allyn Young, revived it in a neglected but profound article in 1928 entitled 'Increasing Returns and Economic Progress'.[1] As Young observed:

> Adam Smith's famous theorem [that the division of labour depends on the extent of the market and the extent of the market depends on the division of labour] amounts to saying that the division of labour depends in large part on the division of labour. [But] this is more than mere tautology. It means that the counter forces which are continually defeating the forces which make for equilibrium are more pervasive and more deeply rooted than we commonly realise . . . Change becomes progressive and propagates itself in a cumulative way.

For Young, increasing returns are not simply confined to factors that raise productivity *within* individual industries, but are related to the output of *all* industries which, he argued, must be viewed as an interrelated whole: what are now sometimes called **macroeconomies of scale**. For example, a larger market for product *x* may make it profitable to use more machinery in its production, which reduces the cost of *x and* the cost of the machinery, which then makes the use of machinery more profitable in other industries, and so on. Under certain conditions change will become progressive and propagate itself in a cumulative way; the precise conditions being increasing returns and an elastic demand for products so that as their relative price falls, proportionately more is bought. Take the example of steel and textiles, both of which are subject to increasing returns and are price elastic. As the supply of steel increases, its relative price (or exchange value) falls. If demand is price elastic, textile producers demand proportionately more steel, and offer proportionately more textiles in exchange. Textile production increases and its exchange value falls. If demand is price elastic, steel producers demand proportionately more textiles, and so on. As Young said, 'under these circumstances there are no limits to the process of expansion except the limits beyond which demand is not elastic and returns do not increase'.

The process described above could not occur with diminishing returns activities with an inelastic price demand, which characterizes most primary products. No wonder rapid development tends to be associated with the process of industrialization. It is true to say, however, that Young's vision was also lost until the 1950s, when economists such as Gunnar Myrdal, Albert Hirschman and Nicholas Kaldor started to challenge equilibrium theory and develop non-equilibrium models of the growth and development process in such books as *Economic Theory and Underdeveloped Regions* (Myrdal, 1957), *Strategy of Economic Development* (Hirschman, 1958), *Strategic Factors in Economic Development* (Kaldor, 1967) and *Economics without Equilibrium* (Kaldor, 1985). Kaldor used to joke that economics went wrong after Chapter 4 of Book I of Smith's *Wealth of Nations*, when Smith abandoned the assumption of increasing returns in favour of constant returns, and the foundations for neoclassical general equilibrium theory were laid. In contrast, it is now Smith and Young's emphasis on increasing returns that lies at the heart of the new endogenous growth theory.

The classical pessimists

The prevailing classical view after Smith was very pessimistic about the process of economic development, focusing on the problems of rapid population growth and the effect exerted on the rate of profit in industry by rising food prices owing to diminishing returns and rising costs in agriculture. One of the foremost pessimists was **Thomas Malthus**, and it might be said that the ghost of

Malthus still haunts many developing countries today with respect to his views on population. But there are two strands to Malthus's writing: his theory of population, and his focus on the importance for development of maintaining 'effective demand' – a concept later borrowed by Keynes, who acknowledged a debt to Malthus. In fact Malthus was the only classical economist to emphasize the importance of demand for the determination of output – all others adhered to **Say's Law**: that supply creates its *own* demand, so that the level and growth of output is a function of the supply of physical inputs alone. For Malthus, effective demand must grow in line with productive potential if profitability as the stimulus to investment is to be maintained, but there is nothing to guarantee this. Malthus focused on the savings of landlords and the possible imbalance between the supply of saving and the planned investment of capitalists, which might impede development. If landlord saving exceeded the amount that capitalists wished to borrow, Malthus suggested the taxation of landlords as one solution.

Malthus is best known, however, for his *Essay on the Principle of Population* (1798), in which he claimed that there is a 'constant tendency in all animated life to increase beyond the nourishment prepared for it'. According to Malthus, 'population goes on doubling itself every twenty five years, or increases in a geometrical ratio', whereas 'it may be fairly said . . . that the means of subsistence increase in an arithmetical ratio'. Taking the world as a whole, therefore, Malthus concluded:

> the human species would increase (if unchecked) as the numbers 1, 2, 4, 8, 16, 32, 64, 128, 256, and subsistence as 1, 2, 3, 4, 5, 6, 7, 8, 9. [This would mean that] in two centuries the population would be to the means of subsistence as 256 to 9; in three centuries as 4096 to 13, and in two thousand years the difference would be incalculable.

If food production only grows at an arithmetic rate, this implies, of course, diminishing returns to agriculture. The imbalance between population growth and growth of the food supply would lead to the per capita income of countries oscillating around the subsistence level, or being caught in what is now sometimes called a '**low-level equilibrium trap**' (see Chapter 9). Any increases in per capita income brought about by technical progress lead to more births, which then reduce per capita income back to subsistence level. Early development models of the 'big push' were designed to lift economies from this trap. Malthus recognized certain checks to the process,

Thomas Malthus

Born 1766, Surrey, England. Died 1834. Professor of History and Political Economy at the East India Company College. Famous for his *An Essay on the Principle of Population* (1798) predicting that population growth will outstrip food supply because of diminishing returns in agriculture. Some communities in developing countries still have Malthusian characteristics, and some 'environmentalists' predict a Malthusian world in the future.

which he divided into 'preventative' and 'positive' checks, some of which still operate today in certain countries. Preventative checks include sexual abstinence or the use of contraception, although Malthus was opposed to the latter. Where preventative checks are weak, positive checks take over in the form of pestilence, disease and famine. Malthus's solution to population growth was the 'postponement of marriage in a viceless society'!

While Malthusian economics may still have relevance in certain parts of Africa and Asia, Malthus's gloomy prognostications have not materialized for the world as a whole, because preventative checks have become stronger and because food production has grown not at an arithmetic rate but at a rate faster than the growth of population (see Chapter 3). Technical progress in agriculture has offset diminishing returns. The underestimation of technical progress in agriculture has confounded all the classical pessimists.

David Ricardo was another of the great classical pessimists. In 1817 he published his *Principles of Political Economy and Taxation,* in which he predicted that capitalist economies would end up in a stationary state, with no growth, also owing to diminishing returns in agriculture. In Ricardo's model, like Smith's, growth and development is a function of capital accumulation, and capital accumulation depends on reinvested profits. However, profits are squeezed between subsistence wages and the payment of rent to landlords, which increases as the price of food rises owing to diminishing returns to land and rising marginal costs. Ricardo thought of the economy as 'one big farm' in which food (or corn) and manufactures are consumed in fixed proportions, so corn can be used as the unit of account. Figure 5.1 illustrates the model.

With the employment of L amount of labour, the total output is $0RZL$. Rent is determined by the difference between the average and marginal product of labour working on the land and is given by the area $PRZY$. Wages are equal to $0WXL$, and profit is the difference between rent and wages, equal to $WPYX$. As output increases and the marginal product of labour falls to the subsistence wage (L_1), profits disappear. In equilibrium, the rate of profit in agriculture must equal the rate of profit in industry. As the profit rate in agriculture falls, capital will shift to industry, causing the rate of profit to decline there. Profits are also squeezed because wages rise in terms of food. But for Ricardo, unlike Malthus, there was no problem of effective demand. Ricardo saw no limit to the amount of capital that could be employed because he accepted Say's Law that supply creates its own demand. The villain of the piece is wages. He writes: 'there is no limit to demand – no limit to the employment of capital while it yields any profit, and that however abundant capital

Figure 5.1 Ricardo's model of the economy

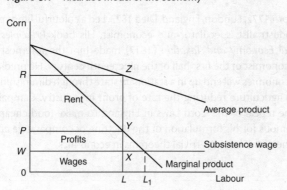

may become, there is no other adequate reason for a fall in profit but a rise in wages'. As profits fall to zero, capital accumulation ceases, heralding the stationary state. As Ricardo put it:

> a real rise of wages is necessarily followed by a real fall in profits, and, therefore, when the land of a country is brought to the highest state of cultivation, when more labour employed upon it will not yield in return more food than what is necessary to support the labourer so employed, that country has come to the limit of its increase both of capital and population.

As discussed in Chapter 6, Arthur Lewis's famous development model, 'Economic Development with Unlimited Supplies of Labour', is a classical Ricardian model, but wages are assumed to stay the same until disguised unemployment on the land is absorbed.

Given the central importance of capital accumulation in Ricardo's vision of economic progress, anything that reduces capital accumulation (including rises in wages) will slow economic growth. Ricardo was thus opposed to all forms of taxes, levies and tariffs on inputs into the productive system, including tariffs on imported food. Indeed, he believed that the importation of cheap food might delay the predicted stationary state indefinitely by holding down wages measured in terms of food:

> a country could go on for an indefinite time increasing its wealth and population, for the only obstacle to this increase would be the scarcity, and consequent high value, of food and other raw produce. Let these be supplied from abroad in exchange for manufactured goods, and it is difficult to say where the limit is at which you would cease to accumulate wealth and to derive profits from its employment.

It was for this reason that Ricardo campaigned for the abolition of the Corn Laws in Britain in the nineteenth century. These laws were eventually repealed in 1846 – to the benefit of industrialists but to the detriment of domestic farmers. In developing countries today, governments often attempt to keep the price of agricultural goods artificially low in order to keep wages low (measured in terms of food). Doing this, however, raises another problem of reducing the incentive of farmers to produce. Determining the equilibrium terms of trade between agriculture and industry, which maximizes the output of both sectors, is a difficult empirical issue (see Chapter 6).

David Ricardo

Born 1772, London, England. Died 1823. Led a colourful life as politician, industrialist, speculator and economist. His book *Principles of Political Economy and Taxation* (1817) made him the foremost classical economist of the first half of the nineteenth century. He predicted that economies will end up in a stationary state through diminishing returns in agriculture reducing the rate of profit in industry. Campaigned for the repeal of the Corn Laws in England to make food cheaper. Most famous for his formulation of the doctrine of comparative advantage; one of the few non-trivial theorems in economics.

Finally we turn to **Karl Marx**, famous for his book *Das Kapital* (1867), and his prediction of the collapse of capitalism. All members of the classical school agreed that the rate of profit on capital would fall as the economy grew, but they differed as to the reason for the fall. Adam Smith saw the decline in profits as the result of competition among capitalists. Ricardo saw the fall as the result of diminishing returns to land, and profits being squeezed between rent and wages, leading to a stationary state. For Marx, the economy does not grow forever, but the end comes not from a stationary state but from 'crises' associated with overproduction and social upheaval. But Marx's model bears many similarities to the other classical economists. The capitalist surplus is the source of capital accumulation and the principal mainspring of growth. Population growth responds to wages in Malthusian fashion, keeping wages down, and the rate of profit has a long-run tendency to fall.

Let us briefly consider Marx's model and his prediction of crisis. Gross output consists of three elements:

- Variable capital or the wage bill (v)
- Constant capital (c), that is, plant and machinery and the raw materials used in production
- Surplus value or profit (s).

The wages of labour are determined by the minimum subsistence level (what Marx called the cost of reproducing the working class), and surplus value (which only labour can create) is the difference between output per worker and the minimum wage per worker. The rate of surplus value, or what Marx called the 'degree of exploitation', is given by s/v. The rate of profit is given by the ratio of surplus value to total capital; that is

$$s/(v+c) = (s/v)/(1 + [c/v])$$ (5.1)

where the ratio of constant to variable capital (c/v) is defined as the '**organic composition of capital**'. As techniques of production become more capital intensive, the organic composition rises through time, and as it does so the rate of profit falls unless surplus value rises. While there is no limit to the rise in c/v, however, there is a limit to s/v. Marx foresaw no major problem as long as surplus labour exists to keep wages down, but he predicted that as capital accumulation continues, the '**reserve army of labour**', as he called it, would disappear, driving wages up and profits down. The capitalist's response is then either to attempt to keep wages down, leading to the '**immiserisation of workers**' and social conflict, or to substitute more capital for labour, which would worsen the problem by raising c/v.

For Marx, the desire and necessity to invest are inherent in the psychological makeup of the capitalist: 'To accumulate, is to conquer the world of social wealth, to increase the mass of human beings exploited by him, and then to extend both the direct and indirect sway of the capitalist.' Thus the capitalist's motto is 'Accumulate, accumulate! That is Moses and the Prophets.' But as capital is substituted for labour there is another problem: labour cannot consume all the goods produced, and a '**realization crisis**' is caused by the failure of effective demand. Capitalism eventually collapses through its own 'inner contradictions', and power passes to the working classes because fewer and fewer people benefit from capitalism. Capitalism is replaced by socialism, whereby workers own the means of production, distribution and exchange, and ultimately the state withers away.

Karl Marx

Born 1818, Trier, Germany. Died 1883. Settled in England in 1848 and supported by Friedrich Engels. His major work, *Das Kapital* (vol. 1, 1868, and three further volumes published posthumously), has inspired generations of left-wing thinkers in their critiques of the inequalities of capitalism. His prediction that capitalism would collapse through a decline in the rate of profit and the immiserisation of workers leading to social revolution has not materialized because in a growing economy with technical progress there is no clash between real wages and the rate of profit.

Marx's analysis contains valuable insights into the functioning of capitalism, but his predictions, like those of his predecessors, have not materialized. There seem to be two basic reasons for this. The first is that there is a confusion in Marx's work between *money wages* and *real wages*. A rise in money wages as surplus labour disappears does not necessarily mean a rise in real wages; but in any case, any rise in real wages could be offset by a rise in labour productivity, leaving the rate of profit unchanged. The second and related reason is that just as the other classical economists underestimated the rate of technical progress in agriculture as an offset to diminishing returns, so Marx underestimated the effect of technical progress in industry on the productivity of labour. It can be seen from (5.1) that even if c/v is rising, the rate of profit can remain unchanged if technical progress exceeds the rate of wage growth by the same amount. Technical progress also means there is no necessary clash between real wages and the rate of profit. Both can rise.

For nearly 60 years after Marx's death in 1883, growth and development theory lay effectively dormant, as economics came to be dominated by static neoclassical value theory under the influence of Alfred Marshall's *Principles of Economics* (1890). Marshall treated growth and development as more or less a 'natural' phenomenon; an evolutionary process akin to biological developments in the natural world. Modern growth theory started with the classic article by the British economist Roy Harrod, 'An Essay in Dynamic Theory' (1939),[2] which led to the development of what is now called the Harrod–Domar growth model.[3] The model has played a major part in thinking about development issues since the Second World War, and is still widely used in development planning (see Chapter 10).

The Harrod–Domar growth model

Harrod's original model is a dynamic extension of Keynes's static equilibrium analysis. In Keynes's *General Theory*, the condition for income and output to be in equilibrium (in the closed economy) is that plans to invest equal plans to save (or injections into the circular flow of income should equal leakages). The question Harrod asked is: if changes in income induce investment, what must be the *rate of growth of income* for plans to invest to equal plans to save in order to ensure a *moving* equilibrium in a growing economy through time? Moreover, is there any guarantee that this required rate of growth will prevail? If not, what will happen? In static Keynesian theory, if equilibrium between saving and investment is disturbed, the economy corrects itself and a new equilibrium is achieved via the multiplier process. If growth equilibrium is disturbed, will it be self-correcting or self-aggravating? Moreover, will this equilibrium rate be equal to the maximum rate of growth that the economy is able to sustain given the rate of growth of productive capacity? If not, what will happen? These are fundamental questions for the understanding of the growth performance of any country, be it developed or underdeveloped, and Harrod's place in the history of economic thought was guaranteed by the insight and simplicity with which he answered them.

To consider the questions posed, Harrod distinguished three different growth rates: what he called the **actual growth rate** (g), the **warranted growth rate** (g_w) and the **natural growth rate** (g_n). The actual growth rate is defined as

$$g = s/c \tag{5.2}$$

where s is the ratio of savings to national income (S/Y) and c is the *actual* incremental capital–output ratio, that is, the ratio of extra capital accumulation or investment to the flow of output ($\Delta K/\Delta Y = I/\Delta Y$). This expression for the actual growth rate (5.2) is by definition true since it expresses the accounting identity that savings equals investment. We can see this if we substitute the expressions for s and c into (5.2) – that is, $s/c = (S/Y)/(I/\Delta Y) = \Delta Y/Y$ given $S = I$, where $\Delta Y/Y$ measures the growth of output.

We need more than a definitional equation, however, to know whether the actual growth rate will provide the basis for steady advance in the future in the sense that it keeps plans to invest and plans to save in line with one another at full employment. This is where the concepts of the warranted rate of growth and the natural rate of growth become important.

Harrod defined the warranted rate of growth as

that rate of growth which, if it occurs, will leave all parties satisfied that they have produced neither more nor less than the right amount. Or, to state matters otherwise, it will put them into a frame of mind which will cause them to give such orders as will maintain the same rate of growth.

In other words, the warranted growth rate is the rate that induces just enough investment to match planned saving and therefore keeps capital fully employed (that is, there is no under-capacity or over-capacity), so that manufacturers are willing to carry on investment in the future at the same rate as in the past. How is this rate determined? Plans to save at any point in time are given by the Keynesian savings function:

$$S = sY \tag{5.3}$$

where s is the propensity to save. This gives the potential supply of investment goods. The demand for investment is given by the **acceleration principle** (or what Harrod calls 'the relation'), where c_r is the accelerator coefficient measured as the *required* amount of extra capital or investment to produce a unit flow of output at a given rate of interest, determined by technological conditions. Thus:

$$c_r = \Delta K_r/\Delta Y = I/\Delta Y \tag{5.4}$$

The demand for investment, given by the accelerator principle, is then

$$I = c_r \Delta Y \tag{5.5}$$

For planned saving to equal planned investment, therefore, we have

$$sY = c_r \Delta Y \tag{5.6}$$

and the required rate of growth for a moving equilibrium through time is

$$\Delta Y/Y = s/c_r = g_w \tag{5.7}$$

This is the warranted rate of growth, g_w. For dynamic equilibrium, output must grow at this rate. At this rate, expenditure on consumption goods will equal the production of consumption goods, and this is the only rate at which entrepreneurs will be satisfied with what they are doing, so that they do not revise their investment plans.

Now suppose there is a departure from this equilibrium rate. What happens? The condition for equilibrium is that $g = g_w$ or, from (5.2) and (5.7), that $gc = g_w c_r$. First suppose that the actual growth rate exceeds the warranted rate. It is easily seen that if $g > g_w$ then $c < c_r$, which means that actual investment falls below the level required to meet the increase in output. There will be a shortage of equipment, a depletion of stocks and an incentive to invest more. The actual growth rate will then depart even further from the warranted rate. Conversely, if the actual growth rate is less than the warranted rate, $g < g_w$, then $c > c_r$, and there will be a surplus of capital goods and investment will be discouraged, causing the actual growth rate to fall even further below the equilibrium rate. Thus, as Harrod points out, we have in the dynamic field a condition opposite to that in the static field. A departure from equilibrium, instead of being self-righting, will be self-aggravating. This is the short-term trade cycle problem in Harrod's growth model.

Roy Harrod

Born 1900, Norfolk, England. Died 1978. He spent all his academic career in Christ Church College, Oxford. One of Keynes's inner circle, who in the late 1930s made static Keynesian theory dynamic, and in doing so pioneered modern growth theory. One of the most original economists of the twentieth century who made important contributions to the theory of the firm, to international economics and to economic dynamics. Authored a book on inductive logic as well as the first biography of Keynes.

The American economist **Evesey Domar**, working independently of Harrod, also arrived at Harrod's central conclusion, although by a slightly different route. Domar recognized that investment is a double-edged sword: it both increases demand via the multiplier, and increases supply via its effect on expanding capacity. The question Domar asked, therefore, is what rate of growth of investment must prevail in order for supply to grow in line with demand (at full employment)? The crucial rate of growth of investment can be derived in the following way. A change in the level of investment increases demand by

$$\Delta Y_d = \Delta I/s \tag{5.8}$$

and investment itself increases supply by

$$\Delta Y_s = I\sigma \tag{5.9}$$

where σ is the productivity of capital or the flow of output per unit of investment ($\Delta Y/I$). For $\Delta Y_d = \Delta Y_s$ we must have

$$\Delta I/s = I\sigma \tag{5.10}$$

or

$$\Delta I/I = s\sigma \tag{5.11}$$

In other words, investment must grow at a rate equal to the product of the savings ratio and the productivity of capital. With a constant savings–investment ratio, this also implies output growth at the rate $s\sigma$. If $\sigma = 1/c_r$ (at full employment), then the Harrod–Domar result for equilibrium growth is the same.

But even if growth proceeds at the rate required for full utilization of the capital stock and a moving equilibrium through time, this still does not guarantee the full employment of labour, which depends on the natural rate of growth. The **natural growth rate** is derived from the identity $Y^* = L^*(Y/L)^*$, where Y^* is the potential level of output, L^* is the potential labour force and $(Y/L)^*$ is the potential level of labour productivity. Taking rates of change of the variables gives $y^* = l + \dot{q}$. The natural rate of growth (g_n) is therefore made up of two components: the growth of the potential labour force (l) and the growth of potential labour productivity ($\dot{q}$) (what Harrod called the rate of growth of the labour force in efficiency units) – both exogenously determined in the Harrod model.[4] The natural rate of growth plays an important role in Harrod's growth model in two ways. First it defines the rate of growth of productive capacity or the long-run full employment equilibrium growth rate. Second, it sets the upper limit to the actual growth rate, which brings cumulative expansion in the Harrod (trade cycle) model to a sticky end. If $g > g_w$, g can continue to diverge from g_w only until it hits g_n, when all available labour has been completely absorbed: g cannot be greater than g_n in the long run. The long-run question for an economy, then, is the relation between g_w and g_n; that is, the relation between the growth of capital and the growth of the labour force (measured in efficiency units). With fixed coefficients of production, the full employment of labour clearly requires $g = g_n$. The full employment of labour *and* capital requires

$$g = g_w = g_n \tag{5.12}$$

a state of affairs that the famous Cambridge economist Joan Robinson once called a 'golden age' to emphasize its mythical nature, because there is nothing in the Harrod model that would automatically generate this happy coincidence.

Let us now consider what happens if the warranted growth rate diverges from the natural rate. If $g_w > g_n$ there will be a chronic tendency towards depression because the actual rate of growth will never be sufficient to stimulate investment demand to match the amount of saving at full-employment equilibrium. There is too much capital and too much saving. This was the worry that economists had in the 1930s, particularly when it was predicted that the size of the population would fall in developed countries because the net reproduction rate had fallen below one (that is, females were not replacing themselves). If $g_w < g_n$, there will be a tendency towards demand inflation because there will be a tendency for the actual rate of growth to exceed that necessary to induce investment to match saving. Inflationary pressure, however, will be accompanied by growing unemployment of the structural variety because the growth of capital falls short of the growth of the effective labour force and there is no change in the techniques of production.

Where do the developing countries fit into this picture? In most developing countries the natural growth rate exceeds the warranted rate. If the population growth is, say, 2 per cent and labour productivity is growing at 3 per cent, this gives a rate of growth of the labour force in efficiency units of 5 per cent. If the net savings ratio is, say, 9 per cent and the required incremental capital–output ratio is 3, this gives a warranted growth rate of 3 per cent. This has two main consequences. First, it means that the effective labour force is growing faster than capital accumulation, which is part of the explanation for growing unemployment in developing countries. Second, it implies plans to invest greater than plans to save, and therefore inflationary pressure. If $g_n = 5$ per cent and $c_r = 3$, there will be profitable investment opportunities for 15 per cent saving, whereas actual saving is only 9 per cent.

The simultaneous existence of inflation and high unemployment in developing countries is therefore not a paradox. It can easily be explained within the framework and assumptions of the Harrod growth model, as can a great deal of development policy. Given the inequality $g_n \neq g_w$, or $1 + \dot{q} \neq s/c_r$, it can be seen that there are basically four ways in which g_n and g_w might be reconciled. If the problem is $g_n > g_w$, the first possibility is to reduce the rate of growth of the labour force. Measures to control population growth can be justified on these grounds, as a contribution to solving the problem of structural unemployment. Second, a reduction in the rate of growth of labour productivity would help, but this would of course reduce the growth of living standards of those in work. There is a clash here between employment and efficiency. Third, a rise in the savings ratio could narrow the gap. This is at the heart of monetary and fiscal reform in developing countries (see Chapter 13). Finally, the natural and warranted growth rates might be brought into line by a reduction in the required capital–output ratio through the use of more labour-intensive techniques. There is an active debate in developing countries over the appropriate choice of techniques, and whether developing countries could move towards the use of more labour-intensive techniques without impairing output and sacrificing saving (see Chapter 7).

All these adjustment mechanisms can be illustrated by a simple diagram (Figure 5.2).

Growth is measured on the vertical axis, and the investment and savings ratios on the horizontal axis. Growth and the investment ratio are related through c_r – the required incremental

Figure 5.2 Adjustment of g_w and g_n

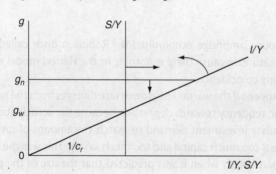

capital–output ratio. The savings ratio is independent of the growth rate. Figure 5.2 depicts a situation in which the natural growth rate (g_n) exceeds the warranted growth rate (g_w). To equalize g_n and g_w we can bring down g_n to g_w by measures to curb labour force growth; we can shift rightwards the S/Y curve through monetary and fiscal policies (and also by foreign borrowing) to raise g_w to g_n, or we can pivot the I/Y curve inwards by reducing c_r through the use of more labour-intensive techniques of production.

The Harrod framework is not only useful for understanding some of the development difficulties of developing countries, it is also useful for planning purposes. If a country sets a target rate of growth of, say, 5 per cent per annum and the required capital–output ratio is 3, it knows it must save and invest 15 per cent of GDP if the target growth rate is to be achieved. If domestic saving is less than 15 per cent of GDP there is an investment–savings gap to fill, which might be done by foreign borrowing (see Chapter 14).

At a theoretical level, there has been a great deal of discussion in the literature of whether *automatic* adjustment mechanisms might not come into play to reconcile the divergence between g_n and g_w. In the Harrod model, the parameters and variables that make up the model, l, $\dot{q}$, s and c_r, are all independently determined. Harrod himself recognized that in the long run the savings ratio may not be fixed, but will adjust. Specifically, in periods of recession, savings may fall, and in periods of demand inflation, savings may rise. One way this may come about is through a change in the functional distribution of income between wages and profits. This is a possible mechanism of adjustment emphasized by the **Keynesian economists of Cambridge, England**, represented by Joan Robinson, Nicholas Kaldor, Richard Kahn, Luigi Pasinetti and others. If $g_w > g_n$, and there is a tendency towards depression, this will tend to reduce the share of profits in national income and increase the share of wages, so that if the propensity to save out of profits is higher than the propensity to save out of wages, this change in the distribution of income will lower the overall savings ratio and reduce g_w towards g_n. There is a limit, however, to which the share of profits can fall, given by the minimum rate of profit acceptable to entrepreneurs. Likewise if $g_w < g_n$, and there is a tendency towards demand inflation, the share of profits in national income will tend to rise, increasing the overall savings ratio and raising g_w towards g_n. There is also a limit, however, to the rise in the profit share, set by the degree to which workers are willing to see their real wages reduced – what Joan Robinson called 'the inflation barrier' (see Chapter 13).

In contrast to the Cambridge, England, school of Keynesian (post-Keynesian) economists, in the USA a formidable group of **economists in Cambridge, Massachusetts**, represented by Robert Solow, Paul Samuelson, Franco Modigliani and others, developed at the same time in the 1950s the so-called neoclassical model of growth as an attack on both Harrod and the post-Keynesian school. They pointed out that the gloomy conclusions of Harrod concerning the possibility of achieving steady growth with full employment assume fixed coefficients of production, and that if the capital–labour ratio is allowed to vary there is the possibility of equilibrium growth at the natural rate. In other words, if capital grows faster than labour ($g_w > g_n$), economies will move smoothly via the price mechanism to more capital-intensive techniques, and growth in the long run will proceed at the exogenously given natural rate. Conversely, if labour grows faster than capital ($g_n > g_w$), the wage rate will fall relative to the price of capital, economies will adopt more labour-intensive techniques, and again growth will proceed at the natural rate.

One central feature of this neoclassical model, which has come under sustained attack in recent years from 'new' growth theory, is that investment does not matter for long-run growth. Any increase in the savings or investment ratio is offset by an increase in the capital–output ratio, because of diminishing returns to capital, leaving the long-run growth rate (at the natural rate) unchanged. The argument depends, however, on the productivity of capital falling (or c_r rising) as the capital–labour ratio rises. This is disputed by the 'new' growth theorists. If there are mechanisms to prevent the productivity of capital from falling as investment increases, then investment does matter for long-run growth and growth is *endogenous* in this sense. Before we turn to new growth theory and the important new studies of the macrodeterminants of growth, however, we need to consider the assumptions and predictions of neoclassical growth theory, and see how it has been used empirically for understanding the sources of growth in developed and developing countries.

Neoclassical growth theory

There are three basic propositions of neoclassical growth theory:

- In the long-run steady state, the growth of output is determined by the *rate of growth of the labour force in efficiency units*, that is, by the rate of growth of the labour force plus the rate of growth of labour productivity (exogenously given as in Harrod's natural rate of growth), and is independent of the ratio of saving and investment to GDP. This is so because a higher savings or investment ratio is offset by a higher capital–output ratio or lower productivity of capital, because of the neoclassical assumption of **diminishing returns to capital**.
- The *level* of per capita income (PCY), however, *does* depend on the ratio of saving and investment to GDP. The level of PCY varies positively with the savings–investment ratio and negatively with the rate of growth of the population.
- If there is an inverse relation across countries between the capital–labour ratio and the productivity of capital, and tastes (i.e. savings behaviour) and technology are the same across countries, poor countries with a small amount of capital per head should grow faster than rich countries with a lot of capital per head, leading to the *convergence* of per capita incomes and living standards across the world.

Let us now consider how these fundamental propositions are arrived at. The basic **neoclassical growth model** was first developed by Robert Solow and Trevor Swan in 1956,[5] and has been very influential in the analysis of growth ever since – particularly the use of the aggregate production function, as we shall see. The model is based on three key assumptions (ignoring for the moment technical progress).

- The labour force grows at a constant exogenous rate, l
- Output is a function of capital and labour: $Y = F(K, L)$; the production function relating output to inputs exhibits constant returns to scale, diminishing returns to individual factors of production, and has a unitary elasticity of substitution between factors (see later)
- All saving is invested: $S = I = sY$; there is no independent investment function.

What the basic neoclassical growth model is designed to show is that an economy will tend towards a long-run equilibrium capital–labour ratio (k^*) at which output (or income) per head (q^*) is also in equilibrium, so that output, capital and labour all grow at the same rate, l. The model therefore predicts long-run growth equilibrium at the natural rate.

Robert Solow

Born 1924, New York City, USA. He has spent all his academic career at the Massachusetts Institute of Technology. Famous for his pioneering work on the theory of economic growth and technical change with his 1956 paper 'A Contribution to the Theory of Economic Growth', which challenged the rigid Harrod model of long-run disequilibrium growth. Also made important contributions to mathematical economics, capital theory and macroeconomics. Received the Nobel Prize for Economics, 1987.

The most commonly used neoclassical production function with constant returns to scale is the so-called **Cobb–Douglas production function**:

$$Y = bK^{\alpha}L^{1-\alpha} \tag{5.13}$$

where α is the elasticity of output with respect to capital, $1-\alpha$ is the elasticity of output with respect to labour, and obviously $\alpha + (1-\alpha) = 1$, that is, a 1 per cent increase in K and L will lead to a 1 per cent increase in Y, which is what is meant by output exhibiting constant returns to scale.

Equation (5.13) can also be written in 'labour-intensive' form by dividing both sides of the equation by L to give output per head as a function of capital per head:

$$\frac{Y}{L} = \frac{bK^{\alpha}L^{1-\alpha}}{L} = b\left(\frac{K}{L}\right)^{\alpha} \tag{5.14}$$

or, for short

$$q = b(k)^{\alpha} \tag{5.15}$$

This is the 'labour-intensive' form of the neoclassical production function, and can be drawn as in Figure 5.3. The diminishing slope of the function represents the diminishing marginal product of capital.

Now impose a ray from the origin along which the rate of growth of capital is equal to the rate of growth of labour, so that the capital–labour ratio is constant and the capital–output ratio is constant. This is given by

$$q = (l/s)k \tag{5.16}[6]$$

where s is the savings ratio. This straight line from the origin with slope l/s shows the level of q that will keep capital per head constant, and the level of k that will keep output per head constant – given the rate of growth of the labour force, l. Superimposing equation (5.16) on Figure 5.3 gives Figure 5.4.

Figure 5.3   The 'labour-intensive' form of the neoclassical production function

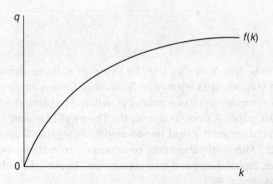

Figure 5.4   Equilibrium capital–labour ratio and output per head

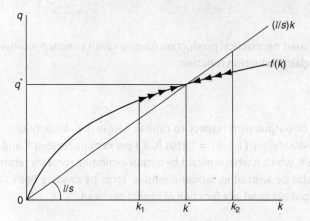

The slope of the ray from the origin to any point on the production function determines the capital–output ratio at that point. It is clear from Figure 5.4 that only where these two lines cross is an equilibrium capital–labour ratio (k^*) and output per head (q^*) defined. To the left of k^* (at k_1), where $q > (l/s)k$, q is greater than necessary to maintain k constant; that is, there is too much saving and capital accumulation relative to the growth of the labour force, and steady growth requires more capital-intensive techniques. There will be a movement from k_1 towards k^*. The capital–output ratio adjusts to bring the rate of growth of capital and labour (or the warranted and natural growth rates) into line. Similarly, to the right of k^* (at k_2), where $q < (l/s)k$, q is less than necessary to maintain k constant; there is too little saving and capital accumulation to keep pace with the rate of growth of the labour force, and steady growth requires more labour-intensive techniques. There will be a movement from k_2 towards k^*. Again, the capital–output ratio adjusts if there is a spectrum of techniques to choose from.

When k reaches an equilibrium, q also reaches an equilibrium, so output must be growing as fast as labour. Thus output, labour and capital must all be growing at the same rate, l, the natural rate of growth, with the capital–output ratio constant. This is the neoclassical story.

We can now see what happens if there is an increase in the ratio of savings and investment to national income (s). If s rises, this lowers the slope of the l/s line in Figure 5.4, *which increases the equilibrium level of* per capita *income and the capital–labour ratio, but leaves the equilibrium growth rate unchanged*. This demonstrates formally the first two basic propositions of neoclassical growth theory stated on p. 146. The reason a higher savings or investment ratio does not affect the long-run equilibrium growth rate is that a higher savings–investment ratio is offset by a higher capital–output ratio. The capital–output ratio adjusts 'passively' to keep the growth of capital in line with the growth of the labour force.

None of these conclusions is altered if technical progress is introduced into the model. If technical progress augments the productivity of labour only (so-called Harrod neutral technical progress, which leaves the capital–output ratio unchanged), the *effective* labour force now grows at the rate $l + \dot{q}$, where $\dot{q}$ is the rate of growth of labour productivity. Equation (5.16), which defines the relation between q and k that keeps the capital–labour ratio and capital–output ratio constant, now becomes:

$$q = \frac{l + \dot{q}}{s}k \qquad (5.17)$$

which means that in Figure 5.4 the l/s line becomes *steeper* because output per head must now be higher to provide the saving and capital accumulation required to keep the capital–labour ratio constant with faster growth of the effective labour force. At equilibrium k^* we now have $\Delta K/K = l + \dot{q}$, and at equilibrium q^* we have $\Delta Y/Y = l + \dot{q}$, so that $\Delta Y/Y = \Delta K/K = l + \dot{q}$, and output per head and capital per head grow at rate $\dot{q}$; that is, by the rate of Harrod neutral technical progress:

$$\Delta Y/Y - l = \Delta K/K - 1 = \dot{q} \qquad (5.18)$$

This is, of course, consistent with what we observe in the real world – output and capital grow faster than the rate of growth of the labour force. But a rise in the ratio of savings and investment to GDP still has no effect on the equilibrium growth of output, unless of course a higher level of investment raises the rate of growth of labour-augmenting technical progress, but this is ruled out by assumption in the neoclassical model, because technical progress is assumed to be exogenously determined.

It now only remains to demonstrate the third basic proposition of neoclassical growth theory: that poor countries should grow faster than rich countries, leading to the convergence of per capita incomes because poor countries with a low ratio of capital to labour will have a higher productivity of capital (or lower capital–output ratio). The capital–output ratio may be written as:

$$\frac{K}{Y} = \frac{K}{L} \cdot \frac{L}{Y} \qquad (5.19)$$

Given diminishing returns to capital (so that Y/L does not rise in the same proportion as K/L) it can be seen that a higher K/L ratio will be associated with a higher K/Y ratio. This means that if the ratio of savings and investment to GDP is the same across countries, capital-rich countries should grow slower than capital-poor countries. Note, however, that if there are *not* diminishing returns to capital, but, say, constant returns to capital, a higher capital–labour ratio will be exactly offset by a higher output–labour ratio, and the capital–output ratio will not be higher in capital-rich countries than in capital-poor countries, so convergence is not to be expected. If there are not diminishing returns to capital, this also means that the capital–output ratio will not rise as more investment takes place, and therefore **the ratio of saving and investment to GDP does**

matter for growth. Growth is endogenously determined in this sense; it is not simply exogenously determined by the rate of growth of the labour force and technical progress. This is the starting point for the 'new' (endogenous) growth theory, which seeks to explain why in practice living standards in the world economy have not converged (see Chapter 2), contrary to the predictions of neoclassical theory. The explanation offered by the new growth theory is that there are forces at work that prevent the marginal product of capital from falling (and the capital–output ratio from rising) as more investment takes place as countries get richer. Before turning to the new growth theory, however, let us first consider how the neoclassical production function can be used to analyse the sources of growth. This requires us to look more closely at the concept of the production function and the properties of the Cobb–Douglas production function, which is still widely used in the analysis of growth in both developed and developing countries.

The production function approach to the analysis of growth

We have already seen that there are several ways in which the growth of income or output of a country may be expressed, but frequently they consist of identities that tell us very little about the causes or sources of growth. For example, in the Harrod–Domar model, growth can be expressed as the product of the ratio of investment to GDP and the productivity of investment, so that by definition slow growth is the product of a low investment ratio and/or a low productivity of capital. By itself, however, this does not further much our understanding of the growth process in different countries. Why do some countries save and invest more than others, and why does the productivity of capital differ? Likewise, we have seen that the growth of output can be expressed as the sum of the rate of growth of the labour force and the rate of growth of labour productivity. By definition, slow growth is attributable to a slow rate of growth of the labour force and/or a slow rate of growth of labour productivity. Again, however, why does growth in labour productivity differ between countries? Is it because of differences in capital accumulation, or is it because of differences in technical progress, broadly defined to include such factors as improvements in the quality of labour, improvements in the quality of capital, economies of scale, advances in knowledge, a better organization of capital and labour in the productive process, and so on? Growth identities cannot distinguish between such competing hypotheses.

The production function approach to the analysis of growth is a response to this challenge. It takes the concept of the aggregate production function and attempts to disaggregate the sources of growth into the contribution of labour, capital, technical progress and any other variable included in the production function that is thought to influence the growth process. In this sense it is a very versatile approach. It is, however, a **supply orientated** approach. It does not tell us *why* the growth of capital, labour, technical progress and so on differs over time or between countries. The sources of growth are treated as *exogenous*. In practice, however, the supply of most resources to an economic system is endogenous, responding to the demand for them. Capital is a produced means of production and comes from the growth of output itself; labour is very elastic in supply from both internal and external sources (migration), and technical progress is itself partly dependent on the growth of output arising from static and dynamic returns to scale.

Thus while the production function approach can disaggregate any measured growth rate into various constituent growth-inducing sources, and can 'explain' growth rate differences in terms of these sources, it cannot answer the more fundamental question of why labour supply, capital accumulation and technical progress grow at different rates in different countries. The answer to this question must lie in differences in the strength of *demand* for countries' products, which in the early stages of development depends largely on the prosperity of agriculture (see Chapter 6), and in the later stages of development depends largely on the country's export performance relative to its import propensity (see Chapter 16).

Having said this, the production function approach can provide a useful **growth accounting** exercise, which is in fact widely used. Apart from deciding which determinants of growth to specify in the production function, and accurately measuring the independent variables, the main problem is a methodological one of fitting the appropriate production function to the data; that is, specifying the function relating output to inputs.

The production function

A desirable property of any macroeconomic hypothesis, apart from being consistent with the observed facts, is that it should be consistent with and derivable from microeconomic theory. What we call the **production function approach to the analysis of growth** in the aggregate possesses, in part, this desirable property in that it borrows the concept of the production function from the theory of the firm. Just as it can be said that, for a firm, output is a function of the factors of production – land, labour, capital and the level of technology (or factor efficiency) – so aggregate output can be written as a function of factor inputs and the prevailing technology:

$$Y = f(R, K, L, T) \tag{5.20}$$

where R is land, K is capital, L is labour and T is technology.[7]

The question is how to separate empirically the contribution to growth of the growth of factor inputs from other factors that can lead to higher output, included in T, such as economies of scale (due both to technical change and to increases in factor supplies), improvements in the quality of factor inputs, advances in knowledge, better organization of factors and so on. The task is to fit an appropriate, correctly specified production function that, if possible, will not only separate the contribution of factor inputs to growth from the contribution of increases in output per unit of inputs (increases in 'total' factor productivity), but will also distinguish between some of the factors that may contribute to increases in the productivity of factors, such as education, improvements in the quality of capital and economies of scale.

Before going on to discuss the types of function that may be employed, however, let us examine in a little more detail the properties of a production function. We have established so far that the aggregate production function expresses the functional relation between aggregate output and the stock of inputs. If land is subsumed into capital, and technology is held constant, we are left with two factors, and the production function may be drawn on a two-dimensional diagram, as in Figure 5.5. Capital (K) is measured on the vertical axis and labour (L) on the horizontal axis,

Figure 5.5   The production function

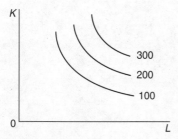

and each function represents a given level of output that can be produced with different combinations of capital and labour. The functions slope negatively from left to right on the assumption that marginal additions of either factor will increase total output – that is, factors have positive marginal products – and they are drawn convex to the origin on the assumption that factors have a diminishing marginal productivity as their supply increases, so that if one unit is withdrawn it needs to be substituted by more and more of the other factor to keep output constant. The position of the functions broadly reflects the level of technology. The more 'advanced' the technology, the greater the level of output per unit of total inputs, and the closer to the origin will be the production function representing a *given* output.

From the simple production function diagram it is easy to see how output may increase. First, there may be a physical increase in factor inputs, L and K, permitting a higher level of production. Either or both factors may increase. If only one factor increases, the movement to a higher production function will involve a change in the combination of factors, and output will not be able to increase forever, because ultimately the marginal product of the variable factor will fall to zero. This is illustrated in Figure 5.6, where, with a given stock of capital $0K_1$, output cannot increase beyond 300 with increases in the supply of labour ($0L_1$, $0L_2$ and so on) beyond the limit indicated. The diminishing productivity of the variable factor, labour, with capital fixed, is shown by the flatter and flatter slope of the production functions at successive points, L_1, L_2, until at the limit the production function is horizontal and the marginal product of labour is zero.

If both factors increase in supply, however, there is no reason why output should not go on increasing indefinitely. In fact, if both factors increase in supply there is a possibility that production may be subject to increasing returns, such that output rises more than proportionately to the increase in combined inputs. If this is the case, output per unit of total inputs will increase and the production functions representing equal additional amounts of production, for example 100, 200, 300 and so on, must be drawn closer and closer together, as in Figure 5.7.

Figure 5.6 Production function diagram

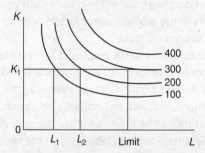

Figure 5.7 The effect of increasing returns

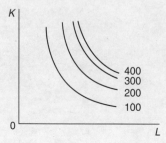

In the opposite case of decreasing returns, the functions would be drawn further and further apart. Finally, in the case of production subject to constant returns, the functions would be drawn equidistant from one another.

Increasing returns may also result from advances in technology, irrespective of increases in factor supplies. These are called **technological economies of scale**. In this case, increases in output per unit of input would have to be represented on a production function diagram either by re-labelling the functions or re-labelling the axes. That is, either the same amount of factor inputs, measured on the axes, would have to be shown to be producing a higher output than before, or the same output could be shown to be produced by lesser amounts of inputs. If the functions are re-labelled and not the axes, this is tantamount to a shift in all the production functions towards the origin. Shifts in the production function towards the origin are implied by all forms of technical progress or any factor that increases the productivity of the physical inputs.

In short, three broad sources of growth can be distinguished using the production function framework:

- Increases in factor supplies
- Increasing returns
- Technical progress, interpreted in the wide sense of anything that increases the productivity of factors other than increasing returns.

The Cobb–Douglas production function

The production function most commonly fitted to aggregate data to distinguish empirically between these three broad sources of growth has been the unconstrained form of the **Cobb–Douglas production function**, named after its two American originators, Charles Cobb (a mathematician) and Paul Douglas (an economist), who pioneered research in the area of applied economic growth in the 1920s and 1930s (Cobb and Douglas, 1928). The Cobb–Douglas function may be written as

$$Y_t = T_t K_t^{\alpha} L_t^{\beta} \tag{5.21}$$

where Y_t is real output at time, t, T_t is an index of technology, or 'total' productivity, K_t is an index of the capital stock, or capital services, at constant prices, L_t is an index of labour input (preferably man-hours), α is the partial elasticity (responsiveness) of output with respect to capital (holding labour constant), and β is the partial elasticity of output with respect to labour (holding capital constant).

It is assumed that changes in technology are exogenous and independent of changes in factor inputs, and that the effect of technical progress is neutral on the factor intensity of production (see p. 233 for a definition of neutral technical progress). T_t, α and β are constants to be estimated empirically if the function is unconstrained. If α and β are assigned values in advance of the use of the function for estimating purposes, the function is said to be constrained. Normally α and β will be less than unity on the assumption of diminishing marginal productivity of factors. The sum of the partial elasticities of output with respect to the factors of production gives the scale of returns, or the degree of homogeneity, of the function: $\alpha + \beta = 1$ represents constant returns, $\alpha + \beta > 1$ represents increasing returns, and $\alpha + \beta < 1$ represents decreasing returns, and the function is said to be homogeneous of degree one, greater than one, and less than one, respectively.

If α and β are not estimated empirically but are assumed to sum to unity, in which case the function will be constrained to constant returns, then increasing or decreasing returns will be reflected in the value of T_t, which is the index of total factor productivity. The existence of increasing returns would bias the value of T_t upwards, and decreasing returns would bias the value of T_t downwards. These points are made because in practice the Cobb–Douglas function is often employed in this constrained form with the sum of α and β put equal to unity. Then values are assigned to α and β according to the share of capital and labour in the national income. The underlying assumption is the perfectly competitive one that if production is subject to constant returns and factors are paid the value of their marginal products, then factor shares will reflect the elasticity of output with respect to each factor.[8]

In order to use (5.21) to separate the influence of the three broad sources of growth mentioned earlier, we must first make it operational by transforming it into *rate-of-growth* form. This can be done by taking logarithms of the variables and differentiating with respect to time, which gives:[9]

$$\frac{d \log Y_t}{dt} = \frac{d \log T_t}{dt} + \alpha \frac{d \log K_t}{dt} + \beta \frac{d \log L_t}{dt} \tag{5.22}$$

or

$$\frac{dY}{dt} \times \frac{1}{Y} = \left(\frac{dT}{dt} \times \frac{1}{T} \right) + \alpha \left(\frac{dK}{dt} \times \frac{1}{K} \right) + \beta \left(\frac{dL}{dt} \times \frac{1}{L} \right)$$

The above equations are in continuous time. The discrete approximation, taking annual rates of change of the variables, may be written as

$$r_Y = r_T + \alpha r_K + \beta r_L \tag{5.23}$$

where r_Y is the annual rate of growth of output per time period, r_T is the annual rate of growth of total productivity, or technical progress, r_K is the annual rate of growth of capital, r_L is the annual rate of growth of labour, and α and β are the partial elasticities of output with respect to capital and labour, respectively, as before.

In other words, equation (5.23) says that the rate of growth of output is equal to the sum of the rate of growth of 'total' productivity, the rate of growth of capital weighted by the partial elasticity of output with respect to capital and the rate of growth of labour weighted by the partial elasticity of output with respect to labour. With knowledge of r_y, r_K, r_L, α and β it becomes possible as a first step to separate out the contribution of factor inputs to growth from increases in output per unit of inputs represented by r_T. Now let us give an illustrative example. Suppose $r_Y = 5$ per cent per annum, $r_K = 5$ per cent per annum, $r_L = 1$ per cent per annum, $\alpha = 0.25$ and $\beta = 0.75$ (decided on the basis of factor shares). Substituting in (5.23) we have

$$5.0 = r_T + 0.25\,(5.0) + 0.75\,(1.0) \tag{5.24}$$

The contribution of capital to measured growth is $0.25\,(5.0) = 1.25$ percentage points; the contribution of labour is $0.75\,(1.0) = 0.75$ percentage points; and r_T is left as a residual with a contribution of 3.0 percentage points. If α and β were estimated empirically and there happened to be increasing returns ($\alpha + \beta > 1$), the significance of the factor contribution would be enhanced and r_T would be smaller.

On the assumption of constant returns to scale, the production function can also be estimated in its so-called labour-intensive form to analyse the **growth of output per head** (see (5.14)). If we subtract r_L from both sides of (5.23) and assume $\alpha + \beta = 1$, so that $\beta = 1 - \alpha$ we get

$$r_Y - r_L = r_T + \alpha\,(r_K - r_L) \qquad\qquad (5.25)$$

which means that the rate of growth of output per head (or labour productivity) is equal to the sum of the rate of growth of total productivity plus the rate of growth of capital per head times the elasticity of output with respect to capital. Taking the illustrative figures above, if $r_y = 5$ per cent and $r_L = 1$ per cent, then the rate of labour productivity growth is 4 per cent. Therefore

$$4.0 = r_T + 0.25\,(5.0 - 1.0) \qquad\qquad (5.26)$$

The contribution of capital per head (capital deepening) to productivity growth is 1 percentage point, leaving r_T with a contribution of 3 percentage points (as before).

Although r_T has been variously called technical progress, advances in knowledge and so on, by definition it is that portion of the growth of output not attributable to increases in the factors of production, and includes the effects not only of the multifarious factors that increase the productivity of labour and capital but also any measurement errors in the capital and labour input series . r_T is perhaps best described as a residual, or, perhaps more appropriately still, a 'coefficient of ignorance' if the analysis proceeds no further.

One important component of r_T, which can be considered the result of measurement errors, is likely to be the effect of **resource shifts** from less productive to more productive activities. Since the analysis is aggregative there is bound to be a confounding of changes in actual output with changes in the composition of output unless the weights used for aggregating inputs are continually revised. Resource shifts from agriculture to industry can be expected to figure prominently in any production function study of developing countries, as they do for studies of many advanced economies.

Limitations of the Cobb–Douglas function

Before considering some of the results of applying the Cobb–Douglas function to empirical data, we must briefly mention some of its limitations. Its use has come under attack on four main counts. First, since only one combination of factor inputs can be observed at any one time, there is an identification problem in attempting to distinguish shifts in the function (technical progress) from movements along the function (changes in factor intensity) unless the assumption of neutral technical progress is made. But technical progress may not be neutral and therefore the effects of technical progress and changing factor intensity become confused, biasing the results of the contribution of factor inputs and technical progress to growth.

Second, the assumption that technical progress is independent of increases in factor inputs has been questioned. This is not a specification error of the function itself, however, and the Cobb–Douglas function can be used, making technical progress a function of the rate of growth of inputs – so-called endogenous models of technical progress.

Third, the Cobb–Douglas function possesses the restrictive property of constant unitary elasticity of substitution between factors, whatever the factor intensity.[10] The assumption of constant elasticity means that the function cannot represent a change in the ease of substitution between capital and labour. The assumption of unitary elasticity may be serious if the elasticity of substitution of factors differs significantly from unity and there are wide discrepancies in the growth rate of factors. For example, if the elasticity of substitution between capital and labour is significantly less than unity, and capital grows faster than labour, this will result in an overestimate of the contribution of capital to growth and an underestimate of the role of other factors. The intuitive explanation of this bias is that the smaller the elasticity of substitution the more difficult it is in practice to obtain increased output just by increasing one factor, because diminishing returns set in strongly. By assuming the elasticity is higher than it is, the importance of the fastest-growing factor is exaggerated. If elasticity is high, diminishing returns are not a problem, and if both capital and labour expand at the same rate, growth is obviously independent of the elasticity of substitution.[11]

A final criticism relates to the measurement of output and inputs. What, argue some, is the meaning of a function that aggregates so many heterogeneous items; in particular, what is the meaning of an aggregation of capital goods built at different times, at different costs and with varying productivities? How are such capital goods to be equated and added in an aggregate measure of capital?

By and large, most of the above-mentioned criticisms are theoretical worries, the practical significance of which is hard to determine. Studies of the nature of technical progress, at least in advanced countries, suggest that the assumption of neutrality is a fair working hypothesis. The fact that technical progress may be dependent on factor accumulation can be accommodated within the Cobb–Douglas framework. Capital and labour would have to grow at very different rates for the elasticity of substitution to matter very much, but in any case studies show that it is quite close to unity. Finally, although the aggregation of heterogeneous outputs and inputs can present severe problems, especially the aggregation of capital, which cannot be measured directly in physical units, there are techniques of aggregation available that various studies have used with some success.

Application of the Cobb–Douglas function

What have been the results of applying the Cobb–Douglas function to empirical data? First, let us consider its application in developed countries and consider the conclusions that emerge. We can start with the pioneering work of Cobb and Douglas themselves. Ironically, the Cobb–Douglas function, as first conceived, was not intended as a device for distinguishing the sources of growth but as a test of neoclassical marginal productivity theory; that is, to see whether elasticities of output with respect to labour and capital corresponded to factor shares. Douglas had observed that the output curve for US manufacturing industry for the period 1899–1922 lay consistently between the two curves for the factors of production, and he suggested to his mathematician friend, Cobb, that they should seek to develop a formula that could measure the relative effect of labour and capital on the growth of output over the period in question. This story is described by Douglas (1948) in his fascinating review article 'Are There Laws of Production?' As an insight into the inductive method the relevant passage is worth quoting in full:

> Having computed indexes for American manufacturing of the number of workers employed by years from 1899 to 1922 as well as indexes of the amounts of fixed capital in manufacturing deflated to dollars of approximately constant purchasing power, and then plotting these on a log scale, together with the Day index of physical production for manufacturing, I observed that the product curve lay consistently between the two curves for the factors of production and tended to be approximately one-quarter of the relative distance between the curve of the index for labour, which showed the least increase in the period, and that of the index of

capital which showed the most. I suggested to my friend Charles Cobb that we seek to develop a formula which could measure the relative effect of labour and capital upon product during this period. At his suggestion the sum of the exponents was tentatively made equal to unity in the formula $Y = TK^{\alpha}L^{1-\alpha}$ [our notation] . . . The fact that on the basis of fairly wide studies there is an appreciable degree of uniformity, and that the sum of the exponents approximates to unity, fairly clearly suggests that there are laws of production which can be approximated by inductive studies and that we are at least approaching them.

(Douglas, 1948, p. 20)

The estimated function derived was $Y = 1.01K^{0.25}L^{0.75}$, which lent support to the neoclassical model of constant returns and marginal product pricing. There was no discussion of the relative importance of factors of production and the T variable in accounting for measured growth. It was not until Abramovitz (1956) and Solow (1957) showed that 80–90 per cent of the growth of output per head in the US economy in the first half of the twentieth century could not be accounted for by increases in capital per head that the production function started to be used in earnest as a technique in the applied economics of growth. Abramovitz (1956, p. 11) remarked that:

This result is surprising in the lop-sided importance which it appears to give to productivity increase and it should be, in a sense, sobering, if not discouraging to students of economic growth. Since we know little about the causes of productivity increase, the indicated importance of this element may be taken to be some sort of measure of our ignorance about the causes of economic growth in the USA, and some sort of indication of where we need to concentrate our attention.

Abramovitz's findings were supported by Solow, who found, when examining the data for the non-farm sector of the US economy for the period 1919–57, that approximately 90 per cent of the growth of output per head could not be accounted for by increases in capital per head; that is, using the notation in (5.25):

$$r_T/(r_y - r_L) = 0.90 \tag{5.27}$$

The findings of Abramovitz and Solow disturbed economists brought up in the belief that investment and capital accumulation played a crucial role in the growth process. Even allowing for the statistical difficulties of computing a series of the capital stock, and the limitations of the function applied to the data (for example, the assumption of constant returns and neutral technical progress, plus the high degree of aggregation), it was difficult to escape from the conclusion that the growth of the capital stock was of relatively minor importance in accounting for the growth of total output.

It would not be misleading to say that much of the subsequent research effort in this field of growth was designed (even before the advent of new growth theory) to reverse this conclusion, or rather to 'assign back' to the factors of production sources of growth that make up the residual factor but are interrelated with, or dependent on, the growth of factor inputs. Work has proceeded on two fronts. On the one hand, attempts have been made to disaggregate the residual factor, measuring factor inputs in the conventional way; on the other hand, attempts have been made to adjust the labour and capital input series for such things as changes in the *quality* of factors and their composition, so that much more measured growth is seen to be attributable to increases in factor inputs in the first place. For example, the labour input series has been adjusted for improvements in its quality due to the growth of education, and for changes in its composition due to age/sex shifts. Likewise the capital stock series has been adjusted to reflect changes in its composition and, more importantly, to allow for the fact that new additions to the capital stock in any line of production are likely to be more productive than the existing capital stock as a result of technical advance. This is the notion of **embodied** or **endogenous technical change** as opposed to the exogenous technical change assumption of the original Cobb–Douglas function, which assumes that all vintages of capital share equally in technical progress.

A distinction is made, therefore, between embodied and disembodied technical progress – embodied technical progress refers to technical improvements that can only be introduced into the productive system by new investment, and disembodied technical progress is exogenous and not dependent on capital accumulation. There are several ways in which embodied technical progress can be isolated from the residual factor by appropriate adjustments to the capital stock series to reflect the greater productivity of the latest investments. The net result is to enhance the role of capital accumulation in the growth process.

Efforts have also been made to overcome one of the problems associated with the aggregation of outputs by taking explicit account of shifts of labour and capital from low-productivity to high-productivity sectors. This, too, reduces the significance of the residual factor and makes the role of labour and capital in the growth process look correspondingly more important.

Since Abramovitz and Solow reported their findings in 1956 and 1957, a substantial body of empirical evidence relating to the sources of growth has accumulated, experimenting with different specifications of the aggregate production function. Unfortunately, it is not systematic. The time periods taken, the data used, the sectors of the economy examined and the methodology employed all vary within and between countries.

Until recently most of the evidence available pertained to fairly advanced economies and it is largely from this evidence, wisely or not, that conclusions have been drawn on development strategy for developing countries. Research in developing countries has been hampered by a shortage of reliable empirical data and perhaps an even greater suspicion of the aggregate production function, and its implicit assumptions, than in developed countries. The assumption that factor shares can be used as weights to measure the relative contribution of labour and capital to growth is probably more dubious in developing countries than in developed countries. The price of labour almost certainly exceeds its marginal product, while the price of capital falls short of it so that the share of income going to labour exceeds the elasticity of output with respect to labour and the share of income going to capital understates the elasticity of output with respect to capital. Second, the aggregation of inputs and outputs is generally more difficult, and there are greater problems of resource underutilization to contend with. The recent past, however, has witnessed a number of production function studies for developing countries.

Production function studies of developing countries

Two of the early production function studies of the sources of growth in developing countries are by Maddison (1970) and Robinson (1971) (surveyed, with others, by Nadiri, 1972). More recent studies include Shaaeldin (1989), World Bank (1991), Young (1995), Hu and Khan (1997), Felipe (1999), Senhadji (2000) and Sala-í-Martin (1997), who surveys other studies. Let us consider these studies and bring out their major conclusions, especially any important contrasts with the conclusions from studies of developed countries.

The major conclusions of the early production function studies of developing countries were:

- Capital accumulation is more important as a source of growth than total productivity growth, and more important than in developed countries.
- Improvements in the *quality* of labour are important through better health, nutrition and education.
- Resource shifts are not so important as might have been expected, perhaps due to the general surplus of labour in developing countries and the low capacity to absorb labour into productive employment in the industrial sector.

Now let us turn to the more recent studies. Shaaeldin (1989) fits equation (5.23) to the industrial sector of four African countries, and shows that between the mid-1960s and the early 1980s total factor productivity growth was *negative* in three of the countries as the result of severe macro-recession. The results are shown in Table 5.1 and confirm the overwhelming importance of the contribution of capital formation to the growth process.

Table 5.2 provides the results of a World Bank study for the period 1960–87, showing the contribution of factor inputs and total productivity growth to the growth of output in various continents. It is clear that the major source of growth is not productivity growth, but the growth of inputs themselves.

Young (1995) has used the production function model to debunk the idea that there has been a 'growth miracle' in the four East Asian countries of Hong Kong, Singapore, South Korea and Taiwan (the so-called 'four little dragons'). Young uses the production function approach and shows that while the growth of output was spectacular over the 1966–90 period, most of

Table 5.1 Contribution of factor inputs and total productivity growth to industrial growth in Kenya, Tanzania, Zambia and Zimbabwe, 1964–81

	Growth of output (% p.a)	Contribution of labour	Contribution of capital	Total productivity growth
Kenya 1964–83	7.99	1.99	6.89	−0.89
Tanzania 1966–80	8.06	3.16	5.41	−0.51
Zambia 1965–80	4.98	1.20	9.38	−6.60
Zimbabwe 1964–81	5.28	1.88	3.39	+0.03

Source: Shaaeldin, 1989.

Table 5.2 Contribution of factor inputs and total productivity growth to economic growth in 68 developing countries, 1960–87

	GDP growth (% p.a.)	Contribution of labour	Contribution of capital	TFP
Africa	3.3	1.0	2.3	0.0
East Asia	6.8	1.1	3.8	1.9
Europe, Middle East and North Africa	5.0	0.7	2.9	1.4
Latin America	3.6	1.2	2.4	0.0
South Asia	4.4	0.9	2.9	0.6
68 Economies	4.2	1.0	2.6	0.6

Source: World Bank, 1991.

Table 5.3 Growth of output and total factor productivity in the East Asian 'dragons', 1966–90 (%)

	Output growth	Total factor productivity growth
Hong Kong	7.3	2.3
Singapore	8.7	0.2
South Korea	8.5	1.7
Taiwan	8.5	2.1

Source: Young, 1995.

the growth can be accounted for by the rapid growth of factor inputs and there was nothing abnormal about the growth of total factor productivity. Table 5.3 presents the figures. Young describes such calculations as 'the tyranny of numbers', by which he means that there is nothing special to explain. On the basis of Young's calculations, Krugman (1994) has described the 'Asian miracle' as a myth. The spectacular growth of inputs, however, does need explaining. The rapid growth of capital and labour is a function of an internal dynamism fuelled by the relentless and successful drive for export markets, partly engineered by deliberate government intervention. East Asia is not the bastion of free market enterprise that is often portrayed. The growth of factor inputs may decelerate in the future, but the performance of these four economies up to 1990 was indeed remarkable, notwithstanding the relatively low rate of growth of total factor productivity.

Hu and Khan (1997) use the production function[12] approach to understand the sources of fast growth in China over the period 1953–94, and the acceleration of growth after the economic reforms and 'open door' policy were introduced in 1978. From 1953 to 1978, GDP grew at 5.8 per cent per annum, and then accelerated to 9.3 per cent per annum from 1979 to 1994. Why was this? To estimate the contribution of labour, capital and total factor productivity (TFP) to measured growth over the periods, factor shares of GDP are taken as the elasticities of output with respect to labour and capital, with labour's elasticity approximately 0.4, and capital's elasticity approximately 0.6. The results are shown in Table 5.4.

To give an example, in the pre-reform period 1953–78, the growth of capital was 6.2 per cent per annum. Multiplying 6.2 by 0.6 (capital's elasticity) gives a contribution of capital to growth of 3.72 percentage points which is approximately 65 per cent of the total growth of output of 5.8 per cent. Capital accumulation was by far the most important contributor to growth in this period. In the post-reform period 1979–94, however, it can be seen that the contribution of productivity growth increases considerably to almost equal importance with capital. The rate of

Table 5.4 Sources of growth in China, 1953–94 (%)

	1953–94	1953–78	1979–94
Output growth	7.2	5.8	9.3
Capital input growth	6.8	6.2	7.7
Labour input growth	2.6	2.5	2.7
TFP growth	2.1	1.1	3.9
Contribution of capital	55.6	65.2	45.6
Contribution of labour	14.9	16.8	12.8
Contribution of productivity growth	29.5	18.0	41.6

Source: Hu and Khan, 1997.

growth of TFP more than triples, from 1.1 per cent per annum to 3.9 per cent, contributing over 40 per cent to measured growth. According to Hu and Khan, the process of reform stimulated productivity growth in a number of ways, including the transfer of resources from agriculture to industry; a reallocation of resources from the public to the private sector; the encouragement of foreign direct investment (FDI), and a faster growth of exports.

Felipe (1999) surveys the studies done of TFP growth in the whole of East Asia, most of which use the production function approach. He is critical of many of them, and shows how estimates of TFP can vary according to the time period taken, the estimates made of the growth of factor inputs and the assumed elasticities of output with respect to labour and capital. Remember that TFP is obtained as a residual after the contribution of the factor inputs has been calculated. The various methodological and conceptual problems associated with the use of production functions discussed earlier are also emphasized, particularly the assumption that technical progress and factor inputs are exogenous and not interrelated.

The most comprehensive recent study of the sources of growth using the aggregate production function comes from Senhadji (2000) at the IMF. He estimates production functions for 66 countries over the period 1960–94 (including 46 developing countries) of the form: $Y = TK^{\alpha}(LH)^{1-\alpha}$ where T is TFP, K is the stock of capital, L is the active population and H is an index of human capital. The function is estimated using both levels of the variables (measured in logarithms) and taking first differences of the log level (i.e. in rate of growth form – see (5.22)). The estimates of the elasticity of output with respect to capital (α) vary considerably across countries (and regions) and also according to whether levels or first differences of the variables are used (which is another problem!). Using levels, the estimates of (α) range from 0.43 in sub-Saharan Africa to 0.63 in the Middle East and North Africa. Using first differences, the estimates of α range from 0.30 in East Asia to 0.62 in Latin America. Using the mean value of α from the equations estimated in levels gives the sources of growth in different regions shown in Table 5.5.

It can be seen again from Table 5.5 that capital accumulation is by far the most important contributor to measured growth in all the regions. The small contribution of TFP in the fastest-growing region of East Asia confirms the conclusions of Young. Notice also, the *negative* contribution of TFP in Africa (which supports Shaaeldin's results), and also in Latin America. Human capital formation makes a positive contribution to growth in all regions, but a relatively minor one.

It is satisfying that the conclusions from a wide range of studies using different techniques and dubious data should all point in roughly the same direction. First, the major source of growth in developing countries is increased factor inputs, aided by improvements in the quality of labour through health improvement and education. Second, the growth of 'total' factor productivity in

Table 5.5   Sources of growth by region of the world, 1960–94

Region	Output growth (%)	Contribution (percentage points) of:			
		Capital	Labour	Human capital	TFP
East Asia	6.49	4.50	1.27	0.44	0.28
South Asia	4.66	2.87	0.99	0.25	0.55
Sub-Saharan Africa	2.83	1.79	1.39	0.22	−0.56
Middle East & North Africa	5.05	3.99	0.84	0.25	−0.03
Latin America	3.42	2.31	1.22	0.28	−0.39

Source: Senhadji, 2000.

developing countries is relatively slow compared with that in developed countries, which may be partly a reflection of the different stage of development reached. Third, resource transfers from agriculture to industry are quite important as a source of growth, but not as important as one might have expected. They will become more important as the ability of the industrial sector to absorb surplus labour increases.

Before ending it should be said again that the aggregate models that produced the above results are rough tools. They do, however, give an important idea of the forces at work and a rough idea of the likely quantitative significance of different factors. The production function approach is also a very versatile tool of analysis. Sala-í-Martin (1997) has surveyed a number of production function studies and found that researchers have included at least 62 different variables in the production function to explain growth, in addition to the growth of capital and labour!

'New' (endogenous) growth theory and the macrodeterminants of growth[13]

Since the mid-1980s there has been an outpouring of literature and research on the applied economics of growth, attempting to understand and explain the differences in the rates of output growth and per capita income growth across the world, many inspired by the so-called 'new' growth theory, or endogenous growth theory. This spate of cross-sectional studies seems to have been prompted by a number of factors:

- Increased concern with the economic performance of the poorer regions of the world, and particularly the striking differences between countries and continents
- The increased availability of standardized data (e.g. Summers and Heston, 1991 and *World Development Indicators* from the World Bank), enabling more reliable econometric work
- Pioneering studies (e.g. Baumol, 1986) that could find no convergence of per capita incomes in the world economy, contrary to the prediction of neoclassical growth theory based on the assumption of diminishing returns to capital, which, given identical preferences and technology across countries, should lead to faster growth in poor countries than in rich ones.

It is the latter finding (although hardly new, as outlined in Chapter 2) that has been the major inspiration behind the development of the 'new' growth theory, which relaxes the assumption of diminishing returns to capital and shows that, with constant or increasing returns, there can be no presumption of the convergence of per capita incomes across the world, or of individual countries reaching a long-run steady-state growth equilibrium at the natural rate. If there are not diminishing returns to capital, investment is important for long-run growth and growth is endogenous in this sense. In these 'new' models of endogenous growth, pioneered by Robert Lucas (1988) and Paul Romer (1986, 1990), there are assumed to be positive externalities associated with human capital formation (for example, education and training) and research and development (R&D) that prevent the marginal product of capital from falling and the capital–output ratio from rising. We have a production function in capital of

$$Y = AK^{\alpha} \tag{5.28}$$

where K is a composite measure of capital (i.e. physical capital plus other types of reproducible capital), and $\alpha = 1$. This is the so-called **AK model** of new growth theory. As Barro and Sala-í-Martin (1995) put it, 'the global absence of diminishing returns may seem unrealistic, but the idea becomes more plausible if we think of K in a broad sense to include [for example] human capital'. It can be seen from the expression for the capital–output ratio, that is

$$\frac{K}{Y} = \frac{K}{L} \cdot \frac{L}{Y} \qquad (5.29)$$

that anything that raises the productivity of labour (Y/L) in the same proportion as K/L will keep the capital–output ratio constant. Learning by doing and embodied technical progress in the spirit of Arrow (1962) and Kaldor (1957), as well as technological spillovers from trade (Grossman and Helpman, 1990, 1991) and FDI (de Mello, 1996), are other possibilities in addition to education and research and development.

The first crude test of the 'new' growth theory is to see whether or not poor countries do grow faster than rich ones, or in other words to see whether there is an inverse relation between the growth of output (or output per head) and the *initial* level of per capita income. If there is, this would provide support for the neoclassical model. If there is not, this would support the new growth theory's assertion that the marginal product of capital does not decline. The equation to be estimated is

$$g_i = a + b_1 (PCY)_i \qquad (5.30)$$

where g_i is the average growth of output per head of country i over a number of years and PCY_i is its initial level of per capita income. A significantly negative estimate of b_1 would be evidence of **unconditional convergence**, or **beta (β) convergence** as it is called in the literature; that is, poor countries growing faster than rich without allowing for any other economic, social or political differences between countries. As we saw in Chapter 2, none of the studies taking large samples of developed and developing countries has been able to find evidence of unconditional convergence. The estimate of b_1 is not significantly negative; in fact it is invariably positive, indicating divergence.[14]

Before jumping to the conclusion that this is a rejection of the neoclassical model, however, it must be remembered that the neoclassical prediction of convergence assumes that the savings or investment ratio, population growth, technology and all factors that affect the productivity of labour are the same across countries. Since these assumptions are manifestly false, there can never be the presumption of unconditional convergence (even if there are diminishing returns to capital), only **conditional convergence**, holding constant all other factors that influence the growth of per capita income, including population growth (p), the investment ratio (I/Y) and variables that affect the productivity of labour, for example education (ED), research and development expenditure ($R+D$), trade (T) and even non-economic variables such as political stability measured by the number of revolutions and coups (PS). The equation to be estimated is therefore

$$g_i = a + b_1(PCY)_i + b_2(p)_i + b_3(I/Y)_i + b_4(ED)_i$$
$$+ b_5(R+D)_i + b_6(T)_i + b_7(PS)_i + \ldots \qquad (5.31)$$

and the question to be asked is what happens to the sign of the initial per capita income variable (PCY) when these other variables are introduced into the equation? If the sign turns negative ($b_1 < 0$) when allowance is made for these other factors, this is supposed to represent a rehabilitation of the neoclassical model (see Barro, 1991); that is, there *would be* convergence if it were not for differences between rich and poor countries in all these other important variables in the growth process. 'New' growth theory would be supported by finding that education, research and development expenditure and so on matter, and it is these factors that keep the marginal product of capital from falling, producing actual divergence in the world economy. A very good empirical illustration of what we have been talking about is given in Table 2.8 (Chapter 2, p. 65).

Note here that if the model of 'new' growth theory is represented by the *AK* model, as in (5.28), this can be shown to be equivalent to the Harrod–Domar growth equation. Assuming $\alpha = 1$, totally differentiate (5.28) and divide by Y. This gives

$$dY/Y = A(dK/Y) = A(I/Y) \qquad (5.32)$$

where dY/Y is the growth rate, I/Y is the investment ratio, and A is the productivity of capital (dY/I) which is the reciprocal of the incremental capital–output ratio. This is the same as the Harrod growth equation $g = s/c$, where s is the savings ratio and c is the incremental capital–output ratio, or the Domar equation $g = s\sigma$, where σ is the productivity of capital.

If the productivity of capital was the same across countries, there would be a perfect correlation between the growth rate of countries and the investment ratio where the slope of the relationship is the reciprocal of the incremental capital–output ratio (c). If there is not a perfect correlation, then by definition, the productivity of capital, or the capital–output ratio, must differ between countries. 'New' growth theory equations that attempt to explain growth rate differences between countries (such as (5.31) – and see empirical studies later) are really asking the question (and hopefully answering it!) why does the productivity of capital differ between countries (assuming I/Y is included in the equations)?

We said above that evidence of **conditional convergence** delights the neoclassical economists because it is interpreted as a rehabilitation of the neoclassical growth model with diminishing returns, but this may be a hasty judgement. Outside the neoclassical paradigm there is another distinct body of literature that argues that economic growth *should be* inversely related to the initial level of per capita income because the more backward the country, the greater the scope for '**catch-up**'; that is, for absorbing a backlog of technology (see Gomulka, 1971, 1990; Abramovitz, 1986; Dowrick and Nguyen, 1989; Dowrick and Gemmell, 1991; Amable, 1993). Thus the negative sign on the per capita income variable could be picking up the effect of catch-up, and the notion of catch-up is conceptually distinct from the *shape* of the production function and whether or not there are diminishing returns to capital. How are the two effects to be distinguished? Also, output growth will be a function of the stage of development because of sectoral differences in the productivity growth rates of agriculture, industry and services, so that convergence may also be partly 'structural', independent of both diminishing returns and catch-up (see Cornwall and Cornwall, 1994). This adds further complications to the interpretation of the coefficient relating country growth rates to the initial level of per capita income.

Now let us turn to the question of the capital–output ratio. Non-diminishing returns to capital, or constancy of the capital–output ratio, lie at the heart of 'new' growth theory, as pioneered by Lucas and Romer who emphasize externalities to education and research. For the historical record, however, it should be mentioned that, many years ago the famous Cambridge economist Nicholas Kaldor pointed out the fact that despite continued capital accumulation and increases in capital per head through time, the capital–output ratio remains broadly the same, implying some form of externalities or constant returns to capital. It is worth quoting Kaldor in full:

> As regards the process of economic change and development in capitalist societies, I suggest the following 'stylised facts' as a starting point for the construction of theoretical models . . . (4) steady capital–output ratios over long periods; at least there are no clear long-term trends, either rising or falling, if differences in the degree of capital utilisation are allowed for. This implies, or reflects, the near identity in the percentage rate of growth of production and of the capital stock i.e. for the economy as a whole, and over long periods, income and capital tend to grow at the same rate.
>
> (Kaldor, 1961)

Kaldor's explanation (as a critique of the neoclassical production function) lay in his innovation of the **technical progress function**, which relates the rate of growth of output per worker ($\dot{q}$) to the rate of growth of capital per worker ($\dot{k}$) as depicted in Figure 5.8.

The position of the function depends on the exogenous rate of technical progress, and the slope of the function depends on the extent to which technical progress is embodied in capital. Along the 45° line the capital–output ratio is constant, and the equilibrium growth of output per head will be at $\dot{q}^*$. An upward shift of the technical progress function – associated, for example, with new discoveries, a technological breakthrough or more education – will shift the curve upwards, causing the growth of output to exceed the growth of capital, raising the rate of profit and inducing more investment to give a new equilibrium growth of output per worker at q_1^*. An increase in capital accumulation *without* an associated upward shift in the schedule will cause the capital–output ratio to rise. 'New' growth theory is precisely anticipated. Kaldor's technical progress function is the true progenitor of endogenous growth theory.

Figure 5.8   Kaldor's technical progress function

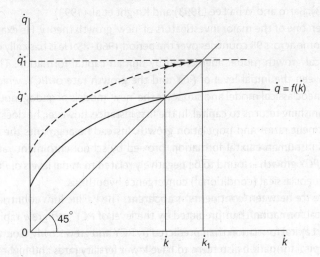

What applies to countries through time applies, *pari passu*, to different countries at a point in time, with differences in growth rates at the same capital–output ratio being associated with different technical progress functions. To quote Kaldor again:

> A lower capital–labour ratio does not necessarily imply a lower capital–output ratio – indeed, the reverse is often the case. The countries with the most highly mechanised industries, such as the USA, do not require a higher ratio of capital to output. The capital–output ratio in the USA has been falling over the past 50 years whilst the capital–labour ratio has been steadily rising; *and it is lower in the United States today than in the manufacturing industries of many underdeveloped countries.*
>
> (Kaldor, 1972, emphasis added)

In other words, rich and poor countries are simply not on the same production function.

Empirical studies

In this section we survey six pioneer studies of inter-country growth rate differences that have been inspired by 'new' growth theory. A summary of the studies is given in Table 5.6. Before turning to the individual studies, it may be mentioned from the outset that only four variables seem to be robust in the sense that they remain statistically significant regardless of what other variables are included in the equation. Consider an equation of the form:

$$Y = b_i I + b_m M + b_z Z + \mu \tag{5.33}$$

where *I* is a set of variables always in the regression, *M* is the variable of interest, and *Z* is a subset of variables added to the regression. As a first step, estimate the regression with the *I* variables (for example, *PCY*) and the variable of interest (say, investment). Then add up to three other variables and observe the significance of the variable of interest. If the variable remains significant without changing its sign, the variable is regarded as robust. Otherwise it is 'fragile'. The only robust variables found in the majority of studies are the ratio of savings and investment to GDP, population growth, the initial level of per capita income, and investment in human capital measured by the secondary school enrolment rate. All other variables are fragile.

The six studies surveyed are Barro (1991), Mankiw et al. (1992), Levine and Renelt (1992), Levine and Zervos (1993), Barro and Wha Lee (1993) and Knight et al. (1993).

Robert Barro has been one of the major investigators of 'new' growth theory. He examines the growth of per capita income across 98 countries over the period 1960–85. He is basically interested in testing the neoclassical growth model augmented by human capital formation. There is no significant relation between the initial level of *PCY* and the growth rate of *PCY*, which on the surface contradicts the neoclassical model and supports the 'new' models of endogenous growth, which assume non-diminishing returns to capital. In the first instance, however, he does not allow for differences in investment ratios and population growth. Instead he augments the model by allowing for differences in human capital formation, proxied by school enrolment ratios. With this additional variable, *PCY* growth is found to be negatively related to initial levels of *PCY* which, he argues, supports the neoclassical (conditional) convergence hypothesis.

An interesting difference between 'continents' is apparent. The Pacific Rim countries in 1960 had higher human capital formation than predicted by the level of *PCY* and grew rapidly, while Africa had lower human capital formation than predicted by PCY and grew slowly. Countries with high ratios of human capital formation also seem to have lower fertility rates and higher ratios of physical investment to GDP, which means that the human capital variable is likely to be picking up differences in population growth and investment ratios.

Table 5.6 The macrodeterminants of growth

Study	Dependent variable	Convergence	Savings – investment ratio	Population growth	Education	Government consumption distortions	Political instability	Monetary and fiscal variables	Trade variables	Inflation
Barro (1991)[1]	Growth of per capita income	Conditional	Not considered	Not considered	Significant (+)	Significant (−)	Not considered	Not considered	Not considered	Not considered
Mankiw et al. (1992)[2]	Level of per capita income	Conditional	Significant (+)	Significant (−)	Significant (+)	Not considered	Not considered	Not considered	Not considered	Not considered
Knight et al. (1993)[3]	Growth of output per worker	Conditional	Significant (+)	Significant (−)	Significant (+)	Not considered	Not considered	Not considered	Significant (+)	Not considered
Barro and Wha Lee (1993)[4]	Growth of per capita income	Conditional	Significant (+)	Not considered	Significant (+)	Significant (−)	Significant (−)	Not considered	Not considered	Not considered
Levine and Renelt (1992)[5]	Growth of per capita income	Conditional	Significant (+)	Not robust	Significant (+)	Not robust	Not robust	Not robust	Not robust	Not robust
Levine and Zervos (1993)[6]	Growth of per capita income	Conditional	Not considered	Not considered	Significant (+)	Not considered	Significant (−)	Weak	Weak	Not significant

Notes:

[1] 98 countries, 1960–85.
[2] 98 countries, 1960–85.
[3] 98 countries, 1960–85.
[4] 116 countries, 1965–85.
[5] 119 countries, 1960–89.
[6] 98 countries, 1960–85.

Mankiw et al. (1992) take three samples of countries over the period 1960–85: 98 non-oil-producing countries, 76 developing countries (excluding small countries and those where data are doubtful), and 22 OECD countries with a population of more than 1 million. First they take the *level* of PCY as the dependent variable and find that differences in savings rates and population growth account for over 50 per cent of income differences in the large sample of countries, which is support for the second basic proposition of neoclassical growth theory (see p. 146). However, the cross-section regression implies a much higher elasticity of output with respect to capital than capital's share of national income, so that the empirical model over-predicts. The authors thus augment the model for differences in human capital formation, proxied by secondary school enrolment rates, and find that the augmented Solow model 'explains' 80 per cent of differences in PCY, and human capital formation is a significant variable in all three samples of countries. Regressing the *growth* of PCY on initial PCY levels shows no tendency for convergence (except in the OECD sample), but there is evidence for conditional convergence in all three samples if differences in investment ratios and population growth are allowed for. It is therefore claimed by the authors that the data give support to the Solow neoclassical model against the 'new' endogenous growth models, which, because of the assumption of non-diminishing returns to capital, predict that differences in PCY between countries will persist indefinitely or even widen.

Knight et al. (1993) extend Mankiw et al.'s study in two ways. First, they use panel data (that is, pooled time-series and cross-section data) to look at country-specific effects. Second, they assume that the rate of technical progress is influenced by the 'outwardness' of trade policy and by the stock of infrastructure investment (proxied by the 'flow' variable, government fixed investment as a proportion of GDP). Trade is assumed to influence technical progress in two ways: through technological transfers, and through greater availability of foreign exchange, which enables countries to purchase technologically superior capital goods. Tests of the model, taking two samples (76 developing countries and 22 OECD countries), show that the growth of output per worker is positively related to the savings ratio, and negatively related to the growth of population and the initial level of PCY; that is, there is evidence of conditional convergence. Human capital investment is significant and raises the productivity of physical investment. The tests of trade 'openness', and the role of infrastructure investment, also show significant positive effects and enhance the coefficient on physical capital.

Barro and Wha Lee (1993) analyse 116 countries over the period 1965–85 and find that five factors differentiate reasonably well slow-growing countries from fast-growing countries:

- The initial level of PCY (relative to educational and health attainment), which has a negative effect (that is, there is evidence of conditional convergence)
- The investment ratio (+)
- The ratio of government consumption to GDP (−)
- Market distortions measured by the black market rate of foreign exchange (−)
- Political instability measured by the number of political 'revolutions' per year (−).

These five variables 'explain' 80 per cent the growth rate differences between countries. No trade variables are included in the analysis.

Levine and Renelt (1992) show that cross-country regression results are 'fragile' to model selection and data sets, but at least two 'robust' results stand out: the relation between investment and growth, and the relation between the investment ratio and the ratio of international trade to GDP. The authors first take 119 countries over the period 1960–89 and use the growth of PCY as the dependent variable. The I (constant) variables used (see (5.33)) are the investment ratio, the initial level of PCY, the initial level of secondary school enrolment and population growth. The pool of Z variables used includes government expenditure, exports, inflation, the variance of inflation, domestic credit expansion and its variance and political instability. When the Z variables are added to the I variables, the investment ratio remains robust, the initial PCY variable remains robust (that is, there is evidence of conditional convergence), the secondary school enrolment rate is robust, but not population growth. None of the Z variables themselves are robust, however; they depend on the conditioning variables, that is, which other Z variables are introduced. The authors repeat the Barro (1991) study and find only the investment ratio and the initial level of PCY to be robust. No fiscal or monetary indicators are robust, and no trade variables. The authors suggest that the importance of trade probably works through investment (rather than through improved resource allocation).

Levine and Zervos (1993) report new evidence on the 'robustness' of variables, taking a different set of I and Z variables. The I (constant) variables used are the Barro (1991) variables of initial PCY, initial secondary school enrolment rate and the number of political revolutions and coups. The results largely support the earlier findings of Levine and Renelt (1992), but no investment variable is included. The authors pay particular attention to financial variables and the role of inflation. Various indicators of financial deepening are robust (which may be standing as a proxy for investment), and apparently there are no Z variables that make growth and inflation negatively correlated. They comment that, 'given the uncharacteristically unified view among economists and policy analysts that countries with high inflation rates should adopt policies that lower inflation in order to promote economic prosperity, the inability to find simple cross-country regressions supporting this contention is both surprising and troubling'.[15]

What have we learned?

These studies (and many others not reported here) have revealed a lot about the sources of inter-country growth rate differences. Interestingly, the variables of significance turn out to be those which have traditionally been at the heart of mainstream growth and development theory, particularly the importance of investment and capital accumulation.

On the other hand, it is often the case that studies reach conflicting conclusions, and a large proportion of inter-country growth rate differences remain unexplained (as much as 40 per cent). Why is this? One set of reasons relate to the availability and quality of data, and the econometric procedures used for testing. Often data are weak and unreliable, and the econometric methodology used not only differs but is also questionable because allowance has not been made for lags in the relationship between variables or inter-correlation between variables. A second set of reasons is that countries are much more heterogeneous in their structure and institutions than most studies allow for. As Kenny and Williams (2001) put it, 'it is because countries are so heterogenous in their make-up and institutions that cross section studies reach contradictory results and produce a lack of robustness'. They argue 'perhaps more energy should be directed towards understanding the complex and varied inner-workings of actual economies rather than trying to assimilate them into abstract universal models'.

A similar point is made by Putterman (2000), who argues that one of the important reasons why countries have grown at different rates over the last 50 years is that the *preconditions* for development were not equal in terms of institutional structure (the strength of government, for example); the tax system; the state of agriculture; the stock of knowledge and ideas and so on, and these factors are not well captured by the initial level of per capita income. Emphasis on preconditions, and why countries have responded differently to the possibilities of industrialization, goes back to Rostow's ideas of the preconditions for take-off. To put it another way: economic history matters! The question is how to measure the level of 'pre-modern' development. Putterman concentrates on conditions prevailing in agriculture such as cultivatable land per head; population density, and the prevalence of irrigation. When these variables are included in regression equations, along with the investment ratio population growth, education, there is an increase in the proportion of the variance in growth rates that is explained.

Another serious weakness of 'new' growth theory is that many of the models are closed economy models, and there are no demand constraints. It is difficult to imagine how growth rate differences between countries can be explained without reference to trade, and without reference to the balance of payments position of countries, which in most developing economies constitutes a major constraint on the growth of demand and output (see Chapter 16). Where a trade variable is included in the models tested, it is invariably insignificant, or loses its significance when combined with other variables. All this is very puzzling, given the rich theoretical and empirical literature that exists on the relation between trade and growth (see Chapter 15). There are at least two possible explanations. First, it could be that trade works through investment. Indeed in some studies that look directly at the determinants of investment, trade and exports are found to be significant. Second, the measure of trade taken is a very static one, usually measured as the share of trade in GDP. This may pick up the static gains from trade but not the dynamic gains. In a growth model, the most obvious trade variable to focus on is the *growth* of exports, which will favourably influence growth from the demand side (particularly by relaxing a balance of payments constraint on domestic demand), and from the supply side by raising import capacity. A study by the present author (Thirlwall and Sanna, 1996) of 65 countries over the period 1960–88 shows the growth of exports to be a highly significant independent determinant of inter-country growth rate differences, together with the investment ratio, population growth and the initial level of per capita income. So, too, does an interesting study by Pugno (1995), which shows catch-up and convergence to be a function of demand-growth driven by exports.

Finally, a more fundamental issue is raised by Pritchett (2000) who argues that it is difficult to characterize the growth of many developing countries by a single time trend because growth is very volatile. Periods of rapid growth are often followed by plateaus and steep declines. Rapid and slow growth are for the most part transitory. Very few countries see their success or failure persist from decade to decade. Correlations of country growth rates across periods (e.g. 5–10 years) show very low correlations. Taking 111 countries over a 25-year period, Pritchett shows that in 55 of them, growth either accelerated or decelerated by more than 3 percentage points on at least one occasion over the period. In 40 per cent of developing countries, trying to estimate a time trend for the growth of output gives a correlation coefficient of less than 0.5; and volatility around the trend is much higher for developing countries than developed countries. So Pritchett asks the question: what aspects of a country's growth is growth theory trying to explain when growth is so ephemeral and volatile? If growth is so volatile, it is no wonder that the variance of growth explained by traditional variables is relatively low. What is important is to analyse and explain the determinants of *shifts* in growth rates from one period to another.

Hausmann et al. (2005) try to do this. They take 106 countries over the period 1957–92, defining a 'growth acceleration' as an increase in PCY growth of 2 per cent or more per annum over an eight-year period with a minimum growth rate of 3.5 per cent per annum. Also the post-acceleration output level must exceed the pre-episode peak level of income (to rule out cases of pure recovery from deep depression). They find 83 episodes of growth accelerations, and 60 countries out of the 106 had at least one. The average growth acceleration is 4.7 percentage points. When they look at the causes of accelerations, however, they are struck by their unpredictability. There is only a weak link between conventional determinants of growth and growth accelerations. Investment, trade and real exchange-rate depreciation are the strongest links, but there seems to be very little association between standard economic reform packages and growth accelerations. **Only 14 per cent of accelerations were associated with economic liberalization**. Only 18 per cent of reform episodes and 14 per cent of political regime change were followed by growth accelerations. The authors conclude that 'growth accelerations seem to be driven largely by idiosyncratic causes'. This may be because the 'binding constraints' on growth are 'idiosyncratic' and for certain time periods get relieved. This leads us to a brief discussion of the topic of growth diagnostics and binding constraints on growth pioneered by Hausmann et al. (2008).

'Growth diagnostics' and binding constraints on growth

A poor growth and development performance may be caused by a multitude of factors, but a sweeping programme of reforms (à la Washington Consensus), including financial and trade liberalization, the privatization of enterprises and reductions in public expenditure, may not be the solution. This is what Hausmann et al. (2008) call the 'spray gun' approach to economic policy-making, which may not hit hard enough the binding constraints on growth and development that really matter, and which in any case are likely to vary from one country to another. Much better, they argue, is to undertake 'growth diagnostics', which locates the binding constraints on economic performance, and to target them directly, giving the most favourable outcomes from the resources expended.

The framework of 'growth diagnostics' encompasses all major strategies of development. Its importance is that it clarifies *which* strategies are most likely to be effective. Since investment is the key to long-run growth, the obvious starting point for growth diagnostics is to answer the question: why is investment low? Is it the high cost or lack of access to finance? Is it an intrinsically low social rate of return to investment, or is it that returns cannot easily be appropriated by private agents? If the problem is the cost and availability of financial resources, this is likely to be associated with low savings rates, high interest rates and large balance of payments deficits. If the social return is low, this could be due to unfavourable geography, lack of infrastructure, poor education and health, and a lack of technological dynamism. If the ability to appropriate returns is difficult, this could be due to an uncertain economic and political climate, high taxes, absence of the rule of law and weak property rights. Once the diagnosis is done, certain policy reforms follow and others can be ruled out, saving time and effort. Policy must then be targeted as close to the distortion and binding constraint as possible.

The authors illustrate their methodology by comparing and contrasting three developing economies: Brazil, El Salvador and the Dominican Republic. According to the identification of binding constraints, policy recommendations differ. Brazil, for example, seems to be constrained by a shortage of finance, not by low returns on investment, so the policy message is to raise domestic saving and to attract foreign funds. By contrast, the binding constraint in El Salvador is not a shortage of investment funds, but a low social return associated with a lack of technological dynamism. It needs new (industrial) activities to invest in. The Dominican Republic tells another different story of inability to cope with shocks. Here, institutional and political reforms are likely to yield the highest return. Institutions to deal with conflict management are very important to cope with the consequences of shocks and change (see Chapter 4).

The World Bank Commission on Growth and Development, chaired by the Nobel laureate Michael Spence, and including Robert Solow, identified 13 countries that have grown at more than 7 per cent per annum for at least 25 years since 1950. They are listed in Case example 5.1. The ingredients of their success are also highlighted: high savings and investment rates; rapid export growth; macroeconomic stability; the import of knowledge and technology, and market-friendly policies.

Case example 5.1   **Findings of the Commission on Growth and Development**

The World Bank Commission on Growth and Development 2008, headed by the Nobel laureate Professor Michael Spence, identified 13 countries that have grown at more than 7 per cent per annum for at least 25 years since 1950. They are listed below.

Economy	Period of high growth	Per capita income	
		At start of growth period	2005
Botswana	1960–2005	210	3,800
Brazil	1950–1980	960	4,000
China	1961–2005	105	1,400
Hong Kong SAR	1960–1997	3,100	29,900
Indonesia	1966–1997	200	900
Japan	1950–1983	3,500	39,600
Korea	1960–2001	1,100	13,200
Malaysia	1967–1997	790	4,400
Malta	1963–1994	1,100	9,600
Oman	1960–1999	950	9,000
Singapore	1967–2002	2,200	25,400
Taiwan Province of China	1965–2002	1,500	16,400
Thailand	1960–1997	330	2,400

The Commission identified six major ingredients of success:

- Commitment to growth, combined with effective governance
- High savings and investment rates
- Fast export growth
- Macroeconomic stability
- Import of knowledge and technology
- Market-friendly policies

Source: World Bank, 2008.

Summary

- All the great classical economists of the eighteenth and nineteenth centuries were development economists in the sense that they were all concerned with the causes and consequences of economic growth during the industrial revolution in Europe at this time.
- Adam Smith was optimistic about the growth and development process based on increasing returns in industry.
- Malthus, Ricardo, Mill and Marx were all pessimistic about the development process because of diminishing returns in agriculture and a declining rate of profit in industry. Classical pessimism has been confounded by rapid technical progress in both agriculture (offsetting diminishing returns) and industry (allowing real wages to rise without the rate of profit falling).
- Modern growth theory originated with Harrod's famous 1939 paper 'An Essay in Dynamic Theory', in which he distinguishes three growth rates: the actual growth rate (g), the warranted growth rate (g_w) and the natural growth rate (g_n). Divergences between g and g_w cause short-run instability. Divergences between g_w and g_n cause secular stagnation if $g_w > g_n$, or growing structural unemployment with inflation if $g_n > g_w$ (which is the case for most developing economies). There were no mechanisms in the Harrod model for equalizing g, g_w and g_n.
- Solow's 1956 neoclassical growth model provided an equilibrating mechanism to bring g_w and g_n together so that all economies in the long run would grow at their natural rate of growth determined by the growth of the labour force and the growth of labour productivity. In Solow's original model, investment did not matter for long-run growth because of the assumption of diminishing returns to capital.
- Solow's model also predicted that poor countries should grow faster than rich countries, leading to a convergence of per capita incomes across the world, but we do not observe a convergence of living standards. 'New' growth theory, or endogenous growth theory, attempts to provide an answer. There are lots of factors that prevent the marginal product of capital from falling as countries get richer and invest more, such as education, R&D expenditure, learning by doing, trade, etc., so that investment does matter for long-run growth and is not simply exogenously determined by the natural rate of growth. The AK model is the simplest 'new' growth theory model which assumes constant returns to capital.
- The neoclassical Cobb–Douglas production function can be used to decompose the sources of growth into the contribution of labour input, capital input and total factor productivity growth. In fact, any variable can be included in a production function and its contribution to output measured.
- 'New' growth theory uses many of the same variables as the production function approach in analysing the sources of growth, but with particular focus on education, R&D effort and institutional variables, and testing for conditional convergence by including in the estimating equation the initial level of per capita income.
- Cross-country analysis, however, is unable to explain the growth and development experience of individual countries, so growth diagnostics become important in identifying the binding constraints on growth in particular economies, and the factors that are associated with growth accelerations within countries.
- The major determinants of rapid growth and development are: high investment, fast export growth (to pay for imports), macroeconomic stability, high levels of human capital formation and an institutional framework conducive to growth (e.g. secure property rights, the rule of law and political stability).

Chapter 5	Discussion questions

1   What did Adam Smith mean when he said that the 'division of labour is limited by the extent of the market' and 'the extent of the market is limited by the division of labour'? What is the economic significance of these propositions?

2   Why were the classical economists after Adam Smith pessimistic about the growth and development process?

3   How does Harrod define the warranted growth rate and the natural growth rate? What are the implications for a country if the natural growth rate exceeds the warranted rate?

4   What is the mechanism in neoclassical growth theory by which the warranted rate of growth adjusts to the natural rate? Do you think it is a realistic mechanism?

5   What are the essential propositions and predictions of neoclassical growth theory, and how is the conclusion reached that investment does not matter for long-run growth?

6   What are the special properties of the Cobb–Douglas production function, and how might the function be used to calculate the sources of growth?

7   What is the difference between exogenous and endogenous technical progress?

8   What factors does the growth of 'total factor productivity' depend on?

9   What have been the major findings of production function studies of the sources of growth in developing countries?

10 Outline the essential propositions of 'new' (endogenous) growth theory.

11 What have we learnt from the major studies of the macro-determinants of growth in developing countries?

12 How useful is the exercise of 'growth diagnostics'?

Notes

1. *Economic Journal*, December 1928.

2. *Economic Journal*, March 1939.

3. The American economist Evesey Domar arrived at Harrod's result independently in 1947, hence the linking of the two names ('Expansion and Employment', *American Economic Review*, March 1947).

4. In practice, g_n may respond to g. This is the idea of the endogeneity of the natural rate of growth (see Leon-Ledesma and Thirlwall, 2002).

5. Robert Solow from the Massachusetts Institute of Technology (MIT) was awarded the Nobel Prize in economics in 1987, partly for his pioneering contribution to growth theory.

6. This can be seen by rearranging the equation to $qs/k = l$, where $q = Y/L$; $s = S/Y = \Delta K/Y$ (since all saving leads to capital accumulation); $k = K/L$, and $l = \Delta L/L$. Therefore $(Y/L)(\Delta K/Y)(L/K) = \Delta L/L$, or $\Delta K/K = \Delta L/L$.

7. For the time being, the formidable problems associated with an aggregate measure of capital are ignored.

8. The proof is as follows. The elasticity of output with respect to capital, α, is $(dY/Y)/(dK/K) = (dYK)/(dKY)$. Now if capital is paid its marginal product, then $dY/dK = r$, where r is the rental on capital. Hence $\alpha = rK/Y$, where rK/Y is capital's share of total output. Thus under perfectly competitive assumptions the elasticity of output with respect to any factor is equal to that factor's share of total output.

9. Alternatively, the total differential of (5.21) can be taken and the result divided by output, which will also convert the equation into rate-of-growth form.

10. The elasticity of substitution (α) relates the proportional change in relative factor inputs to a proportional change in the marginal rate of substitution between labour and capital (MRS) (or the proportional change in the relative factor–price ratio on the basis of marginal productivity theory). The elasticity of substitution may therefore be written as

$$\sigma = \frac{\partial \log(L/K)}{\partial \log MRS}$$

The proof that $\sigma = 1$ is very simple:

$$MRS = \frac{\partial Y}{\partial K} \bigg| \frac{\partial Y}{\partial L} = \frac{\alpha L}{\beta K}$$

$$\log MRS = \log \frac{\alpha}{\beta} + \log \frac{L}{K}$$

Differentiating with respect to log MRS gives

$$1 = \frac{\partial \log(L/K)}{\partial \log MRS} = \sigma$$

11. To overcome the restrictive property of the Cobb–Douglas function when the growth rates of factors differ, it is possible to use the more general constant elasticity of substitution production function, of which the Cobb–Douglas is a special case. We cannot discuss the function here except to say that it, too, is not without its specification errors. There is still the assumption of constancy, which has the drawback that one may be ascribing changes in elasticity to changes in technology that are really due to changes in factor proportions. This limitation can be overcome only with a function possessing the property of variable elasticity of substitution.

12. The production function used here is the translog production function, which allows for the elasticity of substitution between inputs to vary.

13. For a discussion of the origins of endogenous growth theory, and its relevance to developing countries, see Romer (1994), Pack (1994), Ruttan (1998) and Temple (1999). For an advanced textbook treatment of the topic, see Barro and Sala-í-Martin (1995).

14. For an advanced theoretical discussion of convergence issues, see the Symposium in *Economic Journal*, July 1996; also Islam (2003).

15. See Chapter 13 for a discussion of the relation between inflation and growth.

Websites on growth theory

New School for Social Research (New York) http://cepa.newschool.edu/het/home.htm

Economic Growth Resources run by Jon Temple, Bristol University, UK www.bris.ac.uk/Depts/Economics/Growth

Overseas Development Institute www.odi.org
Foundation for Advanced Studies on International Development www.fasid.or.jp/english
Institute of Developing Economies Japan-External Trade Organisation www.ide.go.jp/English/Research/index.html
The Vienna Institute for International Economic Studies www.wiiw.ac.at
Carnegie Endowment for International Peace www.ceip.org

II

FACTORS IN THE DEVELOPMENT PROCESS

6

THE ROLE OF AGRICULTURE AND SURPLUS LABOUR FOR INDUSTRIALIZATION

- Introduction
- The role of agriculture in development
- Barriers to agricultural development
- Land reform
- The supply response of agriculture
- Transforming traditional agriculture
- The growth of the money economy
- Finance for traditional agriculture
- The interdependence of agriculture and industry
- Economic development with unlimited supplies of labour
- A model of the complementarity between agriculture and industry
- Rural–urban migration and urban unemployment
- Disguised unemployment: types and measurement

- Incentives and the costs of labour transfer
- Summary
- Appendix: the functioning of markets in agrarian societies
- The land market
- The labour market
- Credit markets
- Interlocked markets
- Institutions and decision-making in agriculture
- Discussion questions
- Notes
- Websites on agriculture

Introduction

The task of a true theory of economic growth and development must be to explain why some societies developed sooner than others; why some societies have experienced such rapid increases in living standards while others have lagged behind, and why development has not spread.

The answer must be that at different stages of development, different constraints on progress operate. While some of these factors are likely to be sociological and political, the major constraints are likely to be economic. One of the most critical factors in the early stages of development is the health of the agricultural sector, because without a surplus of food production over subsistence needs, little else can be done. There would be no surplus labour, no saving, no investment and no food to feed labour working in alternative activities.

It is no coincidence that the material progress of mankind started 8,000 years ago in the region of Mesopotamia (the cradle of civilization, now Iraq), where for the first time agriculture became settled. Unless agriculture is settled, there is no prospect of agricultural productivity increasing to provide the basis for the development of non-agricultural activities, the building of cities and the enjoyment of leisure. Where shifting agriculture is practised, as by nomadic tribes in the Kalahari Desert of Botswana and Namibia, for example, there is no basis for an agricultural surplus.

Likewise, as the World Bank says in its *World Development Report 2008* devoted to the topic of 'Agriculture for Development':

> agricultural growth was the precursor to the industrial revolutions that spread across the temperate world from England in the mid-18th century to Japan in the late-19th century. More recently, rapid agricultural growth in China, India and Vietnam was the precursor to the rise of industry . . . the special powers of agriculture as the basis for early growth are well established.

In many developing countries today, agriculture is still extremely backward. Low productivity is a major cause of poverty and retards development of the whole economy. Over 3 billion people live in rural areas, and most of them live in households engaged in agriculture earning just a few dollars a day. The World Bank recognizes 'that agriculture must be a prominent part of the development agenda whether for delivering growth in the agricultural-based countries or for reducing rural poverty' (World Bank, 2007). It also recognizes that the state has a role to play in providing core public goods and incentives for investment in the agricultural sector.

In this chapter we consider some of the reasons for agricultural backwardness, and why productivity is so low. We look at the process of transforming traditional agriculture and the growth of the money economy, and model the interrelationship between the growth of agriculture and industry. Then we use Arthur Lewis's famous model of 'Economic Development with Unlimited Supplies of Labour' (1954) to illustrate the important role that surplus labour in agriculture (and other sectors) plays in the development process and fuelling industrial growth. The precise meaning of surplus labour is addressed, as well as the rural–urban migration process. An appendix describes the various markets in agrarian societies – land, labour and credit – and how they interlock.

The role of agriculture in development

Agriculture makes four major contributions to the process of economic development: a **product contribution**, a **factor contribution**, a **market contribution** and a **foreign exchange contribution**.

Product contribution

The product contribution of agriculture refers to the fact that agriculture must supply food above subsistence needs in order to feed labour working in alternative occupations. If other sectors of the economy are to be developed, labour needs to be fed, and this cannot be done by imports until export activities have been developed to provide foreign exchange to pay for the imports. It will be remembered from Chapter 3 that in Rostow's model of economic growth, the take-off stage of development must be preceded by an agricultural revolution. Indeed, as mentioned above in the quote from the World Bank, one of the major reasons why Britain was the first country to industrialize was that it was the first to experience a significant agricultural revolution based on the abolition of serfdom and on the enclosure movement, which raised agricultural productivity and provided surplus labour and food to support industrial expansion.

The difference between total agricultural output and subsistence needs is called the **marketable surplus**. Economic progress in the early stages of development requires an increase in the marketable surplus, which in turn requires an increase in labour productivity. If productivity does not increase naturally or 'voluntarily', a marketable surplus can be forcibly extracted, as it was in Japan at the time of the Meiji Restoration (1868), when landowners were compulsorily taxed, and more dramatically in the Soviet Union in the 1920s, when there was mass genocide of the kulaks (small prosperous landowners) during Stalin's collectivization programme.

Marketable surplus is a very important concept in the neoclassical model of the development process, because unless the marketable surplus rises as the demand for food increases, the price of food will tend to rise. This will turn the terms of trade against industry; higher wages will have to be paid to workers in industry, which will eat into profits and capital accumulation. The marketable surplus therefore becomes the major constraint on industrial growth.

Factor contribution

The factor contribution of agriculture consists of two parts: a labour contribution and a capital contribution. Labour for industry and other activities must come from agriculture, but can be released only if productivity in agriculture rises. The existence of surplus labour (or disguised unemployment) plays a major role in the development process, as we shall see when we consider the famous Lewis model of economic development with unlimited supplies of labour. The lower the cost of industrial labour, the faster the rate of industrial expansion is likely to be, but this depends on the rate at which the agricultural sector is releasing labour. Industrial development today in many of the rapidly growing countries of South-East Asia is being fuelled by cheap labour drawn from agriculture. In this respect, China's industrial potential is enormous.

Agriculture is a source of saving and capital accumulation for industrial development. The saving can be voluntary or involuntary. Examples of voluntary saving are rich landlords voluntarily investing in industrial activities (the industrial revolution in Britain was partly financed in this way), and peasant farmers investing small savings in rural banks. Involuntary saving could take the form of the government taxing the agricultural sector and using the proceeds for investment, or more drastically, the forced extraction of the agricultural surplus through expropriation or collectivization (as in Stalinist Russia).

Another traditional way in which governments have taxed the agricultural sector is through the pricing policies of **marketing boards**, established to market agricultural produce. The prices paid to farmers are lower than the prices at which the goods are sold on the market – the difference providing net revenue to the government.

The general policy in developing countries of keeping agricultural prices low used to be justified on two main grounds: that low prices benefit the industrial sector; and that peasant farmers have limited horizons and do not respond to incentives, so if prices are higher they may actually produce less if all they are interested in is a fixed money income. This is the notion of a **backward-bending supply curve of effort**. It can be said without hesitation that the deliberate policy of keeping agricultural prices low has done enormous damage to the agricultural sector in developing countries. As we shall see later, there is ample evidence that peasant farmers do respond to price incentives. They not only increase supply in response to price rises, but also switch crops as relative prices change.

Market contribution

The market contribution of agriculture refers to the fact that the demand from agriculture must be the major source of autonomous demand for industrial goods. If industry is to grow and prosper, it must be able to sell its goods. In the early stages of development the agricultural sector is likely to provide the largest market for industrial goods. There is a *complementarity* between agricultural and industrial growth. This is well documented in the historical experience of developed countries, and in the contemporary world economy. In his classic study of Japanese economic development, Lockwood (1954) wrote:

> The growth of primary production was interrelated with industrialization and urbanization at every point . . . As industry developed, it offered a widening market for the food and raw material surpluses of the countryside . . . On the other hand, the increasing productivity of the primary industries created a growing home market for manufactures and services.

The World Bank's 1979 *World Development Report* remarked that 'a stagnant rural economy with low purchasing power holds back industrial growth in many developing countries'. The 1982 *World Development Report* documented the close correspondence across countries between agricultural development and industrial growth: 'fast growth of industry and sluggish agriculture were evident *only* in countries with oil or mineral-based economies, such as Algeria, Ecuador, Mexico, Morocco and Nigeria . . . These were exceptions but they prove the rule [emphasis in the original].' In other words, a precondition for rapid industrial growth is a rapidly expanding agricultural sector, at least in terms of purchasing power.

This has implications for the pricing of agricultural goods relative to industrial goods, or what is called the agricultural (or industrial) terms of trade. Low farm prices are good for industry from the point of view of supply potential because this means that industry can obtain cheaper raw material inputs and wage goods, which increases profitability. On the other hand, low farm prices are bad for industry from the demand side because this means low farm purchasing power and therefore a lower demand for industrial goods. There needs to be an equilibrium terms of trade between the two sectors to achieve balanced growth between the two sectors, so that industrial growth is not constrained from the supply side by agricultural prices being too high or constrained from the demand side by agricultural prices being too low. Later in the chapter (p. 206) we bring the two sectors together in an equilibrium framework and derive the equilibrium terms of trade that maximizes the growth rate of the economy as a whole.

Foreign exchange contribution

In the early stages of development, the only source of foreign exchange is likely to be primary commodity exports. Agriculture therefore makes an important foreign exchange contribution.

Foreign exchange is a resource, just like savings. It provides access to goods that either cannot be produced domestically or can be produced only at higher cost in an opportunity cost sense. Either way, the imports made possible by exporting agricultural products will be very productive – the more so if they are investment-type goods necessary for the development process. There are not many countries in the world that could not grow faster given the greater availability of foreign exchange. The link between trade, the balance of payments and growth is explored fully in Chapters 15 and 16.

Barriers to agricultural development

For the agricultural sector to supply food, release labour, provide savings, contribute to the market for industrial goods and earn foreign exchange, it must generate a steadily rising surplus of production in excess of subsistence needs. Since land is relatively fixed in supply, this requires rising agricultural productivity. The 'grass-roots' school of economic development, which came into fashion as a reaction against the emphasis on industrialization at any cost, lays stress on policies to raise the level of productivity in agriculture as the most crucial development priority and an indispensable element of a long-run development strategy. Overall, agricultural productivity in developing countries is less than one-twentieth of the level in developed countries, and there are even bigger differences between countries. Table 6.1 gives figures on agricultural productivity in

Table 6.1 Agricultural productivity, agriculture value-added per worker, 2005 ($)

Albania	1,495
Algeria	2,219
Angola	196
Antigua and Barbuda	2,751
Argentina	10,762
Armenia	4,198
Australia	33,252
Austria	22,775
Azerbaijan	1,212
Bangladesh	346
Barbados	15,533
Belarus	3,445
Belgium	39,812
Belize	6,696
Benin	536
Bhutan	138
Bolivia	783
Bosnia and Herzegovina	10,051
Botswana	367
Brazil	3,218

continued overleaf

Table 6.1   Agricultural productivity, agriculture value-added per worker, 2005 ($) – *continued*

Brunei Darussalam	86,426
Bulgaria	7,239
Burkina Faso	179
Burundi	64
Cambodia	337
Cameroon	666
Canada	47,181
Cape Verde	1,510
Central African Republic	384
Chad	225
Chile	5,720
China	430
Colombia	2,821
Comoros	436
Congo, Dem. Rep.	149
Costa Rica	4,643
Côte d'Ivoire	817
Croatia	10,916
Czech Republic	6,241
Denmark	40,052
Djibouti	65
Dominica	4,817
Dominican Republic	4,943
Ecuador	1,778
Egypt, Arab Rep.	2,128
El Salvador	1,700
Equatorial Guinea	1,198
Eritrea	94
Estonia	3,021
Ethiopia	177
Fiji	1,867
Finland	33,738
France	47,153
Gabon	1,663
Gambia, The	224
Georgia	1,937
Germany	26,418
Ghana	332
Greece	9,105
Grenada	1,522

Table 6.1 Agricultural productivity, agriculture value-added per worker, 2005 ($) – *continued*

Guatemala	2,652
Guinea-Bissau	246
Guinea	193
Guyana	3,383
Honduras	1,489
Hungary	8,102
Iceland	53,483
India	402
Indonesia	596
Iran, Islamic Rep.	2,687
Ireland	14,641
Italy	25,416
Jamaica	1,759
Japan	37,842
Jordan	1,392
Kazakhstan	1,652
Kenya	344
Kiribati	8
Korea, Rep.	12,275
Kyrgyz Republic	966
Lao PDR	457
Latvia	2,974
Lebanon	32,025
Lesotho	427
Lithuania	5,020
Luxembourg	30,035
Macedonia, FYR	3,739
Madagascar	175
Malawi	109
Malaysia	551
Mali	244
Mauritania	356
Mauritius	5,338
Mexico	2,821
Moldova	891
Mongolia	1,030
Morocco	1,623
Mozambique	154
Namibia	1,134

continued overleaf

Table 6.1   Agricultural productivity, agriculture value-added per worker, 2005 ($) – *continued*

Nepal	210
Netherlands	44,232
New Zealand	28,271
Nicaragua	2,172
Norway	38,218
Pakistan	717
Panama	4,004
Papua New Guinea	601
Paraguay	2,047
Peru	1,526
Philippines	1,097
Poland	2,260
Portugal	6,279
Romania	5,294
Russian Federation	2,629
Rwanda	184
Samoa	1,768
Saudi Arabia	16,651
Senegal	227
Seychelles	433
Singapore	46,408
Slovak Republic	5,848
Slovenia	47,995
Solomon Islands	613
South Africa	2,670
Spain	18,054
Sri Lanka	705
St Kitts and Nevis	2,228
St Lucia	1,246
St V. and the Grenadines	2,215
Sudan	661
Suriname	3,166
Swaziland	1,376
Sweden	36,162
Switzerland	24,526
Syrian Arab Republic	3,382
Tajikistan	426
Tanzania	306
Thailand	615
Togo	353

Table 6.1 Agricultural productivity, agriculture value-added per worker, 2005 ($) – *continued*

Tonga	3,340
Trinidad and Tobago	1,408
Tunisia	2,630
Turkey	1,946
Uganda	179
Ukraine	1,872
United Arab Emirates	27,487
United Kingdom	27,701
United States	47,463
Uruguay	8,482
Uzbekistan	1,927
Vanuatu	1,219
Venezuela, RB	6,916
Vietnam	313
Zambia	204
Zimbabwe	205
World	**939**
Low income	**330**
Middle income	**673**
Lower middle income	532
Upper middle income	2,947
Low and middle income	**599**
East Asia & Pacific	458
Europe & Central Asia	2,228
Latin America & Caribbean	3,158
Middle East & North Africa	2,313
South Asia	417
Sub-Saharan Africa	287
High income	**27,680**
Least developed countries	**254**

Source: World Bank, *World Development Indicators*, June 2009, online (Washington: World Bank).

the various countries of the world. In China, labour productivity is $430 per annum; in India, $402 per annum, and in the USA, $47,463 per annum. In many countries output per head is barely enough to meet subsistence needs. The figure for the least developed countries is only $254. Some progress has been made in recent years with particular crops in particular countries, but the performance of the agricultural sector is still disappointing, and the lack of a marketable surplus is holding back development on a wide front. So what impedes agricultural productivity? There are several factors, particularly related to geography and land–labour ratios, the existence of urban bias in the treatment of agriculture and the allocation of resources, and unfair competition in world markets, but the most important factors of all are the structure of rural societies, the organization of agriculture and the land-tenure system that operates.

As far as geographical factors are concerned, climate and terrain determine to a large degree what goods a country can produce, the amount of cultivatable land available per inhabitant and the land's fertility. To some extent the application of capital to land can compensate for unfavourable natural forces, but there are obvious limits. Mountains cannot be easily flattened or deserts readily watered. This is the concept of **geographic determinism**, which can be advanced as a hypothesis of underdevelopment in its own right. Having said this, however, differences in natural conditions and the fertility of the soil can be no more than a partial explanation of low productivity. Poor people are to be found along the highly productive alluvial banks of the Nile, as well as on the barren plateaus of Asia and South America.

Productivity is also affected by land–labour ratios. Low labour productivity may be associated, for example, with a high population density and a high ratio of labour to land. In this case, productivity might be increased substantially with small applications of capital in the form of drainage schemes, fertilizers and so on. On the other hand, low productivity may be associated with the opposite situation of a high ratio of land to labour, in which case the solution to low productivity is likely to involve much larger doses of capital for labour to work with. Most countries in Asia have high ratios of labour to land, while in Latin America and Africa the reverse is true, as was the case in many of today's richest countries at an equivalent stage in their economic history, for example the USA, Canada and Australia.

Urban bias against agriculture takes many forms:

• The holding down of agricultural prices to favour the industrial/urban sector
• The concentration of investment in industry
• Tax incentives and subsidies to industry
• Overvalued exchange rates, which keep the price of industrial inputs, and the domestic price of agricultural exports, low
• Tariff and quota protection for industry, which raises the price of fertilizers, seeds and equipment
• Greater spending in urban areas on education, training, housing, nutrition and medical provision, which all affect productivity and the quality of life.

Unfair competition consists of the subsidies that developed countries give to their farmers, and the tariffs that developed countries impose on imported agricultural products from developing countries. The USA and the European Union (EU) alone spend nearly $400 billion a year (or more than $1 billion a day) on farm subsidies. This has two major consequences. First it leads to over-production, and the surpluses are then frequently dumped on the markets of developing countries, impoverishing domestic farmers. Secondly, farmers in developing countries are not able to compete in their own markets, let alone overseas markets. The situation is made worse by developing countries being forced by international agreements to lower their tariffs against imported agricultural produce, while developed countries continue to protect their own agricultural sectors. The average tariff on agricultural commodities into the EU is over 50 per cent. The maize growers of Mexico cannot compete with cheap maize from the USA; nor can the cotton growers of West Africa compete against subsidies of $4 billion a year given to the 20,000 cotton growers in the southern states of America. Unfair competition between developed and developing countries in the markets for agricultural goods is one of the central issues in ongoing world trade talks under the auspices of the World Trade Organization (WTO).

Geographic factors, the land–labour ratio, urban bias and competition from developed countries can, however, only explain a small part of the low productivity of agriculture in most developing countries. There are more fundamental forces at work concerned with the structure of rural society, the organization of agriculture, the incentives to produce and the supply of inputs (see Binswanger and Deinenger, 1997).

In a typical developing country, rural society consists of rich landowners, peasants, sharecroppers, tenants and labourers. Apart from the landowners, most others in the rural sector are extremely poor. Because they live on the margin of subsistence they tend to be **risk averse**. In all developing countries peasant subsistence farming is a traditional way of life, and attempts to raise productivity will alter that way of life and necessarily involve risk. As Theodore Schultz (1980) perceptively remarked in his Nobel Prize-winning lecture:

> Most of the people in the world are poor, so if we knew the economics of being poor we would know much of the economics that really matters. Most of the world's poor people earn their living from agriculture so if we knew the economics of agriculture we would know much of the economics of being poor. People who are rich find it hard to understand the behaviour of poor people. Economists are no exception, for they, too, find it difficult to comprehend the preferences and scarcity constraints that determine the choices that poor people make. We all know that most of the world's people are poor, that they earn a pittance for their labour, that half and more of their meagre income is spent on food, that they reside predominantly in low-income countries and that most of them are earning their livelihood in agriculture. What many economists fail to understand is that poor people are no less concerned about improving their lot and that of their children than rich people are.

Poor people on the margin of subsistence may be reluctant to make the changes necessary to improve productivity because if things go wrong it will spell disaster. But even if poor people wanted to change the traditional ways of doing things, there is the serious constraint of lack of access to credit to finance the purchase of new inputs such as seeds, fertilizers, pesticides, drainage schemes and so on.

Then there is the question of the incentive to change. Where there are tenant farmers there is little or no security of tenure, and therefore no incentive to invest in improved methods of production. Where there is sharecropping a certain proportion of output must be relinquished to the landowner, which also reduces the incentive to invest. Any serious programme of agrarian reform must provide greater security of tenure for farmers and give incentives to raise agricultural production, coupled with access to credit, water, fertilizers and extension services for advice.

The appendix to this chapter gives a detailed description of the markets for land, labour and credit in rural societies; how they are interlocked, and the inefficiencies that arise as a result of the structure of the agricultural sector of developing countries.

Land reform

The system by which land is held and farmed is a serious impediment to increased productivity in many developing countries. The structure of peasant agriculture differs between countries, largely for historical reasons, but the structures have many common characteristics that keep productivity low. In many countries, land-holding tends to be highly concentrated. The average Gini ratio for the concentration of land-holdings in Latin America is 0.8, and in Asia, 0.4. In Latin America, 1 per cent of landowners own roughly 70 per cent of the land. In Brazil, 15 per cent of landowners own 90 per cent of the land. In many parts of Latin America, agriculture is based on a combina-tion of large estates (*latifundios*), owned by a wealthy few, and small farms (*minifundios*), which are often so small that they cannot support a single family. When land is held and worked in the form of large estates, it is frequently underutilized and farmed inefficiently by peasants, who may have no security of tenure and may have to relinquish to the landowner a large fraction of their output. In these circumstances there is little incentive to increase efficiency and improve productivity.

In Asia the organization of peasant agriculture is also an important determinant of produc-tivity. Because of the high population density, the major problem is that too many small farms are operated by sharecroppers and tenant farmers, the land being owned by absentee landlords. As families multiply and debts rise, land is continually sold and subdivided, leading to a very inefficient structure.

Land reform has two aspects: first, the redistribution of land in favour of landless or near-landless households, and secondly, tenancy reform in favour of sharecroppers and other forms of tenant farming. Such reforms involving land rights, and security for tenants, can contribute both to an increased intensity of land use and to improved efficiency and initiative on the part of the tenant farmers, particularly if they are allowed to reap fully the rewards of their own labour. The pressure for land reform is well illustrated by the example described in Case example 6.1.

Case example 6.1	Land reform

Land is an important and sensitive issue in most developing countries and growing numbers of poor people are demanding reform of its ownership and use after centuries of inequitable distribution.

The Movimento dos Trabalhadores Rurais Sem Terra (MST) in Brazil has an esti-mated 1.5 million members who have occupied and farmed many millions of acres of unproductive land in the last 20 years.

The MST is now mirrored across Latin America with growing peasant and indige-nous groups in Ecuador and Bolivia, Uruguay, Paraguay and Chile taking back land. They are supported by powerful international peasant groups such as Via Campesina which now works in 87 countries where land reform is recognized as a major problem.

Land reform in Africa is led by the Landless People's Movement in South Africa, which argues that the official redistribution process is not fast enough for landless rural people. As in Brazil, land reform in Africa is seen as critical in redressing centuries of dispossession.

Many land reform groups are now linked and an international political move-ment is emerging. Almost all landless movements lobby for the right to grow food for themselves and not for export, for ecological agriculture and for an end to GM farming.

Source: *The Guardian*, 25 October 2007.

There is impressive evidence that where a change in the tenure system has permitted the produc-ers themselves to reap the rewards of new techniques, peasant farmers have been ready to break with custom and tradition. The task of persuading producers to adopt more modern methods of production and to purchase improved seed and fertilizer has been much easier. In a study of China from 1978, Lin (1992) finds that the shift from collective to household farming led to big increases in agricultural productivity related to the acquisition of property and land rights. Likewise, Besley and Burgess (2000) in a study of India find that rural poverty was reduced by land reform, particularly reforms that strengthened property rights over land. In Vietnam, efficiency has increased and poverty has been reduced since the end of collectivization in the 1990s.

As was first discovered by Amartya Sen (1964), using Indian farm data, small farms are more productive (per hectare) than large farms. This has been shown in many other studies subsequently. The reason is that land tends to be more fertile on small farms, and family labour tends to work the land more intensively. In other words, small farms tend to employ more labour per unit of land than large farms. Thus, land redistribution from owners of large estates to smaller family farms can raise agricultural output and employment simultaneously, helping to reduce poverty.

Land reform may be a necessary condition for increased productivity, but it is clearly not a sufficient condition. It needs to be accompanied by other measures of agrarian reform. New landowners must be given access to credit, water, fertilizers and extension services for advice. Farmers need to be brought within the organized money market to improve access to credit and to reduce the role of village moneylenders, who charge exorbitant interest rates. Improved farm implements, irrigation and new social infrastructure are likely to be important. There needs to be improved dissemination of agricultural research. Too often the agricultural extension services available are perfunctory and ineffective because the personnel are ill-trained and ill-equipped. Conditions vary from country to country, but in theory at least, agrarian reform, coupled with the application of complementary inputs, offers substantial scope for increased agricultural productivity.[1]

The supply response of agriculture

What may also be required is a rise in the price of agricultural products relative to industrial products in order to induce extra supply. Traditionally, attempts have been made to 'tax' the agricultural sector by keeping prices low in order to maintain the terms of trade in favour of the industrial sector. This policy was justified by the widespread belief that peasant producers in traditional societies would not respond to price incentives, but this assumption has proved to be wrong. Depressing the agricultural terms of trade has depressed agricultural output and caused problems for the feeding of a growing industrial population.

Many countries have had to introduce a positive price policy to act as a stimulus to agricultural output in general and to alter the composition of agricultural output as circumstances warrant. There is in fact considerable evidence that producers, especially those in close proximity to large markets with good transport facilities, respond positively to price changes, as economic theory would predict. Schultz (1964) gave early warning that 'the doctrine that farmers in poor countries either are indifferent or respond perversely to changes in prices . . . is patently false and harmful. Price policies based on it always impair the efficiency of agriculture.'

When discussing the supply response of agricultural output to price, however, a distinction needs to be made between three types of response:

- A change in the composition of agricultural output to a change in the relative price of individual agricultural commodities
- An increase in total agricultural output with respect to an improvement in the relative price of agricultural commodities compared with industrial goods
- An increase in the marketed surplus in response to an increase in the price of agricultural commodities.

Most of the studies on the supply response in peasant agriculture in developing countries relate to how producers respond to changes in the relative price of different agricultural commodities. But of course it would be quite possible for the supply of any individual commodity to be quite elastic with respect to price, yet the total supply of agricultural output and the marketed surplus to be quite inelastic, or even to fall, in response to a rise in price.

Having said this, however, there are reasons for believing that the other two elasticities are likely to be positive if the supply of individual commodities is positive, especially when crops are not just grown for subsistence purposes. For example, for any crop grown commercially the elasticity of marketed supply will be virtually equal to the output elasticity, and unless inputs are withdrawn from the production of other commodities the elasticity of total agricultural supply will also be positive. Only in cases where peasants are content with a fixed money income, or all increased production of a commodity is consumed within the subsistence sector, will the elasticity of marketed supply be zero or negative at the same time as the price elasticity of supply is positive. These conditions are not likely to prevail.

Empirical research on the supply response of agriculture can be divided into four main categories:

- Cross-country studies that look at output differences in relation to price differences across countries
- Time-series studies that examine output movements in relation to price movements within countries over time
- Cross-section studies that look at output differences in relation to price differences across farms within a country
- Inter-sectoral general equilibrium models that examine how the output of agriculture varies in response to changes in the prices of agricultural goods relative to the price of other goods in the economy.

The evidence shows that aggregate supply elasticities of agricultural output range from 0.3 to 0.9 (Chhibber, 1988).[2] Long-run elasticity is obviously higher than short-run elasticity, and elasticity tends to be higher in the more advanced and land-abundant developing countries. The supply response of farmers to price changes depends crucially on the ability of farmers to respond to price signals, which in turn depends on transport, infrastructure and access to agricultural inputs. In poorer countries with inadequate infrastructure, supply elasticity is low (0.2–0.5). In fact, the supply elasticity of agriculture with respect to non-price factors (for example, the provision of public goods and services) is much higher than it is with respect to price, especially in poorer developing countries with inadequate infrastructure and marketing facilities. In a study of farm households in Ethiopia, Abrar et al. (2004) find a high supply response of different crops to changes in relative prices, but non-price factors such as access to fertilizers, land, infrastructure and marketing are often more important than prices in determining how much of which crops is produced for market.

The International Monetary Fund (IMF) and the World Bank are naturally concerned with the performance of the agricultural sector in countries to which they lend under various adjustment programmes (see Chapters 14 and 16). Three interrelated issues are typically addressed:

- The terms of trade between agriculture and the rest of the economy
- The efficiency of the agricultural sector
- The supply response of agriculture to price changes.

With regard to the agricultural terms of trade, the IMF normally insists that the prices paid by state marketing boards to producers be increased. Traditionally, governments have 'taxed' the agricultural sector through agricultural marketing boards, driving a large wedge between the prices paid to producers and the market prices of the commodities concerned. One implication, therefore, of raising producer prices is that government revenue may fall. This has implications for government expenditure if there is a budget constraint. Only if the elasticity of the supply of output with respect to producer prices is greater than unity will government revenue not fall; but as we saw above, supply elasticity is typically less than unity.

To achieve efficiency within agriculture, the IMF concentrates on such factors as improving storage and transport facilities, increasing the availability of agricultural inputs and improving extension services, and enhancing the efficiency of public enterprises in agriculture by insisting on the economic pricing of output and inputs, and by privatizing marketing and extension services.

We saw earlier that the supply response of farmers to price changes depends a great deal on the ability to respond, which in turn depends on infrastructure, transport, access to inputs and so on. Governments may be in a dilemma here because raising producer prices and reducing their own revenue may impair their ability to spend on infrastructure and other facilities. Given that the elasticity of supply with respect to non-price factors is higher than with respect to price, it would seem unwise to cut public expenditure as far as it affects the agricultural sector.

Transforming traditional agriculture

The task of transforming traditional agriculture is not simply a question of land reform or price policy, however. The transformation of traditional agriculture is also dependent on **new inputs**. The policy issue is to determine the form that the new inputs should take if agriculture is to attract an adequate share of investment resources.

The way to transform traditional agriculture into a dynamic source of growth is by investment to produce a supply of new agricultural inputs that will be profitable for farmers to adopt. What is lacking is not so much an unwillingness on the part of the agricultural sector to accept new ideas, but public expenditure and the organization of particular public activities to serve the agricultural sector. Agricultural research, and investment in people to improve human capabilities in agriculture, has been neglected.

The state of agriculture in Africa is particularly dire. Agricultural yields are low and food shortages and undernourishment are rife. Much of the support in place for agriculture in Africa was dismantled in the 1970s by World Bank Structural Adjustment Programmes (see Chapter 14); for example, subsidies for fertilizers and seeds, guaranteed prices for crops, and research and development – all the policies that supported Asia's so-called **Green Revolution** in the 1960s which tripled and quadrupled yields of crops such as wheat, rice and maize.

The World Bank (2007) is now apologetic for its neglect of agriculture in Africa, but it is too late for any recompense to raise productivity sufficiently to meet some of the specific Millennium Development Goals relating to poverty, nutrition and health by 2015. In 2009, the 58 countries meeting in L'Aquila, Italy announced a $19 billion agricultural investment programme for Africa to help feed itself.

The father of the 1960s Green Revolution (which bypassed Africa) was Norman Borlaug, working in Mexico, who crossed a Japanese dwarf wheat with a disease-resistant local strain to produce a high-yielding hybrid. What came to be known as Mexican dwarf wheat is a prime example of the impact that technology can have on the productivity of agriculture, which at the same time probably saved one billion people from starvation. A similar breakthrough or 'kick-start' is required in Africa. To this end, an Alliance for a Green Revolution in Africa (Agra) was founded in 2006 with a $150 million grant from the Rockefeller Foundation and the Bill Gates Foundation to help raise yields through improved farming methods, new seeds and fertilizers, working with the African Agricultural Technology Foundation based in Nairobi, Kenya. One of the major projects is to develop 'water-efficient' maize to cope with long periods of drought now being experienced in southern Africa.

In general, there is a need for a Second Green Revolution in agriculture to follow the first in the 1960s, which has now run its course (see Case example 6.2). Modern science can help. **Biotechnology (including genetically modified (GM) technology)** has the potential to raise productivity substantially and to reduce the incidence of famine and malnutrition. A GM crop is any crop variety that has had a gene or genes from a different species or variety inserted into its genetic material using genetic engineering techniques.

| Case example 6.2 | **Time for a second Green Revolution** |

How to grow more food on the same amount of land: the challenge has been a constant in human history. New answers have allowed growth in population and in living standards., but with today's surge in food prices the need to raise agricultural productivity is once again pressing. To grow more food is possible – but dogmatism about how or where to do so would be unwise.

The spectacular increase of the 1960s in wheat and rice grown per acre of crop land has slowed to as little as 1 per cent per annum. That is not because innovation has stopped, although because of apparent abundance it has taken a lower priority, but because marginal land has been brought into production while some land has been degraded. The rising price of energy inputs – oil and fertilizer – will inevitably reduce the productivity of a complementary input: land.

Just as the causes of lower productivity growth in agriculture are diverse, so must be the efforts to increase it, and higher productivity in rich countries will help reduce food prices just as much as efficient agriculture in the developing world.

Developing countries must be a particular priority, however, for two reasons. First, it may be easier to boost production from small, subsistence farms, which lack fertilizer, machinery and irrigation, than from agribusinesses in rich countries. Second, high food prices often have the perverse effect of hitting the rural poor, who lack capital and political power, hardest of all. As a result, help for small farmers may be even more effective than usual as a way to alleviate poverty.

Rich countries should, therefore, spend more of their development aid on agriculture, a strategy that has fallen out of fashion. But they must do so carefully – a splurge of poorly targeted spending on rural development would go to waste.

Some methods of the 1960s green revolution – copious use of fertilizer, for example – are also unlikely to be economic today. Husbandry of easy-to-destroy soil and water resources will be part of any 21st century boom in agricultural productivity.

Most crucial of all, however, as they have often been in the past, will be new crops and new farming techniques. Many are in prospect. Biotechnology holds the promise of plants that not only resist pests and disease, but convert scarce water and nutrients into food with great efficiency. One of the biggest obstacles to their development and

Case example 6.2	**Time for a second Green Revolution** – *continued*

use has been the resistance of European consumers and governments to genetically modified crops. The purity of food may cease to be such an issue, however, now that the quantity of food is in doubt.

Source: *Financial Times*, 3 June 2008.

Currently about 10 per cent of the world's farmland (approximately 120 million hectares) is devoted to GM crops. Research is being done on many crops, but virtually all planting covers just five crops: soya beans, maize, cotton, rice and oil-seed rape (canola). There is strong opposition to GM crops from consumers and environmental groups on the grounds of risk to human health, but GM crops are already in the food chain because they are widely used as processed food ingredients and for animal feed. So far, there is no scientific evidence that they are harmful.

The benefit of GM technology is that it can produce crops that are more nutritious, can resist pests, can grow in salty soil, are drought resistant, use nitrogen more efficiently and can be stored for longer. For example, Ingo Potrykus, working in Zurich, has genetically engineered a type of rice ('golden rice') to contain beta-carotene, which is the pigment that produces Vitamin A. This is an important breakthrough since Vitamin A deficiency kills 2 million children a year and blinds many more. This research has been funded not by biotechnology companies, concerned with maximizing returns by patenting and the exercise of intellectual property rights, but by the Swiss government and the Rockefeller Foundation. The plan is for growers to be given the new rice free by national research centres supervised by the International Rice Research Institute in Manila. Agricultural innovation cannot flourish without well-resourced agricultural extension services within countries. Research is now under way to cross 'golden rice' with a grain implanted with three genes boosting iron content to combat anaemia, which many people suffer from in developing countries. A quality protein maize has also been developed by Norman Borlaug, containing many important amino acids which could dramatically reduce the number of children who die of malnutrition. GM cotton has increased yields by nearly 100 per cent in India by being more disease resistant.

Some people argue that GM is the only technology that can prevent future world food crises and rising prices of basic foodstuffs. Malnutrition remains a major scourge in developing countries, and by 2020 there will also be 2 billion more mouths to feed. The application of new technology is urgently required.

What matters most are the incentives and associated opportunities that farm people have to augment production by means of investments that include the contribution of agricultural research and the improvement of human skills. We emphasize again that subsistence agriculture is an uncertain activity and therefore risky, particularly when survival is at stake, and this is another factor that breeds conservatism and makes change difficult, even in the face of opportunities. Poor people prefer to be safe than sorry; they tend to prefer an inferior outcome that is relatively certain to the prospect of a higher average return with a greater degree of risk attached. They are **risk averse**. This is clearly not irrational behaviour for poor people living on the margin of subsistence, even if the greater risk is imagined rather than real. To overcome inertia on this score, an integral element of agrarian reform must be policies designed to minimize risk and uncertainty through the provision of various types of insurance (as discussed in Chapter 2). The challenge of agricultural reform in India is highlighted in Case example 6.3.

Case example 6.3	**The challenge of agricultural reform in India**

With about 75 per cent of India's poor living in rural areas, India's government has recognized that raising agricultural productivity is critical to easing poverty. Agriculture's share of India's GDP has shrunk from around 60 per cent in the 1950s to about 25 per cent today. But farming still offers a livelihood for two-thirds of the country's billion-strong population. Agriculture directly employs around 235 million people, or 58 per cent of India's total workforce.

Economists believe that the government must reform agriculture with more urgency, if only to stem a widening gap between India's rural, agriculture-based states, where average incomes per person are about half those of the richest, more urbanized states.

Indian agriculture today is characterized by growing numbers of independent farmers working alongside landless labourers and subsistence farmers, on plots that are not much larger than two football fields.

In many ways, Indian farming still resembles what Mahatma Gandhi described as 'production by the masses, not mass production'. But with such small-scale farms, there are few incentives for farmers to invest in mechanization or crop diversification, which explains why India's rice yields, for example, are about half those of China.

Economists fear that unless agriculture matches the growth of other sectors, it will shackle the rest of the economy. 'It means we're stuck with a small-farm economy,' says Abhijeet Sen, a senior agricultural economist. 'If you want to have larger farms you have to throw people out. Politically, you're stranded.'

According to Biswajit Dhar, a trade economist, the government should take the initiative to turn agriculture into a 'savvy sector' in the same way that India has focused on developing its information technology and telecommunications industries.

Unless India can modernize agriculture, Dr Dhar says, rural people's disenchantment cannot be contained. 'We'll have social and political discontent and this could lead to insecure life in the cities. We could end up in political turmoil.'

Source: *Financial Times*, 9 December 2003.

The growth of the money economy

The question of the willingness to change customs and traditions leads naturally to a consideration of how peasant subsistence economies, producing goods for consumption only, typically transform themselves into money economies with an export and industrial sector. From historical experience, two factors would appear to be crucial for the expansion of the agricultural sector and the eventual production of goods for exchange at home and abroad:

- The expansion of communications to create outlets and markets for surplus production (and to encourage the production of the surplus itself)
- The emergence of a class of middlemen or export–import merchants acting as agents between world markets and the domestic agricultural sectors.

If these conditions prevail, purely subsistence farming can develop first into mixed agriculture, where part of the crop is retained for subsistence and part is sold in the market, and then into modern agriculture with production entirely for the market, very often based on one crop. In the transition from subsistence agriculture, cash crops can utilize slack labour and land when the subsistence crops are finished; but the transition into mixed farming is possible only if the farmer has the inputs to raise productivity and the credit to purchase those inputs, as well as the marketing facilities.

Modern agriculture, run on strictly commercial lines for profit and based on one crop, must rely on exports since the size of the domestic market will generally be too small. The system of modern commercialized agriculture, upon which many developing countries depend for their export earnings, is often termed **agribusiness**. This is a catch-all phrase referring not only to the production of the commodity in question, but also to the backward and forward linkages associated with the production process: the provision of finance, machinery, fertilizers, seed and so on at the input end, and the processing, manufacturing and marketing of the product at the output end.

Today, the **multinational corporations** have a powerful position and a strong hold over the production and export of major agricultural commodities produced in the developing countries. To give just a few examples: three US firms control over one-half of the global banana trade, five European companies control 90 per cent of the tea sold in the developed countries, and the two largest coffee companies control 20 per cent of the world market.

Both the ability to export and the ability to market internally imply surplus production over subsistence needs, and it is the size of this surplus that will largely determine the speed with which the subsistence sector can be drawn into the money economy. Again we come to the fact that unless productivity in agriculture increases, the expansion of the monetized sector will tend to decelerate as the land for cultivation dries up. When land has been exploited to the full it acts as a constraint on development unless agricultural productivity increases or non-agricultural activities can be established.

The emergence of an export sector provides a powerful stimulus to development and extension of the money economy. Exports create the capacity to import, and the very purchase of foreign products can encourage further export specialization. A population that acquires a taste for imported goods provides the impetus to producers to export more. In the case of new goods, as well as new techniques, there is strong evidence that peasant producers respond to incentives, and are not as different from 'Western economic man' as is sometimes claimed. Imports also provide a stimulus to industrialization. If a market for a foreign-manufactured good becomes established, it becomes easier and less risky, with the aid of tariff protection, for a domestic manufacturer to set up in business because the market is assured. Imports can also substitute for domestic capital and raise the growth rate directly.

When farmers start to specialize in goods for export, and rely on other producers for goods they previously produced themselves, the money economy will spread from the foreign trade sector to the rest of the domestic economy. This is nothing more than the international division of labour giving rise to the need for a means of exchange within a country as well as between countries.

The emergence of an export sector, the spread of the money economy and the establishment of industries typically occur concurrently. What form industrialization takes will depend, in the first instance, on the initial impetus. One stimulus to industrialization that we have already mentioned is imports creating a market for goods that can be produced domestically without much difficulty. A more obvious factor leading naturally to industrialization is the availability of resources from the land, forming an indigenous industrial base. In this case industrialization takes the form of the processing of raw materials. There are few countries that do not possess some natural resource or other, and every country will have a comparative advantage in the production of one or other raw material that can be processed. These are the agribusinesses mentioned earlier.

In many of the present developing countries, formerly under colonial rule, the initiating force behind industrialization was the foreign exploitation of resources. Industrial activity took the form of mining operations and plantation agriculture. The establishment of foreign enclave activities undoubtedly exerted a development impact, but it is sometimes argued that development would have been more rapid if countries had been left to their own devices. Some claim that the long-run development of these countries was impaired because the availability of cheap labour from the subsistence sector discouraged the installation of more modern productive machinery, and also that the foreign ownership and exploitation of countries' resources considerably reduced the potential level of investment through the remittance of profits to the host country. This is the argument of dependency theorists, which is discussed more fully in Chapter 8.

Finance for traditional agriculture

For many years traditional agriculture has been starved of investment resources. While it accounts for approximately 30 per cent of output and 50 per cent of total employment, it attracts little more than 10 per cent of total investment resources. Private capital has no doubt been deterred by the risks involved, and by the low returns in traditional agriculture. But institutional investment has also been meagre. For example, in the early years of the World Bank from 1947 to 1959, only $124 million was spent on agriculture out of total loans of $4 billion. Official Development Assistance (ODA) to agriculture from multilateral and bilateral sources rose sharply in the 1970s, but since 1979 the share of ODA going to agriculture decreased from 18 per cent to 3.5 per cent in 2004. In absolute terms, it reached a peak of $8 billion (measured at 2004 US$) in 1984, falling to only £3.4 billion in 2004 (World Bank, 2007).

Within agriculture-based developing economies, the share of public expenditure spent on agriculture has also decreased from 7 per cent in 1980 to 4 per cent in 2004 (World Bank, 2007). This gives some measure of the neglect of agriculture, which was partly responsible for the world food crisis, and food price rises, in 2007/2008.

The public sectors of developing countries, and multilateral institutions such as the World Bank, have a responsibility to invest in agriculture to raise productivity and combat poverty. Some projects will involve increasing the output of traditional crops through the more effective use of seeds, fertilizers and water. Other projects will involve changing the product mix from subsistence crops to the production of high-value crops.

At present, the largest single component of lending to agriculture is irrigation, which permits the expansion of cultivation and makes more intensive cultivation possible by permitting double cropping. Bank-financed irrigation schemes have had a major impact on rice yields and production in Asia. The World Bank has also become the most important source of financial and technical assistance for the construction of fertilizer plants in developing countries, and these have played an important role in increasing yields and output. The Bank gives credit for rural infrastructure projects such as roads to reduce marketing and supply bottlenecks, and rural electrification schemes. **Agricultural extension** is another important aspect of the Bank's assistance to the rural sector. In India, where 'contact' farmers disseminate knowledge to their neighbours of improved techniques learnt from field agents, over 10 million farm families have been helped. The rural poor now have more extensive and easier access to credit financed by the Bank. In India much of the credit has been used by small farmers to provide supplementary irrigation.

Finally, the World Bank operates various multi-purpose projects that combine a wide range of activities, normally in conjunction with a regional development programme. In Mexico, some 75,000 low-income families have benefited from such a project in about 30 localities through investments in irrigation, soil conservation, electrification, schools, health care, water supplies and marketing services. Each dollar the Bank invests in rural development is supplemented by local investment, and the Bank rightly stresses that its contribution to the total flow of resources can be effective only if appropriate national policies are pursued on pricing, taxation, land reform and so on. The major part of the Bank's programme to reach the rural poor is still in the process of implementation, and is therefore difficult to assess reliably, but indications suggest that a combination of additional resources, institutional reform and national government commitment to improvement in the rural sector can have a major impact.

Apart from the World Bank, other multilateral institutions exist to help traditional agriculture, notably the United Nations International Fund for Agricultural Development (IFAD), which seeks to integrate small farmers and landless people into the development process. IFAD states that its priority is for 'projects which will have a significant impact on improving food production in developing countries, particularly for the benefit of the poorest sections of the rural population'. Up to 2008, nearly $2 billion had been dispersed.

In the absence of external institutional investment, the sources of capital for the expansion of both agriculture and industry are relatively limited in the early stages of development. In a truly subsistence economy, in the sense of an economy producing only what it needs for itself and no more, everyone is a Robinson Crusoe, supplying their own capital by refraining from present consumption. With specialization in the production of goods for export, and the producer's need for capital to expand productive capacity, mechanisms grow up spontaneously to meet the need for credit. It is a good market maxim that demand will create a supplier at a price. The suppliers are generally village moneylenders, shopkeepers, landlords and, not infrequently, the Church – especially in South America – charging rates of interest that often exceed 50 per cent.

The interdependence of agriculture and industry

Once agriculture emerges from its subsistence state and starts to specialize and produce goods for export, and industry develops under the impact of growth in the agricultural sector, the two sectors of agriculture and industry become very interdependent. The industrial sector adds to the demand for goods produced by agriculture and absorbs surplus labour, which may raise productivity in agriculture. In turn, the agricultural sector provides a market for industrial goods out of rising real income, and makes a factor contribution to development through the release of resources if productivity rises faster than the demand for commodities.

Demand coming from agriculture can be a major stimulus to industrialization. Adelman (1984) has described the process as 'agricultural-demand-led-industrialisation'. Vogel (1994) has shown, taking 27 social accounting matrixes for both low- and high-income economies, that the impact of agriculture on industry is much higher than the impact of industry on agriculture, and it increases with the level of income. At low levels of income, a $1 expenditure in agriculture generates a

$2.75 increase in induced demand for non-agricultural inputs and services, and a $10 increase in high-income countries. It is rural household demand that contributes most to the backward multiplier; this leads Vogel to conclude: 'the early development theorists failed to articulate a place for rural household demand for consumer goods. Not recognising the centrality of these institutional feedbacks in agriculture's production linkages in developing economies has been one of the great failures of theories of economic development.' It is true that a stagnant rural sector has held back industrial development in several developing countries.

The transfer of resources from agriculture to industry may be in the form of capital or labour or both. Since labour is in abundant supply in most low-income countries, there is generally no difficulty in releasing labour for industry, except during harvest time. In any case, labour will tend to migrate naturally in response to seemingly better opportunities in the industrial sector and higher real incomes. The real earnings of labour in the industrial sector may be more than twice as much as the agricultural wage. If the industrial sector is to be guaranteed an adequate supply of labour, some wage differential is inevitably required to offset the higher real living costs in an urban environment, to compensate for the forfeit of non-monetary benefits of rural life, and to compensate for greater job uncertainty in the industrial sector. Real earnings may also be higher because of genuinely higher productivity in the industrial sector, where labour has more factors of production to work with. Most models of rural–urban migration make migration a positive function of the *expected* urban–rural wage differential, which is the difference between the urban wage, adjusted for the proportion of the total urban labour force employed (as a proxy for the probability of finding work), and the agricultural real wage (see p. 207 below for an outline of the model).

Capital may be less 'mobile' than labour, and if there is considered to be insufficient lending from the agricultural sector on a voluntary basis it may become necessary for a government to extract savings compulsorily from the agricultural sector by taxation. As mentioned already, this method was resorted to in a harsh manner by Japan at the time of the Meiji restoration and by Soviet Russia after the communist revolution. In Japan between 1880 and 1900 the land tax provided approximately 80 per cent of central government tax revenue, and in Russia forced extraction of the agricultural surplus took the form of expropriation of land and the extermination of labour. Industrialization in Western Europe, and particularly in England, was also financed to a large extent by surpluses generated on the land, but transference of these surpluses was on the whole voluntary through a rapidly expanding banking system. The developing countries today, despite their access to foreign sources of capital, must also rely heavily on extracting the surplus from agriculture to finance industrialization. The difficulty is to decide on the best means of extraction without impairing the incentive to produce, or damaging the growth of productivity, upon which a growing agricultural surplus depends. The financing of economic development will be discussed more fully in Part V of this book.

Economic development with unlimited supplies of labour

The process of the emergence of a money economy from a subsistence state was formalized by Sir Arthur Lewis in his classic paper 'Economic Development with Unlimited Supplies of Labour' (1954).[3] There he presents a 'classical' model of a dual economy with the purpose, as he describes it, of seeing what can be made of the classical framework for understanding the issues of distribution, capital accumulation and growth in developing countries. His ultimate aim is to emphasize the crucial role of the capitalist surplus in the development process.

Arthur Lewis

Born 1915, St Lucia, West Indies. Died 1991. Professor of Economics, Manchester University, University of the West Indies and Princeton University. Vice-Chancellor, University of the West Indies, and Director of the Caribbean Development Bank. Wrote the first textbook on development economics, *The Theory of Economic Growth* (1955), but most famous for his 1954 paper 'Economic Development with Unlimited Supplies of Labour', one of the most influential papers in development economics, still widely consulted today. Lewis was one of the 'fathers' of development economics and was awarded the Nobel Prize for Economics, 1979.

The Lewis model therefore starts with the assumption of a dual economy with a modern exchange (capitalist) sector and an indigenous (non-capitalist) subsistence sector, and assumes that there are unlimited supplies of labour in the subsistence sector in the sense that the supply of labour exceeds the demand for labour at the subsistence wage; that is, the marginal product of workers in the subsistence sector is equal to, or less than, the subsistence or institutional wage.

It has even been argued that the marginal product of labour may be zero or negative in an economy that is still at a fairly low level of development and experiencing a rapid growth of population. Indeed, Lewis himself says 'there are large sectors of [a developing] economy where the marginal productivity of labour is negligible, zero or even negative'.

One of the distinguishing features of agriculture is that it is an activity that is subject to diminishing returns owing to the fixity of the supply of land. If there is rapid population growth and labour has little employment opportunity other than on the land, a stage may be reached where the land cannot provide further workers with a living unless the existing workers drastically reduce their hours of work. These propositions are illustrated in Figure 6.1. The curve drawn represents the marginal product of successive units of labour added to the land. After the employment of X units of labour the marginal product of labour begins to fall owing to diminishing returns; after X_1 units of labour, labour's marginal contribution to output falls below the subsistence wage; and

Figure 6.1   Marginal product of successive units of labour added to the land

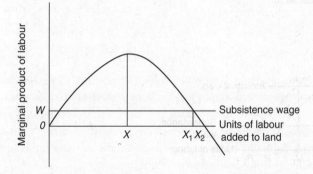

Figure 6.2   Tendency towards diminishing returns

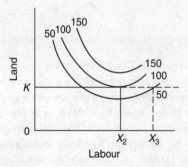

after X_2 units of labour, labour's contribution to output becomes negative and total product will decline with successive additions of labour beyond X_2.

The same tendencies can also be represented using the type of production function diagram introduced in Chapter 5, which is reproduced in Figure 6.2. With more than X_2 labour employed with a fixed amount of land, K, the marginal product of labour becomes negative, and further additions to the labour supply, without corresponding increases in the amount of land, will push the economy on to a lower production function, that is, total output will fall from 100 units to, say, 50 units with X_3 units of labour.

There are three main means of escape from the tendency towards diminishing returns and zero marginal product in agriculture: first, through the absorption of more and more of the agricultural population into industry; second, by technical progress in the agricultural sector increasing labour's marginal product; and third, by capital accumulation, which can raise productivity directly and also be the vehicle for technical progress.

In Lewis's model, labour in excess of X_1 in Figure 6.1 is in completely elastic supply to the industrial sector at whatever the industrial wage.[4] The industrial or capitalist sector is represented in Figure 6.3. The curve NR represents the marginal product of labour in the capitalist sector, W is the industrial wage and, on the profit-maximizing assumption, labour is employed in the capitalist sector up to the point where the marginal product is equal to the wage rate. That is, M will be employed. Workers in excess of M earn what they can in the subsistence sector. The industrial wage is assumed to be determined in some relation to the wage that workers can earn in the subsistence sector. The differential (WW_1) between the industrial wage and the subsistence wage will be a function of many factors, some of which were mentioned earlier, for example higher real living costs in the capitalist sector and greater job uncertainty. Given that the industrial wage is

Figure 6.3   Industrial/capitalist sector

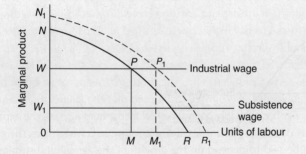

based on earnings in the subsistence sector, capitalists have a direct interest in holding down productivity in the subsistence sector, and Lewis comments that the record of employers in Africa in modern times was one of impoverishing the subsistence economy.

The total product of labour, $0NPM$ in Figure 6.3, is split between the payment to labour in the form of wages, $0WPM$, and the capitalist surplus, WNP. The expansion of the capitalist sector and the rate of absorption of labour from the subsistence sector depends on the use made of the capitalist surplus. If the surplus is reinvested, leading to greater capital formation, this will increase the total product of labour. The marginal product curve will shift upwards to the right, say N_1R_1, which means that if wages remain constant the capitalist sector can now afford to employ more labour and will do so by drawing on labour from the subsistence sector to the extent of MM_1 workers. The size of the capitalist surplus will increase from WNP to WN_1P_1, which is available for further reinvestment, and so the process goes on. This for Lewis is the essence of the development process. The stimulus to investment in the capitalist sector comes from the rate of profit, which must rise over time because all the benefits of increased productivity accrue to capital if the real wage is constant.[5]

According to Lewis, the share of profits in the national income ($P/0$) will also rise. First, the share of profits in the capitalist sector (P/C) will increase, and second, the capitalist sector relative to the national income ($C/0$) will tend to expand; that is, if $P/0 = P/C \times C/0$, then $P/0$ will rise as P/C and $C/0$ increase. For Lewis, the latter is the more important. He says: 'if we ask why the less developed countries save so little, the answer is not because they are so poor but because their capitalist sector is so small'.

The process outlined by Lewis comes to an end when capital accumulation has caught up with population, so that there is no surplus labour in the subsistence sector left to absorb. When all surplus labour is absorbed, the supply of labour to the industrial sector becomes less than perfectly elastic. It is now in the interests of producers in the subsistence sector to compete for labour, since the marginal product of labour is no longer below the institutional wage. When this point is reached, the agricultural sector can be said to have become commercialized. This change in producer behaviour in the subsistence sector has also been defined as the end of the take-off stage (Ranis and Fei, 1961).

Implicit in the Lewis model is the assumption that employment growth in the capitalist sector will be proportional to the rate of capital formation. If profits are reinvested in labour-saving technology, however, this will not be so, and the rate of growth of employment in the industrial sector, as well as the rate of absorption from the agricultural sector, may be very low.

It is also possible that the process of absorption may end prematurely before surplus labour in the subsistence sector is fully exhausted, owing to checks to the expansion of the capitalist surplus. First, capital accumulation and labour absorption may be checked for reasons that are related to the expansion of the capitalist sector itself. For example, as the capitalist sector expands the terms of trade may turn against it. If the demand for food expands faster than agricultural output, the capitalist sector will be forced to pay higher prices for food in exchange for industrial goods, reducing the size of the capitalist surplus. This will have two effects.

First, if the capitalists are forced to pay higher prices for the goods they buy relative to those that they sell, this means less saving for investment. The problem does not arise if productivity in agriculture is expanding rapidly, but Lewis himself recognized that the failure of peasant agriculture to increase its productivity has probably been the chief factor holding back the expansion of the industrial sector in many developing countries. If this is so, argue Lewis's critics, the growth of non-farm employment can be said to depend on the growth of the agricultural surplus. This in fact is the starting point of **neoclassical models of development** (see Jorgenson, 1966), in contrast to classical models with their exclusive stress on capital accumulation.

The second effect arising from the expansion of the capitalist sector if there is a shortage of food is that the real wage may have to rise in industry, further squeezing the capitalist surplus. If labour is needed in agriculture to meet the demand for food, unlimited supplies of labour at a *constant real wage* may be very limited indeed. The assumption of an unlimited supply of labour is the central proposition underlying the classical approach to the theory of development, and Jorgenson has argued that the classical approach stands or falls by this hypothesis. Historically, of course, real wages have risen in agriculture *and* industry, and the capitalist sector has also expanded rapidly, which lends support to a middle view between the classical and neoclassical approaches. Lewis himself recognized the importance of both capital accumulation and food supply, and it is this consideration that forms the basis of his argument for the balanced growth of the agricultural and industrial sectors.

Capital accumulation in the industrial sector may also be checked for reasons unrelated to the expansion of the capitalist sector and its demand for food. For example, real wages may be forced up directly by trade unions, or indirectly through rising real wages in the subsistence sector due to increased agricultural productivity. Lewis (1954) himself states that

> anything which raises the productivity of the subsistence sector (average product per person) will raise real wages in the capitalist sector, and will therefore reduce the capitalist surplus and the rate of capital accumulation, unless it at the same time more than correspondingly moves the terms of trade against the subsistence sector.

Lewis reaches this conclusion because one of the simplifying assumptions of his classical two-sector model is that the expansion of the capitalist sector is limited *only* by a shortage of capital, so that any increase in prices and purchasing power for farmers is not a stimulus to industrialization but an obstacle to the expansion of the capitalist sector. How does this square with the idea of the agricultural sector providing a market for industrial goods, and the view of the World Bank (*World Development Report 1979*) that 'a stagnant rural economy with low purchasing power holds back industrial growth in many developing countries'? The answer is that there does seem to be a contradiction, because the classical approach emphasizes supply to the exclusion of demand, or rather takes for granted that there will always be a market clearing price for industrial goods. In fact there will be a minimum below which the price of industrial goods cannot fall, set by the subsistence level wage in industry.

Johnston and Mellor (1961) recognized this worrying feature of the Lewis model many years ago when they perceptively remarked 'there is clearly a conflict between emphasis on agriculture's essential contribution to the capital requirements for overall development, and emphasis on increased farm purchasing power as a stimulus to industrialization. Nor is there any easy reconciliation of the conflict.' The challenge of reconciliation has never been taken up in a simple way, but there is a resolution of the conflict if the **complementarity** between the two sectors is recognized from the outset, and it is remembered that there must be an equilibrium terms of trade that balances supply and demand in both sectors. The basis of a model of reconciliation is provided by Kaldor (1979).

A model of the complementarity between agriculture and industry[6]

We have seen that agriculture provides the potential for capital accumulation in industry by providing a marketable surplus. The greater the surplus, the cheaper industry can obtain food and

Figure 6.4 Industrial terms of trade and agricultural growth rate

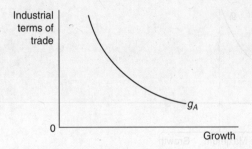

the more saving and capital accumulation can be undertaken. This is the supply side. But industry also needs a market for its industrial goods, which in the early stages of development must largely come from agriculture. This is the demand side, and the higher the price of agricultural goods the greater agricultural purchasing power will be. Given this conflict between low food prices being good for industrial supply and high food prices being good for industrial demand, what is required is a simple model that brings together agriculture and industry in an equilibrium framework, where the terms of trade between agriculture and industry provide the equilibrating mechanism ensuring that supply and demand grow at the same rate in each sector.

Let us first model growth in the agricultural sector in relation to the terms of trade; then growth in the industrial sector; and then bring the two sectors together. Agriculture's growth rate will be a function of how much it invests relative to output and of the productivity of investment. How much investment goods it obtains from industry in exchange for food that it 'saves' depends on the price of industrial goods relative to food; that is, on the terms of trade between industry and agriculture. The higher the price of investment goods, the lower the possible investment for a given amount of food and the lower the growth of supply capacity. This inverse relation between the industrial terms of trade (the price of industrial goods relative to the price of food) and the agricultural growth rate (g_A) is shown in Figure 6.4.

Industry's growth rate will also be a function of its investment ratio and the productivity of investment. But there is a certain minimum to the terms of trade, below which industry would not be able to invest anything because all output would be required to pay for workers' wage goods (food). If all wages are consumed, the cost of food input per unit of output in industry will depend on the real wage rate in industry divided by the productivity of labour, that is $w/(O/L) = (W/O)$, where w is the real wage and W is the wage bill. Industrial prices must cover W/O, and this sets the lower limit to industrial prices relative to food prices. At the other extreme, industrial growth cannot exceed a certain maximum where the price of food is so low relative to industrial goods that all industrial goods are retained for investment in industry. The investment ratio approaches, in effect, 100 per cent, and the upper limit to growth is given by the productivity of investment. The positive relation between the industrial terms of trade and the industrial growth rate (g_I) is shown in Figure 6.5.

If we now assume for simplicity (although without loss of generality) that the income elasticity of demand for agricultural and industrial goods is unity, then at a given terms of trade the rate of growth of agricultural output represents the rate of growth of demand for industrial goods, and the rate of growth of industrial output represents the rate of growth of demand for agricultural output, and where g_A and g_S cross there will be balanced growth of agriculture and industry (g^*) at equilibrium terms of trade (p^*), as shown in Figure 6.6.[7] In this model of the complementarity between agriculture and industry, we can see the implications of what happens if the

Figure 6.5   Industrial terms of trade and industrial growth rate

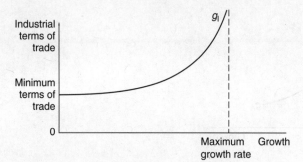

Figure 6.6   Growth equilibrium and disequilibrium

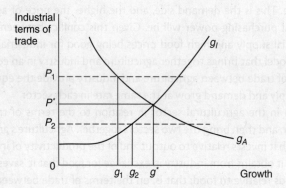

terms of trade are not in equilibrium, as well as the checks to the expansion of industry that Lewis mentions.

If the terms of trade are not in equilibrium – if the price of food is 'too low' or 'too high' in relation to industrial goods – then industrial growth is either demand constrained or supply constrained. For example, if in Figure 6.6 the terms of trade were at P_1, because the price of food was 'too low', industrial growth would be demand constrained to g_1 by a lack of agricultural purchasing power over industrial goods. Industry could accumulate capital, but it could not sell its goods. Alternatively, if the terms of trade were below equilibrium at P_2, industrial growth would be supply constrained to g_2 because the price of food would be 'too high', impairing capital accumulation in industry. Agriculture could buy, but industry could not supply. Growth is maximized at P^*.

We can now examine what happens if there are shifts in the curves. Clearly, shifts in the curves will cause both the growth rates and the equilibrium terms of trade to vary. An improvement in agricultural productivity that shifts g_A outwards will mean both higher industrial growth and an improvement in the industrial terms of trade. The importance of agricultural productivity improvement could not be better illustrated. An improvement in industrial productivity will shift g_I outwards, which will also mean higher industrial growth but at the expense of worse terms of trade for industry.[8] If there is a tendency for real wages in industry to rise commensurately with productivity increases, however, the g_I curve will remain stable and the terms of trade will never move against industry in favour of agriculture unless agricultural productivity falls and the g_A curve shifts inwards.

The checks to industrial expansion in Lewis's model are easily illustrated. A rise in the real wage in industry will shift the g_I curve inwards, which will choke industrial expansion unless an equivalent increase in agricultural productivity shifts the g_A curve outwards (see the quote from Lewis on p. 204).

A final implication of the model is that if through time agriculture is subject to diminishing returns, productivity in agriculture will fall, shifting inwards the g_A curve and reducing the rate of industrial growth. If the g_I curve is relatively stable, industrial growth depends fundamentally on the rate of land-saving innovations (technical progress) in agriculture to offset the effect of diminishing returns.

Rural–urban migration and urban unemployment

Lewis spoke of an urban–rural wage differential of approximately 30 per cent to attract labour to the industrial sector. What has happened in recent years, however, is that the urban–rural wage differential has widened considerably beyond this level – there has been rural–urban migration on an unprecedented scale, but the expansion of the industrial sector has not generated sufficient employment for all those available to work. The urban–rural wage differential in China is over 300 per cent; in Guatemala 300 per cent, and in Vietnam 210 per cent (World Bank, 2007). Migration has thus served to transfer unemployment from rural to urban areas, as described in Chapter 3. In 2008, for the first time in human history, the number of people living in urban areas exceeded those living in the rural sector. The **informal economy** of the urban sector harbours the bulk of unemployed labour in transition from the rural sector into industrial employment. The conclusion to be drawn is that the *expected* value of the urban wage, notwithstanding the probability of long spells of unemployment, still exceeds the wage in the rural sector, and as long as it does so the process of migration will continue. In these changed circumstances, development theory has focused its attention in recent years on **urban unemployment** and policies to combat it. Most of the models of the rural–urban migration process are pessimistic about reducing the level of urban unemployment by conventional means such as subsidies to labour or public-works programmes in the urban areas. The reason is that migration from the land is made to be a function not only of the *actual* urban–rural wage differential but also of the level of employment opportunities. More employment opportunities reduce unemployment immediately but encourage more migration. It thus becomes an empirical question whether increasing the rate of growth of employment in urban areas will actually reduce unemployment. The very real possibility exists, however, that urban areas may be caught in a 'high level unemployment equilibrium trap' as long as surplus labour on the land remains and development policy concentrates new activity in established urban (industrial) centres.

One of the earliest and simplest models of the rural–urban migration process, which is also operational in the sense of being testable, is that of Todaro (1971). Let us consider its main features and implications.

The supply of labour to the urban sector is assumed to be a function of the *expected* urban–rural wage differential (d), where the expected urban–rural wage differential is equal to the actual urban wage times the probability of obtaining a job in the urban sector minus the average rural wage. Thus

$$S = f_s(d) \qquad (6.1)$$

where S is the supply of labour to the urban sector and

$$d = w\pi - r \qquad (6.2)$$

where w is the urban real wage, r is the average rural wage, and π is the probability of obtaining a job in the urban sector.

The probability of obtaining a job in the urban sector is assumed to be directly related to the rate of new job creation and inversely related to the ratio of unemployed job-seekers to the number of existing job opportunities,[9] that is

$$\pi = \frac{\gamma N}{W - N} = \frac{\gamma N}{U} \qquad (6.3)$$

where γ is the net rate of new urban job creation, N is the level of urban employment, W is the total urban labour force,[10] and U is the level of urban unemployment. Substituting (6.3) into (6.2) gives

$$d = \frac{w\gamma N}{U} - r \qquad (6.4)$$

If it is assumed that migration will come to a stop when the *expected* urban wage equals the rural wage (that is, when $d = 0$), we can derive from (6.4) the equilibrium level of unemployment as

$$U^e = \frac{w\gamma N}{r} \qquad (6.5)$$

It can be seen from (6.5) that a reduction in the *actual* urban wage will reduce the equilibrium level of unemployment, and a rise in the rural wage will also reduce it, but (paradoxically) an increase in the rate of new job creation will *raise* the equilibrium level of unemployment by increasing the probability of obtaining a job and encouraging migration. Whether policies such as wage subsidies can reduce unemployment therefore depends on whether the increase in the demand for labour as a result is greater or less than the induced supply.

From (6.5) we can solve for the equilibrium ratio of unemployment to employment and give some quantitative content to the model. Dividing both sides by N gives $U^e/N = w\gamma/r$. Thus, for example, if the industrial wage is twice as high as the rural wage ($w/r = 2$), and $\gamma = 0.05$, the equilibrium ratio of unemployment to employment will be 10 per cent.

To consider the policy implications more fully, and to answer the question 'under what conditions will the actual level of urban unemployment rise?', let us suppose that the rate of urban job creation is a function of the urban wage, w, and a policy parameter, a (for example, a government policy variable to increase employment). Thus

$$\gamma = f_d(w, a) \frac{\partial \gamma}{\partial a} > 0 \qquad (6.6)$$

If the growth of urban labour demand is increased, the response of labour supply can be written as

$$\frac{\partial S}{\partial a} = \frac{\partial S}{\partial d} \frac{\partial d}{\partial \gamma} \frac{\partial \gamma}{\partial a} \qquad (6.7)$$

Now, from (6.4) by partial differentiation, we have

$$\frac{\partial d}{\partial \gamma} = w \frac{N}{U} \tag{6.8}$$

Substituting (6.8) into (6.7) gives

$$\frac{\partial S}{\partial a} = \frac{\partial S}{\partial d} \frac{wN}{U} \frac{\partial \gamma}{\partial a} \tag{6.9}$$

There will be an increase in the absolute level of urban unemployment if the increase in supply in response to a policy change exceeds the increase in the absolute number of new jobs created, that is, if

$$\frac{\partial S}{\partial d} \frac{wN}{U} \frac{\partial \gamma}{\partial a} > N \frac{\partial \gamma}{\partial a} \tag{6.10}$$

Now, cancelling N and $\partial \gamma / \partial a$ from both sides and multiplying both sides by d/w and U/W, the condition for unemployment to increase becomes

$$\frac{\partial S/W}{\partial d/d} > \frac{d}{w} \frac{U}{W} \tag{6.11}$$

or substituting (6.2) into (6.11):

$$\frac{\partial S/W}{\partial d/d} > \frac{w\pi - r}{w} \frac{U}{W} \tag{6.12}$$

In words, (6.12) says that unemployment will increase in the urban sector as a result of a policy change to increase employment if the elasticity of the urban labour supply (by migration) with respect to the urban–rural wage differential exceeds the expected urban–rural wage differential as a proportion of the urban wage times the unemployment rate. Equation (6.12) is clearly testable. It transpires, in fact, that (6.12) is satisfied with a very low elasticity. For example, suppose that the actual urban wage is twice the rural wage,[11] that the probability of obtaining a job in the urban sector is 0.8 and that the unemployment rate is 10 per cent, then the level of unemployment will increase if the elasticity of the urban labour supply with respect to the expected urban–rural wage differential is 0.03.

Note that the growth of total labour supply as a result of migration ($\partial S/W$) is not the same thing as the rate of growth of migration ($\partial S/S$), so that the elasticity of *supply* with respect to a change in job opportunities is not the same as the elasticity of *migration* with respect to a change in job opportunities. We could, however, convert (6.12) into the elasticity of migration with respect to $\partial d/\partial$ by multiplying both sides of (6.10) by U/S instead of U/W. This would give

$$\frac{\partial S/S}{\partial d/d} > \frac{w\pi - r}{w} \frac{U}{S} \tag{6.13}$$

Since the ratio of unemployment to migration (U/S) is much higher than U/W, the elasticity of migration itself would have to be higher than the elasticity of labour supply for unemployment to increase following a job expansion programme. If, as before, we assume that $w/r = 2$, $\pi = 0.8$

and, say, $U/S = 2$, the migration elasticity would have to exceed 0.6 for unemployment to rise. In principle this elasticity is easy to estimate by specifying a migration function in which migration is a function of the expected urban–rural wage differential, holding constant other factors affecting migration. For an interesting case study, see the study of Tanzania by Barnum and Sabot (1977), who estimate an elasticity of migration with respect to the urban wage itself, holding other things constant, of between 0.7 and 2.0.[12]

Disguised unemployment: types and measurement

The higher the marginal product of labour in agriculture, the greater the force of the neoclassical argument that it is the growth of the agricultural surplus that determines the growth of non-farm employment. We must now examine more critically the classical assumption of unlimited supplies of labour, defined as marginal product below the subsistence wage.

If the marginal product of labour in the rural sector is positive (which is not precluded in Lewis's model as long as it is below the subsistence wage), the withdrawal of labour from the subsistence sector will reduce total output. To argue that development via unlimited supplies of labour is feasible and relatively painless one must implicitly assume that the marginal product of labour is virtually zero. The term '**disguised unemployment**' is usually defined loosely in this way. But the question arises of how workers can survive on the land if their marginal product is zero, or even positive but below subsistence. Who would employ such labour? Would output in the subsistence sector really remain unaffected if substantial quantities of labour migrated? In short, what precisely is meant by the term 'disguised unemployment'? Can it be quantified, and what are we to make of the argument that industrial development in surplus-labour economies is a relatively painless process?

Let us redraw Figure 6.1 from the point of diminishing returns and describe more formally three possible interpretations of the concept of disguised unemployment that are commonly found in the literature. Let A in Figure 6.7 be the actual number of workers employable. One possible measure of disguised unemployment is the difference between A and S, or the gap between the number of workers available for work and the amount of employment that equates the marginal product of labour and the subsistence wage. This is the definition of unlimited supplies of labour in Lewis's model where, if the marginal product of labour is below the subsistence wage, landowners have no interest in retaining these workers and therefore do not compete for them with the industrial sector.

Figure 6.7   Disguised unemployment

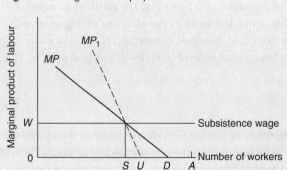

A second possible measure of disguised unemployment is the difference between A and D, or the gap between the actual number of workers available for employment and the level of employment at which the marginal product of labour is zero, which is sometimes referred to as the **static surplus**. This surplus is clearly less than if disguised unemployment is defined as labour with a marginal product below the institutional or subsistence wage.

A third measure of disguised unemployment is the difference between the actual number of workers available and the level of employment at which the marginal product of labour would be zero if some change occurred that enabled the same level of output to be produced with fewer workers. This is represented by a pivoting of the marginal product curve to MP_1. Disguised unemployment is now measured by the difference between A and U, which is sometimes referred to as the **dynamic surplus**. The dynamic surplus clearly embraces many 'types' of disguised unemployment because there are many reasons, particularly in developing countries, why labour productivity may be low and why small changes in technique and organization of production may release substantial quantities of labour.

There are three main ways of ascertaining whether surplus labour exists in the sense that labour's marginal product is zero. The first is to examine instances where substantial numbers of the agricultural labour force have been withdrawn from the land, either to work on some industrialization project or as the result of illness, and to observe whether agricultural output falls or not.

This method was followed by Schultz (1964), who examined the effect of the influenza epidemic in India in 1918–19, which killed approximately 8 per cent of the agricultural labour force. He found that acreage and output during the following year declined, and concluded from this that surplus labour in Indian agriculture did not exist. An important criticism of Schultz's study, however, is that he failed to distinguish between the summer and winter season of the year following the epidemic. Mehra (1966) has shown that summer production, which just followed the epidemic, was not in fact reduced and that the decline in agricultural production in 1919–20 found by Schultz was entirely due to a reduction in the winter crop, which could have resulted from low rainfall. Notwithstanding the criticism, this is one method of approach.

A second method of estimating the static surplus is to take the difference between the labour available and the labour required to produce the current level of agricultural output *with given techniques*, making due allowance for the seasonality of production. The estimate of the magnitude of surplus labour in this case will vary with local conditions, and what is regarded as a normal working day.

A third approach is to estimate agricultural production functions (see Chapter 5) to test whether the elasticity of output with respect to labour input is significantly different from zero. This approach indicates whether or not there is surplus labour, but does not measure its magnitude.

When discussing labour's marginal product in agriculture and the extent of disguised unemployment, two important distinctions need to be made: between harvest and non-harvest time; and between farms that hire labour and those that do not. Within the production function approach this distinction is easily made explicit and is a very fruitful approach for that reason. As far as the distinction between hired and non-hired labour is concerned, the marginal product of family labour can hardly be zero if workers are hired, nor can the marginal product of the hired workers be zero if they are paid.

We now turn to the measurement of the **dynamic surplus**, which is the difference between the actual labour employed and the labour required given some small change in technique (including an increase in the number of hours worked per day).

Unfortunately those investigators who have measured the dynamic surplus have generally not distinguished between the causes of the surplus, or made explicit the assumptions upon which their estimates of labour requirements are based, and this is a major reason why estimates and opinions differ on the extent and existence of disguised unemployment. If the surplus is measured simply by the difference between the amount of labour that, in the investigator's opinion, should be necessary to produce a given output and the amount of labour that there actually is, this does not distinguish between the different causes of low productivity such as poor health, lack of incentive, a preference for leisure, primitive technology or the seasonal nature of production.

The simplest reconciliation between those who argue that there is such a phenomenon of disguised unemployment, in the sense of a very low marginal product of labour in agriculture, and those who disagree, is provided by the distinction between **the amount of labour time employed and the number of persons employed**. In a wage-payment system it is extremely unlikely that labour would be used up to the point where its marginal product is zero. If the wage is positive, the marginal product will be positive too. But profit-maximizing behaviour is quite consistent with redundant labour. Labour is employed up to the point where the marginal product of a unit of *labour time* is equal to the wage, and **disguised unemployment takes the form of a small number of hours worked per person**. It is not that there is too much labour time but too many labourers spending it. Total output would fall if workers were drawn from the land, unless those remaining worked longer hours to compensate. How much disguised unemployment is estimated to exist depends on what is regarded as a normal working day. Estimates may be subjective, but unlimited supplies of labour exist in the classical sense provided those remaining on the land work harder or longer. Let us illustrate these points diagrammatically.

In Figure 6.8 total output is measured on the vertical axis above the origin, and the amount of labour time on the horizontal axis. Let L_1 be the point where the marginal product of labour time is equal to the subsistence wage corresponding to total output, Q. The number of workers is measured on the vertical axis below the origin, so that the tangent of the angle $0YL_1$ (tan a) gives the average number of hours worked by each unit of labour. If the tangent of the angle $0XL_1$ is regarded as the normal length of a working day so that the same output, Q, could be produced by X labour instead of Y, the amount of disguised unemployment would be equal to XY. It can easily be seen that if there was a reduction in the labour force from Y to t and the number of hours worked per worker remained the same (that is, tan $0tS$ = tan $0YL_1$), total output would

Figure 6.8   The dynamic surplus

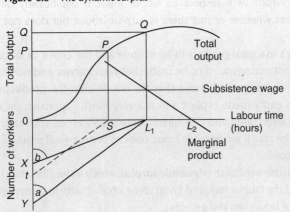

fall from Q to P. If the normal working day is considered to be longer or shorter than the hours given by $\tan b$, the amount of disguised unemployment will be greater or less than XY. Let us now give a practical example. Suppose a producer employs 10 workers ($Y = 10$), each doing 5 hours' work a day ($\tan a = 5$), and that the marginal product of the 50th hour is equal to the subsistence wage ($L_1 = 50$). If one worker leaves (say Yt), total output will fall from Q to P unless the 9 workers now do the 50 hours' work previously done by 10 workers; that is, the working day must be increased by five-ninths of an hour. The amount of disguised unemployment depends on what is considered to be a full day's work. If 10 hours is considered normal, then only 5 workers would be required to do 50 hours' work and 5 could be regarded as disguised unemployed.

The precise conditions under which the remaining labour force would supply more work effort have been formalized by Sen (1966). If workers are rational, they will work up to the point where the marginal utility of income from work (dU/dL) is equal to the marginal disutility of work (dV/dL). Now the marginal utility of income from work can be expressed as

$$\frac{dU}{dL} = \frac{dY}{dL} \cdot \frac{dU}{dY} \tag{6.14}$$

where dY/dL is the marginal product of labour and dU/dY is the marginal utility of income. Welfare maximization therefore implies that

$$\frac{dY}{dL} \cdot \frac{dU}{dY} = \frac{dV}{dL} \tag{6.15}$$

or

$$\frac{dY}{dL} = \frac{dV}{dL} \div \frac{dU}{dY} = \frac{\text{Marginal disutility of work}}{\text{Marginal utility of income}} \tag{6.16}$$

Sen defines the ratio of the marginal disutility of work to the marginal utility of income as the **real cost of labour**. Now consider Figure 6.9.

Equilibrium is at N where the marginal product is equal to the real cost of labour. The removal of one worker reduces total output from $0PXN$ to $0PX_1N_1$, and marginal product rises from X to X_1. Equilibrium will be restored again at N if the real cost of labour remains constant – that is, if the ratio of the marginal disutility of work to the marginal utility of income does not increase. If the real cost of labour rises, there will not be full compensation for output lost. In other words, disguised unemployment in the sense of *zero* marginal product (or full compensation for lost output)

Figure 6.9 Effect of labour withdrawal

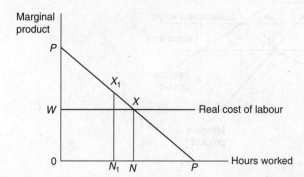

implies a **non-increasing marginal disutility of work and a non-diminishing marginal utility of income**. Sen gives a number of reasons why this may be the case for people near subsistence with little work and a lot of leisure; for example, rising aspirations and more public expenditure on such things as education may prevent the marginal utility of income from falling, and higher incomes may prevent the marginal disutility of work from increasing if people are better fed.

The amount of underutilized labour is likely to be the greater, the less capitalistic the organization of agriculture. In fact, in the extreme situation of no wage-payment system with no competitive pressure and little desire to maximize, the distinction between a unit of labour and a unit of labour time becomes largely redundant, as in the classical model. It is perhaps this type of environment that the originators of the classical model mainly had in mind. In an extended family-type system, for example, the marginal product of both workers and labour time may be below the subsistence wage. It is the *average* product that matters for the group as a whole, not the product of the last worker or hour, and the average product may still be above the subsistence level when the marginal product of labour time is below it. It is difficult to represent both cases on the same diagram, but if the marginal product of labour is zero, the marginal product of labour time is bound to be zero (and probably negative), so we may continue to illustrate the argument in terms of labour time, as in Figure 6.10.

The basis of Figure 6.10 is the same as Figure 6.8. When the marginal product of labour time is zero at L_2 the average product of labour time is P_1, or PP_1 in excess of the subsistence wage P. The amount of labour time could be extended to L_3 without the average product of labour time falling below subsistence, and the amount of labour time could be made up of any combination of workers and hours worked. If the number of workers was Y_1 they could work hours equal to the tangent of $0Y_1L_3$ without the average product of labour time falling below subsistence. Even though the marginal product of labour time, L_2L_3, is negative, all workers can subsist if the total product is equally shared. A zero or negative marginal product of labour time is not inconsistent with rational worker behaviour if positive utility is attached to work regardless of the effect on output.

Suppose, as in Figure 6.11, that the marginal product of a unit of labour time is zero after four hours' work but the marginal disutility of leisure is still negative at this point. The worker may

Figure 6.10   Maximum sustainable labour

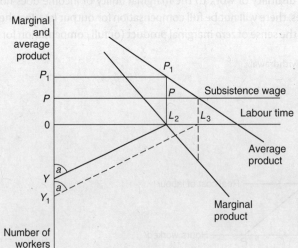

Figure 6.11   The possibility of negative marginal product

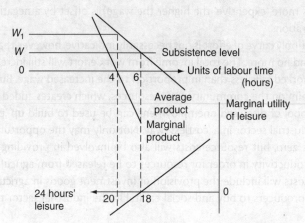

substitute work for leisure, working, say, 6 hours, despite the fact that the marginal product of labour time is negative after the fourth hour. If such behaviour is observed, the presumption must be that the marginal utility attached to working exceeds the loss of utility resulting from a lower average product. The fact that people receive positive utility from work may partly explain why in some societies the time taken to do specific tasks seems to be much longer than in others.

Incentives and the costs of labour transfer

Whether workers are willing to work more intensively to compensate for lost production as labour migrates, or whether capital is substituted for labour to raise productivity, requires some discussion of worker motivation and attitudes towards industrialization in general in a predominantly agricultural economy.

Some economic incentive will almost certainly be required to induce agricultural labour to work extra hours. At the least there will need to be goods with which to exchange their surplus production. It is sometimes argued, however, that peasant producers, accustomed to a traditional way of life, may not respond to such incentives – that their horizons are so limited that they have no desire to increase their surplus either by investing in capital or by working longer hours. The corollary of this argument is that as labour productivity increases, workers will ultimately reduce the number of hours they work. This is the notion of the **backward-bending supply curve of effort**, illustrated in Figure 6.12. SS is the supply curve of effort relating hours worked to the wage, determined by productivity. Total income is equal to the product of hours worked and the wage. Up to income level $SWZX$, supply responds positively to the wage. Beyond the wage SW,

Figure 6.12   Backward-bending supply curve

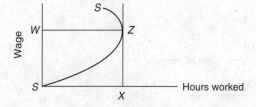

however, fewer hours will be offered. This is the point where the positive substitution effect of work for leisure (leisure is more 'expensive' the higher the wage) is offset by a negative income effect because of low aspirations.

A backward-bending supply curve of effort is not necessarily indicative, however, that peasants work for a fixed income and no more. The total income from work effort will still increase as long as the number of hours worked falls less than in proportion to the increased wage. But the need for incentives implies a claim on the community's real resources, which creates added difficulties for the argument that a pool of disguised unemployment can be used to build up 'productive' goods and expand the industrial sector in a 'costless' way. Not only may the opportunity cost of agricultural labour not be zero, but resource costs will also be involved in providing incentives to increased effort and productivity in order for resources to be released from agriculture in the first place. The resource costs will include the provision of investment goods in agriculture, consumer goods for peasant producers to buy and social capital in the industrial sector to cater for migrants.

All this has an important bearing on the question of the valuation of labour in surplus-labour economies when planning the social optimum allocation of resources and deciding on the degree to which activities in the industrial sector should be labour-intensive. Even if labour's opportunity cost is negligible, the resource costs of labour transference must be considered as a cost to the community in expanding the industrial sector.

There is also the question of increased consumption to consider. If the objective of a surplus-labour economy is to maximize growth, as opposed to the level of current consumption, the transference of labour will also involve a further 'cost' in terms of increased consumption because there will be a reduction in the size of the capitalist surplus if labour is valued at its opportunity cost. Consider Figure 6.13.

The diagram represents the capitalist sector of the economy. On the normal assumption of profit maximization, labour will be employed up to the point where the marginal product is equal to the industrial wage. The capitalist surplus is equal to WNX. But suppose the supply of labour to the industrial sector is assumed to be 'costless' to society and is given, by the planners, a notional (or shadow) wage of zero. In this planned system labour would be employed up to the point L_1. Given the industrial wage, W, and assuming the propensity to consume out of wages is unity, each

Figure 6.13   The social valuation of labour

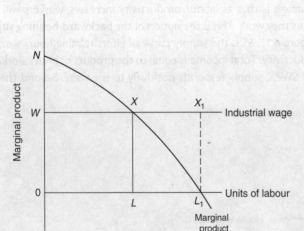

additional unit of labour employed beyond L will involve consumption in excess of production. If LL_1 additional labour is employed, the size of the investible surplus would be reduced by XX_1L_1. It follows that in an economy geared to growth the relationship between the consumption and production of migrant labour must also be taken into account when estimating the costs to society of industrial expansion with surplus labour from agriculture. If at the margin additional saving is valued more than an additional unit of consumption, the cost of a unit of labour transferred from agriculture to industry must include an allowance for increased consumption. These matters are taken up more fully in Chapter 11 in the discussion of social cost–benefit analysis and the determination of the shadow wage.

Summary

- Agriculture plays a crucial role in the early stages of a country's economic development. A surplus of agricultural output over subsistence needs – a marketable surplus – is required to feed labour in alternative activities, to release labour and to provide capital for investment in industry, to buy other domestically produced goods, and to provide foreign exchange to buy imports.

- A necessary condition for agriculture to make these various contributions to economic development is an increase of productivity in agriculture. Agricultural productivity is extremely low in most developing countries, which accounts for why so many people are so poor.

- There are several reasons for low agricultural productivity including poor geographic and climatic conditions, a lack of investment and knowledge, the land tenure system, and urban bias in the allocation of resources for health, education and infrastructure.

- Land reform is needed in many countries in order to break up large inefficient estates, and to provide tenants with security of tenure so that they have the incentive to invest in new inputs.

- Attention needs to be paid to the pricing of agricultural goods to encourage a supply response in agriculture.

- The transformation of traditional agriculture requires new inputs such as new varieties of seeds and proper irrigation. Genetically modified (GM) food is a matter for debate. Finance for the purchase of new inputs is crucial.

- As productivity in agriculture rises, the agricultural sector and other sectors of the economy become more and more interdependent. Industrial growth can be fuelled by the release of cheap labour from agriculture. This is the essence of Arthur Lewis's famous model of 'economic development with unlimited supplies of labour'. The reinvestment of industrial profits drives industrial expansion.

- But industry needs a market for its goods, so the purchasing power of the agricultural sector is important. It is vital to get the terms of trade right between agricultural and industrial goods if the growth of the economy is not to be demand constrained if the prices of agricultural goods are too low, or supply constrained because the prices are too high.

- Surplus labour on the land has led to a vast rural–urban migration process which is swelling the amount of unemployment and underemployment in the cities of developing countries. Todaro's model of rural–urban migration explains why migration is still so high despite the low probability of getting a job in the urban area.

- There are many different definitions of surplus labour, or different measures of so-called disguised unemployment. The most important distinction is between the static surplus which assumes that the marginal product of labour is zero, and the dynamic surplus which is the amount of labour that could be released without agricultural output falling, providing some small compensating changes take place such as the remaining labour working longer hours or small improvements in techniques of production which raise labour productivity.

- The transfer of labour from agriculture to industry or from rural to urban areas is not a costless process either for individuals or society at large. The economic and social costs of congestion and overcrowding are particularly acute.

Appendix: the functioning of markets in agrarian societies[13]

In mature developed countries, markets tend to be specialized; the markets for land, labour and credit are segmented. Each market has its own set of institutions, which have their own special-ized function. In developing countries, at least in poor rural communities, markets are different; transactions of all kinds are interlinked, with the terms of one transaction contingent on another. **The land, labour and credit markets are interlocked**. For example, landlords might provide credit to tenants and labourers in the slack season, when there is no income being generated, in return for a specific amount of labour in the peak season; or traders may grant credit to farm-ers in return for a specific amount of their crop at a pre-agreed discount price. These interlinked transactions make many of the markets very imperfect, not the least because they create serious barriers to the entry of new agents, and inefficiency in one market may be the cause, or con-sequence, of imperfections in another. Inefficiencies arise through lack of information, lack of incentives, the inability to enforce contracts, and so on. Imperfect and inefficient markets are a characteristic feature of the economic functioning of poor developing economies, and they are the basis of informal institutional arrangements that govern economic behaviour in rural societies.

Below there are separate discussions on the markets for land, labour and credit, but as we go along we will see how they interlock. What we shall find is that the contract choices made by peasant farmers depend on the technological, economic and social conditions that exist in different environments which determine risks and transaction costs. Agricultural production has three distinguishing features: (i) production is subject to uncertainty, (ii) production is seasonal and hired labour is required, and (iii) the costs of supervising labour are high. These all play a part in determining the institutional arrangements and the types of contracts reached in different markets.

The land market

One of the characteristics of the market for land is that the volume of land transactions (buying and selling) relative to the stock of land is low. This has to do with the very inegalitarian ownership of land in poor countries, and a lack of property rights for a large number of people who work on the land. The high concentration of land ownership in a few hands, and lack of access to land, can have serious consequences for the overall development of an economy. Land may not be used efficiently, large tracts of land may not be fully utilized, food production is likely to be below potential, and those who might want to farm and work the land become migrants to already overcrowded cities.

The concentration of land, and the size distribution of farms, differs across continents. Latin America has by far the highest concentration of land ownership with Gini ratios of over 0.8 in countries such as Brazil, Peru, Uruguay, Colombia and Venezuela. In Asia the concentration is less, but still high – with a Gini ratio in excess of 0.4 in Bangladesh, India, Thailand, Indonesia and Nepal. Latin America, not surprisingly, also has the largest farms. The proportion of small farms of less than 5 hectares is less than 50 per cent on average, and covers only 2 per cent of the total land area. Ninety per cent of land is cultivated on farms in excess of 50 hectares. In Asia, by contrast, 90 per cent of farms are less than 5 hectares, occupying over 50 per cent of farmland. The figures on land concentration and farm size are summarized in Table A6.1. In Africa, the situation differs because much of the land is communally owned. The predominant form of farming is subsistence agriculture based on the village. On large tracts of land, there is also shifting cultivation, although this type of farming is now on the decline because of increased pressure of population on food supplies. It has been replaced by small owner-occupied plots. There is virtually no sharecropping with large landlords.

There are not many economies of scale in farm production. In fact, it turns out to be the case that small farms produce a higher output per hectare than large farms (see Sen, 1964; Ray, 1998). One explanation is that labour is used more intensively on small (family owned) farms because the opportunity cost of using labour is very low, whereas large farms hire labour and pay a market wage which leads to a lower input of labour per unit of land. Owner-occupied farms using family labour are always found to be more productive than large mechanized farms using hired labour, or tenant farms with no property rights, because the incentive to be efficient is greater (see Biswanger and Deininger, 1997).

If small owner-occupied farms are more productive than large farms, there would be an efficiency or productivity gain if large landowners were to sell their land to small family units and appropriate the surplus. But the market for land doesn't work in this rational way. First, land confers power, and can be used as collateral for other purposes. Secondly, in practice most land

Table A6.1   Land concentration and farm size in Asia and Latin America

Countries	Gini ratio of land concentration	Percentage of farms and farmland				Percentage of sharecroppers on tenanted
		Below 5 hectares		Above 50 hectares		
Asia		Farms	Area	Farms	Area	
Bangladesh	0.42	90.6	62.6	–	–	91.0
India	0.62	88.7	46.7	0.1	3.7	48.0
Indonesia	0.56	92.9	68.7	0	13.6	60.0
Nepal	0.56	97.2	72.1	0	0.8	48.3
Philippines	0.51	84.8	47.8	0.2	13.9	79.3
Thailand	0.45	72.3	39.4	0	0.9	29.0
Latin America						
Brazil	0.84	36.8	1.3	16.3	84.6	–
Costa Rica	0.82	48.9	1.9	14.5	79.7	9.4
Colombia	0.86	59.6	3.7	8.4	77.7	49.4
Peru	0.91	78.0	8.9	1.9	79.1	0
Uruguay	0.82	14.3	0.2	37.6	95.8	4.7
Venezuela	0.91	43.8	0.9	13.6	92.5	–

Source: Otsuka et al., 1992.

sales are not from rich to poor, but from poor to rich because the poor often have to sell land in order to pay debts and survive, and they are credit constrained (see later). This matters for efficiency if land rental and sharecroppers replace owner-operated family farms. This is a collective action problem and the only solution is state involvement in **land reform** which transfers land compulsorily from rich to poor.

Land reform can take three main forms. First, land can be transferred from landowners to tenants who already work the land, as happened historically in South Korea, Japan and Taiwan. South Korea is an interesting case where land reform took place when the country ceased to be a Japanese colony in 1949. Over one-half of agricultural land owned by Japanese and large domestic landowners was transferred to over 60 per cent of the rural population comprising tenant farmers. Second, land reform can take the form of the transfer of large estates to smaller farms as happened in Mexico after the revolution in 1917. Thirdly, there can be expropriation and break-up of large estates for new settlements, as in some countries of Africa in recent times (but often with disastrous results as in Kenya and Zimbabwe). Historically, most land reforms have taken place at the same time as political change which has transferred power from corrupt elites to 'the people' through the creation of democratic institutions. Land reform is an important institutional change conferring property rights and providing incentives to invest.

Where tenant farmers exist, arrangements between tenants and landlords vary in different parts of the world. In Latin America, tenants tend to pay a fixed rent to the landlord for the right to cultivate, but retain 100 per cent of the output. In Asia, tenants tend to be **sharecroppers**, sharing output with the landlord on an agreed percentage basis, depending on circumstances, usually 50:50. With fixed-rent contracts, the tenant bears the risk of fluctuations in output. Poor farmers, however, are risk-averse, and so they tend to be sharecroppers, sharing the risk with the landlord. It is often argued that sharecropping is inefficient compared with fixed-rent tenancies because work incentives are weaker. With fixed rents, tenant farmers keep any extra output produced, whereas sharecroppers have to relinquish a certain share, and thus there will be a tendency for sharecroppers to undersupply effort (unless, of course, their work can be costlessly observed and enforced by the landlord). The empirical evidence shows (see Ray, 1998), however, that productivity on tenant-owned land is higher than on sharecropped land, controlling for other factors.

The question then arises, if sharecropping is inefficient, why is it practised so widely? The answer is that it can be beneficial to both landowner and farmer by reducing risks and costs to both. Stiglitz (1974) was the first to show formally that sharecropping reflects a compromise between risk-sharing and work incentives. From the landlord's point of view, they can use a share-cropping contract as a screening device to choose between more wealthy, high productivity tenants and poorer, lower productivity tenants – the former receiving the fixed-rent contracts and the latter receiving the sharecropping contracts. Also sharecropping is cheaper, compared with self-cultivation using hired labour. Labour recruitment, and the supervision of labour effort, can be costly. This is a classic **principal-agent** example where the interests of the landowner and the worker differ. The principal (the landowner) naturally wants as much effort and output as possible, but work effort generates disutility and the worker may shirk. The landowner has no way of knowing how much of a worker's output is dependent on his effort and how much on exogenous factors. The principal cannot easily monitor and enforce the work effort he wants without employing supervisory staff. Sharecropping may also be the preferred contract if input costs are being shared between landlord and tenant. Cost-sharing inputs is a way of offsetting disincentive effects of applying inputs under output-sharing contracts (Otsuka et al., 1992). Cost sharing can be thought of as production loans to the tenant which are repaid with the output, which is deducted from total output before the output is shared.

From the tenant's point of view, not paying a fixed rent considerably reduces risk because in the event of a bad harvest the tenant could find himself in considerable difficulties, with his livelihood threatened. The landlord also knows this. For the landlord, he can vary the share he gets in order to get the same income as a fixed rent taking good and bad years together. In fact, in recent years the tenant's share has been falling because landlords have been bearing the cost of increased mechanization. But greater overall efficiency will only come with giving sharecroppers a greater share of output, to induce more effort, and providing security of tenure on the land to provide tenants themselves with the incentive to invest.

The labour market

There are two main types of labour working in the rural sector of developing countries. The first is **casual labour**, hired on a daily basis and paid either a daily wage or 'piece rates' for specific tasks. Large landowners need more than family labour to work on their large estates, and if people are landless, or possess only very small farms, they need to earn extra income for nutrition and survival. The second type of labour is **permanent labour** hired by landlords on long-term contracts. The function of the two types of labour is different. Casual labour is used for routine tasks that are easily monitored. It will need a minimum income in order to have enough nutrition and energy to work productively – the so-called **efficiency wage**. If the labour is landless and has no other source of income, this is the minimum wage that will be paid. If the labour has other sources of income, however, either from a small farm or other assets, it can supply labour at a lower threshold wage because the other income buys the nutrition it needs. On the other hand, as non-labour income rises, the minimum at which labour is willing to work rises because it values leisure more highly. Thus, there are conflicting forces working in the labour market (Ray, 1998). At low levels of non-labour income, the availability to work for a lower wage rate dominates, while at higher levels of non-labour income, the willingness to work dominates. This gives rise to two types of unemployment, or categories of surplus labour, in rural areas. The first category is voluntary unemployment among labour able to work but who do not want to because of high non-labour income. The second category is 'involuntary' because the wage rate is not high enough to enable labour to work productively. In these circumstances, land reform and income distribution would increase total agricultural output because if the landless are given land the increase in their non-labour income will increase their ability to work, and a lower level of income for the previously more 'wealthy' will increase the incentive to work. The necessity to pay a minimum efficiency wage is one of the reasons why wages tend to be rigid downwards in rural economies, despite unemployment. Another explanation is the phenomenon of **segmented labour markets**, with village employers hiring local labour even when it is cheaper outside. Institutions and social norms often determine economic outcomes, not the free forces of the market place.

The main drawback of the casual labour market from the point of view of economic development is that employers of labour (landlords) have no interest in improving the working conditions of workers or investing in them by way of health or education because there is no guarantee that they will reap the benefits. Ray (1998) comments, 'a casual labour market creates a deterioration in the nutritional status of the workforce'. The function of permanent labour, and the argument for more permanent labour contracts, is that a lot of agricultural work needs supervising and large landowners require people to supervise and monitor work. One facet of permanent labour is **labour-tying** which, because of the seasonal nature of production, suits both employer and employee. The employer is guaranteed labour in the busy season and the worker is guaranteed work in the off-season. The wage paid to permanent labour will be some margin above the casual wage to provide the incentive to monitor and supervise tasks properly. The premium must be just enough to prevent 'shirking', and also to compensate for the threat of dismissal.

Another way of enforcing work effort is to offer long-term contracts, so that a party not honouring a contract will suffer **loss of reputation**, and find it difficult to work in the future. In small rural communities, reputation matters. If long-term fixed-wage contracts can elicit loyal effort from permanent workers, they may also receive in return fringe benefits and subsidized credit.

According to Ray (1998), however, the amount of permanent labour used on farms relative to casual labour has been falling in recent years. One reason may be that because of multiple cropping the seasonality of production has decreased, and therefore there is less need to offer permanent contracts to ensure labour is available in the harvest season. Secondly, if the casual wage in the harvest season is above the contracted income for permanent labour, it is difficult to enforce 'tied contracts'.

We can summarize this section on labour contracts by saying that when work effort is unenforceable there are three basic predictions from a standard model of landlord and workers both attempting to maximize their utility in the face of production uncertainty and risk (Otsuka et al., 1992):

- If production is uncertain and the worker is risk-averse, the share contract will be optimal. (If the worker is risk-neutral, which is highly unlikely, the fixed rent contract would be chosen.)
- A share or fixed-rent tenancy is superior to a fixed-wage permanent labour contract because the latter is costly, but long-term and interlinked contracts may be observed because they can help to enforce contracts through reputation effects. Permanent labour contracts will also be observed if land tenancy is illegal.
- A share-tenancy is less efficient than a fixed-rent tenancy and owner-cultivation because of reduced work incentives (unless labour can be monitored costlessly).

Where work effort is perfectly enforceable, optimal contracts are, in general, indeterminate. If the worker is risk-neutral and contract enforcement is costless, all forms of contract become equally efficient. If both landlord and workers are risk-averse, the share contract will be chosen to share production risk.

Credit markets

Farmers need credit for three main reasons: first, for fixed capital investment; second, to bridge the gap between financing production (seeds, fertilizers, pesticides) and sales receipts from the harvest (in other words, they need working capital), and third to smooth consumption before the harvest.

Credit markets in the rural sector of developing countries are not well developed, however, for two main reasons. Firstly, due to lack of information, it is difficult for lenders to monitor loans, to know how risky they are, and whether they are going to be used productively. The second reason is that credit contracts are difficult to enforce because the legal system is weak. There is therefore the risk of default. This makes the formal banking sector reluctant to lend to the rural sector. The risk of default means that the formal sector only lends to richer farmers with collateral. The poor may have some collateral in the form of a plot of land, but the formal banking system wants something more.

This means that the rural credit market is dominated by **informal moneylenders**, charging high interest rates either explicit in the form of high money rates of interest, or implicit because the loan is given in return for a share of the borrower's output at a discount price, or an agreed amount of labour service at a lower-than-market wage. The rural credit market is also very segmented. Because moneylenders have much more knowledge of borrowers within a local community, moneylenders tend to become very specialized, dealing with a particular clientele within a village or serving a particular type of person. Segmentation often takes place on occupational lines. Because of these links, lenders in informal markets do not like their borrowers borrowing from another lender, so the existence of many lenders does not necessarily mean there is competition. Rather, the credit market is more like a series of local monopolies, and because of this segmentation, interest rates on loans in the informal market are not only high but can also vary considerably. There is little chance of arbitrage.

High interest rates largely reflect lenders' risk; that is, the risk that the borrowers might not repay either because of adverse circumstance, such as a bad harvest, or because of the difficulties of collecting bad debts. Potential default exists, but in practice it turns out to be quite low. One reason is that in rural communities where everybody knows each other, if someone defaults everybody knows and no one else will lend to them. There is 'peer' pressure to repay. The second reason is that moneylenders devise contracts that minimize the risk of default (which also makes the implicit interest rate high). If the lender is a large landowner, and the landowner knows the farmer, he can minimize the risk of default by making the first claim on the borrower's output, or insist that the borrower supplies labour at a lower-than-market wage (**bonded labour**). If the lender is a trader, he can minimize risk by contracting to buy the output of the borrower at a discount price. Udry (1994) found that over 90 per cent of loans to the rural sector in Northern Nigeria came from the informal sector. Research in the Punjab and Sindh regions of Pakistan shows that landlords are the major source of credit for tenant farmers, while traders are the major source of credit for owner-cultivators (Ray, 1998).

Even though risk of default can be minimized by various practices, credit-rationing still exists because high interest rates may attract too many high-risk customers, and high interest rates which would equilibrate the supply and demand for loans would themselves increase the risk of default. Lenders therefore prefer to ration credit instead.

There is also the issue of risk and insurance to consider. Agricultural production is risky because of the vagaries of the weather, the incidence of disease and many other factors. Peasant farmers somehow need to be able to smooth their income and consumption, so as not to suffer unduly in bad times. This is where insurance mechanisms are important. Self-insurance is one possibility, smoothing consumption using one's own resources, for example, saving grain in good times for use in bad. Mutual insurance is another possibility. If farmers produce different products, and good and bad harvests for different crops are negatively correlated, producers can help each other out in what are bad times for some and good times for others. But mutual insurance may not be easily enforceable. There could be risk pooling within a community through formal insurance markets, but these are not well developed. If there is not risk pooling or mutual insurance, saving and credit have to be used for consumption smoothing. There is evidence from a wide variety of studies (see Bardhan and Udry, 1999) that households in poor, risky agricultural environments engage in both risk pooling and consumption smoothing, although not always successfully because of informational and enforcement difficulties.

Interlocked markets

As we have indicated above, the markets for land, labour and credit in the rural sector of developing countries are closely interlinked. Inefficiency in one market may be both the cause and consequence of inefficiencies in others. The markets for land and labour are interlinked because an imbalance in the market for land (with both large and small holdings) leads to imbalances in the market for labour. If people are landless, or have only very small holdings, they need to sell their labour to large landowners who need more than just family labour.

The markets for land and credit are linked because, as we have outlined before, landlords are a major source of credit for farmers, and their labour or output is used as collateral. Also crop-traders are the main source of credit for cultivators who own land, and loans are provided in advance of crop production. In Muslim countries, where charging interest is against Sharia law, credit contracts which take part of the output of the borrower, or specify the sale of the output at a certain discount, are a substitute for charging interest.

Floro and Yotopoulous (1991), in their study of the Philippines, identify five types of credit market interlinkages:

- Credit in return for the procurement of output
- Credit in return for the sale of output to the lender
- Credit tied to the purchase of inputs or leasing machinery from the lender
- Credit in return for provision of labour to the lender
- Transfer of rights over the usufruct (profits) of the land to the lender.

The authors find that the first three types of interlinkages are most common amongst trader-lenders, while the last two are most prevalent among farmer-lenders.

In conclusion, in rural communities where formal lending is limited by lack of proper collateral, interlinked contracts in the informal money market make sense because the lender has more control over the borrower and saves the cost of monitoring, and reduces the risk of non-repayment. Landlords, or traders, in effect, get their 'interest' immediately if loans are conditional on work for lower wages or output at lower prices.

Institutions and decision-making in agriculture

Agriculture is a neglected sector of the economy in many developing countries, and governments pursue policies that discriminate against agriculture in favour of industry. The explanation is partly historical, but mainly institutional and political. The agricultural sector's potential for collective action is weak because of the unequal relation between landlords and workers within the agricultural sector and the weak bargaining power that the agricultural sector has vis-à-vis other groups in society due to history and initial conditions. It is difficult for owner-operated family farms to act collectively to change things because farmers are dispersed, and lack political clout. If peasant farmers lack education, and cannot vote, they lack the means to promote change. Only by enhancing the poor's potential for collective action, by increasing their potential participation, will there be increased efficiency and sustained and equitable growth in the rural sector (Binswanger and Deininger, 1997).

Chapter 6	Discussion questions

1 What is the importance to economic development of rapid productivity growth in agriculture?

2 What factors hold back productivity growth in agriculture?

3 How could land reform help to raise agricultural productivity?

4 What is meant by 'marketable surplus'?

5 Explain why poor people tend to be risk-averse and reluctant to innovate.

6 In what sense is there disguised unemployment on the land?

7 Does disguised unemployment on the land mean that development using surplus labour is a relatively painless and costless process?

8 Compare and contrast the main features of Lewis's classical model of development with the neoclassical model.

9 Explain the continued process of rural–urban migration despite growing unemployment in urban areas.

10 In what ways do the agricultural and industrial sectors of an economy complement one another?

11 What are the major characteristics of the market for land in the rural sector of developing countries?

12 What is the principal-agent problem facing landlords in the rural sector of poor countries?

13 Why are peasant farmers risk-averse?

14 Why is share-cropping so common in the agricultural sector of many poor countries?

15 In what ways is the credit market linked to the land and labour markets in the rural sector of poor countries?

Notes

1. For an excellent survey of the issues, see Bardhan (1984), Binswanger and Deinenger (1997), Dorner (1992) and Otsuka et al. (1992).
2. See also Askari and Cummings (1976) and Schiff and Montenegro (1999).
3. Lewis (1954, 1958). See also the symposium on the Lewis model to celebrate its 25th anniversary in the *Manchester School*, September 1979, and the symposium on the Lewis model after 50 years, *Manchester School*, December 2004.
4. The capitalist sector is not synonymous with the industrial sector, but it is convenient to think of it in this way. Agribusiness, for example, is also capitalist.

5. The profit rate can be expressed as

$$P/K = \frac{(0/L - w/p)}{(K/L)}$$

where P is profits, K is the quantity of capital, $0/L$ is the productivity of labour, w/p is the real wage and K/L is the capital–labour ratio. The profit rate will rise if $0/L$ rises and w/p remains the same (assuming no offsetting rise in K/L).

6. A formal algebraic model, with various extensions, may be found in Thirlwall (1986).

7. If the income elasticity of demand for industrial goods is greater than unity, and for agricultural goods less than unity, then the equilibrium growth rate for industry will exceed that for agriculture.

8. See Weisdorf (2006) for historical evidence on how industrial growth promoted agriculture by lowering the relative price of industrial goods and buying more goods commercially rather than producing 'non-agricultural' goods within the agricultural sector itself.

9. This is not a statistical probability since π is not bounded between zero and unity. The 'chance' of getting a job would be a better word to use.

10. Todaro (1971) uses the same notation, S, for the total urban labour force as for the supply of migrants. This can be confusing. We therefore use W for the total urban labour force and S for the supply of migrants.

11. Any values can be substituted as long as $w/r = 2$.

12. Barnum and Sabot (1977). Other early studies of the rural–urban migration process include Knight (1972). For a survey of studies, see Todaro (1976), Yap (1977) and Stark (1991). Todaro gives an alternative way of evaluating whether urban unemployment will rise or not. It can be shown that the *level* of unemployment will rise if $\eta > g \times N/S$, where η is the period elasticity of induced migration with respect to the change in modern sector job probabilities, g is the growth of urban employment prior to the increase in job opportunities, N is the level of urban employment and S is the existing level of rural–urban migration. It can also be shown that the rate of urban unemployment will rise if $\eta > g \times W/S$, where W is the urban workforce.

13. This section relies heavily on the works of Otsuka et al. (1992), Binswanger and Deininger (1997), Ray (1998) and Bardhan and Udry (1999).

Websites on agriculture

Food and Agricultural Organization www.fao.org
International Food Policy Research Institute www.ifpri.org
Consultative Group on International Agricultural Research www.cgiar.org
Inter-American Institute for Cooperation on Agriculture www.iicanet.org
Food and Agricultural Policy Research Institute: www.fapri.iastate.edu

7

CAPITAL ACCUMULATION, TECHNICAL PROGRESS AND TECHNIQUES OF PRODUCTION

- Introduction
- The role of capital in development
- Technical progress
- Capital- and labour-saving technical progress
- How societies progress technologically
- Learning
- Investment in human capital: education
- Women's education
- Infrastructure investment
- Technology and the developing countries
- Techniques of production
- The conflict between employment and output and employment and saving in the choice of techniques
- Employment versus output
- Employment versus saving
- Wages and the capital intensity of production

- Different classes' propensity to consume
- Support of the unemployed
- Are consumption and investment distinct?
- Taxes and subsidies
- Future policy
- Summary
- Discussion questions
- Notes
- Websites on technology and investment
- Website on choice of techniques

Introduction

Economic growth and development are impossible without capital accumulation. If all of the output produced by an economy was consumed, there would be no saving, no investment, and the economy would grind to a halt.

In this chapter we identify the different forms that capital accumulation takes, and their role in the development process: physical capital such as plant and machinery; infrastructure such as roads and railways; human capital and social capital that makes humans more productive such as education and good health.

The productivity of capital itself largely depends on the technical progress embodied in it. We identify the different meanings of technical progress and the types of technical progress that take place – whether it is labour-saving, capital-saving or neutral – which has implications for employment and the distribution of income between wages and profits. The process of learning by doing is a form of technical progress because it improves the productivity of factors of production.

We then explore how societies progress technologically by acquiring the capabilities to invest, to innovate, to undertake R&D and to absorb new ideas. Education and skill acquisition play a key role and are important forms of investment with high private and social returns. Some evidence is given of how backward technology is in poor countries, and the challenge of the magnitude of 'catch-up'. Finally, we discuss the important issue of the choice of techniques of production in developing countries and whether labour-abundant economies could move towards the use of more labour-intensive techniques without jeopardizing the level of output and saving for future growth. Theory and evidence suggests that the potential clash between employment and output and employment and saving in the choice of *new* techniques is exaggerated.

The role of capital in development

The capital stock of a country increases through the process of net investment (I), which is the difference between a country's net income in an accounting period (that is, gross income minus depreciation) and how much it consumes out of that income in the same period. The essence of capital accumulation is that it enhances a country's capacity to produce goods in the future and enables it to grow faster.

There are many types of capital goods. First, there are **plant and machinery** used in factories and offices, which yield no utility directly but produce consumption goods and services that do. Second, there is **infrastructure investment**, which partly provides goods and services directly, and at the same time makes other forms of investment more productive; for example transport facilities, telecommunications, power generation, the provision of water facilities and so on. Third, there is expenditure on **research and development (R&D)**, which may improve the productivity of labour or capital, or both. R&D can lead to new inventions and then to innovation – either **process innovation** or **product innovation**. Process innovations make the production of existing products more efficient; product innovations involve the creation of new products that not only add to utility but also enhance productivity by enabling new ways of doing things; for example, information technology. Fourth, there is **social expenditure** such as investment in health and education, which also provides some utility directly but at the same time makes individuals and society more productive. Indeed, if capital is defined as any asset that generates an additional future stream of measurable income to society, many goods and services that might be thought of as primarily consumption goods ought strictly to be included as part of a country's capital stock.

If cars, for example, or other consumer durable goods, save time and make people more efficient, part of the expenditure on them should be considered as an investment. Expenditure on housing is another example where private expenditure may be partly considered as consumption and partly investment; and the public provision of housing might be put in the category of social capital. Similarly, if certain types of consumption goods are necessary as incentives to induce peasant producers in the agricultural sector, or workers elsewhere, to increase their productivity, they too ought to be considered as part of the capital stock.

If it is agreed, therefore, that the only way to build up a country's productive potential and to raise per capita income is to expand the capacity for producing goods, this need not refer simply to the provision of physical capital such as plant and machinery, but also to roads, railways, power lines, water pipes, schools, hospitals, houses and even 'incentive' consumer goods such as consumer durables – all of which can contribute to increased productivity and higher living standards.

When using the production function approach to the study of the sources of growth or the macrodeterminants of growth, as described in Chapter 5, it is important to define capital as broadly as possible if the relation between capital accumulation and growth is to be properly understood. This is in addition to the point, which was also emphasized in Chapter 5, that capital is likely to be the main vehicle for the introduction of technical progress in the productive system. In other words, capital accumulation is not only important in its own right, but is the major conduit for advances in knowledge, which in turn are also a major determinant of productivity growth.

Developing economies lay great emphasis on the importance of capital accumulation, and stress the need to raise the level of investment as a proportion of national output. A glance at any national development plan will testify to this. Development is associated with industrialization and industrialization with capital accumulation. Many famous development economists in the past have picked out investment as the most important single factor in the growth process. As we saw in Chapter 3, Rostow (1960) defines the process of 'take-off' into sustained growth in terms of a critical ratio of investment to national product, and Arthur Lewis (1955) has described the process of development as one of transforming a country from being a 5 per cent saver and investor to a 12 per cent saver and investor. It is common, in fact, for countries to calculate fairly precise ratios of investment to national income that will be required to achieve a particular rate of growth. These calculations involve assumptions about the normal relation between capital and output, a relation that is formally expressed in the concept of the **capital–output ratio** which measures how much capital stock is required to produce a unit flow of output over an accounting period (normally one year). If 300 units of capital (from new investment) are required to produce an annual flow of 100 units of output, the capital–output ratio is 3.

The returns to investment in developing countries are potentially much higher than in developed countries, which already have large quantities of capital per head. In countries where specialization (the division of labour) is minimal, the scope for capital to permit more round-about methods of production and increase productivity will be greater than where specialization has already reached a high level of sophistication. Moreover, in technologically backward countries the rate of growth of capital required to absorb new technology is likely to be greater than in advanced countries. By definition, technologically backward countries also have a backlog of technology to make up. Furthermore, in a labour-abundant economy with a low capital–labour ratio, the very act of *capital deepening* – giving each worker a little more capital to work with – may make a substantial difference to total product, much more so than in countries where the process of capital deepening has been a continuing process for some length of time. All these factors represent important contributions that capital can make to economic progress, which may be relatively more important the smaller is the initial capital stock of a country relative to its population. It is a familiar proposition in economics that the scarcer one factor of production is in relation to another, the higher its productivity is likely to be, all other things being equal.

Capital accumulation is also seen as an escape from the so-called 'vicious circle of poverty' – a circle of low productivity, leading to low per capita income, leading to a low level of saving per head, leading to a low level of capital accumulation per head, leading to low productivity. Low productivity is seen as the source of the 'vicious circle of poverty', and the point where the circle must be broken by capital accumulation. (See Chapters 8 and 9.)

According to recent research by Hulten and Isaksson (2007), the amount of capital per head of the working population in high-income developed countries is $150,000 (in 2000) compared with $3,000 in low-income countries, and this difference is one of the major explanations of why labour productivity is $52,000 in rich countries and only $2,300 in poor countries.

These huge differences in the amount of capital per head are the cumulative effect of much higher levels of savings and investment in rich countries than in poorer countries that cannot, or prefer not to, save. A precondition for raising the level of capital per head in poor countries is a higher level of investment. There needs to be greater incentives for investment. Case example 7.1 contains the conclusions of the World Bank's *World Development Report 2005*, which was devoted to the topic of 'A Better Investment Climate for Everyone'.

| Case example 7.1 | **Main messages from *World Development Report 2005* on investment** |

The investment climate is central to growth and poverty reduction

Improving the opportunities and incentives for firms of all types to invest productively, create jobs and expand should be a top priority for governments. It is not just about increasing the volume of investment but also spurring productivity improvements that are the keys to sustainable growth.

- The goal is to create a better investment climate for everyone. A good investment climate benefits society as a whole, not just firms. And it embraces all firms, not just large or politically connected firms.
- Expanding opportunities for young people is a pressing concern for developing countries, where 53 per cent of people live on less than US$2 a day, youths have more than double the average unemployment rate, and populations are growing rapidly.

Reducing unjustified costs is critical, but policy-related risks and barriers to competition also need to be tackled

All three matter for firms and thus for growth and poverty reduction.

- Costs associated with weak contract enforcement, inadequate infrastructure, crime, corruption and regulation can amount to over 25 per cent of sales – or more than three times what firms typically pay in taxes.
- Firms in developing countries rate policy uncertainty as their top concern. This and other sources of policy-related risk – such as insecure property rights, macroeconomic instability, and arbitrary regulation – chill incentives to invest.

Case example 7.1	**Main messages from *World Development Report* 2005 on investment** – *continued*

Improving policy predictability can increase the likelihood of new investment by over 30 per cent.

- Barriers to competition benefit some firms but deny opportunities and increase costs to other firms and to consumers. They also weaken incentives for protected firms to innovate and improve their productivity. Increasing competitive pressure can increase the probability of firm innovation by more than 50 per cent.

Progress requires more than changes to formal policies

Over 90 per cent of firms claim gaps between formal rules and what happens in practice, and the informal economy accounts for more than half of output in many developing countries. Creating a better investment climate requires governments to bridge these gaps and to tackle deeper sources of policy failure that undermine a sound investment climate. This requires efforts:

- to restrain corruption and other forms of rent seeking that increase costs and distort policies;
- to build policy credibility to give firms the confidence to invest;
- to foster the public trust required to enable and sustain policy improvements; and
- to ensure policy responses are crafted to fit local conditions.

Investment climate improvements are a process, not an event

Government policies and behaviours influencing the investment climate cover a wide field. But everything does not have to be fixed at once, and perfection on even a single policy dimension is not required. Significant progress can be made by addressing important constraints facing firms in a way that gives them the confidence to invest – and by sustaining a process of ongoing improvements.

Because constraints differ widely across and even within countries, priorities need to be assessed in each case. Reform processes benefit from effective public communication and other measures to build consensus and maintain momentum.

Source: World Bank, 2004.

Technical progress

The term 'technical progress' is used in several different senses to describe a variety of phenomena; but three in particular can be singled out. First, economists use the term to refer to the *effects* of changes in technology, and specifically to the role of technical change in the growth process. It is in this sense that the term was used in Chapter 5; that is, as an umbrella term to cover all those factors which contribute to the growth of 'total' productivity. Second, technical progress is used by economists in a narrow specialist sense to describe the *character* of technical improvements, and is often prefaced for this purpose by the adjectives 'labour-saving', 'capital-saving' or 'neutral'. Third, technical progress is used more literally to refer to *changes* in technology itself, defining technology as useful knowledge pertaining to the art of production. Used in this sense, the emphasis is on describing improvements in the design, sophistication and performance of plant and machinery, and the economic activities through which improvements come about – by research and development, invention and innovation.

Having already discussed technical progress in the first sense in Chapter 5, we concentrate here on the narrow specialist descriptions of technical progress, and on how societies progress technologically.

Capital- and labour-saving technical progress

The classification of technical progress as to whether it is capital-saving, labour-saving or neutral owes its origins primarily to the work of Harrod (1948) and Hicks (1932). Their criteria of classification differ, however. **Harrod's classification of technical progress** employs the concept of the capital–output ratio. Given the rate of profit, technical change is said to be capital-saving if it lowers the capital–output ratio, labour-saving if it raises the capital–output ratio, and neutral if it leaves the capital–output ratio unchanged.

The nature of technical progress by this criterion will be an amalgam of the effect of 'pure' technical change on factor combinations on the one hand and the effect of the substitution of capital for labour on the other (as, for example, relative factor prices change). As such, Harrod neutrality at the aggregate level is quite consistent with capital-saving technical progress at the industry level. In fact, most of the evidence for advanced countries suggests that *if* technical progress is neutral in the aggregate in the Harrod sense, this must be due to substitution of capital for labour because 'pure' technical advance has saved capital. The substitution of capital for labour takes place because as countries become richer the price of labour relative to capital tends to rise, which not only induces a 'pure' substitution effect but also encourages inventive effort towards saving labour, which is becoming relatively expensive (and scarce).

Hicks's classification of technical progress takes the concept of the marginal rate of substitution between factors, which is the rate at which one factor must be substituted for another, leaving output unchanged. The marginal rate of substitution is given by the ratio of the marginal products of factors. Holding constant the ratio of labour to capital, technical progress is said to be **capital-saving** if it raises the marginal product of labour in greater proportion than the marginal product of capital; **labour-saving** if it raises the marginal product of capital in greater proportion than the marginal product of labour; and **neutral** if it leaves unchanged the ratio of marginal products. These definitions are illustrated in Figures 7.1, 7.2 and 7.3, respectively.

It will be recalled from Chapter 5 that technical progress on a production function map is represented by shifts in the function towards the origin, showing that the same output can be

Figure 7.1 Capital-saving technical progress

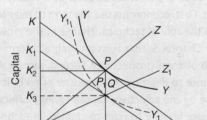

Figure 7.2 Labour-saving technical progress

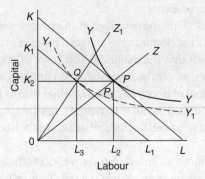

Figure 7.3 Neutral technical progress

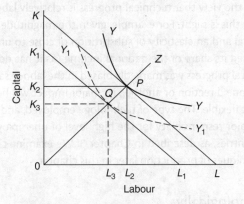

produced with fewer inputs, or that the same volume of inputs can produce a greater output. According to the shape of the new production function, fewer of either one or both factors will be required to produce the same output. In the case of neutral technical progress, a quantity of both factors can be dispensed with. In the case of non-neutral technical progress, if only one factor is saved technical progress is said to be *absolutely* labour- or capital-saving. If fewer of both factors are required, technical progress is said to be *relatively* labour- or capital-saving.

Consider first **neutral technical progress** (Figure 7.3). The ray from the origin, or expansion path, 0Z, goes through the minimum-cost point of tangency between the production function YY and the factor–price ratio line KL. With neutral technical progress the production function shifts such that the new point of tangency at the same factor–price ratio lies on the same expansion path. This means that the ratio of marginal products is the same at the same capital–labour ratio, and equal proportionate amounts of the two factors are saved. The condition for neutral technical progress is simply that the new production function is parallel to the old.

With **labour-saving technical change** (Figure 7.2) the ratio of the marginal product of capital to the marginal product of labour rises such as to shift the minimum-cost point of tangency from the old expansion path 0Z to a new expansion path $0Z_1$. At P_1, where the new production function cuts the old expansion path, the ratio of the marginal product of labour to capital is lower than at P. P_1 is not an equilibrium point and it will pay producers to move to point Q, substituting capital for labour. The ratio of marginal products has not remained unchanged at a constant labour to capital ratio, and L_2L_3 labour is saved. The isoquants have been so drawn as to keep the volume of capital the same, but this is for expositional purposes only.

Capital-saving technical progress (Figure 7.1) may be described in an exactly analogous fashion. In this case the ratio of the marginal product of labour to the marginal product of capital rises and the shift in the production function is such that the minimum-cost point of tangency now lies to the right of the old expansion path. At P_1, where the new production function cuts the old expansion path, the ratio of the marginal product of labour to capital is higher than at P. Again, P_1 is not an equilibrium point and it will pay producers to move to point Q, substituting labour for capital. The ratio of marginal products has not remained unchanged at a constant labour–capital ratio, and in this case K_2K_3 capital is saved.

As with Harrod technical progress, it is difficult to know what form Hicks technical progress takes in practice, largely because of identification problems. While the classification is analytically distinct, how does one distinguish empirically between a change in factor proportions due to a shift in the production function and a change in factor proportions due to a change in relative prices? Hicks himself seemed to be of the view that technical progress is relatively labour-saving, but the indirect evidence we have for this is slight. For example, given the magnitude of the rise in the price of labour relative to capital and an elasticity of substitution of close to unity, labour could not have maintained or increased its share of the national income (as it has done slightly in some advanced countries) if technical progress was markedly biased in the labour-saving direction. If technical progress is biased in one direction or another, its major impact will be on factor utilization if the price of factors is not flexible. The type of technology employed, and the factor proportions it entails, must bear a major responsibility for the high level of unemployment and underemployment in developing countries, as described in Chapter 3. We examine the case for the use of more labour-intensive techniques of production later in this chapter.

How societies progress technologically

Improvements in the art of production, which is the most literal interpretation of technical progress, result from a combination of **research and development, invention** and **innovation**. Research and development and invention are the activities that 'create' knowledge, and innovation is the activity that applies new knowledge to the task of production. These are all basically economic activities. But the study of the way in which societies progress technologically, and the speed of progress, is not only the preserve of the economist.

The economist can identify the mainsprings of progress, but their pervasiveness and acceptance in societies is not a purely economic matter. The spread of new knowledge, for example, depends on its rate of *adoption* and *diffusion* and this raises questions of individual motivation, the willingness of societies to assimilate new ideas and to break with custom and tradition, which impinge heavily on territory occupied by development sociologists. The relative importance of different factors contributing to progress, and the speed of progress itself, will vary from country to country according to stage of development and a whole complex of social and economic forces. Moreover, many of the mainsprings of technological progress are not mutually exclusive. At the risk of excessive simplification, attention here will be confined to four main sources of progress that are of potential significance to any society.

One major source of improvement in technology and progress is the **inventive and innovative activity** of the population. All societies are endowed to some degree with a potential supply of inventors, innovators and risk-takers, and in the absence of imported technology and personnel, it is on the emergence of this class of person that technological progress will primarily depend during the early stages of development. Economic backwardness in many countries may quite legitimately be traced back to a relative shortage of inventors, innovators and risk-takers. It is fairly well established that some cultures and some environments are more amenable to change than others, and in the past have produced a greater supply of entrepreneurs. One of the major sources of growth during Britain's industrial revolution was technological progress fostered by an abundant supply of inventors, innovators, entrepreneurs and risk-takers. The great Austrian economist Joseph Schumpeter (1934, 1943) laid great stress on the role of the entrepreneur and innovation in the development process. Ultimately, however, it is the lag between the creation of knowledge and its adoption, and the rate of dissemination of new knowledge, that most directly affects the rate of measured technical progress between countries; and these two facets of innovation are influenced by the attitudes of society to change.

For Schumpeter, progress results from what he calls the 'process of creative destruction', which is bound up with innovation and instigated by competition. Innovation, in turn, is the driving force behind competition. But innovation requires decision-takers and hence his complementary stress on the role of the entrepreneur. A characteristic of many poor countries is a shortage of decision-takers, a relative lack of competitive spirit and a general aversion to risk-taking. These may be partly cultural traits and also partly, if not mainly, a function of the stage of development itself. The characteristics commonly associated with business dynamism are themselves a function of business, and more particularly the form of organization we call 'capitalism'.

There is an enormous technological divide in the world economy which acts as a serious barrier to narrowing the gap between rich and poor countries. A small number of countries (accounting for about 15 per cent of the world's population) produce nearly 50 per cent of the world's technological innovations. A number of other countries (containing 50 per cent of the world's population) are able to adopt some or all of these technologies. The remaining countries (containing one-third of the world's poorest people) are almost entirely excluded from technological progress. These latter countries are also the areas of the world most affected by low agricultural productivity, malnutrition and disease. They need technology to raise productivity and to improve health, but cannot afford or assimilate it.

To acquire technology, countries can import it embodied in capital and consumer goods; they can obtain it on licence from patent holders, or they can attract foreign direct investment (FDI) which brings technology with it. The spread of technology and ideas may also be expected to come about naturally in the general process of commercial intercourse and the exchange of information through trade. This is one of the dynamic gains from trade (see Chapter 15). But not all countries have equal access to technology. Geography, culture, institutions and the quality of human capital matter. The speed with which modern technology is absorbed by economically backward countries will depend on the same class of factors as the diffusion of knowledge within countries – which in the final analysis amounts to the receptiveness of all sections of the community to change, and the ability to assimilate new ways of doing things. Some economists argue that the World Bank should focus more of its lending to countries specifically for knowledge creation and assimilation.

According to a recent study by Fagerberg et al. (2007), of 90 countries over the period 1980 to 2002, the superior growth of innovative activity is the main factor behind the difference in economic performance between the newly industrializing countries of Asia on the one hand, and Latin America and Africa on the other. Growth rate differences between open economies can be explained in terms of technological competitiveness; the capacity to absorb technology and to exploit knowledge from elsewhere; price competitiveness which is a function of new technologies which reduce costs, and non-price competitiveness which largely depends on product innovation.

Learning

A third means by which societies progress technologically, gradually raising their efficiency and productivity, is through the process of '**learning by doing**', which refers to the accumulation of experience by workers, managers and owners of capital in the course of production, which enables productive efficiency to be improved in the future. It is a learning process that Adam Smith referred to when discussing the benefits of **division of labour** (see Chapter 5). Smith stressed the importance of the division of labour for three main reasons: as a means of improving the dexterity of workers, to save the time lost in the absence of specialization, and to encourage the invention of machines that facilitate and abridge labour to improve the productivity of labour. All these advantages of the division of labour are part of a learning process. Labour improves its skill through specialization and work experience, and becomes more adept at the job in hand. Managers see deficiencies in organization, which can subsequently be remedied; and on the basis of accumulated knowledge they are also able to embody more productive techniques in the capital stock.

Learning may be regarded as either endogenous or exogenous, or both, depending on the factor of production considered. If existing labour and existing capital are subject to a learning process, then learning by doing may be regarded as exogenous and part of disembodied technical progress. If, however, it is assumed that learning enters the productive system only through the addition of new factors, then learning by doing must be regarded as endogenous. This is the basis of Kenneth Arrow's famous capital model (1962), from which the term 'learning by doing' originates. His hypothesis with respect to capital is that at any moment of time new capital goods incorporate all the knowledge then available, based on accumulated experience, but once built their productive efficiency cannot be altered by subsequent learning.

The endogenous model may be appropriate in the case of capital but is much less relevant in the case of labour. It is in relation to labour that most research into the learning process has been conducted. The notion of the **learning curve**, or progress function, which has been found in many industries, relates direct labour input per unit of output to cumulative output as the measure of experience. Typically, labour input per unit of output is found to decline by between 10 and 20 per cent for each doubling of cumulative output, with a corresponding rise in the productivity of labour. For any one product, of course, learning cannot go on at the same rate forever, but since product types are constantly changing it is probably safe to conclude that at the aggregate level, over time, there is no limit to the learning process.

Investment in human capital: education

We turn now to the relation between technological progress and improvements in the health, education and skills of the labour force, or what is commonly called **investment in human capital**.

Investment in human capital takes many different forms, including expenditure on health facilities, on-the-job and institutional training and retraining, formally organized education, study programmes and adult education, and so on. Investment in human capital can overcome many of the characteristics of the labour force that act as impediments to greater productivity, such as poor health, illiteracy, unreceptiveness to new knowledge, fear of change, a lack of incentive and immobility. Improvements in the health, education and skill of labour can increase considerably the productivity and earnings of labour and may be preconditions for the introduction of more sophisticated, advanced technology applied to production. The capacity to absorb physical capital may be limited, among other things, by investment in human capital. It is in this respect that there is likely to be a close interrelationship between the mainsprings of technological progress.

We focus here on the relation between education and growth, and the importance of education in the development process. We then give some estimates of the rates of return to investment in education in developing countries according to type of education and level of per capita income.

There are three main ways in which education can improve growth performance:

- Education improves the quality of labour, and also the quality of physical capital through the application of knowledge.
- Education has spillover effects (externalities) on other sections of society which offset diminishing returns to physical capital.
- Education is one of the most important inputs into R&D and for attracting FDI.

There are three main methods of estimating the contribution of education to growth:

- Measuring the contribution that education makes to the difference in earnings of individuals
- The production function approach
- The use of macrodeterminants of growth equations.

The first method involves constructing a quality-weighted index of the labour force, where quality is measured by the contribution that education makes to the difference in the earnings of individuals as a measure of productivity. The approach, pioneered by Denison (1962), involves two steps. The first entails gathering information on the distribution of the labour force by amounts of schooling at different dates. The second step involves collecting information on income differences between education cohorts with different amounts of schooling embodied in them, which are then used as weights to derive an index of the improvement in the quality of labour due to education on the assumption that a certain percentage of differences in earnings is due to differences in the amount of education.

Suppose, for instance, that the earnings differential between those with eight years' schooling and those with ten years' schooling is 20 per cent, that one-half of the difference is assumed to be due to the extra two years' schooling, and that a person with eight years' schooling is treated as one unit; then the person with ten years' education is counted as $1 + (0.5 \times 0.2) = 1.1$ units. The growth of the quality of labour due to education over a given period can then be estimated and its contribution to measured growth calculated. For example, suppose that the growth in the quality of labour is estimated to be 1 per cent per annum, that the elasticity of output with respect to labour is 0.7, and the annual average growth rate of the economy is 3 per cent. This gives a contribution of education to measured growth of 23 per cent, that is, $(0.7 \times 1.0)/3.0 = 0.23$.

The approach is not without its difficulties. The proportion of earnings differences assumed to be due to differences in the amounts of education between individuals is arbitrary, and if the figure is too high this will give an upward bias to the contribution of education. On the other hand, there are other reasons why the approach underestimates the contribution of education:

- The methodology employed ignores the role of education in maintaining the *average* quality of the labour force.
- No allowance is made for improvements in the *quality* of education.
- There are the '*spillovers*' from education to consider, such as the contribution of education to knowledge and its diffusion throughout society.

The second method for estimating the contribution of education to growth, and also the rate of return to educational expenditure, is to use the production function approach outlined in Chapter 5 (see equation (5.23)). All that is required is a measure of education expansion to include in the production function. The contribution of education to measured growth is then the rate of growth of the education variable multiplied by the elasticity of output with respect to the education variable. In estimating form, the production function with the growth of education included is written as

$$r_Y = r_T + a r_K + \beta r_L + \gamma r_E \tag{7.1}$$

where r_E is the rate of growth of education, and γ is the elasticity of output with respect to education. The rate of return to education can then be measured as

$$\frac{\Delta Y}{\Delta E} = \gamma \frac{\overline{Y}}{\overline{E}} \tag{7.2}$$

where $\overline{Y}$ and $\overline{E}$ are the mean levels of output and the education variable, respectively.

For example, suppose that the mean level of output over a period was £100 million, that the mean level of expenditure on education was £5 million, and that the elasticity of output with respect to education (γ) was 0.01. The rate of return would then be 0.2 or 20 per cent, that is, $(0.01)(100/5) = 0.2$.

The third method for estimating the contribution of education to growth comes from 'new' growth theory, discussed in Chapter 5, in which the stock of education (measured by enrolment rates, or number of years of schooling) is included as a variable to explain differences in growth rates between countries using large samples of countries. A simple cross-section estimating equation would be of the form:

$$g = a + b(PCY) + c(education) \tag{7.3}$$

where g is the average growth rate of countries over, say, a 20-year period; *PCY* is the initial level of per capita income of countries, and (*education*) measures the proportion of the age group enrolled in primary or secondary schools in each country, or the average years of schooling. The coefficient, c, then measures the contribution of a 1 percentage point difference in school enrolment rates, or years of schooling, to the difference in growth rates between countries. Barro's (1991) pioneer study using this approach, and adopted by others (see Table 5.6, p. 167), suggested that each additional year of schooling was associated with a 0.3 percentage point faster growth of per capita income over the period 1960–90. These so-called 'macrodeterminants of growth' studies also include a number of other variables, and the contribution of education to growth sometimes remains a significant variable and sometimes not. The fast growth of the East Asian economies in recent decades is often attributed to their heavy investment in education.

But highlighting the role of education in the growth process pre-dates 'new' growth theory. In the postwar years, it was Denison, and T. W. Schultz in his Presidential address to the American Economic Association in 1961 (see Schultz, 1961), who first drew attention to the importance of education for growth with quantitative evidence. According to Schultz, the stock of education in the USA rose by approximately 850 per cent between 1900 and 1956 compared with an increase in reproducible capital of 450 per cent. He acknowledged the difficulties of estimating the rate of return to education, but argued that even when every conceivable cost is considered, and all expenditure is treated as investment and none as consumption,[1] the return on investment in education is at least as high as, if not higher than, the return on investment in non-human capital. Denison estimated a contribution of education to the growth of per capita income of 40 per cent.

It is the apparent importance of education in the historical growth process of developed countries that has invoked the response that investment in human capital may be as important as investment in physical capital in developing countries. The empirical evidence seems to support this view. In 1980 a World Bank survey concluded that 'studies have shown that economic returns on investment in education seem, in most instances, to exceed returns on alternative kinds of investment, and that developing countries often have higher returns than the developed ones'.[2] Some estimates of the rate of return to education in developing countries are given in Tables 7.1 and 7.2, compiled by Psacharopoulos (1994) from the extensive research done in several developing countries. Table 7.1 shows the social and private returns on investment in primary, secondary and higher education by continent. Table 7.2 gives the same information according to the level of per capita income of countries.

There are several interesting and important conclusions to be derived from the statistics. The first is that the highest rate of return comes from investment in primary education. This is consistent with the observation that one of the strongest associations in developing countries is between the level and rate of growth of per capita income and the proportion of the population in primary education.[3] Traditional customs and attitudes cannot be changed significantly until a large section of the community at a fairly young age is exposed to new ideas and ways of doing things, and there can be very little progress at all without basic literacy and numeracy. The rate of

Table 7.1 Returns on investment in education (%), by continent, early 1990s

Country	Social			Private		
	Prim.	Sec.	Higher	Prim.	Sec.	Higher
Sub-Saharan Africa	24.3	18.2	11.2	41.3	26.6	27.8
Asia*	19.9	13.3	11.7	39.0	18.9	19.9
Europe/Middle East/ North Africa*	15.5	11.2	10.6	17.4	15.9	21.7
Latin America/Caribbean	17.9	12.8	12.3	26.2	16.8	19.7
OECD	14.4	10.2	8.7	21.7	12.4	12.3
World	18.4	13.1	10.9	29.1	18.1	20.3

*Non-OECD

Source: Psacharopoulos, 1994.

Table 7.2   Returns on investment in education (%), by level of per capita income, early 1990s

Country	Mean per capita (US$)	Social			Private		
		Prim.	Sec.	Higher	Prim.	Sec.	Higher
Low-income ($610 or less)	299	23.4	15.2	10.6	35.2	19.3	23.5
Lower middle-income (to $2,449)	1,402	18.2	13.4	11.4	29.9	18.7	18.9
Upper middle-income (to $7,619)	4,184	14.3	10.6	9.5	21.3	12.7	14.8
High-income ($7,620 or more)	13,100	n.a.	10.3	8.2	n.a.	12.8	7.7
World	2,020	20.0	13.5	10.7	30.7	17.7	19.0

Source: Psacharopoulos, 1994.

return then declines with the level of schooling. Primary, secondary and tertiary enrolment rates are shown in Table 3.5 in Chapter 3 (p. 84).

Secondly, it will be noticed that the rate of return on education at all levels tends to decline with the level of development, as measured by per capita income. Since enrolment rates tend to be higher in developed countries than in developing countries, this suggests diminishing returns from expenditure on education at all levels.

A third important observation is that the social return is invariably lower than the private return. This is because most of the costs of education, at least at the primary and secondary level, are not borne by the individual, but by the state. In higher education in high-income countries, however, the private and social returns are close because many of the direct costs are borne by students and there is a high opportunity cost in the form of foregone earnings. The social return on higher education in developed countries is very close to the social discount rate; that is, 8–10 per cent.

Overall, it can be concluded that investment in education in all countries is both privately and socially profitable – the more so, the less developed the country. A social return to investment in primary education in developing countries of 20 per cent or more is very high indeed.

Women's education

The discussion so far has made no distinction between the education of men and women. In most developing countries, however, there is still a big gender gap in the provision of educational opportunities, and in the labour market, with women considerably disadvantaged. This is reflected in the statistics for primary, secondary and tertiary school enrolment rates, and in levels of literacy, as shown in Table 7.3. One of the major Millennium Development Goals outlined in Chapter 1 is to eliminate gender disparity in primary and secondary education, no later than 2015.

The underinvestment in women's education can be explained partly by cultural factors, but also by economic factors. Because women have inferior work opportunities, the costs of educating women are not so easily recouped, and the rate of return is low – at least, the private return. Families see greater returns from investing in the education of boys. From a social point of view, however, the returns to investment in the education of females could be high. The education of

Table 7.3 Educational provision and literacy, females relative to males, 2005

	Adult literacy		Gross primary enrolment		Gross secondary enrolment		Gross tertiary enrolment	
	Female rate (% aged 15 and older) 1995–2005	Ratio of female rate to male rate 1995–2005	Female rate (%) 2005	Ratio of female rate to male rate 2005	Female rate (%) 2005	Ratio of female rate to male rate 2005	Female rate (%) 2005	Ratio of female rate to male rate 2005
Developing countries	69.9	0.91	104	0.94	58	0.93	16	0.91
Least developed countries	44.3	0.80	90	0.89	28	0.81	3	0.63
Arab States	59.4	0.88	88	0.90	65	0.92	21	1.01
East Asia and the Pacific	86.7	0.99	110	0.98	72	1.00	21	0.93
Latin America and the Caribbean	89.7	1.01	115	0.96	91	1.08	32	1.17
South Asia	47.4	0.81	109	0.93	48	0.83	9	0.74
Sub-Saharan Africa	51.2	0.84	92	0.89	28	0.79	4	0.62
Central & Eastern Europe and the CIS	98.7	1.00	107	0.99	90	0.98	63	1.30

Source: UNDP, 2007/2008.

women is not only important in its own right for improving the entitlements and capabilities of women, but it has important direct and indirect effects by leading to reductions in fertility and population growth (see Chapter 9) and improving social welfare in general. As the former Chief Economist of the World Bank, Lawrence Summers, has observed (Summers 1994): 'hard statistical evaluations fairly consistently find that female education is the variable most highly correlated with social indicators. The benefits of [female] education have a multiplier effect because they empower women to bring about other necessary changes.'

To conclude the discussion of education, it needs to be said that the fact that the capacity of a country to absorb physical capital and technological progress may be constrained by the availability of human capital does not necessarily mean education should be given preferential treatment. All types of capital formation need to be considered together and carried out simultaneously. Ultimately, the amount of resources devoted to investment in human capital is an allocative decision that each country must make for itself on the basis of a number of considerations, of which the rate of return would be one. Other important considerations would be the type of educated workforce that might be required in the future to avoid skill bottlenecks on the one hand, and unemployment on the other, if the pattern of demand and the balance between genders is changing.

Infrastructure investment

Another major type of investment that is very important to developing countries is infrastructure investment. Just as the productivity of physical capital depends on investment in human capital, so it also depends on the existence of infrastructure investment – for example, in transport and power facilities. Good infrastructure improves productivity and reduces production costs in the private sector. Apart from this obvious benefit, the adequacy of infrastructure can make a crucial difference to a country's development programme in a number of ways, such as diversifying production, expanding trade, improving environmental conditions and reducing poverty.

For poor farmers, improved infrastructure will reduce input costs, increase agricultural output and reduce traders' monopoly by improving access to markets. Nearly two-thirds of African farmers are cut off from national and world markets because of poor infrastructure and market access. Better transport means greater access to public services, including schools, hospitals and other health facilities. In this way, infrastructure investment can help in meeting some of the Millennium Development Goals in the field of education, health and gender equality. Research at the World Bank (2005) across 73 countries shows that a 10 per cent improvement in a country's infrastructure index is associated with a 5 per cent reduction in child mortality, a 3.5 per cent reduction in infant mortality, and a 7.8 per cent reduction in maternal mortality (linked to safer water supply, sanitation and easier access to hospitals). Piped water promotes gender equality by freeing women who traditionally spend hours a day collecting water from wells. Straub (2008) surveys 64 recent research papers on this topic, and virtually all support a positive and significant link between infrastructure provisions and various aspects of economic development.

Currently, developing countries invest approximately $500 billion a year in new infrastructure – transport, power, water, sanitation, telecommunications, irrigation and so on, equal to 20 per cent of total investment and approximately 5 per cent of GDP – and the need for such investment is still huge. One billion people still lack access to clean water, two billion people lack access to sanitation and electric power, and transport facilities are still very rudimentary in many developing countries.

Most infrastructure investment is undertaken by governments. The public sector owns, operates and finances virtually all infrastructure because it is either regarded as a natural monopoly or a public good. Without competition and accountability, however, there can be a great deal of inefficiency and waste. The underutilization of capacity can be a major problem in transport and power because of lack of maintenance. The World Bank calculates that raising operating efficiency to best-practice levels could save over $50 billion a year, and that the greater private provision of infrastructure and the recoupment of costs from users could reduce government subsidies by over $100 billion.

The Bank has called for a shift of emphasis 'from increasing the quantity of infrastructure stocks to improving the quality of infrastructure services', and a change of thinking from the view that infrastructure services can only be provided by government. It makes three major recommendations: the wider application of commercial principles, including managerial autonomy and the setting of performance targets; the introduction of more competition, for example arranging for suppliers to compete for an entire market; and the increased involvement of users so that suppliers respond to user needs.

Technology and the developing countries

Most technological improvement originates from developed countries. The Organisation for Economic Co-operation and Development (OECD) countries spend over $700 billion a year on R&D, which is more than the GDP of sub-Saharan Africa, and account for more than 90 per cent of patents issued. If developing countries are to develop their own technology, there needs to be the right institutional environment, including an incentive structure through patents, sound infrastructure, political stability to attract investment funds, and the availability of credit. Some of the technological leaders among developing countries include Singapore, Taiwan, India, South Korea, Malaysia, China, Mexico, Thailand, Philippines and Brazil, measured by the share of medium- and high-technology manufactures in total manufacturing value-added.

Technology is currently making a contribution to development in three major fields: agriculture, health, and information and communications. In agriculture, the impact of the Green Revolution in the 1960s and 1970s has now diminished, but on the horizon is biotechnology with the potential to end world hunger through the use of genetically modified (GM) foods and crops. The advantage of GM technology is that it allows the transfer of traits between unrelated species. For example, a gene in one species associated with the ability to resist drought can be directly transferred into the genetic code of another species. We now have GM crops more resistant to viruses and insects and more tolerant of herbicides; in the future we could have food with extra vitamins and protein, and even vaccines to combat malnutrition and disease. In the late 1990s China gave 26 approvals for GM crops, including transgenic peppers, tomatoes, rice and cotton. China has the advantage of being an authoritarian regime. Other countries – including India, China's main economic rival – have had to deal with public protests against GM technology, with invasion of field trials and burning of GM crops.

In health, new technology and advances in medicine have been the biggest single factor in reducing mortality and increasing life expectancy in developing countries. Important discoveries include vaccines against influenza, smallpox, polio, measles, tuberculosis, antibiotics (penicillin), and oral rehydration therapy – which was originally developed in Bangladesh and has saved millions of babies from dying from diarrhoea. Biotechnology and genomics offer new ways to cure disease by altering genes that contribute to cancer, or boosting genes that might fight it.

Information and communications technology (ICT) can provide enormous benefits to developing countries, both as consumers and producers. Any task that can be digitized can now be done at a distance, which gives the opportunity for low-cost countries to develop ICT industries. India's software industry now employs over one million people. Call centres are one of the fastest-growing industries in the subcontinent. For consumers, access to information through the Internet can be of benefit in almost any field – for weather information in agriculture, for the dissemination of knowledge in health care and the tracking of diseases, and for distance learning in education.

Case example 7.2 describes the World Bank's views on bridging the technology divide between rich and poor countries.

| Case example 7.2 | **Bridging the technology divide** |

Technological progress – improvements in the ways that goods and services are produced, marketed, and brought to market – is at the very heart of human advancement and development. It has helped reduce the share of people living in absolute poverty in developing countries from 29 per cent in 1990 to 18 per cent in 2004.

As a result, the technology gap between rich and poor countries has narrowed, although it remains wide. Low-income countries employ only one-fourth the technology used in high-income countries.

Technological progress in developing countries (that is, low-income, lower-middle-income, and upper-middle-income countries) outstripped progress in high-income countries between the early 1990s and 2000s. Of course, the initial level of technology in lower-income countries was much lower to begin with.

The very strong technological progress developing countries have enjoyed has come mainly from adopting and absorbing existing technologies. Compared with the size of their economies, they perform relatively little new-to-the-world innovation.

The diffusion of technology across developing countries has been facilitated by their increased exposure to foreign technologies. Over the past 15 years, foreign direct investment levels and imports of high-technology and capital goods have doubled as a percentage of GDP – in part because of contacts with well-educated migrant populations living abroad.

Slow diffusion within countries means that, although individual cities may be technology leaders, the use of technology in a country as a whole may be low. For instance, while more than one in two urban Indian families has cell [mobile] phone access, only one in 10 in the rural sector does.

Partly as a result of this increased exposure, newer technology – such as cell phones, computers, and the Internet – now spreads much more quickly. In the early 1900s, new technology took more than 50 years to reach most countries; today it takes about 16 years. But technology tends to spread slowly within countries because many developing countries lack the technical skills necessary to master new, or even older, technologies.

Although better macroeconomic and educational policies, as well as the spread of older enabling technologies – such as electrical networks, road infrastructure, telephone land lines, and sanitation networks – have advanced the spread of technology

| Case example 7.2 | **Bridging the technology divide** – *continued* |

in developing countries, progress has been slow and the capacity to absorb new ideas and techniques remains weak.

Closing the gap

To continue catching up with high-income countries, developing countries need to

- maintain exposure to foreign technologies through trade openness, foreign direct investment, and the participation of migrant populations;
- further improve the investment climate to allow innovative firms to grow;
- invest in enabling technologies and basic infrastructure, such as roads, electricity, and telephones;
- improve the quality and increase the quantity of education throughout the economy – not just in major centers; and
- emphasize technology diffusion by reinforcing dissemination systems and the market orientation of R&D programs.

Source: *Finance & Development*, June 2008.

Techniques of production

If labour is more abundant and capital is scarcer in developing countries than in developed countries, we might expect to observe the use of more labour-intensive techniques of production in the industrial sector of developing countries, reflecting a lower price of labour relative to capital. Figure 7.4 shows this. Assuming the same production function in the two sets of countries, labelled '1', and holding everything else constant, the lower relative price of labour in the developing country, given by the price line (or isocost curve), *cb*, gives a more labour-intensive choice of technique than in the developed country, where the relative price of labour is given by the steeper line *ad*.

In the developed country the capital–labour ratio is given by the ray from the origin, *DC*, while in the less-developed country the capital–labour ratio is given by the ray *LDC*; both rays

Figure 7.4   Optimal choice of technique

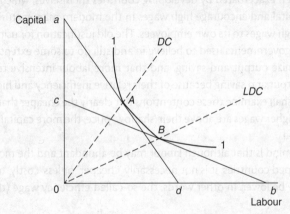

pass through the point of tangency between the price line and production function – A and B, respectively.

In practice, however, it is often the case that for the same outputs produced, the capital intensity of techniques is not very different between the two sets of countries, and that the capital–labour ratio differs between developed and developing countries in the aggregate only to the extent that the composition of output differs; that is, because there are large sectors in developing countries' economies where very little capital is employed at all, as in subsistence farming and petty service activities. In the modern sectors of developing countries, however, techniques are much more capital-intensive than would be predicted on the basis of knowledge of factor endowments. Given the supply of labour available, and given the rate of investment, the more capital-intensive the techniques, the less employment and the more unemployment there will be.

Unemployment and underemployment are major preoccupations in developing countries, and are one reason why the prevailing techniques of production might be regarded as 'inappropriate'.

But what accounts for this relative capital intensity of modern sector techniques, and would the developing countries be better off using more labour-intensive techniques? There are a number of reasons why technological choice sometimes appears to be little different in developing countries than in technologically advanced societies.

First, for a large number of commodities there may not be a spectrum of techniques to choose from; that is, in practice the production function in Figure 7.4 may not be smooth, and a country cannot move from point A to B in accordance with differences in relative factor endowments and relative factor prices. We are talking here, of course, about techniques that are profitable. There may always be more labour-intensive techniques using both more labour and capital, but then the output would not be competitively saleable. If there is not a spectrum of profitable techniques of production, and the coefficients of production are fixed, the production function is L-shaped (sometimes called a **Leontief production function** after Wassily Leontief, the 'father' of input–output analysis, which assumes no substitutability between capital and labour). Whether technology is such that there is only one profitable technique, or whether there are many but developing countries do not have access to them, is an empirical question that we shall consider later in the chapter.

A second reason for the relative capital intensity of production in developing countries is that the market prices of factors of production frequently do not reflect relative abundance or scarcity. This tendency is often exacerbated by developing countries themselves, which give generous subsidies to scarce capital and encourage high wages in the modern manufacturing sector by the government paying high wages to its own employees. The old justification for using capital-intensive techniques, which governments used to believe in and still do to some extent, was that they are necessary to maximize output and saving, and that more labour-intensive techniques would reduce the level of output and saving because of their relative inefficiency and higher wage bills. Later in the chapter we shall examine these contentions but clearly the cheaper that capital is made by subsidies, and the higher wages are above their 'shadow' price, the more capital-intensive the techniques will tend to be.

A third factor to bear in mind is that although labour may be abundant and the money wage may be lower than in developed countries, it is not necessarily 'cheaper' or less 'costly' to employ, because its productivity may be lower. In other words, the so-called **efficiency wage** (that is, the

Figure 7.5 Different wages: same technique

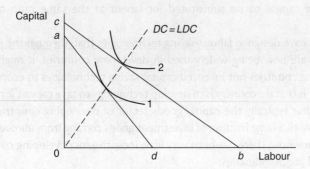

wage rate divided by the productivity of labour), or wage costs per unit of output, may differ very little between the developing and developed countries. This means that the production function for the developing country in Figure 7.4 will lie outside the production function for the developed country in such a way that even if the relative money wage of labour is lower in the developing country, it is profitable to choose a relatively capital-intensive technique. Figure 7.5 shows this. The production function for the developing country is labelled '2'. Even though labour is cheaper relative to capital in the developing country (slope of *cb* < slope of *ad*), nonetheless the most profitable capital–labour ratio will be the same in both countries (given by the ray from the origin, *DC = LDC*). It is probably because abundant labour is not necessarily 'cheap', in a cost per unit of output sense, that accounts for the observation that in trade developing countries' exports are sometimes as capital-intensive as in developed countries, contrary to the prediction of certain trade theories. This apparent paradox (sometimes called the **Leontief Paradox**) could be explained by the fact that it is the 'efficiency' wage that matters, not the money wage, and while the money wage may be low in developing countries, the 'efficiency' wage is relatively high.

Fourth, we may mention the fact that in certain instances capital intensity may be explained by a skill constraint. Typically, labour-intensive techniques require a great deal of skilled labour, compared with capital-intensive techniques which mainly require a preponderance of semi-skilled labour to undertake routine tasks. In developing countries that are short of skilled manpower, capital may substitute for skills and constitute a rational response on the part of decision-makers, whoever they may be.

But perhaps the overriding factor that accounts for the relative capital intensity of the modern sector of developing countries is the fact that many, if not most, of the techniques of production are imported from abroad, with a heavy bias in the labour-saving direction. The techniques may either be employed by indigenous firms or, as increasingly seems to be the case, by large foreign-owned **multinational corporations**, which invest in the country and bring their technology with them. In this case the technology may be 'inappropriate' not because there is not a spectrum of techniques or an inappropriate selection is made, but because the technology available is circumscribed by the global profit-maximizing motives of the companies investing in the developing country concerned. The labour-saving bias of the technology is to be explained by the labour-saving bias of technical progress in advanced countries where labour is relatively scarce and expensive. As we saw earlier (Figure 7.2), labour-saving bias on a production function diagram is represented by a non-uniform inward shift in the production function, causing capital to be substituted for labour at the same ratio of relative factor prices.

If developed countries have designed labour-saving technologies that, through the process of international investment, are now being widely used in developing countries, it might well be asked: why have developing countries not invented capital-saving technologies to economize on scarce capital? The answer is that if a country is to develop technology to save capital, it must have a capital goods industry, but typically the capital goods sector of developing countries is rudimentary or non-existent. With a large fraction of investment goods coming from abroad, coupled with a lack of domestic knowhow, there has been very little incentive for developing countries to establish their own capital goods industries.

Capital goods production is characterized by the ability to specialize, but to do this economically requires a large market – a much larger market than for homogeneous consumer products that can reap economies of scale. Capital saving also comes from improvement in the efficiency of capital goods production itself, but without a capital goods sector there cannot be innovations, and an important source of capital saving and technical progress in the economy as a whole is lost. It is widely recognized that a capital goods sector is essential for innovatory activity in the economy as a whole, and if developing countries are to reduce their dependence on imported technology, priority must be given to the establishment and nurture of an indigenous capital goods sector (Stewart, 1977).[4]

The empirical evidence on multinational corporations and the choice of techniques is mixed. Lall (1978) distinguishes three separate issues:

- Whether the technologies used by multinationals are adaptable to abundant labour and low wage conditions in developing countries
- Whether multinationals do adapt the technologies they transfer
- Whether multinationals adapt better or worse than local firms.

Regarding the first question, the technologies used by multinationals are unlikely to be very flexible because the companies tend to predominate in modern industries where processes are complex, continuous and, by their very nature, capital-intensive. Outside processing, however, ancillary activities, such as the handling of materials and packaging, may be amenable to substitution. On the second issue, it is unlikely that multinationals will undertake major, expensive alterations to technology simply to suit local conditions, and there is not much evidence that they do so.

With regard to the third matter, however, in comparison with local firms, the experience of the multinationals seems to be very mixed. The problem here is that when making comparisons, like must be compared with like; that is, local and foreign firms must be compared in the same market, producing similar products with equal access to technology. Studies must therefore be treated with caution. It is easy to reach the conclusion that multinationals are more capital-intensive than local firms if they operate in different industries producing different products. This in fact is often the case, as they tend to be concentrated in activities that are intrinsically more capital-intensive such as heavy industries and extractive industries. We shall say more about the empirical evidence below, and more about multinational corporations in Chapter 14 where we consider the role of foreign direct investment in the development process.

We turn now to the potential conflict between moving towards the use of more labour-intensive techniques of production and output on the one hand, and saving on the other.

The conflict between employment and output and employment and saving in the choice of techniques

Developing countries have three broad objectives: to raise the level of *present* consumption, to raise the level of *future* consumption (by saving now), and to raise the level of *employment*. In the choice of *new* techniques, a conflict between objectives may arise. First, a technique that maximizes employment *may* involve a sacrifice of output. Second, a technique that maximizes employment *may* involve a sacrifice of saving. As we have mentioned already, certainly one of the justifications for the use of modern capital-intensive technology used to be that labour-intensive techniques would reduce output and the investible surplus. We need to look at this matter theoretically and empirically. We shall argue that while in theory there may be a conflict, the assumptions upon which a potential conflict is based are either invalid or too extreme, and that in practice developing countries could move towards the use of more labour-intensive techniques without sacrificing the level of present or future consumption. Some of the empirical evidence would seem to bear this out.

Employment versus output

A potential conflict between employment and output exists in the choice of new techniques because methods that employ high labour–capital ratios may involve high capital–output ratios because labour productivity is lower.[5] Assume that a fixed amount of capital, £1,000, is to be invested. Technique I employs 100 persons with an incremental capital–output ratio of 5, giving an annual flow of output of £200. Technique II employs 50 persons with an incremental capital–output ratio of 4, giving an annual flow of output of £250. Therefore the technique that maximizes employment has a lower flow of current output.

It should be said straight away that there is very little evidence, if any, to support the view that labour-intensive techniques have higher capital–output ratios than capital-intensive techniques. On the contrary, there is growing evidence that labour can be substituted for capital, provided cooperating factors are available, without the level of output being impaired. One interesting pioneer study is that by Pack (1974), using UN data on capital per unit of output (K/O) and labour per unit of output (L/O) for 6 commodities in 16 firms across 10 countries. Pack plots the observations of (K/O) and (L/O) (as in Figure 7.6) for each commodity from the cross-section data, and then defines the efficiency frontier to estimate the elasticity of substitution along it.

Each scatter point in Figure 7.6 represents country observations for one industry, say cotton textiles, of the relative amounts of capital and labour employed per unit of output. The **efficiency frontier** (or unit isoquant) is drawn through the points closest to the origin and the elasticity of substitution is calculated as

$$\frac{(K/L)_i}{(K/L)_j} = \left[\frac{(w/r)_i}{(w/r)_j} \right]^{\sigma}$$

where w/r is the wage-rental ratio, i and j are the two observations closest to the origin, and α is the elasticity of substitution. For five of the six commodities there is a large difference in the amount of capital per worker year used by countries on the efficiency frontier and a fairly high elasticity of substitution. The results are shown in Table 7.4.

Figure 7.6   Efficiency frontier

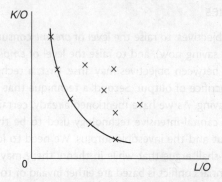

Table 7.4   Capital–labour substitution possibilities

Industry		Countries on the efficiency frontier	Capital per worker year ($)	Elasticity of substitution (σ)
Bicycles	}	India	400	0.24
		Japan	520	
Grain milling	}	Japan	280	3.70
		Israel	6,410	
Paints	}	India	214	1.60
		Middle Europe	2,790	
Tyres	}	Iran	6,240	1.50
		Mexico	10,600	
Cotton textiles	}	India	1,100	2.00
		Mexico	8,240	
Woollen textiles	}	India	260	1.20
		Japan	4,600	

The results suggest that for countries using large amounts of capital per unit of labour there are more labour-intensive techniques available (as used by other countries) that could be adopted without sacrificing output unless the cooperating factors associated with the increased labour intensity are not available. One interesting observation from Pack's work is that India is invariably either on or close to the efficiency frontier, and hence is using labour-intensive techniques effectively.

Pack's study (1976) of 42 plants in Kenyan manufacturing also suggests that there appears to be considerable *ex ante* choice of capital intensity in most industries, particularly outside the processing sector in the auxiliary activities of material receiving, material handling among processes, packaging and storage of the finished products. In fact many auxiliary activities are already very labour-intensive, and contrary to the conventional wisdom it was found that foreign-owned firms generally used more labour-intensive techniques than indigenous firms. Pack ascribes this to the better managerial expertise and technical training of personnel in foreign firms. Forsyth and Solomon (1977), in a study of Ghana, also found scope for capital/labour substitution and could find no conclusive evidence that foreign firms are more capital-intensive than resident expatriate or private indigenous firms. The situation varies from industry to industry. Helleiner (1975) concludes his survey of multinational corporations and technological choice by saying: 'In particular industrial sectors, the multinational firm has often proven more responsive and adaptable in its factor and input use, especially in the ancillary activities associated with the basic production processes, than local firms, and so it perhaps should be with its wide range of experience on which to draw.'

Even if more labour-intensive techniques can be used without a sacrifice of output, there is still the question of whether the investible surplus, and therefore future output, will be impaired. Pack's work suggests otherwise, but let us now consider in more detail the potential conflict between employment and saving, as the traditional argument has it.

Employment versus saving

The potential conflict between employment and saving can be illustrated in its starkest form using a simple production function diagram first used in this context by Dobb (1955) and Sen (1968).

Consider the use of a given amount of investible resources, K, and the possibility of employing those resources with varying amounts of labour to produce output. In Figure 7.7, $0O$ is the production function in the consumption sector, exhibiting diminishing returns to labour. Now take the standard traditional (though not necessarily correct!) assumption that in the industrial sector labour is paid a fixed wage that is all consumed, so that a ray from the origin ($0C$) with a constant slope (w) shows the level of the wage bill and consumption at each level of employment. The difference between $0O$ and $0C$ is profit; and if all profits are saved the difference also shows the level of saving at each capital–labour ratio. Saving is maximized where a line drawn parallel to $0C$ is tangential to the production function – at employment level L in Figure 7.7. Beyond this point, further employment generation would diminish the level of saving and investible surplus.

Figure 7.7 Employment versus saving

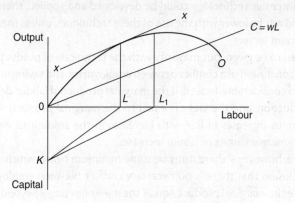

The potential clash between increasing employment and maximizing saving can be seen, however, to be based on several assumptions, the validity of which may be questioned.

- That the wage rate is given and invariant with respect to the technique of production. This assumption would seem to be a hangover from Lewis's influential model of the development process (discussed in Chapter 6), which assumes an elastic supply of labour to the industrial sector at a *constant* wage. If this wage is above the minimum necessary, however, several implications ensue.
- That all profits are saved and all wages are consumed.
- That unemployment resulting from the use of capital-intensive techniques does not reduce community saving by at least as much as with more employment and a higher wage bill.
- That consumption is not productive (that is, it has no investment component), or that present consumption is no more productive than future consumption.
- That governments lack the ability to tax and to subsidize labour to reconcile the potential conflict.

Let us relax these assumptions and see what difference is made.

Wages and the capital intensity of production

Let us first relax the assumption that the wage rate is given and the same for all techniques, regardless of the capital intensity. There are two fundamental points to be made here in the context of a developing country. The first is that a great deal of the technology, at least in the modern industrial sector, is not indigenous but imported. In this case the wage structure is set by the *skill mix* demanded by the technology and the need to keep the labour force well nourished and contented if the capital equipment is to be worked productively and profitably. By and large it may be expected that the greater the degree of capital intensity the higher the average wage paid.

The second point is that with large amounts of disguised and open unemployment in the urban sector of developing countries there is likely to be a big difference between the wage that is being paid with the use of existing technology (imported or indigenous) and the wage at which labour would be willing to work, given the opportunity, with the use of more labour-intensive technology. If more labour-intensive technology could be developed and applied, there is no reason why the wage rate should not be lower with the use of these techniques, unless there is strong trade union resistance in certain sectors.

If the wage is not assumed to be given, but may vary with the technique of production for the reasons outlined above, the conclusion of a conflict between employment and saving in the choice of new techniques is affected considerably. Indeed, if the marginal product of labour declines with the labour intensity of production, and the wage is equal to the marginal product, the conflict disappears entirely. The surplus increases in line with increases in the amount of employment because the surplus on *intra-marginal* units of labour increases.

Wages cannot fall to zero, however – there must be some minimum below which wages cannot fall. This gives the conclusion that there is no necessary conflict between employment and saving up to the point where the marginal product equals the *minimum* wage. Beyond that point there will be a conflict.

Different classes' propensity to consume

The alleged conflict between employment and saving also depends on the assumption that the propensity to save out of profits is higher than the propensity to save out of wages. In Figure 7.7 the difference between employment levels L (which maximizes saving) and L_1 (which maximizes employment) depends on the extreme assumption that all profits are saved and all wages are spent. No one would dispute that the propensity to save out of profits (s_p) is higher than the propensity to save out of wages (s_w) (indeed, there is plenty of empirical evidence to support the assertion), but it would be unrealistic to argue that there is no saving out of wages and no consumption out of profits. Both consumption out of profits and saving out of wages will reduce the conflict between employment and saving and move the point of maximum surplus away from L towards L_1.

The narrower the difference between s_w and s_p the higher the level of employment before a conflict sets in, until at the limit, if $s_w = s_p$, there is no conflict at all. The distribution of income between wages and profits will not affect the aggregate level of saving.

Support of the unemployed

If a particular choice of technology, which is designed to maximize the reinvestible surplus, causes unemployment and the unemployed make claims on society's investible resources, the surplus may ultimately be less than if more labour-intensive techniques had been chosen. There are three main ways in which the unemployed may reduce the investible surplus:

- If the unemployed remain in the agricultural sector they may depress average product and consume more than they produce, thus reducing the agricultural surplus.
- If the unemployed remain in the industrial sector they will absorb family savings to support themselves.
- There may be public support for the unemployed through unemployment insurance programmes, in which case public saving will be reduced below what it otherwise might be.

If 'compensation' to the unemployed in any of the forms outlined above exceeds the difference between the industrial wage and the marginal product using more labour-intensive techniques, it would pay to create extra employment because the difference between consumption and production as a result of expanding employment would be less than the reduction in saving caused by the unemployment. At the limit, of course, if the unemployed 'consumed' resources equal to the value of the industrial wage, it would make no difference if labour was employed up to the point where the marginal product of labour is zero. There is clearly no difference from the point of view of saving between an unemployed person consuming the equivalent of an industrial wage and an employed man with zero marginal product receiving an industrial wage. As long as unemployment absorbs saving, therefore, in whatever form, employment can be higher without reducing the investible surplus to below what it would otherwise have been. Thus as a general proposition it may be said that the extent of the conflict between employment and saving will also depend on the amount of compensation to the unemployed out of the total investible surplus.

Are consumption and investment distinct?

The alleged conflict between employment and saving also assumes either that consumption has no investment component or that present and future consumption are equally productive. Those who argue for techniques to maximize the investible surplus at the expense of employment place no value on present consumption at the margin, and those who argue for techniques to maximize employment are indifferent at the margin between an extra unit of consumption and saving (investment). It can be shown, however, that if consumption has an investment content, and that the productivity of consumption falls as the level of consumption increases, the relative valuation of present consumption increases, favouring more labour-intensive techniques (Thirlwall, 1977). 'Productive' consumption refers to consumption that improves the efficiency of labour, thereby raising the level of income in the same way as normal additions to the capital stock. As long as consumption is productive, therefore, an increase in employment and consumption need not be at the expense of 'investment' for future output.

All too little is known about the precise extent to which low levels of consumption, and particularly food intake, impair working efficiency and productivity. But we do know that the food requirements considered by nutritionists to be necessary for efficient working and healthy living are far greater than the levels achieved by a large minority of the population in developing countries (see Dasgupta, 1993). Calorie deficiency causes loss of body weight, tiredness, listlessness and a deterioration of mental faculties. Protein deficiency causes such conditions as kwashiorkor, and may cause death in children. Vitamin A deficiency causes blindness, and iodine deficiency is a cause of goitre, which leads to cretinism and deaf-mutism. Altogether it has been estimated by the UN Food and Agriculture Organization that at least one billion people in the world suffer from various degrees of malnutrition (see Chapter 3). To the extent that this impairs efficiency and output, and is caused by a lack of consumption, an increase in employment and present consumption may be as valuable at the margin as an extra unit of saving from the point of view of future welfare. The more equal the relative valuation of consumption and saving at the margin, the less the conflict between employment generation in the present and the level of future output.

Taxes and subsidies

It has been assumed so far that savings and employment depend exclusively on the choice of technique. In practice, of course, governments can tax and subsidize to achieve desired ends, and this they can do to reconcile the conflict between employment and saving. As Sen (1969) has remarked:

> the total amount of income to be saved can be determined by the planner in any way he likes . . . If this is true then the link snaps between the choice of techniques and the proportion of income saved. The technical choice may be made with the main purpose of maximising the amount of output, and the proportion of the output to be invested can be decided at a separate stage.

Consider again Figure 7.7, which is redrawn here as Figure 7.8. By the choice of techniques alone, maximization of the surplus XY means a sacrifice of employment L_1L. Or employment L_1 means a sacrifice of savings equal to Y_1Y_2. Now suppose that the government possesses the power to tax and subsidize. To employ L_1 requires a shadow wage of zero: that is, a subsidy to employers equal to the full value of the wage. The employers' surplus will now be X_1L_1, but since workers receive the market wage and all wages are consumed, consumption will still be Y_1L_1, and the investible

Figure 7.8 Preserving the level of saving through taxation

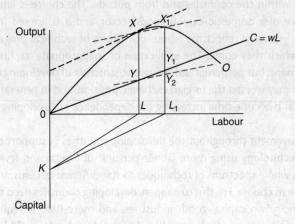

surplus, X_1Y_1. The question is, can tax policy in the new situation preserve the level of the surplus XY generated by the more capital-intensive technology? The answer must be yes, provided the propensity to consume is greater than zero. The total wage bill is Y_1L_1 and it is desired to reduce consumption out of the wage bill by Y_1Y_2. Consumption will fall by the amount of tax times the propensity to consume (c). Hence the level of tax raised must be $T = (Y_1Y_2)/c$. If the wage bill is, say, £1,000, Y_1Y_2 is £100 and c is 0.8, then the tax raised must be £100/0.8 = £125.

In this example the preservation of the level of saving is quite easily accomplished while moving from the more capital-intensive to labour-intensive techniques. If, of course, a fairly high level of taxation already exists, and there is no scope for further taxation, subsidization and taxation will not be a feasible means of reconciliation. In practice, however, the presumption must be that developing countries are not yet at their taxable capacity, and that the subsidization of labour, coupled with appropriate tax policy, is a possible policy.

Some care must be taken, however, over the form of taxation. For example, if the wage is fixed in real terms then indirect taxes that raise prices will reduce the real wage, and the money wage will have to rise to compensate. Since the money wage is the cost to the employer, subsidies will then have to be increased. The imposition of indirect taxes to finance subsidies may lead to a spiral of increased taxation, inflation and subsidization. Direct taxes on workers' incomes may also be counterproductive if workers bid for money-wage increases to maintain disposable income. The only feasible taxes to finance subsidies may be on exports or luxury consumption goods, which will not affect the real income of the broad mass of the working class. While theoretically, therefore, a policy of labour subsidization financed by taxation may reconcile the conflict between employment and saving, it may run into a number of practical difficulties.

All the factors discussed that may lead to an increase in the labour intensity of production without impairing the investible surplus may either be thought of as additive, or any one of them by itself may be powerful enough to push employment close to L_1 in Figure 7.7 without loss of saving or its benefits.

Future policy

It has become part of conventional wisdom, and there may be a good deal of truth in the assertion, that a major cause of the growth of urban unemployment in developing countries lies in the application of 'inappropriate' production techniques because of the limited choice of techniques available, both from within the countries and from outside. The choice is limited from within owing to the absence of a domestic capital goods sector, and it is limited from without because the techniques imported reflect the labour-saving bias of technical progress in the developed countries from which they come. The application of 'inappropriate' technology not only exacerbates unemployment, but perpetuates the dualistic structure of developing countries, increases income inequality, may worsen the foreign exchange position, and in general produces a distorted economy, while at the same time increasing the dependence of developing countries on developed countries.

There is now a strong movement throughout the developing countries in support of the creation of an **intermediate technology** using more labour per unit of capital and fewer foreign inputs. What is required is a whole spectrum of techniques to suit different circumstances, from which developing countries can choose. For this to happen, developing countries need to encourage the establishment of their own capital goods industries, and more R&D is required both within, and on behalf of, poor countries. An **international technology bank** would be a useful starting point, giving countries access to technological blueprints from different sources.

The capital intensity of production is also a function of the composition of output. There are often many ways of meeting a given need, some of which may be more labour-intensive than others. Where this is so, such as in transport, nutrition, housing and so on, serious consideration should be given to the most labour-intensive way of meeting such needs, consistent with other objectives.

Finally, the location of activity needs to be considered. Whatever technology is applied in the modern sector, it will have implications for the rural sector that will rebound on the modern sector. We saw in Chapter 6 that the creation of more modern sector jobs may encourage more migrants than the number of jobs created, thus increasing urban unemployment. This would seem to call for the location of new labour-intensive industries in the rural sector, to curb the flow of migrants and ease urban unemployment.

To conclude our analysis, we have seen that there are many reasons for believing that the potential conflicts inherent in the choice of new techniques between employment and saving on the one hand, and between employment and output on the other, have been exaggerated, and that techniques can be more labour-intensive without impairing the level of the investible surplus or the level of output. **It is in the direction of more rural-based labour-intensive projects that development strategy ought to move for maximization of the general welfare.**

Summary

- There can be no economic growth unless economies invest a proportion of their output. The amount of capital per worker in developing countries is much lower than in developed countries, which partly accounts for the lower productivity of labour in developing countries.
- There are many different types of capital: physical plant and machinery, infrastructure, human capital, and social capital including health expenditure which makes labour more productive.
- The productivity of capital depends to a large extent on the amount of technical progress embodied in it.
- The pace of technical progress depends on the willingness and capacity of societies to be inventive, to innovate, and to devote resources to human capital formation, skill training and R&D expenditure.

- There is a huge technological divide between rich and poor countries, which will take time and effort to bridge.
- The choice of techniques of production is an important issue in developing countries – whether to choose relatively labour-intensive techniques to create more employment, or relatively capital-intensive techniques which embody more technology.
- Theory and evidence suggests that developing countries can move towards the use of more labour-intensive technologies without sacrificing future growth.

Chapter 7	Discussion questions

1   What is meant by the process of capital accumulation?

2   Distinguish between the various forms of investment and capital accumulation that can raise per capita income.

3   Why do developing countries, and many development economists, lay great stress on the role of capital accumulation in the development process?

4   What is meant by the following terms: neutral, capital-saving, and labour-saving technical progress?

5   What are the main means by which societies progress technologically?

6   What is 'learning by doing'?

7   Why is the rate of return on investment in education higher in developing countries than in developed countries?

8   In what senses is infrastructure investment complementary to investment in plant and machinery, and does it have to be provided publicly?

9   What are the major factors that dictate the choice of techniques in the industrial sector in developing countries?

10   Why did early development theory tend to stress the importance of capital-intensive techniques for rapid economic development?

11   Would the use of more labour-intensive techniques necessarily reduce the size of the investible surplus?

12   What do you understand by the 'efficiency wage' of labour, and how does this concept help to explain the relative capital intensity of production and goods traded?

Notes

1. The greater the proportion of expenditure treated as consumption, the higher the rate of return on the investment component.
2. *Education Sector Policy Paper* (Washington, DC: World Bank, 1980).

3. See Colclough (1982).

4. For a lucid discussion of these issues, see Stewart (1977), especially Chapter 6.

5. The capital–output ratio (K/O) may be expressed as the product of the capital–labour ratio and labour requirements per unit of output, that is, $K/O = (K/L)(L/O)$. Techniques with a low K/L may nonetheless have a high K/O because L/O is high – that is, the productivity of labour is low.

Websites on technology and investment

Economic Growth Resources run by Jon Temple, Bristol University, UK www.bris.ac.uk/Economics/Growth

International Institute for Communication www.iicd.org

World Intellectual Property Organization www.wipo.int

Website on choice of techniques

UNIDO www.unido.org

THE PERPETUATION OF UNDERDEVELOPMENT

Introduction

It is easy to argue that poverty and backwardness are due to a general shortage and inefficient use of the key factors of production; it is much harder to determine precisely why there should be a dearth of some factors and an abundance of others, and why development may be a slow and lengthy process. It is certainly impossible to explain current international discrepancies in the level of development with reference to *initial* differences in factor endowments. The present development gap in the world economy has arisen largely through industrial development in certain selected areas of the world, which in turn has generated its *own* factor endowments. The purpose here, however, is not to consider why some countries were able to industrialize sooner than others, but rather to consider some of the mechanisms through which divisions in the world economy, and unequal advantage between developed and developing countries, are perpetuated.

First, the **dualistic structure** of developing countries will be considered. Then we shall examine Gunnar Myrdal's model of the process of **circular and cumulative causation**, which can be applied to regions and countries alike (Myrdal, 1957, 1963). We shall see that Myrdal's model is one of many that can be used to understand the perpetuation of the development gap and divergences between North and South or between the 'centre' (industrialized) countries and the 'periphery' (primary producing) countries.

The pioneering models of *Raúl* Prebisch and Nicholas Kaldor will be examined in this context, and their similarities emphasized. Thirdly, we will discuss the **new economic geography**, which has links with the model of cumulative causation, and the role of geographic factors that seem to be associated with divisions in the world economy. Finally, we shall briefly discuss models of **unequal exchange** and **dependency**, which emphasize alternative institutional and economic mechanisms making for international inequality in the world economy.

Dualism

The term 'dualism' describes a condition in which developing countries usually find themselves in the early stages of development, which can have implications for the future pattern and pace of development. There are a number of possible definitions and interpretations of 'dualism', but the term is used mainly to refer to economic and social divisions in an economy, such as differences in the level of technology between sectors or regions, differences in the degree of geographic development and differences in social customs and attitudes between an indigenous and an imported social system.

Dualism in all its aspects is a concomitant of the growth of a money economy, which, as we saw in Chapter 6, may either arise naturally as a result of specialization or be imposed from outside. Basically, therefore, a dual economy is characterized by a difference in social customs between the subsistence and exchange sectors of the economy, by a gap between the levels of technology in the rural subsistence sector and the industrial monetized sector, and often by a gap in the level of per capita income between regions of a country if the money economy and industrial development are geographically concentrated. In fact it is not unusual for **geographic, social and technological dualism** to occur together, with each type of dualism tending to reinforce the other. Also, the more 'progressive' sectors typically have favourable access to scarce factors of production, which is a major cause of the persistence of dualism. **Urban bias** plays an important part in this process (Lipton, 1977).

If the basic origin of dualism is the introduction of money into a subsistence barter economy, and development depends on the extension of the money economy, development must contend with the existence of dualism in all its aspects. We shall consider here social and technological dualism, leaving geographic dualism until later when we consider Myrdal's hypothesis of cumulative causation, and the new economic geography.

The first question is, what development problems does the existence of dualism pose for an economy, and how can dualism impede and retard development? As far as **social dualism** is concerned, the obstacles are similar to those presented by a traditional society with no modern exchange sector at all. The task is one of providing incentives in the subsistence sector and drawing the subsistence sector into the money economy. The fact that the indigenous subsistence sector may be reluctant to alter its traditional way of life and respond to incentives is not peculiar to a dual economy. It is therefore true that underdevelopment tends to be associated with social dualism, but it would be misleading to regard social dualism as an underlying *cause* of backwardness and poverty. It is difficult to argue that development would be more rapid in the absence of a monetary sector, from which the existence of dualism stems. Even if the growth of the exchange sector makes little impact on attitudes in the indigenous sector, it is difficult to envisage any progress without the growth of the money economy. In short, it seems more realistic to regard social dualism as an inevitable consequence of development rather than as a basic cause of underdevelopment itself.

Similar reservations can be raised over whether it is accurate to describe **technological dualism** as a cause of underdevelopment. As with social dualism, it is probably more realistic to regard it as an inevitable feature of the development process. Two disadvantages are commonly associated with technological dualism. The first is that where technological dualism is the result of a foreign enclave, a proportion of the profits generated in the industrial sector will be remitted to the home country, reducing the level of saving and investment below what it might have been. The second disadvantage is more fundamental, but difficult to avoid. If in the rural, or non-monetized, sector of the economy production processes are characterized by labour-intensive techniques and variable technical coefficients of production, while production processes in the industrial, technologically advanced sector are capital-intensive and possess relatively fixed technical coefficients, it is possible that the technology of the industrial sector may impede the progress of the agricultural sector. First, relatively fixed technical coefficients (that is, a low elasticity of substitution between factors) means that labour can be absorbed from agriculture into industry only as fast as the growth of capital, and second, capital intensity itself will restrict employment opportunities in the industrial sector, contributing to urban unemployment and perpetuating underdevelopment in the rural sector. Hence productivity growth in the agricultural sector, which is recognized as being necessary to establish a secure basis for take-off into sustained growth, may be slowed down.

It is true that if the technology of the modern sector (imported or otherwise) does embody fixed technological coefficients, it may be difficult for an economy to use the socially optimum combination of factors, but this disadvantage must be weighed against the favourable impact on productivity stemming from the more advanced technology. If capital accumulation and technical progress, and the development of an industrial sector – in addition to agricultural development – are essential for raising the level of per capita income, it is difficult to see how technological dualism can be avoided, at least in the early stages of development. The best that can be done is first to encourage the widespread application and rapid assimilation of technical progress throughout all sectors of the economy, and second to ensure the 'proper' pricing of factors of production to prevent the introduction of a technology that may be profitable to private individuals but does not maximize the returns to society at large because factor prices do not adequately reflect relative factor endowments. But even a technology that is socially optimal in this sense may not be the technology that provides the soundest basis for sustained growth in the long run. The question of the choice of techniques was discussed in detail in Chapter 7, and the issue of the 'social' pricing of factors of production is taken up in Chapter 11.

The process of cumulative causation

The hypothesis of cumulative causation as an explanation of the backwardness of developing nations is associated with the famous Swedish economist Gunnar Myrdal (1957, 1963) who won the Nobel Prize for Economics in 1974. Basically, it is a hypothesis of **geographic dualism**, applicable to nations and regions within nations, which can be advanced to account for the persistence of spatial differences in a wide variety of development indices, including wage rates, per capita income, employment growth rates and levels of unemployment. As such, the process of cumulative causation is a direct challenge to static equilibrium theory, which predicts that the working of economic and social forces will cause spatial differences to narrow.

Myrdal contends that in the context of development both economic and social forces produce tendencies towards *disequilibrium*, and that the assumption in economic theory that disequilibrium situations tend towards equilibrium is false. If this were not so, how can the tendency for international and regional differences in living standards to widen be explained? Thus, Myrdal replaces the assumption of stable equilibrium with what he calls the hypothesis of **circular and cumulative causation**, arguing that the use of this hypothesis can go a long way towards explaining why international differences in levels of development, and interregional differences in development within nations, may persist and even widen over time.

He first considers the hypothesis in the context of a geographically dual economy, describing how, through the mechanisms of labour migration, capital movements and trade, the existence of dualism not only retards the development of backward regions but can also slow up the development of the whole economy. To describe the process of circular and cumulative causation, let us start off with a country in which all regions have attained the same stage of development, as measured by the same level of per capita income, or by similar levels of productivity and wages in the same occupations. Then assume that an exogenous shock produces a disequilibrium situation with development proceeding more rapidly in one region than another. The proposition is that economic and social forces will tend to strengthen the disequilibrium situation by leading to cumulative expansion in the favoured region at the expense of other regions, which then become comparatively worse off, retarding their future development.

Gunnar Myrdal

Born 1898, Skattungbyn, Sweden. Died 1987. Politician, economist and prolific writer in several fields of economics. One of the architects of the Swedish welfare state in the 1930s. His early work in macroeconomics anticipated Keynes's *General Theory*. In development economics, he is best known for his challenge to equilibrium theory, and the notion of 'circular and cumulative causation' in such books as *An American Dilemma: The Negro Problem and Modern Democracy* (1944) and *Economic Theory and Underdeveloped Regions* (1957). Also author of a massive three-volume tome *Asian Drama: An Inquiry into the Poverty of Nations* (1968). Awarded the Nobel Prize for Economics, 1974.

This contrasts with neoclassical equilibrium theory, which assumes that, through the process of factor mobility, wage rates and the rate of profit will equalize across regions. According to neoclassical theory, in places where labour is scarce and capital is abundant, labour will flow in and capital will flow out, thus reducing wages and raising the rate of profit, while in less prosperous areas where labour is abundant, labour will flow out and capital will flow in, raising wages and reducing the rate of profit.

In contrast, what Myrdal has in mind is a type of multiplier–accelerator mechanism producing increasing returns in the favoured region. Instead of leading to equality, the forces of supply and demand interact with each other to produce cumulative movements away from spatial equilibrium. Since the wage level is the basic determinant of per capita income, let us take the example of wages and wage differences to illustrate the kind of process that Myrdal has in mind. Take two regions, A and B (for example, northern and southern Italy), and assume that wages are determined by supply and demand, as in Figures 8.1 and 8.2.

Suppose to start with that wage levels are identical in the two regions, that is, $W_A = W_B$. Then assume that a stimulus of some sort causes the demand for labour, and therefore wages, to rise in region A relative to region B; that is, the demand curve for labour in region A shifts to D_1D_1, causing wages to rise to W_{A1}. Since labour tends to respond to differences in economic opportunities of this sort, the wage discrepancy may be assumed to induce labour migration from region B to region A. Equilibrium theory then predicts that there will be a tendency for wage levels to be equalized once more through a *reduction* in labour supply in region B from SS to S_1S_1 and an *increase* in labour supply in region A from SS to S_1S_1, giving a wage in region A of W_{A2}, equal to a wage in B of W_{B1}.

Figure 8.1   Region A

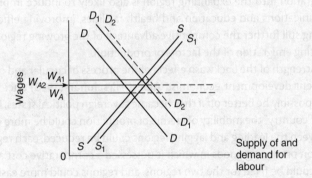

Figure 8.2   Region B

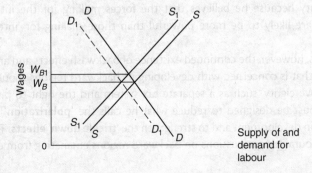

According to the hypothesis of cumulative causation, however, changes in supply may be expected to react on demand in such a way as to counteract the tendency towards equilibrium. Migration from region B denudes the area of human capital and entrepreneurs, and depresses the local demand for goods and services and factors of production, while movements into region A, on the other hand, will tend to stimulate enterprise and the demand for products, adding to the demand for factors of production. In short, migration from region B will cause the demand curve for labour to shift to the left, say to D_1D_1, and migration into region A will cause the demand curve for labour to shift further to the right, say to D_2D_2, causing the initial wage discrepancy at least to persist, if not widen (if the shifts in demand are greater than those assumed). Thus once development differences appear, there is set in motion a chain of cumulative expansion in the favoured region, and this has what Myrdal calls a **'backwash' effect** on other regions, causing development differences in general to persist or even diverge.

Capital movements and **trade** also play a part in the process of cumulative causation. In a free market, capital, like labour, will tend to move to where the prospective return is highest, and this will be to the region where demand is buoyant (not necessarily the region where the wage is lowest, as in neoclassical theory). Capital, labour and entrepreneurship will tend to migrate together. The benefits of trade will also accrue to the host region. Regions within a nation using a common currency cannot have balance-of-payments difficulties in the normal sense, but the maintenance of employment depends on the ability to export, otherwise unemployment will appear. If production is subject to increasing returns, the region experiencing the rapid growth of factor supplies will be able to increase its competitive advantage over the relatively lagging regions containing smaller-scale industries, and increase its real income accordingly. In this same way, the general freeing and widening of international markets and the expansion of world trade will tend to favour the more rapidly growing regions within nation-states.

The impact of immigration into the expanding region is also likely to induce improvements in transport and communications and education and health facilities, improving efficiency and productivity and widening still further the competitive advantage of the growing region over the lagging regions experiencing emigration of the factors of production.

Such is the potential strength of the backwash effects of the process of circular and cumulative causation, that the eminent development economist, **Albert Hirschman** (1958) once suggested that lagging regions may possibly be better off if they became sovereign political states. If a lagging area was an independent 'country', the mobility of factors of production could be more easily controlled, competition between the leading and lagging regions could be reduced, each region could more easily concentrate on producing goods in which it possessed a comparative cost advantage, separate exchange rates could be fixed for the two regions, and regions could more easily protect themselves.

Despite these potential advantages of nationhood for a backward region, however, Hirschman argues against sovereignty because he believes that the forces making for the interregional transmission of growth are likely to be more powerful than those making for 'international' transmission.

Hirschman recognizes, however, the continued existence of backwash effects and argues that, to offset them, a nation that is concerned with developing its backward regions should provide certain equivalents of sovereignty, such as a separate tax system and the right to protect certain activities. Policies must be designed to reduce what he calls the **'polarization' effects** of interregional differences in development and to strengthen the **'trickle down' effects**. The 'trickle down' effects are the favourable repercussions on backward regions emanating from expanding regions, which Myrdal calls **'spread' effects**. These trickle-down or spread effects consist mainly of an increased demand for the backward areas' products and the diffusion of technology and knowledge. In Myrdal's view, the spread effects are weaker than the backwash effects, and if interregional differences are to be narrowed, nations must rely on state intervention through regional policies. The only alternative is to wait for a natural end to the process of cumulative causation, which may be a long time coming.

But the time must eventually come when increasing costs in the expanding region will halt expansion. The higher costs of living, and the external diseconomies produced by congestion, will ultimately outweigh the benefits of greater efficiency and higher money returns to the factors of production. The process of migration will then be halted, and possibly reversed. In some developed countries this stage has now been reached. The question for governments with certain growth and welfare objectives is whether they can afford to let the process take its natural course, and to tolerate the inequalities that may arise before the process ends. High levels of inequality can lead to negative social, economic and political consequences that have a destabilizing effect on societies, causing insecurity and social unrest. In practice, governments in many advanced countries have taken active steps for many years to redress regional imbalances, and this is one reason why regional disparities tend to be less in advanced countries than in developing countries. In the developing countries, however, Myrdal was of the view that, far from lessening regional inequalities, the state has been a positive force in their persistence: 'In many of the poorer countries the natural drift towards inequalities has been supported and magnified by built-in feudal and other inegalitarian institutions and power structures which aid the rich in exploiting the poor' (Myrdal, 1963, p. 40). This is still true in many poor countries today.

Regional inequalities

The international cross-section evidence on regional inequalities, and time-series evidence for individual countries, suggests that the degree of inequality follows an inverted 'U' shape; that is, regional inequalities first rise with the level of development and then decrease. This pattern is not hard to explain. Very poor countries are uniformly poor. Regional differences then first emerge as a result of some favourable shock to one region or set of regions – for example an export enclave or the establishment of industrial activities. Once a difference has emerged, it will tend to be widened by the processes already described. Migration from poor to richer regions will tend to be selective in the early stages of development because only those with skills and education will be able to afford to migrate. Capital will tend to locate in the more dynamic region(s). 'Spread' effects emanating from prosperous regions will be weak owing to a general lack of political and economic integration.

The factors that accentuate differences in the early stages of development, however, will tend to weaken with time as countries get richer. Migration will become less selective; the spread effects will become more powerful; industrialization will tend to spread and the size of the agricultural sector shrink; external diseconomies of expansion and congestion in expanding regions will worsen, curbing capital and labour migration from poor to rich regions; and governments may also attempt to rectify imbalances through the implementation of regional policies.

The empirical evidence shows that regional disparities in output and income per head are much more unequal in developing countries than in developed countries. Table 8.1 gives the unweighted and weighted (by population) Gini ratios for a selection of developed and developing countries estimated by Shankar and Shah (2003), who also distinguish between countries

Table 8.1 Regional disparities within developed and developing countries

Countries	Year	Unweighted Gini ratio	Weighted Gini ratio
Developed countries (federal)			
Canada	1997	0.018	0.067
United States	1997	0.090	0.039
Germany	1997	0.191	0.122
Spain	1997	0.128	0.118
Developed countries (unitary)			
France	1997	0.096	0.126
Italy	1997	0.152	0.145
United Kingdom	1997	0.085	0.083
Developing countries (federal)			
Brazil	1997	0.334	0.267
India	1997	0.226	0.227
Mexico	1997	0.253	0.301
Pakistan	1997	0.113	0.072
Russia	1997	0.283	0.280
Developing countries (unitary)			
Chile	1994	0.267	0.165
China	1997	0.351	0.250
Indonesia	1997	0.378	0.274
Nepal	1996		
Philippines	1997	0.307	0.261
Poland	1996	0.106	0.090
Romania	1996	0.230	0.249
Sri Lanka	1995	0.352	0.341
South Africa	1994		
Thailand	1997	0.438	0.442
Uganda	1997–8		
Uzbekistan	1997	0.155	0.170
Vietnam	1997	0.372	0.410

Source: Shankar and Shah, 2003.

with a federal or unitary political structure. It can be seen that the Gini ratios for developing countries are much higher than for developed countries; also that unitary developing countries are generally more unequal than federal developing countries. Countries with some of the highest measures of regional inequality are large unitary countries such as China, Vietnam, Thailand and Indonesia. There are three main reasons why regional inequalities tend to be lower in federal states: firstly, widening regional disparities pose a greater political risk in federal countries in the sense that disadvantaged regions may decide to break away; secondly, national political parties need to emphasize regional issues more, and thirdly, autonomous regional governments have more concern for their regions than a unitary state.

Shankar and Shah also look at trends in regional inequality over time in 14 developing countries and find inequalities still increasing – or moving up the inverted 'U'. Rodriguez-Pose and Gill (2006) also show this in a study of India, China and Mexico since 1980, and find that the growth of regional inequalities is significantly related to the shift of trade from primary to manufactured exports. This trade effect is greater the larger the share of trade in GDP and the greater the shift. This contrasts to what is happening in most developed countries, including the USA and European Union. In the USA, Barro and Sala-i-Martin (1992) show that a process of regional per capita income convergence has been going on over the last hundred years. Taking personal income data, they find an inverse relation across US states between the average growth of per capita income over the period 1880–1988 and the initial (1880) level of per capita income. Only two sub-periods, 1920–30 and 1980–88, show evidence of divergence.

In Europe, the evidence is more mixed. Across the regions of Europe there is some evidence of per capita income convergence in the postwar years up to 1980, but not thereafter. Regional unemployment rate differences, however, both within Europe as a whole and within industrial countries, have remained very stubborn. Fagerberg and Verspagen (1996) take 70 regions in 6 EU countries and show income convergence up to 1980, but not since. The authors argue that the scope for convergence is not exhausted, but other factors in the 1980s pushed towards divergence, particularly differences in unemployment and the research and development (R&D) effort between industrial and agricultural regions.

Indeed, it appears to be the case from a further study by Fagerberg et al. (1996) that regional differences in per capita income are systematically related to differences in unemployment rates. They take 64 regions in Germany, France, Italy and Spain over the period 1980–90 and find that growth in poor regions is hampered by unfavourable industrial structure and weak R&D effort. There is evidence of convergence, but only after allowing for differences in industrial structure, R&D effort, population density and migration. Interestingly, labour migration is found to have a strong positive impact on per capita income growth, indicating that migration was disequilibrating during this period. The policy implications are that the predominance of agriculture is a barrier to growth in poor regions, mainly because the scope for scale economies and R&D is less than in industry. Greater regional balance requires structural change in favour of industrial activities, but this in turn requires an appropriate physical infrastructure and the provision of human capital.

International inequality and centre–periphery models

The process of circular and cumulative causation is also used by Myrdal in an attempt to explain **widening international differences** in the level of development from similar initial conditions. Through the mechanisms of labour migration, capital movements and trade, international inequalities are perpetuated in exactly the same way as regional inequalities within nations. Myrdal argues that through trade the developing countries have been forced into the production of goods, notably primary products, with inelastic demand with respect to both price and income. This has put the developing countries at a grave disadvantage compared with the developed countries with respect to the balance of payments and the availability of foreign exchange. Moreover, with the tendency for the efficiency wage (that is, the money wage in relation to labour productivity) to fall in faster-growing areas relative to other areas, the developed countries have gained a cumulative competitive trading advantage, especially in manufactured commodities. Myrdal, of course, is not alone in this view, and we shall elaborate below on other models that stress the unequal gains and the balance-of-payments effects of trade as the main mechanisms through which international differences in development are perpetuated, including the contribution of the new economic geography pioneered by Krugman (1991).

Myrdal argues in the same vein in the case of capital movements. Because the risks associated with investment tend to be higher in developing countries, the natural tendency will be for the developing countries to be net exporters of capital. In practice, because of the large volume of capital from international lending organizations, and the favourable tax treatment of foreign direct investment, the developing countries are generally net importers of long-term capital, although the short-term capital account tends to be adverse. The fact remains, however, as Lucas (1990) points out, that capital flows mainly to regions already rich. With regard to foreign direct investment, the richest countries receive over 80 per cent of flows, while the poorest countries (excluding China) receive less than 5 per cent.

The potential weakness of Myrdal's hypothesis at the international level concerns the effects of labour migration. The international migration of labour from developing to developed countries can have beneficial as well as harmful effects on backward economies. The greatest deleterious effect on backward economies is the obvious one of possible loss of human capital, although even here, if the human capital is unemployed, migration may not be a serious loss. But it is not only the skilled and educated that may be induced to leave their native lands. Unskilled labour may also respond to the existence of better employment opportunities elsewhere. If it is argued that developing countries suffer from underemployment, and that productivity is low owing to 'overpopulation', the emigration of unskilled labour could be a substantial benefit to developing countries. It is possible, for example, that emigration has helped to raise per capita income in some countries such as Mexico, Pakistan and Bangladesh, and improved the balance of payments at the same time through remittances by emigrants to their home countries. Migrant remittances now amount to nearly $150 billion a year, exceeding the level of official development assistance to developing countries (see Chapter 15). In this important respect, generous immigration policies in developed countries can provide a valuable means of development assistance.

Even so, any potential gain from unrestricted labour mobility is unlikely to offset the international backwash effects arising from trade and international capital movements. Even with unrestricted migration, therefore, there would still be a tendency for international differences in the level of development to widen through trade and the free movement of capital. The existence of international 'spread' effects gives no reason for modifying this conclusion. International spread effects are relatively weak – certainly weaker than the spread effects within nations.

What, then, should be our verdict on the hypothesis of cumulative causation? Given that the hypothesis assumes free trade and free mobility of the factors of production, it perhaps contains more force with respect to interregional differences in development within countries than international differences between countries. On the other hand it cannot be dismissed lightly when discussing the development gap in the world economy. In view of the fact that there has been no tendency in the recent past for international per capita income levels to converge (see Chapters 2 and 5), the hypothesis is not refuted by the evidence. In particular, the present international trading and payments position of developing countries does not inspire confidence that the total gains from trade between the developed and developing countries are distributed equitably (see Chapters 15 and 16).

The contribution of the hypothesis of cumulative causation to an understanding of development and underdevelopment is its emphasis on economic and social development as a cumulative phenomenon and, more important still, its challenge to static equilibrium theory; that is, that regions or nations that gain an initial advantage may maintain that advantage to the detriment of development elsewhere. At its root is the phenomenon of increasing returns, defined broadly as the accumulation of productive advantages of the type discussed in Chapter 7, relating to how societies progress technologically.

Two models of 'regional' growth rate differences: Prebisch and Kaldor

While the Myrdal model of centre and periphery emphasizes the process of cumulative causation working through increasing returns and competitiveness in favoured regions, other centre–periphery models stress the balance-of-payments implications of the particular pattern of production and trade between rich and poor countries, which arise from the fact that industrial goods produced and traded by rich countries have a higher income elasticity of demand than goods produced and traded by poor countries. One of the earliest models, powerful in its simplicity, is that of Raúl Prebisch, the famous Argentinian economist (1901–86).

Raúl Prebisch

Born 1901, Tucuan, Argentina. Died 1986. Argentina's most famous economist who mixed economics and politics on the national and international stage. He was architect and first President of the Central Bank of Argentina in his early thirties; first Director of the Economic Commission for Latin America, 1948, and first Secretary General of UNCTAD, 1964. He was the 'father' of Latin American 'structuralist' thinking, and worked tirelessly for a fairer deal for poor countries in the world trading system. He was the first to document, with Hans Singer, the historical decline in the terms of trade of primary commodities: the Prebisch–Singer thesis.

The Prebisch Model[1]

Consider a two-country, two-commodity model in which the advanced centre produces and exports manufactured goods with an **income elasticity of demand**[2] greater than unity, and the backward periphery produces and exports primary commodities with an income elasticity of demand less than unity. Let us suppose that the income elasticity of demand for manufactures (e_m) is 1.3, and the income elasticity of demand for primary commodities (e_p) is 0.8. Assume to start with that the growth rates of income of both centre and periphery are equal to 3 per cent, that is, $g_c = g_p = 3.0$. What will be the growth of exports (x) and imports (m) in the centre and periphery? For the centre we have

$$x_c = g_p \times e_m = 3.0 \times 1.3 = 3.9 \text{ per cent}$$
$$m_c = g_c \times e_p = 3.0 \times 0.8 = 2.4 \text{ per cent}$$

For the periphery we have

$$x_p = g_c \times e_p = 3.0 \times 0.8 = 2.4 \text{ per cent}$$

$$m_p = g_p \times e_m = 3.0 \times 1.3 = 3.9 \text{ per cent}$$

With imports growing faster than exports in the periphery, this is not a sustainable position, unless the periphery can finance an ever-growing balance-of-payments deficit on the current account by capital inflows. If it cannot, and balance-of-payments equilibrium on the current account is a requirement, there must be some adjustment to raise the rate of growth of exports or reduce the rate of growth of imports. Now suppose we rule out the possibility that relative prices measured in a common currency (or real exchange rate) can change as an adjustment mechanism, the only adjustment mechanism left (barring protection) is a reduction in the periphery's growth rate to reduce the rate of growth of imports in line with the rate of growth of exports. From the model, we can solve for the necessary growth rate of the periphery to keep trade balanced. On the assumptions outlined, we must have $m_p = x_p$ or $g_p e_m = x_p$ and therefore

$$g_p = \frac{x_p}{e_m} = \frac{2.4}{1.3} = 1.846$$

Thus, the growth rate of the periphery is constrained to 1.846 per cent, compared with 3 per cent in the centre. In these circumstances both the relative and the absolute gap in income between periphery and centre will widen. Notice, in fact, that since the growth of the periphery's exports is equal to $g_c \times e_p$ we can write the above equation as

$$g_p = \frac{g_c \times e_p}{e_m}$$

and dividing through by g_c, we reach the interesting result that the relative growth rates of the periphery and centre will equal the ratio of the income elasticity of demand for the two countries' commodities:

$$\frac{g_p}{g_c} = \frac{e_p}{e_m}$$

This result will hold as long as current account equilibrium on the balance of payments is a requirement, and relative price adjustment in international trade is either ruled out as an adjustment mechanism to rectify balance-of-payments disequilibrium or does not work. To avoid the consequences of this model, Prebisch argued the case for protection and import substitution, which in effect is a policy to reduce e_m, which for the periphery is the propensity to import manufactured goods. We reserve discussion of the relative merits of protection until Chapter 15 on trade policy.

Kaldor's model of regional growth rate differences

It is possible to combine the ideas of Myrdal with the insights of Prebisch in a single model, which focuses on the role of export growth in the development process in an open economy and in which the Prebisch result emerges as a special case if relative prices are fixed and trade is balanced. The model due to Kaldor (1970) is applicable to regions and open developing economies alike.[3] It takes as its starting point the not unreasonable assumption that the output of an open economy is demand-determined, not supply-constrained, and that it is the long-run growth of autonomous demand that governs the long-run rate of growth of output. The main component of autonomous demand in an open economy, in turn, is demand coming from outside the region; that is, the demand for the region's exports. The model is a variant of **export-base models of development**, which stress the importance of exports as a leading sector. The hypothesis is that once a region obtains a growth advantage it will tend to sustain it at the expense of other regions because faster growth leads to faster productivity growth (the so-called '**Verdoorn effect**', see Chapter 3, p. 111), which keeps the region competitive in the export of goods that gave the region its growth advantage in the first place. Success breeds success, and failure breeds failure! In this section attention will be confined to outlining the model. An examination of the international evidence of the relation between the growth of exports and the growth of output in developing countries will be left until Chapter 15.

Let

$$g_t = \gamma(x_t) \tag{8.1}$$

where g_t is the rate of growth of output in time t, x_t is the rate of growth of exports in time t, γ is the (constant) elasticity of output with respect to export growth ($= 1$ if exports are a constant proportion of output) and t is time. Apart from the theoretical considerations underlying the specification of (8.1), that the rate of growth of the economy as a whole will be governed by the rate of growth of autonomous demand, there are a number of practical considerations that make export demand for highly specialized regions (or countries) extremely important for both demand and supply. For most industries in a region, local demand is likely to be trivial compared with the optimum production capacity of the industries. The viability of regional enterprise must largely depend on the strength of demand from outside the region.

There are also a number of important reasons why export demand may be a more potent growth-inducing force than other elements of demand, especially in open, backward areas – regions or countries. The first is that exports allow regional specialization, which may bring dynamic as well as static gains. Second, exports permit imports, and imports may be important in developing areas that lack the capacity to produce development goods themselves. Third, if the exchange of information and technical knowledge is linked to trade, exporting facilitates the flow of technical knowledge, which can improve the area's supply capacity.

Now let us consider the determinants of export demand and the form of the export demand function. It is conventional to specify exports as a multiplicative (or constant elasticity) function of relative prices measured in a common currency and foreign income.

Thus

$$X_t = \left(\frac{P_{dt}}{P_{ft}}\right)^{\eta} z_t^{\varepsilon} \tag{8.2}$$

where X is the quantity of exports in time t, P_d is the domestic price in time t, P_f is the foreign price in time t, Z is foreign income in time t, η is the price elasticity of demand for exports (< 0) and ε is the income elasticity of demand for exports (> 0). Taking logarithms of the variables and differentiating with respect to time gives:

$$x_t = \eta(p_{dt} - p_{ft}) + \varepsilon(z_t) \tag{8.3}$$

where the lower-case letters represent the rates of growth of the variables. The rate of growth of income outside the region (z) and the rate of change of competitors' prices (p_f) may both be taken as exogenous to the region. The rate of growth of domestic (export) prices will be endogenous, however. Let us assume that prices are formed on the basis of a constant 'mark-up' on unit labour costs, so that

$$P_{dt} = \left(\frac{W}{R}\right)_t (T_t) \tag{8.4}$$

where P_d is the domestic price, W is the level of money wages, R is the average product of labour and T is 1+ percentage mark-up on unit labour costs. From (8.4) we can write

$$p_{dt} = w_t - r_t + \tau_t \tag{8.5}$$

where the lower-case letters stand for the rates of change of the variables.

The model becomes 'circular and cumulative' by specifying the growth of labour productivity (r) as partly a function of the growth output itself (Verdoorn's Law). If the function is linear we may write

$$r_t = r_{at} + \lambda\left(g_t\right) \tag{8.6}$$

where r_{at} is the rate of autonomous productivity growth at time t, and λ is the Verdoorn coefficient (> 0). Equation (8.6) provides the link between exports and growth via productivity growth and prices. Fast export growth leads to fast output growth, and fast output growth leads to fast export growth by making goods more competitive. Combining (8.1), (8.3), (8.5) and (8.6) to obtain an expression for the equilibrium growth rate gives

$$g_t = \frac{\gamma\left[\eta(w_t - r_{at} + \tau_t - p_{ft}) + \varepsilon(z_t)\right]}{1 + \gamma\eta\lambda} \tag{8.7}$$

Remembering that $\eta < 0$, the growth rate is shown to vary positively with $r_a, z, \varepsilon, p_f z$ and γ, and negatively with w and τ. The effect of η is ambiguous since it appears in both the numerator and the denominator of the equation. It is clear that it is the assumed dependence of productivity growth on the growth of output that gives rise to the possibility that once a region obtains a growth advantage it will keep it. Suppose, for example, that a region obtains an advantage in the production of goods with a high income elasticity of demand (ε), which causes its growth rate to rise above that of another region. Through the so-called Verdoorn effect, productivity growth will be higher, the rate of change of prices lower (other things being the same) and the rate of growth of exports (and hence the rate of growth of output) higher, and so on. Moreover, the fact that the region with the initial advantage will obtain a competitive advantage in the production of goods with a high income elasticity of demand will mean that it will be difficult for other regions to establish the same activities. This is the essence of the theory of cumulative causation, of divergence between 'centre' and 'periphery' and between industrial (developed) and agricultural (developing) regions (countries). Figure 8.3 illustrates the model graphically.

The distance of each of the linear functions from the origin reflects factors affecting each variable other than the variable specified in the functional relation. From the initial condition, S, the growth rate is shown converging to its equilibrium value E, as determined in (8.7).[4] The link

Figure 8.3   Convergent–divergent growth

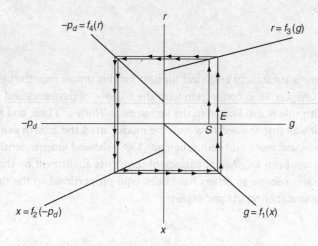

that the Verdoorn relation provides between exports and growth via productivity and prices, and its sustaining influence, is clearly seen. And the greater the dependence of productivity growth on the growth of output (that is, the higher λ), the higher the equilibrium growth rate will be and the greater the divergence between regional growth rates for given differences between regions in the other variables and parameters.

An important implication of the model we have developed is that an autonomous shock will not be sufficient to raise a lagging region's growth rate *permanently* unless the autonomous shock favourably affects the parameters and variables of the model, or is a sustained shock. On these grounds, the relevance of policies of devaluation in a national context, or wage subsidies in a regional context, for improving a region's growth rate may be called into question. What is likely to be required is structural change, in particular structural change to improve the demand characteristics of exports. It is recognition of this point that accounts, among other things, for the emphasis placed by developing countries on industrialization and the restructuring of world trade to provide their manufactured goods with easier access to world markets (see Chapter 15).

Note that it is also a property of the model that if relative prices measured in a common currency do not change (that is, $p_{dt} - p_{ft} = 0$), then export growth is determined solely by income growth outside the region or country, and equation (8.7) would reduce to

$$g_t = \gamma \varepsilon(z_t) \tag{8.8}$$

and if balanced trade is a requirement so that the growth of imports (m) is equal to the growth of exports ($m = x$) we have

$$g_t \pi = \varepsilon(z_t) \tag{8.9}$$

where π is the income elasticity of demand for imports.

Thus with relative prices fixed, the growth elasticity with respect to exports (γ) in equation (8.1) must equal the reciprocal of the income elasticity of demand for imports (π) in a balanced trade model such as Prebisch's. Again we end up with the simple rule that one country's growth rate (g) relative to that of others (z) depends on the ratio of the income elasticity of demand for the country's exports relative to its imports (or the other country's exports in a two-country model), that is, from (8.9):

$$\frac{g_t}{z_t} = \frac{\varepsilon}{\pi} \qquad\qquad (8.10)$$

At the country level there is substantial empirical support for this simple growth rule, which is discussed more fully in Chapter 16 in connection with the balance of payments and economic development. This growth rule is also known in the literature as Thirlwall's Law, and Krugman's 45-degree rule, after Thirlwall first showed how well the model fitted the growth experience of many countries in the postwar years, and Paul Krugman (1989) showed independently that relative price changes have not been an efficient balance-of-payments adjustment mechanism and that countries' growth rates relative to others have been equi-proportional to the ratio of the income elasticities of demand for imports and exports.[5]

Nicholas Kaldor

Born 1908, Budapest, Hungary. Died 1986. Lecturer and Reader at the London School of Economics 1931–49; then a Fellow of King's College, Cambridge from 1950 and Professor of Economics from 1966. Economic adviser to three British Chancellors of the Exchequer between 1964 and 1979, and tax adviser to many developing countries. He was the joint architect with Joan Robinson, Richard Kahn and Luigi Pasinetti of post-Keynesian growth and distribution theory, and a strong critic of neoclassical equilibrium economics. Famous for his sectoral approach to explaining why growth rates differ between countries.

The new economic geography

The **new economic geography**, pioneered by Krugman (1991, 1998), who received the Nobel Prize in Economics for his contribution, is also an attempt to explain the geographic pattern of economic development between countries, and between regions within countries, in terms of **centripetal forces** which lead to industrial concentration and **centrifugal forces** which lead to industrial dispersal. In this sense, there is an affinity with the cumulative causation model of Myrdal, but in the new economic geography, distance and transport costs play a key role.

There is always a tug of war going on between centripetal forces which promote geographic concentration of activities and centrifugal forces which oppose it. The centripetal forces, acting as magnets for activity, are mainly the different types of external economies associated with the size of markets and linkages between activities, labour market externalities (pools of skilled labour) and pure externalities such as knowledge spillovers. The centrifugal forces, resisting concentration, are such factors as the immobility of factors of production, high rents in concentrated areas and pure external diseconomies, such as congestion costs.

Within this framework, the emergence of a 'centre' and 'periphery', and shifts in the geographic pattern of development, can be explained in terms of the changing balance between the pull of the market on the one hand and transport costs on the other. As in the Myrdal model, consider first of all two identical regions. If transport costs are very high, each region will be more or less self-sufficient. Activity will be widely dispersed serving local markets because it is too costly to transport inputs and outputs elsewhere.

Now suppose that transport costs start to fall. It becomes more economical for some regions to supply the needs of others. Those regions with some small initial advantage, as a result of geography or historical accident, will tend to capitalize on that advantage, exporting to the less favoured region and driving out business. Activity becomes concentrated in a core (or centre), leaving a run-down 'periphery' with only agricultural and service-type activities. A small initial difference between regions leads to a much larger difference in outcomes through the forces of cumulative causation based on external economies associated particularly with market size (**agglomeration economies**). At the regional level, Italy is a good case study. When the railway was introduced and transport costs fell, this made it possible for the factories of northern Italy to supply the needs of the less-competitive south of Italy, causing the heavy concentration of industrial activity in the north and deindustrialization of the south.

The periphery, however, will tend to have low production costs, particularly low wage costs because of high unemployment and underemployment. At some point, if transport costs fall even more, it may become economical to shift production from the centre to the periphery because low production costs now outweigh the cost of transport to the market. This is one important reason why, in recent years, there has been a major shift of the world's manufacturing base from the core of Europe and North America to the periphery of South-East Asia.

This set of ideas outlined above helps to explain the historical evolution of divisions between regions and countries of the world which can spontaneously emerge with better communications, and then go into reverse when transport costs fall even lower (Krugman and Venables, 1995). It is not, however, an equilibrium world; it is an ever-changing world in which economic development in some regions or countries may be precluded altogether.

The World Bank's *World Development Report 2009* is devoted to this topic and argues that even though in the present circumstances of the world economy, economic growth will be unbalanced (leading to divergence), development can still be inclusive but governments must promote integration through spatially connective infrastructure, spatially targeted incentives and appropriate institutions. The disadvantaged regions (countries) are those that are too small to reap internal and external economies of scale and to attract investment in labour-intensive manufacturing specializing in some part of the productive chain.

Attempts have been made to quantify the impact of distance and transport costs on the level and growth of per capita income of countries across the world, as well as the effect of other geographic variables (e.g. Gallup et al., 1998). Looking at a map of the world by income, two striking relationships are apparent. The first is that countries located close to the sea have higher per capita incomes (PCY) than landlocked countries. The second is that countries located in the tropics are poorer than countries outside the tropics. A third fact is (although not visible) that the coastal, temperate regions of the northern hemisphere have the highest income per square kilometre (km) of land (i.e. PCY × population density). The regions of North America, Western Europe (and parts of East Asia) that lie within 100 km of the sea contain 13 per cent of the world's population and produce 32 per cent of the world's output of goods and services. The explanation lies in the factors that we discussed above. Regions near the sea have lower transport costs so they can benefit from greater trade and specialization, and the greater densities of population lead to agglomeration economies and increasing returns. Today, the fastest-growing developing countries have based their growth on labour-intensive manufactured exports located in coastal regions.

Gallup et al. (1998) run regressions across a large sample of countries of the level and growth of PCY against several geographic variables including the percentage of land in the tropics; the proportion of the population within 100 km of the coast; the minimum distance of a country to one of three core 'regions' (New York, Rotterdam and Tokyo); the incidence of malaria, and transport costs of a country measured (imperfectly) as the difference between the cost of imports free on board (f.o.b.) and their cost including insurance and freight charges (c.i.f.). The level of PCY is found to be negatively related to location in the tropics, malaria, distance and transport costs; and positively related to the proportion of the population close to the sea. The growth of income (holding other variables constant such as education, trade openness) is shown to be 0.9 percentage points (p.p.) less in tropical countries than non-tropical countries; 1.2 p.p. less in countries severely affected by malaria; and 1.0 p.p. less in landlocked countries compared with coastal countries. Distance also significantly reduces growth if the trade openness variable is excluded from the equations.

Given these findings, it is hardly surprising that Africa has some of the poorest and most stagnant economies in the world. Geography is stacked against it!

Theories of dependence and unequal exchange

Apart from the ideas of circular and cumulative causation and balance-of-payments constrained growth, there are also a number of theories and models in the Marxist tradition (many originating from Latin America and France) concerned with **dependency, exploitation and unequal exchange**. These theories attempt to explain the perpetuation and widening of the differences between centre and periphery, and may be regarded as complementary to, and an integral part of, the mechanisms we have been discussing. For example, part of the dependency and unequal exchange relation is related to the characteristics of trade; but there are many other important dimensions to the argument:

- The dependence of the periphery on foreign capital and the expropriation of the surplus by the centre
- The dependence on foreign technology
- Terms of trade deterioration
- Mechanisms that reduce real wages in developing countries to below what they would otherwise be
- Various socio-cultural aspects of neocolonialism that thwart the drive for independence and self-reliance.

Pioneer writers in this tradition include Dos Santos, Baran, Gunder Frank, Amin and Emmanuel. It should be emphasized at the outset that dependency theory cannot easily be tested empirically; rather it is designed to provide a framework of ideas to accommodate the many aspects and features of the functioning of the world capitalist economy and the many types of dominance and dependency.

Dos Santos (1970) defines dependence thus: 'by dependence we mean a situation in which the economy of certain countries is conditioned by the development and expansion of another economy to which the former is subjected'. The relation is such that 'some countries (the dominant ones) can expand and can be self-sustaining, while others (the dependent ones) can do this only as a reflection of expansion, which can have either a positive or a negative effect on their intermediate development'. **Unequal development must be seen as an integral part of the world capitalist system.** Inequality is inevitable because development of some parts of the system occurs at the expense of others. The monopoly power over trade that is exercised by the centre leads to the transfer of the economic surplus from the dependent countries to the centre, and financial relations that are based on loans and the exportation of capital by the centre ultimately lead to reverse flows and strengthen the position of the dominant country in the dependent country.

Different forms of dependence can be distinguished, as they have evolved historically. First, there is **colonial dependence**, based on trade and the exploitation of natural resources. Second, there is **financial–industrial dependence**, which consolidated itself at the end of the nineteenth century and has geared the economic structure of dependent nations to the needs of the centre. Third, a new type of dependence has emerged from 1945 based on multinational corporations, which began to invest in industries geared to the internal market of developing countries. This is **technological–industrial dependence**. Dos Santos argues that each of these forms of dependence has so conditioned the internal structure of peripheral countries, that this itself has become part of the dependency relation; for example the highly dualistic structure, the income inequality and conspicuous consumption of the wealthy classes, a dependency mentality and the ingrained habit of seeking outside help, and the unholy alliance between the domestic ruling elite and foreign interests all conspire to impede internal development. Thus Dos Santos (1973) maintains that dependency is not simply an external phenomenon; it also has to do with the supportive power groups within the poor countries themselves who find the status quo profitable:

> if dependency defines the internal situation and is structurally linked to it, a country cannot break out of it simply by isolating herself from external influence; such action would simply provoke chaos in a society which is of its essence dependent. The only solution therefore would be to change its internal structure; a course which necessarily leads to confrontation with the existing international structure.

Baran (1957), Frank (1967) and Amin (1974) focus their attention more squarely on the traditional Marxist mechanisms by which capitalism in general, and international capitalism in particular, aid the rich in exploiting the poor. Emphasis is placed on the expropriation and transfer of the surplus produced by labour to the owners of capital, which operates at different levels. Think of a cone, the base of which represents the rural poor producing a surplus from their labours in the fields or down the mines. This surplus is first siphoned off by those in the provincial towns, by small employers and merchants. In turn, the wealth of these towns is sapped by the capital cities, and finally, part of this wealth is siphoned away by foreign investors, who repatriate it to the apex of the cone – the rich world. The multinational corporations are seen as the modern instrument for the expropriation of surplus value. Neo-Marxists allow for a residue of surplus, but argue that if it is reinvested in the periphery or left in the hands of local elites, it will not be used appropriately for development purposes. As in Dos Santos's model, the system hinges on the collaboration of the governing elite who live in the capital city, who think like, and identify with, their ex-colonial masters. So poor countries, despite formal political independence, remain locked into an old system of economic dependence that perpetuates underdevelopment.

For Frank, like Dos Santos, underdevelopment is a natural outcome of the world capitalist system since the development of some countries inevitably means the distorted development or underdevelopment of others. Development itself perpetuates underdevelopment, a process that Frank has called '**the development of underdevelopment**'. Frank sees the origins of the process in colonization, which started as a form of economic exploitation and has distorted the economic structure of Third World countries ever since. The developing countries were forced into the position of being suppliers of raw materials to industrial countries, thus effectively blocking industrial development in the primary producing countries themselves. The whole export orientation and foreign dominance of these countries has limited the growth of the domestic market and the establishment of basic national industries for widespread development throughout the whole economy. The international, national and local capitalist systems alike generate economic development for the few and underdevelopment for the many. The solution would appear to be nothing short of social and political revolution.

Unequal exchange

The theory of unequal exchange owes its name to Emmanuel (1972). Exchange is unequal between rich and poor countries because wages are lower in poor countries, and lower than if the rate of profit in poor countries was not as high as in rich countries. In other words, exchange is unequal in relation to a situation where wages would be equalized: 'Inequality of wages as such, all other things being equal, is alone the cause of the inequality of exchange.' Let us illustrate the model diagrammatically and show its affinity with the ideas of those who stress the terms of trade as the main mechanism through which the gains from exchange are unequally distributed. Let us take two countries and call them 'centre' (c) and 'periphery' (p). Assume that prices in the two countries are based on a percentage mark-up (r) on unit labour costs, so that

$$P_c = w_c \left(\frac{L}{O}\right)_c (1 + r_c)$$

and

$$P_p = w_p \left(\frac{L}{O}\right)_p (1 + r_p)$$

where w is the money wage rate, and wL/O is wage costs per unit of output. Now assume that for institutional reasons $w_c > w_p$ and that the mark-up or rate of profit equalizes between the two countries. The theory of unequal exchange says that because of this, the terms of trade will be worse for the periphery than if wages in the periphery were higher and the rate of profit lower. This can be illustrated diagrammatically, taking the price of the centre's goods as the *numéraire*, so that $P_c = 1$ (Figure 8.4).

In the centre, the given rate of profit ($\bar{r}$) and wage rate (w_c) give a constant price (P_c) which acts as *numéraire* (hence the horizontal line, w_c). In the periphery, at a given wage (w_p), there is a positive relation between the rate of profit and terms of trade (P), given by the upward-sloping line w_p. The equilibrium terms of trade is given at P_1. An increase in periphery wages shifts the periphery curve rightwards to w_p^1, giving a new terms of trade, P_2, at the same rate of profit. Unequal exchange is measured as the difference between the actual terms of trade (P_1) and what it would be if wages were higher in the periphery and the rate of profit was lower at r^1. The 'explanation' of unequal exchange is unequal wage rates.

The model does not get us very far, however, without understanding why there are wage differences between centre and periphery. In Emmanuel's model, the wage differences are institutionally determined outside the model, whereas in practice there are many factors that impinge on wage

Figure 8.4   The theory of unequal exchange

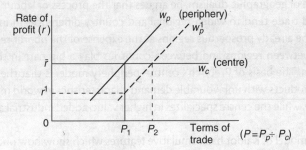

differences within the model itself that need consideration. Moreover, money wage differences may not be the only factor leading to unequal exchange. If money wage differences between centre and periphery reflect differences in labour productivity, the terms of trade between periphery and centre will not be nearly as bad as suggested by money wage differences alone. Indeed, if differences in money wages are exactly matched by differences in productivity, there will be no difference in money wage costs per unit of output and no difference in relative prices 'caused' by differences in money wages. There can still be unequal exchange in the Emmanuel sense by virtue of the way Emmanuel defines the concept, but if the cause of low wages is low productivity it is not a simple institutional matter to raise them.[6]

On the other side of the coin, if there is no good reason why the rate of profit should equalize between the two countries, a higher rate of profit in the centre could be an independent source of unequal exchange between centre and periphery, and also an explanation of why wages are depressed in the periphery. If account is taken of the characteristics of the goods produced by the centre and periphery – manufactured goods in the centre subject to decreasing costs, and primary commodities in the periphery subject to increasing costs – we can predict that oligopolistic structures will develop in the centre, while competitive structures will prevail in the periphery, with a tendency, therefore, for the rate of profit to be higher in the centre. The lower rate of profit in the periphery, and the attempt by capitalists to keep up the rate of profit in the face of competition, leads to the depression of wages in classic Marxist style.

Summary

- Disparities in living standards between countries of the world cannot be explained by initial (God-given) differences in factor endowments (natural resources) between countries. Through time, the process of growth has generated its own factor endowments favouring some countries more than others.
- Geographic differences in living standards between countries and between regions within countries are referred to as geographic dualism.
- Within most developing countries there are other forms of dualism. There is social dualism between how individuals behave and how markets function in the rural subsistence sector on the one hand and the modern capitalist sector on the other. There is technological dualism relating to differences in the level of technology and differences in techniques of production between the rural and modern sectors of the economy.
- Orthodox theory argues that when economic and social differences arise between sectors or regions, forces will come into play to narrow the differences. That is the equilibrium story.

- Myrdal's theory of circular and cumulative causation is a challenge to static equilibrium theory. In particular, in the case of geographic dualism, he argues that the process of labour migration, capital movements and trade tend to widen regional and country differences in income and welfare, by benefiting the already prosperous regions at the expense of the poorer regions.
- Structural differences between regions and between countries play a big part in the process of cumulative causation. The basis of Prebisch's centre–periphery model is that the periphery specializes in primary products with unfavourable demand characteristics in world markets and declining terms of trade, while the centre specializes in higher value-added industrial and service activities.
- The export-led growth model of Kaldor has cumulative features which show how once a region or country gets an advantage in the production and export of particular goods with favourable characteristics, it will sustain it through the impact that growth has on induced productivity growth and competitiveness (Verdoorn's Law).
- The new economic geography pioneered by Krugman shows how centripetal forces (which work towards the spatial concentration of industrial activities) and centrifugal forces (which work towards dispersal) depend on the balance between transport costs of importing inputs and exporting output on the one hand, and increasing returns to geographic specialization (agglomeration economies) on the other.
- The dependence of poor countries on the rich is another explanation given for divisions in the world economy. Dependency theorists focus on various forms of exploitation of poor countries by rich ones: in the old days by colonialism, and today by industrial and financial imperialism. Multinational corporations are criticized for siphoning off profits from the periphery to the centre, and the world's banking system is attacked for serving the needs of global finance rather than global development. Trade can also lead to unequal exchange through a deterioration in the terms of trade between primary commodities and industrial goods.

Chapter 8	Discussion questions

1 What do you understand by the terms 'technological dualism', 'social dualism' and 'geographic dualism'?

2 Is dualism avoidable in the development process?

3 In what ways might dualism impede the functioning of the total economy?

4 In what senses is Myrdal's theory of circular and cumulative causation a challenge to static equilibrium theory?

5 What are the mechanisms through which the process of circular and cumulative causation works?

6 If backward regions suffer 'backwash' effects from regions of expansion, would they be better off as sovereign states?

7 What is the so-called 'Verdoorn effect' and its importance in the process of circular and cumulative causation?

Chapter 8	Discussion questions – *continued*

8   What do the centre–periphery (or North–South) models by Prebisch, Dixon and Thirlwall, and Kaldor all have in common?

9   How does distance, and transport costs, affect the geographical pattern of economic development?

10   What are the various 'Marxist' explanations of the divergence between rich and poor countries?

11   What do you understand by the theory of unequal exchange?

Notes

1. First hinted at in Prebisch, *The Economic Development of Latin America and its Principal Problems* (1950), and developed in 'Commercial Policy in the Underdeveloped Countries', *American Economic Review, Papers and Proceedings*, May 1959.

2. The income elasticity of demand for goods measures the proportionate change in demand for a good with respect to a proportionate change in income, holding other things constant.

3. The model is discussed more fully in Dixon and Thirlwall (1975).

4. Under certain circumstances the growth rate may not converge to its equilibrium level. This depends on the behaviour of the model out of equilibrium. See Dixon and Thirlwall (1975).

5. For a comprehensive review and discussion of the models, see McCombie and Thirlwall (1994).

6. Within this framework, movements in the terms of trade can be seen as the outcome of differences in the movement of productivity on the one hand and whether money wage changes fully match productivity changes on the other. If money wage increases fail to match productivity increases in the periphery, for example, so that real wages do not rise as fast as productivity, whereas they do in the centre, there will be a steady deterioration in the terms of trade of the periphery. This is the essence of the Prebisch argument (see Chapter 15).

9

POPULATION AND DEVELOPMENT

- Introduction
- Facts about world population
- The determinants of fertility
- The costs and benefits of population growth
- Population and the growth of cities
- Simon's challenge
- The 'optimum' population
- A model of the low-level equilibrium trap
- Summary
- Discussion questions
- Notes
- Websites on population

Introduction

The relation between population growth and economic development is a complex one and the historical quantitative evidence is ambiguous, particularly concerning what is cause and what is effect. Does economic development precede population growth, or is population growth a necessary condition for economic development to take place? Is population growth an impediment or a stimulus to economic development? Many people consider rapid population growth in developing countries to be a major obstacle to development, yet there are several ways in which population growth may be a stimulus to progress, and there are several rational reasons why families in developing countries choose to have many children.

In this chapter we first of all consider the facts on world population, which has grown at unprecedented rates in the years since the Second World War, particularly in developing countries – although the growth is now slowing down.

Then we turn to the question of family size and the determinants of fertility. There is a rationale for poor families to have several children, and it is clear that fertility declines as people and countries get richer. This is the theory of demographic transition. The evidence also shows that fertility is heavily influenced by female education and the opportunity for women to work.

The costs to society of rapid population growth are considered, especially the effect of a high young dependency ratio on saving and capital accumulation. The potential benefits of rapid population growth are also considered, including how population pressure can be a stimulus to technical progress, and the fact that young people are more receptive to change and to new ideas and ways of doing things. It turns out that the empirical evidence across countries shows no statistically significant relation (positive or negative) between the growth of population and the growth of living standards.

The question then arises of what is the optimum population of countries? This can be defined in a number of ways; and it is argued that the claim that a country is 'over-populated' or 'underpopulated' needs to be viewed with some caution unless a precise definition of terms is given. The resource base of a country, the size of the country and the level of technology are crucial to any calculations.

The chapter ends with an exposition of Nelson's famous model of the 'low-level equilibrium trap' which shows how a poor region or country may get stuck in a situation where its population growth exceeds its output growth, pushing income per capita down to its minimum subsistence level, and how a 'big push' or 'critical minimum effort' may be necessary to get per capita income to a level where the growth of per capita income becomes self-sustaining. The Nelson 'trap' model is similar to the Malthusian trap in which some communities in developing countries still find themselves with large families, and living standards oscillating around subsistence level.

Facts about world population

The pertinent facts about the level and growth of world population are shown in Table 9.1. Today the world's population is just over 6,600 million, of which more than two-thirds live in the developing countries, and nearly one-half reside in Asia. This level compares with approximately 179 million at the time of Christ, and fewer than 1,000 million as recently as AD 1800. The current rate of growth of the world population is 1.2 per cent per annum, which has no precedent historically. From AD 1 to 1750 the rate was no more than 0.05 per cent per annum; from 1750 to 1850 it was 0.5 per cent per annum; and even between 1900 and 1950 it was only 0.8 per cent per annum.[1]

Table 9.1   Population statistics

	Total population millions 2007	Population growth % 2007	Age dependency ratio of dependants to working-age population		Death rate, crude per 1,000 people 2007	Birth rate, crude per 1,000 people 2007
			old 2007	young 2007		
World	6,610	1.2	11.5	42.6	8.4	20.2
Low income	1,296	2.2	6.3	68.5	11.4	33.2
Middle income	4,258	1.0	10.2	39.8	7.5	18.2
Lower middle income	3,435	1.0	9.6	40.7	7.2	18.6
Upper middle income	824	0.7	12.8	36.2	8.9	16.8
Low & middle income	5,554	1.2	9.4	45.8	8.4	21.7
East Asia & Pacific	1,912	0.8	10.4	33.1	6.7	14.4
Europe & Central Asia	446	0.2	16.6	27.8	11.5	13.8
Latin America & Caribbean	561	1.2	10.0	45.3	6.0	19.8
Middle East & North Africa	313	1.7	6.8	50.8	5.9	23.8
South Asia	1,522	1.5	7.7	52.9	7.7	24.5
Sub-Saharan Africa	800	2.4	5.8	80.2	14.8	38.9
High income	1,056	0.7	22.4	26.4	8.2	12.0

Source: World Bank, *World Development Indicators*, June 2009, online (http://data.worldbank.org/data-catalog/world-development-indicators).

At the present rate of increase the world population will double every 65 years. The current projection from the United Nations (UN) is that by the year 2050 the population will rise to 8 billion if birth rates continue to fall dramatically, or 12 billion if birth rates come down only slowly. The explosive growth of the world population is illustrated in Figure 9.1, which also shows the crude birth and death rates for the developed and developing countries. The gap between the two rates gives the rate of population growth. The past and projected population growth rates are shown in Figure 9.2.

The rates of population growth in developing countries in the recent past have been substantially in excess of the rate of growth for the world as a whole, and they look like continuing in the foreseeable future. The average rate of growth for the low- and middle-income countries since 2000 has been 1.3 per cent per annum, compared with 0.7 per cent in the developed countries. By continent, Africa has experienced the most rapid population growth (2.5 per cent), followed by Asia (1.4 per cent) and Latin America (1.3 per cent).

The country with the largest population is China, with an estimated current population of 1,300 million, followed by India, the USA, Indonesia, Japan, Russia, Brazil, Bangladesh, Nigeria, Pakistan and Mexico, all with populations of over 100 million. China and India alone currently add 25 million people to the world's population every year. In the last minute, approximately 300 babies have been born and 150 people have died, increasing the world's population by 150 persons, giving a yearly increase of 80 million.

The rate of growth of population is the difference between the number of live births per thousand of the population and the number of deaths per thousand. In a country where the birth

Figure 9.1   Past and projected world population, AD 1–2150

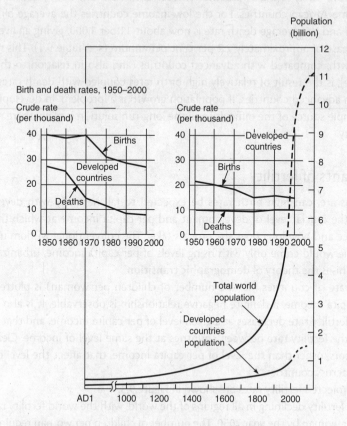

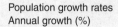

Figure 9.2   Past and projected population growth rates

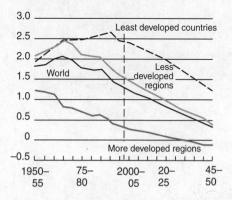

rate is 40 per 1,000 and the death rate is 20 per 1,000, the rate of population growth will there-fore be (40 − 20)/1,000 = 20 per 1,000, or 2 per cent per annum. If (in normal circumstances) a birth rate of 60 per 1,000 is considered to be a 'biological' maximum, and a death rate of 10 per 1,000 is considered a 'medical' minimum, the maximum possible growth rate of population, ignoring immigration, would be about 5 per cent per annum. These birth and death rates are in fact extremes, and are rarely found in practice. The current maximum birth rates recorded are 40 per 1,000 in some African countries. For the low-income countries the average birth rate is about 33 per 1,000 and the average death rate is now about 11 per 1,000, giving an average rate of population increase of approximately 2.2 per cent per annum (see Table 9.1). This rapid rate of population growth, compared with advanced countries (and also in relation to the growth of national income), is the result of relatively high birth rates coupled with death rates that are almost as low as in advanced countries. If population growth is a 'problem' in developing countries, this is the simple source of the difficulty and the long-run solution is plain: there must be a reduction in fertility.

The determinants of fertility

The vital questions are, can high birth rates be expected to fall naturally with development, and if so, what is the crucial level of development and per capita income at which the adjustment will take place and how long does the process take? The conventional wisdom used to be that fertility decline would come only with rising levels of per capita income, urbanization and industrialization. This is the theory of **demographic transition**.

If the fertility rate of countries (i.e. the number of children per woman) is plotted against the level of per capita income, a definite negative relationship is observable. It is also true that through time the fertility rate decreases at a given level of per capita income, and that there are big differences in the fertility rate between countries at the same level of income. Clearly there are important factors, other than the level of per capita income, that affect the level of fertility through time and across countries.

The past and projected fertility rates are shown in Figure 9.3.

The data show fertility declining in all regions of the world, with the world fertility rate falling to two children per woman by the year 2050. The number of children per woman required for the population to replace itself is 2.1. In the developed countries, fertility has already fallen below this critical level with an average of 1.6 children per woman.

Figure 9.3   Past and projected fertility

Total fertility
Children per woman

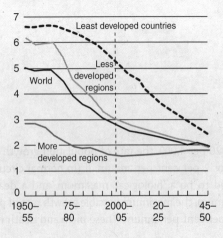

Figure 9.4 Fertility rate and female literacy, 1990

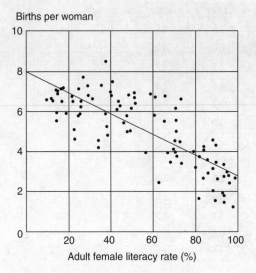

Reductions in fertility can occur with improvement in a wide range of socioeconomic conditions, such as access to family planning services, the provision of health care and a reduction in child mortality, greater employment opportunities for women, and above all the education of women and the promotion of female literacy. Where women are excluded from secondary education the average number of children per woman is six. In countries where half of women go to secondary school, the average number of children is three. Figure 9.4 shows the strong negative relationship between female literacy and the reduction in fertility across 93 countries.

There are a number of reasons why women's education lowers fertility:

- Education improves work opportunities for women, which makes having children more costly in terms of income forgone
- Educated women want their own children to be educated, which raises the cost of having children
- Education and literacy make women more receptive to information about contraception
- Education and employment delay marriage and the time available to rear children
- Education improves the status, bargaining power and independence of women, encouraging and enabling them to make their own choices.

From a **vicious circle** of no education, high fertility, poor health of children and low productivity, the education of women can lead to a **virtuous circle** of lower fertility, better care of children, more educational opportunity and higher productivity. The countries where fertility is declining most rapidly are those with the highest levels of female schooling, the lowest levels of child mortality and the widest availability of family planning services.

The reductions in fertility in different parts of the world over the last two decades are shown in Table 9.2. In developing countries as a whole the reduction has been 30 per cent from 3.8 children per fertile woman in 1987 to 2.7 in 2007. In the low-income countries, however, the number of children is still nearly five. Sub-Saharan Africa has the highest fertility rate and East and Central Asia the lowest.

Table 9.2   Total fertility rate (births per woman)

	1987	1997	2007
World	3.4	2.8	2.5
Low income	5.9	4.9	4.2
Middle income	3.3	2.5	2.2
Lower middle income	3.4	2.6	2.3
Upper middle income	2.9	2.2	2.0
Low & middle income	3.8	3.0	2.7
East Asia & Pacific	2.9	2.1	1.9
Europe & Central Asia	2.6	1.7	1.7
Latin America & Caribbean	3.5	2.8	2.4
Middle East & North Africa	5.4	3.5	2.8
South Asia	4.5	3.7	2.9
Sub-Saharan Africa	6.4	5.8	5.1
High income	1.8	1.7	1.8

Source: World Bank, *World Development Indicators*, June 2009, online
(http://data.worldbank.org/data-catalog/world-development-indicators).

The birth rate of a country is equal to its fertility rate multiplied by the ratio of fertile women to the total population. Even though fertility rates decline, birth rates do not necessarily decline in the same proportion because of the young age structure of the population produced by high fertility levels in the past. Thus, even if fertility continues to decline substantially, it will still take decades for the population level to stabilize because of the sheer number of couples having families. There is a **population momentum** built into the present age structure of the population of most developing countries. It is estimated that even if fertility rates were reduced immediately to the level of replacement (that is, one daughter per woman, which means approximately 2.1 children per family), the population of the developing countries will not stabilize until 2050, at a level of about 9 billion.

Given that there may be a lag between the death rate falling and a subsequent decline in the birth rate, rapid population growth may be considered a transitional or more enduring 'problem' for a country depending on the currently prevailing level of the rate of births and deaths. This proposition is best illustrated by means of a simple diagram (Figure 9.5).

The curves RB and RD represent the time paths of the birth rate and death rate, respectively. Population growth is determined by the gap between the two curves. To save drawing more diagrams, let us suppose that points X and Y in Figure 9.5 represent two countries with the same current rate of population growth ($Pq = St$). In the case of country Y, population growth will soon slow down since the death rate has reached its minimum and the birth rate is falling. In the case of country X, however, which has the same *current* population growth, the population growth rate can be expected to increase in the future as the gap between the birth and death rates widens. The death rate is falling but the birth rate remains constant to the point V; only after this point will population growth decrease. Here, then, are two countries with the same observed population growth at present but with radically different future prospects. When comparing countries, and their population 'problems', the time profile of countries must be borne in mind. But the crucial questions, as we suggested earlier, are what is the length of the time lag between the death rate falling and the downturn of the birth rate? What is the length of the **demographic transition**?

Figure 9.5 Population momentum

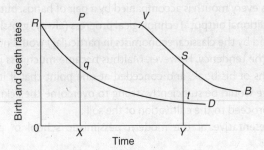

It is the length of this lag that determines the short-run prospects of countries emerging from a transitional state and attempting to 'take-off' into self-sustaining growth.

The experience of the developing countries today has no historical parallel, at least in Western Europe. In nineteenth-century Europe the birth and death rates tended to fall together and population growth never exceeded 1 per cent per annum. It could almost be argued that the 'balance of nature' has been upset in today's developing countries. The introduction of public health measures and medical advances reduced death rates suddenly and dramatically, but the means and know-how to effect an equally dramatic fall in the birth rate were not provided at the same time. Modern science and public health improvements have contributed to the ending of premature death, but have not until recently exerted a significant impact on births.

The costs and benefits of population growth

Population growth plays a conflicting role in the development process. It can act as both a stimulus and an impediment to growth and development. The question, to which there is no easy answer, is at what point do the economic disadvantages begin to outweigh the advantages? Where does the balance lie?

The conventional view is that high levels and rates of growth of population constitute a problem for the world as a whole and for the developing countries in particular. Population growth, it is argued, depresses human welfare because it:

- Uses up scarce (non-renewable) resources and causes environmental degradation
- Puts pressure on food supplies
- Leads to overcrowding and congestion in cities
- Adds to the employment problem
- Reduces the savings ratio and dilutes the quantity of capital per person employed.

There are elements of truth in all these arguments, especially in parts of the world where there are particularly heavy concentrations of population in relation to habitable land. Asia, for example, contains over one-half of the world's population and nearly 2 billion people live in big cities which already suffer the highest levels of air pollution in the world, not to mention the congestion. Asia will be the biggest source of greenhouse gases by the year 2015 (on present trends). As we shall see later in the chapter, however, there are also arguments to be put on the other side.

The pessimistic view of population originated with Malthus (see Chapter 5, p. 136), and in recent years it has been revived by ecologists, environmentalists and various eco-doomsters of different persuasions. The pessimism of Malthus stemmed from the pervasive classical belief in the law of diminishing returns, and the underestimation of humankind's response to the challenge of diminishing productivity with the expansion of numbers through invention and innovation.

According to Malthus there is a 'constant tendency in all animated life to increase beyond the nourishment prepared for it'. Thus every mouth is accompanied by a pair of hands, but every pair of hands produces less and less additional output. Technological progress (always grossly underestimated by pessimists in general and by the classical economists in particular) would not be rapid enough, it was thought, to offset the tendency. However, Malthus became much less pessimistic between the first and fifth editions of his book, and conceded at one point that if it were not for population increase, 'no motive would be sufficiently strong to overcome the acknowledged indolence of man and make him proceed to the cultivation of the soil'.

A fairly typical remark, representative of the modern pessimistic school of population economists, is that by Enke (1971):

> The economic danger of rapid population growth lies in the consequent inability of a country both to increase its stock of capital and to improve its state of art rapidly enough for its *per capita* income not to be less than it otherwise would be. If the rate of technological innovation cannot be forced, and is not advanced by faster population growth, a rapid proportionate growth in population can cause an actual reduction in income per capita. Rapid population growth inhibits an increase in capital per worker, especially if associated with high crude birth rates that make for a young age distribution.

Hoover and Coale (1958), in their classic study of population growth and development based on the Indian experience, remark that:

> While greater numbers in the labour force add to the total product, faster growth of the labour force implies a lower output per worker than slower growth. The reason for this result is that with a faster growing labour force more capital must be directed to provide tools and equipment for the extra workers so that they will be as productive as the existing labour force, and thus less will be available, *ceteris paribus*, for increasing output per worker.

The arguments made do not sound unreasonable but the effect of population growth on savings is a good deal more theoretically complex than the above arguments suggest. The traditional argument is that population growth reduces the community's savings ratio by leading to a **high dependency ratio** of children who consume but do not produce. Ignoring the fact that many young children in developing countries do in fact work, the implication of the argument would seem to be that a reduction in population growth would increase the savings ratio by raising the age structure of the population. In the process, however, it must be remembered that many of the older members of a community also consume without producing and that the proportion of retired members of the community to total population will rise as population growth slows. Thus what happens to the aggregate savings ratio as the population growth rate changes will depend on how the composition of the *total* dependency ratio alters, and on the propensity to save (dissave) of the two groups of dependants. For example, if the propensity to dissave of the retired was greater than that of the inactive young, the aggregate savings ratio might fall with a reduction in the birth rate as the retired dependency ratio rose.

It should also be remembered that the effect of children on a society's total savings works primarily through the family as a unit and depends on how the family reacts to the increase in the number of children. There may just be a substitution of one form of expenditure (on children) for another. Alternatively, the family may work harder to provide for the children, in which case there will be no adverse effect on saving at all. Saving in some families may even increase if there is a sufficient increase in output and a high degree of substitution. The degree of substitution between one form of expenditure and another will depend on the ability to substitute, determined by living standards, and the level of saving already achieved.

The question of an output response to population pressure comes back to the point made earlier of the possibility of a positive relation between population growth and total productivity growth. It may well be that the sheer increase in numbers creates work and production incentives that affect output and productivity favourably. In fact there is a good deal of theory and empirical evidence to suggest a positive relation between population growth and the growth of output per unit of labour, especially in the manufacturing sector, assuming some growth in employment as the population expands. This is **Verdoorn's Law** (discussed in Chapter 3, p. 111), which hypothesizes a positive relation between the growth of the population, employment and output on the one hand and the growth of labour productivity on the other.

The possible explanations for such a relation are numerous. First, it has been argued (see Chapter 7, p. 236) that an economy with a faster rate of growth of employment and output may be able to learn more quickly and hence raise its rate of technical progress. Second, if there are internal and external economies of scale in production, increased employment and output will lead to a faster rate of growth of labour productivity. Third, there are likely to be economies of scale in the use of capital. Capital requirements, in most cases, do not increase in the same proportion as population. There are many important indivisibilities in the provision of capital, especially in the field of transport and other social overhead capital.

It is also possible that population pressure can favourably affect individual motivation and lead to changes in production techniques that can overcome the negative consequences of population growth. In this connection it has been argued that a major stimulus to the 'Green Revolution' in the 1960s and 1970s came from the pressure of population on food supply. The young age structure of a country also makes it more amenable to change, more receptive to new ideas, more willing to shift resources from low-productivity to high-productivity sectors, and so on, all of which may raise income per head. In Hirschman's model of development (see Chapter 10), population growth increases the supply of potential decision-makers, expands markets and leads to development via shortages.

It must not be forgotten that the world as a whole has grown progressively richer while the population has expanded. Would the world be as rich today if the population had remained static? Would Britain have been the first country to industrialize if its population had not grown? Would the USA have become the richest country in the world without the great influx of people from beyond its shores to exploit its abundant natural resources?

All that has really been said so far is that population growth presents a paradox. On the one hand, increases in population may reduce living standards owing to the adverse effect of population growth on savings and capital per head. On the other hand, increases in population and the labour force can raise living standards through the learning, specialization and scale economies that larger numbers, wider markets and a higher volume of output make possible. What may be called the '**paradox of labour**' can be seen more easily by taking the identity $O = P(O/P)$, or in differential form, $(\Delta O/O) = \Delta P/P + \Delta(O/P)/(O/P)$, where O is output, P is population and O/P is output per head of population (and a constant fraction of the population is assumed to work). Decreasing amounts of capital per worker (and possibly diminishing returns to land) imply a negative relation between the terms on the right-hand side of the equations, so that output per head and living standards are lower than they would otherwise be as the population increases. On the other hand, the possibility of increasing returns, due to the factors mentioned, implies a positive relation between the two terms, so that living standards rise as the population increases.

The question is, which forces predominate? The debate as to whether population growth acts as a stimulus or an impediment to the growth of living standards is largely a question of whether the relation between $\Delta P/P$ and $\Delta(O/P)/(O/P)$ is significantly positive or negative. If the relation is negative, then population growth is an impediment to rising living standards. If the relation is positive then the effect of population growth on the growth of output and output per head is unambiguously favourable. Evidence across countries suggests that population growth and the rate of capital accumulation are inversely related which decreases the growth of labour productivity, but population growth and technical progress are positively related which increases the growth of labour productivity. The two effects offset each other, leaving the total effect of population growth on the growth of per capita income roughly neutral.[2]

This indeed is the conclusion of studies that examine *directly* the relation between population growth and the growth of living standards by correlating the two variables for a cross-section of countries to see whether the relation is positive or negative. When this is done, there is very little systematic relation to be found between inter-country rates of population growth and rates of growth of per capita income. As an exercise, students might like to take their own sample of countries and correlate the rate of growth of population with the rate of growth of per capita income, to see what results emerge.

The fact that the international cross-section evidence lends very little support to the notion that curbing population growth will have much impact, if any, on the growth of income per head is not to deny, of course, that curbing population growth may be desirable for other reasons, such as to relieve overcrowding, to relieve pressure on food supplies and, in general, to improve the distribution of income. To be sceptical of an inverse relation between population growth and per capita income growth is not to pour cold water on population-control programmes. On the contrary, given the uncertainty of the population-growth/living-standards relation, and the force of other arguments for limiting numbers, the most sensible strategy is to pursue programmes on the hypothesis that population control increases per capita income. In simulation studies of the gains from population control that use the effect on per capita income as the criterion for success, however, it is important that explicit account should be taken of the positive relation between population growth and technical progress if the gains from population control are not to be exaggerated.

Population and the growth of cities

One of the major consequences of population growth, and the process of rural–urban migration, is the rapid growth of cities in developing countries. At present, just over one-half of the world's population lives in cities, and this is predicted to rise to two-thirds by 2025. In fact, virtually all the predicted increase in world population will live in cities. The urban population of developing countries is already increasing by almost 700 million a year, which puts huge pressure on resources. While cities only occupy 2 per cent of the land's earth surface, they absorb 75 per cent of natural resources: food, energy and water (Reader, 2005).

Currently, the top ten cities in the world (by population) are Tokyo (35.7 m); Mexico City (19 m); New York (19 m); São Paulo (19 m); Mumbai (18.8 m); Delhi (15.9 m); Shanghai (15 m); Kolkata (14.8 m); Dhaka (13.5 m); and Buenos Aires (12.8 m). By 2025 it is predicted that there will be 26 cities in developing countries with more than 10 million people and 400 cities with more than 1 million.

Living conditions in the cities of developing countries are often extremely poor. One-third of city dwellers live in slums, and many are very insecure because of lack of land rights. There is overcrowding, poor sanitation, lack of clean water, pollution and disease. Over 500 million lack access to clean water and 2 million die each year as a result.

Simon's challenge

The most concerted challenge to the view that population growth is uniformly depressing for the material well-being of mankind has come from Julian Simon (1992, 1996). Simon's major thesis is that 'the ultimate resource is people – skilled, spirited and hopeful people – who will exert their wills and imaginations for their own benefit, and so, inevitably, for the benefit of us all'. The English political economist of the seventeenth century, William Petty, was making the same point when he said 'it is more likely that one ingenious, curious man may rather be found among 4 million than among 400 persons' (Petty, 1682). Simon brings together both the theoretical arguments and empirical evidence on both sides of the population debate and presents simulation results on the relation between population growth and living standards. He finds that the initial effects of population increase on per capita income are negative, but that in the longer term the positive feedback effects that result from the stimulus of population growth to technological progress and other factors that improve the rate of growth of productivity outweigh the negative effects. Simulations suggest that for countries already industrialized the initial negative effect of population is offset within 50 years. For less developed countries the conclusion is that moderate population growth is more favourable to the growth of living standards than either a stationary population or very rapid population growth.

An overall judgement of population growth, and whether it is beneficial or not, therefore depends very much on a weighing of the balance between the present and the future. In economic analysis the present and the future are made comparable using the concept of a discount rate. Whether the positive long-run benefits of population growth are considered to outweigh the short-run negative effects depends on the discount rate and the time period taken. The less future benefits are discounted and the longer the time period taken, the more beneficial (less detrimental) population growth appears, and the shorter the time period considered and the more future benefits are discounted, the less beneficial (more detrimental) population growth appears. There will be some time period and some discount rate at which additional population is exactly on the borderline of having a negative or positive value.

What are the positive feedback effects that population increase can have on economic progress that vitiate the classical prediction that population growth is uniformly depressing on living standards? In his simulation model of the relationship between population growth and per capita income in advanced countries, Simon attempts to capture the effect of additional children on such factors as the savings ratio, labour supplied by the parents, scale economies and technical progress. In his simulation model for developing countries Simon considers the following important feedback mechanisms:

- The stimulus to new methods in agriculture
- The supply response of families
- The provision of social infrastructure (particularly transport)
- Scale economies
- Demand-induced investment.

Let us briefly consider some of these factors.

A society under pressure from population growth may be expected to respond by finding new and more efficient ways of meeting given needs. In agriculture, the Malthusian view would be that improvement in agricultural techniques is independent of population and that improvements simply induce population expansion. Others would argue that even if population pressure does not induce the production of new techniques it certainly induces the adoption of new techniques. It is difficult to see how the Green Revolution in Asia in the 1970s would have occurred without the pressure of numbers on food supply.

Agricultural families may respond to the needs of additional children by changing methods, working harder and producing more. Studies suggest that the elasticity of output to increases in the number of children is about 0.5; that is, an increase in family size, say, from four to five (25 per cent) would result in a 12.5 per cent increase in output. Simon argues that population growth also has a large positive effect on agricultural saving, which tends to be overlooked because a large fraction is non-monetized.

Population pressure provides a stimulus to develop social infrastructure, transport and communication facilities, which have far-reaching external repercussions, extending beyond the additional numbers they are designed to serve. Population growth also makes these facilities more economical to provide because of the scale economies involved in their provision. Simon argues, 'if there is a single key element in economic development other than culture and institutions and psychological make-up, that single key element is transportation together with communications'. Adam Smith, an early contemporary of Malthus and much more optimistic about the development process, was impressed by the benefits of communications:

> good roads, canals and navigable rivers, by diminishing the expense of carriage, put the remote parts of the country more nearly upon a level with those in the neighbourhood of the town. They are upon that account the greatest of all improvements – they break down monopolies . . . they open new markets.

To the extent that population growth exerts pressure for these facilities to be provided, a significant output response is to be expected.

Increased population has many other productivity effects that are subtle and indirect, yet nonetheless very important. It is very difficult, for example, to improve health and sanitation in sparsely populated areas, but once sanitation and health improvement become feasible and economical with greater numbers, enormous benefits may result – more than in proportion to the increase in population. A growing population also facilitates change without disrupting the organization and positions of those already established. Thus government and administration may be expected to improve and become more in keeping with the needs of development. Youth itself has positive advantages. Young people are more receptive to change and modernization than older people. The younger a population the more education (or human capital) per head of the population. Young people tend to be more mobile, which is an asset when structural change is required. With a growing population, investment is less risky. Many economists are of the view that one of the major obstacles to development is not a shortage of savings but a lack of willingness to invest. An expanding market resulting from population growth provides an incentive to investment.

The great difference between the results of Simon and those of the pessimists is that all the beneficial feedback effects of population on output mentioned above are not considered. But any of the feedback factors referred to may partially or fully offset the capital-dilution effect of greater numbers in the short run, which is the factor that the predictions of conventional models reflect. A complete analysis of the relation between population and living standards must have due regard to the longer-term benefits that population expansion can confer on societies, as well as the short-term costs. Indeed, only when the benefits are considered is it possible to comprehend why societies are infinitely wealthier today than centuries ago, despite population expansion.

The 'optimum' population

What is the 'optimum' population? The term 'optimum population' is used in several different senses, but four in particular are commonly employed. First, it is sometimes used to refer to the size of population that *maximizes the average product or income per head*. It is in this situation that a society's savings ratio is likely to be maximized. Thus if the total product curve for an economy is drawn as in Figure 9.6, the optimum population is P, where a ray from the origin is tangential to the total product curve. At P, total product (Y) divided by population (P), or average product per head of population, is at its maximum. The condition for maximum average product per head is that the marginal and average product per head should be equal. If the marginal product of an addition to the population is above the average, the average product could be increased by an expansion of the population. Conversely, if the marginal product is below the average, a further increase in population will reduce the average product and the population will exceed the optimum level in the way defined. If there was no saving, the maximization of product per head would maximize welfare per head because consumption per head would then also be at a maximum.

On the surface, this concept of optimum population seems an attractive one upon which to base a population policy. It provides the greatest scope for maximizing savings per head if desired or, in the absence of forced or compulsory saving, it will lead to the maximization of welfare per head. Yet a population policy based on maximizing per capita income has frightening implications (not entirely fanciful) for all submarginal groups in society that may be deemed to be depressing the average standard of life.

A second approach to the concept of optimum population adopts the criterion of *total welfare maximization*. This is the utilitarian approach, adopted by the English economist cum philosopher Henry Sidgwick in his *Methods of Ethics*, originally published in 1874. He argues:

> If the additional population enjoy on the whole positive happiness, we ought to weigh the amount of happiness gained by the extra numbers against the amount lost by the remained. So that, strictly conceived, the point up to which, on utilitarian principles, population ought to be encouraged to increase is not that at which *average* happiness is the greatest possible – as appears to be often assumed by political economists of the school of Malthus – but at which the product formed by multiplying the number of persons living into the amount of average happiness reaches its maximum (emphasis added).

According to this criterion, the population would be suboptimal if the marginal product of labour was above some notional welfare subsistence level, and would reach the optimum when all incomes were equalized at the welfare subsistence level (assuming a diminishing marginal utility of income). But in conditions of poverty, if increments to population reduce the average standard of living still further, it seems perverse to call this an improvement in welfare simply because the number of people 'enjoying' such an impoverished state has risen. As Rawls (1972) argues, however, in his *Theory of Justice*, if a rational observer was asked to choose membership of one or other society from behind a veil of ignorance they would undoubtedly reject the maximization of total welfare and choose the society with the prospect of a higher per capita income.

Figure 9.6   Maximization of average product

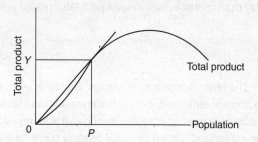

A third definition of optimum population refers to the level of population beyond which the average product in an economy falls below the level necessary for subsistence, on the assumption that the total product is equally shared. In this case the term 'optimum' simply refers to the maximum population that can be supported with existing resources, and is the point of Malthusian equilibrium. In Figure 9.7 a population beyond P_1 could not be supported because the average product of the population would be below the level of subsistence. If total product was not equally shared, a total population of P_1 would not be supportable, for some would have more income than necessary for subsistence and others less. But note that if the product is equally shared, a much larger population can be maintained than the population at which the marginal product falls below subsistence, that is, P. In fact the optimum population, P_1, is consistent with a negative marginal product.

This last point leads us to the fourth sense in which the term 'optimum' population is sometimes used, which is to describe a state of affairs where a country's population is so large that further increases lead to a fall in total output implying a negative marginal product. The population is optimal in this sense when total product is maximized, at P_2 in Figure 9.7. This definition of optimum population is closely linked with the notion of population density, and attempts to define under-population and over-population in terms of the relation between population and resources, and, in particular, land. Since resources such as land vary considerably in quality, however, inter-country comparisons of ratios of population to resources must be treated with great care. One country may be regarded as 'under-populated' in relation to another country even though it has a higher population–resource ratio, simply because the technology it uses to exploit its resources is superior. Technology will influence the position and shape of the total product

Figure 9.7   The 'optimum' population

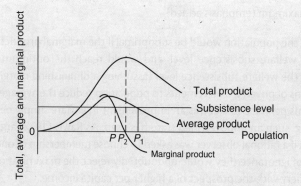

curve – and hence the optimum population – for any given ratio of population to resources. In view of the variety of interpretations of the concept of optimum population, the claim that a country is 'overpopulated' or 'under-populated' needs to be viewed with some scepticism unless a precise definition of the terms is given.

Where does all this leave the welfare basis for population control programmes? A firmer basis than whether or not there are diminishing or increasing returns to population growth is to consider the divergences between the private and social benefits that arise from large numbers of children. For example, individual families may prefer to have fewer children if they know that all other families will have fewer children, but in isolation they are not willing to limit the number of children they have. This is an example of what is known in welfare economics as 'the isolation paradox', and it establishes a case for public intervention. It is the young who suffer from there being more children because most of the costs arise in the future. Present parents may enjoy their children, but their children may wish their parents had had fewer, and they probably would have had fewer if they could have been sure that everybody else would have had fewer too. A further reason for public intervention in the field of population control may be market failure, if it can be shown that families have more children than they actually want and that there is an unmet need for family planning services.

It is interesting to note that surveys of desired family size in developing countries consistently put the figure at one or two lower than the actual family size. Apart from this, it could be argued that it is a basic human right to be able to choose freely and responsibly the number of children to have and how far apart to have them. This indeed was the resolution endorsed by the Bucharest World Population Conference in 1974, which laid the foundation for the World Bank's increased support for population control programmes throughout the Third World, and reiterated by the UN Conference on Population and Development in Cairo in 1994. The Cairo Conference emphasized the right of women to control the number and timing of their children and urged countries to provide universal access to family planning services. It is estimated that only 50 per cent of married women in developing countries use any form of birth control. As we saw earlier, however (p. 289), the education of women is the major determinant of fertility, and a necessary condition for a reduction in fertility is the expansion of educational and work opportunities for women.

A model of the low-level equilibrium trap

To repeat, there are two main interrelated reasons why rapid population growth may be regarded as a retarding influence on development. First, rapid population growth may not permit a sufficiently large rise in per capita incomes to provide the savings necessary for the required amount of capital formation for growth. Second, if population growth outstrips the capacity of industry to absorb new labour, either urban unemployment will develop or rural underemployment will be exacerbated, depressing productivity in the agricultural sector. It is not inconceivable, moreover, that rises in per capita income in the early stages of development may be accompanied by, or even induce, population growth in excess of income growth, holding down per capita incomes to a subsistence level. Today's falling death rates (associated with development) are contributing to population pressure; and presumably for centuries past the population of most countries has been oscillating around the subsistence level, with small gains in living standards (due to 'technical progress') being wiped out either by higher birth rates or such factors as disease, famine and war.

This is the notion of a **low-level equilibrium trap** illustrated in Figure 9.8.

Figure 9.8 Low-level equilibrium trap

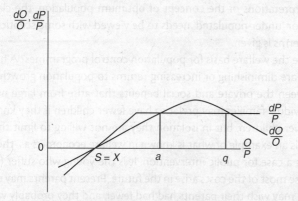

The figure shows the relationship between the growth of population (dP/P) and the growth of output (dO/O) on the one hand (measured on the vertical axis), against the level of per capita income (O/P) on the other (measured on the horizontal axis). $S = X$ represents the subsistence level of per capita income at which population growth is zero and output growth is also zero because at the subsistence level there is no saving and investment. Population growth rises with per capita income and then levels off at a biological maximum. Output growth rises with per capita income because the savings ratio also rises with per capita income, but then levels off (and even declines). Output growth eventually falls as the capital–labour ratio falls. If the output growth curve cuts the population growth curve from above at point S=X, it can be seen that any increase in per capita income above the subsistence level up to a point a will lead to population growth in excess of output growth pushing income per head back to the subsistence level. Conversely, any per capita income level beyond a will mean a sustained rise in per capita income until the two curves cut again at q. This would be a new stable equilibrium with the output growth curve again cutting the population growth curve from above.

To escape from the low-level equilibrium trap, per capita income must either be raised to a, or the dO/O and dP/P curves must be shifted favourably. The origin of '**big push**' theories of development (see Chapter 10, p. 322), and the concept of a '**critical minimum effort**', was the belief that to escape from the 'trap' it would be necessary to raise per capita income to a in one go through a massive investment programme. If countries are in a trap situation, however, much greater hope probably lies in the dO/O curve drifting upwards over time, through technical progress, or in a sudden drop in the dP/P curve from a reduction in the birth rate. Capital from abroad, raising the dO/O curve, and emigration, lowering the dP/P curve, could also free an economy from such a trap.

To take account of factors other than population growth that may depress per capita income, and factors other than increases in capital per head that may raise per capita income, the low-level equilibrium trap model can be extended and generalized by adopting Leibenstein's terminology of income-depressing forces and income-raising forces (Leibenstein, 1957). Leibenstein's approach is illustrated in Figure 9.9. The curve representing income-depressing forces, Z_t, is measured horizontally from the 45-degree line, and the curve representing income-raising forces , X_t, is measured vertically from the 45-degree line. Per capita income level a is the only point of stable equilibrium. Between a and q, income-depressing forces are greater than income-raising forces and per capita income will slip back to a. Only beyond q are income-raising forces greater than

Figure 9.9 Leibenstein's approach

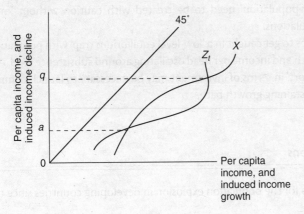

income-depressing forces such that a sustained increase in per capita income becomes possible. q is the critical per capita income level necessary to escape from the low-level equilibrium trap.

Most developing countries in the world today are experiencing income growth faster than population growth. Whether income growth would be faster if population growth was reduced is an open question. It is possible to conceive of a low-level equilibrium trap, but its level almost certainly rises over time owing largely to technical progress before a reduction in birth rates sets in.[3]

Summary

- Since the 1950s, the world's population has grown at an unprecedented rate, more than doubling from just over 3 billion in 1950 to 6.8 billion today. The pace of growth is slowing but population growth in developing countries is still nearly three times faster than in developed countries (1.8 per cent compared with 0.7 per cent per annum). The world's population is forecast to stabilize at around 11 billion in 2050.
- The cause of this population explosion has been a dramatic fall in the death rate due to advances in medical knowledge and improved sanitation, without a commensurate fall in the birth rate (until recently).
- Fertility rates are high in poor countries, but decline with the level of per capita income. This is the theory of demographic transition. Fertility also declines with the years of education women receive and with female employment opportunities.
- The costs of rapid population growth include: pressure on food supplies, the congestion of cities, environmental degradation, the depletion of non-renewable resources, and a reduction in the savings ratio of countries.
- The potential benefits of population growth include: the stimulus to new methods in agriculture to raise output (e.g. the Green Revolution of the 1970s and 1980s); demand-induced investment; scale economies, and the provision of social infrastructure which confers positive externalities (e.g. transport).
- There is no statistically significant correlation (negative or positive) between the growth of population and the growth of living standards across countries.
- The term 'optimum population' is used in several different senses including: maximizing income per head; maximizing total welfare; the maximum population that can be supported with

existing resources, and the population level that maximizes total output. The terms 'over-population' and 'under-population' need to be treated with caution without knowing the precise basis of the calculations.

• It is possible for countries to get caught in a 'low-level equilibrium trap' with population growth exceeding income growth and income per head oscillating around subsistence level. A 'big push' or 'critical minimum effort' in terms of investment may be necessary to launch communities in this state on to a self-sustaining growth path.

Chapter 9	Discussion questions

1 What accounts for the population explosion in developing countries since the 1970s?

2 Why do poor people have large families?

3 What are the major determinants of fertility?

4 It has been said that 'affluence is its own prophylactic'. Does this mean that it is futile to attempt to control the size of the population before living standards rise?

5 Why will the population continue to grow rapidly even if fertility rates in developing countries fall rapidly?

6 In what ways may rapid population growth impair development?

7 What are the stimuli that rapid population growth might give to development?

8 How would you do a cost–benefit analysis of population growth?

9 What do you understand by the concept of the 'low-level equilibrium trap'?

10 Is it possible to define an 'optimum' population?

Notes

1. For a history of world population, see Kremer (1993).
2. For an early study, see Thirlwall (1972).
3. For good surveys of many of the issues discussed in this chapter, see Cassen (1976), Kelley (1988) and Simon (1997).

Websites on population

World Bank, World Development Indicators www.worldbank.org/data/onlinedatabases/online databases.html

United Nations www.un.org/popin/wdtrends

UNDP www.undp.org/popin.htm

UN Population Division www.un.org/esa/population/unpop.htm

UN Population Fund www.unfpa.org

UN Population Information Network www.un.org/popin/

IV

THE ROLE OF THE STATE, THE ALLOCATION OF RESOURCES, AND SUSTAINABLE DEVELOPMENT

10

RESOURCE ALLOCATION IN DEVELOPING COUNTRIES, AND SUSTAINABLE DEVELOPMENT

- Introduction
- The market mechanism and market failures
- The role of the state
- Corruption
- Failed states
- Development plans
- The allocation of resources: the broad policy choices
- Industry versus agriculture
- The comparative cost doctrine
- Present versus future consumption
- Choice of techniques
- Balanced versus unbalanced growth
- Investment criteria
- Summary
- Discussion questions
- Notes
- Websites on government and corruption

Introduction

The central issue facing all economies is how to allocate resources among competing uses. This question takes on more significance in developing countries than in developed countries because resources are scarcer, the basic needs of people are greater and the market mechanism as a device for resource allocation has many more imperfections. In this part of the book we turn to some of the major topics of development strategy concerning the use of investment criteria for the allocation of resources (particularly the use of social cost–benefit analysis for the appraisal of public sector projects), and the concept of sustainable development, relating to how economic development affects the environment and climate change, and how the latter affects development. Separate chapters are devoted to each of these subjects.

In this preliminary chapter we first review the role of the market mechanism as an efficient device for resource allocation, and the various imperfections and failures that markets may suffer from which might be corrected by the state. Four roles for the state are identified: to provide public goods, to eliminate divergences between private and social costs and benefits (which arise because market prices do not reflect the social costs and benefits of goods and factors of production), to protect the vulnerable because the market mechanism does not guarantee an equitable distribution of income, and to provide an institutional environment in which markets can flourish.

But there can be state failures as well as market failures. Corruption is endemic in many poor countries, and there are at least 50 countries in the world classified as 'failed states' that hardly function at all, politically or economically.

Finally, the role of planning in developing countries is discussed, and some of the broader policy issues confronting decision-makers, including types of planning, the balance between agriculture and industry, the choice between consumption today and consumption tomorrow, pursuing (or not) the law of comparative advantage, techniques of production, and the debate over whether growth should be balanced or deliberately 'unbalanced'.

The market mechanism and market failures

In free-enterprise market economies, resources are allocated by Adam Smith's 'invisible hand' of the market in accordance with consumer demand. The market is the organizational framework that brings together those who supply and those who demand a product, who then trade at an agreed price. In a completely free market, the price will clear the market so there are no unsatisfied buyers and sellers. Decision-making about what is produced is decentralized and left to the market, comprising the decisions of myriad private individuals. If the demand for a good increases, the price will rise and producers will be induced to supply more; if demand falls, the price will fall and producers will supply less. Market prices act as **signals** to producers to supply more or less of a commodity according to the changing profitability of production. The efficiency of markets relies on prices acting as signals, on suppliers responding, and on the mobility of the factors of production enabling supply to be forthcoming.

This brings us to one of the most important theorems in welfare economics: if consumers consume to the point where the marginal utility of consumption is equal to the price of a good, and producers produce to the point where the marginal cost of production is equal to price, then resources will be optimally allocated since the marginal utility of production will just equal the marginal cost. Society will have reached its highest level of utility consistent with its production possibilities. This is illustrated in Figure 10.1.

Figure 10.1 Welfare maximization

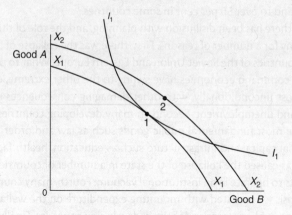

The curve I_1I_1 is society's indifference curve between two goods, A and B, representing the highest utility attainable, and X_1X_1 is a country's production possibility curve between the two goods, A and B. Point 1 represents the optimum allocation of resources between the two goods. Any point to the left or right of point 1, or inside the production possibility curve, would represent a lower level of utility.

The allocation role of markets, however, is only one of the functions of the market mechanism. To use a distinction introduced by Kaldor (1972), the market also has a *creative* function, to provide an environment for change that expands production possibilities – that is, which shifts the production possibility curve outwards to X_2X_2, enabling a higher level of utility at point 2. An environment for change means all the dynamic forces that lead to technical progress, innovation and ultimately investment. In the early stages of development, the creative function of markets, producing new opportunities for growth, may be just as important as the allocative function of markets.

The conditions required for markets to perform their allocative and creative functions in an optimal manner are very stringent, and are unlikely to be satisfied in any economy, let alone developing countries. The true benefit of output may not be reflected in price because of **externalities**; price may not reflect marginal cost because of **market imperfections**; and many developmental goods and services may not be produced at all because **markets are incomplete or missing** entirely, and therefore cannot perform their creative function. In other words, there are likely to be **market failures**.

In addition, there is the problem that there is nothing in the market mechanism that guarantees an equitable distribution of income in society, or that will direct adequate resources away from present consumption to build up the means of production for a higher level of consumption in the future.

In the past, all these types of market failure have led development economists to argue for government intervention in the development process, as well as leading most developing countries to interfere with the market mechanism and to adopt various forms of planning for the allocation of resources. In the former Soviet Union and the countries of Eastern Europe, planning superseded the market mechanism entirely, and output and resource allocation was decided by bureaucrats, not by consumers. In other countries, governments produced plans for the sectoral allocation of resources, and took on more and more functions. In the latter half of the twentieth century there was an explosion of government expenditure in developing countries, rising to over 30 per cent of national income on average and to over 50 per cent in some countries.[1]

In recent years, however, there has been disillusion with planning, and the role of the state has come under increased scrutiny for a number of reasons. First, there was the collapse of the former state-planned, communist countries of the Soviet Union and Eastern Europe. What to put in their place? Most of these former command economies have swung to the other extreme, embracing the market mechanism almost unconditionally, with other damaging consequences relating to growing income inequality and unemployment. Second, in many developing countries the state has failed to deliver even the most fundamental public goods such as law and order and property rights, and essential social capital and infrastructure such as education, health facilities and transport. Third, civil strife has caused the collapse of the state in a number of countries, particularly in Africa, leaving markets to operate in an institutional vacuum. Fourth, many countries have found themselves in fiscal crisis – associated with mounting expenditure on the welfare state in developed countries, and huge public enterprise deficits in developing countries. Finally, there is a fascination with the enabling role that the state has played in the successful developing countries of South-East Asia – in Japan and the Asian Tigers of Hong Kong, Singapore, Taiwan and South Korea. Can the East Asian model be copied?

Surveying the experience of the developed and developing countries in the years since 1945, the message would seem to be that the state has a vital role to play in economic development, but not so much as a direct provider of goods and services; rather as the agency through which market failures can be rectified and as the architect of a framework in which markets can flourish and evolve. History shows that markets can come into existence without government intervention, but markets work incrementally. It takes time for price signals to be recognized, for people to respond to incentives and for resources to be (re)allocated efficiently. This does not mean that the state should step in and do everything. There is a middle way between state-led, central planning on the one hand, and the minimal state espoused by extreme free-marketeers on the other. The bad experience of government planning in Eastern Europe should not blind us to the market failures mentioned earlier. The way forward in most developing countries must be a judicious mix of market capitalism combined with state intervention. Let us now consider in more detail the role the state can play in correcting these market failures.

The role of the state

The state has four key roles to play in the development process:

- To provide public goods
- To correct market imperfections
- To protect the vulnerable and ensure an equitable distribution of income, both intratemporally (between people at a point in time) and intertemporally (between generations over time)
- To provide an institutional environment in which markets can flourish (including the maintenance of macroeconomic stability).

Public goods are goods that have certain characteristics that make it difficult, if not impossible, to charge for them, and therefore private suppliers will not provide them. These characteristics are (1) consumption by one user does not reduce the supply available for others (the good is **non-rival**), and (2) users cannot be prevented from consuming the good (the good is **non-excludable**). There are not many *pure* public goods (air is perhaps the purest of all) but there are others that come close and are important for economic development, such as defence, law and order, and the provision of basic infrastructure such as roads, railways, power supply, sewers and clean water. A market in defence, or laws governing property rights which benefit the whole nation, is not conceivable. Markets in some infrastructural facilities are conceivable, but not very likely because of the high fixed costs. Also, the providers might have difficulty in charging for, and capturing, the externalities. The market would either not provide at all, or it would underprovide.

Market imperfections refer to three important phenomena. First, market prices may provide a very imperfect guide to the *social* optimum allocation of resources because they do not reflect the opportunity costs to society of using factors of production, or the value to society of the production of commodities. The price of labour may be above its opportunity cost and therefore used too little. The price of capital and foreign exchange may be below the opportunity cost and therefore used too much from a social point of view. Likewise, the price of goods may not reflect the marginal cost of production. Monopolies, tariffs, subsidies and other imperfections in the market all distort free market prices, upon which private producers base their production decisions. There is more on this topic in Chapter 11, where social cost–benefit analysis is discussed in detail.

Second, there is the existence of **externalities**, both positive and negative, which means that some goods may be underprovided and others overprovided from a social point of view because the positive or negative externality is not reflected in the price. Most infrastructure projects, such as transport facilities, power generation, irrigation schemes and so on, and social capital, such as education and health facilities, will have greater social returns than the private return and will therefore be underprovided from a social point of view unless private suppliers in the market are compensated or subsidized. Other activities may produce negative externalities by imposing costs on society that are not paid for by the provider, and therefore the market oversupplies from a social point of view. Governments can curb negative externalities through regulation or taxation, and promote positive externalities through subsidies or providing the output itself, as with education and health care.

Third, markets may be incomplete or missing altogether. One good reason why markets may be missing in the case of public goods is the inability of suppliers to exclude 'free-riders', that is, to exclude people from consuming the good once it is provided. But there are other important reasons for incomplete or missing markets. For example, high transaction costs can prevent markets from developing, particularly in developing countries, where poor communications make information costs high and there is an absence of futures markets to compensate for risk in conditions of uncertainty. The actual cost of providing a good or service may be less than individuals are willing to pay, but imperfect information on the part of consumers leads to an undervaluation of the product and therefore restricted supply; for example, preventive health care. In this sense the market is incomplete.

Asymmetric information, adverse selection and **moral hazard** can also lead to market inefficiency. 'Asymmetric information' refers to the imbalance of knowledge in a market between buyers and sellers. In the market for bank loans, for example, the borrowers know more about their own circumstances than the lenders. Banks could make bad loans (adverse selection), which makes them cautious and leads to credit rationing. It would be very costly for banks to obtain all the information they require on high-risk customers. The informal money market compensates by charging very high interest rates for all. Another example would be the health insurance market, where individuals know more about their health than the suppliers of insurance. Those who know they are prone to illness are more likely to take out insurance, and more likely to be turned down. 'Moral hazard' is present when the possession of insurance encourages the activity that is insured against, leading to resource waste and higher costs (and higher insurance premiums for all). Governments may step in by regulating private insurance, or providing the service themselves at lower cost.

As far as **equity** is concerned, the state has an important role to play in protecting the vulnerable and ensuring an equitable distribution of income between people, between groups in society, between regions and across generations. There is not only a moral case for the state to help those in absolute poverty, but also a strong political and economic one. Poor, vulnerable and disaffected people can be a major cause of civil unrest and political instability (Stewart, 2001). This deters investment and growth. It is also important for the state to keep an eye on the welfare of future generations, which may require altering the balance between consumption and investment in the present. There are a number of ways in which governments can intervene to discourage present consumption and raise the level of investment for higher future consumption; examples are taxation, subsidized interest rates and public investment on society's behalf. We talk more about altering the balance between consumption and investment in Chapter 11.

Finally, the state is essential for providing the appropriate **institutional environment** for markets to flourish and operate efficiently (see Chapter 4). In this sense, markets and government intervention are complementary. The World Bank devoted its *World Development Report 1997* to the topic 'the state in a changing world'. It conveys three principal messages:

- Development (economic, social and sustainable) without an effective state is impossible. It is increasingly recognized that an effective state – not a minimal one – is central to economic and social development, but more as partner and facilitator than director. States should work to complement markets, not replace them.
- A rich body of evidence shows the importance of good economic policies (including the promotion of macroeconomic stability), well-developed human capital and openness to the world economy for broad-based, sustainable growth and the reduction of poverty. But as our understanding of the ingredients of development improves, a deeper set of questions emerges: why have some societies pursued these actions with greater success than others, and how precisely did the state contribute to these differing outcomes?
- The historical record suggests the importance of building on the relative strengths of the market, the state and civil society to improve the state's effectiveness. This suggests a two-part strategy of matching the role of the state to its capability, and then improving that capability.

The *World Development Report 1997* argues that many developing countries are not performing their core functions properly. They are failing to protect property, to ensure law and order, and to protect the vulnerable, all of which causes unrest and leads to a lack of government **credibility**. A survey of 69 countries shows that government credibility is highest in South and South-East Asia, and lowest in sub-Saharan Africa and the states of the former Soviet Union. Investment and growth are positively related to credibility. The Report says of Africa that many countries are 'trapped in a vicious circle of declining state capability and thus declining credibility in the eyes of their citizens – leading to increased crime and an absence of security affecting investment and growth'. It refers to a 'crisis of statehood' in Africa, and a lower 'state capability' than 50 years ago. In contrast, it praises the countries of South-East Asia because they have paid attention to the institutional framework for markets to fulfil their various roles in allocating and augmenting resources. State credibility is particularly important if developing countries are to attract private foreign investment.

The World Bank outlines a two-pronged strategy for governments to increase both their credibility and the effectiveness of the state: first, governments must match the role of the state to its capabilities and not try to do too much, and second, they must try to improve capabilities by reinvigorating state institutions.

With regard to the first prong of the strategy, the state should concentrate on getting the basics right, such as safeguarding property rights and guaranteeing the rule of law, rather than trying to do too much. In many countries there is overregulation and excessive state consumption. Governments should decide more carefully what to do and how to do it. The basics should be:

- Law and order
- Maintaining macroeconomic stability
- Investing in basic social services and infrastructure
- Protecting the vulnerable
- Protecting the environment.

But the state does not have to be the *sole* provider of all infrastructure and social services. It can contract these services out to the private sector and introduce competition into their provision, coupled with a regulatory framework to protect consumers and workers. Neither does the state have to be the monopoly supplier of public utilities such as electricity, gas and telecommunications. These activities can be **privatized** with state supervision. Privatization has gathered pace throughout the world in recent years. There have been thousands of divestitures of state companies in developing countries, and in the former communist countries of Eastern Europe. The motivation has been the generally poor economic performance of state-owned companies, the large deficits of public enterprises, and the promotion of competition to improve the delivery of services.

Beyond the basics, the state may want to intervene strategically – in industrial policy, for example, if it has the capability, as the successful Asian Tiger economies have done. The past success of Hong Kong, Singapore, Taiwan and South Korea has depended on the state and the private sector working in harmony with each other, with the state providing the economic and legal environment for markets to flourish but with the government taking an entrepreneurial role and intervening where it thought necessary. In Hong Kong the state took a leading role in planning infrastructure and providing subsidized housing to maintain social stability and to reduce the cost of labour. Singapore, Taiwan and South Korea targeted financial assistance to specific industries and even specific companies (with an emphasis on exports), with spectacular success.

On the second strategy of improving the capabilities of the state and reinvigorating state institutions, the task is to provide incentives for public officials to perform better and reduce the scope for arbitrary action that could lead to poor decision-making and corruption.

Corruption

Corruption is a serious issue in many developing countries. An organization based in Germany called Transparency International publishes a corruption perception index based on surveys of business people, risk analysts and perceptions of the general public, ranked on a scale 0 to 10 (the lower the index, the more corrupt). The results for 180 countries in 2008 are shown in Table 10.1.

Developing countries appear to be the most corrupt, although the same level of income (or development) is often associated with different levels of corruption. In general, poverty breeds corruption, and corruption can lead to severe inefficiencies in the functioning of economies.[2]

Table 10.1 Transparency International's corruption perception index, 2008

Country rank	Country	Index	Country rank	Country	Index	Country rank	Country	Index
1	Denmark	9.3	36	Botswana	5.8	70	Romania	3.8
1	New Zealand	9.3	36	Malta	5.8	72	Bulgaria	3.6
1	Sweden	9.3	36	puerto Rico	5.8	72	China	3.6
4	Singapore	9.2	39	Taiwan	5.7	72	Macedonia	3.6
5	Finland	9.0	40	South Korea	5.6	72	Mexico	3.6
5	Switzerland	9.0	41	Mauritius	5.5	72	Peru	3.6
7	Iceland	8.9	40	Oman	5.5	72	Suriname	3.6
7	Netherlands	8.9	43	Bahrain	5.4	72	Swaziland	3.6
9	Australia	8.7	43	Macau	5.4	72	Trinidad and Tobago	3.6
9	Canada	8.7	45	Bhutan	5.2	80	Brazil	3.5
11	Luxembourg	8.3	45	Czech Republic	5.2	80	Burkina Faso	3.5
12	Austria	8.1	47	Cape Verde	5.1	80	Morocco	3.5
12	Hong Kong	8.1	47	Costa Rica	5.1	80	Saudi Arabia	3.5
14	Germany	7.9	47	Hungary	5.1	80	Thailand	3.5
14	Norway	7.9	47	Jordan	5.1	85	Albania	3.4
16	Ireland	7.7	47	Malaysia	5.1	85	India	3.4
16	United Kingdom	7.7	52	Latvia	5.0	85	Madagascar	3.4
18	Belgium	7.3	52	Slovakia	5.0	85	Montenegro	3.4
18	Japan	7.3	54	South Africa	4.9	85	Panama	3.4
18	USA	7.3	55	Italy	4.8	85	Senegal	3.4
21	Saint Lucia	7.1	55	Seychelles	4.8	85	Serbia	3.4
22	Barbados	7.0	57	Greece	4.7	92	Algeria	3.2
23	Chile	6.9	58	Lithuania	4.6	92	Bosnia and Herzegovina	3.2
23	France	6.9	58	Poland	4.6	92	Lesotho	3.2
23	Uruguay	6.9	58	Turkey	4.6	92	Sri Lanka	3.2
26	Slovenia	6.7	61	Namibia	4.5	96	Benin	3.1
27	Estonia	6.6	62	Croatia	4.4	96	Gabon	3.1
28	Qatar	6.5	62	Samoa	4.4	96	Guatemala	3.1
28	St Vincent and the Grenadines	6.5	62	Tunisia	4.4	96	Jamaica	3.1
28	Spain	6.5	65	Cuba	4.3	96	Kiribati	3.1
31	Cyprus	6.4	65	Kuwait	4.3	96	Mali	3.1
32	Portugal	6.1	67	El Salvador	3.9	102	Bolivia	3.9
33	Dominica	6.0	67	Georgia	3.9	102	Djibouti	3.0
33	Israel	6.0	67	Ghana	3.9	102	Dominican Republic	3.0
35	United Arab Emirates	5.9	70	Colombia	3.8	102	Lebanon	3.0

Table 10.1 Transparency International's corruption perception index, 2008 – *continued*

Country rank	Country	Index	Country rank	Country	Index	Country rank	Country	Index
102	Mongolia	3.0	134	Comoros	2.5	158	Gambia	1.9
102	Rwanda	3.0	134	Nicaragua	2.5	158	Guinea-Bissau	1.9
102	Tanzania	3.0	134	Pakistan	2.5	158	Sierra Leone	1.9
109	Argentina	2.9	134	Ukraine	2.5	158	Venezuela	1.9
109	Armenia	2.9	138	Liberia	2.4	166	Cambodia	1.8
109	Belize	2.9	138	Paraguay	2.4	166	Kyrgyzstan	1.8
109	Moldova	2.9	138	Tonga	2.4	166	Turkmenistan	1.8
109	Solomon Islands	2.9	141	Cameroon	2.3	166	Uzbekistan	1.8
109	Vanuatu	2.9	141	Iran	2.3	166	Zimbabwe	1.8
115	Egypt	2.8	141	Philippines	2.3	171	Congo. Dem. Rep.	1.7
115	Malawi	2.8	141	Yemen	2.3	171	Equatorial Guinea	1.7
115	Maldives	2.8	145	Kazakhstan	2.2	173	Chad	1.6
115	Mauritania		145	Timor-Leste	2.2	173	Guinea	1.6
115	Niger		147	Bangladesh	2.1	173	Sudan	1.6
115	Zambia		147	Kenya	2.1	176	Afghanistan	1.5
121	Nepal		147	Russia	2.1	177	Haiti	1.4
121	Nigeria		147	Syria	2.1	178	Iraq	1.3
121	São Tomé and Principe		151	Belarus	2.0	178	Myanmar	1.3
121	Togo		151	Central African Republic	2.0	180	Somalia	1.0
121	Vietnam		151	Côte d'Ivoire	2.0			
126	Eritrea		151	Ecuador	2.0			
126	Ethiopia	2.6	151	Laos	2.0			
126	Guyana	2.6	151	Papua New Guinea	2.0			
126	Honduras	2.6	151	Tajikistan	2.0			
126	Indonesia	2.6	158	Angola	1.9			
126	Libya	2.6	158	Azerbaijan	1.9			
126	Mozambique	2.6	158	Burundi	1.9			
126	Uganda	2.6	158	Congo. Republic	1.9			

Source: Transparency International: http://www.transparency.org/news_room/in_focus/2008/cpi2008/cpi_2008_table.

Daniel Kaufmann (2005) at the World Bank reckons that a country that improves its governance from a low average level (and reduces corruption) could triple its average per capita income in the long run, and tackle effectively illiteracy and infant mortality at the same time.

The World Bank defines corruption as 'the abuse of public office for private gain', including bribery, threats and 'kickbacks'. These are all aspects of **rent-seeking** behaviour that arise primarily because decisions over the allocation of resources are in the hands of politicians and government officials. The existence of licences, permits, regulations, subsidies and, of course, taxes all offer scope for corruption. Corruption not only leads to inefficiency – particularly the discouragement of investment – but can undermine the legitimacy of government itself. Where corruption is endemic, policy-making in other areas is less effective and it makes it more difficult for governments to enforce laws in such areas as taxation or control of environmental damage.[3]

The International Monetary Fund (IMF) now specifies anti-corruption measures as one of the conditions for loan support. For example, the IMF recently got tough with the Kenyan government, insisting first on a 'wealth declaration law' that all government ministers and senior civil servants declare the full range of their assets and liabilities every year, and secondly on a weekly inspection by IMF officials in Washington of the Kenyan Central Bank's balance sheet to prevent foreign aid being used for private gain.

Removing unnecessary regulations and bureaucracy, increasing transparency and paying officials higher salaries reduce the scope for corruption, but vested interests involved in corruption make the reform process more difficult. The *World Development Report 1997* outlines three essential ingredients for improving the capabilities of the state (and rooting out corruption):

- There must be effective rules and restraints to check public authority and prevent corruption. Independence of the judiciary is important, and an independent Commission against corruption would be helpful.
- Public officials should be appointed on merit, not on the basis of political patronage, and can be encouraged to perform effectively through a merit-based promotion system and adequate remuneration. Opening up competition in employment in the delivery of services is necessary to reduce the discretionary power of state officials to minimize **rent-seeking** behaviour, which is the basis of bribery and corruption.
- Decision-making needs to be brought closer to the people so that they have more confidence in the state. All government programmes are likely to work better if there is democracy, if power is devolved, and if users are consulted.

Figure 10.2 shows the functions of the state in tabular form, distinguishing between the roles of addressing market failure and improving equity on the one hand, and the provision of minimal functions through to activist functions on the other, according to capability.

Countries with a low state capability should concentrate first on basic functions such as the provision of pure public goods, macroeconomic stability and anti-poverty programmes. Going beyond these basic services are intermediate functions such as the management of externalities, regulating monopoly, improving information and providing social insurance. Finally, states with a strong capability can take on more active functions, as mentioned above in the case of the Asian Tigers, particularly promoting new markets through active industrial and financial policy.

The state also has a duty to reduce bureaucracy and regulation to allow markets to flourish. According to a World Bank (2004) study of laws and regulations in 133 countries, the costs in time, effort and money in setting up businesses in developing countries are colossal compared with developed countries because of bureaucratic delays and institutional inefficiencies. In Indonesia it takes 168 days to set up a business and in Brazil 152 days, but it takes only 2 days in New Zealand. In some developing countries, the average bureaucratic cost of setting up a business can be four times the average income per head; in developed countries it is as little as 1 per cent of average income per head. The consequences of poor and inappropriate regulations are that business is discouraged; a higher proportion of businesses operates outside the law, so the tax base is lower and corruption is more widespread. It is estimated that excessive regulations, inadequate enforcement of contracts, corruption and crime reduce the sales of firms by at least 25 per cent.

315

Figure 10.2 Functions of the state

	Addressing market failure			Improving equity
Minimal functions	*Providing pure public goods:* Defence Law and order Property rights Macroeconomic management Public health			*Protecting the poor:* Antipoverty programmes Disaster relief
Intermediate functions	*Addressing externalities:* Basic education Environmental protection	*Regulating monopoly:* Utility regulation Antitrust policy	*Overcoming imperfect information:* Insurance (health, life, pensions) Financial regulation Consumer protection	*Providing social insurance:* Redistributive pensions Family allowances Unemployment insurance
Activist functions	*Coordinating private activity:* Fostering markets Cluster initiatives			*Redistribution:* Asset redistribution

Source: World Bank, 1997.

Failed states

There are some 50 to 60 countries in the world, many in Africa, that hardly function at all, politically or economically, because their institutions and the rule of law have broken down. These are **failed states**. Within these countries, people are disenfranchised and trapped in poverty at the mercy of vicious networks of criminality, violence and drugs. The world pretends, or behaves as if, they are sovereign states, but in reality they have collapsed and are unable to provide even the most basic services and protection for their people.

Ghani and Lockhart (2008) in their powerful book *Fixing Failed States* outline ten key functions that the state should perform if its citizens are to survive and thrive.

- To make laws, and to enforce the rule of law, to allow all sections of society to live in harmony
- The control of violence
- The appointment of uncorrupt administrators to oversee public bodies
- The sound management of the public finances
- Investment in human capital
- The creation of citizenship rights through social policy to ensure equal opportunities for all
- The provision of infrastructure services
- The creation and expansion of markets
- The management of public assets, such as land, water rights and other 'natural' capital
- Effective public borrowing.

If all these functions are performed well, a virtuous circle of growth and development is possible. If some of the functions are performed badly, a vicious circle can start, ending ultimately in the failure of the state, and any prospect of sustained economic and social development. The UK government is intending to spend one-half of its bilateral aid budget on 20 or so countries, mainly in Africa, where the state has virtually collapsed.[4]

Development plans

In its *World Development Report 1997* the World Bank does not address the role of development planning, but almost all developing countries, whatever their political ideology, publish development plans.[5] A **development plan** is an ideal way for a government to set out its development objectives and demonstrate initiative in tackling the country's development problems. A development plan can serve to stimulate effort throughout the country, and also act as a catalyst for foreign investment and loans from international institutions.

As an example, the Tongan 6th Development Plan (1991–95) stated that:

> The ultimate aim of government policy is to induce improvements in the standard of living of Tongans in an equitable manner with a view to protecting natural resources and preserving cultural assets – Government policy will also pursue an equitable distribution of public investment and services between rural and urban areas, and between the capital [city], islands and outer regions.

Four economic and social objectives were set out:

- To achieve sustainable economic growth conducive to higher per capita income
- To achieve a more equitable distribution of income
- To generate more employment opportunities
- To restore and control external financial imbalances.

Depending on the politics of a country and its available expertise, a development plan will vary in its ambitiousness from a mere statement of aims to detailed calculations (and proposals for action) of the resources needed, and the amount of output that each sector of the economy must generate, in order to achieve a stipulated target rate of growth of output or per capita income. Anything more than a statement of aims inevitably involves some form of model building, if only to delineate the relationship between sectors of the economy and between the key variables in the growth process.

Four basic types of model are typically used in development planning:

- **Macro or aggregate models** of the economy, which may either be of the simple Harrod–Domar type (see Chapter 5) or of a more econometric nature, consisting of a series of equations that represent the basic structural relations in an economy between, say, factor inputs and product outputs, saving and income, imports and expenditure, and so on.
- **Sector models**, which isolate the major sectors of an economy and give the structural relations within each sector, and also specify the interrelationships between sectors, for example between agriculture and industry, between capital- and consumer-goods industries, and between the government and the rest of the economy.
- **Inter-industry models**, which show the transactions and interrelationships between producing sectors of an economy, normally in the form of an input–output table.
- Models and techniques for **project appraisal** to decide on the allocation of resources between activities (see Chapter 11).

Models such as these serve a twofold purpose. In the first place they enable planners to reach decisions on how to achieve specified goals. They highlight the strategic choices open to the policy-maker in the knowledge that not all desirable goals are achievable simultaneously. Only with an understanding of the interrelationship between the different parts of the economy, and a knowledge of the parameters of the economic system, is it possible for meaningful and consistent policy decisions to be reached. Without detailed information upon which to base planning (or what has been called 'planning without facts'), the case for decentralized decision-making becomes overwhelming.

Second, models of the type described above can perform an equally valuable function of enabling the future to be projected with a greater degree of certainty than would otherwise be possible, thereby providing some knowledge of what resources are likely to be available in relation to requirements within a stipulated planning period. Various types of model may be classified, therefore, according to whether they are required for policy or decision purposes or for the purpose of projection and forecasting. The necessary constituents of a plan containing both types of model are a statement of economic goals, a specification of policy instruments, an estimation of structural relationships, historical data, the recognition of exogenous variables, and last but not least, a set of national accounts for national income and expenditure, foreign trade and even manpower to ensure consistency between demand and the supply of resources available.

The allocation of resources: the broad policy choices

Given the scarcity of resources in developing countries in relation to development needs, one of the central issues in development economics is the allocation of resources among competing ends. For most developing countries the two major constraints on the growth of output are the ability to invest and the ability to import, and most theories of resource allocation and most public investment criteria reflect this fact. A common starting point in the consideration of resource allocation is how to maximize the level or growth of output with the domestic resources available, and how to minimize the use of foreign exchange.

Apart from the decision of how much to invest, three broad types of allocation decision may be distinguished:

- Which sectors to invest in
- Which projects should receive priority given the factor endowments of a country and its development goals
- Which combination of factors of production should be used to produce a given vector of goods and services, which will determine the technology of production.

While these decisions may look independent, in fact they are not. In practice, interdependence between decisions on output and decisions on technology is inevitable. Deciding which goods to produce will, to a certain extent, dictate factor proportions if technical coefficients are relatively fixed, and decisions about technology will influence the types of goods and services that are produced, insofar as factor proportions cannot be varied. Some goods and services are obviously more labour-intensive than others. The choice of technology, in turn, will be particularly influenced by factor endowments and the price of factors of production, and by the relative valuation given to present versus future consumption and welfare.

Because of the interdependence between the choice of goods and the choice of technology, a country that decides to use relatively labour-intensive techniques within the framework of goods chosen may nonetheless have a greater capital intensity than another country using relatively capital-intensive techniques with a different mix of goods. When discussing resource allocation and the choice of techniques a sharp distinction needs to be made between investment criteria that relate to the pattern of output on the one hand, and the choice of technology to produce the given vector of outputs on the other.

Investment decisions of the micro-type outlined above will also be influenced to a certain degree by the nature of the development strategy intended – that is, by broader policy issues such as whether emphasis is to be given to agriculture or industry, whether resources are to be used to build up complementary activities or whether imbalances are to be deliberately created in order to induce investment and influence decision-making, and whether emphasis is to be on static short-term efficiency in the allocation of resources or on laying the foundations for faster growth in the future. And in an open economy, the potential clash between efficiency and growth also requires a consideration of the implications of adherence to different versions of the comparative cost doctrine. In short, the question of resource allocation between projects cannot be divorced from consideration of the wider policy issues of industry versus agriculture, balanced versus unbalanced growth, foreign trade strategy and so on. And influencing all these decisions will be the underlying objectives of the development strategy: whether the aim is to maximize *current welfare* or to maximize consumption at *some future point in time*.

The choice of development strategy itself will be subject to political, social and economic constraints. A particular strategy, for example, may conflict with the desired income distribution or other social objectives. Other strategies may involve political repercussions inimical to development. One factor that cannot be ignored is the regional distribution of political power. Spatial considerations of this sort add a further dimension to the allocation problem. The pursuit of balanced growth or massive investment in social-overhead capital may imply a large public sector in the economy, which may not be politically possible. Certain development plans may antagonize foreign investors or multilateral aid-giving agencies such that if the plans are carried out, foreign capital or 'agency' capital dries up. Bearing in mind these constraints, let us first consider some of the broader aspects of development strategy and briefly discuss development goals, before examining a number of specific investment criteria that have been recommended for determining the allocation of resources and the pattern of output.

Industry versus agriculture

The issue of the choice between industry and agriculture, and where the emphasis should lie, can be discussed very quickly because, as we saw in Chapter 6, the two sectors are very much complementary to each other. In practice the fortunes of agriculture and industry are closely interwoven in that the expansion of industry depends to a large extent on improvements in agricultural productivity, and improvements in agricultural productivity depend on adequate supplies of industrial 'inputs', including the provision of consumer goods acting as incentives to peasant farmers to increase the agricultural surplus. It is worth mentioning, however, that the emphasis on *balance* between industry and agriculture is of fairly recent origin. On the one hand it represents a shift of emphasis away from the 'modern' view of an all-out drive for industrialization by developing countries, and at the same time it represents a reaction against the traditional doctrine of comparative cost advantage which, when applied to many developing countries, may lead to the production of primary commodities and a pattern of trade that puts these countries at a relative development disadvantage.

The comparative cost doctrine

Whether the static comparative cost doctrine should be adhered to is itself a question of development strategy, which is closely bound up with the goals of developing countries (that is, what they are trying to maximize), and with the controversy over whether trade should be looked at more from the point of view of the balance of payments than from that of the allocation of real resources. Assuming the full employment of resources, and that the price of a commodity reflects its opportunity cost (admittedly bold assumptions in any country), adherence to the comparative cost doctrine will produce the optimum pattern of production and trade for a country (see Chapter 15). Efficiency will be maximized when no commodity is produced that could be imported at a lower cost, measured by the resources that would have to be sacrificed to produce it at home. In a free trade world this would rule out the production of a wide range of industrial commodities in developing countries.

If the objective is faster economic *growth*, however, as opposed to static efficiency, the theory of growth suggests investment criteria that are quite different from those derived from the theory of comparative advantage. If growth depends on increases in investment, for example, it may not be wise to channel resources into activities that are too labour-intensive, where the income generated is all consumed and none is saved, or where there is no scope for increasing returns. Similarly, if growth is constrained by the balance of payments, it may be equally unwise to develop activities producing goods with a low price and income elasticity of demand in world markets, such as primary commodities. A low-price elasticity of demand can cause fluctuations in export earnings with shifts in supply, and cause the terms of trade to move adversely. A low-income elasticity of demand will mean that for any given growth of world income, countries producing these commodities will be put at a permanent balance-of-payments disadvantage compared with other countries producing goods with a higher income elasticity of demand (see Chapters 15 and 16).

The question ultimately boils down to one of the relative valuation of present versus future output and consumption (or welfare) – between consumption today and consumption tomorrow. Efficiency in resource allocation will maximize present output and consumption from a given amount of resources, but may impair growth and future consumption. Focusing on growth may lower present welfare but provide greater output and welfare in the future.

Present versus future consumption

The choice between present and future consumption is the same as the choice between consumption and investment in the present. How much investment should be undertaken in the present depends on the time interval over which society wants to maximize consumption and what value it places on consumption in the future compared with consumption in the present – that is, on the rate at which it discounts future consumption gains. Time affects both the accumulation of consumption gains and the effect that discounting has. Investment should take place so as to maximize consumption over the planning period. The investment ratio that maximizes consumption will vary according to the planning period, with and without discounting.

Let us illustrate this with a numerical example. Consider three different investment ratios – 0 per cent, 10 per cent and 50 per cent of national income – and three different planning periods – 3 years, 6 years and 10 years. Further assume that the capital–output ratio is 2, and that, for simplicity, there is no depreciation and no discounting. Let the initial capital stock equal 200, producing 100 units of output. The time paths of output, consumption, investment and the capital stock for the three different investment strategies and three different planning horizons can now be shown, as in Table 10.2. Over the three-year planning period, the first policy of no investment maximizes consumption. Over the six-year planning period, the second policy of a 10 per cent investment ratio maximizes consumption, and over the ten-year planning period the third policy of a 50 per cent investment ratio maximizes consumption.

The calculations in Table 10.2, and the conclusions drawn from them about the time period over which consumption will be maximized, will be affected by discounting and the discount rate chosen, because the present value of future consumption gains becomes less and less the further into the future they accrue, and their value is also lower the higher the discount rate chosen. What we illustrate, then, is that the answer to the question of how much to invest depends crucially on the *planning horizon* taken and the *discount rate* chosen. The longer the planning horizon and the less the stream of future consumption benefits is discounted, the more investment there should be in the present. The shorter the planning horizon and the higher the discount rate, the less investment there will be.

We also illustrate that countries with low initial stocks of capital and low levels of consumption must invest heavily if high future living standards are to be attained. But to invest heavily countries must take long planning horizons. One of the arguments for planning is, in fact, to lengthen the planning horizon beyond that chosen by individuals maximizing privately. Any finite planning horizon, however, only takes care of the people living within the planning period. To take account of generations living beyond the horizon, certain constraints must be built into the investment model such that, for example, the level of consumption at the end of the period should not be above a specified level, otherwise maximization of consumption within the horizon would mean consuming all income at the end of the horizon, leaving no saving for future investment and consumption.

Table 10.2 Consumption benefits with different investment ratios over different planning horizons

Time	Policy 1 (no investment)				Policy 2 (10% investment)				Policy 3 (50% investment)			
	K	Y	I	C	K	Y	I	C	K	Y	I	C
1	200	100	0	00	200.00	100.00	10.00	90.00	200.00	100.00	50.00	50.00
2	200	100	0	100	210.00	105.00	10.50	94.50	250.00	125.00	62.50	62.50
3	200	100	0	100	220.50	110.25	11.03	99.22	312.50	156.25	78.12	78.12
4	200	100	0	100	231.53	115.76	11.57	104.19	390.62	195.31	97.65	97.65
5	200	100	0	100	243.10	121.55	12.15	109.40	488.27	244.13	122.07	122.07
6	200	100	0	100	255.25	127.62	12.76	114.86	610.34	305.17	152.58	152.58
7	200	100	0	100	268.01	134.00	13.40	120.60	762.92	381.46	190.73	190.73
8	200	100	0	100	281.41	140.70	14.07	126.61	953.65	476.82	238.41	238.41
9	200	100	0	100	295.48	147.74	14.77	132.97	1192.06	596.03	298.01	298.01
10	200	100	0	100	310.25	155.12	15.51	139.61	1490.07	745.03	372.51	372.51

Key: K = capital stock; Y = output; I = the level of investment; C = consumption.

Choice of techniques

In a planning framework, the valuation of present versus future welfare is also the central issue regarding the choice of technology – whether techniques should be capital- or labour-intensive. At first sight it would seem sensible, in a labour-abundant economy, to use labour-intensive techniques of production, and to encourage activities that use factors of production that are in abundance. Doing so, however, may lead to a conflict between efficiency and growth; a clash between the maximization of present consumption and the level of consumption in the future. The problem is that if the wage rate is given, and invariant with respect to the technique of production, the more labour-intensive the technique the less saving that is likely to be generated for future reinvestment. Specifically, if the workers' propensity to consume is higher than that of the owners of capital, the total surplus, and the surplus per unit of capital invested, left for reinvestment will be smaller than if the technology were more capital-intensive. On the other hand, the more capital-intensive the technology, the lower the level of consumption and employment in the present.[6] In general, we reach the conclusion that the higher the valuation placed on raising the present level of employment and consumption as compared with future output, the more that labour-intensive techniques should be favoured. At the same time, the greater the valuation placed on future output in relation to present welfare, the more that capital-intensive methods of production should be favoured.

There is not only a potential conflict between employment and saving in the choice of techniques, but also a conflict between employment and output. The conflict arises not in the utilization of existing equipment but in the choice of *new* techniques. Techniques of production that are labour-intensive may have higher capital–output ratios than techniques that are more capital-intensive. A simple example will illustrate the point. Assume a fixed amount of capital to be invested of £1,000. One technique of production could employ 100 units of labour with £1,000 of capital, but the capital–output ratio is 5. This would give a flow of output of 200 with the employment of 100 persons. A second technique of production employs 50 units of labour but has a capital–output ratio of 4. This would give a flow of output of 250 with the employment of 50 persons. Thus maximizing both the current level of employment and output are consistent only if the more labour-intensive techniques also have the lowest capital–output ratios. These issues are discussed fully in Chapter 7.

Balanced versus unbalanced growth

Another broad choice of development strategy is between so-called balanced and unbalanced growth. The term 'balanced growth' is used in many different senses, but the original exponents of the balanced growth doctrine had in mind the scale of investment necessary to overcome indivisibilities on both the supply and the demand side of the development process (see, e.g., Rosenstein-Rodan, 1943; Nurkse, 1953). Indivisibilities on the supply side refer to the 'lumpiness' of capital (especially social-overhead capital), and the fact that only investment in a large number of activities simultaneously can take advantage of various external economies of scale. Indivisibilities on the demand side refer to the limitations imposed by the size of the market on the profitability, and hence feasibility, of economic activities. This was the original interpretation of the doctrine of balanced growth: that the large-scale expansion of activities or **'big push'** was necessary to overcome divergences between the private and social returns to investment. The doctrine was later extended, however, to refer to the *path* of economic development and the *pattern* of investment necessary to keep the different sectors of the economy in balance, so that lack of development in one sector does not impede development in others – for example necessity to strike a balance between such sectors as agriculture and industry, between the capital-goods and consumer-goods industries, and between social capital and directly productive activities (see also Lewis, 1955).

On the demand side, the argument is akin to Adam Smith's famous dictum that specialization, or the division of labour, is limited by the extent of the market, and that if the market is limited certain activities may not be economically viable (see Chapter 5). If, however, several activities are established simultaneously, each could provide a market for the other's products, so that activities that are not profitable when considered in isolation would become profitable when considered in the context of a large-scale development programme.

On the supply side, the argument for a 'big push' is related to the existence of **external economies of scale** whereby the production function of one activity may be favourably altered by the existence of other activities (for example those in close proximity), so that the social return of an activity will exceed the private return. The way to eliminate this divergence is to make each activity part of an overall programme of investment expansion. Enterprises that are not, or do not appear to be, profitable in isolation become profitable when considered as part of an overall plan for industrial expansion embracing several activities.

A major criticism of the balanced growth doctrine, however, is that it fails to come to grips with one of the fundamental obstacles to development in developing countries, namely a shortage of resources of all kinds. Critics of balanced growth do not deny the importance of a large-scale investment programme and the expansion of complementary activities. Their argument is that in the absence of sufficient resources, especially capital, entrepreneurs and decision-makers, the striving for balanced growth may not provide sufficient stimulus to the spontaneous mobilization of resources or the inducement to invest, and will certainly not economize on decision-taking if planning is required.

One of the most provocative books ever written on development strategy is that by Hirschman (1958), whose argument is along the above lines. Hirschman was then the foremost exponent of the doctrine of **unbalanced growth**, and we must briefly consider his views as these are still relevant today. The question he attempts to answer is this: given a limited amount of investment resources and a series of proposed investment projects whose total cost exceeds the available resources, how do we pick out the projects that will make the greatest contribution to development relative to their cost? And how should 'contribution' be measured?

Albert Hirschman

Born 1915, Berlin, Germany. Appointed Professor of Social Science, Institute for Advanced Study, Princeton, in 1974. Best known for his book *Strategy of Economic Development* (1958) which challenges the conventional view that developing countries should strive for balanced growth. Imbalances create incentives and economize on the decision-making process. Governments should deliberately target activities with high backward and forward linkages. Also an expert on Latin American economies and economic history with such books as *Journeys Towards Progress: Studies of Economic Policy-Making in Latin America* (1963) and *A Basis for Hope: Essays on Development and Latin America* (1971).

Hirschman distinguishes two types of investment choices – *substitution choices* and *postponement choices*. Substitution choices are those that involve a decision as to whether project A or B should be undertaken. Postponement choices are those that involve a decision as to the sequence of projects A and B – that is, which should precede the other. Hirschman is mainly concerned with postponement choices and how they are made. His fundamental thesis is that the question of priority must be resolved on the basis of a comparative appraisal of the strength with which progress in one area will induce progress in another. The efficient sequence of projects will necessarily vary from region to region and from country to country, depending on the nature of the obstacles to development, but the basic case for the approach remains the same – that is, to economize on decision-making. In Hirschman's view, the real scarcity in developing countries is not the resources themselves but the means and ability to bring them into play. Preference should be given to that sequence of projects which maximizes **'induced' decision-making**.

He illustrates his argument by considering the relation between social capital (SC) and directly productive activities (DPA). The case in which SC precedes DPA he calls 'development via excess capacity', and the case in which DPA precedes SC he labels 'development via shortages'. Both sequences create inducements and pressures conducive to development; the question is, which sequence should be adopted, if it is not possible to pursue a 'balanced' growth path, to produce DPA output at minimum cost in terms of inputs into both DPA and SC? The question can be made clearer with the aid of a diagram (Figure 10.3).

If the total cost of DPA output is measured on the vertical axis, and the availability and cost of SC is measured on the horizontal axis, curves can be drawn (a, b, c) showing the cost of producing a given full-capacity output of DPA from a given amount of investment in DPA, as a function of the availability of SC. The successive curves, a, b, c, represent different levels of DPA output from successively higher investment in DPA. The curves are negatively sloped and convex to the origin because DPA costs will decrease the greater the availability of social capital, but there is a minimum amount of SC necessary for any level of DPA output (for example 0S1, corresponding to curve a), and as SC increases, its impact on the cost of DPA output becomes less and less.

Now assume that the objective of the economy is to obtain increasing outputs of DPA with the minimum use of resources devoted to both DPA and SC. On each curve, a, b, c, the point where the sum of the coordinates is smallest will represent the most desirable combination of DPA and SC on this criterion. The line 0X connects the optimal points on the different curves and this represents the most 'efficient' expansion path, or 'balanced' growth path, between SC and DPA.

Figure 10.3 Induced decision-making

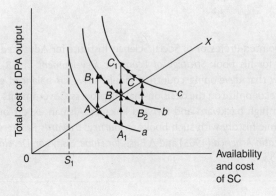

But suppose that 'optimal' amounts of SC and DPA cannot be expanded simultaneously to keep in balance with one another. On what criteria is that postponement choice made? One possibility is the sequence AA_1BB_2C, where the initial expansionary step is always taken by social capital. This sequence is called 'development via excess capacity'. The other (opposite) possibility is the sequence AB_1BC_1C, where the initial expansionary step is taken by DPA. This sequence is called 'development via shortages'. According to Hirschman, the preference should go to the sequence of expansion that maximizes 'induced' decision-making. It is difficult to tell *a priori* which sequence this is likely to be. If SC is expanded, existing DPA becomes less costly, encouraging further DPA. If DPA is expanded first, costs will rise but pressures will arise for SC facilities to be provided. Both sequences set up incentives and pressures, and ultimately, in Hirschman's view, the sequence chosen must depend on the relative strength of entrepreneurial motivations on the one hand, and on the response to public pressure of the authorities responsible for social capital on the other.

In general, however, Hirschman has some harsh things to say about the traditional view that SC must precede, or even be kept in balance with, DPA if development is to progress smoothly. While he admits that a certain minimum of social capital is a prerequisite to the establishment of DPA, he argues that development via excess capacity is purely permissive, and that to strive for balance is equally dangerous because there will be no incentive to induced investment (or induced decision-making). On the other hand, development via shortages will compel further investment, and hence the most 'efficient' sequence as far as 'induced' decision-making is concerned is likely to be that where DPA precedes SC.

It is true that where there is strong social and economic resistance to change, 'permissive' acts such as the construction of social-overhead capital are not likely to provide much impetus to development. On the other hand, Hirschman's analysis leaves several questions unanswered. He concedes that the objective must be to obtain increasing outputs of directly productive activities at minimum cost in terms of resources devoted to both DPA and SC, and that the cost of producing any given output of DPA will be higher the more inadequate is SC, but what is the *minimum* amount of SC required in a developing economy? Is this minimum so high as to contradict the argument that DPA should precede SC, at least in the earlier stages of development? Furthermore, what is the guarantee that SC will subsequently be provided once DPA has been established? Indivisibilities with respect to social capital may be so large that private investors are not induced to supply at any price. Reliance would then be on the government.

Hirschman applies the same criterion of 'induced decision-making' to the choice and sequence of projects *within* the directly productive sector. Here inducements stem from interdependencies between activities, or what Hirschman calls **'backward' and 'forward' linkage effects**. Backward linkages measure the proportion of an activity's output that represents purchases from other domestic activities. Forward linkages measure the proportion of an activity's output that does not go to meet final demand but is used as an input into other activities. With knowledge of inter-industry flows in an economy, with the help of an **input–output table**, it is possible to rank activities according to the magnitude of their combined linkage effects. Hirschman is suggesting that within the directly productive sector a useful development strategy would be to encourage those activities with the potentially highest combined linkages, because this will provide the greatest inducement and incentive to other activities to develop.

Unfortunately, one of the typical characteristics of developing countries is a lack of interdependence between activities. Primary product production has only limited backward linkages with other activities, while forward linkages, although potentially greater, also tend to be limited in practice. Agriculture's demands on other sectors are minimal, and only a comparatively small fraction of total agricultural output in developing countries is processed domestically; most is exported. The fact that manufacturing activities possess greater backward and forward linkages, strengthening the cumulative nature of development, is another powerful argument for industrialization. Hirschman advocates the expansion of industry through the transformation of semi-manufactures into goods required for final demand, or what he calls 'enclave import' industries.

In general Hirschman lays great stress on the role of imports in the development process, seeing imports as part of the inducement mechanism. For not only can semi-manufactured imports be processed into goods for final demand, but final-demand imports themselves can then be readily produced at home once the market has attained a certain size (or production threshold). If one of the major obstacles to development is a shortage of decision-makers, coupled with uncertainty and a limited market, the existence of imports provides conclusive proof that the market is there. As imports increase, so too do the chances that domestic production will one day be profitable. Hirschman criticizes developing countries for restricting imports prematurely, and argues that infant industry protection should only be given after imports have reached such a level as to guarantee domestic producers a market for their goods.

Investment criteria

Traditional micro-theory teaches that under perfect competition, resources will be optimally allocated when each factor of production is employed up to the point where its marginal product is equal to its price, and that society's output (welfare) will be maximized when the marginal products of factors are equated in all their uses. This is the so-called 'marginal rule' for resource allocation, and implies 'efficiency' in the sense that a society's total output of goods and services could not be increased by any redistribution of resources between activities because each factor of production is equally productive in existing activities. In static analysis, therefore, 'efficiency' in resource allocation implies maximizing the national product, and this is achieved when the marginal products of factors are equated in their different uses.

If the application of the marginal rule leads to an efficient allocation of resources, what is the allocation 'problem' in developing countries? Why seek other criteria to decide on the allocation of resources? One good reason is that the assumptions of traditional micro-theory do not accord with the realities or with the aspirations of developing countries. Two major drawbacks of the application of the marginal rule may be cited. One is that the marginal rule is a static criterion, and as we have said before, it is by no means certain that the aim of developing countries is, or ought to be, the maximization of the *present* level of output, consumption or welfare. Second, traditional static theory ignores many factors that may have a bearing on the *social* optimum allocation of resources. In countries characterized by fundamental structural disequilibria and extreme imperfections in the market, it cannot be assumed that the market prices of goods and factors of production reflect the social costs and benefits of production. The application of the marginal rule will only lead to a *socially* optimal allocation of resources in the absence of divergences between market prices and social costs and benefits, or if market prices are corrected to reflect social values.

Several factors can lead to divergences between market prices and the social valuation of goods and factors of production. First, if external economies and increasing returns are attached to some projects, their social value will exceed their private value, and the application of the marginal rule must make allowances for this if output is to be maximized from a given endowment of factors.

Second, if perfect competition does not prevail in the product market, product prices will not reflect society's valuation of those products, and market prices must somehow be adjusted to achieve a social optimum. Similarly, if perfect competition does not prevail in the factor market, the price of factors will not reflect their opportunity cost to society so that employing factors up to the point where their marginal product equals their price will not produce a social optimum. Underemployed resources such as labour will be overvalued, and scarce resources such as capital and foreign exchange will be undervalued, and market prices must therefore be corrected to reflect the value of these resources to society.

Third, static analysis ignores the future structure of product and factor prices arising from the choice of projects in the present. An optimum resource allocation in the present may not produce an optimal allocation of resources in the future. The only way of coping with this difficulty is through what is called **the programming approach to resource allocation**, by which the repercussions of one activity on others are explicitly considered and due allowance is made for time.

Finally, the application of the marginal rule can only lead to optimal resource allocation if income distribution is 'optimal' and remains unaffected by whatever programme is decided on. If a new pattern of resource allocation alters income distribution, output may be maximized but welfare diminished because of 'undesirable' changes in the distribution of income gains. To say anything concrete on this score requires an explicit statement of societal objectives, or a **social welfare function**, if interpersonal comparisons of utility are to be avoided. Presumably there might be a fair degree of consensus that an income distribution that leaves half the population unemployed and starving is 'inferior' to one that does not. Only the conditions for Pareto optimality would deny it![7]

For all the above reasons, there has been a prolonged debate for many years over the most appropriate criterion for resource allocation in the light of the development obstacles of developing countries and their aspirations. The different criteria that have been suggested reflect, by and large, differences of opinion as to what developing countries ought to attempt to maximize, the broad choice being between present and future levels of output and consumption. Most of the criteria discussed by early writers in this field refer to the allocation of capital, reflecting the view of domestic saving as the primary scarce resource. Increasingly, however, attention has been paid to the effects of resource allocation decisions on the balance of payments in recognition of foreign exchange as an equally scarce resource. This leads us on to Chapter 11, which explores social cost–benefit analysis.

Summary

- In free market economies, the market mechanism allocates resources among competing ends, but markets in developing countries have many imperfections which need correcting for a social optimum allocation of resources.
- Prices of goods and factors of production may not reflect their social benefit and social cost, respectively, because of positive and negative externalities. Markets may be incomplete or missing entirely. This provides a role for the state.
- The state has four key functions: to correct market imperfections; to provide public goods (such as health and education); to protect the vulnerable, and to provide an institutional environment in which markets can flourish.

- The state may also fail through corruption and rent-seeking behaviour. There are many 'failed states' in the world in which institutions and the rule of law have broken down.
- Many developing countries practise development planning, with various degrees of success.
- The central question facing all developing countries is how to allocate resources to maximize the level or growth of per capita output with the domestic resources available, and how to minimize the use of foreign exchange (which is a scarce resource).
- Apart from the decision of how much to invest, there are three broad types of allocation decisions: which sectors to invest in, which projects should receive priority, and which combination of factors of production should be used, which will determine the technology of production.
- In addition, countries need to decide on the balance between agriculture and industry, the extent to which static comparative advantage is allowed to dictate production, the balance between present and future consumption, and whether growth should be 'balanced' (between sectors) or deliberately unbalanced.

Chapter 10	Discussion questions

1 What is the role of markets in the development process?

2 Distinguish the different types of market failure, and the role that governments can play in rectifying market failures.

3 According to the World Bank (1997), what are the key roles of the state in developing countries, and how can the role of the state be made more effective?

4 What causes corruption, and how can it be reduced?

5 What are the major causes of divergences between the market prices of goods and the value of those goods to society?

6 What are the characteristics of failed states?

7 What are the major causes of divergences between the market prices of factors of production and their cost to society?

8 Why do developing countries construct development plans?

9 Why is there a clash between present and future consumption, and how can it be reconciled?

10 What do you understand by the concept of 'balanced growth'?

11 What is Hirschman's major criticism of the doctrine of balanced growth?

Notes

1. In many developed countries the state is even more pervasive in terms of expenditure, although a much higher proportion represents social security transfer payments, not expenditure on real resources.

2. For a comprehensive survey, see Abed and Gupta (2002).

3. For a collection of case studies on corruption see Elliott (1997); also Tanzi (1998) and Bardhan (1997).
4. See the website www.dfid.gov.uk/commonfuture
5. Students should familiarize themselves with a plan for a country of their choosing.
6. This conclusion depends on, among other things, the wage rate being invariant with respect to the technique of production. If the wage is higher the more capital-intensive the technique, this conclusion would have to be modified. For a discussion of this point, and other considerations that may lessen the conflict between employment and saving in the choice of techniques, see Chapter 7.
7. A situation is said to be Pareto optimal only if a change that benefits some does not harm others.

Websites on government and corruption

Role of the state

World Bank www.worldbank.org/publicsector
The International Development Department Research (University of Birmingham) www.idd.bham.ac. uk/research/Projects/Role_of_gov/role_of_gov.htm

Corruption

Transparency International www.transparency.org
Internet Centre for Corruption Research www.gwdg.de/ruwvw/icr.htm

11

PROJECT APPRAISAL, SOCIAL COST–BENEFIT ANALYSIS AND SHADOW WAGES

- Introduction
- Project appraisal
- Financial appraisal
- Economic appraisal
- Divergences between market prices and social values
- Economic prices for goods
- Non-traded goods and conversion factors
- Traded goods
- Shadow prices for factors of production
- The social rate of discount
- The social cost of investment
- The shadow wage rate
- A closer examination of the change in consumption in industry and agriculture
- The valuation of production forgone and the increase in consumption
- A numerical calculation of the shadow wage

- Social appraisal
- The equivalence of the Little–Mirrlees formulation of the shadow wage and the UNIDO approach
- Is it worth valuing all goods at world prices?
- The application of the Little–Mirrlees and UNIDO approaches to project appraisal
- Summary
- Discussion questions
- Notes
- Websites on project appraisal

Introduction

The literature and discussion about project choice and the allocation of resources have been dominated since the 1970s by **social cost–benefit analysis**. Social cost–benefit analysis is really the public analogue or equivalent of the **present value method** of private investment appraisal, but it has to take many things into account, which adds to its complexity. The technique is recommended for the appraisal of publicly financed investment projects in order to allocate resources in a way that is most profitable to society, recognizing that the market prices of goods and factors of production do not necessarily reflect their social value and costs, respectively, and, given that society is concerned with the *future* level of consumption as well as the present, the level of current saving may be suboptimal.

In this chapter we first distinguish between the financial, economic and social appraisal of projects. **Financial appraisal** is concerned with the financial benefits and costs of projects at market prices. We show how the net present value of a project is calculated. **Economic appraisal** adjusts the costs and benefits at market prices to reflect their social values, and takes into account the indirect effects that a project may have on the economy as well. We discuss the various divergences between market prices and social values; how the economic prices of traded and non-traded goods may be calculated; how the economic (or social) prices of factors of production may be calculated (with emphasis on the shadow wage), and how the social rate of discount may be derived. **Social appraisal** has to do with the distributional consequences of project choices, both inter-temporal (over time) and intra-temporal (that is, between groups at a point in time).

In making calculations, the question arises of what prices to use (domestic or world), and what *numéraire* benefits and costs should be expressed in. We compare two different approaches, called the UNIDO approach and the Little–Mirrlees approach. The UNIDO approach takes consumption as *numéraire* and measures benefits and costs at domestic market prices with adjustments made for divergences between market prices and social values and making domestic and foreign resources comparable using a shadow exchange rate. The Little–Mirrlees approach takes public saving measured in foreign exchange as *numéraire*, and measures all prices at world prices (including the price of non-traded goods).

At the end of the chapter there is a numerical example of how the two approaches are used and the condition for their equivalence.

Project appraisal

When we talk about 'public investment' we are talking mainly about *public infrastructure projects* (such as roads and water supplies) and *public enterprise projects* (such as steel mills, power plants and so on). But there are other categories of state-supported investment where social cost–benefit analysis may be applied, such as private sector projects financed by public credit (for example, small-scale industries financed through state development banks) and private sector projects subject to public control (for example, transport and mining ventures).

When discussing project appraisal there is a distinction to be made between financial, economic and social appraisal.

- **Financial appraisal** has to do with the financial flows generated by the project itself and the direct costs of the project measured at market prices.

- **Economic appraisal** has to do with adjusting costs and benefits to take account of costs and benefits to the economy at large, including the indirect effects of projects that are not captured by the price mechanism.
- **Social appraisal** has to do with the distributional consequences of project choices, both intertemporal (that is, over time) and intratemporal (that is, between groups in society at a point in time).

A typical **project appraisal report** would consist of the following:

- The terms of reference
- An engineering study to see whether the project is technically feasible
- A financial study to ascertain how much the project will cost in budgetary terms, at market prices
- An appraisal of the economic costs and benefits, valuing outputs and inputs at social prices and including secondary impacts on the economy and the effect on the distribution of income
- Details of the administrative requirements of the project
- Conclusions and recommendations.

Project appraisal or project planning must be thought of as a process of decision-making over time, starting with the **identification** of projects (in relation to the planning process, which may have set a target growth rate), and going through **stages** of various **feasibility** studies (for example engineering, financial and so on), then the **investment** phase, and finally **evaluation**. This is the notion of the **project cycle**.

Financial appraisal

We first turn to financial appraisal and consider how to calculate the **net present value** of an investment. The first step in project (investment) appraisal is always to identify the *flows* involved. First there is the investment cost in the initial period. Second, there are the operating costs, for example labour and raw materials. Third, there is the value of the output (sales volume multiplied by price). Fourth, there is the question of the life of the project. The value of the flows must then be **discounted** to obtain their **present value** because everything has an opportunity cost. To have £100 next year is not the same as having £100 at the present, because £100 now could be invested at a rate of interest, say 10 per cent, to give £110 next year. The future and the present are made equivalent by discounting future sums by the rate of interest. The present value (PV) of any future value (FV) in period t is $FV_t/(1+r)^t$, where r is the rate of interest (or discount rate). We can show this with a simple algebraic example: The value of a present sum after 1 year invested at rate, r, is $FV_1 = PV(1+r)$. After 2 years the sum is worth $FV_2 = [PV(1+r)](1+r) = PV(1+r)^2$ and so on. Therefore $FV_t = PV(1+r)^t$, and hence $PV = FV_t/(1+r)^t$.

The NPV formula is then

$$NPV = \sum_{t=0}^{T} \left(\frac{V_t - C_t}{(1+r)^t} \right) - K_0 \qquad (11.1)$$

where K_0 is the initial cost of the project in the base period, V_t is the value of output at time t, C_t are the operating costs at time t, r is the rate of discount and T is the life of the project. If NPV > 0, the project yields a positive return.

Table 11.1 Numerical example of the calculation of NPV

Year (t)	Net cash flow $(V_t - C_t)$		Discount factor $1/(1 + 0.08)^t$	Discounted cash flow
0	−5		−	−5.00
1	2	×	0.926	+1.85
2	2	×	0.857	+1.71
3	2	×	0.794	+1.59
4	2	×	0.735	+1.47
5	2	×	0.681	+1.36
			NPV =	+2.98

Let us give a numerical example of a small shoe factory, the initial cost of which is £5 million and which yields a net cash flow over 5 years of £2 million per annum, with a rate of interest of 8 per cent. Table 11.1 gives the calculation of net present value. The project yields a net present value of £2.98 million.

Economic appraisal

First let us consider the secondary (or indirect) costs and benefits that may arise from public projects, and then consider how to adjust the market prices of goods and services and factors of production in order to take account of their **economic** value to society at large. There are three major indirect effects to consider:

1. First there is the economic impact of the project on the immediate vicinity of the project. Some projects, of course, such as an irrigation scheme, are designed to have an impact on the immediate vicinity, and their benefits would be counted as direct benefits, but other projects will have incidental indirect effects, both positive and negative. A new road, for example, which is designed to cut travel time, may raise output in the immediate vicinity. This is a positive benefit. On the other hand, a new dam to generate electricity may flood arable land and reduce agricultural production. This is a negative indirect effect.
2. Second, there are the price effects upon local markets. If, for example, prices fall as a result of a project, this represents a gain in consumer surplus, and this needs to be added to the value of the project. A new road that reduces supply costs will reduce the price of local supplies; this will represent an indirect benefit of the road.
3. Third, there are the consequences of a project for other sectors that supply inputs to the project. If a project demands more inputs, this is income to the supplier. For example a new dam will require local materials; a new factory will demand steel, and so on. These repercussions need to be taken account of.

Beyond the secondary (or indirect) effects of projects, the market prices of goods produced and the factors of production used may not reflect their value to the economy as a whole. The prices need adjusting to reflect their true economic value to society.

In **economic** appraisal (as opposed to financial appraisal), we now have to redefine the variables in the net present value formula in (11.1) to ascertain whether a project is profitable to society at large.

- V_t is the flow of social benefit **measured at economic (or efficiency) prices**
- C_t is the **social** cost of inputs (measured by opportunity cost)
- r is the **social** rate of discount
- K_0 is the **social** cost of the investment.

A project will be profitable to society if the social benefits of the project exceed the social costs – or, to put it another way, if the net present value of the project to society is greater than zero.

The question is, how should a project's social benefits and costs be measured, and what common unit of account (or *numéraire*) should the benefits and costs be expressed in, given a society's objectives and the fact that it has trading opportunities with the rest of the world so that it can sell and buy outputs and inputs abroad (so that domestic and foreign goods need to be made comparable)? There are two broad approaches to this question.

1. First, benefits and costs may be measured at domestic market prices using consumption as the *numéraire*, with adjustments made for divergences between market prices and social values, and making domestic and foreign resources comparable using a shadow foreign exchange rate. This is sometimes referred to as the **UNIDO approach** (see Dasgupta et al., 1972).
2. Second, benefits and costs may be measured at **world prices** to reflect the true opportunity cost of outputs and inputs (also obviating the need to use a shadow foreign exchange rate), using public saving measured in foreign exchange as the *numéraire* (that is, converting everything into its foreign exchange equivalent). This is referred to as the **Little–Mirrlees approach** (see Little and Mirrlees, 1969, 1974). The fact that foreign exchange is taken as the *numéraire* does not mean that project accounts are necessarily expressed in foreign currency. The unit of account can remain the domestic currency, but the values recorded are the foreign exchange equivalent – that is, how much net foreign exchange is earned.

Before proceeding to contrast the approaches and to look at the problems of measurement, let us consider the important divergences that require correction between the market prices of goods and factors of production and their value to society.

Divergences between market prices and social values

The market prices of goods may not reflect their social value for a number of reasons:

1. First, government-imposed taxes, subsidies, tariffs and controls of various kinds distort free market prices. Opportunity cost must be measured *net* of taxes and subsidies.
2. Second, imperfections in the market will raise prices above the marginal cost of production. Prices set by private monopolists and public utilities may be particularly distorted.
3. Third, the existence of externalities, both positive and negative, will mean that the prices of goods do not reflect their true value to society.

The market prices of factors of production may not reflect their true cost to society – that is, the opportunity cost of using them measured by their marginal product in alternative uses – because:

- Labour's market price in the industrial sector (that is, the industrial wage) is likely to exceed the cost to society of using labour if there is disguised unemployment on the land or in the petty service sector.
- Capital's market price will be below its social cost if it is subsidized.

- Foreign exchange may also be too cheap from a social point of view if the exchange rate (measured as the domestic price of foreign currency) is kept artificially low by exchange controls of one form or another.

The existence of external economies and diseconomies may also cause divergences between the market price of inputs and their social cost. If, for example, a project purchases inputs from decreasing cost industries, the social cost is not equal to the price based on average cost but to the lesser figure of marginal cost.

It is also possible that aggregate saving and investment in an economy is less than socially desirable, but the market does not allow individuals to express a preference for a higher rate of investment and capital accumulation for growth and future welfare. This is another example of the **isolation paradox** – one solution to which is for the government to use a lower social discount rate than the market rate of interest to encourage more investment than if the market rate of interest was used for calculating net present value.

Market prices adjusted for these various divergences and distortions are called **shadow, social, economic** or **accounting** prices. Adjusted market prices for goods we shall call 'economic prices', and adjusted market prices for factors of production (including foreign exchange) we shall call 'shadow prices'.

Economic prices for goods

The first divergence mentioned above requires the economic prices for goods to be found. As already stated, either domestic market prices may be corrected for the various distortions and imperfections, with domestic and foreign goods made comparable using a shadow price of foreign exchange (the UNIDO approach), or goods may be valued at world prices, as recommended by Little and Mirrlees. Doing the latter, it is argued, will give a truer measure of the social valuation of goods than the first alternative of measuring some goods at domestic prices (with adjustments), traded goods at their international price, and then making domestic and foreign goods comparable using a shadow foreign exchange rate that may itself be subject to distortions.

The stimulus to valuing output (and inputs) at world prices (as a measure of true economic benefit) originally came in the context of **import substitution policies** pursued by many developing countries in the 1950s and 1960s, when it became clear that a large number of commercially profitable industries were producing goods at a much higher price than the alternatives available on the international market. At the same time, these industries were high-cost, devoting more resources to new investment than embodied in alternative sources of supply on the world market. It was thought that if a project was analysed at world prices, this would give an indication first of whether it could survive in the long term in the face of international competition, and secondly of whether its output could be obtained more cheaply from international sources.

If world prices are used, the economic price at which to value a project's output is its export price if it adds to exports, or its import price if domestic production leads to a saving in imports. Similarly, on the cost side, the price at which to value a project input is its import price if it has to be imported, or its export price if greater domestic use leads to a reduction in exports.

To give a simple example: suppose the purpose of a project to produce more wheat for domestic use is to reduce wheat imports. The true economic value of wheat output is the border price of imports whatever the domestic price is (that is, what is saved in foreign exchange). The same argument applies if the wheat is exported; its true economic value is its border price; that is, what the foreign exchange will buy in world markets.

For imports, the **border price** corresponds to the amount of foreign currency needed to pay for the good at the border, including cost, insurance and freight (c.i.f.). For exports, the **border price** corresponds to the amount of foreign currency received at the border, free on board (f.o.b.).

However, since projects are not usually located at the border, the prices must be adjusted for handling and transport costs between project locations and the border. This is called **border parity pricing**.

Thus the **economic price of imports** is the c.i.f. price of imports *plus* transport and handling costs, and the **economic price of exports** is the f.o.b. price of exports *minus* transport and handling costs.

The Little–Mirrlees approach of using world prices for measurement presents no major problems when goods are tradable. The problem comes with **non-traded goods**, which by definition do not have world prices. Some method has to be found of converting non-traded goods prices into their foreign exchange equivalent.

Non-traded goods and conversion factors

The method used for converting non-traded goods prices into world prices is to use **conversion factors**. A conversion factor (CF) is the ratio of the economic (or shadow) price to the market price, that is

$$CF = \frac{\text{economic price}}{\text{market price}} \tag{11.2}$$

so that the economic price for a non-traded good is its market price multiplied by the conversion factor.

How are conversion factors derived? The true economic cost of any good is its *marginal cost to society*. In principle, to find the world price of non-traded goods, each good could be decomposed into its traded and non-traded components in successive rounds – backwards through the chain of production. A detailed input–output table would be required for the job to be done properly. By this method, each good would be treated separately and have a specific conversion factor. In practice, however, only special outputs (and inputs) are treated in this way because the procedure is difficult, time consuming and costly. Major non-traded outputs and inputs include roads and railways, electricity and water supplies, buildings and labour.

For most goods, it is convenient to have a **standard conversion factor** (SCF) to convert non-traded goods prices into border (world) prices. What we can show is that the standard conversion factor is equal to the reciprocal of the shadow price of foreign exchange, and if this is so, the Little–Mirrlees and UNIDO approaches to project appraisal amount to the same thing.

The SCF translates domestic prices into border prices (measured at the official exchange rate), that is

$$(SCF)P_d = P_w(OER) \tag{11.3}$$

where P_d is domestic prices, P_w is world prices and OER is the official exchange rate measured as the domestic price of foreign currency. In this sense, the standard conversion factor (SCF) is the reciprocal of the shadow price of foreign exchange (P_F). To show this, from (11.3) we have

$$SCF = \frac{P_w}{P_d}(OER) \tag{11.4}$$

or

$$SCF = \frac{1}{P_d/P_w(OER)} \qquad (11.5)$$

where P_d/P_w is the shadow exchange rate (SER), that is, the price of goods in domestic currency relative to their world prices:

$$SCF = \frac{1}{SER/OER} = \frac{1}{P_F} \qquad (11.6)$$

where SER/OER is the shadow price of foreign exchange (P_F). This means that the standard conversion factor is effectively measured by estimating the shadow price of foreign exchange.

To calculate the shadow price of foreign exchange let us do a simple numerical example for one commodity: a bicycle. Suppose that in India the official exchange rate is 2 rupees per US$, and that the world price of a bicycle is $100. Therefore in India the border price of a bicycle costing $100 is 200 rupees. But suppose the price of the bicycle in India is 250 rupees. According to the formula in (11.5), the standard conversion factor will be $1/(250/200) = 0.8$. Also, the fact that a bicycle for 200 at the official exchange rate sells for 250 rupees indicates that the domestic price of foreign exchange is too low (that is, the currency is overvalued). In other words, the shadow exchange rate is higher than the official exchange rate. For bicycles alone it is 2.5 rupees per dollar. The shadow price of foreign exchange (P_F) is therefore $2.5/2.0 = 1.25$, and we know that the SCF is the reciprocal of P_F, that is, $SCF = 1/P_F = 1/1.25 = 0.8$.

Extending this line of argument to many commodities, the shadow price of foreign exchange may be written as

$$P_F = \sum_{i=1}^{n} f_i \left(\frac{P_{di}}{P_{wi}(OER)} \right) \qquad (11.7)$$

where i is the ith good and f_i are the weights. The SCF is the reciprocal of (11.7).

We can now show that if the SCF is the reciprocal of the shadow price of foreign exchange, the Little−Mirrlees and UNIDO approaches to the social profitability of projects amount to the same thing. Let us give a simple illustration. Suppose we have a project producing exports that uses both foreign and domestic inputs. Using the UNIDO methodology, the net benefit (ignoring discounting) would be estimated as

$$\text{Net benefit} = (SER)(X - M) - D \qquad (11.8)$$

where X is the border price of exports, M is the border price of imported inputs, D is domestic inputs and SER is the shadow exchange rate (assuming the official exchange rate does not accurately reflect the true value of foreign exchange to the economy). Goods are all valued at domestic prices, but revalued by the shadow exchange rate. If the net benefit is greater than zero the project will be acceptable.

In contrast, Little and Mirrlees use world prices so that

$$\text{Net benefit} = (OER)(X - M) - (SCF)D \qquad (11.9)$$

where *OER* is the official exchange rate, and *SCF* is the standard conversion factor which converts the value of domestic inputs into their foreign exchange equivalent and is defined as the ratio of *OER/SER*.

It is clear that the two approaches are equivalent since multiplying (11.8) by *OER/SER* yields (11.9).

Note that if *OER* is less than *SER* because the currency is overvalued, then the standard conversion factor will always be less than unity, and the foreign exchange equivalent of using domestic inputs will be less than their value in domestic prices. This will favour the use of domestic inputs and save foreign exchange.[1]

Traded goods

As far as traded goods are concerned, Little and Mirrlees distinguish three categories:

- Commodities that are being exported and imported with infinite elasticities of demand and supply, respectively
- Commodities traded with less than infinitely elastic demand and supply
- Commodities that are not currently traded but which are potentially tradable if the country adopts optimal trade policies.

For commodities in the first category, in principle the valuation is straightforward. Exports and imports should be valued at border prices, *net* of taxes, tariffs, transport and distribution costs, and so on. If import supply is infinite (the small country assumption), the foreign price of imports will not change as import demand rises. Likewise, if the demand for exports is infinite, the export price will not be affected if more exports are supplied.

For commodities in the second category, the supply of imports can be assumed to be infinite, but the demand for exports may be less than infinite. In this case the foreign exchange impact will be less than the border price times the quantity sold. In other words, marginal revenue is less than price. In this case the economic price of the good is the border price multiplied by $(1 - 1/\eta)$, where η is the price elasticity of demand. If $\eta = \infty$, the economic price is the border price; if $\eta = 1$, the economic price is zero, and if $\eta < 1$, the economic price is negative.

Commodities in the third category that are potentially tradable can be treated as traded goods for all practical purposes.

Shadow prices for factors of production

The second divergence mentioned above between market prices and social values requires the shadow prices of the factors of production to be found. We shall spend some time below considering the Little–Mirrlees derivation of the shadow price of labour, which in many ways is the most important price to calculate. It is through the valuation of labour that projects using domestic inputs as opposed to foreign inputs are encouraged or discouraged. Moreover, as we shall see, the shadow price of labour can take into account *both* the opportunity cost of labour *and* the effect of new projects on saving, if saving is suboptimal. It can thus incorporate distributional considerations over time and between social groups. **In this way, the shadow price of labour bridges economic and social appraisal.** The output forgone from the employment of additional labour on projects and the increased consumption (or lost saving) must, of course, be valued at world prices using the Little–Mirrlees methodology.

The social rate of discount

The choice of discount rate depends on the *numéraire* taken. If consumption is taken as the *numéraire*, the appropriate discount rate is the **consumption rate of interest** (CRI), measured as the rate at which the marginal utility of income declines, which may be approximated by the market rate of interest.

If public saving (measured by foreign exchange) is taken as the *numéraire*, the appropriate discount rate is the rate at which the marginal utility of public saving falls. This rate is termed the **accounting rate of interest** (ARI), which should equal the rate of return on public money. In practice the ARI is determined by trial and error, such that its value does not pass more projects as profitable than the investment budget allows. The alternative would be to take the marginal rate of return on private capital as a measure of opportunity cost, on the grounds that public investment ought to produce benefits at least equal to the rate of return forgone if the resources had been invested privately. This assumes, however, that public and private investment compete for funds.

For the UNIDO and Little–Mirrlees approaches to project appraisal to give the same result, clearly the CRI and the ARI must be equal, which will be the case if the relative valuation of saving compared with consumption stays unchanged. This can be shown as follows. Let U_I be the utility weight of public money (saving) and V_c be the utility weight of consumption. Thus $S = U_I/V_c$ is the relative valuation of saving compared with consumption. It then follows that (taking small rates of change):

$$\frac{dS}{S} = \frac{dU_I}{U_I} - \frac{dV_c}{V_c} = ARI - CRI \qquad (11.10)$$

If S is constant (so that $dS/S = 0$), the accounting rate of interest will equal the consumption rate of interest. If S is falling through time, however, which seems likely as countries get richer, then $dS/S < 0$ and $ARI < CRI$.

The social cost of investment

If investment is wholly at the expense of consumption, the social cost of the investment may be measured by the current sacrifice of consumption, if consumption is the *numéraire*. If investment in one project is partly at the expense of another investment, part of the costs of the sacrifice of consumption is deferred until the time at which the displaced investment would itself have yielded consumption.

If saving expressed in foreign exchange is taken as the *numéraire*, the cost of the investment must be valued at world prices.

A numerical example comparing the Little–Mirrlees and UNIDO approaches, applying (11.1), will be given after we have considered the economic cost of the variable inputs (C_t), the chief input being that of labour. We turn now, therefore, to the important topic of the valuation of labour and determination of the shadow wage rate.

The shadow wage rate[2]

In a dual economy, such as the typical developing country, where the marginal product of labour differs between sectors and in which saving is suboptimal, there are two aspects to the measurement of the social cost of the use of more labour in projects:

- The **opportunity cost of the labour in alternative uses**, which could be the marginal product in agriculture, or perhaps the earnings to be had on the fringe of the industrial sector in the informal service sector (P_A).
- The **present value of the sacrificed saving** that results if an attempt is made to maximize present output by equating the marginal products in the different sectors.

Consider Figure 11.1, which depicts the industrial sector of the economy.

Total output in the economy will be maximized when labour is employed in industry up to the point where the marginal product in industry is equal to that in alternative uses (say, agriculture), that is, up to L_1 in Figure 11.1. But at this employment level the industrial wage exceeds the marginal product of labour, and if all wages are consumed there will be a loss of saving equal to the shaded area. If saving is suboptimal, the optimal shadow wage cannot be the marginal product of labour in alternative uses. Savings will be maximized at employment level L, where the marginal product of labour in industry is exactly equal to the industrial wage, but at the expense of employment and present consumption. No society places an infinite value on saving at the margin. Thus the optimal shadow wage cannot be the industrial wage. Clearly the shadow wage is going to lie somewhere between the limits of the opportunity cost of labour on the one hand, and the industrial wage on the other, depending on the relative valuation of saving and consumption. We may derive the optimal shadow wage by making the cost of using an additional unit of labour equal to the benefits. The social cost of the labour is

$$P_A + (C - m) \tag{11.11}$$

where P_A is the opportunity cost of labour and $(C - m)$ is the *total* net increase in consumption (C is the increase in consumption in industry and $-m$ is the fall in consumption in agriculture as labour migrates).

The social benefit of the labour used on the project is its marginal product (P_I), plus that part of the increase in consumption that is valued, which we may write as $(C - m)/S_o$, where S_o is

Figure 11.1 The optimal shadow wage

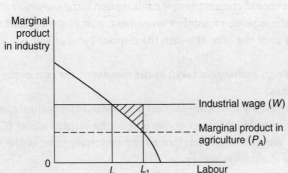

the valuation of saving (or future consumption) relative to present consumption. The total social benefit is thus

$$P_I + \frac{(C - m)}{S_0} \tag{11.12}$$

Labour should be employed up to the point where the social benefit is equal to the social cost; that is, up to the point where

$$P_I + \frac{(C - m)}{S_0} = P_A + (C - m) \tag{11.13}$$

or

$$P_I = P_A + (C - m)\left(1 - \frac{1}{S_0}\right) \tag{11.14}$$

This defines the optimum shadow wage rate (W^*). That is, the shadow wage is equal to the loss of agricultural output (P_A), plus the increase in consumption ($C - m$) less that part of the increase in consumption that is treated as a benefit ($C - m)/S_0$.

Within this framework we can see the two bounds between which the shadow wage will lie. If societies are indifferent between the present and the future, the valuation coefficient of saving relative to consumption will equal unity ($S_0 = 1$) and the shadow wage from (11.14) will be

$$W^* = P_A \tag{11.15}$$

which is the opportunity cost of labour in alternative uses. This is the standard, static result. If the opportunity cost of labour is zero, the shadow wage would be zero. If it is positive, as in Figure 11.1, the shadow wage would give employment level, L_1.

At the other extreme, if societies place an infinite value on the future and none on the present, then the valuation coefficient of saving relative to present consumption would be infinite ($S_0 = 1$) and the shadow wage from (11.14) will be

$$W^* = P_A + (C - m) \tag{11.16}$$

If workers' consumption in agriculture (m) is equal to their marginal product (P_A), and the increased consumption in industry (C) represents increased workers' consumption out of the wage (W),[3] so that $C = W$, then the shadow wage is equal to the industrial wage:

$$W^* = W \tag{11.17}$$

In Figure 11.1, this would give employment level, L, where savings are maximized.

In practice the shadow wage will lie somewhere between P_A and W, depending on the value of S_0. How do we measure the relative value of future versus present consumption? An approach originally suggested by Sen (1968), and embraced by Little and Mirrlees, is to take a time horizon acceptable to society and to calculate the present value of the future consumption gains arising from investment now, relative to the current consumption sacrifice. Thus

$$S_o = \frac{\frac{C_1}{(1+i)} + \frac{C_2}{(1+i)^2} + \ldots + \frac{C_t}{(1+i)^t}}{C_o}$$

$$= \frac{\sum_{t=1}^{T} \frac{C_t}{(1+i)^t}}{C_o} \tag{11.18}$$

The value of S_0 will depend on the marginal product of capital, the length of the time horizon (T) taken and the discount rate (i) chosen. The longer the time horizon and the lower the discount rate, the higher S_0 and the higher the shadow wage rate. If $S_0 = 3$, for example, then assuming P_A and m to be very small, the shadow wage would be approximately two-thirds of the industrial wage. In the Little–Mirrlees approach to project appraisal, the shadow wage is the principal means by which the scarcity of foreign exchange is allowed for. The lower the shadow wage, the greater the use of domestic resources.

A closer examination of the change in consumption in industry and agriculture

Until now it has been assumed that the marginal propensity to consume out of wages is unity and that all 'profits' are saved. It has also been assumed that consumption falls in agriculture to the extent of the migrants' consumption. In practice the marginal propensity to consume out of wages may be less than unity; the marginal propensity to save out of 'profits' may be less than unity; and consumption in agriculture may not fall by the extent of the migrant's consumption. A more general formulation of the shadow wage is required to allow for these possibilities.

The change in consumption in industry as more labour is employed may be written as

$$C = Wc + c^*(P_l - W) \tag{11.19}$$

where W is the industrial wage, $(P_l - W)$ is 'profit' per worker, c is the marginal propensity to consume out of wages and c^* is the marginal propensity to consume out of profits (or government income).

The change in consumption in agriculture as labour is drawn away may be written as

$$m = d(1 - c') \tag{11.20}$$

where d is the consumption of the migrants from agriculture and c' is the propensity to consume of those remaining in agriculture. Clearly if those remaining increase their consumption by as much consumption as the migrants 'release', so that $c' = 1$, agricultural consumption will not fall as labour migrates.

Substituting for C and m in the standard formulation for the shadow wage in (11.14), we obtain

$$P_l = P_A + [Wc + c^*(P_l - W) \tag{11.21}$$
$$- d(1 - c')][1 - (1/S_o)]$$

as the optimal shadow wage (W^*).

The valuation of production forgone and the increase in consumption

Using the Little–Mirrlees approach, the value of agricultural production forgone (P_A) and increased consumption ($C - m$) must be measured at world prices. To value agricultural production forgone, a bundle of goods must be taken to represent the marginal physical product, which must then be priced according to whether they are traded or non-traded, as described earlier. To value the increased consumption also requires taking a bundle of goods, and distinguishing between traded and non-traded goods. To recap, **standard conversion factors** are recommended to reprice non-traded goods, which are calculated as the ratio of the weighted average of the world prices of all exports and imports to the value of their domestic prices (see p. 337).

As we saw earlier, it is generally accepted in the comparison of the Little–Mirrlees and UNIDO approaches to project evaluation that the standard conversion factor (SCF) should be the inverse of the shadow price of foreign exchange (P_F). The reason is that both approaches advocate the use of border prices to value traded goods, so while in the Little–Mirrlees method they are automatically expressed in the *numéraire*, in the UNIDO approach they need to be converted into domestic prices using a shadow exchange rate. The opposite is the case with non-traded goods, and the Little–Mirrlees approach must convert the domestic prices of these goods into border prices using the standard conversion factor. As the one process is the reverse of the other, it is accepted by both methodologies that SCF $= 1/P_F$ (see p. 337).

A numerical calculation of the shadow wage

Now let us do a simple numerical example of the calculation of the shadow wage using the simple formula in (11.14) for illustration:

$$W^* = P_A + (C - m)(1 - 1/S_o)$$

Consider a project in India where the market wage is 70 rupees and all wages are consumed ($C = 70$). The marginal product in agriculture is 10 rupees ($P_A = 10$), and the worker consumed 10 rupees of output in agriculture before working on the project ($m = 10$). All goods are non-traded and the standard conversion factor is 0.8. The relative valuation of future to present consumption is 4 ($S_o = 4$). Therefore, the shadow wage is:

$$W^* = [10 + (70 - 10)(1 - ¼)]0.8 = 44 \text{ rupees}$$

Note that all the values for the lost output in agriculture and net increases in consumption are multiplied by the standard conversion factor of 0.8 to measure the foreign exchange equivalent of using more labour. The market price of labour is 70 rupees but the shadow price is only 44 rupees. This will encourage the use of more domestic labour on projects and save foreign exchange.

There are two additional considerations. The first is that more employment on projects in urban areas may bring additional migration from the rural sector, so that the loss of output in alternative uses is greater than the marginal product of the person employed. For example, if five extra jobs pulled in ten extra people, the loss of output would be $2P_A$ – double the marginal product of labour in agriculture. In this case, the shadow wage would be 52 rupees.

The second consideration is the distributional consequences of project choice to which we now turn. We will see that the formula for the shadow wage changes when distributional weights are included to take account of who gains from the project – the rich or the poor.

Social appraisal

Distributional considerations in project appraisal[4]

So far, we have ignored the effect of project choice on the distribution of income. The distributional consequences of projects can be included in the estimation of the shadow wage by altering the valuation of present to future consumption $(1/S_o)$ – increasing the value if the consumption gain is to the poor, and decreasing the value if the consumption gain is to the rich. **The distribution-weighted relative valuation of present to future consumption** may be thought of as being composed of two parts. The first is the value of a marginal increase in consumption to someone at a level of consumption, C, divided by the value of a marginal increase in consumption accruing to someone at the average level of consumption, $\bar{C}$. Let us denote this as

$$\frac{W_c}{W_{\bar{c}}}(=d) \tag{11.22}$$

The second part is the value of a marginal increase in consumption to someone at the average level of consumption divided by the value of a marginal increase in public income (saving). Let us denote this as

$$\frac{W_{\bar{c}}}{W_g} = \frac{1}{S_o} \tag{11.23}$$

Therefore the distribution-weighted relative valuation of present versus future consumption is

$$\frac{W_c}{W_{\bar{c}}} \cdot \frac{W_{\bar{c}}}{W_g} = \frac{d}{S_o} \tag{11.24}$$

The ratio d/S_o can be thought of as the trade-off between raising the consumption levels of the poor and accelerating economic growth.

Up to now it has been implicitly assumed that $d = 1$, as if it is the average person who always gains from projects or that the gains to all individuals are valued equally. If greater weight is given to the consumption gains of the poor $(d > 1)$ than to the rich $(d < 1)$, however, it can be seen from (11.21) or (11.14) that the substitution of d/S_o for $1/S_o$ will alter the shadow wage. A high d will lower the shadow price of labour and favour projects that provide consumption gains to the poor, and a low d will raise the shadow price of labour and favour projects that benefit the wealthy.

The question is, how is d determined? To derive distribution weights, a utility function must be specified. One possible utility function, with the underlying assumption of diminishing marginal utility of consumption, is

$$U_c = C^{-n} = \frac{1}{C^n} \tag{11.25}$$

where C is consumption and n is a parameter of the utility function. n is a reflection of the rate at which the marginal utility of consumption decreases, and is measured as the intertemporal elasticity of substitution between present and future consumption. The higher that n is, the higher the rate of diminishing marginal utility.

The question is, how should the value of n be decided? This is not an easy question to answer. Squire and Van der Tak (1975) say that for most governments, n would probably centre around 1. One justification for this would be to make the simple assumption that if a poor person's income is only one-half of the average level of income, then a dollar increase in income to the poor person is twice more valuable. It can be seen from (11.25) that if the utility of the consumption of a person with twice as much consumption as another person is only one-half, then $n = 1$. So, if $n = 1$, the utility of consumption for a person with double consumption of another $(C = 2)$ is one-half. If $n = 2$, the utility of consumption for a person with double the consumption of another is one-quarter, and so on. To compare the value of consumption to different people (or groups), some standard needs to be taken, and it makes sense to take the average. Thus

$$d = \frac{U_c}{U_{\bar{c}}} = \left(\frac{\bar{C}}{C}\right)^n \tag{11.26}$$

where $\bar{C}$ is the average level of consumption (and utility and consumption at the margin are inversely related).

Equation (11.26) says, for example, that the marginal utility of consumption to someone with a level of consumption of half the average $(0.5\bar{C})$ is $(2)^n$. If $n = 1$, $d = 2$. The lower the level of consumption relative to the average, and the higher that n is, the higher the distributional weight will be, and the greater the egalitarian bias in project selection. Table 11.2 shows how the value of the distribution weight changes with n and $\bar{C}/C$, for representative values of n and $\bar{C}/C$ with $(\bar{C} = 100)$. The values of $\bar{C}$ and n are not project-specific, but country-specific, and must be provided by the planning office.

Having discussed the determination of d in (11.24), we must return to the valuation of S_o. We have already discussed one method of valuing S_o (see (11.18)). We now have some independent check of whether the value of S_o is plausible. One test is to estimate, at the chosen value of S_o, the value of $\bar{C}/C$ at which the government is indifferent between its own income (saving) and consumption, so that the costs and benefits of increased consumption are assumed to be equal and the shadow price of labour is measured simply as the efficiency price or opportunity cost. In other words, what is the value of $\bar{C}/C$ at which $d/S_o = 1$, so that $1 - d/S_o = 0$?

If S_o is assumed to be 4, then d must equal 4. With $n = 1$ (say), this required value for d implies an existing level of consumption equal to one-quarter of the average (see Table 11.2). In this case the value of S_o used by the planners would imply that the government is indifferent between

Table 11.2 Values of the consumption distribution weight (d) for marginal changes in consumption

At existing consumption level (C)	At relative consumption level ($\bar{C}/C$)	Values of distribution weight (d) And when n equals				
		0	0.5	1.0	1.5	2
10	10.00	1.00	3.16	10.00	31.62	100.00
25	4.00	1.00	2.00	4.00	8.00	16.00
50	2.00	1.00	1.41	2.00	2.83	4.00
75	1.33	1.00	1.15	1.33	1.53	1.77
100	1.00	1.00	1.00	1.00	1.00	1.00
150	0.66	1.00	0.81	0.66	0.54	0.44
300	0.33	1.00	0.57	0.33	0.19	0.11
600	0.17	1.00	0.41	0.17	0.07	0.03
1000	0.10	1.00	0.32	0.10	0.03	0.01

Source: Squire and Van der Tak, 1975.

additions to its own income and additions to the consumption of those currently consuming one-quarter of the average level. This may not seem plausible in the light of other policies. For example, the government may be distributing various forms of subsidies at this level of consumption, which suggests it values consumption more highly than public income or saving. In this case it should lower S_o and put a higher value on present consumption to give a lower shadow wage. An S_o that implied some starvation level of consumption could be immediately ruled out.

If we go to our numerical calculation of the shadow wage, we can now replace $1/S_o$ with d/S_o. If $d = 4$ and $S_o = 4$, then the shadow wage becomes simply $W^* = 10 \times 0.8 = 8$ rupees compared with a market wage of 70 rupees. Attaching a high value to the benefit of the project to the poor has made the social use of labour virtually costless and therefore much more profitable to undertake from society's point of view.

The equivalence of the Little–Mirrlees formulation of the shadow wage and the UNIDO approach

In the UNIDO approach, the optimal shadow wage is given by

$$W^* = P_A + s^*(P^{INV} - 1)W \tag{11.27}$$

where s^* is the propensity to save out of public income, W is the wage and P^{INV} measures the price of investment in terms of consumption. Assuming that the propensity to save out of public income is unity ($s^* = 1$) and all wages are consumed, (11.27) may be written as

$$W^* = P_A + (P^{INV} - 1)C \tag{11.28}$$

where $(P^{INV} - 1)C$ represents the *present* value of aggregate consumption lost (assuming $P^{INV} > 1$) because of the increased consumption of workers, which reduces saving for future consumption.

Now, for the two approaches to give equivalent cash flows, whichever *numéraire* is taken, P^{INV} must equal S_o so that (11.28) may be written as

$$W^* = P_A + (S_o - 1)C \tag{11.29}$$

Now the Little–Mirrlees formulation of the shadow wage from (11.14) is

$$W^* = P_A + (C - m)\left(1 - \frac{1}{S_o}\right)$$

which, assuming that $P_A = m$, may be written as

$$W^* = \frac{P_A}{S_o} + C\left(1 - \frac{1}{S_o}\right) \tag{11.30}$$

Comparing (11.30) with the UNIDO (11.29), it can be seen that the UNIDO formula is S_o times the Little–Mirrlees formula because the UNIDO *numéraire* is $1/S_o$ times as valuable as the Little–Mirrlees *numéraire*.

The calculation of the shadow wage will be different according to the two approaches (assuming that $P^{INV} = S_o$) only to the extent that they classify goods into traded and non-traded in a different way and that the standard conversion factor (SCF) to convert non-traded goods into world prices is not the reciprocal of the shadow price of foreign exchange (P_F) to convert traded goods prices into domestic prices.

Is it worth valuing all goods at world prices?

The justification in the Little–Mirrlees approach for valuing all goods at world prices is that it avoids the use of a shadow exchange rate in order to value in a single currency some goods that are measured at world prices (traded goods) and others that are measured at domestic prices (non-traded goods). The question is: how much trouble is it worth to avoid using a shadow foreign exchange rate? Some economists feel it is a lot of trouble for doubtful accuracy because of the need to disaggregate non-traded goods into their traded and non-traded inputs, which requires input–output data that do not exist in many cases. It may be just as accurate, it is argued, to convert the prices of non-traded goods into a single currency by the exchange rate appropriately adjusted for under- or over-valuation. Baldwin (1972) concludes his layman's guide to Little–Mirrlees by saying that 'their essential ideas are not new and their new ideas are not essential . . . the world pricing of non-traded inputs that has caused so much argument is a tempest in a teapot. I doubt it will catch on and it will not matter much if it doesn't'! Baldwin's first prediction has not proved accurate. There are now many case studies that have used the Little–Mirrlees methodology and students are encouraged to read some for themselves.[5] In his second prediction, Baldwin may be right. Below we give a simple hypothetical example of the application of the UNIDO and Little–Mirrlees approaches, assuming that the standard conversion factor and the shadow price of foreign exchange are the reciprocal of each other.

The application of the Little–Mirrlees and UNIDO approaches to project appraisal

Assume that world prices are measured in dollars and domestic prices in rupees (R), that the official exchange rate is 1 rupee per dollar, that the shadow exchange rate is 1.25 rupees per dollar, that the shadow price of foreign exchange (P_F) = 1.25 and that the standard conversion factor for converting non-traded goods prices into world prices is 0.8, that is, 1/1.25. Assume further that:

- All output is exported with an annual value of $3,000
- The cost of the investment has a foreign component of $1,000 and a local (non-traded) component of 1,000 rupees
- There are traded inputs of $1,000 and non-traded inputs of 1,000 rupees
- The accounting rate of interest is equal to the consumption rate of interest.

We can now apply our net present value formula in (11.1) using the two approaches. Remember that with the Little–Mirrlees approach we convert world prices into domestic prices at the official exchange rate and the prices of non-traded goods into world prices using the standard conversion factor of 0.8. With the UNIDO approach we convert all values at world prices ($) into domestic prices using the shadow exchange rate of 1.25. We shall do the analysis for three periods only (see Table 11.3).

We can see that the results obtained using the Little–Mirrlees approach and those obtained using the UNIDO approach differ only to the extent that the shadow exchange rate is different from the actual exchange rate. To obtain NPV the net benefit streams in years 1 and 2 must be

Table 11.3   Comparison of the Little–Mirrlees and UNIDO approaches to project appraisal

	Little–Mirrlees				UNIDO		
	Year 0	Year 1	Year 2		Year 0	Year 1	Year 2
Cost of investment (K)							
1. Foreign component	R1,000			1. Foreign cost converted into rupees at shadow exchange rate of 1.25	R1,250		
2. Local component = 1,000 rupees × conversion factor of 0.8	R800			2. Local component	R1,000		
Input costs (C)							
1. Traded inputs		R1,000	R1,000	1. Traded inputs converted into rupees at shadow exchange rate of 1.25		R1,250	R1,250
2. Non-traded inputs = 1,000 rupees × conversion factor of 0.8		R800	R800	2. Non-traded inputs		R1,000	R1,000
Benefit flow (V)		R3,000	R3,000	Benefit flow in rupees		R3,750	R3,750
Net benefit	R−1,800	R1,200	R1,200	Net benefit	R−2,250	R1,500	R1,500

discounted by the appropriate discount factors, which we assume here to be the same in both approaches. Assuming a discount rate of 10 per cent we have the following:

Using Little–Mirrlees $\text{NPV} = \dfrac{\text{R1,200}}{(1.1)} + \dfrac{\text{R1,200}}{(1.1)^2} - \text{R1,800} = \text{R282.6}$

Using UNIDO $\text{NPV} = \dfrac{\text{R1,500}}{(1.1)} + \dfrac{\text{R1,500}}{(1.1)^2} - \text{R2,250} = \text{R353.2}$

The Little–Mirrlees result would yield the same rupee value if the actual exchange rate of dollars into rupees was equal to the shadow exchange rate of 1.25.

Little and Mirrlees (1974) conclude their own evaluation of the two approaches by saying:

> there is no doubt that the two works adopt basically the same approach to project evaluation. Both treatments single out the values of foreign exchange, savings and unskilled labour, as crucial sources of a distorted price mechanism. Both go on to calculate accounting prices which will correct these distortions, and both carry out these corrections in an essentially similar manner. Both advocate DCF (Discounted Cash Flow) analysis and the use of PSVs (Present Social Values).

Finally, both works advocate making explicit allowance for inequality and distributional considerations in project choice through manipulation of the shadow wage. In the UNIDO approach this is done by giving greater weight to the increased consumption of the poor than of the rich, which reduces the present value of lost consumption. In the Little–Mirrlees approach distributional con-siderations are taken account of by working out the value of S_o taking account of the standard of living of the particular extra workers employed, as described above.

Summary

- Governments need techniques to evaluate the social profitability of projects they undertake. The technique they use is called social cost–benefit analysis.
- Social cost–benefit analysis is the public equivalent of private net present value calculations to measure the private profitability of projects, but in which market prices of goods and factors of production are adjusted to reflect social values and the indirect effect of projects, as well as distributional consequences.
- There are two main approaches to the measurement of benefits and costs. One is the UNIDO approach which uses consumption as *numéraire* and adjusts market prices for various dis-tortions, making domestic and foreign resources comparable using a shadow exchange rate. The other approach is the Little–Mirrlees method, which takes public saving measured in for-eign exchange as *numéraire* and measures everything at world prices. For non-traded goods (including labour), a standard conversion factor is used to estimate their world price.
- The social (or shadow) price given to labour is of great importance because it is a major cost of projects and will determine the extent of domestic resource use. The lower the shadow wage, the greater the use of domestic resources, and the more foreign exchange saved.
- Distributional consequences of projects can be included in the estimation of the shadow wage by altering the valuation of present to future consumption – increasing the value if the con-sumption gain of the project is to the poor (giving the project a higher profitability) and decreasing the value if the consumption gain is to the rich.
- The UNIDO and Little–Mirrlees approaches to the appraisal of public projects can be shown to be equivalent if the standard conversion factor in the Little–Mirrlees approach to reprice non-traded goods to world prices is the reciprocal of the shadow exchange rate in the UNIDO approach to make domestic and foreign resources comparable.

Chapter 11	Discussion questions

1 What is the meaning of social cost–benefit analysis?

2 Explain how the costs and benefits of a project to society may differ from the costs and benefits to the private entrepreneur.

3 Why are the future net benefits of a project discounted?

4 Why do Little and Mirrlees choose to measure the net benefits of a project in terms of saving rather than consumption?

5 Why do Little and Mirrlees measure benefits and costs of a project using world prices rather than domestic prices?

6 How is it possible to measure non-traded goods at world prices?

| Chapter 11 | Discussion questions – *continued* |

7   What is the relationship between the standard conversion factor and the shadow price of foreign exchange?

8   What factors need to be taken into account when measuring the shadow wage (or the social opportunity cost) of labour?

9   Evaluate the relative merits of the Little–Mirrlees and UNIDO approaches to social cost–benefit analysis.

10 How would you measure the relative value of investment (or future consumption) compared with present consumption?

Notes

1. The domestic inputs referred to are goods not labour. We shall consider the valuation of labour below, p. 340.
2. The discussion here takes the approach of Little and Mirrlees, the origin of which can be found in Sen (1968) and Little (1961). See also Little and Mirrlees (1974) and Squire and Van der Tak (1975). See below, p. 346, for the equivalence of the Little–Mirrlees and UNIDO approaches.
3. Implicitly assuming for the time being that the propensity to consume out of profits is zero and the propensity to consume of workers out of wages is unity. We shall relax this assumption below, p. 342.
4. This section relies heavily on the exposition given in Squire and Van der Tak (1975) and Brent (1998).
5. See, for example, Lal (1980), Scott et al. (1976), Stewart (1978) and the Symposium in the *Oxford Bulletin of Economics and Statistics*, February 1972.

Websites on project appraisal

OECD Development Centre www.oecd.org/department
UNIDO www.unido.org

12

DEVELOPMENT AND THE ENVIRONMENT*

- Introduction
- A model of the environment and economic activity
- The market-based approach to environmental analysis
- Externalities
- Common property rights
- The discount rate
- The harvesting of renewable resources
- Non-renewable resources
- Other environmental values
- Measuring environmental values
- National income accounting
- Risk and uncertainty
- Economic growth and the environment
- Sustainable development
- Natural capital, equity and environmental values

- Economic thought and the environment
- Climate change and the Stern Review
- Climate change and the poor
- International agencies, agreements and the environment
- Summary
- Discussion questions
- Notes
- Websites on the environment

* This chapter has been written by my colleague Dr John Peirson. He is grateful to Michael Common and the late Douglas Peirson for helpful comments.

Introduction

The environment is vital to supporting life, absorbing waste and providing inputs for production. Since the 1960s, there has been increasing concern about the effects of economic activity on the environment. In particular it has been argued that economic growth has caused serious environmental damage and that the current state of the environment will constrain future economic development. For example, it is now widely, but not universally, accepted that recent economic development has led to climate changes, and that changes will, unless adapted to, seriously disrupt economic activity and society in the future. The poor in developing countries are often dependent on the natural environment for their livelihood, and even their continued existence. Thus, damage to the environment and the relationship between the environment and the economy are often thought to be of more importance to developing than to developed countries. Figure 12.1 shows how selected environmental indicators vary with economic development, as measured by per capita income. This chapter provides an introduction to the economic analysis of the relationship between the environment (including the climate), development and the economy.

First, a simple model is developed that explains the services the environment provides for economic activity and the effects of the economy on the environment.

Second, the market-based approach to analysing the interactions of the environment and the economy is examined. This approach emphasizes the efficient use of the environment and considers market failures to be the main, and perhaps the only, cause of market economies' difficulties in allowing for environmental concerns in economic development. Drawing on the material on social cost–benefit analysis in Chapter 11, it is shown how this approach can be used to provide valuations of environmental services and to improve the efficiency of the use of the environment. The neoclassical analysis of equity within and between generations is considered and its importance in the context of the environment is examined.

Figure 12.1 Environmental indicators at different country income levels

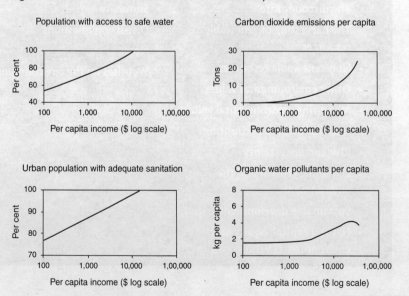

Note: The estimates are based on cross-country data for the year 2000.

Source: World Bank, 2004.

Third, the concept of **sustainable development** is explained. This idea defines forms of development that meet the needs of the present generation whilst maintaining the potential to meet the needs of future generations.

Fourth, there is a discussion of the recent **Stern Review on climate change**, and the effect of climate change on the poor.

Finally, there is a brief review of how environmentalists, economists and international agencies have approached the analysis of the environment, climate change and the economy.

A model of the environment and economic activity

There are many different models of the relationship between the environment and the economy. The simple model depicted in Figure 12.2 illustrates the four functions of the environment in supporting economic activity and the effects of this activity on the environment.[1] These four functions are life support, supply of natural resources, absorption of waste products and supply of amenity services. The economy is represented in Figure 12.2 by households consuming goods and services and firms producing with natural resources provided by the environment, with labour and man-made capital provided by households.

The environment provides a **biological, chemical and physical system** that enables human life to exist. This system includes, for example, the atmosphere, river systems, the fertility of the soil and the diversity of plant and animal life. These environmental services are consumed by households and are essential to life. Large reductions in these services, for example through major climate change, would have catastrophic consequences for life.

The environment provides **raw materials and energy** for economic production and household activity. These natural resources are either renewable, for example forests and fisheries, or non-renewable, for example minerals. Renewable resources can be used in a sustainable manner, though excessive use or mismanagement can result in the complete loss of the resources, for

Figure 12.2   A simple model of the relationships between the economy and the environment

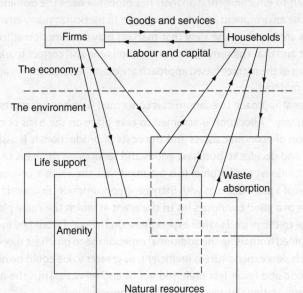

example desertification following deforestation. The ability to use renewable resources sustainably and to increase the stock of renewable resources is represented in Figure 12.2 by the flow from firms to natural resources. However, the use of a non-renewable resource reduces the finite stock of the resource forever.

The **waste products** of economic and household activity are absorbed by the environment. This sink function allows some of this waste to be disposed of safely. However, there are certain wastes that are difficult or impossible for the environment to dispose of safely. For example, the global warming gas, carbon dioxide, is captured through the growth of forests and absorption in the oceans. Deforestation and physical limits to absorption in the oceans mean that the absorptive capacity of these processes has been reduced. Consequently, because of the effect of rising levels of carbon dioxide on climate change, it has been argued that the world economy has to change through reducing carbon dioxide emissions, seeking alternative means of capturing these emissions and adapting to climate change.

The environment also provides **amenity services**: for example, natural beauty and space for outdoor pursuits, which are consumed, but are not crucial to the continued existence of life.

Parts of the environment may serve more than one function: for example the oceans are important in determining the life-support systems provided by the global and microclimates; they are sources of many minerals and other resources; they assimilate many different wastes; and they provide the space and opportunity for marine pastimes. Thus, in Figure 12.2, the four blocks representing the different functions of the environment overlap. The functions of the environment may be competitive. For example, excessive discharges of waste materials into the oceans will reduce their capacity to provide a habitat for fish stocks. Alternatively, environmental functions can be complementary. For example, appropriate forestry policies can provide a sustainable source of timber (a natural resource function), reduce soil erosion (an improvement in the life-support function) and capture carbon dioxide emissions (a waste absorption function).

The market-based approach to environmental analysis

The market-based approach to environmental analysis has probably been the dominant view of the relationship between the environment and the economy.[2] In particular, many environmental policies and much analysis are based on the view that markets may not function efficiently with regard to the environment and that the state has a duty to intervene and correct market failures. The underlying assumptions of the market-based approach are examined and various applications to the environment are considered.

The market or neoclassical approach to economics is concerned with how scarce resources are allocated in a market economy.[3] Allocation is assumed to take place on the basis of consumers' preferences, the distribution of economic assets and the costs of production. It is assumed that each consumer is rational and decides to purchase goods and services on the basis of prices and economic assets, which include labour income. It is assumed that the value a consumer places on additional consumption of a good declines with increasing consumption. Economic rationality dictates that consumption of a good continues up to the point at which the value placed on an additional unit is just equal to the price. Further expenditure on the good would be inefficient as greater value could be obtained from using the additional expenditure to purchase more preferred goods and services. Similarly, less expenditure is inefficient, as greater value could be obtained by purchasing more of the good and fewer less preferred goods and services. Thus the neoclassical model assumes that economic rationality gives efficiency in consumption.

The neoclassical view assumes that firms are profit maximizers. This implies that firms minimize costs. This gives efficiency in production.

Finally, it is assumed that competition among firms forces them to charge prices that are equal to their marginal costs of production. As consumption decisions are based on prices, the equality between prices and marginal costs means that these decisions are based upon the marginal costs of production. This ensures efficiency between consumption and production.

The neoclassical view has various important implications for the analysis of the relationship between the environment and the economy. First, it is implicitly assumed that the value of consumption is determined by the individual consuming the good. The value of consumption is not determined by the state or some higher authority. Additionally, it is assumed that individual consumers and producers do not consider the effects of their decisions on other economic agents. Consequently, there is no difference between private and social costs or private and social benefits. Second, economic rationality implies that the value of marginal consumption of a good or service can be measured by price. Third, the neoclassical analysis of the market is based upon considering small changes in consumption and production. This view extends to the neoclassical view of the environment. Fourth, the outcome of a market economy, in terms of prices, quantities and the distribution of economic welfare, depends on the initial distribution of economic assets. Different distributions or reallocations of assets give different outcomes. It is frequently pointed out that under certain conditions the operation of the market may be efficient, but it may not be equitable. It may be possible to assess the efficiency of a market economy in an objective manner, but evaluation of the equity of a market outcome is a value judgement.

Externalities

The idea of externalities can be used to analyse many, but not all, types of environmental degradation. Externalities occur when the actions of one economic agent affect other economic agents and the actions are not controlled through the operation of the market. Externalities have two related causes: lack of individual property rights, and jointness in either production or consumption (Baumol and Oates, 1988). Individual property rights are exercised over goods, services and factors of production and allow markets to function efficiently. With a complete set of individual property rights, all the effects of an action are controlled by the market, since consumption of a good or service and use of a factor require payment to the owner. Beneficial or positive externalities are likely to be undersupplied by a market, and negative externalities are likely to be oversupplied. For an externality to continue to exist, it is usually presumed that jointness in either production or consumption is involved.

An example of environmental externalities and economic development can be seen in the building and operation of the Manantali and Diama hydroelectric dams in Mali.[4] These dams generate cheap electricity which is distributed to the countries of Mali, Senegal and Mauritania. Downstream from the dams, the annual floods have been reduced and this has decreased agricultural productivity. Additionally, the elimination of salt water intrusion through the building of these dams has led to an increased incidence of bilharzia and other health problems. Thus, the building and operation of these hydroelectric dams has imposed external costs on those living and working downstream of the dams.

These (negative) externalities are caused by jointness in production of electricity. At the same time as electricity is being generated, the water system is being altered and this causes health and productivity effects. The economic cause of the externalities is that no markets exist in

Figure 12.3 Marginal benefits and environmental costs of a dam

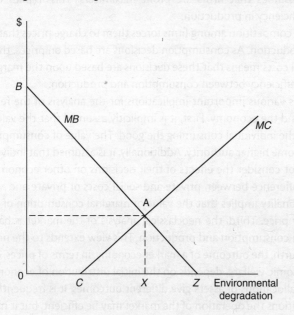

the management of water systems. In particular, there are not clear, legally enforceable rights to the ownership and services of the water system downstream. A simple model is developed in Figure 12.3 of the interests of the electricity generators and the downstream population. The downstream environmental degradation by the generators produces a benefit to the economy as it allows the production of electricity. This is denoted by the marginal benefit curve MB (measured in dollars) and is assumed to be downward sloping. The downward slope can be justified by a lower price being obtained for the sale of electricity as more is produced.

The environmental effects are mostly negative and are represented by an upward sloping marginal cost of environmental degradation curve (MC). There is a threshold effect below which there is no environmental damage as the environment can absorb a minor change in the water system without any cost. The curve then slopes upwards as the environment has difficulty in coping with the increased environmental degradation.

The neoclassical view is that there is an optimal level of environmental degradation at which the marginal benefit is equal to the marginal cost, point X in Figure 12.3. Whether this level of degradation is small or large depends on the shape of the marginal benefit and cost functions. This conclusion considers environmental effects purely from the point of view of efficiency. However, it should be remembered that outcome X may be efficient, but if the costs imposed on the inhabitants are relatively large, the resulting distribution of welfare may not be desirable.

The operation of a market economy is unlikely to lead to an efficient outcome. The downstream inhabitants' environment is being degraded by the actions of the generators. In an economy with a complete set of individual property rights over all economic assets, the inhabitants or the generators would own the property rights to the environment. If the inhabitants owned the rights, the generators would have to pay to be allowed to degrade the environment. In the case of the generators owning the rights, the inhabitants would have to pay the generators to restrict environmental degradation. In reality, such property rights are likely to be ill-defined, particularly across national boundaries. It might be expected that no market controls this environmental degradation. Generators are likely to continue to degrade the environment until the marginal benefit to them of continuing production is zero, point Z in Figure 12.3.

This analysis is one of **market failure.** A conventional reaction to market failure is to suggest the intervention of the state to secure a more efficient outcome. There are four feasible policies that have been suggested as solutions to this type of externality problem: **Pigovian taxes and subsidies** (named after the famous Cambridge economist A. C. Pigou); **Coasian bargains** (named after the Nobel Prize-winning economist Ronald Coase); **marketable permits**; and **administrative action and legislation** (see Perman et al., 2003).

The **Pigovian tax solution** imposes an environmental-use tax on the generators of the value of the marginal cost of degradation at the point of the optimal outcome X. This forces the generators to take account of the costs they impose on the inhabitants. This is shown in Figure 12.4, where the generators face a new marginal benefit of environmental degradation schedule (MB′) that includes the tax. Generators will, out of self-interest, choose the efficient level of degradation. A Pigovian subsidy could be given to generators to reduce environmental degradation and a similar solution occurs.

However, the Pigovian solution suffers from a number of problems. First, it is very difficult to quantify and value the costs and benefits of environmental degradation (this point will be discussed further later in this chapter, p. 364). The benefits and costs are not likely to be uniform across different dams, and this implies the complication of different tax rates. Second, many of the downstream inhabitants are not part of the cash economy and the state is unlikely to be able to tax and regulate generators or afford the cost of subsidies.

The **Coasian bargain solution** assumes that individual property rights are established and economic agents bargain an efficient outcome. If individual property rights over the environment are given to the inhabitants, then generators have an incentive to bargain and pay to be allowed the right to degrade the environment, as their marginal benefit exceeds the inhabitants' marginal cost at the origin in Figure 12.3. The potential efficiency gains of this bargaining are

Figure 12.4 Taxation, marginal benefits and costs of a dam

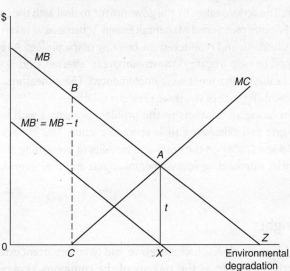

represented by the area *ABC*. Similarly, if the generators are given the property right, there are incentives for the inhabitants to pay the generators to reduce degradation from the point Z. The Coasian solution suffers from the major problem of how property rights are established. Additionally, there are incentives for individuals to **free ride** on the contributions that others make to reduce externalities. It is difficult to see how bargains can be enforced when there are many inhabitants. Finally, in many cases the transactions costs of negotiating a Coasian bargain may be high and are likely to prevent such solutions from emerging.

In the real world, it may be rare for Coasian bargains to occur as solutions to environmental problems. **The Global Environment Facility** could be interpreted as such an example. This Facility is a partnership of many countries and international organizations to address global environmental issues, and receives donations from the countries. The Facility provides grants to countries to address such global problems as climate change and pollution of international waters. The Facility was charged with funding mechanisms to help achieve the Climate Change and Biodiversity Conventions of the 1992 Rio Earth Summit.

The issuing of **marketable permits** that give the bearers the right to pollute is a potentially elegant and efficient means of solving the problem of pollution and externalities such as global warming and gas emissions. The size of the issue of permits directly controls the level of total pollution. Potential polluters have to decide whether to reduce their pollution or use their own or purchased permits. This should result in the set level of pollution being obtained at the least cost. Tietenberg and Johnstone's review (2004) shows that the use of different types of tradable permit schemes has increased and they are often regarded as a valuable policy tool. The tradable permit scheme 'cap and trade' lies behind the operation of the **Kyoto Protocol** to reduce global warming gas emissions. The operation of tradable permit schemes does not have universal support, however. There has been little investigation of the use of schemes by developing countries, and experience suggests problems with their operation and outcomes; for example, the European Commission in 2008 responded to criticism of the European Carbon Trading System by implementing major changes.

The fourth solution to the externality problem is **command and control.** This approach takes action to ensure that the externality is reduced to a lower level. The usual examples of this solution are fixed standards backed up by legal sanctions, for example maximum allowable levels of environmental degradation. The actions taken by the government to deal with the environmental problems caused by the previously mentioned Manantali Energy Scheme have taken many forms. The government enforced standards and monitored the building of the project. A reservoir management plan was developed to help irrigate downstream areas, affected land was purchased, people were resettled and health programmes were implemented. These measures are practical, but do not have the theoretical elegance of the three previous solutions.

The one major problem facing all solutions to the problem of dealing with externalities is assessing their physical nature and calculating their economic value. This is discussed later in the section on the Stern Review (2006) on the costs and benefits of preventing climate change. In particular, the uncertainties surrounding environmental effects and their economic value are discussed.

Common property rights

The common ownership of a renewable resource is likely to lead to an important externality. Such circumstances are frequently referred to as **the tragedy of the commons**. However, Dasgupta

(1982) has forcefully argued that there has been considerable confusion over the economic analysis of this problem.[5] The analysis is considered in terms of the example of cattle farmers grazing their animals on commonly owned land. The rational individual farmer will use common land without regard to the cost this use imposes on other farmers. This behaviour is a negative externality and is inefficient. The cost imposed on other farmers is the exhaustion of the fertility of the soil. This effect will decrease the future value of the resource to farmers. In this sense, the problem of the commons is an **intertemporal externality**. However, it is not the case that use of the common property resource of grazing land necessarily destroys the usefulness of the land. The extent of overgrazing depends on the private cost of rearing animals, their market value and the ability of the land to support a large number of animals. However, appropriate cooperative action by farmers to reduce overgrazing would increase the economic welfare of farmers as a group.

The discount rate

Degradation of the environment reduces the supply of environmental services in the future. Economic analysis of the environment requires a means of comparing the benefits and costs of environmental effects in the present and the future. This comparison is usually made through a weighting device called **the discount factor** (see Chapter 11). The practice of discounting environmental costs and benefits has caused much confusion and dispute.

In a neoclassical model of the behaviour of individual economic agents with finite lives, the discount rate is simply the market rate of interest. The level of the market rate of interest is the outcome of the preferences of individuals for present consumption over future consumption and the physical possibilities of transforming present consumption into future consumption. However, even with a set of perfect capital markets, the resulting intertemporal allocation of resources is unlikely to be socially efficient for a number of reasons.

First, the outcome of perfect capital markets reflects the preferences and actions of those presently alive. All individuals will eventually die, and they presumably value their own consumption more highly than that of their descendants. This implies the market outcome may underweight the consumption of future generations. It might be argued that the state should decide upon a distribution of economic welfare over time that favours future generations more. Alternatively, it has been argued that technical progress will increase future incomes and fairness requires redistribution from future generations to the present. However, it is unclear how the state can easily decide which distribution should be preferred (see Hanley and Spash, 1993).

Second, even with regard to the preferences of the present generation, the market outcome may be inefficient. The present generation may wish to save for the benefit of future generations. This can lead to two types of market failure, called the **assurance problem** and the **isolation paradox** (Sen, 1967). Both phenomena are examples of externalities. The assurance problem concerns saving by one individual for future generations, which benefits all other individuals in the present who place a value on the consumption of future generations. Thus the market aggregate level of saving is inefficient and the market rate of interest undervalues future consumption. Aggregate saving would be increased if individuals were assured that their additional savings would be matched by other altruistic individuals.

The isolation paradox concerns the value individuals place on their descendants' consumption compared with that of the rest of future generations. If the return from saving for the benefit of future generations cannot be captured entirely by an individual's descendants, then it is likely that even perfect capital markets will provide an inefficient level of saving.

Imperfections in the capital market are widespread and there is no unique interest rate or discount rate. Instead of the use of an observed market interest rate, the social opportunity cost of capital has been used as a measure to discount the future. The social opportunity cost of capital measures the social value of a loss of one unit of capital in the economy to fund the proposed investment. If resources to fund a project displace other investments, rather than consumption, the social opportunity cost of capital is the correct measure of the cost of capital. However, there are practical difficulties in calculating the social opportunity cost of capital.

The effect of the discount rate on environmental degradation is unclear. A low discount rate weights future consumption more heavily and might be thought to give a better future environment than a higher rate. However, most investments have costs at the beginning of their life and benefits thereafter. Thus a lower discount rate will make these investments appear more attractive as weighted future benefits will increase relative to present costs (see equation (11.1) (p. 332). Increased investment and the consequent economic growth may lead to more environmental degradation. The importance of discount rates in evaluating environmental policies is discussed later in the context of climate change and the Stern Review (2006).

The harvesting of renewable resources

Renewable resources are those whose stock is capable of growth as well as depletion. Renewable resources are usually thought of as experiencing growth and regeneration through a biological process. Fisheries, forests and the previous example of common pasture land are all examples of renewable resources. The neoclassical analysis of renewable resources considers efficient harvesting, whilst biologists are often concerned with the **maximum sustainable yield** (MSY) that can be obtained from the resource. These two ideas are examined in the context of a fisheries example.

The growth of the stock of fish, ΔX, depends on the stock, X. This relationship is shown in Figure 12.5. Below a critical level, X_c, the stock is in danger of terminal decline as it is not capable of replication. The existence of a critical level may be explained by difficulties in reproduction. Above this level, growth is positive. Eventually the growth declines because of competition for food supplies or the effects of predators. The MSY occurs at the point of greatest absolute growth.

Figure 12.5 Relation between the growth and stock of a renewable resource

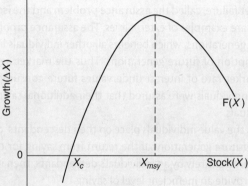

The efficient use of the fish stock is examined by considering a simple model in which harvesting is costless. The objective is to maximize the social value of the stock over time. The social gain is examined in connection with reducing the harvesting of fish and allowing the present stock to increase by one unit. The present marginal social value of one unit of fish is denoted by v. The marginal productivity of the stock, $F'(X)$, represents the change in growth from increasing the stock by one unit. The social value of this gain is $vF'(X)$. The marginal social value of an additional unit of fish in the second period is $(v + \Delta v)$, where Δv is the change in social value between the first and second periods. With a discount rate of r, the present value of an additional unit of stock in the next period is

$$\frac{vF'(X) + (v + \Delta v)}{1 + r} \tag{12.1}$$

The marginal social value of consuming one unit of fish in the present period is v. Thus if (12.1) exceeds v, an increase in social welfare can be obtained by reducing the level of harvesting. This condition can be written more simply as

$$F'(X) + \Delta v/v > r \tag{12.2}$$

This condition has a simple interpretation. If the marginal productivity of the stock plus the proportionate gain in the value of the stock over time exceeds the discount rate, then it is efficient to reduce harvesting. A reduction in the harvest increases the stock, which is likely to decrease $F'(X)$ (see Figure 12.5). A reduction in the harvest means consumption will fall and the marginal social value of present consumption compared with future consumption will increase. These two effects may be expected eventually to give equality in (12.2), and thus efficiency.

Equation (12.2) has two important implications. First, the efficient outcome is not the same as the MSY, as the latter is given by $F'(X) = 0$. Second, for species that have a low marginal productivity of stock and whose value does not increase appreciably with decreasing stock, extinction may be an efficient outcome!

The present analysis is concerned with maximizing the social value of the fishery stock over time. It is appropriate to consider whether the efficient outcome can be achieved through a market system. The fisheries example is another case of common property rights. In the discussion of common property rights, it was seen that it can be difficult to establish individual property rights for renewable resources such as fisheries, forests and pasture land. Thus the market use of such renewable resources is likely to be inefficient.

If the property rights for the resource are given to a few individuals, this will affect the distribution of economic welfare and will result in monopoly power. Private monopoly control of a renewable resource may result in its inefficient use, as marginal (private) revenue rather than social value would appear in (12.2) and, in order to maximize profits, the monopolist may restrict the use of the resource below the efficient level (see Hanley et al., 2006).

Non-renewable resources

Non-renewable resources cannot be regenerated over time. The present use of one unit of such a resource prevents it from being used in the future. The finite levels of these resources means that they are often referred to as **exhaustible resources.** This suggests that non-renewable resources should be used with care.

There are many estimates of the stocks of non-renewable resources. Calculation of the known reserves of a non-renewable resource has to be made in the context of the extraction cost and the price of the resource. It is considered inappropriate to include in estimates of reserves sources for which the cost of recovery exceeds the current price or for which there is no proven extraction technology. Proven reserves refer to those sources that are presently known. It is likely that there are sources yet to be discovered. However, uncertainty means that it is difficult to calculate meaningful estimates for unproven reserves.

The depletion of a non-renewable resource can be analysed in terms of the objective of maximizing the social value of the stock. Figure 12.6 considers a one-period model and the maximization of the economic rent from extracting a mineral that has a price P. The economic rent is the area between the price and the marginal cost curve. If the price is equal to the marginal social value of consumption, a perfectly competitive industry will extract the resource up to the point Q_0 and this is a socially efficient outcome. A monopoly faced with a downward sloping demand curve is likely to restrict output below Q_0, which is inefficient.

The **optimal depletion** of a non-renewable resource over time can be analysed in a very similar manner to the harvesting of a renewable resource. Again the objective is maximization of the social value of the stock over time. The decision to extract a non-renewable resource is simpler in that there is no marginal productivity of the stock to consider. It is assumed that the extraction of the resource is costless. The resource should be further conserved if

$$\frac{\Delta v}{v} > r \tag{12.3}$$

Equation (12.3) has a simple interpretation. If the relative appreciation of the social value of the resource is greater than the discount rate, then more of the resource should be saved for the future.

For an efficient outcome, the social value of marginal consumption should be increasing at the rate r. This implies (through integration) that v is given by the function $v_o e^{rt}$, where v_0 is the social

Figure 12.6 Economic rent and the use of a non-renewable resource

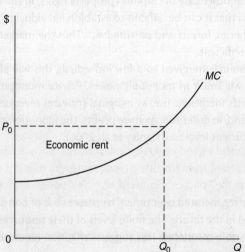

value at time zero. If a constant marginal cost of extraction (mc) is introduced into the analysis, the efficient outcome gives a final equation:

$$v(t) = mc + v_0 e^{rt} \tag{12.4}$$

Equation (12.4) reflects the optimal depletion path. It is possible for a perfect market to give this outcome. In this case, the optimal price path is given by

$$p(t) = mc + r_0 e^{rt} \tag{12.5}$$

The $r_0 e^{rt}$ term is referred to as the **discounted rental premium**. It may be interpreted as the social cost of consuming the resource in the present rather than in the future.

As before, if the price is equal to the marginal social value of consumption, a perfectly competitive market will maximize social welfare over time. A monopoly may restrict the use of the resource below the efficient level and the price path will be inefficient (see Hanley et al., 1997).

It has been pointed out by Kay and Mirrlees (1975) that, for reasonable discount rates, one would expect the optimal price to be close to marginal cost for most of the lifetime of a non-renewable resource.

Other environmental values

It is a central tenet of neoclassical economics that prices should reflect the marginal costs of production. In a competitive economy, prices may reflect private marginal costs, but there are a number of other types of social costs that should be taken into consideration (see Garrod and Willis, 1999). First, the external costs imposed on other individuals should be taken into account.[6]

Second, the economic rent in the use of non-renewable resources should be included in social marginal costs. As noted before, the economic rent may be regarded as a premium that has to be paid for the use of the resource in the present rather than in the future.

There are four other types of value that have not yet been considered: **option**, **quasi-option**, **existence** and **bequest values**. An option value is the value placed on an option that allows use to be made of the environment in the future. Option values depend on attitudes to uncertainty, such as risk averseness. The option is not necessarily taken up, but it gives value. An example of an option value is **biodiversity**. Protection of species of animals and plants may be desired in order to allow possible future uses of these species as inputs to production, and because many individuals may wish to have the opportunity of seeing these species in the future. **Quasi-option values** are the values placed on an option given an expectation that there will be increases in knowledge. For example, the value of certain plant species may depend on the development of knowledge of new uses of the plants.

Existence value is the value placed on a good or service independent of any actual or possible future consumption. This value is different from the other types of value in that it is unrelated to use. An example of existence value is the concern expressed by many individuals for the preservation of elephants, even though they are unlikely ever to see them at first hand, or use this resource.

The final type of value is the self-explanatory **bequest value**, when an economic agent wishes to pass on resources to members of future generations.

Thus the total social cost is composed of seven components:

$$
\begin{aligned}
\text{Social cost} = \ & \text{private cost} \\
& + \text{external cost} \\
& + \text{rental premium} \\
& + \text{option value} \\
& + \text{quasi-option value} \\
& + \text{existence value} \\
& + \text{bequest value}
\end{aligned}
\tag{12.6}
$$

Efficient allocation requires consideration of all seven components of social costs.

Measuring environmental values

The analysis of this chapter suggests that a market economy will not value all aspects of the environment appropriately. This view is widely held and has led to much intellectual and practical effort being applied to the problem of how to introduce appropriate environmental values into economic decision-making. The following discussion considers the introduction of environmental considerations into social cost–benefit analysis and national income accounting.

Appraisals of many investment projects in developing countries now include **environmental impact assessments** (EIAs), which estimate the environmental effects of the projects. This should be the first stage of the introduction of the environmental effects of a project into social cost–benefit analysis. Often it is very difficult to assess a project's physical effects on the environment. For example, the British government's *Review of Climate Change* in 2008 argued that the Stern Review (2006) had underestimated the physical impacts of climate change. EIAs can rarely firmly establish the type and extent of environmental effects of projects. Thus the introduction of previously unconsidered environmental effects into economic decision-making should take account of this uncertainty.

Once the environmental effects of a project have been estimated, there are three approaches to placing economic values on the effects.[7] First, the basic valuation technique in social cost–benefit analysis is to use market prices. This is justified by the neoclassical assumption that prices reflect the social value of goods and services. In the case of environmental effects in developing countries, markets and prices may not exist for many of the effects that require valuation. For large environmental effects, the project may actually alter prices. In this case, the changes in the values placed on environmental effects should be modelled. In practice, this is often impossible.

The second approach calculates the value of environmental effects indirectly through observed economic behaviour. Within this approach, there are a number of different techniques. One is the **preventive expenditure technique**, which takes the expenditure that people are prepared to undertake to prevent degradation as a measure of the value of the environmental effects. Another is the **replacement cost technique**, which estimates the expenditure people are prepared to undertake to restore the environment to its previous state after degradation has occurred.[8] These techniques can be very similar. The full long-term consequences of environmental effects may not be understood. Not all environmental effects can be fully offset by preventive expenditure and the environment cannot always be restored after degradation. Such problems may be particularly important for large changes in the environment, for example changes in the ecology of a large watershed, and climate change. The ability of individuals to fund these expenditures may be limited by imperfect capital markets. For these reasons, it is usually thought that the two techniques may underestimate environmental costs.

In the absence of a market for an environmental effect, it is sometimes possible to derive the value placed on the effect by the prices paid for other goods and services that implicitly value the effect. For example, property values vary with location, and this may in part reflect differences in the environment. The method of **hedonic prices** can produce estimates of the contribution of differences in the environment to the prices of property. This can be used to give an estimate of the implied value of certain environmental qualities. In developing countries, there are often significant imperfections in markets, for example rent controls, which affect the validity of the technique. The hedonic price method requires large amounts of data. It is often difficult to measure the environmental quality that is being considered. The importance of the environmental variable may not be properly understood by individuals. These problems limit the usefulness of this technique, particularly in developing countries.

The production function approach values environmental impacts by their effects on production. Thus part of the environmental impact of a change in climate conditions could be valued through the effects on agricultural output. Another example is the valuation of environmental health effects by estimating changes in the productivity of affected individuals. This implies that the value of life is only determined by production and there are no psychic costs to ill-health and early death.

The **travel cost method** values the time and costs that people are willing to incur in travelling to areas with more pleasant environments. Thus the method gives an implied value of environmental quality. The formal assumptions of the model and its applicability to developing countries have been criticized (see Garrod and Willis, 1999). The method implicitly considers the environment in terms of the provision of recreational services rather than basic life-support services.

The third approach to valuing environmental effects is that of **contingent valuation**. A subset of the population is surveyed and asked for their valuation of the environment. There are two ways in which this question can be asked. Individuals can be asked either about their willingness to pay for an environmental benefit or about their willingness to accept compensation for a loss of environmental quality. Economic theory suggests that the answers to the two types of question should be similar. In many surveys, willingness to accept compensation questions receive much higher responses. The questions asked are hypothetical and those surveyed may not be familiar with the environmental effect/resource being surveyed. Respondents may respond to questions strategically, and there is evidence of other forms of bias in the replies to surveys. The responses of individuals may reflect the context of the survey question. Thus, for example, individuals could, with appropriate questions, be induced to respond as citizens concerned with the public interest rather than as consumers pursuing their own self-interest. It is not always clear how to gross up the response from a survey to represent the general population's valuation of an environmental effect.

Chapter 11 considered the importance to social cost–benefit analysis of the distribution of costs and benefits. There are many environmental effects that imply major changes in the distribution of economic welfare; for example, the resettlement of an indigenous population following the construction of a dam. The distribution of environmental benefits and costs can affect the desirability of a project. Simple social cost–benefit analysis is concerned with improving the efficiency of economic decision-making. The prices used in social cost–benefit analysis reflect the distribution of welfare. If this distribution is unfair, the use of the resulting prices may be inappropriate. The introduction of distributional issues means that value judgements have to be made explicitly.

The valuation of environmental costs is essential to improving economic decision-making on the environment, and social cost–benefit analysis has developed various techniques to this end. However, there remain theoretical and practical problems with the use of these techniques.

National income accounting

The neoclassical approach to economic analysis assumes that consumption in its widest sense is, and should be, the objective of economic activity. The ethical issues concerning whose consumption should be considered were examined in Chapter 9 on population. The conventional approach is to measure economic welfare in terms of per capita income. This approach has been widely criticized and alternative measures have been proposed, many of which emphasize the importance of accounting for the environment.

Measures of economic welfare have to be judged in terms of their theoretical definition and practical application. The most obvious measure of current economic welfare is per capita current consumption. Current consumption can be increased by reducing investment, and thus future consumption. This suggests that economic welfare in one period should be defined relative to a fixed capital stock. Thus additions to capital stock, though not increasing current consumption, should be reflected in a measure of economic welfare as they allow increases in future consumption. This idea underlies the conventional definition of income (see Hicks, 1946):

> A person's income is what he can consume during the week and still be as well off at the end
> of the week as he was at the beginning.

There are many conceptual and practical problems with the definition of income. Only those directly concerned with accounting for the environment are examined here. Environmental degradation can be mitigated by the actions of economic agents; for example soil erosion can be reduced by planting forests. In national income accounts, such **defensive expenditures** are taken as giving rise to increases in economic welfare rather than as attempts to maintain the environment. It is commonly argued that these expenditures should be excluded from measures of economic welfare and account be taken of the environmental effects that give rise to these expenditures.

Environmental degradation affects economic welfare as individuals directly consume environmental services, for example unpolluted air. As there is not always a market in such services, or only an indirect one, they are not recorded in national income accounts. Degradation also reduces the productive potential of the environment, for example non-natural causes of soil erosion and reductions in the ability of the environment to absorb waste products. Reductions in the productive potential of the environment are examples of the depreciation of the stock of natural capital. These types of change are not recorded in national income accounts.

The use of non-renewable resources, for example fossil fuels, is not allowed for in a correct manner in national income accounts. These resources are part of the natural capital of the environment. Their use in the present reduces the supply available for future generations. National income accounts consider the use of non-renewable resources as a simple productive activity. It should also be considered as a depreciation of natural capital.[9]

There have been three responses to the failure of national income measures to account for the environment. The first method follows Nordhaus and Tobin's (1972) calculations of **measures of economic welfare** which attempt to recalculate national income accounts allowing for environmental effects. Progress on developing measures of national income that allow for use of natural capital and environmental degradation has been slow for most developing countries, though the World Bank now reports the value of natural capital in many developing countries. A report in *Nature* (1998) suggests that adjusting for environmental effects may have reduced national income for Brazil, India and Indonesia by 12–17 per cent in the mid-1990s, but a more recent estimate using World Bank data on adjusted national income for Taiwan suggests a reduction of only 1 per cent. Allowing for the environment can often give quite different estimates of economic welfare and economic growth.

The second method of accounting for the environment follows the weak sustainability view that total capital should be at least maintained. In this approach, the level of saving is calculated and the depreciation of natural, man-made and other forms of capital is deducted. If the resulting number is negative, this may be taken as evidence of unsustainable development. The method is explained in World Bank (2002). Adjusted net savings allowing for the environment is reported for many developing countries and is sometimes negative (see World Bank website).

A third method of accounting for the environment in economic growth is to construct *physical*, rather than monetary, accounts of the environment. These accounts divide up the environment into different sectors and estimate the changes that have taken place over time. For example, the use and discovery of mineral and energy resources would be recorded. The World Bank has argued for the collection of indicators across time of the effect of human activities on the environment and of the effect of the environment on human activities (see the World Bank website).

The three methods of accounting for the environment are not substitutes. The monetary approach of the first two methods requires the calculation of physical accounts. Physical environmental accounts are useful for considering ecological and environmental issues. Monetary environmental accounts are useful as they reduce all effects to a common measure and estimate a net figure for the use of the environment. However, because of the difficulty of doing this, they have been criticized on theoretical and practical grounds (see Perman et al., 2003, and Hanley and Atkinson, 2003).

Risk and uncertainty

Risk exists where there is doubt about a future outcome and it is possible to estimate objective probabilities of the occurrence of different possible future outcomes. The outcome of a throw of a dice is an example of risk. Uncertainty exists where there is doubt about the outcome and it is not possible to estimate probabilities of the occurrence of the different possible future outcomes. It is difficult to analyse uncertain events and most environmental analysis that considers risk and uncertainty assumes, either explicitly or implicitly, that it is possible to estimate probabilities with some degree of objectivity – that is, the circumstances are assumed to be those of risk rather than uncertainty.

Uncertainty about the relationship between the environment and the economy complicates analysis. As previous examples have shown, there is scientific dispute about many important environmental effects. In the analysis of environmental policies, it is possible to distinguish two approaches to managing this uncertainty.

First, the different possible outcomes of a policy are predicted. Then probabilities are estimated for these different outcomes, though these probabilities are necessarily subjective. It could be argued that the notion of estimating probabilities for events such as global warming is not appropriate, as they cannot be considered as repeated probabilistic events like the throwing of a dice. However, recent studies have attempted to provide probability estimates of different levels of global warming and Stern (2006) suggests that there is a 63–99 per cent chance of warming exceeding two degrees centigrade after a doubling of greenhouse gas concentrations. Notwithstanding this, policy analysis could proceed by selecting the most preferred policy on the basis of the probabilities of the different outcomes of the policies. If society is averse to taking risks, it can be shown that uncertain costs should be given more weight than the expected value of costs, and uncertain benefits should be given less weight than their expected value.

The alternative procedure is to select the average estimates of the effects of different environmental policies. These estimates are then used to decide the most preferred policy. This procedure is often used. The choice of the average estimates is highly subjective. More importantly, this approach does not take account of either risk or uncertainty.

Economic growth and the environment

Figure 12.2 indicates that the environment is essential for economic activity and growth, and shows the importance of the effects of economic growth on the environment. Environmentalists have argued that unconstrained economic growth will lead to the exhaustion of non-renewable resources and to levels of environmental degradation and climate change that will seriously affect economic production and the quality and existence of life (Meadows et al., 1972; Forrester, 1971). Economists who believe in the effectiveness of the market-based policy instruments have responded to these arguments (see Sterner, 2003).

If markets operate effectively, increased scarcity of non-renewable resources will increase their prices. These higher prices will give incentives for changes in economic behaviour:

- The direct consumption of these resources may fall – for example lower consumption of scarce fossil fuels
- There will be incentives to search for new supplies of these resources – for example the level of exploration for new oilfields will increase
- The use of higher-priced non-renewable resources in production will decline through substitution towards techniques of production that are less intensive in these inputs – for example production will become less fossil-fuel-intensive
- Higher prices will encourage the development of new technologies that provide substitutes for the scarce resources – for example non-fossil fuels such as 'biomass' or wind power, or utilize it more efficiently – for example fuel-efficient cars.

Thus efficient markets may provide a solution to the running down of non-renewable resources.

Supporters of economic growth often argue that its contribution to environmental degradation has been overestimated. Alternatively, there is a common view of the existence of opportunities for simultaneous economic development and improvement in the environment, as argued by the World Bank (2001). However, the pursuit of these twin goals is usually assumed to require the state to intervene and improve the operation of markets with regard to the environment.

It has been suggested by Grossman and Krueger (1995) that in the early stages of economic development the level of environmental degradation increases, but after this phase the environment improves with economic development; however, it is important to note that carbon dioxide emissions increase with the level of development (see Figure 12.1). This proposition is in line with the World Bank (1992) and the results that are reported at the beginning of this chapter. However, there is an extensive debate on the relationship between the environment and economic development (see de Bruyn, 2001; Cole, 2003). This relation between the environment and economic development could be explained by changes in the mix of output at different levels of development, changes in the demand for the environment at different levels of income and the policy responses to these demands, and the availability and use of more environmentally friendly technologies in developed countries.

All the different views of economic growth and environmental degradation considered here are likely to be true in part. It is unlikely that the debates on the relationships between the environment and the economy can be resolved through exhaustive scientific and economic investigation. Economic and environmental policies have to be formulated and carried out on the basis of existing uncertain and disputed evidence. For example, the validity of the modelling used by the Stern Review (2006) has been criticized as both over- and underestimating the impacts of economic activity on global warming (see discussion below, p. 373).

Sustainable development

Much of the vast literature on the environment and the economy could be interpreted as a response to the concern that present patterns of economic growth may seriously degrade the environment and may be unsustainable, as the environment cannot support economic growth forever. This proposition may or may not be substantially true. At its heart lies the view that past and present economic policies have usually been concerned with providing the conditions for equilibrium economic growth, as measured by standard national accounting methods. Many environmentalists are concerned that these policies have not attempted to ensure 'the existence of ecological conditions necessary to support human life at a specified level of well-being through future generations' (Lele, 1991). This concern is of major importance in the concept of **sustainable development**. Sustainable development has become perhaps the most important approach to considering the environment and development.

There is a wide range of definitions and interpretations of the meaning of 'sustainable development'. The term first came to prominence in the *World Conservation Strategy*, presented in 1980 by the International Union for the Conservation of Nature and Natural Resources. It was popularized by the World Commission on the Environment and Development's study *Our Common Future* (1987), which is also known as the Brundtland Report, named in honour of its chairperson, the Norwegian prime minister. These and other studies have defined sustainable development in different ways. The most frequently quoted definition comes from the latter study:

> Sustainable development seeks to meet the needs and aspirations of the present without compromising the ability of future generations to meet their own needs.

This definition would appear uncontroversial and is remarkably similar to the neoclassical definition of income that we gave earlier by Hicks (1946). However, the interpretation differs in that *Our Common Future* examined how sustainable development can be achieved. This inevitably requires the making of value judgements that link the definition and the operational objectives that it has been suggested will result in the attainment of sustainable development. For this reason, there has been criticism of the connection between the definition and the operational objectives. The objectives are increasing economic growth, meeting basic needs, involving more of the population in decision-making and development, controlling population growth, conserving and improving the environment, accounting for the environment in economic decision-making, changing technology, managing risk and changing international economic relationships.

The concept of sustainable development has gained very wide acceptance and has become a standard model for thinking about the environment, development and the economy. Most countries attending the Rio Earth Summit in 1992 accepted the general idea of sustainable development, for example as enshrined in the *Agenda 22* process agreed at this summit (United Nations, 1993). The United Nations 2005 World Summit 'reaffirmed [its] commitment to achieve the goal of sustainable development [and its] three components ... economic development, social development and environmental protection' (United Nations, 2005). However, as suggested above, what the concept of sustainable development should imply for economic and environmental policies is disputed. In particular, the concern for equity between and within generations is central to most interpretations of the concept, but it is unclear how the welfare of individuals can be compared. One of the major controversies concerning the approach of the Stern Review (2006) is the low discount rate which is used to compare costs and benefits for different generations. This is a central problem in neoclassical economics and the concept of sustainable development does not appear to provide a solution to the problem.

Natural capital, equity and environmental values

In defining the notion of sustainable development, it is common to require that the stock of capital be non-declining through time. A constant or increasing stock of capital allows consumption levels to be maintained or increased. However, there are major differences of opinion over the capital stock that must be held constant or increased. The weak sustainability view considers all the different forms of capital (for example, man-made, human, natural and social capital) to be substitutes and that they can be aggregated into total capital. Thus, for example, degrading the natural fertility of the soil can be compensated for through using fertilizers and the methods of agricultural science to maintain crop yields. In this example, human and man-made capital are used to substitute for natural capital.

The alternative view of strong sustainability takes the position that it is only natural capital that needs to be held constant or increased. In this view, the focus is often on critical natural capital which is either required for human survival or cannot be substituted for other forms of capital. Thus, one might take atmospheric global warming gas levels that cause climate change as critical natural capital as higher levels cannot be offset by other capital. For an economic comparison and analysis of weak and strong sustainability, see Hanley and Atkinson (2003). However it might be argued that some of the effects of climate change resulting from higher global warming gas levels can be adapted to through additional sea defences and migration of population (see the discussion of the Stern Review later in this chapter, p. 373).

Underlying the analysis of the environment and development, and the importance of natural capital, are views about environmental values. The study of environmental values suggests three possible ways in which these values could be generated. First, the preferences of individuals give rise to values that, with a complete set of perfect markets, are reflected in the prices of goods and services. This is the neoclassical approach to valuation, and examples of market failure have already been examined. Market failures suggest that the environment will not be adequately accounted for in the operation of market economies.

The second source of environmental values is that of social preferences. Sagoff (1988) has suggested that individuals are capable of considering issues, in particular those concerning the environment, from the point of view of society. It is not clear how such values could be established in the psyche of individuals. A possible explanation is a socio-biological one in that individuals behave as social organisms for the benefit of the species (Dawkins, 1976). Environmental choices are so complex that even if social preferences exist it is difficult to assume that, apart from in a tautological sense, they will result in decisions that improve social welfare. However, it has been suggested that the poor in developing countries are the most dependent on the environment. Thus if social preferences are to give weight to the circumstances of the poor, the environment should be given greater weight than would occur from simple aggregation of the individual values placed on the environment.

The third source of environmental values follows from the belief that ecological systems have an intrinsic value independent of any value placed on them by humans (see Booth, 1994; Common and Stagl, 2005). The individual-preferences basis for values considers only human beings to have rights. The ecological view represents the extension of rights to other species. How these rights can be measured is a difficult problem. The ecological-values view suggests that greater weight should be attached to the environment than would be given by taking just social values or simple aggregation of individual values.

Preserving or increasing the stock of natural capital has important effects on intergenerational equity. If it is believed that present levels of environmental degradation and resource use will substantially alter future human economic welfare, then intergenerational equity may be improved by the constraint that the stock of natural capital should be preserved. This is the strong sustainability view. However, the substitution of this constraint by a more flexible approach that allows some use of natural capital could conceivably increase economic welfare measured across all present and future generations. This is the weak sustainability view.

The use of a positive discount rate weights future environmental effects less heavily than those effects occurring in the present. This has been criticized as underestimating the importance of environmental degradation and resource use. This criticism is misplaced. If the arguments are accepted of a social preference for the present compared with the future, then discounting is appropriate. If it is felt that too little weight is being attached to future environmental effects, their estimated values should be adjusted, but not the discount rate.

Many environmental effects are irreversible – for example, the extinction of a species. Irreversibility has been used as an argument for maintaining the natural capital stock. However, the dislike of irreversible losses in natural capital can be captured by the concepts of option, quasi-option and existence values.

The resilience of an ecosystem is its ability to maintain its normal functions after an external disturbance (Common and Stagl, 2005). It has been suggested that the larger the stock of natural capital, the more resilient an ecosystem is likely to be. This argument is justified on the basis of the idea that the diversity of the ecosystem increases its resilience. However, the notion of resilience and the related concept of stability have been criticized, as no ecosystem is likely to be globally stable and constant through time. This implies that the size of the external disturbance is important (Norton, 1987).

As discussed previously, uncertainty is crucial to the analysis of the relation between the environment and the economy. A possible policy response to such uncertainty is to adopt policies that provide insurance against possibly disastrous future outcomes. This risk-averse strategy of emphasizing the worst possible outcome might be justified by, say, the worst forecasts of the disastrous outcomes of global warming. This argument supports the setting of a constraint that keeps the stock of natural capital fixed. Alternatively, it has been argued (e.g. see Lomberg, 2001) that the vast expenditure necessary to reduce global warming, the long period before such effects become important and the lack of absolutely clear scientific proof of the size of these effects suggest that a conservative approach ought to be adopted. It is unclear how uncertainty should be included in environmental decision-making, but it *is* clear that the treatment of uncertainty has a very important effect on the actual decisions that have been or will be taken.

Arguments about weak and strong sustainability, sources of environmental values, discounting, irreversibility, uncertainty and resilience suggest a higher value should perhaps be placed on the environment than the operation of a market economy would give. Strictly, this is not the same as suggesting that the stock of natural capital should be maintained. However, the complexity of decision-making on the environment might require a very approximate constraint on the use of environment such as preserving the stock of natural capital.

This critical discussion of the concept of sustainable development suggests that the environment has an important role in economic development and this may not have been fully understood in the past. The concept of sustainable development has won many academic and political adherents. However, there are differences in opinion whether natural capital deserves special protection in economic development or whether it can be traded off against man-made and human capital. These differences are important in determining how the environment enters into economic decision-making.

There are also practical difficulties with the implementation of a constraint that keeps the stock of natural capital fixed. The environment is made up of many different resources and services. Constancy of the stock of natural capital could be interpreted as constancy of all types of natural capital. This interpretation implies that any positive use of non-renewable resources would not be compatible with sustainable development and is difficult to justify.

The alternative interpretation is to consider a single measure of natural capital that appropriately weights the different types of natural capital. The obvious weights are the values of the various types of natural capital. These values may not only reflect the ideas considered in equation (12.6), but also the distributional views that are often associated with the idea of sustainable development. However, placing values on the different types of natural capital would appear to deny the special role of such capital. If different forms of natural capital can be valued so as to give a single measure, this suggests that it can be traded off against man-made and human capital and requires no special protection in the process of development.

It may be the case that a single measure of most types of natural capital would be desirable, with individual measures for the remaining and critical types of natural capital, for example atmospheric levels of greenhouse gases.

If the view is taken that the environment must be preserved, then social cost–benefit analysis of a project should be carried out subject to the additional constraint that the net effects on the environment are zero or positive. The strength of this additional constraint can be weakened by adding environmentally friendly investments to the project that allow the constraint to be met. If it is considered necessary to preserve the different types of natural stock, then there must be an additional constraint for each type of natural capital.

The constraint of preservation of all aspects of the environment implies that national income accounting methods cannot be altered to allow the calculation of one measure of economic welfare that includes environmental effects. Thus it has been suggested that measures of economic welfare be presented alongside a set of indicators of the state of the environment.

The less restrictive interpretation of the concept of sustainable development allows substitution between different forms of capital and the simple inclusion of the environment in social cost–benefit analysis and national income accounting (see World Bank website). The inclusion of the environment simply requires the correct valuation of environmental effects.

Economic thought and the environment[10]

Classical economists such as Malthus, Ricardo and Mill were generally pessimistic about the possibility of continued economic progress.[11] These economists assumed that there were diminishing returns to factors of production and the supply of land was fixed. The growth in population, and thus the labour force, would lead to reductions in the marginal product of labour and a declining average product of labour. Malthus and Ricardo assumed a constant technology, with the inevitable result that average agricultural production per unit of labour would decline. Mill considered that technical progress could offset the effect of diminishing returns to a factor, but was unlikely to do so in the long run. Marshall (1890) invented the idea of an externality and it was developed by Pigou (1920). However, in general, environmental externalities were considered to be unimportant.

The start of the debate about the environment and the economy is usually attributed to Rachel Carson and her book *Silent Spring* (1962). Other early contributions to the environmental debate were made by Boulding (1966), the Ehrlichs (1970), Goldsmith et al. (1972), Forrester (1971), Schumacher (1973) and Commoner (1972). A most influential environmental publication was *The Limits to Growth* by Meadows et al. (1972). The basic point of this study was that there are a number of non-renewable resources whose present levels of consumption are such that the known reserves will be exhausted in the not so distant future. The study was heavily criticized for not allowing for the effects of the price mechanism to reduce consumption and provide incentives to explore for new reserves and develop new technologies.

These environmental contributions to the debate stimulated economic interest in the relation between the environment and the economy. Barnett and Morse (1963) could find little evidence of resource scarcity in the US economy in the period 1850–1957. Dasgupta and Heal (1979) provided a rigorous neoclassical analysis of the depletion of exhaustible natural resources. Kneese et al.'s (1970) development of the **materials balance approach** changed the view that some economists had of how the economic system dealt with the environment's waste absorption function. This simple principle states that all resources that flow into an economic system must eventually end up as waste products.

The debate about the environment and the economy has changed public views, and in particular the views of international agencies have changed.

Climate change and the Stern Review

Climate change occurs because the earth absorbs energy from the sun and re-emits this energy. Some of this energy is absorbed by greenhouse gases and warms the earth. The existence of the greenhouse effect and the warming of the planet since the middle of the twentieth century are universally agreed. The extent of the contribution to climate change from man-made greenhouse gas emissions, however, has been disputed by some scientists and is difficult to prove beyond doubt.

The impacts on nature of global warming are: sea-level rises; loss of land; species and ecosystem changes in agriculture, relocation of forests and fisheries; changes in water availability; changes in local climates, and more unpredictable weather episodes. The impacts on humans are: increased mortality and morbidity from climate-related diseases; lack of food; air pollution, and weather-related disasters. Climate change also increases costs to society related to human migrations; changes in economic activity; adaptation to climate changes, and measures to reduce greenhouse gas emissions. The World Meterological Organization and United Nations Environment Programme set up the **Intergovernmental Panel on Climate Change (IPCC)**, which has reported over the period 1990–2007 on the scientific and economic research literature on climate change. These reports suggest that global temperatures could rise by between one and six degrees centigrade during the twenty-first century. The variation in the estimates is due to the differing assumptions concerning the complex mechanisms and feedback systems that cause global warming.

The **Stern Review** (2006) on the economics of climate change was commissioned by the UK government to review the possible impacts of global climate change, to investigate the costs of these impacts, and to advise on policy actions. This review is the most widely quoted report on the economic effects of climate change, and possible policy responses. The review concludes on the scientific evidence that climate change is a serious threat, with many of the impacts being irreversible, and requires an urgent global response. The review estimates that compared with a 'business as usual' scenario, the overall costs of climate change to the world economy will be in the region of 5 per cent of total world GDP for each year over the next two centuries. Stern suggests that with alternative modelling assumptions, the costs may be as high as 20 per cent of GDP for each year.

Stern calculated that a two-degree rise in global temperatures would cost about 1 per cent of GDP. More recently Stern (2008) has increased this estimate to 2 per cent of GDP because of faster than expected climate change. The 2010 *World Development Report* puts the cost to Africa at 4 per cent of GDP and India 5 per cent. At present global CO_2 emissions are 50 billion tons a year and are forecast to rise to 70 billion tons by 2050. To prevent the temperature rising by two degrees centigrade by 2050, emissions need to be cut to 20 billion tons, or by 70 per cent of the forecast level. The Stern Review argues that the majority of these cuts must be borne by developed countries, but developing countries must also take significant action. It is suggested that such policies can help promote growth and development, but it is important that they '[do] not cap the aspirations for the growth of poor countries' (Stern, 2006).

The different sources of global CO_2 emissions are given in Figure 12.7. The biggest polluters are power-generators and industry.

Estimates of the use of energy and emission of greenhouse gases per capita and per $1,000 of GDP are shown in Table 12.1.

It is clear who the big energy users are and where the greenhouse gases come from. The USA uses by far the most energy per capita and is the biggest polluter per capita. Developed countries produce five times more CO_2 emissions per capita than developing countries. This is why poor countries think it is unfair that they should bear as much of the burden of adjustment to global warming as the rich countries.

However, energy use and greenhouse gas emissions measured relative to GDP are slightly higher for developing countries compared with developed countries, with the transition economies faring the worst. This suggests that economic development is associated with energy and emission-intensive economic activity, and this is most apparent in the intermediate and later stages of economic development. Thus while the higher per capita use of energy and emission

Figure 12.7 Sources of CO₂ emissions

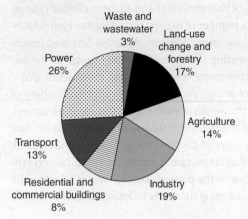

Source: World Bank (2010).

Table 12.1 Energy use and CO₂ emissions, 2006

	Energy use per capita (tons of oil equivalent)	Energy use per $1,000 GDP	CO₂ emissions per capita (tons)	CO₂ emissions per $1,000 GDP
World	1.80	0.20	4.4	0.5
Developed countries	4.70	0.18	10.9	0.4
Europe	3.49	0.15	7.6	0.3
Japan	4.13	0.15	9.5	0.3
United States	7.74	0.21	15.2	0.5
Transition economies	3.87	0.48	8.1	1.3
Developing countries	0.97	0.21	2.3	0.5
Africa	0.66	0.28	1.0	0.4
Latin America	1.17	0.15	2.2	0.3
West Asia	2.76	0.36	6.8	0.9
Other Asia, excl. China	0.63	0.17	1.3	0.4
India	0.51	0.15	1.1	0.3
China	1.44	0.21	4.3	0.6

Source: UNCTAD, 2009.

in developed countries indicates that they should bear the major burden of reducing CO₂ emissions, the developing and transition economies also need to take significant action to become more energy efficient.

The Stern Review believes that emissions can be reduced through the trading of emission permits; the pricing of carbon; the development and use of low-carbon technologies (e.g. carbon capture), and action to reduce deforestation. Throughout the Review it is emphasized that the poorest countries are the most vulnerable to climate change. The World Bank (2010) estimates that developing countries will bear 75 to 80 per cent of the cost of damage because of their dependence on ecosystem services and natural capital for their livelihoods. Stern concludes that it is the duty of rich countries to bear the majority of the emission reductions and provide technical and financial assistance to developing countries to reduce their emissions and adapt to climate change.

The Review has received strong support from a number of experts including five Nobel Prize-winning economists: Kenneth Arrow, Robert Solow, James Mirrlees, Amartya Sen and Joseph Stiglitz. But it has also been criticized for overestimating the costs of climate change, for under-estimating the costs of reducing emissions, and, conversely, underestimating the costs of global warming to the environment. These criticisms are important, and, as the range and variety of view in the debate shows, it is difficult to evaluate the weight of evidence on this complex subject.

A more technical, but important, criticism of the Review is its use of a low discount rate over time for estimating the present value of the costs of climate change (see Nordhaus, 2007; Dasgupta, 2007). As discussed earlier, the choice of discount rate is a complex technical and eth-ical issue concerning how to value the future relative to the present. The low values taken by the Review results in greater estimated costs of global warming than may be found in less pessimistic studies, for example Nordhaus (2007).

The Stern Review is undoubtedly the most important report on probably the most pressing economic issue that faces the world in the future. It has many detractors and as many supporters. Either way, the importance of climate change to future economic development requires expensive decisions to be made by the world economic community in the short term. The World Bank (2010) calculates that to keep global warming down to an increase of two degrees centigrade by 2050 will cost developing countries alone a minimum of US$140 billion a year (compared with $8 billion they are currently receiving for climate change mitigation). The cost of adapting to global warming (as opposed to trying to stop it) would be $75 billion, compared with the $1 billion now available.

Climate change and the poor

It is now widely acknowledged that climate change is taking place in a serious way, and that poorer countries are most vulnerable to the impacts of such change (Stern, 2006; World Bank, 2003, 2010). This vulnerability results from the close dependence of poor countries and poor people on the natural environment and their limited human, institutional and economic capacity to respond to the effects of climate change. The World Bank, in its *World Development Report 2010* (which is devoted to climate change), gives four major reasons why the poor are more vulnerable to climate change than the rich:

- First, natural disasters, such as hurricanes and floods, hurt them more because of poor hous-ing, poor health and inadequate health care. In the early 1980s, fewer than 500 million people required international disaster assistance. In the early 2000s, the number was 1.5 billion.
- Second, and related to the above, global warming increases the chances of catching life-threatening diseases such as malaria, meningitis, dengue fever and diarrhoea. It is estimated that by 2030, 90 million extra people in Africa alone may be exposed to malaria as the temperature rises.
- Third, poor countries are particularly prone to flooding. Of the 15 largest cities in the developing world, 10 are in low-lying coastal areas, including such cities as Shanghai, Dhaka and Cairo, all with over 10 million inhabitants.
- Fourth, climate change affects agriculture and fishing on which many poor countries still rely for everyday living. The climate, by becoming more extreme, with more drought and more flooding,

is starting to affect agricultural productivity. In the short term, some countries may benefit from being able to grow new products, but for most developing countries, agricultural productivity is predicted to fall as a result of climate change. This is likely to lead to greater hunger and famine. The number of malnourished children could rise by 25 million. The IPCC's Fourth Annual Report (2007) predicts that yields in agriculture may fall by up to 50 per cent by 2050, and the price of staples such as wheat and rice could more than double. Africa is regarded as the most vulnerable continent because of climate variability and its weak capacity to adapt. Warren et al. (2006) estimate an additional 600 million people in poor countries are at risk from starvation by 2050 if nothing is done.

As a consequence of this vulnerability, it has been suggested that it is critical that developing countries adapt to the consequences of climate change (see Nyong, 2008; Brainard et al., 2009). This adaptation includes increased foreign financial and technical assistance, improved governance, better planning and information, the sharing of information between similar regions and countries, and increasing the resilience of the present types of economic activity and infrastructure to climate change. A particular concern is that climate change will result in substantial migration within and between countries and increased pressure on scarce natural resources such as water. The World Bank (2010) estimates that between 200 million and 1 billion people may have to migrate and relocate. The impact of this is likely to result in increased conflict between and within countries.[12]

One policy to mitigate fossil fuel carbon dioxide emissions is to grow biomass (e.g. maize or oil crops) that can be converted into liquid fuels (see World Bank, 2007). The effect of the shift in the use of land to biomass production has been to reduce food production. The low supply elasticity of food production has led to large food price increases and a consequent increase in poverty (World Bank, 2007). In terms of the mitigation of the effects of climate change, this outcome was not intended and has led to policies encouraging the use of biofuels being reconsidered.

The Millennium Development Goals of ensuring environmental sustainability and eradicating extreme poverty and hunger are closely linked. Unfortunately, 'the plight of the poor is directly linked to natural resources around them [and as] total emissions continue to grow . . . the expected repercussions of climate change will affect [them]' (United Nations, 2005).

International agencies, agreements and the environment[13]

Since 1990, international agencies have begun to accept the importance of allowing for the environment in economic development and have started to change their practices.

The World Bank has accepted that the environment is directly relevant to the Bank's mission of supporting development (see World Bank, 1992). The World Bank supports the sustainable development view. There are various aspects to the Bank's new policy view. First, it is accepted that there is a need for appropriate valuation of environmental effects. Since 1989, the World Bank has formally required environmental assessments of all projects that are expected to have a significant adverse environmental impact. However, there have been criticisms of whether these assessments contribute to actual project decision-making (see Lawrence, 2003). The World Bank (2001) has recognized that the environment has yet to be fully incorporated into the Bank's operations, but they argue that the environment has a 'core task in supporting development and poverty reduction'.

Second, poverty is seen as a major cause of environmental damage and the poor are regarded as being heavily dependent on the environment (see the section above on climate change and the poor). Third, it is argued that high-income countries must accept financial responsibility and take the initiative for dealing with major worldwide environmental problems. However, it is also clear that the World Bank disagrees with the view that economic development should take place under the constraint that the stock of natural capital should not be depleted. The Bank does now lend explicitly for environmental projects, and through the **Global Environment Fund** makes grants to protect the environment. By 2007, the Fund had provided $38 billion of capital for active environmental projects and funded many other projects with clear environmental objectives. However, the benefits to the environment and native peoples of this lending have been disputed (World Bank, 2001).

Similarly, the IMF has slowly begun to recognize the need to take account of the environment in its structural adjustment programmes (SAPs) (see IMF website). The IMF has been criticized for only making token and superficial changes in policy (see Friends of the Earth website). Both the World Bank and the IMF are large international agencies where change is difficult to implement, and whether there is a commitment to implement changes in policies properly to protect the environment and the most disadvantaged persons in developing countries remains to be seen.

The World Trade Organization (WTO) (and its predecessor, the General Agreement on Tariffs and Trade, GATT) exists to promote the liberalization of world trade. The WTO's position is that sustainable development and environmental protection are important goals of the organization. The WTO's rules allow for trade-related measures to be adopted in order to protect the environment. However, the WTO believes that such measures are best managed through multilateral environmental agreements. Though the WTO has a dispute settlement procedure, it has not been used to deal with fundamental environmental issues such as climate change. An important environment and trade issue is when developed countries reduce their production of goods which generate large levels of global warming gases and instead import such goods from developing countries. This helps developed countries meet their UN climate change obligations but it is likely to increase total global warming gas emissions This complex and important subject is only just beginning to be considered by the WTO (2009) (see WTO website). The WTO believes that it is not appropriate for it to set environmental policies and standards. It believes that such issues should be considered by specialist agencies and international negotiation. However, the WTO supports the objective of sustainable development and has been involved in assisting multilateral environmental agreements and increasing the awareness of links between trade and the environment (see Stokke and Thommessen, 2003).

The United Nations has been responsible for the two reports – *World Conservation Strategy* and *Our Common Future* – that have greatly influenced world opinion in favour of sustainable development. The UN Development Programme (UNDP) and the World Bank, as we have seen, set up the Global Environment Facility in 1991.

The United Nations Framework on Climate Change was signed in June 1992 at the Rio Earth Summit. Its purpose is to stabilize greenhouse gas concentrations at levels low enough to prevent serious change to the climate systems. The Kyoto Protocol of 1997 established legally binding commitments to reduce greenhouse gas emissions. The intention was to reduce by 2012 emissions of industrial countries to an average 5.2 per cent below 1990 levels (the exact targets varied between countries). China, India and other developing countries were not given targets by the Kyoto Protocol but were expected to take responsibility for reducing emissions of greenhouse gases, while their share of global emissions would be allowed to rise in order for them to meet their development needs. The negotiations of the arrangements for the trading systems have been very difficult and it is not clear how effective the present proposals are, and will be, in reducing global warming. The successor to the Kyoto Protocol was the **Copenhagen Conference** at the end of 2009, which ended in failure to agree new targets.

There is general agreement on the Rio Declaration's support of sustainable global development, and *Agenda 21* considers specific programmes to achieve sustainable development in the twenty-first century (United Nations, 1993). The **United Nations Commission on Sustainable Development** was set up with the objective of promoting, investigating and monitoring sustainable development. But by the UN's own admission, the Millennium Development Goal of environmental sustainability by 2015 is not likely to be met (United Nations, 2009).

The Rio Earth Summit was criticized for its failure to secure a binding commitment to increase aid, reduce debt and fundamentally shift resources from rich to poor countries. Since then the UN has linked the goal of sustainable development to the goal of eradicating extreme poverty and hunger. The Stern Review (2006) suggests that economic growth in developing countries can still be achieved in the face of climate change. However, for this to happen, it is necessary for the state and international organizations to intervene and improve the operation of markets with regard to the environment, and in particular with regard to the impacts of climate change on developing countries.

Summary

- Economic development in the past has caused serious environmental damage and the current state of the environment will constrain future economic development in developing countries. The environment provides four major functions for the economy and society: life support; amenity; natural resources and waste absorption.
- The neoclassical view of the economy is that markets allocate scarce resources efficiently. Many environmental economists argue that markets fail to allocate efficiently and fairly, and the state should intervene to correct these market failures.
- Externalities occur when the actions of one economic agent affect other economic agents and the actions are not controlled through the operation of the market. The burning of fossil fuels and the release of global warming gases is an example of an externality. The effects of externalities and, in particular pollution, can be corrected to an extent by taxation, subsidization, bargaining, marketable permits and regulation.
- Economic analysis of the environment requires the comparison of the costs and benefits of environmental effects in the present and future, and this is achieved using the device of the discount rate.
- The efficient use of renewable and non-renewable resources across time depends upon their social value, the growth of renewable resources, the reserves of non-renewable resources and the discount rate. The market will not necessarily use renewable and non-renewable resources efficiently.
- Economic analysis of market failures suggests that they can be corrected for in environmental decision-making by estimating and allowing for additional environmental values: external costs; a premium on the prices of non-renewable resources such as oil; value placed on the existence of environmental goods and services by the present generation and its wish to pass on the environment to future generations; and the impact of uncertainty on the value of the environment.

- The World Bank and other agencies have attempted to adjust measures of national income for environmental degradation caused by increased economic activity. The relation between economic development and the environment is complex and the subject of dispute.
- The major idea of sustainable development has emerged since the 1980s, in which the well-being of future generations is not compromised by meeting the material needs of the present generation. This idea places an emphasis on the natural environment supporting economic activity and suggests the world should be very cautious in depleting natural capital.

Chapter 12	Discussion questions

1   What are the functions of the environment in supporting economic activity?

2   What are the different possible solutions to externalities?

3   Explain the causes of 'the tragedy of the commons'.

4   What conditions determine the efficient use of renewable and non-renewable resources?

5   What are the different types of value that should be included in social costs?

6   How might one allow for environmental effects in social cost–benefit analysis and national income accounting practices?

7   Define and explain the idea of sustainable development.

8   What are the arguments for and against keeping the stock of natural capital fixed?

9   What are the physical and economic impacts of climate change?

10   How are the poor in developing countries affected by climate change?

11   How have international organizations responded to the ideas of sustainable development and the economic importance of the environment?

Notes

1. This discussion of the relationships between the environment and the economy is very general and simple. A good introduction to earth sciences and the interaction of humans and the environment can be found in Tarbuck et al. (2008)
2. For a good introduction to this subject, see Common (1996).
3. Explanations of the neoclassical approach to economics can be found in most intermediate microeconomics textbooks: see Varian (2002).
4. See Bond et al. (2001) for details and evaluation of the external effects of this hydroelectric facility.
5. See the discussion of 'the problem of the commons' in Dasgupta (1982).
6. The remaining values could strictly be classified as private or external costs, but for the purpose of exposition they are separated into different categories.
7. More precise details and discussion of economic valuation can be found in Garrod and Willis (1999).

8. These expenditures and costs may be difficult to observe and both techniques often require experts to estimate them.

9. A similar analysis applies in the case of renewable resources, as regeneration can require time and investment, and thus present consumption of renewable resources can impose costs on future generations.

10. See Barbier (1989) for a good survey of the history of economic thought on the environment and development.

11. Malthus (1798); Ricardo (1817); Mill (1856). See also Chapter 5.

12. See Bushby (2009) for an analysis of the security implications in developing countries of climate change.

13. For a good clear summary of the objectives and activities of most international agencies that work in the environmental and development fields see Stokke and Thommessen (2003).

Websites on the environment

Amazing Environmental Organisation Web Directory www.webdirectory.com
International Institute for Environment and Development www.iied.org
World Watch Institute www.worldwatch.org
World Resources Institute www.wri.org
United Nations Environmental Program www.unep.org
UN Commission on Sustainable Development www.un.org/esa/sustdev
World Bank www.world bank.org.
World Trade Organization www.wto.org
International Monetary Fund www imf.org
Friends of the Earth www.foe.org

V

FINANCING ECONOMIC DEVELOPMENT

13

FINANCING DEVELOPMENT FROM DOMESTIC RESOURCES

- Introduction
- Forms of saving
- The prior-savings approach
- The capacity to save
- The willingness to save
- Financial systems and economic development
- The informal financial sector
- Monetization and money market integration
- Developing a banking system
- Rural financial intermediaries and micro-credit
- Development banks
- Financial intermediaries
- Financial liberalization
- Fiscal policy and taxation
- Tax reform in developing countries
- Inflation, saving and growth

- The Keynesian approach to the financing of development
- Reconciling the prior-saving and forced-saving approaches to development
- The quantity theory approach to the financing of development
- The dangers of inflation
- Inflation targeting
- Inflation and growth: the empirical evidence
- The inflationary experience
- The structuralist–monetarist debate in Latin America
- Summary
- Discussion questions
- Notes
- Websites on banking and finance

Introduction

The topic of financing development from domestic resources has two major aspects. The first concerns the ways in which **savings** can be encouraged in developing countries, because only if society is willing to save can resources be devoted to the production of capital goods. Saving is necessary to *fund* investment. In a primitive subsistence economy, without money or monetary assets, saving and investment will tend to be simultaneous acts, in the sense that saving and investment will be done by the same people, and saving will be invested in the sector in which the saving takes place. In a more sophisticated money exchange economy, however, there is no guarantee that saving will necessarily be converted into investment. With the existence of money and monetary assets, the act of saving becomes divorced from the act of investing. Those who want to do the investing may be different from those who want to do the saving, and the process of capital accumulation is likely to require financial and credit mechanisms to 'redistribute' resources from savers to investors. Indeed, with a banking system with the power to create credit, investment can take place *without* prior saving through the process of borrowing. In other words, saving funds investment, but does not necessarily *finance* it. Investment generates its own saving through increases in output and profits. In fact, in the early stages of development, savings may not be the major barrier to capital formation but rather an unwillingness or inability to invest.

Unwillingness to invest may stem from cultural attitudes or simply from a realistic assessment of the risks involved. We analysed in Chapter 6 why poor people may be risk-averse. The inability to invest, on the other hand, may result from shortages of cooperating factors of production (including foreign exchange), or lack of access to credit because of the underdeveloped state of the financial system. The second important aspect of financing development from domestic resources, therefore, has to do with the role of the banking and financial system in promoting and financing investment. **The financial system is important for encouraging saving, financing investment and allocating savings in the most productive manner**.

This chapter starts by distinguishing the different types of saving – voluntary, involuntary and forced – and then distinguishes the different analytical approaches to the finance of development which have different policy implications. The **prior savings approach** focuses on policies to raise the level of voluntary and involuntary saving as a prerequisite for investment. The **Keynesian approach** focuses on incentives to investment which will generate its own saving. The **quantity theory approach** emphasizes the role of government in appropriating resources for development through monetary expansion and forced saving through inflation (the inflation tax).

Raising the level of voluntary and involuntary saving involves the use of monetary and fiscal policy. The chapter discusses the financial systems of developing countries, including the informal financial sector, which dominates in rural areas; the formal banking system and financial intermediaries, and the various forms of **financial repression** that exist which have led in recent years to extensive programmes of **financial liberalization**. The case for and against financial liberalization, and the empirical evidence, is presented. The role of **micro-credit** and **development banks** in helping people out of poverty is also examined.

We then consider fiscal policy and taxation; the tax effort of countries, and the need for fiscal reform to raise tax revenue as a proportion of GDP.

If voluntary and involuntary saving are inadequate for the development effort, inflationary policies that redistribute income between wages and profits, and between the private sector and the government, are alternative possibilities.

The former possibility is the Keynesian approach to the finance of development which argues that stimulating investment can generate its own saving by raising the level of income if the economy is operating below capacity, and by redistributing income from wage earners with a low propensity to save to profit earners with a higher propensity to save if the economy is working at full capacity.

The latter possibility is the quantity theory approach to the finance of development (so named after the quantity theory of money). One of the ways a government can divert more resources to investment is to invest on society's behalf, financing the investment by expanding the money supply. At full employment, monetary expansion will be inflationary. The 'tax' on money consists of a reduction in the real purchasing power of money, and the real resources that holders of money must forgo to restore the real value of their money holdings (forced saving).

The dangers of inflationary finance are recognized, and the extensive empirical research on the relation between inflation and growth is evaluated.

Forms of saving

There are three broad groups in society that save: the household sector, the business sector and the government. The household sector saves out of personal disposable income (personal saving), the business sector saves out of profits, and the government can save out of tax revenues if it spends less than it receives (that is, runs a budget surplus on current account). Household and business saving is sometimes referred to as **private saving**, while government saving is **public saving**. Each of the sectors' motives for saving will differ, and we shall consider the determinants of saving later in this chapter, p. 393.

As far as the nature of saving is concerned, three broad 'types' may be distinguished: voluntary, involuntary and 'forced'. The nature of these 'types' of saving is fairly self-explanatory:

- **Voluntary savings** are savings that arise through voluntary reductions in consumption out of disposable income. Both the household and the business sector may be a source of voluntary savings.
- **Involuntary savings** are savings brought about through involuntary reductions in consumption. All forms of taxation, social insurance contributions and schemes for compulsory lending to governments are traditional measures involving involuntary reductions in consumption.
- Consumption may be reduced because of rising prices. This is referred to as **'forced' saving**[1] and may happen for a number of reasons. People may spend the same amount in money terms, but because prices have risen this means they spend less in *real* terms (money illusion). People may want to keep the *real* value of their holdings of money constant, so they accumulate more money as prices rise (**the real balance effect**). Also, inflation may redistribute income to those with a higher propensity to save, such as profit earners.

For a variety of reasons, which will be considered below (p. 420), inflation is likely to be a natural concomitant of development, but it can also be deliberately induced by governments financing budget deficits at full employment by monetary expansion. This is the idea of **'inflation as a tax on money'**. It should also be remembered that if an economy is at less than full employment, there can always be more saving by activating unemployed or underemployed resources, provided not all of the increase in output is consumed.

Domestic savings for investment can also be supplemented from abroad. Private foreign investment is a direct source of capital formation and provides a direct addition to domestic investment. It can also be a source of savings by stimulating income and employing previously underutilized resources. Second, borrowing from abroad provides resources for investment by enabling imports to exceed exports, which in the national accounts shows up as investment in excess of domestic saving. Foreign assistance may be from multilateral or bilateral sources and may take a variety of forms, ranging from loans at commercial rates of interest to outright gifts of goods and services and technical assistance (see Chapter 14). Remittances from abroad also augment domestic saving.

Finally, a country's commercial policy can stimulate savings and release resources for investment purposes. Trade itself, and an improvement in a country's terms of trade, can provide additional resources for investment if the resulting increase in real income is not fully consumed. Likewise, policies to restrict imports of consumption goods can release additional resources for investment, provided that domestic saving is not reduced by the purchasing power released being switched to home-consumption goods.

The amount that countries save and invest as a proportion of their gross domestic product (GDP) differs enormously, affected by differences in the ability and willingness to save and invest. Some countries dissave, consuming more than they produce. Some countries save more than they invest domestically, which means they are investing abroad, and other countries invest more than they save, which means they are net importers of capital. The experience by country and by continent for 2009 is shown in Table 13.1. The first thing to note is that the savings ratio is much lower in poor countries than in rich ones, but that the savings ratio does not continue to rise forever as countries grow richer. It tends to level off in the middle-income group of countries and then stabilize. The weighted average savings ratio in the low-income countries is 16.5 per cent of GDP compared with 31.6 per cent in the middle-income countries and 19 per cent in high-income countries.[2] Some countries in the low-income category dissave, for example Eritrea and Nicaragua. Most of the low-income countries also have investment ratios that are higher than their domestic savings ratios, indicating that they are net capital importers. The most notable exception is China, which for many years has been saving over 40 per cent of GDP and exporting capital, mainly to the United States. Not only is personal saving high to compensate for a lack of a state social security system, but so also is the corporate saving of state-owned enterprises, amounting to 30 per cent of GDP.

The second important observation is the enormous disparity in saving performance between continents, particularly between the high savings ratios of the highly successful East Asian countries and the much lower savings ratios in the less successful economies of Latin America and sub-Saharan Africa. The ratio in East Asia (46 per cent) is double that of Latin America (23 per cent), and more than double that of sub-Saharan Africa (15 per cent). The question that naturally arises is: did high savings precede rapid growth in East Asia, or did rapid growth generate its own high savings ratio? Some might argue that it was policies to stimulate saving that were important, including financial liberalization. Some might say it was policies to stimulate investment, partly through control of the banking system, that generated growth and therefore saving. Others might say it was the deliberate involvement of the government in generating and reallocating new resources.

There is no easy answer to the question, but the different replies that might be given highlight the differences in the three broad analytical approaches to the study of financing development

Table 13.1 Investment and savings as a percentage of GDP

	Gross capital formation % of GDP 2007	Gross domestic savings % of GDP 2007		Gross capital formation % of GDP 2007	Gross domestic savings % of GDP 2007		Gross capital formation % of GDP 2007	Gross domestic savings % of GDP 2007
Albania	29.9	3.5	Cambodia	20.8	13.2	El Salvador	20.4	−3.5
Algeria	33.4	56.9	Cameroon	17.3	18.1	Equatorial Guinea	46.7	82.8
Angola	13.9	46.2	Cape Verde	40.6	5.4	Eritrea	10.6	−17.7
Argentina	24.2	28.5	Central African Republic	8.9	1.5	Estonia	37.9	27.0
Armenia	37.2	17.3	Chad	19.1	34.2	Ethiopia	25.0	5.5
Australia	27.4	26.2	Chile	21.1	34.8	Fiji	16.2	0.6
Austria	20.8	28.1	China	43.3	52.9	Finland	22.3	26.9
Azerbaijan	21.3	63.2	Colombia	24.3	20.2	France	22.1	20.2
Bangladesh	24.5	17.5	Comoros	14.3	−11.8	Gabon	26.2	55.0
Belarus	33.2	27.1	Congo, Dem. Rep.	20.2	9.1	Gambia	23.2	6.7
Belgium	22.3	25.2	Congo, Rep.	27.1	57.2	Georgia	34.6	8.4
Belize	19.3	17.5	Costa Rica	24.6	19.8	Germany	18.3	25.3
Bhutan	52.5	60.1	Côte d'Ivoire	8.6	14.3	Ghana	33.7	7.5
Bolivia	15.2	22.7	Croatia	32.7	24.1	Greece	25.7	12.5
Bosnia & Herzegovina	22.7	−11.9	Czech Republic	26.9	31.9	Guatemala	20.7	3.8
Botswana	40.7	51.1	Denmark	23.4	24.5	Guinea-Bissau	17.2	13.3
Brazil	17.9	19.5	Djibouti	38.3	17.8	Guinea	12.6	10.4
Brunei Darussalam	12.9	52.8	Ecuador	23.7	23.0	Haiti	25.7	2.3
Bulgaria	36.8	14.7	Egypt, Arab Rep.	20.9	16.3	Honduras	33.5	6.6

continued overleaf

Table 13.1 Investment and savings as a percentage of GDP – continued

	Gross capital formation % of GDP 2007	Gross domestic savings % of GDP 2007		Gross capital formation % of GDP 2007	Gross domestic savings % of GDP 2007		Gross capital formation % of GDP 2007	Gross domestic savings % of GDP 2007
Hong Kong, China	21.3	32.2	Liberia	20.0	−30.5	Nepal	28.0	9.7
Hungary	22.3	23.8	Lithuania	29.5	17.5	Netherlands	19.7	27.7
Iceland	27.7	17.1	Luxembourg	19.1	49.7	Nicaragua	31.8	−2.2
India	38.7	35.6	Macedonia, FYR	23.2	3.4	Norway	23.1	38.7
Indonesia	24.9	28.9	Madagascar	27.3	11.0	Pakistan	22.9	15.8
Iran, Islamic Rep.	33.2	43.8	Malawi	26.0	4.9	Panama	23.5	28.5
Israel	20.1	18.4	Malaysia	21.9	42.2	Papua New Guinea	19.7	41.2
Italy	21.5	21.2	Mali	23.3	13.5	Paraguay	18.0	15.0
Jordan	27.4	−14.1	Malta	21.6	19.4	Peru	22.9	29.4
Kazakhstan	35.6	42.5	Mauritania	25.9	18.7	Philippines	15.3	15.7
Kenya	20.2	9.0	Mauritius	26.8	17.5	Poland	23.8	21.1
Korea, Rep.	29.4	30.2	Mexico	26.0	24.3	Portugal	22.2	15.1
Kuwait	19.7	55.0	Moldova	38.2	−14.1	Romania	29.6	17.2
Kyrgyz Rep.	26.0	−19.2	Mongolia	40.2	38.8	Russian Fed.	24.6	33.3
Lao PDR	39.8	23.9	Montenegro	27.4	−15.3	Rwanda	21.2	2.8
Latvia	37.2	17.0	Morocco	32.5	23.4	Saudi Arabia	21.8	49.2
Lebanon	17.9	−6.6	Mozambique	19.2	12.3	Senegal	32.5	12.3
Lesotho	27.9	−24.1	Namibia	30.1	25.4	Serbia	23.1	1.0

continued overleaf

Table 13.1 Investment and savings as a percentage of GDP – *continued*

	Gross capital formation % of GDP 2007	Gross domestic savings % of GDP 2007		Gross capital formation % of GDP 2007	Gross domestic savings % of GDP 2007		Gross capital formation % of GDP 2007	Gross domestic savings % of GDP 2007
Seychelles	41.6	–2.4	Trinidad & Tobago	13.4	33.9	Upper middle income	23.0	24.2
Sierra Leone	13.4	6.1	Tunisia	24.8	22.4	Low & middle income	28.8	30.9
Singapore	22.6	51.4	Turkey	21.6	16.5	East Asia & Pacific	37.7	46.3
Slovak Rep.	27.8	26.8	Uganda	22.3	8.3	Europe & Central Asia	24.9	23.6
Slovenia	31.4	30.1	Ukraine	26.9	21.4	Latin America & Caribbean	22.4	23.5
South Africa	21.4	18.3	United Kingdom	18.7	15.2	Middle East & North Africa	27.7	29.7
Spain	31.3	24.8	Uruguay	15.1	14.4	South Asia	35.4	31.2
Sri Lanka	27.2	16.9	Uzbekistan	19.4	29.5	Sub-Saharan Africa	21.9	17.9
Sudan	24.2	20.5	Venezuela, RB	28.0	34.3	Least developed countries	23.8	15.5
Swaziland	13.0	11.6	Vietnam	41.6	28.2			
Sweden	19.7	27.4	Zambia	24.1	30.6			
Syrian Arab Rep.	19.8	20.7	Low income	24.9	16.5			
Tajikistan	22.0	–23.8	Middle income	29.0	31.6			
Thailand	26.8	34.5	Lower middle income	35.3	39.4			

Source: World Bank, *World Development Indicators*, June 2009, online (http://data.worldbank.org/data-catalog/world-development-indicators).

from domestic resources, which we will use as the organizing framework for the rest of the chapter. The three approaches are as follows:

- The **prior-savings approach** to the financing of development, which stresses the importance of prior savings for investment and the need for policies to raise the level of savings either voluntarily or involuntarily, or both. The approach is very classical in conception, emphasizing saving as a prerequisite of investment. The approach is also characterized by a strong aversion to inflation and a belief that saving will readily find investment outlets.
- The **Keynesian approach**, which rejects the idea that saving determines investment and argues instead that the encouragement of investment will generate its own saving, either through increases in output if resources are unemployed, or through income redistribution from groups with a low propensity to save to groups with a higher propensity to save as a result of inflation if resources are fully employed.
- The so-called **quantity theory approach**, which emphasizes the role of government monetary expansion in appropriating resources for development through forced saving or the inflation tax.[3]

If developing countries are characterized as fully employed in the Keynesian sense (with no spare capacity in the consumption-goods industries), both the Keynesian and the quantity theory approach to the financing of development will involve inflation. Plans to invest in excess of plans to save at full employment will drive up the price level, and so will monetary expansion by government. In this sense there is an important practical, as well as a theoretical, difference between the prior-savings approach and the other two approaches. In the prior-savings approach the resources released for investment come from voluntary and involuntary saving and no inflation is involved. In the Keynesian and quantity theory approaches the resources are partly released through the process of inflation, by income redistribution from classes with low propensities to save to those with higher propensities to save, and by inflation as a 'tax' on money.

The prior-savings approach

In classical theory saving and investment are one and the same thing. All saving finds investment outlets through variations in the rate of interest. Investment and the development process are led by savings. It is this classical view of the development process that underlies such phrases in the development literature as the 'mobilization of savings for development', and also underlies the policy recommendation of high real interest rates to encourage voluntary saving. Lewis's influential model of the development process, which was considered in Chapter 6, is a classical model stressing the importance for development of reinvesting the capitalist surplus.

The level of saving and the ratio of saving to national income in developing countries are likely to be a function of many variables affecting the ability and willingness to save. The main determinants of the **capacity or ability to save** are the average level of per capita income, the rate of growth of income, the distribution of income between rich and poor and the age composition of the population (or dependency ratio). In turn, the **willingness to save** depends mainly on monetary factors such as the rate of interest, the range and availability of financial institutions and assets (financial deepening), and the rate of inflation. Differences in cultural attitudes towards saving may also be important, but are not easily measured.

The capacity to save

Income is the major determinant of the capacity or the ability to save. It was Keynes who first introduced into economics the idea of the consumption function (and therefore savings function), making consumption and saving primarily a function of income rather than a function of the rate of interest as in classical theory. Saving as a function of income is known as the Keynesian **absolute income hypothesis**. We can derive the savings ratio as a function of the level of per capita income (PCY) in the following way: If we write the Keynesian savings function as $S = -a_0 + b_0(Y)$, where b_0 is the marginal propensity to save and $-a_0$ represents dissaving (or positive consumption) when income is zero, and divide by the population level (P), we have:

$$S/P = -a_1 + b_1(Y/P) \qquad (13.1)$$

Then to obtain an expression for the savings ratio, multiply (13.1) by P and divide by Y:

$$S/Y = b_1 - a_1(Y/P)^{-1} \qquad (13.2)$$

The Keynesian absolute income hypothesis therefore predicts that savings per head (S/P) is a linear (but non-proportional) function of income per head (Y/P), and that the savings ratio (S/Y) is a hyperbolic function of the level of income per head; that is, that the savings ratio will rise with the level of per capita income but at a decreasing rate. As $Y/P \to \infty$, $S/Y \to$ to the asymptote b_1. This is shown in Figure 13.1.

The data on the savings ratio in Table 13.1 suggest this type of relation, as already discussed. The savings ratio is lower in poor countries than in richer countries, but the ratio does not continue rising linearly (for ever) as PCY rises. It increases at a diminishing rate and then levels off. Indeed, there is even some indication that it starts falling at high levels of income, as we shall see when we come to examine the empirical evidence.

The reason why the savings ratio should rise as per capita income increases and then level off is not clear-cut. It is as if saving is a luxury good in the early stages of development but then loses its appeal. Part of the reason may be purely 'statistical', arising from the way saving is normally defined in developing countries as the difference between investment and foreign capital inflows. As investment expenditure becomes more faithfully and accurately recorded as development proceeds (as per capita income rises) the savings ratio is also shown to increase. But there are also a number of economic factors that probably play a contributory role in explaining the relation. One is the growth of the money economy. As money replaces barter for transactions, the public will

Figure 13.1 The Keynesian absolute income hypothesis

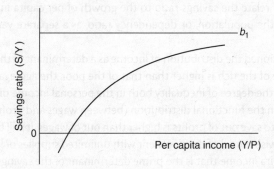

wish to hold a higher proportion of their income in the form of money, which they can do only by reducing consumption as a proportion of income. This hypothesis is supported by what we know about the income elasticity of demand for money in developing countries, which exceeds unity.

A second possible explanation is that population growth decreases with increases in the level of per capita income, so that population growth absorbs household saving to a lesser and lesser extent. Another plausible hypothesis is that in the early stages of development the distribution of income, both personal and functional, grows more unequal but at a decreasing rate. If higher-income groups have higher propensities to save than lower-income groups, and profit earners have a higher propensity to save than wage earners, the savings ratio will be positively related to the degree of inequality in income distribution (personal income distribution) and to the share of profits in total income (functional income distribution). Some evidence of the widening distribution of income in the early stages of development was given in Chapter 3.

A second major determinant of the capacity of a country to save is the growth of income as suggested by the **life-cycle hypothesis of saving**. The basis of the hypothesis, as originally formu-lated by Modigliani and Brumberg (1954), is that individuals and households attempt to spread out consumption evenly over their lifetime so that decisions to save are assumed to be a func-tion of total lifetime earnings and the stage reached in the earnings cycle. A typical pattern of behaviour would be dissaving in youth, positive saving in middle-age and dissaving in retirement. Consider now the effect of income growth within this framework. If income is rising over time, this means that the life earnings and consumption of each successive age group will be higher than the preceding one. If each successive age group is aiming for a higher level of consumption in retirement, the volume of saving of the active households will exceed the dissaving of the cur-rently retired households with a lower level of lifetime consumption. The saving ratio will then tend to rise with the rate of growth of income because the higher the growth rate, the greater the gap between the target future consumption level of the current generation of working households and the dissaving of retired people from a less prosperous generation. Thus, countries with higher growth rates might be expected to have at least higher personal savings ratios than countries with lower growth rates.

But income growth comprises two components: the growth of income per head (PCY) and the growth of population. Income growth due to population growth will affect the savings ratio according to how population growth affects the ratio of active to non-active households. Thus, a third major determinant of the savings ratio is the **dependency ratio**. If population growth rises suddenly this will lead to a higher ratio of young dependants who consume but do not produce, and this will tend to reduce saving. Equally, however, if population growth slows for a long period this will lead to a higher ratio of retired people, who also consume but do not produce. Thus, both high and low population growth may be associated with a low savings ratio. To test the life-cycle hypothesis of saving it is best to relate the savings ratio to the growth of per capita income and to include the age structure of the population, or dependency ratio, as a separate variable (see Hussein and Thirlwall, 1999).

Finally, we have already mentioned the distribution of income as a determinant of the capacity to save. If the propensity to save of the rich is higher than that of the poor, the aggregate savings ratio will be positively related to the degree of inequality both in the personal income distribution (between individuals), and also in the functional distribution (between wages and profits) on the assumption that the propensity to save out of profits is higher than out of wages. It will be remem-bered from Chapter 6 that in Lewis's model of development with unlimited supplies of labour, it is not the absolute level of per capita income that is the prime determinant of the savings ratio but the size of the capitalist surplus and the distribution of income between entrepreneurial profits and other income. According to Lewis (1955): 'if we ask why the less developed countries save so little the answer is not because they are so poor but because their capitalist sector is so small'.

Empirical studies

There have been four major recent studies of the determinants of saving across countries which include all or some of the variables discussed above, and also other variables measuring the willingness to save that we will discuss below. These are Edwards (1996), Masson et al. (1998), Hussein and Thirlwall (1999) and Loayza et al. (2000). Edwards takes panel data for 36 countries over the period 1970–92, distinguishing between private and government savings. Masson et al. use panel data for 21 developed countries (1971–93) and 40 less developed countries (1982–93) to explain the ratio of private saving to GDP. Hussein and Thirlwall take 62 countries over the period 1967–95, taking the domestic savings ratio as the dependent variable. Finally, Loayza et al. use a data set of 160 countries from 1964 to 1994, taking four different measures of private saving (all highly correlated). All the studies find the level and growth of per capita income highly significant as determinants of intercountry differences in the savings ratio. Masson et al. and Hussein and Thirlwall use a non-linear specification for the level of PCY, as discussed above, and find it more significant than the linear specification, thus supporting the shape of the curve in Figure 13.1. Indeed, in the Masson study, a quadratic term for PCY is used so that the savings ratio is first assumed to rise and then fall. For both developed and developing countries the quadratic term turns out to be significantly negative, with the savings ratio peaking at 60 per cent of the US level of PCY. The Loayza et al. study does separate analyses of developing countries and OECD countries and finds the impact of PCY on the savings ratio larger in developing countries than in developed countries, which is also evidence of non-linearity. For the sample as a whole, the authors find that a 10 per cent difference in PCY is associated with a 0.47 percentage point difference in the savings ratio. The authors conclude that 'policies that spur development are an indirect but most effective way to raise saving' and 'successful growth policies may be able to set in motion a virtuous cycle of saving, capital accumulation and growth'. The question is how to get this cumulative process started of rising income, more saving and faster growth, leading to more saving. Monetary and fiscal policy, and the sophistication of the financial system, is likely to play an important part in this process. This leads us on to the topic of the willingness to save and the role of the financial system in promoting saving and allocating resources in the most efficient manner. All of the studies mentioned above include financial variables in their equations.

The willingness to save

Saving represents an intertemporal choice between consumption today and consumption tomorrow. It might be expected, therefore, that the price of present consumption, namely the real rate of interest, will affect saving positively. The higher the rate of interest, the greater the amount of saving. This assumed positive relation also reflects the classical idea of the rate of interest as the reward for waiting, and lies behind the financial liberalization programmes in developing countries which seek to raise the real interest rate in order to encourage saving, investment and growth. Since the 1970s there has been extensive testing of the **financial liberalization hypothesis**, and the role of the **interest rate**, in promoting saving, with mixed and largely inconclusive results. Perhaps this is not surprising since the financial liberalization argument largely refers to *financial* saving, but financial saving is only one component of total saving. If interest rates rise, financial saving may rise but at the expense of other assets, leaving total saving unchanged (see Warman and Thirlwall, 1994). It is also standard theory that any price change has both *income* and *substitution* effects. The substitution effect promotes saving, but the income effect reduces saving (because the same level of income can now be generated by less saving) and the two effects may cancel each other out.

Probably a more important determinant of the willingness to save is **the existence of financial institutions and the range and availability of financial assets to suit savers**. There is no *single* measure that can capture those institutional determinants of the willingness to save. The number, proximity and diversity of financial institutions serving the different needs of savers could be important. Equally, the volume and range of financial assets might matter as a measure of financial deepening. Such measures include: money and quasi-money as a percentage of GDP, money and quasi-money growth, and quasi-liquid liabilities as a percentage of GDP. Domestic credit provided by the banking system as a percentage of GDP is also a measure of financial deepening, but its effect on saving is ambiguous. On the one hand, if bank credit finances investment and growth, this will have a positive effect on saving. On the other hand, an increase in bank credit will relax a liquidity constraint on consumption, resulting in a decline in saving.

Finally, the rate of inflation can be expected to affect the willingness to save, but the effect is ambiguous. On the one hand, inflation acts as a tax on money balance holdings. If individuals wish to restore the real value of their money balance holdings (the so-called **real balance effect**), saving will rise with the rate of inflation. On the other hand, it is natural to expect individuals to avoid the tax if it becomes burdensome in relation to the convenience of holding money. Even if private saving does increase, however, total saving may not increase if the government fully consumes the proceeds of the inflation tax. Inflation will also redistribute income from wages to profits within the private sector if the wage–price coefficient is less than unity. This will increase saving if the propensity to save out of profits is higher than out of wages (as discussed above, p. 393), but this process can last only as long as there is money illusion and workers do not bid for wage increases to match price increases. The most likely relation between inflation and the savings ratio is an inverted U-shape (quadratic function) showing saving rising with mild inflation and then falling as inflation becomes excessive. This type of non-linear relation is also suggested by the evidence available on the relation between inflation and growth (see below, p. 429).

The evidence from the four studies cited above (and others) is that financial variables matter for the performance of saving, but financial deepening and credit availability are much more significant than interest rates. Edwards, and Masson et al., find that the level of financial development is an important determinant of private saving. Hussein and Thirlwall experiment with different measures of financial deepening and find a strong positive relation between the domestic savings ratio of countries and the ratio of quasi-liquid liabilities of the banking system to GDP. Loayza et al. take the ratio of M_2 money to GNP as a measure of financial deepening but find it only weakly significant. More interesting, they find that both higher interest rates and larger private domestic credit flows exert a *negative* effect on the private savings ratio. The authors conclude that 'these results provide a bleaker view of the savings effects of financial liberalization than previous studies suggested'. The process and effects of financial liberalization are discussed later in this chapter.

The overall conclusion would be that while financial variables may not be as important as income variables in determining savings behaviour, economic development itself is dependent

Table 13.2   Interest sensitivity of saving

Country groupings	Initial real interest rate		
	3%	4%	5%
Low-income			
Average for group	0.312	0.306	0.300
Average for 10 poorest	0.177	0.174	0.171
Lower-middle-income	0.532	0.522	0.512
Upper-middle-income	0.560	0.549	0.539
High-income	0.584	0.573	0.562

Note: The data refer to the change (in percentage points) in the saving rate owing to a 1 percentage point increase in the real interest rate. For example, in high-income countries with a real interest rate of 3 per cent, a 1 percentage point rise in the real interest rate would raise the saving rate by nearly two-thirds of a percentage point (0.584 of a percentage point). At higher baseline levels of the real interest rate, the saving response diminishes slightly.

Source: Ogaki et al., 1996.

on the sophistication of the financial system, and there is evidence that saving may be more responsive to interest rates when the level of income rises above subsistence. Research on this topic by Ogaki et al. (1996) is reported in Table 13.2.

It appears that saving is very unresponsive to interest rates in low-income countries where there is little margin of income over subsistence needs, but its responsiveness increases as consumption rises above subsistence needs and people can exercise choice about increasing their present or future consumption.

This leads us to the extensive topic of financial systems, financial policy and economic development.

Financial systems and economic development

One of the characteristic features of developing countries is that quite large sections of the economy are either non-monetized or transactions take place outside the formal financial sector. In other words, the economies of developing countries have a large sector where money is not used as the primary means of exchange, as well as having a large **informal financial sector** or **unorganized money market**. This has a number of consequences that are not conducive to development:

- If transactions take the form of barter, this is both costly in time and wasteful of resources. Sellers must spend time and effort finding buyers who have things they want. Money as a means of exchange avoids the problem of the double coincidence of wants. In this sense money is a resource and its introduction and use in an economy can be highly productive.
- Without a convenient and acceptable means of payment, the division of labour or specialization is impeded, which hinders the process of capital accumulation and reduces productivity. Remember that for Adam Smith (see Chapter 5) it is the division of labour that is the source of increasing returns by allowing complex processes to be broken up into simpler operations

that permit the use of machinery and mass production. Specialization is not worthwhile if the market is limited by the difficulty of exchanging goods.

- Saving takes the form of the acquisition of real assets as opposed to monetary assets – for example land, cattle, gold, jewellery and so on – which absorb resources and may not be used productively.
- Without the existence of financial institutions issuing monetary assets, investment will tend to take place in the sector in which the saving takes place, and this may not be the most productive sector.
- Much of the lending in the informal sector is for consumption purposes and interest rates are very high, both of which can adversely affect total investment. The informal financial sector has an important role to play in the development process, but its integration with the formal financial sector is desirable for a number of reasons.

The informal financial sector

The **informal financial sector** refers to all institutions and transactions that take place outside a country's authorized banking system. The sector plays a significant role in the financing of economic development, although exactly how significant no one really knows. Within the informal sector there are a wide variety of institutions and multifarious arrangements between depositors, lenders and borrowers, some dating back for centuries, rooted in custom and tradition. Others are evolving constantly in response to changing economic and social conditions. The sector is characterized by a high degree of spontaneity and flexibility, with demand creating its own supply. The major participants are moneylenders, merchants, loan brokers, savings groups, and friends and relatives.

Moneylenders have a long tradition in the rural areas of developing countries. They may be landlords, merchants, shopkeepers and pawnbrokers. Loans are typically for short periods at high rates of interest, reflecting the scarcity of funds and the high demand for short-period loans to finance both consumption and investment, for example the holding of stocks (inventories). Merchants often provide loans to clients based on the future sale or purchase of commodities (see Appendix to Chapter 6). Loan brokers act as intermediaries between agents who have surplus funds and those who require credit. The loans tend to be larger and the duration longer than for other sectors in the informal market.

Savings groups take different forms and have different names in various countries, and are also important sources of finance and credit in rural areas. In some cases the savings group consists of individuals who deposit money on a regular basis with a group leader or treasurer, sometimes for special purposes such as tax payments, investment or paying for festivities. If the savings are invested, the returns may be shared by the members. Rules and regulations are shaped by local conditions and traditions. In other cases, members of the savings group take turns to borrow the collected sums of money. One particular type of savings group with a long history in Africa is the Rotating Savings and Credit Association (ROSCA). ROSCAs operate like miniature credit unions based on the 'mutuality' principle, whereby members of the association make a fixed contribution to the savings fund on a periodic basis and are entitled to withdraw money on a rotational basis. Individuals can decide on the cycle of payments and withdrawals that suit their needs. The advantage is that large expenditures can be undertaken by members sooner than if they had to rely on their own personal savings.

Rural financial intermediaries (RFIs), including **micro-credit institutions,** have grown in importance in recent years, operating mainly in the rural sector providing small, unsecured, short-term loans to individuals (mainly women), households and small entrepreneurs. These intermediaries are discussed in greater detail below (p. 402).

Finally, **friends and relatives** are major providers of credit. The credit is flexible and interest-free, and repayment is open-ended.

Despite the growth of the formal financial sector in the majority of developing countries, the informal financial sector continues to flourish because it fulfils needs that are not met elsewhere. First, many rural areas have no ready access to financial institutions, either because they are non-existent or because they are not in the immediate vicinity. The formal financial sector is predominantly urban-based. Second, where banks do exist, there are a number of institutional barriers to their use, in the form of rules of procedure for obtaining financial assistance. The conditions for obtaining loans can be stringent and hard to satisfy for a number of people. It is difficult, for instance, for the poor and illiterate to provide collateral for loans, which is usually required by the formal sector. In practice the formal financial sector tends to be out of reach of peasant farmers, small-scale entrepreneurs and ordinary households, so the informal financial sector fills the gap in the market. Third, the informal sector sometimes acts as a complement to the formal sector. Individuals may borrow from the formal sector but find such credits inadequate and therefore resort to the informal sector to augment their borrowing. In recent years the World Bank Structural Adjustment Programmes, implemented in several countries, have reduced the flow of credit from the formal sector and demand has switched to the informal sector.

A well-developed financial system serving the whole community has five main requisites, each of which can contribute to the process of **financial deepening**, as well as to raising the level of saving and investment, the productivity of capital and the growth of output:

- Full monetization of the economy and the replacement of barter as a means of exchange
- Integration of the informal and formal money markets
- Development of a commercial banking system with central bank supervision
- The creation of development banks and micro-credit facilities for small-scale borrowing
- Development of financial markets and financial intermediaries, issuing and dealing in financial assets.

Monetization and money market integration

Monetization of an economy provides the potential to generate a real investible surplus in several ways. As fiat (paper) money replaces barter in transactions, the demand for money relative to income rises, which releases real resources of equivalent value. The increase in real saving is equal to the increase in the real stock of money held. The issuer of money can appropriate the released resources and increase the level of investment accordingly. In a growing economy monetary expansion is also required to allow an increased volume of transactions to take place. Monetary expansion for this purpose can also be appropriated by governments for development purposes.

The increased use of money not only releases resources, but it also saves and generates resources. It saves resources by replacing barter objects, or commodity money, which may be costly to produce, with money which is virtually costless to produce. It also saves time – which is a resource if the marginal product of labour time is positive – by avoiding the double coincidence of wants necessitated by barter. Money generates resources by facilitating exchange and thereby permitting the greater division of labour (and specialization).

Historically, the growth of the money economy has also been a powerful stimulus to the development of banking and credit mechanisms, which can themselves act as a stimulus to saving and investment. When the range of financial assets is narrow, saving tends to take the form of the acquisition of physical assets. While, in principle, this need not mean that the level of saving is reduced, in practice it depends on how sellers of physical assets dispose of the sale proceeds. If a portion of the proceeds is consumed, the saving of one person is offset by the dissaving of another, and less resources are released for investment than if financial assets had been acquired, issued by financial institutions with an investment function.

For a number of reasons, there is also the need to promote links between the informal and formal financial sectors. The high interest rates charged in the informal sector add to costs and add to household debt, and these could be reduced if the informal sector was exposed to greater competition from the formal sector. This could be done by transforming informal institutions into more formal ones, or using the informal sector as a conduit for formal funds, taking advantage of the low transaction costs, local knowledge and greater flexibility in the informal sector. There could also be support mechanisms to guarantee loans from the informal sector.

It is also important that the capital market should be integrated, in the sense that the interest-rate structure is unified. The consequence of a fragmented capital market in which interest rates vary from one sector to another because of a lack of information and factor immobility is that some sectors of the economy may be able to borrow funds far below the rate of interest prevailing in other sectors where the productivity of capital is higher. The allocation of capital is distorted and inefficient and the capital–output ratio is higher than it would otherwise be: the solution is to encourage funds into the organized money market, and to extend the provision of financial institutions into sectors of the economy that lack them.

Paradoxically (on a classical view of the world), development of the organized money market can both *lower* average interest rates in the economy at large and *raise* the level of saving because the unorganized money market tends to charge higher interest rates and lends mainly for consumption purposes, whereas in the organized money market interest rates are lower and lending is more for investment purposes.

Developing a banking system

Developing a national banking system, comprising a central bank, a commercial banking system and special development banks, is one of the first priorities of development strategy. The functions of **a central bank** include the following:

- Issuing currency and lending to government, whereby real resources are transferred to the government in the manner described earlier (with a strong central bank it is very much easier to give priority to the needs of the government and the public sector).
- Developing a fractional reserve banking system through which it can provide liquidity and control credit (a central bank can require member banks to hold reserves in government bonds, and the growth of the bond market itself can aid development without excessive monetary expansion).
- Developing other financial institutions, especially institutions that provide long-term loan finance for development, and a market for government securities.

- Maintaining a high level of demand, through the appropriate use of monetary policy, to achieve capacity growth.
- Applying selective credit controls when necessary, in the interests of developing particular sectors of the economy.

The **commercial banking system** has two important functions: to create credit, and to encourage thrift and allocate saving in the most socially productive manner. The ability of an economic system to create credit is important for two main reasons. First, it can compensate for the failure of the economic system to generate enough investment to match planned saving. Second, it provides the means by which growth is financed. This is the real significance of the invention of paper money and credit – permitting the economic system to expand in response to the continual opportunities for growth provided by technical progress, which a barter system or a purely metallic currency do not allow.

Banks can encourage thrift and allocate savings more productively than would otherwise be the case, by offering a return on savings and enabling savings to be used outside the sector in which they originate. Banks can help to break down sectoral bottlenecks and to unify interest rates. But commercial banking is still rudimentary in many developing economies. The ratio of bank deposits to national income averages approximately 20 per cent and the proportion of demand deposits to the total money supply averages between 30 and 40 per cent. In developed countries, in contrast, the ratio of bank deposits to national income usually exceeds 50 per cent and the money supply consists largely of the deposits of commercial banks. The number of banks relative to population size is also small. In the developing countries as a whole, the average number of banks per million of the population is about 20 compared with 200 in developed countries. Banks need to be numerous and dispersed if they are to act as catalysts for small savings. The case for **branch banking** is that it can tap small savings. If savings institutions are pushed under people's noses they will save more than if the nearest savings institution is some distance away! Case example 13.1 describes Vietnam's Bank on Wheels, which is also an example of micro-credit as discussed in the next section.

Case example 13.1	**Vietnam's Bank on Wheels**

Ma Seo Sang, a Hmong widow living on less than 25 cents a day in the mountainous region of Vietnam, needed help. She had sold a pig to pay for her husband's funeral, paid a fine incurred by her son by selling one of her buffalo, and redeemed a debt with the other. She had borrowed all she could from relatives. Moneylenders, if they would even lend to her, would charge exorbitant interest (up to 10 per cent per month). She needed money to survive.

Sang's plight raises many issues related to extreme poverty, of which lack of access to credit is one. Part of the solution is microfinance – the provision of basic financial services to the poor. Microfinance can offer a path out of poverty. But how long is the path, and can it be shortened? Vietnam's experiment with the Mobile Banking Programme under the World Bank's Rural Finance Project provides a partial answer to those questions. It suggests that creative ways can be found not only for lenders to reach out to the poor but also for the poor to 'reach in' to lenders.

continued overleaf

Case example 13.1	Vietnam's Bank on Wheels – *continued*

In 1998 the Vietnam Bank for Agriculture and Rural Development (Agribank) initiated a mobile banking programme modelled after similar programmes in Bangladesh and Malaysia. It procured 159 vehicles equipped to travel on dirt roads and hilly pathways, enabling loan officers to reach remote areas to process loan applications, disburse money, collect payments, and mobilize savings deposits. The visits followed a fixed calendar and were announced in advance.

Once the programme was launched, it became clear that more than just difficult access prevented the poorest from taking advantage of its services. Their isolation caused them to have feelings of helplessness and fear. In the upland ethnic group, the higher up a mountain people lived and the longer their isolation, the more they seemed to believe that they could not get credit. Suspicion was another issue. What if the lender offered a loan and then, if a payment were late, took a farmer's buffalo, as had happened to Sang?

Above all, the poorest people lacked confidence and self-esteem. For example, the illiterate poor would wonder how they could fill in applications and receipts. Others felt they could do nothing to earn extra income to repay a loan. Many were afraid to venture into activities other than cultivation and animal husbandry, even though opportunities existed.

For mobile banking to work for borrowers, the following services had to be made available: **offering appropriate loan products; linking lending and saving; combining credit and human asset building.**

For lenders, it was necessary that the mobile banking experiment be financially self-sustaining. It thus required the following ingredients: **group-based lending; linking formal and informal credit; reasonable interest rates.**

Barely five years in operation, the Mobile Banking Programme has proved to be relatively cost-effective, providing financial services to 315,000 poor households. Preliminary data show that, on average, each mobile bank disbursed 1,921 loans, collected 1,387 payments, and transported cash on 75 occasions to 16 local points monthly. The excellent repayment rate suggests that the poor are good credit risks. The programme also mobilized 1983 small savings accounts every month, showing that the poor can be good savers.

As for Ma Seo Sang, she received a loan of about $300 and used the money to buy some chickens and pigs to raise. The income she made from selling her animals helped her earn a living.

Source: G. Nguyen Tien Hung (2004), 'Bank on Wheels', *Finance and Development*, June.

Rural financial intermediaries and micro-credit[4]

Rural financial intermediaries (RFIs) and micro-credit institutions play a crucial role in helping the poor and fostering the growth of small business where potential entrepreneurs are precluded from borrowing from the banking system because they are too poor and lack collateral. Within the structure of RFIs there is a diversity of organizations and financial services. In the rural sector where most RFIs operate, and where most lending takes place, there are different niches and markets to be served. There are several case studies of successful RFIs. One such study is for Indonesia (Chaves and Gonzalez-Vega, 1995). In the 1980s and 1990s the Indonesian government established a network of semi-independent, locally operated RFIs which have been highly successful, largely through the recruitment of local agents to gather information on borrowers, monitor their actions and enforce loan contracts. This has kept down loan defaults to less than 2 per cent of lending. In the early 1990s there were 13,000 such intermediaries reaching out to over four million people, dispensing loans of between $50 and $600. Most of the RFIs made accounting profits because fixed costs are kept low, and the effective interest rate is high, ranging from 30 to 84 per cent per annum. Interestingly, the loans are not group-based; they are to individuals, and the pressure to repay comes from the local agents who are given appropriate incentives not to shirk, or to collude with the borrower or be bribed.

This contrasts with the micro-credit movement where most lending is through **joint-liability lending** which makes all members of the group jointly liable for any loan given to its members. If the group does not repay, there is no further access to loans. Thus, joint liability group lending stimulates screening, monitoring and enforcement of contracts among borrowers, reducing costs to the lenders. Because of the close proximity of borrowers within a group, information asymmetries between lenders and borrowers are reduced. Evidence shows (see Hermes and Lensik, 2007) that groups with stronger group ties have better repayment records, as do groups with written rules and a strong group leader, and which are more open geographically with no other access to credit.

There are now over 3,000 micro-finance institutions across the world (some now also in developed countries), and it is estimated that at least 100 million poor people have benefited. The lobby group Microcredit Summit Campaign wants to see a vast expansion of such institutions, particularly to achieve the 2015 Millennium Development Goals.

The bank that pioneered the concept of micro-credit in developing countries was the Grameen (meaning 'village') Bank in Bangladesh. It was formally established in 1983 (seven years after the initial idea) by Muhammad Yunus, an economics professor at Chittagong University in Bangladesh, who instead of teaching the economics of poverty from an ivory tower decided to do something practical about it, based on the philosophy that everyone has the right to credit, but the poor are excluded from the conventional banking system. But the best way for people to help themselves out of poverty is to be able to borrow to set up small businesses. Thus, the Grameen Bank was founded as a micro-credit organization to lend to the rural poor, especially women, without collateral – sums as little as $10. A poor woman may obtain a micro-loan to buy an oven in order to sell hot food. She repays the loan with interest; others can borrow; she can borrow more to buy another oven and ultimately become a prosperous trader. Another poor woman uses her micro-loan to buy chickens; starts selling eggs; repays the loan; borrows more and becomes a chicken farmer. These are simple, real-life stories of what is possible. Lending and repayment take place within a group context (usually five people) where members of the group agree to monitor one another, so that there is peer pressure to use loans wisely and to repay. Each member of the group normally comes from the same village and members have a similar economic and social background. Loans are first given to two members of the group, who are closely observed for two months and must repay the loan in weekly instalments. If the repayments are made, then two others can borrow. Loan use is monitored by the staff of the Grameen Bank and groups meet collectively to discuss the choice of new projects. All credit transactions are discussed openly, so there is complete transparency concerning what is going on. There can be no 'cover-ups' and no corruption. The record of repayment to the Grameen Bank is close to 98 per cent of loans; far better than the record of repayment to the commercial banking system where bad debts are rife.

Muhammad Yunus

Born 1940, Chittagong, Bangladesh. Professor of Economics at Chittagong University, and founder of the Grameen Bank in 1983 lending small sums mainly to groups of poor women, with the philosophy that everyone has the right to credit, not just the rich with collateral. The micro-credit movement has now spread throughout the developing world and has lifted millions of families out of poverty. He and the Grameen Bank were awarded the Nobel Prize for Peace in 2006.

The conventional explanation for the low default rate is the peer pressure from the group, but research shows (Pankaj, 1996) that the explanation is much deeper than this; it lies within the culture and ethos that the Bank has developed amongst its employees, and the relationship between the Bank's employees and the client borrowers. Pankaj could find no evidence of members of a group not being able to borrow if one member defaulted. The main explanation for the very high repayment rate seems to be that the Bank is very tightly structured, with checks on clients and borrowings at every stage. Each borrowing Group has five members, and six Groups make a Centre which meets weekly at a fixed time. Each Centre is supervised by an employee from a Grameen branch bank who may look after between 10 and 15 Centres. Each branch bank is answerable to an area manager. The line of command is clear and there is supervision at every stage. It is this organizational structure of the Bank that lies at the heart of its success. Other banks serving the poor in rural communities could learn lessons from the Grameen structure.

The Grameen Bank also involves itself in social development programmes in the villages to improve the quality of life, such as encouraging members to build houses and sanitation facilities, planting trees and kitchen gardens. There is also a comprehensive training programme in maternal health, nutrition and child care. In Bangladesh alone there are over 1,000 branches of the bank serving 36,000 villages, which have lent more than $6 billion to 8 million people. In 2006 Muhammad Yunus and the Grameen Bank were awarded the Nobel Prize for Peace.

The Grameen idea has now spread to over 100 countries. Not all micro-credit banks operate in the same way, but all are designed to lend to poor people denied access to credit from the commercial banking system because they have no collateral. Other well-known micro-credit institutions across the world are Banco Sol in Bolivia (the first micro-credit bank to be set up in Latin America in 1992), Banco Compartamos in Mexico (lending mainly to women), Acción Internacional based in the United States with affiliates in 13 Latin American countries (including Mibanco in Peru), Kenya's Rural Enterprise Programme (K-Rep) and Bank Rakyat in Indonesia.

At the beginning of the micro-credit movement, almost all the banks relied on public subsidies to operate because of the high overhead costs of administering very small loans – despite high interest rates on loans of 20 to 30 per cent. In the last ten years alone, micro-credit institutions (many run by NGOs) have received public subsidies of $10 billion. Commercially operated micro-credit institutions have lower operating costs and charge lower interest rates, but the size of the loans is larger and the borrowers are not so poor.

The challenge for the future is to see whether micro-finance can be extended more on a commercial basis without long-term subsidies, but without compromising the basic purpose of micro-credit – which is to lend to the very poorest who are cut off from the normal banking system. At present, the evidence is that there seems to be a trade-off between the commercialization of micro-finance and reaching out to the poor. Cull et al. (2007) attempt to examine this issue rigorously by taking a sample of 124 micro-credit institutions in 49 countries to see whether there is any significant relation between the profitability of banks and their outreach to the poor. Three types of bank are distinguished: (i) those that lend to groups (48), (ii) those that lend to individuals (56), and (iii) village lenders (20). What the evidence shows is that individual-based lenders seem to have higher profitability than group-based institutions, but the fraction of poor (and female) borrowers in the loan portfolio is lower in the latter case. The authors conclude:

> we find examples of institutions that have managed to achieve profitability together with notable outreach to the poor – achieving the ultimate promise of micro-finance. *But they are so far the exceptions.* (emphasis added)

Cull et al. (2009) have also used data from the Microfinance Information Exchange covering 364 institutions with £25 billion of assets and 10 million borrowers in the period 2002 to 2004, distinguishing between the activities of the commercial micro-banks on the one hand and the NGOs on the other. They find that:

- Commercial micro-banks account for more assets, but NGOs reach out to more people
- More micro-banks are profitable (73 per cent) than NGOs (54 per cent)
- Most micro-banks lend to individuals while most NGOs lend to groups
- NGOs give much smaller loans than micro-banks
- NGOs charge higher interest rates (25 per cent a year for the median bank) than micro-banks (13 per cent) because operating costs are higher (26 cents per $ lent for NGOs compared with 12 cents per $ for micro-banks)
- Default rates don't differ between the two types of micro-credit institution.

The authors remark, however, that evidence on the social returns to micro-lending, and by how much people have been lifted out of poverty, is scant. This is the research challenge for the future.

Development banks

Development banks play a particularly important role in the development process because it is not the explicit function of the private commercial banking system to have development priorities in mind when making loans, unless directed by the government. The function of commercial banks is to make a profit for their shareholders. This means that commercial banks are generally risk-averse and have short time horizons. It also means that they are only interested in their own cash flows and have no particular interest in the *social* profitability of the projects that they lend for, or in lending to poor people. Development banks can afford to have longer time horizons, take more risks, pursue development objectives and focus on the social profitability of lending, as well as encouraging saving.

The activities of the Tonga Development Bank provide an interesting case study.[5] The Bank was established in 1977 'to promote the expansion of Tonga for the economic advancement of the people of Tonga'. The Bank's lending policy gives priority to projects that have the potential to increase exports or reduce imports, involve local entrepreneurship, use local inputs, contribute to increased employment opportunities, particularly for women, and increase income for the poorer sections of the community in rural areas and the outer islands. Regarding exports, if economic growth is constrained by a shortage of foreign exchange, any project financed by the bank that earns net foreign exchange will give a higher social return than private return because the growth of output will be higher than would otherwise have been the case. In Tonga, the commercial banking system would not lend to producers wishing to grow the vegetable squash, because the venture was regarded as too risky. However the Tonga Development Bank lent nearly $10 million to squash producers, and squash now accounts for 80 per cent of the country's export earnings. The Bank reaches out to nearly 50 per cent of households in Tonga, and 70 per cent of all loans to the private sector are funded by the Bank. The Bank fills an important gap in the market for small loans because commercial banks will not lend for projects of less than $5,000. There can be little doubt that the Tonga Development Bank is playing a pivotal role in the development of the economy of Tonga and is able to do things that the private sector would not contemplate. The positive externalities conferred fully justify interest rate subsidies.

All development banks have a role to play in stimulating the capital market. They can do this by selling their own stocks and bonds to raise finance, by helping enterprises to float or place their own securities, and by selling from their own portfolio of investments.

Financial intermediaries

The importance of having a wide variety of financial intermediaries is that they can offer a diversity of financial assets with different yields, maturities and divisibilities to suit savers and investors with different requirements and different time horizons. This can increase the level of both saving and investment, and also improve the efficiency of resource allocation.

As far as the level of saving and investment is concerned, financial intermediaries offer four major advantages:

- In general, savers wish to lend for only a short period of time (to remain liquid), while investors wish to borrow for a longer period of time. Direct lending from savers to investors, without financial intermediation, would involve savers committing themselves for longer periods than they really would like because investment does not generally generate returns immediately. Financial intermediaries, however, are able to pool risks and can borrow short and lend long, thus suiting both savers and investors.
- The use of financial intermediaries reduces transaction costs. Direct lending, whereby savers have to find suitable borrowers or investors have to find suitable lenders, is both time consuming and costly. Reduced transaction costs encourage both saving and investment.
- Financial intermediaries can specialize in particular areas of business, which reduces information costs by accumulating knowledge of various markets. This lessens the credit risks associated with lending, and also encourages greater saving and investment.
- Investment projects are invariably larger than the savings of any one individual or group of individuals. The existence of financial intermediaries overcomes the problem of indivisibilities.

As far as the *efficiency* of resource allocation is concerned, the great advantage of financial intermediaries is that the creation of financial assets and liabilities allows savers to hold part of their wealth in financial form. This means that investment is no longer confined to the sector where the saving takes place, thereby facilitating the allocation of resources to the most productive sectors of the economy.

Financial liberalization

The formal financial sector, consisting of a central bank, a commercial banking system and various other financial intermediaries, typically suffers from various forms of **financial repression**, which may thwart the development process. For example, the government may have a near-monopoly of the banking system and restrict the growth of financial institutions. Private sector banks may have to keep high reserve requirements and lend compulsorily to the government to finance its deficits. The central bank may impose credit rationing on the commercial banks, or insist that the banks lend to certain priority sectors. Nominal interest rates may be kept artificially low, so that with inflation the *real* rate of interest is negative, discouraging the acquisition of interest-bearing financial assets. These are all examples of financial repression.

The argument for **financial liberalization** is that the various forms of financial repression impede the development of financial markets. The consequences, it is argued, are a reduction of the flow of funds to the formal financial sector and distortion of the allocation of resources, leading to lower levels of saving, investment and output growth than otherwise would be the case.

The importance of the growth of the money economy and financial deepening for economic development along the lines indicated above has been stressed in the development literature for a long time,[6] but it was McKinnon (1973) and Shaw (1973) who independently in 1973 first highlighted the dangers of financial repression in a rigorous way, and argued the case for maximum financial liberalization. Their views became highly influential in the thinking of the IMF and the World Bank in the design of programmes for the financial restructuring of countries as part of structural adjustment programmes. Their arguments, however, emphasize different points:

- **McKinnon's argument** is that money holdings and capital accumulation are complementary in the development process. Because of the lumpiness of investment expenditure and the reliance on self-financing, agents need to accumulate money balances before investment takes place. Positive (and high) real interest rates are necessary to encourage agents to accumulate money balances, and investment will take place as long as the real rate of return on investment exceeds the real rate of interest.
- **Shaw's argument**, on the other hand, stresses the importance of financial liberalization for financial deepening, and the beneficial effect of high interest rates on encouragement to save and discouragement to invest in low-yielding projects. The increased liabilities of the banking system, resulting from higher real interest rates, enable the banking system to lend more resources for productive investment in a more efficient way. A simple diagram (Figure 13.2) can illustrate the McKinnon–Shaw argument.

Figure 13.2 is a standard classical savings and investment diagram showing saving as a positive function of the real interest rate (reflecting the idea of time preference and the interest rate as the reward for abstaining from present consumption), and investment as a negative function of the real interest rate (reflecting the diminishing marginal efficiency of investment). With no interest

Figure 13.2   The McKinnon–Shaw argument

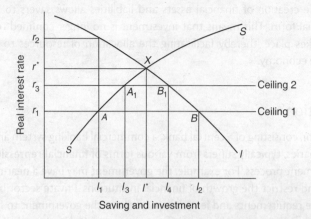

rate controls, the equilibrium rate of interest would be r^* and the level of saving and investment would be I^*.

Now suppose that the government imposes a ceiling on the *nominal deposit rate* for savers, giving a *real* rate of interest of r_1. This would mean that saving is I_1, and on classical assumptions that prior saving is necessary for investment, this also constrains investment to I_1. If there was no ceiling on the *loan* rate of interest, the banks could charge interest rate r_2 to investors and the gap between r_1 and r_2 would give substantial profits to banks, which they could use for various forms of non-price competition. At r_2 there is no unsatisfied demand for investment funds.

Suppose, however, that the interest rate ceiling applies to loans as well as deposits. This means that saving is still I_1, but investment demand is now I_2 and there is an excess demand for investment funds equal to AB. Credit will have to be rationed. There will be a tendency for banks to favour less risky projects with lower rates of return. This will lower the overall productivity of investment.

If the interest rate ceiling is raised so that real interest rates rise to r_3, this encourages saving from I_1 to I_3. This leads to more investment, credit rationing is reduced and the productivity of investment rises. From this argument, it would seem to follow that saving and investment will be optimal and credit rationing will disappear when the market is fully liberalized and the real rate of interest is left to find its market clearing level at r^*.

Critics of financial liberalization and empirical evidence

Many of the arguments for financial liberalization sound convincing on the surface, but a number of qualifications need to be made. The experience of financial liberalization across the globe has been very mixed, and we shall consider some of the empirical evidence relating to the effect of liberalization on saving, investment and growth as we examine some of the major criticisms of the financial liberalization argument.[7]

First, the argument refers to *financial* saving, but financial saving is only one type of saving. Financial saving may increase as interest rates are liberalized, but there may simply be a substitution between financial assets and other assets, leaving total saving unchanged. It is also well known that any price change (in this case the interest rate) has income as well as substitution effects. The substitution effect promotes saving by making current consumption more 'expensive', but the income effect deters saving because at higher interest rates the same income can be obtained with less saving, and the two effects may cancel each other out. This being so, it is perhaps surprising, as Dornbusch and Reynoso (1989) once remarked, 'to find so strong a belief in the ability of higher interest rates to mobilise saving'.

In fact, many of the empirical studies and surveys of the results of financial liberalization in various countries are extremely cautious in their conclusions. Research by Gupta (1987) on 22 Asian and Latin American countries over the period 1967–76 suggests that there is little support for the 'repressionist' hypothesis that the positive substitution effect of real interest rates on savings dominates the negative income effect. The most important determinant of saving is real income. Giovannini (1983) concludes from his research on eight Asian countries that his results 'cast serious doubts on the view that the interest elasticity of savings is significantly positive and easy to detect in developing countries'. Similarly, a study by two World Bank economists (Cho and Khatkhate, 1990) of the financial liberalization experience of five Asian countries concluded that:

> financial reform, whether comprehensive and sweeping or measured and gradual, does not seem to have made any significant difference to the saving and investment activities in the liberalised countries. It was believed until recently that removal of the repressive policies would boost saving. The survey in this paper of the consequences of reform does not reveal any systematic trend or pattern in regard to saving . . . it lends support to the conclusion that decisions to save are determined by several factors and the relationship between saving and real interest rates is at best ambiguous.

Bandiera et al. (2000) examine the liberalization experience of eight countries (Chile, Ghana, Indonesia, South Korea, Malaysia, Mexico, Turkey and Zimbabwe) over 25 years and conclude 'our results cannot offer support for the hypothesis that financial liberalization will increase saving. On the contrary, the indications are that liberalization overall – and in particular those elements that relax liquidity constraints – may be associated with a fall in saving.' Maxwell Fry (1995), a leading authority on finance and development and an ardent advocate of financial liberalization, has conceded that 'what is agreed . . . is that if an effect [on saving] exists at all, it is relatively small' and that 'positive interest effects are easier to find in Asia than in other parts of the world, but even in Asia the effects appear to have diminished over the past two decades'.

If financial liberalization does not increase aggregate saving, its positive impact on development must come through a more efficient allocation of resources, which raises the productivity of investment. In other words, as stressed by Shaw, financial liberalization should concentrate on the quality of investment rather than the quantity. There is not much evidence on this point, but the World Bank, which devoted its *World Development Report 1989* to the topic of financial systems and economic development, claims that in countries with positive real interest rates, the average productivity of investment (as measured by the incremental output–capital ratio) was four times higher than in countries with strongly negative real interest rates. Bandiera et al. also conclude their study by saying that even if financial liberalization does not increase private saving, it does not follow that the process contracts the volume of funds applied to productive investment. For one thing, financial liberalization can increase the flow of capital from abroad, and secondly the reform process can have the effect of eliminating less productive uses of loanable funds. This is an area where more research needs to be done.

A second major criticism of the financial liberalization argument is that the model seems to treat banks simply as savings depositories, with the presumption that the supply of loans from the banking system depends on deposits held by the banks, and if deposits increase, loans will automatically increase. In short, the supply of credit is treated as exogenously determined. However, if banks have the power to create credit (which they do), backed by a central bank acting as lender of last resort, the supply of loans will depend on the demand for loans, not on the supply of deposits. The supply of loans becomes endogenous. Within this framework, what is important is not so much incentives for saving, but incentives for investment, which may require lower interest rates. This is part of the **Keynesian and post-Keynesian** critique of the financial liberalization school. The work of the foremost post-Keynesian, Paul Davidson (1986), is representative of this line of argument. Davidson argues that all that is needed to initiate additional real investment is finance provided by an increase in total bank loans and there is no need for prior savings, 'as long as the banks can create new finance via acceptable bank accounting practices'.

How the supply of credit responds to the interest rate, and how investment is affected by the supply of credit and the rate of interest, becomes very much an empirical matter that can only be settled by an appeal to the facts. Warman and Thirlwall (1994) found that for Mexico, over the period 1960–90, financial saving responded positively to the rate of interest, and this led to an increase in the supply of credit from the banking system to the private sector. However, while the increased supply of credit affects investment positively, there is a strong negative effect of interest rates on the level of investment, holding the supply of credit constant, and the *net* effect of higher real interest rates on investment is adverse. This is also the central conclusion of Demetriades and Devereux (1992) from research on 63 developing countries over the period 1961–90. They find that the negative effect of a high cost of capital on investment outweighs the effect of a greater supply of investible funds. Greene and Villanueva (1991), in a sample of 23 developing countries over the period 1975–87, likewise show a negative effect of real interest rates on investment.

This leads to a third worry about the financial liberalization model, which is that it ignores the adverse effect that high real interest rates can have on costs and the level of demand in an economy, which may lead to stagflation (a combination of cost inflation and rising unemployment). This is another aspect of the post-Keynesian critique of the financial liberalization model (see Dutt, 1990–91). High interest rates not only discourage investment, but may also lead to currency overvaluation by attracting capital from overseas, which leads to a fall in exports, and also increases the cost of servicing government debt, which leads to cuts in government expenditure. This has occurred in Africa (see *African Development Report*, 1994). Currency overvaluation and cuts in government expenditure are both deflationary. In Latin America in the 1970s, financial liberalization went wrong because there was an explosion of government debt, economic instability and excessively high real interest rates, which led to bankruptcies, bank failures and prolonged recession. In the immortal words of Diaz-Alejandro (1985): 'Goodbye financial repression, hello financial crash'! Financial liberalization programmes were abandoned (temporarily).

A fourth critique of the financial liberalization school concerns the relationship between the formal and the informal financial sectors. Higher real interest rates are likely to attract funds away from the informal money market, or **curb market**, where there is no regulation over the use of funds. If banks are subject to reserve requirements and are forced to lend compulsorily to governments, the diversion of funds away from the informal sector may lead to the total supply of loans to the private sector being reduced. This is part of the argument of the **neostructuralist school** (see Buffie, 1984). The hypothesis is very difficult to test directly without information on the supply and composition of credit from the curb market. To the extent that curb loans are mainly for consumption purposes and the government uses the reserve requirements of the banks for productive investment, the problem may not be serious. If, however, the curb loans are for investment and the government uses the banks to finance current account budget deficits, the reallocation of funds between the sectors will adversely affect the total level of saving and investment.

A final point to make is that it does not follow that credit rationing will necessarily be eliminated and resources allocated more 'efficiently' if interest rates are not controlled and are allowed to reach their market clearing level. As Stiglitz[8] and Weiss (1981) showed in a classic paper, banks suffer from the problem of **adverse selection** because of **asymmetric information** on the part of borrowers and lenders. Borrowers know more than lenders about the risks involved in a loan transaction. A rational profit-maximizing bank may therefore be expected to practise credit rationing to reduce risk, and not simply lend to those projects that seem to offer the highest return but with more risk attached.

Where do these various criticisms leave the financial liberalization argument? Clearly, the existence of financial repression has to be taken seriously, but it does not follow that the more liberalization there is the better, when we know that financial markets have many imperfections, and that competition between banks and other financial institutions can lead to **financial distress** if there are not institutional structures in place with adequate standards of accounting and auditing to prevent bad loans. Governments will always need to intervene for prudential reasons, and also for strategic reasons either as a major borrower or to direct credit. Particular care needs to be exercised in the liberalization of interest rates because of their impact on costs, investment demand, the exchange rate and the cost of financing government deficits. This raises the intriguing question of what is the 'optimum' real rate of interest for a country? This is virtually impossible to answer (see Clarke, 1996), but even in classical terms it is not clear that the optimum real interest rate (r^* in Figure 13.2) is necessarily positive. The savings and investment curves could cut below the horizontal axis if liquidity preference is very high and investment demand is very weak.

Ultimately, financial liberalization has to be judged by its impact on economic growth and development, and here the evidence is very mixed. In a major cross-section study of 80 countries over the period 1960–89, King and Levine (1993) conclude that 'higher levels of financial development are significantly and robustly correlated with faster current and future rates of economic growth, physical capital accumulation and economic efficiency improvements'. Using cross-section analysis, however, it is difficult to test for causality. It could be that financial development is itself the product of growth and economic development. In fact Demetriades and Hussein (1996), taking time-series data for 16 countries, find considerable evidence of bidirectional causality between levels of financial deepening and economic development, and conclude that different countries exhibit different causality patterns, reflecting differences in financial sector policies and institutional structures. Arestis and Demetriades (1997) find that in South Korea the real interest rate and growth performance have been negatively related, and South Korea, despite financial liberalization, has deliberately pursued a policy of keeping real interest rates low in order to encourage investment. This is also the message from the World Bank's analysis of the *East Asian Miracle* (World Bank, 1993). It says 'a policy of moderate financial repression at positive real interest rates may have boosted aggregate investment and growth in the HPAEs [high-performing Asian economies] by transferring income from depositors, primarily households, to borrowers, primarily firms'.

De Gregorio and Guidotti (1995) suggest that the relationship between real interest rates and growth is likely to be an inverted U-shape because negative real interest rates are not conducive to financial development and growth, and very high real interest rates are also likely to reduce growth by adversely affecting investment and leading to a concentration on risky projects. Somewhere in between, growth is likely to be maximized. Fry (1997) tests this hypothesis across 85 countries for the period 1971–95 and finds broad support for the idea, with the growth rate maximized with the real interest rate at zero!

What is clear from all the evidence across countries and continents is that if financial reforms are to succeed, they must be implemented in an appropriate macroeconomic, financial and institutional framework, with proper sequencing between internal and external liberalization. Sequencing is important because if countries liberalize their external sector before or at the same time as internal liberalization, it could have severe repercussions for the exchange rate. If there is no confidence in the country, the relaxation of capital controls could lead to capital flight and downward pressure on the exchange rate. On the other hand, higher real interest rates could attract massive capital inflows, leading to excessive currency appreciation. Either way, exchange rate instability is not conducive to macroeconomic stability.

Liberalization has been more successful in Asia than in Latin America and Africa because it has taken place in an environment of greater macroeconomic stability with a sounder institutional framework of regulation and supervision of the banking system. Macroeconomic stability means manageable fiscal and balance-of-payments deficits and low inflation to encourage the holding of financial assets and to allow funds to be devoted to the private sector. Confidence in the banking system is also important and requires the restructuring of bank balance sheets, the removal of bad debts and a strengthening of the management and risk evaluation capabilities of bank managers in order to avoid bankruptcies. Governments need to strengthen banking regulation and supervision at the same time that liberalization takes place. For successful liberalization, Fry (1997) outlines the following five prerequisites:

- Adequate prudential regulation and supervision of commercial banks, implying some minimal levels of accounting and legal infrastructure
- A reasonable degree of price stability
- Fiscal discipline
- Profit maximizing, competitive behaviour by the commercial banks
- A tax system that does not impose discriminatory explicit or implicit taxes on financial intermediation.

Two brief contrasting case studies of financial liberalization are presented in Case example 13.2.

| Case example 13.2 | **Financial liberalization in Indonesia and Kenya, mid-1990s** |

Indonesia

Foreign exchange controls were eliminated in Indonesia in 1971, partly at the urging of the IMF but also because these controls reduced the efficiency of international trade and payments, and were extremely difficult to enforce given Indonesia's proximity to an open international financial centre in Singapore. However, extensive controls on the domestic financial system remained in place until 1983. Only then were interest rates liberalized and controls on credit allocation relaxed. Prudential supervision was strengthened in 1984, after the initial liberalization of the banking system. Similarly,

Case example 13.2	Financial liberalization in Indonesia and Kenya, mid-1990s – *continued*

after relaxing controls on the entry of new banks and easing restrictions on the extension of bank branches in 1988–89, stricter prudential regulations were introduced by the central bank to constrain the explosion of bank credit that followed deregulation.

Indonesia's experience is therefore characterized by the implementation of several large reforms, each followed by retrenchment and consolidation. Although problems have emerged because institutional development, especially in the area of prudential supervision, has tended to lag behind deregulation measures, the overall success of reform has been considerable. Real interest rates have been positive since 1983, and financial deepening has been extensive. Privately owned banks now constitute a much larger proportion of the banking sector, as the relative importance of publicly owned banks has declined, and securities markets, especially the Jakarta Stock Exchange, have become more important. Although there have been occasional setbacks, and institutional weaknesses in the accounting and legal systems remain, overall the financial liberalization strategy pursued in Indonesia has been supportive of wider economic development.

Kenya

Financial liberalization in Kenya is much more recent. Ceilings on bank lending rates were not removed until July 1991. The central bank continued to announce guidelines for the sectoral composition of bank credit expansion, although these were not strictly enforced after interest rate liberalization. International financial liberalization is even more recent. Offshore borrowing by domestic residents has been permitted only since early 1994, and portfolio capital inflows from abroad were restricted until January 1995. Supporting structural and institutional reforms have yet to be fully implemented. Many banks remain publicly owned and competition among them is limited.

Deregulation of interest rates in this monopolistic environment permitted banks to widen their margins such that real interest rates on bank deposits fell substantially. Partly in consequence, financial deepening has been modest, especially when measured by the ratio of private sector credit to national income. Although it is too early to evaluate the success of financial liberalization, the lack of accompanying institutional and structural reforms suggests that financial sector reforms will provide only modest benefits to the overall Kenyan development strategy.

Source: *Finance and Development*, June 1997.

Fiscal policy and taxation[9]

There is another arm of the prior-savings approach to the financing of development from domestic resources that needs to be considered, and that is the use of fiscal policy and taxation. Fiscal policy has two major roles in the financing of development. The first is to maintain the economy at full employment so that the savings capacity of the economy is not impaired. The second is to design a tax policy to raise the marginal propensity to save of the economy as far above the average as possible without discouraging work effort and consistent with an equitable distribution of the tax burden.

Using fiscal policy to maintain full employment will involve deficit finance if unemployed or underused real resources exist in the Keynesian sense due to a deficiency of aggregate demand. While deficit finance may be inflationary in the short run until supply has had time to adjust, there is an important analytical distinction between the means by which resources are made available for investment through deficit finance at less than full employment and the means by which savings are generated by inflation. In the former case savings are generated by an increase in real output; in the latter case by a reduction in real consumption through a combination of factors, including a real balance effect on outside money,[10] income redistribution from low savers to high savers, and money illusion.

Fiscal policy to raise the marginal propensity to save above the average is concerned with the implementation of taxes to reduce consumption in the private sector. Saving brought about by taxation is **involuntary saving**. How much taxation a country raises as a proportion of national income depends on two major factors: the **taxable capacity** of the country, and the **tax effort** made by the country in relation to its taxable capacity. The taxable capacity of a country depends on such factors as the overall level of per capita income of the country, the distribution of income, the level of literacy and urbanization, the size of the industrial sector, the importance of trade, whether the country has mineral resources, and the amount of foreign investment. In turn, the tax effort depends on the extent to which a country exploits these various tax bases and on the rates of tax applied to the bases.

The overall **buoyancy** of a tax system is measured by the proportional change in total tax revenue ($\Delta T/T$) with respect to the proportional change in national income ($\Delta Y/Y$), and is composed of two parts: the elasticity of tax revenue ($\Delta T/T$) with respect to the tax base ($\Delta B/B$); and the elasticity of the base ($\Delta B/B$) with respect to income ($\Delta Y/Y$), that is

$$(\Delta T/T)/(\Delta Y/Y) = (\Delta T/T)/(\Delta B/B) \times (\Delta B/B)/(\Delta Y/Y) \qquad (13.3)$$

If the tax system is progressive (with higher tax rates applied to higher levels of income or expenditure), then the elasticity of tax revenue with respect to the base will be greater than unity, and buoyancy will be greater than unity provided the elasticity of the base with respect to income is at least unity. If buoyancy is greater than unity, then tax revenue as a proportion of national income will rise as national income rises. The buoyancy of the tax system can be increased by increasing the rates of tax or extending the base.

Any measured change in tax revenue with respect to income is likely to consist both of an automatic increase in tax revenue as income increases if the rate structure is progressive, and the effect of discretionary changes in tax rates and extension of the tax base. The **elasticity** of a tax system is measured as buoyancy minus the effect of discretionary tax changes. There are techniques for estimating the elasticity of the tax system but we will not describe them here – suffice it to say that the greater the elasticity, the more that tax revenue and saving can increase without the need for discretionary changes. This is a desirable feature of tax systems in circumstances where it may be difficult to implement discretionary changes.

Tax effort depends on the elasticity of the system and overall buoyancy, and needs to be measured in relation to capacity. One way of doing this, pioneered by the IMF (see Tait et al., 1979), is to take a cross-section of countries and relate their ratios of tax revenue to national income to the various measures of tax capacity mentioned earlier, namely per capita income, the importance of trade and industry and so on. Estimating such an international tax function gives an equation of the form:

$$T/GDP = a + b_1(PCY) + b_2(X/GDP) + b_3(I/GDP) + \text{other variables} \qquad (13.4)$$

where T/GDP is a country's ratio of tax revenue to national income, PCY is per capita income, X/GDP is the ratio of trade to GDP, I/GDP is the ratio of industrial output to GDP, and the coefficients b_1, b_2, b_3 etc. measure the *average* effect of each of the variables on the tax ratio across countries. For example, if b_2 was estimated as 0.5, this would mean that a country with a trade ratio that is 1 per cent above the average for all countries will have a tax ratio that is 0.5 percentage points above the average for all countries, other things remaining the same.

By this method, a country's tax effort can be measured by substituting its values for PCY, X/GDP, I/GDP and so on in (13.4), predicting what the tax ratio *should be* and then comparing the predicted value with the actual value of the tax ratio. If the actual value is greater than predicted, the country can be said to be making a good effort; if it is less, then the tax effort can be regarded as weak. A study of this nature has been made by Piancastelli (2001) for 75 developed and developing countries over the period 1985–95, and the results are shown in Table 13.3. Any country with a tax effort index greater than 1 has a tax ratio greater than predicted. It can be seen from Table 13.3 that there are several developing countries making a good tax effort, including some of the largest and poorest such as India, Pakistan and Ghana. Equally, however, there are other developing countries making a very poor effort, including many countries in Latin America, notably Mexico, Argentina, Venezuela, Colombia, Bolivia and Peru.

The facts on tax revenue in developing countries are that tax revenue as a percentage of national income is typically low, averaging less than 20 per cent compared with nearly 30 per cent in high-income countries, and taxes on income are a minor source of tax revenue compared with indirect taxes. The proportion of the population that pays income tax in developing countries is correspondingly low, averaging about 20 per cent, compared with the vast majority of the working population in developed countries, who constitute over 40 per cent of the total population.

On the surface there would appear to be a great deal of scope for using tax policy to raise the level of community saving relative to income. Two important points must be borne in mind, however. The first is that the rudimentary nature of the tax system in developing countries is partly a reflection of the stage of development itself. Thus the scope for increasing tax revenue as a proportion of income may in practice be severely circumscribed. There are the difficulties of defining and measuring the tax base and of assessing and collecting taxes in circumstances where the population is dispersed and primarily engaged in producing for subsistence, and where illiteracy is also rife. And there is also the fact that, as far as income tax is concerned, the income of the majority of the population is so low anyway that it falls outside the scope of the tax system. Whereas 70 per cent of national income is subject to income tax in developed countries, only about 30 per cent is subject to income tax in developing countries.

Even if there is scope for raising considerably more revenue by means of taxation, whether the *total* level of saving will rise depends on how tax payments are financed – whether out of consumption or saving – and how income (output) is affected. It is often the case that taxes that make tax revenue highly elastic with respect to income are taxes that are met mainly out of saving or have the most discouraging effect on incentives. For example, very progressive income tax will discourage work effort if the substitution effect of the tax outweighs the income effect; and to the extent that high marginal rates of tax fall primarily on the upper-income groups with a low propensity to consume, saving may fall by nearly as much as tax revenue rises.

To avoid such large reductions in private saving, an **expenditure tax** on upper-income groups, which exempts saving from taxation, is an alternative to a progressive income tax, but the

Table 13.3 Tax effort indices estimated over 1985–95

Countries	Actual tax ratio (a)	Predicted tax ratio (b)	Tax effort index ((c)=(a)/(b))	Countries	Actual tax ratio (a)	Predicted tax ratio (b)	Tax effort index ((c)=(a)/(b))	Countries	Actual tax ratio (a)	Predicted tax ratio (b)	Tax effort index ((c)=(a)/(b))
Fiji	20.595	9.023	2.283	Botswana	26.766	22.224	1.204	Peru	10.728	12.223	0.878
Kenya	19.991	10.497	1.908	PN Guinea	18.825	15.774	1.193	Jordan	17.733	20.938	0.847
Belgium	42.357	23.774	1.782	UK	32.752	27.542	1.189	Panama	17.881	22.197	0.806
South Africa	25.182	15.297	1.646	Luxembourg	39.923	33.653	1.186	Philippines	13.696	17.218	0.795
Netherlands	44.273	27.228	1.626	Portugal	28.667	24.307	1.179	Madagascar	9.174	11.641	0.788
Ethiopia	11.665	7.502	1.555	Sweden	34.721	29.484	1.178	Japan	15.856	20.236	0.784
Ghana	11.760	7.776	1.512	Costa Rica	20.903	17.913	1.167	Dominican Rep.	12.677	16.432	0.772
France	37.808	25.785	1.466	Cameroon	12.784	11.011	1.161	Colombia	11.895	15.431	0.771
India	10.645	7.279	1.462	Spain	28.326	24.437	1.159	El Salvador	12.265	15.979	0.768
Lesotho	23.370	16.058	1.455	Belize	21.649	18.685	1.159	Mexico	13.752	18.431	0.746
Italy	37.482	26.176	1.432	Finland	28.219	24.777	1.139	USA	18.020	24.251	0.743
Zimbabwe	21.449	15.062	1.424	Austria	32.210	28.559	1.128	Turkey	12.452	16.899	0.737
Uruguay	25.515	18.089	1.411	Syria	16.334	14.576	1.121	Congo (Dem. Rep.)	6.885	9.379	0.734

Table 13.3 Tax effort indices estimated over 1985–95 – *continued*

Countries	Actual tax ratio (a)	Predicted tax ratio (b)	Tax effort index ((c)=(a)/(b))	Countries	Actual tax ratio (a)	Predicted tax ratio (b)	Tax effort index ((c)=(a)/(b))	Countries	Actual tax ratio (a)	Predicted tax ratio (b)	Tax effort index ((c)=(a)/(b))
Morocco	22.534	16.027	1.406	Iceland	24.347	22.018	1.106	Switzerland	19.878	28.015	0.710
Namibia	27.595	19.957	1.383	Indonesia	15.737	14.533	1.083	Nepal	7.160	10.387	0.689
Egypt	20.704	15.121	1.369	Greece	23.093	21.862	1.056	Venezuela	16.119	23.675	0.681
Romania	21.053	15.797	1.333	Brazil	17.103	16.273	1.051	Argentina	11.401	17.434	0.654
Tunisia	24.165	18.171	1.330	Malaysia	20.016	20.417	0.980	Canada	18.008	27.743	0.649
New Zealand	32.996	24.815	1.330	Chile	18.801	19.451	0.967	Bolivia	9.451	14.620	0.646
Ireland	34.487	26.496	1.302	Thailand	15.620	16.450	0.950	Sierra Leone	6.789	10.772	0.630
Norway	32.860	25.263	1.301	Mauritius	19.667	20.720	0.949	South Korea	15.619	25.678	0.608
Pakistan	12.999	10.058	1.292	Malta	25.688	27.647	0.929	Paraguay	9.139	15.754	0.580
Denmark	33.840	26.369	1.283	Germany	23.485	26.413	0.889	Guatemala	8.024	14.269	0.562
Sri Lanka	17.886	14.422	1.240	Australia	22.017	24.904	0.884	Iran	7.423	13.702	0.542
Zambia	18.286	15.133	1.208	Ecuador	14.836	16.819	0.882	Singapore	15.672	38.905	0.403

Source: Piancastelli, 2001.

disincentive effect on work effort is not necessarily avoided. This is so because if the expenditure tax encourages saving, the tax rate must be higher to yield the same revenue as the income tax. If people work to consume and the price of consumption is raised, work effort will be curtailed if the substitution effect of the change outweighs the income effect. The more successful the expenditure tax is in stimulating saving out of a given income, the higher must be the rate of tax to keep the yields from the two taxes equal, and the greater the disincentive to work effort is likely to be. If the expenditure tax is in addition to the income tax, however, there is no reason to expect any substitution effect in favour of private saving, so that whether aggregate community saving increases depends on how much work effort is discouraged and on the relative propensities to consume and save of those who pay the tax compared with those of the government. In general the most effective tax policy to raise the level of saving relative to income is to impose taxes on those with a high marginal propensity to consume, namely the poor, but there are obvious considerations of equity to bear in mind in pursuing such a policy, as well as the practical consideration of political feasibility.

The prominence of agriculture in developing countries makes agricultural taxation a potentially significant source of tax revenue and a means of transferring resources into investment. There are a great variety of tax instruments for taxing agriculture, including taxes on land area, on land value, on net income, marketing taxes, export taxes, land transfer taxes and so on. If revenue is the aim, then marketing and export taxes are probably the most efficient and the easiest to collect. As far as exports are concerned, two main systems may be adopted. Either the state-controlled marketing board may pay the producer a price that is lower than the international price received, or the government may require that all foreign exchange receipts be surrendered, with compensation given in local currency at an exchange rate that overvalues the local currency.

Export taxes may, however, have disincentive effects. The substitution effect of export taxes will be to discourage production, or to switch production to the home market if the home market is not saturated. Either way, the yield from tax will fall if the tax base (the level of exports) falls more than in proportion to the rise in the export tax. Trade taxes have also been shown to be very unstable because of the volatility of primary product exports (and of imports), which can lead to severe budgetary problems for countries that rely on them (see Bleaney et al., 1995).

In theory, land taxes are probably the most desirable way to transfer resources from agriculture, but in practice land taxes are not important as a source of tax revenue. It is also worth mentioning that no developing country has yet successfully applied a conventional income tax to agricultural income. The nearest that countries have come to this is to tax the value of land, the imputed income from land or the potential physical yield from land.

The balance between direct taxes on income and indirect taxation on expenditures and trade in the economy at large is heavily weighted in the direction of the latter, particularly in the form of import duties and sales taxes. The emphasis on indirect taxes reflects the difficulties already mentioned of levying direct taxes, and the disincentive effects that direct taxes can have. This is not to say that indirect taxes are totally devoid of disincentive effects, but they are probably less, especially if taxes such as sales taxes and import duties can be levied on necessities without too much social hardship. Indirect taxes on luxuries will raise revenue, the more so the more price inelastic the demand, but the taxes may largely be paid out of saving to the extent that luxuries are consumed by upper-income groups with a low propensity to consume. The equity grounds for such taxation, however, are still strong.

Taxes on business are relatively easy to collect and administer, but again business taxation may merely replace one form of saving with another. The marginal propensity to save out of profits is typically high. The main justification for company taxation must be to retain control of resources that might otherwise leave the country if the business is foreign-owned, or to substitute public for private investment on the grounds that public investment is more socially productive than its private counterpart.

Tax reform in developing countries[11]

Efficient utilization of the tax potential of developing countries raises problems that vary with the circumstances of each country, but there are certain fundamental changes in most of these countries that if adopted would make it possible to increase public revenue and reduce some of the inequities that now exist. In particular, if a tax system is to be accepted by a poor community it must be seen to be administered honestly and efficiently, which means that every attempt must be made to minimize the scope for avoidance (legal) and evasion (illegal).

According to the classical canons of taxation, a tax system is to be judged by the standards of equity, efficiency and administrative convenience. In most developing countries the tax system is neither equitable nor efficient and is administratively cumbersome. Avoidance and evasion are rife.

Equity requires a comprehensive definition of income and non-discrimination between income sources. A major deficiency of tax systems all over the world, and particularly in developing countries, is that there is no single comprehensive tax on all income. Typically there is a 'cedular' system, with separate taxes on different sources of income. Wage and salary earners ('earned' incomes) tend to be discriminated against vis-à-vis the owners of property and capital and the self-employed (professional people and small traders). An equitable system should also be such that it discourages luxury consumption and makes it difficult to avoid and evade taxation.

Taxable capacity is not measured by income alone, but also by wealth. Equity therefore also requires the taxation of wealth. The ownership of wealth endows the owner with an inherent taxable capacity, irrespective of the money income that the asset yields. Consider the case of a beggar with nothing and a rich man who holds all his wealth in the form of jewellery and gold, which yields no money income. Judged by income their taxable capacity is the same: nil! No one could claim, however, that their ability to pay was the same, and that for tax purposes they should be treated equally.

Income tax is not only inequitable between those with property and those without, but also *between* property holders. For example, two property holders may derive the same income from property but the value of their property may differ greatly. One has a greater taxable capacity than the other. Only a combination of income and property taxes can achieve equity according to ability to pay. This is the case for a **wealth tax**.

Equity also requires that gifts between individuals be taxed, on death and *inter vivos*.

Efficiency requires that the entire tax system be self-reinforcing and self-checking so that the attempt to escape one tax increases the liability to other taxes. The system should also, as far as possible, be based on a comprehensive annual tax return.

The above considerations suggest at least four major reforms of the tax system in developing countries, which at the same time would release resources for investment and act as an incentive to effort:

- That *all* income (including capital gains) be aggregated and taxed in the same way, at a progressive rate but not exceeding a maximum marginal rate of, say, 50 per cent. Marginal rates above this level may not only discourage incentive but may also be counterproductive by encouraging evasion and avoidance

- The institution of a progressive personal expenditure tax levied on rich individuals who reach the maximum marginal rate of income tax
- The institution of a wealth tax
- The institution of a gifts tax.

Inflation, saving and growth

If voluntary and involuntary saving are inadequate, inflationary policies that 'force' saving by 'taxing' money and redistributing income between classes within the private sector are an alternative possibility. The price of financial conservatism may well be economic stagnation. The potential benefits of inflationary finance, which embrace both the Keynesian and the quantity theory approach to development finance, have been discussed by economists[12] at least since David Hume in the eighteenth century; and several economic historians (including Keynes) claim to have discerned a relationship in history between periods of inflation and rapid economic development. Hamilton (1952) claims that inflation was a powerful stimulant to growth in a wide number of historical contexts through the favourable effect of excess demand on profits, saving and investment, for example in England and France in the sixteenth and seventeenth centuries and in England in the latter half of the eighteenth century. Rostow (1960) also claims that inflation was important for several industrial take-offs.

Keynes, in his *Treatise on Money* (1930), similarly remarked on the apparent extraordinary correspondence in history between periods of inflation and deflation and national rise and decline, respectively. Keynes was certainly more predisposed to inflation than to deflation. He described inflation as unjust and deflation as inexpedient, but of the two inflation is to be preferred because 'it is worse in an impoverished world to provoke unemployment than to disappoint the rentier' (Keynes, 1931). While recognizing that inflation to increase capital accumulation may have regressive distributional consequences, he further argued (Keynes, 1930) that the long-run gains to wage earners can outweigh the short-term losses:

> the working class may benefit far more in the long run from the forced abstinence which a profit inflation imposes on them than they lose in the first instance in the shape of diminished consumption so long as wealth and its fruits are not consumed by the nominal owner but are accumulated.

The Keynesian approach to the financing of development

The Keynesian approach to the financing of development by inflationary means stresses, first, that investment can generate its own saving by raising the level of income when the economy is operating below capacity, and by redistributing income from wage earners with a low propensity to save to profit earners with a higher propensity to save when the economy is working at full capacity. Second, inflation itself can encourage investment by raising the nominal rate of return on investment and reducing the real rate of interest. Only the first of these two aspects of the Keynesian approach will be considered here.

Unemployed resources provide the classic argument for Keynesian policies of inflationary finance. If resources are unemployed or underused, real output and real savings can be increased by governments running budget deficits financed either by printing money or by issuing government bonds to the banking system and the public.

In a situation of genuine 'Keynesian' unemployment, any tendency towards inflation, whatever method of deficit finance is used, should burn itself out as the supply of goods rises to meet the additional purchasing power created. Some economists have questioned, however, whether the observed unemployment of labour in developing countries is strictly of the Keynesian variety, and whether the supply of output would respond very much to increased demand. It is probably true that most unemployment in developing countries results not from a shortage of demand, but from a lack of cooperating factors of production to work with (mainly capital); and the direct multiplier effects of government expenditure may be low, but some deficit-financed projects (e.g. infrastructure projects) may have considerable secondary repercussions on output if they eliminate production and marketing bottlenecks at the same time.

In the agricultural sector of developing countries, and in the production of consumer goods in the industrial sector, there are many opportunities for investment that can yield outputs several times more than the money value of capital invested in a very short space of time. In agriculture, the use of fertilizers and the provision of transport facilities are good examples. Credit expansion for these activities can soon generate sufficient output to absorb the demand-creating effects of the new money in circulation.

Thus, while it may be true that much of the unemployment in developing countries is not of the Keynesian variety, it does not follow that monetary expansion cannot generate secondary employment and output effects. The capacity-generating effects need to be considered in conjunction with the emphasis on demand in Keynesian static multiplier theory.

Let us now turn to the Keynesian full-employment case. At full employment, inflation is the inevitable result of the Keynesian approach to development. In contrast to classical and neoclassical theory, Keynesian theory specifies independent saving and investment functions and allows price changes in response to excess demand in the goods market to raise saving by redistributing income. Inflation is the means by which resources are redistributed between consumption and investment. In Keynesian models, investment is not constrained by saving, but by the inflation rate willing to be tolerated by wage earners who have had their real wages cut.

If plans to invest exceed plans to save it is reasonable to suppose that both investors and consumers will have their plans thwarted. Investment is less than firms desire, but greater than consumers plan to save. Let us assume, therefore, that the actual growth of capital is a linear combination of planned saving and planned investment:

$$\frac{dK}{K} = \alpha \frac{I}{K} + (1-\alpha)\frac{S}{K}, \quad \alpha < 1 \tag{13.5}$$

where K is the quantity of capital, I is planned investment and S is planned saving. Now assume that the rate of inflation is proportional to the degree of excess demand as measured by the difference between plans to invest and save:

$$\frac{dP}{P} = \lambda\left(\frac{I}{K} - \frac{S}{K}\right), \quad \lambda > 0 \tag{13.6}$$

where P is the price level. Substituting the expression for I/K into (13.5) gives

$$\frac{dK}{K} = \frac{\alpha(dP/P)}{\lambda} + \frac{S}{K} \tag{13.7}$$

S/K is planned saving, and $\alpha(dP/P)/\lambda$ is forced saving, per unit of capital. Forced saving results from the inability of consumers to fulfil their planned consumption in conditions of excess demand. The underlying mechanism that thwarts the plans of consumers is inflation, which redistributes income from wage earners to profits. Other things remaining the same, if prices rise faster than wages, real consumption will fall and real saving increase as long as the propensity to save out of profits is higher than the propensity to save out of wages.

In Keynesian models, therefore, the effect of inflation on saving depends on two factors: the extent to which income is redistributed between wages and profits, and the extent of the difference in the propensity to save out of wages and profits. The relation between wages, prices and profits, and the consequent effect of income redistribution on saving, is best illustrated using simple algebra. Let Z be labour's share of national income so that

$$Z = \frac{W}{PY} = \frac{wL}{PY} = \frac{w}{Pr} \tag{13.8}$$

where W is the wage bill, w is the wage rate, P is price per unit of output, Y is income and $r = Y/L$ is the productivity of labour. Hence the rate of change of labour's share may be written as

$$\frac{dZ}{Z} = \left(\frac{dw}{w} - \frac{dP}{P}\right) - \frac{dr}{r} \tag{13.9}$$

From this equation it can be seen that given a positive rate of growth of productivity, a sufficient condition for a redistribution of income from wages to profits is that prices rise faster than wages. Note, however, that in a growing economy (with positive productivity growth) it is not a *necessary* condition. Labour's share will fall and the share of profits rise as long as $(dw/w - dP/P) < dr/r$; that is, as long as the real wage rises less than the growth of labour productivity. In a growing economy, therefore, there is no necessary clash between the real wage and profits. The real wage can rise and the share of profits in income can also rise as long as some of the gains in labour productivity are appropriated by the capitalists.

It is also obvious that on the classical savings assumption that all wages are consumed and all profits are saved, the savings ratio will rise by exactly the same amount as the wage share falls.

The basic Keynesian notion that investment determines saving forms the backbone of **neo-Keynesian growth theory**, as originally expounded by Robinson (1962) and Kaldor (1955–56). Variations in the savings ratio resulting from inflation and income redistribution is one of the many possible adjustment mechanisms for raising the warranted growth rate towards the natural rate (see Chapter 5). As Robinson used to argue, in response to the neoclassical adjustment mechanisms of variations in interest rates and the capital–output ratio, there is nothing in the laws of nature to guarantee growth at the natural rate, but if entrepreneurs wish to invest sufficient to grow at the natural rate then saving will adapt, subject to an **inflation barrier**.[13] When there is a steady rate of growth, the share of savings adapts to it. In effect, the actual growth rate pulls up the warranted growth rate by forcing saving. Saving adapts to investment through the dependence of saving on the share of profits in income, which rises with the level of investment relative to income in the way that has been described. Profits in turn depend on what happens to real wages when the system is out of equilibrium. The basic equation of Robinson's model is the distribution equation:

$$PY = wL + \pi PK \tag{13.10}$$

where π is the gross profit rate R/K, and P, Y, w, L and K are as before. Dividing by P and rearranging to obtain an expression for the profit rate, gives

$$\pi = \frac{(Y/L) - (w/P)}{(K/L)} = \frac{R/L}{K/L} = \frac{R}{K} \tag{13.11}$$

Given the capital–labour ratio (K/L), the rate of profit depends on the relationship between output per head and the real wage. If all wages are consumed and all profits are saved, the rate of profit gives the rate of capital accumulation and the rate of growth. This follows since $S = I = \pi K$, and $\Delta K = \pi K$; therefore $\Delta K/K = \pi$. And if the capital–output ratio is fixed, $\Delta K/K = \Delta Y/Y$; hence $\pi = \Delta K/K = \Delta Y/Y$.

Variations in the rate of profit and corresponding variations in the real wage provide the mechanism that equilibrates plans to save and invest and the actual and warranted growth rates. If the actual growth rate equals the natural rate, the warranted and natural growth rates will also be equalized. If the real wage remains unchanged as investment takes place, however, saving cannot adapt and a greater volume of real investment cannot be funded. This is the inflation barrier in a static model. It appears, in fact, that in a static context the growth rate can only be raised at the expense of the real wage, which comes close to the pessimistic development theories of Ricardo and Marx as discussed in Chapter 5. In a growing economy, however, such pessimism would be unfounded because it can be seen from equation (13.11) that the rate of profit and capital accumulation can rise even if the real wage is rising, as long as the growth in labour productivity exceeds the increase in the real wage.

Kaldor's model also makes saving adjust to the desired level of investment through a rise in the share of profits in national income. The model consists of three basic equations:

$$Y = W + R \tag{13.12}$$

$$I = S \tag{13.13}$$

$$S = s_w W + s_r R \tag{13.14}$$

where R is profits, W is wages, s_w is the propensity to save out of wages and s_r is the propensity to save out of profits. Using the three equations we can write

$$I = s_w(Y - R) + s_r R$$
$$= (s_r - s_w)R + s_w Y \tag{13.15}$$

Making investment the independent variable in the system, and dividing by Y gives

$$\frac{R}{Y} = \left(\frac{1}{s_r - s_w}\right)\frac{I}{Y} - \frac{s_w}{(s_r - s_w)} \tag{13.16}$$

The ratio of profits to income and the investment ratio are positively related as long as the propensity to save out of profits exceeds the propensity to save out of wages. The investment ratio must clearly be the independent variable in the system. Capitalists can decide how much they are going to consume and invest but they cannot decide how much profit they are going to make. If $s_r = 1$ and $s_w = 0$, then $I/Y = R/Y$, and, multiplying both sides of (13.16) by Y/K we have Robinson's result that the rate of profit, the rate of capital accumulation and the rate of growth are all equal. A higher level of investment can raise the rate of capital accumulation by raising the profit rate and the share of saving in total income, subject, of course, to the inflation barrier. The mechanism that gives this result is rising prices relative to wages.

The Kaldor model can be used for estimating how much inflation is necessary to raise the savings ratio by a given amount (see Thirlwall, 1974 for the model). The inflation rate required depends on three main factors:

- Labour's initial share of national income
- The difference in the propensity to save out of wages (s_w) and profits (s_{rp})
- How fast wages chase prices (the wage–price coefficient).

If wages chase prices equi-proportionately, and there is no difference in the propensity to save out of wages and profits, there can be no redistribution effects on saving by generating inflation. If there is a big difference in the savings propensities, and the wage–price coefficient is quite low, mild inflation of approximately 3 per cent can increase the savings ratio by one percentage point. If there is only a small difference in the savings propensities, and the wage–price coefficient is very high (close to unity), over 100 per cent inflation would be required to raise the savings ratio by one percentage point. Even Keynesians might regard such a rate as a high price to pay for extra growth![14]

Reconciling the prior-saving and forced-saving approaches to development

There can be little doubt that the traditional development literature and the governments of most developing countries have veered towards the classical view of development when making policy prescriptions and formulating plans. But there is scope for a more eclectic approach. It is not necessary to be a classicist to recognize the importance of voluntary saving in capital-scarce economies, and it should not be necessary to be a Keynesian to admit that investors may lay claim on real resources in excess of the community's plans to save. Keynesians welcome prior saving. What they dispute is that saving is necessary for investment; that investment is constrained by saving. As Robinson (1960, vol. II) said when discussing the relation between savings and investment at full employment: 'We cannot return to the pre-Keynesian view that savings governs investment. The essential point of Keynes' teaching remains. It is decisions about how much investment is to be made that governs the rate at which wealth will accumulate, not decisions about savings.' A start at reconciliation would be for the prior-savings school to admit the possibility of forced saving and to reduce their aversion to demand inflation. Equally, the Keynesians could admit that saving depends on factors other than the functional distribution of income, and that for any desired savings or investment ratio, inflation will fall as voluntary saving rises.

The quantity theory approach to the financing of development

The quantity theory approach to the financing of development stresses the effect of inflation as a tax on real money balances. Suppose a government wishes to divert more of a country's resources to investment; one of the ways it can do so is to invest on society's behalf, financing the investment by expanding the money supply. In conditions where capital is already fully employed, monetary expansion will be inflationary.

Inflation is the means by which resources are effectively transferred to government. Inflation imposes a **tax on money holdings** and consists of a reduction in the real purchasing power of money and of the real resources that the holders of money must forego to restore the real value of their money holdings. The base of the tax is the level of real cash balances (M/P), and the tax rate is the rate at which the real value of money is deteriorating, which is equal to the rate of inflation (dP/P). The real yield from the tax is the product of the tax base and the tax rate; that is $(M/P)(dP/P)$, which will be maximized (as in standard tax theory) when the elasticity of the base with respect to the rate of tax is equal to -1. If the rate of inflation is equal to the rate of monetary expansion, the real tax yield (R) will equal the real value of the new money issued; that is, $(M/P)(dM/M) = dM/P$. If $dP/P > . dM/M$, some of the potential tax yield will be lost owing to a reduction in the tax base.

The inflation tax can be illustrated diagrammatically, as in Figure 13.3. DD is the demand for real money balances in relation to the rate of inflation. When prices are stable, the demand for real balances is D. At inflation rate P, however, which is expected to continue, the demand for real balances falls to M. The area $0PXM$ thus represents the amount of real income that holders of real money balances must substitute for money balances to keep real balances intact at level M. Since money balances must be accumulated and real income forgone at the same rate as the rate of inflation, the rate of tax is equal to the rate of inflation.

Inflation as a tax on money redistributes resources from the private sector to the government as the issuer of money – resources that are just as real as those obtained by more conventional means of taxation. Keynes was fully aware of this other aspect of inflation, as well as the tendency for demand inflation to transfer income from wages to profits. In his *Tract on Monetary Reform* (1923) he describes inflation as 'a form of taxation that the public finds hard to evade and even the weakest government can enforce when it can enforce nothing else'.

The real yield from the inflation tax available for investment as a proportion of income (R_I/Y) will be the product of the money–income ratio, $(M/P)/Y$, the rate of inflation, $dP/P = dM/M$, and the proportion of the increase in the real money supply captured for investment (R_I)/(dM/P), that is

$$\frac{R_I}{Y} = \left(\frac{M}{PY}\right)\left(\frac{dM}{M}\right)\left(\frac{R_I}{dM/P}\right) \tag{13.17}$$

Suppose that the money–income ratio is 0.4 and 50 per cent of new money issued is used for investment purposes, then a 10 per cent expansion of the money supply leading to a 10 per cent rate of inflation would yield 2 per cent of the national income for the development programme.

Figure 13.3 Inflation tax

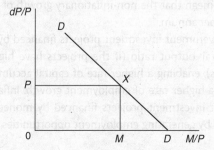

If all the new money is used for investment purposes, the real yield from the tax is simply the ratio of the real value of the new money issued to income (our earlier result), which in this example would be 2.5 per cent. These calculations assume, however, that the desired ratio of money holdings to income remains unchanged regardless of the rate of inflation. In practice the ratio is likely to be a decreasing function of the rate of inflation because the opportunity cost of holding real money balances rises. Only if the base of the tax falls more than in proportion to the inflation rate, however, will the yield from the inflation tax actually decline.

From the limited evidence available, it appears that the elasticity of the money–income ratio with respect to the rate of inflation is quite low even in high-inflation countries. This suggests that inflation can operate effectively as a tax on money even in countries that have been experiencing high rates of inflation for many years. It should also be remembered that while inflation may reduce the desired ratio of money holdings to income, the ratio will have a continual tendency to rise with the gradual monetization and development of the economy. On balance the ratio may be very little affected by monetary expansion.

The fact that the demand to hold money relative to income rises as development proceeds, and output is growing, also means that some government investment can be financed without any increase in the price level. This is easily seen taking the fundamental equation of exchange:

$$MV = PY$$

or

$$M = K_d PY \tag{13.18}$$

where M is the nominal money supply, V is the income velocity of circulation of money, $K_d (= 1/V)$ is the demand to hold money per unit of money income, P is the average price of final goods and services, and Y is real income.

Taking rates of growth of the variables, denoted by lower-case letters, gives

$$m = k_d + p + y \tag{13.19}$$

It can be seen that if the demand for money per unit of income is increasing ($k_d > 0$), m can be positive without the price level rising. Similarly, if the economy is growing ($y > 0$), m can also be positive without the price level rising. The government's proceeds from monetary expansion will equal $m - p$. In several developing countries the rate of growth of the demand for money per unit of income seems to be in the order of 5 per cent per annum. This, combined with a growth rate of output of 3 per cent per annum, would mean that the non-inflationary growth of the money supply would be in the order of 8 per cent per annum.

Finally, it should also be added that government investment projects financed by monetary expansion can reduce an economy's capital–output ratio (if the projects have high output–labour ratios and low capital–labour ratios), enabling a higher rate of capital accumulation for any given investment ratio, and therefore a higher rate of employment growth. Inflation is not necessarily inegalitarian if the government investment projects financed by monetary expansion help the poor in rural and urban areas by generating employment opportunities and raising productivity.

The dangers of inflation

Some of the benefits of inflation have been considered, especially the ability of inflation to release resources for development by redistributing income between classes within the private sector and from the private sector to the government. Inflation is not without its dangers, however, and these must be emphasized.

First, a distinction needs to be made between the different types of inflation that may be experienced by a developing country: **demand inflation**, **cost inflation** and **structural inflation**. The argument for inflationary finance is an argument for demand inflation. Cost inflation, by reducing profits, will not be conducive to development. Structural inflation may be the inevitable price of development, but there is nothing in the process of structural inflation itself that will necessarily accelerate the development process.

There are also certain dangers and costs involved in deliberately pursuing an inflationary policy to stimulate development. The most serious threats to growth from inflation come from the effect on the balance of payments if foreign exchange is a scarce resource, and from the possibility that voluntary saving, productive investment and the use of money as a medium of exchange may be discouraged if inflation becomes excessive. If one country inflates at a faster rate than others its balance of payments may suffer severely, leading to protection and exchange controls, and hence inefficiency in resource allocation. As far as investment is concerned, if inflation becomes excessive, investment in physical plant and equipment may become unattractive relative to speculative investment in inventories, overseas assets, property and artefacts that absorb a society's real resources. If the real rate of interest becomes negative (that is, the rate of inflation exceeds the nominal rate of interest) it may even become attractive to claim real resources and not to use them.

Inflation clearly reduces the purchasing power of money. If inflation becomes excessive, not only may voluntary saving be discouraged but the use of money as a medium of exchange may be discouraged, involving society in real resource costs and welfare losses. Since inflation reduces the purchasing power of money, holders may be expected to avoid losses by cutting down their holdings of money for transactions purposes. The cost of inflation arises from the fact that cash balances yield utility and contribute to production, and inflation causes energy, time and resources to be devoted to minimizing the use of cash balances that are costless to produce; for example the frequency of trips to the bank may increase, which absorbs labour time, and credit mechanisms may be resorted to, which absorb society's resources.

There are also the distributional consequences of inflation to consider. These are difficult to assess, but the following can be said with some confidence:

- Debtors benefit at the expense of creditors
- Profit earners gain at the expense of wage earners in times of demand inflation and lose at the expense of wage earners in times of wage inflation
- Real-asset holders probably gain relative to money-asset holders
- The strong (in a bargaining sense) probably gain relative to the weak; and the young gain relative to the old, who tend to live on fixed contractual incomes.

In developing countries the possible inegalitarian distributional consequences of demand inflation should not be allowed, however, to constitute an argument against the use of mildly inflationary policies if one of the aims is to create additional employment. The major beneficiaries of inflationary finance should be the unemployed and the underemployed, which represents a move towards a more egalitarian structure of household incomes.

Having considered some of the potential dangers of inflation it can be seen that there is plenty of room for disagreement over whether inflation is a help or a hindrance to development. We have seen that it can help to raise the level of real saving and encourage investment; on the other hand it may stimulate the 'wrong' type of investment, and inflation may get out of control and retard development through its adverse effects on productive investment and the balance of payments. A lot clearly depends on the type of inflation under discussion and its rate.

Inflation targeting

Because of the perceived dangers of inflation – that inflation is harmful to growth and development – many developing countries have recently copied developed countries, such as the United Kingdom and the countries of the European Union under the direction of the European Central Bank, and adopted inflation targeting to control the rate of inflation. Countries such as Brazil, Chile, Colombia, Mexico, Peru, Korea, the Philippines and Thailand all started the process in the late 1990s and early 2000s. Targeting a specific inflation rate, such as 5 per cent, or a range between 4 and 6 per cent, is a way of dampening inflationary expectations in an economy and of lending credibility to a government's monetary and fiscal policies for controlling the economy. The question is: does it work, without sacrificing growth and employment? To evaluate this properly, the countries adopting inflation targeting need to be compared with a control group. When this is done, the evidence for developed countries is that targeting has no significant effect on either inflation or its variability (see Lin and Ye, 2007). On the other hand, given that the credibility of central banks in developing countries is significantly less than in developed countries, it might be expected that the credibility gain from explicitly announcing an inflation target would be much more substantial in developing countries. Goncalves and Salles (2008) find this to be so in a sample of 36 emerging economies, but they do not compare their results with a control group. Lin and Ye (2009) rectify this deficiency by comparing 13 developing countries that adopted inflation targeting up to 2004, using 39 other countries as a control group. The central conclusion of the authors is that inflation targeting has reduced the inflation rate by about 3 percentage points on average, but the experience varies between countries according to the length of time the policy has been adopted, fiscal discipline, exchange rate variability and governments' commitment to meet the preconditions for the policy of adopting a target inflation rate. Whether any costs have been incurred, however, in terms of slower growth or higher unemployment, is not explored. But what does the empirical evidence show of the relation between inflation and growth across countries? We examine this in the next section.

Inflation and growth: the empirical evidence

The discussion so far suggests that the relation between inflation and growth is likely to be non-linear, with growth positively related to inflation up to a certain rate of inflation and then negatively related as the disadvantages of inflation outweigh the advantages. This is in line with recent empirical evidence from large data sets across developing and developed countries.

A study by Bruno (1995) at the World Bank, taking pooled annual observations for 127 countries over the years 1960–92, produced the pattern depicted in Figure 13.4. Inflation and growth are positively related up to 5 per cent inflation, and then 'diminishing returns' to inflation set in.

Figure 13.4   Inflation and per capita income growth, 1960–92 (pooled annual observations, 127 countries)

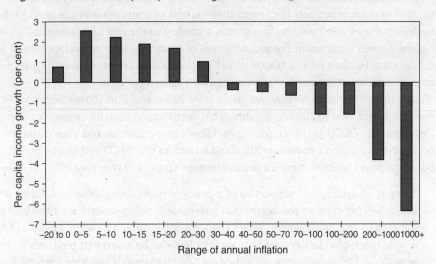

Inflation and growth are strongly negative once inflation rises above 30 per cent, but for inflation rates below 20 per cent Bruno concludes 'there is no obvious empirical evidence for significant long-run growth costs'.

A study by Sarel (1996) at the IMF has produced a similar result. He takes 87 countries over the period 1970–90 and divides the observations into 12 inflation groupings using the inflation rate of group 6 as the standard of reference. He then estimates the effect that differential inflation has on the growth rate in the other groups. The results are shown in Figure 13.5. It can be seen that inflation has a generally positive effect on growth up to group 7, with inflation averaging 8 per cent. Thereafter, inflation and growth are negatively related. When inflation is very high (in group 12) the difference in the effect of inflation on growth compared with group 6 is close to 4 percentage points (holding all other factors constant).[15]

Ghosh and Phillips (1998), also at the IMF, show the growth of GDP to be highest in the range of inflation 3–5 per cent for developed countries, and in the range 5–10 per cent for developing countries (no doubt reflecting greater structural inflation).

Figure 13.5   Effects of different inflation rates on growth

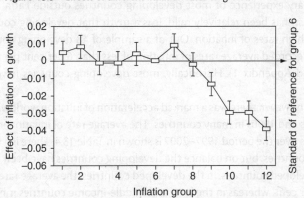

Evidence of non-linearity between inflation and growth is also found by Stanners (1993) in a study of nine countries over the period 1948–86 and 44 countries over the period 1980–88. First he divides the 44 countries into four groups according to the rate of inflation and shows that the highest growth occurred in the second group of countries, with an average rate of inflation of 8.2 per cent. He then takes a scatter of 342 points for nine countries over 38 years and shows a positive correlation between inflation and growth up to 8 per cent.

The most recent comprehensive study is by Pollin and Zhu (2006) who take 80 countries over the period 1961 to 2000 distinguishing between Organisation for Economic Cooperation and Development (OECD (rich)) countries, middle-income countries and poor countries. They find no significant relation between inflation and growth in the OECD and middle-income countries, but in the poor countries there is a positive relation up to 15–23 per cent inflation. They conclude:

> There is no evidence . . . supportive of a policy of maintaining inflation within a low band of about 3–5 per cent, to the degree that government policy-makers are interested in promoting growth and employment, rather than low inflation as an end in itself. . . . [T]here is still a wide range of inflation rates that are very likely to be associated positively with economic growth. . . . This is most especially the case when inflation is resulting from, as Bruno (1995) puts it, 'investment demand pressure in an expanding economy'.

It is not surprising from this evidence that Temple (2000) concludes his survey of inflation by saying: 'since there is not yet robust evidence that moderate inflation has an adverse impact on growth, any case for price stability which relies on a positive growth effect should continue to be regarded with considerable suspicion'. Similarly, Levine and Zervos (1993), in a review of studies of the macrodeterminants of growth, conclude that 'given the uncharacteristically unified view among economists and policy analysts that countries with high inflation rates should adopt policies that lower inflation in order to promote economic prosperity, the inability to find simple cross-country regressions supporting this contention is both surprising and troubling'. Indeed, we can be more categorical and say that there is *no* scientific evidence to suggest that a necessary condition for faster growth is that inflation should be as low as possible. The evidence suggests that mild inflation, up to 5–8 per cent, is positively beneficial for growth. After that, however, the effects of inflation can be seriously damaging, certainly at rates in excess of 20 per cent.

The inflationary experience

Having discussed the advantages of inflation and warned of the dangers of excessive inflation, the fact is that the inflationary experience of most developing countries outside Latin America, at least until the recent past, has been relatively mild. It is a myth that developing countries have been typically prone to high rates of inflation. Out of a sample of 48 developing countries over the period 1958–68, 38 recorded average rates of inflation of less than 6 per cent per annum (see Thirlwall, 1974, p. 35 and Appendix 1). Historically, most developing countries have been very financially conservative.

From the mid-1970s, however, there was a marked acceleration of inflation worldwide, and this continued into the 1980s and 1990s in many countries. The average rate of inflation in developed and developing countries over the period 1997–2007 is shown in Table 13.4. There is a wide variety of experience between countries, but on balance the developing countries have been more prone to inflation than the developed countries. In the developed countries, the average rate of inflation has been less than 10 per cent, whereas in the low- and middle-income countries it has averaged

Table 13.4 Inflation

	GDP implicit deflator average annual growth 1997–2007		GDP implicit deflator average annual growth 1997–2007		GDP implicit deflator average annual growth 1997–2007
Afghanistan	4.1	Cameroon	2.6	Finland	1.6
Albania	5.6	Canada	1.6	France	1.7
Algeria	8.7	Cape Verde	3.6	French Polynesia	0.3
Angola	139.5	Central African Republic	2.0	Gabon	5.5
Antigua and Barbuda	1.0	Chad	5.9	Gambia, The	8.8
Argentina	7.5	Channel Islands	3.0	Georgia	7.0
Armenia	5.1	Chile	5.4	Germany	0.8
Aruba	1.7	China	2.6	Ghana	20.1
Australia	2.9	Colombia	10.7	Greece	3.7
Austria	1.4	Comoros	3.5	Grenada	3.6
Azerbaijan	7.7	Congo, Dem. Rep.	151.3	Guatemala	5.4
Bahamas, The	2.7	Congo, Rep.	8.3	Guinea-Bissau	5.4
Bahrain	3.2	Costa Rica	10.7	Guinea	12.9
Bangladesh	4.1	Côte d'Ivoire	3.0	Guyana	6.0
Barbados	1.0	Croatia	4.6	Haiti	15.1
Belarus	79.1	Cuba	2.9	Honduras	11.0
Belgium	1.8	Cyprus	3.0	Hong Kong, China	−1.3
Belize	0.9	Czech Republic	3.7	Hungary	8.2
Benin	3.3	Denmark	2.1	Iceland	4.5
Bermuda	3.2	Djibouti	2.5	India	4.7
Bhutan	5.5	Dominica	1.3	Indonesia	17.9
Bolivia	6.0	Dominican Republic	12.6	Iran, Islamic Rep.	18.4
Bosnia and Herzegovina	6.7	Ecuador	4.3	Iraq	9.2
Botswana	8.1	Egypt, Arab Rep.	6.3	Ireland	3.8
Brazil	7.6	El Salvador	3.2	Isle of Man	2.7
Brunei Darussalam	7.6	Equatorial Guinea	13.6	Israel	2.8
Bulgaria	92.8	Eritrea	14.8	Italy	2.4
Burkina Faso	2.7	Estonia	6.2	Jamaica	11.0
Burundi	11.6	Ethiopia	5.2	Japan	−1.0
Cambodia	3.7	Fiji	4.5	Jordan	2.5

continued overleaf

Table 13.4   Inflation – *continued*

	GDP implicit deflator average annual growth 1997–2007		GDP implicit deflator average annual growth 1997–2007		GDP implicit deflator average annual growth 1997–2007
Kazakhstan	13.8	Mongolia	13.5	Rwanda	6.7
Kenya	5.6	Montenegro	5.2	Samoa	4.6
Kiribati	0.9	Morocco	2.2	San Marino	1.3
Korea, Rep.	2.1	Mozambique	8.1	São Tomé and Principe	6.4
Kuwait	6.2	Myanmar	18.9	Saudi Arabia	5.4
Kyrgyz Republic	12.9	Namibia	6.6	Senegal	2.3
Lao PDR	29.1	Nepal	6.2	Serbia	30.3
Latvia	6.3	Netherlands	2.5	Seychelles	3.6
Lebanon	2.3	New Caledonia	0.2	Sierra Leone	11.9
Lesotho	5.8	New Zealand	2.5	Singapore	0.3
Liberia	350.8	Nicaragua	8.7	Slovak Republic	4.8
Libya	13.9	Nigeria	15.0	Slovenia	5.5
Lithuania	3.9	Niger	2.6	Solomon Islands	6.4
Luxembourg	2.4	Norway	4.6	South Africa	7.4
Macao, China	0.9	Oman	4.3	Spain	3.5
Macedonia, FYR	3.5	Pakistan	9.1	Sri Lanka	9.5
Madagascar	10.2	Palau	2.8	St Kitts and Nevis	3.3
Malawi	24.8	Panama	1.3	St Lucia	2.6
Malaysia	4.1	Papua New Guinea	8.9	St Vincent and the Grenadines	1.4
Maldives	1.5	Paraguay	9.7	Sudan	13.7
Mali	2.8	Peru	4.0	Suriname	27.6
Malta	3.4	Philippines	6.0	Swaziland	6.7
Marshall Islands	2.6	Poland	5.1	Sweden	1.5
Mauritania	8.7	Portugal	3.2	Switzerland	0.7
Mauritius	5.5	Puerto Rico	1.6	Syrian Arab Republic	5.8
Mexico	10.6	Qatar	4.9	Tajikistan	32.3
Micronesia, Fed. Sts.	2.0	Romania	38.9	Tanzania	10.3
Moldova	15.8	Russian Federation	23.5	Thailand	2.8

Table 13.4 Inflation – *continued*

	GDP implicit deflator average annual growth 1997–2007		GDP implicit deflator average annual growth 1997–2007		GDP implicit deflator average annual growth 1997–2007
Timor-Leste	2.3	Ukraine	16.4	Vietnam	6.3
Togo	1.7	United Arab Emirates	6.1	West Bank and Gaza	3.2
Tonga	6.0	United Kingdom	2.6	Yemen, Rep.	13.3
Trinidad and Tobago	5.6	United States	2.2	Zambia	20.3
Tunisia	2.9	Uruguay	9.3	Zimbabwe	124.6
Turkey	37.1	Uzbekistan	36.0		
Turkmenistan	10.2	Vanuatu	2.6		
Uganda	4.9	Venezuela, RB	25.9		

Source: World Bank, *World Development Indicators*, June 2009, online (http://data.worldbank.org/data-catalog/world-development-indicators).

over 20 per cent, even excluding the higher inflation countries (with rates over 100 per cent) and the inflation-prone countries of Latin America. In Latin America, inflation has been endemic for many years, almost from the start of the industrialization process, and we conclude this chapter with a brief discussion of the Latin American experience and of the 'structuralist–monetarist' controversy over the causes of rapid inflation.

The structuralist–monetarist debate in Latin America

The inflation rate in countries such as Argentina, Brazil, Peru, Bolivia, Chile and Uruguay has reached over 100 per cent at times since the Second World War. In the early postwar years a heated debate developed, that still smoulders today, over the major cause of rapid price increases. The participants in the debate polarized into two schools, frequently referred to as **the 'structuralists' and the 'monetarists'**. Although the debate is set in the Latin American context, it is nonetheless of general interest and in many ways is analogous to the Keynesian–monetarist debate that took place in the 1970s and 1980s over the causes of inflation in developed countries. It might also be said that the two debates have been equally inconclusive.

The essence of the structuralist argument is that the basic forces of inflation are structural in nature; that inflation is a supply phenomenon, and can only be remedied by monetary and fiscal means at the expense of the underutilization of resources. The role of monetary expansion in propagating inflation is not denied; what is disputed is that inflation has its *origins* in monetary factors. In the structuralists' view, monetary policy can only attack the symptoms of inflation, not its root causes.

In support of the argument that inflation emanates from the supply side, the structuralists point to the characteristic features of developing countries: the rapid structural changes taking place in the economy and supply inelasticities leading to bottlenecks, and refer back to the pre-industrialization era of Latin America when inflation was much less severe than it has been in the recent past. Prior to 1930 there was relative price stability due to fairly elastic supplies of agricultural output and low population growth. But Latin America then entered the industrialization era with a capitalist class that was reluctant to invest, and with growing population pressure on food supplies, which together contributed to bottlenecks and the beginnings of inflation, subsequently exacerbated by a wage–price spiral, and currency depreciation.

There is some dispute about whether this picture is accurate for the whole of Latin America, however. According to some observers the sequence of events described by the structuralist school is more a description of a particular country, Chile. Indeed, Campos (1961) went as far as to say that any visitor to the Economic Commission for Latin America in Santiago could not help but feel that the thinking of the structuralist school had been affected by the peculiarities of Chilean inflation. But Campos was a confessed monetarist! For even in the Chilean case he claims that the bottlenecks observed were induced by inflation itself and were not causal elements in the process. This is a more general claim of the monetarist school. They argue that supply bottlenecks are created by policies that discourage investment; for example, price controls. Thus they maintain that the act of repressing inflation, instead of tackling the monetary causes of inflation, creates bottlenecks that subsequently feed the inflation. But in the first instance inflation is caused by excess demand due to monetary expansion. In support of the monetarists, it does seem to be the case that in countries where prices have risen the fastest the money supply has also grown most rapidly, but this does not answer the question of whether monetary expansion initiates inflation or simply 'finances' inflationary tendencies already present on the supply side. Moreover, if there was tighter monetary control, would it be inflation or output that would fall the most? There is no consensus, but a majority of observers seem to pinpoint supply factors as the main contributors to rising prices – particularly agricultural bottlenecks and exchange rate depreciation due to balance-of-payments difficulties. It is possible to argue, of course, that all balance-of-payments deficits are a monetary phenomenon, but the more relevant question is, what is the cause of deficits in the first place? Most balance-of-payments difficulties in Latin America have to do with a high income elasticity of demand for imports and low export growth because of the poor supply characteristics of domestic goods (see Chapter 16).[16]

Summary

- Development requires investment, and saving is necessary to *fund* investment (although not necessarily to finance it)
- There are three main analytical approaches to the finance of development from domestic resources: the prior-saving approach, the Keynesian approach and the quantity theory approach, which all focus on the ways in which saving and investment can be raised.
- The prior-saving approach focuses on raising voluntary and involuntary saving through monetary and fiscal policy. The Keynesian approach emphasizes incentives to invest which can generate its own saving. The quantity theory approach focuses on 'forcing' saving through inflationary policies.
- Voluntary saving depends on the capacity and willingness to save determined by the level of income, the growth of income, the rate of interest and the availability of financial assets.
- Most developing countries have a dual financial structure with a large informal financial sector serving the poor, rural, subsistence sector, and a formal financial sector serving those with collateral to borrow.
- Rural financial intermediaries and micro-credit play an important role in the lending and borrowing activities of poor people.

- The formal financial sector often suffers various forms of financial repression impeding the growth of the financial system.
- Financial liberalization programmes have been implemented in many developing countries, often under pressure, with mixed results.
- Involuntary saving depends on tax policy. Tax effort is weak in many developing countries.
- Investment can generate its own saving through a rise in income if the economy is at less than full employment, or through a redistribution of income by inflation from wage earners with a low propensity to save to profit earners with a higher propensity to save if the economy is at full employment (this is the Keynesian argument).
- Governments can invest on society's behalf and finance the investment by monetary expansion. If this is inflationary, this will 'force' saving (the idea of inflation as a tax on money).
- Inflation poses some dangers, but the empirical evidence shows a positive relation between inflation and growth up to about 5 per cent inflation.
- Many Latin American countries have experienced high inflation in the past, but the monetarist–structuralist debate which originated there is largely inconclusive.

Chapter 13	Discussion questions

1 What is the difference between voluntary saving, compulsory saving and 'forced' saving?

2 What are the main determinants of voluntary saving?

3 How can 'monetization' of the economy help to raise the level and productivity of capital accumulation in developing economies?

4 What are the essential features of the informal financial sector in developing countries?

5 Outline the main requisites of a well-developed financial system.

6 What forms do financial repression take in developing countries?

7 What are the dangers of financial liberalization, and on what factors does the success of liberalization depend?

8 What role do special development banks and micro-credit play in financing development?

9 Suggest reforms to the tax system in developing countries that would promote both equity and more saving for investment.

10 What is meant by 'inflation as a tax on money'?

11 In what ways is demand inflation conducive to growth and development?

12 What conclusions would you draw from the recent empirical evidence on the relation between inflation and growth?

Notes

1. Some inflation-induced saving may be voluntary, some involuntary.
2. Excluding China and India from the low-income countries, the savings ratio is only 9 per cent.
3. The approach gets its name from the quantity theory of money, which predicts that increases in the quantity of money will always lead eventually to increases in the price level.
4. For a survey of micro-credit, see Morduch (1999) and 'Symposium' in the *Economic Journal*, February 2007 (Hermes and Lensink, 2007).
5. The author was a consultant to the Tonga Development Bank in 1995.
6. See, for example, Schumpeter (1911), Gurley and Shaw (1960) and Tun Wai (1972).
7. For an excellent comprehensive survey of the issues involved, see Gibson and Tsakolotos (1994).
8. A Nobel Prize-winner in 2001.
9. For a comprehensive discussion of the general issues in this field, see Bird (1991) and Burgess and Stern (1993).
10. The 'real balance effect on outside money' refers to the attempt by holders of money assets to restore the real value of their money balances, eroded by inflation, by reducing their consumption. For a fuller discussion, see below, p. 425.
11. For an excellent discussion of general issues, and with specific reference to Pakistan, see Ahmad and Stern (1991).
12. Including Malthus, Bentham, Thornton, Robertson and, more recently, Kaldor.
13. In a static economy the inflation barrier means a real wage so low that wage earners react to price increases to prevent the real wage from falling further. In a growing economy, it is the point at which labour resists any further reduction in its share of national income; that is, where labour appropriates all increases in labour productivity itself in the form of increased real wages.
14. For a full range of estimates, see Thirlwall (1974).
15. These results support the early work of the present author (Thirlwall, 1974) which also showed a non-linear relation between inflation and the savings ratio, and inflation and the investment ratio. For a survey of models of inflation and growth, and some of the early empirical evidence, see Johnson (1984). For an up-to-date overview, see Temple (2000).
16. For a 'structural' interpretation of Bolivian hyperinflation, see Pastor (1991).

Websites on banking and finance

Micro-credit

Grameen Development Bank www.grameen-info.org
www.mixmarket.org
www.microcreditsummit.org

Banking statistics

Search engine for central banks of countries www.directhit.com

14

FOREIGN ASSISTANCE, AID, DEBT AND DEVELOPMENT

- Introduction
- The role of foreign borrowing
- Dual-gap analysis and foreign borrowing
- Models of capital imports and growth
- Capital imports, domestic saving and the capital–output ratio
- Types of international capital flows
- The debate over international assistance to developing countries
- The motives for official assistance
- The critics of international aid
- The macroeconomic impact of aid
- The total net flow of financial resources to developing countries
- Official development assistance (ODA)
- Total net flow of financial resources from DAC countries
- UK assistance to developing countries
- The recipients of official assistance
- Aid tying
- Remittances
- Multilateral assistance
- World Bank activities
- Structural adjustment lending
- Poverty Reduction Strategy Papers
- Estimating the aid component of international assistance
- The distribution of international assistance
- Schemes for increasing the flow of revenue
- Foreign direct investment and multinational corporations
- International debt and debt–service problems
- Optimal borrowing and sustainable debt
- The debt crisis of the 1980s
- Debt relief
- The highly indebted poor country initiative (HIPC)
- Debt rescheduling
- Debt–service capping
- Debt buy-backs and debt swaps
- Long-term solutions
- Summary
- Discussion questions
- Notes
- Websites on aid, remittances, debt and FDI

Introduction

In an open economy, domestic savings can be supplemented by many kinds of external assistance. This chapter considers the role of foreign borrowing in the development process. The emphasis is on longer-term resource flows to developing countries rather than on the provision of short-term balance of payments support, which is the traditional function of the International Monetary Fund (IMF), and is considered in Chapter 16.

The chapter starts by showing how the need for foreign resource inflows can be quantified, using the concept of **dual-gap analysis**, and then outlines the conditions under which foreign capital inflows will raise the growth of national income and the growth of national output.

The various magnitudes of resource inflows to developing countries are given including: official bilateral and multilateral aid flows (official development assistance, ODA); foreign direct investment (FDI) and remittances. The various donors and country recipients are identified.

We consider the debate over international assistance to developing countries; the motives for giving aid; the macroeconomic impact of aid on economies, and the critics of aid who say that it can do more harm than good.

The World Bank is a major multilateral donor, and its programmes of **Structural Adjustment Lending** come under scrutiny.

Some resource flows, such as FDI and remittances, do not create debt, but loans from international organizations and the private banking system do, and we look at the debt burden of developing countries and the debt-servicing difficulties that they face because debt has to be repaid with interest in foreign exchange, which is scarce and badly needed for imports. We ask the question: is it possible to define an optimal level of borrowing and sustainable debt?

The 1980s witnessed a severe debt crisis for developing countries which still lingers today, and we explore the various solutions that have been put forward for relieving the debt burden of poor, developing countries, including the **Highly Indebted Poor Country Initiative (HIPC)** of the World Bank.

The role of foreign borrowing

It is important to understand that lending and borrowing are natural features of capitalist economic activity, and without them capital accumulation would be confined to sectors of economic activity that have a surplus of income over current requirements, which would be inefficient and suboptimal from a growth point of view. Very often the factors that cause the supply of capital to increase create their own demand. The most obvious example of this, at the international level, are increases in the price of oil which create large surpluses for oil-exporting countries and the need to borrow by oil-importing countries to maintain economic growth without curtailing imports. Going back into history, sovereign lending (and the problems associated with it) has been a feature of international economic life at least since the Medicis of Florence started to make loans to the English and Spanish monarchs in the fourteenth century. Historically, the international lending and borrowing process has played an integral part in the development of most major industrialized countries, and continues to play a significant role in the economic transformation of today's developing countries.

Traditionally, the role of foreign borrowing has been seen by countries as a supplement to domestic saving to bridge an investment–savings gap and achieve faster growth. The concept of

dual-gap analysis, however, pioneered by Hollis Chenery and his collaborators, shows that for-eign borrowing may also be viewed as a supplement to foreign exchange if, to achieve a faster rate of growth and development, the gap between foreign exchange earnings from exports and necessary imports is larger than the domestic investment–savings gap, and domestic and foreign resources are not easily substitutable for one another. Foreign borrowing must fill the larger of the two gaps if the target growth rate is to be achieved. The historical sequence of experience orig-inally suggested by Chenery was that countries in the pre-take-off stage of development would have a dominant investment–savings gap, followed by a dominant foreign exchange gap, with the possibility of a skill constraint at any stage. Most of today's developing countries, apart from China and the oil-exporting countries, have a dominant foreign exchange gap, which manifests itself in a chronic balance-of-payments deficit on the current account, while domestic resources lie idle. These deficits require financing not only in the interests of the countries themselves, but for the sake of the growth momentum of the whole world economy. There is an interdependence in the world economic system because countries are linked through trade. The alternative to the financ-ing of deficits is adjustment by deflation to reduce imports, which means slower growth in the world economy as a whole.

If the historical experience of the developed countries is considered, in cases where borrowing took place (mainly from Britain as the major creditor) the borrowing was ultimately converted into an export surplus, which enabled the borrowing country to repay its debt and become a net creditor. The condition for this to happen is that the marginal savings ratio should exceed the average in order to eliminate the investment–savings gap, if that is the dominant constraint, or that the marginal propensity to export should exceed the marginal propensity to import if foreign exchange is the dominant constraint. For most developing countries today there is little evidence that they have either the desire or the option to reduce the level of net resource inflows without a major disruption of their economies. The need for resources is as acute as ever, because of a dominant foreign exchange gap to meet development requirements and to pay interest and amortization on past borrowing. The countries find it difficult to convert domestic resources into foreign exchange in adequate quantities, not only cyclically when the world economy is depressed, but also secularly owing to their economic structure; that is, they produce goods whose demand tends to be both price and income inelastic in world trade.

In the first edition of this book (Thirlwall, 1972) I predicted that 'unless something is done the debt-servicing problem arising from mounting resource flows may well become unmanage-able in the not too distant future. It will certainly be a long time before these countries become net exporters of capital even in the absence of a investment–savings gap.' The prediction has turned out to be true. Developing countries continue to borrow extensively; Third World debt now stands at over \$3,000 billion, and over \$200 billion flows out of the developing countries each year to service the debts.

Dual-gap analysis and foreign borrowing

In national income accounting an excess of investment over domestic saving is equivalent to a sur-plus of imports over exports. The national income equation can be written from the expenditure side as

$$\text{Income} = \text{Consumption} + \text{Investment} + \text{Exports} - \text{Imports}$$

Since saving is equal to income minus consumption, we have

$$\text{Saving} = \text{Investment} + \text{Exports} - \text{Imports}$$

or

$$\text{Investment} - \text{Savings} = \text{Imports} - \text{Exports}$$

A surplus of imports over exports financed by foreign borrowing allows a country to spend more than it produces or to invest more than it saves.

Note that in accounting terms the amount of foreign borrowing required to supplement domestic savings is the same whether the need is just for more resources for capital formation or for imports as well. The identity between the two gaps, the investment–savings $(I - S)$ gap and the import–export $(M - X)$ gap, follows from the nature of the accounting procedures. It is a matter of arithmetic that if a country invests more than it saves this will show up in the national accounts as a balance-of-payments deficit. Or to put it another way, an excess of imports over exports necessarily implies an excess of the resources used by an economy over the resources supplied by it, or an excess of investment over saving. There is no reason in principle, however, why the two gaps should be equal *ex ante* (in a planned sense); that is, that *plans* to invest in excess of *planned* saving should exactly equal *plans* to import in excess of *plans* to export. This is the starting point of dual-gap analysis.

Before going into dual-gap analysis in more detail, a reminder of elementary growth theory is in order. Growth requires investment goods, which may either be provided domestically or be purchased from abroad. The domestic provision requires saving; the foreign provision requires foreign exchange. If it is assumed that some investment goods for growth can be provided only from abroad, a minimum amount of foreign exchange is always required to sustain the growth process. In the Harrod model of growth (see Chapter 5), it will be remembered, the relation between growth and saving is given by the incremental capital–output ratio (c), which is the reciprocal of the productivity of capital (p), that is, $g = s/c$ or $g = sp$, where g is the growth rate and s is the saving ratio. Likewise the growth rate can be expressed as the product of the incremental output–import ratio $(\Delta Y/M = m')$ and the ratio of investment-good imports to income $([M/Y] = i)$, that is, $g = im'$.

If there is a lack of substitutability between domestic and foreign resources, growth will be constrained by whatever factor is the most limiting – domestic saving or foreign exchange. Suppose, for example, that the growth rate permitted by domestic saving is less than the growth rate permitted by the availability of foreign exchange. In this case, **growth will be savings-limited** and if the constraint is not lifted a proportion of foreign exchange will go unused. For example, suppose that the product of the savings ratio (s) and the productivity of capital (p) gives a permissible growth rate of 5 per cent, and the product of the import ratio (i) and the productivity of imports (m') gives a permissible growth rate of 6 per cent. Growth is constrained to 5 per cent, and for a given m' a proportion of the foreign exchange available cannot be absorbed (at least for the purposes of growth). Some oil-exporting countries fall into this category; they cannot use all their foreign exchange. Conversely, suppose that the growth rate permitted by domestic savings is higher than that permitted by the availability of foreign exchange. In this case the country will be **foreign exchange constrained** and a proportion of domestic saving will go unused. Most developing countries fall into this category. The policy implications are clear: there will be *resource* *waste* as long as one resource constraint is dominant. If foreign exchange is the dominant constraint, ways must be found of using unused domestic resources to earn more foreign exchange and/or raise the productivity of imports. If domestic saving is the dominant constraint, ways must be found of using foreign exchange to augment domestic saving and/or raise the productivity of domestic resources (by relaxing a skill constraint, for example).[1]

Suppose now a country sets a target rate of growth, r. From our simple growth equations (identities), the required savings ratio (s^*) to achieve the target is $s^* = rc$, and the required import ratio (i^*) is $i^* = r/m'$. If domestic saving is calculated to be less than the level required to achieve the target rate of growth, there is said to exist an investment–savings gap equal at time t to

$$I_t - S_t = s^* Y_t - s Y_t = (rc)Y_t - s Y_t \tag{14.1}$$

Similarly, if minimum import requirements to achieve the growth target are calculated to be greater than the maximum level of export earnings available for investment purposes, there is said to exist an import–export gap, or foreign exchange gap, equal at time t to

$$M_t - X_t = i^* Y_t - i Y_t = (r/m')Y_t - i Y_t, \tag{14.2}$$

where i is the ratio of imports to output that is permitted by export earnings. If the target growth rate is to be achieved, foreign capital flows must fill the larger of the two gaps. The two gaps are not additive. If the import–export gap is the larger, then foreign borrowing to fill it will also fill the investment–savings gap. If the investment–savings gap is the larger, foreign borrowing to fill it will obviously cover the smaller foreign exchange gap.

The distinctive contribution of dual-gap analysis to development theory is that if foreign exchange is the dominant constraint, it points to the dual role of foreign borrowing in supplementing not only deficient domestic saving but also foreign exchange. Dual-gap theory thus performs the valuable service of emphasizing the role of imports and foreign exchange in the development process. It synthesizes traditional and more modern views concerning aid, trade and development. On the one hand it embraces the traditional view of foreign assistance as merely a boost to domestic saving; on the other hand it takes the more modern view that many of the goods necessary for development cannot be produced by the developing countries themselves and must therefore be imported with the aid of foreign assistance. Indeed if foreign exchange is truly the dominant constraint, it can be argued that dual-gap analysis also presents a more relevant theory of trade for developing countries that justifies selective protection and import substitution. If growth is constrained by a lack of foreign exchange, free trade cannot guarantee simultaneous internal and external equilibrium, and the efficiency gains from trade may be offset by the underutilization of domestic resources. We shall take up this matter in Chapter 15.

A practical example of dual-gap analysis

Now let us give a practical example of how dual-gap analysis may be applied to a country. We shall be applying equation (14.1) to estimate the investment–savings gap, and (14.2) to estimate the import–export gap. Suppose that the target rate of growth (r) set by the government over a five-year planning period 2010–15 is 5 per cent per annum and the capital–output ratio is 3. The investment requirements in time t may be written as:

$$I_t = cr Y_t = c\Delta Y = 3\Delta Y$$

Table 14.1   Estimates of investment–savings and import–export gaps assuming a 5% growth of GDP, 2010–2015 ($ million)

	Y_0	Y_1	Y_2	Y_3	Y_4	Y_5
	Base year 2010	**2011**	**2012**	**2013**	**2014**	**2015**
GDP	1,000	1,050	1,102.5	1,157.6	1,215.5	1,276.3
Savings	100	105	110.2	115.8	121.5	127.6
Investment	140	150	157.5	165.3	173.7	182.4
Investment–savings gap	**40**	**45**	**47.3**	**49.5**	**52.2**	**54.8**
Exports	210	216.3	222.8	229.4	236.3	243.4
Imports	250	262.5	275.6	289.4	303.9	319.0
Import–export gap	**40**	**46.2**	**52.8**	**60.0**	**67.6**	**75.6**

Note: The base level of investment and exports will be given by the country's national accounts and balance of payments statistics.

Now assume that 10 per cent of income is saved, so that

$$S_t = 0.1\, Y_t$$

Given this information and the target level of income, Y_t, for each year ($t = 1 - 5$), obtained from applying the target rate of growth to the base level of income ($Y_0 = 1,000$), the $I - S$ gap can be calculated for each year in the future. The results are shown in Table 14.1. All values are in dollars at constant (base year) prices.

For import requirements, let us assume that the incremental output–import ratio (m') is 0.2. Therefore

$$M_t = (r/m')Y_t = i^* Y_t = (0.05/0.2)Y_t = 0.25\, Y_t$$

Finally, assume a forecast exponential rate of growth of exports of 3 per cent a year, namely,

$$X_t = X_0\, e^{0.03t}$$

The calculated import–export gap is also shown in Table 14.1. The results show that while the two gaps are equal in the 2010 base year from the national accounts, the forecast gaps, *ex ante*, diverge through time, with the import–export gap dominant. For the target rate of growth of 5 per cent per annum to be achieved there would have to be foreign borrowing each year to fill the larger of the two gaps. The analysis here is brief and mechanistic, but it illustrates the principle and what can be done in a simple way as a first approach to calculating foreign resource requirements for growth and development.[2]

Models of capital imports and growth

It has been established that foreign borrowing can raise the growth rate, but we have not considered how capital imports are financed and how the terms of borrowing may affect the growth rate. A model that incorporates these considerations is developed below. It is shown that:

• **The rate of growth of output** will be faster with capital imports, provided new inflows of foreign capital exceed the loss of domestic saving to pay interest – if, however, interest charges are met by new borrowing, capital imports must always have a favourable effect on the growth rate of output.

- **The rate of growth of income** will be faster as long as the productivity of capital imports exceeds the rate of interest.

The model is as follows. Let

$$O = Y + rD \tag{14.3}$$

where O is output, Y is income, r is the interest rate and D is debt. The difference between domestic output and national income is net factor payments abroad (including interest, profits and dividends). From (14.3) we have

$$\Delta O = \Delta Y + r\Delta D \tag{14.4}$$

Now

$$\Delta O = \sigma I \tag{14.5}$$

where σ is the productivity of capital, and

$$I = sO + \Delta D - srD \tag{14.6}$$

where s is the propensity to save. Substituting (14.6) into (14.5) and dividing by O gives an expression for output growth of

$$\frac{\Delta O}{O} = \sigma \left(s + \frac{\Delta D - srD}{O} \right) \tag{14.7}$$

Equation (14.7) shows that the growth of output will be higher than the rate obtainable from domestic saving alone as long a $\Delta D > srD$, that is, as long as new inflows of capital exceed the amount of outflow on past loans that would otherwise have been saved. This is a fairly stringent condition unless it is assumed that the interest payments due are met by creating new debt. It can be seen from (14.7) that if $rD = \Delta D$, the rate of growth of output with capital imports will always be higher than without capital imports as long as $s < 1$ (which is the normal case to consider). It may be concluded, then, that if interest payments on past loans can be borrowed in perpetuity, there is a permanent gain to be had from running an import surplus. In practice, however, a country that continually reschedules its debts might ultimately be classified by the international community as uncreditworthy and therefore not be able to borrow continually.

Now let us consider the rate of growth of income as the dependent variable. From (14.3):

$$\Delta Y = \Delta O - r\Delta D \tag{14.8}$$

Substituting (14.6) into (14.5) and the result into (14.8) gives

$$\Delta Y = \sigma(sO + \Delta D - srD) - r\Delta D \tag{14.9}$$

Now since $Y = O - rD$, we can also write (14.9) as

$$\Delta Y = \sigma s Y + \Delta D(\sigma - r) \tag{14.10}$$

and dividing by Y we have the following expression for the rate of growth of income:

$$\frac{\Delta Y}{Y} = \sigma s + (\sigma - r)\frac{\Delta D}{Y} \tag{14.11}$$

Equation (14.11) shows that the growth rate of income with capital imports will be higher than that obtained from domestic saving alone as long as the productivity of capital imports (σ) exceeds the rate of interest on foreign borrowing (r). This is a standard result showing that investment is profitable as long as the rate of return exceeds the rate of interest. In some circumstances, however, this condition may also be a fairly stringent one.

Capital imports, domestic saving and the capital–output ratio

From the discussion above it would appear that import surpluses have great potential in the development process. It is sometimes argued, however, that import surpluses financed by foreign capital inflows increase the capital–output ratio (that is, reduce the productivity of capital) and discourage domestic saving; and that a large fraction of capital inflows is consumed rather than invested. The net result may be no extra growth at all or even a reduction in the growth rate.[3] In terms of (14.7) and (14.11), the inflow of capital ΔD may reduce s and σ and only a fraction of ΔD may be invested.

As far as the relation between capital imports and domestic saving is concerned, many studies find a negative relation. Care must be taken in interpreting the relation, however, because owing to the way saving is defined, a negative relation is bound to be found as long as a proportion of capital imports is consumed. As we said before, domestic saving is normally defined in developing countries as investment minus foreign capital inflows: $S = I - F$. If F rises and I rises by less than F, S must fall for the equality to hold. Thus, a negative statistical relation between foreign capital inflows and domestic saving cannot necessarily be interpreted as a weakening of the development effort; it may simply reflect the fact that a proportion of foreign capital inflows is consumed. The important point is that no studies find a negative relation between capital inflows and the investment ratio. This means that capital inflows must finance some additional growth unless the productivity of capital falls drastically.

Some economists argue that foreign capital inflows do lower the productivity of capital and raise the capital–output ratio because of the tendency for international assistance to be used for prestige projects and because of a bias towards the use of international resource flows for infrastructure projects and social-overhead capital. It should be remembered, however, that there is an important distinction to be made between the capital–output ratio of a particular project on the one hand and the capital–output ratio for the economy as a whole, which is the ratio relevant to the model. It is quite possible for the overall capital–output ratio to fall even if projects financed by capital inflows are relatively capital-intensive because the projects financed confer externalities on the rest of the economy and relax a foreign exchange constraint on demand at the same time. There is no convincing evidence that countries with a high ratio of capital inflows to national income have a higher capital–output ratio than other countries, and no convincing evidence either that the productivity of foreign resource inflows is lower than the productivity of domestic saving.

Types of international capital flows

The main types of international capital flows to developing countries consist of:

- Official flows from **bilateral** sources and **multilateral** sources (such as the World Bank and its two affiliates, the International Development Association (IDA) and the International Finance Corporation (IFC)), on concessional and non-concessional terms
- Aid provided by non-governmental organizations (NGOs)
- Humanitarian and emergency aid
- Foreign direct investment (FDI), and portfolio investment
- Remittances from migrant labour.

Because of the different types of capital flow and the different terms of borrowing, there is an important distinction between the nominal value of capital flows and their worth in terms of the increased command over goods and services that they represent to the recipient. There is also a distinction between the **return** to international assistance, the **benefit** of international assistance (in a cost–benefit sense) and the **value** of international assistance.

The **return** to international assistance is the difference between the nominal value of assistance and any repayments due, discounted by the productivity of the assistance in the recipient country. In other words, the rate of return to assistance is measured in the same way as the return to any other investment.

The **benefit** of assistance is the difference between the nominal value of assistance and repayments discounted by the rate of interest at which the country *would have had to borrow* in the capital market. It is this calculation that we shall later refer to as the '**grant element**' or '**aid component**' of the capital flow, representing 'something for nothing' to the recipient country. Clearly, if the terms on which the country borrows from the donor are no different from those prevailing in the free market, there is no grant element or aid attached to the capital transfer and the benefit of assistance in this sense is zero.

The **value** of the assistance may in turn differ from its benefit if the assistance is tied to the purchase of donor goods that differ in price from the world market price. If the prices are higher, this reduces the value of the grant element of assistance to below what it would otherwise have been.[4]

Not all foreign resource inflows create **debt**; only those flows that involve a repayment obligation. The aid component of official flows, for example, does not create debt; nor do remittances from migrant workers or foreign direct investment – although the latter may involve an outflow of profits.

Now let us turn to a discussion of the various types of international capital flows, and the magnitudes involved. We start with a discussion of official development assistance, or international aid, and the motives behind it.

The debate over international assistance to developing countries

As indicated above, capital flows to developing countries come in many different forms: from grants or pure aid from bilateral and multilateral donors and NGOs, to loans, to portfolio investment and foreign direct investment by multinational companies. The magnitude of these various flows will be given later in the chapter. Donor countries and institutions provide aid, loans and investment, and the developing countries accept the flows, for a mixture of reasons. But the motives of the donors and recipients, and the wider interests of the developing countries as a whole, may not always coincide. The rationale and relevance of financial assistance to developing countries are very much a matter of subjective assessment, depending on the meaning and vision of the development process held by the protagonists. There is a substantial body of opinion on both the right and the left of the political spectrum that argues that not only are financial resource transfers unnecessary for development, but may even be counterproductive and inimical to development by fostering dependence, weakening the domestic development effort and leading to a distorted structure of consumption and production (as well as to debt-servicing problems and profit outflows). These criticisms are levelled both at official assistance and at private investment, particularly at the activities of multinational companies. We shall consider some of these concerns later, but first let us examine the motives for assistance and why developing countries accept the transfers.

The motives for official assistance[5]

There are several motives that inspire financial assistance from bilateral and multilateral sources on concessionary terms, but they can be grouped under three headings.

- The **moral, humanitarian motive** to assist poor countries, and particularly poor people in poor countries (see Opeskin, 1996). The same arguments that provide the basis for income redistribution within nations can also be applied at the global level, namely that absolute poverty is morally unacceptable and that if the marginal utility of income diminishes, total welfare will be increased by a redistribution of income from rich to poor. From a moral and welfare point of view, national boundaries are quite artificial constructions. Developing countries accept assistance with this concern in mind not only from national governments and international organizations as part of their regular aid programmes, but also from many voluntary and charitable organizations (NGOs), and from emergency and disaster relief funds.

- The **political, military and historical motives** for granting assistance. A large part of the US aid programme was originally designed as a bulwark against the spread of communism, and the regional and country distribution of international assistance can still be partly explained in these terms. British and French assistance tends to be concentrated on ex-colonial territories, reflecting strong historical ties and perhaps some recompense for former colonial neglect. Most developing countries are willing to accept assistance on this basis to assist their development effort, particularly when governments are threatened by hostile forces from within or without.

- The **economic motives** of developed countries to invest in developing countries are not only to raise the growth rate of the developing countries, but also to improve their own welfare. Hence international assistance is seen as mutually beneficial. If the rate of interest on loans is higher than the productivity of capital in the developed donor country and lower than the productivity of capital in the developing recipient country, both parties will gain. If there are underutilized resources in the developed country that could not otherwise be activated because of balance-of-payments constraints, international assistance will be mutually profitable by adding to the resources in the developing country and enabling fuller utilization of the resources in the developed country. This is the strong Keynesian argument for international assistance, and forcefully recommended in the Brandt Report (discussed in Chapter 1). Developing countries accept these financial flows because most are desperately short of foreign exchange (see Chapter 16), and judge the benefits of the international programmes and the projects that they finance to be greater than the costs of servicing the borrowing and any unfavourable side-effects.

The critics of international aid

Despite the many worthy motives for giving international assistance to developing countries, there are many critics of international aid. One extreme view is that aid has no effect on the growth performance of poor countries and can undermine development by fostering a dependency culture. This was the view of early critics such as Bauer (1971) and Friedman (1958), and has recently been revived in polemical books such as Easterly's *The White Man's Burden* (2006), and Moyo's *Dead Aid* (2009). Both argue that aid to Africa has been wasted, and Moyo argues that there should be a programme of aid withdrawal from Africa, and that all future capital inflows should come from the private sector. This would lead to a more responsible and efficient use of resource inflows, she argues.

It is true that international assistance may be wasted. If not directed wisely, it may help to support governments that are corrupt and profligate. It may encourage irresponsible financial policies; and if the assistance is free (pure aid) there may be no incentive to use resources productively. The critics argue that billions of dollars have been invested in Africa over the past half century, but still Africa is extremely poor.

There are several counter-arguments, however, to this extreme view. Firstly, it needs to be remembered that the amount of aid received *per head of population* in developing countries (and Africa) is very low, and poor countries have many depressive cumulative forces working against them, so that expectations relating to the impact of aid should not be exaggerated. Secondly, much aid has been used for humanitarian purposes; for social investment in hospitals, public health and schools, the benefits of which are not disputed. Thirdly, as far as corrupt governments, and irresponsible economic policy-making, are concerned, it is not clear that the same scenario would not prevail without aid. Indeed, the alternatives might be worse because with international assistance comes a certain amount of 'leverage', which can be used for the promotion of good governance and more enlightened policy-making. The challenge is not to stop aid, but to make it more effective.

The most valid criticism of aid is that it may lead to a weakening of the domestic development effort by supporting a culture of dependency. In particular, it may weaken a country's tax effort. In many poor developing countries the value of aid exceeds tax revenue. To cope with this issue, one suggestion by the Oxford economist Adrian Wood (2008), is for donors collectively to set an upper limit to the aid to tax ratio (say 50 per cent), above which aid would be phased out, but below which donors would give 50 cents more aid for every extra dollar raised in taxes. This would encourage developing countries to raise more tax, and at the same time encourage governments to pay more attention to what their citizens want (because they are paying!) rather than what donors want the aid used for.

Another, less extreme, view of aid is that aid can have a positive effect on growth and development on average, but not in every country, and is conditional on absorptive capacity, good governance and the policies of donor countries. Some countries may not have the administrative or technical capacity to absorb much aid, in which case there will be diminishing returns to aid. There is evidence on this, which will be discussed below (p. 450). There is also evidence that aid only works in good policy environments, where there is good governance and sound macroeconomic policy-making. The practices of donor countries also make a difference to the productivity of aid, whether the aid is multilateral or bilateral, whether it is tied to the purchase of donor goods or untied, and how the aid is monitored. The consensus now is that recipient countries themselves should have 'ownership' of aid programmes, and that the heavy hand of donors can be counterproductive.

There are valid criticisms of aid, and how it has been administered in the past, but the fact that it can be wasted; that it doesn't help the people that it is meant to, and that recipients of aid still remain poor and underdeveloped, is more a challenge to the use of aid than an argument that resource flows to poor countries cannot be productive. That would defy economic logic. Some flavour of the contrast in country experience on the successes and failures of aid is given in Case example 14.1.

| Case example 14.1 | **Successes and failures of aid, 1970–1990s** |

Foreign aid has at times been a spectacular success. Botswana and the Republic of Korea in the 1960s, Indonesia in the 1970s, Bolivia and Ghana in the late 1980s, and Uganda and Vietnam in the 1990s are all examples of countries that have gone from crisis to rapid development. Foreign aid played a significant role in each transformation, contributing ideas about development policy, training for public policy-makers, and finance to support reform and an expansion of public services. Foreign aid has also transformed entire sectors. The agricultural innovations, investments and policies that created the 'Green Revolution' – improving the lives of millions of poor people around the world – were financed, supported and disseminated through alliances of bilateral and multilateral donors. Internationally funded and coordinated programmes have dramatically reduced such diseases as river blindness and vastly expanded immunization against key childhood diseases. Hundreds of millions of people have had their lives touched, if not transformed, by access to schools, clean water, sanitation, electric power, health clinics, roads and irrigation – all financed by foreign aid.

On the flip side, foreign aid has also been, at times, an unmitigated failure. While the former Zaire's Mobutu Sese Seko was reportedly amassing one of the world's largest personal fortunes (invested, naturally, outside his own country), decades of large-scale foreign assistance left not a trace of progress. Zaire (now the Democratic Republic of Congo) is just one of several examples where a steady flow of aid ignored, if not encouraged, incompetence, corruption and misguided policies. Consider Tanzania, where donors poured a colossal $2 billion into building roads over 20 years. Did the road network improve? No. For lack of maintenance, roads often deteriorated faster than they were built.

Sadly, experience has long since undermined the rosy optimism of aid-financed, government-led, accumulationist strategies for development. Suppose that development aid only financed investment and investment really played the crucial role projected by early models. In that case aid to Zambia should have financed rapid growth that would have pushed per capita income above $20,000, while in reality per capita income stagnated at around $600.

Foreign aid in different times and different places has thus been highly effective, totally ineffective, and everything in between. The chequered history of assistance has already led to improvements in foreign aid, and there is scope for further reform.

Source: *World Bank Policy and Research Bulletin*, October–December 1998.

The macroeconomic impact of aid

When a country receives aid, it can do one of two things, or a combination of both. It can either spend the aid directly on imports, in which case there are no serious domestic implications (e.g. there will be no change in the exchange rate or change in foreign exchange reserves), or the government can sell the extra foreign exchange to the Central Bank and then use the local currency to buy domestic goods. This does have domestic implications depending on the response of governments and the Central Bank. Aiyar et al. (2005) consider four responses. The first is to **absorb and spend** which involves government spending on domestic goods, and the Central Bank selling foreign exchange, which neutralizes the increase in local currency spent by the government and finances the current account balance of payments deficit due to rising imports. The second response is **neither absorb nor spend**, in which case the government keeps the new foreign exchange in the Central Bank to add to reserves. This does not assist development directly, but can act as a buffer against aid volatility in the future. The third response is **absorb but not spend**. In this case aid acts as a substitute for the domestic finance of government budget deficits. The government reduces the money supply at the same time as the Central Bank sells the foreign exchange. Finally, the last response is to **spend but not absorb**. In this case, the government increases its expenditure but keeps aid in the Central Bank as reserves. This is equivalent to a fiscal stimulus financed by selling bonds or printing money. There is no real resource transfer to the developing country because no aid has been used to import more. This policy can be highly inflationary and lead to the currency depreciating unless the Central Bank sells foreign exchange to stop it.

If aid is not spent directly on imports, the first best response is to absorb and spend, but according to Aiyar et al. it is surprisingly rare, at least in the five countries studied in detail (Ethiopia, Ghana, Mozambique, Tanzania and Uganda). In four of the countries, less than one-third of aid was absorbed.

If aid is not spent directly on imports, there is the strong possibility of exchange rate appreciation, or what is sometimes called the **Dutch disease**,[6] which can have damaging effects on the tradable goods sector of the economy, by making exports more expensive and imports cheaper. To prevent appreciation, governments can buy up foreign exchange which adds to reserves, but then the Central Bank has to sell bonds if it wants to absorb the excess liquidity arising from such purchases (to prevent inflation, for example). This may lead to a rise in interest rates, which can also damage the real economy. Some studies of the impact of aid find evidence of the Dutch disease (see Rajan and Subramanian, 2005) but the important point to make is that it is not inevitable if the aid is spent on the purchase of tradable goods which, in principle, is the best policy. There are so many goods needed for development that poor developing countries cannot produce themselves. Aid gives the chance to import them.

To assess the impact of aid on growth and development, there are two main approaches that can be taken. The first is to do detailed case studies. As representative of this approach, a study by Cassen (1994) of seven countries (Bangladesh, Colombia, India, Kenya, Korea, Malawi and Mali) shows that most aid achieves its development objectives, although in several instances the performance could have been improved. The provision of aid played a major part in the 'Green Revolution' in South-East Asia, in the building of infrastructure in southern Africa and in the direct provision of basic needs and the relief of poverty in many countries. The study also found, however, that aid performance appears to be least satisfactory where it is most needed, and that, above all, improved performance requires better collaboration between aid agencies.

The second approach to assessing the impact of aid is to conduct a detailed statistical analysis of the relation between the growth of GDP or living standards and the amount of aid (as a proportion of GDP) received by each country, controlling for other variables. A typical estimating equation, taking a large sample of developing countries, would be:

$$y = a + b\,(\text{AID}) + (V_i)$$

where y is the growth of per capita income, AID is the ratio of official development assistance (ODA) to GDP and V_i is a vector of control variables ($i = 1 \cdots n$). Hansen and Tarp (2001) review 131 cross-section studies and conclude that most of them show a positive relation between aid and growth. Their own research shows that aid has a positive effect on growth with a coefficient (b) of approximately 0.25, although not when investment is included in the equations as one of the control variables. The implication is that aid promotes growth by encouraging investment, and this is confirmed by equations relating the ratio of investment to GDP with the ratio of aid to GDP. Dalgaard et al. (2004) also show that aid has a positive effect on the growth of living standards with a 1 percentage point difference in the aid variable leading to (approximately) a 0.5 percentage point difference in the growth of per capita income. The impact is lower, however, in tropical countries. The authors conclude, 'we have confidence . . . that aid has a positive impact on growth, and that the impact depends on climate-related differences'.

Addison et al. (2005) survey studies conducted between 1997 and 2005 and conclude that growth of developing countries would have been slower without aid, and that the criticism of aid that it is counterproductive is not supported by the bulk of statistical evidence.

Clements et al. (2004) distinguish different types of aid, and focus on the impact of aid specifically meant for development purposes, as opposed to aid given for political and humanitarian reasons. They take a cross-section of 67 countries over the period 1974 to 2001, and use a non-linear specification of the aid–growth relationship to allow for the possibility of diminishing returns to aid. Their central estimate is that an increase in aid of 1 per cent of GDP leads to a 0.31 percentage point increase in growth, and diminishing returns to aid seem to set in at about 8–9 per cent of GDP (which implies 16–18 per cent of total aid to GDP because only one-half of total aid is specifically for development purposes). These figures are three times the amount of aid actually given.

In recent years the World Bank has been heavily involved in attempting to assess the impact of aid, and one of its major researchers is David Dollar. The World Bank (1998) and Burnside and Dollar (2000) take a panel of 56 developing countries over the period 1970–93 and try to disentangle the circumstances in which aid 'works' and in which it does not. The major findings are that, on average, aid has had only a minor impact on the growth of GDP per head (partly because aid as a percentage of GDP is so small), but that it can be extremely effective in promoting growth and reducing poverty in the right economic and political environment where there are democratic governments pursuing sensible macroeconomic policies. In countries with good economic management, a 1 percentage point increase in aid raises the growth rate by 0.5 per cent and reduces poverty by 1 per cent. The Bank calculates that an extra $10 billion of aid could lift 25 million people out of poverty if the aid is directed to countries that manage their economies well. In countries with poor management, aid is entirely wasted. There are also diminishing returns to aid. Even in good environments, the returns to aid peak when aid reaches about 10 per cent of GDP.

The Bank emphasizes five major points from its analysis, and indicates five policy reforms for making aid more effective:

• Analysis

  – Financial aid works in a good policy environment.
  – Improvements in economic institutions and policies are the key to reducing poverty.
  – Effective aid and private investment are complementary.
  – The value of development projects is to strengthen institutions and policies so that services can be delivered effectively.
  – Aid can nurture reform even in the most distorted environments – but it requires patience and a focus on ideas, not money.

• Reforms

  – Financial assistance must be targeted more effectively to low-income countries with sound economic management.
  – Policy-based aid should be provided to nurture policy reform where needed.
  – The mix of aid activities should be tailored to suit the needs of the country and sectoral conditions.
  – Projects need to focus on creating and transmitting knowledge and capacity.
  – Aid agencies need to find alternative approaches to helping highly distorted countries.

Research also shows that the **unpredictability** and **volatility** of the flow of aid also affects the impact of aid on growth because it affects the composition and effectiveness of government expenditure and can deter private investment. Aid is unpredictable if recipients cannot be confident about the amount and timing of aid disbursements. Aid is volatile if it fluctuates significantly (predictably or unpredictably). Measuring the predictability of aid is not easy, but it can be done with detailed data on aid commitments and disbursements by donor agencies, such as the Development Assistance Committee of the OECD. It has been found by Celasun and Walliser (2008) that on average over the period 1993–2005, disbursed budget aid differed from the amount expected by 30 per cent, or roughly 1 per cent of GDP. Total aid disbursements to sub-Saharan Africa deviated from aid commitments by 3.4 per cent of GDP. Aid shortfalls cut investment, while aid windfalls encourage consumption. This aid unpredictability affects the composition of expenditure in favour of consumption. The authors find that an aid shortfall of 1 per cent of GDP is associated with a cut of investment expenditure of about 0.1 to 0.2 per cent of GDP, while a 1 per cent aid windfall is associated with an increase in consumption of about 0.6 per cent of GDP. In other words, more predictable aid would lead to more investment.

Aid volatility can be measured by the standard deviation of aid flows. Lensink and Morrissey (2000) take 75 countries over the period 1970–95 and find that volatility negatively affects growth performance, but when volatility is controlled for, aid itself has a positive and significant effect on growth performance.

Since the fundamental purpose of international aid is the relief of primary poverty, there is a strong case for arguing (as part of the reform of aid programmes) that assistance should be given only to countries that are committed to poverty reduction programmes and make progress towards certain targets, such as literacy, basic health care provision, reducing infant mortality and so on. As incentives for governments to embark on and continue the programmes, donor countries could, in turn, commit themselves to funding as long as the recipients continue to support them. This would improve the certainty of aid flows.

The World Bank is moving in these directions. In its *World Development Report* 2000/2001 it refers to the new consensus on how aid can be made more effective: by linking aid to policy reforms; by improving coordination between donors and, above all, by getting people in the recipient countries to believe that the projects or reforms will bring benefits, so that countries feel they 'own' the programmes (see below on the reform of World Bank lending). The Bank now has a **Comprehensive Development Framework** which addresses these various issues. One new approach is the sectorwide approach where donors sign on to finance a *sector* (not individual projects), and the country itself does the work. An example is given in Case example 14.2.

| Case example 14.2 | **Sectorwide development cooperation, mid-1990s** |

To address problems of ownership, donor coordination, and fungibility, donors are experimenting with pooling their resources to support sectorwide strategies designed and implemented by the recipient government. The country, in consultation with key stakeholders, designs a sector strategy and a budget framework extending several years forward, and donors put their money into the central expenditure pool for the sector. The approach encourages country ownership of sector strategies and programmes. It also links sector expenditure with the overall macroeconomic framework. And it ensures coordination of donor and recipient activities.

Some benefits of a sectorwide programme are evident in the Zambian health sector. In 1994 the government presented its national health policy and strategy to donors and – to ensure equitable distribution of services and coherent implementation of the strategy – asked them not to fund specific provinces or projects but to fund the Ministry of Health centrally. Hesitant at first, donors began to comply. An independent evaluation in 1997 found that 'health workers are better motivated; clinics are functioning; funds are flowing to the districts; some modicum of decentralization is in place; [and] an important part of the private sector has become formally involved'.

The approach ensures full ownership by the country and eliminates problems of donor coordination. With the country having more ownership and control over what happens, the use of resources can be much more efficient. But it also means great changes in donor–recipient relations and perhaps greater difficulties in implementation. Several sectorwide programmes have stumbled because of the recipient country's inadequate institutional capacity. Lack of consistency with the macroeconomic programme has been another problem. And donors often have too many requirements and thus too much of a problem (or too little interest) in harmonizing them. . . . Furthermore, these arrangements greatly diminish donor control and monitoring of exactly how money is spent.

The changes required imply that gaining support for the approach will be difficult. The recipient government has to be very confident, because strict adherence to a sectorwide approach means donors that do not participate in common implementation arrangements are not allowed to act in the sector (that is, they do not have their own projects). The result may be less donor funding for a sector. Governments might therefore opt for less strict sectorwide programmes, choosing instead to allow donors to implement projects as long as they fit into the overall sector strategy.

Source: *World Bank, World Development Report 2000/2001: Attacking Poverty*
(New York: Oxford University Press, 2000).

The total net flow of financial resources to developing countries

The total net flow of financial resources to developing countries is the total of all official and private flows to developing countries *net* of repayments of past loans (amortization). It includes flows given **bilaterally** by individual donor countries and **multilaterally** through international organizations, and includes flows both with and without concessionary terms. Most official flows are given on concessionary terms and are referred to as **official development assistance**. To qualify as such, the concessional (or grant) element of the flow must be at least 25 per cent. Only the concessional element of international financial flows really qualifies for the term 'aid'. The major donors of official development assistance are the 22 developed countries that form the **Development Assistance Committee (DAC)** of the OECD, and the various multilateral agencies. In addition, the OPEC countries have lent substantial sums on concessional terms in recent years. Also included are net grants by NGOs.

Non-concessional flows are primarily bilateral, and consist mainly of foreign direct investment (FDI), export credits and syndicated bank loans.

The magnitude of all these various types of flow from 2004 to 2007 is shown in Table 14.2. The total net flows of financial resources from DAC countries to developing countries and multilateral

Table 14.2　Total net flow of financial resources from DAC countries to developing countries and multilateral organizations, by type of flow ($ million)

	2004	2005	2006	2007
I. Official development assistance	79,432	107,078	104,370	103,491
1. Bilateral grants and grant-like flows	57,246	83,432	79,440	75,326
of which: Technical cooperation	18,672	20,732	22,242	14,779
Developmental food aid	1,169	887	956	1,051
Humanitarian aid	5,193	7,121	6,751	6,278
Debt forgiveness	7,134	24,999	18,600	9,624
Administrative costs	4,032	4,115	4,250	4,618
2. Bilateral loans	−2,942	−1,008	−2,531	−2,433
3. Contributions to multilateral institutions	25,127	24,653	27,461	30,598
of which: UN	5,129	5,469	5239	5801
EC	8,906	9,258	9,931	11,714
IDA	5,690	4,827	6,787	5,609
Regional development banks	2,274	2,096	2,466	2,361
II. Other official flows	−5,601	1,430	−10,728	−6,438
1. Bilateral	−5,349	2,262	−10,551	−6,962
2. Multilateral	−252	−832	−177	524
III. Private flows at market terms	75,262	179,559	194,761	325,350
1. Direct investment	76,901	100,622	127,925	188,696
2. Bilateral portfolio investment	−3,544	73,335	60,910	133,199
3. Multilateral portfolio investment	−4,657	40	2,789	−9,727
4. Export credits	6,561	5,563	3,137	13,182
IV. Net grants by NGOs	11,320	14,712	14,648	18,508
TOTAL NET FLOWS	**160,412**	**302,779**	**303,051**	**440,912**

Source: OECD, 2009.

institutions in 2007 amounted to $440 billion, of which $103 billion was official development assistance and $325 billion consisted of non-concessional flows, mainly FDI.

The aid targets set for the developed countries of 1 per cent of their national incomes refer to the total net flow of financial resources, while the target for official development assistance alone is 0.7 per cent of donor countries' national incomes. It must also be remembered that the net flow of financial resources is not the same thing as the flow of *real resources*, since the former does not take account of interest payments and profit repatriation. If the terms of lending are steady over time, the net transfer of resources in any one year (that is, the gross capital inflow net of amortization *and* interest and profit payments) will be approximately equal to the estimated grant equivalent or aid component of assistance, the measurement of which is discussed later (see p. 471).

Official development assistance (ODA)

The total flow of ODA from the DAC countries in 2007 was $103 billion, of which approximately $75 billion consisted of grants, including $15 billion for technical assistance. $30 billion was disbursed by multilateral institutions.

The evolution of official development assistance in current and constant (2004) prices, and as a ratio of national income, is shown in Figures 14.1 and 14.2. The total value of ODA rose from less than $10 billion a year from 1950 to 1973 to over $100 billion today. The real value of ODA has also increased almost continuously except for a dip in the first half of the 1990s. On the other hand, the ratio of ODA to national income fell more or less continuously from 1960 to 2000, despite the commitment in the 1970s to the 0.7 per cent aid target, and it has only started to rise in the past decade.

The recent record of individual DAC countries as providers of ODA is shown in Table 14.3, together with the flow measured as a proportion of the donor's GNI. It can be seen that only the Netherlands, Denmark, Norway, Luxembourg and Sweden met the aid target of 0.7 per cent of GNI. The USA is the richest country but contributes the lowest proportion of GNI. The ratio for all DAC countries fell during the 1990s and now averages only 0.28 per cent.

Figure 14.1   Official development assistance (ODA), 1950–2010

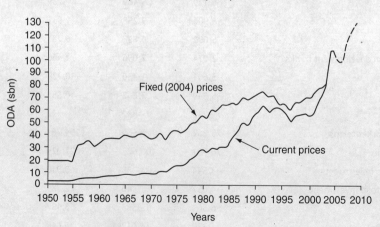

Note: 2006–10 figures are OECD projections.

Source: Riddell, 2007.

Figure 14.2   Ratio of ODA to GNI, 1960–2005

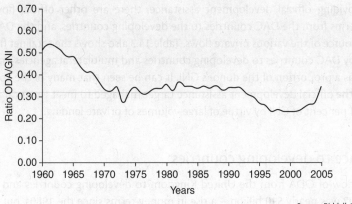

Source: Riddell, 2007.

Table 14.3   ODA and total net flow of financial resources from DAC countries to developing countries and multilateral agencies, 2007

	ODA		Total net flows by DAC country	
	US$ million	% of GNI	US$ million	% of GNI
Australia	2,669	0.32	10,307	1.25
Austria	1,808	0.50	20,553	5.66
Belgium	1,953	0.43	3,820	0.83
Canada	4,080	0.29	17,161	1.22
Denmark	2,562	0.81	4,807	1.51
Finland	981	0.39	2,149	0.86
France	9,884	0.38	43,126	1.66
Germany	12,291	0.37	39,339	1.17
Greece	501	0.16	3,391	1.10
Ireland	1,192	0.55	5,840	2.70
Italy	3,971	0.19	4,422	0.21
Japan	7,679	0.17	30,315	0.67
Luxembourg	376	0.91	384	0.93
Netherlands	6,224	0.81	18,142	2.35
New Zealand	320	0.27	404	0.34
Norway	3,728	0.95	5,221	1.33
Portugal	471	0.22	2,215	1.03
Spain	5,140	0.37	21,662	1.55
Sweden	4,339	0.93	6,911	1.49
Switzerland	1,689	0.37	12,561	2.73
United Kingdom	9,849	0.36	58,319	2.10
United States	21,787	0.16	129,862	0.93
TOTAL DAC	**103,491**	**0.28**	**440,912**	**1.18**

Source: OECD, 2009.

Total net flow of financial resources from DAC countries

As well as providing official development assistance, there are other official flows on non-concessional terms from the DAC countries to the developing countries, and the DAC countries are the major source of the various private flows. Table 14.3 also shows the total net flow of financial resources by DAC countries to developing countries and multilateral agencies, together with the total flow as a proportion of the donor's GNI. It can be seen that many of the countries that failed to meet the official development assistance target managed to meet the total net financial flow target of 1 per cent of GNI by virtue of large volumes of private lending.

UK assistance to developing countries

The total net flow of ODA from the United Kingdom to developing countries and multilateral agencies in 2007 was nearly $10 billion – a rise in money terms since the 1980s, but roughly the same as a proportion of Gross National Income: 0.33 per cent in the mid-1980s and 0.36 per cent in 2007 (see Table 14.4). This is well below the UN target of 0.7 per cent, although the UK is committed to reaching the target by 2013.

Table 14.4   Total net flow of financial resources from the United Kingdom to developing countries and multilateral agencies, 2007

	$ million
NET DISBURSEMENTS	
I. Official development assistance (ODA) (A + B)	9,849
ODA as % of GNI	**0.36**
A. Bilateral official development assistance (1 + 2)	5,602
1. Grants and grant-like contributions	6,572
of which: Technical cooperation	888
Developmental food aid	90
Humanitarian aid	352
Contributions to NGOs	669
Administrative costs	545
2. Development lending and capital	−71
of which: New development lending	−20
B. Contributions to multilateral institutions	4,247
Grants and capital subscriptions, Total	4,247
of which: EC	2,143
IDA	987
Regional development banks	188
II. Other official flows (OOF) net (C + D)	−43
C. Bilateral other official flows (1 + 2)	−43
1. Official export credits (a)	−8
2. Equities and other bilateral assets	−35
D. Multilateral institutions	—
III. Grants by private voluntary agencies	667

Table 14.4 Total net flow of financial resources from the United Kingdom to developing countries and multilateral agencies, 2007 – *continued*

	$ million
IV. Private flows at market terms (long-term) (1 to 4)	47,846
1. Direct investment	31,043
2. Private export credits	217
3. Securities of multilateral agencies	—
4. Bilateral portfolio investment	16,587
V. Total resource flows (long-term) (I to IV)	58,319
Total resource flows as % of GNI	2.10

Source: OECD, 2009.

Most of the bilateral development assistance is now given in the form of grants. This represents a softening of the terms of assistance over the years, when in the past assistance was largely in the form of loans at near market rates of interest. Nearly two-thirds of assistance is bilateral and the remainder goes to multilateral institutions. Of total bilateral aid, most is financial aid, of which approximately 15 per cent represents technical assistance. Technical assistance is an integral part of the UK aid programme and now amounts to nearly $1 billion. Over 75 per cent of bilateral aid goes to the poorest countries with per capita incomes of less than $1,500.

The UK aid programme is administered by the Department for International Development (DFID), and its Mission Statement is given in Case example 14.3.

Case example 14.3	**DFID Mission Statement**

DFID, the Department for International Development: leading the British government's fight against world poverty.

One in five people in the world today, over 1 billion people, live in poverty on less than one dollar a day. In an increasingly inter-dependent world, many problems – like conflict, crime, pollution, and diseases such as HIV and AIDS – are caused or made worse by poverty.

DFID supports long-term programmes to help tackle the underlying causes of poverty.

DFID also responds to emergencies, both natural and man-made.

DFID's work forms part of a global promise to

- halve the number of people living in extreme poverty and hunger
- ensure that all children receive primary education
- promote gender equality and give women a stronger voice
- reduce child death rates
- improve the health of mothers
- combat HIV & AIDS, malaria and other diseases
- make sure the environment is protected
- build a global partnership for those working in development.

Together, these form the United Nations' eight 'Millennium Development Goals', with a 2015 deadline. Each of these Goals has its own, measurable, targets.

continued overleaf

Case example 14.3   **DFID Mission Statement** – *continued*

DFID works in partnership with governments, civil society, the private sector and others. It also works with multilateral institutions, including the World Bank, United Nations agencies, and the European Commission.

Source: Department for International Development (DFID), London.

The focus is very much on poverty reduction through social expenditure on health and education. Part of doctors' salaries in Africa are paid out of the aid budget, as well as user fees for medicines and various forms of hospital care. The aid budget is also increasingly being used to improve security in 'fragile states' (see Chapter 10).

Perhaps the most significant recent development, however, is that DFID tries not to tell the aid-receiving countries what to do; rather it listens to what countries want to achieve and tries to help them to do so by ensuring that aid strengthens a country's system for planning, budgeting and accounting. As much aid as possible is channelled through countries' budgets so that they can assess resources and plan spending. Aid conditionality has been abandoned (see Case example 14.4).

Case example 14.4   **Rethinking conditionality**

Traditional conditionality, under which donors link aid to the implementation of particular policies by developing countries, is not compatible with the guiding principles of the country-led approach. It limits governments' freedom to design poverty reduction plans suited to the circumstances of their countries, and it compromises their accountability to their own citizens. It also undermines efforts to make aid more predictable. Conditionality has been particularly criticized when applied to privatization and trade liberalization. But even where it has been less controversial, there is little evidence that conditionality has been effective in promoting long-term policy reform. The UK has therefore adopted a new approach, in which the key purpose is to safeguard donor resources from misuse, rather than to promote policy change in partner countries. Good policy remains vital for development, and we will continue to discuss policy options with partner countries. But we will not attempt to impose policies on them by making aid conditional on specific policy decisions. Our aid relationships will be based on three shared commitments – to poverty reduction, to human rights and other international obligations, and to sound financial management and accountability. Only if countries veer substantially away from these commitments will we consider reducing or withdrawing agreed aid.

To specify what our aid is intended to achieve, and as a basis for measuring progress, we will agree on benchmarks with partner countries, drawn from national poverty reduction plans. They will focus on outcomes and results, rather than on particular policies, and will be the basis for both partners to be accountable to their citizens for the effective use of aid. Although aid will not be conditional on the achievement of any particular benchmark, the rate and pattern of a country's progress will contribute to our assessment of its continuing commitment to poverty reduction and may be reflected in our subsequent aid allocation decisions.

Source: Department for International Development (DFID), London.

The recipients of official assistance

We end this statistical section by showing the distribution of external capital by recipient country for 2007. It is important to remember that while ODA in 2007 amounted to approximately $100 billion, it was spread over nearly 5 billion people in developing countries, giving an annual average per capita receipt of $19. In India, the largest developing country in receipt of ODA from the DAC countries, assistance per head is approximately $1 per annum. The aggregate amounts of net official development assistance and ODA per head, and aid as a percentage of recipients' GNI, are shown in Table 14.5. It can be seen that in several poor countries, the amount of ODA per head is paltry and in the low-income countries as a whole, ODA represents only 5.2 per cent of their GNI.

Table 14.5   The recipients of aid, 2007

Country/Group	Official development assistance ($ million)	Aid per capita (current US$)	Aid (% of GNI)
Afghanistan	3,951	–	–
Albania	305	96	2.7
Algeria	390	12	0.3
Angola	241	14	0.5
Antigua and Barbuda	4	49	0.4
Argentina	82	2	0.0
Armenia	352	117	3.7
Azerbaijan	225	26	0.9
Bangladesh	1,502	9	2.0
Barbados	14	46	–
Belarus	83	9	0.2
Belize	23	77	2.0
Benin	470	52	8.7
Bhutan	89	136	7.9
Bolivia	476	50	3.7
Bosnia and Herzegovina	443	117	2.8
Botswana	104	56	0.9
Brazil	297	2	0.0
Burkina Faso	930	63	13.8
Burundi	466	55	49.5
Cambodia	672	46	8.4
Cameroon	1,933	104	9.4
Cape Verde	163	308	11.8
Central African Republic	176	41	10.4
Chad	352	33	5.7
Chile	120	7	0.1
China	1,439	1	0.0

continued overleaf

Table 14.5   The recipients of aid, 2007 – *continued*

Country/Group	Official development assistance ($ million)	Aid per capita (current US$)	Aid (% of GNI)
Colombia	731	17	0.4
Comoros	44	71	9.9
Congo, Dem. Rep.	1,217	19	14.2
Congo, Rep.	127	34	2.1
Costa Rica	53	12	0.2
Côte d'Ivoire	165	9	0.9
Croatia	164	37	0.3
Cuba	92	8	–
Djibouti	112	135	12.3
Dominica	19	267	–
Dominican Republic	128	13	0.4
Ecuador	215	16	0.5
Egypt, Arab Rep.	1,083	14	0.8
El Salvador	88	13	0.4
Equatorial Guinea	31	62	0.5
Eritrea	155	32	11.3
Ethiopia	2,422	31	12.5
Fiji	57	69	1.7
Gabon	48	36	0.5
Gambia, The	72	42	12.1
Georgia	382	87	3.7
Ghana	1,151	49	7.7
Grenada	23	215	5.0
Guatemala	450	34	1.3
Guinea-Bissau	123	73	35.4
Guinea	224	24	5.0
Guyana	124	168	12.4
Haiti	701	73	11.4
Honduras	464	65	4.0
India	1,298	1	0.1
Indonesia	796	4	0.2
Iran, Islamic Rep.	102	1	0.0
Iraq	9,115	–	–
Jamaica	26	10	0.3
Jordan	504	88	3.0
Kazakhstan	202	13	0.2
Kenya	1,275	34	5.3
Kiribati	27	285	22.2
Korea, Dem. Rep.	98	4	–

Table 14.5 The recipients of aid, 2007 – *continued*

Country/Group	Official development assistance ($ million)	Aid per capita (current US$)	Aid (% of GNI)
Kyrgyz Republic	274	52	7.4
Lao PDR	396	68	10.0
Lebanon	939	229	3.9
Lesotho	130	65	6.4
Liberia	696	187	124.3
Libya	19	3	0.0
Macedonia, FYR	213	105	2.8
Madagascar	892	45	12.2
Malawi	735	53	20.8
Malaysia	200	8	0.1
Maldives	37	122	3.7
Mali	1,017	82	15.4
Marshall Islands	52	894	28.3
Mauritania	364	117	13.2
Mauritius	75	59	1.1
Mayotte	407	2,189	—
Mexico	121	1	0.0
Micronesia, Fed. Sts.	115	1,035	45.3
Moldova	269	71	5.6
Mongolia	228	87	5.9
Montenegro	106	177	3.0
Morocco	1,090	35	1.5
Mozambique	1,777	83	25.2
Myanmar	190	4	—
Namibia	205	99	3.0
Nepal	598	21	5.7
Nicaragua	834	149	14.9
Nigeria	2,042	14	1.4
Niger	542	38	12.8
Oman	−31	−12	—
Pakistan	2,212	14	1.5
Palau	22	1,108	13.4
Panama	−135	−40	−0.7
Papua New Guinea	317	50	5.7
Paraguay	108	18	0.9
Peru	263	9	0.3
Philippines	634	7	0.4
Rwanda	713	73	21.5

continued overleaf

Table 14.5 The recipients of aid, 2007 – *continued*

Country/Group	Official development assistance ($ million)	Aid per capita (current US$)	Aid (% of GNI)
Samoa	37	204	7.2
São Tomé and Principe	36	228	25.0
Saudi Arabia	−131	−5	0.0
Senegal	843	68	7.6
Serbia	834	113	2.2
Seychelles	3	33	0.4
Sierra Leone	535	92	32.9
Solomon Islands	248	501	64.6
Somalia	384	44	—
South Africa	794	17	0.3
Sri Lanka	589	29	1.8
St Kitts and Nevis	3	59	0.6
St Lucia	24	141	2.6
St V and Grenadines	66	545	12.7
Sudan	2,104	55	5.0
Suriname	151	330	6.9
Swaziland	63	55	2.1
Syrian Arab Republic	75	4	0.2
Tajikistan	221	33	6.1
Tanzania	2,811	70	17.4
Thailand	−312	−5	−0.1
Timor-Leste	278	262	16.3
Togo	121	18	4.9
Tonga	30	298	11.6
Trinidad and Tobago	18	14	0.1
Tunisia	310	30	0.9
Turkey	797	11	0.1
Turkmenistan	28	6	0.2
Uganda	1,728	56	15.0
Ukraine	405	9	0.3
Uruguay	34	10	0.1
Uzbekistan	166	6	0.7
Vanuatu	57	251	13.5
Venezuela, RB	71	3	0.0
Vietnam	2,497	29	3.7
West Bank and Gaza	1,868	504	—
Yemen, Rep.	225	10	1.1
Zambia	1,045	88	10.5
Zimbabwe	465	35	—

Table 14.5   The recipients of aid, 2007 – *continued*

Country/Group	Official development assistance ($ million)	Aid per capita (current US$)	Aid (% of GNI)
World	105,056	16	0.2
Low income	40,259	31	5.2
Middle income	38,538	9	0.3
Lower middle income	31,700	9	0.5
Upper middle income	6,011	7	0.1
Low & middle income	105,130	19	0.7
East Asia & Pacific	8,611	5	0.2
Europe & Central Asia	5,785	13	0.2
Latin America & Caribbean	6,826	12	0.2
Middle East & North Africa	17,578	56	1.8
South Asia	10,379	7	0.7
Sub-Saharan Africa	35,362	44	4.5

Source: World Bank, *World Development Indicators 2009* (http://data.worldbank.org/data-catalog/world-development-indicators).

Aid tying

About $15 billion of DAC aid to developing countries (or roughly one-fifth of total bilateral aid) is tied to the purchase of donors' goods. In this sense, capital inflows are not worth as much as they might be as the recipients have to pay higher prices for goods and services bought with aid money than the prices prevailing in the free market. Tying tends to be of two kinds: restrictions on where the recipients can spend the aid money, and restrictions on how the aid is used. Spending restrictions take the form of tying assistance to purchases in the donor country – so-called 'procurement tying'. This reduces the real worth of aid because it prevents recipients from shopping around to find the precise goods they want in the cheapest markets. Use restrictions normally mean that the aid must be used to cover the foreign exchange costs of a defined project. Restricting the use of aid to particular projects as well as to the donor country's goods amounts to double tying. Tying can be expensive.

The price of tied goods can be 20 per cent or more above the price of the same goods in the free market (see Jepma, 1991; Morrissey and White, 1993). Moreover there are other costs of tying apart from the inability of the recipient to buy in the cheapest market. If there is double tying, the project for which assistance is given might not fit perfectly into the recipient's development programme, the technology might be inappropriate, the donor may raise the import content unnecessarily, the suppliers may engage in exploitation, knowing that they have a captive consumer, and servicing over the life of the investment may be expensive.

The excess cost of imported goods from the tied source represents a form of export subsidy to suppliers in the donor country in the sense that if the aid was not tied and the suppliers had to remain competitive, the subsidy would have to be paid by the donor country itself. This subsidy to exporters in DAC countries through aid-tying amounts to about $2 billion a year, or 2 per cent of DAC assistance.

The one mitigating factor in all this is that the project for which assistance is given in tied form may have been undertaken anyway using the same source of supplies, in which case the assistance releases resources for another purpose. In other words, assistance to a certain extent is fungible because of resource switching. The fungibility of assistance also means that the balance-of-payments gain to the donor from tying may be quite small in practice because one form of purchase is substituted for another. This could be used as a bargaining weapon to reduce the extent of tying, the major reason for which seems to be balance-of-payments protection of the donors.

Remittances

Remittances from migrant workers are a growing source of resource transfer to many poor developing countries, supporting their balance of payments, and allowing the countries to grow faster than otherwise would be the case. In 2005, nearly 200 million migrant workers across the world remitted back to their homelands (developing countries) over $160 billion, more than 50 per cent higher than the volume of ODA. And these are just official remittances; informal flows may be as high as formal flows. The estimated workers' remittances to developing countries by region are shown in Figure 14.3.

East Asia and the Pacific, and Latin America and the Caribbean, receive the most, and Mexico is the largest individual country recipient with an inflow of $16 billion (Fajnzylbu et al., 2008). Each migrant on average remits $2,000–$5,000, or 20–30 per cent of their earnings.

Remittances support the balance of payments of recipient countries and can be used either for consumption purposes or used productively to set up small businesses, to build houses, to invest in health and education. There is evidence that the children of families that receive remittances stay longer in school, and infant mortality is lower. In general, remittances help to reduce poverty.

The long-run growth effects are more controversial. The IMF (2003), using data for 100 developing countries over the period 1975 to 2002, finds that remittances boost growth in countries with less developed financial systems by providing an alternative way to finance investment, but remittances don't seem to impact on growth in countries with already well-functioning credit markets. Catrinescu et al. (2008) find in their study across 162 countries over 34 years that the impact of remittances on growth depends on the quality of a country's institutions; specifically that 'low level of ethnic tension; good governance; prevalence of law and order and good socio-economic conditions are preconditions for a successful use of migrant remittances'. Their

Figure 14.3   Estimated workers' remittances to developing countries by region in 2005 (US$ billion)

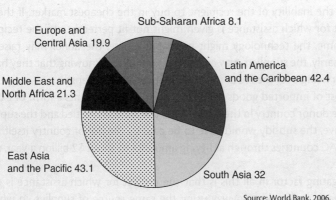

Source: World Bank, 2006.

central estimate is that a 1 per cent increase in the remittances/GDP ratio leads to a 0.04–0.05 percentage point increase in growth on average. Findings of a negative relation between remittances and growth are due to the failure to take into account the institutional structure of countries.

Multilateral assistance

The major sources of multilateral assistance to developing countries are the World Bank (the International Bank for Reconstruction and Development, IBRD) and its two affiliates, the International Development Association (IDA) and the International Finance Corporation (IFC), as well as the United Nations and various regional development banks.

The total disbursement in 2007 was $72 billion, of which $36 billion was on concessional terms. A detailed breakdown of the lending by the various multilateral agencies from 2004 to 2007 is given in Table 14.6.

Table 14.6 Concessional and non-concessional flows by multilateral organizations, US$ million, at current prices and exchange rates

	Gross disbursements			
	2004	2005	2006	2007
Concessional flows				
International Financial Institutions				
AfDF	1,057	988	6,041	1,313
AsDF	1,084	1,293	1,488	1,768
Caribbean Dev. Bank	60	45	47	59
EBRD	53	50	11	8
IDA	9,188	8,673	40,219	10,002
IDB	560	535	514	4,452
IMF	1,440	1,048	4,718	521
Nordic Dev. Fund	74	68	73	74
Total IFIs	**13,516**	**12,699**	**53,111**	**18,198**
United Nations				
IFAD	281	317	348	461
UNAIDS	—	123	181	193
UNDP	374	399	437	439
UNFPA	195	201	212	216
UNHCR	347	322	289	289
UNICEF	650	711	740	984
UNRWA	449	508	600	700
UNTA	434	580	371	462
WFP	253	555	473	233
Total UN	**2,982**	**3,715**	**3,651**	**3,977**

continued overleaf

Table 14.6 Concessional and non-concessional flows by multilateral organizations, US$ million, at current prices and exchange rates – *continued*

	Gross disbursements			
	2004	**2005**	**2006**	**2007**
EC	8,335	9,022	9,922	11,546
Global Environment Facility	138	181	190	193
Global Fund	584	1,006	1,252	1,627
Montreal Protocol Fund	59	83	81	94
Arab Funds	536	491	680	751
Total concessional	**26,150**	**27,197**	**68,887**	**36,386**
Non-concessional flows				
African Dev. Bank	979	851	825	1,398
Asian Dev. Bank	2,508	3,498	4,420	5,234
Caribbean Dev. Bank	60	35	84	102
EBRD	1,698	1,547	1,349	2,227
EC	2,391	2,618	3,286	5,515
IBRD	9,214	8,591	11,533	9,990
IFC	2,301	2,478	3,768	4,322
IDB	3,764	4,894	6,080	6,715
IFAD	31	27	39	40
Total non-concessional	**22,945**	**24,539**	**31,385**	**35,543**

Source: OECD, DAC Journal Development Cooperation 2009 Report (Paris: OECD).

The disbursements by multilateral agencies to developing countries consist not only of the contributions of developed countries but also of funds raised on the international capital market and repayments of previous loans. As can be seen from Table 14.6, the World Bank is essentially a commercial institution lending on non-concessional terms, and it raises large sums of money on the world's capital markets.

The IDA is the 'soft' loan affiliate of the World Bank and dispenses loans at very low rates of interest with long repayment periods. It is the most important provider of concessional multilateral assistance. Since 1960 it has lent over $150 billion to over 100 countries. Only countries with less than a certain level of per capita income are eligible to receive assistance but this currently includes at least 80 countries with over 3 billion people. The European Community (EC) has also become a major provider of concessional assistance through the European Development Fund (EDF). In 2007, it dispensed over £11 billion – a little more than the IDA.

The major providers of non-concessional assistance in recent years (apart from the World Bank) have been the two regional development banks – the IDB (the Inter-American Development Bank, lending to Latin America) and the ADB (Asian Development Bank).

World Bank activities

The activities of the World Bank since its creation in 1946 have broadly reflected changes in thinking about development policy and development priorities – changes that the World Bank itself has played a large part in promoting. In the early years, and throughout the 1960s, the major emphasis of the Bank was on financing infrastructure projects in the field of power generation and distribution, transportation, ports, telecommunications and irrigation. There was very little support for agriculture and rural development, or industry and tourism; and programme loans (as opposed to project assistance) were largely confined to countries outside those classified as less developed.

The Bank began to realize, however, that investment in infrastructure was not enough; that it had a role to play in lending to support directly productive activities. It also recognized the need for investment in education and managerial skills, and became increasingly aware that the development taking place in the countries it was supporting was not trickling down to the vast masses of the poor. In the late 1960s and throughout the 1970s, the Bank began to play a more active role in agriculture and in helping both the rural and urban poor. Robert McNamara, the President of the Bank from 1968 to 1981, inaugurated this radical change of emphasis in his annual address to the Bank in Nairobi in 1973. He defined absolute poverty as 'a condition of life so degraded by disease, illiteracy, malnutrition and squalor as to deny its victims basic human necessities', and he pledged that the Bank would make a concerted attack on rural poverty in order to raise the productivity of the poor and improve the incomes of small farmers. The objective was to provide most of the benefits of lending to those in the bottom 40 per cent of the income distribution. In 1975 the Bank announced that it would also attempt to deal with the problems of the urban poor by promoting productive employment opportunities on labour-intensive projects, and by developing basic services to serve the poor at low cost, for example water supplies, sanitation and family planning services.

Successive presidents of the World Bank have reiterated the Bank's commitment to helping the poor. It was mentioned in Chapter 2 that Lewis Preston announced in May 1992 that poverty reduction will be the 'benchmark by which our performance as a development institution will be measured', and this was reaffirmed by his successor, James Wolfensohn, who wrote in the *World Development Report 2000/2001*: 'poverty amidst plenty is the world's greatest challenge. We at the Bank have made it our mission to fight poverty with passion and professionalism, putting it at the centre of all the work that we do.' The current President of the Bank, Robert Zoellich, has said 'it is the vision of the World Bank Group to contribute to inclusive and sustainable globalization – to overcome poverty, enhance growth with care for the environment, and create individual opportunity and hope'.

The Bank itself sees four major challenges:

- To spur growth and overcome poverty, particularly in Africa, by provision of infrastructure, tackling corruption and raising agricultural productivity
- To help countries coming out of conflict, and failed states
- To foster regional and global public goods, for example disease control, dissemination of technology and combating global warming
- To advance development and opportunities in the Arab World, and to reduce social tensions particularly among young people who cannot find jobs.

The Bank is committed to the Millennium Development Goal of halving the proportion of people living in poverty by 2015 compared with the level in 1990.

The distribution of World Bank assistance for various purposes is shown in Table 14.7. Apart from programme assistance, the majority of lending goes to transport and communications, and education.

Table 14.7   Distribution of World Bank lending, 2007

Area	% of total
Social and administrative infrastructure	31.8
Education	7.7
Health and population	3.6
Water supply and sanitation	10.5
Government and civil society	5.3
Other social infrastructures	4.8
Economic infrastructure	31.8
Transport and communications	17.0
Energy	11.2
Other	3.7
Production	9.1
Agriculture	8.1
Industry	0.7
Trade and tourism	0.3
Programme assistance, including emergency relief	25.8

Source: OECD, 2009.

Structural adjustment lending

Another initiative was introduced by the World Bank in October 1979: **structural adjustment lending** to countries in order to support their balance of payments. To qualify for structural adjustment loans, a country has to adopt policies that are acceptable to the Bank and designed to secure external equilibrium in the longer run without sacrificing growth. The emphasis is on improving the supply-side capacity of the economy.

The World Bank defines structural adjustment loans as 'non-project lending to support programmes of policy and institutional change to modify the structure of the economy so that it can maintain both its growth rate and viability of its balance of payments in the medium term'. The loans are geared to seven main areas:

- Supply-side reforms, for example improving the efficiency with which markets operate
- Price reforms
- Changing the price of tradable goods relative to non-tradables
- Getting the 'correct' terms of trade between agricultural goods and industrial goods
- Reducing the size of the public sector
- Financial reforms
- Tax reforms.

Governments must commit themselves to policy reform in order to qualify for a loan.

Balance-of-payments support has been the traditional preserve of the International Monetary Fund (see Chapter 16), but there is a difference of emphasis between the IMF and the World Bank. Whereas the policies of the IMF focus primarily on balance-of-payments management, the World Bank is more concerned with promoting policies to increase efficiency and providing incentives to raise export earnings and reduce import payments. Clearly, however, the roles of the two

institutions now overlap and will do so increasingly as the IMF itself insists on supply-side policies as a condition for assistance, as well as on the traditional demand-side policies of devaluation
and monetary contraction.[7] The distinct roles of the IMF and the World Bank are outlined in
Case example 14.5.

Case example 14.5	The IMF and the World Bank – what's the difference?

The IMF and the World Bank were conceived at the Bretton Woods conference in July
1944 to strengthen international economic cooperation and to help create a more stable and prosperous global economy. Although these goals have remained central to
both institutions, their mandates and functions differ, and their work has evolved in
response to new economic developments and challenges.

The IMF promotes international monetary cooperation and provides member
countries with policy advice, temporary loans and technical assistance so they can
establish and maintain financial stability and external viability, and build and maintain strong economies. The IMF's loans are provided in support of policy programmes
designed to solve balance of payments problems – that is, situations in which a country
cannot obtain sufficient financing on affordable terms to meet international payment obligations. Some IMF loans are relatively short term and funded by the pool of
quota contributions provided by its members. Others are for longer periods, including
concessional loans provided to low-income members on the basis of subsidies financed
by past IMF gold sales and members' contributions. In its work in low-income countries,
the IMF's main focus is on how macroeconomic and financial policies can contribute
to laying a basis for sustainable growth and poverty reduction. Most IMF professional
staff are economists.

The World Bank promotes long-term economic development and poverty reduction by providing technical and financial support, including by helping countries
reform particular sectors or implement specific projects – for example, building schools
and health centres, providing water and electricity, fighting disease, and protecting the
environment. World Bank financial assistance is generally long term and is funded both
by member country contributions and through bond issuance. World Bank staff have
qualifications that embrace a broader range of disciplines than those of IMF staff. The
IMF and the World Bank collaborate in a variety of areas, particularly in supporting
governments in implementing poverty reduction strategies in low-income countries,
providing debt relief for the poorest countries, and assessing the financial sectors of
countries. The two institutions hold joint meetings twice a year.

Source: *IMF in Focus*, September 2006.

Since the purpose of structural adjustment lending and the **structural adjustment programmes
(SAPs)** is to improve the growth potential of countries, evaluations of these lending programmes
by independent investigators and the World Bank itself have focused on the key macro variables of GDP growth, savings, investment, exports and the balance of payments. In a World Bank
symposium on adjustment lending, Corbo, Fischer and Webb (1992) single out the following as
indicators of country performance: real GDP growth, the ratio of savings to GDP, the ratio of
investment to GDP and the export ratio. Their methodology is to compare countries that have

SAP programmes with other countries that have less intensive adjustment lending programmes and with countries that had received no adjustment loans. The performance of the three sets of countries is then compared relative to their performance in a base period before any loans were dispensed (that is, pre-1979). It appears that only the export ratio was superior in the SAP countries, and the investment ratio was much worse. This was also the conclusion of another World Bank study (1990), which found that structural adjustment lending had achieved a modest degree of success in helping countries to improve their balance of payments, but had failed to lead to an upsurge in investment or to enable countries to 'grow out of debt'. Another major study of 40 countries (Harrigan and Mosley, 1991) found that the effect on GDP growth had been negligible; export growth and the balance of payments had improved, but investment had declined. The main reason for the disappointing results appears to be the heavy requirements (or conditionality) placed on recipient governments, which have served to depress demand and confidence. There is a general consensus that the requirements should be less stringent and more selective, and more sensitive to each country's circumstances (see Mosley et al., 1991).

Structural adjustment programmes have particularly hit the poor in many countries. Cornia et al. (1987, 1988) called for 'adjustment with a human face', but the record is still not good. A major study by Noorbakhsh (1999), comparing the periods 1970–85 and 1986–92 in countries with SAPs and those without, found that virtually all the indicators of the standard of living – for example, infant mortality, life expectancy, adult literacy, primary school enrolment and per capita calorie supply – fared worse in countries with structural adjustment loans.

It would seem that much more care is required in the design of structural adjustment programmes if they are to achieve growth with equity (see Bourguignon and Morrisson, 1992), and if the World Bank is to avoid the charge of being an anti-developmental institution, like its sister institution, the IMF (see Chapter 16). In fact, one of the most damning indictments of SAPs comes from Joseph Stiglitz (2002), a former chief economist of the World Bank, in his powerful book *Globalization and its Discontents*, who attacks IMF policy-making at the same time. We leave the discussion until Chapter 16.

Joseph Stiglitz

Born 1943, Gary, Indiana, USA. He has taught at several universities including MIT, Yale, Stanford, Princeton and Oxford. Now Professor of Economics at Columbia University. Former Chairman of the Council of Economic Advisers under President Clinton (1995–97), and Chief Economist of the World Bank (1997–2000). The most prolific economist of his generation, with major contributions to virtually every branch of economics. Highly critical of the global trade and financial architecture in such books as *Globalization and its Discontents* (2002) and *Making Globalization Work* (2006). Awarded the Nobel Prize for Economics in 2001.

The imposition of harsh conditionality, which has not worked, and the relative failure of SAPs, has led to calls for reform of World Bank lending. Gilbert et al. (1999) suggest that *ex ante* conditionality should be abandoned altogether. Instead, the Bank should say to countries, 'If you get your own house in order you can borrow from us without conditions, and can continue to do so as long as sensible economic policies are pursued and good governance prevails.' This amounts to a form of *ex post* conditionality, but the countries would 'own' the policies rather than be dictated to by the Bank. For countries without good governance and the ability to reform, the Bank should stop lending. Instead, it should act as a knowledge bank for the dissemination of best practice techniques in economic management and policy reform. This would require more World Bank staff in the countries concerned, fulfilling a training role.

Poverty Reduction Strategy Papers

World Bank policy is already moving in the direction suggested above. In a new approach announced by the World Bank and IMF in 1999, national governments are offered a role in shaping and implementing anti-poverty strategies as part of its new focus on tackling poverty directly and making debt relief conditional on countries producing **Poverty Reduction Strategy Papers (PRSPs)**. According to the Bank, the focus of PRSPs should be on 'identifying in a participatory manner the poverty reduction outcomes a country wishes to achieve and the key public actions – policy changes, institutional reforms, programmes and projects – that are needed to achieve the desired outcomes'. The idea is that the attack on poverty should be based on partnership between governments and all sections of society concerned with poverty reduction, with governments leading the process of setting the goals and monitoring the process. Already a few poor countries have developed their own broad-based anti-poverty programmes. Uganda has instituted a successful 'Poverty Eradication Action Plan'; Mozambique has a countrywide poverty plan, and Guinea has what it calls a 'National Strategic Vision'.

Estimating the aid component of international assistance

Because of the different nature of the various capital flows, a common procedure is required for measuring the equivalence of the different flows. Clearly grants and loans are not equivalent since the latter have to be repaid and the former do not.

A standard procedure for making the flows equivalent is to estimate the **grant equivalent or aid component** of the different flows by taking the difference between the nominal flow and future repayments discounted by the free market rate of interest, which was our earlier measure of the benefit of assistance. A capital inflow that is a pure grant (with no repayment obligations) is 'worth' its face value. A capital inflow that has to be repaid with interest is not worth its face value. How much less it is worth than its face value depends on the rate at which the repayments are discounted:

- If the rate of interest at which the country would have had to borrow in the free market is greater than the actual rate of interest it has to pay, the worth or benefit will be *positive*.
- If the rate of interest at which it would have had to borrow is less than the actual rate, the worth or benefit will be *negative* because the recipient would have had to pay back more than it need to have done (this is unlikely to happen).

The grant equivalent or aid component of assistance is measured in this differential benefit sense. The rate of return on the assistance may of course be much greater than the benefit if the productivity of the assistance is higher than the free market rate of interest.

Other factors determine the grant equivalent of a loan as well as the effective interest rate subsidy. First, there is the **grace period** between the disbursement of the loan and the first repayment. The longer the grace period for a loan of a given maturity, the less the present value of the future discounted repayments. Second, there is the **maturity of the loan** to consider. This is important because the longer the maturity, the longer the concessionary interest rate is enjoyed and the less the present value of the future discounted repayments. Through the technique of discounting, any combination of repayment terms can be brought to a common measure.

All three factors referred to – the interest rate subsidy, the grace period and the maturity of the loan – can be incorporated into a simple formula for calculating the grant equivalent of a loan. The grant equivalent or aid component of a loan (as a percentage of its face value) is called the **grant element** and is equal to

$$\frac{G}{F} = \left[\frac{F - \left(\sum_{t=1}^{T} \frac{P_t}{(1+r)^t} \right)}{F} \right] 100$$

where F is the face value of the loan, P_t is the total repayment of principal and interest in year t, T is the maturity of the loan and r is the rate of discount. Since P_t includes interest charges it can be seen that the lower the interest rate relative to the rate of discount (r), and the more that repayments can be delayed through time, the greater the grant element of the loan.

The grant element can be worked out for different combinations of interest rates, discount rates, grace periods and length of maturity. At the two extremes, if the financial flow is a pure grant, then $P_t = 0$ and the grant element is 100 per cent. If the financial flow is at a rate of interest equal to the market rate of interest, and the grace period and maturity of the loan are the same as in the free market, the sum of the discounted future repayments will equal the face value of the flow and the grant element will be zero.

For combinations of conditions between the two extremes, Table 14.8 provides some illustrative calculations. For example the grant element of a 10-year loan at 5 per cent interest with a grace period of 5 years, with the recipient discounting repayments at 10 per cent, would be 26.1 per cent. It can be seen that the grant element is quite sensitive to small changes in the interest rate and the discount rate but relatively insensitive to variations in the grace period and the length of maturity. Long maturities and grace periods are mainly means of providing liquidity rather than aid.

The terms of official development assistance from the DAC members in 2007 are shown in Table 14.9. The average rate of interest charged was 1.3 per cent; the average grace period was 9 years and the average maturity of loans was 29 years. The discount rate normally applied is 10 per cent, giving a grant element of approximately 69 per cent. In 2007 the grant element of total official development assistance was 74 per cent. The grant element of major forms of multilateral assistance is approximately 50 per cent.

The moral of the foregoing discussion on the grant element of loans is that identifying the real worth of assistance depends on knowledge of the alternatives. Loans that look generous on the surface because they have a lower interest rate attached may be less valuable than the alternatives if they have shorter lives and grace periods. There is also the question of the freedom of the recipient country to use the loan as it wishes, which we considered earlier in connection with aid tying.

Table 14.8 Grant element in loans at different discount rates

Rate of interest and maturity period	5%			6%			7%			10%		
	No grace period G=0	5 years' grace G=5	10 years' grace G=10	G=0	G=5	G=10	G=0	G=5	G=10	G=0	G=5	G=10
2% interest												
10 years	12.9	21.2		16.7	24.0		20.0	28.9		29.5	41.8	
20 years	22.1	27.1	31.3	27.8	34.0	39.0	32.8	40.1	45.7	39.8	48.0	53.7
30 years	28.9	34.0	37.0	35.7	40.6	45.4	41.5	47.5	52.4	54.7	62.3	67.3
40 years	34.2	38.0	41.2	41.5	46.2	49.4	47.5	52.7	56.6	60.5	61.6	73.0
3% interest												
10 years	8.6	14.1		12.5	18.0		16.0	23.2		25.8	36.6	
20 years	14.7	18.1	20.9	20.8	25.5	29.2	21.3	32.2	36.6	31.3	38.1	43.1
30 years	19.3	22.6	24.6	26.8	30.5	34.9	33.2	38.1	42.0	47.8	54.5	58.9
40 years	22.8	25.4	27.4	31.1	34.6	37.0	38.0	42.2	45.4	52.9	58.2	63.8
4% interest												
10 years	4.3	7.1		8.1	12.0		12.0	17.4		22.1	31.4	
20 years	7.4	9.0	10.4	13.9	17.0	19.4	19.8	24.2	27.5	34.1	41.1	46.0
30 years	9.6	11.3	12.3	17.8	20.3	22.8	24.9	28.6	31.5	41.0	46.7	50.5
40 years	11.4	12.7	13.7	20.7	23.0	24.6	28.6	31.7	34.1	45.3	50.0	54.6

continued overleaf

Table 14.8 Grant element in loans at different discount rates – *continued*

Rate of interest and maturity period	5% No grace period G = 0	5% 5 years' grace G = 5	5% 10 years' grace G = 10	6% G = 0	6% G = 5	6% G = 10	7% G = 0	7% G = 5	7% G = 10	10% G = 0	10% G = 5	10% G = 10
5% interest												
10 years	0	0	0	4.2	6.0		8.0	11.5		18.4	26.1*	
20 years	0	0	0	6.9	8.5	9.7	13.1	16.2	18.3	28.4	34.2	38.4
30 years	0	0	0	8.9	10.2	11.3	16.6	19.0	20.9	34.2	38.9	42.0
40 years	0	0	0	10.4	11.5	12.1	19.0	21.0	22.6	37.7	41.6	45.5
6% interest												
10 years	a	a	a	0	0	0	4.0	5.8		14.7	20.9	
20 years	a	a	a	0	0	0	6.6	8.1	9.2	22.7	27.4	30.7
30 years	a	a	a	0	0	0	8.4	9.6	10.6	27.4	31.1	33.6
40 years	a	a	a	0	0	0	9.6	10.6	11.4	30.1	33.3	36.4
7% interest												
10 years	a	a	a	a	a	a	0	0	0	11.1	15.7	
20 years	a	a	a	a	a	a	0	0	0	17.1	21.6	23.0
30 years	a	a	a	a	a	a	0	0	0	20.5	23.3	25.2
40 years	a	a	a	a	a	a	0	0	0	22.6	25.0	27.3

Note: a indicates negative aid value.
* Illustrative calculation referred to in the text.

Source: Ohlin, 1965, appendix.

Table 14.9 DAC members' ODA terms, 2007

	Loan share of total ODA (%)	Terms of total bilateral loans			
		Average maturity (years)	Average grace period (years)	Average interest rate (%)	Grant element (%)
Australia	—	—	—	—	—
Austria	—	—	—	—	—
Belgium	1.2	29.3	10.3	0.5	79.3
Canada	—	—	—	—	—
Denmark	—	—	—	—	—
Finland	4.2	8.7	7.6	1.7	48.9
France	13.1	18.8	6.6	2.3	51.8
Germany	8.0	25.5	7.8	2.2	55.8
Greece	—	—	—	—	—
Ireland	—	—	—	—	—
Italy	5.4	28.7	15.8	0.1	83.3
Japan	48.0	33.3	9.5	0.9	74.9
Luxembourg	—	—	—	—	—
Netherlands	—	—	—	—	—
New Zealand	—	—	—	—	—
Norway	—	—	—	—	—
Portugal	5.2	29.9	16.2	2.2	67.4
Spain	7.1	21.3	10.3	1.5	62.6
Sweden	0.5	0.6	0.2	0.0	92.7
Switzerland	—	—	—	—	—
United Kingdom	—	—	—	—	—
United States	—	—	—	—	—
TOTAL DAC	**8.3**	**29.4**	**9.3**	**1.3**	**68.8**

Source: OECD, 2009.

The distribution of international assistance

The distribution of international assistance will affect the comparative rates of growth of developing countries if aid is a positive growth-inducing force. At present, the distribution of assistance in relation to the population of developing countries is extremely unequal. Whereas some countries receive less than $5 per head per annum, others receive over $100 per head. Assistance as a proportion of national income also differs widely between countries (see Table 14.5).

Most bilateral donors refrain from making explicit the criteria on which they distribute assistance. In practice, the criteria employed often tend to be as much non-economic as economic, reflecting historical relations between countries, as well as military and political objectives. It is often said that it pays a country to be a small island of ex-colonial status in a politically sensitive part of the world. High levels of per capita assistance seem to be closely associated with these characteristics. It is difficult to discern any significant relationship between the distribution of assistance and developmental considerations such as low per capita income, slow growth, balance-of-payments problems or even good governance. Dictators and corrupt governments also seem to be rewarded.

One recent comprehensive study by Burnside and Dollar (2000) takes a sample of 56 countries over the period 1970–93 and tries to explain the distribution of aid as a percentage of GDP in terms of such variables as the level of per capita income of the recipient countries (as a measure of need), population size, various strategic (political and military) interests, and whether there is good governance. There seems to be no tendency for either total aid or bilateral aid to be related to the level of poverty, or to favour countries pursuing 'good policies', although multilateral aid is more 'wisely' distributed (see also Alesina and Dollar, 2000).

Individual donor countries will continue to pursue their own objectives and set their own criteria, although there is evidence that more and more donor countries are focusing directly on the attack on poverty and favouring poor countries with sound policies in line with World Bank thinking.

The criteria governing the distribution of multilateral assistance through international agencies, to which rich countries contribute, are of wider concern. Since loans have to be repaid in foreign exchange, one obvious criterion for distribution would be a productivity criterion measured in terms of foreign exchange, but then all sorts of questions arise concerning the measurement of productivity, the time horizon to be taken and whether this would lead to a distribution of assistance in relation to need. Without an economically objective and value-free criterion, need is as good a criterion as any and meets the main direct objective of the World Bank which is the 'attack on poverty' (see Chapter 2). One possibility in this connection would be to distribute assistance on a per capita basis according to some target level of per capita income, which would operate rather like an **international negative income tax**. Certain graduated rates of per capita income assistance could be applied to the gap between the actual level of per capita income and the target level. A country that fell way below the target would receive a greater amount of assistance per head of the population than a country that was closer to the target or exceeded it. Given knowledge of the total amount of resources available, rates could be fixed to ensure a wide spread of assistance across countries while not making demands on resources in excess of supply. All this would be conditional, of course, on the new guiding principle of 'good governance'.

Schemes for increasing the flow of revenue

There are two ways of increasing the net flow of financial resources to developing countries: either nominal assistance can be left unchanged and repayment obligations reduced, or nominal assistance can be increased, leaving the terms of repayments unchanged. Reducing repayment obligations means cutting interest rates, lengthening repayment periods and generally increasing the grant element of international assistance. Other possibilities would be to allow countries to repay in local currency rather than foreign currency and to reduce the level of aid tying, as discussed earlier. We shall concentrate here, however, on measures that might be taken to increase the volume of nominal assistance.

One quick way to increase the flow would be for *all* the developed countries to meet their development assistance targets of 1 per cent of national income for total assistance and 0.7 per cent of national income for official development assistance. A significant increase in the resource flow by a deliberate budget decision in the developed countries is only likely to occur, however, if there is widespread public support for the programme. In recent years there have been signs of diminished public support for aid, based on the belief that a good deal of assistance is wasted and misused. If there is disillusion with assistance – or **aid 'fatigue'** as it has been called – an increased flow of assistance in the future is unlikely in the absence of some recognizable improvement in the efficiency with which current assistance is used. It is difficult to convince people in developed countries whose standard of living is not that high, to acquiesce to programmes that transfer resources from themselves if these resources are then perceived to be wasted or end up in the hands of people in recipient countries who are richer than themselves. The major reasons for the waste and misuse of resources in the past have been inefficiency and corruption on the part of recipient governments and interference from donor countries in the administration of programme assistance.

Given the political difficulties of increasing aid budgets, what the global economy needs are schemes and forms of international taxation that would raise revenue automatically, free of political debate and budgetary pressure in donor countries. The 1980 Brandt Report first raised the issue of the need for automatic revenue to support global development needs, and the United Nations Development Programme (UNDP) has called for more work on global taxes. There is no shortage of suggestions as to how more global finance might be raised, particularly through the taxation of global transactions. The schemes can be divided into three (overlapping) groups:

- Taxes and charges on various international transactions and external diseconomies that damage human welfare in various ways
- Taxes or charges on unexploited resources over which no state has sovereignty (for example, deep sea minerals)
- International income taxes earmarked for development purposes.

A useful and interesting list of the various suggestions made has been compiled by the Overseas Development Institute in London (ODI Briefing Paper: ODI, 1996).

Twenty recent suggestions for global revenue

- A tax on all or some international financial transactions (the 'Tobin Tax'); variants include a tax on bond turnover, or on derivatives
- A general surcharge on international trade
- Taxes on specified traded commodities such as fuel
- A tax on the international arms trade
- Surcharges on post and telecommunications revenues
- An international lottery
- A surcharge on domestic taxation (usually expressed as a progressive share of income tax)
- Dedication of some part of national or local taxes, for example on luxuries (or surcharges on them)
- Parking charges for satellites placed in geostationary orbit
- Royalties on minerals mined in international waters
- Charges for exploration in, or exploitation of, Antarctica
- Charges for fishing in international waters
- Charges for use of the electromagnetic spectrum
- A tax or charge on international flights (or alternatively, on flights in congested sectors); a variant is a tax on aviation kerosene
- A tax or charge on international shipping
- Pollution charges (for example, for dumping at sea)

- A tax on traded pollution permits
- A voluntary local tax paid to a central global agency
- A new issue of Special Drawing Rights (SDRs), distributed to the poorer developing countries (or used for peacekeeping or other global public goods)
- Sale of part of the IMF gold stock.

These are only suggestions and possibilities. There has been no sustained discussion of any of them at the intergovernmental level, and none of them has been taken up in a serious way by any of the major aid-giving countries.[8]

Apart from the idea of various taxes and charges, one of the most attractive ideas is to involve individuals in the spirit of international aid giving and to foster their interest in the challenge of development by allowing them to pay a proportion of their tax obligations in the form of donations to various development funds concerned with poverty eradication, the environment, education and so on. This already happens in a small way with tax relief on donations to charities and non-governmental organizations (NGOs) working in developing countries, but the principle needs to be expanded if the idea of voluntary taxation in support of development is to have a significant impact.

The proposal for new issues of SDRs and the sale of IMF gold for development purposes is discussed in Chapter 16.

Foreign direct investment and multinational corporations

Apart from ODA, another major source of development finance is private capital flows that allow countries to import more than they export and to invest more than they save. Private capital flows are of three main types: FDI and portfolio investment, which are non-debt-creating flows, and commercial bank lending, which creates debt. In this section we focus on foreign direct investment in developing countries. Bank lending, and the debt problems to which it gives rise, are considered in the final section.

There has been a vast increase in the amount of FDI going to developing countries in recent years, fuelled by three major factors: the rise of multinational corporations and the search for global profits, the liberalization of global capital markets and economic liberalization within developing countries.[9] But these flows are highly concentrated in a few countries. Total flows of FDI into developing countries are now running at over $300 billion a year, compared with under $20 billion in the early 1980s, but 80 per cent goes to only ten countries located in South America and South-East Asia (including China), as shown in Table 14.10. Overall, FDI accounts for about 10 per cent of total investment in developing countries and roughly 2 per cent of GDP. In discussing the costs and benefits of FDI, the relatively small contribution of FDI to economic activity in the majority of developing countries needs to be borne in mind.

Research into the determinants of FDI shows that cost structures, differential returns, market growth and the institutional characteristics of the host country are of prime importance. Companies wishing to invest overseas are looking for a favourable trade and investment regime, good infrastructure, property rights, political stability, macroeconomic stability and an educated and committed workforce. Much depends on the capacity of the country to absorb the investment, which in turn depends on its growth prospects and ability to export.

FDI brings many advantages to recipient countries, but there are also many potential dangers and disadvantages from a development point of view. We shall first list the advantages. FDI raises

Table 14.10   FDI net inflows to top ten developing countries

	Total 2007 ($ million)
China	138,413
Brazil	34,585
Mexico	24,686
Singapore	24,137
India	22,950
Turkey	22,195
Chile	14,457
Egypt, Arab Rep.	11,578
Thailand	9,498
Colombia	9,040

Source: World Bank, *World Development Indicators 2009*
(http://data.worldbank.org/data-catalog/world-development-indicators).

the investment ratio above the domestic savings ratio, which is good for growth if nothing adverse happens to the productivity of investment. The investment brings with it knowledge, technology and management skills, which can have positive externalities on the rest of the economy. Foreign investment can often be a catalyst for domestic investment in the same or related fields. It requires the training of labour, which is another positive externality. It is estimated that over 30 million workers are employed directly or indirectly by multinational corporations in developing countries. Finally, a great deal of FDI goes into the tradable goods sector of the recipient countries, which improves the export performance of these countries and earns them valuable foreign exchange.

Recent research shows a positive relation between FDI, domestic investment and the growth of GDP. Bosworth and Collins (1999) take a sample of 58 developing countries over the period 1978–95 and find that FDI brings about a one-to-one increase in domestic investment, while capital inflows as a whole increase domestic investment by only half the amount. Coe et al. (1997) examine the empirical evidence between international research and development (R&D) spillovers and economic growth for a sample of 77 countries. They find that the variation in total factor productivity growth between countries is related to the foreign stock of R&D capital, and that East Asian countries have benefited most from foreign R&D. It has been estimated by Borensztein et al. (1995) that a 1 percentage point increase in the ratio of FDI to GDP in developing countries over the period 1971–89 was associated with a 0.4–0.7 percentage point increase in the growth of per capita GDP, with the impact varying positively with educational attainment as an indicator of a country's ability to absorb technology. But there is also evidence of bidirectional causality (see de Mello, 1997). FDI affects growth positively, at least above a certain threshold, but growth also affects FDI positively; another example of a virtuous circle. Pacheco-López (2005) also finds evidence of bidirectional causality in a study of FDI in Mexico.

Now let us turn to some of the potential dangers of FDI. As we have indicated, investment by multinational corporations with headquarters in developed countries involves not only a transfer of funds (including the reinvestment of profits) but also a whole package of physical capital, techniques of production, managerial and marketing expertise, products, advertising and business practices for the maximization of global profits. There is no doubt that such investment augments real resources directly; the question is whether such investment contributes to the broader aspects of development relating to the pattern of development and the distribution of income.

The activities of the multinationals come under attack on a variety of grounds. First, because they tend to locate in urban areas they widen the income gap between the urban and rural sectors, thus perpetuating dualism. This criticism, however, cannot be levelled exclusively against multinationals because any new industrial activity establishing in existing urban centres will have the same effect.

A second and more serious criticism is the way in which they encourage and manipulate consumption. Not only do they tend to cater for the tastes of the already well-to-do, which itself acts as a divisive force, but also they tend to encourage forms of consumption among the broad mass of people, particularly in the urban areas, that are inappropriate to the stage of development and often nutritionally damaging. Prime examples are powdered baby milk and Coca-Cola. These tendencies are not only wasteful, but they encourage acquisitiveness, reduce domestic saving and can worsen balance-of-payments difficulties by encouraging expensive tastes.

A third criticism, which we have already dealt with in Chapter 7, is that they may introduce inappropriate technology and retard the development of an indigenous capital-goods industry. Related to this is the possibility that the multinationals may stifle indigenous entrepreneurship and destroy domestic firms, so that the net addition to capital accumulation is much less than the investment provided by the multinationals themselves.

Another aspect of the multinationals is that because of their large size and the power they wield, the developing countries in which they operate lose aspects of their national sovereignty and control over economic policy. The companies may easily avoid the effects of domestic monetary policy because of easy access to foreign capital markets and their own internal resources. They can avoid tax by shifting profits abroad. Countries may wish a multinational company to do one thing, but it may not readily comply because the action may conflict with the global profit objectives of the company as a whole. Firms may exploit resources more quickly than is desirable, and exploit consumers and workers through the exercise of monopoly and monopsony power.

There is also the question of the repatriation of profits. FDI has the potential disadvantage, even compared with loan finance, that there may be an outflow of profits that lasts much longer than the outflow of debt–service payments on a loan of equivalent amount. While a loan only creates repayment obligations for a definite number of years, FDI may involve an unending commitment. This has serious implications for the balance of payments and for domestic resource utilization if foreign exchange is a scarce resource. We can show with a numerical example that, in the long run, if profits are repatriated the impact of continuous foreign direct investment on the balance of payments must be negative unless the *gross* inflow of foreign investment grows substantially from year to year. This, of course, then increases the power and influence of the foreign interests within the country concerned.

Suppose that there is a steady gross inflow of 100 units of foreign capital per annum; that the productivity of capital is 20 per cent; and that one-half of the profits are reinvested and the other half are repatriated. Table 14.11 shows that on these assumptions the balance-of-payments effect turns negative after the eighth year. To keep the net inflow of resources positive requires a steadily rising *gross* flow of private foreign investment, with all the implications that this may have for the pattern of development in the future.

It is extremely difficult to measure the full impact and real costs of multinational investment using economic calculus alone, but this is what the developing countries must do. What would

Table 14.11 Balance-of-payments effects of private foreign investment

Year	Gross inflow	Foreign investment at beginning of period	Foreign investment at end of period	Outflow of profits	Net inflow
1	100	100.0	110.0	10.0	90.0
2	100	210.0	231.0	21.0	79.0
3	100	331.0	364.1	33.1	66.9
4	100	464.1	510.5	46.4	53.6
5	100	610.5	671.6	61.1	38.9
6	100	771.5	848.7	77.2	22.8
7	100	948.7	1,043.6	94.9	5.1
8	100	1,143.6	1,258.0	114.4	−14.4

be the real income gains and losses of controlling the free mobility of FDI? Other ways of taking advantage of FDI might be actively explored, including **joint ventures** and **turn-key projects**, whereby the foreign investor pays for and builds the project in collaboration with the host country, which is then run by host-country nationals. There is already evidence that this is the direction in which developing countries are moving. Developing countries must lay down very clearly the conditions under which they will accept multinational investments and monitor the companies' operations so that distorted development and exploitation are avoided.

International debt and debt–service problems

Developing countries not only borrow from donor countries and multilateral agencies but also commercially from the international banking system. All borrowing, whether official or private, involves repayment obligations, unless the loans are gifts or written off. First, the loan has to be repaid over a certain number of years (**amortization repayments**), and secondly, **interest payments** will be charged on the loan. Amortization and interest payments constitute **debt–service** payments. All loans that have to be repaid with interest are **debt-creating flows**.

There has been a massive increase in debt-creating flows to developing countries since the early 1970s, particularly after the oil price increase in 1973–74. The total volume of debt in 2007, the debt burden measured by various indicators – such as the debt–export ratio, the debt to national income ratio and the ratio of debt–service payments to export earnings (**the debt–service ratio**) – is shown in Table 14.12 for individual countries and groups of countries. The total debt of developing countries is now a colossal $3,500 billion (or roughly $700 per head of population) and debt–service payments absorb $250 billion of foreign exchange or 10 per cent of total export earnings. In the severely indebted low-income countries, the debt–service ratio is higher at approximately 25 per cent. The debt–service ratio is particularly crucial because this measures the amount of foreign exchange earnings that cannot be used to purchase imports and is therefore some measure of the extent to which a country might decide to default on its repayment obligations. The greater the debt–service payments, the more that development is thwarted. Some of the largest debtor countries of the world, such as Brazil and Turkey, have the highest debt–service ratios.

To judge whether a country's level of debt is sustainable, the World Bank takes a present value of debt–export ratio of 150 per cent. This is the main criterion for relief under the **highly**

Table 14.12 The debt burden of developing countries, 2007

Country/Group	Present value of external debt (current US$)	Present value of external debt (% of exports of goods and services)	Present value of external debt (% of GNI)	Total debt service (% of exports of goods and services)
Afghanistan	1,425	80	18	—
Albania	2,117	61	22	4
Algeria	5,087	9	4	—
Angola	12,077	35	32	10
Argentina	135,691	219	63	13
Armenia	2,672	117	38	7
Azerbaijan	2,592	16	14	1
Bangladesh	15,142	84	22	4
Belarus	9,132	40	25	4
Belize	968	119	89	69
Benin	569	58	12	—
Bhutan	742	178	77	—
Bolivia	2,599	52	24	12
Bosnia and Herzegovina	5,602	80	42	8
Botswana	316	5	3	1
Brazil	261,702	155	25	28
Bulgaria	32,516	144	100	15
Burkina Faso	815	108	14	—
Burundi	838	882	97	43
Cambodia	3,222	63	46	0
Cameroon	886	19	5	10
Cape Verde	400	61	34	4
Central African Republic	720	325	48	—
Chad	998	28	19	—
Chile	57,202	85	45	14
China	363,630	32	13	2
Colombia	45,908	133	28	22
Comoros	186	157	45	—
Congo, Dem. Rep.	8,731	326	111	—
Congo, Rep.	5,113	88	93	1
Costa Rica	7,817	62	35	4
Côte d'Ivoire	11,445	123	67	4
Croatia	46,784	197	109	33
Djibouti	326	91	38	—
Dominica	254	154	90	12
Dominican Republic	10,157	70	33	9
Ecuador	19,493	115	50	19
Egypt, Arab Rep.	27,297	60	25	4

Table 14.12   The debt burden of developing countries, 2007 – *continued*

Country/Group	Present value of external debt (current US$)	Present value of external debt (% of exports of goods and services)	Present value of external debt (% of GNI)	Total debt service (% of exports of goods and services)
El Salvador	9,049	104	50	11
Eritrea	524	660	41	–
Ethiopia	1,208	47	8	4
Fiji	387	22	12	–
Gabon	6,405	99	73	–
Gambia, The	167	63	34	12
Georgia	1,658	52	20	5
Ghana	2,849	55	22	3
Grenada	614	294	136	8
Guatemala	6,361	54	21	5
Guinea-Bissau	820	529	263	–
Guinea	2,327	210	64	13
Guyana	422	43	49	2
Haiti	1,017	57	20	5
Honduras	2,173	26	21	4
India	194,337	82	20	–
Indonesia	147,835	120	43	10
Iran, Islamic Rep.	18,200	22	8	–
Jamaica	12,401	183	131	17
Jordan	7,965	69	54	6
Kazakhstan	94,263	218	131	50
Kenya	5,694	85	26	6
Kyrgyz Republic	1,275	65	43	7
Lao PDR	2,784	267	84	19
Latvia	39,262	373	192	73
Lebanon	25,218	115	111	19
Lesotho	429	35	23	7
Liberia	4,632	976	978	112
Macedonia, FYR	3,568	100	54	–
Madagascar	1,240	70	21	–
Malawi	297	37	9	–
Malaysia	52,738	28	34	5
Maldives	468	65	54	5
Mali	926	51	16	–
Mauritania	2,103	150	85	–
Mauritius	4,220	94	65	5
Mexico	181,722	62	20	13

continued overleaf

Table 14.12   The debt burden of developing countries, 2007 – *continued*

Country/Group	Present value of external debt (current US$)	Present value of external debt (% of exports of goods and services)	Present value of external debt (% of GNI)	Total debt service (% of exports of goods and services)
Moldova	2,878	98	72	9
Mongolia	1,140	52	37	—
Montenegro	1,154	73	41	—
Morocco	19,134	66	29	11
Mozambique	940	34	15	1
Myanmar	5,930	119	46	—
Nepal	2,001	70	22	4
Nicaragua	1,583	52	31	12
Nigeria	8,028	12	6	1
Niger	456	70	12	—
Pakistan	32,807	123	25	9
Panama	11,299	81	70	5
Papua New Guinea	2,102	47	42	—
Paraguay	3,464	60	35	6
Peru	35,864	125	42	25
Philippines	66,459	97	51	14
Poland	184,939	121	53	26
Romania	85,293	175	67	19
Russian Federation	381,401	105	39	9
Rwanda	241	69	8	3
Samoa	1,030	701	228	27
São Tomé and Principe	23	110	19	39
Senegal	2,043	59	21	—
Serbia	26,637	198	86	—
Seychelles	1,348	162	193	11
Sierra Leone	143	37	10	3
Solomon Islands	141	68	42	—
Somalia	3,628	—	—	—
South Africa	48,323	58	19	6
Sri Lanka	11,638	105	42	7
St Kitts and Nevis	259	96	58	17
St Lucia	392	79	46	8
St V. and the Grenadines	237	95	52	11
Sudan	31,071	382	93	3
Swaziland	390	17	14	2
Tajikistan	856	33	30	2
Tanzania	2,186	62	15	3

Table 14.12   The debt burden of developing countries, 2007 – *continued*

Country/Group	Present value of external debt (current US$)	Present value of external debt (% of exports of goods and services)	Present value of external debt (% of GNI)	Total debt service (% of exports of goods and services)
Thailand	58,506	37	29	8
Togo	1,789	148	80	–
Tonga	64	49	27	3
Tunisia	19,672	106	65	11
Turkey	257,109	200	47	32
Turkmenistan	727	10	7	–
Uganda	925	37	9	2
Ukraine	73,134	131	66	17
Uruguay	13,181	196	69	19
Uzbekistan	3,605	51	20	–
Vanuatu	77	34	20	1
Venezuela, RB	48,087	66	26	7
Vietnam	20,558	45	35	2
Yemen, Rep.	4,135	46	23	3
Zambia	629	16	7	2
Zimbabwe	6,228	326	121	–
Low income	171,347	72	29	4
Middle income	3,255,268	65	25	11
Lower middle income	1,225,993	45	19	6
Upper middle income	2,029,274	92	31	16
East Asia & Pacific	726,600	35	17	4
Europe & Central Asia	1,259,175	108	41	19
Latin America & Caribbean	869,919	85	24	16
Middle East & North Africa	127,034	41	19	6
South Asia	258,558	87	21	13
Sub-Saharan Africa	185,328	57	25	5

Source: World Bank, *World Development Indicators 2009* (http://data.worldbank.org/data-catalog/world-development-indicators) and *Global Development Finance 2009* (http://siteresources.worldbank.org/INTGDF2009/Resources/gdf_combined_web.pdf).

indebted poor country initiative (HIPC) (see below, p. 490). By this criterion, it is mainly African countries that constitute the severely indebted low-income countries with debt–export ratios of 200 per cent or more in some cases.

Before turning to the origins of this massive volume of debt, however, let us consider in more detail the nature of the debt-servicing problem. At the beginning of the chapter it was shown that it is profitable for a country to borrow as long as the rate of return on the borrowing exceeds the rate of interest. In these circumstances, the rate of growth of income is higher than it would otherwise be. This gives no indication, however, of whether the borrowing can be serviced or repaid since the loan must be repaid with interest in *foreign* currency. Thus the profitability of borrowing and the capacity to service debt are conceptually distinct. The ability to service debt depends on whether additional foreign exchange can be earned or saved by the borrowing. This depends on the domestic economic policy pursued by the country concerned, and on the ability to export, which depends to a large extent on world economic conditions.

The debt-servicing difficulties that have arisen in recent years have had as much to do with deteriorating world economic conditions (which have depressed the foreign exchange earnings of developing countries) as with the miscalculation of rates of return on investment, the misuse of investment funds or the use of capital inflows to increase present consumption. There was a parallel in the 1980s with the Great Depression of the 1930s when the collapse of the world prices of key commodities and a general shrinkage of world trade caused major debt defaults (which subsequently dried up the flow of private capital to developing countries for the next 40 years). The trouble started in 1982 when the volume of world trade fell by 2.5 per cent, and the terms of trade for developing countries as a whole deteriorated by over 10 per cent. The decline in many commodities that developing countries export has continued (see Chapter 16, p. 544).

Not even the most prudent borrower or cautious lender can foresee such events, which may occur halfway through the life of a loan commitment that was entered into under quite different economic circumstances. Lenders and borrowers can allow for risk – that is, the statistical probability that the expected outcome will not materialize – but not uncertainty, and what happened in the world economy in the 1980s was a whole shift in the probability distribution of outcomes that could not be insured against. When such unforeseen events occur, beyond the borrower's control, that make it difficult for loans to be repaid and serviced without severe economic disruption, two questions arise: what is the optimal degree of debt rescheduling, and who should bear the cost?

It is naturally in the interests of private banks that loans be repaid on schedule, but it is not necessarily in the global interest if this leads to a contraction of imports by the borrowing country, which then reduces the exports of other (lending) countries, leading to a deflationary spiral in the whole world economy.

Optimal borrowing and sustainable debt

The benefits of borrowing to individual countries, and to the world economy at large, are clear. The question is: how far should borrowing go? Is it possible that after a certain point, even though a developing country still requires resources for development, the disadvantages of further borrowing outweigh the advantages? This raises the question of **optimal borrowing and the sustainability of debt**. Reasonable levels of debt are likely to enhance growth in countries short of capital if borrowing is used productively and earns foreign exchange so that debt can be serviced without deflating the economy to save imports. Debt becomes unsustainable when it accumulates at a faster rate than the borrower's capacity to service it. Expected debt–service costs then discourage domestic and foreign investment, because potential investors fear the economy will be deflated or that they will be 'taxed' to service the debts.

Working out what level of debt is sustainable requires an assessment of how outstanding stocks of debt are likely to evolve over time, together with forecasts about the future interest rates, exchange rates and foreign exchange earnings. The IMF has recently developed a standardized framework for assessing debt sustainability which takes account of a country's future growth rate, interest rate and exchange rate, and applies sensitivity analysis based on each country's history.

Several debt indicators and measures of sustainability can be used. One is the ratio of debt to GDP. There has been a progressive rise in the **ratio of debt to GDP** among developing countries, from less than 20 per cent in the early 1970s to nearly 30 per cent today, but it is not clear what economic significance should be attached to this ratio as a measure of the ability to service debt and therefore as a measure of debt sustainability. It is true that to service more and more debt, export earnings as a proportion of national income should rise, but this suggests more direct measures of sustainability: either the **debt–export ratio** or the **debt–service ratio** which measures the ratio of amortization and interest payments to export earnings.

To answer the question of the sustainability of debt, Kraay and Nehru (2006) at the World Bank take 132 low- and middle-income countries over the period 1970–2002, and use probit analysis to predict debt distress defined as the inability to service debt from the Paris Club of OECD countries and from the IMF. They find that the debt–export ratio is one important factor, but that the level of debt that can be sustained depends on the quality of country institutions and policies. For a country with an average institutional/policy score, a 100 per cent debt–export ratio would be sustainable with a 39 per cent probability of distress (the mean of the sample for low-income countries), while for countries with very good institutions and policies, a debt–export ratio of 400 per cent would be sustainable.

On the relationship between the debt–export ratio and the growth of per capita income, Patillo et al. (2002) find a non-linear relation. They take a sample of 93 developing countries over the period 1969 to 1998 and, controlling for other variables, find that the per capita income growth of countries is maximized when the debt–export ratio is approximately 80 per cent, and debt impacts negatively on growth when the debt–export ratio exceeds 160 per cent – as shown in Figure 14.4. The growth differential between countries with low indebtedness (with an export–debt ratio < 100%) and those with high indebtedness (with an export–debt ratio > 367 per cent) is, on average, more than 2 percentage points. It appears that the relationship between debt and growth is non-linear (an inverted 'U' shape) and that the level of sustainable debt is, on average, close to the ratio of 150 per cent of export earnings which is the ratio at which countries become eligible for debt relief under the highly indebted poor country (HIPC) initiative launched by the World Bank in 1996 (see later).

These results have been corroborated by Bhattacharya and Clements (2004), who take 55 low-income countries over the period 1970–99 and find a positive relation between the debt–export

Figure 14.4   Debt–export ratio and growth

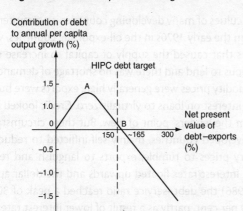

ratio and per capita income growth up to a ratio of nearly 200 per cent (and for the debt–GDP ratio up to 50 per cent). They calculate that if the net present value of debt–GDP ratio for the most heavily indebted countries was reduced from say 100 per cent to 50 per cent, this could raise the annual growth of per capita income by 2.8 percentage points. They also calculate that a 1 percentage point reduction in the debt–service ratio could raise the investment to GDP ratio of countries by about 0.2 percentage points.

The debt crisis of the 1980s[10]

The world debt crisis erupted in the summer of 1982, when Mexico became the first country to suspend the repayment of loans due to the private banking system and sovereign lenders. The crisis has smouldered ever since, with more and more countries, particularly in Africa, finding it difficult to service accumulated debts out of foreign exchange earnings. In 1987 Brazil became the first country to suspend interest payments to foreign creditors.

The 'crisis' aspects of debt can be looked at from different standpoints: from the point of view of the individual borrowing countries, or that of the lenders (private and sovereign governments), or that of the entire world economy. As far as borrowers are concerned, when the crisis first erupted there were essentially two types of 'problem' countries. First, there were a number of *poor commodity-dependent countries*, mainly in Africa but also elsewhere, where private banks were not heavily involved. It became a crisis for these countries when they had to cut back on essential imports in order to service their debts, but not a crisis for the banking system or the world economy, even if they had defaulted.

Second, there was a set of large *newly industrializing countries*, mainly in Latin America, which borrowed from the commercial banking system at floating rates of interest, but then their export markets became depressed. The sums of money involved were huge. In the early 1980s, 16 countries accounted for over half of the total debt of nearly $1,000 billion and for nearly 90 per cent of the debt owed to the private banking system. In this case the non-repayment of debt would have caused a crisis for the private banking system (which in retrospect had clearly overextended itself), and a crisis for individual countries if the threat of default had dried up the flow of new capital. There would also have been a crisis for the world economy if there had been a major default that led to a massive contraction of bank lending throughout the system; but this did not happen. Lending did contract sharply in the early 1980s, but then rose again as the difficulties were resolved by various forms of international cooperation and the rescheduling of debt.

The origin of the current debt difficulties of many developing countries is no mystery. Massive balance-of-payments surpluses arose in the early 1970s in the oil-exporting countries, with counterpart deficits elsewhere. The factors that caused the supply of capital to increase created its own demand. Private banks were anxious to lend and there was no shortage of demand. Demand was particularly strong because commodity prices were generally high, exports were buoyant and inflation had reduced the real rate of interest on loans to virtually zero. Credit looked cheap and borrowers looked like good risks from the lenders' point of view. But these circumstances suddenly changed. Depression in the developed countries, mainly self-inflicted to reduce the rate of inflation, caused world commodity prices to tumble, exports to languish and real interest rates to rise. On top of this, nominal interest rates floated upwards and the dollar appreciated. At the height of the debt crisis (in 1986) the debt–service ratio reached a peak of 30 per cent. This has since fallen back to under 20 per cent, partly as a result of lower interest rates and debt rescheduling and partly as a result of increased export earnings following the recovery of the world economy.

The world debt problem is a foreign exchange problem. It represents the inability of debtors to earn enough foreign exchange through exports to service foreign debts, and at the same time to sustain the growth of output (which requires foreign exchange to pay for imports). Either debt–service payments have to be suspended or growth curtailed, or a combination of both. Unfortunately for many debtor countries it is living standards that have suffered. Many indebted developing countries have stagnated under a total burden of debt that has now reached $3,500 billion, with resource transfers to service the debt close to $250 billion per annum.

All this is part of the **transfer problem** analysed by Keynes in 1919 in the wake of the controversy over the reparation payments imposed on Germany after the First World War by the Treaty of Versailles in 1919 (Keynes, 1919). Keynes mocked the folly and futility of the whole exercise on the grounds that it was likely to be self-defeating, and so it turned out to be. Today the attempt to extract large transfers, particularly in Africa, is also leading nowhere. Their economies continue to suffer, and the poor become progressively poorer.

There are two aspects of the transfer problem: the **budgetary problem** for governments of acquiring domestic resources for the repayment of debt, and the problem of turning the resources into foreign exchange – or the **'pure' transfer problem** as Keynes called it. The **transfer burden** is the export surplus that has to be generated to acquire the necessary foreign exchange, plus the possibility of a deterioration in the terms of trade if, in order to sell more exports, prices must be reduced. Even if prices do fall there is still no guarantee that export *earnings* will increase if the quantity sold does not rise in proportion to the fall in price. In these circumstances the transfer becomes impossible without a contraction of domestic output to compress imports. There is substantial evidence that the indebted countries collectively are caught in this trap, since for a large part of their trade they compete with each other; and competitive price reductions leave total earnings unchanged. It is the contraction of living standards that generates the export surplus by reducing the import bill. This is not good for the developing countries, or for the health of the world economy.

The debt crisis of the early 1980s has subsided, but the debt problem has not gone away. Lenders have been as irresponsible as borrowers. The developed countries must accept a large share of the responsibility for the world recession of the 1980s, as should the private banks for voluntarily overextending themselves. Shared blame requires shared solutions.

Debt relief

Debt in many ways is like a cancer – once it gets a grip on a country it is very hard to eradicate and may spread unless the rest of the economy can be reinforced to overcome it.

There are no easy solutions to the debt-servicing problem short of a massive programme of **debt forgiveness**, which leaves a manageable debt that the debtors can service. There has to be debt relief if there is to be any easing of the transfer burden. Without relief, further borrowing increases the size of the debt–service payments and simply makes matters worse, creating what might be called a **debt trap**. Since lenders, borrowers and the whole world community have benefited from the debt-creation process, there is a strong case for saying that the same three parties should share the burden of relief. It is not fair that the debtor countries (the borrowers) should bear the whole of the adjustment burden. Up to now the world community (including the creditor countries) has done very little to ease the plight of the debtors, although there are three reasons why it should:

- The world community received an external benefit when the debt was created by the on-lending process in the 1970s, preventing output contraction in countries with balance-of-payments deficits, and thereby avoiding a world slump
- Much of the debt problem arose in the first place through no fault of the developing countries themselves, but as a result of events in the world economy – rising oil prices, rising interest rates, world recession and falling commodity prices
- Relief could actually confer a global benefit by easing the deflationary forces associated with the huge debt overhang.

The highly indebted poor country initiative (HIPC)

The most recent and publicized global scheme for debt relief is the **highly indebted poor country initiative (HIPC)** launched by the World Bank in 1996, designed to help the world's poorest indebted countries. The World Bank has always been hostile to the write-off of debt, but the share of debt–service payments going to multilateral creditors has increased in recent years and now accounts for over 50 per cent of debt–service payments by some African countries. This new World Bank initiative therefore marked a radical departure in thinking and attitude. At the time the President of the Bank, James Wolfensohn, described the initiative as 'a breakthrough – it deals with debt in a comprehensive way to give countries the possibility of exiting from unsustainable debt. It is very good news for the poor of the world'. To qualify for debt relief, a country had to have a debt–export ratio in excess of 220 per cent or a debt to government revenue ratio of more than 280 per cent. Forty-one countries, mainly in Africa, originally met the criteria with a combined debt of nearly $200 billion. In the first three years of the initiative, however, progress was painfully slow. Only seven countries satisfied the stringent conditions laid down by the World Bank in order to receive help, and only $10 billion of relief was dispensed.

Dissatisfaction with the original initiative led the Group of Seven (G-7) rich industrialized countries to launch a new enhanced HIPC initiative in Cologne in 1999, which was later endorsed by the World Bank and IMF and called **the Enhanced HIPC Debt Relief Initiative** intended to be 'deeper, broader and faster' (to use the World Bank's words). To be eligible for debt relief under this new initiative, countries had to satisfy three conditions:

- A country must be very poor, defined as eligible for concessional assistance from the International Development Association (IDA) of the World Bank and eligible for support from the IMF's Poverty Reduction and Growth Facility (formerly the Enhanced Structural Adjustment Facility) (see Chapter 16)
- A country must have an unsustainable debt burden, defined as a present value of debt–export ratio of more than 150 per cent or a debt–government expenditure ratio in excess of 250 per cent
- A country must have good governance consistent with sustained growth and poverty reduction with its anti-poverty strategy outlined in a Poverty Reduction Strategy Paper (PRSP).

To see how the HIPC initiative works, see Case example 14.6.

By 2010, debt relief programmes had been approved for 35 countries, 29 in Africa, providing $51 billion of debt service relief over future years. Five other countries are potentially eligible.

So far, 24 countries are receiving full debt relief. Uganda was the first country to receive debt relief under the Enhanced HIPC Initiative in May 2000, based on several years of progress in implementing poverty relief programmes (see Case example 14.7).

In 2005, to help accelerate progress towards the Millennium Development Goals, the HIPC was supplemented by the **Multilateral Debt Relief Initiative (MDRI)**, which allows for 100 per cent relief on eligible debts to the World Bank, the IMF and the African Development Bank.

Progress since 1996 under all the initiatives has been slow. Many African countries continue to pay more in debt–service payments than they spend on education and health. The World Bank seems to be unduly harsh and bureaucratic in applying the criteria for relief and disbursement.

| Case example 14.6 | **The highly indebted poor country initiative** |

The highly indebted poor country (HIPC) initiative, launched in 1996 by the International Monetary Fund (IMF) and the World Bank and endorsed by 180 governments, has two main objectives. The first is to relieve certain low-income countries of their unsustainable debt to donors. The second is to promote reform and sound policies for growth, human development and poverty reduction.

The enhanced HIPC framework, approved in 1999, introduces broader eligibility criteria and increases debt relief. To qualify, countries must be eligible for highly concessional assistance such as from the World Bank's International Development Association and the IMF's Poverty Reduction and Growth Facility. In addition, countries must face unsustainable debt even after the full application of traditional debt relief mechanisms. They must also have a proven track record in implementing strategies focused on reducing poverty and building the foundations for sustainable economic growth.

Debt relief occurs in two steps:

- At the decision point the country gets debt *service* relief after having demonstrated adherence to an IMF programme and progress in developing a national poverty strategy.
- At the completion point the country gets debt *stock* relief upon approval by the World Bank and the IMF of its Poverty Reduction Strategy Paper. The country is entitled to at least 90 per cent debt relief from bilateral and multilateral creditors to make debt levels sustainable.

Of the 42 countries participating in the initiative, 34 are in sub-Saharan Africa. None had a per capita income above $1,500 (in purchasing power parity terms) in 2001, and all rank low on the Human Development Index. Between 1990 and 2001, HIPCs grew by an average of just 0.5 per cent a year.

HIPCs have been overindebted for at least 20 years: by poor country standards their ratios of debt–exports were already high in the 1980s. At the same time, HIPCs have received considerable official development assistance. Net transfers of such aid averaged about 10 per cent of their GNP in the 1990s, compared with about 2 per cent for all poor countries. To date 16 HIPCs have reached the decision point and eight have reached the completion point (Benin, Bolivia, Burkina Faso, Mali, Mauritania, Mozambique, Tanzania, Uganda).

Source: UNDP, 2003.

Case example 14.7

How debt relief fits into a poverty-reduction strategy: Uganda's Poverty Action Fund

Improving the overall allocation of resources, including those from debt relief, through more poverty-oriented and transparent budgets, is fundamental in the fight against poverty. There are many ways of achieving this end, and in Uganda a special fund to use the savings from debt relief is proving useful.

The government chose to create the Poverty Action Fund as a conduit for the savings from debt relief under the HIPC initiative (about $37 million a year; the Enhanced HIPC initiative is expected to double this amount). The fund has been earmarked for priorities of the poverty eradication action plan adopted in 1997 to address poverty and social conditions. The plan emphasizes maintaining macroeconomic stability while increasing the incomes and the quality of life of poor people by developing rural infrastructure, promoting small businesses and microenterprises, creating jobs and improving health services and education. The Poverty Action Fund focuses on schools, rural feeder roads, agricultural extension, and district-level water and sanitation. Specific outcome targets have been identified, such as the construction of 1,000 additional classrooms to support the primary education programme.

Two crucial features of the Poverty Action Fund are its integration into the overall budget and the Ugandan government's effort to create a transparent and accountable structure of management. Reports on financial allocation are released at quarterly meetings attended by donors and NGOs. The Inspector General's office monitors the use of funds at the district and national levels. This self-imposed conditionality reflects the government's strong commitment to tackling corruption. But it is also an attempt to address creditor concerns about the capacity of a debtor country to link debt relief to poverty reduction. Several measures have been proposed for improving monitoring, ranging from including district-level officials in the quarterly meetings to having local NGOs do community-based monitoring of the poverty fund's spending.

Apart from bold, imaginative, global schemes of debt relief, there have been a number of piecemeal, case-by-case initiatives in which the burden on the debtor developing countries has been ameliorated.

Debt rescheduling

The initial US response to the 1980s debt crisis was to attempt to increase **liquidity**, to give developing countries more breathing space to 'grow out' of their debt problems. This was the thinking behind the so-called **Baker Plan** of October 1988, which made provision for $20 billion of additional lending from the commercial banks and $9 billion of multilateral lending to the 15 or so most severely indebted countries, contingent on market-friendly, growth-oriented structural adjustment programmes being adopted. There was no acceptance of debt reduction by banks, and the sums of money were a drop in the ocean. In the event, most of the money was not lent because of the continued vulnerability of the banks and the deteriorating external situation.

The abortive Baker Plan was followed by the so-called **Brady Plan** of 1989, which did accept debt reduction and was more successful. The two main elements of the plan were (1) providing funds via the IMF and the World Bank for various forms of debt relief to those middle-income debtor countries that were willing to adopt policy reforms, and (2) encouraging countries to buy back debt from banks at a discount, thereby reducing future obligations. One possibility was for countries to swap old loans for new long-term (30-year) bonds at a discount of some 35 per cent and an interest rate only marginally above the market rate – the bonds were guaranteed by the IMF. Agreements of this type were reached with Mexico, the Philippines, Costa Rica, Venezuela and Uruguay. The deal with Mexico relieved it of $20 billion of debt–service payments.

Other multilateral initiatives focused on the poorest debtor countries. The governments of OECD countries representing the so-called Paris Club adopted two major initiatives in 1988 and 1990 – the **Toronto Terms** (September 1988) and the **Trinidad Terms** (September 1990). These initiatives were related to official debt (that is, debt owed to governments) and first of all made provision for the cancellation of a substantial proportion of the debt. For the remainder of the debt, substantial restructuring was offered.

Under the Toronto terms, eligible countries were those receiving concessional assistance from the soft-loan affiliate of the World Bank, the International Development Association, and a distinction was made between official development assistance (ODA) and non-ODA. For ODA, countries were given 25 years to pay with a grace period of 14 years, with no change in the interest rate. For non-ODA, three options were offered of different combinations of rescheduling, relief and interest rates.

Under the Trinidad terms, heavily indebted countries with a per capita income of less than $1,195 were eligible. For ODA, countries were given 20 years to pay with a grace period of 10 years. For non-ODA, countries were given 15 years to pay with a grace period of 8 years and a market rate of interest.

In 1996 and 1999 the HIPCs initiatives were launched, as discussed above, which concentrate more on debt relief than debt rescheduling.

Apart from these official initiatives, a great deal of other debt rescheduling has been arranged privately between individual countries and the creditor banks. These ease the short-term pressure but do not reduce future repayment obligations, unless the rescheduled debt is on softer terms.

Debt–service capping

Several schemes have been suggested to prevent debt–service payments becoming excessive. One is for **variable maturity loans** to be issued, so that debt–service payments would remain unaltered as interest rates floated upwards on private debt (rather like mortgage loans are variable in the housing market). Alternatively, maturities could be varied automatically in order to keep the debt–service ratio unchanged. This would also accommodate fluctuations in foreign exchange receipts from exports. These schemes are equivalent to capping interest payments above a certain level. In 1985 Peru unilaterally imposed a 10 per cent ceiling on debt–service payments as a proportion of export earnings.

Another possibility is to offer **zero coupon bonds**, which would delay interest payments until a loan had matured. This would reduce the present value of interest payments, but more importantly it would allow investment to be fully productive before there was any commitment of foreign exchange. It would not insure, however, against the bunching of repayment commitments when foreign exchange earnings might be low.

Debt buy-backs and debt swaps

Another solution to the debt–service problem that has gained favour in recent years is for countries to buy back their debt at a discount, or to exchange the debt in various ways that fully or partially relieve the burden of interest and principal repayments. Third World debt trades in a secondary market, where some countries' debts can be bought at a discount of more than 50 per cent. At one time Sudanese debt could be bought in the secondary market for $2 per $100. If Sudan had been able and willing to use its foreign exchange reserves to buy its own debt, it could have wiped out, say, $1 million of debt for as little as $20,000. The secondary market, however, is generally thin, and heavy buying is likely to raise the price considerably. Even so, the use of foreign exchange reserves to buy back debt at a discount of 20–30 per cent can make a useful contribution to debt relief. In 1995 Peru spent $600 million in the secondary market, buying $1.2 billion of its debt accumulated in the late 1970s and early 1980s at an estimated saving of $1 billion in interest payments.

Debt–equity swaps are a way of eliminating debt–service payments altogether. In a debt–equity swap the debt held by the creditor is converted into an equity stake in enterprises within the debtor country. The creditors have a claim on future profits, but the debtor countries are relieved of interest payments. Such swaps can be profitable to all parties involved. A classic example was the Nissan motor company's purchase of Mexican debt for investment in its Mexican subsidiary in 1982. Nissan bought $60 million of Mexican debt held by the Citicorp Bank at a price of $40 million – a discount of one-third. Nissan redeemed the debt certificates at the Mexican central bank for $54 million in Mexican pesos, which were then invested in its subsidiary. The bank unloaded its debt at the 'market' price, Nissan made a profit in dollars, and Mexico was relieved of interest payments in foreign currency. There have been several other debt–equity swaps since 1986, and they are increasingly linked to privatization programmes in the debtor countries, but the absolute magnitude of the sums involved is still relatively small in relation to the size of the debt burden.

Debt for nature and debt for development swaps work in the same way as debt–equity swaps, except the debt is bought by a governmental or charitable organization and the proceeds are used for environmental or developmental purposes within the debtor country. The World Wide Fund for Nature (WWF) has bought Third World debt at a considerable discount and exchanged it for local currency for use on environmental projects within the developing countries. In 1988 the UNICEF bought Sudanese debt from the Midland Bank, and this was redeemed by the Sudanese government to finance water sanitation programmes in central Sudan.

Debt for bonds is a swap scheme whereby debtor countries offer fixed-interest, long-term bonds in exchange for debt held by the banks. They can be advantageous if the debt can be exchanged at a discount at a more favourable rate of interest. In 1988 Mexico launched a scheme offering $10 billion of bonds to its creditor banks, hoping to sell at a discount of 50 per cent. The sale turned out to be disappointing, however. Only 100 out of the 500 banks bid for the bonds, and the debt was discounted by only 30 per cent. Even so, some saving was made by the Mexican government.

Exit bonds are a particular type of bond that give a bank a lower rate of interest than on the original debt, but end the bank's liability to provide new money. One way of encouraging this type of arrangement would be for the IMF to guarantee interest payments on the exit bonds, which would encourage the banks to swap debt for this type of bond.

Long-term solutions

On a longer-term basis, developed countries might set up machinery to guarantee loans from private sources (in addition to export credit guarantees) and establish a fund from which commercial interest rates could be subsidized. Such a scheme would mean that private lenders would not be deterred from lending through fear of default, developing countries would receive cheaper credit and the donor's contribution in the form of payments to private lenders would not burden the balance of payments (if this was regarded as an obstacle to a higher level of official assistance).

Secondly, ODA might be given as grants rather than loans. The grant element of official assistance is already high, and this further step would not only give extra marginal help but would also eliminate the need to haggle over debt renegotiations if the need for rescheduling arose.

Finally, there is an urgent need to devise schemes to stabilize the price or terms of trade for primary commodities. A large part of the 1980s debt crisis resulted from the collapse of primary product prices and large fluctuations in primary product prices continue to pose problems for poor countries today (see Chapter 15).

To stabilize the terms of trade, indexation may be appropriate for some commodities, for example oil. For other primary commodities, credit creation to finance merchants' stocks would assist. Special drawing rights (see Chapter 16) might play a useful role here for buying up surplus stocks of primary commodities that are storable, or for income compensation for commodities that are not. It seems incredible that so many years have passed since Keynes's wartime plan for an international agency for stabilizing commodity prices,[11] yet the world still lacks the requisite international agreement and institutional structures for greater stability and a fairer deal for developing countries that live by exporting primary commodities.

Summary

- Domestic saving and investment for growth and development can be supplemented by various types of foreign resource inflows such as loans from bilateral and multilateral sources, pure aid, foreign direct investment (FDI) and remittances.
- The amount of foreign resource inflows required to support a particular target rate of economic growth can be estimated using dual-gap analysis.
- Foreign borrowing will raise the growth of national income if the productivity of capital imports is greater than the rate of interest on loans, and will raise the growth of national output if new foreign borrowing exceeds the loss of domestic saving to pay interest on past borrowing.
- The total amount of foreign resource inflows into developing countries is approximately $600 billion, including $100 billion of aid, $300 billion of FDI and $150 billion of remittances.
- The motives for aid-giving are humanitarian and economic, but there are many critics of aid who argue that it weakens the domestic savings effort and fosters a 'dependency' culture.
- The macroeconomic impact of aid depends on whether it is spent directly on imports or whether the government sells the foreign exchange to the Central Bank and then uses the local currency to buy domestic goods.
- The World Bank is a major multilateral lender to developing countries, but its structural adjustment programmes have been criticized for being too deflationary and 'anti-developmental'.
- Foreign direct investment has benefits, particularly knowledge spillovers, but it also has costs in terms of continual profit outflows and the use of inappropriate techniques of production.
- Migrant remittances are now greater than official aid, and are non-debt-creating.
- Loans create debt which have to be repaid in foreign currency. The debt burden of developing countries is a foreign exchange problem. The volume of international debt is approximately $3,500 billion.
- Empirically, the optimal level of country debt seems to be about 80 per cent of the value of exports, and the impact of debt on growth becomes negative if debt grows to 160 per cent of exports.

- The debt crisis of the 1980s, which still lingers today, was largely caused by unfavourable external circumstances including a collapse of commodity prices and a doubling of interest rates.
- There is no solution to the debt burden of the highly indebted countries without debt forgiveness. Some poor countries qualify for the World Bank's HIPC, which allows debt to be written off if the proceeds are used for Poverty Reduction Programmes approved by the Bank.

Chapter 14	Discussion questions

1 What is the distinctive contribution of dual-gap analysis to the theory of development?

2 Under what circumstances will foreign borrowing (a) raise the rate of growth of income, and (b) raise the rate of growth of output?

3 What are the characteristics of the different types of financial flow to developing countries?

4 What factors determine the grant element of a financial flow?

5 How might the flow of resources to developing countries be augmented, and what criteria should govern their distribution between countries?

6 What is the purpose of World Bank structural adjustment lending, and how successful has it been?

7 What are the advantages and disadvantages of FDI to developing countries?

8 Discuss the view that foreign lending is merely a pernicious device for transferring resources from poor to rich countries.

9 Can countries borrow too much? What is the sustainable level of borrowing?

10 What is the nature of the debt problem in developing countries?

11 What imaginative schemes can you think of to relieve the debt-servicing burden of developing countries?

12 How successful have the World Bank's HIPC debt-relief programmes been?

Notes

1. If there were complete substitutability between imports and domestic resources, any surplus of domestic resources could be immediately converted into foreign exchange, and any surplus of foreign exchange could be immediately converted into domestic resources, and there could only be one gap, *ex ante*, as well as *ex post*.
2. See El-Shibley and Thirlwall (1981) for a case study of Sudan. Chenery's pioneer study of dual-gap analysis is in Chenery and Bruno (1962).
3. The argument was first put forward by Griffin (1970) and has since been the subject of continual scrutiny. See the survey by White (1992).
4. For calculations of the grant element, see p. 472.

5. By far the most comprehensive book on foreign aid is by Riddell (2007).
6. So called after what happened to the Dutch currency after the discovery of natural gas in the Netherlands in the 1970s.
7. See Taylor (1997) for a trenchant summary and critique of IMF and World Bank policies in poor countries.
8. A $100 billion increase in SDRs was announced in 2009 in the wake of the international financial crisis that erupted across the world in 2008 (see Chapter 16).
9. For a comprehensive survey of the causes and effects of FDI, see de Mello (1997).
10. Useful books on the 1980s debt crisis include Cline (1984, 1995); Claudon (1986); Lomax (1986); Lever and Huhne (1985); Griffith-Jones and Sunkel (1986).
11. See Thirlwall (1987). See Chapter 15 for partial schemes already in existence.

Websites on aid, remittances, debt and FDI

Debt

World Bank, Global Development Finance http://publications.worldbank.org
OECD, Development Assistance Committee www.oecd.org/dac/stats
HIPC Initiative www.worldbank.org/hipc

Non-governmental organizations

NGO Global Network www.ngo.org
Links via the UN www.un.org/MoreInfo/ngolink/ngodir.htm
Jubilee Debt Campaign www.jubileedebtcampaign.org.uk

Foreign direct investment

UNCTAD www.unctad.org

International migration and remittances

econ.worldbank.org/programs/migration
www.gcim.org
www.iadb.org/mif/remittances
www/iom.int

VI

INTERNATIONAL TRADE, THE BALANCE OF PAYMENTS AND DEVELOPMENT

VI

15

TRADE THEORY, TRADE POLICY AND ECONOMIC DEVELOPMENT

- Introduction
- Trade and growth
- The gains from trade
- The static gains from trade
- The dynamic gains from trade
- Trade as a vent for surplus
- Theory of customs unions and free trade areas
- Free trade enthusiasm in the modern era
- Measurement and process of trade liberalization
- Models of export-led growth
- What you export matters
- Trade liberalization and export growth
- Trade liberalization, import growth and the balance of payments
- Trade liberalization and economic performance
- Trade liberalization, poverty and domestic inequality
- Trade liberalization and international inequality

- Disadvantages of free trade for development
- Theory of protection: tariffs versus subsidies
- Effective protection
- Import substitution versus export promotion
- The Prebisch doctrine
- Technical progress and the terms of trade
- The income elasticity of demand for products and the balance of payments
- Recent trends in the terms of trade
- Fair trade not free trade
- Trade strategy for development
- International commodity agreements
- Trade versus aid
- Summary
- Discussion questions
- Notes
- Websites on trade

Introduction

In Chapter 14 we discussed the important role of foreign borrowing and foreign resources inflows in the development process. Using dual-gap analysis, it was shown that foreign borrowing can be used to bridge either a domestic investment–savings gap or a foreign exchange gap, whichever is the larger. We saw that the policy issue is deciding how far borrowing should go without leading to unmanageable international debt.

The empirical evidence indicates a serious conflict in many poor countries between maintaining an adequate growth rate and a sustainable balance of payments on current account. The ultimate solution must lie in improving the balance of payments through trade and faster export growth.

In this chapter, we do a number of things. First we discuss the general relation between trade and economic growth, and establish the precise nature of the benefits from trade, including the formation of customs unions and regional trade agreements (RTAs). The static and dynamic gains from trade are distinguished, and the role of trade as a vent for surplus commodities.

We go on to outline the enthusiasm for trade liberalization in the modern era; the way the process of trade liberalization is measured, and the empirical evidence of the impact of trade liberalization on export growth, import growth, the balance of payments and overall economic performance of poor developing economies. There are separate sections on trade liberalization, poverty and domestic inequality, and on trade liberalization and international inequality.

The disadvantages of free trade for development are then explored. We examine critically the underlying assumptions of the comparative advantage doctrine and free trade theory, and ask the question whether poor countries might fare better in a more protected environment. This leads on to the theory of protection; the debate over import substitution versus export promotion, and the use of tariffs and subsidies as protective devices.

We then turn to the issues originally raised by the famous Latin American economist Raúl Prebisch, concerning the terms of trade between primary commodities and manufactured goods and the balance of payments consequences of free trade for developing economies. The empirical evidence of trends and cycles in the terms of trade of primary commodities is documented, and the case for international commodity agreements to stabilize the price of primary commodities.

We conclude that what developing countries need is 'fair trade' not free trade, and that the slogan 'trade not aid' may be misleading from an economic point of view.

Trade and growth

The growth rates of individual developing countries correlate better with their export performance than with almost any other single economic indicator, and there is a strong correlation across countries between the growth of exports and the growth of GDP as shown in Figure 15.1, taking 133 countries over the period 1995–2006. For much of the period since 1950, the export performance of developing countries lagged behind that of the developed industrial countries, with their share of world trade falling, but in recent years there has been a reversal of fortunes for some developing countries as trade barriers have come down, and with a switch in the composition of exports towards manufactured goods.

Table 15.1 shows the developing countries' share of world manufacturing exports in 1981 and 2006, distinguishing between resource-based exports (RB); low-technology exports (LT);

Figure 15.1   The relation between export growth and GDP growth across 133 countries, 1995–2006

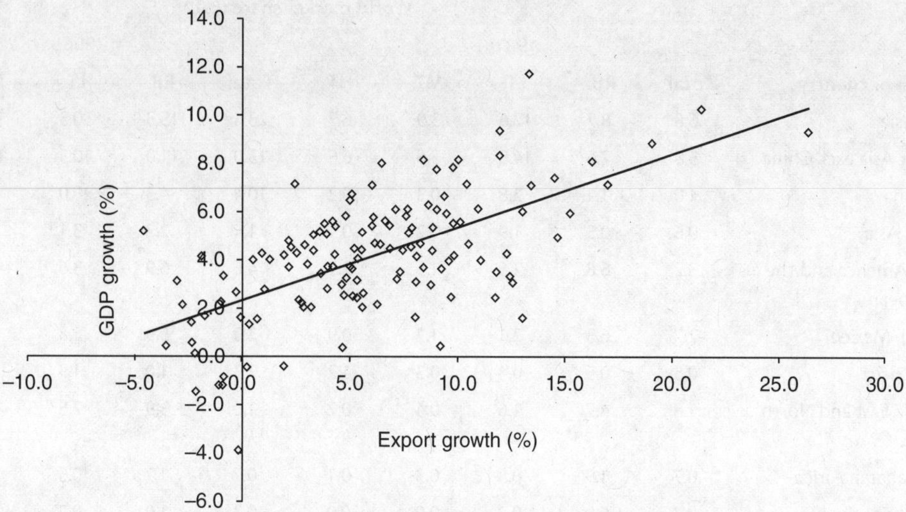

Source: United Nations Statistical Division (New York: United Nations).

medium-technology exports (MT), and high-technology exports (HT). The developing countries as a whole have more than doubled their share of world manufacturing exports from 1981 to 2006, but the share of 32.1 per cent is still relatively low. Without China, the share is only 22.1 per cent. East Asia has been most successful in expanding its share, while Africa's share is still less than 1 per cent. Despite the fast growth of manufactured exports from some developing countries, it must be remembered that they are starting from a very low base, and the export trade of many poor countries, particularly in Africa, is still dominated by primary commodities. Twenty-two countries rely on just one crop or product for over 50 per cent of export earnings (e.g. Zambia (copper), Malawi (tobacco), Uganda, Burundi, Ethiopia (coffee), plus many countries dependent on oil), and over 50 countries rely on one primary commodity for at least 20 per cent of exports. This is a very heavy dependence, particularly if prices are volatile or decline (see later below, p. 543).

Taking the developing countries together, however, it is not true that the world as a whole is neatly polarized into two camps: the developing countries, producing and exporting *solely* primary products in exchange for manufactures from developed countries, and the developed world, producing and exporting *solely* manufactures in exchange for primary commodities from developing countries. In practice a good deal of trade in both manufactures and primary products goes on among the developed and developing countries alike, with the developed countries exporting substantial quantities of primary commodities (especially temperate-zone foodstuffs) and the developing countries exporting some manufactured goods. Developed countries, in fact, account for about 50 per cent of the world's supply of primary products, and developing countries just over 30 per cent of world trade in manufactures. In short, the distinction between developing and developed countries is not wholly synonymous with the distinction between primary producers and producers of manufactured goods. This needs to be borne in mind later when we discuss the terms of trade – the ratio of export to import prices. There is a distinction to be made between the terms of trade for developing and developed countries

Table 15.1   World market shares of manufactured exports of developing regions, 1981 and 2006

Region or country	World market share (%)									
	1981					2006				
	Total	RB	LT	MT	HT	Total	RB	LT	MT	HT
East Asia	6.8	8.7	17.6	3.9	6.7	23.4	15.3	30.3	16.9	36.3
East Asia excl. China	5.8	7.6	14.8	3.6	6.5	13.0	11.0	10.3	10.0	22.0
China	1.0	1.1	2.8	0.3	0.2	10.4	4.3	20.0	6.9	14.3
South Asia	0.6	0.5	1.9	0.2	0.1	1.4	2.7	3.1	0.6	0.3
Latin America and the Caribbean	3.2	6.8	2.5	1.5	2.1	4.6	6.9	3.6	5.0	2.6
excl. Mexico	2.7	6.3	2.1	1.2	0.9	2.3	5.9	1.8	1.7	0.7
Mexico	0.5	0.5	0.4	0.3	1.2	2.3	1.0	1.9	3.3	1.9
Middle East and North Africa	1.8	4.7	1.6	0.4	0.2	1.6	3.9	2.5	0.8	0.1
Sub-Saharan Africa	0.7	1.9	0.5	0.3	0.1	0.7	1.7	0.5	0.5	0.2
excl. South Africa	0.3	0.9	0.2	0.0	0.0	0.3	1.0	0.2	0.0	0.1
South Africa	0.4	0.9	0.4	0.2	0.1	0.4	0.7	0.3	0.4	0.1
All developing economies	13.1	22.5	24.2	6.2	9.2	32.1	31.6	40.5	24.0	40.0

Note: RB (resource-based exports), LT (low-tech exports), MT (medium-tech exports, HT high-tech exports).

Source: UNIDO, 2008.

on the one hand and the terms of trade for primary products and manufactured goods on the other.

Historically, trade has acted as a powerful engine of growth, not only by contributing to a more efficient allocation of resources within countries, but also because it transmitted growth from one part of the world to another. In the nineteenth century, the demand in Europe, and in Britain in particular, for food and raw materials brought prosperity to such countries as Canada, Argentina, South Africa, Australia and New Zealand. As the demand for their commodities increased, investment in these countries also increased. Trade was mutually profitable. As Alfred Marshall wrote in the nineteenth century: **'the causes which determine the economic progress of nations belong to the study of international trade'** (Marshall, 1890).

Not all countries benefited equally, however, and today the situation is somewhat different. Most world trade takes place in industrial commodities, in which many poor developing countries find it difficult to compete, and the demand for developing countries' traditional exports grows slowly relative to the demand for industrial goods. Except for spasmodic commodity booms, trade does not seem to work to the equal advantage of both sets of countries.

Three distinct factors have slowed the growth of the traditional exports of the developing countries.

- The pattern of demand has shifted to types of manufactured goods with a relatively low import content of primary commodities.
- Technological change has led to the development of synthetic substitutes for raw materials.

- Developed countries have pursued protectionist policies that have retarded the growth of their imports of both primary commodities and low value-added manufactured goods from developing countries, particularly textiles.

In view of these trading developments and the emergence of a foreign exchange gap as a constraint on growth in developing countries, there has been a rethinking by some economists in recent years about the basis on which the gains from trade should be evaluated. The slow growth and balance-of-payments difficulties of developing countries has led to a shift of emphasis from viewing the effects of trade solely from the traditional classical standpoint of efficient resource allocation to viewing the impact of trade on growth and foreign exchange earnings. It is balance-of-payments difficulties, necessitating foreign borrowing if growth is to be sustained, that have led to the cry in recent years of '**trade, not aid**'. The relevance of this slogan is examined later in this chapter. The problem facing developing countries is not so much *whether* to trade but *in what commodities* to trade, and to ensure that the terms on which they trade with the developed countries are favourable. There is no dispute that there are both static and dynamic gains from trade. The issue is whether the overall gains would be greater, and the distribution of gains between countries fairer, if the pattern of trade were different from its present structure, and if the developed countries modified their trading policies towards the developing world.

So what should developing countries do? The answer would appear to be structural change in favour of the production and export of manufactured goods which have more favourable demand characteristics in world markets; in particular, a higher income elasticity of demand. These dynamic considerations and the need for diversification out of primary products do not diminish the case for international specialization. What is involved is a recognition of the distinction between **natural comparative advantage** on the one hand (the classical, static basis for trade) and **acquired comparative advantage** on the other, and whether developing countries can acquire new comparative advantage on the basis of free trade. If not, what form of protection would be welfare-enhancing? Before considering these controversial, and highly topical, issues, let us first establish more firmly the static and dynamic gains from trade that are stressed by traditional theory.

The gains from trade

The benefits from trade in traditional trade theory are measured by the increase in the value of output and real income from domestic resources that international specialization and trade permit. This is quite distinct from the balance of payments effects of trade. The resource gains from trade can be divided into static and dynamic gains. **Static gains** are those which accrue from international specialization according to the doctrine of comparative advantage. **Dynamic gains** are those which result from the impact of trade on production possibilities at large. Economies of scale, foreign investment and the transmission of technical knowledge are examples of dynamic gains. In addition, trade can provide a **vent for surplus** commodities, which brings otherwise unemployed resources into employment. It also enables countries to purchase goods from abroad, which can be important for two reasons: first, if there are no domestic substitutes, the ability to import can relieve domestic bottlenecks in production, and, secondly, imports may simply be more productive than domestic resources.

The static gains from trade

Ricardo

The static gains from trade are based on the **law of comparative advantage**, first outlined by the English classical economist David Ricardo (1772–1823) in his *Principles of Political Economy and Taxation* (1817). What Ricardo showed in his remarkable theorem is that even though a country may have an absolute productivity (cost) advantage in the production of *every* good, it will still pay a country to specialize in those commodities in which it has a *comparative* advantage – that is, in those commodities in which *relative* labour productivity is the highest or for which the *opportunity cost* of production is lowest. Ricardo is not explicit about what determines relative differences in productivity and costs, but clearly resource endowments will be the major determinants: natural resources, labour and human capital and the level of technology.

To illustrate the gains from trade, according to the law of comparative advantage, Ricardo used the example of England and Portugal, both with the capacity to produce cloth and wine, but with England having a comparative advantage in cloth and Portugal in wine. Suppose, for example, with its given resources, England can produce 10,000 yards of cloth or 2,000 bottles of wine. The opportunity cost ratio of cloth to wine is 10:2. Portugal, on the other hand, with its resources can produce 10,000 yards of cloth and 8,000 bottles of wine. The opportunity cost ratio is 10:8. England has to sacrifice 5 yards of cloth to produce one bottle of wine, whereas Portugal only has to sacrifice 1.25 yards of cloth. Clearly, the opportunity cost of producing wine in Portugal is less than in England. However, England has to sacrifice one-fifth of a bottle of wine to produce 1 yard of cloth, whereas Portugal has to sacrifice four-fifths of a bottle of wine. The opportunity cost of producing cloth in England is lower.

What we can now show is that if there is an international rate of exchange between England and Portugal which is between the two domestic rates of exchange of 10:2 and 10:8, both countries can benefit by specializing in what they are best at producing in an opportunity cost sense, and exchanging goods at a more favourable rate of transformation internationally than domestically. Consider Figure 15.2.

The solid linear lines show the production possibility curves (or the marginal rate of transformation between the two goods) in the two countries: 10,000 yards of cloth and 2,000 bottles of wine in England, and 10,000 yards of cloth and 8,000 bottles of wine in Portugal. Before trade, each country produces combinations of cloth and wine that give the maximum utility represented by indifference curve I. The two countries produce at a and b, respectively, where the slope of the production possibility curve is tangential to the slope of the indifference curve. Now assume that with the opening of trade, there is an international price ratio of 10:5, shown by the broken line. England, if it specializes in cloth, can now exchange cloth for wine more favourably, and likewise Portugal can exchange wine for cloth more favourably. For example, in trading 5,000 yards of cloth England can now consume 2,500 bottles of wine instead of 1,000, while Portugal, trading 4,000 bottles of wine, can now consume 8,000 yards of cloth instead of 5,000. Both countries move to higher levels of welfare at point c on indifference curve II. As a result of the international division of labour, world production increases (in this example, wine production increases from 5,000 to 8,000 bottles and cloth production stays the same) and world welfare increases.

Ricardo's theorem is a very powerful one, and has been extremely influential because it lies at the heart of the free trade doctrine that countries will always benefit if they liberalize trade. There

Figure 15.2   Gains from trade

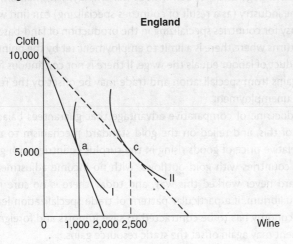

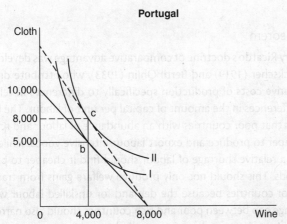

are four important caveats, however, that need to be remembered in discussing the merits of free trade:

- There is nothing in the comparative cost doctrine that ensures equality in the distribution of the gains from trade. This depends on where the international price ratio lies between the two opportunity cost ratios. One country may lose absolutely if a decline in its terms of trade (the ratio of its export price to its import price) offsets the efficiency resource gain from specialization. This is the concept of **immiserising growth** made famous by Bhagwati (1958).
- The gains from trade are 'once for all'. They do not recur. Once the process of resource reallocation through trade has taken place, there are no further gains. The law of comparative advantage, therefore, has nothing to say about the growth effects of trade. The law is static. The growth effects of trade will depend on the types of goods countries specialize in – whether they are subject to increasing returns or diminishing returns, and whether they are income elastic or inelastic in demand.

- The law of comparative advantage assumes continuous full employment, namely, that those thrown out of work in one industry (as a result of countries specializing) can find work in others. This may not be so easy for countries specializing in the production of land-based activities subject to diminishing returns where there is a limit to employment set by the point where the diminishing marginal product of labour equals the wage. If there is not continuous full employment, the real resource gains from specialization and trade may be offset by the real resource (and welfare) losses from unemployment.
- There is nothing in the doctrine of comparative advantage that guarantees balanced trade. Ricardo was fully aware of this, and relied on the gold standard mechanism to produce an equilibrium – with the relative price of goods rising in the surplus countries with gold inflows and falling in the deficit countries with gold outflows, with no income adjustment. But the international gold standard never worked this way, and today there is no sure mechanism that guarantees trade equilibrium. If a particular pattern of trade specialization leads to payments deficits, and the economy has to be contracted to save imports and foreign exchange, the resulting unemployment may again offset the static resource gains.

The Heckscher–Ohlin theorem

In the early twentieth century Ricardo's doctrine of comparative advantage was developed by two Swedish economists, Eli Heckscher (1919) and Bertil Ohlin (1933), who attribute differences in labour productivity and relative costs of production specifically to differences in relative factor endowments – that is, to differences in the amount of capital per unit of labour. The Heckscher–Ohlin (H–O) theorem states that poor countries with an abundance of labour and scarce capital should find it relatively cheaper to produce and export labour-intensive goods, while rich countries with more capital and a relative shortage of labour should find it cheaper to produce and export capital-intensive goods. This should not only produce welfare gains from trade, but also greater wage equality in poor countries because the demand for unskilled labour will rise relative to skilled labour. The wage gap between poor and rich countries should also narrow. As with Ricardo's theorem, however, there are a number of caveats to be made:

- Abundant labour in poor countries is not necessarily cheap labour in an economic sense, if the productivity of labour is correspondingly lower. It is the efficiency wage (the money wage divided by labour productivity) that determines the combination of factors used in production. Labour-abundant economies may still therefore export relatively capital-intensive goods, and capital-abundant economies may export relatively labour-intensive goods (the so-called **Leontief Paradox**, named after Wassily Leontief, 1953, who first discovered that contrary to the H–O theorem, US exports were relatively labour-intensive compared with import substitutes).
- The theorem takes only two groups of countries – poor developing countries and rich developed countries – but poor countries not only trade with rich countries but also with each other. As the demand for labour-intensive exports from poor countries rises in rich countries, wages in poor countries may rise, but may also fall as a result of competitive imports from other poor countries. Mexico, for example, benefits from exporting labour-intensive products to the USA, but suffers from labour-intensive imports from China. What happens to the wages of unskilled labour in poor countries is the outcome of a balance of forces.
- The theorem ignores the flow of capital from rich to poor countries as trade takes place. The inflow of foreign direct investment into poor countries may increase the demand for skilled

labour relative to unskilled labour, and increase the degree of wage inequality, contrary to the predictions of the H–O theorem.

The dynamic gains from trade

The major dynamic benefit of trade is that export markets widen the total market for a country's producers, thereby allowing greater specialization, or division of labour. Specialization, in turn, stimulates capital accumulation and 'learning by doing'. Historically, Adam Smith recognized this benefit of trade in his famous book *The Wealth of Nations* (1776), as did John Stuart Mill in his *Principles of Political Economy* (1848) in which he wrote: 'a country which produces for a larger market than its own can introduce a more extended division of labour, can make greater use of machinery, and is more likely to make inventions and improvements in the process of production'. Mill also stressed the role of trade as a conduit for the international dissemination of ideas and technology through a number of mechanisms: first, a domestic buyer of an imported good may imitate the production technique, or adapt the new technique if it is patented, and second, there may be a direct exchange of ideas for further varieties of goods which increase welfare. 'New' growth theory (see Chapter 5) which incorporates trade, as pioneered by Grossman and Helpman (1991a, 1991b), encapsulates many of these original ideas of Mill.

Mill also recognized that the growth effects of trade depend on what a country specializes in: natural resource activities or manufacturing industries. It is the production of industrial goods, and particularly research-intensive goods, that produces technical dynamism and rapid growth. Stiglitz (2006) makes the same enduring point:

> a country whose static comparative advantage lies in, say, agriculture, risks stagnation . . . with limited growth prospects; . . . the industrial sector is almost everywhere the source of innovation, [and] many of these advances spill over into the rest of the economy as do the benefits from the development of institutions, like financial markets, that accompany the growth of an industrial sector.

As alluded to above, there is a close association between the size of markets and the accumulation of capital. The larger the market, the easier capital accumulation becomes. For a small country with no trade there is very little scope for large-scale investment in advanced capital equipment. Trade offers some escape, but a minimum size of domestic market in the first place is important to make trade viable. In this respect larger countries such as China and India are in a more favourable position than smaller countries such as Fiji, Mauritius or the Gambia. India and China's large populations offer the basis for the establishment of capital-goods industries and the production of manufactured goods, since production can take place on an economic basis before trade. The smaller country may need substantial protection for a commodity before it can be produced economically and compete in world markets. At least 60 countries classified as 'developing' have populations below 15 million. In terms of Figure 15.2, the dynamic benefits of trade are represented by an outward shift of the production possibility curves of both countries, leading to a higher level of community welfare.

Dynamic gains from trade are at the heart of **'new' trade theory** pioneered by Paul Krugman (1979, 1980, 1986), with its emphasis on increasing returns and positive externalities associated with the geographic concentration of production for trade (also providing an argument for strategic protection).

Paul Krugman

Born 1953, New York, USA. Has taught at the Universities of Yale, the Massachusetts Institute of Technology, and California (Berkeley), and is now Professor of Economics at Princeton University. He has made many important contributions to economics, but is best known for his pioneering work on the role of increasing returns in explaining trade patterns ('new' trade theory) and the spatial concentration of industrial activities ('new' economic geography). He is also an influential columnist of the *New York Times*. He was awarded the Nobel Prize for Economics in 2008.

Trade as a vent for surplus

Another important potential gain from trade is the provision of an outlet for a country's surplus production which would otherwise go unsold and represent a waste of resources. This is the so-called 'vent for surplus' gain from trade, first articulated by Adam Smith in his *Wealth of Nations* (1776). He writes:

> between whatever places foreign trade is carried on, they all of them derive two distinct benefits from it. It carries the surplus part of the product of their land and labour for which there is no demand among them, and brings back in return something else, which may satisfy part of their wants and increase their enjoyment.

In Figure 15.2 this vent for surplus argument is represented by a movement from a point inside the production possibility frontier to a point on the frontier which represents a higher level of welfare. The gain implies that the 'surplus' export resources have no alternative uses and cannot be switched to domestic use. This is not an unreasonable assumption in many natural resource-rich countries. Oil wells, mines and fishing grounds, for example, have no alternative uses, and the market for their products would soon become saturated if demand was confined to domestic consumption alone. The vent for surplus theory is a much more plausible explanation for the start of trade than the comparative cost doctrine of specialization.

Theory of customs unions and free trade areas

Because of the various gains to be had from trade, **regional trade agreements** (RTAs) have become very fashionable in recent years, in the form of **customs unions and free trade areas**. The WTO lists nearly 100 that have been established or modified since 1948. The major ones are the European Union (EU); the North American Free Trade Agreement (NAFTA); MERCOSUR covering Argentina, Brazil, Paraguay, Uruguay and Chile; APEC, covering countries in the Asia and Pacific region; ASEAN covering South-East Asian countries, and SACU, covering countries in southern Africa.

The essence of a customs union is that it frees trade between members and imposes a *common external tariff* (CET) on imported goods from the rest of the world. In a free trade area (FTA), by contrast, barriers to trade are brought down within the area, but there is no CET. Countries are free to impose their own specific tariffs on goods from outside the area, although often subject to agreement over the proportion of goods that must be purchased from within the area. Customs unions therefore *create* trade, but also *divert* it from lower-cost suppliers outside the Union. The interesting question is always whether the benefits of trade creation exceed the costs of trade diversion. FTAs also create trade, but the extent of trade diversion is likely to be much less, with the presumption that on narrow economic grounds, at least, FTAs are superior. For the same reason, customs unions are likely to be inferior to a policy of unilateral tariff reductions, and therefore need to be justified on other economic or non-economic grounds.

Before we look at the empirical evidence on these matters, however, let us consider theoretically the gains and losses of customs unions. The analysis makes the same assumptions as orthodox trade theory: perfect competition; prices reflect opportunity cost; factors of production are immobile between countries; trade is balanced (i.e. no balance of payments problems), and the full employment of resources. The **trade creation** effect of a Union is composed of two parts: first, a production effect which consists of the substitution of cheaper 'foreign' goods for domestic goods from within the union, and secondly, a consumption effect consisting of the gain in consumer surplus from cheaper goods. The **trade diversion** effect is also composed of two parts: first, the substitution of higher-priced goods from within the union for goods outside the union, and secondly, the loss of consumer surplus that this entails. The gains and losses for two partner countries within the union are illustrated in Figure 15.3. To simplify the analysis, scale economies and terms of trade effects are ignored.[1]

D_1 and D_2 are the demand curves for a good in the two countries; S_1 and S_2 are the domestic supply curves; $S_1 + M_1$ is the supply curve in country 1 consisting of the domestic supply curve and the supply of the good from the partner country which is assumed to enter duty free; and P_w is the world price. Now suppose that before the union of the two countries, a tariff of $P_w T_1$ was imposed in country 1 and $P_w T_2$ in country 2. In this case, it can be seen that demand equals supply in both markets; there are no imports from the rest of the world, and we can focus first of all on the process of trade creation. A customs union is now formed with a CET that balances supply and demand of the two partners (equal to $P_w CET$). The CET is lower than OT_1 in country 1 and higher than OT_2 in country 2. This has consumption and production effects in the two countries.

In country 1 domestic consumption increases from N to Q, and domestic production decreases from N to L. In country 2, domestic production increases from S to T; domestic consumption decreases from S to R, and the difference between supply and demand is exported to country 1. For country 1 there has been a cost saving equal to the area ABD, and an increase in consumer surplus equal to the area ADC. The total gain of trade creation is equal to $ABD + ADC$. In country 2, there has been a loss of consumer surplus equal to area 'd' and an increased production cost equal to area 'e', but this is more than offset by the increased export revenue of $LFGQ$, so country 2 is also better off.

Now let us consider the case where there is also trade diversion from the rest of the world. Suppose that in country 1 the initial tariff level was lower than $P_w T_1$ – say $P_w T^*$, so that demand exceeded supply and the excess demand was filled by imports from the rest of the world, MP, at price P_w. If a CET was now introduced of $P_w CET$, demand would increase from P to Q with an increase in consumer surplus of area 'c'. Production would fall from M to L with a reduction in production cost equal to area 'a'. There would be trade creation gains equal to 'a' + 'c', but now there is also trade diversion. Imports, previously from outside the union, would now come from the higher-cost partner. MP imports from abroad would be replaced at the increased cost of $MP + P_w CET$. This is the cost of trade diversion.

Figure 15.3   Gains and losses within a customs union

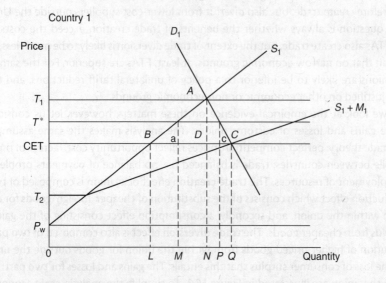

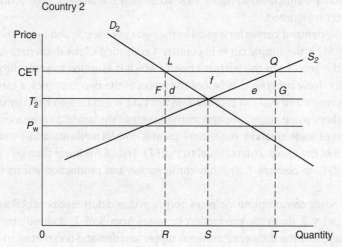

In evaluating the net gains from a customs union, trade creation needs to be compared with trade diversion. In general, trade creation is likely to predominate over trade diversion, the larger is the union and the lower is the CET. The larger the union, the greater the scope for trade creation, and the lower the CET, the less trade diversion there is likely to be. It is possible, however, even if the union as a whole is, on balance, trade-creating, that at least one country may lose. Likewise, it is possible for at least one country to gain even if the union as a whole is, on balance, trade-diverting. Everything depends on circumstances. A customs union can be devised, however, which raises the welfare of all members. This requires first that the CET of the union is set so that the level of post-union trade with the rest of the world does not fall below its pre-union level, and secondly that lump-sum compensatory taxes and transfers are imposed to offset individual country losses.

Apart from trade creation and trade diversion, customs unions may also have other important effects associated with the enlargement of the market which are neglected by the static analysis presented above. First, the larger market may generate economies of scale. If there are economies of scale, the supply curves in Figure 15.3 will slope downwards, and the CET can be lower than the original tariff in *both* partner countries. There will be a normal trade-creation effect and a cost saving in both countries. Secondly, integration is likely to promote increased competition which is likely to favourably affect prices and costs, and the growth of output. Thirdly, the widening of markets within a customs union is likely to attract international investment. Producers will prefer to produce within the union rather than face a CET from outside. Finally, if the world supply of output is not infinitely elastic, there are terms of trade effects to consider. Specifically, if there is trade diversion, the world price of the good will fall, moving the terms of trade in favour of the customs union. This terms of trade effect represents a welfare gain which may partly offset the welfare loss of trade diversion. It was mentioned earlier, however, that because customs unions impose a CET, they are likely to be inferior, in terms of welfare improvement, to a policy of *unilateral* tariff reductions (continuing to make the standard assumptions, of course, e.g. of trade balance, full employment). We can now illustrate this using Figure 15.3. Suppose country 1 has an initial tariff level of P_wT^*. It enters a customs union with country 2 with a common external tariff CET, and trade creation takes place equal to 'a' + 'c' (as before). Country 1 could also, however, reduce its tariff to P_wT^* on a non-discriminatory basis. It would enjoy the same trade creation gains, but now would be able to obtain imports cheaper from the rest of the world. This means an additional gain equal to the difference between the total expenditure on imports from the union compared with the rest of the world. At a simple level, the conclusion from this theoretical analysis is that the formation of customs unions represents a movement towards free trade, but even freer trade (i.e. no trade diversion) is better.

The general experience of RTAs in developing countries has been disappointing because they have been inward looking and protectionist, with trade diversion exceeding trade creation. Typically, the existing ratio of trade to GDP has been high in the member countries, and the ratio of trade with the rest of the world has also been high, so that the scope for trade creation has been minimal and the potential for trade diversion has been great. In the Economic Community of West African States (ECOWAS), founded in 1975, the amount of interregional trade is still less than 15 per cent of total exports. Forouton (1993) concludes his study of regional integration in sub-Saharan Africa (SSA) by saying, 'the structural characteristics of the SSA economies, the pursuit of import-substitution policies, and the very uneven distribution of costs and benefits of integration arising from economic differences among the partner countries, have thus far prevented any meaningful trade integration in SSA'. Of the various groupings in sub-Saharan Africa, only SACU has achieved any noticeable degree of integration in the market for goods. Otherwise, intra-group trade has remained limited. This conclusion is echoed by the authors of many of the applied papers in Oyejide et al. (1997), which examine the experience of regional integration and trade liberalization in sub-Saharan Africa.

Research by Vamvakidis (1999) across developing countries as a whole supports this pessimistic conclusion. He takes 109 cases of participation in 18 RTAs over the period 1950–92, and regresses the growth of per capita income of countries on the growth of world income, the initial level of per capita income, education level, trade openness, plus a dummy variable if a country belongs to an RTA. The dummy variable is significantly negative. He also finds that membership of an RTA lowers the share of investment in GDP.

In related work, Vamvakidis (1998) and Arora and Vamvakidis (2005) also try to estimate the effect on a country's growth rate of the size, income and growth of neighbouring countries. They find, perhaps not surprisingly, that it pays to have neighbours that are relatively rich, open to trade and growing fast. A 1 percentage point change in the growth of a country's trading partners is associated with a 0.8 percentage point increase in its own domestic growth. In a customs union, the countries swim or sink together!

Free trade enthusiasm in the modern era

Despite the arguments for free trade laid down by classical economic theory, it was never seriously practised by countries (except by Britain post-1850) until after the Second World War (see Chang, 2002, 2005, 2007; Reinert, 2007), with the establishment of the General Agreement on Tariffs and Trade (GATT) in 1947 and the general commitment by developed countries to the freeing of international trade in the wake of the protectionism and 'beggar-thy-neighbour' policies practised in the inter-war depression years between 1919 and 1939. Even so, the process of liberalization took a long time to gather momentum. Many developed countries maintained quite high tariff levels, and non-tariff barriers, until the early 1970s, and many developing countries, freed from their colonial past, adopted protection, particularly in Latin America and parts of Asia. It is only since the 1970s that both developed and developing countries have made a concerted effort to liberalize trade between themselves under various pressures from GATT (and the World Trade Organization since 1995 – the successor to GATT), the World Bank, the IMF and other international organizations, and in view of the alleged poor economic performance of countries pursuing protection.

Overall, the liberalization of trade has led to a massive growth of world trade relative to world output. While world output (or GDP) has expanded nearly sevenfold, the volume of world trade has grown 25 times at an annual compound rate of nearly 8 per cent per annum. In some individual countries, notably in South-East Asia, the growth of exports has exceeded 10 per cent per annum, and in China, 20 per cent per annum. The evolution of world trade as a proportion of world output is shown in Figure 15.4, rising from 25 per cent in 1960 to nearly 60 per cent today.

Figure 15.4   The share of world trade in world output, 1960–2006

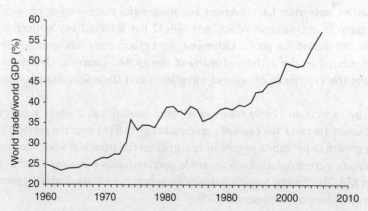

Note: Trade is measured as the sum of exports and imports of goods and services.

Source: World Bank, *World Development Indicators*, June 2009, online (Washington: World Bank).

Measurement and process of trade liberalization

To measure the degree and process of trade liberalization, it must be borne in mind that there are many different measures and types of protection, such as tariffs, quotas, licences, technical and environmental restrictions, and many different measures and concepts of trade liberalization and trade openness. The first thing to make clear, however, is that trade liberalization is not the same thing as trade openness. For example, a country may be very open in the sense that it has a high ratio of trade to GDP because it has abundant natural resources which it can only export, but may operate a very illiberal trade regime which makes trade difficult in other activities. Equally, a country with a low ratio of total trade to GDP, because it is a large country and relatively self-sufficient, may be very liberal in its trading practices.

The most common measure of trade liberalization focuses on what is happening to tariffs and non-tariff barriers (NTBs) to trade, whether trade is biased against exports in favour of import substitutes, and the general micro- and macro-environment of a country in which trade takes place, including the level of the exchange rate, whether the state has a monopoly of major exports, and monetary and fiscal conditions. Average tariff rates, export taxes, total taxes on international trade and indices of NTBs are all obvious measures of protection, but there are difficulties in using any one of these indices as a measure of trade liberalization. For one thing, a country may substitute one type of protection for another. For example, it may reduce NTBs, but raise tariffs to compensate, and vice versa. Secondly, *nominal* tariffs on goods are not the appropriate basis for assessing the restrictive effect of a tariff structure on trade. The nominal rate does not measure how inefficient (or costly) producers can be without incurring competition and losing market share. This is measured by the protection of value-added. This is the so-called *effective rate of protection* (see p. 537 below). A third point to make is that average tariff rates are often measured in empirical work by the ratio of tariff revenues to the value of imports, but this is not a measure of the official tariff rate, but of the collected rate. In the extreme, if a very high tariff discouraged imports completely, there would be no imports, and the measured tariff rate would be zero!

It is more useful to devise measures of trade regimes which can then be ranked from illiberal to liberal, or from protectionist to liberalized, and to look at the various indices through time. One approach is to measure the extent to which the structure of protection and incentives is biased against exports. The easiest way to measure this, outlined by Krueger (1998), is by the extent to which the ratio of domestic price of import competing goods (P_{md}) to their international (world) price (P_{mw}), relative to the ratio of the domestic price of importables (P_{xd}) compared with their international price (P_{xw}), deviates from unity, that is

$$B = \frac{P_{md}/P_{mw}}{P_{xd}/P_{xw}} \tag{15.1}$$

If we assume that $P_{mw}/P_{xw} = 1$, then if $P_{md}/P_{xd} > 1$, the trade regime is biased against exports in favour of import substitutes, and if $P_{md}/P_{xd} < 1$, the trade regime favours export promotion.

Greenaway et al. (1998), in their major study of trade liberalization and growth across 73 countries, construct a similar index to Krueger's which also measures the relative distortion (D) of the price of exportables to importables. It is calculated as:

$$D = \frac{(1+t)}{(1+s)} \tag{15.2}$$

where t is the tariff on imports and s is the rate of subsidy to exports. A ratio of unity implies trade neutrality; $D > 1$ implies anti-export bias in favour of import substitution, while $D < 1$ implies an export-oriented trade strategy.

David Greenaway was very influential in the first World Bank classification of trade regimes in its *World Development Report 1987*. Four categories were identified:

- **Strongly outward-oriented** countries, where there are very few trade or foreign exchange controls and trade and industrial policies do not discriminate between production for the home market and exports, and between purchases of domestic goods and foreign goods
- **Moderately outward-oriented** countries, where the overall incentive structure is moderately biased towards the production of goods for the home market rather than for export, and favours the purchase of domestic goods
- **Moderately inward-oriented** countries, where there is a more definite bias against exports and in favour of import substitution
- **Strongly inward-oriented** countries, where trade controls and the incentive structures strongly favour production for the domestic market and discriminate strongly against imports.

Many investigators and international organizations devise their own measures of protection and liberalization, using multiple criteria. One is the **Sachs and Warner (1995) Openness Index**. Countries are classified as 'open' or 'closed' according to five criteria. A country is regarded as 'closed' if at least one of the following criteria is satisfied: an average tariff rate higher than 40 per cent; non-tariff barriers covering more than 40 per cent of imports; a socialist economic system; a state monopoly of major exports, or a black market exchange-rate premium in excess of 20 per cent. The criteria are arbitrary, of course, but nonetheless many investigators have used this index to classify countries, and to measure the timing of liberalization (although, as we said above, openness and liberalization are not the same).

Another measure is the **Index of Economic Freedom** published since 1995 by the Heritage Foundation in Washington, which considers a broad array of institutional factors, one of which is trade policies. A trade policy score of 1 to 5 is given to countries based on their average tariff rate, the extent of non-tariff barriers, and the degree of corruption in the customs service. Five broad levels of protection are distinguished: very low (free); low; moderate; high, and very high (repressed). Countries can be classified according to category, and their economic performance analysed.

The process of trade liberalization can take many forms, but as Michaely et al. (1991) say in their massive volume of case studies of trade liberalization in developing countries: 'very little is known about essential attributes of a change from one [trade] regime to another; of a move away from a distorted trade policy regime towards a more neutral one'. On the other hand, we know that the issues of timing, phasing and sequencing are likely to be important in the design and implementation of a successful trade liberalization policy (see Rodrik, 1996, 2001).

Often the first stage of liberalization is the dismantling of non-tariff barriers to trade in the form of quotas and licences, not necessarily the reduction of tariffs. In fact, tariffs often rise to compensate for the removal of quantitative restrictions on imports. This makes protection more transparent and reduces rent-seeking behaviour. When protection is removed from an industry, production is likely to decline and unemployment rise. Capital is specific and will be left unutilized, and labour may not be mobile enough to be employed in other activities. This is a serious worry and can undermine the static welfare gains from trade liberalization. It is certainly an argument against liberalizing imports too rapidly. As the relative prices of factors of production and goods change, there is also likely to be considerable redistribution effects which need taking account of in the process of liberalization (see below, p. 526).

The other big worry is the effect of trade liberalization on the balance of payments. If imports rise faster than exports, balance-of-payments difficulties may arise, which have negative growth consequences. This has implications for the sequencing of trade liberalization. Imports should not be liberalized before the export sector has had time to adjust or respond in order for foreign exchange to be available to meet the higher import bill. In terms of policy, it means that anti-export bias needs removing, or export subsidies given, before serious import liberalization takes place (as was the case in Japan and South Korea, for example). East Asia provides an interesting case study of how countries should proceed, where the process of trade liberalization was gradual and export-oriented, in contrast to many Latin American countries where the process of liberalization was sudden and no attention was paid to the sequencing.

Another message from the experience of liberalization is that liberalization is much more likely to be successful in an environment of internal and external stability. It is particularly important not to allow the exchange rate to appreciate, which otherwise worsens the balance between export and import growth. This means that countries need to retain control of the capital account of the balance of payments, and not to liberalize capital flows at the same time as trade. Unfortunately, many Latin American countries, such as Mexico, Argentina and Peru, when they liberalized in the 1980s and early 1990s, allowed their exchange rate to appreciate which damaged the trade balance and impacted negatively on growth.

In short, if trade liberalization is to be successful in promoting economic development, it needs to avoid adjustment costs as a result of the poor timing and sequencing of liberalization, and it needs to avoid inegalitarian distributional consequences.

Models of export-led growth

The impact of trade liberalization on economic performance works mainly through improving the efficiency of resource allocation, allowing greater scope for specialization, and stimulating exports which have powerful effects on both supply and demand within an economy. Before examining the empirical evidence on the relation between trade liberalization, trade performance and the economic growth of countries, it is first important to understand why exports are so crucial for economic development.

There are three main models of export-led growth:

- The neoclassical supply-side model
- The balance-of-payments-constrained growth model
- The virtuous circle model.

The first is the orthodox model which fits neatly into mainstream neoclassical growth theory. The latter two models are rarely articulated in the trade and growth literature, and yet may be of greater importance for understanding growth rate differences in open developing economies, especially if most developing countries are constrained in their economic performance by a shortage of foreign exchange. Moreover, orthodox growth and trade theory predicts the convergence of per capita incomes across countries (see Chapter 5), which is at variance with what we observe in the real world. What appears to happen in practice is that once a country gains an advantage through the capture of export markets, it tends to sustain that advantage through the operation of various cumulative forces which generate 'virtuous circles' of success for favoured countries (and regions), and 'vicious circles' of slow growth and underemployment for those countries that are left behind (see Chapter 8). When studies are conducted of the relation between exports and growth, either across countries or over time, it is not always clear whether the relation found is picking up supply-side factors; demand-side influences; cumulative forces interacting with each other; or a combination of all three.

The neoclassical supply-side model

The neoclassical supply-side model of the relation between exports and growth assumes that the export sector, because of its exposure to foreign competition, confers externalities on the non-export sector, and also that the export sector has a higher level of productivity than the non-export sector. Thus, the share of exports in GDP, and the growth of exports, matters for overall growth performance. Feder (1983) was the first to provide a formal model of this type to explain the relation between export growth and output growth. The output of the export sector is assumed to be a function of labour and capital in the sector; the output of the non-export sector is assumed to be a function of labour, capital and the output of the export sector (to capture externalities); and the ratio of respective marginal factor productivities in the two sectors is assumed to deviate from unity by a factor δ. These assumptions produce an augmented neoclassical growth equation of the form:

$$G = a(I/Y) + b(dL/L) + [\delta/(1 + \delta) + F_x](X/Y)(dX/X) \qquad (15.3)$$

where I/Y is the investment ratio; dL/L is the growth of the labour force; dX/X is the growth of exports; X/Y is the share of exports in GDP; $\delta/(1 + \delta)$ is the differential productivity effect; and F_x is the externality effect. Feder originally tested the model taking a cross-section of 19 semi-industrialized countries and a larger sample of 31 countries over the period 1964–73. First he tested the model without export growth, and then with the growth of exports included. The inclusion of dX/X considerably improves the explanatory power of the equation, and the effect of export growth is always statistically significant. The coefficient on export growth, however, is an amalgam of an externality effect and a productivity differential effect. To decompose the two, (15.3) can be fitted excluding the export share term (X/Y) which then isolates the externality effect. The difference between the total effect of export growth and the externality effect is the productivity differential effect. When this is done, Feder found substantial differences in productivity between the export and non-export sectors and also evidence of externalities. The results should not surprise. The export sector is likely to be more 'modern' and capital-intensive than the non-export sector, which to a large extent consists of low productivity agriculture and petty service activities. The externalities conferred are part of the dynamic gains from trade discussed at the beginning of the chapter, associated with the transmission and diffusion of new ideas from abroad relating to both production techniques and efficient management practices.

The Feder model is a pure supply-side argument which has plausibility, but there are other (non-neoclassical) supply-side arguments, and also demand-side considerations which would also be consistent with finding export growth and GDP growth positively correlated over the long term. From the supply side, export growth may raise output growth through externalities, but also faster export growth permits faster import growth. If countries are short of foreign exchange, and domestic and foreign resources are not fully substitutable, more imports permit a fuller use of domestic resources. In particular, more foreign exchange allows the greater import of capital goods which may not be produced domestically.

The balance-of-payments-constrained growth model

The major weakness of the orthodox supply-side model of the role of exports is that it doesn't go far enough; it neglects the importance of demand for the growth of output. All components of domestic demand – consumption, investment, government expenditure and exports themselves – have an import content that must be paid for. Exports are unique in this respect, because exports are the only component of demand that provide the foreign exchange to pay for the other components of demand, which otherwise would be constrained. It is important to stress this, because this insight lies at the heart of demand-oriented theories of growth and development in an open economy.

Most factors of production in the growth and development process are *endogenous* to demand and not exogenously determined as neoclassical growth theory assumes. Capital is a produced means of production and is as much a consequence of the growth of output as its cause. The demand for labour is a derived demand from output. Labour input responds to demand in a variety of ways through reductions in unemployment; increases in labour force participation; increases in hours worked; shifts of labour from low productivity to high productivity sectors; and in the last resort, through international migration. In labour surplus economies, such as most developing countries, it stretches credulity to assume an exogenously given supply of labour that determines output in a *causal* sense. Productivity growth is also largely endogenous to output growth working through induced capital accumulation, embodied technical progress and static and dynamic returns to scale. To understand growth rate differences between countries, it is necessary to understand why demand growth differs between countries, and the constraints on demand that exist within countries.

In most developing countries, the major constraint on the growth of demand is the current balance of payments and the shortage of foreign exchange. Export growth relaxes a balance-of-payments constraint on demand and allows all other components of demand (consumption, investment and government expenditure) to grow faster without running into balance-of-payments difficulties. This is the simplest of all explanations of the relationship between export growth and output growth. The fact is that in the long run, no country can grow faster than that rate consistent with balance-of-payments equilibrium on current account unless it can finance ever-growing deficits which, in general, it cannot. Ratios of payments deficit to GDP of more than 2–3 per cent start to make the international financial markets nervous (witness the experience of Mexico, Brazil and the countries of East Asia in recent years), and *all* borrowing *eventually* has to be repaid. We will show in Chapter 16 that if relative price (or exchange rate) changes do not act as an efficient balance-of-payments-adjustment mechanism, the rate of growth of output of a country (g) can be approximated by the simple formula:

$$g = x/\pi \qquad (15.4)$$

where x is the growth of export volume (determined by the growth of 'world' income and the income elasticity of demand for exports) and π is the income elasticity of demand for imports. The correlation between g and x is immediately apparent.

The virtuous circle model of export-led growth

Finally, it needs to be recognized that exports and growth may be interrelated in a cumulative process. This raises the question of causality but, more important, such models provide an explanation of why growth and development through trade tends to be concentrated in particular areas of the world, while other regions and countries have been left behind. These models provide a challenge to both orthodox growth theory and trade theory which predict the long-run convergence of living standards across the world. In neoclassical growth theory, capital is assumed to be subject to diminishing returns so that rich countries should grow slower than poor countries for the same amount of investment undertaken (see Chapter 5). Neoclassical trade theory predicts convergence through the assumption of factor price equalization. The empirical evidence is at odds with the theory: there is no evidence that living standards across the world are converging. A simple cumulative model, driven by exports as the major component of autonomous demand, was outlined in Chapter 8, p. 272. Output growth is a function of export growth; export growth is a function of price competitiveness and foreign income growth; price competitiveness is a function of wage growth and productivity growth, and productivity growth is a function of output growth – the so-called Verdoorn Law working through static and dynamic returns to scale, including learning by doing. It is this induced productivity growth that makes the model 'circular and cumulative' since if fast output growth (caused by export growth) induces faster productivity growth, this makes goods more competitive and therefore induces faster export growth. The Verdoorn relation not only makes the model 'circular and cumulative', but also gives rise to the possibility that once an economy obtains a growth advantage it will tend to keep it. Suppose, for example, that an economy obtains an advantage in the production of goods with a high income elasticity of demand in world markets, such as high-technology goods, which raises its growth rate above other countries. Through the Verdoorn effect, productivity growth will be higher and the economy will retain its competitive advantage in these goods, making it difficult, without protection or exceptional industrial enterprise, to establish the same commodities. In such a cumulative model, it is the difference between the income elasticity characteristics of exports (and imports, if balance-of-payments equilibrium is a requirement, as argued earlier) which is the essence of divergence between industrial and agricultural economies, or between 'centre' and 'periphery'. This simple model can go a long way in explaining differences in the level of development between countries and the forces that perpetuate divergences in the world economy. The forces are *structural*, relating to the production and demand characteristics of the goods produced and traded.

What you export matters

The argument that what a country exports matters for its growth performance can be formally tested using a procedure developed by Hausmann et al. (2007). First they measure what is called the 'productivity' (PRODY) of each commodity (i) exported to see what country income level the good is associated with. Secondly, they calculate an EXPY for each country which is the weighted sum of all the PRODYs that the country exports. If a country is specializing in high-income goods, it will have a high EXPY, and if it is specializing in low-income goods the EXPY will be low. Cross-country analysis shows a high correlation between a country's EXPY and its growth and export performance.

The calculation of PRODY is:

$$PRODY_i = \sum_j \left(\frac{(x_{ij}/X_j)}{\sum_j (x_{ij}/X_j)} \right) Y_j$$

where x_{ij} is the export of commodity i from country j

X_j is the country's total exports

x_{ij}/X_j represents a country's specialization in commodity i

$\sum_i$ is the share of commodity i in total world exports

Y_j is the income per capita of each country exporting the good i.

$PRODY_i$ will be low if low-income countries specialize in that good, and high if high-income countries specialize in that good.

$$EXPY_j = \sum_i PRODY_i(x_{ij}/X_j)$$

This is simply the weighted average of the PRODYs for that country where the weights are the value shares in the country's total exports. As would be expected, the relationship between the level of per capita income of countries and EXPY is strong, but more significantly there is a strong relation between EXPY, output growth and export growth across countries (controlling for the other determinants of GDP growth). Some developing countries such as China have an EXPY higher than would be expected on the basis of their level of per capita income, indicating that they are producing and exporting sophisticated goods more associated with high-income countries. This is one reason why China is so successful (see also Felipe, 2009). A 10 per cent higher level of EXPY gives a country extra growth of about 0.4 percentage points. The calculations are picking up the higher income elasticity of demand for more sophisticated goods, and this is why the structure of exports matters for economic performance.

Trade liberalization and export growth

What is the empirical evidence on the relation between trade liberalization and export growth? Because various forms of trade restrictions, including export duties, cause anti-export bias, the presumption must be that trade liberalization will raise the growth of exports, but by how much?

There are two broad types of empirical work on the relationship between trade liberalization and export performance. Firstly, there are large multi-country studies that examine in detail the process of trade policy reforms within individual countries and its consequences. Pioneer studies of this type include Little et al. (1970); Balassa (1971), and Michaely et al. (1991). Secondly, there are econometric studies using time-series, cross-section or panel data analysis (pooling time-series and cross-section data). The evidence gives mixed and conflicting results, which suggests that the context in which trade liberalization takes place is of primary importance, particularly world economic conditions and domestic economic policies being pursued at the same time, especially with regard to the exchange rate.

Individual country (or industry) case studies that show a positive effect of liberalization on export performance include Joshi and Little's (1996) analysis of India's trade reforms in 1991; Ahmed's (2000) study of Bangladesh: Jenkins's (1996) study of manufactured exports from Bolivia, and Pacheco-López's (2005) study of Mexico after the trade reforms of 1985/86. Multi-country case studies that show a positive impact of liberalization on export growth include the cross-section analysis by Thomas et al. (1991); Helleiner's (1994) collection of theoretical and empirical studies, and Bleaney's (1999) panel data study of manufactured exports for ten countries of Latin America.

The most comprehensive recent study is that by Santos-Paulino and Thirlwall (2004) (see also Santos-Paulino, 2002a), who take a panel of 22 countries that have adopted trade liberalization policies since the mid-1970s. A dummy variable for the year(s) of liberalization is included in an export growth equation using between 350 and 500 observations (depending on the method of estimation), and the central conclusion is that, controlling for other variables, liberalization has raised export growth by nearly 2 percentage points compared with the pre-liberalization period. The impact appears to have been the greatest in Africa (3.6 percentage points) and the least in Latin America (1.6 percentage points). There is also evidence that liberalization has increased the sensitivity of export growth to world income growth; that is, liberalization has increased the income elasticity of demand for exports by inducing structural change.

The high-performance Asian countries are perhaps the most spectacular examples of economic success linked to export performance, but, interestingly, this has not always been based on free trade. The economies of Japan, South Korea, Taiwan, Singapore, Hong Kong, Malaysia, Indonesia and Thailand have recorded some of the highest GDP growth rates in the world since 1965 (averaging as a group nearly 6 per cent per annum) and also some of the highest rates of growth of exports (averaging more than 10 per cent per annum). While some of the countries have been very laissez-faire, however, others have been very interventionist, for example Japan and South Korea, pursuing relentless export promotion but import substitution at the same time.

Another interesting case study is China, which still restricts trade, but is now the world's second-largest exporter after Germany. Since China launched its 'open door' policy in 1978, after three decades of inward-oriented trade, its exports have been growing at over 10 per cent per annum and its average GDP growth rate has been 8 per cent. This is another classic example of export-led growth deliberately promoted by the government through the establishment of special economic zones and 'open cities' (originally in the provinces of Guangdong and Fujian) which act as magnets for investment and provide incentives for exporters. Typical incentives for exporters in all export-orientated economies consist of:

• Exemption from duties and tariffs on inputs that go into exports
• Investment grants
• Tax holidays
• Favourable retention rights over foreign exchange if exports are in certain sectors
• Favourable treatment of foreign investment.

In China a 25 per cent investment share was enough to give joint venture status to foreign investors, who then qualified for tax incentives, and no limit was placed on foreign equity investment in Chinese companies.

For a country's overall economic performance to improve, however, it is not enough for export growth to accelerate. Export growth must be shown to outpace import growth, otherwise balance-of-payments difficulties will arise.

Trade liberalization, import growth and the balance of payments

The main function of tariffs and non-tariff barriers, such as quantitative import controls, quality standards and government procurement policies, is to control the level and growth of imports in order to protect and promote domestic industry. If tariffs are reduced, and quantitative restrictions are lifted, imports can be expected to increase. There will be an 'autonomous' increase, and in addition imports are likely to become more sensitive to income and relative price changes domestically. If the income elasticity of demand for imports increases, this tightens the balance-of-payments constraint on growth (see equation (15.4) and Chapter 16). Country studies by Melo and Vogt (1984) for Venezuela; Mah (1999) for Thailand, and Bertola and Faini (1991) for Morocco all show a significant impact of trade liberalization on import growth and the sensitivity of imports to domestic income growth.

The most comprehensive, recent, study to date is by Santos-Paulino and Thirlwall (2004) (see also Santos-Paulino, 2002b) who take the same 22 countries as for export growth, discussed previously, and find that trade liberalization, by itself, controlling for other factors, has increased the growth of imports by between 5 and 6 percentage points (more in countries initially highly protected and less in others), and also increased the income elasticity of demand for imports by between 0.2 and 0.5 percentage points. Pacheco-López and Thirlwall (2006) have also examined the direct effect of liberalization on the income elasticity of demand for imports in 17 Latin American countries over the period 1977 to 2002 and find a rise from 2.08 in the pre-liberalization period to 2.63 in the post-liberalization period.

If trade liberalization raises the growth of imports by more than exports, or raises the income elasticity of demand for imports by more than in proportion to the growth of exports, the balance of trade (or payments) will worsen for a given growth of output, unless the currency can be manipulated to raise the value of exports relative to imports. The consequence is that the growth of output may have to be constrained to avoid balance-of-payments crises.

The first major studies of this topic were by Parikh for UNCTAD (1999) and for WIDER (Parikh, 2002). The first study examined 16 countries over the period 1970–95, with the main conclusion that trade liberalization seems to have worsened the trade balance by 2.7 per cent of GDP, which is substantial. The second study extends the analysis to 64 countries with the general conclusion:

> the exports of most of the liberalizing countries have not grown fast enough after trade liberalization to compensate for the rapid growth of imports during the years immediately following trade liberalization. The evidence suggests that trade liberalization in developing countries has tended to lead to a deterioration in the trade account.

Santos-Paulino and Thirlwall (2004) take the same sample of 22 developing countries as for the impact of liberalization on export and import growth previously discussed and find that the switch to a more liberal trading regime worsened, on average, the trade balance by 2 per cent of GDP (which is similar to the Parikh estimate), and the current account by 1 per cent of GDP. For a separate group of 17 Least Developed Countries, Santos-Paulino (2007) finds a deterioration in the trade balance ratio of 4 per cent of GDP. For a sample of 17 Latin American countries over the period 1997–2002, Pacheco-López and Thirlwall (2007) find a deterioration in the trade balance of between 1.3 and 2.3 per cent of GDP (depending on the method of estimation used).

All these results show that trade liberalization has impacted unfavourably on the trade balance and current account balance of liberalizing countries. Such a deterioration, if it cannot be financed by sustainable capital inflows, may either trigger a currency crisis or necessitate a severe deflation of domestic demand (and therefore growth) to control imports. As UNCTAD (2004) argues in its *Least Developed Countries Report 2004* on the theme of linking international trade with poverty reduction: 'this critical [balance-of-payments] constraint on development and sustained poverty reduction is conspicuously absent in the current debate on trade and poverty'.

Indeed, the ultimate test of successful trade liberalization, at least at the macro-level, ignoring distributional effects, is whether it lifts a country on to a higher growth path consistent with a sustainable balance of payment; or, in other words, whether it improves the trade-off between growth and the balance of payments, as illustrated in Figure 15.5.

Figure 15.5   The trade-off between growth and the balance of payments

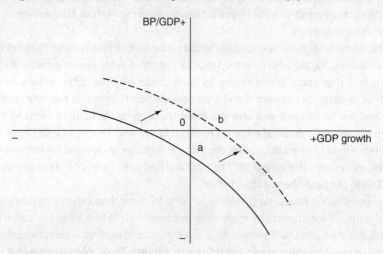

The ratio of the current balance (or trade balance) to GDP (BP/GDP) is measured on the vertical axis, and the growth of GDP on the horizontal axis. The solid line curve gives the negative trade-off curve showing how the balance of payments deteriorates as growth accelerates. The curve is deliberately drawn here to represent a serious situation where the balance of payments is in deficit (point a) even at zero growth. The objective of trade policy should be to shift the curve upwards to, say, point b on the horizontal axis so that some positive growth is possible without running into payments difficulties. It is possible to estimate such a trade-off curve and see whether liberalization has shifted it favourably. Pacheco-López and Thirlwall (2007) do this for 17 Latin American countries using pooled time-series/cross-section data over the period 1977–2002 and find that trade liberalization *worsened* the trade-off by 3.6 percentage points. Before liberalization the curve cut the vertical axis at a deficit of 1.39 per cent; after liberalization it cuts the curve at a −4.99 deficit/GDP ratio. This may be one of the reasons why it is difficult to find robust results showing that trade liberalization has improved the growth performance of countries.

Trade liberalization and economic performance

It is fairly clear that trade liberalization has improved export performance, but liberalization and export growth are not the same and should not be confused in the discussion of trade liberalization and economic growth. As Stiglitz (2006) notes:

> Advocates of liberalization cite statistical studies claiming that liberalization enhances growth. But a careful look at the evidence shows something quite different ... It is exports – not the removal of trade barriers – that is the driving force of growth. Studies that focus directly on the removal of trade barriers show little relationship between liberalization and growth. The advocates of quick liberalization tried an intellectual sleight of hand, hoping that the broad-brush discussion of the benefits of globalization would suffice to make their case.

The early work of Edwards (1992, 1993, 1998) and Dollar (1992) showed a positive relation between the outward orientation of countries, the removal of trade distortions and the growth of countries. This work, however, has been heavily criticized by Rodriguez and Rodrik (2000) both on methodological grounds and for lack of robustness. They themselves find no significant relationship between either import duties or the percentage of imports covered by non-tariff barriers and the growth of per capita income (controlling for other variables).

The work of Dollar and Kraay (2004) has been highly influential, especially with the World Bank. They take a sample of 73 developing countries from the 1970s to the 1990s and rank them according to their share of trade (exports plus imports) in GDP. The top one-third of countries are called 'the post-1980s globalizers', and these countries (24 in all) are compared with the rest of the sample. Per capita income in the 'globalizer' countries is shown to have grown much more rapidly decade by decade compared with the 'non-globalizers'. The influence of Dollar and Kraay on the views of the World Bank can be vividly seen in its 2002 report on *Globalization, Growth and Poverty* in which it claims:

> Some 24 developing countries – with 3 million people – have doubled their ratio of trade to income over the past two decades. The rest of the developing world trades less than 20 years ago. The more globalizing developing countries have increased their per capita growth rate from 1 percent in the 1960s to 3 percent in the 1970s, 4 percent in the 1980s and 5 per cent in the 1990s; . . . much of the rest of the developing world – with about 2 billion people – is becoming marginalized.

The results of Dollar and Kraay, however, need to be treated with some care. Dowrick and Golley (2004) show that the faster growth of the 'globalizing' countries is entirely due to the fast growth of China and India. If these two countries are excluded from the sample, the remaining 22 'globalized' countries grew slower over the period 1980–2000 than the 'non-globalized' ones. They also show that the 'globalizing' countries were not the most open or liberal. Their share of trade in GDP rose the most, but the countries started from a low base and were still less open economies than the 'non-globalizers', at least until the 1990s. In the 1990s the tariffs of the 'globalizers' were still higher than the 'non-globalizers'.

Another major influential study of trade orientation and growth is that by Sachs and Warner (1995), which takes 79 countries over the period 1979 to 1989. They find that open economies (see p. 516 for the definitions of 'open' and 'closed') grew on average 2.44 percentage points faster than closed economies. Rodriguez and Rodrik (2000) argue, however, that it is not tariffs and non-tariff barriers that distinguish the two sets of countries but a combination of the black market exchange rate-premium and the state monopoly of exports. The black market exchange rate is highly correlated with turbulent macroeconomic conditions – debt, terms of trade deterioration and wars – and this was the major cause of their slower economic growth. Wacziard and Welch (2008) extend the Sachs–Warner study into the 1990s when 78 countries are classified as open and 27 closed (compared with 31 open and 74 closed during the period studied by Sachs and Warner), and find that there appears to be no significant effect of openness on economic growth.

Greenaway et al. (1998, 2002) examine the relationship between trade liberalization and growth within a 'new' growth theory framework (see Chapter 5) using panel data analysis for up to 73 countries over the period 1975–93. Different measures of liberalization are used, and they also look for lagged effects. What they find is that in the first year of liberalization the impact is negative (although not significantly so); in the second year it is positive but not significant, but in the third year it is positive and significant. This suggests a J-curve type effect of liberalization on growth, with the effects taking time to come through. On the other hand, there is no indication of whether the positive impact lasts.

In conclusion, we see that there is some evidence that trade liberalization promotes growth and a higher growth of living standards; on the other hand, the results are not always robust, and depend on the measure of liberalization used, the time period taken and the estimation method. Rodriguez and Rodrik (2000) conclude their evaluation of trade orientation and economic growth by saying that indicators of openness and liberalization used are either poor measures of trade barriers or are highly correlated with other determinants of domestic performance. They are particularly concerned that the priority given to trade policy reforms has generated expectations that are unlikely to be met, and may preclude other institutional reforms which would have a greater impact on economic performance. In other words, trade liberalization cannot be regarded as a substitute for a comprehensive trade and development strategy. To quote Rodrik (2001): 'deep trade liberalization cannot be relied upon to deliver high rates of economic growth and therefore does not deserve the high priority it typically receives in the development strategies pushed by leading organisations'.

Trade liberalization, poverty and domestic inequality

Poverty

There may be static efficiency gains from trade liberalization and a greater volume of trade, but there will also be welfare losses if domestic firms cannot compete as trade barriers fall and those thrown out of work cannot find alternative employment. In other words, the gains from trade to a country may not be equally distributed between people within a country, and some may lose absolutely. George (2010) cites production losses in some poor countries of more than 20 per cent as a result of liberalization.

If more trade leads to faster economic growth, this should lift more people out of poverty and reduce the poverty rate, depending on the elasticity of the poverty rate with respect to growth (see Chapter 2, p. 46), but as we saw earlier, trade liberalization does not guarantee faster economic growth, and even if the poverty rate declines the income distribution may still become more unequal if the richest in the country gain relative to the poorest.

The impact of trade liberalization on poverty depends mainly on its effects on employment and prices. Two main groups in society need distinguishing: workers (or wage earners) on the one hand and producers (or profit earners) on the other. In the latter category are included not only firms and enterprises, but also the self-employed who are consumers as well as producers, such as peasant farmers in rural areas, and those working in the petty service sector in urban areas.

Wage earners will be affected by trade liberalization in three main ways: by what happens to the wage rate, to employment and to the prices of goods they consume. There are many possibilities. If liberalization increases productivity, and real wages rise, workers will benefit. Increased competition in import-competing activities, however, may destroy jobs and lower wages. In Kenya, cotton farming and textile production have been badly hit by liberalization. Cotton production fell by 70 per cent between the mid-1980s and the mid-1990s and textile employment fell from 120,000 to 85,000 in ten years (Christian Aid, 2005). Two million Mexican maize farmers have lost their jobs since the NAFTA free trade agreement was signed in 1994 because they cannot compete with subsidized maize from the USA. For a fuller discussion of the research on the effect of trade liberalization on labour markets see Case example 15.1.

Case example 15.1	**Globalization and manufacturing employment**

Globalization creates winners and losers among workers and from this, two immediate questions arise: in terms of employment, are there more winners than losers? And who are the winners and losers likely to be?

Research carried out by the University of East Anglia and local researchers in Bangladesh, Kenya, South Africa and Vietnam looked at the impact of changes in trade flows and foreign investment on manufacturing employment in the four countries. All four economies became increasingly open during the 1990s. However, their experience in terms of manufacturing employment contrasts sharply. In Vietnam, more than 900,000 new jobs were created in manufacturing between 1990 and 2000, with a similar number being created in Bangladesh during the first half of the 1990s. In contrast, in South Africa manufacturing employment (in the formal sector, at least) actually fell during the 1990s while unemployment rose. Manufacturing employment rose gradually in Kenya but remained at relatively low levels.

Imports and exports

The research estimated the impact of increased exports and increased import penetration on employment. It confirmed that export growth made a significant contribution to increased employment in both Vietnam and Bangladesh during the 1990s. In South Africa, however, although export expansion did contribute to employment, this was not enough to offset the overall decline in employment. In Kenya, manufactured exports made no contribution to employment growth. All four countries experienced increased import penetration during the 1990s, which means that the overall impact of greater openness was less positive (or more negative) in terms of employment than might appear from looking only at exports. However, in the case of Vietnam and, to a more modest extent, Bangladesh, the net employment created by trade changes was still significant.

Skill and gender impacts

The research also looked at the skill and gender impacts of the globalization of manufacturing. Evidence from Kenya and South Africa suggested that there was a skill-bias associated with greater openness in that there was a tendency for the demand for more skilled labour to increase faster than that for unskilled labour. Yet in Vietnam and Bangladesh, the growth in demand was mainly concentrated on unskilled labour. In the two Asian countries, the bulk of export jobs were filled by women and exports employed far more women per US dollar of output than import-competing industries. In contrast in Africa, women workers were far less prominent in the industries that were the main exporters. The research highlights the impact that globalization can have on labour markets in the south. It found that:

- Integration with the global economy has led to a significant increase in the number of unskilled jobs, particularly for women, in Bangladesh and Vietnam.
- Job creation as a result of greater openness has been minimal in Kenya and South Africa and is biased towards more skilled workers.

continued overleaf

| Case example 15.1 | **Globalization and manufacturing employment** – *continued* |

- Where export growth is limited, increased competition from imports can significantly depress the employment impact.
- Unless a significant number of unskilled jobs is created, globalization is unlikely to lead to poverty reduction.

These findings suggest that:

- Greater openness does not necessarily – but can – lead to increased employment and is not a cure-all in terms of poverty reduction.
- The specific context in terms of resource endowments, market access and geographical location plays a part in determining the likely impact of globalization on poverty.
- Trade policy can also play a part in ensuring that the gains from increased employment in export industries are not offset totally by increased import penetration.

Source: Jenkins and Sen, 2003.

Real income also depends on the price of consumption goods. Price changes will have distributional effects depending on the weight of each good in each worker's basket. If the price of food falls, the poor will gain more than the rich because they spend a higher proportion of their income on food. If liberalization raises the price of food, however, because of the removal of subsidies for example, the poor are likely to suffer severely.

Producers will also be affected in a variety of ways, in particular by what happens to output prices, to input prices, and to the prices of the basket of goods bought for consumption in the case of self-employed producers. Producer prices are likely to fall with trade liberalization. In Senegal, after liberalization, the price farmers received for their tomatoes fell by 50 per cent, and tomato production fell by 70 per cent, leaving many farmers without a cash crop (Christian Aid, 2005). But the price of inputs is also likely to fall, so whether producers gain or lose depends on the prevailing protective structure of their output and inputs.

If any generalization can be made from case studies it seems that when all price and wage effects are taken into account, rural families tend to lose, and urban households tend to gain at least in circumstances where workers retain their jobs. Ravallion (2006) concludes, on the basis of his micro-case studies of trade liberalization in Morocco and China, that 'the most vulnerable households tend to be rural dependent on agriculture, with relatively few workers, and with weak links to the outside economy through migration'. Ravallion also looks at the relationship between trade liberalization and the poverty rate across 75 countries in which there have been at least two household surveys on poverty (giving 178 cases in all), and finds no significant relation, positive or negative. He concludes, 'it remains clear that there is considerable variation in the rates of poverty reduction at a given rate of expansion of trade volume'. Equally, however, he says, 'based on the data available from cross-country comparison, it is hard to maintain the view that expanding trade, in general, is a powerful force for poverty reduction in developing countries'.

Winters et al. (2004) likewise conclude their major survey on trade liberalization and poverty by saying there can be no simple relationship between trade liberalization and poverty. Theory provides strong presumption that trade liberalization [should] be poverty-alleviating in the long run and on average ... equally, however, it does not assert that the static and microeconomic effects of liberalization will always be beneficial to the poor. Trade liberalization necessarily implies distributional changes; it may well reduce the well-being of some people (at least in the short term) and some of these may be poor.[2]

To protect the poor as trade liberalization takes place, countries need to consider a number of policy issues:

- The sequencing of liberalization. To ameliorate the costs of adjustment, great care needs to be taken with the sequencing of liberalization, so that vulnerable sectors are given time to adjust.
- The provision of social safety nets. For those already poor, and adversely affected by liberalization, governments need to put in place social safety nets in the form of, for example, unemployment and income insurance. These could be supported by World Bank Programmes.
- Labour mobility and training. Improved worker mobility and worker training can help those who lose jobs to find new ones.
- The development of markets. To take advantage of new market opportunities, the poor and other disadvantaged groups require training and technical assistance in both traditional and non-traditional activities. Access to credit is particularly important for the start of new businesses.
- Infrastructure development. In agriculture, improved and cheaper transport is important to allow poor farmers to take advantage of new market opportunities. They should be a core component of 'aid for trade' programmes.
- Poverty Reduction Strategy Papers. A conscious effort needs to be made to integrate pro-poor trade strategies into Poverty Reduction Strategy Papers (see p. 471) that have to be prepared by countries for international organizations, such as the World Bank, to qualify for debt relief (see UNCTAD, 2004).

Income inequality

Let us now turn specifically to the issue of the impact of trade liberalization on wage and income inequality within countries, which is not necessarily the same as the impact on poverty or the poverty rate. Poverty can fall, but wage and income inequality can rise because the share of income going to the top income recipients rises by more than the share going to the bottom. In general, what will happen to the income distribution as trade liberalization takes place will depend on how the wage distribution is affected, how the distribution of assets changes and what happens to the rate of return on assets. Goldberg and Pavcnik (2007), in their survey of the distributional effects of globalization in developing countries, say: 'while inequality has many different dimensions, all existing measures of inequality for developing countries seem to point to an increase in inequality which in some cases is severe'. Table 15.2 gives the Gini ratios (as a measure of distribution – see Chapter 2, p. 28) for a selection of developing countries in the 1990s, and the latest figures available from the World Bank. Gini ratios are generally higher in Latin America than in Asia or Africa, but it can be seen that in most countries in the last decade or so, inequality has continued to increase. Brazil and Venezuela are notable exceptions where deliberate income redistribution policies have been implemented to raise the income of the poor.

Table 15.2   Income inequality in selected developing countries measured by the Gini ratio

Country	Earliest date in the 1990s[1]	Latest date in the 2000s[2]
Bangladesh	28.3	33.4
Bolivia	42.0	60.1
Brazil	63.4	57.0
Chile	56.5	54.9
China	41.5	46.9
Colombia	51.3	58.6
Dominican Republic	50.5	51.6
Egypt	32.0	34.4
Ghana	33.9	40.8
Honduras	52.7	53.8
India	33.8	36.8
Indonesia	31.7	34.3
Jamaica	41.1	45.5
Mexico	50.3	46.1
Nigeria	37.5	43.7
Pakistan	31.2	30.6
Peru	44.9	52.0
Philippines	40.7	44.5
Sri Lanka	30.1	40.2
Thailand	46.2	42.0
Venezuela	53.8	48.2
Zambia	46.2	50.8

Source: 1. World Bank, *World Development Indicators 1997*, Table 2.6 (Washington, DC: World Bank).
2. World Bank, *World Development Indicators 2007*, Table 2.7 (Washington, DC: World Bank).

The major cause of income inequality is wage inequality between skilled and unskilled workers. Orthodox trade theory (e.g. the Heckscher–Ohlin theory) predicts a narrowing of wage inequality in poor countries because their comparative advantage lies in the production and export of goods using abundant unskilled labour, which should raise wages of unskilled workers relative to skilled. But this narrowing has not happened. Robbins (1996), Freeman and Oostendrop (2001), Zhu and Trefler (2005) and Anderson (2005) all give extensive evidence of a worldwide trend towards greater wage inequality between skilled and unskilled labour in poor countries. There are four major reasons for this:

- Competition between poor countries themselves. Orthodox theory takes a two-country world – rich and poor. But poor countries trade with each other – for example, Mexico and China. Mexico's trade with the USA may raise the wages of unskilled relative to skilled labour in Mexico, but trading with China may reduce the wages of unskilled labour in Mexico.
- Flows of foreign direct investment to poor countries, and rich developed countries shifting the production of inputs to poor countries, or outsourcing (see the model of Feenstra and Hanson, 1997). This increases the demand for skilled labour in poor countries.

- Trade-related skill-biased technical change in poor countries either as a result of increased competition, and trying to 'catch up', or arising from the increased import of machinery from rich countries which increases the demand for skilled labour (see Wood, 1993, 1995, 1997).
- If trade liberalization causes balance-of-payments problems and the economy has contracted, this depresses the demand for unskilled labour and reduces relative wages (see Arbache et al., 2004 for a case study of Brazil).

Wage differences between skilled and unskilled workers are not the only source of income inequality, although according to Goldberg and Pavcnik (2007) income inequality tends to move in the same direction as wage inequality. Greater trade openness may alter the gap in earnings between men and women, between regions within a country and between rural and urban areas, and also change the rate of return on assets – all of which affect a measure of income inequality such as the Gini ratio. What is the evidence?

The most highly publicized and 'rose-tinted' view that trade openness has not worsened the income distribution and that 'growth is good for the poor', is the study by Dollar and Kraay (2002, 2004). First, they plot changes in the Gini ratio against changes in trade shares for more than 100 developed and developing countries, and find no relation. Secondly, they take 80 countries over 40 years and regress the growth of per capita income of the poorest 20 per cent of the population on the growth of average income per head, and find the relation is 1:1, that is, an elasticity of unity, and that the level of openness makes no difference to the coefficient. The authors express some surprise that they do not find a negative effect of openness on the poor, given all the assertions and adverse publicity of the anti-globalization movement. They do various tests of robustness and stick with their original conclusion, which is that 'openness to trade increases the income of the poor to the same extent that it increases the income of the other households in society'.

This is not the general consensus, however, of most other studies in this field. One direct contrary study is by Edward (2006), who uses world consumption data and finds that for roughly 1 billion people between the 50th and 70th percentile of the consumption distribution, consumption hardly changed between 1993 and 2001, and among the $2 a day poor, the ratio of their consumption growth to average growth was not 1:1 but 1:2. He concluded that 'growth is good for the poor but much better for the rich'.

The most detailed study of the impact of trade liberalization on the distribution of income is by Milanovic (2005). In his introductory survey of the existing literature, he remarks:

> The conclusions run nearly the full gamut, from openness reducing the real income of the poor to openness raising the income of the poor proportionately less than the income of the rich to raising both the same in relative terms. Note, however, that there are *no* results that show openness reducing inequality; that is raising the income of the poor more than the income of the rich – let alone raising the absolute income of the poor by more.

Milanovic's own research takes 321 household income surveys from 95 countries in 1988, and 113 countries in 1993 and 1998 covering 90 per cent of the world's population. The income is divided up into deciles, and inequality is measured by the income of the ith decile (i=1 to 10) of the population relative to the mean level of income of the whole population. For each decile, income inequality is then related to trade openness measured by the ratio of total trade to GDP, and also to openness interacted with the level of income to test whether the effect of openness on inequality varies with the level of income. Two striking results emerge. First, increased openness *reduces* the income share of the bottom six deciles. Secondly, the adverse effect of openness on inequality is greater the lower a country's per capita income. The poor only start to benefit relative to the rich at an income per capita of about $7,500 at 1990 prices. Barro (2000) and Spilimbergo et al. (1999) also find that openness worsens income inequality up to a certain point, and then the effect diminishes. Milanovic concludes: 'openness would therefore seem to have a particularly negative impact on poor and middle income groups in poor countries – directly opposite to what would be expected from the standard Heckscher–Ohlin framework'.

Trade liberalization and international inequality

Not only has the distribution of income within poor countries been increasing over time, but also the distribution of income between poor and rich countries. We showed the evidence in Chapter 2. The unweighted Gini ratio for international inequality (taking each country's average per capita income as a single observation unweighted by population size) shows a steady historical rise from 1820, and also in the postwar period of trade liberalization from 1952. The population-weighted Gini ratio of international inequality shows a slight decline in recent years due to the fast growth of populous countries such as China and India. If China is taken from the sample, the population-weighted Gini ratio also shows a rise. The Gini ratio for global inequality (which takes account of the distribution of income within countries, as well as between countries) has increased over time but has been relatively static in recent years because while between-country inequality (population-weighted) has fallen slightly, income inequality within countries has increased, particularly in China between the rural and urban sector.

The question is: how much of this rising and persistent inequality across the world is due to trade liberalization? Is freer trade equilibrating or disequilibrating? This is not an easy question to answer, but attempts can be made. One methodological approach is to interact a measure of trade openness with the level of per capita income (PCY) to test whether the impact of openness varies with the level of development. This is what Dowrick and Golley (2004) do, taking over 100 countries for two separate time periods 1960–80 and 1980–2000. For the first period, a higher trade share of one percentage point (p.p.) is associated with 0.11 per cent faster growth, and the poorer the country, the slightly greater the benefit from openness, meaning that trade liberalization was a force for convergence. But for the second period, this result is reversed. The impact of the trade share on the growth of PCY is now negative, and poor countries suffered more than rich countries, leading to divergence. Dividing the 1980–2000 sample of countries into 30 poorest countries and the rest shows no significant effect of the trade share on growth in the poorest countries, but the richer countries gained about 0.012 per cent growth for a 1 percentage point increase in the trade share. Specialization in primary products had a strong negative effect on growth in the 1980–2000 period, reducing it on average by nearly 1 per cent; and the impact was even stronger in the poor country group, a difference of 1.7 per cent. Dowrick and Golley's conclusion is that 'trade has promoted strong divergence in productivity [between countries] since 1980'.

Ghose (2004) has also examined this issue, and reaches a more neutral conclusion. He takes 96 countries over the period 1981–1997, and examines the relationship between the rate of change of the trade/GDP ratio (as a measure of trade liberalization) and both the level of PCY in 1981 and the size of population. Overall, he finds that the effect of trade liberalization on growth performance has been much the same for poor and rich countries, and that, therefore, trade liberalization has had no discernible effect on international inequality. On the other hand, there seems to be a positive relationship between trade performance and population size, and this may have contributed to the decline in the population-weighted Gini ratio mentioned above. The result is heavily influenced by China and India, the two most populous countries in the world, both of which started with a very low trade base in 1981. In both cases, however, export growth has been the driving force, not trade liberalization per se.

All we can say with some confidence is that there is little evidence that free trade has contributed to a narrowing of the income gap between countries, as predicted by orthodox trade and growth theory. Despite growing trade between countries, income disparities are as wide as ever.

Disadvantages of free trade for development

Even if trade-liberalized countries did perform (on average) better than non-liberalized countries, this does not mean that all developing countries should liberalize as quickly as possible, and that there is no role for protection and government intervention to improve trade and growth performance. Indeed, we have seen that this is exactly what many successful East Asian countries have done. It is also worth remembering that historically no country developed on the basis of free trade. The countries of Europe, North America and Scandinavia all developed their industrial sectors with the aid of tariff and non-tariff protection (see Chang, 2002, 2005, 2008; Reinert, 2007). Trade liberalization is not a substitute for a trade and development strategy.

Now let us consider, therefore, the potential disadvantages of free trade, and the weaknesses of the comparative cost doctrine that underlies it. Like most micro-welfare theories, the comparative advantage/free trade argument is a *static* one based on restrictive and very often unrealistic assumptions. The doctrine assumes, for example, the existence of full employment in each country (otherwise there would be no opportunity cost involved in expanding the production of commodities), that the prices of resources and goods reflect their opportunity cost (that is, that perfect competition exists), and that factor endowments are given and unalterable. Moreover, the doctrine ignores the effect of free trade on the terms of trade (movements in which affect real income), and the balance-of-payments consequences of free trade. As a result it can be argued that the principle of comparative advantage is not very useful in the context of developing countries, which are in need of rapid structural change and are as much concerned with long-term development as with short-term efficiency. As many economists have commented, the doctrine of comparative advantage is more useful in explaining the *past* pattern of trade than in providing a guide as to what the future pattern of trade should be as a stimulus to development.

The question is not whether there should be trade but whether there should be *free trade*, as the doctrine of comparative advantage implies. Perhaps the long-run needs of developing countries would be better served, at least initially, by various forms of protection.

The development considerations that the doctrine of free trade overlooks are numerous. First, it ignores the balance-of-payments effects of free trade and the effect of free trade on the terms of trade. If the demands for different commodities grow at different rates owing to differences in their price and income elasticity of demand, free trade will work to the benefit of some countries and to the relative detriment of others. In classical theory, Torrens, J. S. Mill, Marshall, Edgeworth and Taussig all conceded that unilateral substitution by a country of free trade for protection would move the terms of trade against the country. But most 'free traders' ignored the issue. In general, the implicit assumption was that moving from protection to free trade would not alter the commodity terms of trade, or if it did, the gains from trade would more than offset any unfavourable terms of trade effect. If the terms of trade effect does offset the gains from trade, this is a valid argument for protection (see below, p. 535).

A second factor that the free trade doctrine tends to overlook is that some activities are subject to increasing returns while others are subject to diminishing returns. The commodities most susceptible to diminishing returns are primary products, where the scope for technical progress may also be less than in the case of manufactured goods. This being so, one might expect a rise in the ratio of primary to manufactured goods prices, and diminishing returns would not matter so much if the goods were price inelastic. In practice, however, there has been a substitution of synthetic alternatives for primary products, and the terms of trade have deteriorated (see below), partly because of substitution and partly because of the fact that the demand for primary commodities in general, in relation to supply, has expanded much less than for manufactured commodities. But whatever the movement in the terms of trade, it would surely be perverse to base a trade and development strategy on activities subject to diminishing returns, particularly in light of the theory of cumulative causation, which we discussed in Chapter 8.

A third disadvantage of adherence to the comparative advantage doctrine is that it could lead to excessive specialization in a narrow range of products, putting the economy at the mercy of outside influences. The possibility exists of severe balance-of-payments instability arising from specialization, which could be damaging to development.

Fourth, static comparative cost analysis ignores the fact that comparative advantage can be altered by deliberate policies to promote certain activities. There is no reason why countries should be condemned to the production and export of the same commodities forever. No country was endowed with the *natural* ability to produce industrial goods. Now that technology and capital accumulation, rather than natural resources, are the basis for trade, comparative advantage is no longer predetermined or predictable. Hausmann and Rodrik (2003) document how countries somehow stumble on lucrative niche markets almost by accident: hats in Bangladesh, cut flowers in Colombia, footballs and bed sheets in Pakistan and software in India, to give just a few examples. If there is any explanation at all, it is entrepreneurial trial and error. If comparative advantage is not given by nature but can be altered, the case for initial protection is strengthened (the classic infant industry argument).

It should also be remembered that the concept of comparative advantage is based on calculations of private cost. But we observed in Chapter 11 that social costs in developing countries may diverge markedly from private costs, and that social benefits may exceed private benefits because of externalities. If private costs exceed social costs in industry (because wage rates are artificially high, for example), and social benefits from industrial projects exceed private benefits, there is a strong argument for protecting industry in order to encourage the transfer of labour from other activities into industry to equate private and social cost and private and social benefit.

Finally, it may be mentioned that the export growth of some activities has relatively little secondary impact on other activities. Primary commodities fall into this category. There is abundant evidence that the export growth of primary commodities has not had the development impact that might have been expected from the expansion of industrial exports. The reasons for this are not hard to understand. Primary production has very few backward or forward linkages; and historically it has tended to be undertaken by foreign enterprises, with a consequent outflow of profits. The secondary repercussions of the pattern of trade are overlooked by the free trade doctrine.

Theory of protection: tariffs versus subsidies

We have seen that trade brings substantial benefits, but it does not follow that the freer the trade the better. There are many disadvantages that the doctrine of free trade overlooks when trade is considered in a long-run development context, as opposed to the static short-run context of the doctrine of comparative advantage. Furthermore, free trade does not guarantee an equal distribution of the gains from trade, and this is an important consideration for countries that naturally look to their relative position compared with others, and not only at their absolute performance.

We can summarize the **arguments for protection** as follows (see Johnson, 1964). First there are purely **economic arguments** that comprise all arguments in favour of protection as a means of increasing real output or income above what it would otherwise be. These include the following:

- The infant industry argument – allowing industries to reach their optimum size in terms of minimum average costs of production
- The existence of external economies in production, where the social cost of production is less than the private cost
- Distortions in the labour market that make the social cost of using labour less than the private cost
- International distortions that cause the domestic rate of transformation between goods to diverge from the foreign rate of transformation; due, for, example, to monopoly power in international trade. This argument for protection is often referred to as the **optimum tariff argument**.

This category of economic arguments might also include two factors previously stressed: terms of trade deterioration and balance-of-payments difficulties arising from the pattern of trade. Johnson (1964) and others of neoclassical persuasion have argued that these are non-arguments because in the case of the terms of trade, the restriction of imports will not reduce import prices for a small country; and in the case of the balance of payments, equilibrium can be achieved automatically by letting the exchange rate float freely.

The terms of trade argument may be correct, but the balance-of-payments argument suffers from confusion between a balance-of-payments equilibrium on the current account, which affects the real economy, and balance in the foreign exchange market. The two are not the same. A floating exchange rate by definition will equilibrate the foreign exchange market, but will not necessarily equilibrate the balance of payments on current account. If both terms of trade deterioration and balance-of-payments difficulties constrain growth and lead to unemployment, the social cost of labour will be less than the private cost, which is a domestic distortion and an economic argument for protection.

Second, **non-economic arguments** for protection tend to be arguments in favour of protection for its own sake rather than to increase output or income above what it would otherwise be. Industrialization at any price and self-sufficiency for strategic reasons are examples of this type of argument.

Having summarized the arguments in favour of protection, the question then is, what is the best means of protection? It can be shown that tariffs are appropriate only under special circumstances: when the distortions are international (the optimum tariff argument) and when self-sufficiency is the objective. All other arguments for protection are arguments for subsidies, the reason being that when distortions are domestic a tariff will introduce further distortions,

Figure 15.6   Welfare gains and losses from protection

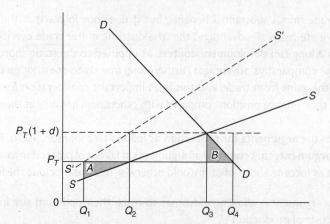

and according to the **theory of the second best** there is no way of knowing *a priori* whether the situation will be made better or worse.

The argument can be illustrated with a diagram. Consider Figure 15.6, where a good that is producible domestically is subject to a domestic distortion such that the private cost of production ($S'S'$) is d per cent above the social cost (SS). The demand curve is DD and the good is also importable at the international price, P_t. Under free trade, domestic producers will produce up to Q_1 and Q_1 to Q_4 will be imported. Q_1 to Q_2 imports could be replaced, however, by additional domestic production, with real savings equal to the shaded area A, if domestic producers were given a subsidy of d per cent. The same real income gain could be achieved by a tariff of the same percentage, but because the domestic price rises to $P_T(1 + d)$, there will be a loss of consumer surplus equal to the shaded area B owing to the restriction of consumption by Q_3Q_4. The loss of consumer surplus may be greater than the real income gain reducing total welfare. The balance of advantage depends on the relative slopes of the supply and demand curves. In these circumstances a subsidy to labour is unequivocally first-best.

Now let us consider the relative merits of tariffs and subsidies where the arguments in favour of protection are non-economic. Suppose, for example, the objective of protection is simply to increase domestic output. Here subsidies are also superior to tariffs because tariffs impose a consumption cost and add nothing more to the achievement of increased production. Consider Figure 15.7. We assume that there is no domestic distortion, so the SS curve represents both the private and the social cost of production. Now suppose that the object is to raise domestic production from Q_1 to Q_2. This can be done with a tariff or subsidy of d per cent that uses extra resources equal to the shaded area A. The tariff, however, imposes an extra consumption cost equal to area B as a result of a rise in the price from P_T to $P_T(1 + d)$.

On the other hand, if the objective is self-sufficiency and to cut back imports, we can show that tariffs are the least costly. The reason for this is that it is more efficient to reduce imports by jointly restricting consumption and increasing domestic production, than by doing either of these on their own. Consider Figure 15.7 again. A tariff of d per cent reduces imports to Q_2Q_3 at a cost of $A + B$. To get the same reduction with a subsidy requires a subsidy in excess of d per cent in order to induce extra domestic production Q_2Q_5 (equal to the cutback in consumption through the tariff of Q_3Q_4). This involves an extra cost equal to the area $C + D$. Since $C > B$, the cost of the subsidy policy is obviously greater than the cost of the tariff.

Figure 15.7   Tariffs and subsidies

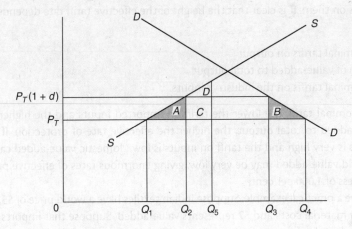

If subsidies are first-best they may be effectively granted by exemption from taxation. If this exemption is from existing taxes, it will have revenue implications for the government budget. In the long run, however, subsidies can be 'self-financing' by the increased output they stimulate.

A further argument against tariffs and in favour of subsidies is that tariffs are very 'inward-looking', whereas protection through subsidies is much more 'outward-looking'. Tariffs adjust the internal price structure to the (high) internal cost structure. This may lead to inefficiencies and make it difficult for exports to compete when the effects of import-substitution policies cease. Subsidies, in contrast, adjust the internal cost structure to the (low) external price structure and make it possible for exports to compete more easily in world markets.

Effective protection

In assessing the restrictive effect that a tariff structure has on trade, however, it is not enough just to look at the nominal tariff on finished goods.[3] The nominal rate does not measure how inefficient (or costly) producers can be without incurring competition and losing their market. This is measured by the protection of **value-added**, which is the difference between the value of output and the value of inputs. The protection of value-added is the so-called **effective rate of protection**. Since value-added is the difference between the value of output and inputs, not only is the tariff on output important when measuring the degree of protection, but also the tariff on inputs.

Formally, the effective rate of protection is measured as the excess of domestic value-added over value-added at world prices, expressed as a percentage of the latter. Thus the effective rate of protection of industry X may be defined as:

$$EP_x = \frac{V'_x - V_x}{V_x} = \frac{V'_x}{V_x} - 1$$

where V'_x is domestic value-added under protection and V_x is value-added under free market conditions (at world prices). Domestic value-added is equal to the sale of the industry's product minus the sum of intermediate inputs, all valued at domestic market prices; that is, including the effect of tariffs on the finished good and on the inputs into the finished good. The free market value-added can be defined identically, but with the final product and input prices measured exclusive of tariffs on them. It is clear that the height of the effective tariff rate depends on three variables:

- The level of nominal tariffs on output
- The proportion of value-added to total output
- The level of nominal tariffs on the industry's inputs.

The higher the nominal tariff, the lower the tariff on imported inputs and the higher the proportion of value-added to total output, the higher the effective rate of protection. If the tariff on finished goods is very high and the tariff on inputs is low, domestic value-added can be very high; in turn, world value-added may be very low, giving enormous rates of effective protection, sometimes in excess of 1,000 per cent.

Let us now give a practical example. Suppose Indian textiles have a world price of $5, of which $3 represents raw material costs and $2 represents value-added. Suppose that imports of Indian textiles into a developed country are subject to a tariff of 20 per cent while domestic producers must pay a tariff of 10 per cent on textile raw materials. To remain competitive, the domestic producer must produce the commodity for not more than $6. The value-added can be $6 minus the cost of raw materials plus the tariff on raw materials, that is, $6 − ($3 + $0.30) = $2.70. The effective rate of protection is the difference between domestic value-added and Indian value-added (that is, value-added at world prices), expressed as a percentage of Indian value-added, that is, (2.70 − 2)/2 = 35 per cent. This is the effective rate of protection, equal to the difference between the gross subsidy on value-added provided by the tariff on the final product ($(1/2) = 50 per cent) and the implicit tax on value-added as a result of the tariff on raw materials ($(0.30/2) = 15 per cent). This is the extent (35 per cent) to which production can be more costly in the developed country without losing competitive advantage; or, to put it another way, it is the degree to which Indian textile producers would have to be more productive to compete in the developed country market.

Effective rates of protection almost always exceed nominal rates. At one extreme, if a country obtains raw material inputs that are duty free (at world prices) but puts a tariff on the final good, the effective rate must be higher than the nominal rate. At the other extreme, if a country puts a tariff on inputs but no tariff on the finished good, the effective rate of protection is negative.[4]

Calculation of the effective rate of protection also depends on the exchange rate. If the exchange rate of a country in the protected situation is overvalued, the price of imported inputs measured in domestic currency will be undervalued, and this will affect the calculation of the domestic value-added and the value-added at world market prices. Without adjustment for this factor, effective rates of protection are described as 'gross'; with adjustment they are referred to as 'net'.

Our example of the effective rate of protection also assumes that all inputs are traded. Some inputs will be non-traded, however, and their price enters into the value of both total output and total inputs. If the effect of protection on the price of non-traded goods is ignored, the rates of effective protection will be overestimated. In practice it is not easy to estimate the effect of protection on the price of non-traded goods.

The theory of effective protection suggests that the same *nominal* tariff cuts mean different degrees of change in effective rates of protection, and it may thus be unwise for the developing countries to press for across-the-board tariff cuts on all commodities. *Reductions in tariffs against their primary products will increase the effective rate of protection against their manufactures,* which, we have argued, are the more important exports as far as long-run development prospects are concerned. The average nominal level of protection in developed countries is about 4 per cent, but effective protection against the goods of developing countries may well be in the region of 30 per cent or more. Developing countries themselves may give their own producers very high rates of effective protection.

Import substitution versus export promotion

In the early stages of production, the protectionist strategy of import substitution using tariffs is undoubtedly the easiest and many countries have pursued it, particularly in Latin America in the 1950s to the 1970s. However, there are different stages of import substitution, and some are easier than others. The first easy stage involves the replacement by domestic production of imports of non-durable consumption goods such as clothing, footwear, leather and wood products. Countries in the early stages of industrialization are naturally suited to these products and relatively little protection is required. Once this stage is over, the maintenance of high growth rates then requires the import substitution of other goods if the strategy is to be continued.

The problem with this second stage of import substitution is that relatively high rates of protection are required, because intermediate goods such as steel and producer durables are subject to substantial economies of scale, both internal and external, so that unit costs are very high if output is low. The problem with high rates of protection is that they breed inefficiency, and more importantly act as a tax on exports by keeping costs and the exchange rate high. The catalogue of costs and distortions introduced by protective import-substitution policies is formidable. Import substitution tends to shift the distribution of income in favour of the urban sector and the higher-income groups with a higher propensity to import, thereby worsening the balance of payments. Protection taxes agriculture since it raises the price of industrial goods relative to agricultural goods. Furthermore, since protection maintains an artificially high exchange rate it reduces receipts in terms of domestic currency from a given quantity of agricultural exports, which may discourage agricultural production. Import substitution may also worsen unemployment by encouraging capital-intensive activities.

Despite the dangers of the second stage of import substitution, this is the strategy that many Latin American, South-East Asian and Eastern European countries adopted in the immediate postwar years. The consequence was that the export of manufactures was discouraged and the terms of trade turned against agriculture within the countries, discouraging agricultural output and reducing the growth of demand for industrial products internally. In the 1960s reforms were undertaken in several countries, but there was a distinct difference in emphasis and approach between Latin America and South-East Asia. In Latin America, policies became more 'outward-looking' but still favoured production for the domestic market. Although subsidies were given to exports, exporters were still required to use domestic inputs produced under protection, and the subsidies were generally insufficient to provide an incentive to export that was comparable to the protection of domestic markets, and thus there was a continued bias in favour of import substitution. In East and South-East Asia, in contrast, the policy has always been one of relentless export expansion – in Japan, South Korea, Singapore, Taiwan and other countries, as outlined earlier. Now most developing countries are attempting to follow this route with varying degrees of success.

The Prebisch doctrine[5]

An alternative approach to trade in developing countries

Raúl Prebisch (1901–86) was one of the first development economists to question the mutual profitability of the international division of labour for developing countries on existing lines. He looked at the relation between trade and development from the standpoint of the balance of payments rather than the augmentation of real resources. His major claim was that the unfavourable impact of unrestricted trade on the terms of trade and balance of payments of developing countries can far outweigh any advantages with respect to a more efficient allocation of resources. His concern was with two distinct, but not unrelated, phenomena. One is the transference of the benefits of technical progress from the developing to the developed countries through terms of trade deterioration. The second is the balance-of-payments effects of differences in the income elasticity of demand for different types of products. He divided the world into industrial 'centres' and 'peripheral' countries, and then conducted his analysis within the framework of the traditional two-country, two-commodity case of international trade theory – equating the developing countries with primary producers (the 'periphery') and the developed countries with industrial producers (the 'centre').

Technical progress and the terms of trade

As stated earlier, in theory the barter terms of trade might be expected to move in favour of the developing countries. For one thing, primary-product production tends to be subject to diminishing returns, and for another, technical progress tends to be more rapid in manufacturing industry than in agriculture. If prices are related to costs one would expect that in theory the ratio of primary-product prices to industrial-good prices would rise. According to Prebisch (1950), however, the ratio had shown a long-run historical tendency to fall. He advanced two explanations of this and hence why the benefits of technical progress tend to flow from the developing to developed countries and not the other way round. His first explanation concerns the relation between incomes and productivity. He suggested that whereas factor incomes tend to rise with productivity increases in developed countries, they rise more slowly than productivity in the developing countries owing to surplus labour. Thus there is a greater upward pressure on final goods' prices in developed than in developing countries, causing the ratio of prices to move in the opposite direction to that suggested by the pace of technical progress. All this is on the supply side.

On the demand side is the fact that the demand for primary products grows more slowly than that for industrial products as world income grows, for two major reasons: (1) many primary commodities have intrinsically low-income elasticities of demand because they are necessities; and (2) many primary commodities have been substituted by synthetics, for example natural rubber. Putting these demand and supply factors together gives the picture in Figure 15.8, which shows what is likely to happen to the terms of trade of primary commodities through time.

In the centre, the supply and demand curves for industrial goods are relatively elastic, and in the periphery, the supply and demand curves for primary products are relatively inelastic. Assume initially that the supply and demand curves intersect at the same point in both sectors, so that the prices of industrial and primary products are 'equal' (that is, the terms of trade = 1). In the centre,

Figure 15.8   Movements in the terms of trade

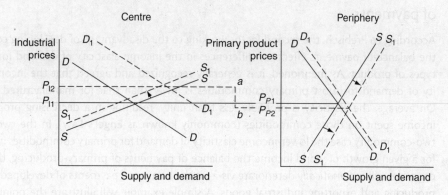

technical progress will first shift the supply curve (SS) outwards, but let us assume that increases in wage costs push it back inwards to S_1S_1. In the periphery, in contrast, technical progress shifts the supply curve outwards to S_1S_1, but there is no inward shift due to rising wage costs. In the centre, the demand for industrial goods grows strongly from DD to D_1D_1, while in the periphery the demand for primary products grows only slowly. The price of industrial goods rises to P_{I2}, while the price of primary products in this example has actually fallen to P_{p2}. The terms of trade of primary products has deteriorated by the amount ab for fundamental economic reasons associated with the characteristics of the products and the institutional structures of the countries that produce them.

Prebisch also put forward a separate independent hypothesis of the secular deterioration in the terms of trade of primary products: the operation of a ratchet effect, with the prices of primary products *relative* to those of manufactured goods falling during cyclical downturns by more than they rise *relative* to the prices of manufactures on the upturns. Such asymmetrical cycles, illustrated in Figure 15.9, would produce a secular trend deterioration.

However, the asymmetry hypothesis does not seem to be supported in the years since the Second World War (see Thirlwall and Bergevin, 1985), or for the longer period since 1900 (see Diakosavvas and Scandizzo, 1991), except for a few commodities such as rice, cotton, rubber and coffee, and even then the difference between the elasticity of prices on the downswing and on the upswing is quite small.

Figure 15.9   Asymmetrical cycles

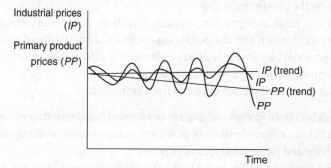

The income elasticity of demand for products and the balance of payments

According to Prebisch, the second factor working to the disadvantage of developing countries is the balance-of-payments effects of differences in the income elasticity of demand for different types of product. As mentioned, it is generally recognized and agreed that the income elasticity of demand for most primary commodities is lower than that for manufactured products. On average, the elasticity is probably less than unity, resulting in a decreasing proportion of income spent on those commodities (commonly known as **Engel's Law**). In the two-country, two-commodity case the lower-income elasticity of demand for primary commodities means that for a given growth of world income the balance of payments of primary-producing, developing countries will *automatically* deteriorate vis-à-vis the balance of payments of developed countries producing and exporting industrial goods. A simple example will illustrate the point (see also Chapter 8, p. 271).

Suppose that the income elasticity of demand for the exports of the developing countries is 0.8 and that the growth of world income is 3.0 per cent: exports will then grow at 2.4 per cent. Now suppose that the income elasticity of demand for the exports of developed countries is 1.3 and the growth of world income is 3.0 per cent; exports of developed countries will then grow at 3.9 per cent. Since there are only two sets of countries, the developing countries' exports are the imports of developed countries and the exports of developed countries are the imports of the developing countries. Thus developing countries' exports grow at 2.4 per cent but imports grow at 3.9 per cent; developed countries' exports grow at 3.9 per cent and imports at 2.4 per cent. Starting from equilibrium, the balance of payments of the developing countries automatically worsens while that of the developed countries shows a surplus. This has further repercussions on the terms of trade. With imports growing faster than exports in developing countries, and the balance of payments deteriorating, the terms of trade will also deteriorate through depreciation of the currency, which may cause the balance of payments to deteriorate even more if imports and exports are price inelastic.

It is easily seen that the price of balance-of-payments equilibrium is slower growth for the developing countries. If their exports are growing at 2.4 per cent, import growth must be constrained to 2.4 per cent, which means that with an income elasticity of demand for imports of 1.3, income growth in the developing countries must be restrained to 2.4/1.3 = 1.85 per cent for balance-of-payments equilibrium. In the absence of foreign borrowing to bridge the foreign exchange gap, or a change in the structure of exports, the result of different income elasticities of demand for primary and manufactured products is slower growth in the primary-producing countries – perpetuating the development 'gap'.

For terms of trade and balance-of-payments reasons (which are connected), Prebisch therefore argued for import substitution and the protection of certain domestically produced goods. Prebisch's balance-of-payments argument reinforces the classical infant industry and optimum-tariff (terms of trade improvement) argument for protection.

There are several benefits that Prebisch expected from protection:

- Protection would enable scarce foreign exchange to be rationed between different categories of imports, and could help to correct balance-of-payments disequilibrium resulting from a high-income elasticity of demand for certain types of imports.
- It could help to arrest the deterioration in the terms of trade by damping down the demand for imports.

- It could provide the opportunity to diversify products and to start producing and exporting goods with a much higher-income elasticity of demand in world markets.
- Following our earlier analysis, however, protection by tariffs is only appropriate if the arguments for protection do not arise from domestic distortions.

Recent trends in the terms of trade

Primary commodities

Whether the terms of trade have moved unfavourably against primary commodities and the developing countries is an empirical question. Prebisch originally suggested an average deterioration of the terms of trade of primary commodities between 1876 and 1938 of 0.9 per cent per annum. Work by Hans Singer at the United Nations in 1949 also suggested a trend deterioration of 0.64 per cent per annum over the same period, and thus the **Prebisch–Singer thesis** of the declining terms of trade for primary commodities was born (see Singer, 1950). In a detailed reappraisal of Prebisch's work, Spraos (1980) confirmed the historical trend deterioration, but at the lower rate of approximately 0.5 per cent, having corrected the statistics for the changing quality of goods, shipping costs and other factors. Extending the data to 1970, however, Spraos concluded that there had been no significant trend deterioration. Sapsford (1985, 1988), however, shows that it is the 'wartime' structural improvement (1940–51) that makes the whole series look trendless. If the series is divided into two subperiods – pre- and post-Second World War – there is a trend deterioration in both subperiods and the estimated trend deterioration over the whole period 1900–82 is 1.2 per cent per annum, allowing for the wartime structural break.

Hans Singer

Born 1910, Elberfield, Germany. Died 2006. He came to England in 1933 as a refugee to work on his Ph.D. with Keynes at Cambridge. He joined the United Nations in 1947 and was instrumental in the establishment of bodies such as the International Development Association of the World Bank; the United Nations Development Programme, and the World Food Programme. At the same time he taught at the New School for Social Research in New York. In 1969 he joined the Institute for Development Studies at the University of Sussex from where he travelled and lectured widely, advising several countries and development institutions. Through his prolific writing, he championed the world's poor, and was a passionate advocate of international aid. Linked with the name of Prebisch and the thesis of a declining terms of trade of primary commodities.

Since the original Spraos and Sapsford evaluations of the Prebisch–Singer thesis, there has been an outpouring of further studies using different time periods and different statistical estimating techniques. Grilli and Yang (1988) at the World Bank constructed their own series of the terms of trade and also looked at individual commodities, but reached similar conclusions to Sapsford.

Over the period 1900–83 they put the percentage terms of trade deterioration of all primary commodities at 0.5 per cent per annum, and 0.6 per cent per annum for non-fuel commodities (allowing for a wartime structural break). For individual commodities the trend deterioration is estimated as follows: food, −0.3 per cent per annum; cereals, −0.6 per cent per annum; non-food agricultural commodities, −0.8 per cent per annum; and metals, −0.8 per cent per annum. Only tropical beverages registered an improvement of 0.6 per cent per annum. Bleaney and Greenaway (1993) updated the Grilli–Yang series to 1991 and estimated a trend deterioration of 0.8 per cent per annum, with a big structural break in the early 1980s associated with world recession and the supply response of developing countries attempting to export themselves out of debt difficulties.

Another study is by Cashin and McDermott (2002) at the IMF, who look at trends and cycles in both the nominal and real price (i.e. the terms of trade) of non-food commodities over the period 1862 to 1999. The graphs of both indices are shown in Figure 15.10.

Nominal prices were relatively stable from 1862 to 1932 (except during the First World War), but since then have been very volatile around a rising trend. The real price index, however, or the terms of trade of primary commodities, has always been very volatile around a generally declining trend. The average trend decline over the whole period 1862–1999 is 1.3 per cent per annum. From an index of 120 in 1862 to an index of 20 in 1999, real commodity prices lost 85 per cent of their value. Or, to put it another way, in 1999 primary commodities could only buy 20 per cent of the industrial goods that they could buy in 1862. This represents a substantial real income loss. The estimated trend decline is even more serious if the commodity boom years of 1951 or 1973 are taken as the starting point for analysis.

Cashin and McDermott also focus on the magnitude and length of the cycles in real commodity prices, which they believe to be more serious than the trend decline. They find 13 occasions since 1913 when the annual price change was more than 20 per cent in one year. This is

Figure 15.10   Nominal and real price indices of non-food primary commodities, 1862–1999

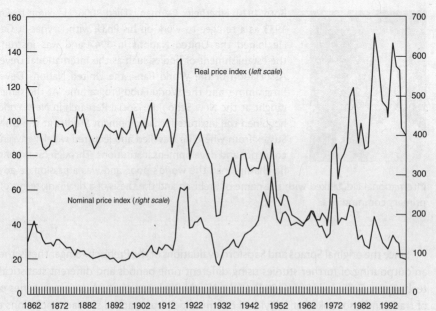

serious volatility. They also find that average price slumps last longer than price booms (4.2 years compared with 3.6 years).

The authors conclude their study by saying:

> Although there is a downward trend in real commodity prices, this is of little policy relevance, because it is small compared with the variability of prices. In contrast, rapid, unexpected and often large movements in commodity prices are an important feature of their behaviour. Such movements can have serious consequences for the terms of trade, real incomes, and fiscal positions of commodity-dependent countries, and have profound implications for the achievement of macroeconomic stabilisation.

Blattman et al. (2007) have looked historically at the relationship between terms of trade volatility and growth, taking 35 countries over the period 1870–1939 and finding a negative relationship, and this is one of the major reasons why the income gap between the 'periphery' primary producing countries and the industrial countries widened during this period. One major adverse effect of volatility was the deterrent to foreign direct investment.

Developing countries

As already indicated, the terms of trade of primary commodities relative to manufactures is not necessarily the same as the terms of trade of developing countries relative to developed countries, because both sets of countries export and import both types of goods (albeit in different ratios), but in practice there is likely to be a close overlap and parallel movement between the two. Sarkar (1986) has looked at the export prices of developing countries relative to those of developed countries, and also at the prices of exports from developing to developed countries relative to the prices of imports from developed countries into developing countries (both excluding fuel). In the first case the trend deterioration was 0.51 per cent per annum; in the second case the relative deterioration was 0.93 per cent per annum.

Bleaney and Greenaway (1993) find that over the period 1955–89 a 1 per cent deterioration in the terms of trade of primary products translated into a 0.3 per cent deterioration in the terms of trade for developing countries as a whole, although this would have been substantially greater for Africa and Latin America, which are more commodity-dependent than Asia.

Sarkar and Singer (1991, 1993) have also looked at the terms of trade of *manufactures* exported by developing countries relative to those of developed countries over the period 1970–87, and find a deterioration of approximately 1 per cent per annum. If this is the case,[6] it would appear that the developing countries suffer double jeopardy. Not only do the prices of their primary products decline relative to those of manufactured goods, but also the prices of their manufactured exports decline relative to those of developed countries; reflecting, no doubt, the commodity composition of these exports – their lower value-added and lower income elasticity of demand in world markets. This is confirmed by Erten (2010), who has carefully examined the terms of trade for different groups of developing countries using UNCTAD data (e.g. countries exporting mainly primary commodities; countries exporting mainly manufactures; the least developed countries; the highly indebted countries), and finds in all cases a decline in their terms of trade from 1960 to 2006 of between 1 and 3 per cent per annum, with a severe structural break in the mid-1970s.

Finally, it must be mentioned that there is a distinction between the **barter (or commodity) terms of trade**, which measures the ratio of export to import prices, and the **income terms of trade**, which is the ratio of export to import prices times the quantity of exports, that is, $(Px/Pm) \times Qx$. The income terms of trade is thus a measure of the total purchasing power of exports over imports. From the point of view of development, measured by per capita income, the income terms of trade is perhaps the more relevant concept to consider than the barter terms of trade. It may well be, for instance, that the prices of exports fall relative to those of imports owing to increased efficiency in the exporting country, and this releases resources for further exports, which subsequently expand more than proportionately to the fall in price. The barter terms of trade will have worsened, but the country will be better off. It is also worth remembering that when a country devalues its currency it deliberately worsens its barter terms of trade in the hope that the balance of payments will improve, providing scope for a faster growth of real income through a rapid improvement in the income terms of trade. On the other hand, if the demand for a country's exports is price inelastic, then a decline in the barter terms of trade will also mean a deterioration in the income terms of trade.

In the long run, if world trade is buoyant, all countries can experience an improvement in their income terms of trade. The question is not who are the gainers and who are the losers, as in the case of the barter terms of trade, but what are the *relative* rates of improvement in the income terms of trade?

Fair trade not free trade

Trade policies towards developing countries

Developed countries, supported by multilateral institutions such as the IMF, World Bank and the World Trade Organization (WTO), preach the virtues of trade liberalization and free trade for developing countries, but fail to practise it themselves. In particular, the rich countries still protect their agricultural sectors with subsidies and tariffs which make it difficult, and sometimes impossible, for poor developing countries to compete in world markets. The case of cotton is highlighted in Case example 15.2. Agricultural subsidies in the European Union (EU) and the USA amount to over $400 billion per annum, which is over half the GDP of Africa. Each cow in the EU earns a subsidy of $800 per annum, which is more than the average income per head of at least 2 billion people living in developing countries. Developed countries also impose tariffs on agricultural imports from developing countries, and subsidize exports. The average tariff against agricultural imports into developed countries is 23 per cent. US rice farmers receive a 72 per cent subsidy. Dumping of artificially cheap crops from rich country agribusiness has destroyed thousands of small farmers in developing countries.

Case example 15.2	**Unfair trade in cotton**

The USA spends $3.3 billion a year on subsidies to 25,000 cotton farmers which profoundly affects the livelihoods of 10 million cotton farmers in the west and central African countries of Burkina Faso, Benin, Chad and Mali. This subsidy to US cotton producers is three times the US aid budget to the whole of Africa. The tragedy is that the World Bank has encouraged these African countries to produce more cotton on the pretext of comparative advantage, but they find it impossible to compete against such subsidies. The US Trade Representative at the Doha Round of WTO trade negotiations in 2002 had the audacity to tell the cotton farmers of Africa that 'they should do something else'.

The protection afforded to agriculture is also given to many low value-added manufactured goods in which developing countries have a static comparative advantage – particularly for a wide range of textile goods. Trade barriers against the exports of developing countries cost these countries approximately $100 billion a year, which is equal to the amount they receive in official development assistance.

When it comes to the reality of free trade, as opposed to the rhetoric, there appears to be one law for the rich developed nations and another for the poor. As long as the terms of trade of primary products continue to decline, and the agricultural products of developing countries are discriminated against in world markets, trade between the developed and developing countries cannot be fair. The playing field between rich and poor countries is not level, and the rich countries seem to want to keep it that way. What developing countries want is fair trade not free trade.[7]

The **World Trade Organization**, established in 1995 (formerly the General Agreement on Tariffs and Trade – the GATT – founded in 1947) is the major international body that negotiates multilateral tariff reductions between countries. Up to now, however, it has been singularly unsuccessful in freeing trade in agricultural commodities. The **Kennedy Round** of trade negotiations (1964–67), the **Tokyo Round** (1973–79) and the **Uruguay Round** (1986–93) all focused mainly on reducing tariffs on trade in manufactures (with some preferential treatment for developing countries). It was in Seattle in 1999 that the developing countries began to raise their voice concerning agricultural protection, but the talks ended in failure. The rich countries refused to make any concessions over agriculture, and the trade round collapsed amid recriminations and violent street protests. In November 2001, the **Doha Round** was launched. This was supposed to be a 'development' round (to help poor countries), but in 2009 the talks ended with no agreement being reached because of the insistence by rich countries that they will only cut farm subsidies and trade barriers if the developing countries allow them access to their markets for manufactured goods and the financial services sector, and enforce stricter competition rules and transparency in government procurement. The United States' reaction to the breakdown of the Doha Round has been to start bilateral trade deals with countries that it favours politically.

The main multilateral pressure group for a fairer trading deal between developed and developing countries is the **United Nations Conference on Trade and Development (UNCTAD)**, which was first convened in Geneva in 1964 with Raúl Prebisch as Secretary General. The organization exists as a continuous pressure group with the aim of assisting developing countries through fairer trade, and also aid. Among its stated objectives are:

- Greater access to the markets of developed countries through the reduction in trade barriers
- More stable commodity prices
- Raising the level of aid from developed countries to the UN target of 0.7 per cent of donors' GNP
- Compensation to developing countries for fluctuations in export earnings and terms of trade deterioration.

It has had some limited success in persuading developed countries to grant preferential access to the exports of developing countries, but mainly in the field of manufactured goods, benefiting the larger and more advanced developing countries.

Perhaps the most significant trade agreement negotiated to date to help poorer developing nations is the **Lomé Convention** which was signed in 1975 by the European Economic Community (EEC, now the European Union, EU) and 46 (now 77) developing countries in Africa, the Caribbean and the Pacific (the so-called ACP countries). The Lomé Convention provides for free access to the

European market for all the developing countries' manufactured goods and 90 per cent of their agricultural exports. In addition, agreement was reached to stabilize the foreign exchange earnings of 12 key commodities (the so-called **Stabex scheme**). The Lomé Convention also dispenses aid to the ACP countries through the **European Development Fund (EDF)**. Since 1975, the Convention has been renegotiated five times. The latest agreement reached in Cotonou (Benin) in 2000 is designed to last for 20 years, with revisions possible every 5 years. In 2000 the Stabex scheme was discontinued. Instead, support for fluctuations in export earnings will come from the EDF as part of a **Country Support Strategy** drawn up for each ACP state.

In the voluntary sector, the **Fair Trade movement** is gathering widespread support, and is making a difference to the lives of poor farmers in many developing countries. The movement was founded in 1979 with the main objective of guaranteeing a price to producers above the world price with a sufficient premium above the cost of production to allow producer cooperatives to invest in community projects such as housing, health care and public utilities. More than 7 million farmers and their families in over 60 countries participate and benefit. Importers of fair trade products such as coffee, tea, chocolate, sugar, bananas, fruit juices and so on must buy directly from Fair Trade-certified producers, and agree to establish long-term and stable relationships with them. This cuts out the middleman, or monopsonist – often a large multinational corporation in the case of many primary commodities. The Fair Trade movement has encouraged farmers to join cooperatives which have much greater bargaining power in dealing with buyers. Many supermarkets and other retail outlets now stock a range of Fair Trade products. The value of retail sales is still a drop in the ocean, but is forecast to rise to over £600 billion in the UK alone by the year 2015. Global sales of Fair Trade products exceed $1.5 billion. Unfortunately, however, the Fair Trade movement cannot alter the fundamental economic forces which drive down the price of commodities relative to the prices of manufactured goods and services. The only long-run solution to this dilemma is structural change which requires the protection of new industries; and this is what the rich, developed countries do not like. They want access to poor countries' markets, while continuing to protect their own. The Fair Trade movement can, however, make a major contribution to raising public awareness of the inequities in the global trading system which, in turn, can exert pressure on the governments of rich developed countries for fundamental reform of the terms on which developed and developing countries trade with each other.

Trade strategy for development

So what trade strategy should poor countries pursue? The overriding objective must be to acquire dynamic comparative advantage. For this, the private sector of an economy needs the support of the government in the form of incentives and various types of 'protection' to mitigate investment risks. It is one thing to argue against anti-export bias; it is another to argue that the poor countries should abandon all forms of protection of domestic industry. Improved market access to developed countries for poor-country exports merely perpetuates static comparative advantage. As Rodrik (2001) argued in the lead-up to the Doha round of trade negotiations, 'the exchange of reduced policy autonomy in the South for improved market access in the North is a bad bargain where development is concerned'. Poor countries need time and policy space to nurture new (infant) industrial activities as developed countries did historically, and as many newly industrializing economies still do today. As Hausmann and Rodrik (2003) say in their important work on the concept of 'self discovery':

the fact that the world's most successful economies during the last few decades prospered doing things that are most commonly associated with failure (e.g. protection) is something that cannot easily be dismissed.

Dani Rodrik

Born 1957, Istanbul, Turkey. He is Professor of Political Economy, Harvard University, and one of the foremost development economists of his generation, working on the importance of institutions for economic development and on the relation between trade and development. In his book *The Global Governance of Trade as if Development Really Mattered* he is a strong critic of free trade orthodoxy, and of the World Trade Organization. He has also pioneered, with Ricardo Hausmann and others, new thinking in development economics relating to 'self-discovery' and 'growth diagnostics', and important work on the analysis of 'growth accelerations'. Many of his ideas are included in his latest book, *One Economics: Many Recipes*.

Hausmann and Rodrik's argument is that there is much randomness in the process of a country discovering what it is best at producing, and a lack of protection reduces the incentive to invest in discovering which goods and services they are. Poor, labour-abundant economies have thousands of things they could produce and trade, but in practice their exports are highly concentrated. Sometimes, over 50 per cent of exports are accounted for by less than ten products. Bangladesh and Pakistan are countries at similar levels of development, but Bangladesh specializes in hats and Pakistan in bed sheets. This specialization is not the result of resource endowment; it is the result of chance choice by enterprising entrepreneurs who 'discovered' (*ex post*) where relative costs were. Other 'chance' investments include cut flowers in Colombia for export to North America, camel cheese in Mauritania for export to the European Union, high-yield maize in Malawi, and squash in Tonga. The policy implications of the Haussmann and Rodrik observation and model are that governments need to encourage entrepreneurship and invest in new activities *ex ante*, but push out unproductive firms and sectors *ex post*. Intervention needs to discriminate as far as possible between innovators and imitators. Normal forms of trade protection turn out not to be the ideal policy instruments because they do not discriminate, and earn profits only for those selling in the domestic market. Export subsidies avoid anti-export bias, but still do not discriminate between the innovators and the copycats, and in any case are illegal under the rules of the WTO. The first-best policy is public sector credit or guarantees which can discriminate in favour of the innovator, and be used as a 'stick' if firms do not perform well.

There is much that the international community can also do to promote trade for development, as opposed to pursuing trade liberalization for its own sake. The whole world trade system works against the majority of poor developing countries, firstly because of their dependence on primary commodities (the 'curse' of natural resources) and low value-added manufactures; secondly because the 'rules of the game' governing trade between rich and poor countries are biased in favour of the rich, and thirdly because the agenda for trade reform is largely set by the rich developed countries. The only permanent solution to primary-commodity dependence is structural change which requires the establishment of new, non-traditional industries; but the rich developed nations are hostile to this move. They want free access to poor countries' markets while continuing to protect their own. The most recent example of this is the ongoing debate between the European Union (EU) and the African, Caribbean and Pacific (ACP) countries over **Economic Partnership Agreements (EPAs)** to replace the trade preferences that the ACP countries used to enjoy under the Lomé Convention. The EU is insisting that poor developing countries reduce restrictions on imports of manufactured goods and service activities in return for continued access to the EU market for their agricultural products. The EU is refusing to look at alternatives to free trade EPAs, but by its own admission it concedes that EPAs could lead to the collapse of the manufacturing sector in many poor countries. As Stiglitz (2006) remarks in his powerful book *Making Globalization Work*, 'the US and Europe have perfected the art of arguing for free trade while simultaneously working for trade agreements that protect themselves against imports from developing countries'. If developed countries really wanted to help poor developing countries they could reduce and eliminate tariffs and barriers against all their goods. In addition, developing countries might be allowed 'infant *country* protection' which would be equivalent to a currency devaluation, but has the advantage of raising revenue for spending on public goods. One of the severe drawbacks of tariff reductions in poor countries is a loss of tax revenue.

If trade is to promote development, the World Trade Organization (WTO), which now governs world trade, needs radical reform and rethinking (Wade, 2003). The Agreement establishing the WTO (1995) lists as one of its purposes:

> Raising standards of living, ensuring full employment and a large and steady growing volume of real income and effective demand, and expanding the production of, and trade in, goods and services, while allowing for the objective of sustainable development, seeking both to protect and preserve the environment and to enhance the means of doing so in a manner consistent with their respective needs and concerns at different levels of development.

The aim is laudable, but unfortunately there is a divorce between rhetoric and reality because the WTO treats trade liberalization and economic development as synonymous. As we have seen, however, the historical and contemporary evidence is that domestic economic policy, institution-building and the promotion of investment opportunities are far more important than trade liberalization and trade openness in determining economic success in the early stages of economic development. Rodrik (2001) reminds us (like Chang 2002, 2005, 2008 and Reinert, 2007) that:

> No country has [ever] developed simply by opening itself up to foreign trade and investment. The trick has been to combine the opportunities offered by world markets with a domestic investment and institution-building strategy to stimulate the animal spirits of domestic entrepreneurs.

But now, under WTO rules, all the things that, for example, South Korea, Taiwan and other East Asian countries did to promote economic development in the 1960s, 1970s and 1980s are severely restricted. Some countries that break the rules are succeeding spectacularly. China is one obvious example, but another would be Vietnam which, while promoting FDI and exports, also protects its domestic market, maintains import monopolies and engages in state trading. The WTO should shift away from trying to maximize the flow of trade to understanding and evaluating what trade regime will maximize the possibility of development for individual poor countries. A new world trade order is required that acts on behalf of poor countries; and poor developing countries need a louder voice in any reformed structure.

International commodity agreements[8]

The developing countries in particular, and the world economy in general, suffer several problems from the uncontrolled movement of primary commodity prices. First there is the fact already mentioned of the gradual trend deterioration in the prices of primary commodities relative to industrial goods, which reduces the real income and welfare of the developing countries directly. Second, the prices of primary products are much more cyclically volatile than those of industrial goods.

This volatility has a number of detrimental consequences. First, it leads to a great deal of instability in the foreign exchange earnings and balance-of-payments position of developing countries, which makes investment planning and economic management much more difficult than would otherwise be the case.

Second, because of asymmetries in the economic system, volatility imparts inflationary bias combined with tendencies to depression in the world economy at large. When the prices of primary products fall, the demand for industrial goods falls but their prices are sticky downwards. When the prices of primary products rise, prices of industrial goods are quick to follow suit and governments depress demand to control inflation. The result is stagflation.

Third, the price volatility of primary products leads to volatility in the terms of trade, which may not reflect movements in the equilibrium terms of trade between primary products and industrial goods in the sense that supply and demand are equated in both markets. In these circumstances world economic growth becomes either supply constrained if the prices of primary products are 'too high', or demand constrained if they are 'too low' (see Chapter 6, p. 206). On all these macroeconomic grounds there is a prima facie case for attempting to introduce a greater degree of stability into markets for primary commodities (including, I believe, oil).

Price falls, however, can be dramatic and persistent. Cashin et al. (2000) look at shocks to the prices of 60 commodities over the period 1957–98 and find them typically long-lasting and not just temporary blips: 17 of the commodities experienced price shocks that persisted for longer than five years. This means depressed prices for a long time, and makes price stabilization and income compensation schemes more difficult and costly to manage (see below, p. 555).

The issue of primary product price instability is not something new. It preoccupied Keynes both before and during the Second World War. In a Memorandum in 1942 on the 'International Regulation of Primary Commodities' he remarked: 'one of the greatest evils in international trade before the war was the wide and rapid fluctuations in the world price of primary commodities . . . It must be the primary purpose of control to prevent these wide fluctuations' (Moggridge, 1980).

Keynes followed up his observations and proposals with a more detailed plan for what he called '**commod control**' – an international body representing leading producers and consumers that would stand ready to buy 'commods' (Keynes's name for typical commodities), and store them, at a price (say) 10 per cent below the fixed basic price and sell them at 10 per cent above (Moggridge, 1980). Figure 15.11 illustrates how the scheme would operate.

P_n is the fixed basic price. When the price rises outside the 10 per cent upper range, the commod-control scheme would sell, pushing the price downwards towards the 'normal' price. Similarly, when the price falls outside the 10 per cent lower range, the commod-control scheme would buy, pushing price upwards within the range. The basic price would have to be adjusted

Figure 15.11   Keynes's commod-control scheme

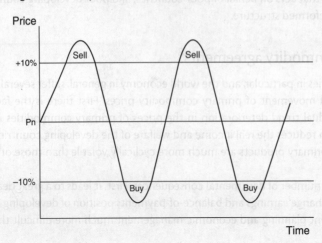

according to whether there was a gradual run-down or build-up of stocks, indicating that the price was either 'too low' or 'too high'. If production did not adjust (at least downwards), Keynes recognized that production quotas might have to be implemented. Commodities should be stored as widely as possible across producing and consuming centres.

This proposal is of some contemporary relevance as a means of responding quickly to conditions of famine. For example, there could be a system of granaries strategically placed across the world under international supervision to store surpluses and release them in times of need. The finance for the storage and holding of 'commods' in Keynes's scheme would have been provided through his proposal for an international clearing union, acting like a world central bank, with which 'commod controls' would keep accounts.

The finance for storage and holding could now be provided through the issue of Special Drawing Rights (SDRs) by the IMF (see Chapter 16). A scheme such as 'commod control' could make a major contribution to curing the international trade cycle, with all its attendant implications. Nearly 70 years have passed since Keynes's wartime proposal, but primary product price fluctuations still plague the world economy. The world still lacks the requisite international mechanisms to rectify what is a major source of instability for the world economy.

In the recent past there have been five main international commodity agreements in operation – for sugar, tin, rubber, coffee and cocoa, and accounting for some 35 per cent of non-oil exports of the developing countries – but all have had their difficulties.[9]

The basic problem with all agreements is getting suppliers to abide by quotas to restrict output in the face of declining prices. Participants must share a common purpose. The most successful 'commodity agreement' of all is the Common Agricultural Policy (CAP) of the European Union, but this does not help developing countries.

Small fluctuations in the export earnings of developing countries, arising from falling prices, are capable of offsetting the entire value of foreign assistance to developing countries in any one year. A 10 per cent fall in export earnings is approximately equivalent to the annual flow of official development assistance. Stable export earnings, it would appear, are at least as important as foreign assistance.[10] In general, unstable export proceeds are the product of variations in both price and quantity. Large fluctuations in earnings may be causally related to four factors:

- Excessive variability of supply and demand
- Low price elasticity of supply and demand
- Excessive specialization in one or two commodities
- A concentration of exports in particular markets.

If the source of instability does come from the supply side, stabilizing prices will not, of course, sta-bilize earnings. It will reduce them in times of scarcity and boost them in periods of glut. If there is a tendency towards perpetual oversupply, and demand is price inelastic, price stabilization will maintain earnings, but price stabilization will further encourage supply, which may then necessi-tate production quotas and lead to inefficiency in production if producing countries are allocated quotas to satisfy equity rather than efficiency.

This is not to argue that there is not a case for compensation, but that methods should be avoided that encourage overproduction or inefficiency. It may be better to let prices find their own market level and for the producing countries to be compensated by the beneficiaries under long-term agreements, the compensation being used to encourage some producers into other activities. Alternatively, income-compensation schemes could be worked out, especially in cases where export instability results from variations in domestic supply. Several alterna-tive methods of price stabilization have been tried or recommended, including buffer stock schemes, export restriction schemes and price compensation schemes. These are examined briefly below.

Buffer stock schemes involve buying up the stock of a commodity when its price is abnormally low and selling the commodity when its price is unusually high. The success of such schemes rests on the foresight of those who manage them. Purchases must be made when prices are low rela-tive to future prices and sold when prices are high relative to future prices. Clearly, buffer stock schemes are only suitable for evening out price fluctuations. They cannot cope with persistent downward trends in price without accumulating large stocks of the commodity, which must be paid for – and presumably sold in the future at still lower prices. Storage schemes are only appro-priate for goods that can easily be stored, and for which the cost of storage is not excessive. Apart from internationally managed buffer stock schemes, governments of individual countries often take an active role in stabilizing prices via commodity boards. Again the problem arises, however, that if there is excess supply, the government will acquire large stocks of the commodity and the budgetary burden of maintaining the price becomes prohibitive.

Restriction schemes are concerned with maintaining prices by restricting supply to the market. The essence of a restriction scheme is that major producers or nations (on behalf of pro-ducers) get together and agree to restrict the production and export of a good whose price is falling, thus maintaining or increasing (if demand is inelastic) revenue from a smaller volume of output. In practice it is very difficult to maintain and supervise schemes of this nature, because it becomes extremely attractive for any one producer or nation to break away from, or refuse to join, the scheme.

The disadvantages of restriction schemes are, first, that demand may not be inelastic in the long run, so that raising the price by restricting supply may reduce export earnings in the long run. Restriction schemes may ultimately lead to substitution for the product and falling sales. Second, restriction schemes can lead to serious resource allocation inefficiencies stemming from the arbitrary allocation of export quotas between countries and production quotas between pro-ducers within countries, unless the quotas are revised regularly to take account of changes in the efficiency of production between producers and between regions of the world. Restriction schemes are often operated by producer cartels, the classic example being the oil-producing countries belonging to the Organization of Petroleum Exporting Countries (OPEC), which managed to raised the price of crude oil by 800 per cent between 1973 and 1980 (although it has not been so successful since then at stabilizing prices at a consistently high level).

Developing countries are not only producers of raw materials, however; they are also consumers, and what some countries gain with respect to the production and exportation of one commodity they may lose with respect to the importation and consumption of another. Developing countries that are poor in all raw materials may not benefit at all. It is not clear, except in the case of a few special commodities such as oil, that cartelization and monopoly pricing of the product will necessarily redistribute income from the developed to the developing countries taken as a whole. If this is so, bilateral commodity agreements between poor-country producers and rich-country users are probably preferable as a means of ensuring that all developing countries benefit.

Price compensation agreements lend themselves to the above form of bilateral arrangement. For example, if the price of a commodity falls, two countries could agree upon a sliding scale of compensation such that the importing country pays an increasing sum of money to the exporter as the price falls below a 'normal' price specified in advance. The sliding scale of compensation could be applied to deviations of the actual price from the 'normal' price. Since restrictions on output and quotas are not part of the scheme, arrangements of this kind have the beauty of divorcing the efficiency aspects of pricing and commodity arrangements from the distributional aspects. The commodity would be traded at world prices, and the lack of full compensation would ensure that if world prices were falling some countries would decide to shift resources, so maintaining some degree of allocative efficiency.

There is no reason why price compensation schemes should not run concurrently with other types of international commodity agreement. Indeed, if the price of a commodity continually declines it may be necessary to couple a restriction scheme with a price compensation scheme, otherwise importing countries will be *persistently* subsidizing the exporting countries. There is also the danger in this case, and also in the case of price-support schemes, that one form of assistance will replace another. If developed countries continually have to pay more than the market prices for their primary products, and argue at the same time that the major constraint on financial assistance to developing countries is their balance of payments, they might use price compensation agreements as an excuse for cutting other forms of assistance. If so, what primary producers gain in the form of higher prices or higher export earnings than if the market were free, they lose in other ways.

If fluctuations in price emanate from the supply side and not from changes in demand, price compensation will operate perversely on the stabilization of *export earnings*. This is illustrated in Figure 15.12. Price in the market is determined by the intersection of the supply and demand curves, D_1D_1 and S_1S_1, giving equilibrium price, P_1. Now suppose that there is a decrease in demand to D_2D_2, causing price to fall to P_2. Earnings before the price fall were $0P_1XS_1$; after the price fall they are $0P_2X_1S_1$. Assume that P_1 is the 'normal' price agreed under the price compensation scheme, and that P_2C represents the appropriate amount of price compensation in relation to the deviation from the 'normal' price following the decrease in demand. Total revenue under the price compensation scheme will be $0CC_1S_1$, which is not far short of total revenue before the fall in price. Consider, however, an equivalent fall in price from P_1 to P_2 as a result of an increase in supply from S_1S_1 to S_2S_2. Under the same price

Figure 15.12   Price compensation and export earnings

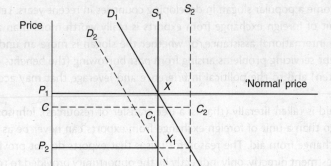

compensation scheme total revenue is now $0CC_2S_2$, which is greatly in excess of the original total revenue (before the price fall) of $0P_1XS_1$. Conversely, if the supply falls, and the price rises above the 'normal' price, revenue will be less than before the price rise since the exporting country will presumably be compensating the importing country – unless the scheme works only one way!

The only way to overcome the induced instability of price compensation schemes is to formulate an **income compensation scheme** that takes account of both price and quantity changes. The practical difficulty is reaching agreement on a 'normal' level of income. If the trend rate of growth of output is positive for most commodities, to settle for a fixed level of 'normal' income would be unjust.

The way that most income compensation schemes work is that each year's compensation is based on deviations of actual export earnings from the moving average of a series of previous years. The IMF's Compensatory and Contingency Financing Facility operates along these lines, and we shall discuss this in the next chapter. The Stabex scheme – once operated by the European Union under the Lomé Convention – was another example of an income compensation scheme. But there must be sufficient funds available. Furthermore, the compensation is paid to governments, so producers do not necessarily reap the benefits.

For stability and a greater degree of certainty over export earnings, producers and governments are increasingly looking to **futures markets** for risk management. To be able to sell forward in futures markets guarantees the producer a price and therefore earnings, depending on supply. Futures markets are not well developed, however, and very often cover is not available for more than one year in advance. Where private risk management is not available, there is a case for publicly subsidized agencies to increase the access of commodity producers in poor countries to insurance against price volatility – perhaps offering price floor guarantees to producers. This may be cheaper in the long run than compensating countries for commodity price fluctuations.

Trade versus aid

'Trade not aid' has become a popular slogan in developing countries in recent years. Let us now consider whether a unit of foreign exchange from exports is really worth more than a unit of foreign exchange from international assistance, or whether the slogan is more an understandable reaction to the debt-servicing problems arising from *past* borrowing (the benefits of which may have been forgotten) and to the political interference and leverage that may accompany international assistance.

If the meaning of aid is taken literally (that is, a free transfer of resources), Johnson (1967) showed a long time ago than a unit of foreign exchange from exports can never be as valuable as a unit of foreign exchange from aid. The reason for this is that exports do not provide additional resources for investment directly, only indirectly by the opportunity provided to transform domestic resources into goods and services more cheaply than if the transformation had to be done domestically. Aid, on the other hand, not only provides resources directly, but also indirectly by *saving the excess cost of import substitution*. The relative worth of exports compared with pure aid can therefore be expressed as

$$\frac{cX}{(1+c)A} \tag{15.5}$$

where X is the value of exports, A is the value of pure aid and c is the proportional excess cost of import substitution. The relative worth of exports will rise with the excess cost of import substitution, but it is clear that the worth of exports can never match the worth of an *equal* amount of pure aid ($X = A$) since $c < (1+c)$. The fact that aid may be tied to higher-priced goods makes some difference to the argument, but it can be shown that the excess cost of import substitution and the excess cost of tied goods would have to be relatively high for the worth of aid not to exceed the worth of trade. Let r be the ratio of the price of tied goods to the price of the same goods in the free market. The relative worth of exports may then be written as

$$\frac{cX}{(1+c)A} \times r \tag{15.6}$$

Now exports will be worth more than aid if $cr > (1+c)$. Different combinations of c and r could be thought of to satisfy this condition, but both c and r would have to be quite high, for example $c = 2.0$ and $r = 1.5$.

The more important consideration, however, is that the term 'aid' in the slogan 'trade not aid' should probably not be interpreted literally. The comparison that developing countries are making is not between trade and pure aid, but either between trade and the **aid component** of an equal amount of foreign assistance, or simply between trade and an equal amount of foreign assistance. If these are the comparisons being made in practice, two interesting questions arise. First, under what circumstances will trade be more valuable? And second, which is the most appropriate comparison to make?

Consider first the comparison between exports and the aid component of an equal amount of foreign assistance. If this is the comparison that is being made by the developing countries, the Johnson formula can be modified by letting $A = Fg$, where A is the aid component of assistance (see Chapter 14, p. 471), F is the nominal amount of foreign assistance and g is the aid component as a proportion of nominal assistance (that is, the grant element). Substituting Fg for A in (15.5) gives the relative worth of exports compared with the aid component of an equal amount of foreign assistance:

$$\frac{cX}{(1+c)Fg} \tag{15.7}$$

or, if the aid is tied:

$$\frac{cX}{(1+c)Fg} \times r \tag{15.8}$$

From (15.7) the value of exports will exceed the value of the aid component of an *equal* amount of foreign assistance ($X = F$) if $c > g(1+c)$, and, from (15.8), if $cr > g(1+c)$. The relative worth of exports is the greater, the higher the excess cost of import substitution, the higher the excess cost of tied aid and the lower the grant element of assistance. It is still the case, however, that c and r would have to be quite high and g relatively low for the worth of exports to exceed the worth of the aid component of an equal amount of foreign assistance.

But even if a comparison of exports with the aid component of an equal amount of foreign assistance showed exports to be worth more, it is not clear that this is the correct comparison to make when justifying the slogan 'trade not aid'. Equations (15.7) and (15.8) assume that only the aid component of assistance saves the excess cost of import substitution. In fact, foreign borrowing *on any terms* saves the excess cost of import substitution. This being so, there are strong grounds for arguing that the comparison that should underlie the slogan 'trade not aid' is a comparison of the worth of exports with the worth of foreign assistance itself of equal amount, which provides resources directly equal to Fg and indirectly equal to Fc. The relative worth of exports compared with foreign assistance can thus be expressed as

$$\frac{cX}{Fg + Fc} = \frac{cX}{(g+c)F} \tag{15.9}$$

or, with tied assistance:

$$\frac{cX}{(g+c)F} \times r \tag{15.10}$$

The conditions for the worth of exports to exceed that of foreign assistance are clearly more stringent than for the worth of exports to exceed the worth of the aid component of an equal amount of foreign assistance. Now, ignoring the potential excess cost of tying, foreign assistance is always worth more than an equal value of exports as long as some grant element is attached to the assistance (that is, as long as $g > 0$).

The values of g, c and r give a practical guide to any country of the relevance of the slogan 'trade not aid', ignoring the secondary repercussions and the side-effects of the two resource flows.[11] The values of g, c and r for most developing countries are probably not such as to justify the slogan 'trade not aid' on narrow economic grounds. As far as secondary repercussions are concerned, however, there is the question of the productivity of resources from abroad compared with those released by exports, and of the additional saving generated by the two means of resource augmentation. There is little evidence on the first point, but on the second it is sometimes claimed, as we saw in Chapter 14, that foreign assistance discourages saving, while export earnings contribute positively to saving. There is no disputing that some foreign assistance may be 'consumed', but this is not the important consideration. The question is, which resource flow leads to the most investment? If 50 per cent of the foreign assistance is 'saved' and the propensity to save of the export sector is 50 per cent, the contribution of the two sources of foreign exchange to growth is exactly the same.

There is no evidence to suggest that the propensity to 'save' out of foreign assistance is less than the propensity to 'save' out of exports. Given that export income may be highly concentrated in the hands of the government or multinational firms, the propensity to save out of export income could be high. If the propensity was, say, 0.6, then 40 per cent of foreign assistance would have to be 'consumed' for foreign assistance not to contribute as much to saving as exports. This is unlikely. If anything, therefore, the economic secondary repercussions of exports and assistance favour assistance.

Summary

- Trade (or more accurately export growth) has been the 'engine' of growth for many countries, both historically and in the contemporary world economy since the Second World War.
- There is nothing in the theory of free trade, however, to guarantee an equitable distribution of the gains from trade between rich and poor countries. This depends on the terms of trade and the balance-of-payments consequences of different patterns of specialization.
- There are static gains from trade based on the law of comparative advantage, dynamic gains from trade from wider markets and the flow of knowledge, and gains by allowing surplus production over domestic consumption to be exported (e.g. many natural resource products).
- There has been extensive trade liberalization and growth in trade in the years since the Second World War, under the auspices of GATT since 1947 and the WTO since 1995.
- Trade liberalization in developing countries has boosted export growth, but raised import growth by more and worsened the balance of payments.
- The overall effect of trade liberalization on the performance of developing countries has been disappointing. Positive growth effects are hard to discern; the impact on reducing poverty has been minimal, and the income distribution within countries has worsened.
- There are many disadvantages of free trade for development. The law of comparative advantage is static and does not consider the supply and demand characteristics of goods produced and traded which affect the future growth performance of countries. There are several respectable economic arguments for protection, including the infant industry argument.
- Structural change is important for developing countries to acquire new comparative advantage in non-traditional goods. *What* you export matters.
- Ideally, import substitution and export promotion should be pursued together, as happened in most successful South-East Asian countries, and now in China.
- The long-run deterioration in the terms of trade of primary commodities (first outlined by Prebisch and Singer in 1950), and the cyclicality of primary product prices, damages the economies of many developing countries. There is a case for international commodity price stabilization schemes.
- What developing countries need is fair trade, not free trade.
- Trade is not necessarily more beneficial than 'aid' in providing resources for development. It depends on the terms of capital inflows, and the excess cost of import substitution.

Chapter 15	Discussion questions

1 What is the essence of the distinction between static and dynamic gains from trade?

2 What fundamental assumptions of free trade theory may be violated in the context of developing countries?

3 Why might there be a tendency for the terms of trade to move against primary products and primary-producing countries, and what does the empirical evidence show?

4 Outline the various arguments for protection.

5 Under what conditions are tariffs a first-best policy of protection?

6 Discuss the relative merits of import substitution versus export promotion.

7 Why are regional trade agreements (RTAs) inferior to the generalized freeing of trade?

8 What has been the impact of trade liberalization on exports and economic growth in developing countries?

9 To what extent do you think that the 'East Asian miracle' has been based on export-led growth?

10 Why do some economists argue that the gains from trade should be looked at more from the point of view of the effect of trade on the balance of payments than from the traditional viewpoint of real resource augmentation?

11 In what ways is trade not 'fair' between developed and developing countries?

12 What do you understand by the concept of 'effective protection', and how is it measured?

13 What problems do unstable commodity prices pose for a country and for the world economy?

14 What are the theoretical and practical difficulties of stabilizing the price and export earnings of primary products?

Notes

1. The analysis to follow relies heavily on Robson (1988).
2. See also the Special Issue of *World Development* (Thorbecke and Nissanke, 2006) on the transmission mechanisms through which trade liberalization can affect poverty.
3. For one of the original theoretical expositions, see Corden (1966). See also the pioneering work of Balassa et al. (1971).
4. Students might like to prove these propositions for themselves, using the formula for the effective rate of protection.

5. Prebisch (1950). See also his later work (1959). Prebisch was Executive Secretary of the Economic Commission for Latin America (ECLA) from 1950 to 1963 and Secretary General of UNCTAD from 1963 to 1969.

6. This result has been challenged by Bleaney (1993), and particularly by Athukorala (1993), who show that the result apparently depends on the inclusion of non-ferrous metals in the manufacturing export price series. But see the reply of Sarkar and Singer (1991, 1993).

7. See Oxfam's compelling indictment of the world's unfair trading system 'Rigged Rules and Double Standards: Trade, Globalization and the Fight Against Poverty' (2002).

8. For a discussion of the issues involved in this section, see Maizels (1987) and Gilbert (1996).

9. For a comprehensive discussion of international commodity agreements and commodity problems in general, see Maizels (1992) and Gilbert (1996).

10. For a good summary of the measures of instability and the empirical evidence of the effects of instability on the economies of developing countries, see Lim (1991) and Love (1987).

11. For some illustrative calculations see Thirlwall (1976). Morrissey and White (1993) argue that only the face value of assistance should be deflated by the excess cost of tying and not the repayments, but this makes little practical difference.

Websites on trade

Trade negotiations

WTO www.wto.org

Fair trade

Oxfam www.maketradefair.com
Fair Trade Foundation www.fairtrade.org.uk
New Economics Foundation www.neweconomics.org.gen/

Trade agreements

Mercosur www.mercosur.org
NAFTA www.mac.doc.gov/nafta
WTO WATCH www.wtowatch.org

16

THE BALANCE OF PAYMENTS, INTERNATIONAL MONETARY ASSISTANCE AND DEVELOPMENT

- Introduction
- Balance-of-payments-constrained growth
- The terms of trade
- The exchange rate and devaluation
- The IMF supply-side approach to devaluation
- The growth of world income and structural change
- Application of the balance-of-payments-constrained growth model
- Capital flows
- Exchange-rate systems for developing countries
- The East Asian financial crisis: a cautionary tale
- The international monetary system and developing countries
- How the IMF works
- Ordinary drawing rights
- Extended Fund Facility (EFF)

- Special facilities
- Other IMF activities
- Criticisms of the IMF
- The results of IMF programmes
- Special Drawing Rights and the developing countries
- Summary
- Discussion questions
- Notes
- Websites on balance of payments and the IMF

Introduction

We have seen how the composition of trade of developing countries can lead to severe balance-of-payments difficulties, which can act as a constraint on growth, and how vulnerable many developing countries are to exogenous shocks that adversely affect their export earnings and import payments.

In this chapter we develop a simple model of balance-of-payments-constrained growth, first of all without capital flows and then allowing current account deficits to be financed by capital inflows. It is shown that growth consistent with current account equilibrium depends on four major factors: (i) what is happening to the real terms of trade (or real exchange rate) and the price elasticities of demand for exports and imports, (ii) the growth of world income, (iii) the income elasticity of demand for a country's exports, and (iv) the income elasticity of demand for imports. We show that if the real terms of trade are constant, a country's growth rate can be approximated by the ratio of export growth to the income elasticity of demand for imports.

The model has several policy implications relating to exchange-rate policy, industrial policy to improve the income elasticity of demand for exports, and trade policy to reduce the income elasticity of demand for imports. Different types of exchange-rate regimes are considered from fixed pegs to free floating, and a cautionary tale is told from the East Asian financial crisis of 1997.

The model with capital flows shows how capital inflows can relax the constraint of current account equilibrium, but the extra growth is minimal because there are limits to the current account deficit to GDP ratio (and the international debt to GDP ratio).

The original purpose of the IMF was to provide short-term balance-of-payments support to countries and it does this through various facilities such as: Ordinary Drawing Rights; the Extended Fund Facility; Compensatory Financing Facility; Exogenous Shocks Facility; Poverty Reduction and Growth Facility; and other special facilities. But the IMF imposes conditions on lending, and the more lending, the harsher the conditions. We examine the results of the Fund's programmes in developing countries and the criticisms of the policies imposed.

The chapter ends with a discussion of the potential of Special Drawing Rights (SDRs) to aid developing countries without them having to adjust to balance-of-payments difficulties by deflating their economies.

Balance-of-payments-constrained growth

Poor countries are in balance-of-payments deficit most of the time, but the deficits fluctuate according to internal and external economic circumstances. In the 1970s, for example, owing to the oil shocks in 1973 and 1979 and the slowdown of world growth, the deficits grew considerably, despite a slowdown of internal growth that reduced the demand for non-oil imports. In the early 1980s the deficits contracted because most developing countries were forced to adjust (that is, deflate their economies) in order to repay debt out of diminished export earnings. In the late 1980s, the deficits increased again, with some internal recovery and a greater willingness of the international capital markets to resume lending. By 1996, the deficits totalled $98 billion, over half of which was accounted for by Thailand, Indonesia, the Philippines, Malaysia and South Korea, which all experienced serious financial crisis in 1997. These countries had to readjust, and since 2002 East Asia and the Pacific have been in big surplus. Today, China has a huge surplus, but many African countries have deficits in excess of 10 per cent of GDP. For any country or continent, the observed deficit (*ex post*) measures the extent to which it has been able and willing to finance the difference between the value of import payments and the value of export receipts.

All countries have a growth rate that is consistent with balance-of-payments equilibrium on the current account, and with its overall balance on the current and capital account. What determines the growth rate that is consistent with current account balance on the one hand, and overall balance on the other? If we specify the equilibrium equations and the determinants of import and export demand, we can immediately see the major factors of importance, and we can appreciate in turn the various policy measures taken by individual countries and the international community to raise the growth rate of less developed countries consistent with balance-of-payments equilibrium.[1]

The current account balance of payments of a country, measured in its own *domestic* currency, may be written as

$$P_d X = P_f M E \tag{16.1}$$

where X measures the quantity of exports and P_d is the average price of exports, so $P_d X$ is the value of exports in domestic currency. M is the quantity of imports, P_f is the average (foreign) price of imports and E is the nominal exchange rate measured as the domestic price of foreign currency, which thus converts the value of imports measured in foreign currency ($P_f M$) into a domestic currency equivalent.

The condition for the balance of payments to remain in equilibrium in a *growing* economy through time is that the *rate of growth* of export earnings should equal the *rate of growth* of import payments, that is

$$(p_d + x) = (p_f + m + e) \tag{16.2}$$

where the lower-case letters represent rates of change of the variables.

Now let us consider what the growth of export and import volume depends on. Export demand may be expected to depend primarily on the price of a country's exports relative to the foreign price of similar goods (expressed in a common currency) and on the level of 'world' income, which determines the purchasing power over a country's goods. Similarly, import demand may be expected to depend on the price of imports relative to domestic substitutes and on the level of domestic income. If the price and income elasticities of demand for exports and imports are assumed to be constant, we may write the export and import functions in the following (multiplicative) way:

$$X = A \left(\frac{P_d}{P_f E} \right)^\eta Z^\varepsilon \tag{16.3}$$

and

$$M = B \left(\frac{P_f E}{P_d} \right)^\psi Y^\pi \tag{16.4}$$

where Z measures 'world' income; Y measures domestic income; η is the price elasticity of demand for exports (< 0); ε is the income elasticity of demand for exports (> 0); ψ is the price elasticity of demand for imports (< 0); π is the income elasticity of demand for imports (> 0); and A and B are constants.

Taking small rates of change of the variables in (16.3) and (16.4), we can see what the growth of exports and imports depends on:

$$x = \eta(p_d - p_f - e) + \varepsilon(z) \tag{16.5}$$

and

$$m = \psi(p_f + e - p_d) + \pi(y) \tag{16.6}$$

In other words, **export growth** depends on (1) how fast domestic prices are changing relative to foreign prices, taking into account variations in the exchange rate (e), multiplied by the price elasticity of demand for exports; and (2) how fast world income is changing, together with the value of the income elasticity of demand for exports. We rule out here the possibility that developing countries can sell any amount of their goods on world markets at the going price, which would mean that the income elasticity of demand, and what is happening to world purchasing power, does not matter, and that export growth is simply supply determined. This may be true in the case of *some* commodities from some *small* countries, but the proposition that demand conditions do not matter for export performance does not stand up to empirical scrutiny as a general rule. There are very few pure price-takers in international trade.

Likewise, **import growth** depends on (1) how fast import prices are changing relative to domestic substitutes (taking account of exchange-rate changes), multiplied by the price elasticity of demand for imports; and (2) how fast domestic income (as a proxy for expenditure) is changing, together with the income elasticity of demand for imports.

Since the growth of imports depends on the growth of domestic income, if we substitute equations (16.5) and (16.6) into (16.2) (which gives the condition for a moving balance-of-payments equilibrium through time), we can derive an expression for a country's growth of income that is consistent with current account equilibrium, which depends on certain key variables and parameters. Substitution of (16.5) and (16.6) into (16.2) gives

$$p_d + \eta(p_d - p_f - e) + \varepsilon(z) = p_f + \psi(p_f + e - p_d) + \pi(y) + e \tag{16.7}$$

so that

$$y = \frac{(1 + \eta + \psi)(p_d - p_f - e) + \varepsilon(z)}{\pi} \tag{16.8}$$

Before embarking on discussion, let us identify in words what this growth rate depends on, which must be binding if current account deficits cannot be financed:

- First, it depends on the rate at which the real terms of trade are changing ($p_d - p_f - e$). The real terms of trade are the ratio of export to import prices measured in a common currency ($P_d/P_f E$). A rise in this ratio, that is ($p_d - p_f - e) > 0$, raises real income growth consistent with current account equilibrium (other things being constant), and a fall in this ratio lowers the balance-of-payments equilibrium growth rate. This is the **pure terms of trade** effect on income growth.

- Second, if the real terms of trade are changing, the growth rate depends on the **price elasticities of demand** for exports (η) and imports (ψ), which determine the magnitude of the volume response of exports and imports to relative price changes.[2]
- Third, one country's growth depends on the growth rates of other countries (z) – which illustrates nicely the **interdependence of the world economy** – but the rate at which one country grows relative to others depends crucially on the income elasticity of demand for its exports (ε), which depends on the tastes of foreign consumers, the characteristics of goods, and a whole host of **non-price factors** that determine the demand for goods in international trade. One of the main reasons why some countries have a healthier balance of payments and a higher growth rate than others is related to the characteristics of the goods that they produce and export in world trade.
- Fourth, the growth rate depends on a country's **appetite for imports**, as measured by π, the income elasticity of demand for imports. The higher is π, the lower the growth rate that is consistent with balance-of-payments equilibrium on the current account.

One can see in these factors the rationale for agreements to prevent the terms of trade deteriorating for developing countries, for exchange-rate policy, for international Keynesianism to maintain the growth of world income, and for policies to induce structural change – through export promotion or import substitution – in order to raise the income elasticity of demand for exports and to reduce the income elasticity of demand for imports. Let us take up some of these issues in turn.

The terms of trade

The effect of terms of trade deterioration (import prices rising faster than export prices, other things remaining the same) is to worsen the balance of payments at a given rate of growth or, what amounts to the same thing, to reduce the rate of growth of income consistent with current account equilibrium. For example, if in equation (16.8), import prices were rising at 10 per cent per annum while the price of exports was rising at only 5 per cent per annum, this would mean a lower y than if the terms of trade were constant. In theory this 'terms of trade effect' could be offset by a continual **appreciation** of the currency; that is, by a continual percentage fall in $E(e < 0)$, but very few developing countries, if any, are in a position to appreciate their currencies even if they wanted to. Terms of trade stability in real terms must depend, or rely, on international commodity agreements to stabilize the prices of the exports of developing countries relative to the prices of the goods they import. Within this framework of analysis the rationale for terms of trade agreements is apparent.

It is not clear, however, that terms of trade deterioration is always a bad thing, because what happens to export earnings and import payments, and hence to the balance-of-payments equilibrium growth rate, depends not only on changes in relative prices but also on the volume response of exports and imports to price changes. Since the price elasticities, η and ψ, are defined as negative, it can be seen from equation (16.8) that if their sum exceeds -1, $p_d < p_f$ will mean that y is higher than would be the case if $p_d > p_f$. In other words the export and import volume response to domestic export prices rising more slowly than import prices is sufficient to offset the fact that more has to be paid for a given volume of imports relative to exports. If, however, the price elasticity of demand for the exports of a developing country is low because of the nature of the product in question (for example, a primary product), and the price elasticity of demand for imports is also low because the imports are necessities, the balance of payments will *worsen* if the terms of trade deteriorate, and growth will have to be constrained for the preservation of balance-of-payments equilibrium. In these circumstances, commodity agreements assume great importance and it would be beneficial if the ratio of export prices to import prices were to rise. In Chapter 15 we considered various commodity schemes aimed at stabilizing export prices, or changing the relative price of exports and imports. We also noted that this will not necessarily stabilize export earnings if there are fluctuations in export supply. The international response to this has been to devise schemes to compensate for loss of export earnings. The only major scheme now in existence is the IMF's Compensatory and Contingency Financing Facility (see below, p. 587).

Another argument for stabilizing the export prices of developing countries and maintaining their incomes is that price and income instability tends to depress the world economy as a whole and the developing countries with it, given the interdependence between countries in the world economy. Falling prices and incomes in developing countries reduce the purchasing power over industrial goods, inducing recession, while rising commodity prices may also induce recession by raising the price of manufactured goods and inducing deflation in the developed countries. For the smooth growth of the world economy, there is a lot to be said for attempting to stabilize the prices of primary products so that the purchasing power of the producers and exporters of these commodities grows in line with supply. One suggestion is that Special Drawing Rights (SDRs) (see below, p. 596) might be used to purchase primary products in order to stabilize their price in times of glut on the lines of Keynes's 'commod control' scheme discussed in Chapter 15 (p. 551).

The exchange rate and devaluation

Now suppose that export prices do rise more quickly than import prices, improving the terms of trade, but that the sum of the price elasticities of demand for exports and imports exceeds unity, what then? This will worsen the balance of payments and reduce the balance-of-payments equilibrium growth rate. It is in these circumstances that **exchange-rate depreciation** may become relevant, and is often resorted to. It can be seen from equation (16.8) that if a country's rate of price increase is above that of other countries ($p_d > p_f$), this can in principle be compensated for by allowing the exchange rate to depreciate continually ($e > 0$) by the difference between p_d and p_f in order to hold 'competitiveness' steady. The conventional approach to balance-of-payments adjustment, and the policy pursued relentlessly by the IMF in countries experiencing balance-of-payments difficulties, is downward adjustment of the exchange rate. Note well, however, that the rationale of such a policy presupposes a number of things:

- That the source of the difficulties is price uncompetitiveness
- That the price elasticities are 'right' (that is, they sum to greater than unity) for a depreciation to reduce the imbalance
- That the *real* terms of trade (or the *real* exchange rate) can be changed by devaluation.

A fall in the nominal exchange rate, however, that is, $e > 0$, may either lead to a fall in $P_f(p_f < 0)$ or a rise in $P_d(p_d > 0)$, both of which would nullify the effect of the devaluation (see (16.8)). A fall in P_f might come about if foreign suppliers desired to maintain their competitiveness as the devaluing country became more competitive. This is known as **pricing to market**; that is, foreign exporters reduce their markups in response to nominal exchange-rate changes in order to remain competitive in world markets. A rise in P_d may come about as the domestic price of imports rises as a result of devaluation, which is then followed by a domestic wage–price spiral. Either way, within a short space of time, relative prices measured in a common currency may revert to their former level and devaluation will have been ineffective in this respect. Edwards (1989) has looked at the effectiveness of devaluation in reducing a country's *real* exchange rate. He studied 39 cases of devaluation in 25 developing countries between 1962 and 1982, and found that in most cases devaluation had been eroded by domestic inflation within three years. Devaluation must be backed by restrictive monetary and fiscal policies if it is to be effective, but this can lead to unemployment. A detailed case study of Mexico by Kamin and Rogers (2000) shows that devaluation has nearly always been associated with high inflation and economic contraction.

Note also that a *once-and-for-all* devaluation or depreciation of the currency cannot put a country on a *permanently higher growth path* that is consistent with balance-of-payments equilibrium. Currency depreciation would have to be continuous (that is, $e > 0$ permanently) for this to happen, unless devaluation can somehow induce favourable structural changes at the same time. Countries must look very carefully at the prevailing conditions before embracing currency devaluation as a panacea for the relief of balance-of-payments-constrained growth. There are three major worries.

First, raising the domestic price of imported goods can be a highly inflationary policy for an open economy that is heavily dependent on imports, as many developing countries have discovered to their cost, particularly in Latin America, and some countries have had the courage to resist IMF support, which has been conditional on devaluation. In the eyes of some, the acronym IMF stands for (I)nflation, (M)isery and (F)amine!

Second, depreciation can be dangerous because it shifts prematurely resources into the tradable goods sector, where productivity may be lower than in the non-tradable goods sector. This is argued forcefully by Yotopoulos (1996), who believes that there is a tendency for the real exchange rate to be *undervalued* because of weakness on the capital account of the balance of payments, depressing the nominal exchange rate. In the early stages of development, developing countries should therefore protect the nominal exchange rate from depreciation through the use of controls and intervention in the foreign exchange market, and only start to liberalize once the foreign exchange market has become more fully developed and currencies are not regarded as 'soft' by the outside world. In the 33 countries studied by Yotopoulos there was a *negative* relation between changes in the real exchange rate and the growth of per capita income for most of the 1970s and 1980s (holding other factors constant).

Third, the effect of currency devaluation is to make countries more competitive in the range of goods that were the source of their balance-of-payments difficulties in the first place. A devalued currency might encourage export sales of new (manufactured) goods with a high price elasticity in world trade, but it might be inappropriate for the traditional range of goods produced and exported with a low price elasticity of demand. For example, if a country is a large supplier and a price maker in world markets, currency devaluation coupled with low price elasticity will *reduce* export earnings. If the country is a price taker, devaluation will raise the domestic price of the commodity and cause inflation. It is true that production for export will become more profitable and might encourage a greater supply response, but there are other less inflationary ways to encourage supply than devaluation. Different types of exchange-rate systems available in developing countries are discussed below (p. 573).

The IMF supply-side approach to devaluation

Devaluation, as well as permitting a reduction in the foreign currency price of exports, may also increase the profitability of exporting, by raising the price of tradable goods relative to the price of non-tradables, and by providing exporters with more domestic currency per unit of foreign exchange earned. The IMF, having conceded that the price elasticity of demand for many of the goods exported and imported by developing countries (particularly as a group) is low, now increasingly uses this supply-side argument as a justification for devaluation. If output is stimulated, this will also mitigate to a certain extent the contraction of aggregate monetary demand that results from devaluation and any accompanying expenditure-reducing policies.

The IMF supply-side approach to devaluation was first articulated in print by Nashashibi (1980) with reference to the Sudan. The approach first requires the calculation of foreign exchange earnings per unit of domestic resources employed for a range of tradable goods. Export (and import substitute) activities can then be arranged on a profitability scale and, according to the supply-side argument, the appropriate devaluation is the one that goes down the scale far enough to ensure the profitability of traditional exports, as well as (perhaps) to encourage new activities. Thus if the current exchange rate for the Sudan was, say, US$2 to S£1, and foreign exchange earnings per unit of domestic resources were calculated to be less than this for most commodities, it would clearly be unprofitable to produce for export, and the exchange rate should be devalued to bring the production of tradables within the margin of profitability. Foreign exchange earnings per unit of domestic resources are measured as

$$C = \frac{(P_x X - P_m M)r}{P_d D} \qquad (16.9)$$

where X refers to exports, P_x is the world price of exports in domestic currency, M is the quantity of imported inputs, P_m is the price of imported inputs in domestic currency, D is the amount of domestic resources used in production, P_d is the price of domestic inputs and r is the exchange rate measured as the foreign price of domestic currency. If $C > r$, production is not profitable at the existing exchange rate.

It is clear from equation (16.9) that if devaluation is to improve profitability, the rise in $(P_x X - P_m M)/P_d D$ must be more than the reduction in r. Unfortunately this cannot be taken for granted. It depends on the response of $P_x X$, $P_m M$, P_d and D to the change in r. The implicit assumptions underlying the approach are that developing countries are price takers, so that P_x will rise in proportion to the devaluation, that X will increase, that M will decrease, and that these favourable effects will not be offset by rises in P_m and $P_d D$. In practice, there may not be a complete 'pass through' of devaluation to export prices (P_x); the elasticity of export supply may be very low because of structural rigidities and factor immobility, and the elasticity of import prices and domestic prices may be very high. The end result may be that the profitability of exporting remains largely unchanged. This was the conclusion of a detailed study of devaluations in the Sudan by Nureldin-Hussain and Thirlwall (1984), which looked at the profitability of cotton, groundnuts, sesame and gum arabic.

The Sudan and many other developing countries fall into the 'rigid country' classification distinguished by Branson (1983) in his useful taxonomic discussion of trade structures and devaluation. 'Rigid' countries are those that produce agricultural-based raw materials with low supply elasticities and whose demand for imports is very inelastic in the short run, particularly for imports used as intermediate inputs. In addition, the price elasticity of demand for exports may be high but not infinite, and real wages may be sticky. In these circumstances, devaluation may be a second-best policy compared with 'structural' intervention to raise foreign exchange earnings per unit of domestic inputs.

The growth of world income and structural change

Now let us turn to the growth of world income: z in equation (16.8). There is nothing that individual poor countries themselves can do about the growth of world income, but since all countries are linked through trade, the interdependence of countries and the importance of global prosperity is only too apparent. This should be the overriding function of supranational institutions and mechanisms: to keep world income and trade buoyant in the face of exogenous shocks and to avoid the beggar-thy-neighbour policies that characterized the 1930s, when the whole world economy slumped. The purpose of the IMF was to avoid a repetition of the 1930s – to help countries in balance-of-payments difficulties and to avoid recourse to widespread protectionism, which can export unemployment from one country to another in a downward spiral. This is the same purpose that underlies various schemes for the recycling of export surpluses and for managed trade; that is, to relieve the balance-of-payments constraint on growth in countries that tend to have a chronic deficit while other countries are in perpetual surplus. This was a major theme of the Brandt Report discussed in Chapter 1, and the major concern of countries during the financial and economic crisis that hit the world economy in 2008.

While individual countries have no control over the growth of world income, they do have some control over the income elasticity of demand for their exports, which determines how fast exports grow as a result of world income growth. Likewise countries have some control over the income elasticity of demand for imports, because both these parameters are a function of the type and characteristics of the goods being produced for sale in international trade. Thus they are a function of the industrial and trade strategy being pursued.

We discussed in Chapter 15 export promotion versus import-substitution strategies. Import substitution is designed to lower the import elasticity, but there is a limit to import substitution, and the policy itself may lower the export elasticity at the same time by creating a rigid and inefficient industrial structure. A much more fruitful strategy, which has been pursued relentlessly and successfully by several South-East Asian countries, is to concentrate on raising the export elasticity, which at the same time may reduce the import elasticity if the goods produced for export also compete with imports.

Application of the balance-of-payments-constrained growth model

How well does the balance-of-payments-constrained growth model outlined in equations (16.1)–(16.8) fit the growth experience of developing countries? Or, to put it another way, how well does equation (16.8) predict the growth performance of the developing countries? To answer this question, it is convenient to simplify the model by assuming either that the sum of the price elasticities of demand $(\eta + \psi)$ does not differ significantly from unity, in which case equation (16.8) reduces to $y = \varepsilon z/\pi$, and/or that relative prices in international trade do not change in the long run (or the real exchange rate remains constant), in which case (16.8) reduces to $y = \varepsilon z/\pi = x/\pi$. This latter result is often referred to as the **dynamic Harrod trade multiplier result** because it is the dynamic analogue of the static Harrod trade multiplier result $Y = X/m$, where Y is the *level* of income, X is the *level* of exports, m is the marginal propensity to import, and $1/m$ is the foreign trade multiplier (Harrod, 1933). Prima facie evidence that a country is balance-of-payments constrained in its growth performance would be to find that its actual growth is close to or just above its balance-of-payments equilibrium growth rate (financed by sustainable long-run capital inflows – see below, p. 572), combined with unemployed domestic resources.

There have been a number of studies that have applied this simple model to individual, or groups of, developing countries, for example that of Ansari et al. (2000) for a selection of South-East Asian countries; Moreno-Brid and Perez (1999) for Central American countries; Perraton (2003) for several developing countries; Moreno-Brid (1998) and Pacheco-López (2005) for Mexico; Nell (2003) for South Africa; and Razmi (2005) for India.[3] The results from some Asian and Latin American countries are shown in Table 16.1. In most cases, it is not possible to reject the hypothesis that the actual growth rate y is equal to the balance-of-payments equilibrium growth rate (x/π). This is particularly true of Mexico which shows the slowdown of growth post-liberalization in 1985/6 as a result of a dramatic increase in the income elasticity of demand for imports without a corresponding increase in the rate of growth of exports. Export growth stayed roughly the same; the income elasticity of demand for imports more than doubled, and the sustainable growth rate fell by one-half.

Table 16.1   Application of the balance-of-payments-constrained growth model to developing countries

Countries	Actual GDP growth (y) (%)	Export growth (x) (%)	Income elasticity of imports (π)	Predicted balance-of-payments-constrained growth rate (%)
Asian countries[a]				
(1970–96)				
Indonesia	6.90	16.3	2.98	5.47
Malaysia	7.40	14.5	2.25	6.44
Philippines	3.70	9.9	1.92	5.16
Thailand	7.60	13.0	2.86	4.55
Latin American countries[b]				
(1950–96)				
Costa Rica	4.7	5.8	1.10	5.26
El Salvador	3.4	3.3	1.75	1.88
Guatemala	3.8	4.4	1.35	3.34
Honduras	3.8	2.7	3.70	0.73
Nicaragua	2.6	3.4	2.04	2.10
Mexico[c] (1968–83)	5.52	9.17	1.57	5.85
Mexico[c] (1984–99)	2.79	9.14	3.14	2.91
Mexico[d] (1973–85)	5.0	9.0	1.3	6.9
Mexico[d] (1986–98)	2.8	9.2	3.1	2.9

Sources:
[a] Ansari, Hashemzadeh and Xi, 2000
[b] Moreno-Brid and Perez, 1999
[c] Moreno-Brid, 1998
[d] Pacheco-López, 2005.

Perraton (2003) tests the model for a sample of 51 developing countries over the period 1973–95. Import and export demand functions are estimated (equations (16.5) and (16.6)) from which long-run estimates of income and price elasticities are derived. It was only possible, however, to derive stable estimates of the income elasticity of demand for imports (π) for 27 of the countries. For these countries, the dynamic Harrod foreign trade multiplier (x/π) is a good predictor of actual growth performance. Using estimates of the income elasticity of demand for imports made by Senhadji (1998) gives even stronger results. The results of these studies add weight to the ideas and importance of export-led growth that we discussed in the previous chapter.

Capital flows

So far we have assumed growth to be constrained by the necessity to preserve current account equilibrium on the balance of payments. In practice, of course, countries are allowed to run deficits, sometimes for substantial periods of time, financed by capital inflows from abroad from a variety of sources. The extent to which the value of imports can exceed the value of exports to finance a correspondingly higher level of income is determined by the *net* level of capital inflows. Thus we may write the equation for the overall balance of payments as

$$P_d X + C = P_f ME \tag{16.10}$$

where C measures net capital inflows (including reductions in foreign exchange reserves) in domestic currency. Taking the rates of change of this identity gives

$$\frac{E}{R}(p_d + x) + \frac{C}{R}(c) = p_f + m + e \tag{16.11}$$

where E/R and C/R represent the proportion of total receipts to finance the import bill that come from export earnings (E) and capital inflows (C), respectively. If we now substitute our expressions for x and m (equations (16.5) and (16.6)) into (16.11), we can solve for the growth rate associated with overall balance-of-payments equilibrium. This rate will depend on all the factors already mentioned, and on the rate of growth of *real* capital inflows ($c - p_d$). On substitution we obtain:

$$y = \frac{(1 + \frac{E}{R}\eta + \psi)(p_d - p_f - e) + \frac{E}{R}(\varepsilon[z]) + \frac{C}{R}(c - p_d)}{\pi} \tag{16.12}$$

This model is known as the **extended version of the dynamic Harrod trade multiplier result** (that is, extended to allow for capital flows). Apart from the weight, E/R, attached to the two export elasticities, η and ε, the only difference between (16.12) and our earlier result in (16.8) is the addition of the last term ($c - p_d$) which measures the growth of *real* capital inflows (the growth of the nominal flows, c, minus the rate of domestic inflation, p_d). A positive growth of capital inflows will allow a country to grow faster than would be the case if it was constrained to maintain balance-of-payments equilibrium on the current account. On the other hand, it must be said that a continually positive rate of growth of capital inflows implies an *ever-growing* burden of debt, which is not sustainable in the long run. Thus running current account deficits to finance growth is not a feasible option in the long run, and other long-run strategies must be pursued that relate to the determinants of the growth rate consistent with current account equilibrium.[4]

This model has been applied by Nureldin-Hussain (1999) to a sample of African and Asian countries over the period 1970–90, with interesting results (Table 16.2). Each country's growth

Table 16.2   Estimates of extended version of dynamic Harrod foreign trade multiplier, 1970–90 (annual percentage average)

	Actual growth rate (1)	Terms of trade effect (A) (2)	Export volume effect (B) (3)	Real capital inflow effect (C) (4)	Predicted growth rate = ((A) + (B) + (C)) (5)
African countries					
Egypt	6.90	−2.37	4.36	7.31	9.30
Congo, Dem. Rep.	6.59	0.42	3.88	2.38	6.67
Kenya	6.24	−0.50	1.62	5.59	6.71
Mauritius	5.80	0.92	5.13	0.19	6.23
Tunisia	5.69	0.87	5.24	1.48	7.59
Burundi	5.60	1.69	3.21	−1.26	3.65
Cameroon	5.50	−1.12	7.08	0.00	5.97
Gabon	5.10	0.49	6.81	−0.04	7.33
Algeria	4.90	10.15	4.21	−8.72	5.64
Morocco	4.62	−1.34	2.83	3.47	4.96
Côte d'Ivoire	4.50	0.39	4.23	0.81	5.43
Lesotho	4.40	−3.43	6.62	1.55	4.74
Burkina Faso	4.20	−5.17	3.03	5.63	3.50
Somalia	3.40	−1.10	0.18	5.00	4.07
Zimbabwe	3.23	−2.40	2.23	−1.24	−1.41
Sudan	3.10	0.14	1.13	1.92	3.20
Benin	2.90	1.44	0.96	1.35	3.75
Tanzania	2.90	0.33	−0.55	5.01	4.79
Togo	2.90	0.08	2.31	0.61	3.00
Senegal	2.67	0.23	1.56	1.05	2.83
Nigeria	2.50	2.37	1.28	−1.17	2.48
South Africa	2.42	−1.03	1.32	7.74	8.03
Mauritania	2.30	0.68	1.58	0.42	2.69
Ethiopia	2.20	−0.09	0.74	2.53	3.17
Sierra Leone	1.58	−0.23	−0.67	2.65	1.75
Zambia	1.40	−0.31	−1.29	0.58	−1.02
Ghana	1.40	−3.81	0.15	2.88	−0.79
Niger	0.81	−5.07	1.79	3.47	0.20
Madagascar	0.48	−0.10	0.06	0.95	0.91
Average	3.66	−0.27	2.45	1.80	3.98
Average excluding oil exporters	3.40	−0.84	1.99	2.49	3.64
Asian countries					
Korea, Rep. of	9.11	−0.81	13.47	−2.49	10.17
Hong Kong	9.07	−0.07	8.34	1.01	9.28
Indonesia	10.76	1.82	3.18	5.76	7.58

Table 16.2   Estimates of extended version of dynamic Harrod foreign trade multiplier, 1970–90 (annual percentage average) – *continued*

	Actual growth rate (1)	Terms of trade effect (A) (2)	Export volume effect (B) (3)	Real capital inflow effect (C) (4)	Predicted growth rate = ((A) + (B) + (C)) (5)
China	8.20	−0.02	6.43	0.26	6.67
Malaysia	7.08	−0.69	6.60	2.21	8.12
Thailand	6.80	0.96	5.45	2.61	9.02
Pakistan	5.04	−0.44	4.28	4.40	8.24
India	4.31	−0.85	3.16	1.96	4.27
Sri Lanka	4.30	−0.65	2.33	3.00	4.68
Japan	4.20	−1.42	9.73	−4.63	3.68
Philippines	3.70	0.22	2.00	0.26	2.48
Average	6.60	−0.18	5.91	1.31	6.74
Average excluding Japan and Korea	6.58	0.03	4.46	2.39	6.70

Source: Nureldin-Hussain, 1999.

rate (column (1)) is disaggregated into three components according to equation (16.12). The first is the terms of trade effect, the second is the export volume effect, and the third is the effect on growth of real capital inflows. It can be seen that the model fits remarkably well for most countries, but the contribution of the different effects differs between countries, and between the two continents of Africa and Asia. Africa has grown much more slowly than Asia, on average, and over one-half of Africa's growth (excluding that arising from oil exports) has been financed by capital inflows. Movements in the terms of trade have also had an adverse effect on growth in Africa. In Asia, by contrast, a much higher proportion of growth has been permitted by the rapid growth of exports, and terms of trade movements have had a favourable effect on growth.

Nureldin-Hussain (2001) has also used this balance-of-payments-constrained growth model with capital inflows as an alternative to the Harrod–Domar model for calculating the financing requirements if poverty in Africa is to be halved by the year 2015. He concludes that the growth rates required are simply not achievable given the current account deficits implied and the capital inflows required. On average, capital inflows would have to be over 20 per cent of GDP.

Exchange-rate systems for developing countries

All countries have a wide choice of exchange-rate systems, ranging from completely fixed to freely floating, with a number of options in between. Which system a developing country chooses must depend on its circumstances at the time; on what exchange-rate arrangements other countries are using, and on the long-run goals of economic policy. For example, a country may wish to pursue exchange-rate stability because of the instability and perceived disadvantages of floating rates, in which case it will wish to choose some form of fixed exchange-rate regime. Alternatively, a country may wish to use its exchange rate to achieve various real objectives in the domestic economy, such as a faster rate of growth and full employment, and therefore sets a target for the *real* exchange rate. With changing domestic and foreign prices, a real exchange-rate target will require frequent variations in the nominal exchange rate, in which case the country will wish to choose some form of flexible exchange-rate regime. On the other hand, if inflation is the most serious problem within a country, currency depreciation to maintain a given real exchange rate may simply exacerbate inflation, and a country may wish to anchor its currency to that of another country or even adopt the currency of another country in order to gain monetary credibility. This would be an extreme form of exchange-rate pegging. Also there is the question of capital flows. If a country has liberalized its capital markets and the capital account of the balance of payments, and capital is free to move in and out, it will be difficult, if not impossible, for a country to pursue an exchange-rate target and operate an independent monetary policy at the same time. Capital outflows, for example, will cause a currency to depreciate in value. The only effective way to stop this is to raise domestic interest rates which depress the internal economy. The reverse dilemma occurs with capital inflows. The only way to reconcile internal and external equilibrium is either to control capital movements, or to allow the exchange rate to float. Theoretically, free floating allows a country to pursue a completely independent monetary policy geared to the goals of the domestic economy, but in practice no country is completely indifferent to the value of its exchange rate, particularly as it is a characteristic of the foreign exchange market that exchange rates may considerably overshoot their true 'equilibrium' value. These are just a few examples of the considerations and conditions that countries need to bear in mind in choosing an exchange-rate regime.[5] The spectrum of alternatives, from hard pegs to floating, is given in Table 16.3.

Each country must find its own solution, in the light of its own circumstances. The IMF generally respects a country's choice of exchange-rate regime, and gives advice to support that choice. The different options are discussed below, but the historical experience of the last 30 years or so points to three broad policy conclusions (Fischer, 2001):

- Intermediate positions between hard pegs and floating (what might be called 'soft' pegs) are not sustainable without capital controls.
- While countries have shifted from intermediate regimes to either end of the spectrum (more towards floating than hard pegs), a wide range of flexible rate arrangements still remains possible.
- Countries are not indifferent to exchange-rate movements, so independent floating is not an option and can be dangerous.

Let us now briefly consider the different types of exchange-rate regime listed in Table 16.3, and their advantages and disadvantages.

A **currency board** is an extreme form of hard peg that requires each unit of a country's currency to be backed by an equal amount of a reserve currency, such as the US dollar. The currency board system was widely practised in Africa under British rule before independence, and more recently Argentina decided to anchor its currency to the US dollar in this way but ultimately

Table 16.3   Types of exchange-rate regime

Hard pegs	Intermediate regimes	Floating
Currency Boards	Pegged exchange rates	Free float
Currency Unions	Crawling peg	Managed float
Dollarization (or adopting the currency of another country)	Exchange-rate band Crawling band	

unsuccessfully. Linking a weak currency to a stronger currency can be a useful anti-inflation device to gain monetary credibility. Indeed, the system is reminiscent of the old Gold Standard system where the currency had to be backed up by gold, with the money supply expanding and contracting according to the balance of payments and changes in international reserves. The two major serious disadvantages of currency board systems are first that credit for entrepreneurs to invest is not elastic to the needs of trade (because it depends on the availability of dollar reserves), and secondly if the reserve currency appreciates in value, so too does the currency that is linked to it. This can cause serious problems of competitiveness with other trading partners, and damage exports and the balance of payments. Argentina went into serious recession with the appreciation of the US dollar in 2000–01, and the currency board was eventually abandoned.

Another extreme form of hard peg is a **currency union** where countries decide to adopt a common currency, so that by definition exchange rates between member countries of the union disappear. Countries may decide to enter a currency union if they feel that multiple currencies, exchange-rate volatility and uncertainty are seriously damaging trade, and that the overall benefits of surrendering monetary independence exceed the costs. The conditions for an **optimal currency area** in which the benefits to the members exceed the costs are that (1) economic cycles should be synchronized and economic shocks symmetrical so that a single monetary policy is suitable for all members; (2) labour and capital are freely mobile; (3) fiscal transfer mechanisms exist to help disadvantaged regions; and (4) multiple currencies are seriously damaging trade. It is never easy for a country to know whether the benefits will exceed the costs, and decisions are often taken on political, as well as economic, grounds. It is important to stress, however, that the fact that a country has no exchange rate to defend vis-à-vis its partners does not mean that the country avoids balance-of-payments problems; they just show up in a different form (Thirlwall, 1980). If plans to import exceed plans to export, balance-of-payments difficulties will manifest themselves in falling output and rising unemployment, unless there are compensating capital transfers between the members of the currency union. The francophone countries of West Africa are part of a currency union that now uses the euro as the common currency, and the largest currency union in the world is now formed by sixteen countries of the EU using the euro as its common currency.

Another form of hard peg is to simply adopt the currency of another country, referred to as **dollarization** in the case of adopting the US dollar. As far as monetary and exchange-rate policy is concerned, the country becomes an adjunct to the country issuing the currency. This is a last resort for countries unable to manage their own affairs. In recent years, Ecuador and El Salvador have dollarized.

Pegged exchange rates are fixed exchange rates, but adjustable. This was the system set up at Bretton Woods in 1944 by which each country's currency was pegged to the US dollar, so that all bilateral rates of exchange between countries were also pegged. The system was called the 'adjustable peg system', however, because if countries found themselves in fundamental balance-of-payments disequilibrium, with unsustainable deficits, they were allowed to adjust the rate of exchange with the dollar and therefore other currencies too. The system gave exchange-rate stability, and avoided competitive devaluation by countries that characterized the beggar-thy-neighbour policies of the 1930s, but proved difficult to sustain in a world of increasing capital mobility. This is the problem for any country wishing to peg its exchange rate. If a currency is under pressure, the existence of a peg gives a one-way option for speculators. The currency markets anticipate that the peg can be adjusted only downwards, which then makes the currency vulnerable to speculative attacks. With large amounts of capital freely mobile it is very difficult to maintain a pegged rate while at the same time attempting to pursue an independent monetary policy, because the interest rate has to be used to defend the currency. It was largely speculative capital flows, and the inability of the USA to meet the promise of exchanging dollars for gold, that caused the international monetary system established at Bretton Woods to break down in 1972. Since then, other countries that have tried to peg rates have met with a similar fate. To quote Fischer (2001): 'in recent years, fixed or pegged exchange rates have been a major factor in every major emerging market financial crisis – Mexico at the end of 1994; Thailand, Indonesia and Korea in 1997; Russia and Brazil in 1998; Argentina and Turkey in 2000 . . . and 2001'.

If countries do decide to peg their exchange rate, there are three broad choices of peg: (1) pegging to a single currency such as the dollar, pound or euro; (2) pegging to an individually tailored basket of currencies reflecting the trade of the country concerned; and (3) pegging to a common basket of currencies such as the SDR (Special Drawing Rights), which since 2001 has been a weighted basket of the world's four major currencies – the dollar, yen, euro and pound. The question is, which peg to choose? This will depend on what the country is trying to achieve. If it is macroeconomic stability, pegging against just one currency is unlikely to be optimal since movements in a country's exchange rate may bear no relation to its own balance of payments, but instead will move according to the balance of payments of the country that the currency is pegged to. Ideally, the pegged rate needs to balance out the effect of individual *bilateral* exchange-rate changes over the economy as a whole. This requires pegging to a basket of currencies where the weights should reflect the direction and elasticity of total trade (exports and imports) between the country and its trading partners. Pegging to a common basket of currencies, such as the SDR, is likely to be superior to pegging to just one currency, but inferior to an individually tailored basket of currencies.

To preserve the advantages of a fixed exchange rate, but to minimize the speculative pressures that can build up with the prospect of currency depreciation, there are various, more flexible, intermediate exchange-rate regimes.

One possibility is a **crawling peg**. Under a crawling peg, a country maintains its pegged exchange rate within agreed margins at a level equal to the moving average of the market exchange rate over an agreed previous time period. This allows a country's currency to drift gradually lower if circumstances warrant, and at the same time avoids both the upheaval of devaluation under an adjustable peg system and the possibility of excessive depreciation under free floating. To avoid speculation against the currency, the interest rate can be raised by a margin equal to the permitted rate of depreciation.

A variant of the crawling peg is an **exchange-rate band** whereby the country allows the exchange rate to vary within a specified range. A **crawling band** allows the exchange-rate band itself to move over time.

At the furthest extreme of flexibility is to allow a currency to float completely independently without any intervention at all. This implies that the country is completely indifferent to its exchange rate. In practice, no country can be indifferent if it is concerned with macro-stability. Exchange rates can overshoot wildly, which can be very disruptive, and a rapidly depreciating currency can be a serious source of inflation by raising the domestic price of imports. It also needs to be stressed that although free floating guarantees equilibrium in the foreign exchange market by definition (because the exchange rate is the price that equilibrates the supply and demand for foreign exchange), it does *not* guarantee equilibrium on the current account of the balance of payments because the demand elasticities for imports and exports may not be of the right order of magnitude. This may then involve the unsustainable build-up of debt if deficits are financed by foreign borrowing.

Although many countries claim to have moved towards greater exchange-rate flexibility in recent years, in practice they intervene. This is called **managed floating**. Countries have no target rate of exchange, no peg, no official band, but they intervene on a daily basis according to circumstances. Managing the exchange rate is easier when there are controls on capital flows. Capital controls insulated China from the exchange-rate turmoil that hit many countries in South-East Asia in 1997 (see below). In 1998, Malaysia imposed capital controls in order to be able to manage its exchange rate more effectively (see Athukorala, 2001). Chile imposed for a short time a tax on capital inflows so that it could operate a policy of monetary contraction to control inflation without leading to destabilizing capital inflows.

Finally, it needs to be said that an optimal exchange-rate strategy for a developing country ought to recognize the **dual structure** of most countries and that a single exchange rate for all commodities may not be appropriate. Either a **dual exchange rate** is required, or some system of taxes and subsidies to achieve the same effect.[6] Under a dual exchange-rate system a fixed (official) rate could apply to primary commodity exports (and to essential imports to keep their domestic price low) and a free (devalued) rate could apply to manufactured exports with a high price elasticity of demand (and to inessential imports). With a foreign exchange shortage, the free rate would produce a domestic price of foreign exchange well above the official rate. The higher the free rate, or the greater the degree of devaluation, the greater the stimulation of manufactured exports and the greater the discouragement of inessential imports.

The main administrative problem with dual exchange rates is to separate the two markets, to ensure that export proceeds from primary commodity exports are surrendered at the official rate and that foreign exchange bought at the official rate is used for essential imports. The former can be achieved through state marketing boards, the latter through strict licensing. Currency auctions – selling foreign exchange for non-essential purposes to the highest bidder – is another form of dual (or multiple) exchange-rate policy. In the early days of the IMF, dual and multiple exchange rates were discouraged and frowned upon as interfering with free trade and exchange, but in more recent years greater tolerance has been shown.

Recent research on the relation between the exchange-rate regime adopted by countries and the functioning of the real economy shows the following:

- Under pegged regimes, inflation is lower, the growth of output is not affected, but output volatility is higher than under flexible exchange-rate regimes (Ghosh et al. 2002).
- Pegged regimes are more prone to currency crises than floating exchange-rate regimes, particularly in countries more integrated with international financial markets, but intermediate regimes are even more prone to crisis than the bipolar extremes of hard pegs or free floating (Bubala and Otker-Robe, 2004)
- Countries with flexible exchange-rate regimes absorb terms of trade shocks more easily than countries with fixed exchange-rate regimes, so that output is less volatile (Broda, 2004).

The countries currently pursuing different types of exchange-rate regime are shown in Table 16.4.

The East Asian financial crisis: a cautionary tale[7]

The financial crisis in East Asia erupted in July 1997 when pressure on the Thai baht became so severe that the government was compelled to cease defending the fixed exchange rate

Table 16.4   Countries classified by exchange-rate regime

Exchange-rate arrangement (number of countries)	Exchange-rate anchor				
Exchange arrangement with no separate legal tender (10)	US dollar		Euro	Composite	Other
	Ecuador	Palau	Montenegro		Kiribati
	El Salvador	Panama	San Marino		
	Marshall Islands	Timor-Leste			
	Micronesia, Fed. States of				
Currency board arrangement (14)	Antigua and Barbuda	St Lucia	Bosnia and Herzegovina		Brunei
	Djibouti	St Vincent and the Grenadines	Bulgaria		Darussalam
	Dominica		Estonia		
	Grenada		Lithuania		
	Hong Kong SAR				
	St Kitts and Nevis				
Other conventional pegged arrangement (68)	Angola	Seychelles	Benin	Fiji	Bhutan
	Argentina	Sierra Leone	Burkina Faso	Kuwait	Lesotho
	Aruba	Solomon Islands	Cameroon	Libya	Namibia
	Bahamas, The	Sri Lanka	Cape Verde	Morocco	Nepal
	Bahrain	Suriname	Central African Rep.	Russian Federation	Swaziland
	Bangladesh	Tajikistan	Chad	Samoa	
	Barbados	Trinidad and Tobago	Comoros	Tunisia	
	Belarus	Turkmenistan	Congo, Rep. of		
	Belize	United Arab Emirates	Côte d'Ivoire		
	Eritrea	Venezuela, Rep. Bolivariana de	Croatia		
	Guyana	Vietnam	Denmark		
	Honduras	Yemen, Rep. of	Equatorial Guinea		
	Jordan	Zimbabwe	Gabon		
	Kazakhstan		Guinea-Bissau		
	Lebanon		Latvia		
	Malawi		Macedonia, FYR		
	Maldives		Mali		
	Mongolia		Niger		
	Netherlands Antilles		Senegal		
	Oman		Togo		
	Qatar				
	Rwanda				
	Saudi Arabia				

Table 16.4   Countries classified by exchange-rate regime – *continued*

Exchange-rate arrangement (number of countries)	Exchange-rate anchor				
Pegged exchange rate within horizontal bands (3)	US dollar		Euro	Composite	
			Slovak Rep.	Syria	
				Tonga	
Crawling peg (8)	Bolivia	Iraq		Botswana	
	China	Nicaragua		Iran, I.R. of	
	Ethiopia	Uzbekistan			
Crawling band (2)	Costa Rica			Azerbaijan	
Managed floating with no predetermined path for the exchange rate (44)	Afghanistan, I.R. of	Georgia	Kenya	Myanmar	Peru
	Algeria	Guinea	Lao PDR	Nigeria	Romania
	Armenia	Guatemala	Liberia	Pakistan	São Tomé and Principe
	Burundi	Ghana	Madagascar	Papua New Guinea	Serbia
	Cambodia	Haiti	Malaysia	Paraguay	Singapore
	Colombia	India	Mauritania	Uganda	Sudan
	Dominican Rep.	Indonesia	Mauritius	Ukraine	Tanzania
	Egypt	Jamaica	Moldova	Uruguay	Thailand
	Gambia, The	Kyrgyz Republic	Mozambique	Vanuatu	
Independently floating (40)	Albania	Cyprus	Ireland	Netherlands	South Africa
	Australia	Czech Republic	Israel	New Zealand	Spain
	Austria	Finland	Italy	Norway	Sweden
	Belgium	France	Japan	Philippines	Switzerland
	Brazil	Germany	Korea, Rep. of	Poland	Turkey
	Canada	Greece	Luxembourg	Portugal	United Kingdom
	Chile	Hungary	Malta	Somalia	United States
	Congo, Dem. Rep. of	Iceland	Mexico	Slovenia	Zambia

Source: IMF, 2008.

and to allow the currency to float, in order to avoid defaulting on its international obligations. There was rapid contagion throughout the region leading to a collapse of the currencies of Thailand, Indonesia, Malaysia, the Philippines and Korea (the Asia-5) within a matter of weeks. Accompanying the currency collapse were steep falls in the stock markets of these countries, which spread to other economies such as Singapore and Hong Kong, whose currencies remained relatively stable. The turmoil rapidly turned into a major world financial crisis and not only had a dramatic effect on the region's growth performance, but also substantially reduced world economic growth. What happened in East Asia in 1997 provides an illuminating case study, and cautionary tale, of the danger to countries of attempting to run large balance-of-payments deficits financed by short-term capital inflows, while at the same time trying to maintain a fixed exchange rate. Even more remarkable is that the IMF did not see the crisis looming.

The question is, why did this region, previously described by economists and commentators as representing a 'growth miracle', plunge into one of the world's most serious recessions of the postwar period? The traditional explanations of fiscal profligacy and macroeconomic instability, which plagued Latin America in the 1980s and 1990s, can be ruled out. In East Asia, most of the important macroeconomic indicators were generally healthy. The fiscal balance was generally in surplus; inflation was low, and domestic savings and investment as a proportion of GDP were among the highest in the world. There had been for some time, however, a major imbalance in the external accounts of the Asia-5 countries. As we argued earlier in the chapter, no country in the long run can grow faster than that rate compatible with equilibrium on the current account of the balance of payments unless it can finance ever-growing deficits – which, in general, it cannot. The East Asian crisis was mainly the result of unsustainable balance-of-payments deficits financed by short-term, volatile capital inflows, and exacerbated by weak (internal) financial structures and imprudent lending.

The balance-of-payments deficits (and the deficits as a proportion of GDP) of the Asia-5 countries from 1992 to 1998 are shown in Table 16.5.

It can be seen that the deficits as a percentage of GDP were averaging between 2 and 10 per cent in the years preceding the crisis. From historical experience, and more recent experience in Latin America, the maximum sustainable deficit to GDP ratio seems to be of the order of 2–3 per cent (depending on circumstances), beyond which the financial markets start to get nervous, for understandable reasons. If the deficits are financed by debt-creating flows (such as commercial bank lending, and non-bank private lending), the external debt to GDP ratio will start to rise, and the ratio of debt-service payments to export earnings is also likely to increase. Countries become increasingly vulnerable to external shocks, with the possibility of capital flight if the debt is privately held, and the prospect of debt default if the debt is publicly held. Ultimately, all debt must be repaid which requires balance-of-payments surpluses.

The prevailing academic orthodoxy in the 1980s, and endorsed by the IMF, used to be that current account balance-of-payments deficits should not be regarded as a problem as long as they are not associated with a government fiscal deficit. In these circumstances, international payments

Table 16.5 Balance of payments on current account, 1992–98 ($ million and % of GDP)

Countries	1992	1993	1994	1995	1996	1997	1998
Thailand	−6,304	−6,159	−7,862	−13,248	−14,380	−3,130	13,500
	(−5.7)	(−4.9)	(−5.4)	(−7.9)	(−7.9)	(−2.0)	(11.5)
Indonesia	−2,780	−2,940	−3,488	−6,987	−8,069	−1,698	1,423
	(−2.0)	(−1.9)	(−2.0)	(−3.4)	(−3.4)	(−1.4)	(1.1)
Philippines	−858	−3,016	−2,950	−1,980	−3,953	−4,351	1,300
	(−1.6)	(−5.5)	(−4.6)	(−2.7)	(−4.7)	(−5.3)	(2.0)
Malaysia	−2,167	−2,991	−4,521	−8,470	−4,956	−4,791	5,113
	(−3.7)	(−4.7)	(−6.2)	(−9.7)	(−5.0)	(−5.3)	(8.1)
Korea	−3,939	939	−3,868	−8,507	−23,005	−8,167	40,039
	(−1.3)	(−0.3)	(−1.0)	(−1.9)	(−4.7)	(−1.8)	(13.2)

Source: Asian Development Bank, 1998.

deficits are merely a private matter among consenting agents concerning the intertemporal distribution of consumption. The crisis in East Asia has shown this view to be grossly misleading. In the four years preceding the crisis year of 1997, there was no fiscal deficit in any of the Asia-5 countries. What the orthodoxy always ignored was the fragility of situations in which the fast growth of output is fuelled by debt-creating flows which must be serviced and repaid in *foreign* currency, and in which capital can flow out as quickly as it flows in, with all the implications this has for the stability of the currency and the high interest rates necessary to contain currency contagion which have such damaging effects on the real economy. The degree to which balance-of-payments deficits are sustainable will partly depend on the nature of the capital inflows. There are at least four major types of capital inflows each with their own characteristics and associated problems: official flows; foreign direct investment (FDI); portfolio investment; and commercial lending by banks and other institutions. Table 16.6 gives figures on the relative importance of these flows in the Asia-5 countries in the lead-up to the crisis.

Official flows are the most helpful in financing deficits because the repayment terms are the most favourable, but they played only a minor role up to 1997, and were negative in 1996. But when the crisis hit in 1997, they predominated. FDI can also be advantageous because it represents more stable, longer-term investment which does not involve any fixed future repayment obligation as with borrowing. In the high growth period of the early 1990s and right up to 1997, all the Asia-5 countries, and particularly Malaysia, were receiving considerable inflows of direct investment which helped to sustain deficits. The other two categories of flow are much more volatile. During the 1990s there was a massive influx of short-term capital inflows into the Asia-5 countries, made possible by financial liberalization. These flows – portfolio investment and various types of private lending – rose from $36 billion in 1994 to $86 billion in 1996. Volatile flows constituted over 60 per cent of external financing in the years prior to 1997. **The proximate cause of the financial crisis was the rapid reversal of these short-term capital inflows**. Thus, two questions need to be answered for an understanding of the crisis and the future. First, what was the cause of the increasingly large capital flows in the years immediately preceding the crisis – or to put it another way, how were these countries able to finance ever-growing balance-of-payments deficits (at least for a time!)? Secondly, why was there sudden capital flight?

The answer to the first question is that in the early 1990s East Asia proved to be an attractive location for foreign capital, for a number of reasons. The countries had either implicitly or explicitly linked their exchange rate to the US dollar and were committed to defending this relationship. This had, in the eyes of many foreign lenders and East Asian borrowers, removed the element of risk arising from a fall in the exchange rate. There was also an expectation that the

Table 16.6   External financing of deficits in Asia-5 countries, 1994–97 ($ billion)

	1994	1995	1996	1997
Net external financing	47.4	80.9	92.8	15.2
FDI	4.7	4.9	7.0	7.2
Portfolio flows	7.6	10.6	12.1	−11.6
Commercial bank lending	24.0	49.4	55.5	−21.3
Non-bank lending	4.2	12.4	18.4	13.7
Net official flows	7.0	3.6	−0.2	27.2

Source: UNCTAD, 1998.

governments would always bail out any of the large financial institutions or firms that got into trouble. Financial crises in Thailand and Malaysia in the mid-1980s and Indonesia in 1994 had been resolved by government intervention and bailouts, which confirmed the view that the governments were implicitly underwriting the domestic financial institutions and firms. This weakened market discipline on the banks – if the government implicitly guarantees deposits, there is no need for investors to withdraw them even if they believe the bank is behaving recklessly in, say, its lending policies.

The perception of the region as one subject to sustained fast growth with high rates of return led to a flood of foreign capital. Liberalization also led to greater borrowing from abroad by East Asian banks and firms. The belief that the exchange rate was fixed meant that there was no need to hedge, and created a bias towards short-term borrowing. The large borrowing from abroad by the East Asian corporations was also due to the high cost of intermediation by the region's domestic banking system. It was cheaper to raise funds from abroad.

The problem, which was not appreciated until it was too late, was that the rapid liberalization of the capital markets exposed some severe shortcomings of the East Asian financial system that became apparent only with the benefit of hindsight. The problem was that much of the financial intermediation was through the banking system. There were well-developed stock markets, but bond and other security markets were underdeveloped and thus external corporate financing was largely through the banking system. The debt–equity ratios were high throughout the region, and in the case of Korea reached 3.55 in 1996–97. The problem was that the banking system showed some fundamental weaknesses that in earlier years had been papered over by fast growth and had not been subject to the sentiments of the international capital markets. The capital-adequacy ratios of the banks were low, the legal limits on lending to single individuals or a related group were unsatisfactory and not strictly enforced, and there was a lack of transparency in the banks' operations. As the World Bank (1998) commented:

> Weak governance of banks, often influenced directly or indirectly by government policies, added to the poor performance. Perhaps the most important weakness was the limited institutional development of banks. Much lending, for example, was done on a collateral basis, rather than on a cash flow basis, thus obfuscating the need to analyse the profitability and riskiness of the underlying projects. Credit tended to flow to borrowers with relationships to government or private bank owners and to favoured sectors, rather than on the basis of projected cash flows, realistic sensitivity analysis and recoverable collateral values.

The problem was concealed to a certain extent by the fact that the banks appeared to be profitable. The World Bank noted that the 'costs to income ratios . . . did not suggest gross inefficiencies'. However, the fact that there were explicit government guarantees leads to the problem of 'moral hazard'. Since banks and companies are not likely to bear the cost of any failure, there is the temptation for them to go for high return but risky investments. If the investments fail, they will not have to bear the cost, which will be picked up by the government.[8]

Thus, the explanation of the crisis is that in the early 1990s the massive capital inflows led to imprudent lending by the domestic banks, and a rapid expansion in credit, leading to asset and real estate bubbles. The latter encouraged even further capital inflows. However, once market sentiment changed, a self-fulfilling prophecy developed leading to a vicious circle of capital flight, falling exchange rates and a collapse in the regional stock exchanges. Once capital begins to move out of the region and the exchange rate begins to fall, no one wants to be caught holding assets valued in domestic currency. The capital loss caused by a depreciating currency can far outweigh any possible gains in higher returns, or in higher interest rates that are imposed to try to restore confidence. The fact that much of the foreign borrowing was short-term meant that the outflows were rapid. Moreover, they could not be covered by reserves. The ratio of short-term debt to reserves was 2:1 in Korea, 1:7 in Indonesia, 1:5 in Thailand, 0:8 in the Philippines and 0:6 in Malaysia.

A powder keg was being built, ready to explode at the slightest provocation. All that was required for the crisis was a trigger: and Thailand provided the trigger. First, through economic mismanagement Thailand had locked up most of its foreign reserves in forward contracts so that instead of $30 billion at their disposal, as the markets initially thought, there was only $1.4 billion available, equal to just two days' imports. Secondly, the country's struggling financial institutions had outstanding loans of over $8 billion from the Central Bank. The costs of supporting these institutions became so high that, at the end of June, the Thai government announced that it would no longer continue to support Finance One, the country's largest finance house that had been absorbing vast amounts of government loans. At a stroke, this announcement effectively revoked the government's commitment to act as a lender of last resort and sent the risk premium sky high. It is no coincidence that five days after this announcement the Thai government was forced to float the baht rather than default on its international loans. Once one country has abandoned its commitment to defending its exchange rate and bailing out its poorly performing banks, it becomes easier for other countries to do the same (the international opprobrium on subsequent countries' reputations is greatly reduced). Thus, the international markets also became increasingly nervous about the other countries, and the crisis spread.

This, in a nutshell, is the story. What the East Asian financial crisis exposed was some fundamental weaknesses in the Asian growth process, although not the underlying factors that gave rise to rapid growth rates in the first place. Particularly it showed the danger (and this is a warning to other countries) of the rapid liberalization of international capital flows before the domestic banking system has developed sufficient regulatory control, and of financing ever-growing balance-of-payments deficits relative to GDP by increasingly short-term capital flows. The balance of payments becomes the ultimate constraint on the growth performance of nations.

The international monetary system and developing countries

The world's international monetary system is governed largely by the **International Monetary Fund**, which was established at Bretton Woods in 1944 in the aftermath of the Great Depression of the 1920s and 1930s and in preparation for the peace after the Second World War. There was a fear that the protectionism and beggar-thy-neighbour policies that characterized the period after the First World War would rear their ugly heads again, to the detriment of the world economy at large, if not all the individual countries within it. Thus the IMF was originally conceived as an institution for stabilizing the world economy, rather than as an agency for development, providing short-term loans to member countries in temporary balance-of-payments difficulties. Responsibility for development was given to the IMF's sister institution, the **World Bank**, established at the same time. Because the IMF was not allowed to create money, John Maynard Keynes (one of the architects of the IMF) used to complain (and joke) that his proposal for a bank had become a fund, and what was in fact a fund had been called a bank!

Over the years, however, and particularly in recent years, the role of the IMF has changed. It has increasingly become the bank manager of the poor countries, and much more of a development agency, advancing longer-term loans to cover what are now perceived as longer-term structural balance-of-payments difficulties. The role of the World Bank has also been changing, and now it too provides loans as a means of balance-of-payments support (the traditional preserve of the IMF), for programmes of structural adjustment (see Chapter 14). In turn, the IMF instituted a Structural Adjustment Facility in 1986, and in 1987 an Enhanced Structural Adjustment Facility (see below, p. 588). The roles of the IMF and the World Bank have almost merged, reflecting the fact that the balance of payments is the principal long-run constraint on the growth of output in developing countries.

The IMF and World Bank also roughly agree on the same policies and reforms that should be applied in developing countries – often referred to as the **Washington Consensus**. The term 'Washington Consensus' was originally coined by John Williamson of the Institute for International Economics in 1989 to refer to an agenda for reform in Latin America which he believed the IMF and World Bank would endorse (see Williamson 1990, 1993). The reforms quickly came to be seen as a model for the wider developing world. The package of reforms suggested by Williamson consisted of the following:

- Fiscal discipline
- Redirection of public expenditure towards education, health and infrastructure investment
- Tax reform – broadening the tax base and cutting marginal tax rates
- Interest rates that are market determined and positive (but moderate) in real terms
- Competitive exchange rates
- Trade liberalization – replacement of quantitative restrictions with low and uniform tariffs
- Openness to foreign direct investment
- Privatization of state enterprises
- Deregulation – abolition of regulations that impede entry or restrict competition, except for those justified on safety, environmental and consumer protection grounds, and prudential oversight of financial institutions
- Legal security for property rights.

The Consensus extols the virtues of the free market and free trade for the achievement of more rapid economic progress (see Taylor, 1997), but Williamson objects to the interpretation of the Consensus as 'neoliberal' because neoliberalism also embraces a political ideology relating to minimal state interference in economic and social affairs; low tax rates; individualism, and a general indifference to the income distribution produced by market forces.

The wisdom of the Consensus was always a matter of dispute among economists, but its initial appeal did not last long because in the 1990s several developing countries that adopted the package of reforms, under pressure from the IMF and World Bank, suffered severe financial and economic crises which toppled governments, reduced living standards and left millions of people worse off. Free market forces turned out to be as disruptive and destructive as government regulations and controls. Economists now question the pace and sequencing of deregulation and the liberalization of markets, and call for stronger domestic institutions and policies to be put in place before countries open up to floods of imports and capital inflows. The need to mix institution-building with the freeing of markets is sometimes called the **Post-Washington Consensus**. The ideology, and practical policy-making, of the IMF and World Bank, however, have hardly changed.

One country that has resisted the pressure of the Washington Consensus is China. It has forged its own development strategy, which does not allow the economy to be buffeted by the unfettered forces of free market capitalism, either domestic or international. It is called the **Beijing Consensus,** and is becoming increasingly attractive to other (large) developing countries (e.g. Brazil) looking for an alternative approach to economic policy-making which puts the needs of people first, not the interests of bankers and international speculators. China's declared goal is to achieve fast, sustainable growth, combined with equity and poverty reduction. China recognizes that to achieve this requires a degree of economic independence to insulate it from turbulence in the world economy. This makes it cautious about free trade and the free movement of international capital, although not about attracting long-term foreign direct investment. China is fortunate to be large enough (and stable enough) to go its own way. Many developing countries are either too small, too vulnerable or too unstable to resist the orthodoxy because they are dependent on loan support from the IMF and World Bank.

How the IMF works

The IMF is primarily a lending institution. It is a source of four main forms of financial assistance, or liquidity, to developing countries:

- Drawings from the ordinary facilities provided by the IMF
- Drawings made under special facilities
- Facilities for low-income countries
- The periodic issue of Special Drawing Rights (SDRs).

Members' drawing rights, their share of SDR allocations, and indeed their subscription to the IMF and voting power are all based on **quotas**. Every member must subscribe to the IMF an amount equal to its quota – 25 per cent in the form of reserve assets and the remainder in local currency. Initial quotas are based on a formula relating to the economic circumstances of individual countries, such as living standards, importance in world trade and so forth, and are then modified in various ways in the light of the conditions and quotas of other countries. The USA has the largest quota, amounting at present to 37 billion SDRs out of the total value of quota subscriptions of 212 billion SDRs. When countries draw on the Fund they buy the currency they need with their own currency, and when they repay they repurchase their own currency with foreign currency acceptable to the IMF. The size of the quotas comes under continual review. The 13th General Review of Quotas in 2008 proposed no increase. In fact, there has been no increase since 1998.

The IMF may supplement its quota resources by borrowing any country's currency. This was institutionalized by the **General Agreement to Borrow (GAB)** in January 1962, which was a four-year arrangement concluded with ten industrialized countries. Since then the General Agreement to Borrow has been extended several times. The IMF also borrows from the private capital market and makes bilateral deals with countries.

The IMF also borrows to finance special facilities as a means of recycling the balance-of-payments surpluses of some member countries. The IMF argues that while it has no desire to supplant ordinary commercial banks in the recycling process, its ability to advocate adjustment policies effectively and convincingly in deficit countries is enhanced by the capacity to make substantial financial resources available to member countries. Thus while the IMF continues to place reliance on quota subscriptions as the main source of its finance, it is also in the market to borrow. Now that the IMF sees its role as providing larger amounts of finance over longer and longer periods for countries with chronically weak balance of payments in relation to their growth objectives, it has an ever-growing need for resources.

A country making use of the IMF's resources is generally required to carry out a programme of balance-of-payments adjustment as a condition of support. This requirement is known as **conditionality** and reflects the IMF principle that financing and adjustment must go hand in hand. What constitutes balance-of-payments equilibrium is not rigidly defined. It need not mean current-account equilibrium, but the measure must be defined free of restrictions on trade and payments in keeping with the underlying liberal free trade philosophy of the IMF. The enforced programmes of balance-of-payments adjustment typically consist of currency devaluation and restrictions on government expenditure and the money supply, coupled with the liberalization of trade and capital movements.

These conditionality practices, which were developed during the 1950s and 1960s under pressure from the USA, have been severely criticized (see below, p. 593) and have undergone continual review. They are harsh, but perhaps less harsh than they were. Countries are encouraged to approach the IMF early before payments problems become acute, and the Fund recognizes the need for a longer adjustment period. When helping countries to design adjustment programmes, the Fund is supposed to have due regard to the social, economic and political characteristics of the country concerned (although there is still not much evidence of this). The Fund now recognizes that balance-of-payments difficulties associated with an acceptable growth of output may have as much to do with the structural characteristics of a country as with relative price distortions and excessive government expenditure. The emphasis has also shifted from demand contraction to supply-side policies to increase the efficiency of resource allocation and supply potential.[9]

Ordinary drawing rights

Ordinary IMF drawing rights consist of two elements:

- The **gold or reserve tranche**, which usually represents 25 per cent of a member's quota and is equivalent to that part of its quota not paid in its own currency.
- The **credit tranche**, which is officially equal to 100 per cent of a member's quota, but can go beyond.

The credit tranche is split into four parts, and access to higher tranches becomes progressively more difficult and expensive. No conditionality is attached to reserve tranche drawings, except balance-of-payments need. In the case of credit tranche drawings, the conditions attached to the first tranche normally consist of devising a programme that demonstrates a reasonable attempt to overcome balance-of-payments difficulties. Requests for purchases of currency in the higher credit tranches require substantial justification. The purchases here are almost always made under **standby arrangements** rather than directly, and certain performance criteria relating to government expenditure and money supply targets must normally be met before resources are released. A strong programme is required to rectify a balance-of-payments disequilibrium. Typically, standby arrangements cover a 12–18-month period (although they can extend up to 3 years) and repayments are made within 3–5 years of each drawing.

Extended Fund Facility (EFF)

The Extended Fund Facility (EFF) was established in 1974 to allow developing countries to borrow beyond their quotas over longer periods than are allowed under ordinary drawing rights. The EFF arrangement gives members assistance for up to three years, with repayment provisions extending over a range of four to ten years. Drawings under the EFF may be more than 100 per cent of

Table 16.7   Outstanding IMF credit by facility and policy, 2000–2008

	2000	2002	2004	2006	2008
Standby arrangements	21,410	28,612	42,100	11,666	5,171
Extended arrangements	16,808	15,538	13,751	7,477	687
Supplemental Reserve Facility	—	5,875	6,028	—	—
Compensatory and Financing Facility	3,032	745	120	84	38
Systemic Transformation Facility	2,718	1,311	154	8	—
Subtotal (GRA)	**43,968**	**52,081**	**62,153**	**19,227**	**5,896**
SAF arrangements	456	341	86	9	9
PRGF arrangements	5,857	6,188	6,703	3,819	3,873
Trust fund	89	89	89	89	66
Total	**50,370**	**58,699**	**69,031**	**23,144**	**9,844**

Source: IMF, 2008.

a country's quota over a three-year period, but the conditions are stringent. The country must provide a detailed statement of policies and measures every 12 months. The resources are provided in instalments, with performance criteria attached. Nonetheless the facility represented an important and significant shift in emphasis from viewing the balance of payments as a stabilization problem, to recognizing the balance of payments as a fundamental long-term constraint on growth that cannot be rectified in a short period of time, if ever. Drawings since 2000 have amounted to over 50 billion SDRs.

Standby and extended arrangements are the most important source of IMF support for developing countries' balance of payments, but other special IMF facilities have become increasingly important. Total outstanding credit under each facility from 2000 to 2008 is shown in Table 16.7.

Special facilities

Apart from the ordinary drawing rights, developing countries have access to a number of special facilities that may exist at a particular time to assist them with development difficulties arising from balance-of-payments problems. At present there are three main special facilities – the Compensatory Financing Facility (CFF); the Supplemental Reserve Facility (SRF) and Emergency Assistance. In addition, there is the Poverty Reduction and Growth Facility (PRGF) and Exogenous Shocks Facility (ESF) for low-income countries.

As of 2009, the guidelines on the scale of IMF assistance allow member countries annual access to fund resources of up to 100 per cent of their quotas, and cumulative access, net of scheduled repayments, of up to 300 per cent of their quotas. These drawings exclude drawings under all the various special facilities. All assistance is related to quotas, but quotas, of course, may bear no relation to need. Let us now consider the working of these special facilities.

Compensatory Financing Facility (CFF)

The CFF was the first special facility established by the IMF to compensate developing countries for shortfalls of export earnings below a five-year trend centred on the middle year. In 1988 it changed its name to the Compensatory and Contingency Financing Facility, but 'Contingency' was dropped in 2000. Originally the facility enabled a country to draw up to 25 per cent of its quota, provided the shortfall was temporary, but now it can draw up to 45 per cent, in addition to drawings made under tranche facilities.

In 1979 shortfalls in receipts from travel and workers' remittances were included in the compensation scheme, and in 1981 it was extended to cover the increased cost of imported cereals, calculated as the cost of such imports in a given year less their average cost for five years, centred on that year. An optional tranche is also available to cover other unforeseen contingencies. Between 1963 and 1996 over 20 billion SDRs were drawn in total, but since the mid-1990s the Facility has not been used much. Table 16.7 shows the drawings between 2000 and 2008.

Supplemental Reserve Facility (SRF)

The SRF was established in 1997 in response to the East Asian financial crisis discussed above. Its focus is on the capital account of the balance of payments, and it is intended to help member countries experiencing exceptional balance-of-payments problems resulting from a sudden loss of market confidence. Access under the SRF is not subject to the usual quota limits but is based on a country's financing needs, its ability to repay the IMF, and the policies it is pursuing to restore confidence. Repayment must be made within three years of drawing.

Emergency assistance

Since 1962 the fund has provided quick, medium-term assistance to countries with balance-of-payments difficulties related to natural disasters; and since 1995 to countries suffering from the aftermath of civil unrest or international armed conflict.

Poverty Reduction and Growth Facility (PRGF)

The PRGF was established in 1999 to replace the **Enhanced Structural Adjustment Facility (ESAF)** which was the IMF's concessional financing facility to assist poor countries facing persistent balance-of-payments problems. The idea was to give the ESAF a more explicit anti-poverty focus in keeping with the new emphasis of the IMF and World Bank on poverty reduction – hence the change of name. Programmes supported under the PRGF are expected to be based on a strategy designed by the borrower to reduce poverty in collaboration with civil society and the various organizations concerned with development. It is designed to work alongside the Highly Indebted Poor Country (HIPC) initiative of the IMF and World Bank (see Chapter 14, p. 490) for debt relief for poor countries that require the preparation of Poverty Reduction Strategy Papers. Under the PRGF facility, low-income countries may borrow up to 140 per cent of quota under a 3-year arrangement, with an interest rate of 0.5 per cent and repayments made between $5\frac{1}{2}$ and 10 years after disbursement. By 2008, 37 countries were already being supported by borrowings of over 30 billion SDRs.

The amount of drawing under each of the facilities mentioned above, as a percentage of each member's quota, is shown in Table 16.8. In Case example 16.1 there is a summary of the financial assistance that the IMF gives and the conditions it imposes.

Table 16.8 Access limits to IMF facilities, 2008 (% of member's quota)

Standby and extended arrangements[1]	
Annual	100
Cumulative	300
Special Facilities	
Supplemental Reserve Facility	None
Compensatory Financing Facility	
Export earnings shortfall	45
Excess cereal import costs	45
Poverty Reduction and Growth Facility	
3-year access	
Regular	140
Exceptional	185

[1] Under exceptional circumstances, these limits may be exceeded.

Source: IMF, 2008.

Case example 16.1	**IMF lending facilities**

Credit facility (years established)	Purpose	Conditions	Access limits
Credit tranches and Extended Fund Facility			
Standby arrangements (1952)	Medium-term assistance for countries with balance-of-payments difficulties of a short-term character.	Adopt policies that provide confidence that the member's balance-of-payments difficulties will be resolved within a reasonable period.	Annual: 100% of quota; cumulative: 300% of quota.
Extended Fund Facility (1974) (extended arrangements)	Longer-term assistance to support members' structural reforms to address balance-of-payments difficulties of a long-term character.	Adopt three-year programme, with structural agenda, with annual detailed statement of policies for the next 12 months.	Annual: 100% of quota; cumulative: 300% of quota.

continued overleaf

Case example 16.1	IMF lending facilities – *continued*

Credit facility (years established)	Purpose	Conditions	Access limits
Special facilities			
Supplemental Reserve Facility (1997)	Short-term assistance for balance-of-payments difficulties related to crises of market confidence.	Available only in context of standby or extended arrangements with associated programme and with strengthened policies to address loss of market confidence.	No access limits; access under the facility only when access under associated regular arrangement would otherwise exceed either annual or cumulative limit.
Compensatory Financing Facility (1963)	Medium-term assistance for temporary export shortfalls or cereal import excesses.	Available only when the shortfall/excess is largely beyond the control of the authorities and a member has an arrangement with upper credit tranche conditionality, or when its balance-of-payments position excluding the shortfall/excess is satisfactory.	45% of quota each for export and cereal components. Combined limit of 55% of quota for both components.
Emergency assistance	Assistance for balance-of-payments difficulties related to the following:		Generally limited to 25% of quota, though larger amounts can be made available in exceptional cases.
(1) Natural disasters (1962)	Natural disasters.	Reasonable efforts to overcome balance-of-payments difficulties.	
(2) Post-conflict (1995)	The aftermath of civil unrest, political turmoil, or international armed conflict.	Focus on institutional and administrative capacity building to pave the way toward an upper credit tranche arrangement or PRGF.	

Case example 16.1	IMF lending facilities – *continued*

Credit facility (years established)	Purpose	Conditions	Access limits
Facilities for low-income members			
Poverty Reduction and Growth Facility (1999)	Longer-term assistance for protracted balance-of-payments problems of structural nature; aims at poverty-reducing growth.	Adopt three-year PRGF arrangements. PRGF-supported programmes are based on a Poverty Reduction Strategy prepared by the country in a participatory process and integrating macroeconomic, structural, and poverty reduction policies.	140% of quota; 185% of quota in exceptional circumstances.
Exogenous Shocks Facility (2006)	Short-term assistance to address a temporary balance-of-payments need that is due to a sudden shock.	Adopt a 1–2-year programme involving macroeconomic adjustments allowing the member to adjust to the shock and structural reform considered important for adjustment to the shock, or for mitigating the impact of future shocks.	Annual: 25% of quota (norm for annual access); cumulative: 50% of quota except in exceptional circumstances.

Source: IMF, 2008.

Exogenous Shocks Facility (ESF)

This was established in 2005, but is still not fully funded. It provides policy support and financial assistance to low-income countries facing exogenous shocks such as commodity price changes, natural disasters and trade disruption caused by events in a neighbouring country. It is available to countries eligible to use the Poverty Reduction and Growth Facility but without a PRGF-supported programme in place. ESF programmes are designed to be of one to two years in length with no expectation of early repayment.

Other IMF activities

As well as providing finance and loans to member countries, the IMF has a number of other responsibilities connected with the smooth functioning of the world economy, including the surveillance of exchange rates and promoting the health of the world financial system.

One of the mandates of the IMF is to monitor the exchange-rate policies of countries. Article IV, Section I of the original (1947) IMF Charter states that member countries should 'avoid manipulating exchange rates . . . to prevent effective balance-of-payments adjustment or to gain an unfair advantage over other members'. By manipulating the exchange rate, the IMF means countries indulging in practices which keep an exchange rate undervalued in order to maintain large balance-of-payments surpluses. The assessment of exchange-rate levels, however, is not easy because an 'equilibrium' rate depends on how the internal balance of a country is defined, and what is regarded as the optimal level of international reserves. There are different 'equilibrium' exchange rates for different levels of employment and unemployment; different growth rates, and reserves to import ratios. But in any case, the Fund lacks any power to influence the exchange-rate policy of countries, except persuasion. The sanction of fining countries in persistent surpluses, that Keynes proposed at Bretton Woods, was never adopted. On promoting the soundness of financial systems, see Case example 16.2.

Case example 16.2	Promoting financial system soundness

The IMF's main channels for promoting financial system soundness in member countries are its ongoing multilateral and bilateral surveillance, the design of its lending programmes, and technical assistance. *The Financial Sector Assessment Handbook*, published by the IMF and the World Bank in September 2005, provides information on key issues and sound practices in assessing financial systems, and designing policy responses.

The IMF has been working to improve the surveillance process by deepening its coverage of financial system issues to better identify financial system strengths and weaknesses, and thereby lessen the frequency and diminish the intensity of potential financial system problems.

IMF-supported programmes often include measures to strengthen member countries' financial systems. In addition to providing financial assistance, the IMF helps members in identifying and diagnosing financial system problems; designing strategies for systemic reforms and bank restructuring; and ensuring that such strategies are consistent with, and supported by, appropriate macroeconomic and other structural policies.

Technical assistance provided by the IMF helps member countries implement specific measures that will strengthen their financial infrastructure. This assistance may include advice and training on improving monetary and fiscal management; foreign exchange and capital market development; the design of payment systems and deposit insurance arrangements; the development of the legal framework for banking as well as prudential regulations and supervisory capabilities; and strategies for systemic bank restructuring.

Source: *IMF in Focus*, September 2006.

Criticisms of the IMF

The policy prescriptions of the IMF in developing countries have been, and still are, based on a blend of finance and adjustment. Few would dispute the need for international institutions to provide finance to ease the burden of balance-of-payments adjustment. In its adjustment policies, however, the IMF has come in for severe criticism; so much so that it has been described as **'anti-developmental'**. In its approach to adjustment the IMF is conditioned both by the beliefs and philosophy of the organization itself and the prevailing orthodoxy of neoclassical economic theory. The IMF denies that it has a rigid doctrinaire approach to economic policy, but it clearly has a particular philosophy based on the Washington Consensus (see p. 584). It is a major bastion of support of an international economic system that prefers capitalism to socialism, favours private investment over public investment, extols the virtues of free trade and the operation of the price mechanism, and encourages the free flow of private capital to and from developing countries. Gore (2000) argues that this consensus that emerged within the IMF (and World Bank) was more than just a paradigm shift from the idea of state-led development to market-orientated policies. There was a deeper shift in the way development problems were perceived in an increasingly globalized world, and the IMF's policies have been a response to these changes in the world economy. The fact remains, however, that a particular orthodoxy has been applied to the vast majority of developing countries as if they were one homogeneous mass and can be properly treated in exactly the same way.

Joseph Stiglitz (2002), formerly chief economist of the World Bank, has severely criticized the IMF for serving the needs of global finance, rather than the needs of global stability, by encouraging premature internal and external financial liberalization. He has satirized the methods of the IMF by describing what he calls a four-step programme for every country, regardless of circumstances and already 'pre-drafted' by IMF officials before they reach the country, for 'voluntary' signature by the country concerned. No signature, no help! The four core elements of each programme consist of: (1) privatization of state industries; (2) capital market liberalization; (3) market-based pricing; and (4) free trade.

Capital market liberalization has been disastrous for many countries not ready and able to cope with volatile capital inflows and outflows. The IMF has, in fact, admitted that opening economies prematurely to free flows of capital constituted 'an accident waiting to happen', and now concedes that capital controls are justified in some circumstances. The Fund was undoubtedly shaken by the 1997 East Asian crisis, which it did not foresee even though there was a massive build-up of current account deficits and capital had started to flow out of South-East Asia long before the crisis hit.

Market-based pricing has also been disastrous in many instances, leading to civil unrest. When food and fuel subsidies for the poor were lifted in Indonesia in 1998, the country exploded into riots.

Free trade, we saw in Chapter 15, is not optimal from a development point of view. If imports grow faster than exports, the balance of payments worsens.

The neoliberal, neoclassical approach to economic thinking and policy-making colours to a large extent the IMF's diagnosis of balance-of-payments problems and their appropriate solution. Deficits are invariably seen as related to, or caused by, price uncompetitiveness and excess monetary demand, to be 'cured' by devaluation and demand contraction. But the IMF still lacks a comprehensive theoretical apparatus to deal with two basic questions regarding devaluation: firstly, how is the degree of *overvaluation* of a currency determined, and secondly, how is the optimal pace of adjustment from the overvalued to the equilibrium rate of exchange decided? In keeping with the IMF's philosophy, devaluation and retrenchment are coupled with other measures that, from a balance-of-payments point of view, work in the opposite direction – namely the relaxation of foreign exchange controls, the removal of import restrictions and the dismantling of subsidies and price controls.

Critics of the IMF argue with some justification that there is one law for the poor and another for the rich. While the poor countries must remove controls over foreign exchange and imports as a condition of assistance, the rich countries continue to impose restrictions on imports from developing countries. To support the liberalization programme, the country then has to depress aggregate demand sufficiently to accommodate devaluation in the attempt to achieve balance-of-payments equilibrium, which leads to slow growth and unemployment. The symptoms of balance-of-payments disequilibrium are tackled, but not the root causes of the perpetual tendency towards disequilibrium. As we argued in Chapter 15, the balance-of-payments problems of most developing countries must be regarded as primarily *structural* in nature, relating to the characteristics of the goods produced and traded. This implies a very different approach to balance-of-payments adjustment than one of continual devaluation, demand contraction and dismantling of the public sector. At the very least it calls for policies – using a judicious mix of subsidies and controls – to alter the *structure* of production.

Another criticism of the IMF is that it ignores 'structural' *surpluses* on the balance of payments – the counterpart of 'structural' deficits – and critics argue that the burden of adjustment ought to be shared more equitably between deficit and surplus countries, instead of the major part of the burden being shouldered by debtor developing countries, as at present. If surplus countries do not attempt to adjust by expanding their own economies, or by appreciating their currencies, they should be penalized, and deficit countries ought to be allowed to discriminate against the goods of these countries. This would be a revival of the idea of 'scarce currencies', and of the right of countries to control imports from 'scarce currency' countries, that is, from those with surpluses.

Critics would also argue that if the IMF is genuinely concerned with development as well as providing balance-of-payments support, it could distribute all new issues of SDRs to developing countries to spend in developed countries. After all, if the developed countries were not able to earn their reserves by selling goods to developing countries in exchange for SDRs, they would have to earn them in some other way. We shall return to this matter below.

The IMF has become sensitive to some of these criticisms in recent years, particularly to the charge that it is 'anti-developmental'. Along with the World Bank, the IMF now declares itself committed to poverty reduction and allowing countries to 'own' their own policies through the formulation of PRSPs. Instead of countries having to fulfil a mass of individual conditions for loan support, governments can now specify just a few broad outcomes relating to poverty reduction, health and education. To what extent it will change its attitude to balance-of-payments difficulties and the need for devaluation and deflation, however, is still an open question.

The IMF also now has an **Independent Evaluation Office (IEO)**, established in 2001, to monitor its lending activities and to do research on the effects of its lending policies. The IEO chose three subjects for its first studies: fiscal adjustment in IMF-supported programmes; the role of the IMF in three capital-account crises (Indonesia and Korea in 1997–98 and Brazil 1998–99), and prolonged use of IMF resources. Kenen (2004) surveys the results of the studies so far. On fiscal policy, the IEO criticizes IMF programmes for not paying enough attention to raising income and property taxes, and combating tax evasion, and for focusing too heavily on cutting public employment or capping wages in periods of fiscal crisis. In general, fiscal policy has not been 'too tight', although the fiscal outcome has normally been tighter than forecast. In Korea and Indonesia, however, in 1997–98, there was too much fiscal stringency because the IMF did not foresee the collapse of investment and output, so that IMF policies made the situation worse. On the third issue, the prolonged use of IMF resources has increased in recent years because, as Keynes once said, 'if you owe a bank a little, the bank owns you, but if you owe the bank a lot *you* own the bank'! The IMF has been reluctant to pull out of countries in case they don't get repaid at all. The evaluation reaches some interesting findings which have general lessons:

- Excessively detailed conditionality does not appear to be effective.
- Conditionality which is focused on policy rules or procedures, rather than on discretionary one-time actions, seems to be most effective.

The Meltzer Commission, appointed by the US Congress, which reported in 2000, recommended that the IMF should withdraw from the development field entirely and concentrate on the role of lender of last resort to emerging economies facing financial crisis. This would be a return to its original function of lending to countries in short-term balance-of-payments difficulties. Likewise, the World Bank should pare down its activities, lending only to really poor countries, and not to countries able to attract private capital. In line with the focus on poverty reduction, lending should be confined to countries with an income of less than $4,000 per head with low credit ratings. For the poorest countries, there should be grants not loans. Lending to Asia and Latin America could largely be left to the Regional Development Banks in those regions. In general, there should be a much clearer distinction between the activities of the IMF and World Bank. If accepted, this would indeed be a return to the original conception at Bretton Woods that the World Bank would act as the development agency and the Fund would be like a bank to be used in emergencies only, but not get involved in detailed policy-making itself in the countries concerned. A move in this direction would disarm many of the IMF's critics.

The results of IMF programmes

The effects of the IMF's programmes on countries' economic performance have been very mixed. In an early study Reichmann and Stillson (1978) examined the effects of IMF programmes in both developed and developing countries in the period 1963–72, comparing the two years after the implementation of the programme with the two years before. Taking the balance of payments as a whole (current plus capital account), of the 75 cases examined, only 18 showed a statistically significant improvement and 4 showed an actual worsening. In the 29 cases where the inflation rate had exceeded 5 per cent before the programme, it had worsened in 6 cases and in 16 cases there was no significant change. As far as GDP growth is concerned, of the 70 cases examined the performance had improved in 33 but deteriorated in 28. A study by Donavan (1982) of the non-oil-developing countries for the period 1971–80 revealed a similar pattern: some improvement in the balance of payments, mixed effects on growth and some tendency towards inflation.

Following a major analysis of over 30 IMF stabilization programmes supported by upper-tranche credits between 1964 and 1979, Killick and his associates (1984) advocated what they call a 'real economy approach to balance of payments' or 'adjustment with growth', which would be a more flexible supply-orientated approach with demand management subservient.

One of the purposes of the Extended Fund Facility and the (now defunct) Structural Adjustment Facility was to permit the IMF to deal with structural disequilibrium, but as far as the former facility is concerned, the programmes were no different from conventional demand management programmes built around monetary and fiscal contraction coupled with trade liberalization and some production incentives.

In a follow-up study of IMF programmes in developing countries, Killick (1995) criticized the IMF's over-reliance on conditionality and performance criteria, which invariably leads to the breakdown of IMF programmes. To avoid breakdowns and pressure on IMF resources, he calls for the relaxation of standardized reform packages and a greater emphasis on locally initiated programmes of stabilization and reform. Above all, the programmes should set a growth target of at least 1 per cent above population growth, and sufficient financing for this should be mobilized. Killick finds that the main victim of IMF programmes is investment, and that there is no evidence that IMF financing acts as a catalyst for private investment.

Lance Taylor (1988) reports the results of studies of 18 countries, conducted under the auspices of the World Institute for Development Economics Research (WIDER) in Helsinki. The principal finding of the authors of the country studies is that 'past policies could have been designed to better effect, and that programmes of the Fund/Bank type are optimal for neither stabilization nor growth and income redistribution in the Third World'. This is a serious indictment of policy from some of the world's leading development economists. There are alternative programmes to those implemented by the IMF, but they would be more interventionist and more directly concerned with the targets than with the precise instruments. There is a role for selective import controls, export subsidies, multiple exchange rates, low interest rates and so forth, but these are all frowned on by the IMF.

The IMF conducts its own in-house studies of programmes and is naturally more sanguine, but is conscious that the design of programmes can be improved. In a study of 45 IMF lending arrangements approved between mid-1988 and mid-1991, Schadler (1996) reports striking gains on the external accounts, but virtually no improvement in inflation, investment and growth. Four explanations are given:

- Countries coming to the IMF too late
- Too much emphasis on the external objective of balance-of-payments equilibrium rather than domestic objectives
- The breaking of monetary targets
- Not enough emphasis on raising domestic saving.

The latest research on the effect of IMF programmes on the growth of per capita income by Przeworksi and Vreeland (2000) and Dreher (2006) shows a negative effect. The latter study examines data for 98 countries over the period 1970–2000 and finds overall a negative effect of 1.7 percentage points per annum (on average), although the compliance with conditionality mitigated the negative effect. Dreher's conjecture is that 'the short-term effect of demand compression takes place very quickly, while the compliance measures pick up later adherence to the more structural aspects of policy conditions'.

Special Drawing Rights and the developing countries

One possibility for increasing the flow of resources to developing countries is to distribute to them most, if not all, of the saving accruing to developed countries from the issue of costless SDRs as a means of international payment.

The Special Drawing Account of the IMF was established in July 1969. To date there have been only four allocations of SDRs: 9.3 billion between 1970 and 1972; 12.1 billion between 1979 and 1981; 161.2 billion in 2009, and a one-off injection of 21.5 billion in the wake of the financial crisis and world economic recession in 2008–09, allocated mainly to the low-income countries.

The normal basis of allocation of SDRs between countries is the member countries' quota subscriptions to the IMF. This means that approximately 70 per cent of the new international money created has been distributed to the world's richest countries, while the poorest countries have received only 30 per cent. If the SDRs had been distributed on a per capita basis, the distribution would have been almost exactly the reverse.

There can be no doubt about the potential benefits of international money, such as SDRs, for the world as a whole, but there are several objections to the present distribution, and reasons to believe that a redistribution of SDRs in favour of the developing countries could increase world welfare. For one thing, the balance-of-payments adjustment costs of developing countries are generally higher than those of developed countries, and this in itself constitutes an economic argument for revising the present allocation rules. But secondly, SDRs represent a social saving because they are costless to produce (unlike gold), and do not have to be earned by exporting (unlike dollars). The view that the social saving to SDRs should be distributed to the developing countries has spawned several proposals for a so-called **link between development assistance and SDRs** which would have several advantages.

First, if there was a regular expansion of SDRs a link would provide a useful mechanism by which total development aid could be guaranteed to rise with the long-term growth of world trade and production. At present there is no guarantee that aid will rise in proportion to world income. Aid programmes are chopped and changed according to the balance-of-payments situation of donor countries.

Second, a link scheme would increase the proportion of total international aid that is untied, and this would not impose any reserve losses on the donor, as when a country unties its aid unilaterally. All donor countries would gain reserves in exchange for the exports they provide to the developing countries.

Third, if the link scheme operated through such international financial institutions as the World Bank or one of its affiliates, these multilateral institutions would be provided with a regular flow of resources without the necessity of entering into time-consuming negotiations with national governments.

The historical origin of the link idea can be traced back to Keynes's plan for an International Clearing Union (ICU) with the power to issue international money for collectively agreed purposes. The function of the ICU was not only to be a world central bank but also to lend to international organizations pursuing internationally agreed objectives, in particular, at that time, for postwar relief work and the management of international commodities.

The variety of link proposals that have been put forward can be classified into three types:

- A direct link
- An organic link
- An inorganic (or indirect, voluntary) link.

As far as a **direct link** is concerned, the simplest method would be to allocate more SDRs directly to the developing countries, as was done in 2009. Alternatively, the IMF quotas to developing countries could be increased.

An **organic link** refers to the possibility of channelling SDRs to the developing countries via the developed countries, via development agencies, or via both.

The direct allocation of SDRs to development agencies probably has the most advantages and the least drawbacks among the organic-link proposals. Development agencies would have accounts with the IMF to which SDRs would be credited. The development agencies would then lend in the normal way. When goods were purchased from exporters by the developing countries, the IMF would then transfer the SDRs from the account of the development agencies to the account of the exporting country. The country would then pay its exporters in its domestic currency. The scheme has the advantage of being simple and could be introduced with minimal amendments to the IMF Articles of Agreement.

A tied version of the organic link was Scitovsky's (1966) plan for a new international currency to be issued to deficit countries with unemployed resources, which would relinquish domestic currency in exchange. This could then be lent to the developing countries, but could only be spent in the issuing country. This would serve several purposes. It would provide the developing countries with unrequited imports at no opportunity cost to the developed countries and remedy the deficits of the developed countries at the same time. This is also a way of eliminating deflationary bias in the world economy.

An **inorganic link** would involve the developed countries agreeing to make voluntary contributions to the multilateral aid-giving agencies whenever new SDRs were allocated. The contributions would be in national currencies but would represent a uniform proportion of each contributor's SDR allocation. The drawback of the proposal is its voluntary nature – one or two major countries might not contribute or might make their contribution dependent on their balance of payments. This would introduce a great deal of uncertainty into the scheme. Also, national governments would have to agree appropriations and this would create the same difficulties as regular foreign-aid appropriations. There do not seem to be many advantages in an inorganic link.

Several objections have been raised against the link proposals but none is very convincing. Some have argued against the link on the grounds that the creation of reserves should be kept separate from the transfer of real resources. But this has never been the case historically. Resource transfers have always been involved in the acquisition of gold and dollars. Since SDRs save real resources, it is entirely appropriate that in the process of reserve creation the saving should be distributed to the developing countries.

A second objection to the link is that it would mean the loss of control over the granting and distribution of assistance by national governments. Under the link scheme, the distribution of the burden of assistance would depend on where the SDRs were spent, which, it is argued, could not be accurately forecast. This is a weak argument for two reasons. The same objection may be levelled against *all* forms of untied bilateral aid. There is never an automatic correspondence between the financial burden of aid and the real resource burden of aid. It all depends on whether the national governments that grant aid allow the resources to be transferred, which depends primarily on their policy towards the balance of payments.

A further objection is that the link is likely to be inflationary. It is true that developing countries will tend to spend new international money rather than add to their reserves, but whether or not the resulting claims on the developed countries are inflationary will depend on whether the developed countries are willing to release resources to the extent of the claims on them. In practice, SDRs could be less inflationary than the dollar standard by instituting multilateral control over international liquidity rather than unilateral control by the USA, which, because of the need for dollars, has not been subject to the anti-inflationary discipline that is normally present in other countries.

A final objection is that development assistance is not likely to increase under the link because governments will cut down on their normal budgetary aid appropriations. Critics argue that it is highly unlikely that developed countries would be willing to give extra aid through the link but not in other forms. This objection can also be challenged. For one thing the reserve effects of the two forms of assistance are not the same. Conventional aid worsens the donor's balance of payments, whereas the link scheme would improve the balance of payments of countries where SDRs were spent and thus improve the reserve position. Second, governments often wish to provide aid for specific purposes and this desire would not be undermined by a link. Moreover, since it is very difficult for a country to know how much aid it is providing through the link, it would be very difficult for a country to offset it. The link deserves much more consideration in international monetary circles than it has received to date. To paraphrase Pirandello, if ever there were an instrument in search of a policy, it is SDRs!

Summary

- A major constraint on the growth of output in many developing countries is a deficit on the current account of the balance of payments, or, in other words, a shortage of foreign exchange to pay for imports.
- The International Monetary Fund (IMF) was established at the Bretton Woods conference in 1944 to give financial support to countries in temporary balance-of-payments difficulties, but the deficits of developing countries are structural and long term relating to the nature of the goods they export and import.
- A country's growth rate consistent with balance-of-payments equilibrium on current account depends on changes in the real exchange rate; the price elasticities of demand for exports and imports; the growth of world income, and the income elasticity of demand for exports and imports.
- If the real exchange rate is constant over time, the long-run growth of GDP can be approximated by the ratio of the growth of export volume and the income elasticity of demand for imports.
- Capital inflows can lift a balance-of-payments constraint on growth, but only by a small amount for realistic values of the sustainable ratio of deficits (or international debt) to GDP.
- Currency depreciation needs to be continuous to raise a country's growth rate permanently consistent with balance-of-payments equilibrium – but currency depreciation can be very inflationary.
- No single exchange-rate regime can be prescribed for all developing countries. Each country needs to choose its own regime consistent with other economic objectives.
- The IMF has many lending Facilities, but they are all related to the size of a country's quota with the Fund, not to the scale of difficulties confronting the country.
- IMF conditionality has been severely criticized as deflationary, and insensitive to the circumstances and needs of countries. The results of IMF policies have been disappointing.
- Special Drawing Rights (SDRs) could be distributed to developing countries as a means of financial support, to be spent in developed countries. This would increase the reserves of the latter countries and transfer resources to developing countries.

Chapter 16	Discussion questions

1   What factors determine the demand for a country's exports and imports?

2   Can the devaluation of a country's currency guarantee balance-of-payments equilibrium on the current account?

3   What factors determine the income elasticity of demand for a country's exports?

4   Why are developing countries more prone to balance-of-payments disequilibrium than developed countries?

5   What do you understand by the IMF's 'supply-side approach to devaluation' in developing countries?

6   What factors need to be taken into account in choosing a country's exchange-rate regime?

7   What are the lessons of the financial crisis in South-East Asia in 1997?

8   How do the ordinary and special facilities of the IMF work? What do you understand by 'conditionality'?

9   What criticisms have been levelled against the IMF in its policies of support to developing countries?

10 What have been the effects of IMF policies in developing countries?

11 How could Special Drawing Rights (SDRs) be used simultaneously as an instrument of aid to developing countries and as a means of employment creation in developed countries?

Notes

1. For the original development of this model, see Thirlwall (1979). For an overview of the literature, see McCombie and Thirlwall (1997 and 2004).
2. For an up-to-date survey of estimating export- and import-demand functions, see Senhadji and Montenegro (1999) and Senhadji (1998).
3. For a collection of these papers and others, see McCombie and Thirlwall (2004).
4. For the original development of this model, see Thirlwall and Nureldin-Hussain (1982).
5. For useful surveys of exchange-rate policy in developing countries, see Argy (1990); Frenkel (1999); Fischer (2001); Ghosh, Gulde and Wolf (2002).
6. A classic early reference arguing the case for dual exchange rates is Kaldor (1964).
7. This section relies heavily on McCombie and Thirlwall (1999).
8. The World Bank, *East Asia: The Road to Recovery* (Washington, DC: World Bank, 1998).
9. For a comprehensive review of the evolution of the conditionality practices of the IMF, see Guitian (1982) and Dell (1981).

Websites on balance of payments and the IMF

IMF www.imf.org
UNCTAD Handbook of Statistics http://stats.unctad.org/

1997 South-East Asia Crisis

Nouriel Roubini's websites www.stern.nyu.edu/~nroubini/asia/AsiaHomePage.html

REFERENCES AND FURTHER READING

Chapter 1   The study of economic development

Bardhan, P. (1993) 'Economics of Development and the Development of Economics', *Journal of Economic Perspectives*, Spring.

Black, R and H. White (2006) *Targeting Development: Critical Perspectives on the Millennium Development Goals* (London: Routledge).

Brandt Commission (1983) *Common Crisis: North–South Co-operation for World Recovery* (London: Pan).

Brandt Report (1980) *North–South: A Programme for Survival* (London: Pan).

Chang, Ha-Joon (2002) *Kicking Away the Ladder: Development Strategy in Historical Perspective* (London: Anthem Press).

Domar, E. (1947) 'Expansion and Employment', *American Economic Review*, March.

Fischer, S. (2003) 'Globalization and its Challenges', *American Economic Review*, March.

Furtado, C. (1964) *Development and Underdevelopment* (Berkeley: University of California Press).

Galbraith, J.K. (1980) *The Nature of Mass Poverty* (Harmondsworth: Penguin).

Goulet, D. (1971) *The Cruel Choice: A New Concept in the Theory of Development* (New York: Atheneum).

Goulet, D. (2006) *Development Ethics at Work* (London: Routledge).

Harrod, R. (1939) 'An Essay in Dynamic Theory', *Economic Journal*, March.

Harrod, R. (1948) *Towards a Dynamic Economics* (London: Macmillan).

Hirschman, A. (1981) 'The Rise and Decline of Development Economics', in *Essays in Trespassing: Economics to Politics and Beyond* (Cambridge: Cambridge University Press).

Krugman, P. (1992) 'Towards a Counter-Revolution in Development Theory', *World Bank Economic Review (Supplement): Proceedings of the World Bank Annual Conference on Development Economics* (Washington, DC: World Bank).

Lal, D. (1983) *The Poverty of Development Economics* (London: Hobart).

Lewis, W.A. (1984) 'The State of Development Theory', *American Economic Review*, March.

Lipton, M. (1977) *Why Poor People Stay Poor* (London: Temple Smith).

Little, I.M.D. (1982) *Economic Development: Theory, Policies and International Relations* (New York: Basic Books).

Myrdal, G. (1957) *Economic Theory and Underdeveloped Regions* (London: Duckworth).

Naqvi, S.N.H. (1995) 'The Nature of Economic Development', *World Development*, April.

Naqvi, S.N.H. (1996) 'The Significance of Development Economics', *World Development*, June.

Patel, S.J. (1964) 'The Economic Distance between Nations: Its Origins, Measurement and Outlook', *Economic Journal*, March.

Pearson Report (1969) *Partners in Development*. Report of the Commission on International Development (London: Pall Mall Press).

Rawls, J. (1972) *A Theory of Justice* (Oxford: Oxford University Press).

Reinert, E. (2007) *How Rich Countries Got Rich and Why Poor Countries Stay Poor* (London: Constable and Robinson).

Sen, A.K. (1981) *Poverty and Famines: An Essay on Entitlement and Deprivation* (Oxford: Clarendon Press).

Sen, A.K. (1983) 'Development: Which Way Now?', *Economic Journal*, December.

Sen, A.K. (1999) *Development as Freedom* (Oxford: Oxford University Press).

Thirlwall, A.P. (1995) 'In Praise of Development Economics', *METU Studies in Development*, 1 and 2 (1984), repr. in A.P. Thirlwall, *The Economics of Growth and Development: Selected Essays*, Vol. 1 (Aldershot: Edward Elgar).

Todaro, M. and S.C. Smith (2008) *Economic Development in the Third World* (London: Longman).

UNDP (United Nations Development Programme) (2002) *Human Development Report* (New York: Oxford University Press).

World Bank (2000) *World Development Report 2000/2001: Attacking Poverty* (New York: Oxford University Press).

World Bank (2008) *Global Monitoring Report* (Washington, DC: World Bank).

Chapter 2   The development gap and the measurement of poverty

Baumol, W. (1986) 'Productivity Growth, Convergence and Welfare: What the Long-run Data Show', *American Economic Review*, December.

Basu, K. (2006) 'Globalization, Poverty and Inequality: What is the Relationship? What Can be Done?', *World Development*, August.

Besley, T. and R. Burgess (2003) 'Halving Global Poverty', *Journal of Economic Perspectives*, Summer.

Bourguignon, F. and C. Morrisson (2002) 'Inequality Among World Citizens: 1820–1992', *American Economic Review*, September.

Chen, S. and M. Ravallion (2008) 'The Developing World is Poorer than we Thought, but no Less Successful in the Fight Against Poverty', Policy Research Paper 4703 (Washington, DC: World Bank).

Collier, P. (2007) *The Bottom Billion* (Oxford: Oxford University Press).

Dollar, D. and A. Kraay (2000) *Growth is Good for the Poor* (Washington, DC: World Bank).

Dowrick, S. (1992) 'Technological Catch-up and Diverging Incomes: Patterns of Economic Growth 1960–1988', *Economic Journal*, May.

Easterlin, R. (2000) 'The Worldwide Standard of Living Since 1800', *Journal of Economic Perspectives*, Winter.

Edward, P. (2006) 'Examining Inequality: Who Really Benefits from Global Growth?', *World Development*, October.

Ghose, A.K. (2004) 'Global Inequality and International Trade', *Cambridge Journal of Economics*, March.

Jones, C. (1997) 'On the Evolution of the World Income Distribution', *Journal of Economic Perspectives*, Summer.

Kravis, I.B. et al. (1975) *A System of International Comparisons of Gross Product and Purchasing Power* (Baltimore: Johns Hopkins Press for the World Bank).

Kravis, I.B. et al. (1978) 'Real GDP Per Capita for More than One Hundred Countries', *Economic Journal*, June.

Maddison, A. (2003) *The World Economy: Historical Statistics*, Development Studies Centre (Paris: OECD).

Maddison, A. (2001) *The World Economy: A Millennial Perspective* (Paris: OECD).

Milanovic, B. (2002) 'True World Income Distribution 1988 and 1993: First Calculations Based on Household Surveys Alone', *Economic Journal*, January.

Milanovic, B. (2005) *Worlds Apart: Measuring International and Global Inequality* (Princeton, NJ: Princeton University Press).

Norwegian Institute of International Affairs (2000) *Globalisation and Inequality: World Income Distribution and Livings Standards, 1960–1998* (Report to the Norwegian Ministry of Foreign Affairs: Report 6b: 2000).

Pritchett, L. (1997) 'Divergence: Big Time', *Journal of Economic Perspectives*, Summer.

Ravallion, M. (1997) 'Good and Bad Growth: Human Development Reports', *World Development*, May.

Ravallion, M. (2001) 'Growth, Inequality and Poverty: Looking Beyond Averages', *World Development*, November.

Sala-í-Martin, X. (2002) 'The Disturbing Rise of Global Income Inequality', NBER Working Paper 8940 (New York: NBER).

Summers, R. and A. Heston (1988) 'A New Set of International Comparisons of Real Product and Price Levels: Estimates for 130 Countries 1950–1985', *Review of Income and Wealth*, March.

Summers, R. and A. Heston (1991) 'The Penn World Table (Mark 5): An Expanded Set of International Comparisons, 1950–1985', *Quarterly Journal of Economics*, May.

Sutcliffe, R. (1971) *Industry and Underdevelopment* (Reading, MA: Addison-Wesley).

Sutcliffe, R. (2004) 'World Inequality and Globalization', *Oxford Review of Economic Policy*, Spring.

Svedberg, P. (2004) 'World Income Distribution: Which Way?', *Journal of Development Studies*, June.

Thorbecke, E. and M. Nissanke (2006) 'Introduction: The Impact of Globalization on the World's Poor', *World Development*, August.

UNDP (United Nations Development Programme) (1997) *Human Development Report* (New York: Oxford University Press).

UNDP (United Nations Development Programme) (2001) *Human Development Report 2000* (New York: United Nations).

UNDP (United Nations Development Programme) (2003) *Human Development Report* (New York: Oxford University Press).

UNDP (United Nations Development Programme) (2004) *Human Development Report 2004* (New York: Oxford University Press).

Wade, R. (2001) 'The Rising Inequality of World Income Distribution', *Finance and Development*, December.

Wade, R. (2004) 'Is Globalization Reducing Poverty and Inequality?' *World Development*, April.

World Bank (1990) *World Development Report 1990* (Oxford: Oxford University Press).

World Bank (2000) *World Development Report 2000/2001: Attacking Poverty* (New York: Oxford University Press).

World Bank (2001) *World Development Report 2002* (Oxford: Oxford University Press).

World Bank (2004) *World Development Indicators, 2004* (Washington, DC: World Bank).

World Bank (2008) *The Growth Report: Strategies for Sustained Growth and Inclusive Development* (Washington, DC: Commission on Growth and Development, World Bank).

Zind, R. G. (1991) 'Income Convergence and Divergence within and between LDC Groups', *World Development*, June.

Chapter 3   The characteristics of underdevelopment and structural change

Acemoglu, D. (2003) 'Root Causes: A Historical Approach to Assessing the Role of Institutions in Economic Development', *Finance and Development*, June.

Acemoglu, D., S. Johnson and J. Robinson (2001) 'The Colonial Origins of Comparative Development: An Empirical Investigation', *American Economic Review*, December.

Adelman, I. and C.T. Morris (1971) 'An Anatomy of Income Distribution Patterns in Developing Countries', *AID Development Digest*, October.

Ahluwalia, M.S., N. Carter and H. Chenery (1979) 'Growth and Poverty in Developing Countries', *Journal of Development Economics*, September.

Bairam, E. (1991) 'Economic Growth and Kaldor's Law: The Case of Turkey 1925–78', *Applied Economics*, August.

Baldacci, E., B. Clements, Q. Cui and S. Gupta (2005) 'What does it Take to Help the Poor?', *Finance and Development*, June.

Behrman, J.R. (1993) 'The Economic Rationale for Investing in Nutrition in Developing Countries', *World Development*, November.

Bliss, C. and N. Stern (1978) 'Productivity, Wages and Nutrition, Parts I and II', *Journal of Development Economics*, December.

Chang, Ha-Joon (2002) *Kicking Away the Ladder: Development Strategy in Historical Perspective* (London: Anthem Press).

Chang, Ha-Joon (ed.) (2003) *Rethinking Development Economics* (London: Anthem Press).

Chatterji, M., B. Gilmore, K. Strunk and J. Vanasin (1993) 'Political Economy, Growth and Convergence in Less Developed Countries', *World Development*, December.

Chenery, H., M. Ahluwalia, C. Bell, J. Duloy and R. Jolly (eds) (1974) *Redistribution with Growth* (Oxford: Oxford University Press).

Chenery, H. and M. Syrquin (1975) *Patterns of Development 1950–1970* (Oxford: Oxford University Press).

Chenery, H. and L. Taylor (1968) 'Development Patterns: Among Countries and Over Time', *Review of Economics and Statistics*, November.

Chenery, H., S. Robinson and M. Syrquin (1986) *Industrialisation and Growth: A Comparative Study* (New York: Oxford University Press).

Clark, C. (1940) *The Conditions of Economic Progress* (London: Macmillan).

Collier, P. (2007) *The Bottom Billion* (Oxford: Oxford University Press)

Dasgupta, P. (1993) *An Inquiry into Well-Being and Destitution* (Oxford: Clarendon Press).

Deininger, K. and L. Squire (1996) 'A New Data Set Measuring Income Inequalities', *World Bank Economic Review*, September.

Dollar, D. and A. Kraay (2000) *Growth is Good for the Poor* (Washington, DC: World Bank).

Drakopoulos, S.A. and I. Theodossiou (1991) 'Kaldorian Approach to Greek Economic Growth', *Applied Economics*, October.

Dreze, J. (ed.) (1999) *The Economics of Famine* (Cheltenham: Edward Elgar).

Drèze, J. and A.K. Sen (1989) *Hunger and Public Action* (Oxford: Clarendon Press).

Dyson, T. (1996) *Population and Food: Global Trends and Future Prospects* (London: Routledge).

Easterly, W. and R. Levine (2002) 'Tropics, Germs and Crops: How Endowments Influence Economic Development', *NBER Working Paper 9106*, August.

Edwards, E.O. (ed.) (1974) *Employment in Developing Nations* (New York: Columbia University Press).

Felipe, J. (2009) *Inclusive Growth, Full Employment and Structural Change* (London: Anthem Press).

Felipe, J. and R. Hasan (eds) (2006) *Labour Markets in Asia: Issues and Perspectives* (London: Macmillan).

Finance and Development (2005) 'Cultivating Minds: How Investing in Education Boosts Development' (Washington, DC: IMF).

Fisher, A.G.B. (1939) 'Production: Primary, Secondary and Tertiary', *Economic Record*, June.

Forbes, K.J. (2000) 'A Reassessment of the Relationship between Inequality and Growth', *American Economic Review*, September.

Godfrey, M. (1986) *Global Unemployment: The New Challenge to Economic Theory* (Brighton: Wheatsheaf).

Gylfason, J. (1999) *Principles of Economic Growth* (Oxford: Oxford University Press).

Gylfason, J. (2001) 'Nature, Power and Growth', *Scottish Journal of Political Economy*, November.

Hansen, J.D. and J. Zhang (1996) 'A Kaldorian Approach to Regional Economic Growth in China', *Applied Economics*, June.

Harris, J., J. Hunter and C.M. Lewis (eds) (1996) *The New Institutional Economics and Third World Development* (London: Routledge).

Imbs, J. and R. Wacziarg (2003) 'Stages of Diversification', *American Economic Review*, March.

Institute for Development Studies (2002) 'The New Famines', *IDS Bulletin*, 33(4)

ILO (International Labour Organization) (1977) *Meeting Basic Needs* (Geneva: ILO).

ILO (International Labour Organization) (1995) *World Employment 1995* (Geneva: ILO).

ILO (International Labour Organization) (1996) *Annual Employment Report* (Geneva: ILO).

ILO (International Labour Organization) (2002) *Labour Force Statistics* (Geneva: ILO).

ILO (International Labour Organization) (2009) *Labour Force Statistics* (Geneva: ILO).

Kaldor, N. (1966) *Causes of the Slow Rate of Economic Growth of the United Kingdom* (Cambridge: Cambridge University Press).

Kaldor, N. (1967) *Strategic Factors in Economic Development* (New York: Ithaca).

Kuznets, S. (1955) 'Economic Growth and Income Inequality', *American Economic Review*, March.

Kuznets, S. (1963) 'Quantitative Aspects of the Economic Growth of Nations: Distribution of Income by Size', *Economic Development and Cultural Change*, Part II, January.

Maddison, A. (1991) *Dynamic Forces in Capitalist Development* (Oxford: Oxford University Press).

Mauro, P. (1995) 'Corruption and Growth', *Quarterly Journal of Economics*, August.

Morawetz, D. (1974) 'Employment Implications of Industrialisation in Developing Countries', *Economic Journal*, December.

Myrdal, G. (1957) (1963) *Economic Theory and Underdeveloped Regions* (London: Duckworth) (paperback edn, London: Methuen).

Naqvi, S.N.H. (1995) 'The Nature of Economic Development', *World Development*, April.

O'Grada, C. (2007) 'Making Famine History', *Journal of Economic Literature*, March.

Oxfam (2007) *Africa's Missing Billions*, Briefing Paper 107, October (IANSA, Oxfam and a Safer World).

Paukert, E. (1973) 'Income Distribution at Different Levels of Development: A Survey of Evidence', *International Labour Review*, August.

Pieper, U. (2003) 'Sectoral Regularities of Productivity Growth in Developing Countries: A Kaldorian Interpretation', *Cambridge Journal of Economics*, June.

Ravallion, M. (1997) 'Famines and Economics', *Journal of Economic Literature*, September.

Reinert, E. (2007) *How Rich Countries Got Rich and Why Poor Countries Stay Poor* (London: Constable and Robinson).

Rodrik, D. (2007) *One Economics: Many Recipes* (Princeton, NJ: Princeton University Press).

Rodrik, D., A. Subramanian and F. Trebbi (2002) 'Institutions Rule: The Primacy of Institutions over Geography and Integration in Economic Development', *NBER Working Paper 9305*, October.

Rostow, W.W. (1960) *The Stages of Economic Growth* (Cambridge: Cambridge University Press).

Rowthorn, R. and R. Ramswamy (1999) 'Growth, Trade and Deindustrialisation', *IMF Staff Papers*, March.

Sachs, J. (2003) 'Institutions Matter, But Not for Everything', *Finance and Development*, June.

Sachs, J. and A. Warner (2001) 'The Curse of Natural Resources', *European Economic Review*, May.

Sen, A.K. (1981a) *Poverty and Famines: An Essay on Entitlement and Deprivation* (Oxford: Clarendon Press).

Sen, A.K. (1981b) 'Ingredients of Famine Analysis: Availability and Entitlements', *Quarterly Journal of Economics*, August.

Stewart, F. (1985) *Planning to Meet Basic Needs* (London: Macmillan).

Stewart, F. (2001) *Horizontal Inequalities: A Neglected Dimension of Development* (WIDER: Helsinki).

Streeten, P. et al. (1981) *First Things First: Meeting Basic Human Needs in the Developing Countries* (Oxford: Oxford University Press for the World Bank).

Thirlwall, A.P. (ed.) (1983) 'Symposium on Kaldor's Growth Laws', *Journal of Post Keynesian Economics*, Spring.

Thorbecke, E. (1973) 'The Employment Problem: A Critical Evaluation of Four ILO Comprehensive Country Reports', *International Labour Review*, May.

Tregenna, F. (2009) 'Characterising Deindustrialisation: An Analysis of Changes in Manufacturing Employment and Output Internationally', *Cambridge Journal of Economics*, May.

Turnham, T. (1971) *The Employment Problem in Less Developed Countries* (Paris: OECD).

Wade, R. (1990) *Governing the Market: Economic Theory and the Role of Government in East Asian Industrialisation* (Princeton, NJ: Princeton University Press).

Wells, H. and A.P. Thirlwall (2003) 'Testing Kaldor's Growth Laws Across the Countries of Africa', *African Development Review*, December.

White, A. and E. Anderson (1991) 'Growth versus Distribution: Does the Pattern of Growth Matter?', *Development Policy Review*, 19(3).

World Bank (1991) *World Development Report 1991* (Washington, DC: World Bank).

World Bank (1995) *World Development Report 1995: Workers in an Integrating World* (Oxford: Oxford University Press for the World Bank).

World Bank (1997) *World Development Report* (Washington, DC: World Bank).

World Bank (2000) *World Development Report 2000/2001: Attacking Poverty* (New York: Oxford University Press).

World Bank (2001a) *World Development Indicators 2001* (Washington, DC: World Bank).

World Bank (2001b) *World Development Report 2002* (Washington, DC: World Bank).

World Bank (2004) *World Development Indicators, 2004* (Washington, DC: World Bank).

World Bank (2009) *World Development Indicators, 2009* (Washington, DC: World Bank).

WHO (World Health Organization) (2001) *Macroeconomics and Health: Investing in Health for Economic Development* (Geneva: WTO).

Chapter 4   The role of institutions in economic development

Acemoglu, D. (2008) 'Root Causes: An Historical Approach to Assessing the Role of Institutions in Economic Development', in G. Secondi (ed.) *The Development Economics Reader* (London: Routledge).

Acemoglu, D., S. Johnson and J. Robinson (2001) 'The Colonial Origins of Comparative Development: An Empirical Investigation', *American Economic Review*, December.

Acemoglu, D., S. Johnson and J. Robinson (2002) 'Reversal of Fortune: Geography and Institutions in the Making of the Modern World Income Distribution', *Quarterly Journal of Economics*, November.

Alesina, A. and D. Rodrik (1994) 'Distributive Politics and Economic Growth', *Quarterly Journal of Economics*, May.

Alesina, A. and R. Perotti (1994) 'The Political Economy of Growth: A Critical Survey of the Recent Literature', *The World Bank Economic Review*, 8(3).

Aron, J. (2000) 'Growth and Institutions: A Review of the Evidence', *The World Bank Research Observer*, February.

Bardhan, P. (1993) 'Symposium on Democracy and Development', *Journal of Economic Perspectives*, Summer.

Bardhan, P. (2005a) 'Institutions Matter, But Which Ones?', *Economics of Transition*, July.

Bardhan, P. (2005b) *Conflicts and Cooperation: Essays in the Political and Institutional Economics of Development* (Cambridge, MA: MIT Press).

Bardhan, P. and C. Udry (1999) *Development Microeconomics* (New York: Oxford University Press).

Barro, R. (1991) 'Economic Growth in a Cross Section of Countries' *Quarterly Journal of Economics*, May.

Barro, R. (1996a) 'Democracy and Growth', *Journal of Economic Growth*, January.

Barro, R. (1996b) 'Institutions and Growth: An Introductory Essay', *Journal of Economic Growth*, June.

Barro, R. (2008) 'Democracy and Growth', in G. Secondi (ed.) *The Development Economics Reader* (London: Routledge).

Chang, Ha-Joon (ed.) (2003) *Rethinking Development Economics*, (London: Anthem Press).

Gastil, R.D. (1983, 1986) *Freedom in the World* (Westport, CT: Greenwood).

Hausmann, R., L. Pritchett and D. Rodrik (2005) 'Growth Accelerations', *Journal of Economic Growth*, December.

Hoff, K. (2003) 'Paths of Institutional Development: A View from Economic History', *The World Bank Research Observer*, Fall.

Keefer, P. and S. Knack (1995) 'Institutions and Economic Performance: Cross-Country Tests Using Alternative Institutional Measures', *Economic and Politics*, November.

Kaufman, D., A. Kraay and P. Zoido-Lobaton (1999) *Governance Matters*, Policy Research Working Papers 2196, World Bank, October.

Lin, J.V. and J. Nugent (1995) 'Institutions and Economic Development', in J. Behrman and T. Srinivasan (eds), *Handbook of Development Economics* (Amsterdam: North Holland).

Mauro, P. (1995) 'Corruption and Growth', *Quarterly Journal of Economics*, August.

North, D. (1990) *Institutions, Institutional Change and Economic Performance* (New York: Cambridge University Press).

North, D. (1994) 'Economic Performance Through Time', *American Economic Review*, June.

Olson, M. (1982) *The Rise and Decline of Nations* (New Haven: Yale University Press).

Rodrik, D. (2000) 'Institutions for High Quality Growth and How to Acquire Them', *Studies in Comparative International Development*, Fall.

Rodrik, D. (2008) *One Economics: Many Recipes* (Princeton, NJ: Princeton University Press).

Rodrik, D. and A. Subramanian (2008) 'The Primacy of Institutions and What This Does and Does Not Mean', in G. Secondi (ed.) *The Development Economics Reader* (London: Routledge).

Rodrik, D., A. Subramanian and E. Trebbi (2004) 'Institutions Rule: The Primacy of Institutions over Geography and Integration in Economic Development', *Journal of Economic Growth*, June.

Sachs, J. (2008) 'Institutions Matter but not for Everything: The Role of Geography and Resource Endowments in Development Shouldn't be Underestimated', in G. Secondi (ed.) *The Development Economics Reader* (London: Routledge).

Secondi, G. (ed.) (2008) *The Development Economics Reader* (London: Routledge).

Shirley, M. (2008) *Institutions and Development* (Cheltenham: Edward Elgar).

World Bank (2002) *World Development Report 2002: Building Institutions for Markets* (Washington, DC: World Bank).

World Bank (2007) *World Development Report 2008* (Washington, DC: World Bank).

Chapter 5   Theories of economic growth: why growth rates differ between countries

Abramovitz, M. (1956) 'Resource and Output Trends in the United States since 1870', *American Economic Review, Papers and Proceedings*, May.

Abramovitz, M. (1986) 'Catching-up, Forging Ahead and Falling Behind', *Journal of Economic History*, June.

Adelman, I. (1961) *Theories of Economic Growth and Development* (Stanford University Press).

Amable, B. (1993) 'Catch-up and Convergence: A Model of Cumulative Growth', *International Review of Applied Economics*, January.

Arrow, K. (1962) 'The Economic Implications of Learning by Doing', *Review of Economic Studies*, June.

Barro, R. (1991) 'Economic Growth in a Cross-Section of Countries', *Quarterly Journal of Economics*, May.

Barro, R. (1998) *Determinants of Economic Growth*. Lionel Robbins Lectures (Cambridge, MA: MIT Press).

Barro, R. and X. Sala-i-Martin (2003) *Economic Growth*, 2nd edn (New York: McGraw Hill).

Barro, R. and J. Wha Lee (1993) 'Losers and Winners in Economic Growth', *Proceedings of the World Bank Conference on Development Economics* (Washington, DC: World Bank, 1994).

Baumol, W. (1986) 'Productivity Growth, Convergence and Welfare', *American Economic Review*, December.

Blaug, M. (1996) *Economic Theory in Retrospect*, 5th edn (Cambridge: Cambridge University Press).

Bosworth, B. and S. Collins (2007) 'Accounting for Growth: Comparing China and India', NBER Working Paper 12943 (Cambridge, MA: NBER).

Brown, M. (1966) *On the Theory and Measurement of Technical Change* (Cambridge: Cambridge University Press).

Chaudhuri, P. (1989) *Economic Theory of Growth* (Iowa: Iowa State University Press).

Cobb, C. and P. Douglas (1928) 'A Theory of Production', *American Economic Review*, Supplement, March.

Collier, P. and J.W. Gunning (1999) 'Explaining African Economic Performance', *Journal of Economic Literature*, March.

Cornwall, J. and W. Cornwall (1994) 'Structural Change and Productivity in the OECD', in P. Davidson and J. Kregel (eds), *Employment Growth and Finance: Economic Reality and Economic Theory* (Aldershot: Edward Elgar).

De Gregorio, J. (1992) 'Economic Growth in Latin America', *Journal of Development Economics*, July.

de Mello, L. (1996) *Foreign Direct Investment, International Knowledge Transfers and Endogenous Growth: Times Series Evidence* (Department of Economics, University of Kent, Studies in Economics).

Denison, E. (1962) *The Sources of Economic Growth in the US and the Alternatives before Us* (New York: Committee for Economic Development, Library of Congress).

Domar, E. (1947) 'Expansion and Employment, *American Economic Review*, March.

Douglas, P. (1948) 'Are There Laws of Production?', *American Economic Review*, March.

Dowrick, S. and N. Gemmell (1991) 'Industrialisation, Catching-up and Economic Growth: A Comparative Study across the World's Capitalist Economies', *Economic Journal*, March.

Dowrick, S. and D.T. Nguyen (1989) 'OECD Comparative Economic Growth 1950–85: Catch-Up and Convergence', *American Economic Review*, December.

Easterly, W. and R. Levine (2001) 'It's not Factor Accumulation: Stylised Facts and Growth Models', *The World Bank Economic Review*, 15(2).

Easterly, W. and L. Pritchett (1993) 'The Determinants of Economic Success: Luck and Policy', *Finance and Development*, December.

Eltis, W. (1984) *The Classical Theory of Economic Growth* (London: Macmillan).

Felipe, J. (1999) 'Total Factor Productivity Growth in East Asia: A Critical Survey', *Journal of Development Studies*, April.

Gomulka, S. (1971) *Inventive Activity, Diffusion and the Stages of Economic Growth* (Aarhus: Aarhus University Press).

Gomulka, S. (1990) *The Theory of Technological Change and Economic Growth* (London: Routledge).

Grossman, G. and E. Helpman (1990) 'Trade, Innovation and Growth', *American Economic Review Papers and Proceedings*, May.

Grossman, G. and E. Helpman (1991) *Innovation and Growth in the Global Economy* (Cambridge, MA: MIT Press).

Harrod, R. (1939) 'An Essay in Dynamic Theory', *Economic Journal*, March.

Hausmann, R., L. Pritchett and D. Rodrik (2005) 'Growth Accelerations', *Journal of Economic Growth*, December.

Hausmann, R., D. Rodrik and A. Velasco (2008) 'Growth Diagnostics', in J. Stiglitz and N.Serra (eds) *The Washington Consensus Reconsidered: Towards a New Global Governance* (New York: Oxford University Press).

Hirschman, A. (1958) *Strategy of Economic Development* (New Haven, CT: Yale University Press).

Hu, Z.F. and M.S. Khan (1997) 'Why is China Growing So Fast?', *IMF Staff Papers*, March.

Hulten, C. and A. Isaksson (2007) 'Why do Development Levels Differ: The Sources of Differential Growth in a Panel of High and Low Income Countries', NBER Working Paper 13469 (Cambridge, MA: NBER).

Islam, N. (2003) 'What Have we Learnt from the Convergence Debate?' *Journal of Economic Surveys*, July.

Kaldor, N. (1957) 'A Model of Economic Growth', *Economic Journal*, December.

Kaldor, N. (1961) 'Capital Accumulation and Economic Growth', in F. Lutz (ed.), *The Theory of Capital* (London: Macmillan).

Kaldor, N. (1967) *Strategic Factors in Economic Development* (Ithaca: Cornell University Press).

Kaldor, N. (1972) 'Advanced Technology in a Strategy for Development: Some Lessons from Britain's Experience', in *Automation and Developing Countries* (Geneva: ILO).

Kaldor, N. (1985) *Economics without Equilibrium* (Cardiff: University College Cardiff Press).

Kennedy, C. and A.P. Thirlwall (1972) 'Surveys in Applied Economics: Technical Progress', *Economic Journal*, March.

Kenny, C. and D. Williams (2001) 'What Do We Know About Economic Growth? Or, Why Don't We Know Very Much?', *World Development*, January.

Keynes, J.M. (1936) *The General Theory of Employment, Interest and Money* (London: Macmillan).

Knight, M., N. Loayza and D. Villanueva (1993) 'Testing the Neoclassical Theory of Economic Growth', *IMF Staff Papers*, September.

Krugman, P. (1994) 'The Myth of Asia's Miracle', *Foreign Affairs*, November–December.

Leon-Ledesma, M. and A.P. Thirlwall (2002) 'The Endogeneity of the Natural Rate of Growth', *Cambridge Journal of Economics*, July.

Levine, R. and D. Renelt (1992) 'A Sensitivity Analysis of Cross-Country Growth Regressions', *American Economic Review*, September.

Levine, R. and S. Zervos (1993) 'What We Have Learned About Policy and Growth From Cross-Country Regressions', *American Economic Review, Papers and Proceedings*, May.

Lucas, R. (1988) 'On the Mechanics of Economic Development', *Journal of Monetary Economics*, July.

Maddison, A. (1970) *Economic Progress and Policy in Developing Countries* (London: Allen & Unwin).

Malthus, T. (1798) *Essay on the Principle of Population* (London: Penguin, 1983).

Mankiw, N.G., D. Romer and D.N. Weil (1992) 'A Contribution to the Empirics of Economic Growth', *Quarterly Journal of Economics*, May.

Marshall, A. (1890) *Principles of Economics* (London: Macmillan).

Marx, K. (1867) *Capital: A Critique of Political Economy, Vol. 1* (New York: International Publishers, 1967).

Myrdal, G. (1957) *Economic Theory and Underdeveloped Regions* (London: Duckworth).

Nadiri, M. (1972) 'International Studies of Factor Inputs and Total Factor Productivity: A Brief Survey', *Review of Income and Wealth*, June.

Pack, H. (1994) 'Endogenous Growth: Intellectual Appeal and Empirical Shortcomings', *Journal of Economic Perspectives*, Winter.

Pritchett, L. (2000) 'Understanding Patterns of Growth: Searching for Hills among Plateaus, Mountains and Plains', *World Bank Economic Review*, May.

Pugno, M. (1995) 'On Competing Theories of Economic Growth: Cross-Country Evidence', *International Review of Applied Economics*, 9(3).

Putterman, L. (2000) 'Can an Evolutionary Approach to Development Predict Post-War Economic Growth?', *Journal of Development Studies*, February.

Ricardo, D. (1817) *Principles of Political Economy and Taxation* (London: Everyman, 1992).

Robinson, S. (1971) 'The Sources of Growth in Less Developed Countries: A Cross-Section Study', *Quarterly Journal of Economics*, August.

Romer, P.M. (1986) 'Increasing Returns and Long Run Growth', *Journal of Political Economy*, October.

Romer, P.M. (1990) 'Endogenous Technical Change', *Journal of Political Economy*, October.

Romer, P.M. (1994) 'The Origins of Endogenous Growth', *Journal of Economic Perspectives*, Winter.

Ruttan, V. (1998) 'New Growth Theory and Development Economics: A Survey', *Journal of Development Studies*, December.

Sala-í-Martin, X. (1997) 'I Just Ran Two Million Regressions', *American Economic Review*, May.

Senhadji, A. (2000) 'Sources of Economic Growth: An Extensive Growth Accounting Exercise', *IMF Staff Papers*, March.

Shaaeldin, E. (1989) 'Sources of Industrial Growth in Kenya, Tanzania, Zambia and Zimbabwe: Some Estimates', *African Development Review*, June.

Smith, A. (1776) *An Inquiry into the Nature and Causes of the Wealth of Nations* (London: Strahan & Caddell).

Solow, R. (1956) 'A Contribution to the Theory of Economic Growth', *Quarterly Journal of Economics*, February.

Solow, R. (1957) 'Technical Change and the Aggregate Production Function', *Review of Economics and Statistics*, August.

Solow, R. (1962) 'Technical Progress, Capital Formation and Growth', *American Economic Review*, Papers and Proceedings, May.

Summers, R. and A. Heston (1991) 'The Penn World Table (Mark 5): An Expanded Set of International Comparisons, 1950–1988', *Quarterly Journal of Economics*, May.

Swan, T. (1956) 'Economic Growth and Capital Accumulation', *Economic Record*, November.

Symposium on Convergence (1996) *Economic Journal*, July.

Symposium on Slow Growth in Africa (1999) *Journal of Economic Perspectives*, Summer.

Temple, J. (1999) 'The New Growth Evidence', *Journal of Economic Literature*, March.

Thirlwall, A.P. and G. Sanna (1996) ' "New" Growth Theory and the Macrodeterminants of Growth: An Evaluation and Further Evidence', in P. Arestis (ed.), *Employment, Economic Growth and the Tyranny of the Market* (Aldershot: Edward Elgar).

Williamson, J.G. (1968) 'Production Functions, Technological Change and the Developing Economies: A Review Article', *Malayan Economic Review*, October.

World Bank (1991) *World Development Report 1991* (Washington, DC: World Bank).

World Bank (2008) *The Growth Report: Strategies for Sustained Growth and Inclusive Development* (Washington, DC: World Bank)

Young, A. (1995) 'The Tyranny of Numbers: Confronting the Statistical Realities of the East Asian Growth Experience', *Quarterly Journal of Economics*, August.

Young, A.A. (1928) 'Increasing Returns and Economic Progress', *Economic Journal*, December.

Chapter 6   The role of agriculture and surplus labour for industrialization

Abrar, S., O. Morrissey and A. Rayner (2004) 'Crop-Level Supply Response by Agro-Climate Regions in Ethiopia', *Journal of Agricultural Economics*, July.

Adelman, I. (1984) 'Beyond Export Led Growth', *World Development*, September.

Askari, H. and J. Cummings (1976) *Agricultural Supply Response: A Survey of the Econometric Evidence* (New York: Praeger).

Bardhan, P. (1980) 'Interlocking Factor Markets and Agrarian Development: A Review of the Issues', *Oxford Economic Papers*, March.

Bardhan, P. (1984) *Land, Labour and Rural Poverty: Essays in Development Economics* (Oxford: Oxford University Press).

Bardhan, P. and C. Udry (1999) *Development Microeconomics* (New York: Oxford University Press).

Barnum, A.N. and R.H. Sabot (1977) 'Education, Employment Probabilities and Rural–Urban Migration in Tanzania', *Oxford Bulletin of Economics and Statistics*, May.

Besley, T. and R. Burgess (2000) 'Land Reform, Poverty and Growth: Evidence from India', *Quarterly Journal of Economics*, May.

Binswanger, H. and K. Deininger (1997) 'Explaining Agricultural and Agrarian Policies in Developing Countries', *Journal of Economic Literature*, December.

Chhibber, A. (1988) 'Raising Agricultural Output: Price and Non-Price Factors', *Finance and Development*, June.

Dorner, P. (1972) *Land Reform and Economic Development* (Harmondsworth: Penguin).

Dorner, P. (1992) *Latin American Land Reform in Theory and in Practice: A Retrospective Analysis* (Madison: University of Wisconsin Press).

Floro, M. and D. Ray (1997), 'Vertical Links between Formal and Informal Financial Institutions', *Review of Development Economics*, Vol. 1.

Floro, M. and P. Yotopoulos (1991) *Informal Credit Markets and the New Institutional Economics: The Case of Philippine Agriculture* (Boulder, CO: Westview Press).

Duranton, G. (1998) 'Agricultural Productivity, Trade and Industrialisation', *Oxford Economic Papers*, April.

Ghatak, S. and K. Ingersent (1984) *Agriculture and Economic Development* (Brighton: Wheatsheaf).

Gollin, D., S. Parente and R. Rogerson (1997) 'The Role of Agriculture in Development', *American Economic Review, Papers and Proceedings*, May.

Johnston, B.F. (1970) 'Agriculture and Structural Transformation in Developing Countries: A Survey of Research', *Journal of Economic Literature*, June.

Johnston, B.F. and J. Mellor (1961) 'The Role of Agriculture in Economic Development', *American Economic Review*, September.

Jorgenson, D. (1966) 'Testing Alternative Theories of the Development of a Dual Economy', in I. Adelman and E. Thorbecke (eds), *The Theory and Design of Economic Development* (Baltimore, MD: Johns Hopkins University Press).

Kaldor, N. (1979) 'Equilibrium Theory and Growth Theory', in M. Baskia (ed.), *Economics and Human Welfare: Essays in Honor of Tibor Scitovsky* (New York: Academic Press).

Kirkpatrick, C. and R. Barrientos (2004) 'The Lewis Model After 50 Years', *Manchester School*, December.

Knight, J.B. (1972) 'Rural–Urban Income Comparisons and Migration in Ghana', *Oxford Bulletin of Economics and Statistics*, May.

Lehmann, D. (ed.) (1974) *Agrarian Reform and Agrarian Reformism: Studies of Peru, Chile, China and India* (London: Faber & Faber).

Levi, J.S.F. (1973) 'Migration from the Land and Urban Unemployment in Sierra Leone', *Oxford Bulletin of Economics and Statistics*, November.

Lewis, A. (1954) 'Economic Development with Unlimited Supplies of Labour', *Manchester School*, May.

Lewis, A. (1958) 'Unlimited Supplies of Labour: Further Notes', *Manchester School*, January.

Lin, J.Y. (1992) 'Rural Reforms and Agricultural Growth in China', *American Economic Review*, March.

Lockwood, W.W. (1954) *The Economic Development of Japan: Growth and Structural Change 1868–1938* (Princeton, NJ: Princeton University Press).

Mehra, S. (1966) 'Surplus Labour in Indian Agriculture', *Indian Economic Review*, April.

Otsuka, K., H. Chuma and Y. Hayami (1992) 'Land and Labour Contracts in Agrarian Economies', *Journal of Economic Literature*, December.

Powelson J.P. and R. Stock (1987) *The Peasant Betrayed: Agriculture and Land Reform in the Third World* (Boston, MA: Oelgeschlager, Gunn and Hain).

Ranis, G. (2004) 'Arthur Lewis's Contribution to Development Thinking and Policy', *Manchester School*, December.

Ranis, G. and J. Fei (1961) 'A Theory of Economic Development', *American Economic Review*, September.

Ray, D. (1998) *Development Economics* (Princeton, NJ: Princeton University Press).

Schiff, M. and C.E. Montenegro (1997) 'Aggregate Agricultural Supply Response in Developing Countries: A Survey of Selected Issues', *Economic Development and Cultural Change*, January.

Schultz, T.W. (1964) *Transforming Traditional Agriculture* (New Haven, CT: Yale University Press).

Schultz, T.W. (1968) *Economic Growth and Agriculture* (New York: McGraw-Hill).

Schultz, T.W. (1980) 'The Economics of Being Poor', *Journal of Political Economy*, August.

Sen, A.K. (1964) 'Size of Holdings and Productivity', *Economic and Political Weekly*, February.

Sen, A.K. (1966) 'Peasants and Dualism: With and Without Surplus Labour', *Journal of Political Economy*, October.

Sen, A.K. (1981) 'Market Failure and Control of Labour Power: Towards an Explanation of 'Structure' and Change in Indian Agriculture: Part 1', *Cambridge Journal of Economics*, September.

Southworth, H. and B.F. Johnston (eds) (1967) *Agricultural Development and Economic Growth* (Ithaca: Cornell University Press).

Stark, O. (1991) *The Migration of Labour* (Oxford: Blackwell).

Stiglitz, J. (1974) 'Incentives and Risk Sharing in Sharecropping', *Review of Economic Studies*, 41(2): 2.

'Symposium on Lewis' Model' (1979) *Manchester School*, September.

'Symposium on Lewis' Model after 50 years' (2004) *Manchester School*, December.

Thirlwall, A.P. (1986) 'A General Model of Growth and Development on Kaldorian Lines', *Oxford Economic Papers*, July.

Todaro, M. (1969) 'A Model of Labour Migration and Urban Unemployment in Less Developed Countries', *American Economic Review*, March.

Todaro, M. (1971) 'Income Expectations, Rural–Urban Migration and Employment in Africa', *International Labour Review*, November.

Todaro, M. (1976) *Internal Migration in Developing Countries* (ILO: Geneva).

Vogel, S. (1994) 'Structural Change in Agriculture: Production Linkages and Agriculture: Production Linkages and Agricultural Demand-Led Industrialisation', *Oxford Economic Papers*, January.

Udry, C. (1994) 'Risk and Insurance in a Rural Credit Market: An Empirical Investigation, *Review of Economic Studies*, 61(3).

Weisdorf, J. (2006) 'From Domestic Manufacture to Industrial Revolution: Long Run Growth and Agricultural Development', *Oxford Economic Papers*, April.

World Bank (1979) *World Development Report 1979* (Washington, DC: World Bank).

World Bank (1982) *World Development Report 1982* (Washington, DC: World Bank).

World Bank (2000) *World Development Report 2000/2001: Attacking Poverty* (New York: Oxford University Press).

World Bank (2007) *World Development Report 2008: Agriculture for Development* (Oxford: Oxford University Press for the World Bank).

Yap, L.Y.L. (1977) 'The Attraction of Cities: A Review of the Migration Literature', *Journal of Development Economics*, September.

Chapter 7   Capital accumulation, technical progress and techniques of production

Ahiakpor, J. (1989) 'Do Firms Choose Inappropriate Technology in LDCs?', *Economic Development and Cultural Change*, April.

Arrow, K. (1962) 'The Economic Implications of Learning by Doing', *Review of Economic Studies*, June.

Bagachwa, M. (1992) 'The Economic Implications of Learning by Doing', *Review of Economic Studies*, June.

Barro, R. (1991) 'Economic Growth in a Cross-Section of Countries', *Quarterly Journal of Economics*, May.

Bell, M. and K. Pavitt (1992) 'Accumulating Technological Capability in Developing Countries', *The World Bank Economic Review, Supplement*.

Bliss, C. and N. Stern (1978) 'Productivity, Wages and Nutrition, Parts I and II', *Journal of Development Economics*, December.

Bruton, H. (1987) 'Technology Choice and Factor Proportions Problems in LDCs', in N. Gemmell (ed.), *Surveys in Development Economics* (Oxford: Blackwell).

Colclough, C. (1982) 'The Impact of Primary Schooling on Economic Development: A Review of the Evidence', *World Development*, April.

Dasgupta, P. (1993) *An Inquiry into Well-Being and Destitution* (Oxford: Clarendon Press).

Denison, E. (1962) *The Sources of Economic Growth in the US and the Alternatives Before Us* (New York: Committee for Economic Development, Library of Congress).

Dobb, M. (1955) 'A Note on the so-called Degree of Capital Intensity of Investment in Underdeveloped Countries', in *On Economic Theory and Socialism* (London: Routledge & Kegan Paul).

Fagerberg, J., M. Scholec and M. Knell (2007) 'The Competitiveness of Nations: Why Some Countries Prosper While Others Fall Behind', *World Development*, October.

Forsyth, D. and R. Solomon (1977) 'Choice of Technology and Nationality of Ownership in a Developing Country', *Oxford Economic Papers*, July.

Harrod, R. (1948) *Towards a Dynamic Economics* (London: Macmillan).

Helleiner, G.K. (1975) 'The Role of Multinational Corporations in the Less Developed Countries' Trade in Technology', *World Development*, April.

Hicks, J. (1932) *The Theory of Wages* (London: Macmillan).

Hulten, C. and A. Isaksson (2007) 'Why Development Levels Differ: The Sources of Differential Income Growth in a Panel of High and Low Income Countries', NBER Working Paper 13469 (Cambridge, MA: NBER).

Jenkins, R. (1990) 'Comparing Foreign Subsidiaries and Local Firms in LDCs', *Journal of Development Studies*, January.

Lall, S. (1978) 'Transnationals, Domestic Enterprises and Industrial Structures in Host LDCs: A Survey', *Oxford Economic Papers*, July.

Lall, S. (1992) 'Technological Capabilities and Industrialisation', *World Development*, February.

Lewis, A. (1955) *The Theory of Economic Growth* (London: Allen & Unwin).

Navaretti, G.B. and D.G. Tarr (2000) 'International Knowledge Flows and Economic Performance: A Review of the Evidence', *World Bank Economic Review*, January.

Pack, H. (1974) 'The Employment-Output Trade-Off in LDCs – A Microeconomic Approach', *Oxford Economic Papers*, November.

Pack, H. (1976) 'The Substitution of Labour for Capital in Kenyan Manufacturing', *Economic Journal*, March.

Psacharopoulos, G. (1985) 'Returns to Education: A Further International Update and Implications', *Journal of Human Resources*, April.

Psacharopoulos, G. (1991) *Education for Development* (Washington, DC: World Bank).

Psacharopoulos, G. (1994) 'Returns to Investment in Education: A Global Update', *World Development*, September.

Rostow, W.W. (1960) *The Stages of Economic Growth* (Cambridge: Cambridge University Press).

Schultz, T. Paul (1988) 'Education Investments and Returns', in H. Chenery and T. Srinivasan (eds), *Handbook of Development Economics, Vol. 1*, (Amsterdam: North-Holland).

Schultz, T.W. (1961) 'Investment in Human Capital', *American Economic Review*, March.

Schumpeter, J. (1934) *The Theory of Economic Development* (Cambridge, MA: Harvard University Press).

Schumpeter, J. (1943) *Capitalism, Socialism and Democracy* (London: Allen & Unwin).

Straub, S. (2008) 'Infrastructure and Growth in Developing Countries: Recent Advances and Research Challenges', Policy Research Working Paper 4460 (Washington, DC: World Bank).

Sen, A.K. (1968) *Choice of Techniques*, 3rd edn (Oxford: Basil Blackwell).

Sen, A.K. (1969) 'Choice of Technology: A Critical Survey of a Class of Debates', in UNIDO, *Planning for Advanced Skills and Technology* (New York: UNIDO).

Sen, A.K. (1975) *Employment, Technology and Development* (Oxford: Clarendon Press).

Stewart, F. (1977) *Technology and Underdevelopment* (London: Macmillan).

Summers, L. (1994) 'Investing in All the People', World Bank Policy Research Working Paper Series No 905 (Washington, DC: World Bank).

Thirlwall, A.P. (1974) *Inflation, Saving and Growth in Developing Economies* (London:Macmillan).

Thirlwall, A.P. (1977) 'The Shadow Wage when Consumption is Productive', *Bangladesh Development Studies*, October–December.

Thirlwall, A.P. (1978) 'Reconciling the Conflict between Employment and Saving and Employment and Output in the Choice of Techniques in Developing Countries', *Rivista Internazionale di Scienze Economiche e Commerciali*, February.

UNDP (United Nations Development Programme), *Human Development Report 2007/2008* (New York: United Nations).

UN (United Nations) (1999) Human Development Report 1999 (New York: UNDP).

White, L. (1978) The Evidence on Appropriate Factor Proportions for Manufacturing in LDCs: A Survey', *Economic Development and Cultural Change*, October.

World Bank (1994) *World Development Report 1994: Infrastructure for Development* (Oxford: Oxford University Press).

World Bank (2004) *World Development Report 2005: A Better Investment Climate for Everyone* (Washington, DC: World Bank).

World Bank (2005) *World Development Report 2006: Equity and Development* (Washington, DC: World Bank).

Chapter 8   Dualism, centre–periphery models and the process of cumulative causation

Amin, S. (1974) *Accumulation on a World Scale: A Critique of the Theory of Underdevelopment* (New York: Monthly Review Press).

Baran, P. (1957) *The Political Economy of Growth* (New York: Monthly Review Press).

Barro R. and X. Sala-í-Martin (1992) 'Convergence', *Journal of Political Economy*, April.

Dixon, R. and A.P. Thirlwall (1975) 'A Model of Regional Growth Rate Differences on Kaldorian Lines', *Oxford Economic Papers*, July.

Dos Santos, T. (1970) 'The Structure of Dependence', *American Economic Review, Papers and Proceedings*, May.

Dos Santos, T. (1973) 'The Crisis of Development Theory and the Problem of Dependence in Latin America', in H. Bernstein (ed.), *Underdevelopment and Development* (Harmondsworth: Penguin).

Emmanuel, A. (1972) *Unequal Exchange: A Study of the Imperialism of Trade* (New York: Monthly Review Press, translated from the French).

Fagerberg, J. and B. Verspagen (1996) 'Heading for Divergence? Regional Growth in Europe Reconsidered', *Journal of Common Market Studies*, September.

Fagerberg, J., B. Verspagen and M. Caniels (1996) *Technology, Growth, and Unemployment Across European Regions*, Working Paper, 565 (Norwegian Institute of International Affairs), December.

Frank, G. (1967) *Capitalism and Underdevelopment in Latin America* (New York: Monthly Review Press).

Gallup, J., J. Sachs and A. Mellinger (1998), 'Geography and Economic Development', in B. Pleskovic and J. Stiglitz (eds), *Annual World Bank Conference on Development Economics 1998* (Washington, DC: World Bank).

Higgins, B. (1956) 'The "Dualistic Theory" of Underdeveloped Areas', *Economic Development and Cultural Change*, January.

Hirschman, A. (1958) *Strategy of Economic Development* (Yale University Press).

Kaldor, N. (1970) 'The Case for Regional Policies', *Scottish Journal of Political Economy*, November.

Krugman, P. (1989) 'Differences in Income Elasticities and Trends in Real Exchange Rates', *European Economic Review*, May.

Krugman, P. (1991) *Geography and Trade* (Cambridge, MA: MIT Press).

Krugman, P. (1995) *Development, Geography and Economic Theory* (Cambridge, MA: MIT Press).

Krugman, P. (1998) 'The Role of Geography in Development', in B. Pleskovic and J. Stiglitz (eds), *Annual World Bank Conference on Development Economics 1998* (Washington, DC: World Bank).

Krugman, P. and A. Venables (1995) 'Globalisation and the Inequality of Nations', *Quarterly Journal of Economics*, November.

Lipton, M. (1977) *Why Poor People Stay Poor* (London: Temple Smith).

Lucas, R. (1990) 'Why Doesn't Capital Flow from Rich to Poor Countries?' *American Economic Review, Papers and Proceedings*, May.

McCombie, J.S.L. and A.P. Thirlwall (1994) *Economic Growth and the Balance of Payments Constraint* (London: Macmillan).

Myrdal, G. (1957, 1963) *Economic Theory and Underdeveloped Regions* (London: Duckworth; paper, London: Methuen).

Prebisch, R. (1950) *The Economic Development of Latin America and its Principal Problems* (New York: ECLA, UN Dept of Economic Affairs).

Prebisch, R. (1959) 'Commercial Policy in the Underdeveloped Countries', *American Economic Review, Papers and Proceedings*, May.

Rodriguez-Pose, A. and N. Gill (2006) 'How Does Trade Affect Regional Disparities?', *World Development*, July.

Shankar, R. and A. Shah (2003) 'Bridging the Economic Divide within Countries: A Scorecard on the Performance of Regional Policies in Reducing Income Disparities', *World Development*, August.

Thirlwall, A.P. (1983) 'Foreign Trade Elasticities in Centre–Periphery Models of Growth and Development', *Banca Nazionale del Lavoro Quarterly Review*, September.

Toner, P. (1999) *Main Currents in Cumulative Causation* (London: Macmillan).

World Bank (2009) *World Development Report: Reshaping Economic Geography* (Washington, DC: World Bank).

Chapter 9　Population and development

Cassen, R. (1976) 'Population and Development: A Survey', *World Development*, October.

Cassen, R. et al. (1994) *Population and Development: Old Debates, New Conclusions* (Washington, DC: Overseas Development Council).

Enke, S. (1971) 'Economic Consequences of Rapid Population Growth', *Economic Journal*, December.

Finlay, A. and A. Finlay (1995) *Population and Development in the Third World* (Suffolk: Metheun and Co.).

Hoover, E. and A. Coale (1958) *Population Growth and Economic Development in Low Income Countries* (Princeton: Princeton University Press).

Kelley, A.C. (1988) 'Economic Consequences of Population Change in the Third World', *Journal of Economic Literature*, December.

Kremer, M. (1993) 'Population Growth and Technology Change: One Million BC to 1990', *Quarterly Journal of Economics*, August.

Leibenstein, H. (1957) *Economic Backwardness and Economic Growth* (New York: Wiley).

Meade, J. (1967) 'Population Explosion, Standard of Living and Social Conflict', *Economic Journal*, June.

Modigliani, F. (1970) 'The Life Cycle Hypothesis of Saving and Inter-Country Differences in the Savings Ratio', in W. Eltis et al. (eds), *Induction, Growth and Trade: Essays in Honour of Sir Roy Harrod* (Oxford University Press).

Neher, P.A. (1971) 'Peasants, Procreation and Pensions', *American Economic Review*, June.

Ohlin, G. (1967) *Population Control and Economic Development* (Paris: OECD).

Petty, W. (1682) *Essay Concerning the Multiplication of Mankind* (London: Mark Pardoe).

Rawls, J. (1972) *A Theory of Justice* (Oxford: Oxford University Press).

Reader, J. (2005) *Cities* (London: Heinemann).

Sidgwick, H. (1874) *Methods of Ethics* (London: Macmillan).

Simon, J. (ed.) (1992) *Population and Development in Poor Countries* (Princeton, NJ: Princeton University Press).

Simon, J. (1996) *The Ultimate Resource 2* (Princeton, NJ: Princeton University Press).

Simon, J. (1997) *The Economics of Population: Key Modern Writings, Vols 1 and 2* (Aldershot: Edward Elgar).

Thirlwall, A.P. (1972) 'A Cross Section Study of Population Growth and the Growth of Output and Per Capita Income in a Production Function Framework', *Manchester School*, December.

Thirlwall, A.P. (1988) 'Population Growth and Development', in D. Ironmonger, J.O.N. Perkins and T.V. Hoa (eds), *National Income and Economic Progress: Essays in Honour of Colin Clark* (London: Macmillan).

UN Population Fund (2003) *State of World Population 2002* (New York: United Nations).

UNDP (United Nations Development Programme) (1999) *Human Development Report* (New York: United Nations).

World Bank (1984) *World Development Report 1984: Population Change and Development* (New York: Oxford University Press for the World Bank).

World Bank (2000) *World Development Report 2000/2001: Attacking Poverty* (Oxford: Oxford University Press).

Chapter 10   Resource allocation in developing countries, and sustainable development

Abed, G. and S. Gupta (eds) (2002) *Governance, Corruption and Economic Performance* (Washington, DC: IMF).

Arndt, H. W. (1988) ' "Market Failure" and Underdevelopment', *World Development*, February.

Bardhan, P. (1997) 'Corruption and Development: A Review of Issues', *Journal of Economic Literature*, September.

Bhatt, V.V. (1964) 'Theories of Balanced and Unbalanced Growth: A Critical Appraisal', *Kyklos*, November.

Chang, Ha-Joon and R. Rowthorn (eds) (1995) *The Role of the State in Economic Change* (New York: Oxford University Press).

Crabtree, D. and A.P. Thirlwall (eds) (1993) *Keynes and the Role of the State* (London: Macmillan).

Eckaus, R. (1955) 'The Factor Proportions Problem in Underdeveloped Areas', *American Economic Review*, September.

Eckstein, O. (1957) 'Investment Criteria for Economic Development and the Theory of Intertemporal Welfare Economics', *Quarterly Journal of Economics*, February.

Elliott, K.A. (ed.) (1997) *Corruption and the Global Economy* (Washington, DC: Institute for International Economics).

Galenson, W. and H. Leibenstein (1955) 'Investment Criteria, Productivity and Economic Development', *Quarterly Journal of Economics*, August.

Ghani, A. and C. Lockhart (2008) *Fixing Failed States: A Framework for Rebuilding a Fractured World* (Oxford: Oxford University Press).

Ghosh, P.K. (ed.) (1984) *Development Policy and Planning: A Third World Perspective* (Westport, CT: Greenwood Press).

Griffin, K. and J. Enos (1970) *Planning Development* (Reading, MA: Addison-Wesley).

Hagen, E. (1963) *Planning Economic Development* (Homewood, IL: Irwin).

Hirschman, A. (1958) *Strategy of Economic Development* (New Haven, CT: Yale University Press).

Kahn, A. (1951) 'Investment Criteria in Development Programmes', *Quarterly Journal of Economics*, February.

Kaldor, N. (1972) 'The Irrelevance of Equilibrium Economics', *Economic Journal*, December.

Kaufmann, D. (2005) 'Ten Myths About Governance and Corruption', *Finance and Development*, September.

Killick, T. (1977) 'The Possibilities of Development Planning', *Oxford Economic Papers*, July.

Killick, T. (1989) *A Reaction Too Far: Economic Theory and the Role of the State in Developing Countries* (London: Overseas Development Institute).

Leibenstein, H. (1978) *General X-Efficiency Theory and Economic Development* (New York: Oxford University Press).

Lewis, A. (1955) *The Theory of Economic Growth* (London: Allen & Unwin).

Lewis, A. (1966) *Development Planning* (London: Allen & Unwin).

Lipton, M. (1962) 'Balanced and Unbalanced Growth in Underdeveloped Countries', *Economic Journal*, September.

Little, I.M.D. (1982) *Economic Development: Theory, Policies and International Relations* (New York: Basic Books).

Meier, R. (1965) *Developmental Planning* (New York: McGraw-Hill).

Nurkse, R. (1953) *Problems of Capital Formation in Underdeveloped Countries* (Oxford: Oxford University Press).

Ranis, G. (1962) 'Investment Criteria, Productivity and Economic Development: An Empirical Comment', *Quarterly Journal of Economics*, May.

Rosenstein-Rodan, P. (1943) 'Problems of Industrialisation of East and South-East Europe', *Economic Journal*, June–September.

Scitovsky, T. (1954) 'Two Concepts of External Economies', *Journal of Political Economy*, April.

Sen, A.K. (1957) 'Some Notes on the Choice of Capital Intensity in Development Planning', *Quarterly Journal of Economics*, November.

Sen, A.K. (1968) *Choice of Techniques*, 3rd edn (Oxford: Basil Blackwell).

Stern, N. (1989) 'The Economics of Development: A Survey', *Economic Journal*, September.

Stewart, F. (2001) *Horizontal Inequality: A Neglected Dimension of Development* (WIDER: Helsinki).

Stewart, F. and Ghani, E. (1991) 'How Significant are Externalities for Development?', *World Development*, June.

Stiglitz, J. (1990) *Economic Role of the State* (London: Allen & Unwin).

Streeten, P. (1993) 'Markets and States: Against Minimalism', *World Development*, August.

Sutcliffe, R. (1964) 'Balanced and Unbalanced Growth', *Quarterly Journal of Economics*, November.

Tanzi, V. (1998) 'Corruption around the World', *IMF Staff Papers*, 43(4).

Wade, R. (1990) *Governing the Market: Economic Theory and the Role of Government in East Asian Industrialisation* (Princeton, NJ: Princeton University Press).

Waterson, A. (1966) *Development Planning: Lessons of Experience* (Oxford: Oxford University Press).

World Bank (1997) *World Development Report 1997: The State in a Changing World* (New York: Oxford University Press).

World Bank (2004) *Doing Business in 2004: Understanding Regulation* (New York: Oxford University Press).

Chapter 11 Project appraisal, social cost–benefit analysis and shadow wages

Baldwin, G.B. (1972) 'A Layman's Guide to Little–Mirrlees', *Finance and Development*, March.

Brent, R. (1998) *Cost–Benefit Analysis for Developing Countries* (Cheltenham: Edward Elgar).

Curry, S. and J. Weiss (1993) *Project Analysis in Developing Countries* (London: Macmillan).

Dasgupta, P., S. Marglin and A.K. Sen (1972) *Guidelines for Project Evaluation* (New York: United Nations).

Dinwiddy, C. and F. Teal (1996) *Principles of Cost–Benefit Analysis for Developing Countries* (Cambridge: Cambridge University Press).

Fitzgerald, E.V.K. (1978) *Public Sector Investment Planning for Developing Countries* (London: Macmillan).

Hansen, J.R. (1979) *A Guide to the UNIDO Guidelines* (Vienna: UNIDO).

Kirkpatrick, C. and J. Weiss (eds) (1996) *Cost–Benefit Analysis and Project Appraisal in Developing Countries* (Cheltenham: Edward Elgar).

Lal, D. (1980) *Prices for Planning: Towards the Reform of Indian Planning* (London: Heinemann).

Little, I.M.D. (1961) 'The Real Cost of Labour and the Choice between Consumption and Investment', *Quarterly Journal of Economics*, February.

Little, I.M.D. and J. Mirrlees (1969) *Manual of Industrial Project Analysis in Developing Countries*, Vol. II: *Social Cost–Benefit Analysis* (Paris: OECD).

Little, I.M.D. and J. Mirrlees (1974) *Project Appraisal and Planning for Developing Countries* (London: Heinemann).

Overseas Development Administration (1972) *A Guide to Project Appraisal in Developing Countries* (London: HMSO).

Papps, I. (1987) 'Techniques of Project Appraisal', in N. Gemmell (ed.), *Surveys in Development Economics* (Oxford: Blackwell).

Pearce, D.W. (1971) *Cost–Benefit Analysis* (London: Macmillan).

Scott, M., J. MacArthur and D. Newbery (1976) *Project Appraisal in Practice* (London: Heinemann).

Sen, A.K. (1968) *Choice of Techniques*, 3rd edn (Oxford: Basil Blackwell).

Squire, L. and H.G. van der Tak (1975) *Economic Analysis of Projects* (Baltimore, MD: Johns Hopkins University Press).

Stewart, F. (1978) 'Social Cost–Benefit Analysis in Practice: Some Reflections in the Light of Case Studies Using Little–Mirrlees Techniques', *World Development*, February.

Symposium on Little–Mirrlees (1972) *Oxford Bulletin of Economics and Statistics*, February.

Thirlwall, A.P. (1970) 'An Extension of Sen's Model of the Valuation of Labour in Surplus Labour Economies', *Pakistan Development Review*, Autumn.

Thirlwall, A.P. (1977) 'The Shadow Wage when Consumption is Productive', *Bangladesh Development Studies*, October–December.

Chapter 12   Development and the environment

Barbier, E.R. (1989) *Economics, Natural Resource Scarcity and Development* (London: Earthscan).

Barnett, H.J. and C. Morse (1963) *Scarcity and Growth: The Economics of Natural Resource Availability* (Baltimore, MD: Johns Hopkins University Press).

Baumol, W. and W. Oates (1988) *The Theory of Environmental Policy*, 2nd edn (Cambridge: Cambridge University Press).

Blackman, A., M. Mathis and P. Nelson (2001) *The Greening of Development Economics* (Washington, DC: Resources for the Future).

Blowers, A. and P. Glasbergen (1996) *Environmental Policy in an International Context* (Chichester: John Wiley).

Bond, R., J. Curran, C. Kirkpatrick, N. Lee and P. Francis (2001) 'Integrated Impact Assessment for Sustainable Development: A Case Study Approach', *World Development*, June.

Booth, D.E. (1994) 'Ethics and the Limits of Environmental Economics' *Ecological Economics*, April.

Boulding, K.E. (1966) 'The Economics of the Coming Spaceship Earth', in H. Jarrett (ed.), *Environmental Quality in a Growing Economy* (Baltimore, MD: Johns Hopkins University Press).

Bowers, J. (1997) *Sustainability and Environmental Economics: An Alternative Text* (Harlow: Longman).

Bushby, J.W. (2009) 'The Climate Security Connection: What it Means for the Poor', in Brainard, L., A. Jones and M. Purvis (eds) *Climate Change and Global Poverty: A Billion of Lives in the Balance* (Washington, DC: Brooking Institution Press).

Brainard, L., A. Jones and M. Purvis (eds) (2009) *Climate Change and Global Poverty: A Billion Lives in the Balance* (Washington, DC: Brookings Institution Press).

Carson, R. (1962) *Silent Spring* (Boston: Houghton-Mifflin).

Cole, M.A. (2003) 'Development, Trade and the Environment: How Robust is the Environmental Kuznets Curve?' *Environment and Development Economics*, 8.

Common, M. (1996) *Environmental and Resource Economics: An Introduction*, 2nd edn (London: Longman).

Common, M. and S. Stagl (2005) *Ecological Economics: An Introduction* (Cambridge: Cambridge University Press).

Commoner, B. (1972) *The Closing Circle* (London: Cape).

Conable, B. (1989) 'Development and the Environment: A Global Balance', *Finance and Development*, December.

Dasgupta, P. (1982) *The Control of Resources* (Oxford: Blackwell).

Dasgupta, P. (2007) 'Comments on the Stern Review's Economics of Climate Change' *National Institute Economic Review*, January.

Dasgupta, P. (2008) 'Creative Accounting' *Nature*, October.

Dasgupta, P. and G.M. Heal (1979) *Economic Theory and Exhaustible Resources* (Cambridge: Cambridge University Press).

Dawkins, R. (1976) *The Selfish Gene* (Oxford: Oxford University Press).

de Bruyn, S. (2001) *Economic Growth and the Environment* (Dordrecht: Kluwer).

Ehrlich, P.R. and A.H. Ehrlich (1970) *Population, Resources, Environment: Issues in Human Ecology* (San Francisco: Freeman).

Fankhauser, S. (1995) *Valuing Climate Change: The Economics of the Greenhouse* (London: Earthscan).

Forrester, J. (1971) *World Dynamics* (Cambridge: Wright-Allen Press).

Garnaut, R. (2008) *The Garnaut Climate Change Review* (Cambridge: Cambridge University Press).

Garrod, G.D. and K. Willis (1999) *Economic Valuation of the Environment* (Cheltenham: Edward Elgar).

Goldsmith, E., R. Allen, M. Allaby, J. Davoli, and S. Lawrence (1972) *BluePrint for Survival* (London: Penguin).

Grossman, G. and A. Krueger (1995) 'Economic Growth and the Environment', *Quarterly Journal of Economics*, May.

Hanley, N. and G. Atkinson (2003) 'Economics and Sustainable Development: What Have we Learnt, and What do we Still Need to Learn?', in F. Berkhout, M. Leach and I. Scoones (eds) *Negotiating Environmental Change* (Cheltenham: Earthscan).

Hanley, N., J. Shogren and B. White (2006) *Environmental Economics: In Theory and Practice* (Basingstoke: Palgrave Macmillan).

Hanley, N. and C. Spash (1993) *Cost Benefit Analysis and the Environment* (Aldershot: Edward Elgar).

Hicks, J. (1946) *Value and Capital*, 2nd edn (Oxford: Oxford University Press).

Horta, K. (1996) 'The World Bank and International Monetary Fund', in J. Werksman, *Greening International Institutions* (London: Earthscan).

IMF (International Monetary Fund) (1993) 'Seminar Explores Links between Macro Policy and Environment' (Washington, DC: IMF).

IMF (International Monetary Fund) (2008) *Climate Change, the Environment and the Work of the IMF* (Washington, DC: IMF).

IPCC (Intergovernmental Panel on Climate Change) (1990) *First Assessment Report* (Cambridge: Cambridge University Press). Second Report 1995; Third Report 2001; Fourth Report 2007.

International Union for the Conservation of Nature and Natural Resources (1980) *World Conservation Strategy* (Gland: United Nations Environment and World Wildlife Fund).

Kay, J. and J. Mirrlees (1975) 'The Desirability of Natural Resource Depletion', in D. W. Pearce (ed.), *The Economics of Natural Resource Depletion* (London: Macmillan).

Kneese, A.V., R.V. Ayres and R.C. D'Arge (1970) *Economics and the Environment: A Materials Balance Approach* (Baltimore, MD: Johns Hopkins University Press).

Lawrence, D.P. (2003) *Environmental Impact Assessment: Practical Solutions to Recurrent Problems* (Oxford: Wiley).

Lele, S. (1991) 'Sustainable Development: A Critical Review', *World Development*, June.

Lomberg, B. (2001) *The Skeptical Environmentalist: Measuring the Real State of the World* (Cambridge: Cambridge University Press).

Makuch, Z. (1996) 'The World Trade Organisation and the General Agreement on Tariffs and Trade', in J. Werksman, *Greening International Institutions* (London: Earthscan).

Malthus, T. (1798) *Essay on the Principle of Population* (London: Penguin 1983).

Marshall, A. (1890) *Principles of Economics* (London: Macmillan).

Meadows, D.H., D.L. Meadows, R. Randers and W.W. Behrens (1972) *The Limits to Growth* (New York: Universe Books).

Mill, J.S. (1856) *The Principles of Political Economy* (London: Penguin, 1986).

Nature (1998) 'When Self Interest is a Key to a Better Environment' *Nature*, October.

Nordhaus, W. (2007) 'A Review of the Stern Review of Economics of Climate Change', *Journal of Economic Literature*, September.

Nordhaus, W.D. and J. Tobin (1972) 'Is Growth Obsolete?', in National Bureau of Economic Research, *Economic Growth* (Columbia: Columbia University Press).

Norton, B.G. (1987) *Why Preserve Natural Variety?* (Princeton, NJ: Princeton University Press).

Nyong, A. (2009) 'Climate Change Impacts in Developing Countries: Implications for Sustainable Development', in Brainard, L., A. Jones and M. Purvis (eds) *Climate Change and Global Poverty: A Billion Lives in the Balance* (Washington, DC: Brookings Institution Press).

OECD (Organisation for Economic Co-operation and Development) (1994) *Environmental Indicators: OECD Core Set* (Paris: OECD).

OECD (Organisation for Economic Co-operation and Development) (1999) *Economic Instruments for the Pollution Control and Natural Resource Management in OECD Countries: A Survey* (Paris: OECD).

Pearce, D. and R.K. Turner (1990) *Economics of Natural Resources and the Environment* (Hemel Hempstead: Harvester Wheatsheaf).

Perman, R., Y. Ma, J. McGilvray and M. Common (2003) *Natural Resource and Environmental Economics*, 3rd edn (Harlow: Pearson Education).

Pigou, A.C. (1920) *The Economics of Welfare* (London: Macmillan).

Ricardo, D. (1817) *Principles of Political Economy and Taxation* (London: Everyman 1992).

Sagoff, M. (1988) *The Economy of the Earth* (Cambridge: Cambridge University Press).

Schumacher, E. (1973) *Small is Beautiful: Economics as if People Mattered* (London: Blond & Briggs).

Sen, A.K. (1967) 'Isolation, Assurance and the Social Rate of Discount', *Quarterly Journal of Economics*, February.

Stern, N. (2006) *The Economics of Climate Change: The Stern Review* (Cambridge: Cambridge University Press).

Stern, N. (2008) 'The Cost of Tackling Global Climate Change Has Doubled Warns Stern', *Guardian* 26 June.

Sterner, T. (2003) *Policy Instruments for Environmental and Natural Resource Management* (Washington, DC: World Bank).

Stokke, O.S. and O.B. Thommessen (2003) *Yearbook of International Co-operation on Environment and Development 2003/2004* (London: Earthscan).

Tarbuck, E.J., F. Lutgens and D. Tusa (2008) *Earth Science*, 12th edn (London: Pearson Education).

Tietenberg, T. and N. Johnstone (2004) 'Ex Post Evaluation of Tradable Permits: Methodological Issues and Literature Review', in Tietenberg, T. and N. Johnstone (eds) *Tradable Permits: Policy Evaluation, Design and Reform* (Paris: OECD).

Tietenberg, T. and L. Lewis (2008) *Environmental and Natural Resource Economics*, 8th edn (London: Pearson Education).

UN (United Nations) (1993) *Earth's Summit: Agenda 21, United Nations Programme of Action from Rio* (New York: United Nations Department of Public Information).

UN (United Nations) (2005) *World Summit Outcome 2005* (New York: United Nations).

UN (United Nations) (2009) *The Millennium Development Goals Report 2009* (New York: United Nations).

Varian, H. (2005) *Intermediate Microeconomics: A Modern Approach*, 5th edn (New York: Norton).

Warren, R.N., W. Arnell, R. Nicholls, P.E. Levy and J. Price (2006) 'Understanding the Regional Impacts of Climate Change: Research Report Prepared for the Stern Review on the Economics of Climate Change' (Norwich: Tyndall Working Papers 90).

World Bank (1992) *World Development Report 1992* (New York: Oxford University Press).

World Bank (2001) *Making Sustainable Commitments: An Environment Strategy for the World Bank* (Washington, DC: World Bank).

World Bank (2002) *World Development Report: Sustainable Development in a Dynamic World* (Washington, DC: World Bank).

World Bank (2003) *Poverty and Climate Change: Reducing the Vulnerability of the Poor through Adaptation* (Washington, DC: World Bank).

World Bank (2004) *World Development Indicators, 2004* (Washington, DC: World Bank).

World Bank (2007) *World Development Report 2008* (Washington, DC: World Bank).

World Bank (2010) *World Development Report 2010: Development and Climate Change* (Washington, DC: World Bank).

World Commission on Environment and Development (1987) *Our Common Future* (Brundtland Report) (Oxford: Oxford University Press).

Chapter 13   Financing development from domestic resources

Adam, D. and J.D. Von Pischke (1992) 'Micro-enterprise Credit Programmes: Déjà vu', *World Development*, October.

African Development Report 1994: Financial Structures, Reforms and Economic Development in Africa (Abidjan: African Development Bank).

Ahmad, E. and N. Stern (1991) *The Theory and Practice of Tax Reform in Developing Countries* (Cambridge: Cambridge University Press).

Arestis, P. and P. Demetriades (1997) 'Financial Development and Economic Growth: Assessing the Evidence', *Economic Journal*, May.

Athukorala, P. (1998) 'Interest Rates, Savings and Investment: Evidence from India', *Oxford Development Studies*, June.

Balkenhol, B. (ed.) (2007) *Microfinance and Public Policy* (Geneva: International Labour Office).

Bandiera, O., G. Caprio, P. Honohan and F. Schiantarelli (2000) 'Does Financial Reform Raise or Reduce Saving?', *Review of Economics and Statistics*, May.

Barro, R. (1995) 'Inflation and Economic Growth', *Bank of England Quarterly Bulletin*, 2.

Beck, T. and A. Demirguc-Kunt (2009) 'Access to Finance: An Unfinished Agenda' *Journal of Economic Perspectives*, March.

Bird, R.M. (1991) *Tax Policy and Economic Development* (Baltimore, MD: Johns Hopkins University Press).

Bleaney, M. et al. (1995) 'Tax Revenue Instability with Particular Reference to Sub-Saharan Africa', *Journal of Development Studies*, August.

Braverman, A. and J. Guasch (1986) 'Rural Credit Markets and Institutions in Developing Countries: Lessons for Policy Analysis from Practice and Modern Theory' *World Development*, October.

Bruno, M. (1995) 'Does Inflation Really Lower Growth?', *Finance and Development*, September.

Bruno, M. and W. Easterly (1998) 'Inflation Crises and Long Run Growth', *Journal of Monetary Economics*, February.

Buffie, E.F. (1984) 'Financial Repression, the New Structuralists and Stabilisation Policy in Semi-industrialised Economies', *Journal of Development Economics*, April.

Burgess, R. and N. Stern (1993) 'Taxation and Development', *Journal of Economic Literature*, June.

Campos, R. (1961) 'Two Views on Inflation in Latin America', in A. Hirschman (ed.), *Latin American Issues* (New Haven, Conn.: Yale University Press).

Chaves, R. and C. Gonzales-Vega (1996) 'The Design of Successful Rural Intermediaries: Evidence from Indonesia', *World Development*, January.

Chelliah, R.J., H.J. Bass and M.R. Kelly (1975) 'Tax Ratios and Tax Effort in Developing Countries 1969–71', *IMF Staff Papers*, March.

Cho, Y.C. and D. Khatkhate (1990) 'Financial Liberalisation: Issues and Evidence', *Economic and Political Weekly*, May.

Clarke, R. (1996) 'Equilibrium Interest Rates and Financial Liberalisation in Developing Countries', *Journal of Development Studies*, February.

Cull, R., A. Demirguc-Kunt and J. Morduch (2007) 'Financial Performance and Outreach: A Global Analysis of Leading Microbanks', *Economic Journal*, February.

Cull, R.A., A. Demirguc-Kunt and J. Morduch (2009) 'Microfinance Meets the Market', *Journal of Economic Perspectives*, Winter.

Davidson, P. (1986) 'Finance, Funding, Saving and Investment', *Journal of Post Keynesian Economics*, Fall.

De Aghion, B. and J. Morduch (2005) *The Economics of Microfinance* (London: MIT Press).

De Gregorio, J. and P. Guidotti (1995) 'Financial Development and Economic Growth', *World Development*, March.

Demetriades, P.O. and P. Devereux (1992) 'Investment and "Financial Repression", Theory and Evidence from 63 LDCs', *Working Paper in Economics*, 92/16, Keele University.

Demetriades, P.O. and K.A. Hussein (1996) 'Does Financial Development Cause Economic Growth? Time Series Evidence from 16 Countries', *Journal of Development Economics*, December.

Diaz-Alejandro, C. (1985) 'Good-bye Financial Repression, Hello Financial Crash', *Journal of Development Economics*, September–October.

Dornbusch, R. and A. Reynoso (1989) 'Financial Factors in Economic Development', *American Economic Review, Papers and Proceedings*, May.

Drake, P.J. (1980) *Money, Finance and Development* (London: Martin Robertson).

Dutt, A. (1990–91) 'Interest Rate Policy in LDCs: A Post Keynesian View', *Journal of Post Keynesian Economics*, Winter.

Edwards, S. (1996) 'Why are Latin America's Savings Rates so Low? An International Comparative Analysis', *Journal of Development Economics*, October.

Eshag, E. (1983) *Fiscal and Monetary Policies and Problems in Developing Countries* (Cambridge: Cambridge University Press).

Fitzgerald, E.V.K. (1993) *The Macroeconomics of Development Finance: A Kaleckian Approach* (London: Macmillan).

Fry, M. (1989) 'Financial Development: Theories and Recent Experience', *Oxford Review of Economic Policy*, Winter.

Fry, M. (1995) *Money, Interest and Banking in Economic Development* (Baltimore, MD: Johns Hopkins University Press).

Fry, M. (1997) 'In Favour of Financial Liberalisation', *Economic Journal*, May.

Ghatak, S. and J. Sanchez-Fung (2006) *Monetary Economics in Developing Countries* (London: Macmillan).

Ghosh, A. and S. Phillips (1998) 'Inflation may be Harmful to Your Growth', *IMF Staff Papers*, December.

Gibson, H. and E. Tsakolotos (1994) 'The Scope and Limits of Financial Liberalisation in Developing Countries: A Critical Survey', *Journal of Development Studies*, April.

Gillis, M. (ed.) (1989) *Tax Reform in Developing Countries* (Durham, NC: Duke University Press).

Giovannini, A. (1983) 'The Interest Rate Elasticity of Savings in Developing Countries', *World Development*, July.

Giovannini, A. (1985) 'Saving and the Real Interest Rate in LDCs', *Journal of Development Economics*, August.

Goncalves, C. and J. Salles (2008) 'Inflation Targeting in Emerging Economies: What do the Data Say?', *Journal of Development Economics*, February.

Goode, R. (1993) 'Tax Advice to Developing Countries: An Historical Survey', *World Development*, January.

Greene, J. and D. Villanueva (1991) 'Private Investment in Developing Countries: An Empirical Analysis', *IMF Staff Papers*, March.

Gupta, K.L. (1987) 'Aggregate Savings, Financial Intermediation and Interest Rates', *Review of Economics and Statistics*, May.

Gurley, G.J. and E. Shaw (1960) *Money in a Theory of Finance* (Washington, DC: Brookings Institution).

Hamilton, E. (1952) 'Prices as a Factor in Business Growth', *Journal of Economic History*, Autumn.

Hermes, N. and R. Lensik (2007) 'The Empirics of Microfinance: What Do We Know?', *Economic Journal*, February.

Hossain, A. and A. Chowdhury (1996) 'Monetary and Financial Policies', in *Developing Countries: Growth and Stabilisation* (London: Routledge).

Hulme, D. and A. Thankom (eds) (2008) *Microfinance: A Reader* (London: Routledge).

Hussein, K. and A.P. Thirlwall (1999) 'Explaining Differences in the Domestic Savings Ratio across Countries: A Panel Data Study', *Journal of Development Studies*, October.

Johnson, O.E.G. (1984) 'On Growth and Inflation in Developing Countries', *IMF Staff Papers*, December.

Kaldor, N. (1955–56) 'Alternative Theories of Distribution', *Review of Economic Studies*, 23(2).

Kaldor, N. (1956) *Indian Tax Reform* (Delhi: Ministry of Finance).

Kaldor, N. (1980) *Reports on Taxation II, Collected Economic Essays, Vol. 8* (London: Duckworth).

Keynes, J.M. (1930) *Treatise on Money, Vol. 2* (London: Macmillan).

Keynes, J.M. (1931) *Essays in Persuasion* (London: Macmillan).

King, R.G. and R. Levine (1993) 'Finance and Growth: Schumpeter Might be Right', *Quarterly Journal of Economics*, August.

Kirkpatrick, C.H. and F.I. Nixson (1981) 'The Origins of Inflation in Less Developed Countries: A Selective Review', in I. Livingstone (ed.), *Development Economics and Policy: Readings* (London: Allen & Unwin).

Levine, R. (1997) 'Financial Development and Economic Growth: Views and Agenda', *Journal of Economic Literature*, June.

Levine, R. and S. Zervos (1993) 'What we have Learned About Policy and Growth From Cross-Country Regressions', *American Economic Review, Papers and Proceedings*, May.

Lewis, A. (1955) *The Theory of Economic Growth* (London: Allen & Unwin).

Lin, S. and H. Ye (2007) 'Does Inflation Targeting Really Make a Difference? Evaluating the Treatment Effect of Inflation Targeting in Seven Industrial Countries', *Journal of Monetary Economics*, November.

Lin, S. and H. Ye (2009) 'Does Inflation Targeting Make a Difference in Developing Countries?', *Journal of Development Economics*, May.

Loayza, N., K. Schmidt-Hebbel and L. Serven (2000) 'What Drives Private Saving Across the World?', *Review of Economics and Statistics*, May.

McKinnon, R. (1973) *Money and Capital in Economic Development* (Washington, DC: Brookings Institution).

McKinnon, R. (1991) *The Order of Economic Liberalisation: Financial Control in the Transition to the Market Economy* (Baltimore, MD: Johns Hopkins University Press).

Masson, P., J. Bayoumi and H. Samiei (1998) 'International Evidence on the Determinants of Private Saving', *World Bank Economic Review*, September.

Mikesell, R. and J. Zinser (1973) 'The Nature of the Savings Function in Developing Countries: A Survey of the Theoretical and Empirical Literature', *Journal of Economic Literature*, March.

Modigliani, F. and R. Brumberg (1954) 'Utility Analysis and the Consumption Function: An Integration of Cross Section Data', in K.K. Kurihara (ed.), *Post-Keynesian Economics* (New Brunswick: Rutgers University Press).

Molho, L.E. (1986) 'Interest Rates, Saving and Investment in Developing Countries: A Re-examination of the McKinnon–Shaw Hypothesis, *IMF Staff Papers*, March.

Morduch, J. (1999) 'The Microfinance Promise', *Journal of Economic Literature*, December.

Newbery, D. and N. Stern (1987) *The Theory of Taxation for Developing Countries* (Oxford: Oxford University Press for the World Bank).

Ogaki, M., J.D. Ostry and C.M. Reinhart (1996) 'Savings Behaviour in Low and Middle Income Developing Countries', *IMF Staff Papers*, March.

Ostry, J.D. and C.M. Reinhart (1995) 'Savings and the Real Interest Rate in Developing Countries', *Finance and Development*, December.

Pankaj, J. (1996) 'Managing Credit for Rural Poor': Lessons from the Grameen Bank', *World Development*, January.

Pastor, M. (1991) 'Bolivia: Hyperinflation, Stabilisation and Beyond', *Journal of Development Studies*, January.

Piancastelli, M. (2001) 'Measuring the Tax Effort of Developed and Developing Countries: Cross Country Panel Data Analysis 1985–95', mimeo, University of Kent at Canterbury.

Pollin, R. and A. Zhu (2006) 'Inflation and Economic Growth: A Cross-Country Non-Linear Anaysis', *Journal of Post Keynesian Economics*, Summer.

Robinson, J. (1960) 'Notes on the Theory of Economic Development', in *Collected Economic Papers* (Oxford: Blackwell).

Robinson, J. (1962) 'A Model of Accumulation', in *Essays in the Theory of Economic Growth* (London: Macmillan).

Rostow, W.W. (1960) *The Stages of Economic Growth* (Cambridge: Cambridge University Press).

Sarel, M. (1996) 'Nonlinear Effects of Inflation on Economic Growth', *IMF Staff Papers*, March.

Schumpeter, J. (1911) *The Theory of Economic Development* (Cambridge, MA: Harvard University Press).

Shaw, E. (1973) *Financial Deepening in Economic Development* (London: Oxford University Press).

Spratt, S. (2008) *Development Finance* (London: Routledge).

Stanners, W. (1993) 'Is Low Inflation an Important Condition for High Growth?' *Cambridge Journal of Economics*, March.

Stiglitz, J.E. and A. Weiss (1981) 'Credit Rationing in Markets with Imperfect Information', *American Economic Review*, June.

Tait, A.A. et al. (1979) 'International Comparisons of Taxation for Selected Developing Countries', *IMF Staff Papers*, March.

Tanzi, V. (1987) 'Quantitative Characteristics of the Tax System of Developing Countries', in D. Newbery and N. Stern (eds), *The Theory of Taxation for Developing Countries* (Oxford: Oxford University Press for the World Bank).

Tanzi, V. (1991) *Public Finance in Developing Countries* (Aldershot: Edward Elgar).

Temple, J. (2000) 'Inflation and Growth: Stories Short and Tall', *Journal of Economic Surveys*, September.

Thirlwall, A.P. (1974) *Inflation, Saving and Growth in Developing Economies* (London: Macmillan).

Thirlwall, A.P. (1976) *Financing Economic Development* (London: Macmillan).

Thirlwall, A.P. (1987) *Nicholas Kaldor* (Brighton: Wheatsheaf).

Tun Wai, U. (1972) *Financial Intermediaries and National Savings in Developing Countries* (New York: Praeger).

Warman, F. and A.P. Thirlwall (1994) 'Interest Rates, Savings, Investment and Growth in Mexico 1960–90: Tests of the Financial Liberalisation Hypothesis', *Journal of Development Studies*, April.

Williamson, J. and M. Mohar (1999) 'A Survey of Financial Liberalisation', *Princeton Essays in International Finance*, 211.

Woo Jung, S. (1986) 'Financial Development and Economic Growth: International Evidence', *Economic Development and Cultural Change*, January.

World Bank (1989) 'Financial Systems and Development: An Overview', *World Development Report* (Washington, DC: World Bank).

World Bank (1990) *Adjustment Lending: Ten Years of Experience* (Washington, DC: World Bank).

World Bank (1993) *The East Asian Miracle: Economic Growth and Public Policies* (Oxford: Oxford University Press).

World Bank (2000) *World Development Report 2000/2001: Attacking Poverty* (New York: Oxford University Press).

World Bank (2001) *World Development Report 2002* (Oxford: Oxford University Press).

Chapter 14   Foreign assistance, aid, debt and development

Adams, R. and J. Page (2005) 'Do International Migration and Remittances Reduce Poverty in Developing Countries', *World Development*, October.

Addison, T., G. Mavrotas and M. McGillivray (2005) 'Development Assistance and Development Finance: Evidence and Global Policy Agendas', WIDER Research Paper 23 (Helsinki: WIDER).

Aiyar, S., A. Berg and M. Hussain (2005) 'The Macroeconomic Challenge of Aid', *Finance and Development*, September.

Alesina, A. and D. Dollar (2000) 'Who Gives Foreign Aid to Whom and Why?', *Journal of Economic Growth*, March.

Allsopp, C. and V. Joshi (1991) 'The Assessment: the International Debt Crisis', *Oxford Review of Economic Policy*, Spring.

Bauer, P. (1971) *Dissent on Development* (London: Weidenfeld & Nicolson).

Bhattacharya, R. and B. Clements (2004) 'Calculating the Benefits of Debt Relief', *Finance and Development*, December.

Borensztein, E., J. De Gregorio and J.Wha. Lee (1995) 'How Does Foreign Investment Affect Growth?', NBER Working Paper 5057 (Cambridge, MA: NBER).

Bosworth, S. and S. Collins (1999) 'Capital Flows to Developing Economies: Implications for Savings and Investment', *Brookings Papers on Economic Activity*, 1.

Bourguignon, F. and C. Morrisson (1992) *Adjustment and Equality in Developing Countries: A New Approach* (Paris: OECD).

Burnside, C. and D. Dollar (2000) 'Aid, Policies and Growth', *American Economic Review*, September.

Cassen, R. (1994) *Does Aid Work?*, 2nd edn (Oxford: Clarendon Press).

Catrinescu, N., M. Leon-Ledesma, M. Piracha and B. Quillin (2008) 'Remittances, Institutions and Economic Growth', *World Development*, January.

Celasun, O and J. Walliser (2008) 'Managing Aid Surprises', *Finance and Development*, September.

Chenery, H. and M. Bruno (1962) 'Development Alternatives in an Open Economy: The Case of Israel', *Economic Journal*, March.

Claudon, M.P. (ed.) (1986) *World Debt Crisis* (Cambridge, MA: Ballinger).

Clements, M., S. Radelet and R. Bhavnani (2004) 'Counting Chickens When they Hatch: The Short Term Effect of Aid on Growth', Centre for Global Development Working Paper 44 (Washington, DC).

Cline, W.R. (1984) *International Debt: Systematic Risk and Policy Response* (Washington, DC: MIT Press for the Institute for International Economics).

Cline, W. (1995) *International Debt* (Harlow: Longman).

Coe, D., E. Helpman and A. Hoffmaister (1997) 'North–South R&D Spillovers', *Economic Journal*, January.

Collier, P. and D. Dollar (2000) *Aid Allocation and Poverty Reduction* (Washington, DC: World Bank).

Collier, P. and D. Dollar (2004) 'Development Effectiveness: What Have We Learnt?', *Economic Journal*, June.

Corbo, V., S. Fischer and S.B. Webb (1992) in *Adjustment Lending Revisited: Policies to Restore Growth* (Washington, DC: World Bank).

Cornia, G., R. Jolly and F. Stewart (1987, 1988) *Adjustment with a Human Face*, Vols I and II (Oxford: Oxford University Press).

Dalgaard, C.J., H. Hansen and F. Tarp (2004) 'On the Empirics of Foreign Aid and Growth', *Economic Journal*, June.

Daseking, C. (2002) 'Debt: How Much is too Much?', *Finance and Development*, December.

Davidson, P. (1992) *International Money and the Real World*, 2nd edn (London: Macmillan).

de Mello, L. (1997) 'Foreign Investment in Developing Countries and Growth: A Selective Survey', *Journal of Development Studies*, October.

Easterly, W. (2002) 'How Did Heavily Indebted Poor Countries Become Heavily Indebted? Reviewing Two Decades of Debt Relief', *World Development*, October.

Easterly, W. (2006) *The White Man's Burden* (Oxford: University Press).

El Shibley, M. and A.P. Thirlwall (1981) 'Dual-Gap Analysis for the Sudan', *World Development*, February.

Fajnzylbu, P. and J. Humberto Lopez (eds) (2008) *Remittances and Economic Development: Lessons from Latin America* (Washington, DC: World Bank).

Frank, A.G. (1981) *Crisis in the Third World* (London: Heinemann).

Friedman, M. (1958) 'Economic Aid: Means and Objectives', *Yale Review*, Summer.

Gibson, H.D. and A.P. Thirlwall (1989) 'An International Comparison of the Causes of Changes in the Debt Service Ratio 1980–85', *Banca Nazionale del Lavoro Quarterly Review*, March.

Gilbert, C., A. Powell and D. Vines (1999) 'Positioning the World Bank', *Economic Journal*, November.

Gilbert, C. and D. Vines (eds) (2000) *The World Bank: Structure and Policies* (Cambridge: Cambridge University Press).

Greenaway, D. and O. Morrissey (1993) 'Structural Adjustment and Liberalisation in Developing Countries: What Lessons Have We Learnt?' *Kyklos*, 46(2).

Griffin, K. (1970) 'Foreign Capital, Domestic Savings and Economic Development', *Bulletin of the Oxford Institute of Economics and Statistics*, May.

Griffith-Jones, S. and O. Sunkel (1986) *Debt and Development Crisis in Latin America* (Oxford: Clarendon Press).

Hansen, H. and F. Tarp (2001) 'Aid and Growth Regressions', *Journal of Development Economics*, April.

Harrigan, J. and P. Mosley (1991) 'Evaluating the Impact of World Bank Structural Adjustment Lending 1980–87', *Journal of Development Studies*, April.

Hermes, N. and R. Lensink (eds) (2001) 'Changing the Conditions for Development Aid', *Journal of Development Studies*, August.

IMF (International Monetary Fund) (2003) *World Economic Outlook: Growth and Institutions* (Washington, DC: IMF)

Jepma, C. (1991) *The Tying of Aid* (Paris: OECD).

Kennedy, C. (1968) 'Restraints and the Allocation of Resources', *Oxford Economic Papers*, July.

Kennedy, C. and A.P. Thirlwall (1971) 'Foreign Capital, Domestic Savings and Economic Development: Some Comments', *Bulletin of the Oxford Institute of Economics and Statistics*, May.

Keynes, J.M. (1919) *Economic Consequences of the Peace* (London: Macmillan).

Kraay, A. and V. Nehru (2006) 'When is External Debt Sustainable?', *The World Bank Economic Review*, 20(3).

Lall, S. (1974) 'Less Developed Countries and Private Foreign Direct Investment: A Review Article', *World Development*, 2(4,5).

Lensink, R. and O. Morrissey (2000) 'Aid Instability as a Measure of Uncertainty and the Positive Impact of Aid on Growth', *Journal of Development Studies*, February.

Lever, H. and C. Huhne (1985) *Debt and Danger: The World Financial Crisis* (Harmondsworth: Penguin).

Lomax, D.F. (1986) *The Developing Country Debt Crisis* (London: Macmillan).

Morrissey, O. and H. White (1993) 'How Concessional is Tied Aid?', *CREDIT Research Paper*, 93/13 (University of Nottingham).

Mosley, P. (1987) *Overseas Aid: Its Defence and Reform* (Brighton: Wheatsheaf).

Mosley, P., J. Harrigan and J. Toye (1991) *Aid and Power: The World Bank and Policy Lending: Vol. 1, Analysis and Policy Proposals; Vol. 2, Case Studies* (London: Routledge).

Mosley, P., J. Hudson and A. Verschoos (2004) 'Aid, Poverty and the "New Conditionality"', *Economic Journal*, June.

Moyo, D. (2009) *Dead Aid* (London: Allen Lane).

Noorbakhsh, F. (1997) 'Structural Adjustment and Standards of Living in Developing Countries', *Discussion Papers in Economics*, 9701 (Centre for Development Studies, Department of Economics, University of Glasgow).

Noorbakhsh, F. (1999) 'Standards of Living, Human Development Indices and Structural Adjustment in Developing Countries: An Empirical Investigation', *Journal of International Development*, January/February.

OECD (Organisation for Economic Co-operation and Development) (2000) *Development Cooperation 1999 Report* (Paris: OECD).

OECD (Organisation for Economic Co-operation and Development) (2001) *Development Cooperation 2000 Report* (Paris: OECD).

Ohlin, E. (1965) *Foreign Aid Policies Reconsidered* (Paris: OECD).

Omlin, C. (1965) 'The Evolution of Aid Doctrine', in *Foreign Aid Policies Reconsidered* (Paris: OECD).

Opeskin, B.R. (1996) 'The Moral Foundation of Foreign Aid', *World Development*, January.

Overseas Development Institute (ODI) (1996) *ODI Briefing Paper* (London: ODI, February).

Pacheco-López, P. (2005) 'Foreign Direct Investment, Exports and Imports in Mexico', *World Economy*, August.

Pattillo, C., C.H. Poirson and L. Ricci (2002) 'External Debt and Growth', *Finance and Development*, June.

Pearson Report (1969) *Partners in Development, Report of the Commission on International Development* (London: Pall Mall Press).

Pesmazoglu, J. (1972) 'Growth, Investment and Savings Ratios: Some Long and Medium Term Associations by Groups of Countries', *Bulletin of the Oxford Institute of Economics and Statistics*, November.

Raffer, K. and H. Singer (1994) *The Foreign Aid Business* (Aldershot: Edward Elgar).

Rajan, R. and A. Subramanian (2005) 'Aid and Growth: What Does the Cross-Country Evidence Show', IMF Working Paper 05/127 (Washington, DC: IMF).

Riddell, R. (2007) *Does Foreign Aid Really Work?* (Oxford: Oxford University Press).

Sachs, J.D. (1990) 'A Strategy for Efficient Debt Reduction', *Journal of Economic Perspectives*, Winter.

Sahn, D.E., P.A. Dorosh and S.D. Younger (2000) *Structural Adjustment Reconsidered* (Cambridge: Cambridge University Press).

Sharpe, S., A. Wood and E. Wratten (2005) 'UK: More Country Ownership', *Finance and Development*, September.

Singer, H. (1950) 'The Distribution of Gains between Investing and Borrowing Countries', *American Economic Review*, May.

Stiglitz, J. (1999) 'The World Bank at the Millennium', *Economic Journal*, November.

Stiglitz, J. (2002) *Globalisation and its Discontents* (London: Allen Lane).

Streeten, P. (1973) 'The Multinational Enterprise and the Theory of Development Policy', *World Development*, October.

Taylor, L. (1997) 'The Revival of the Liberal Creed – the IMF and the World Bank in a Global Economy', *World Development*, February.

Thirlwall, A.P. (1986) 'Foreign Debt and Economic Development', *Studies in Banking and Finance* (Supplement to the Journal of Banking and Finance), 4.

Thirlwall, A.P. (ed.) (1987) *Keynes and Economic Development* (London: Macmillan).

Trumbull, W. and H. Wall (1994) 'Estimating Aid-Allocation Criteria with Panel Data', *Economic Journal*, July.

UN (United Nations) (2000) *World Investment Report 2000* (New York: United Nations).

UNDP (United Nations Development Programme) (2003) *Human Development Report* (New York: Oxford University Press).

Weeks, J. (ed.) (1989) *Debt Disaster? Banks, Governments and Multilaterals Confront the Crisis* (New York: New York University Press).

White, H. (1992) 'The Macroeconomic Impact of Development Aid: A Critical Survey', *Journal of Development Studies*, January.

Wood, A. (2008) 'How Donors Should Cap Aid to Africa', *Financial Times* 4 September.

World Bank (1987) *World Development Report 1987* (Washington, DC: World Bank).

World Bank (1990) *Adjustment Lending: Ten Years of Experience* (Washington, DC: World Bank).

World Bank (1998) *Assessing Aid: What Works, What Doesn't, and Why* (New York: Oxford University Press).

World Bank (2000) *Global Development Finance 2000* (Washington, DC: World Bank).

World Bank (2001) *World Development Report 2002* (Oxford: Oxford University Press).

Chapter 15 Trade theory, trade policy and economic development

Ahmed, N. (2000) 'Export Responses to Trade Liberalisation in Bangladesh: A Cointegration Analysis', *Applied Economics*, 30.

Anderson, E. (2005) 'Openness and Inequality in Developing Countries: A Review of Theory and Recent Evidence', *World Development*, July.

Arbache, J., A. Dickerson and F. Green (2004) 'Trade Liberalisation and Wages in Developing Countries', *Economic Journal*, February.

Arora, V. and A. Vamvakidis (2005) 'How Much do Trading Partners Matter for Economic Growth?', *IMF Staff Papers*, April.

Athukorala, P. (1993) 'Manufactured Exports from Developing Countries and Their Terms of Trade: A Reexamination of the Sarkar–Singer Results', *World Development*, October.

Athukorala, P. (2000) 'Manufactured Exports and Terms of Trade of Developing Countries: Evidence from Sri Lanka', *Journal of Development Studies*, June.

Balassa, B. et al. (1971) *The Structure of Protection in Developing Countries* (Baltimore, MD: World Bank).

Barro, R. (2000) 'Inequality and Growth in a Panel of Countries', *Journal of Economic Growth*, March.

Barros, A.R. and A. Amazonas (1993) 'On the Deterioration of the Net Barter Terms of Trade for Primary Commodities', *UNCTAD Review*, 4.

Bertola, G. and R. Faini (1991) 'Import Demand and Non-Tariff Barriers: the Impact of Trade Liberalisation', *Journal of Development Economics*, November.

Bhagwati, J. (1958) 'Immiserising Growth: A Geometrical Note', *Review of Economic Studies*, June.

Bhagwati, J. (1962) 'The Theory of Comparative Advantage in the Context of Underdevelopment and Growth', *Pakistan Development Review*, Autumn.

Blattman, C., J. Hwang and J.G. Williamson (2007) 'Winners and Losers in the Commodity Lottery: The Impact of Terms of Trade Growth and Volatility in the Periphery 1870–1939', *Journal of Development Economics*, January.

Bleaney, M. (1993) 'Manufactured Exports of Developing Countries and their Terms of Trade since 1965: A Comment', *World Development*, October.

Bleaney, M. (1999) 'Trade Reform, Macroeconomic Performance and Export Growth in Ten Latin American Countries 1979–95', *Journal of International Trade and Economic Development*, 8(1).

Bleaney, M. and D. Greenaway (1993) 'Long Run Trends in the Relative Prices of Primary Commodities and in the Terms of Trade of Developing Countries', *Oxford Economic Papers*, July.

Cashin, P., H. Liang and C.J. McDermott (2000) 'How Persistent are Shocks to World Commodity Prices?', *IMF Staff Papers*, June.

Cashin, P. and C.J. McDermott (2002) 'The Long-Run Behavior of Commodity Prices: Small Trends and Big Variability', *IMF Staff Papers*, July.

Cashin, P., C.J. McDermott and A. Scott (2002) 'Booms and Slumps in World Commodity Prices', *Journal of Development Economics*, October.

Chang Ha-Joon (2002) *Kicking Away the Ladder: Development Strategy in Historical Perspective* (London: Anthem).

Chang, Ha-Joon (2005) *Why Developing Countries Need Tariffs* (Geneva: South Centre).

Chang, Ha-Joon (2007) *Bad Samaritans: Rich Nations, Poor Policies and the Threat to the Developing World* (New York: Random House Business Books).

Chenery, H. and A. Strout (1966) 'Foreign Assistance and Economic Development', *American Economic Review*, September.

Christian Aid (2005) 'The Economics of Failure: The Real Cost of Free Trade for Poor Countries', Briefing Paper, June.

Cline, W. (1997) *Trade and Income Distribution* (Washington, DC: Institute for International Economics).

Corden, W.M. (1966) 'The Structure of a Tariff System and the Effective Rate of Protection', *Journal of Political Economy*, June.

Darity, W. and L. Davis (2005) 'Growth, Trade and Uneven Development', *Cambridge Journal of Economics*, January.

de Mello, J. and A. Panagariya (eds) (1993) *New Dimensions in Regional Integration* (Cambridge: Cambridge University Press).

de Mello, J., J. Panagariya and D. Rodrik (1993) 'The New Regionalism: A Country Perspective', in J. de Mello and A. Panagariya (eds), *New Dimensions in Regional Integration* (Cambridge: Cambridge University Press).

Diakosavvas, D. and P.L. Scandizzo (1991) 'Trends in the Terms of Trade of Primary Commodities, 1900–1982: The Controversy and Its Origin', *Economic Development and Cultural Change*, January.

Dollar, D. (1992) 'Outward-Oriented Developing Countries Really Do Grow More Rapidly: Evidence from 95 LDCs 1976–1985', *Economic Development and Cultural Change*, April.

Dollar, D. and A. Kraay (2002) 'Growth is Good for the Poor', *Journal of Economic Growth*, September.

Dollar, D. and A. Kraay (2004) 'Trade, Growth and Poverty', *Economic Journal*, February.

Dowrick, S. and J. Golley (2004) 'Trade Openness and Growth: Who Benefits?', *Oxford Review of Economic Policy*, Spring.

Edward, P. (2006) 'Examining Inequality: Who Really Benefits from Global Growth?', *World Development*, October.

Edwards, S. (1992) 'Trade Orientation, Distortions and Growth in Developing Countries', *Journal of Development Economics*, July.

Edwards, S. (1993) 'Openness, Trade Liberalisation and Growth in Developing Countries', *Journal of Economic Literature*, September.

Edwards, S. (1998) 'Openness, Productivity and Growth: What do we Really Know', *Economic Journal*, March.

Erten, B. (2010) 'North-South Terms of Trade from 1960 to 2006', *International Review of Applied Economics*,

Feder, G. (1983) 'On Exports and Economic Growth', *Journal of Development Economics*, February–April.

Felipe, J. (2009) *Inclusive Growth, Full Employment and Structural Change* (London: Anthem Press).

Feenstra, R. and R. Hanson (1997) 'Foreign Direct Investment and Relative Wages: Evidence from Mexico's Maquiladoras', *Journal of International Economics*, May.

Forouton, F. (1993) 'Regional Integration in Sub-Saharan Africa: Past Experience and Future Prospects', in J. de Melo and A. Panagariya (eds), *New Dimensions in Regional Integration* (Cambridge: Cambridge University Press).

Freeman, R. and R. Oostendrop (2001) 'The Occupational Wages Around the World Data', *international Labour Review*, 140(4).

George, C. (2010) *The Truth About Trade: The Real Impact of Liberalization* (London: Zed Books).

Ghose, A. (2004) 'Global Inequality and International Trade', *Cambridge Journal of Economics*, March.

Gilbert, C. (1987) 'International Commodity Agreements: Design and Performance', *World Development*, May.

Gilbert, C. (1996) 'International Commodity Agreements: An Obituary Notice', *World Development*, January.

Goldberg, P. and N. Pavcnik (2007) 'Distributional Effects of Globalisation in Developing Countries', *Journal of Economic Literature*, March.

Greenaway, D. and C. Milner (1993) *Trade and Industrial Policy in Developing Countries* (London: Macmillan).

Greenaway, D. and D. Sapsford (1994) 'What Does Liberalisation do for Exports and Growth?', *Weltwirtschaftliches Archives*, 1.

Greenaway, D., W. Morgan and P. Wright (1998) 'Trade Reform, Adjustment and Growth: What Does the Evidence Tell Us?', *Economic Journal*, September.

Greenaway, D., W. Morgan and P. Wright (2002) 'Trade Liberalisation and Growth in Developing Countries', *Journal of Development Economics*, February.

Grilli, E.R. and M.C. Yang (1988) 'Primary Product Prices, Manufactured Goods Prices, and Terms of Trade of Developing Countries: What the Long Run Evidence Shows', *World Bank Economic Review*, January.

Grossman, G. and E. Helpman (1991a) *Innovation and Growth in the Global Economy* (Cambridge, MA: MIT Press).

Grossman, G. and E. Helpman (1991b) 'Trade, Knowledge Spillovers and Growth', *European Economic Review*, April.

Hanson, G.H. and A. Harrison (1999) 'Trade Liberalisation and Wage Inequality in Mexico', *Industrial and Labour Relations Review*, 52(2).

Hausmann, R. and D. Rodrik (2003) 'Economic Development as Self-Discovery', *Journal of Development Economics*, December.

Hausmann, R., J. Hwang and D. Rodrik (2007) 'What You Export Matters', *Journal of Economic Growth*, March.

Heckscher, E. (1919) 'The Effect of Foreign Trade on the Distribution of Income', *Ekonomisk Tidskrift*, 21.

Helleiner, G. (ed.) (1994) *Trade Policy and Industrialisation in Turbulent Times* (London: Routledge).

Jenkins, R. (1996) 'Trade Liberalisation and Export Performance in Bolivia', *Development and Change*, April.

Jenkins, R. and K. Sen (2003) 'Globalization and Manufacturing Employment', *Development Research Insights*, Institute of Development Studies, Sussex, June.

Johnson, H.G. (1964) 'Tariffs and Economic Development: Some Theoretical Issues', *Journal of Development Studies*, October.

Johnson, H.G. (1967) *Economic Policies Towards Less Developed Countries* (London: Allen & Unwin).

Joshi, V. and I.M.D. Little (1996) *India's Economic Reforms 1991–2001* (Oxford: Oxford University Press).

Krueger, A. (1997) 'Trade Policy and Economic Development: How We Learn', *American Economic Review*, March.

Krueger, A. (1998) 'Why Trade Liberalisation is Good for Growth', *Economic Journal*, September.

Krugman, P. (1979) 'Increasing Returns, Monopolistic Competition and International Trade' *Journal of International Economics*, November.

Krugman, P. (1980) 'Scale Economies, Product Differentiation and the Pattern of Trade' *American Economic Review*, December.

Krugman, P. (1986) *Strategic Trade Policy and the New International Economics* (Cambridge, MA: MIT Press).

Leamer, E. (1988) 'Measures of Openness', in R. Baldwin (ed.), *Trade Policy and Empirical Analysis* (Chicago: Chicago University Press).

Leontief, W. (1953) 'Domestic Production and Foreign Trade: the American Position Re-examined', *Proceedings of the American Philosophic Society*, September.

Lim, D. (1991), *Export Instability and Compensatory Finance* (London: Routledge).

Little, I., T. Scitovsky and M. Scott (1970) *Industry and Trade in Some Developing Countries* (Oxford University Press).

Love, J. (1987), 'Export Instability in Less Developed Countries', *Journal of Economic Studies*, 14(2).

McCulloch, N., A. Winters and X. Cirera (2001) *Trade Liberalisation and Poverty: A Handbook* (London: Centre for Economic Policy Research).

Mah, J. (1994) 'Import Demand, Liberalisation and Economic Development', *Journal of Policy Modeling*, July.

Maizels, A. (ed.) (1987) 'Primary Commodities in the World Economy: Problems and Policies', *World Development*, May.

Maizels, A. (1992) *Commodities in Crisis* (Oxford: Oxford University Press).

Marshall, A. (1890) *Principles of Economics* (London: Macmillan).

Melo, O. and M. Vogt (1984) 'Determinants of Demand for Imports in Venezuala', *Journal of Development Economics*, April.

Michaely, M., D. Papageorgiou and A. Choksi (eds) (1991) *Liberalising Foreign Trade, Vol. 7: Lessons from Experience in the Developing World* (Oxford: Basil Blackwell).

Milanovic, B. (2005) 'Can we Discern the Effects of Globalization on Income Distribution?', *The World Bank Economic Review*, January.

Mill, J.S. (1848) *Principles of Political Economy* (London: Longmans, Green and Co.).

Moggridge, D. (ed.) (1980) *The Collected Writings of J.M. Keynes, Vol. XXVII: Activities 1940–1946 Shaping the Post-War World: Employment and Commodities* (London: Macmillan).

Morrissey, O. and H. White (1993) 'How Concessional is Tied Aid?', *CREDIT Research Paper*, 93/13 (University of Nottingham).

Ohlin, B. (1933) *Interregional and International Trade* (Cambridge, MA: Harvard University Press).

Oxfam (2002) *Rigged Rules and Double Standards: Trade, Globalization and the Fight Against Poverty* (Oxford: Oxfam).

Oyejide, A., I. Elbadawi and P. Collier (1997) *Regional Integration and Trade Liberalisation in Sub-Saharan Africa, Vol. 1: Framework Issues and Methodological Perspectives* (London: Macmillan).

Pacheco-López, P. (2005) 'The Impact of Trade Liberalisation on Exports, Imports, the Balance of Payments and Growth: the Case of Mexico', *Journal of Post Keynesian Economics*, Summer.

Pacheco-López, P. and A.P. Thirlwall (2007) 'Trade Liberalisation and the Trade-off between Growth and the Balance of Payments in Latin America', *International Review of Applied Economics*, September.

Pacheco-López, P. and A.P. Thirlwall (2006) 'Trade Liberalization, the Income Elasticity of Demand for Imports and Growth in Latin America', *Journal of Post Keynesian Economics*, Fall.

Parikh, A. (2002) 'Impact of Liberalisation, Economic Growth and Trade Policies on Current Accounts of Developing Countries: An Econometric Study', WDP 2002/63 (Helsinki: WIDER).

Prebisch, R. (1950) *The Economic Development of Latin America and its Principal Problems* (New York: ECLA, UN Dept of Economic Affairs).

Prebisch, R. (1959) 'Commercial Policy in the Underdeveloped Countries', *American Economic Review, Papers and Proceedings*, May.

Ram, R. (1987) 'Exports and Economic Growth in Developing Countries: Evidence from Time Series and Cross Section Data', *Economic Development and Cultural Change*, October.

Ravallion, M. (2001) 'Growth, Inequality and Poverty: Looking Beyond Averages', *World Development*, November.

Ravallion, M. (2006) 'Looking Beyond Averages in the Trade and Poverty Debate', *World Development*, August.

Reinert, E. (2007) *How Rich Countries Got Rich and Why Poor Countries Stay Poor* (London: Constable and Robinson).

Ricardo, D. (1817), *On the Principles of Political Economy and Taxation* (P. Sraffa, ed.) (Cambridge: Cambridge University Press).

Robbins, D.J. (1994) 'Worsening Relative Wage Dispersion in Chile during Trade Liberalisation and its Causes: Is Supply at Fault?', Development Discussion Papers no. 484, Harvard Institute for International Development, Harvard University.

Robbins, D.J. (1996) 'Evidence on Trade and Wages in the Developing World', OECD Development Centre Technical Paper 119, December.

Robbins, D.J. and T.H. Gindling (1999) 'Trade Liberalisation and the Relative Wages for More-Skilled Workers in Costa Rica', *Review of Development Economics*, 3.

Robson, P. (1968) *Economic Integration in Africa* (London: Allen & Unwin).

Robson, P. (1980) *The Economics of International Integration*, 4th edn, 1998 (London: Routledge).

Robson, P. (1988) *Integration, Development and Equity: Economic Integration in West Africa* (London: Allen & Unwin).

Rodriguez, F. and D. Rodrik (2000) 'Trade Policy and Economic Growth: A Skeptic's Guide to the Cross-National Evidence', in B. Bernanke and K. Rogoff (eds) *Macroeconomics Annual 2000* (Cambridge, MA: MIT Press).

Rodrik, D. (1996) 'Understanding Economic Policy Reform', *Journal of Economic Literature*, March.

Rodrik, D. (2001) *The Global Governance of Trade: As if Development Really Mattered* (New York: UNDP).

Sachs, J. and A. Warner (1995) 'Economic Reform and the Process of Global Integration', *Brookings Papers on Economic Activity*, 1.

Sachs, J.D. and A. Warner (1997) 'Sources of Slow Growth in African Economies', *Journal of African Economies*, 6(3).

Salvatore, D. and T. Hatcher (1991) 'Inward Oriented and Outward Oriented Trade Strategies', *Journal of Development Studies*, April.

Santos-Paulino, A. (2002a) 'Trade Liberalisation and Export Performance in Selected Developing Countries', *Journal of Development Studies*, October.

Santos-Paulino, A. (2002b) 'The Effects of Trade Liberalisation on Imports in Selected Developing Countries', *World Development*, June.

Santos-Paulino, A. (2007) 'Aid and Trade Sustainability under Liberalisation in Least Developed Countries', *World Economy*, June.

Santos-Paulino, A. and A.P. Thirlwall (2004) 'The Impact of Trade Liberalisation on Export Growth, Import Growth, and the Balance of Payments of Developing Countries', *Economic Journal*, February.

Sapsford, D. (1985) 'The Statistical Debate on the Net Barter Terms of Trade between Primary Commodities and Manufactures', *Economic Journal*, September.

Sapsford, D. (1988) 'The Debate over Trends in the Terms of Trade', in D. Greenaway (ed.), *Economic Development and International Trade* (London: Macmillan).

Sapsford, D. and V.N. Balasubramanyam (1994) 'The Long-Run Behaviour of the Relative Price of Primary Commodities: Statistical Evidence and Policy Implications', *World Development*, November.

Sarkar, P. (1986) 'The Singer–Prebisch Hypothesis: A Statistical Evaluation', *Cambridge Journal of Economics*, December.

Sarkar, P. and H. Singer (1991, 1993) 'Manufactured Exports of Developing Countries and their Terms of Trade since 1965', *World Development*, April and October.

Singer, H. (1950) 'The Distribution of Gains between Investing and Borrowing Countries', *American Economic Review*, May.

Skarstein, R. (2007) 'Free Trade: A Dead End for Underdeveloped Countries', *Review of Political Economy*, July

Smith, A. (1776) *An Inquiry into the Nature and Causes of the Wealth of Nations* (London: Strahan & Caddell).

Spilimbergo, A., J. Londono and M. Szekely (1999) 'Income Distribution, Factor Endowments and Trade Openness', *Journal of Development Economics*, June.

Spraos, J. (1980) 'The Statistical Debate on the Net Barter Terms of Trade between Primary Commodities and Manufactures', *Economic Journal*, March.

Stiglitz, J. (2006) *Making Globalization Work* (New York: W.W. Norton and Co.).

Thirlwall, A.P. (1976) 'When is Trade More Valuable than Aid?', *Journal of Development Studies*, October.

Thirlwall, A.P. (1986) 'A General Model of Growth and Development on Kaldorian Lines', *Oxford Economic Papers*, July.

Thirlwall, A.P. (2000) 'Trade Agreements, Trade Liberalisation and Economic Growth: A Selective Survey', *African Development Review*, December.

Thirlwall, A.P. and J. Bergevin (1985) 'Trends, Cycles and Asymmetries in the Terms of Trade of Primary Commodities from Developed and Less Developed Countries', *World Development*, July.

Thirlwall, A.P. and P. Pacheco-López (2008) *Trade Liberalisation and The Poverty of Nations* (Cheltenham: Edward Elgar).

Thomas, V., J. Nash and S. Edwards (1991) *Best Practices in Trade Policy Reform* (Oxford: Oxford University Press for the World Bank).

Thorbecke, E. and M. Nissanke (eds) (2006) 'Introduction: The Impact of Globalization on the World's Poor', *World Development*, August.

UNCTAD (United Nations Conference on Trade and Development) (1999) *Trade and Development Report* (Geneva: United Nations).

UNCTAD (United Nations Conference on Trade and Development) (2004) *The Least Developed Countries Report 2004* (Geneva: United Nations).

Vamvakidis, A. (1998) 'Regional Integration and Economic Growth', *The World Bank Economic Review*, May.

Vamvakidis, A. (1999) 'Regional Trade Agreements or Broad Liberalisation: Which Path Leads to Faster Growth?', *IMF Staff Papers*, March.

Wacziard, R. (2001) 'Measuring the Dynamic Gains from Trade', *The World Bank Economic Review*, 15(3).

Wacziard, R. and K. Welch (2008) 'Trade Liberalisation and Growth: New Evidence', *The World Bank Economic Review*, 22(2).

Wade, R. (2003) 'What Strategies are Viable for Developing Countries Today? The World Trade Organisation and the Shrinking of "Development Space" ', *Review of International Political Economy*, November.

Winters, A., N. McCulloch and A. McKay (2004) 'Trade Liberalisation and Poverty: The Evidence So Far', *Journal of Economic Literature*, March.

Wood, A. (1993) *North–South Trade: Employment and Inequality* (Oxford: Clarendon Press).

Wood, A. (1995) 'How Trade Hurt Unskilled Workers', *Journal of Economic Perspectives*, Summer.

Wood, A. (1997) 'Openness and Wage Inequality in Developing Countries: The Latin American Challenge to East Asian Conventional Wisdom', *The World Bank Economic Review*, January.

Wolf, M. (2005) *Why Globalization Works* (New Haven: Yale University Press).

World Bank (1987) *World Development Report* (Washington, DC: World Bank).

World Bank (2001a) *World Development Report 2002* (Oxford: Oxford University Press).

World Bank (2001b) *World Development Indicators 2001* (Washington, DC: World Bank).

World Bank (2002) *Globalization, Growth and Poverty* (Washington, DC: Oxford University Press).

Zhu, S. and D. Trefler (2005) 'Trade and Inequality in Developing Countries: A General Equilibrium Analysis' *Journal of International Economics*, January.

Chapter 16   The balance of payments, international monetary assistance and development

Ansari, M., N. Hashemzadeh and L. Xi (2000) 'The Chronicle of Economic Growth in Southeast Asian Countries: Does Thirlwall's Law Provide an Adequate Explanation?', *Journal of Post Keynesian Economics*, Summer.

Argy, V. (ed.) (1990) *Choosing an Exchange Rate Regime: The Challenge for Smaller Industrial Countries* (Washington, DC: IMF).

Asian Development Bank (1998) *Asian Development Outlook, 1998* (Manila: Asian Development Bank).

Athukorala, P. (2001) *Crisis and Recovery in Malaysia: The Role of Capital Controls* (Cheltenham: Edward Elgar).

Bairam, E. (1993) 'Income Elasticities of Exports and Imports: A Reexamination of the Empirical Evidence', *Applied Economics*, January.

Bird, G. (1982) *The International Monetary System and the Less Developed Countries*, 2nd edn (London: Macmillan).

Bird, G. (1987) *International Financial Policy and Economic Development* (London: Macmillan).

Bird, G. (1995) *IMF Lending to Developing Countries: Issues and Evidence* (London: Routledge).

Bird, G. (2001) 'IMF Programs: Do They Work? Can They be Made to Work Better?', *World Development*, November.

Bird, G. (2003) *The IMF and the Future: Issues and Options Facing the Fund* (London: Routledge).

Branson, W. (1983) 'Economic Structure and Policy for External Balance', *IMF Staff Papers*, March.

Broda, C. (2004) 'Terms of Trade and Exchange Rate Regimes in Developing Countries', *Journal of International Economics*, May.

Bubula, A. and I. Otker-Robe (2004) 'The Continuing Bi-Polar Conundrum', *Finance and Development*, March.

Collier, P. and J. Gunning (1999) 'The IMF's Role in Structural Adjustment', *Economic Journal*, November.

Corden, W.M. (1993) 'Exchange Rate Policies for Developing Countries', *Economic Journal*, January.

Crockett, A. (1977) 'Exchange Rate Policies for Developing Countries', *Journal of Development Studies*, January.

Dell, S. (1981) 'On Being Grandmotherly: The Evolution of IMF Conditionality', *Essays in International Finance*, 144 (Princeton University, October).

Dell, S. and R. Lawrence (1980) *The Balance of Payments Adjustment Process in Developing Countries* (New York: Pergamon).

Donavan, D.J. (1982) 'Macroeconomic Performance and Adjustment under Fund-Supported Programs: The Experience of the Seventies', *IMF Staff Papers*, June.

Dreher, A. (2006) 'IMF and Economic Growth: The Effects of Programs, Loans and Compliance with Conditionality', *World Development*, May.

Edwards, S. (1989) *Real Exchange Rates, Devaluation and Adjustment: Exchange Rate Policy in Developing Countries* (Cambridge, MA: MIT Press).

Fischer, S. (2001) 'Exchange Rate Regimes: Is the Bipolar View Correct?', *Journal of Economic Perspectives*, Spring.

Frenkel, J. (1999) 'No Single Currency Regime is Right for all Countries at all Times', *Princeton University Essays in International Finance*, 215.

Ghosh, A., A. Gulde and H. Wolf (2002) *Exchange Rate Regimes: Choices and Consequences* (Cambridge, MA: MIT Press).

Gore, C. (2000) 'The Rise and Fall of the Washington Consensus as a Paradigm for Developing Countries', *World Development*, May.

Guitian, M. (1982) *Fund Conditionality: Evolution of Principles and Practices* (Washington, DC: IMF).

Harrod, R. (1933) *International Economics* (Cambridge: Cambridge University Press).

Helleiner, G. K. (1983) *The IMF and Africa in the 1960s* (Princeton University: Essays in International Finance, 152), July.

IMF (International Monetary Fund) (2000) *IMF Annual Report 2000* (Washington, DC: IMF).

IMF (International Monetary Fund) (2001) *IMF Annual Report 2001* (Washington, DC: IMF).

IMF (International Monetary Fund) (2008) *Annual Report 2008* (Washington, DC: IMF).

Johnson, O.E.G. (1976) 'The Exchange Rate as an Instrument of Policy in a Developing Country', *IMF Staff Papers*, July.

Kaldor, N. (1964) 'Dual Exchange Rates and Economic Development', *Economic Bulletin for Latin America*, September (reprinted in *Collected Economic Essays*, II, London: Duckworth, 1981).

Kamin, S. and J.H. Rogers (2000) 'Output and the Real Exchange Rate in Developing Countries: an Application to Mexico', *Journal of Development Economics*, February.

Kenen, P. (2004) 'Appraising the IMF's Performance', *Finance and Development*, March.

Khan, M. (1990) 'The Macroeconomic Effects of Fund-supported Adjustment Programs', *IMF Staff Papers*, June.

Killick, T. (1995) *IMF Programmes in Developing Countries: Design and Impact* (London: Routledge).

Killick, T. (ed.) (1982) *Adjustment and Financing in the Developing World* (Washington, DC: IMF).

Killick, T. (ed.) (1984) *The Quest for Economic Stabilisation: The IMF and the Third World* and *The IMF and Stabilisation: Developing Country Experiences* (London: Heinemann for the Overseas Development Institute).

Lim, D. (1991) *Export Instability and Compensatory Financing* (London: Routledge).

Love, J. (1987) 'Export Instability in Less Developed Countries: Consequences and Causes', *Journal of Economic Studies*, 2.

McCombie, J.S.L. and A.P. Thirlwall (1997) 'The Dynamic Harrod Foreign Trade Multiplier and the Demand Oriented Approach to Economic Growth: An Evaluation', *International Review of Applied Economics*, January.

McCombie, J. and A.P. Thirlwall (1999) 'The East Asian Crisis: Retrospect and Prospect', *Economic Intelligence Unit Asia and Australasia Regional Overview*, 3rd Quarter.

McCombie, J. and A.P. Thirlwall (2004) *Essays on Balance of Payments Constrained Growth: Theory and Evidence* (London: Routledge).

Moreno-Brid, J.C. (1998) 'Balance of Payments Constrained Economic Growth: The Case of Mexico', *Banca Nazionale del Lavoro Quarterly Review*, 207.

Moreno-Brid, J.C. and E. Perez (1999) 'Balance of Payments Constrained Growth in Central America', *Journal of Post Keynesian Economics*, Fall.

Nashashibi, K. (1980) 'A Supply Framework for the Exchange Reform in Developing Countries: The Experience of Sudan', *IMF Staff Papers*, March.

Nell, K. (2003) 'A "Generalised" Version of the Balance of Payments Constrained Growth Model: An Application to Neighbouring Regions', *International Review of Applied Economics*, July.

Nowzad, B. (1981) 'The IMF and its Critics', *Princeton University Essays in International Finance*, 146, December.

Nureldin-Hussain, M. (1999) 'The Balance of Payments Constraint and Growth Rate Differences among African and East Asian Economies', *African Development Review*, June.

Nureldin-Hussain, M. (2001) ' "Exorcising the Ghost": An Alternate Model for Measuring the Finance Gap in Developing Countries', *Journal of Post Keynesian Economics*, Fall.

Nureldin-Hussain, M. and A.P. Thirlwall (1984) 'The IMF Supply-Side Approach to Devaluation: An Assessment with Reference to the Sudan', *Oxford Bulletin of Economics and Statistics*, May.

Pacheco-López, P. (2005) 'The Impact of Trade Liberalisation on Exports, Imports, the Balance of Payments and Growth: The Case of Mexico', *Journal of Post Keynesian Economics*, Summer.

Pastor, M. (1987) 'The Effects of IMF Programs in the Third World: Debate and Evidence from Latin America', *World Development*, February.

Payer, C. (1974) *The Debt Trap* (Harmondsworth: Penguin).

Perraton, J. (2003) 'Balance of Payments Constrained Growth and Developing Countries: An Examination of Thirlwall's Hypothesis', *International Review of Applied Economics*, January.

Razmi, A. (2005) 'Balance of Payments Constrained Growth Model: the Case of India', *Journal of Post Keynesian Economics*, Summer.

Przeworski, A. and J. Vreeland (2000) 'The Effect of IMF Programs on Economic Growth', *Journal of Development Economics*, August.

Reichmann, T.M. and R. Stillson (1978) 'Experience with Programs of Balance of Payments Adjustment: Stand-by Arrangements in the Higher Tranches, 1963–72', *IMF Staff Papers*, June.

Schadler, S. (1996) 'How Successful are IMF Supported Adjustment Programs?', *Finance and Development*, June.

Scitovsky, T. (1966) 'A New Approach to International Liquidity', *American Economic Review*, December.

Senhadji, A. (1988) 'Time Series Estimation of Structural Import Demand Equations: A Cross-Country Analysis', *IMF Staff Papers*, June.

Senhadji, A. and C. Montenegro (1999) 'Time Series Analysis of Export Demand Equations: A Cross-Country Analysis', *IMF Staff Papers*, September–December.

Spraos, J. (1986) 'IMF Conditionality: Ineffectual, Inefficient, Mistargeted', *Princeton University Essays in International Finance*, 166, December.

Stiglitz, J. (2002) *Globalisation and its Discontents* (London: Allen Lane, the Penguin Press).

Taylor, L. (1988) *Varieties of Stabilisation Experience* (Oxford: Clarendon Press).

Taylor, L. (1997) 'The Revival of the Liberal Creed – the IMF and the World Bank in a Global Economy', *World Development*, February.

Thirlwall, A.P. (1979) 'The Balance of Payments Constraint as an Explanation of International Growth Rate Differences', *Banca Nazionale del Lavoro Quarterly Review*, March.

Thirlwall, A.P. (2007) 'Regional Problems are Balance of Payments Problems', *Regional Studies*, September.

Thirlwall, A.P. (2003) *Trade, the Balance of Payments and Exchange Rate Policy in Developing Countries* (Cheltenham: Edward Elgar).

Thirlwall, A.P. and M. Nureldin-Hussain (1982) 'The Balance of Payments Constraint, Capital Flows and Growth Rate Differences between Developing Countries', *Oxford Economic Papers*, November.

Triffin, R. (1971) 'The Use of SDR Finance for Collectively Agreed Purposes', *Banca Naziónale del Lavoro Quarterly Review*, March.

UNCTAD (United Nations Conference on Trade and Development) (1998) *Trade and Development Report* (Geneva: UNCTAD).

Vreeland, J.R. (2003) *The IMF and Economic Development* (Cambridge: Cambridge University Press).

Williamson, J. (1990) 'What Washington Means by Policy Reform', in J. Williamson (ed.), *Latin American Adjustment: How Much Has Happened?* (Washington, DC: Institute for International Economics).

Williamson, J. (1993) 'Democracy and the "Washington Consensus"', *World Development*, August.

Williamson, J. (2000) *Exchange Rate Regimes for Emerging Markets: Reviving the Intermediate Option* (Washington, DC: Institute for International Economics).

Williamson, J. (ed.) (1983) *IMF Conditionality* (Washington, DC: Institute for International Economics).

World Bank (1987) *World Development Report 1987* (Washington, DC: World Bank).

World Bank (1998) *East Asia: The Road to Recovery* (Washington, DC: World Bank).

World Bank (2000) *Global Development Finance 2000* (Washington, DC: World Bank).

Yotopoulos, P. (1996) *Exchange Rate Parity for Trade and Development: Theory, Tests and Measurement* (Cambridge: Cambridge University Press).

Other introductory texts and reading

Chenery, H. and T.N. Srinivasan (eds) (1988) *Handbook of Development Economics*, Vols 1 and 2 (Amsterdam: North-Holland).

Clunies-Ross, A., D. Forsyth and M. Huq (2009) *Development Economics* (London: McGraw-Hill).

Colman, D. and F. Nixson (1986) *Economics of Change in Less Developed Countries* (Oxford: Philip Allan).

Cypher, J.M and J.L. Dietz (2004) *The Process of Economic Development* (London: Routledge).

Gemmell, N. (ed.) (1987) *Surveys in Development Economics* (Oxford: Blackwell).

Ghatak, S. (2003) *Introduction to Development Economics* (London: Longman).

Herrick, B. and C. Kindleberger (1983) *Economic Development* (New York: McGraw-Hill).

Lynn, S.R. (2003) *Economic Development* (New Jersey: Prentice Hall).

Meier, G. and J.E. Rauch (2000) *Leading Issues in Economic Development*, 7th edn (Oxford: Oxford University Press).

Nafziger, E.W. (1997) *The Economics of Developing Countries* 3rd edn (Englewood Cliffs, NJ: Prentice-Hall).

Perkins, D., S. Radelet and D. Lindauer (2006) *Economics of Development*, 6th edn (New York: W.W. Norton).

Ray, D. (1998) *Development Economics* (Princeton, NJ: Princeton University Press).

Secondi, G. (ed.) (2008) *The Development Economics Reader* (London: Routledge).

Thirlwall, A.P. (2002) *The Nature of Economic Growth: An Alternative Framework for Understanding the Performance of Nations* (Cheltenham: Edward Elgar).

Todaro, M.P. and S.C. Smith (2008) *Economic Development in the Third World* (London: Longman).

Van Den Berg, H. (2001) *Economic Growth and Development* (New York: McGraw-Hill).

NAME INDEX

Abed, G. 328n2, 616
Abramovitz, M. 157, 158, 164, 608
Abrar, S. et al. 192, 610
Acemoglu, D. 79, 118, 122, 124, 128, 604, 607
  et al. 79, 122, 123, 124, 604, 607
Adam, D. 620
Adams, R. 624
Addison, T. et al. 450, 624
Adelman, I. 85, 199, 604, 608, 610
Ahiakpor, J. 612
Ahluwalia, M.S.
  et al. 92, 604
  see also Chenery, H. et al. (1974)
Ahmad, E. 436n11, 620
Ahmed, N. 521, 627
Aiyar, S. et al. 449, 624
Alesina, A. 125, 126, 476, 607, 624
Allaby, M. see Goldsmith, E.R. et al.
Allen, R. see Goldsmith, E.R. et al.
Allsopp, C. 624
Amable, B. 164, 608
Amazonas, A. 627
Amin, Idi 90c
Amin, S. 278, 279, 614
Anderson, E. 530, 606, 627
Ansari, M. et al. 565t, 570, 632
Arbache, J. et al. 531, 627
Arestis, P. 411, 620
Argy, V. 600n5, 632
Arndt, H.W. 616
Arnell, W. see Warren, R.N. et al.
Aron, J. 607
Arora, V. 513, 627
Arrow, K. 11, 163, 236, 376, 608, 512
Askari, H. 225n2, 610
Athukorala, P. 560n6, 577, 620, 627, 632
Atkinson, G. 367, 370, 618
Ayres, R.V. see Kneese, A.V. et al.

Bagachwa, M. 612
Bairam, E. 116n9, 604, 632
Baker, J. 492
Balassa, B. et al. 521, 559n3, 627
Balasubramanyam, V.N. 631
Baldacci, E.B. et al. 84, 97, 604
Baldwin, G.B. 347, 617
Balkenhol, B. 620
Bandiera, O. et al. 409, 620
Baran, P. 278, 279, 614
Barbier, E.R. 381n10, 618
Bardhan, P. 6, 10, 119, 120, 124–5, 223, 225n1, 226n13, 329n3, 602, 607, 610, 616
Barnett, H.J. 373, 618
Barnum, A.N. 210, 226n12, 611
Barrientos, R. 611
Barro, R. 122, 125, 126, 162, 164, 166, 167t, 168, 169, 175n13, 238, 269, 532, 607, 608, 612, 614, 620, 627
Barros, A.R. 627
Baskia, M. 611
Bass, H.J. see Chelliah, R.J. et al.
Basu, K. 37, 603
Bauer, P. 447, 624
Baumol, W. 64, 162, 355, 603, 608, 618
Bayoumi, J. see Masson P. et al.
Beck, T. 620
Behrens, W.W. see Meadows, D.H. et al.
Behrman, J.R. 115n5, 604
Bell, C. 612
  see also Chenery, H. et al. (1974)
Bentham, J. 436n12
Berg, A. see Aiyar, S. et al.
Bergevin, J. 541, 631
Bertola, G. 523, 627
Besley, T. 46, 47t, 190–1, 603, 611

Bhagwati, J. 6, 507, 627
Bhatt, V.V. 616
Bhattacharya, R. 487, 624
Bhavnani, R. see Clements, M. et al.
Binswanger, H. 189, 219, 224, 225n1, 226n13, 611
Bird, G. 632
Bird, R.M. 436n9, 620
Bismarck, Otto von 107
Black, R. 602
Blackman, A. et al. 618
Blattman, C. et al. 545, 627
Blaug, M. 608
Bleaney, M. 521, 544, 545, 560n6, 621, 627
  et al. 418
Bliss, C. 93, 604, 612
Blowers, A. 618
Bond, R. et al. 380n4, 618
Booth, D.E. 371, 618
Borensztein, E. et al. 479, 624
Borlaug, N. 193, 195
Bosworth, S. 479, 608, 624
Boulding, K.E. 373, 618
Bourguignon, F. 34, 36, 470, 603, 624
Bowers, J. 618
Brady, N. 492
Brainard, L.A. et al. 377, 618
Brandt, W. 446, 477, 570, 602
Branson, W. 569, 632
Braverman, A. 621
Brent, R. 350n4, 617
Broda, C. 577, 632
Brown, L. 100
Brown, M. 608
Brumberg, R. 394, 623
Bruno, M. 428, 429, 430, 496n2, 621, 624
Bruntland, G.H. 369
Bruton, H. 612

Bubula, A. 577, 632
Buffie, E.F. 410, 621
Burgess, R. 46, 47t, 191, 436n9, 603, 611, 621
Burnside, D. 450, 476, 624
Bushby, J.W. 381n12, 618

Campos, R. 40, 434, 621
Caniels, M. *see* Fagerberg, J. et al. (1996)
Caprio, G. *see* Bandiera, O. et al.
Carlyle, T. 132
Carson, R. 373, 618
Carter, N. *see* Ahluwalia, M.S. et al.
Cashin, P. 544–5
    et al. (2000) 627
    et al. (2002) 551, 627
Cassen, R. 302n3, 449, 615, 624
Catrinescu, N. et al. 464, 624
Celasun, O. 451, 624
Chang, Ha-Joon 21, 113, 126–7, 128, 514, 533, 550, 602, 604, 607, 616, 627
Chatterji, M. et al. 605
Chaudhuri, P. 608
Chaves, R. 402, 621
Chelliah, R.J. et al. 621
Chen, S. 43, 46t, 47, 603
Chenery, H. 6, 116n8, 439, 496n2, 605, 624, 627, 634
    et al. (1974) 605
    et al. (1986) 605
    see also Ahluwalia, M.S. et al.
Chhibber, A. 192, 611
Cho, Y.C. 409, 621
Choksi, A. *see* Michealy, M. et al.
Chowdhury, A. 622
Chuma, H. *see* Otsuka, K. et al.
Cirera, X. *see* McCulloch, N. et al.
Clark, C. 102, 605
Clarke, R. 411
Claudon, M.P. 497n10, 624
Clements, B. 487, 624
    see also Baldacci, E.B. et al.
Clements, M. et al. 450, 624
Cline, W. 497n10, 624, 627
Clinton, W. 470
Clunies-Ross, A. et al. 634
Coale, A. 292, 615
Coase, R. 357, 358
Cobb, C. 147, 150, **153–8**, 173, 175n11, 608
Coe, D. et al. 479, 624
Colclough, C. 258n3, 612
Cole, M.A. 369, 618

Collier, P. 6, 43, 80, 603, 605, 608, 624, 632
    see also Oyejide, A. et al.
Collins, S. 479, 608, 624
Colman, D. 634
Common, M. 351, 371, 380n2, 618
    see also Perman, R. et al.
Commoner, B. 373, 618
Conable, B. 618
Corbo, V. et al. 469, 624
Corden, W.M. 559n3, 627, 632
Cornia, G. et al. 470, 624
Cornwall, J. 164, 608
Cornwall, W. 164, 608
Crabtree, D. 616
Crockett, A. 632
Cui, Q. *see* Baldacci, E.B. et al.
Cull, R.A. et al. 405
Cummings, J. 225n2, 610
Curran, J. *see* Bond, R. et al.
Curry, S. 617
Cypher, J.M. 634

Dalgaard, C.J. et al. 450, 624
D'Arge, R.C. *see* Kneese, A.V. et al.
Darity, W. 627
Daseking, C. 624
Dasgupta, P. 6, 92, 93, 254, 334, 358–9, 373, 376, 380n5, 605, 612, 618
    et al. 617
Davidson, P. 410, 621, 624
Davis, L. 627
Davoli, J. *see* Goldsmith, E.R. et al.
Dawkins, R. 371, 618
De Aghion, B. 621
de Bruyn, S. 369, 618
De Gregorio, J. 411, 608, 621
    see also Borensztein, E. et al.
de Mello, J. 628
    et al. 627
de Mello, L. 163, 479, 497n9, 608, 625
Deininger, K. 85, 85–8t, 188, 219, 224, 225n1, 226n13, 605, 611
Dell, S. 600n9, 632
Demetriades, P.O. 410, 411, 620, 621
Demirguc-Kunt, A. 620
    see also Cull, R.A. et al.
Denison, E. 237, 239, 608, 613
Devereux, P. 410, 621
Dhar, B. 196c
Diakosavvas, D. 541, 628
Diaz-Alejandro, C. 410, 621
Dickerson, A. *see* Arbache, J. et al.

Dietz, J.L. 634
Dinwiddy, C. 617
Dixon, R. 283n3–4, 614
Dobb, M. 251, 613
Dollar, D. 91, 450, 476, 524, 525, 531, 603, 605, 624, 628
Domar, E. 8, 140, 602, 608
Donavan, D.J. 595, 632
Dornbusch, R. 409, 621
Dorner, P. 225n1, 611
Dorosh, P.A. *see* Sahn, D.E. et al.
Dos Santos, T. 278–9, 614
Douglas, P., production function 147, 150, **153–8**, 173, 175n11, 608
Dowrick, S. 64, 164, 525, 532, 603, 608, 628
Drake, P.J. 621
Drakopoulos, S.A. 116n9, 605
Dreher, A. 596, 632
Drèze, J. 115n7, 605
Duloy, J. *see* Chenery, H. et al. (1974)
Duranton, G. 611
Dutt, A. 621
Dyson, T. 100, 605

Easterlin, R. 35, 603
Easterly, W. 79, 605, 608, 621, 625
Echaus, R. 616
Eckstein, O. 616
Edgeworth, F.Y. 533
Edward, P. 37, 531, 603, 628
Edwards, E.O. 605
Edwards, S. 395, 396, 524, 567, 621, 628, 632
    see also Thomas, V. et al.
Ehrlich, A.H. 373, 618
Ehrlich, P.R. 373, 618
El Shibley, M. 496n2, 625
Elbadawi, I. *see* Oyejide, A. et al.
Elliott, K.A. 329, 616
Eltis, W. 608
Emmanuel, A. xxx, 278, 280–1, 614
Engels, Friedrich 140, 542
Enke, S. xxx, 292, 615
Enos, J. 616
Erten, B. 545, 628
Eshag, E. 621

Fagerberg, J. 269, 614
    et al. (1996) 614
    et al. (2007) 235, 269, 613
Faini, R. 523, 627
Fajnzylbu, P. et al. 464, 625
Fankhauser, S. 618
Feder, G. 518

Feenstra, R. 628
Fei, J. 203, 611
Felipe, J. 83, 108, 158, 161, 521, 605, 608, 628
Finlay, A. 615
Fischer, S. 15, 602, 632
   see also Corbo, V. et al.
Fisher, A.G.B. 102, 605
Fitzgerald, E.V.K. 617, 621
Floro, M. 224, 611
Forbes, K.J. 91, 605
Forouton, F. 513, 628
Forrester, J.J. 368, 618
Forsyth, D. 251, 613
   see also Clunies-Ross, A. et al.
Francis, P. see Bond, R. et al.
Frank, A.G. 625
Frank, G. 278, 279–80, 614
Freeman, R. 530, 628
Frenkel, J. 600n5, 632
Friedman, M. 447, 625
Fry, M. 409, 412, 621
Furtado, C. 602

Galbraith, J.K. 19, 21, 602
Galenson, W. 616
Gallup, J. et al. 277, 278, 614
Gandhi, M.K. 66, 196
Garnaut, R. 618
Garrod, G.D. 363, 365, 370n7, 618
Gastil, R.D. 122, 125, 126, 607
Gates, Bill 194
Gemmell, N. 164, 608, 635
George, C. 526, 628
Gerschenkron, A. 10
Ghani, A. 316, 616, 617
Ghatak, S. 611, 621, 635
Ghose, A.K. 34, 603, 628
Ghosh, A. 429, 621
   et al. 560n5, 577, 632
Ghosh, P.K. 616
Gibson, H. 436n7, 622, 625
Gilbert, C. 625, 628
   et al. 470–1, 560n9, 625
Gill, N. 269, 615
Gillis, M. 622
Gilmore, B. see Chatterji, M. et al.
Gindling, T.H. 630
Giovannini, A. 409, 622
Glasbergen, P. 618
Godfrey, M. 605
Goldberg, P. 529, 531, 628
Goldsmith, E.R. et al. 373, 618
Golley, J. 525, 532, 628
Gollin, D. et al. 611
Gomulka, S. 164, 608

Goncalves, C. 428, 622
Gonzales-Vega, C. 402, 621
Goode, R. 622
Gore, C. 632
Goulet, D. 4, 18, 19, 20, 602
Green, F. see Arbache, J. et al.
Greenaway, D. 516, 544, 545, 625, 628
   et al. 515, 525, 628
Greene, J. 410, 622
Griffin, K. 496n3, 616, 625
Griffith-Jones, S. 497n10, 625
Grilli, E.R. 543, 544, 628
Grossman, G. 163, 369, 509, 609, 618, 628
Guasch, J. 621
Guidotti, P. 411, 621
Guitian, M. 600n9, 633
Gulde, A. see Ghosh, A. et al.
Gunning, J.W. 608, 632
Gupta, K.L. 409, 622
Gupta, S. 328n2, 616
   see also Baldacci, E.B. et al.
Gurley, G.J. 436n6, 622
Gylfason, J. 77, 78, 605

Hagen, E. 616
Hamilton, E. 420, 622
Hanley, N. 359, 367, 370, 618, 619
   et al. 361, 363, 618
Hansen, H. 625
   see also Dalgaard, C.J. et al.
Hansen, J.D. 111, 116n9, 605
Hansen, J.R. 617
Hanson, G.H. 628
Hanson, R. 628
Harrigan, J. 470, 625
   see also Mosley, P. et al. (1991)
Harris, J. et al. 605
Harrison, A. 628
Harrod, R. 8, 131, 140, **142**, 149, 173, 602, 609, 613, 633
Hasan, R. 83, 605
Hashemzadeh, N. see Ansari, M. et al.
Hatcher, T. 630
Hausmann, R. xxx, 534, 548, 549, 629
   et al. (2005) 127, 170, 171, 607, 609
   et al. (2007) 520, 629
   et al. (2008) 609
Hayami, Y. see Otsuka, K. et al.
Heal, G.M. 373, 618
Heckscher, E. **508–9**, 530, 532, 629
Helleiner, G. 251, 521, 613, 629, 633

Helpman, E. 163, 509, 609, 628
   see also Coe, D. et al.
Hermes, M. 403, 436n5, 622, 625
Herrick, B. 635
Heston, A. 40, 162, 604, 610
Hicks, J. 366, 369, 613, 619
Higgins, B. 614
Hirschman, A. 6, 8, 10, 135, **266**, 293, **323**, 324–6, 602, 609, 614, 616
Hoff, K. 607
Hoffmaister, A. see Coe, D. et al.
Honohan, P. see Bandiera, O. et al.
Hoover, E. 292, 615
Horta, K. 619
Hossain, A. 622
Hu, Z.F. 158, 160–1, 160t, 609
Hudson, J. see Mosley, P. (2004) et al.
Huhne, C. 497n10, 625
Hulme, D. 622
Hulton, C. 230, 609, 613
Humberto Lopez, J. see Fajnzylbu et al.
Hume, D. 420
Hunter, J. see Harris, J. et al.
Huq, M. see Clunies-Ross, A. et al.
Hussain, M. see Aiyar, S. et al.
Hussein, K. 394, 395, 396, 411, 622
Hwang, J. see Blattman, C. et al.; Hausmann, R. et al. (2007)

Imbs, J. 108, 605
Ingersent, K. 611
Isaksson, A. 230, 609, 613
Islam, N. 609

Jenkins, R. 521, 527–8c, 613, 629
Jepma, C. 463, 625
Johnson, H.G. 6, 535, 556, 629
Johnson, O.E.G. 436n15, 622, 633
Johnson, S. 118, 128
   see also Acemoglu, D. et al.
Johnston, B.F. 204, 611, 612
Johnstone, N. 620
Jolly, R. see Chenery, H. et al. (1974); Cornia, G. et al.
Jones, A. see Brainard, L.A. et al.
Jones, C. 603
Jorgenson, D. 204, 611
Joshi, V. 521, 624, 629

Kahn, A. 616
Kahn, R. 145, 276
Kaldor, N. xxx, 6, 11, 71, 135, 145, 163, 204, 262, **276**, 436n12, 600n6, 605, 609, 611, 614, 616, 622, 633

Kalecki, M. 6
Kamin, S. 567, 633
Kaufmann, D. 313, 616
    et al. 121
Kay, J. 363, 619
Keefer, P. 122, 123, 129n1, 607
Kelley, A.C. 302n3, 615
Kelly, M.R. see Chelliah, R.J. et al.
Kenen, P. 594, 633
Kennedy, C. 609, 625
Kenny, C. 169, 609
Keynes, J.M. 6, 131, 136, 140, 420,
    433, 495, 543, 565, 583, 592,
    595, 597, 609, 622, 625
Khan, M.S. 158, 160–1, 160t, 609,
    633
Khatkhate, D. 409, 621
Killick, T. 595, 596, 616, 633
Kindleberger, C. 635
King, R.G. 411, 622
Kirkpatrick, C. 611, 617, 622
    see also Bond, R. et al.
Knack, S. 122, 123, 129n1, 607
Kneese, A, V. et al. 373, 619
Knell, M. see Fagerberg, J. et al.
Knight, J.B. 611
Knight, M. et al. 166, 167t, 168, 609
Kraay, A. 91, 487, 525, 531, 603, 605,
    625, 628
    see also Kaufmann, D. et al.
Kravis, I.B. 40, 603
Kremer, M. 302n1, 615
Krueger, A. 369, 515, 618, 629
Krugman, P. xxx, 6, 10–11, 160, 270,
    276, 277, 282, **510**, 602, 609,
    614, 629
Kuznets, S. 6, 85, 605

Lal, D. 8, 350n5, 602, 617
Lall, S. 248, 613, 625
Lawrence, D.P. 377, 619
Lawrence, R. 632
Lawrence, S. see Goldsmith, E.R. et al.
Leamer, E. 629
Lee, N. see Bond, R. et al.
Lefeber, L. 617
Lehmann, D. 611
Leibenstein, H. 6, 615, 616
Lele, S. 369, 619
Lensink, R. 403, 436n5, 451, 622,
    625
Leon-Ledesma, M. 174n4, 609
    see also Catrinescu, N. et al.
Leontief, W. 246, 247, **508**, 629
Lever, H. 497n10, 625
Levi, J.S.F. 611

Levine, R. 79, 166, 167t, 168, 169,
    411, 430, 605, 608, 609, 622
Levy, P. see Warren, R.N. et al.
Lewis, A. xxx, 6, 9, 10, 74, **201**, 229,
    613, 616, 622
Lewis, C.M. see Harris, J. et al.
Lewis, W.A. 602
Liang, H. see Cashin, P. et al. (2000)
Lim, D. 560n10, 629, 633
Lin, J.V. 118, 607
Lin, J.Y. 190, 611
Lin, S. 428, 622
Lindauer, D. see Perkins, D. et al.
Lipton, M. 21, 262, 602, 614, 616
Little, I.M.D. xxxi, 8, 331, 334, 335,
    336, 337, 338, 339, 341, 342,
    343, **346–9**, 348t, 350n2, 521,
    602, 616, 617, 629
    et al. 521, 629
Loayza, N.
    et al. 395, 396, 622
    see also Knight, M. et al.
Lockhart, C. 316, 616
Lockwood, W.W. 182, 611
Lomax, D.F. 497n10, 625
Lomberg, B. 372, 619
Londono, J. see Spilimbergo, A. et al.
Love, J. 560n10, 629, 633
Lucas, R. 162, 164, 270, 609, 614
Lutgens, F. see Tarbuck, E.J. et al.
Lynn, S.R. 635

Ma, Y. see Perman, R. et al.
MacArthur, J. see Scott, M. et al.
McCombie, J.S.L. 283n5, 600n1, 3, 7,
    614, 633
McCulloch, N.
    et al. 629
    see also Winters, A. et al.
McDermott, C.J. 544–5, 627
    see also Cashin, P. et al. (2000);
    Cashin, P. et al. (2002)
McGillivray, M. see Addison, T. et al.
McGilvray, J. see Perman, R. et al.
McKay, A. see Winters, A. et al.
McKinnon, R. **407**, 408f, 622
McNamara, R. 45, 467
Maddison, A. 34, 35, 158, 603, 605,
    609
Mah, J. 523, 629
Maizels, A. 560n9, 629
Makuch, Z. 619
Malthus, T. xxix, 4, 6, 7, 22, 100,
    131, 132, 134, **135–7**, 285,
    291–2, 295, 296, 297, 298, 373,
    381n11, 436n12, 609, 619

Mankiw, N.G. et al. 166, 167t, 168,
    609
Marglin, S. see Dasgupta, P. et al.
Marshall, A. 140, 373, 504, 533, 609,
    629
Marx, K. xxix, 4, 6, 22, 131, 132, 134,
    139–40, 173, 423, 609
Masson P. et al. 395, 396, 622
Mathis, M. see Blackman, A. et al.
Mauro, P. 605, 607
Mavrotas, G. see Addison, T. et al.
Meade, J. 615
Meadows, D.H. et al. 368, 373, 619
Meadows, D.L. see Meadows, D.H.
    et al.
Medici family 438
Mehra, S. 211, 212, 611
Meier, G. 635
Meier, R. 616
Mellinger, A. see Gallup, J. et al.
Mellor, J. 204, 611
Melo, O. 522, 629
Meltzer, A. 595
Michealy, M. et al. 516, 521, 629
Mikesell, R. 622
Milanovic, B. 34, 35, 35t, 36–7,
    531–2, 603, 629
Mill, J.S. 4, 6, 7, 22, 131, 173,
    373, 381n11, 509, 533,
    619, 629
Mirrlees, J. xxxi, 6, 331, 334, 335,
    336, 337, 338, 339, 341, 342,
    343, **346–9**, 348t, 350n2, 363,
    376, 617, 619
Mobuto Sese Seko 448c
Modigliani, F. 145, 394, 615, 623
Moggridge, D. 551, 629
Mohar, M. 623
Molho, L.E. 623
Montenegro, C.E. 225n2, 600n2,
    611, 634
Morawetz, D. 606
Morduch, J. 436n5, 621, 623
    see also Cull, R.A. et al.
Moreno-Brid, J.C. 565t, 570, 633
Morgan, W. see Greenaway, D.
    et al.
Morris, C.T. 85, 604
Morrison, C. 34, 36, 470, 603, 624
Morrissey, O. 451, 463, 560n11, 625,
    629
    see also Abrar, S. et al.
Morse, C. 373, 618
Mosley, P. 470, 625
    et al. (1991) 470, 625
    et al. (2004) 625

Moyo, D.   447, 625
Myrdal, G.   xxx, 6, 21, 135, **264**, 271, 272, 602, 606, 609, 614

Nadiri, M.   158, 609
Nafziger, E.W.   635
Naqvi, S.   8, 9, 91, 116n8, 602, 606
Nash, J. *see* Thomas, V. et al.
Nashashibi, K.   568, 633
Navaretti, G.B.   613
Neher, P.A.   615
Nehru, V.   487, 625
Nell, K.   570, 633
Nelson, P.   285
    see also Blackman, A. et al.
Newbery, D.   623
    see also Scott, M. et al.
Nguyen, D.T.   164, 608
Nicholls, R. *see* Warren, R.N. et al.
Nissanke, M.   559n2, 604
Nixson, F.I.   622, 634
Noorbakhsh, F.   470, 625, 626
Nordhaus, W.D.   367, 376, 619
North, D.   118
Norton, B.G.   371, 619
Nowzad, B.   633
Nugent, J.   118, 607
Nureldin-Hussain, M.   569, 571–2t, 573, 600n4, 633, 634
Nurske, R.   322, 616
Nyong, A.   377, 619

Oates, W.   355, 618
Ogaki, M. et al.   397, 397t, 623
O'Grada, C.   97, 99, 606
Ohlin, B.   **508–9**, 530, 532, 615, 629
Ohlin, E.   626
Olson, M.   118, 607
Omlin, C.   626
Oostendorp, R.   530, 628
Opeskin, B.R.   446, 626
Ostry, J.D.   623
    see also Ogaki, M. et al.
Otker-Robe, I.   577, 632
Otsuka, K. et al.   219t, 221, 222, 225n1, 226n13, 611
Oyejide, A. et al.   513, 629

Pacheco-López, P.   xxxii, xxxiv, 479, 521, 523, 524, 565t, 570, 626, 630, 631, 633
Pack, H.   175n13, 249, 250–1, 609, 613
Page, J.   624
Panagariya, A.   628
    see also de Mello, J. et al.
Pankaj, J.   404, 623

Papageorgiou, D. *see* Michealy, M. et al.
Papps, I.   617
Parente, S. *see* Gollin, D. et al.
Pareto, V.   329n7
Parikh, A.   523, 630
Pasinetti, L.   145, 276
Pastor, M.   436n16, 623, 633
Patel, S.J.   602
Patillo, C. et al.   487, 626
Paukert, E.   85, 606
Pavcnik, N.   529, 531, 628
Pavitt, K.   612
Payer, C.   633
Pearce, D.W.   617, 619
Pearson, W.B.   5, 602, 626
Peirson, D.   351
Peirson, J.   xxxi, 351
Perez, E.   565t, 570, 633
Perkins, D. et al.   635
Perman, R. et al.   357, 367, 619
Perotti, R.   125, 126, 607
Perraton, J.   634
Pesmazoglu, J.   626
Petty, W.   295, 615
Phillips, S.   429, 621
Piancastelli, M.   415, 416–17t, 623
Pieper, U.   104, 606
Pigou, A.C.   357, 373, 619
Piot, P.   95
Piracha, M. *see* Catrinescu, N. et al.
Poirson, C.H. *see* Patillo, C. et al.
Pollin, R.   430, 623
Potrykus, I.   195
Powell, A. *see* Gilbert, C. et al.
Powelson, J.P.   611
Prebisch, R.   xxx, 6, 76, 262, **271**, 283n1, 502, 547, 560n5, 615, 630
Preston, L.   45, 467
Price, J. *see* Warren, R.N. et al.
Pritchett, L.   64–5, 65t, 170, 603, 608
    see also Hausmann, R. et al. (2005)
Przeworski, A.   596, 634
Psacharopoulos, G.   239, 239–40t, 613
Pugno, M.   170, 609
Purvis, M. *see* Brainard, L.A. et al.
Putterman, L.   169–70, 610

Quillin, B. *see* Catrinescu, N. et al.

Radelet, S. *see* Clements, M. et al.; Perkins, D. et al.
Raffer, K.   626
Rajan, R.   626

Ram, R.   630
Ramswamy, R.   104
Randers, R. *see* Meadows, D.H. et al.
Ranis, G.   203, 611, 616
Rauch, J.E.   635
Ravallion, M.   43, 46t, 47, 98, 99–100, 528, 603, 606, 630
Rawls, J.   4, 298, 602, 615
Ray, D.   219, 220, 221, 222, 223, 226n13, 611, 635
Rayner, A. *see* Abrar, S. et al.
Razmi, A.   570, 634
Reader, J.   294, 615
Reichmann, T.M.   595, 634
Reinert, E.   21, 113, 514, 533, 550, 603, 606, 630
Reinhart, C.M.   623
    see also Ogaki, M. et al.
Renelt, D.   166, 167t, 168, 609
Reynoso, A.   409, 621
Ricardo, D.   xxix, 4, 6, 7, 22, 131, 132, 134, **137–8**, 173, 373, 381n11, 423, 549, 610, 619, 630
Ricci, L. *see* Patillo, C. et al.
Riddell, R.   497n5, 626
Robbins, D.J.   530, 630
Robertson, D.   436n12
Robinson, J.   6, 118, 128, 143, 145, 276, 422, 424, 623
    see also Acemoglu, D. et al.
Robinson, S.   116n8, 158, 610
    see also Chenery, H. et al. (1986)
Robson, P.   559n1, 630
Rodriguez, F.   525, 526, 630
Rodriguez-Pose, A.   269, 615
Rodrik, D.   xxx, 6, 79, 118, 119, 120, 121, 122, 124, 125, 126, 127, 128, 516, 525, 526, 534, 548, **549**, 550, 606, 607, 630
    et al.   124, 606
    see also de Mello, J. et al.; Hausmann, R. et al. (2005, 2007, 2008)
Rogers, J.H.   567
Rogerson, R. *see* Gollin, D. et al.
Romer, D. *see* Mankiw, N.G. et al.
Romer, P.M.   162, 164, 175n13, 610
Rosenstein-Rodan, P.   6, 322, 616
Rostow, W.W.   6, 10, 74, **105–8**, 114, 170, 181, 229, 420, 606, 613, 623
Rowthorn, R.   104, 606, 616
Ruttan, V.   175n13, 610

Sabot, R.H.   210, 226n12, 611
Sachs, J.   6, 77, 78, 79–80, 96, 115n6,
    124, 525, 606, 607, 626, 630
        Sachs and Warner (1995)
            Openness Index   516
    see also Gallup, J. et al.
Sagoff, M.   371, 619
Sahn, D.E. et al.   626
Sala-í-Martin, X.   34, 36, 37, 158, 162,
    175n13, 269, 604, 608, 610, 614
Salles, J.   428, 622
Salvatore, D.   630
Samiei, H. see Masson P. et al.
Samuelson, P.   145
Sanchez-Fung, J.   621
Sanna, G.   170, 610
Santos-Paulino, A.   521, 523, 630
Sapsford, D.   543, 628, 631
Sarel, M.   623
Sarkar, P.   545, 560n6, 631
Scandizzo, P.   541, 628
Schadler, S.   596, 634
Schiantarelli, F. see Bandiera, O. et al.
Schiff, M.   225n2, 611
Schmidt-Hebbel, K. see Loayza, N.
    et al.
Scholec, M. see Fagerberg, J. et al.
Schultz, T.P.   613
Schultz, T.W.   xxvii, 6, 189, 191, 211,
    239, 611, 612, 613
Schumacher, E.   373, 619
Schumpeter, J.   235, 436n6, 613, 623
Scitovsky, T.   598, 616, 634
    see also Little, I.M.D. et al.
Scott, A. see Cashin, P. et al. (2002)
Scott, M.
    et al.   350n5, 617
    see also Little, I.M.D. et al.
Secondi, G.   607, 635
Sen, Abhijeet   196c
Sen, A.K.   4, 6, 8, 19, 20, 22, 98–9,
    114, 115n7, 191, 213–14, 251,
    254, 350n2, 359, 376, 527–8c,
    603, 605, 606, 612, 613, 616,
    617, 619
    see also Dasgupta, P. et al.
Sen, K.   629
Senhadji, A.   158, 161, 161t, 572,
    600n2, 610, 634
Serra, N.   609
Serven, L. see Loayza, N. et al.
Shaaeldin, E.   158, 159, 159t, 610
Shah, A.   267–9, 268t, 615
Shankar, R.   267–9, 268t, 615
Sharpe, S. et al.   626
Shaw, E.   407, 408f, 436n6, 622, 623

Shirley, M.   607
Shogren, J. see Hanley, N. et al.
Sidgwick, H.   297, 615
Simon, J.   xxx, 295, 296, 302n3, 615
Singer, H.   6, 76, 271, 543, 545, 558,
    560n6, 626, 631
Singh, A.   113
Skarstein, R.   631
Smith, A.   xxix, 4, 6, 22, 131, 132–5,
    173, 236, 296, 306, 323, 397,
    509, 510, 610, 631
Smith, S.C.   603
Solomon, R.   251, 613
Solow, R.   131, 145, 146, 147, 157,
    158, 168, 172, 173, 174n5, 376,
    610
Southworth, H.   612
Spash, C.   359, 619
Spence, M.   172
Spilimbergo, A. et al.   532, 631
Spraos, J.   543, 631, 634
Spratt, S.   623
Squire, L.   85, 85–8t, 344, 345t,
    350n2, 350n4, 605, 617
Srinivasan, T.N.   634
Stagl, S.   371, 618
Stalin, J.   66, 107, 181
Stanners, W.   430, 623
Stark, O.   226n12, 612
Stern, N.   xxxi, 6, 93, 353, 358, 360,
    364, 368, 369, 370, 373–6, 378,
    436n9, 436n11, 604, 612, 616,
    619, 620, 621, 623
Sterner, T.   368, 620
Stewart, F.   89, 248, 258n4, 310,
    350n5, 606, 613, 617
    see also Cornia, G. et al.
Stiglitz, J.   6, 220, 376, 411, 470, 524,
    550, 593, 609, 612, 617, 623,
    626, 631, 634
Stillson, R.   595, 634
Stock, R.   611, 620
Stokke, O.S.   378, 381n13
Straub, S.   242, 613
Streeten, P.   617, 626
    et al.   606
Strout, A.   627
Strunk, K. see Chatterji, M. et al.
Subramanian, A.   119, 120, 124, 607,
    626
    see also Rodrik, D. et al.
Summers, L.   242, 613
Summers, R.   40, 162, 604, 610
Sunkel, O.   497n10, 625
Sutcliffe, R.   34, 66, 604, 617
Svedberg, P.   34, 604

Swan, T.   146, 610
Syrquin, M.   116n8, 605
    see also Chenery, H. et al. (1986)
Szekely, M. see Spilimbergo, A.
    et al.

Tait, V.   623
Tanzi, V.   329n3, 617, 623
Tarbuck, E.J. et al.   380n1, 620
Tarp, F.   625
    see also Dalgaard, C.J. et al.
Tarr, D.G.   613
Taussig, F.W.   533
Taylor, L.   497n7, 584, 596, 605, 626,
    634
Teal, F.   617
Temple, J.   175n13, 430, 436n15,
    610, 623
Thankom, A.   622
Theodossiou, I.   116n9
Thirlwall, A.P.   109f, 113–14c,
    116n9, 170, 174n4, 226n6, 254,
    283n3–5, 302n2, 394, 395, 396,
    410, 424, 430, 436n14-15, 439,
    496n2, 497n11, 521, 523, 524,
    541, 560n11, 569, 600n1, 3, 4,
    7, 603, 606, 609, 610, 612, 613,
    614, 615, 616, 617, 622, 623,
    625, 626, 630, 631, 633, 634,
    635
Thomas, V. et al.   521, 631
Thommessen, O.B.   378, 381n13
Thorbecke, E.   115n4, 559n2, 604,
    606, 631
Thornton, H.   436n12
Tietenberg, T.   620
Tinbergen, J.   6
Tobin, J.   367, 477, 619
Todaro, M.   207, 217, 226n10,
    226n12, 603, 612, 635
Toner, P.   615
Torrens, R.   533
Toye, J. see Mosley, P. et al.
    (1991)
Trebbi, E. see Rodrik, D. et al.
Trefler, D.   530, 632
Tregenna, F.   104, 606
Triffin, R.   634
Trumbull, W.   626
Tsakolotos, E.   436n7, 622
Tun Wai, U.   436n6, 623
Turner, R.K.   619
Turnham, T.   606
Tusa, D. see Tarbuck, E.J. et al.

Udry, C.   119, 120, 223, 226n13, 607,
    610, 612

Vamvakidis, A.   513, 627, 631
Van Den Berg, H.   635
Van der Tak, H.G.   344, 345t, 350n2, 350n4, 617
Vanasin, J. *see* Chatterji, M. et al.
Varian, H.   380n3, 620
Velasco, A. *see* Hausmann, R. et al. (2008)
Venables, A.   277, 614
Verdoorn, P.J.   112, 273, 274, 275, 282, 293, 520
Verschoos, A. *see* Mosley, P. (2004) et al.
Verspagen, B.   269, 614
   see also Fagerberg, J. et al. (1996)
Villanueva, D.   410, 622
   see also Knight, M. et al.
Vines, D.   625
   see also Gilbert, C. et al.
Vogel, S.   199–200, 612
Vogt, M.   523, 629
Von Pischke, J.D.   620
Vreeland, J.   596, 634

Wacziard, R.   525, 631
Wacziarg, R.   108, 605
Wade, R.   37, 113, 550, 604, 606, 617, 631
Wall, H.   626
Walliser, J.   450, 624

Warman, F.   396, 410, 623
Warner, A.   77, 78, 525, 606, 630
   Sachs and Warner (1995)
      Openness Index   516
Warren, R.N. et al.   377, 620
Waterson, A.   617
Webb, S.B. *see* Corbo, V. et al.
Weeks, J.   626
Weil, D.N. *see* Mankiw, N.G. et al.
Weisdorf, J.   226n8, 612
Weiss, A.   411, 617, 623
Welch, K.   525, 631
Wells, H.   113–14c, 116n9, 606
Wha Lee, J.   166, 167t, 168, 608
   see also Borensztein, E. et al.
White, A.   606
White, B. *see* Hanley, N. et al.
White, H.   463, 496n3, 560n11, 602, 625, 626, 629
White, L.   614
Williams, D.   169, 609
Williamson, J.   584, 623, 634
Williamson, J.G.   610
   see also Blattman, C. et al.
Willis, K.   363, 365, 380n7, 618
Winters, A.
   et al.   528–9, 631
   see also McCulloch, N. et al.
Wolf, H. *see* Ghosh, A. et al.

Wolfensohn, J.   45, 467, 490
Woo Jung, S.   623
Wood, A.   447, 531, 626, 631
   see also Sharpe, S. et al.
Woolf, M.   631
Wratten, E. *see* Sharpe, S. et al.
Wright, P. *see* Greenaway, D. et al.

Xi, L. *see* Ansari, M. et al.

Yang, M.C.   543, 544, 628
Yap, L.Y.L.   226n12, 612
Ye, H.   428, 622
Yotopoulous, P.   224, 568, 611, 634
Young, A.   158, 159–60, 160t, 610
Young, A.A.   135, 610
Younger, S.D. *see* Sahn, D.E. et al.
Yunus, Muhammad   403, **404**

Zervos, S.   166, 167t, 169, 430, 609, 622
Zhang, J.   111, 116n9, 605
Zhu, A.   430, 623
Zhu, S.   530, 632
Zind, R.G.   64, 604
Zinser, J.   622
Zoellich, R.   467
Zoido-Lobaton, P. *see* Kaufmann, D. et al.

SUBJECT INDEX

In this index c denotes case example, f figure, n note and t table. Page references in bold indicate extended discussion or heading emphasized in main text.

absolute income gap 27
absolute income hypothesis
  (Keynesian) **393–4**, 393f
absolute poverty **12–13**, 13c, 43,
  44t, 89, 244, 310
  McNamara's definition 45, 467
  Millennium Goal **45–7**
  World Bank measure 43
  see also primary poverty
acceleration principle **141–2**
Accion International (USA) 404
'accommodation to poverty'
  (Galbraith) 21
accounting prices **335**
accounting rate of interest (ARI)
  339
ACP countries 547–8, 550
acquired comparative advantage
  505
actual growth rate (Harrod) **142**,
  143
adverse selection **309, 411**
African Development Bank 466t,
  491
African Development Report (1994)
  410
agglomeration benefits 108
agglomeration economies **277**
aggregate governance index
  (Kaufman et al., 1999) **121**
aggregate production function
  (neoclassical growth model)
  146, 158
agrarian reform 189, 196c
agrarian societies, functioning of
  markets **218–24**
agribusiness **197**, 198, 546

agricultural extension services 191,
  193, **198–9**, 492c
agricultural productivity 41,
  183–7t
agricultural research 50
agricultural sector 102–4, 112, 203,
  263
  distribution of labour 102–3,
    103f
  distribution of output 103–4,
    103f
  efficiency 192
  Fair Trade Movement **548**
  protectionism (rich countries)
    546–7
agricultural surplus 180, 196, 200,
  253
  neoclassical argument 201
agriculture xxx, 11, 17, 20, 21, 41,
  49c, 134, 151, 169–70, 295–6,
  326, 374, 376, 529
  aggregate supply elasticities 192
  barrier to growth in poor regions
    169
  and climate change 376–7
  commercialization 203
  complementarity with industry
    204–7
  developmental prerequisites
    108
  diminishing returns 133, 136,
    137, 138, 139, 140, 373
  dominance **71–3**
  factor contribution **181–2**
  finance **198–9**
  foreign exchange contribution
    182–3
  industry versus 306, 318, **319**

  interdependence with industry
    199–200
  market contribution **182**
  need for reform 101
  organization of agriculture and
    land reform **189–91**
  product contribution **181**
  rapid productivity growth
    (importance to economic
    development) **180–3**
  rapid productivity growth
    (obstacles) **183–9**
  role in development **180–3**
  seasonality of production 211
  subsidies 546–7
  supply response **191–3**
  surplus labour 73
  taxation 191, 193, 418
  transformation **193–6**
  valuation of production forgone
    343
  websites 226
  World Bank role 467
  see also Green Revolution
aid 18, 50, 94, 316
  conditionality **458c, 585–6,**
    589–91t, 596, 600n9
  financial 456
  flows 451
  impact on development xxxi
  per head of population 447
  percentage of GDP 476
  and social factors 12, 447
  trade versus **556–8,** 560n11
  untied 597, 598
  volatility **451**
  websites 497
  see also international assistance

aid administration   447
aid agencies   449
    multilateral   319
aid component/grant element   **445**,
    496n4, **556–7**
aid donors   445–8, 476–7, 597–9
    bilateral   448c, 453, 475
    coordination   452c
    multilateral   448c, 453
aid 'fatigue'   **477**
'aid for trade' programmes   529
aid tying   **463–4**, 476, 560n11, 597,
    598
    double tying   463
    procurement tying   463
AIDS/HIV   13, **14c**, 15, 16, **94**, **95c**,
    96, 457
    life expectancy   95c
air travel, taxation   477
AK model   **162**, 164
Alliance for a Green Revolution in
    Africa (Agra)   194
American Economic Association
    xxxiv, 9
amortization   454, **481**, 487
anaemia   92, 94
anti-globalization movement   531
antibiotics   95, 243
APEC (Asia–Pacific Economic
    Cooperation)   510
Arab Funds   466t
'Are There Laws of Production?'
    (Douglas, 1948)   156
arms (weapons)   15, 477
Arusha Declaration (1980)   12
ASEAN   510
Asian Development Bank (ADB)
    466, 466t, 580t
Asian Tigers   308, 311, 550
assurance problem   **359**
asymmetric information   **309, 411**
asymmetrical cycles   541, 541f
Attacking Poverty see World
    Development Report
    (2000/2001)
average product of labour   214f,
    215f, 274, 298f
    maximization   297, 297f

baby milk, powdered   480
backward-bending supply curve of
    effort   **182**, **215–16**, 215f
'backwash' effect (Myrdal)   266,
    267, 270
bad debts/loans   223, 309, 403, 411,
    412

Baker Plan (1988)   **492**
balance of payments
    'adjustment with growth' (Killick)
        595
    aid-donor countries   464
    capital account   270, 517, 563,
        568, 574, 588, 594, 595
    constraints   17, 319, 446, 522
    current account   272, 287, 411,
        439, 449, 502, 519, 523, 535,
        562, 563, 564, 565, 566, 572,
        573, 576, 580, 586, 593,
        595, 599
    dangers of deficits financed by
        short-term capital inflows
        583
    deficits   16, 171, 439, 490, 562,
        579, 581
    difficulties/problems   xxxi, 77,
        434, 480, 505, 535, 551, 562,
        568, 569, 586, 590–1t, 593
    disequilibrium   542, 593, 594
    dual-gap analysis   439–41
    effects of FDI   480, 481t
    effects of free trade   502
    equilibrium   519, 520, 535, 542,
        563, 566, 570, 586, 594, 596
    equilibrium growth rate   566
    IMF management   468, 470c
    income elasticity of demand for
        products and   **542–3**
    instability   533
    recycling of surpluses   17, 585
    relief of temporary difficulties
        583
    stability   17
    structural problems   594
    surpluses   488, 592, 594
    and trade liberalization   517,
        523–4, 524f, 531
    trade-off between growth and
        524f
    'ultimate constraint on growth
        performance of nations'
        583, 584
    websites   601
balance-of-payments-constrained
    growth model   xxxi, **562–6**,
    565t, 600n1–2
    application   **570–2**, 600n3
    export-led growth   517, **519–20**
balanced growth   134, 182, 204, 205,
    306, 318, **322–6**
    Hirschman's major criticism
        323–6
    see also big push

bananas   197
Banco Compartamos (Mexico)   404
Banco Sol (Bolivia 1992–)   404
Bank for Agriculture and Rural
    Development (Agribank,
    Vietnam)   402c
bank credit   396
Bank Rakyat (Indonesia)   404
Bank on Wheels (Vietnam)   **401–2c**
banking crisis (2007/2008)   15
banking system   120, 200, 223, 386,
    399, 400, **400–2**
    domestic   582
    international   582
    regulation   127, 412, 412–13c,
        583
    websites   436
bankruptcy   75c, 412
banks   309, 582
    branch   **401**
    capital adequacy   582
    central   **400–1**
    commercial   **401**, 492–3
    private   488, 489
    profit-maximization   412
    publicly owned   413c
barter   399–400
barter (or commodity) terms of
    trade   76, 540, **545–6**
basic needs   19, 20, 449, 467
basic needs approach   **80**, 97
beggar-thy-neighbour policies   569,
    583
Beijing Consensus   **594–5**
bequest value   **363**
beta convergence   **64**, 163, 175n14
'Better Investment Climate for
    Everyone, A' (World Bank,
    2005)   **230–1c**
big push theory   9, 136, **300**, **322**
    see also balanced growth
bilharzia   355
Bill Gates Foundation   194
binding constraints on growth
    171–2
biodiversity   **363**
biomass   368, 377
biotechnology   **194–5**, 243–4
birth control   76, 299
birth rates   41, 286–8, 286t, 287f,
    289, 290–1
black market   196c
blindness   92, 93, 94, 254
    river blindness   95, 448c
bonded labour   **223**
bonds   400, 449, 477, 493, 494

border parity pricing **336**
border price **335–6**, 337, 338
borrowing 486, 488
   abroad 388
   debt crisis of 1980s **488–9**,
     497n10
   excessive **481–6**
   informal 50c
   offshore 413c
   optimal **486–8**
   public 316
   rate of return 485
   short-term 583
bottlenecks 198, 242, 401, 421, 433,
   434, 505
Bottom Billion **43**, 80
BP (British Petroleum) 110c
Brady Plan (1989) **492**
brain damage/cretinism 93, 94, 254
branch banking **401**
Brandt Commission (1983) 16
Brandt Report (1980) **16–17**, 477,
   570
   sequel (1983) 16
Bretton Woods system (1944–72)
   27, 469, 576, 583, 592
Britain *see* United Kingdom
budgetary problem **489**
buffer stock schemes **553**
buoyancy of a tax system **414**
bureaucracy, reduction of 314
Business Environmental Risk
   Intelligence (BERI) 121–2
business start-ups 75c, 314

calories 93, 254
capabilities (Sen) **19**
capacity to save **392, 393–5**
capital
   aggregate measure 175n7
   in agriculture 222–4
   allocation 400
   application to land 186
   commercial 447
   constant returns 165
   definition 229
   diminishing returns (neoclassical
     assumption) 64, 65, **146**,
     149, 162, 163, 164
   factor contribution of agriculture
     to development **181–2**
   foreign 106, 278, 319m393, 409,
     438, 441, 442, 444, 480,
     581, 582
   free movement 270

inflows 74, 272, 393, 412, 413,
   438, 444, 447, 454, 463, 471,
   479, 486, 523, 558, 562,
   571–2t, 572–3, 574, 577,
   579, 580, 581, 582, 584, 593
international movements 270
long-term 270
'lumpiness' 322
non-diminishing returns 167
per head 165
price relative to labour 232
private 198, 339, 478, 486, 585,
   593, 595
productivity 142–3, 146, 149,
   150, 154, 164, 480
quality 150, 151
rate of profit 139
role in development **228–30**
scarcity 508
shift from agriculture to industry
   (Ricardo) 137
short-term 270
social overhead 293
capital accumulation 8, 73, 169,
   228, 229, 230, 386, 420, 424,
   426, 509
   escape from 'vicious circle of
     poverty' 230
   for industrial development 181
   low level **73–4, 74–5c**, 76
   role in development process
     xxx, 106–7
   way of raising per capita income
     106–7
capital controls 412, 574, 577, 593
capital deepening 155, **229**
capital equipment 509, 525
capital flight 412, 580, 581, 582
capital flows 15, **572–3**, 600n4
   international **445**
   private 478
   volatile 593
capital formation xxix, 21, 71, 81,
   159, 203, 242, 299, 386, 388,
   389–91t, 440
capital gains 419
capital goods 142, 156, 168, 228,
   244c, 248, 323, 386, 509
   aggregation 155, 156
   domestic 256
   imported 518
   indigenous 480
   new 236
   types **228**
capital imports/inflow 74, 272, 393,
   412, 413, 438, 444, **444**, 447,

   454, 463, 471, 479, 486, 523,
   558, 562, 571–2t, 572–3, 574,
   577, 579, 580, 581, 581–2, 581t,
   582, 584, 593
   and economic growth **442–4**
   real effect 571–2t
capital intensity 246, 247, 250, **252**,
   256, 263, 318
   developing countries **245–8**
capital markets 15, 406, 445, 592
   foreign 480
   fragmented 400
   global 15
   imperfect 120, 360, 365
   international 466, 562, 582
   liberalization 478, 574, 582,
     593
   perfect 359
   private 585
   stimulating 406
capital mobility/migration 575
capital movements **266**, 270
capital stock 153, 157, 158, 160–1,
   165, 228–9, 321t, 370
capital-goods industries 323
capital–labour substitution
   possibilities 250–1, 250t
capital–output ratio 229, 245–6,
   300, 400, 441, **444**
   effect of technical progress
     232
capitalism 134, 137, 308, 593
   collapse predicted by Marx **139**,
     140
   'inner contradictions' 132
   international 279
   reasons for survival 140
capitalist sector 203, 204, 216, 216f,
   395
   size relative to total economy
     203
capitalist surplus 203, 204, 216,
   395
   role in development process
     200
carbon dioxide emissions (CO_2)
   352f, 354, 358, 368, 369,
   372, 374–6, 375f, 375t,
   377, 378
Caribbean Development Bank
   465–6t
cash crops 101, 197
cash flow 333t, 582
caste 90c
catch-up 164, 531
cell phones 244c

central banks 400, 412–13c, 449
    functions 400–1
    lender of last resort 410
    Mexico 494
    websites 436
    world 597
centre–periphery models xxx, 9,
    113, 133, 269–71, 283n1–5,
    540–1, 541f
    export growth model 272–6,
        283n3–5
    international inequality
        269–71, 271
    new economic geography
        276–8
    Prebisch model 271–2,
        283n1–2
    theories of dependence and
        unequal exchange
        278–81, 283n6
centrifugal forces 276
centripetal forces 276
cereals 100, 544, 588, 589–90t
Chagas disease 96
characteristics of underdevelopment
    and structural change
    71–115
charitable organizations 446, 478,
    494
charity, tax relief on donations 478
cheap labour 110c, 198
child mortality 12, 13c, 50c, 242,
    254, 457c
childhood diseases (immunization)
    448c
children 13c, 49c, 51c, 78, 292, 295,
    296, 299
    girls 12, 13
    underweight 63t
choice of techniques (of production)
    322, 329n6, 345–56
    optimal 345–6, 345f
Christian Aid 526, 528
Christians/'the Church' 18, 49,
    90c, 199
circular and cumulative causation
    (Myrdal) xxx, 9, 21, 262, 263,
    264–7, 269–70, 271, 278
    challenge to static equilibrium
        theory 264, 269–71
Citicorp bank 494
cities see urban areas/cities
civil liberties/rights 19, 121, 122
civil servants/bureaucrats 78, 90c
civil service 112, 314
civil society 91, 310, 458, 468t, 588

civil unrest 308, 310, 590t
civil war 90c
class 85, 89
classical economics 7–8, 204, 373
    savings assumption 424
    trade theory 326
classical economists 6, 373
classical growth theory 131,
    132–46
    Adam Smith and increasing
        returns 132–5
classical pessimists 132, 135–40,
    291–2, 423
climate 78, 79, 123, 364
climate change xxxi, 306, 352, 353,
    354, 358, 365, 368, 369, 373–9
Coasian bargains 357–8
Cobb–Douglas production function
    147, 150, 153–8
    application 156–8
    limitations 155–6, 175n9
    use in calculation of sources of
        growth 153–8, 175n8–11
coefficient of variation 28
coffee 197, 541
Cold War 5
collateral 48, 219, 223, 224, 339,
    402, 403, 404, 434, 582
collective action problem 120,
    125, 220
collective farming 191
collectivization (Stalinist) 181
colonial dependence 279
colonialism 5, 22, 90c, 198, 279, 280
    and institutional development
        122–5
colonization 11, 79, 279–80
command and control approach to
    externalities 358
commercial bank lending/loans
    580, 581t
commercial banking system 401,
    406, 412
commercial policy 388
'Commercial Policy in
    Underdeveloped Countries'
    (Prebisch, 1959) 283n1
'commod-control' scheme (Keynes)
    551–2, 552f, 567
commodities 338
    industrial 504
    multinational buyers 101
    non-food agricultural 544
    non-fuel 544
    vent for surplus 502, 505, 510
    see also primary commodities

commodity agreements, bilateral
    554
commodity boards 553
commodity policy 12
commodity prices 488, 551
    falling 490
    instability (problems posed for
        countries/world economy)
        551–5, 555, 560n8–10
    nominal 544, 544f
    real 544–5, 544f
    rising 15, 566
    stabilization 495, 497n11,
        560n8–10
Common Agricultural Policy (CAP,
    EU) 546, 552
Common Crisis: North-South
    Cooperation for World
    Recovery (Brandt Commission,
    1983) 16
common external tariff (CET)
    510–13
common land 358–9, 360
communications 14c, 15, 196, 266,
    296, 467, 468t
communism 5, 308
companies/firms 353, 353f
    foreign-owned 110c
    pharmaceutical 14c, 95
    state-owned 311
comparative advantage
    doctrine/comparative cost
        doctrine 102, 198, 306,
        319–20, 506–9
    acquired comparative advantage
        505
    disadvantages 533, 534
    natural comparative advantage
        505
Compensatory Financing Facility
    (CFF) 555, 562, 566, 587–8,
    587t, 589t, 590t
competition 15, 16, 75c, 132, 134,
    139, 189, 223, 235, 243, 266,
    281, 311, 314, 400, 513, 515,
    526, 528, 530, 531, 537, 547,
    584
    barriers to 230–1c
    between banks 411, 413
    between poor countries 530
    and innovation 235
    international 335
    non-price 408
    perfect 326, 327, 511, 533
    unfair 187, 188

competitive advantage 266, 269, 273, 274

competitiveness 75c, 113, 267, 271, 275, 282
  non-price 236
  price 236, 520, 567, 593
  technological 235

complementarity (between sectors) 11, 182, 204–7

compulsory/involuntary saving 386, 387, 414, 436n1

conditionality 314, 458c, 585–6, 589–91t, 596, 600n9
  ex post 471
  self-imposed (Uganda) 492c

conflict 89–90c, 590t

conflict management institutions 119, 120, 126, 172

'conflict trap' 80

conservation, energy 17

conspicuous consumption 380

constant returns 135, 146, 147, 154, 155, 157, 162, 165

consumer goods/products 200, 216, 229, 235, 248, 317, 319, 323, 421

consumer surplus 333, 511, 536

consumption 480
  agriculture 342
  change in industry and agriculture (closer look) 342
  distorted structure 466
  domestic 510, 511
  effects of customs unions 511
  efficiency in 354
  future 249, 252, 254, 310, 318, 320, 328, 341, 342, 344, 346, 349, 359, 360, 361, 363, 366, 394, 397
  and investment 254, 310
  maximization at some future point in time 318
  planning horizon 320
  present 249, 252, 254, 318, 320, 328, 344, 349, 359, 361, 397
  present to future (distribution-weighted relative valuation) 344–6
  present versus future 306, 320, 321t, 359, 395
  value of 354–5, 359

consumption function (Keynes) 392

consumption goods 388, 528

consumption poverty line 43

consumption rate of interest (CRI) 339, 347

contingent valuation 365

contraception 137

contracts
  in different markets 218
  labour 222
  legally binding 118, 119
  long-term 222
  output-sharing 221
  weak enforcement 230c, 314

'Contribution to the Theory of Economic Growth (Solow, 1956) 147

convergence 11, 131, 269
  conditional 64, 65t, 163, 164, 167t, 168
  neoclassical growth theory 64, 146, 150, 162, 163, 167t, 168, 175n14, 520

conversion factors (CFs) 336–8, 350n1

coordinating institutions 124

Copenhagen Conference (2009) 379

Copenhagen Declaration (1995) 12

Corn Laws (repealed 1846) 138

corporate governance structures 126–7

corruption 50, 118, 119, 122, 125, 230c, 231, 306, 311–14, 328n2, 329n3, 448c, 476, 477, 492c, 516
  case studies 329n3
  and international assistance 447
  means of reduction 314
  'more widespread in natural-resource-abundant countries' 78
  websites 329
  World Bank definition 313

cost inflation 427

cost–benefit analysis see social cost–benefit analysis

cotton 188, 249, 526, 541
  unfair trade 546, 546c

Country Support Strategy 548

crawling band 574t, 576, 579t

crawling peg 574t, 576, 579t

'creative destruction' (Schumpeter) 235

credit 6, 398–9, 412–13c, 488, 492c
  access 48, 189, 191, 199, 218, 243, 401c, 529
  combined with human asset building 402c
  for entrepreneurs 575

formal linked with informal 401–2c

outstanding (IMF, 2000–2008) 587, 587t

credit markets 218, 222–4

credit rating 595

credit rationing/controls 401, 411

crime 15, 48c, 51c, 230c, 310, 314, 316

critical minimum effort 285, 300

crop diversification 196c

crop failures 50, 50c, 50c

crop yields 193, 196c, 198, 370

'crowding out' hypothesis 78

cultural barriers 15, 90

cumulative causation see circular and cumulative causation

curb market (informal money market) 410

currency 400, 574
  appreciation 566
  baskets of 576
  common 266, 272, 273, 275, 563, 567, 575
  devaluation 550
  domestic 37, 334, 337, 538, 539, 563, 568, 569, 572, 582, 598
  foreign 334, 335, 336, 476, 485, 494, 495, 563, 568, 581, 585
  international (Scitovsky's 1966 plan) 598
  local 37, 40, 418, 449, 476, 494, 585
  overvaluation 410, 593
  scarce 594
  single 576
  see also exchange rates

currency appreciation 412, 566

currency auctions 577

currency boards 574, 574t, 578t

currency devaluation 275, 567–8, 569, 576, 593–4

currency overvaluation 593

currency unions 574t, 575

custom (tradition) 50, 234

customs unions 502
  gains and losses 512f
  theory 510–14
  trade-creation and trade-diversion 511–14

DAC see OECD: Development Assistance Committee

DAC Journal Development Cooperation 2009 Report (OECD, 2009) 465–6t

Das Kapital (Marx, 1867)　139, 140
Dead Aid (Moyo)　447
deaf mutism　94, 254
death rates　41, 75, 286t, 287, 287f,
　　290–1
debt　111, 445, 544, 577
　ability to service　403–4
　buy-back　492, **493–4**
　ever-growing burden　573
　external (2007)　482–5t
　and growth　487
　household　400
　international　**481–6**
　non-linear relationship with
　　　economic growth　487
　sustainable　14c, 481, **486–8**
　Third World　16
　websites　497
debt crisis (1980s)　xxxi, 15, 16,
　　488–9, 497n10
　'foreign exchange problem'　**489**
debt problem
　long-term solutions　**494–5**,
　　497n11
　nature　**481–6**
　solutions required　489–90
debt service relief　491c
debt stock relief　491c
debt trap　**489**
debt-creating flows　**481**, 581
debt-forgiveness　453t, **489**
debt-reduction　378
debt-relief　12, 14c, 50, **489–90**, 492,
　　492c, 529, 588
　linked with poverty-reduction
　　492c
debt-repayment　562
　foreign currency　581
debt-rescheduling　486, 488–9,
　　492–3
debt–service ratios　481, **487**, 488
　2007　482–5t
debt-servicing　xxxi, 439
　capping　**493**
　difficulties　**481–6**, 488
debt-swaps　**493–4**
　debt for bonds　**494**
　debt for development　**494**
　debt for equity　**494**
　debt for nature　**494**
decision-makers/policy-makers
　　235, 306, 314, 317, 326, 370,
　　447
　agricultural　**224**
　environmental considerations
　　364, 366, 372, 377

'induced' decision-making　**324**,
　　324f, 325
decolonization　111
defensive expenditures　**366**
deficit finance　414, 421
deflation　420, 486, 490, 566
deindustrialization　104
demand　6, **150**, 243, 593
　autonomous　182, 273, 520
　balance-of-payments
　　constraint　17
　constraints　170
　indivisibilities　322
demand inflation　143, 145, 427, **427**
demand management　595, 596
democracy/democratization　xxix,
　　7, 50, 121, 122, **125–7**, 314
demographic transition　285, **288**,
　　291
dengue fever　376
dependence　49c, 446
　definition　278
　forms　**279**
　theories　**278–80**
dependency　10, **21–2**, 198, 262,
　　278, 447
dependency ratio　**394**
　consumption without production
　　292
　dependents as proportion of
　　working age population
　　286t
deposit rate, nominal　408
deregulation　584
derivative markets　477
desertification　354
devaluation　275, **567–8**, 569, 576,
　　593–4
　IMF's 'supply-side approach'
　　568–9
developed countries
　aid targets　454, 455t
　birth and death rates　285–7,
　　286f
　and global warming　374–6, 375t
　inflation　131–3t
　not synonymous with
　　'high-income
　　countries'　40
　pervasiveness of state　328n1
　and world poverty　18
developing countries ('Third World')
　advantages and disadvantages of
　　FDI　**478–81**, 497n9
　alternative approaches to trade
　　560n5

birth and death rates　285–7,
　　286f
capital intensity of techniques
　　345–8
constraints on growth　231c
dangers of inflation　**427–8**
debt burden　**481–95**, 482–5t
debt-servicing burden
　　(imaginative relief
　　schemes)　**492–5**, 497n11
disadvantage of free trade for
　　development　**533–4**
dual economy　340
dual exchange-rate system　577
educational provision and literacy
　　(1997)　241t
effects of export earnings
　　instability　560n10
exchange-rate systems　**573–7**,
　　578–9t
fair trade not free trade　502,
　　546–8
financial system　xxxi
foreign direct investment
　　478–81, 479t
　and global warming　374–6, 375t
Human Development Index
　　(UNDP)　54–62t, 63t
IMF's supply-side approach to
　　devaluation　**568–9**
income distribution　**84–91**
inflation　431–3t
informal financial sector　**398–9**
international assistance　**445–6**
international monetary system
　　583–5
market share of manufactured
　　exports (1981–2006)
　　504t
Prebisch doctrine　**540**, 560n5
production function studies
　　158–62, 175n12
regional disparities　268t
results of IMF programmes
　　595–6
savings　386
small islands　14c
state credibility　310
tax reform　**419–20**, 436n11
　and technology　**243–5**
terms of trade (recent trends)
　　545–6, 560n6
total fertility rate (1987–2007)
　　290t
total net flow of financial
　　resources　**453–4**, 455t

trade liberalization 523
trade orientation (World Bank
classification, 1987) 516
trade policies towards 546–8,
560n7
UK assistance 456–8, 456–7t
development 16
academic interest 5–11
associated with industrialization
229
core components 18–19
disadvantages of free trade 502,
532–4
Doha Round (2000–) 546c, 547,
548
and the environment 253–81
financed from domestic sources
xxxi, 386–436
financed from external sources
xxxi, 438–97
and growth 41–2
interregional differences 270
long process 6–7
meaning 18–20
obstacles to xxix, 27, 259–302
per capita income as index
40–2
and population 285–302
prerequisites 108
'prior-saving' and 'forced saving'
approaches reconciled
424
raison d'être 41
role of capital 228–31
role of capital accumulation
229–30
role of democracy 125–7
role of institutions 118–29
role of state 308–11, 593
structural change 102–5, 104t,
113
and trade liberalization 550
of underdevelopment 279–80
development agencies 101, 598
development assistance 18
link with SDRs 597
Development Assistance Committee
see OECD
development banks 386, 405–6
regional 453t, 456–7t
role in financing development
436n4–5
development economics 4
new models, concepts, ideas
9–11
'obituaries' 8

separateness of discipline 9–11
subject matter xxix, 4, 5–22
websites 23–4
years of high development
theory 10
development finance (Keynesian
approach) 420–4
development gap xxix, 5, 27–68,
80–4, 270, 542
income distribution in world
economy 27–42
measurement of poverty 26–69
development plans 316–17, 329n5
inter-industry models 317
macro or aggregate models 317
projects appraisal 317
sector models 317
development and
underdevelopment 1–176
characteristics of
underdevelopment and
structural change
71–115
development gap and
measurement of poverty
26–69
study of economic development
4–24
theories of economic growth
131–76
'development of underdevelopment'
(Frank) 279–80
'development via shortages'
(Hirschman) 325
diarrhoea 92, 244, 376
diminishing returns 72, 72f, 133,
135, 136, 138, 207, 237, 291,
373, 428, 508, 520, 533
labour 251
offset 137, 140, 146
directly productive activities (DPA)
324–5, 324f
disaster relief 376
discount factors 348, 359
discount rate 295, 320, 332,
359–60, 363, 371, 376, 472,
473–4t
social 334
Discounted Cash Flow (DFC) 333t,
348
discounted rental premium 363
discrimination 49–50, 90c
disease 13, 14c, 15, 45, 50, 79–80,
92, 93–6, 99, 123, 124, 125, 137,
243–4, 295, 376, 448
prevention 94, 95

disguised unemployment 73, 80,
138, 181, 210f, 334
'costless expansion' of industrial
sector 216
definition 210
rural 89
types and measurement
210–15
dissaving 388, 393, 394, 400
diversification 108
division of labour/specialization
132, 236, 323, 397–8, 507, 508,
549
excessive 553
increasing returns 133–4
international (static gains from
trade) 505
'limited by extent of market'
(Smith) 133, 134–5
trade liberalization and economic
growth 517, 532
dollarization 574t, 575
Domar's model 8, 142–3, 164
domestic resources, financing
economic development from
386–436
Keynesian approach 386, 392
prior-savings approach 392,
408, 413, 424
quantity theory approach 386,
387, 392, 424–6, 436n3
domestic violence 51c
drought 99, 376
drugs
medicines 14c, 96
narcotics 15, 316
dual economy 41, 89, 201
dual exchange rates 577
dual-gap analysis 10, 496n2, 502
foreign borrowing 438, 439–42
practical example 441–2, 496n2
dualism xxx, 10, 256, 262–4
models 9
rural–urban 480
Dutch disease 71, 78, 449
dynamic Harrod trade multiplier
570–2
extended version 571–2t, 573
dynamic returns to scale 150
dynamic surplus 211–12

early warning systems, famine 99
East Asian financial crisis (1997) 15,
51c, 562, 577–83, 580t, 581t,
600n7
East Asian model 308, 479

EBRD (European Bank for
Reconstruction and
Development) 465–6t
ecology 365, 371
economic appraisal 331, 333–4,
338
Economic Commission for Latin
America (ECLA) 434, 560n5
Economic Community of West
African States (ECOWAS,
1975–) 513
economic development
and financial deepening
(bidirectional causality)
411
and financial systems 397–8
'grass-roots' school 183
importance of rapid productivity
growth in agriculture
180–3
relationship with financial
development xxxi
study of 4–24
and trade liberalization 550
Economic Development and Cultural
Change (journal) xxxii
Economic Development of Latin
America and its Principal
Problems (Prebisch, 1950)
283n1
'Economic Development with
Unlimited Supplies of Labour'
(Lewis's model, 1954) xxx,
138, 180, 200–4, 207, 210,
225n3, 252, 392, 394
constant returns and marginal
product of labour 203
critics 203–4
economic freedom 122
economic growth
accelerations 171
balance-of-payments-constrained
562–6, 600n1–2
and capital imports 442–4
convergent–divergent 274, 275f
and debt 487
and democracy 125–7
and devaluation 567
and development 41–2, 135,
169
and education 84, 236–42
endogenously determined 150
and environment 352
and the environment 368–9
and FDI (bidirectional causality)
479

and financial liberalization
411–12
foreign-exchange-constrained
440, 441
growth diagnostics and binding
constrains 171–2
income distribution 91
and industrialization 73,
108–10
and inflation xxxi, 169, 175n15,
420, 428–33, 429f, 431–3t,
436n15
and infrastructure 242–3
investment central to 230c
Keynesian theory 131, 132
long-run equilibrium rate 146,
147–8, 162
macrodeterminants 146,
162–71, 167t
neoclassical theory 146–50,
175n7–11
and population 285, 291
and poverty 47t
and poverty reduction 49, 531
production function approach
150–8, 175n7–11
and remittances 464–5
savings-limited 440
self-sustaining 106
and technical progress 231,
235–6
theory xxix–xxx, 6, 131–76
and trade 502–5, 517–20
see also GDP growth;
Harrod–Domar model
economic growth models, export-led
517–20
balance-of-payment-constrained
517, 562–6
identification of causal
mechanism 519
neoclassical supply-side 517,
518
virtuous circle 517, 519–20
Economic Partnership Agreements
(EPAs) 550
economic prices 335–6
economic rationality 354, 355
Economic Theory and
Underdeveloped Regions
(Myrdal, 1957) 135, 264
economic welfare 366, 367, 371,
373
economics
'dismal science' (Carlyle) 132
subdisciplines 9–10

Economics without Equilibrium
(Kaldor, 1985) 135
economies of scale 112, 150, 151,
219, 295, 512–13, 539
dynamic 109
external 293, 323
internal 293
static 109
technological 153
economists
Adam Smith 132
Amartya Sen 20
Arthur Lewis 201
Dani Rodrik 549
David Ricardo 138
Gunnar Myrdal 262
Hans Singer 543
Joseph Stiglitz 470
Karl Marx 140
Keynesian/post-Keynesian 145
Muhammad Yunus 404
neoclassical 145
Nicholas Kaldor 276
Raúl Prebisch 271
Robert Solow 147
Roy Harrod 142
Thomas Malthus 136
Walt Rostow 105
ecosystems 371
education
access to 12, 42, 54–62t, 64, 71,
97, 126, 159, 199, 448
attainment 52, 168, 479
contribution to earnings 237
contribution to economic growth
236–42, 257n2
and development gap 83–4
distance learning 244
enrolment 12, 13, 54–62t, 83,
84t, 240, 241t, 470
investment in 228, 236–42, 266,
315f
lending 467, 468t
primary 12, 13, 13c, 64, 83, 84t,
239, 239t, 240, 240t, 241t,
470
rate of return on investment
239–40, 239t, 240t, 257n1
secondary 83, 84, 84t, 239, 239t,
240, 240t, 241t, 289
tertiary 84t, 239, 239t, 240, 240t,
241t
websites 116
women 240–2, 241t, 285,
288–9, 289f

'effective demand' (Malthus) 136
  failure 139
  'no problem' for Ricardo 137
effective protection 550–1,
    559n3–4
efficiency 144, 326
  conflict with economic growth
    322
  short-term 318, 533
  static 7, 319, 526
  static short-term 318
efficiency frontier 249, 250, 250t
efficiency wage 221, 246–7, 508
elasticity of demand 102, 320, 338,
    505
  for exports 567, 576
  for imports 434, 542, 567, 576
elasticity of migration 209–10,
    226n12
elasticity of output 154, 168, 211,
    296
  with respect to capital 147, 153,
    156, 158, 161, 175n8
  with respect to education 238
  with respect to export growth
    273
  with respect to labour 147, 156,
    158, 161, 238
elasticity of poverty rate 45, 46, 47t,
    526
elasticity of substitution 146, 234,
    249, 250t
  between factors 155–6,
    175n10
  between inputs 175n12
  constant 155, 175n11
  unitary 155
  variable 175n11
elasticity of supply 338, 569
  agricultural 192, 193
  export 569
  urban labour 209–10
elasticity of tax revenue 414
electricity 198, 199, 355–6, 356f,
    448c
elites 79, 106, 125, 279
emergency aid 456t, 457c, 468t
Emergency Assistance (IMF) 588,
    589t, 590t
emerging markets, financial crises
    576
emigration 270
emission permits 375
employment
  conflict with saving 329n6
  distribution by sector 71t

full 12, 141, 142, 143, 145,
    392, 414, 421, 508, 533,
    573
  manufacturing sector 527–8c
  non-farm (neoclassical argument)
    210
  and population growth 291
  public 594
  and trade 527–8
  and trade liberalization 526
  versus output 249–51, 322
  versus saving 249, 251–2, 251f
  see also unemployment
employment opportunities 126,
    201, 209, 270, 316
  women 76
'enclave import' industries
    (Hirschman) 325
enclosure movement (UK) 181
energy (food intake) 93, 93f
energy (power) 16, 110c, 353, 374,
    468t
  international strategy 17
  price 16
  resources 368
  use 374–5, 375t
Engel's Law 542
Enhanced HIPC Debt Relief Initiative
    (1999–) 490–1
  completion point 491c
  decision point 491c
  eligibility 490, 491c
  Uganda 491, 491c, 492, 492c
enhancing security 47, 50
entitlements (Sen) 19, 98–9,
    115n7
entrepreneurs/entrepreneurship
    78, 118, 119, 235, 266, 311, 323,
    399, 549
environment xxxi, 12, 13, 306, 311,
    315f, 353–81, 457c
  biological, chemical and physical
    system 353
  economic thought 373,
    381n10–11
  functions in supporting economic
    activity 352, 353–4, 353f,
    380n1
  international agencies 377–9,
    381n13
  market-based approach 354–5,
    380n1–2
  websites 381
environment and economic activity
    (model) 353–4, 380n1

environmental
  degradation/destruction 5,
    14, 314, 352, 352f, 355–8, 356f,
    366, 368–9, 371
  discount rate 359–60
  marketable permits 358
  optimal level 356
environmental impact assessments
    (EIAs) 364
environmental protection 314,
    315f, 502
environmental sustainability 14c
environmental values 363–6,
    370–3, 380n6
  contingent valuation 365
  measurement 364–6, 380n7,
    381n8
  preventive expenditure technique
    364, 381n8
  three ways of generation 370–1
  travel cost method 365
equilibrium theory (neoclassical)
    265, 266
  challenged 135
equity (fairness) 16, 310, 315f, 418,
    419
  intergenerational 371
'Essay in Dynamic Theory' (Harrod,
    1939) 131, 140
Essay on Principle of Population
    (Malthus, 1798) 136
ethics 16
Ethiopian famine (1973–5) 98
ethnic groups/ethnicity 50, 90c,
    122
ethnic tension 464
European Carbon Trading System
    358
European Central Bank 428
European Community (EC) 466,
    466t
European Development Fund (EDF)
    466, 548
European Economic Community
    (EEC) 547, 552
European Union (EU) 510, 546, 550
exchange controls 427
exchange-rate regimes 574t
exchange-rate systems xxxi, 573–7,
    578–9t, 600n5–6
  adjustable peg 575
  country classification 578–9t
  crawling band 574t, 576, 579t
  crawling peg 574t, 576, 579t
  currency board 574–5, 574t,
    578t

exchange-rate systems – *continued*
　　currency union　574t, **575**
　　for developing countries　573–7
　　dollarization　574t, **575**
　　dual　**577**, 600n6
　　exchange arrangements with no
　　　　separate legal tender
　　　　578t
　　exchange-rate band　**576**, 578t
　　fixed　573, 577, 578t
　　flexible　574, 577
　　floating　535, 574, 574t, 577
　　free float　574, 574t, 577, 579t,
　　　　583
　　hard pegs　574, 574t, 577
　　intermediate regimes　574t, 577
　　managed float　574t, **577**, 579t
　　pegged　574, 574t, 575, 577
　　soft pegs　574
exchange rate/s
　　black market　168, 516, 525
　　competitive　584
　　depreciation　**567**
　　devaluation　**567–8**
　　Dutch disease　71, 449
　　equilibrium　592, 594
　　nominal　574
　　official (OER)　336–8, 347
　　overvaluation　410, 593
　　PPP　38–9
　　and protection　539
　　real　**39**, 574
exhaustible resources　**361**
existence value　**363**
exit bonds　**494**
Exogenous Shocks Facility (ESF)
　　562, **591**, 591t
expenditure tax　**415–18**
exploitation　**278**, 279, 280
　　Marx　139
export credits　453t, 456–7t
export demand function　572
export earnings　468, **489**, 555f,
　　557–8, 562, 563, 566
　　fluctuations　552–3
　　instability　552–3, 560n10
　　and price compensation　555–6,
　　　　555f
　　rate of growth　172, 563–4
　　shortfalls　589t
export enclave　267
export growth　273, 275, 502,
　　517–20, 534, **564**, 565t
　　and GDP growth　502–3, 503f
　　and trade liberalization　**521–2**,
　　　　533

export prices, stabilizing　566
export restriction schemes　**553–4**
export surplus, recycling　569
export taxes　418
export–import merchants　196
export-led growth models　**517–20**
export-promotion, versus
　　import-substitution　**539**, 570
exports
　　agricultural　182–3, 199
　　economic price　**336**
　　factors determining demand
　　　　273, 564–5
　　foreign currency price　568
　　industrial　534
　　labour-intensive manufactured
　　　　508
　　low-, medium-, high-technology
　　　　502–3, 504t
　　manufactured goods　502–3,
　　　　504t, 539, 545
　　primary commodities　**76–7**, 503
　　primary products　41
　　protection as tax on　539
　　resource-based　502, 504t
　　role in development process
　　　　(Smith)　134
　　tariff and quota-free access　14c
　　trade liberalization　**521–2**
　　what you export matters　**520–1**
expropriation risk　123, 124
Extended Fund Facility (EFF, IMF,
　　1974–)　561, **586–7**, 587t,
　　589t, 595–6
external diseconomies of expansion
　　267
external economies　11, 335
external economies of scale　277
externalities (spillover effects)　**16**,
　　162, 164, 165, 237, 276, **307**,
　　309, 314, 315f, 334, **355–8**, 359,
　　373, 380n5, 518
　　dynamic　9
　　intertemporal　**359**
　　negative　309
　　positive　406, 479, 509
　　see also spillover effects
extinction (of species)　371

facilitating empowerment (World
　　Bank)　**47**, 49–50
factor contribution of agriculture
　　180, **181–2**
factor endowments　246, 262, 318,
　　327
factor immobility　400

factor inputs　159t, 161
factor intensity　155
factor mobility　265
factor prices　327
factor substitution　232
factors in development process
　　177–258
　　agriculture and surplus labour
　　　　180–226
　　capital accumulation, technical
　　　　progress and techniques of
　　　　production　**228–58**
factors of production　146, 151, 154,
　　156, 246, 318, 326, 334, 355,
　　386
　　endogenous to demand　**519**
　　free mobility　270
　　initial differences in endowment
　　　　262
　　mobility　266
　　quality　157
　　shadow prices　**338–9**
failed states *see* states, failed
fair trade　**546–8**, 560, 560n7
Fair Trade Movement (1979–)　548
family planning　288, 289, 299, 467
family size　136–7
family/families　292, 295
famine/starvation　20, **97–100**, 101,
　　137
　　'distributional problem, not one
　　　　of food shortage'　100
farm size　218–19, 219t
feasibility studies　332
fertility (human)　167, 242, 288t,
　　289f, 290t
　　determinants　285, **288–91**
fertilizers　181, 188, 189, 193, 194,
　　197, 198
feudalism　106
Fifth Development Decade
　　(2000–2010)　18
Finance and Development (IMF)
　　xxxii, 244–5c, 412–13c
Finance One (finance house,
　　Thailand)　583
financial appraisal　**331**, 332–3
financial assets, availability of　**396**,
　　399, 400, 406, 407
financial assistance　11, 399
　　special　469c
financial deepening　169, 396, **399**,
　　407
　　and economic development
　　　　(bi-directional causality)
　　　　411

financial distress   411

financial and economic crisis (2008–)
   15, 544, 570

financial flows
   factors determining grant
      element   471–5
   types (developing countries)
      445

financial institutions   396, **398–402**,
   583
   prudential oversight   584

financial intermediaries   406–7

financial liberalization   xxxi, **386**,
   388, **395**, 396, **407–13**, 436n6,
   583
   critics and empirical evidence
      408–12, 436n7–8
   dangers   396, **408–12**
   impact on economic growth
      411–12
   Indonesia versus Kenya
      412–13c
   Keynesian and post-Keynesian
      critique   410
   McKinnon's argument   407, 408f
   prerequisites for success (Fry)
      412
   sequencing   412
   Shaw's argument   407, 408f
   Stiglitz's critique   593

financial markets   15, 120, 399, 407,
   411, 509, 519, 577, 580

financial reform   409, 468

financial repression   **386**, **407**, 409,
   410, 411

financial resources
   total net flow from DAC countries
      453t, 455t, 456
   total net flow to developing
      countries   453–4, 453t,
      455t

financial restructuring   407

financial saving   **395**

*Financial Sector Assessment
   Handbook* (IMF/World Bank,
   2005)   592

financial services sector   400

financial stability, global   50, 469

financial system   **386**
   and economic development
      xxxi, **397–8**
   IMF and promotion of soundness
      592c

Financial Times   xxxiv, 74–5c, 75c,
   110c, 194–5c, 196c

financial-industrial dependence
   279

financing economic development
   383–497
   domestic resources   **386–54**
   foreign assistance, debt, and
      development   **437–97**

First Development Decade
   (1960–70)   18

fiscal adjustment   594

fiscal crises   308

fiscal discipline   584

fiscal policy   xxxi, 386, 395, 594
   and taxation   **413–19**, 436n9–10

fiscal profligacy   579

fiscal reform   386

fisheries/fishing   353, 354, 360–1,
   374, 376, 477

floods   376

food   16, 48–9c, 136–7, 137f
   developmental aid   453t, 456t
   entitlement   98, 99, 100
   global programme   17
   imported   138
   international programme   12
   price fluctuations   50, **52c**, 98–9,
      101, 528
   websites   116
   see also famine

food availability decline (FAD)
   97, 98

food energy   **93**
   poverty line calculation   42–3

food energy method   **26, 42**

food production   **100–1**, 199

food security   **100**, 101

food supply   76, 100, **100–1**, 181
   'arithmetical' growth (Malthus)
      136
   and population growth   100–1,
      291

food surplus (basis for industrial
   expansion)   181

forced saving   xxxi, **387**, 420, 422,
   424, 436n1

forecasting   486

foreign assistance *see* international
   assistance

foreign borrowing   144, 438, 502,
   542, 557, 583
   dual-gap analysis   **439–42**, 442
   rate of growth of income   442–4
   rate of growth of output   442–4
   role of   **438–9**

foreign direct investment (FDI)
   xxxi, 15, 161, 171, 235, 237,

245c, 270, 310, 319, 388, 453t,
   454, 581, 581t, 584
   advantages and disadvantages in
      developing countries
      478–81, 479t, 497n9
   balance-of-payments effects
      480, 481t
   causes and effects   497n9
   and economic growth
      (bidirectional causality)
      479
   websites   497

foreign exchange
   black market rate   168, 516, 525
   constraints   440, 441
   contribution of agriculture to
      economic development
      180, **182–3**
   debt crisis of 1980s   **489**
   rationing   542
   retention rights   522
   shadow price   331, 347
   shortage   446, 577

foreign exchange controls   594

foreign exchange earnings   556, 569
   instability   551

foreign exchange gap   439, 441,
   505, 542

forests/forestry   353, 354, 374
   deforestation   354

fossil fuels   368, 377
   non-fossil fuels   368

fractional reserve banking system
   400

fraud   119, 120

free riders   **120, 309, 358**

free trade   7, 134, 270, 441, 536, 550,
   586, 593
   categories of trade regimes   **516**
   classical doctrine (Ricardo/Smith)
      506
   customs unions and free trade
      areas   **510–14**
   disadvantages for development
      502, **533–4**
   fair trade not free trade   **546–8**
   modern era enthusiasm for   **514**

free trade areas   510–14

freedom   7, 11
   from graft   121
   'from want, ignorance,
      squalor'   19
   Goulet   18, **19**
   Sen   **19**

Freedom House Index of Political Rights and Civil Liberties 122, 125
friends and relatives, credit from **399**
full employment 12, 141, 142, 143, 145, 414, 508, 533, 573
    'Keynesian' 392, 421
fungibility 452c, 464
futures market **555**

gains from trade xxxi, 77, 270, **505–9**, 507t
    dynamic 273, 505, **509**
    static 273, 505, **506–9**
GATT see General Agreement on Tariffs and Trade
GDP (Gross Domestic Product) 8
    cost of climate change 374
    deflator 431–3t
    index 54–62t
    per capita (PPP) 53, 54–62t
GDP growth 159t, 470, 479, 518, 595
    actual 565t
    and aid 450, 451
    and export growth 502–3, 503f, 522
    and growth of industry 108–10, 109f
    Kaldor's first growth law 111, 113c
    per capita 65t
    see also economic growth
gender 13, **13c**, 85, 89, 242
    education 12, 13, 240
    equality 12, 13c, 457c
    literacy 84, 84t
General Agreement on Tariffs and Trade (GATT, 1947–94) 514
    Kennedy Round (1964–7) **547**
    Tokyo Round (1973–9) **547**
    Uruguay Round (1986–93) **547**
    see also World Trade Organization
General Agreement to Borrow (GAB, 1962) **585**
General Theory of Employment, Interest and Money (Keynes, 1936) 140–1
genetically modified (GM) technology 100, 190c, **194–5**, 243
genomics 244
geographic dualism **262**, **264**
geographical determinism 188

geography 78, 79, 80, 119, **121–5**, 187, 528c
    see also new economic geography
gifts tax 420
Gini coefficient/ratio 26, 65, 108, 189, 218–19, 267, 268t
    income inequality 28, 33–4, 35, 35t, 36, 37, 85, 85–8t, 89, 529, 530t, 531, 532, 533
    relative income and economic growth 91
Global Development Finance 2009 (World Bank) 482–5t
Global Environment Facility (UNDP/UNEP/World Bank, 1991–) **358**, 378, 466t
Global Governance of Trade as if Development Really Mattered, The (Rodrik, 2001) 549
Global Health Resource Fund (Sachs Report recommendation, 2001) 96
global inequality (of income) 26, **28**, 35t, **36–7**, 532
Global Monitoring Report (World Bank) 13
global partnership for development **14c**
global revenue, twenty suggestions **477–8**
global warming 358, 368, 369, **373–9**
    greenhouse gas emissions 352, 352f, 368, 372, 373, 374, 375f
Globalization and its Discontents (Stiglitz) 470
globalization xxix, 4, 5, 9, **14–18**, 524, 525, 531
    definition (Fischer) 15
    major eras of 14–15
    manufacturing employment **527–8c**
    UNDP proposals **16**
    websites 24
Globalization and Manufacturing Employment (Jenkins and Sen, 2003) 528c
GNI (Gross National Income), ratio of ODA to 454, 455f
goitre (hypothyroidism) 94
gold 398, 419, 469, 478, 508, 575, 576, 586, 597, 598
Gold Standard 508, 575
governance 14, 79

aggregate governance index **121**
    global 17
    good 6, 14c, 91, 118, 119, 447, 464, 476, 478
    poor 80
government bonds 400
government budget 387
government consumption distortions 167t
government credibility 310
government effectiveness 121, **310–11**
government securities 400
governments 193, 268, 307–8, 400, 452c, 549, 583
    encouragement of labour-intensive techniques **254–5**
    expenditure 76, 169, 193, 308, 410, 421, 451, 490, 519, 586
    and investment climate 231
grace period **472**, 473–4t, 475t
Grameen Bank (Bangladesh, 1983–) 403–4
granaries 101
grant element/aid component **445**, **471–5**, 473–4t, 475t, 496n4, **556–7**
grants 454, 456t
Great Bengal Famine (1943) 98
Great Depression (1930s) 5, 6, 486, 583
Green Revolution 100, **193–4**, 194–5c, 243, 293, 296, 448c, 449
Group of Seven (G–7) 490
growth see economic growth; GDP growth
growth accelerations xxx
growth accounting **151**
growth diagnostics xxx, **171–2**, 549
growth pole analysis 10
Guardian, the 190c

happiness 297
Harrod growth model 74, **140–2**, 440
    neoclassical critique 145–6
Harrod trade multiplier result, dynamic **570–2**, 571–2t
    extended version **573**
Harrod–Domar growth model (Keynesian) 8, **140–6**, 150, 164, 174n3, 573
harvest failure 50, **52c**, 98, 99

harvest time 200, 211
head count index **26, 43**
health 48c, 71, **92–7**, 96t, 126, 159, 199, 212, 228, 236, 243–4, 266, 448, 452c, 457c, 458, 468t
  effect on economic performance **92**
  websites 116
health care/health services 13–14, 97, 492c
  access to 12
  reproductive 12
health clinics 448c
health expenditure 96–7t
health indicators 96–7t
health insurance 309–10
Heckscher–Ohlin theorem **508–9**, 530, 532
hedonic prices **365**
Heritage Foundation 122
high mass-consumption stage (Rostow) **105**, 107, 108
high-income countries (World Bank classification) 27, 33t, 40, 108
  education and adult literacy 84t
  fertility rate (1987–2007) 290t
  health indicators 97t
  inflation (1997–2007) 431–3t
  interest sensitivity of saving 397, 397t
  labour force distribution 103f
  not synonymous with developed countries 40
  population growth 76t, 286t
  recipients of aid 463t
  returns on investment in education (early 1990s) 240t
  savings and investments as percentage of GDP (2009) 388, 389–91t
  share of output (2009) 104, 104t
high-performing Asian economies (HPAEs) 411
Highly-Indebted Poor Country (HIPC) Initiative (1996–9) **438, 481–5**, 487, **490–2**, 588
  debt target 487f
  objectives 491c
  see also Enhanced HIPC Initiative
Hirschman's model of development 8, 293
historical motives, official assistance **446**, 475

horizontal inequality (HI) **85, 89**
hours worked 201, 215, 216
  disguised unemployment 211, **212–13**, 214–15, 214f, 215f
households 353, 353f, 354, 387, 394
  savings 387
  surveys 36–7
housing 19, 97, 229
  shelter 48c
HPAEs (high-performing Asian economies) 411
human asset building combined with credit **402c**
human capital 21, 41, 51c, 83, 161, 161t, 166, 228, 266, 269, 270, 296, 316, 370
  correlation with growth performance 162, 163, 166, 167, 168
  definition 73
  education (contribution to economic growth) **236–42**, 257n2
human development 491c
  high 54–7t, 62t
  low 60–1t, 62t, 63t
  medium 57–60t, 62t
  UNDP definition 52
Human Development Index (HDI) xxix, 26–7, **42**, **52–3**, 54–63t, 491c
Human Development Report (UNDP) xxxii
  1999 16, 241t
  2002 **13–14c**
  2004 52, 63t, 89–90c
  2007 54–61t
  2009 62–3t, 63t
Human Poverty Index (HPI) (UNDP) xxix, 26–7, **42**, **52–3**, 63t
human rights 14, 458c
human security 16
humanitarianism 5, 18
  official assistance to developing countries **446**, 447
hunger 13c, 16
hydroelectricity 355, 356f, 380n4
hygiene 13, 93
hyperinflation, 'structural' interpretation (Bolivia) 436n16
hypothyroidism (goitre) 94

IBRD *see* World Bank
ICOR *see* incremental capital–output ratio

ICT 244
IFAD *see* United Nations International Fund for Agricultural Development
illiteracy 45, 53
illness 50
IMF *see* International Monetary Fund
immigration 266, 270
immiserisation of workers (Marx) **139**, 140
immiserising growth 10, 507
import demand function 572
import duties 525
import growth 502, **564**
  and trade liberalization **522–3**
import liberalization 517
import payments 468, 563
import prices 535
import restrictions 594
import substitution **335**, 441, 542, 556, 566, 568
  versus export promotion **539**, 570
import surpluses (in development process) 443, 496n3
import–export gap, dual-gap analysis 439–42, 442t
imports
  appetite for **565**
  demand for 542
  and development process 326
  economic price **336**
  factors determining demand 565
  low-value manufactured goods 505
  manufactured goods 41, 76
  primary commodities 505
  selective controls 596
incentives 212, 220
  and costs of labour transfer **215–17**
income
  conventional definition 366
  disposable 388
  growth 275, 523
  low 92
  neoclassical definition (Hicks) 369
  problem of definition 366
  rate of growth (Keynes) **140**, **443**
  real 42, 528, 531, 533
income compensation schemes 553, **555**

income distribution   318, 394
    and democracy   125
    economic growth   **91**
    equitable   306, 307, 308, 316
    functional   394
    more unequal in developing
        countries   **84–9**
    optimal   327
    personal   394
    websites   69, 116
    world economy   **27–34**
income elasticity of demand   102,
        105, 205, **271–2**, 274, 275,
        283n2, 540, 570
    agricultural products   72
    and balance of payments
        542–3
    for exports   275–6, 519, 562,
        563–4
    for imports   273, 275, 519, 522,
        562, 563–4, 565t, 572
    manufactured goods   77, 542
    for money (developing countries)
        394
    for products   77, **542–3**
    for sophisticated products   521
    world markets   543
income equality   18
income inequality   26, **27–34**, 34f,
        49, 85, 85–8t, 308, 530t
    barriers to narrowing   89
    and trade liberalization   **529–32**
income measure of unemployment
        82–3
income per capita   27, 29–33t,
        29–33t, 394
    growth   172c
    'optimum' population   297
    quintiles   37, 38f
income quintiles   85–8t
income redistribution   420, 529
    between wages and profits   422
income tax   135, 415, 418, 420, 594
    international   **477**
    international negative   **476**
    international progressive   17
income terms of trade   546
income-depressing/raising forces
        (Leibenstein)   300, 301f
increasing returns   **11, 132**, 153,
        153f
    Smith   **132–5**
    Young   **135**
'Increasing Returns and Economic
    Progress' (Young, 1928)   135

incremental capital–output ratio
    (ICOR)   144, 164, 409
Independent Evaluation Office (IEO)
    594
Index of Economic Freedom   **516**
indifference curves   506
indivisibilities   293, 322, 325, 406
industrial growth
    complementarity with
        agricultural growth   182
    link with GDP growth   108–10,
        109f
    non-industrial growth (Kaldor)
        111, 112, 113–14c
industrial revolution   6, 21, 66, 110c,
        180, 181
industrial sector   21, 102–5, 162,
        216, 334
    'costless expansion'   216
    distribution of labour   102–3,
        103f
    distribution of output   103–4,
        103f
    low capacity to absorb labour
        159
    optimal shadow wage   340,
        340f
industrialization   **8**, 20–1, 66–7,
        73, 85, 102, 110c, 113, 124, 135,
        169, 180, 182, 197–8,
        199–200, 204, 215, 262, 267,
        319, 433
    agricultural surplus required
        134, 180
    'blocked by colonialism'   280
    and economic growth   **108–10**
industry   xxx, 64, 104, 104t, 134,
        137, 468t
    complementarity with agriculture
        204–7
    growth-rate   205–6, 206f
    increasing returns activity   73
    interdependence with agriculture
        199–200
    versus agriculture   318, **319**
inequality   49
    absolute   **90**
    centre–periphery models
        (international)   **270**
    domestic   502
    global   36–7
    'integral part' of capitalist system
        279
    international   **34–6, 269–71**,
        502
    measures of   **27–34**

relative   90
    vertical and horizontal   **84–9**
infant industry   113, 534, 542
infant mortality   42, 50c, 92, 95c,
        96–7t, 244, 470
    child mortality   12, **13c**, 50c, 242,
        254, 457c
inflation   16, 575, 598
    dangers   **427–8**
    and economic growth   xxxi,
        169, 175n15, 396, **420**,
        428–33, 429f, 431–3t,
        436n15
    Keynesian approach   **420–4**
    and per capita income growth
        429t
    and saving and growth   **420**
    structural   10, **427**, 429
    structuralist–monetarist
        controversy in Latin
        America   430, **433–4**,
        436n16
    'tax on money'   387, 392, **424–6**,
        425f
'inflation barrier' (Robinson)   145,
        422–3, **422**, 436n13
inflation rate   396
inflation targeting   xxxi, **428**
inflation 'tax'   387, 392, 396, 425f,
        436n3
inflationary experience   **430–3**
inflationary finance   386, 420
influenza   211, 243
informal financial sector   223, **397**,
        400
    essential features (developing
        countries)   **398–9**
informal money market   223, 309
informal sector   51c, 73, **82, 207**,
        400
information   314, 315f, 377
information technology (IT)   14c,
        15, 196c
infrastructure   75c, 108, 168, 192,
        193, 230c, 244–5c, 269, 296,
        308, 309, 311, 316, **331**, 448,
        449, 467, 478
    economic   468t
    investment   xxx, **228**, 229,
        242–3, 467, 468t, 529
    rural   198, 492c
    social   468t
innovation   **234–5**, 244c, 291, 549
input–output analysis   246
    data   347
input–output tables   **325**

inputs
    agricultural 192, 193
    domestic 338, 350n1
    labour 211
    measurement 156
    new **193**
    non-traded 347, 348t, 538
    social costs 334
    world pricing/prices 347
Inquiry into Nature and Causes of
    Wealth of Nations (Smith,
    1776) 131, 135
Inquiry into Well-Being and
    Destitution (Dasgupta,
    1993) 92
institutes of development studies,
    websites 23
institutional environment 306, 308,
    310, 311
institutional reform 127, 413c
institutional reversal 123
institutional structure/framework
    169, 412, 451, 465
institutional vacuums 308
institutions
    agricultural **224**
    definition of 118
    in different markets 218
    evolution of 122–3
    facilitating empowerment
    49–50
    measuring 121–4
    multilateral 50, 198, 199
    role in development xxix,
    118–29
    supranational 18
    weak **78–80**
    websites 129
insurance 223, 253, 309–10, 314,
    315f
intellectual property 15, 119, 126–7
Inter-American Development Bank
    (IDB) 465t, 466
inter-industry models **317**
interdependence of world economy
    4, 5, 9, 14, 15, **565**, 566
interest payments **481**
    suspended (Brazil) 488
interest rates
    commercial 388
    effect on investment 410
    floating 488
    free market level 471
    high 171, 199, 223, 309, 398,
    408–9
    liberalization 413

nominal 408, 427
observed market 360
optimum real 411
organized money market 400
real xxxi, 407–8, 408f, 410–12,
    413c, 427, 488, 584
reasonable **402c**
and saving **395–6**, 397, 397t
sensitivity of saving (scenarios)
    396
subsidies 406, 472, 473–4t, 475t
Intergovernmental Panel on Climate
    Change (IPCC) **374**, 377
intermediate technology **256**
international agencies, and the
    natural environment 353,
    373, **377–9**, 381n13
international assistance 50, 376
    benefit **445**
    critics **467–8**
    debate **445–6**
    distribution **475–6**
    effectiveness (five policy reforms)
    450–1
    grant element/aid component
    445, 471–5, 496n4
    impact assessment **448–52**
    macroeconomic impact of aid
    449–52
    motives **446–7**
    multilateral **465–6**, 465–6t
    'ownership' 448, 452c, 594
    recipients **459–63**, 459–63t
    return **445**
    schemes for increasing the flow of
    revenue **476–8**
    successes and failures (1970s–90s)
    448c
    trade versus aid **556–8**
    value **445**
    see also official assistance
International Bank for
    Reconstruction and
    Development (IBRD) *see*
    World Bank
international capital flows
    bilateral 388, **445**, 448c, **453**,
    453t, 456–7t, 457, 475t
    multilateral 388, **445**, 448c, **453**,
    453t, 456
    schemes for increasing **476–8**
    types (developing countries)
    445, 496n4
International Clearing Union (ICU)
    (Keynes' plan) 597

international commodity agreements
    502, **551–5**, 560n8–10
International Country Risk Guide
    (ICRG) 121–2
International Development
    Association (IDA) 445, 453t,
    456t, 465, 465t, 466, 490, 491c,
    493, 543
    'soft' loans 466
international dollar (Kravis
    et al.) 40
International Finance Corporation
    (IFC) 445, 465, 466t
International Financial Institutions
    (IFIs) 465–6t
international inequality 26, **28**,
    34–6, 35t, **269–71**
    and trade liberalization **532–3**
International Labour Organization
    (ILO) 23, 71t, 80–1, 83, 103f,
    108, 115n2
international monetary cooperation
    469
    websites 601
international monetary disorder 16
International Monetary Fund xxxi,
    4, 11, 12, 23, 50
    activities 546, **592**
    adjustment programmes 585
    and agriculture 192–3
    anti-corruption measures 314
    'anti-developmental' **593**, 594
    Articles of Agreement 598
    balance-of-payments support
    xxxi, 438, 468, 469c, 562
    changing role 583
    Charter 592
    Compensatory Financing Facility
    (CFF) 555, 562, 566,
    587–8, 587t, 589t, 590t
    conditionality 314, 585–6,
    589–91t, 596, 600n9
    criticisms 568, 583–5, 586,
    593–5
    and debt sustainability 486
    East Asian financial crisis (1997)
    580
    emergency assistance **588**
    Enhanced Structural Adjustment
    Facility (ESAF, 1987–99)
    584, 588
    facilities for low-income countries
    583
    financial facilities (2002) 592c
    gold stock 478
    HIPC initiative 491

International Monetary Fund –
    continued
    'ignores structural surpluses on
        balance of payments' **594**
    IMF-supported programmes
        592c
    lending   465–6t
    lending facilities   589–91t
    'one law for poor, another for rich'
        594
    ordinary facilities   **586**
    Poverty Reduction and Growth
        Facility   490, 491c
    promoting financial system
        soundness   **592c**
    purpose   562, 569
    quotas   **585**, 597
    reform   11, 586
    results of programmes   **595–6**
    role   **469c**
    special facilities   562, **587–91**
    stabilization programmes   595,
        596
    Structural Adjustment Facility
        (1986–7)   584, 595
    supply-side approach to
        devaluation   **568–9**
    technical assistance   592c
    workings   **585–6**
    see also Highly-Indebted Poor
        Country Initiative; Special
        Drawing Rights; Structural
        Adjustment Programmes
international monetary reform   17
international monetary system   **583–5**
international organizations   453
    websites   23–4
'International Regulation of Primary
    Commodities' (Keynes, 1942)
    551
International Rice Research Institute
    195
international technology bank   **256**
International Union for the
    Conservation of Nature and
    Natural Resources   369
international waters   477
Internet   xxxii, 244
intertemporal externalities   **359**
invention   **234–5**, 291
investible surplus   253, 256, 399
investment   xxxi, 71, 118, 440, 596
    in agriculture   198, 222
    allocation decisions   318
    central to growth and poverty
        reduction   **230–1c**

China   73–4, **74–5c**
and consumption   **254**, 310, 320,
    321t
and corruption   314
criteria   319, **326–7**, 329n7
demand-induced   295
'determines saving' (basic
    Keynesian notion)   422
discouraged by corruption   314
diversification   108
'does not matter for long-run
    growth'   145, 149
domestic   73, 78, 479
environmentally friendly   372
financial intermediaries   **406–7**
and financial system   386
foreign   78, 110c
human capital   236–42
India   **74–5c**
induced   325
infrastructure   242–3
Keynesian approach   387, **392**
'lumpiness'   407
prior savings approach   386, **392**,
    424
private   451
productivity   205
public   316, 419
rate of return   135, 171
ratio to GDP (2009)   73, 73t
ratio to national product   229
risks   548
and savings   386, 407–8, 408f
social cost   334, **339**
substitution choices versus
    postponement choices
    324
investment ratio   73t, 163, 166–9
    consumption benefits   320, 321t
    raised by FDI   479
investment–savings gap   145, 439,
    442t, 502
    dual-gap analysis   **439–42**
involuntary saving   **414**
iodine deficiency   92, 93–4
irreversibility (environmental)   371
irrigation   52c, 170, 191, 198, 199,
    242, 309, 448, 448c
isolation paradox   **299**, **335**, **359**
ivermectin (drug)   96

Jakarta Stock Exchange   413
Japanese dwarf wheat   193
job creation   82
joint ventures   **481**

Journal of Development Economics
    xxxii
Journal of Development Studies
    xxxii
Journal of International Development
    xxxii
Journal of Post Keynesian Economics
    116n9

Kaldor's growth laws   71, **110**,
    111–13, **113–14c**, 116n9, 423
Kenyan Central Bank   314
Keynesianism
    absolute income hypothesis
        393–4, 393f
    commodity price stabilization
        495, 551–2, 552f, 567
    critique of financial liberalization
        school   **410**
    financing development from
        domestic resources   386,
        387, **392**, **420–4**
    global   17
    international   565
    international assistance   446
    underused real resources   414
knowledge   169, 172, 479
    adoption and diffusion   234, 235,
        238
    application   237
    creation   235
    dissemination   50, 199, 244–5,
        244c, 267, 451
    receptiveness   237
    spillovers   276
Krugman's 45 degree rule   276
kulaks   181
Kuznets curve   **85**
Kwashiorkor   93
Kyoto Protocol   **358**, 378–9

labour
    abundant   508
    bonded   **223**
    casual   **221**
    dynamic surplus   **211–12**, 212f
    effect of withdrawal   213f
    factor contribution of agriculture
        to development   181
    forced   79
    industrial   181
    low-skilled   51c
    market price   334
    maximum sustainable   214f
    opportunity cost of alternative
        uses   340

permanent **221–2**
price relative to capital 232
real cost (Sen) **213**, 213f
semi-skilled 247
shadow price 338–9
skilled 270, 530
social cost 340, 535
social valuation 216, 216f
static surplus **211**
unlimited supplies (classical
assumption) **200–4**
unskilled 270, 530
valuation 339
websites 116
labour force 78, 143, 144, 147, 292
distribution 102–3, 103f
effective 149
rate of growth 146–7, 150
rate of growth in efficiency units
146
Labour Force Statistics (ILO, 2009)
71t
labour markets
distortions 535
rural sector 218, **221–2**
segmented **221**
labour migration 15, 264, 269
labour mobility 270, 529
labour productivity 71, 73, 144,
146, 149, 155, 181, 188, 204,
216, 294, 436n13
rate of growth 150
labour quality 150, **159**
improvement due to education
237
labour supply 151, 152, 246
labour transfer 216
labour-tying 222
laissez-faire 134
land 48, 138, 151, 170, 207, 211, 316
diminishing returns (Ricardo)
137, 138, 201, 202f
marginal product of successive
units of labour added to
201f
land concentration 218–19, 219t
land market **218–21**
land reform 121, **189–91**, 190c,
199, **220**
land taxes 418
land tenure 188
landlocked countries 14c, 43, 80,
277, 278
landlords/landowners 106,
181, 189–90, 210, 218,
220–1, 224

language 85, 89, 90c
latifundios (large estates) 190
law of comparative advantage
506
law of diminishing returns **72**, 72f,
133
law and order 50, 309, 310, 311,
314, 315f, 316
learning **236**
'learning by doing' 133, 163, **236**
learning curve (progress function)
236
*Least Developed Countries
Report 2004* (UNCTAD)
xxxii, 523
least-developed countries 14c, 63t
educational provision and literacy
(1997) 241t
population growth rates 260f
total fertility rate (1987–2007)
290t
legal system 50, 118, 119, 126–7,
309, 413c
leisure 102, 180, 212, 214, 215, 215f,
354
lender of last resort 583
lending
commercial bank 580, 581t
group-based **402c**
joint-liability **403**
linked with saving **402c**
non-bank 580, 581t
private 494–5, 581
lending, foreign
debt crisis of 1980s **488–9**,
497n10
'device for transferring resources
from poor to rich
countries' **481–8**
'shared blame' 489–90
Leontief Paradox 247, **508**
Leontief production function **246**
leprosy 96
Lewis's model *see* 'Economic
Development with Unlimited
Supplies of Labour'
licences 313, 515
life expectancy 42, 52, 53, **95c**,
243–4, 470
life expectancy index 52, 54–63t,
63t
life support 353, 353f
life-cycle hypothesis of saving
(Modigliani) **394**
life-support systems 354
life-sustenance (Goulet) **18–19**

Lima Declaration (UNIDO,
1975) 12
Limits to Growth, The (Meadows
et al.) 373
link between development assistance
and SDRs **597–9**
direct **597**
inorganic **598**
organic **598**
linkages **11**
backward/forward (Hirschman)
325
liquidity **492**
literacy 239
adult 54–63t, 84, 84t, 241t,
470
female 84t, 289, 289f
Little–Mirrlees approach
application to project appraisal
331, 334, 335, 336, 337,
338–9, 341, 343, **346–9**,
348t
'essential ideas not new, new ideas
not essential' (Baldwin)
347
livestock 101, 359
living standards 17, 39, 40, 41,
42, 52, 67, 126, 229, 299, 316,
470
and aid 450
average 298
in cities 294–5
convergence (neoclassical theory)
131, 146, 150, 162, 163,
175n14, 520
divergence 64
impact of population growth
285, 295, 296
inequality 180
meaningful international
comparisons 40
minimum 42
population control **299**
and population growth 294, 295
real 37, 52
and structural change 71
'tolerable' 66
understatement (developing
countries) **39–40**
loan brokers 398
loan maturity **472**, 473–4t, 475t
loan products **402c**
loans 403, 438
agricultural sector 223
balance-of-payments support
583–4

loans – *continued*
    curb 410–11
    governmental 583
    international 583
    long-term 400
    short-term 583
    supply and demand 409–10
    suspended repayment 488
    variable maturity **493**
Lomé Convention (1975) **547–8**, 550
Lorenz curve (income inequality) **28**, **33–4**, 34f
lottery 477
low-carbon technologies 375
low-income countries (World Bank classification) xxviii, xxix, 27, 33t, 40, 52c, 108, 491c
    debt burden (2007) 485t
    distribution of output (2005) 103t, 104
    education and adult literacy 84t
    effectiveness of aid 451
    fertility rate 290t
    health indicators 97t
    IMF work 469
    inflation (1997–2007) 431–3t
    interest sensitivity of saving 397, 397t
    labour force distribution 103f
    population growth 76t, 286, 286t
    recipients of aid 463t
    returns on investment in education (early 1990s) 240t
    savings and investment as percentage of GDP (2009) 388, 389–91t, 436n2
    technological progress 244
low-level equilibrium trap 9, **136**, 285, **299–301**, 300f
lymphatic filariasis 96

M_2 money 396
machinery/machines 66, 133, 135, 197, 198, 509, 531
McKinnon–Shaw argument **407–8**, 408f
macroeconomies of scale **135**
macrodeterminants of growth 167t, 430
macroeconomic impact of aid xxxi, **449–52**
macroeconomic policy 447

macroeconomic stability 91, 119, 172, 308, 310, 311, 314, 315f, 412, 492c, 576
    instability 579
    institutions for **120**
maize 188, 193, 195, 526
Making Globalization Work (Stiglitz, 2006) 550
malaria 13, **14c**, 80, **94**, 96, 99, 124, 278, 376, 457c
malnutrition 45, 195, 254, 377
    'distributional problem, not one of food shortage' **92–101**
    'undernourishment' 42–3
Malthusianism **135–7**, 285, 291–2, 295–6, 297
managed float 547t, **577**, 579t
Manantali hydroelectric dam (Mali) 355, 358
Manchester School (journal) 225n3
manufactured goods 77, 138, 272, 275, 509, 534, 542
    exports 502–4, 504t, 545
    low value-added 547
    terms of trade **545**, 560n6
manufacturing 102, 156
    case for protectionism 535, 542
    China (PRC) 110c
    employment **527–8c**
    Kaldor growth laws 111, 112, 113–14c
    Lima Declaration (1975) 12
marginal capital–output ratio *see* incremental capital–output ratio
marginal cost
    of degradation 357
    of extraction 363
    of production 306, 309, 334, 355
    to society 336
marginal disutility of work 213, **214**
marginal product
    in agriculture 343
    of capital 147, 150, 158, 164, 175n8, 233
    of factors of production 326–7
    of family labour 211
    of labour 133, 137, 152, 158, 216f, 233, 252, 298, 340
    of labour (agricultural) 72, 76, 210, 210–15, 210f, 212f, 214f, 215f
    of labour time 214
    negative 215f

marginal productivity 175n10
    factors of production 152, 153, 154, 233
marginal propensity
    to consume out of profits (government income) 342
    to consume out of wages 342
    to import 272
    to save 413, 414
marginal rate of substitution (MRS)
    between labour and capital 175n10
'marginal rule' for resource allocation 326–7
marginal social value of consumption 361, 362, 363
marginal utility
    of consumption 306, 345
    of income from work **214**
    of public saving 339
market access 11, 50, 528c
market contribution of agriculture 180, **182**
market failures 7, **307–8**, 314, 315f, 328n1, 357, 370–1
market forces 7, 113
market imperfections **307**, 308, **309**
    three phenomena **309**
market liberalization 52c, 171
market mechanism 7, 19, **306–7**, 308, 328n1
market prices 306, 331
    adjusted 335
    agricultural 193
    divergences from social values 326–7, **334–5**
    domestic 331, 334
market rate of interest 335, 339, 359, 471, 472, 493
market regulation xxix
market, the, 'limited by division of labour' (Smith) **133**, 135
market-based approach (to environmental analysis) **354–5**, 380n1–2
market-legitimizing institutions 119
marketable permits **357**, **358**
marketable surplus (agricultural) **181**, 187, 191–2, 204
marketing 418
    agricultural 192–3
marketing boards **181**, 193, 418
markets 135
    creation and expansion 316
    creative function 307

functioning in agrarian society
218–24
incomplete or missing **307**, 309
institutions and function of
118–29
interlocked **224**
international 583
unfair competition 187, 188
world 197, 546
Marxism xxx, 131, 132, **139–40**,
278–81, 283n6
Massachusetts Institute of
Technology (MIT) 174n5
materials balance approach (Kneese
et al.) **373**
maturity (Rostow) **105**, **107**
political features 107
maximum sustainable yield (MSY)
360–1
measles 99, 243
Meltzer Commission (2000) 595
meningitis 376
MERCOSUR 510
Mexican dwarf wheat 193
Mibanco (Peru) 404
micro-credit/micro-finance
institutions **399**, 401c
role in financing development
386, **399**, **401–2c, 402–5**,
436n4–5
websites 436
Microcredit Summit Campaign 403
Microfinance Information Exchange
405
micronutrient projects **94**
middle-income countries (World
Bank classification) 27, 33t,
40, 52c, 108
debt burden (2007) 485t
education and adult literacy 84t
fertility rate 290t
health indicators 97t
inflation (1997–2007) 431–3t
interest sensitivity of saving 397,
397t
labour force distribution 103f
lower middle-income 33t, 40,
84t, 97t, 104t, 240t, 286t,
391t, 397t, 463t
population growth 71t, 286,
286t
recipients of aid 463t
returns on investment in
education (early 1990s)
240t

savings and investment as
percentage of GDP (2009)
388, 389–91t
share of output (2009) 104, 104t
upper middle-income 33t, 40,
84t, 97t, 104t, 240t, 286t,
391t, 463t
migration 15, 150, 266, 267, 342
labour 264, 270
pull factors **81, 82**
push factors **81–2**
remittances **464–5**, 464f, 497
rural–urban 10, 73, 80, 83, 89,
180, 216, 217, 294, 343
rural–urban and urban
unemployment **207–10**,
226n10–12
military motives, official assistance
446, 475, 476
Millennium Development Goals
xxix, 4, **12–13, 13–14c**, 26, 96,
193, 377, 378, 403, 457c, 467
education 240
poverty reduction target **45–7**
minerals 79, 182, 477
see also natural resources
minifundios (small farms) 190
missing markets (theory) 10
Mobile Banking Program 401–2c
monetarists **433–4**, 436n16
monetary environmental accounts
367
monetary policy 395, 401
monetary system, international
469c
reform 17
monetary targets 596
monetization **399–400**, 426
money 49c, 396, 397
new international (Brandt
Commission) 17
money economy/cash economy
262, 400
growth **196–8**
money holdings tax **425**
money illusion 414
money market integration
399–400
money market, unorganized **397**
moneylenders 199, **223, 398**, 401c
monoeconomics 8, 9
monopoly 309, 314, 315f, 334, 407,
515, 535, 550
Montreal Protocol Fund 466t
moral hazard **309**
moral obligation 18, 446

mortality 12, 13, 79–80
colonial settlers 122, 123, 125
maternal 12, 13, **13c**
see also infant mortality
Motorola 110c
moving equilibrium **140**, 143
multilateral assistance **465–6**, 465–6t
concessional terms 465–6t, 466
Multilateral Debt Relief Initiative
(MDRI) **491**
multinational corporations xxx, 15,
101, **197, 247–8**, 251, 279,
479–81, 497n9
multiplier process 141
multiplier–accelerator mechanism
(Myrdal) 265
mutual insurance 223

nation-states 266
national accounts 317
national income 145, 154, 229, 288,
308, 436n13
equation 439
national income accounting 37, 38,
366–8, 372, 381n9
natural capital 316, 366, **370–3**,
372, 378, 381n9
natural comparative advantage **505**
natural disasters 50, 50c, 376, 590t
natural gas 78
natural growth rate (Harrod) **141**,
143, 144–6
natural resources 79, 353, 353f, 509
curse of xxix, 43, 71, **77–8**
economic growth 77f
endowments 549
non-renewable 353–4
renewable 353, 360f
neo-Keynesian growth theory **422**
neo-Marxism/neo-Marxists 8, 279
neoclassical economics 8, 11, 210,
354–5, 360, 366, 370, 380n3,
593
constant returns and marginal
product pricing 157
counter-revolution 11
general equilibrium theory 135,
265
marginal productivity theory
(Cobb-Douglas test) 157
marketable surplus concept 181
models of development **204**
predicts convergence 64, 163,
175n14
production function 146, 147,
148f, 150

neoclassical economics – *continued*
  supply-side model of export-led
    growth 517, **518**
  trade theory 520
  value theory 140
neoclassical growth theory 64, 131,
  145, **146–50**, 167, 174n5–6,
  519
  assumptions 146
  attacked by 'new' endogenous
    growth theory 145
  convergence hypothesis 520
  propositions 146
neocolonialism 278
neoliberalism 593
neostructuralist school **410**
net present value (NPV) **332**, 333,
  333t, 347–8
new economic geography (Krugman)
  xxx, 262, 263, 270, **276–8**, 509,
  510
'new' endogenous growth theory
  xxix–xxx, 6, 10, 11, 131, 157,
  509, 525
  attack on neoclassical theory 145
  country-specific effects 166–7
  empirical studies **166–71**,
    175n15
  essential propositions **162–71**,
    175n13
  macrodeterminants of growth
    166–71
  starting point 150
  weaknesses 170
new international economic order
  4, **11–12**
  programme of action (1974)
    11–12
'new' trade theory (Krugman) **509**,
  510
newly industrialized countries (NICs)
  21, 40, 112, **488**
Nissan motor company 494
Nobel Prize-winners (Economics)
  Coase, R. 537
  Krugman, P. (2008) 510
  Kuznets, S. 85
  Lewis, Arthur **201**
  Myrdal, Gunnar **262**
  Schultz, T. 189
  Sen, A. 19, **20**
  Solow, R. **147**, 174n5
  Stiglitz, J.E. 436n8, **470**
Nobel Prize-winners (Peace),
  Muhammad, Yunus 404
Nokia 110c
nomadic tribes 180

non-concessional flows **453**, 466,
  466t
non-governmental organizations
  (NGOs) 404–5, 453t, 456t,
  478, 492c
  websites 497
non-oil producing countries 167
non-price factors **565**
non-renewable resources 353–4,
  361–3, 362f, 366, 368
  fossil fuels 368
  known reserves 362, 373
  optimal depletion **362**, 363
non-tariff barriers (NTBs) 515, 516,
  522, 525, 533
non-traded goods 39, **336–8**,
  346–7, 350n1, 468
  world-price conversion 336
Nordic Development Fund 465t
North American Free Trade
  Agreement (NAFTA) 510,
  526
North–South: Programme for Survival
  (Brandt Report, 1980) 16
North–South divide 27, 548
Norwegian Institute of Economic
  Affairs 34
numéraire (common unit of
  account) 280, 331, 334,
  339, 346
nutrition 42, 71, **92–7**, 159, 193,
  221, 254, 480
  programmes **100**
  requirements **93**

oceans 354
ODA *see* official development
  assistance
OECD 110, 168, 243
  research and development 243
OECD Development Assistance
  Committee (DAC) 451, **453t**,
  454–6, 459
  aid tying 463
  net ODA (2007) 455t
  ODA terms (2007) 472, 475t
  total net flow of financial
    resources 455f, **456**
official development assistance
  (ODA) 101, 198, 438, **453**,
  453t, **454–5**, 454f, 491c, 493,
  495, 552
  aid component 453, 454
  more than offset by trade barriers
    in developed countries
    546c, 547
  'non-ODA' 493

ratio to GNI 455f
recipients of **459–63**, 459–63t
see also international assistance
official flows 581, 581t
oil-producing/exporting countries
  17, 438, 439, 554
  balance-of-payments surpluses
    488
oil/petroleum 16, 17, 167, 182, 194,
  495, 562
  price rises/shocks (1973,
    1979–80) 438, 490
old people/old age **51c**, 292
  retirement 394
open economies/openness 235,
  272–3, 318, 438, 519, 525, 528,
  531–2, 550, 568, 584
opportunity cost 216, 309, 334,
  507, 533
  labour **340**
optimal borrowing **486–8**
optimal currency area **575**
optimal depletion **362**, 363
optimum population (concept)
  285, **297–9**, 298f
optimum tariff argument **535**, 542
option values **363**
ordinary drawing rights (IMF) 562,
  586
  credit tranche **586**, 589t
  gold or reserve tranche **586**
  standby arrangements **586**,
    587t, 589t
organic composition of capital
  (Marx) **139**
Organization of Petroleum-Exporting
  Countries (OPEC) 453, 554
Our Common Future (Brundtland
  Report, 1987) 369, 378
output
  agricultural 113c, 212, 219
  distribution of 103f
  growth per head **155**
  maximization of present level
    326
  measurement 156
  non-traded 336
  present versus future 320
  sectoral distribution **102–5**,
    104t
  share of 104, 104t
  share of world trade in world
    output 514f
  versus employment **249–51**
output growth 19, 74, 160t, 161t,
  165, 273, 293, 317–18, 519, 520
  per head 71, **155**

per worker 167t, 168, 292
rate 154, 175n9, **442–3**
overpopulation 270, 299
overproduction 139, 553
overregulation 311
Overseas Development Institute
(ODI, London) 477
Oxfam 80
Oxford Development Studies xxxii

paradox of labour **293–4**
Pareto optimality 327, 329n7
Paris Club 487, 493
participatory political institutions
121
patents 243
Pearson Report (1969) 5
peasantry/peasant farmers 189–90,
215–16
incentives 215
Russian 66
see also subsistence agriculture
pegged exchange rates 574, 574t,
575–6, 578t
penicillin 243
per capita income growth 162,
166–7, 167t, 525
beta convergence **64**, 175n14
conditional convergence 64,
164, 167, 167t
and debt–export ratio 487–8
and inflation 429t
target rate 8
unconditional convergence **163**,
175n14
per capita income (PYC)
and corruption 313
distribution within countries 34
equilibrium level **148**
explaining growth (1960–88)
65t
and fertility rate 288
former colonies 123–4
as index of development **40–2**
initial level 64, 65t, 166, 168–9
measurement and comparability
37–8
multilateral comparisons (Kravis)
40
no presumption of convergence
163
per square kilometre of land
277
and population growth 293,
294, 295, 299–300
quality of institutions and 124
rate of growth 64

real 37, 40, 53
regional differences 269
and saving 395
and trade liberalization 531–2
unit of account (difficulties) 37–8
perfect competition 175n8, 326,
327, 511, 533
peripheral countries *see*
centre-periphery relations
permits 313
pesticides 52c
pests 52c
petty services **71–3**, 246, 334, 526
Philips 110c
physical capital 168, 228, 237, 242,
479
definition 73
physical environmental accounts
367
Pigovian taxes and subsidies **357**
planning 7–8, 77, 306, 307–8, **440**
planning horizon 320
'planning without facts' 317
plant disease 52c
plant and machinery **228**
plantation agriculture 198
polarization effects (Hirschman)
266
Policy and Research Bulletin (World
Bank, 1998) 448c
political motives, official assistance
446, 475, 476
political power, regional distribution
318
political revolution 280
political rights 122
political stability 108, 118, 121, 243,
478
instability 90c, 122, 125, 167t,
168, 169, 310
regime change 171
pollution 16, 295, 352, 352f, 358,
374, 477–8
see also environmental
degradation
poor countries 4–5, 149
catch-up mechanisms **53–67**
commodity-dependent **488**
and global warming/climate
change 374, 375, **376–7**
methods of analysing whether
catching up with rich
countries 64, 65
trade strategy for development
548–51
poor people 279, 352, 492c
consumption gains 344

consumption levels 344
'good credit risks' (Vietnam)
402c
impact of climate change 353,
376–7
well-being and ill-being 48–9c
population 21, **29–33t**, 35, 468t
age structure 292, 293
control 294, 299
density 123, 170, 269
and development xxx, **285–302**
facts 2, **285–8**, 286t
growth *see below*
and growth of cities **294–5**
history 285, 287f, 302n1
India and China 74c
momentum **290–1**, 290f
optimum 285, **297–9**, 298f
pressure 293, 296
replacement rate 288, 290
size 143, 533
statistics 286t
websites 302
Population and Food (Dyson, 1996)
100
population growth 74, 76t, 136–7,
139, 163, 166, 169, 201, 242,
285–8, 286t, 287f, 394, 596
costs and benefits
(impairment/stimuli)
291–4
low-level equilibrium trap
299–301
Malthus 136–7
models 10
optimum **297–9**
rapid 71, **75–6**
rates 285, 287f
Simon's challenge **295–7**
portfolio flows 581, 581t
portfolio investment 413c, 453t,
457t, 478
post-conflict lending 590t
post-Keynesianism, critique of
financial liberalization school
410
Post-Washington Consensus **584**
poverty xxix, xxx, 16, 63t, 180, 193,
298
and climate change 377
and corruption 311
definition of 4, 42, 43
economics of xxviii
eradication of 5, 13c, 41, 43
fall in rate 13
growth relationship 91
halving of 12, 13c, 467, 573

poverty – *continued*
  as major cause of environmental
      damage 378
  measuring 26, **42–5**
  rural 191, 279, 467
  tackled from 'grass-roots'
      47–52
  and trade 528
  and trade liberalization **526–9**
  urban 85
  vicious circle of 230
  websites 69
  see also absolute poverty
Poverty Action Fund (Uganda)
  492c
poverty gap **26**, **43**, 45, 46t
poverty line 42
  food energy method **42–3**
  PPP method **42**
poverty rate **43**, 44t
  elasticity of 45, 46, 47t
Poverty Reduction and Growth
    Facility (PRGF, 1999–) 562,
    588, 589t
Poverty Reduction Strategy Papers
    (PRSPs, 1999–) **471**, 490,
    529, 588, 591t, 594
poverty-measurement **42–5**,
    68n2–5
  food energy method **42–3**
  head count index **43**
  PPP method **42**
poverty-reduction 13c, 314, 315f,
    377, 449, 451, 457–8c, 458c,
    467, 469, **526–32**, 594
  anti-poverty policies/programmes
    80, 314, 315f, **471**
  and globalization **527–8c**
  investment climate central to
    230c
  linked with debt-relief 492c
  three-pronged strategy (World
    Bank) **47–50**
poverty-weighted indices of growth
    91–2
power (energy) 228, 242, 243, 309
power (political) 106
  constraints on 78
PPP *see* purchasing power parity
Prebisch doctrine **540**, 541, 542,
    560n5
Prebisch–Singer thesis **76**, **543**
Present Social Values (PSVs) 348
present value **332**
  sacrificed saving **340**
present value method **331**

preventive expenditure technique
  364
price compensation agreements
  554–5, 555f
price controls 594
price elasticity
  of demand 338, 553, 568
  of demand for exports 273, 562,
    565, 569
  of demand for imports 562,
    565, 600n2
  of supply 553
price reforms 468
price stability 412, 553
prices 192–3, 204, 306, 387, 422,
    540–1, 552f
  aid tying 463
  border **335–6**, 337, 338
  domestic 78, 188, 273, 274, 335,
    336, 337, 338, 343, 347, 515,
    535, 563, 564, 567, 568, 569,
    576, 577
  foreign 273, 338, 563, 564, 569,
    574
  free market 463
  future 553
  hedonic **365**
  imports 535
  industrial 541, 541f
  international 418
  labour relative to capital 234
  non-renewable resources 368
  non-traded goods 39
  primary products 541f
  relative 135, 275
  and trade liberalization 526
  traded goods 39, 468
  world 331, **334**, 335, 336, 337,
    339, 343, 347, 486, 511, 513,
    515, 537, 538, 548, 551, 554,
    569
  see also commodity prices
pricing
  market-based 593
  to market **567**
primary commodities 182, 271,
    495, 502, 534, 540, 542
  boom and slump 444–5
  export domination **76–7**, 76t,
    503
  nominal and real price indexes
    (1862–1999) 544, 544f
  price volatility 77, 544–5, 551
  terms of trade (recent trends)
    543–5
  see also commodities

primary poverty 5, 7, 18, 451
  see also absolute poverty
primary products 79, 102, 135, 280,
    325, 532, 540–1, 545
  prices 540–1, 541f, 551, 566
  stabilizing export earnings
    546–55, 560n8–10
primary sector 78
principal-agent **220**
Principles of Economics (Marshall,
    1890) 140, 504
Principles of Political Economy (Mill,
    1848) 509
*Principles of Political Economy and
    Taxation* (Ricardo, 1817) 137,
    506
prior-savings approach, financing
    development from domestic
    resources 386, **392**, 410, 413,
    424
private sector 14c, 242, 311, 386,
    447, 452c
privatization **311**, 584, 593
probit analysis 487
problem/tragedy of the commons
    358, 380n5
process innovation **228**
procurement policies 522
procurement tying 463
producer prices 192, 528
  agricultural 182, 193
product contribution of agriculture
    180, **181**
product diversification 543
product innovation **228**
production 38, 217, 418, 468f
  agricultural 218, 223
  capital-intensive 139, 145, 147,
    318, 322, 329n6
  domestic 99, 326, 335, 511, 536,
    539
  dynamic gains from trade **509**
  effects of customs unions 502,
    510–14
  external economies 11, 335
  improvements in process 509
  labour-intensive xxx, 144, 145,
    147, 148f, 234, 245, 250–1,
    278, 322
  primary 7, 78, **102**, 182, 534
  private cost 535, 536
  seasonal 218
  secondary **102**
  service sector/tertiary **102**
  social costs and benefits
    326–7

structure **594**
techniques of **245–8**, 245f
production function 131, 151f,
      152f, 165, 175n12, 234, 246, 323
   agricultural 211
production function approach (to
      analysis of growth) **150–8**,
      175n7–11, 229, 365
   Cobb–Douglas **153–8**,
      175n8–11
   developing countries **158–62**,
      175n12
   education's contribution to
      earnings 237–8
   production function 151–3
   'supply-orientated' approach
      150
production function diagram/map
      251
production function, neoclassical,
   Kaldor's critique 165
production methods, labour-saving
      256
production possibility curve 307,
      506, 509
production quotas 552, 553
production techniques xxx, 479
   capital-intensive **245–8, 252,**
      255–6, 322
   labour-intensive 322, 345–8
productivity
   agricultural 41, **180–9**, 204,
      206–7
   of commodities 520–1
   energy (food) intake 93, 93f
   Kaldor's growth laws 111, 112,
      113–14c
   of labour 163, 508
   low 41
   and population growth 296
productivity growth 64, 273, 274,
      293, 520
   autonomous 274
   induced 282, 520
productivity rates, agriculture,
   industry, services 164
profit rate 134, 137f, 140, 226n5,
      265, 280, 281f
profit-maximization 216, 247, 355,
      412
profitability 136, 182, 306, 322, 405,
      485, 540, 568, 569, 582
profits 139, 145, 387, 394, 427
   all saved (assumption) 251, 252
   from industry 134
   global 478, 479, 480

ploughed-back 107
private 349
reinvestment 137
remittance 198
repatriation 480
   see also surplus value
Programme of Action for Sustainable
      Development of Small Island
      Developing States 14c
programme aid 447
programme assistance 468t, 476, 477
progress function (learning curve)
      236
project aid 447
project appraisal xxxi, **331–2**
   application of Little–Mirrlees and
      UNIDO approaches xxxi,
      331, 334, 335, 336, 337,
      338–9, 339, 341, **346–9**,
      348t
   distributional considerations
      344–6, 345t
   economic appraisal 333–4
   financial appraisal **332–3**
   websites 350
project appraisal report **332**
project choice 331
project cycle 332
project identification **331**
project planning see project appraisal
projection models 317
promoting opportunity (World
      Bank) **47–9**
propensity to consume 253, 418
   different classes **253**
   out of profits 350n3
   out of wages 216, 342, 350n3
propensity to import 539
propensity to save 292, 393–7, 418
   export sector 558
   higher out of profits than out of
      wages 145
   out of profits 342, 394, 424
   out of public income 346
   out of wages 394, 420, 424
property rights 78, 91, 118, **119**,
      126, 129n1, 171, 190–1, 220,
      309, 311, 315f, 355, 356–7, 358,
      478, 584
   common **358–9**, 380n5
   measure of **121–2**, 123, 124
property taxes 594
prostitution 15
protection xxxi, 16, 502, 515, 533,
      539, 548
   agriculture 546–7

arguments for **535**, 542
benefits expected by Prebisch
      542–3
domestic industry 522
economic arguments **535**
effective rate of 515, **537–9**
infant country 550
infant industry argument 542
levels of 516
non-economic arguments
      535–6
'not whether to, but how to
      protect industry' 113
optimum tariff argument **535**
selective 441
strategic 509
tariffs versus subsidies **535–7**
theory of **535–7**
theory of the second best **536**
welfare gains and losses 536f
'protection against
   expropriation' 79
protectionism 17, 35, 513, 514, 569,
      583
   developed countries 505
protein 92, 93, 254
public enterprise projects **331**
public expenditure 193, 214, 328n1,
      594
   on agriculture 198
   government expenditure 76,
      169, 193, 308, 410, 421, 451,
      490, 519, 586
public finances, management 316
public goods **16**, 50, 64, 306, **308–9**
   non-excludable **308**
   non-rival **308**
   pure **308**, 314, 315f
public health 315f
public officials 314
public projects 333–5
public sector 52c, 243, 400
   reduction 468
public services, access to 242, 448
public utilities 311, 315f, 334
purchasing power 21, 204, 388, 427
   agricultural 205, 206
   exports over imports 345–6
purchasing power parity (PPP) 26,
      29–33t, **38–40**, 491c
   methods of constructing
      ratios 39
   poverty lines 42
pure aid 447
pure terms of trade **564**
'pure' transfer problem **489**

quality of life   40, 492c
quantity theory (of money)
     approach, financing
     development from domestic
     resources   386, 387, **392**,
     424–6, 436n3
quasi-money   396
quasi-option values   **363**
quotas   515, 553, 585, 597

race   85, 89, 90c
ratios
     balance-of-payments deficit to
          GDP   583
     capital to labour   145, 146–7,
          148, 148f, 149, 166, 245–6,
          247, 251, 300
     capital to output   75c, 146–50,
          162–6, **229**, 232, 249, 441,
          444
     consumption to man-hours
          worked   42
     costs to income   582
     debt to equity   582
     debt to exports   481, 482–5t,
          487, 487f, 491c
     debt to GDP   **487**, 488, 562
     debt to GNP   482–5t
     debt service   481, 487, 488
     debt-service payments to GDP
          580
     domestic savings and investment
          to GDP   580
     export to import prices (terms of
          trade)   77, 503, 507
     exports to GDP   518
     external debt to GDP   580
     extra capital accumulation to
          flow of output   141
     FDI to GDP   478
     government consumption to
          GDP   168
     government fixed investment of
          GDP   167
     income per capita   28
     international trade to GDP   168
     investment to consumption
          320, 321t
     investment to GDP   150, 469
     investment to national income
          320, 321t
     investment to national product
          229
     labour to capital   229, 233, 234
     land to labour   187
     M_2 money to GDP   396

marginal product of capital to
     marginal product of labour
     233
marginal product of labour to
     marginal product of capital
     234
money holdings to income   427
ODA to GNI   455f
official to shadow exchange rate
     338
physical investment to GDP   166
population to resources   298
private saving to GDP   396
private sector credit to national
     income   413c
rate of growth of output per
     worker to rate of growth of
     capital per worker (Kaldor)
     166
remittances to GDP   465
savings and investment to GDP
     73t, 146, 148, **149**, 166, 388,
     389–91t
savings to GDP   469
savings to income   141
short-term debt to reserves   583
tariff revenues to value of imports
     515
tax revenue to national income
     414, 415, 416–17t
trade balance to GDP   524, 524f
trade to GDP   513, 515
raw materials   16, 138, 182, 198, 280,
     353, 504, 538, 554
real balance effect   **387**, **396**
     outside money   386n10
realization crisis (Marx)   **139**
recession, world   15, 544, 570
redistribution
     from savers to investors   386
     of land   190, 191
Regional Development Banks   595
'regional' growth rate differences
     271–6, 283n1–5
     export growth model   **272–6**,
          283n3–5
regional inequalities   **267–9**
     'lower in federal states'   268
regional trade agreements (RTAs)
     502, **510**
regions (intra-country)
     new economic geography
          (Krugman)   276
     potential advantages of separate
          nationhood (Hirschman)
          266

regulation   118, 119, 309, 313, 314,
     315f, 334, 412
regulatory burden   121
regulatory institutions   119, **120**
'relation' (Harrod)   141
relative income gap   **28**
religion   79, 85, 89, 90c, 123
remittances   xxxi, 270, 388, **464–5**,
     464f
     websites   497
renewable resources   353
     harvesting   **360–1**
     present consumption and future
          generations   381n9
     relation between growth and
          stock of   360f
rent (economic)   **78**, 362f, 363
rent (paid to landlords)   137, 220,
     221
rent-seeking   10, **313**, **314**
replacement cost technique   **364**,
     381n8
Report of Commission on
     Macroeconomics and Health
     (Sachs Report, 2001)   96,
     115n6
research and development   11,
     110c, 131, 162, 164, **228**, **234**,
     237, 243, 245c, 269, 479
reserve army of labour (Marx)   **139**
reserve assets   585
reserve currency   574, 575
resource allocation   xxx, 7, 9, 102,
     169, 187, 306, 492c
     broad policy choices   **317–19**
     central issue facing all economies
          306
     efficiency   326, **406**, 586
     marginal rule   326
     optimum   309, 327
     programming approach   **327**
resource shifts/transfers   17, 50,
     155, 159, 418, 568
     agriculture to industry   64, 106,
          108, 155, 161, 162, 198, 200
resources   6, 528c
     real   454, 508
     unexploited/unutilized   477
     see also domestic resources
restriction schemes   **553–4**
Review of Climate Change (UK, 2008)
     364
rice   101, 193, 195, 196c, 198, 243,
     541
riots   90c

risk   20, 78, 270, **367–8**, 411,
    411–12, 486
    policy-related   230–1c
    political   268
    poor people's exposure   **50–2c**
risk management   555
risk-aversion   xxx, 363, 368, 372, 408
    rural subsistence sector   **189,
    195–6**
risk-takers   108, 118, 120, 234–5
roads   448c
    rural   492c
Rockefeller Foundation   195
Rotating Savings and Credit
    Association (ROSCA)   398
royalties, mineral   477
rubber   540, 541
rule of law   78–9, 121, 122
rules of behaviour   118–19
rural areas   401–2c, 528
    development   102, 198–9
    problems of measuring PCY   38
    social structure   **189**
    see also migration/rural-urban
Rural Enterprise Programme (K-Rep,
    Kenya, 1999–)   404
rural financial intermediaries (RFIs)
    399, **402–3**

Sachs Report (2001)   96, 115n6
Sachs and Warner (1995) Openness
    Index   **516**, 525
SACU   510, 513
SAF arrangements   587t
sanitation   13, 96–7t, 97, 242, 243,
    295, 352f, 448, 448c, 467, 468t,
    492c
satellites, parking charges   477
saving function (Keynesian)   141,
    392
savings   xxxi, 41, 71, 118, 386, 440,
    557–8
    capacity or ability to save   **392,
    393–5**
    China   **74–5c**
    conflict with employment
    329n6
    domestic   388, 395, 438, 440,
    444, 596
    dual-gap analysis   439–42
    effect of population growth
    292, 394
    empirical studies   **395**
    employment versus   249, **251–2**,
    251f, 322
    financial   395–6, **408**, 410

financial intermediaries   **406–7**
    and financial liberalization
    408–9
    forced   xxxi, **387**, 392, 420, 422,
    424
    forms   **387–92**, 436n1–3
    government   395
    India   **74–5c**
    inflation-induced   387, 436n1
    interest sensitivity   397t
    and investment   407–8, 408f
    life-cycle hypothesis (Modigliani)
    394
    linked with lending   **402c**
    private   **387**, 395, 409
    productive allocation   **386**
    public   **387**
    real   420
    sacrificed   **340**
    taxation and preservation of
    255, 255f
    voluntary and involuntary   386,
    387, 414
    willingness to save   **392, 395–7**
savings groups   **398**
savings rates   167, 171, 172
savings ratio   73–4, 73t, 144, 145,
    163, 168, 291, 292, 295, 297,
    300, 388, 389–91t, 393f, 394,
    395, 424, 436n2
    personal   394
Say's law   136, 137
'scarce currencies'   594
schools/schooling   42, 64, 199, 237,
    448c
    enrolment rates   52, 54–62t
    secondary school enrolment
    166, 169
science/scientists   110c
sector models   **317**
    classical two-sector   204
    intersectional general equilibrium
    models   192
sector thesis (Fisher and Clark)   102
seeds   188, 193
self-discovery   548–9
self-esteem   11
    Goulet   18, **19**
self-sufficiency   101, 535
semi-feudalism   21
semi-industrialization   21
serfdom   181
service sector   20, 102–4, 103f, 104t,
    113c
    'three broad categories of
    activities'   102

shadow exchange rate (SER)   xxxi,
    331, 334, 336–8, 347, 348t
shadow price of labour   **338**
shadow prices   246, **335**
    factors of production   **338–9**
shadow wage   216, 217
    equivalence of Little–Mirrlees
    formulation and UNIDO
    approach   346–9
    numerical calculation   **343**, 346
shadow wage rate   **340–2**, 350n2–3
    optimal   340–2, 340f
sharecroppers/sharecropping   190,
    219t, **220–1**
shifting agriculture   219
shipping, taxation   477
shocks   5, 15, 22, 50, 99, 101, 118,
    125, 172, 275, 486, 562, 569
Siemens   110c
signals (market prices)   **306**
Silent Spring (Carson, 1962)   373
skill constraint   247, 439
skill mix   **252**
skills   51c, 228, 236
slavery   79
slum dwellers   14c, 294–5
small businesses/firms   52c, 403,
    464
small countries   167, 338
small farmers   196c, 219–20, 546
'small is beautiful' (aphorism)   66
smallpox   243
social appraisal   **331, 332, 338,
    344–6**
    distributional considerations in
    project appraisal   344–6,
    350n4
social benefits   334, 534
social capital (SC)   50c, 216, 228,
    308, 324–5, 324f, 370
    indivisibilities   325
social conflict   119, 126
social cooperation   119
social cost
    of investment   **339–40**
    of production   535
social cost–benefit analysis   xxxi, 10,
    217, 306, 309, 326–7, **331**, 334
    environmental   364, 365–6, 373
    Little–Mirrlees and UNIDO
    approach   **334**, 337, 338,
    346–9, 348t, 350n2
    see also project appraisal
social costs   534
    environmental   364
    of investment   334, **339**

social division 122
social dualism **262, 263**
social expenditure **228**
social groups 338
   conflict and tension **89–90c**
social infrastructure 295, 296
social insurance 314, 315f
   institutions 119, **120**
social justice 28
social marginal costs 363
social opportunity cost 360
social preferences 371
social prices **335**
social profitability 405
social protection 118
social rate of discount **339**
social safety nets 529
social saving 597
social security 100
   institutions 127
   transfer payments 328n1
social services 311
social structure 125
social tensions 467
social value and costs 331
social value of stock, divergences
      from market prices 326,
      334–5
social welfare 8, 327
social-overhead capital 318, 322,
   325, 444
socialism 593
software 244
soil 79, 123, 188, 199, 353, 354, 366,
   370
Solow neoclassical growth model
   131, 147, 167
   augmented 167
Special Drawing Rights (SDRs, IMF,
   1969–) xxxii, 478, 552, 562,
   567, 576, 588, 594
   developing countries **596–9**
   link with development assistance
      597
specialization *see* division of labour
speculation/speculators 98, 101
spillover effects 237, 238
   see also externalities
'spread' effects **267**, 270
Stabex scheme **548**
stages of development **102–5**, 119,
   235
Stages of Economic Growth (Rostow,
    1960) 74, **105–8**
   critique 107–8
stagflation 410, 551

Stalinism 66, 107
standby arrangements **586**, 589t
standard conversion factor (SCF)
   xxxi, **336–8**, 343, 347
standard deviation **28**
state antiquity **125**
state capability 310–11, 314
state credibility 310–11
state intervention 8, 113, 160,
   307–8, 311, 334, 368, 549
state marketing boards 577
   government revenue raising 193
state role xxx, 113, 306, **308–11**,
   316
   in agriculture 224
   capabilities 311–12, 314
   functions 314, 315f
   improved effectiveness (World
      Bank prescription)
      313–14, 315f
   websites 329
state, the 48, 78–9, 240, 328n1
state trading 550
states, failed xxx, 306, **316**, 467
static equilibrium theory xxviii, 20
   challenged by cumulative
      causation theory 264–7,
      271
static returns 150
stationary state (Ricardo) 137, 138
Stern Review of Climate Change
   (2006) xxxi, 353, 358, 364,
   368, 369, 370, **373–6**, 378
stock markets 413, 579, 582
*Strategic Factors in Economic
   Development* (Kaldor, 1967)
   135
Strategy of Economic Development
   (Hirschman, 1958) 135
structural adjustment lending/loans
   xxxi, **468–71**
   definition 468
   IMF's difference of emphasis
      469c, 497n7
   purpose (World Bank, 1979–)
      468–71, 497n7
Structural Adjustment Programmes
   (SAPs) 193, 378, 407, **438**,
   469–70, 595
structural breaks 543, 544
structural change 91, 269, 275, 533
   development and **102–14**, 104t
   and living standards 71
   only long-run solution 550
   world income growth **569–70**
structural inflation 10, **427**, 429

structural transformation 91
structuralist theory **21**
structuralist–monetarist controversy
   (causes of rapid inflation),
   Latin America 430, **433–4**,
   436n16
subsidies 193, 243, **254–5**, 275, 309,
   313, 334, 538, 594
   agricultural 546–7, 546c
   tariffs versus **535–7**, 537f
subsistence 38, 52c, 66, 106, 136,
   180, 181, 189, 192, 194, 198,
   214, 262, 285, 298, 299, 386,
   397
subsistence agriculture/farming 67,
   219, 246
subsistence sector 38, 198, 201,
   202, 203, 204, 210, 263
suffrage 126
Supplemental Reserve Facility (SRF,
   1997–) 587t, **588**, 589t, 590t
supply
   'creates its own demand' (Say's
      Law) 136, 137
   domestic 511, 553
   excess 134, 553
   exports 566, 569
   indivisibilities 322
   restriction **553**
   see also production function
      approach
supply and demand 39, 204, 265,
   273, 540–1, 541f, 553
   Domar 142
   excessive variability 553
   labour 265f
   price elasticity 553
supply-side 517, 518, 586
   IMF approach to devaluation
      568–9
   reforms 468
surplus labour xxx, 8, 80, 139, 162,
   180, 210, 216
   agricultural 8, 72–3, 216, 221
   fuelled industrial growth 180
   Indian agriculture 211
   methods of ascertaining existence
      211
surplus value (Marx) 139, 279
sustainable debt 481, **486–8**
sustainable development 12,
   14c, 16, 18, 306, 310, 316,
   353, 367, **369–70**, 372, 377,
   378
   definitions and interpretations
      369–70

objectives 370
    supported by international
        agencies 377–9
synthetic substitutes 504, 533, 540
Systemic Transformation Facility
    587t

take-off stage (Rostow) **74, 105,
    106–7,** 108, 170, 181, 229, 291
tariff barriers 522
tariffs 138, 188, 309, 334, 338, 515,
    516, 533, 538–9, 546
    nominal 515, 537–8, 559n3
    optimum tariff argument **535,**
        542
    unilateral reductions 513
    versus subsidies **535–7,** 537f
tax avoidance 420
tax base 415, 425
tax effort **414–15**
tax effort index 416–17t
tax evasion 420, 594
tax exemptions/incentives 188, 522
tax on money holdings (inflation)
    425–6, 425f
tax rates 357, 414, 418, 425, 584
tax ratio 415, 416–17t
tax reform 468, 594
    developing countries **419–20,**
        436n11
tax revenue/yield 77, 415, 418
tax system 169, 412
    buoyancy **414**
    efficiency 419
    elasticity **414**
    taxable capacity **414,** 419
taxation xxxi, 137, 138, 200, 252,
    254–5, 270, 309, 313, 334, 338,
    386, 387
    agricultural 191, 193, 418
    business 418–19
    direct 418
    environmental 357, 357f
    fiscal policy and **413–19,**
        436n9–10
    global 477–8
    indirect 418
    international 418, **477–8**
    money holdings **425–6,** 425f
    and preservation of level of saving
        255, 255f
    voluntary 478
    wealth 419
technical assistance 388, 457, **592**
technical cooperation 12, 453t, 456t

technical progress 15, 66, 106–7,
    124, 228, 229, **231–6,** 263, 292,
    293, 368, 373, 504, 509
    absolutely labour- or
        capital-saving **233**
    agricultural 193
    assumption of neutrality 156,
        157
    beneficial role underestimated 7
    capital-saving 228, 232, 232f,
        234
    character 231
    different senses **231–2**
    effect on capital-output ratio
        232
    embodied **158,** 163
    endogenous 11, 155, **158**
    exogenous 153, 158, 162
    four main sources 234–5
    Harrod-neutral 149, 232
    Harrod's classification **232,** 234
    Hicks's classification **232,** 234
    investment in human capital
        237–42
    labour-augmenting 149
    labour-saving 228, 231, 232,
        233–4, 233f, 256
    neutral 153, 228, 232, **233,** 233f
    and population growth 285,
        292, 294, 295
    societal **234–6**
    and terms of trade **540–1**
technical progress function (Kaldor)
    165, 165f
technological dualism **262, 263**
technological–industrial dependence
    279
technology 64, 134, 150, 152, 153,
    163, 164, 171, 172, 175n11, 212,
    229, 298, 318, 479
    access to 14c
    bridging the divide **244–5c**
    changes **231–2**
    constant 373
    definition **231–2**
    diffusion of 267
    exports 502–3, 504t
    foreign 278
    inappropriate 256, 480
    intermediate **256**
    labour-intensive 252
    labour-saving 248
    see also production techniques
technology divide **244–5c**
technology transfer 168

telecommunications 110c, 228,
    242, 244–5c, 311, 477
tenants (agricultural) 189–90, 218,
    220–1
terms of trade 77, 78, 205–6f, 278,
    319, 495, 503–4, 533, **535,** 542,
    562, **566–7,** 573
    agriculture and rest of economy
        193
    agriculture–industry xxx, 139,
        181, 182, 191, 193, 204,
        204–7
    centre–periphery 280, 281, 281f,
        283n6, 540–1, 541f
    deterioration 535
    equilibrium 182, 205–6, 206f
    movements 540–1, 541f
    optimum tariff argument **535,**
        542
    pure **564**
    recent trends **543–6,** 560n6
    secular deterioration (Prebisch)
        541
    structural breaks 543, 544
    and technical progress **540–1**
    tendency to move against
        primary-producers 542
    volatility 551
'terms of trade effect' 571–2t
textiles 106, 249, 505, 507f, 526
    relative price 135
Theory of Justice (Rawls, 1972) 298
theory of second best **536**
Third World *see* developing countries
Thirlwall's Law 276, 283n5
    see also name index
timber 106, 354
time 6–7, 41, 154
    available for child-rearing 289
    harvest versus non-harvest 211
    history/past **10**
    life-cycle hypothesis of saving
        394
    planning horizons 320
The Times xxxiv, 95c
Tobin Tax 477
Tonga Development Bank **406,**
    436n4
Tongan 6th Development Plan
    316
Toronto Terms (1988) **493**
total factor productivity (TFP) 151,
    154, 159, 160t, 292
    dependent factors **159–62**
total productivity 159, 159–60t,
    231

total welfare maximization
    (utilitarianism) **297–8**
tourism 468t
Tract on Monetary Reform (Keynes,
    1923) 425
trade 7, 11, 78, 79, 170, 197, **266**,
    270, 279, 388, 439, 468t, 478
    balance-of-payments effects
        505
    balanced 275, 508
    benefits from 502
    classification of regimes **516**
    and economic growth **502–5**
    equilibrium 508
    freeing of 15
    'not fair' between developed and
        developing countries
        548–51, 560n7
    Prebisch doctrine 540, 560n5
    strategy for development
        548–51
    surcharge 477
    technological spillovers 163
    vent for surplus 502, **505**, **510**
    versus aid **556–8**
    websites 560
    see also gains from trade
trade barriers 75, 502, 524, 547
trade creation **511**, 512
trade cycle (Harrod model) 41, 142,
    143, 552
trade and development xxxi,
    501–60
Trade and Development Report
    (UNCTAD) xxxii
trade distortion 524
trade diversion **511**, 512
trade liberalization xxxi, 15, 101,
    171, 378, 502, 513, 514, 549,
    550, 594
    and economic performance
        524–6
    and export growth **521–2**
    and growth 524, 526
    ideal conditions for 517, 529, 533
    and international inequality
        532–3
    measurement and process of
        515–17
    and poverty and domestic
        inequality **526–32**
'trade not aid' (slogan) **505**, **556–8**,
    560n11
trade openness 245c, 278, 515
trade policy xxxi, **516**, 528c
    'outwardness' 167, 539

trade promotion 12
trade taxes 77
trade theory xxxi, 540
traded goods/tradable goods **338**,
    347, 468t, 479
    three categories (Little and
        Mirrlees) 338
traditional societies (Rostow)
    105–6
tragedy of the commons 358–9
training 237, 479
transaction costs 406
transfer burden **489**
transfer problem (Keynes) **489**
    'pure' transfer problem (Keynes)
        489
transitional stage (Rostow) **105–6**,
    108
transparency 314, 403, 492c
Transparency International 122,
    311, 312–13t
transport/transportation 15, 106,
    107, 108, 193, 228, 242, 243,
    266, 295, 296, 309, 467, 468t,
    529
    costs 276–8, 338
travel cost method **365**
Treatise on Money (Keynes, 1930)
    420
trickle-down effects **266–7**
Trinidad Terms (1990) **493**
tropics 20, 278
Trust Fund (IMF) 587t
tuberculosis 50c, **94**, 96, 244
turn-key projects **481**

UNAIDS (Joint UN programme on
    HIV/AIDS) 94, 95c
unbalanced growth 306, **322–6**
uncertainty **367–8**
unconditional convergence **163**,
    175n14
under-population 298, 299
underdevelopment
    characteristics of
        underdevelopment and
        structural change xxix,
        71–116
    development of **279–80**
    geographic determinism **188**
    major reasons why some
        countries are rich and
        others poor 71–80
    perpetuation xxx, 4–5, 18, **20–2**
    structuralist and dependency
        theories **21–2**

weak institutional structures
    78–80
underemployment 80, 82, 89, 270,
    387, 428
unemployment 6, 16, 51–2c,
    80–3, 256, 270, 308, 387, 428,
    508, 535, 569
    income measure **82**
    insurance 50
    'Keynesian' 420–1
    risks **51–2c**
    seasonal 211, 212
    support of the unemployed **253**
    'technological' 212
    urban 255–6
    voluntary and involuntary 221
unequal exchange 22, **262**, **278**,
    280–1, 283n6
    Emmanuel's model xxx, 280–1
unfair competition **187–8**
'unfreedoms' (Sen) 19
United Kingdom
    assistance to developing countries
        456–8, 456–7t
    Department for International
        Development (DFID)
        457, 457–8c
    Overseas Development
        Administration 456–7
United Nations 4, 5, 11, 12, 286, 465
United Nations Children's Fund
    (UNICEF) 465t
United Nations Commission on
    Sustainable Development
    379
United Nations Conference on
    Environment and
    Development (Rio Earth
    Summit, June 1992) 358,
    370, 378
United Nations Conference on
    International Money and
    Finance 12
United Nations Conference on
    Population and Development
    (Cairo, 1994) 299
United Nations Conference on
    Trade and Development
    (UNCTAD, 1964–) xxxii,
    12, 23, **457**, 523, 529, 545,
    560n5
United Nations Development
    Programme (UNDP) xxix,
    xxxii, 13–14c, 16, 23, 26, 37, 42,
    52, 53, 67, 68n1, 68n3, 89–90c,
    241t, 378, 465t, 477

United Nations Food and Agriculture
    Organization (FAO)   23, 43,
    92, 254
United Nations Framework on
    Climate Change   378
United Nations General Assembly
    Sixth Special Session (1974)
    111
United Nations High Commission for
    Refugees (UNHCR)   465t
United Nations Industrial
    Development Organization
    (UNIDO)   12, 23, 108
    project appraisal   331, 334, 335,
        336, 337, 339, **346–9**, 348t
United Nations International Fund
    for Agricultural Development
    (IFAD)   199, 465t
United Nations Population Fund
    (UNFPA)   465t
United Nations Relief and Works
    Agency in Palestine (UNWRA)
    465t
United Nations Statistics Division
    (UNSD)   109f
United Nations World Development
    Summit (Copenhagen
    1995)   12
United Nations World Food
    Programme (WFP)   **100–1**,
    465t
United Nations World Summit
    (2005)   370
Universal Declaration of Human
    Rights (1948)   xxxiii
University of Sussex: Institute of
    Development Studies   xxxiv
UNTA   465t
urban areas/cities   108, 180, 480,
    528
    effect of population on growth
        291, **294–5**
urban bias   **21**, 187, **188, 262**
urban sector   209
urban unemployment   80–1, **207**,
    255–6
    rural-urban migration and   78,
        195–8, 226n9–12
urbanization   123
US dollar
    cross-country PCY measurement
        problems   37–40
    reserve currency   574
    unit of account   38–9, 40
    world prices   347
utilitarianism   297

valuation of agricultural production
    forgone and increase in
    consumption   343
value-added   108, 537–8, 549
    definition   537
value chains (global)   15
variable capital (Marx)   139
vent for surplus   502, **505, 510**
Verdoorn's Law/coefficient   **111**,
    112, 113c, **273**, 274, **293**, 520
Versailles, Treaty of (1919)   489
vertical inequality   **84–9**
vicious circles   5, 9, 22, 92, 230, 289,
    310, 316, 518, 582
Vietnam Bank for Agriculture and
    Development (Agribank)
    402c
violence   48c, **89–90c**, 316
virtuous circles   9
    of growth   **112**, 316
    model of export-led growth
        517, **519–20**
    saving, capital accumulation,
        growth   395
vitamin A deficiency   92, 93, 94, 195,
    254
'Voices of Poor' (World Bank)   47,
    48–9c
    'well-being' and 'ill-being'   48–9c
voluntary agencies/organizations
    18, 456t
voluntary saving   386, **387**, 414,
    436n1
vulnerable people   50, 308, 310, 311,
    315f

wage inequality   529, 530–1
wage rate   202–3, 265, 265f, 280,
    281, 281f, 283n6, 329n6
wage-earners   419, 420, 422, 436n13
wage-price coefficient   396
wages   51c, 110c, 134, 145,
    246–7, 247f, 251, 269, 274,
    394, 534
    all consumed (assumption)   252
    capital intensity of production
        252
    capping   595
    casual   222
    industrial   202, 216f, 334, 340–2,
        340f
    Marx's confusion   140
    minimum   73
    piece rates   221
    public officials   314

real   **140**, 205, 206, 207, 226n5,
    278, 283n6, 436n13, 526
rural   208
rural–urban differential   200,
    207
subsidized   275
subsistence   137–8, 201, 204,
    210, 210f, 211, 212, 212f,
    213, 214, 215f
urban–rural differential   207,
    209–10
urban–rural differential (actual)
    207–8
urban–rural differential
    (expected)   **207–8**,
    209–10
war   **80**, 99
warranted growth rate (Harrod)
    144–5
Washington Consensus (1989–)
    584, 593
waste absorption   353, 353f, **354**,
    366
water   13, 14c, 53, 63t, 92, 96–7t,
    97, 228, 242, 295, 316, 352f,
    355–6, 356f, 374, 448c, 467,
    468t, 492c
    agricultural   189, 191, 199
Wealth of Nations (Smith, 1776)
    509, 510
wealth tax   **419**, 420
weather   52c, 101, 244
websites   xxxii
    agriculture   226
    aid, remittances, debt and FDI   497
    author's   xxxii
    balance of payments   601
    banking   436
    choice of techniques   258
    development economics   23–4
    environment   381
    food production and statistics
        116
    globalization   24
    government and corruption
        329
    growth theory   175
    health   116
    IMF   601
    income distribution   116
    institutes of development
        studies   23
    institutions and market behaviour
        129
    international organizations   23–4
    labour market statistics   116

websites – *continued*
  micro-credit 436
  population 302
  poverty and income distribution 69
  project appraisal 350
  South-East Asia Crisis 601
  technology and investment 258
  trade 560
welfare 11, 42, 366
  gains and losses from protection
    536f
  maximization of general 256,
    297
  measured growth 92
  and population control 299
  and population growth 291
  and trade 509, 516, 526
welfare economics 306, 366, 367,
    371, 373
welfare maximization 306, 307f,
    318
welfare state 107, 264, 308
wheat 193, 335
White Man's Burden, The (Easterly)
    447
wind power 368
women 49c, 51c, 52c, 90c, 403
  education 84t, **240–2**, 241t
  education and rates of fertility
    285, 288–9, 289f, 299
  empowerment **13c**
work effort 418
workers 118
  migrant 464–5
  white-collar 108
working class, cost of reproducing
    (Marx) 139
World Bank Commission on Growth
    and Development (2008) 49,
    172, 172c
World Bank Comprehensive
    Development Framework
    452
World Bank Conference on
    Population and Development
    299
World Bank Economic Review xxxii
*World Bank Global Monitoring
    Report* 13
World Bank (International Bank for
    Reconstruction and
    Development, IBRD, 1946–)
  activities 198–9, **465**, **466–8**,
    469c, 546, 594
  capital flows 445
  changing role 583, 584
  classification of countries 27, 33

definition of poverty 42–3
development loans (agricultural)
    198
distribution of lending (2007)
    465–6t, 468t
and environmental issues 368,
    377–8
'essentially a commercial
    institution' 466
and impact of aid **450–1**
purpose of structural adjustment
    lending **468–71**, 497n7
responsibility for development
    583
role **469c**, 583, 584
and role of the state 311
sectorwide approach **452c**
structural adjustment lending
    468–71
study of laws and regulations
    314
see also Highly-Indebted Poor
    Country (HIPC) Initiative
*World Bank Policy and Research
    Bulletin* 448c
World Bank Rural Finance Project
    401c
World Bank Structural Adjustment
    Programmes 193, 407, 438
World Commission on the
    Environment and
    Development 369
World Conservation Strategy (UN)
    369, 378
World Development Fund
    (proposed) 17
World Development Indicators
    (World Bank) 103f, 162
  (2007) 29–33t, 389–91t
  (2008) 45t
  (2009) 76t, 84t, 97t, 104t,
    183–7t, 286t, 290t, 431–3t,
    479t, 482–5n, 514f
World Development (journal) xxxii
World Development Report
    (World Bank) xxx, xxxi,
    xxxii, 27
  (1979) xxxii, 27, 182, 204
  (1982) 182
  (1987) 516
  (1989) 409
  (1990) 49, 68n2
  (1991) 159t
  (1992) xxxi
  (1995) 81, 115n3
  (1997) *State in a Changing World*
    xxx, 310, 314, 315f, 316

(2000/2001) *Attacking Poverty*
    xxix, 19, 26, 45, 50–2c,
    66, 68n2, 452, 452c,
    467
  (2002) xxxi
  (2004) 230–1c
  (2005) **230–1c**
  (2008) xxx, 180
  (2009) 277
  (2010) xxxi, 374, 375, 376, 377
World Economic Forum 15
world economy 162, 164, 486, 490,
    551, 570, 583, 593
  income distribution **27–34**,
    68n2–3
  integration 8
  interdependence 5, 9, **14–18**,
    565
World Health Organization (WHO)
    23, 94, 96, 115n6
world income 562, 565
  growth (structural change)
    569–70
World Institute for Development and
    Economics Research (WIDER)
    523, 596
  Hunger and Poverty project
    115n7
world population *see* population
World Population Conference
    (Bucharest, 1974) 299
world trade 549
  decline (1982) 486
  growth 514, 514f
  market share of manufactured
    exports (1981–2000)
    504t
World Trade Organization (WTO)
    (1995–) 15, 23, 50, 95, 188,
    378, 510, 514, 546
  Doha Round (2001–) 546c, **547**,
    548
  need for reform 550–1
  Seattle conference (1999) 547
  see also GATT
world wars
  inter-war era 489
  post-war era (1945–) 7, 15, 279,
    285, 541, 583
  World War I 15, 489, 544
  World War II 15, 543, 551
World Wide Fund for Nature 494

youth 14c, 285, 289, 292, 293, 296,
    299, 467

zero coupon bonds **493**

GEOGRAPHIC INDEX

ACP (Africa, Caribbean and Pacific) countries 547–8, 550
Afghanistan 61t, 63t, 313t, 431t, 459t, 482t, 579t
Africa 13, 16, 27, 41, 45, 47, 51c, 67, 76, 79, 80, 83, 84, 94, 95c, 96, 98, 100, 101, 102, 104, 111, 112, 113–14c, 122, 123, 125, 128, 137, 159, 166, 188, 193, 194, 219, 220, 235, 278, 286, 287, 308, 310, 374, 377, 398, 411, 447, 449, 458, 467, 485, 489, 490, 503, 522, 527c, 529, 545, 546, 573
  contribution of factor inputs and total productivity to industrial growth 159t
  energy use and CO_2 emissions (2006) 375t
  estimates of extended version of dynamic Harrod foreign trade multiplier 571t
  land reform 190c
  see also individual countries by name; Middle East and North Africa; Sub-Saharan Africa
Albania 29t, 56t, 183t, 312t, 389t, 431t, 459t, 482t, 579t
Algeria 29t, 58t, 87t, 182, 183t, 312t, 389t, 431t, 459t, 482t, 571t, 579t
Amazonia 105
Andorra 55t
Angola 29t, 53, 59t, 95c, 183t, 312t, 389t, 431t, 459t, 482t, 578t
Antigua and Barbuda 55t, 183t, 431t, 459t, 578t
APEC 510
Arab States 17

educational provision and literacy, females relative to males 241t
Human Development Index (2007) 61t
Argentina 29t, 41, 48c, 56t, 107, 183t, 313t, 389t, 415, 417t, 431t, 459t, 482t, 504, 510, 517, 574, 575, 576
Armenia 29t, 57t, 87t, 183t, 313t, 389t, 431t, 459t, 482t, 579t
Aruba 431t, 578t
ASEAN 510
Asia 27, 41, 96, 125, 137, 188, 189, 190, 193, 218–19, 220, 235, 286, 291, 296, 409, 411, 514, 522, 527c, 529, 545, 570, 573
  application of balance-of-payments-constrained growth model 565t
  energy use and CO_2 emissions (2006) 375t
  estimates of extended version of dynamic Harrod foreign trade multiplier 571–2t
  financial crisis (1997) 15, 51c
  returns on investment in education 239t
  tiger economies 91, 113, 160, 160t, 308, 311, 314, 411
  see also East Asia; East Asia and Pacific; individual countries by name; South-East Asia
Australia 29t, 40, 54t, 79, 88t, 108, 122, 123, 128, 183t, 188, 312t, 417t, 431t, 455t, 475t, 504, 579t
Austria 29t, 54t, 183t, 312t, 389t, 416t, 431t, 455t, 475t, 579t
Azerbaijan 29t, 57t, 183t, 312t, 389t, 416t, 431t, 459t, 482t, 579t

Bahamas 56t, 88t, 431t, 578t
Bahrain 55t, 313t, 431t, 578t
Bangladesh 29t, 48c, 60t, 86t, 98, 183t, 219, 219t, 243, 270, 286, 312t, 389t, 402c, 431t, 449, 459t, 482t, 521, 527c, 530t, 534, 549, 578t
  Grameen Bank 403–4
Barbados 55t, 87t, 183t, 312t, 431t, 459t, 578t
Beijing 584
Belarus 29t, 56t, 87t, 183t, 312t, 389t, 431t, 459t, 482t, 578t
Belgium 29t, 54t, 88t, 183t, 312t, 389t, 416t, 431t, 455t, 475t, 579t
Belize 57t, 183t, 313t, 389t, 416t, 431t, 459t, 482t, 578t
Benin 29t, 60t, 63t, 183t, 312t, 431t, 459t, 482t, 491c, 546c, 548, 571t, 578t
Bhutan 29t, 59t, 183t, 313t, 389t, 431t, 459t, 482t, 578t
Bolivia 29t, 58t, 87t, 183t, 190c, 313t, 389t, 404, 415, 417t, 431t, 436n16, 448c, 459t, 482t, 491c, 521, 530t, 579t
Bosnia and Herzegovina 29t, 57t, 183t, 312t, 389t, 431t, 459t, 482t, 578t
Botswana 29t, 53, 59t, 78, 85t, 94, 95c, 113c, 172c, 180, 183t, 313t, 389t, 416t, 431t, 448c, 459t, 482t, 579t
Brazil 29t, 35, 40, 51c, 57t, 85t, 87t, 89, 125, 171, 172c, 183t, 189–90, 190c, 218, 219t, 243, 268t, 286, 312t, 314, 367, 389t, 417t, 428, 431t, 459t, 479t, 481, 482t, 510, 519, 529, 530t, 531, 576, 579t, 594

Britain *see* United Kingdom
Brunei Darussalam   55t, 184t, 389t,
    431t, 578t
Buenos Aires   294
Bulgaria   29t, 49c, 56t, 87t, 184t,
    312t, 389t, 431t, 482t, 578t
Burkina Faso   29t, 61t, 63t, 184t,
    312t, 431t, 459t, 482t, 491c,
    546c, 571t, 578t
Burundi   4, 27, 29t, 61t, 63t, 80,
    184t, 312t, 431t, 459t, 482t,
    503, 571t, 579t

Cairo   299, 376
Cambodia   29t, 59t, 184t, 313t,
    390t, 431t, 459t, 482t, 579t
Cambridge (England)   145
Cambridge (Massachusetts)   145
Cameroon   29t, 60t, 85t, 184t, 312t,
    390t, 416t, 432t, 459t, 482t,
    571t, 578t
Canada   29t, 54t, 88t, 106, 107, 108,
    123, 184t, 188, 268t, 312t, 417t,
    432t, 455t, 475t, 504, 579t
Cape Verde   59t, 113c, 184t, 313t,
    432t, 459t, 482t, 578t
Central African Republic   29t, 61t,
    63t, 85t, 184t, 312t, 390t, 432t,
    459t, 482t, 578t
Central America   570
Central Asia   289
Central and Eastern Europe and
    the CIS
    educational provision and
        literacy, females relative to
        males   241t
    Human Development Index
        (2007)   61t
Chad   29t, 43, 61t, 63t, 184t, 313t,
    390t, 432t, 459t, 482t, 546c,
    578t
Chile   29t, 55t, 87t, 184t, 190c, 268t,
    312t, 390t, 409, 417t, 428, 432t,
    434, 459t, 479t, 482t, 510, 530t,
    577, 579t
China   8, 17, 27, 29t, 35, 36, 43, 47,
    57t, 73–4, 84, 85, 86t, 95c, 101,
    105, 107, 111, 119, 125, 160–1,
    160t, 172c, 180, 181, 184t, 187,
    190, 196c, 207, 243, 268, 268t,
    269, 270, 286, 312t, 378, 388,
    390t, 432t, 459t, 479t, 482t,
    503, 504t, 508, 509, 514, 521,
    525, 528, 530, 530t, 532, 533,
    550, 558, 562, 572t, 577, 579t,
    584–5
    absolute poverty and poverty
        rates   44t

energy use and CO_2 emissions
    (2006)   375t
famine   98, 99, 100
industrial revolution   110c
poverty gap index   46t
savings and investment   74–5c
trade policy   522
Chittagong   403
Cologne   490
Colombia   29t, 57t, 87t, 184t, 218,
    219t, 312t, 390t, 415, 416t, 428,
    432t, 449, 460t, 479t, 482t,
    530t, 534, 549, 579t
Comoros   29t, 59t, 184t, 312t, 390t,
    432t, 460t, 482t, 578t
Congo, Democratic Republic   29t,
    61t, 63t, 80, 125, 184t, 313t,
    390t, 416t, 432t, 460t, 482t,
    571t, 579t
Congo, Republic   29t, 59t, 125, 312t,
    390t, 432t, 460t, 482t, 578t
Copenhagen   379
Costa Rica   29t, 56t, 87t, 184t, 219t,
    313t, 390t, 416t, 432t, 460t,
    482t, 493, 565t, 579t
Côte d'Ivoire   29t, 60t, 63t, 86t,
    184t, 312t, 390t, 432t, 460t,
    482t, 571t, 578t
Cotonou (Benin)   548
Croatia   29t, 55t, 184t, 313t, 390t,
    432t, 460t, 482t, 578t
Cuba   53, 56t, 312t, 432t, 460t
Cyprus   29t, 55t, 312t, 432t, 579t
Czech Republic   29t, 55t, 87t, 184t,
    313t, 390t, 432t, 579t
Czechoslovakia   87t

Darussalam *see* Brunei Darussalem
Delhi   294
Denmark   29t, 54t, 88t, 184t, 312t,
    390t, 417t, 432t, 454, 455t,
    475t, 578t
Dhaka   294, 376
Diama hydroelectric dam (Mali)
    355
Djibouti   30t, 60t, 184t, 313t, 390t,
    432t, 460t, 482t, 578t
Dominica   57t, 184t, 312t, 432t,
    460t, 482t, 578t
Dominican Republic   30t, 57t, 87t,
    171–2, 184t, 313t, 416t, 432t,
    460t, 482t, 530t, 579t

East Africa   80
East Asia   80, 161, 277, 289, 308, 378,
    479, 503, 517, 519, 539, 550,
    577, 579, 580, 581–2, 581t, 583,
    588, 593, 600n8

contribution of factor inputs and
    total productivity to
    industrial growth   159t
growth of output and total factor
    productivity   160t
miracle countries   8, 411
sources of growth   161t
world market share of
    manufactured exports
    504t
East Asia and Pacific   43, 45, 46, 104,
    464, 562
absolute poverty and poverty
    rates   44t
agricultural productivity,
    agriculture value-added per
    worker   187t
debt burden (2007)   485t
education   84
educational provision and
    literacy, females relative to
    males   241t
estimated workers' remittances
    464f
growth and poverty   47t
Human Development Index
    (2007)   61t
income inequality   85, 86t
income per capita and
    population   33t
investment and savings as
    percentage of GDP   391t
population statistics   286t
poverty gap index   46t
recipients of aid   463t
share of output in GDP   104t
total fertility rate   290t
Eastern Europe   7, 51c, 80, 85, 307,
    308, 539
income inequality   87t
Eastern Europe and Central Asia
absolute poverty and poverty
    rates   44t
growth and poverty   47t
poverty gap index   46t
ECOWAS   513
Ecuador   30t, 49c, 51c, 53, 57t, 88t,
    182, 184t, 190c, 312t, 391t, 417t,
    432t, 460t, 482t, 575, 578t
Egypt   30t, 49c, 59t, 87t, 184t, 313t,
    391t, 417t, 432t, 479t, 482t,
    530t, 571t, 579t
El Salvador   30t, 58t, 88t, 171, 184t,
    312t, 391t, 416t, 432t, 460t,
    483t, 565t, 575, 578t
England   420, 506, 507f
Equatorial Guinea   30t, 53, 59t, 113c,
    184t, 313t, 391t, 432t, 460t, 578t

Eritrea 30t, 60t, 63t, 184t, 313t, 391t, 432t, 460t, 483t, 578t

Estonia 30t, 55t, 87t, 184t, 312t, 391t, 432t, 578t

Ethiopia 30t, 43, 48c, 61t, 63t, 98, 125, 184t, 192, 312t, 391t, 416t, 433t, 449, 460t, 483t, 503, 571t, 579t

Europe 6, 15, 27, 73, 79, 105, 269, 277, 291, 504, 533
  energy use and CO_2 emissions (2006) 375t
  see also Eastern Europe; Western Europe

Europe and Central Asia
  agricultural productivity, agriculture value-added per worker 187t
  debt burden (2007) 485t
  education 84t
  estimated workers' remittances 464f
  health 97t
  income per capita and population 33t
  investment and savings as percentage of GDP 391t
  population statistics 286t
  recipients of aid 463t
  share of output in GDP 104t
  total fertility rate 290t

Europe, Middle East and North Africa
  contribution of factor inputs and total productivity growth to economic growth 159t
  returns on investment in education 239t

European Community (EC) 466, 466t

European Economic Community (EEC) 547

European Union 62t, 188, 269, 428, 510, 546, 547, 549, 550, 552, 575

Fiji 30t, 58t, 86t, 89, 90c, 184t, 391t, 416t, 433t, 460t, 483t, 509, 578t

Finland 30t, 54t, 88t, 184t, 312t, 391t, 416t, 433t, 455t, 475t, 579t

France 30t, 54t, 88t, 107, 184t, 268t, 269, 312t, 391t, 416t, 420, 433t, 455t, 475t, 579t

French Polynesia 433t

Fujian 522

Gabon 30t, 58t, 86t, 184t, 312t, 391t, 433t, 460t, 483t, 571t, 578t

Gambia 30t, 43, 61t, 63t, 184t, 313t, 391t, 433t, 460t, 483t, 509, 579t

Geneva 547

Georgia 30t, 57t, 184t, 312t, 391t, 433t, 460t, 483t, 579t

Germany 30t, 54t, 88t, 107, 184t, 268t, 269, 311, 312t, 391t, 417t, 431t, 455t, 475t, 489, 522, 579t

Ghana 30t, 43, 60t, 86t, 184t, 251, 312t, 391t, 409, 415, 416t, 431t, 448c, 449, 460t, 483t, 530t, 571t, 579t

Greece 30t, 55t, 88t, 184t, 313t, 391t, 417t, 431t, 455t, 475t, 579t

Grenada 57t, 184t, 431t, 460t, 483t, 578t

Guangdong 522

Guatemala 30t, 59t, 88t, 90c, 185t, 207, 312t, 389t, 417t, 431t, 460t, 483t, 565t, 579t

Guinea 30t, 61t, 63t, 185t, 313t, 389t, 431t, 460t, 471, 483t, 579t

Guinea-Bissau 30t, 43, 61t, 63t, 86t, 185t, 313t, 389t, 431t, 460t, 483t, 578t

Guyana 30t, 58t, 88t, 185t, 312t, 431t, 460t, 483t, 578t

Haiti 30t, 60t, 313t, 389t, 431t, 460t, 483t, 579t

Honduras 30t, 58t, 88t, 185t, 312t, 389t, 431t, 460t, 483t, 530t, 565t, 578t

Hong Kong 8, 12, 30t, 40, 55t, 86t, 159, 160t, 172c, 308, 311, 312t, 389t, 431t, 522, 571t, 578t, 579t

Hungary 30t, 51c, 55t, 87t, 185t, 313t, 389t, 431t, 579t

Iceland 54t, 185t, 312t, 389t, 417t, 431t, 579t

India 27, 30t, 35, 36, 39, 40, 50c, 59t, 85, 86t, 95c, 100, 101, 107, 125, 180, 185t, 191, 199, 219, 219t, 243, 250t, 268t, 286, 312t, 367, 374, 378, 389t, 416t, 431t, 449, 460t, 479t, 483t, 509, 525, 530t, 532, 533, 538, 570, 572t, 579t
  absolute poverty and poverty rates 44t
  challenge of agricultural reform 196c
  energy use and CO_2 emissions (2006) 375t
  famine 98, 99
  poverty gap index 46t
  savings and investment 74–5c

Indonesia 30t, 58t, 78, 86t, 90c, 172c, 185t, 219, 219t, 268t, 312t, 367, 389t, 402–3, 404, 409, 417t, 431t, 448c, 460t, 483t, 522, 530t, 562, 565t, 571t, 576, 579, 579t, 580t, 583, 594, 595
  financial liberalization 412–13c

Iran 30t, 53, 57t, 87t, 185t, 250t, 312t, 389t, 417t, 431t, 460t, 483t, 579t

Iraq 180, 313t, 431t, 460t, 579t

Ireland 30t, 54t, 88t, 90c, 185t, 312t, 417t, 431t, 455t, 475t, 579t

Isle of Man 431t

Israel 30t, 55t, 250t, 312t, 389t, 431t, 579t

Italy 30t, 54t, 88t, 185t, 268t, 269, 277, 313t, 389t, 416t, 431t, 455t, 475t, 579t

Jakarta 413c

Jamaica 30t, 48c, 58t, 88t, 185t, 313t, 413t, 460t, 483t, 530t, 579t

Japan 30t, 35, 54t, 86t, 106, 107, 113, 172c, 181, 182, 185t, 200, 220, 250t, 286, 312t, 375t, 413t, 416t, 455t, 475t, 517, 522, 539, 572t, 579t

Jordan 30t, 58t, 87t, 185t, 313t, 389t, 416t, 460t, 578t

Kalahari Desert 180

Kazakhstan 30t, 57t, 87t, 185t, 312t, 389t, 431t, 460t, 483t, 578t

Kenya 30t, 40, 48c, 60t, 86t, 159t, 185t, 194, 220, 250t, 312t, 314, 389t, 404, 416t, 431t, 449, 460t, 483t, 526, 527c, 571t, 579t
  financial liberalization 413c

Kiribati 185t, 313t, 431t, 460t, 578t

Kolkata 294

Korea, Republic 30t, 55t, 86t, 185t, 389t, 428, 431t, 448c, 449, 460t, 571t, 579t

Kuwait 31t, 55t, 312t, 389t, 431t, 578t

Kyoto 358, 378–9

Kyrgyzstan 31t, 59t, 87t, 185t, 313t, 389t, 431t, 461t, 483t, 579t

Lao PDR 31t, 59t, 86t, 185t, 312t, 390t, 432t, 461t, 483t, 579t

Latin America 21, 27, 35, 41, 49, 51c, 79, 96, 104, 123, 125, 161, 188, 189–90, 199, 218, 220, 235, 283n1, 286, 378, 404, 409, 410, 411, 415, 430, 466, 478, 514, 517, 521, 522, 523, 529, 539, 545, 568, 570, 580, 584

Latin America – *continued*
  application of balance-of-
    payments-constrained
    growth model   565t
  contribution of factor inputs and
    total productivity growth
    to economic growth   159t
  energy use and CO_2 emissions
    (2006)   375t
  land reform   190c
  sources of growth   161t
  structuralist-monetarist debate
    433–4
Latin America and Caribbean   43,
  464
  absolute poverty and poverty
    rates   44t
  agricultural productivity,
    agriculture value-added per
    worker   187t
  debt burden (2007)   485t
  education   84t
  educational provision and
    literacy, females relative to
    males   241t
  estimated workers' remittances
    464f
  growth and poverty   47t
  health   97t
  Human Development Index
    (2007)   61t
  income inequality   87–8t
  income per capita and
    population   33t
  investment and savings as
    percentage of GDP   391t
  population statistics   286t
  poverty gap index   46t
  recipients of aid   463t
  returns on investment in
    education   239t
  share of output in GDP   104t
  total fertility rate   290t
  trade   76
  world market share of
    manufactured exports
    504t
Latvia   31t, 48c, 55t, 87t, 185t, 313t,
  390t, 432t, 483t, 578t
Lebanon   31t, 57t, 185t, 313t, 390t,
  432t, 461t, 483t, 578t
Lesotho   31t, 60t, 86t, 95c, 185t,
  312t, 390t, 416t, 432t, 461t,
  483t, 571t, 578t
Liberia   31t, 61t, 63t, 312t, 390t,
  432t, 461t, 483t, 579t

Libya   31t, 56t, 312t, 432t, 461t, 578t
Liechtenstein   54t
Lithuania   31t, 55t, 87t, 185t, 313t,
  390t, 432t, 578t
London   477
Luxembourg   54t, 88t, 185t, 312t,
  390t, 416t, 432t, 454, 455t,
  475t, 579t

Macao   31t, 313t, 432t
Macedonia   31t, 57t, 185t, 312t,
  390t, 432t, 461t, 483t, 578t
Madagascar   31t, 60t, 86t, 185t,
  312t, 390t, 416t, 432t, 461t,
  483t, 571t, 579t
Malawi   31t, 43, 60t, 63t, 95c, 98,
  185t, 313t, 390t, 432t, 449,
  461t, 483t, 503, 549, 578t
Malaysia   31t, 56t, 78, 86t, 89, 90c,
  172c, 185t, 243, 313t, 390t,
  402c, 409, 417t, 432t, 461t, 522,
  562, 565t, 572t, 577, 579t, 580t,
  581, 582, 583
Maldives   58t, 313t, 432t, 461t, 483t,
  578t
Mali   31t, 43, 61t, 63t, 185t, 313t,
  355, 358, 390t, 432t, 449, 461t,
  483t, 491c, 546c, 578t
Malta   55t, 172c, 313t, 390t, 417t,
  432t, 579t
Manantali hydroelectric dam (Mali)
  355, 358
Manila   195
Marshall Islands   432t, 461t, 578t
Mauritania   31t, 60t, 86t, 185t, 313t,
  390t, 432t, 461t, 483t, 491c,
  549, 571t, 579t
Mauritius   31t, 57t, 86t, 113c, 185t,
  313t, 390t, 417t, 432t, 461t,
  483t, 509, 571t, 579t
Mayotte   461t
MERCOSUR   510
Mesopotamia   180
Mexico   31t, 35, 40, 56t, 85, 88t, 89,
  90c, 182, 185t, 188, 193–4, 199,
  220, 243, 250t, 268t, 269, 270,
  286, 312t, 390t, 404, 409, 415,
  416t, 428, 432t, 461t, 464, 479t,
  480, 483t, 493, 494, 504t, 508,
  517, 519, 521, 526, 530, 530t,
  565t, 567, 570, 576, 579t
Micronesia   432t, 461t, 578t
Middle East   76, 105
Middle East and North Africa   161
  absolute poverty and poverty
    rates   44t

  agricultural productivity,
    agriculture value-added per
    worker   187t
  contribution of factor inputs and
    total productivity growth
    to economic growth   159t
  debt burden (2007)   485t
  education   84t
  estimated workers' remittances
    464f
  growth and poverty   47t
  health   97t
  income inequality   87t
  income per capita and
    population   33t
  investment and savings as
    percentage of GDP   391t
  population statistics   286t
  poverty gap index   46t
  recipients of aid   463t
  share of output in GDP   104t
  sources of growth   161t
  total fertility rate   290t
  world market share of
    manufactured exports
    504t
Middle Europe   250t
Moldova   31t, 59t, 87t, 185t, 313t,
  390t, 432t, 461t, 484t, 579t
Mongolia   31t, 58t, 185t, 313t, 391t,
  432t, 461t, 484t, 578t
Montenegro   31t, 56t, 312t, 391t,
  432t, 461t, 484t, 578t
Morocco   31t, 59t, 87t, 182, 185t,
  312t, 391t, 417t, 432t, 461t,
  484t, 523, 528, 571t, 578t
Mozambique   31t, 43, 61t, 63t, 95c,
  185t, 312t, 391t, 432t, 449,
  461t, 471, 484t, 491c, 579t
Mumbai   294
Myanmar   53, 59t, 313t, 432t, 461t,
  484t, 579t

Nairobi   467
Namibia   31t, 59t, 95c, 180, 185t,
  313t, 391t, 417t, 432t, 461t,
  578t
Nepal   31t, 43, 60t, 87t, 90c, 186t,
  219, 219t, 268t, 391t, 417t,
  433t, 461t, 484t, 578t
Netherlands   31t, 54t, 78, 88t, 186t,
  312t, 391t, 416t, 433t, 454,
  455t, 475t, 497n6, 579t
Netherlands Antilles   578t
New Caledonia   433t
New York   278, 294

New Zealand 31t, 40, 54t, 79, 88t,
        108, 123, 186t, 312t, 314, 417t,
        433t, 455t, 475t, 504, 579t
Nicaragua 31t, 59t, 88t, 186t, 312t,
        391t, 433t, 461t, 484t, 565t,
        579t
Niger 31t, 43, 61t, 63t, 86t, 98, 313t,
        433t, 461t, 484t, 571t, 578t
Nigeria 31t, 60t, 86t, 98, 182, 286,
        433t, 461t, 484t, 530t, 571t,
        579t
North Africa see Middle East and
        North Africa
North America 15, 27, 73, 79, 277,
        533, 549
North American Free Trade
        Agreement (NAFTA) 510
Northern Ireland 90c
Norway 4, 27, 31t, 40, 54t, 88t, 186t,
        312t, 391t, 417t, 433t, 454,
        455t, 475t, 579t

Occupied Palestinian Territories
        58t
OECD 61t, 62t, 168, 430
    returns on investment in
        education 239t
Oman 56t, 172c, 313t, 431t, 461t,
        578t
Organization of Petroleum Exporting
        Countries (OPEC) 554

Pacific Rim 166
Pakistan 31t, 59t, 87t, 186t, 223,
        268t, 270, 286, 312t, 391t, 415,
        417t, 431t, 436n11, 461t, 484t,
        530t, 534, 549, 572t, 579t
Palau 431t, 461t, 578t
Panama 31t, 56t, 88t, 186t, 312t,
        391t, 416t, 431t, 461t, 484t,
        578t
Papua New Guinea 31t, 60t, 105,
        186t, 391t, 416t, 431t, 461t,
        484t, 579t
Paraguay 31t, 58t, 186t, 190c, 312t,
        391t, 417t, 431t, 461t, 484t,
        510, 579t
Peru 31t, 57t, 88t, 186t, 218, 219t,
        312t, 391t, 404, 415, 416t, 428,
        431t, 461t, 484t, 494, 517, 530t,
        579t
Philippines 31t, 51c, 58t, 86t, 186t,
        219, 219t, 224, 243, 268t, 312t,
        391t, 416t, 428, 431t, 461t,
        484t, 493, 530t, 562, 565t, 572t,
        579, 579t, 580t, 583

Poland 32t, 55t, 87t, 186t, 268t,
        313t, 391t, 431t, 484t, 579t
Portugal 32t, 55t, 88t, 186t, 312t,
        389t, 416t, 431t, 455t, 475t,
        506, 507f, 579t
Puerto Rico 88t, 313t, 431t
Punjab 223

Qatar 55t, 312t, 431t, 578t

Rio de Janeiro 358, 370, 379
Romania 32t, 56t, 87t, 186t, 268t,
        312t, 389t, 417t, 431t, 484t,
        579t
Rotterdam 278
Russia (Tsarist) 106, 107
Russian Federation 32t, 48c, 57t,
        106, 186t, 268t, 286, 312t, 389t,
        431t, 484t, 576t, 578t
    see also Soviet Union
Rwanda 32t, 43, 61t, 63t, 80, 86t,
        95c, 186t, 313t, 389t, 461t,
        484t, 578t

SACU 510, 513
St Kitts and Nevis 56t, 186t, 432t,
        462t, 484t, 578t
St Lucia 56t, 186t, 312t, 432t, 462t,
        484t, 578t
St Vincent and the Grenadines 57t,
        186t, 312t, 432t, 462t, 484t,
        578t
Samoa 58t, 186t, 313t, 462t, 484t,
        578t
San Marino 578t
Santiago (Chile) 434
São Paulo 51c, 294
São Tomé and Principe 59t, 313t,
        431t, 462t, 484t, 579t
Saudi Arabia 32t, 53, 56t, 186t,
        312t, 389t, 431t, 462t, 578t
Scandinavia 533
Senegal 32t, 61t, 63t, 86t, 186t,
        312t, 389t, 431t, 462t, 484t,
        528, 571t, 578t
Serbia 32t, 56t, 312t, 389t, 431t,
        462t, 484t, 579t
Seychelles 56t, 86t, 186t, 313t, 389t,
        431t, 462t, 484t, 578t
Shanghai 294, 376
Sierra Leone 32t, 43, 61t, 63t, 86t,
        313t, 389t, 417t, 431t, 462t,
        484t, 571t, 578t
Sindh 223
Singapore 8, 32t, 40, 54t, 86t, 113,
        123, 159, 160t, 172c, 186t, 243,

        308, 311, 312t, 389t, 412c, 417t,
        431t, 479t, 522, 539, 579, 579t
Slovak Republic 32t, 55t, 87t, 186t,
        313t, 389t, 431t, 579t
Slovenia 32t, 55t, 87t, 186t, 312t,
        389t, 431t, 579t
Solomon Islands 59t, 186t, 313t,
        431t, 462t, 484t, 578t
Somalia 49c, 313t, 462t, 484t, 571t,
        579t
South Africa 32t, 53, 59t, 61t, 85,
        86t, 89, 90c, 94, 95c, 186t, 190c,
        268t, 313t, 389t, 416t, 431t,
        462t, 484t, 504, 504t, 527c, 570,
        571t, 579t
South Asia 43, 47, 310
    absolute poverty and poverty
        rates 44t
    agricultural productivity,
        agriculture value-added per
        worker 187t
    contribution of factor inputs and
        total productivity growth
        to economic growth 159t
    debt burden (2007) 485t
    education 84t
    educational provision and
        literacy, females relative to
        males 241t
    estimated workers' remittances
        464f
    growth and poverty 47t
    health 97t
    Human Development Index
        (2007) 61t
    income inequality 86–7t
    income per capita and
        population 33t
    investment and savings as
        percentage of GDP 391t
    population statistics 286t
    poverty gap index 46t
    recipients of aid 463t
    share of output in GDP 104t
    sources of growth 161t
    total fertility rate 290t
    world market share of
        manufactured exports
        504t
South Korea 8, 35, 113, 159, 160t,
        172c, 220, 243, 308, 311, 313t,
        409, 417t, 517, 522, 539, 550,
        562, 576, 579, 580t, 583, 594,
        595

South-East Asia   21, 27, 95c, 112,
      181, 277, 308, 310, 478, 510,
      514, 539, 558, 570, 577, 593
Soviet Union   7, 51c, 80, 87t, 99,
      181, 200, 307, 308, 310
   see also Russia (Tsarist); Russian
      Federation
Spain   32t, 54t, 88t, 186t, 268t, 269,
      312t, 389t, 416t, 431t, 455t,
      475t, 579t
Sri Lanka   32t, 58t, 87t, 90c, 186t,
      268t, 312t, 389t, 417t, 431t,
      462t, 484t, 530t, 572t
Sub-Saharan Africa   43, 49, 52c, 80,
      161, 243, 289, 310, 378, 491c,
      513
   absolute poverty and poverty
      rates   44t
   agricultural productivity,
      agriculture value-added per
      worker   187t
   AIDS   95c
   debt burden (2007)   485t
   education   84t
   educational provision and
      literacy, females relative to
      males   241t
   estimated workers' remittances
      464f
   growth and poverty   47t
   health   97t
   Human Development Index
      (2007)   61t
   income inequality   85, 85–6t
   income per capita and
      population   33t
   investment and savings as
      percentage of GDP   391t
   population statistics   286t
   poverty gap index   46t
   recipients of aid   463t
   returns on investment in
      education   239t
   share of output in GDP   104t
   sources of growth   161t
   total fertility rate   290t
   world market share of
      manufactured exports
      504t
Sudan   32t, 60t, 86t, 98, 186t, 313t,
      389t, 432t, 462t, 484t, 494,
      496n2, 568, 569, 571t, 579t
Suriname   32t, 58t, 186t, 312t, 432t,
      462t, 578t

Swaziland   32t, 59t, 95c, 113c, 186t,
      312t, 389t, 432t, 462t, 484t,
      578t
Sweden   32t, 54t, 88t, 106, 107,
      186t, 312t, 389t, 416t, 432t,
      454, 455t, 475t, 579t
Switzerland   15, 32t, 54t, 186t, 195,
      312t, 417t, 432t, 455t, 475t,
      579t
Syria   32t, 58t, 186t, 312t, 389t,
      416t, 432t, 462t, 579t

Taiwan   8, 86t, 159, 160t, 172c, 220,
      243, 308, 311, 313t, 367, 522,
      539, 550
Tajikistan   32t, 43, 59t, 186t, 312t,
      390t, 432t, 462t, 484t, 578t
Tanzania   32t, 43, 60t, 86t, 159t,
      186t, 210, 313t, 432t, 448c, 449,
      462t, 484t, 491c, 571t, 579t
Thailand   32t, 57t, 78, 86t, 125,
      172c, 186t, 219, 219t, 243, 268,
      268t, 312t, 390t, 417t, 428,
      432t, 462t, 479t, 485t, 522, 523,
      530t, 562, 565t, 572t, 576, 577,
      579, 579t, 580t, 582, 583
Timor-Leste   32t, 60t, 63t, 312t,
      432t, 462t, 578t
Togo   32t, 60t, 63t, 186t, 313t, 432t,
      462t, 485t, 571t, 578t
Tokyo   278, 294
Tonga   58t, 187t, 312t, 316, **406**,
      432t, 436n4, 462t, 485t, 549,
      579t
Toronto   493
Trinidad and Tobago   32t, 56t, 88t,
      187t, 312t, 390t, 432t, 462t,
      493, 578t
Tunisia   32t, 58t, 87t, 187t, 312t,
      390t, 417t, 462t, 485t, 571t,
      578t
Turkey   32t, 57t, 88t, 187t, 313t,
      390t, 409, 416t, 417t, 462t,
      479t, 481, 485t, 576, 579t
Turkmenistan   32t, 58t, 313t, 417t,
      462t, 485t, 578t

Uganda   32t, 43, 60t, 86t, 90c, 113c,
      187t, 268t, 312t, 390t, 417t,
      448c, 449, 462t, 471, 485t, 491,
      491c, 503, 579t
   Poverty Action Fund   **492c**
Ukraine   32t, 57t, 87t, 187t, 312t,
      390t, 417t, 462t, 485t, 579t
United Arab Emirates   55t, 187t,
      312t, 417t, 578t

United Kingdom   6, 32t, 54t, 66, 88t,
      90c, 106, 107, 138, 181, 187t,
      200, 235, 268t, 293, 312t, 364,
      390t, 416t, 417t, 428, 475t, 504,
      514, 574, 579t
   assistance to developing countries
      456–8, 456–7t, 457–8c
   see also England; Northern Ireland
United States   32t, 39, 40, 54t, 88t,
      101, 106, 107, 122, 123, 128,
      156–7, 187t, 188, 268t, 269,
      286, 293, 312t, 374, 378, 404,
      416t, 428, 446, 454, 455t, 475t,
      508, 526, 530, 546, 546c, 547,
      574, 575, 576, 579t
   energy use and CO_2 emissions
      (2006)   375t
Uruguay   6t, 32t, 56t, 187t, 190c,
      218, 219t, 312t, 390t, 416t, 428,
      462t, 485t, 493, 510, 579t
USSR see Soviet Union
Uzbekistan   32t, 59t, 187t, 268t,
      313t, 390t, 462t, 485t, 579t

Vanuatu   59t, 187t, 313t, 390t, 462t,
      485t, 579t
Venezuela   32t, 56t, 88t, 187t, 218,
      219t, 313t, 390t, 415, 417t,
      462t, 485t, 493, 523, 529, 530t,
      578t
Vietnam   32t, 58t, 86t, 180, 187t,
      191, 207, 268, 268t, 313t, 390t,
      433t, 448c, 462t, 485t, 527c,
      550
   Bank on Wheels   **401–2c**

Washington, D.C.   314, 516, 584, 593
West Africa   96, 188, 513, 575
West Asia   375t
West Bank and Gaza   433t, 462t
Western Europe   9, 66, 200, 277, 291

Yemen   33t, 59t, 312t, 433t, 462t,
      485t, 578t
Yugoslavia   87t

Zaire   448c
   see also Congo, Democratic
      Republic
Zambia   33t, 51c, 60t, 63t, 86t, 94,
      95c, 159t, 187t, 313t, 390t,
      417t, 433t, 448c, 452c, 462t,
      485t, 503, 530t, 571t, 579t
Zimbabwe   86t, 94, 95c, 159t, 187t,
      220, 313t, 409, 416t, 433t, 462t,
      485t, 571t, 578t
Zurich   195